Introducing

Math Expressions

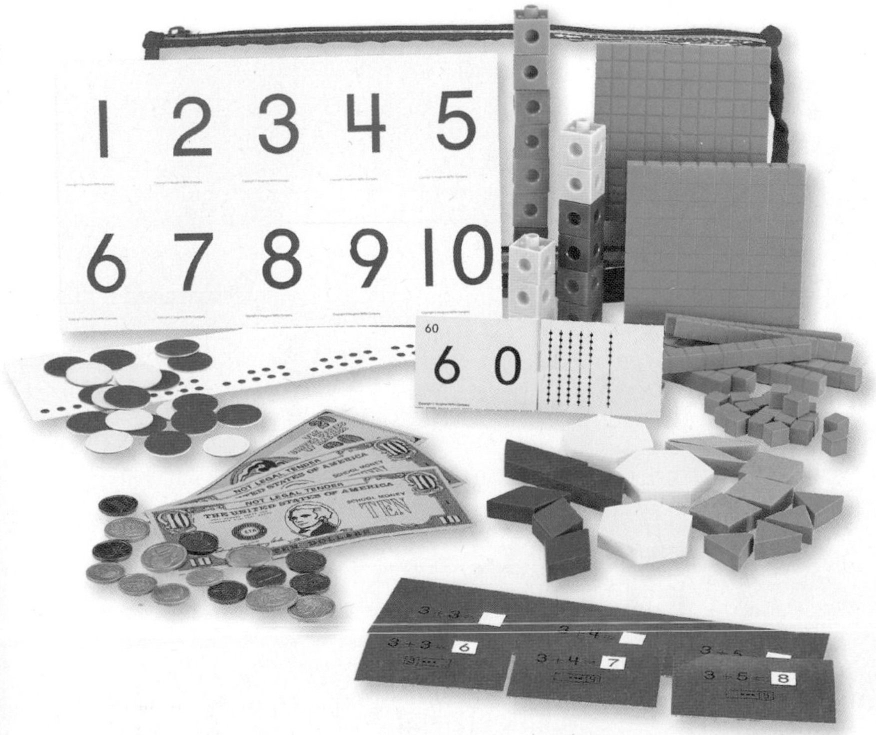

A Fresh Approach to

Math Expressions is a comprehensive Kindergarten–Grade 5 mathematics curriculum that offers new ways to teach and learn mathematics. Combining the most powerful

Standards-Based Instruction

elements of standards-based instruction with the best of traditional approaches, ***Math Expressions*** uses objects, drawings, conceptual language, and real-world situations to help students build mathematical ideas that make sense to them.

Math Expressions implements state standards as well as the recommendations and findings from recent reports on math learning:

Curriculum Focal Points (NCTM, 2007)

Principles and Standards for School Mathematics (NCTM, 2000)

Adding It Up
(National Research Council, 2001)

How Students Learn Mathematics in the Classroom
(National Research Council, 2005)

HOUGHTON MIFFLIN HARCOURT

Math Expressions

Focused on Understanding

In ***Math Expressions,*** teachers create an inquiry environment and encourage constructive discussion. Students invent, question, and explore, but also learn

Math Expressions

Teacher Edition • Volume 2

Developed by
The Children's Math Worlds Research Project

PROJECT DIRECTOR AND AUTHOR
Dr. Karen C. Fuson

This material is based upon work supported by the
National Science Foundation
under Grant Numbers
ESI-9816320, REC-9806020, and RED-935373.

Any opinions, findings, and conclusions, or recommendations expressed in this material are those of the author and do not necessarily reflect the views of the National Science Foundation.

HOUGHTON MIFFLIN HARCOURT

Teacher Reviewers

Kindergarten
Patricia Stroh Sugiyama
Wilmette, Illinois

Barbara Wahle
Evanston, Illinois

Grade 1
Sandra Budson
Newton, Massachusetts

Janet Pecci
Chicago, Illinois

Megan Rees
Chicago, Illinois

Grade 2
Molly Dunn
Danvers, Massachusetts

Agnes Lesnick
Hillside, Illinois

Rita Soto
Chicago, Illinois

Grade 3
Jane Curran
Honesdale, Pennsylvania

Sandra Tucker
Chicago, Illinois

Grade 4
Sara Stoneberg Llibre
Chicago, Illinois

Sheri Roedel
Chicago, Illinois

Grade 5
Todd Atler
Chicago, Illinois

Leah Barry
Norfolk, Massachusetts

Special Thanks
Special thanks to the many teachers, students, parents, principals, writers, researchers, and work-study students who participated in the Children's Math Worlds Research Project over the years.

Credits
(t) © Charles Cormany/Workbook Stock/Jupiter Images, (b) Noah Strycker/Shutterstock

Illustrative art: Robin Boyer/Deborah Wolfe, LTD; Dave Clegg, Geoff Smith, Tim Johnson
Technical art: Nesbitt Graphics, Inc.
Photos: Nesbitt Graphics, Inc.; Page 309 © Anna Clopet/Corbis; Page 366 (i) © David Hancock/Alamy, © Halfdark/Getty Images, (r) © Brooke Fasani/Corbis

Printed in China

ISBN: 978-0-547-06040-8

4 5 6 7 8 9 NPC 17 16 15 14 13 12 11 10 09

and Fluency

and practice important math strategies. Through daily Math Talk students explain their methods and, in turn, become more fluent in them.

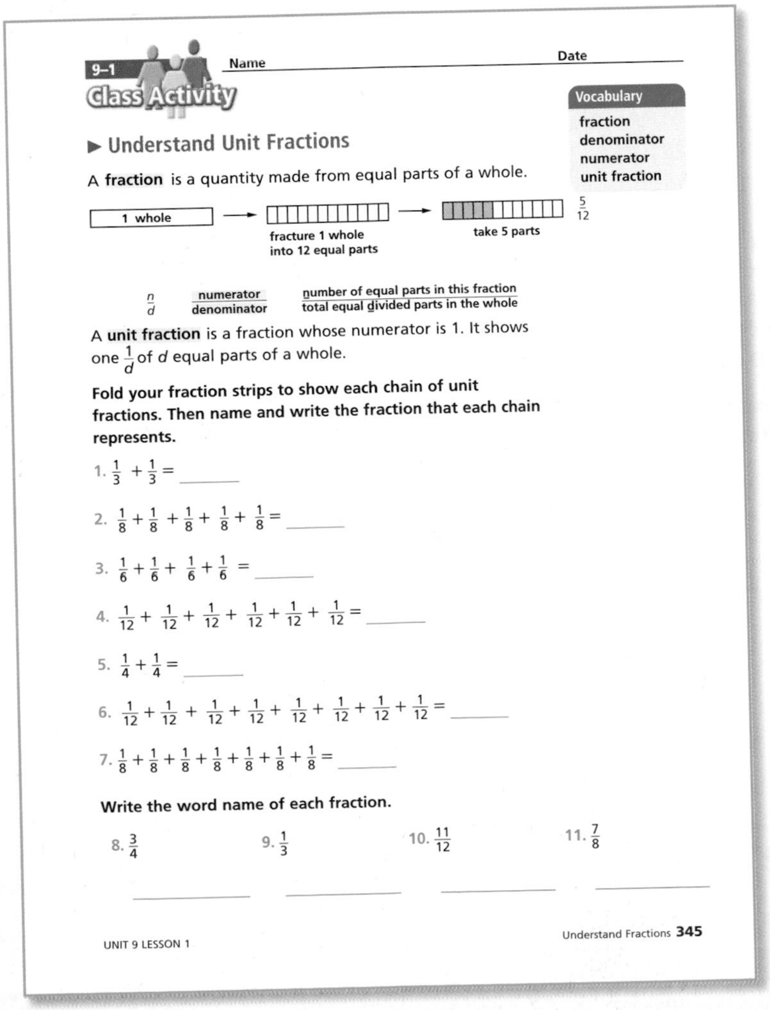
9–1 Class Activity Name ______ Date ______

Vocabulary: fraction, denominator, numerator, unit fraction

▶ Understand Unit Fractions

A **fraction** is a quantity made from equal parts of a whole.

$\frac{n}{d}$ $\frac{\text{numerator}}{\text{denominator}}$ $\frac{\text{number of equal parts in this fraction}}{\text{total equal divided parts in the whole}}$

A **unit fraction** is a fraction whose numerator is 1. It shows one $\frac{1}{d}$ of d equal parts of a whole.

Fold your fraction strips to show each chain of unit fractions. Then name and write the fraction that each chain represents.

1. $\frac{1}{3} + \frac{1}{3} =$ ______
2. $\frac{1}{8} + \frac{1}{8} + \frac{1}{8} + \frac{1}{8} + \frac{1}{8} =$ ______
3. $\frac{1}{6} + \frac{1}{6} + \frac{1}{6} + \frac{1}{6} =$ ______
4. $\frac{1}{12} + \frac{1}{12} + \frac{1}{12} + \frac{1}{12} + \frac{1}{12} + \frac{1}{12} =$ ______
5. $\frac{1}{4} + \frac{1}{4} =$ ______
6. $\frac{1}{12} + \frac{1}{12} + \frac{1}{12} + \frac{1}{12} + \frac{1}{12} + \frac{1}{12} + \frac{1}{12} + \frac{1}{12} =$ ______
7. $\frac{1}{8} + \frac{1}{8} + \frac{1}{8} + \frac{1}{8} + \frac{1}{8} + \frac{1}{8} + \frac{1}{8} =$ ______

Write the word name of each fraction.

8. $\frac{3}{4}$ ______ 9. $\frac{1}{3}$ ______ 10. $\frac{11}{12}$ ______ 11. $\frac{7}{8}$ ______

UNIT 9 LESSON 1 Understand Fractions 345

"As students are asked to communicate about the mathematics they are studying ... they gain insights into their thinking to others, students naturally reflect on their learning and organize and consolidate their thinking about mathematics."

- *Principles and Standards for School Mathematics*, National Council of Teachers of Mathematics (2000), p. 12

HOUGHTON MIFFLIN HARCOURT

Math Expressions

Organized for

Math Expressions is organized around five crucial classroom structures that allow children to develop deep conceptual

Quick Practice

Routines involve whole-class responses or individual partner practice.

Math Talk

Students share strategies and solutions orally and through proof drawings.

Building Concepts

Objects, drawings, conceptua language, and real-world situations strengthen mathematical ideas and understanding.

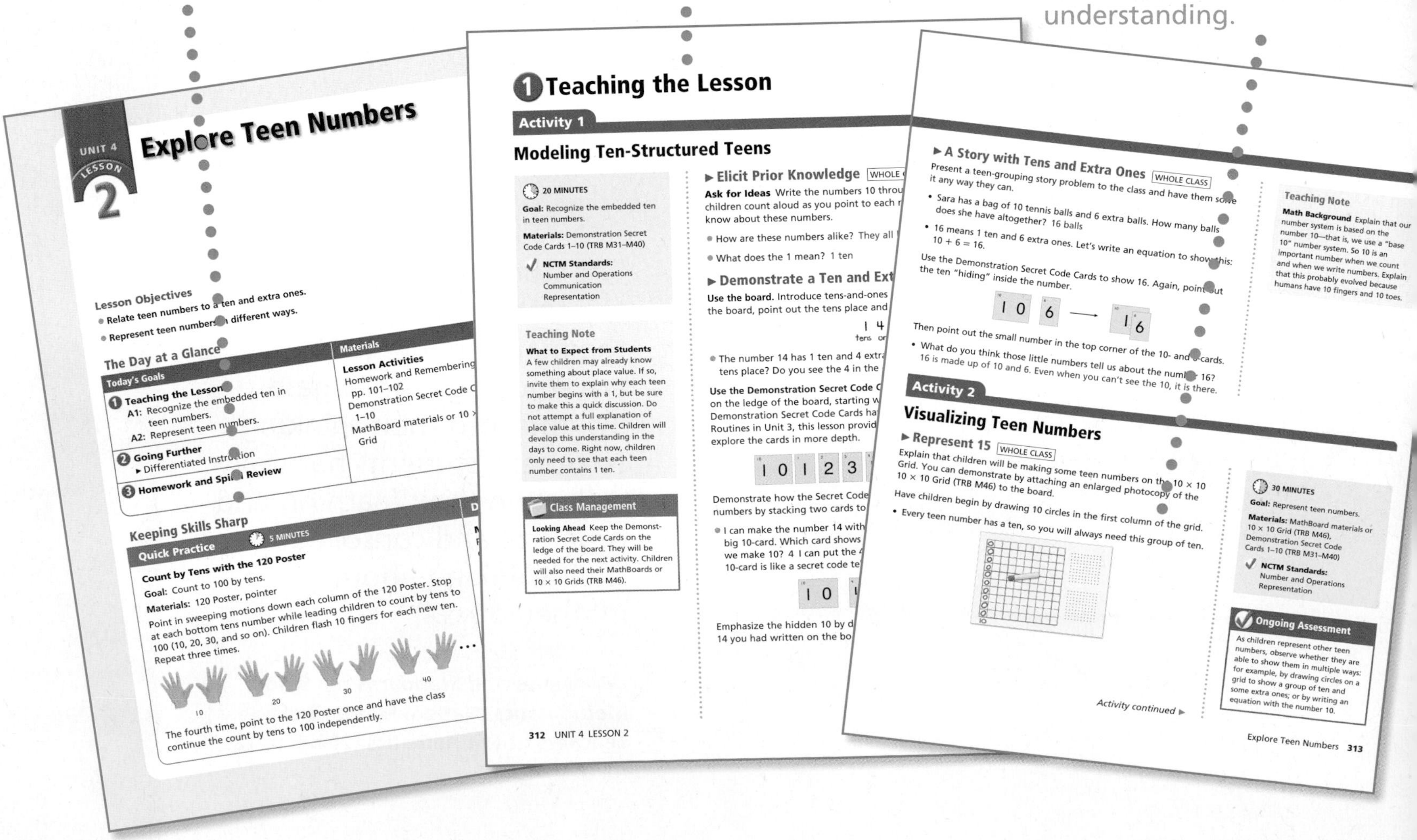

UNIT 4 LESSON 2

Explore Teen Numbers

Lesson Objectives
- Relate teen numbers to a ten and extra ones.
- Represent teen numbers in different ways.

The Day at a Glance

Today's Goals	Materials
1 Teaching the Lesson A1: Recognize the embedded ten in teen numbers. A2: Represent teen numbers.	Lesson Activities Homework and Remembering pp. 101–102 Demonstration Secret Code Cards 1–10 MathBoard materials or 10 × 10 Grid
2 Going Further ▸ Differentiated Instruction	
3 Homework and Spiral Review	

Keeping Skills Sharp

Quick Practice 5 MINUTES

Count by Tens with the 120 Poster
Goal: Count to 100 by tens.
Materials: 120 Poster, pointer
Point in sweeping motions down each column of the 120 Poster. Stop at each bottom tens number while leading children to count by tens to 100 (10, 20, 30, and so on). Children flash 10 fingers for each new ten. Repeat three times.

The fourth time, point to the 120 Poster once and have the class continue the count by tens to 100 independently.

1 Teaching the Lesson

Activity 1

Modeling Ten-Structured Teens

20 MINUTES
Goal: Recognize the embedded ten in teen numbers.
Materials: Demonstration Secret Code Cards 1–10 (TRB M31–M40)
NCTM Standards: Number and Operations, Communication, Representation

▸ Elicit Prior Knowledge
Ask for Ideas Write the numbers 10 throu... children count aloud as you point to each ... know about these numbers.
- How are these numbers alike? They all ...
- What does the 1 mean? 1 ten

▸ Demonstrate a Ten and Ext...
Use the board. Introduce tens-and-ones ... the board, point out the tens place and ...
- The number 14 has 1 ten and 4 extra ... tens place? Do you see the 4 in the ...

Use the Demonstration Secret Code C... on the ledge of the board, starting w... Demonstration Secret Code Cards ha... Routines in Unit 3, this lesson provid... explore the cards in more depth.

Demonstrate how the Secret Code ... numbers by stacking two cards to ...
- I can make the number 14 with ... big 10-card. Which card shows ... we make 10? 4 I can put the 4 ... 10-card is like a secret code te...

Emphasize the hidden 10 by d... 14 you had written on the bo...

Teaching Note
What to Expect from Students A few children may already know something about place value. If so, invite them to explain why each teen number begins with a 1, but be sure to make this a quick discussion. Do not attempt a full explanation of place value at this time. Children will develop this understanding in the days to come. Right now, children only need to see that each teen number contains 1 ten.

Class Management
Looking Ahead Keep the Demonstration Secret Code Cards on the ledge of the board. They will be needed for the next activity. Children will also need their MathBoards or 10 × 10 Grids (TRB M46).

312 UNIT 4 LESSON 2

▸ A Story with Tens and Extra Ones WHOLE CLASS
Present a teen-grouping story problem to the class and have them solve it any way they can.
- Sara has a bag of 10 tennis balls and 6 extra balls. How many balls does she have altogether? 16 balls
- 16 means 1 ten and 6 extra ones. Let's write an equation to show this: 10 + 6 = 16.

Use the Demonstration Secret Code Cards to show 16. Again, point out the ten "hiding" inside the number.

Then point out the small number in the top corner of the 10- and 6-cards.
- What do you think those little numbers tell us about the number 16? 16 is made up of 10 and 6. Even when you can't see the 10, it is there.

Activity 2

Visualizing Teen Numbers

▸ Represent 15 WHOLE CLASS
Explain that children will be making some teen numbers on the 10 × 10 Grid. You can demonstrate by attaching an enlarged photocopy of the 10 × 10 Grid (TRB M46) to the board.
Have children begin by drawing 10 circles in the first column of the grid.
- Every teen number has a ten, so you will always need this group of ten.

Activity continued ▸

Teaching Note
Math Background Explain that our number system is based on the number 10—that is, we use a "base 10" number system. So 10 is an important number when we count and when we write numbers. Explain that this probably evolved because humans have 10 fingers and 10 toes.

30 MINUTES
Goal: Represent teen numbers.
Materials: MathBoard materials or 10 × 10 Grid (TRB M46), Demonstration Secret Code Cards 1–10 (TRB M31–M40)
NCTM Standards: Number and Operations, Representation

Ongoing Assessment
As children represent other teen numbers, observe whether they are able to show them in multiple ways: for example, by drawing circles on a grid to show a group of ten and some extra ones; or by writing an equation with the number 10.

Explore Teen Numbers 313

Classroom Success

understanding, and then practice, apply, and discuss what they know with skill and confidence.

Helping Community

A classroom in which everyone is both a teacher and a learner enhances mathematical understanding, competence, and confidence.

Student Leaders

Teachers facilitate students' growth by helping them learn to lead practice and discussion routines.

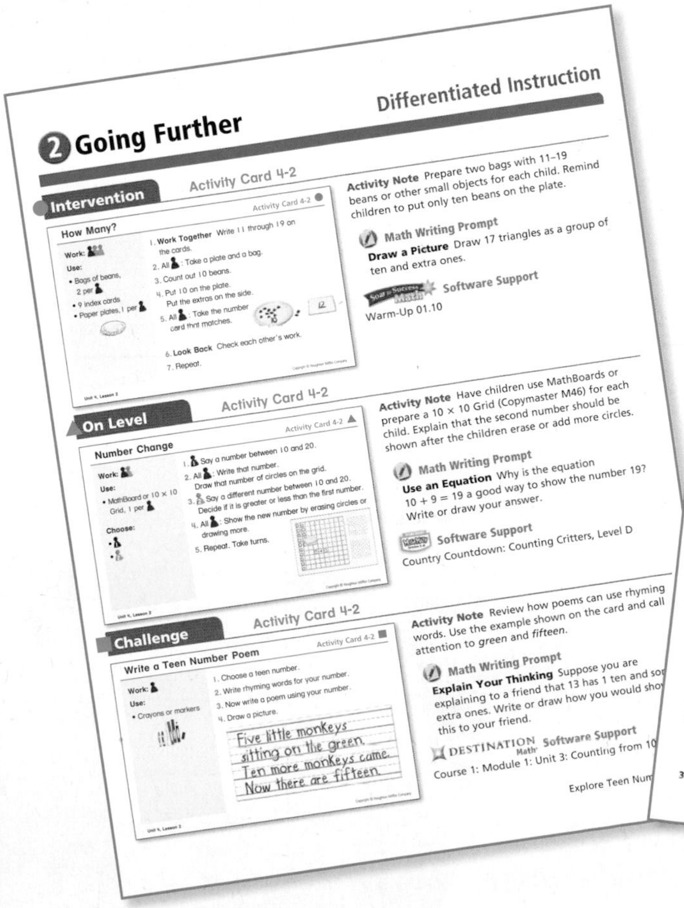

2 Going Further — Differentiated Instruction

Intervention — Activity Card 4-2

How Many?

Work: Use: • Bags of beans, 2 per • 9 index cards • Paper plates, 1 per

1. Work Together Write 11 through 19 on the cards.
2. All: Take a plate and a bag.
3. Count out 10 beans.
4. Put 10 on the plate. Put the extras on the side.
5. All: Take the number card that matches.
6. Look Back Check each other's work.
7. Repeat.

Activity Note Prepare two bags with 11–19 beans or other small objects for each child. Remind children to put only ten beans on the plate.

Math Writing Prompt

Draw a Picture Draw 17 triangles as a group of ten and extra ones.

Software Support

Warm-Up 01.10

On Level — Activity Card 4-2

Number Change

Work: Use: • MathBoard or 10 × 10 Grid, 1 per Choose:

1. Say a number between 10 and 20.
2. All: Write that number. Draw that number of circles on the grid.
3. Say a different number between 10 and 20. Decide if it is greater or less than the first number.
4. All: Show the new number by erasing circles or drawing more.
5. Repeat. Take turns.

Activity Note Have children use MathBoards or prepare a 10 × 10 Grid (Copymaster M46) for each child. Explain that the second number should be shown after the children erase or add more circles.

Math Writing Prompt

Use an Equation Why is the equation 10 + 9 = 19 a good way to show the number 19? Write or draw your answer.

Software Support

Country Countdown: Counting Critters, Level D

Challenge — Activity Card 4-2

Write a Teen Number Poem

Work: Use: • Crayons or markers

1. Choose a teen number.
2. Write rhyming words for your number.
3. Now write a poem using your number.
4. Draw a picture.

Five little monkeys sitting on the green. Ten more monkeys came. Now there are fifteen.

Activity Note Review how poems can use rhyming words. Use the example shown on the card and call attention to *green* and *fifteen*.

Math Writing Prompt

Explain Your Thinking Suppose you are explaining to a friend that 13 has 1 ten and so… explaining to a friend that 13 has 1 ten and so… extra ones. Write or draw how you would sho… this to your friend.

DESTINATION Math Software Support

Course 1: Module 1: Unit 3: Counting from 10…

Explore Teen Num…

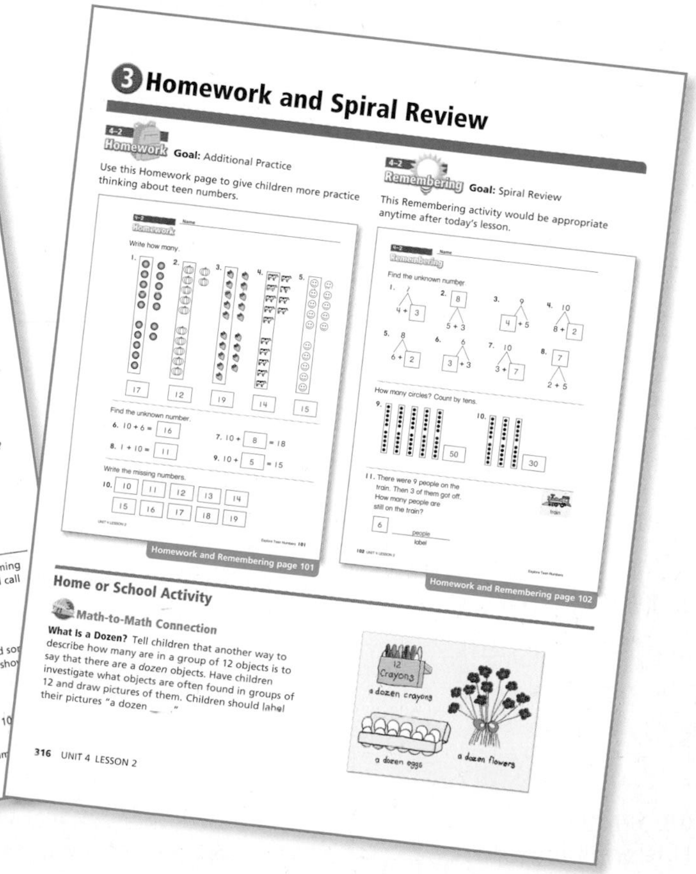

3 Homework and Spiral Review

4-2 Homework **Goal:** Additional Practice

Use this Homework page to give children more practice thinking about teen numbers.

Homework and Remembering page 101

4-2 Remembering **Goal:** Spiral Review

This Remembering activity would be appropriate anytime after today's lesson.

Homework and Remembering page 102

Home or School Activity

Math-to-Math Connection

What Is a Dozen? Tell children that another way to describe how many are in a group of 12 objects is to say that there are a *dozen* objects. Have children investigate what objects are often found in groups of 12 and draw pictures of them. Children should label their pictures "a dozen ___."

a dozen crayons

a dozen eggs

a dozen flowers

316 UNIT 4 LESSON 2

Differentiated for

Every ***Math Expressions*** lesson includes intervention, on level, and challenge differentiation to support classroom needs. Leveled Math Writing Prompts provide opportunities for in–depth thinking and analysis, and help prepare students for high-stakes tests.

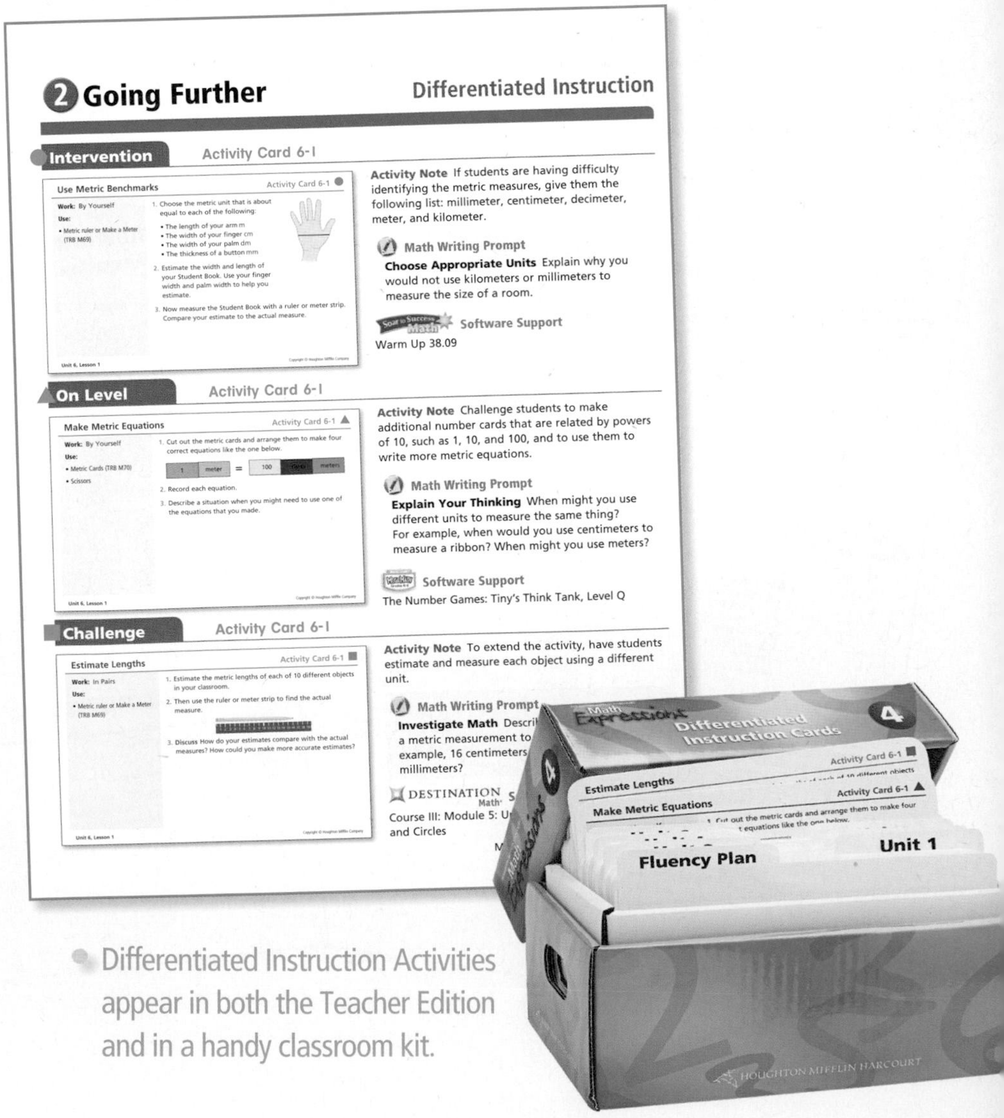

Differentiated Instruction Activities appear in both the Teacher Edition and in a handy classroom kit.

"Activities and strategies should be developed and incorporated into instructional materials to assist teachers in helping all students become proficient in mathematics."

- *Adding It Up: Helping Children Learn Mathematics*, National Research Council (2001), p. 421

All Learners

Support for English Language Learners is included in each lesson. A special Math Center Challenge Easel with activities, projects, and puzzlers helps the highest math achievers reach their potential.

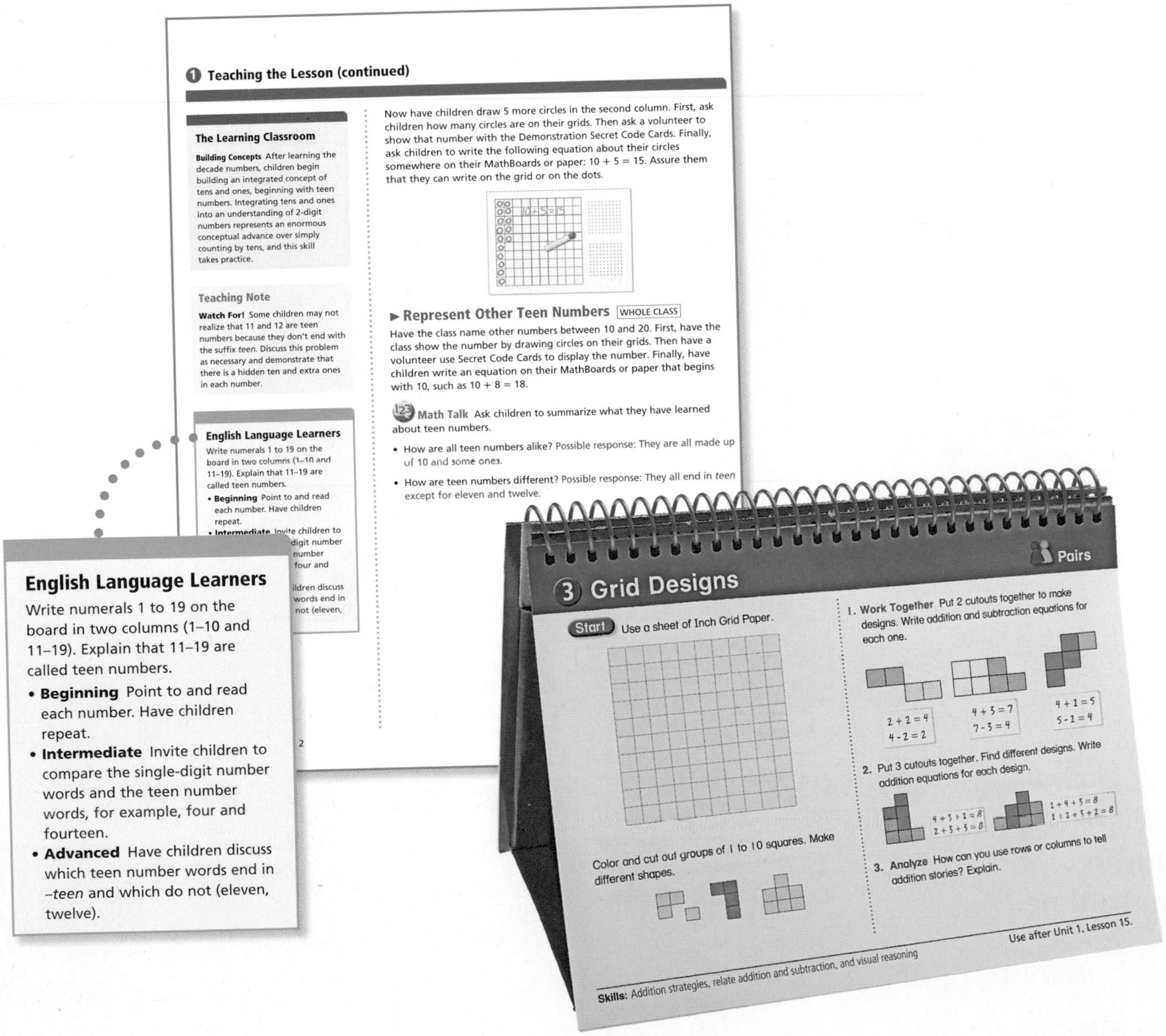

Validated Through Ten

For twenty-five years, Dr. Karen Fuson, Professor Emeritus of Education and Psychology at Northwestern University, researched effective methods of teaching and learning mathematics.

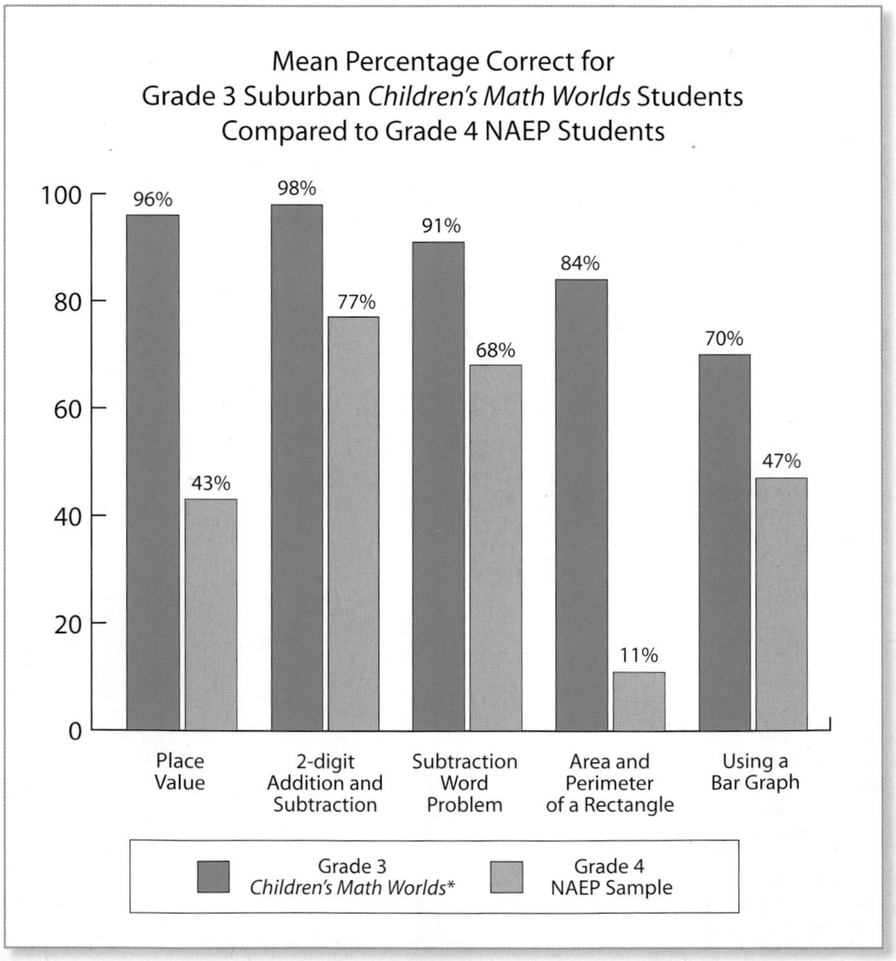

"I have many children who cheer when it's math time."
- Grade 2 Teacher

Years of Research

During the last ten years, with the support of the National Science Foundation for the Children's Math Worlds research Project, Dr. Fuson began development of what is now the ***Math Expressions*** curriculum in real classrooms across the country.

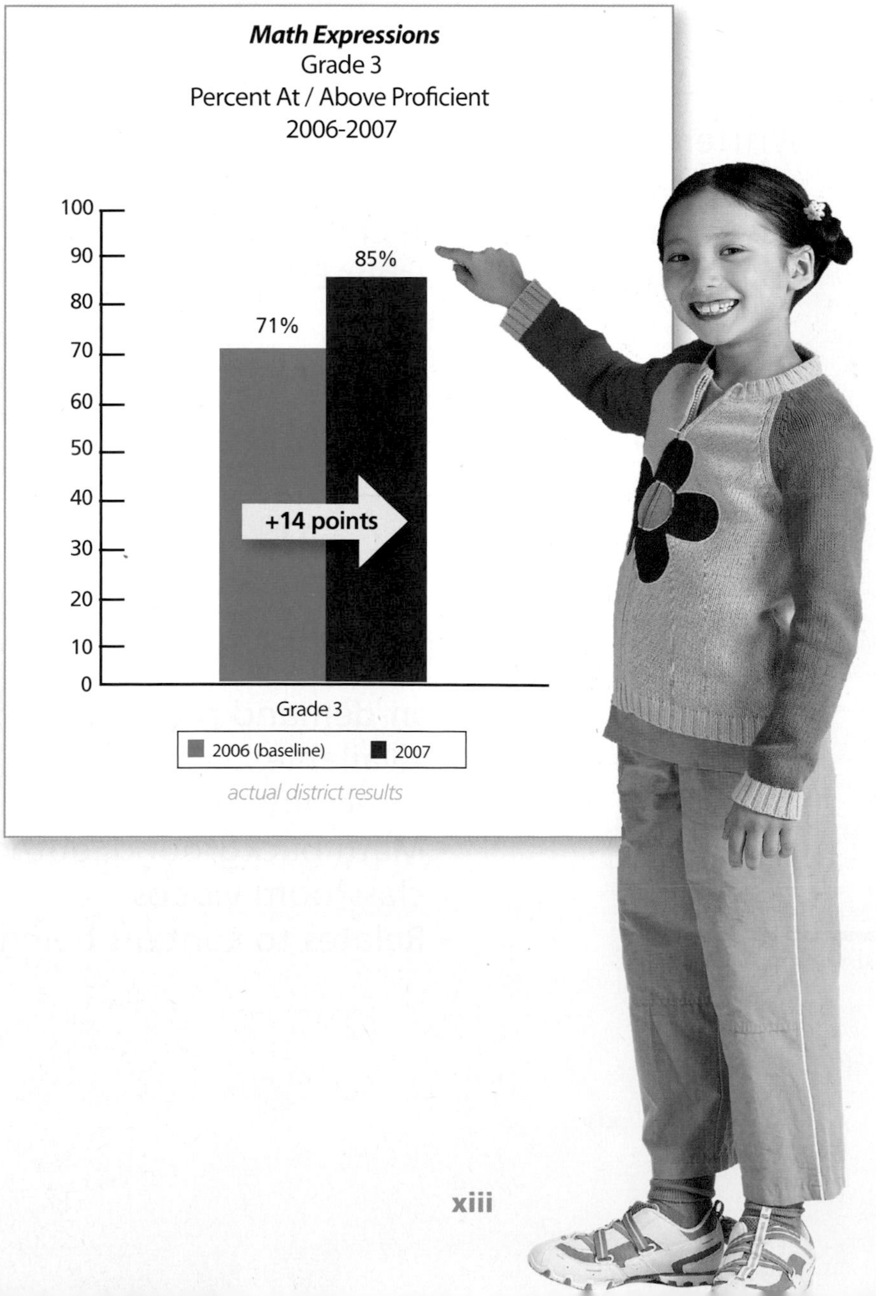

HOUGHTON MIFFLIN HARCOURT
Math Expressions

Powered by

Math Expressions is highly accessible by all teachers. To ensure the program gets off to the right start, our educational consultants are available to support districts implementing ***Math Expressions.*** Unique Teacher Edition support and professional development options are also provided.

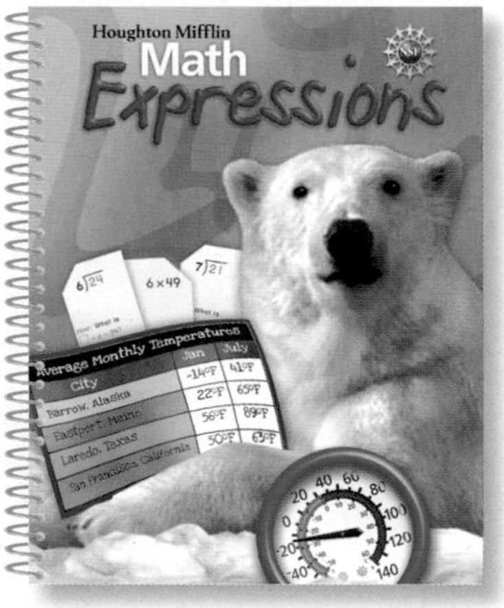

Teacher Edition

Written in a learn while teaching style, math background and learning in the classroom resources are embedded at point of use in the Teacher Edition.

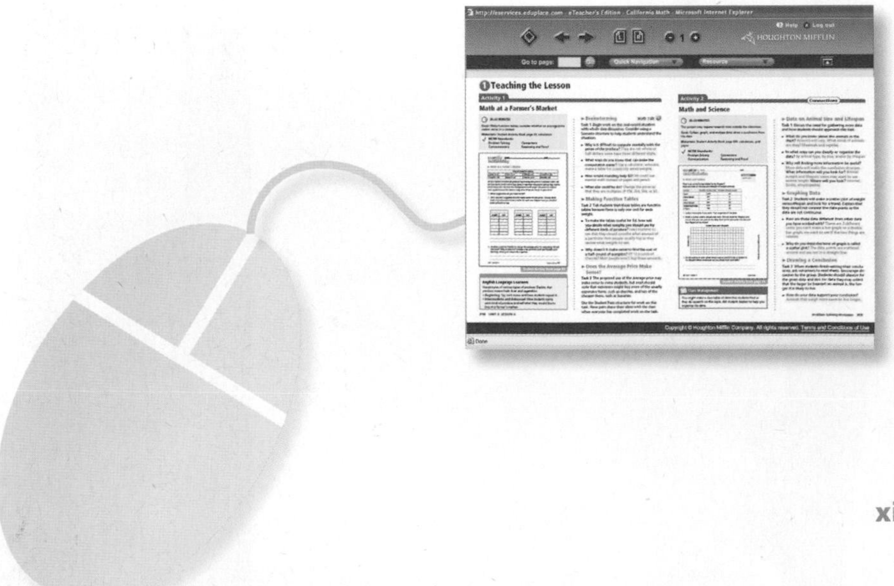

eTeacher Edition

Offers on-demand professional development

- Available 24/7
- Direct links in the eTE
- Math background, author talks, and classroom videos
- Relates to content being taught

Professional Development

Special in depth ***Math Expressions*** seminars are also available.

- **Administrator Institute**
  For administrators with school-based curriculum responsibilities.

- **Level I Institute**
  For teachers who are new to *Math Expressions*

- **Level II Institute**
  For teachers who have at least 6 months' experience teaching *Math Expressions*

Components

New Hardcover Version Grades 3–5

	K	1	2	3	4	5
Core Components						
Teacher Edition	•	•	•	•	•	•
Student Activity Book*	•	•	•	•	•	•
Homework and Remembering	•	•	•	•	•	•
Assessment Guide	•	•	•	•	•	•
Teacher's Resource Book	•	•	•	•	•	•
MathBoards		•	•	•	•	•
Ready-Made Classroom Resources						
Individual Student Manipulatives Kit	•	•	•	•	•	•
Materials and Manipulatives Kit	•	•	•	•	•	•
Custom Manipulatives Kit	•	•	•	•	•	•
Math Center Challenge Easel	•	•	•	•	•	•
Differentiated Instruction Activities Kit	•	•	•	•	•	•
Literature Library	•	•	•	•	•	•
Anno's Counting Book Big Book	•					
Technology						
eTeacher Edition	•	•	•	•	•	•
eStudent Activity Book	•	•	•	•	•	•
Lesson Planner CD-ROM	•	•	•	•	•	•
ExamView Ways to Assess	•	•	•	•	•	•
Houghton Mifflin Harcourt Online Assessment System	•	•	•	•	•	•
MegaMath	•	•	•	•	•	•
Destination Math®	•	•	•	•	•	•
Soar to Success Math		•	•	•	•	•
Education Place	•	•	•	•	•	•

*Grades K–5 available as consumable workbook; Grades 3–5 available as Hardcover book with companion Activity Workbook.

Materials and Manipulatives for Grade 2

The essential materials needed for teaching *Math Expressions* are provided in the Student Activity Book and/or can be made from copymasters in the Teacher's Resource Book. However, many teachers prefer to use the more sturdy materials from the materials and manipulatives kits. This allows the students to take home the paper materials (from the Student Activity Book) or the cardstock materials (made from the copymasters) to facilitate the connection between home and school.

Material or Manipulative in Grade 2	Pages in Student Activity Book	Copymasters in Teacher's Resource Book
Demonstration Secret Code Cards*		M7–M22
Secret Code Cards*	11–14	M3–M6
Count-On Cards*	27–28; 33–36	M25–M26; M29–M32
Make-a-Ten Cards*	39–42; 47–50	M35–M42
Math Mountain Cards	51–54	M43–M44
120 Poster*		M60–M61
Time Poster*		
Money Flip Chart*		Dime and Nickel Strips (M1), Dollar Bills (M67)
Pointer		
Math Expressions 25-cm rulers*		M47–M48
Math Expressions Inch Rulers*		M96
Play Coins (pennies, nickels, dimes, and quarters)	9–10; 271	M1, M73
Play Bills (1-dollar)	339	M67–M68
Two-Color Counters		
Connecting Cubes		
Number Cubes		
Base Ten Blocks		
Pattern Blocks		
3-D Shapes		M58
Sticky Board		
MathBoards		M51, M62–M63

* These materials were developed specifically for this program under the leadership of Dr. Karen C. Fuson, director of the Children's Math Worlds Research Project and author of *Math Expressions*.

Using Materials and Manipulatives for Each Unit

Material or Manipulative in Grade 2	Daily Routines	Unit													
		1	2	3	4	5	6	7	8	9	10	11	12	13	14
Demonstration Secret Code Cards	•	•				•				•		•			
Secret Code Cards		•		•		•				•		•			
Count-On Cards		•		•		•									
Make-a-Ten Cards						•		•		•					
Math Mountain Cards				•				•				•			
120 Poster	•					•				•				•	
Time Poster	•						•								
Money Flip Chart	•														
Pointer	•	•	•	•	•	•	•	•	•	•	•	•	•	•	•
Math Expressions 25-cm rulers		•	•		•	•			•	•	•		•		
Math Expressions Inch Rulers															•
Play Coins (pennies, nickels, dimes, and quarters)	•	•				•		•		•		•	•	•	•
Play Bills (1-dollar)												•			
Two-Color Counters		•		•		•			•					•	
Connecting Cubes		•		•				•			•			•	
Number Cubes		•				•		•		•				•	
Base Ten Blocks			•			•				•		•	•		
Pattern Blocks					•						•				
3-D Shapes													•		
Sticky Board	•									•		•			
MathBoards	•	•	•	•	•	•	•	•	•	•	•	•	•	•	•

All materials for each unit (including those not in the kits) are listed in the planning chart for that unit.

Introduction

History and Development

Math Expressions is a K–5 mathematics program, developed from the Children's Math Worlds (CMW) Research Project conducted by Dr. Karen Fuson, Professor Emeritus at Northwestern University. This project was funded in part by the National Science Foundation.

The Research Project

The project studied the ways children around the world understand mathematical concepts, approach problem solving, and learn to do computation; it included ten years of classroom research and incorporated the ideas of participating students and teachers into the developing curriculum.

The research focused on building conceptual supports that include special language, drawings, manipulatives, and classroom communication methods that facilitate mathematical competence.

Curriculum Design

Within the curriculum, a series of learning progressions reflect recent research regarding children's natural stages when mastering concepts such as addition, subtraction, multiplication, and problem solving. These learning stages help determine the order of concepts, the sequence of units, and the positioning of topics.

The curriculum is designed to help teachers apply the most effective conceptual supports so that each child progresses as rapidly as possible.

During the research, students showed increases in standardized test scores as well as in broader measures of student understanding. These results were found for a wide range of both urban and suburban students from a variety of socio-economic groups.

Philosophy

Math Expressions incorporates the best practices of both traditional and reform mathematics curricula. The program strikes a balance between promoting children's natural solution methods and introducing effective procedures.

Building on Children's Knowledge

Because research has demonstrated that premature instruction in formalized procedures can lead to mechanical, unthinking behavior, established procedures for solving problems are not introduced until students have developed a solid conceptual foundation. Children begin by using their own knowledge to solve problems and then are introduced to research-based accessible methods.

In order to promote children's natural solution methods, as well as to encourage students to become reflective and resourceful problem solvers, teachers need to develop a helping and explaining culture in their classrooms.

Student Interactions

Collaboration and peer helping deepen children's commitment to values such as responsibility and respect for others. *Math Expressions* offers opportunities for students to interact in pairs, small groups, whole-class activities, and special scenarios.

As students collaboratively investigate math situations, they develop communication skills, sharpen their mathematical reasoning, and enhance their social awareness. Integrating students' social and cultural worlds into their emerging math worlds helps them to find their own voices and to connect real-world experiences to math concepts.

Main Concept Streams

Math Expressions focuses on crucially important core concepts. These core topics are placed at grade levels that enable students to do well on standardized tests. The main related concept streams at all grade levels are number concepts and an algebraic approach to word problems.

Breaking apart numbers, or finding the embedded numbers, is a key concept running through the number concept units.

- Kindergartners and first-graders find the numbers embedded within single-digit numbers and find the tens and ones in multi-digit numbers.
- Second- and third-graders continue breaking apart multi-digit numbers into ones and groups of tens, hundreds, and thousands. This activity facilitates their understanding of multi-digit addition and subtraction as well as solving word problems.
- Second-, third-, and fourth-graders work on seeing the repeated groups within numbers, and this awareness helps them to master multiplication and division.
- Fourth- and fifth-graders approach fractions as sums of unit fractions using length models. This permits them to see and comprehend operations on fractions.

Students work with story problems early in kindergarten and continue throughout the other grades. They not only solve but also construct word problems. As a result, they become comfortable and flexible with mathematical language and can connect concepts and terminology with meaningful referents from their own lives. As part of this process, students learn to make math drawings that enable teachers to see student thinking and facilitate communication.

Concepts and skills in algebra, geometry, measurement, and graphing are woven in between these two main streams throughout the grades. In grades two through five, geometry and measurement mini-units follow each regular unit.

Program Features

Many special features and approaches contribute to the effectiveness of ***Math Expressions.***

Quick Practice

The opening 5 minutes of each math period are dedicated to activities (often student-led) that allow students to practice newly acquired knowledge. These *consolidating activities* help students to become faster and more accurate with the concepts. Occasionally, *leading activities* prepare the ground for new concepts before they are introduced. Quick Practice activities are repeated so that they become familiar routines that students can do quickly and confidently.

Drawn Models

Special manipulatives are used at key points. However, students move toward math drawings as rapidly as possible.

These drawn models help students relate to the math situation, facilitate students' explanations of the steps they took to solve the problem, and help listeners comprehend these explanations.

The drawings also give teachers insight into students' mathematical thinking, and leave a durable record of student work.

Language Development

Math Expressions offers a wealth of learning activities that directly support language development. In addition to verbalizing procedures and explanations, students are encouraged to write their own problems and describe their problem-solving strategies in writing as soon as they are able.

Homework Assignments

To help students achieve a high level of mathematical performance, students complete homework assignments every night. Families are expected to identify a homework helper to be responsible for monitoring the student's homework completion and to help if necessary.

Remembering Activities

Remembering Activities provide practice with the important concepts covered in all the units to date. They are ideal for spare classroom moments when students need a quick refresher of what they have learned so far. These pages are also valuable as extra homework pages that promote cumulative review as an ongoing synthesis of concepts.

Student Leaders

Student Leaders lead Quick Practice activities and can help as needed during the solving phase of Solve and Discuss. Such experiences build independence and confidence.

Math Talk

A significant part of the collaborative classroom culture is the frequent exchange of mathematical ideas and problem-solving strategies, or Math Talk. There are multiple benefits of Math Talk:

- Describing one's methods to another person can clarify one's own thinking as well as clarify the matter for others.
- Another person's approach can supply a new perspective, and frequent exposure to different approaches tends to engender flexible thinking.
- In the collaborative Math Talk classroom, students can ask for and receive help, and errors can be identified, discussed, and corrected.
- Student math drawings accompany early explanations in all domains, so that all students can understand and participate in the discussion.
- Math Talk permits teachers to assess students' understanding on an ongoing basis. It encourages students to develop their language skills, both in math and in everyday English.
- Math Talk enables students to become active helpers and questioners, creating student-to-student talk that stimulates engagement and community.

The key supports for Math Talk are the various participant structures, or ways of organizing class members as they interact. The teacher always guides the activity to help students to work both as a community and also independently. Descriptions of the most common participant structures follow.

Math Talk Participant Structures

Solve and Discuss (Solve, Explain, Question, and Justify) at the Board

The teacher selects 4 to 5 students (or as many as space allows) to go to the classroom board and solve a problem, using any method they choose. Their classmates work on the same problem at their desks. Then the teacher picks 2 or 3 students to explain their methods. Students at their desks are encouraged to ask questions and to assist their classmates in understanding.

Benefits: Board work reveals multiple methods of solving a problem, making comparisons possible and communicating to students that different methods are acceptable. The teacher can select methods to highlight in subsequent discussions. Spontaneous helping occurs frequently by students working next to each other at the board. Time is used efficiently because everyone in the class is working. In addition, errors can be identified in a supportive way and corrected and understood by students.

Student Pairs

Two students work together to solve a problem, to explain a solution method to each other, to role play within a mathematical situation (for example, buying and selling), to play a math game, or to help a partner having difficulties. They are called helping pairs when more advanced students are matched with students who are struggling. Pairs may be organized formally, or they may occur spontaneously as help is needed. Initially, it is useful to model pair activities, contrasting effective and ineffective helping.

Benefits: Pair work supports students in learning from each other, particularly in applying and practicing concepts introduced

Math Talk (continued)

Student Pairs (continued)

applying and practicing concepts introduced in whole-class discussion. Helping pairs often foster learning by both students as the helper strives to adopt the perspective of the novice. Helping almost always enables the helper to understand more deeply.

Whole-Class Practice and Student Leaders

This structure can be either teacher-led or student-led. When students lead it, it is usually at the consolidation stage, when children understand the concept and are beginning to achieve speed and automaticity. It is an excellent way for students to work together and learn from each other.

Benefits: Whole-class practice lets the less advanced students benefit from the knowledge of the more advanced students without having to ask for help directly. It also provides the teacher with a quick and easy means of assessing the progress of the class as a whole.

Scenarios

The main purpose of scenarios is to demonstrate mathematical relationships in a visual and memorable way. In scenario-based activities, a group of students is called to the front of the classroom to act out a particular situation. Scenarios are useful when a new concept is being introduced for the first time. They are especially valuable for demonstrating the physical reality that underlies such math concepts as embedded numbers (break-aparts) and regrouping.

Benefits: Because of its active and dramatic nature, the scenario structure often fosters a sense of intense involvement among children. In addition, scenarios create meaningful contexts in which students can reason about numbers and relate math to their everyday lives.

Step-by-Step at the Board

This is a variation of the Solve and Discuss structure. Again, several children go to the board to solve a problem. This time, however, a different student performs each step of the problem, describing the step before everyone does it. Everyone else at the board and at their desks carries out that step. This approach is particularly useful in learning multi-digit addition, subtraction, multiplication, and division. It assists the least-advanced students the most, providing them with accessible, systematic methods.

Benefits: This structure is especially effective when students are having trouble solving certain kinds of problems. The step-by-step structure allows students to grasp a method more easily than doing the whole method at once. It also helps students learn to verbalize their methods more clearly, as they can focus on describing just their own step.

Small Groups

Unstructured groups can form spontaneously if physical arrangements allow (for example, desks arranged in groups of four or children working at tables). Spontaneous helping between and among students as they work on problems individually can be encouraged.

For more structured projects, assign students to specific groups. It is usually a good idea to include a range of students and to have a strong reader in each group. Explain the problem or project and guide the groups as necessary. When students have finished, call a pair from each group to present and explain the results of their work or have the entire group present the results, with each member explaining one part of the solution or project. Having lower-performing students present first allows them to contribute, while higher-performing students expand on their efforts and give the fuller presentation.

Benefits: Students learn different strategies from each other for approaching a problem or task. They are invested in their classmates' learning because the presentation will be on behalf of the whole group.

Daily Routines for Volume 2

See pages xvii and xviii for information about materials for Daily Routines.

The Money Routine

(Use throughout the Year.)

Materials: 120 Poster, pointer, Money Flip Chart, sticky notes, MathBoard materials, Demonstration Secret Code Cards

The Money Routine reinforces fundamental money and multi-digit number concepts. It provides visual practice with these concepts that are built incrementally from day to day. This routine helps children learn to say 2- and 3-digit numbers, become skilled at counting, and helps them link money values with numeric values. This routine should be done every day while working on the numbered units and may be continued during the mini units as well. You should introduce the routine and lead it for 2 or 3 days and then help Student Leaders take over. Have more advanced and socially confident children lead first to act as models. Using four Student Leaders will help the routine move quickly.

Each day, a new total is created by adding a number from 5–9 to the total from the previous day. (The blue box below shows how the number to be added is determined.) The new total is then represented in various ways.

Plan for Using the Money Routine Throughout the Year

Cycle A (about 20 days)

- Add 5, 6, or 7 (randomly chosen by a student volunteer or the teacher) each day until 120 is reached.
- Use pennies and dollars only.

Cycle B (about 30 days)

- Start again. Add 7, 8, or 9 each day until 100 is reached.
- Then add 5, 6, 7, 8, or 9 each day until 240 is reached.
- Use pennies, dimes, and dollars.

Cycle C

- Start again. Add 5, 6, 7, 8, or 9 each day until the end of the year.
- Use pennies, nickels, dimes, and dollars.

Using the 120 Poster

Student Leader 1 draws new circles on the 120 Poster to represent the number being added and, if there is a new ten, erases the circles on that ten and makes a bracket on the bottom of the column.

For example, if the previous total was 25 and 7 is being added:

- I am adding 7. So, 25 plus 7 is *(circling the numbers as saying them)* 26, 27, 28, 29, 30, 31, 32. I have a new ten, so I am going to erase all of the circles on these twenties and mark the ten at the bottom. *(Saying as writing this)* 32 = 30 + 2.

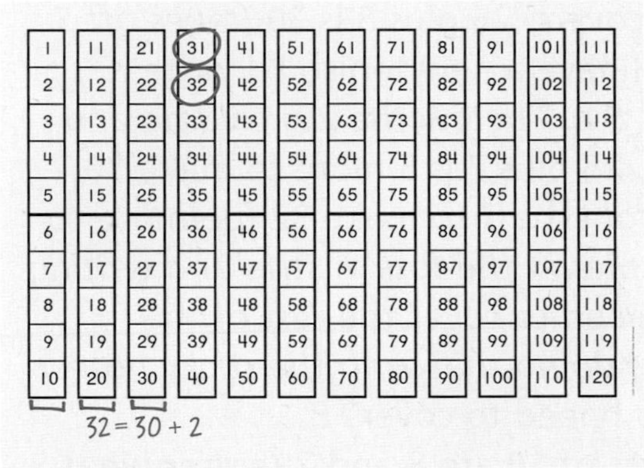

120 Poster

(Numbers 121–240 are on the back of the 120 Poster. This part of the routine is discontinued when the total *exceeds* 240.)

Count to the New Total Student Leader 1 then leads the class to count to the new total. If the total is ≤ 20, the class counts by ones. The Student Leader points to the numbers on the 120 Poster as the class counts. After 20, the children count by tens and ones. For example, to count to 32, children say 10, 20, 30, *freeze*, 31, 32. Children flash ten fingers all at once for each ten and show one finger for each one they count after that. Saying *freeze* helps children shift from counting by tens to counting by ones. You can stop when all children no longer need the signal.

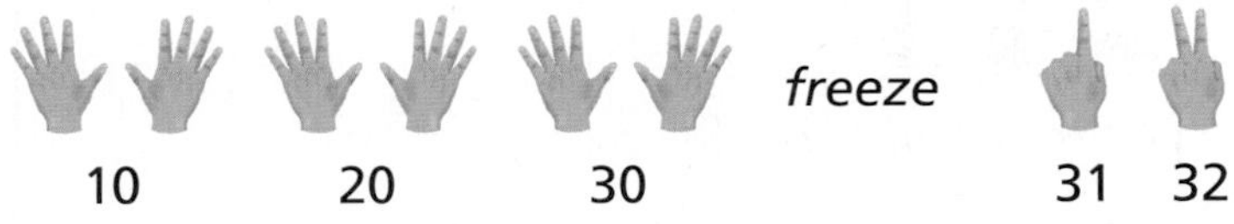

Daily Routines for Volume 2 (Continued)

As the class counts, the Student Leader moves the pointer down each column as 10, 20, 30 are said and then points to each single number as 31, 32 are said.

Using the Money Flip Chart
Student Leader 2 directs the next part of the routine. On the first day, cover the 10 pennies in the first column using sticky notes. *(Keep all other columns covered with the flaps.)* Each day new pennies are uncovered to make the new total. When a new ten is made, another column of pennies and sticky notes is used.

- We have 25 pennies. I'm adding 7 pennies. Will I make a ten? Yes!! So, I'll flip over the covers on the next column so we can see the pennies. *(Flipping the covers)* 25 plus 5 is 30 *(takes off 5 sticky notes).* I have a new ten so I'll write it below *(erases the 5 below the 20s column and writes 10).* So, 25 plus 7 is 5 more to make 30 and 2 more from the 7 to make 32 *(pointing to the top 2 pennies in the fourth strip and writing + 2 below.)* I need to cover the rest of the pennies *(starts doing that with the sticky notes).* How many do I need to cover? 8
- So, my partners of 10 are 8 and 2 *(erases what was there and writes 8 + 2 to the right of the sticky note rectangles, pointing to the 8 empty rectangles and the 2 sticky notes).*
- Let's read the tens and ones. *(Pointing to the 10s written below the penny strips)* 10 plus 10 plus 10 plus 2. That's 3 tens and 2 ones equals 32. *(Writing 30 + 2 in vertical form in the upper right corner of the board)* 30 plus 2 is 32.

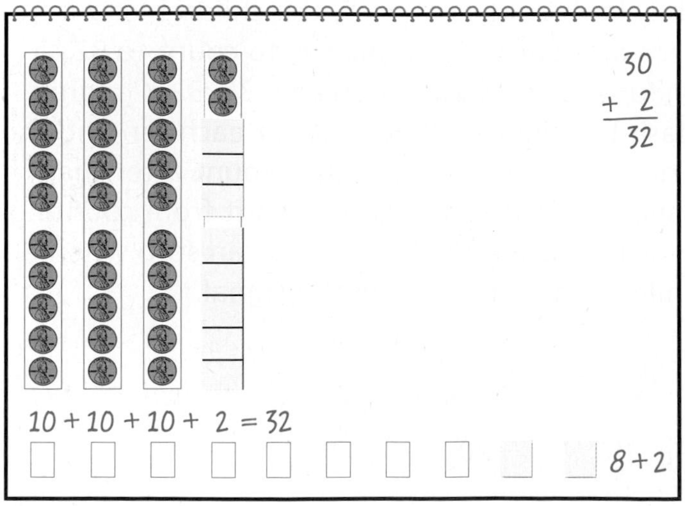

For numbers ≥ 100, the dollars are flipped to show dollar bills to the left of the Coin Strips. In Cycles B and C (see blue box), Dime Strips are flipped over to replace 10 pennies or 2 nickels and Nickel Strips are flipped over to replace 5 pennies.

Using the Number Path
Student Leader 3 leads the next part of the routine. Use a student MathBoard that can stay on display all day. Each day add the new number of circles on the Number Path. When a new ten is made, draw a line through all ten circles to show a 10-stick. (This part of the routine is discontinued when the total exceeds 100.)

Show the Addition Two Ways In the middle of the MathBoard, show in vertical form the addition of the previous day's total and today's new number resulting in today's new total. Then show the new total by adding sticks (Quick Tens) and circles to the drawing from the previous day and then redrawing the number if necessary just with Quick Tens. Be sure to show the 5-groups. (See page 307.)

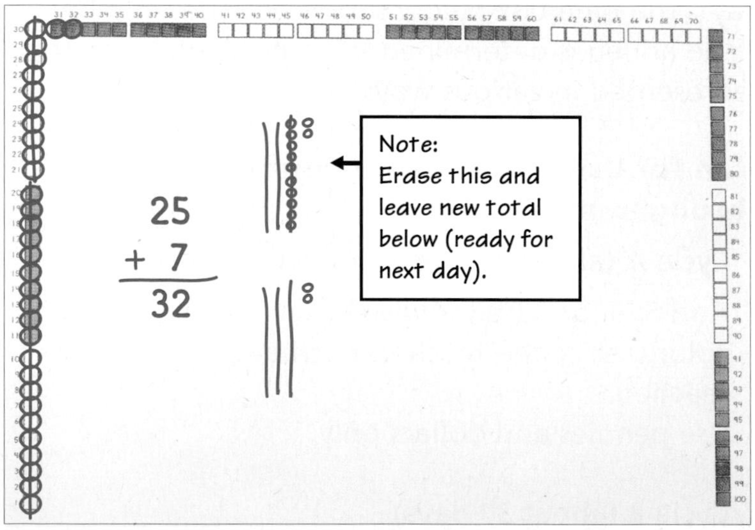

For numbers over 100, Quick Hundreds are also used; for example

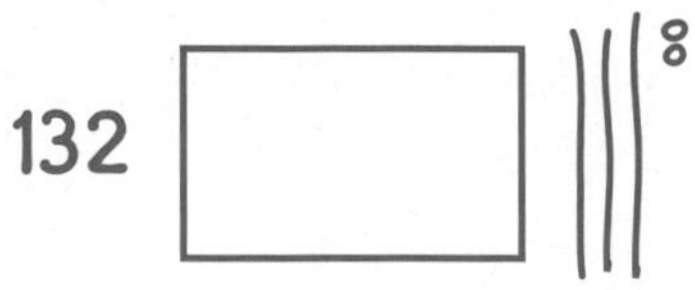

Using Secret Code Cards

Student Leader 4 shows the new total using the Demonstration Secret Code Cards.

- 30 *(shows 30 card)* plus 2 *(shows 2 card).*
- *(Class responds)* 30 plus 2 makes *(puts 2 card over the 0)* 32.

Teaching Note

Some teachers choose to drop the Money Routine during Units 9 and 11 in order to focus more on the coin counting routines for those units. If you do this, you can return to this routine again during Unit 13.

Telling Time

(Use with Units 7 and 8.)

Materials: Demonstration clock or Time Poster and dry erase markers, pointer

This routine reinforces time concepts, the topic of Unit 6. This routine is intended to achieve the following goals for children: tell time to the hour, half hour, quarter hour, and 5 minutes; translate digital time to the analog clock; write the time shown on an analog clock in digital format; and link daily activities to times of the day.

Five Student Leaders lead this routine if you do all of the parts. Part 1 (Name the Hands) can be dropped after children have mastered the concepts. Telling time to 5-minute intervals can be added after the first week or so.

Name the Hands

Write 5, 10, 15 and so on around the outside of the clock on the Time Poster as shown. The class says the minute numbers as Student Leader 1 points to these 5-multiples.

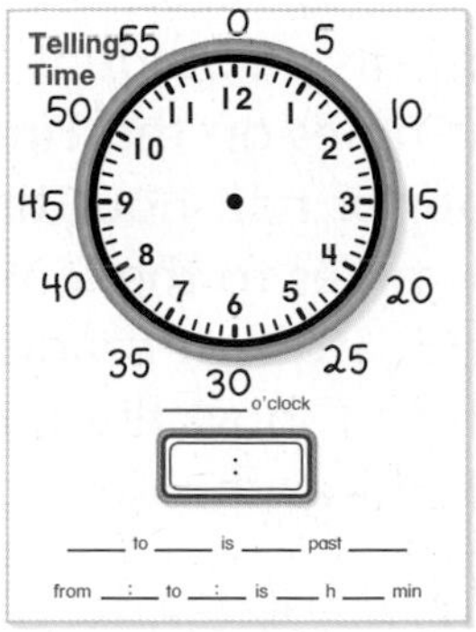

The leader then asks the class to name the clock hands. "What hand is the short hand?" The class responds: "The short hand points to the hours." "What hand is the long hand?" The class responds: "The long hand points to minutes." Drop this part of the routine when all (or nearly all) children have mastered these concepts.

Telling Time on the Time Poster

Student Leader 2 draws hands to show an hour time (for example, 3:00) on the Time Poster. At a signal, the class says the time.

The leader then changes the placement of both the hour and minute hands to show the next half-hour (for example, 3:30). As the leader points (using a pointer) to the 5-minute marks, the class counts by 5s from the hour and to the new time: 5, 10, 15, 20, 25, 30—3:30! The leader sweeps the pointer from 3:00 to 3:30 and says: "The minute hand moved from the o'clock to the half-past time (or the half-hour time)."

The leader then moves the minute hand back 15 minutes and moves the hour hand back a little bit to indicate 15 minutes past the hour. The leader then points to the 5-minute marks as the class counts by 5s from the hour to the new time: "5, 10, 15—3:15! 15 minutes past 3:00!" or "A quarter past 3!"

The leader then moves the hands ahead to show 45 minutes past the hour (for example, 3:45). The leader then points to the 5-minute marks as the class counts by 5s from the hour to the new time: "5, 10, 15, 20, 25, 30, 35, 40, 45—3:45! When you think the class is ready, they can also state the time as "15 minutes before 4!" and as "A quarter to 4!"

Student Leader 3 calls on Student Leaders 4 and 5 to show different times on the Time Poster. These should not be hour or half-hour times. Rather, they should show times to the 5 minutes such as 12:10, 3:40, or 7:35. Student Leader 4 draws hands on the Time Poster to show the time while Student Leader 5 writes the time on the digital clock on the poster.

Student Leader 5 then asks one or two classmates what they were doing at that hour, for example, "What were you doing at 7:35 this morning? Did you see the sun?" Later in the unit the leader can also ask classmates what they will be doing at some hour on a future day, for example, "What will you be doing at 7:35 P.M. two days from now?"

Quarters and Other Coins

(Use with Units 9 and 10.)

Materials: Sticky board or classroom board and tape), Coin Cards (from Student Activity Book page 253 or TRB M77), two sets of Quarter Squares (made from Student Activity Book pages 255 and 256 or TRB M73–M74), real or play coins (pennies, nickels, dimes, quarters), pointer, MathBoard materials

This special money routine is a follow up to Lesson 1 in Unit 9 in which children make quarter amounts with real or paper coins. Keep doing the ongoing Money Routine began in Unit 1 as you do this routine. This routine is intended to help children learn to make combinations of pennies, nickels, and dimes equal to 25¢ (one quarter); count coins to 25¢ (one quarter) and say the coins; count by 25¢ (quarters) to 200¢ (two dollars); make 3-digit money amounts (for example, 372¢ and $3.72) with pennies, nickels, dimes, and quarters; and count up to 3-digit money amounts.

The routine requires 4 Student Leaders.

Making and Counting Coins that Make a Quarter

Student Leader 1 holds the Quarter Squares so the class sees only the quarter side. The leader asks a volunteer to give a combination of coins that equal 25¢ (one quarter): "Tell me some coins that make 25¢." The volunteer can give any possible combination of pennies, nickels, and dimes that make the amount. The 12 possible combinations are on the back of the Quarter Squares. The leader then puts the card that shows that combination on the sticky board and repeats this process with two more volunteers.

The leader points to the coins on each card while leading the class in counting up to 25 cents and then in saying the coins on each card, for example:

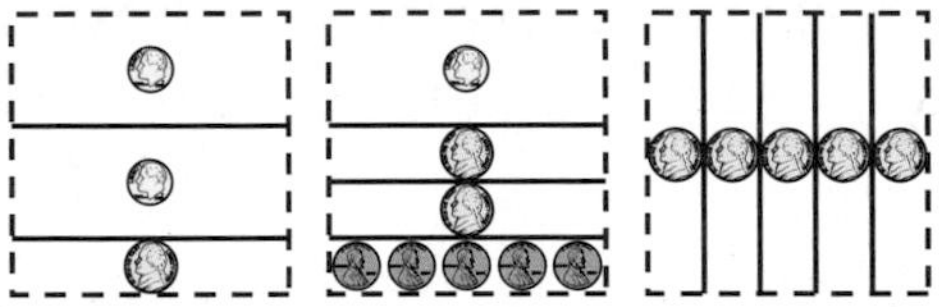

Card 1: "10¢, 20¢, 25¢. 1 quarter equals 2 dimes and 1 nickel."

Card 2: "10¢, 15¢, 20¢, 21¢, 22¢, 23¢, 24¢, 25¢. 1 quarter equals 1 dime, 2 nickels, and 5 pennies."

Card 3: "5¢, 10¢, 15¢, 20¢, 25¢. 1 quarter equals 5 nickels."

Try to have children name all 12 combinations at least once over the course of the unit.

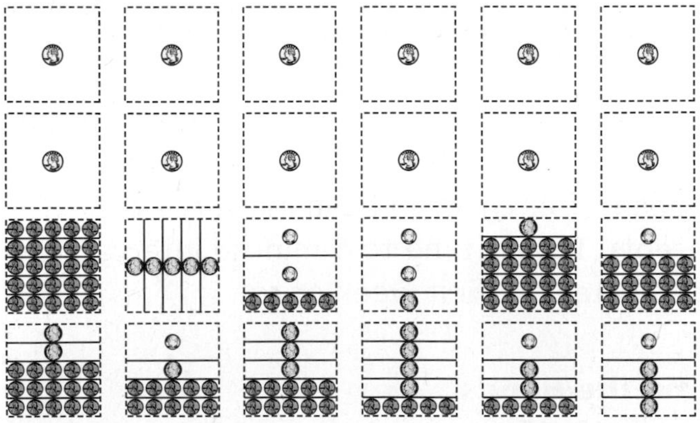

The parts of the routine described above can be dropped when all (or nearly all) children have mastered them. After they are dropped, the role of Student Leader 1 changes. While the class is doing the parts of the routine described below, Student Leader 1 can write a quarter chain on the classroom board or a MathBoard, trying to include all combinations. After doing the rest of the routine, the class checks if the quarter chain is correct. For example:

1Q = 25¢ = 25P = 2D + 1N = 2D + 5P = 5N = 1N + 20P = 4N + 5P = 1D + 15P = 1D + 1N + 10P = 3N + 10P = 1D + 2N + 5P = 1D + 3N = 2N +15P

The leader forgot: 2N + 15P

Counting to 200¢ by 25¢
Student Leader 2 then leads the class in counting to 200¢ by 25¢. The class should use the "cents" word when counting. At 100¢ they say: "100¢. 100¢ is one dollar." They do the same at 200¢: "200¢. 200¢ is two dollars." They should count to 200¢ by 25¢ three times.

This portion of the routine can be dropped when all (or nearly all) children have mastered it.

Making and Counting Dollars and Cents: 3-Digit Numbers as Dollars and Cents
While children are doing the earlier parts of the routine, Student Leader 3 makes a 3-digit money amount on the sticky board with the Coin Cards (quarters, dimes, nickels, and pennies) and writes the amount on a student MathBoard hung near the sticky board. Example: 372¢ ($3.72.) After the rest of the routine is done, he/she leads the class in counting the Coin Cards up to the amount written on the MathBoard.

Student Leader 4 makes the same amount differently with play (or real) coins and then leads the class in counting this amount.

Making Change and Counting Coins
(Use with Units 11 and 12.)

Materials: Sticky board or classroom board and tape, pointer, dollar bills, real or play coins or Coin Cards (from Student Activity Book page 253 or TRB M77)

In this routine children count up to make change, combine coins and dollars to show change from $5.00, and combine coins and dollars to make money amounts more than $1.00 and less than $10.00.

This routine requires 4 Student Leaders.

Making Change from $5.00
Before the routine begins, write an amount between $1.00 and $4.99 on the classroom board. This is the amount spent. If desired, during this routine, the class or a pair of students can make up a word problem and write it on the classroom board for the amount.

Amount I spent = $3.72.

Student Leader 1 makes the change with dollars and coins (or Coin Cards) on the sticky board leading the class to count up as the change is made.

"372 plus 8 is 380, plus 20 is 400 plus 100 is 500. 8 plus 20 plus 100 is 128."

or

"$3.72 plus 8 cents is $3.80, plus 20 cents is $4.00 plus $1 is $5.00. 8 cents plus 20 cents plus $1 is $1.28."

Student Leader 2 draws a Math Mountain on the classroom board to show the total, the amount spent, and the change.

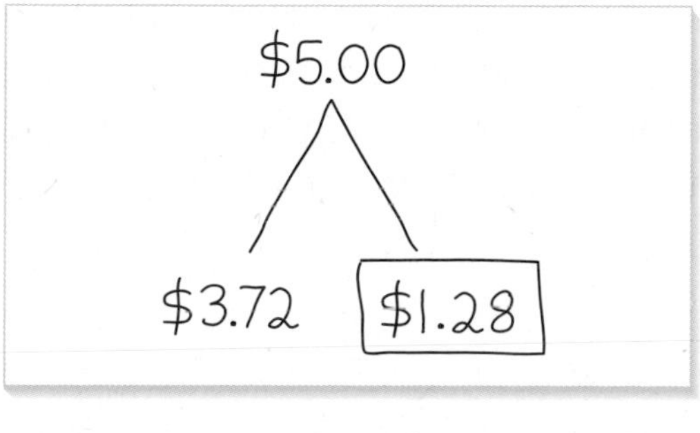

Combining Coins and Counting Money

As Student Leaders 1 and 2 and the class do the first part of this routine, Student Leaders 3 and 4 work together to make money amounts more than $1.00 and less than $10.00 with different combinations of coins. They display the amounts on the sticky board.

When the class has finished the first part of the routine, Student Leaders 3 and 4 use a pointer and lead the class counting the coins. They should start the counting with the larger coins (or dollars), then count the next larger coins, and so on until they reach the total.

Example for $2.06

Dollars and coins on sticky board:

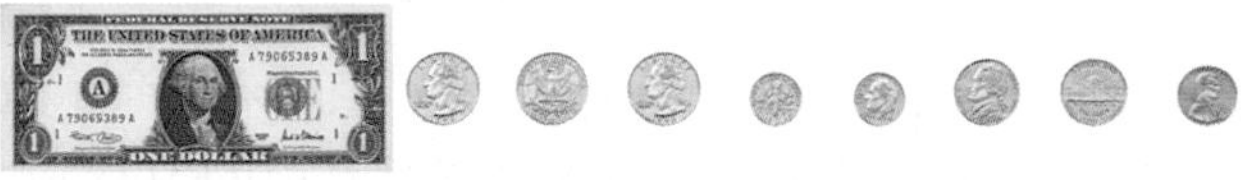

The class says: $1.00 $1.25 $1.50 $1.75 $1.85 $1.95 $2.00 $2.05 $2.06

2s, 3s, and 4s Count-bys

(Use with Units 13 and 14.)

Materials: 120 Poster, MathBoard materials, pointer

In this routine, children practice their count-bys and draw arrays to show products. This routine helps them understand simple multiplication as equal groups and as arrays and learn count-bys for 2s, 3s, and 4s.

It is important that all children have an opportunity to lead this routine or go to the classroom board. On each day, the routine requires 8 Student Leaders. The first three days focus on groups of 2 (for example, 5 × 2, 4 × 2), the second four days focus on groups of 3, and the last four days focus on groups of 4.

Draw Arrays

Three pairs of students (Student Leaders 1–6) draw arrays on the classroom board for three specified multiplication problems (see blue box).

Plan for Groups and Arrays

Day 1: 6 × 2; 3 × 2; 5 × 2
Day 2: 8 × 2; 7 × 2; 4 × 2
Day 3: 9 × 2; 2 × 2; 10 × 2

Day 4: 4 × 3; 6 × 3; 2 × 3
Day 5: 10 × 3; 5 × 3; 8 × 3
Day 6: 9 × 3; 7 × 3; 3 × 3
Day 7: 4 × 3; 7 × 3; 3 × 3

Day 8: 10 × 4; 7× 4; 3 × 4
Day 9: 2 × 4; 5 × 4; 8 × 4
Day 10: 9 × 4; 6 × 4; 4 × 4
Day 11: 10 × 4; 7 × 4; 3 × 4

One member of each pair draws a horizontal array and the other draws a vertical array. The class should see that two arrays for a problem have the same number of dots because you can just turn one array to fit on top of the other array.

Example for 6 × 2

2 × 6 6 × 2

Draw Groups on the 120 Poster

While student pairs are drawing arrays, Student Leader 7 circles groups of 2 (or 3 or 4) on the 120 Poster. The leader then leads the class in counting by 2s (or 3s or 4s) up to the product of the largest array on the classroom board. All students raise one finger with each count to show how many groups they have counted so far.

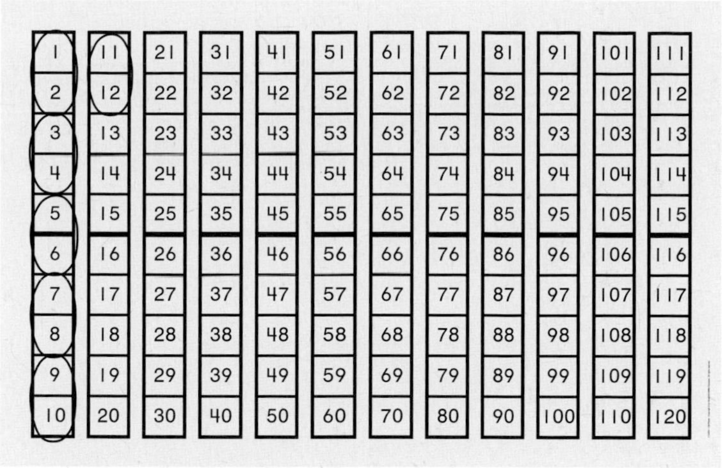

Draw Groups on the Number Path

Student Leader 8 does the routine described above, using circles drawn on the Number Path rather than the 120 Poster.

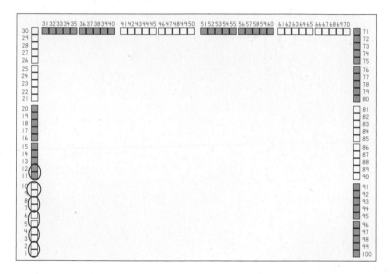

Student Leaders 7 and 8 should draw their groups while the other Student Leaders are drawing their arrays. Then this whole routine can move quite quickly.

Volume 1 Contents

Unit 1 Understanding Addition and Subtraction

Big Idea Add and Subtract Using 10

Big Idea Relate Addition and Subtraction

Big Idea Understand Equations and Inequalities

MINI UNIT

Unit 2 Measurement and Shapes

Big Idea Linear Measurement of 2-D Shapes

Unit 3 Solving Story Problems

Unit 5 Addition to 200

Big Idea Money, Sequences, and 100 Matrix

MINI UNIT

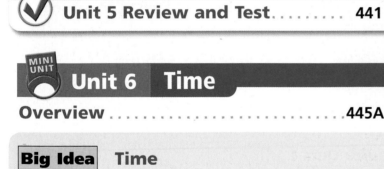

Unit 6 Time

Big Idea Time

Big Idea Bar Graphs, Circle Graphs, and Word Problems

Volume 2 Contents

Big Idea Multi-Digit Subtraction Strategies

Big Idea Relating Addition and Subtraction Strategies

Unit 11 3-Digit Addition and Subtraction

MINI UNIT Unit 12 Metric Measurement and 3-D Shapes

Unit 13 Multiplication and Fractions

Big Idea Symmetry and Fractions

Big Idea The Nature of Chance

MINI UNIT

Unit 14 Non-Standard and Standard Units of Measure

Extension Lessons

Pacing Guide

Unit 1 is designed as a review of topics from Grade 1 but includes skills and understandings for Grade 2. Units 11 and 13 build strong conceptual development and skill fluency at a level often seen in the curricula of other countries that rank high in math performance. In the first year many classes may not cover all of the content of the later unit(s). But as more children experience *Math Expressions* in the previous grade(s) and teachers become familiar with *Math Expressions,* movement through the earlier units is more rapid and classes are able to do more of the later material in greater depth.

Some lessons in every unit, but especially the geometry and measurement mini-units, can be omitted if they do not focus on important state or district goals.

Be sure to do the Quick Practice activities with Student Leaders that begin each lesson, as they provide needed practice on core grade-level skills as well as support the growth of children as they lead these activities. Also be sure to do the Daily Routines on pages xxiii-xxvii to provide crucial grade-level practice for fluency with counting, place value, money, time, and other concepts.

	First Year		Later Years	
Unit	Pacing Suggestions	Days	Pacing Suggestions	Days
1	The first 2 lessons are introductory. Unit 1 focuses on numerical strategies, understanding partners, and teen numbers as tens and ones.	30	Many ideas are review for children who had Math Expressions in Grade 1. Move as quickly as you can while eliciting children's ideas and building community.	20
2	Be sure that children understand these ideas.	6	These are important Grade 2 geometry concepts.	6
3	These are core Grade 2 topics for mastery, except for two-step problems, which will continue in later units.	22	Unit 3 will go faster if children had Grade 1 *Math Expressions* story problem experiences.	14
4	These are important Grade 2 geometry concepts.	5	These are important Grade 2 geometry concepts.	4
5	Spend extra time for understanding these core concepts and use Math Talk with children on a regular basis.	29	Unit 5 will go faster if children had Grade 1 *Math Expressions* place-value experiences.	21
6	This introduction to time needs to be followed by the practice in the Daily Routines for mastery to occur.	6	This introduction to time needs to be followed by the practice in the Daily Routines for mastery to occur.	6
7	Teach only important district and state goals. Comparison language is important but difficult.	18	Teach only important district and state goals. Comparison language is important but difficult.	15
8	Teach only important district and state goals.	2	Teach only important district and state goals.	3
9	These are core Grade 2 topics for mastery. Be sure that children are able to explain ungrouping and the Ungroup First method.	25	Continue to focus on the core Grade 2 mastery topics of explaining ungrouping and the Ungroup First method.	20
10	Teach only important district and state goals.	4	Teach only important district and state goals.	4
11	Extend place-value ideas to 1,000 and money ideas through $10.00.	8	Finishing this unit will prepare children to move rapidly through Units 1 and 2 in Grade 3.	24
12	Teach only important district and state goals.	2	Teach only important district and state goals.	5
13	Lessons 1–5 will introduce multiplication.	2	Explore multiplication to 5 and unit fractions.	10
14	Teach only important district and state goals.	1	Teach only important district and state goals.	2
All Units	**Total Days**	**160**	**Total Days**	**154**

Correlation to NCTM Curriculum Focal Points and Connections for Grade 2

Grade 2 Curriculum Focal Points

1 *Number and Operations:* Developing an understanding of the base-ten numeration system and place-value concepts

Children develop an understanding of the base-ten numeration system and place-value concepts (at least to 1000). Their understanding of base-ten numeration includes ideas of counting in units and multiples of hundreds, tens, and ones, as well as a grasp of number relationships, which they demonstrate in a variety of ways, including comparing and ordering numbers. They understand multidigit numbers in terms of place value, recognizing that place-value notation is a shorthand for the sums of multiples of powers of 10 (e.g., 853 as 8 hundreds + 5 tens + 3 ones).

1.1 count in units	U1 L4, L9, L10; U5 L17; U11 L1, L3
1.2 count in multiples of hundreds, tens, and ones	U5 L1; U11 L1, L3
1.3 compare and order numbers	U1 L21; U3 L1; U7 L2–4, L13
1.4 understand multidigit numbers in terms of place value	U1 L5, L11, L12; U5 L1–3, L5, L12; U11 L2, L4
1.5 recognize that place-value notation is a shorthand for the sums of multiples of powers of 10 (e.g., 853 as 8 hundreds + 5 tens + 3 ones)	U5 L1–3; U11 L2

2 *Number and Operations* and *Algebra:* Developing quick recall of addition facts and related subtraction facts and fluency with multidigit addition and subtraction

Children use their understanding of addition to develop quick recall of basic addition facts and related subtraction facts. They solve arithmetic problems by applying their understanding of models of addition and subtraction (such as combining or separating sets or using number lines), relationships and properties of number (such as place value), and properties of addition (commutativity and associativity). Children develop, discuss, and use efficient, accurate, and generalizable methods to add and subtract multidigit whole numbers. They select and apply appropriate methods to estimate sums and differences or calculate them mentally, depending on the context and numbers involved. They develop fluency with efficient procedures, including standard algorithms, for adding and subtracting whole numbers, understand why the procedures work (on the basis of place value and properties of operations), and use them to solve problems.

2.1 use understanding of addition to develop quick recall of basic addition facts and related subtraction facts	U1 L2, L3, L6–8, L13–19; U3 L1–13
2.2 solve problems by combining and separating sets	U1 L1, L2; U3 L3, L4, L8–14
2.3 solve problems by using a number line	U1 L17
2.4 solve problems by using place value	U5 L1–6, L9–12; U9 L3–6; U11 L2, L4, L5
2.5 solve problems by using properties of addition	U1 L3, L6, L22
2.6 use efficient, accurate, and generalizable methods to add multidigit whole numbers	U5 L5, L6, L9, L10, L12–16; U11 L9–12, L19, L21
2.7 use efficient, accurate, and generalizable methods to subtract multidigit whole numbers	U9 L3–13, L15; U11 L14–19, L21; U13 L7
2.8 select and apply appropriate methods to estimate sums and differences	U5 L11, L18; U9 L6, L11; U11 L4, L22

Grade 2 Curriculum Focal Points (cont.)	
2.9 calculate sums and differences mentally	U1 L13, L16, L20; U5 L4, L11, L12; U9 L12
2.10 develop fluency with efficient procedures including standard algorithms for adding whole numbers	U5 L5, L6, L9, L10, L12–15; U9 L14, L16; U11 L9, L10, L12, L13, L19, L21
2.11 develop fluency with efficient procedures including standard algorithms for subtracting whole numbers	U9 L3–16; U11 L14–19, L21; U13 L7

3 *Measurement:* Developing an understanding of linear measurement and facility in measuring lengths
Children develop an understanding of the meaning and processes of measurement, including such underlying concepts as partitioning (the mental activity of slicing the length of an object into equal-sized units) and transitivity (e.g., if object A is longer than object B and object B is longer than object C, then object A is longer than object C). They understand linear measure as an iteration of units and use rulers and other measurement tools with that understanding. They understand the need for equal-length units, the use of standard units of measure (centimeter and inch), and the inverse relationship between the size of a unit and the number of units used in a particular measurement (i.e., children recognize that the smaller the unit, the more iterations they need to cover a given length).

3.1 understand the concept of partitioning	U2 L1; U12, L1; U14, L1
3.2 understand the concept of transitivity	U12 L3
3.3 understand linear measure as an iteration of units	U2 L1; U12 L1; U14, L1
3.4 use rulers and other linear measurement tools	U2 L1, L3, L4; U4 L1; U5 L14; U8 L2; U12 L1–3; U14 L2
3.5 understand the need for equal-length units	U2 L1; U14 L1
3.6 use standard units of measure (centimeter and inch)	U2 L1, L3, L4; U5 L14; U8 L2; U12 L1–3, L5; U14 L2
3.7 understand inverse relationship between the size of a unit and the number of units used in a particular measurement	U12 L2; U14 L2

Connections to the Focal Points

4 *Number and Operations:* Children use place value and properties of operations to create equivalent representations of given numbers (such as 35 represented by 35 ones, 3 tens and 5 ones, or 2 tens and 15 ones) and to write, compare, and order multidigit numbers. They use these ideas to compose and decompose multidigit numbers. Children add and subtract to solve a variety of problems, including applications involving measurement, geometry, and data, as well as nonroutine problems. In preparation for grade 3, they solve problems involving multiplicative situations, developing initial understandings of multiplication as repeated addition.

4.1 use place value and properties of operations to create equivalent representations	U5 L1–4, L9, L15; U11 L1, L2, L4
4.2 use place value to write multidigit numbers	U5 L1–3; U11 L2
4.3 use place value to order and compare multidigit numbers	Daily Routines, Vol. 1, pp. xxv–xxvi; U1 L21; U3 L1–3
4.4 compose and decompose multidigit numbers	U5 L5, L9, L18; U9 L3–5, L12
4.5 add and subtract to solve measurement problems	U2 L3, L4; U5 L14; U10 L5; U12 L1, L3, L4
4.6 add and subtract to solve geometry problems	U2 L3, L4; U5 L14; U10 L5

Correlation to NCTM Curriculum Focal Points and Connections for Grade 2 (cont.)

Connections to the Focal Points (cont.)	
4.7 add and subtract to solve data problems	U7 L1–5, L7–14; U11 L11; U13 L13
4.8 add and subtract to solve nonroutine problems	U3 L1, L4; U5 L20; U11 L5–7; L13, L14
4.9 solve problems involving multiplicative situations	U13 L1–5
4.10 understand multiplication as repeated addition	U13 L1, L12
5 *Geometry* and *Measurement:* Children estimate, measure, and compute lengths as they solve problems involving data, space, and movement through space. By composing and decomposing two-dimensional shapes (intentionally substituting arrangements of smaller shapes for larger shapes or substituting larger shapes for many smaller shapes), they use geometric knowledge and spatial reasoning to develop foundations for understanding area, fractions, and proportions.	
5.1 estimate length to solve problems	U8 L2; U12 L1, L2; U14 L2
5.2 measure length to solve problems	U2 L1, L3, L4; U5 L14
5.3 compute length to solve problems	U2 L1, L3, L4; U5 L14
5.4 compose and decompose two-dimensional shapes	U2 L2; U4 L2, L3; U8 L1–3; U10 L1–3; U11 L23
6 *Algebra:* Children use number patterns to extend their knowledge of properties of numbers and operations. For example, when skip counting, they build foundations for understanding multiples and factors.	
6.1 use number patterns, including skip counting	U1 L9, L23; U5 L17, L19; U6 L2, L3, L5; U7 L15; U9 L1, L2; U11 L3; U13 L1–5; Extension L2

NCTM Standards and Expectations Correlation for Grade 2

Number and Operations Standard	
Understand numbers, ways of representing numbers, relationships among numbers, and number systems	
• count with understanding and recognize "how many" in sets of objects;	Unit 1, Lesson 2; Unit 5, Lesson 8; Lesson 16; Unit 6, Lesson 4; Unit 9, Lesson 1–Lesson 2; Unit 11, Lesson 1–Lesson 5; Lesson 7; Unit 13, Lesson 1–Lesson 4, Extension Lesson 2
• use multiple models to develop initial understandings of place value and the base-ten number system;	Unit 5, Lesson 1–Lesson 6; Unit 11, Lesson 1–Lesson 2; Lesson 5, Extension Lesson 1
• develop understanding of the relative position and magnitude of whole numbers and of ordinal and cardinal numbers and their connections;	Unit 1, Lesson 21; Unit 3, Lesson 14; Unit 6, Lesson 5; Unit 7, Lesson 3
• develop a sense of whole numbers and represent and use them in flexible ways, including relating, composing, and decomposing numbers;	Unit 1, Lesson 2; Lesson 4–Lesson 8; Unit 5, Lesson 1–Lesson 7; Lesson 15; Lesson 19; Unit 9, Lesson 1–Lesson 2; Unit 11, Lesson 2; Lesson 6; Lesson 24
• connect number words and numerals to the quantities they represent, using various physical models and representations;	Unit 1, Lesson 2; Lesson 4–Lesson 8; Unit 5, Lesson 1–Lesson 7; Lesson 15; Unit 7, Lesson 7; Unit 9, Lesson 1–Lesson 2; Unit 11, Lesson 1–Lesson 3
• understand and represent commonly used fractions, such as $\frac{1}{4}$, $\frac{1}{3}$, and $\frac{1}{2}$.	Unit 13, Lesson 9–Lesson 10; Lesson 13
Understand meanings of operations and how they relate to one another	
• understand various meanings of addition and subtraction of whole numbers and the relationship between the two operations;	Unit 1, Lesson 10; Lesson 14–Lesson 20; Unit 9, Lesson 3; Lesson 11–Lesson 14; Unit 11, Lesson 8; Lesson 14; Lesson 19
• understand the effects of adding and subtracting whole numbers;	Unit 1, Lesson 10; Lesson 14–Lesson 20; Unit 3, Lesson 1–Lesson 13; Unit 5, Lesson 9–Lesson 13; Unit 9, Lesson 3–Lesson 4; Lesson 7–Lesson 8; Lesson 11; Unit 11, Lesson 9, Lesson 19
• understand situations that entail multiplication and division, such as equal groupings of objects and sharing equally.	Unit 13, Lesson 1–Lesson 7

NCTM Standards and Expectations Correlation for Grade 2 (cont.)

Number and Operations Standard (cont.)	
Compute fluently and make reasonable estimates	
• develop and use strategies for whole-number computations, with a focus on addition and subtraction;	Unit 1, Lesson 2; Lesson 9–Lesson 17; Lesson 19–Lesson 20; Lesson 22; Unit 3, Lesson 1–Lesson 13; Unit 5, Lesson 2; Lesson 4–Lesson 6; Lesson 9–Lesson 14; Lesson 16–Lesson 17; Lesson 19; Unit 7, Lesson 14; Unit 9, Lesson 3–Lesson 16; Unit 11, Lesson 5; Lesson 8–Lesson 10
• develop fluency with basic number combinations for addition and subtraction;	Unit 1, Lesson 2; Lesson 9–Lesson 17; Lesson 19–Lesson 20; Lesson 22; Unit 3, Lesson 1–Lesson 13; Unit 5, Lesson 13; Unit 7, Lesson 1–Lesson 5; Lesson 9–Lesson 13; Unit 9, Lesson 4–Lesson 5; Lesson 12; Unit 11, Lesson 10; Lesson 14
• use a variety of methods and tools to compute, including objects, mental computation, estimation, paper and pencil, and calculators.	Unit 1, Lesson 2; Lesson 9–Lesson 17; Lesson 19–Lesson 20; Lesson 22; Unit 3, Lesson 1–Lesson 13; Unit 5, Lesson 2, Lesson 4–Lesson 6; Lesson 9–Lesson 14; Lesson 16–Lesson 17; Lesson 19; Unit 7, Lesson 14; Unit 9, Lesson 3–Lesson 16; Unit 11, Lesson 5; Lesson 8–Lesson 22
Algebra Standard	
Understand patterns, relations, and functions	
• sort, classify, and order objects by size, number, and other properties;	Unit 3, Lesson 4; Unit 7, Lesson 10; Unit 10, Lesson 1
• recognize, describe, and extend patterns such as sequences of sounds and shapes or simple numeric patterns and translate from one representation to another;	Unit 1, Lesson 6; Lesson 23; Unit 5, Lesson 17; Unit 6, Lesson 5; Unit 11, Lesson 24
• analyze how both repeating and growing patterns are generated.	Unit 1, Lesson 6; Lesson 23; Unit 5, Lesson 17
Represent and analyze mathematical situations and structures using algebraic symbols	
• illustrate general principles and properties of operations, such as commutativity, using specific numbers;	Unit 1, Lesson 6; Lesson 20; Lesson 22
• use concrete, pictorial, and verbal representations to develop an understanding of invented and conventional symbolic notations.	Unit 1, Lesson 18; Unit 5, Lesson 1–Lesson 6; Unit 7, Lesson 1–Lesson 2; Unit 11, Lesson 14
Use mathematical models to represent and understand quantitative relationships	
• model situations that involve the addition and subtraction of whole numbers, using objects, pictures, and symbols.	Unit 1, Lesson 6–Lesson 11; Lesson 18; Lesson 20; Unit 5, Lesson 15; Unit 11, Lesson 14

Algebra Standard (cont.)	
Analyze change in various contexts	
• describe qualitative change, such as a student's growing taller;	Unit 6, Lesson 5; Extension Lesson 3
• describe quantitative change, such as a student's growing two inches in one year.	Unit 6, Lesson 5; Unit 11, Lesson 11; Lesson 13–Lesson 14; Extension Lesson 3
Geometry Standard	
Analyze characteristics and properties of two- and three-dimensional geometric shapes and develop mathematical arguments about geometric relationships	
• recognize, name, build, draw, compare, and sort two- and three-dimensional shapes;	Unit 2, Lesson 2–Lesson 4; Unit 4, Lesson 1–Lesson 3; Unit 8, Lesson 1; Unit 10, Lesson 1–Lesson 3; Unit 12, Lesson 5–Lesson 6
• describe attributes and parts of two- and three-dimensional shapes;	Unit 2, Lesson 2–Lesson 4; Unit 4, Lesson 1–Lesson 3; Unit 8, Lesson 1; Unit 10, Lesson 1–Lesson 3; Unit 12, Lesson 5–Lesson 6
• investigate and predict the results of putting together and taking apart two- and three-dimensional shapes.	Unit 7, Lesson 16; Unit 8, Lesson 1–Lesson 3; Unit 10, Lesson 2; Unit 12, Lesson 6, Extension Lesson 4
Specify locations and describe spatial relationships using coordinate geometry and other representational systems	
• describe, name, and interpret relative positions in space and apply ideas about relative position;	Unit 5, Lesson 20; Unit 7, Lesson 12
• describe, name, and interpret direction and distance in navigating space and apply ideas about direction and distance;	Unit 7, Lesson 12
• find and name locations with simple relationships such as "near to" and in coordinate systems such as maps.	Unit 7, Lesson 12
Apply transformations and use symmetry to analyze mathematical situations	
• recognize and apply slides, flips, and turns;	Unit 10, Lesson 1; Lesson 3–Lesson 4
• recognize and create shapes that have symmetry.	Unit 8, Lesson 3; Unit 10, Lesson 3; Unit 13, Lesson 8

NCTM Standards and Expectations Correlation for Grade 2 (cont.)

Geometry Standard (cont.)	
Use visualization, spatial reasoning, and geometric modeling to solve problems	
• create mental images of geometric shapes using spatial memory and spatial visualization;	Unit 4, Lesson 2; Unit 8, Lesson 2; Unit 12, Lesson 5
• recognize and represent shapes from different perspectives;	Unit 12, Lesson 5–Lesson 6
• relate ideas in geometry to ideas in number and measurement;	Unit 2, Lesson 3–Lesson 4; Unit 4, Lesson 1; Unit 5, Lesson 13; Unit 11, Lesson 24; Unit 12, Lesson 5
• recognize geometric shapes and structures in the environment and specify their location.	Unit 2, Lesson 3; Unit 4, Lesson 2; Unit 12, Lesson 5–Lesson 6

Measurement Standard	
Understand measurable attributes of objects and the units, systems, and processes of measurement	
• recognize the attributes of length, volume, weight, area, and time;	Unit 2, Lesson 2–Lesson 4; Unit 4, Lesson 2; Unit 5, Lesson 14; Unit 6, Lesson 1–Lesson 5; Unit 10, Lesson 1; Lesson 5; Unit 12, Lesson 1–Lesson 3; Lesson 5; Unit 14, Lesson 1–Lesson 3
• compare and order objects according to these attributes;	Unit 8, Lesson 1; Unit 10, Lesson 1; Lesson 5; Unit 14, Lesson 1; Lesson 3
• understand how to measure using non-standard and standard units;	Unit 2, Lesson 1–Lesson 4; Unit 10, Lesson 5; Unit 12, Lesson 1–Lesson 3; Unit 14, Lesson 1–Lesson 2
• select an appropriate unit and tool for the attribute being measured.	Unit 6, Lesson 4; Unit 10, Lesson 5; Unit 14, Lesson 1–Lesson 3
Apply appropriate techniques, tools, and formulas to determine measurements	
• measure with multiple copies of units of the same size, such as paper clips laid end to end;	Unit 2, Lesson 1; Unit 10, Lesson 5; Unit 12, Lesson 1–Lesson 2; Unit 14, Lesson 1
• use repetition of a single unit to measure something larger than the unit, for instance, measuring the length of a room with a single meterstick;	Unit 2, Lesson 1; Unit 14, Lesson 1–Lesson 2
• use tools to measure;	Unit 2, Lesson 1–Lesson 4; Unit 4, Lesson 1; Unit 6, Lesson 1; Lesson 2; Lesson 5; Unit 8, Lesson 2; Unit 10, Lesson 5; Unit 12, Lesson 1–Lesson 2; Unit 14, Lesson 1–Lesson 3
• develop common referents for measures to make comparisons and estimates.	Unit 6, Lesson 4; Unit 10, Lesson 5; Unit 12, Lesson 1–Lesson 4; Unit 11, Lesson 1–Lesson 3

Data Analysis and Probability Standard	
Formulate questions that can be addressed with data and collect, organize, and display relevant data to answer them	
• pose questions and gather data about themselves and their surroundings;	Unit 7, Lesson 1–Lesson 2; Lesson 5–Lesson 6; Lesson 8; Lesson 16; Unit 12, Lesson 1–Lesson 2
• sort and classify objects according to their attributes and organize data about the objects;	Unit 3, Lesson 4; Unit 7, Lesson 10; Unit 10, Lesson 1; Extension Lesson 3
• represent data using concrete objects, pictures, and graphs.	Unit 3, Lesson 4; Unit 7, Lesson 1–Lesson 11; Lesson 13; Lesson 15–Lesson 16
Select and use appropriate statistical methods to analyze data	
• describe parts of the data and the set of data as a whole to determine what the data show.	Unit 1, Lesson 23; Unit 3, Lesson 4; Unit 7, Lesson 1–Lesson 5; Lesson 7–Lesson 15; Unit 13, Lesson 6; Lesson 13
Develop and evaluate inferences and predictions that are based on data	
• discuss events related to students' experiences as likely or unlikely.	Unit 13, Lesson 11–Lesson 13
Problem Solving Standard	
• build new mathematical knowledge through problem solving;	Unit 1, Lesson 1; Lesson 3; Lesson 23; Unit 3, Lesson 3; Lesson 7–Lesson 10; Lesson 14; Unit 5, Lesson 9–Lesson 10; Unit 7, Lesson 9; Lesson 14; Unit 9, Lesson 4; Lesson 12; Unit 11, Lesson 6; Unit 7, Lesson 1–Lesson 5, Lesson 12–Lesson 13
• solve problems that arise in mathematics and in other contexts;	Unit 1, Lesson 1–Lesson 3; Lesson 15; Unit 3, Lesson 1–Lesson 10; Unit 5, Lesson 9–Lesson 10; Unit 6, Lesson 4; Unit 4, Lesson 4; Lesson 9–Lesson 10; Lesson 14; Lesson 16; Unit 9, Lesson 4; Lesson 11–Lesson 17; Unit 11, Lesson 6–Lesson 8; Lesson 14; Lesson 24; Unit 13, Lesson 1–Lesson 5; Lesson 12–Lesson 13
• apply and adapt a variety of appropriate strategies to solve problems;	Unit 1, Lesson 1–Lesson 3; Lesson 15; Unit 3, Lesson 1–Lesson 10; Unit 5, Lesson 9–Lesson 10; Unit 7, Lesson 4; Lesson 9–Lesson 10; Lesson 14; Unit 9, Lesson 4; Lesson 11–Lesson 17; Unit 11, Lesson 6–Lesson 8; Lesson 14; Unit 13, Lesson 1–Lesson 5; Lesson 12
• monitor and reflect on the process of mathematical problem solving.	Unit 1, Lesson 1–Lesson 3; Lesson 15; Unit 3, Lesson 1–Lesson 10; Lesson 14; Unit 5, Lesson 9–Lesson 10; Lesson 20; Unit 7, Lesson 4; Lesson 9–Lesson 10; Lesson 14; Unit 9, Lesson 4; Lesson 11–Lesson 16; Unit 11, Lesson 6–Lesson 8; Lesson 14; Unit 13, Lesson 1–Lesson 5; Lesson 12

NCTM Standards and Expectations Correlation for Grade 2 (cont.)

Reasoning and Proof Standard	
• recognize reasoning and proof as fundamental aspects of mathematics;	Unit 1, Lesson 1–Lesson 4; Lesson 8; Lesson 12; Unit 3, Lesson 1–Lesson 12; Unit 5, Lesson 2–Lesson 6; Lesson 9–Lesson 14; Lesson 19; Unit 9, Lesson 5–Lesson 6; Lesson 9; Lesson 16; Unit 11, Lesson 1–Lesson 2; Lesson 4–Lesson 5; Lesson 9–Lesson 10; Lesson 14–Lesson 17; Lesson 19–Lesson 22; Unit 13, Lesson 6; Lesson 8; Lesson 13
• make and investigate mathematical conjectures;	Unit 5, Lesson 9; Unit 7, Lesson 16; Unit 9, Lesson 17; Unit 10, Lesson 1; Unit 11, Lesson 24; Unit 13, Lesson 11
• develop and evaluate mathematical arguments and proofs;	Unit 3, Lesson 4, Unit 5, Lesson 20; Unit 13, Lesson 13
• select and use various types of reasoning and methods of proof.	Unit 1, Lesson 23; Unit 3, Lesson 4; Lesson 14; Unit 9, Lesson 17
Communication Standard	
• communicate their mathematical thinking coherently and clearly to peers, teachers, and others;	Unit 1, Lesson 1–Lesson 3; Lesson 22; Unit 3, Lesson 2–Lesson 7; Lesson 10–Lesson 14; Unit 4, Lesson 1; Lesson 3; Unit 5, Lesson 1–Lesson 2; Lesson 4; Lesson 6; Lesson 9; Lesson 15; Lesson 19; Unit 7, Lesson 1–Lesson 7; Lesson 16; Unit 8, Lesson 1–Lesson 3; Unit 9, Lesson 4; Lesson 6–Lesson 10; Lesson 13; Unit 11, Lesson 10; Lesson 12–Lesson 13; Lesson 19–Lesson 22; Lesson 24; Unit 12, Lesson 3; Unit 13, Lesson 6–Lesson 13
• analyze and evaluate the mathematical thinking and strategies of others;	Unit 1, Lesson 1–Lesson 3; Lesson 12–Lesson 13; Lesson 18; Lesson 22; Unit 3, Lesson 2–Lesson 3; Lesson 5-Lesson 7; Lesson 10–Lesson 13; Unit 5, Lesson 1–Lesson 2; Lesson 6; Lesson 9; Lesson 19; Unit 7, Lesson 1–Lesson 7; Unit 8, Lesson 2; Unit 9, Lesson 4; Lesson 6–Lesson 10; Unit 11, Lesson 10; Lesson 13; Lesson 19–Lesson 22; Unit 13, Lesson 8–Lesson 9; Lesson 11–Lesson 12
• use the language of mathematics to express mathematical ideas precisely.	Unit 1, Lesson 1–Lesson 3; Lesson 12–Lesson 13; Lesson 22; Unit 3, Lesson 3; Lesson 5–Lesson 6; Lesson 11; Lesson 13; Unit 5, Lesson 1–Lesson 2; Lesson 4–Lesson 6; Lesson 8; Lesson 17; Lesson 20; Unit 7, Lesson 1–Lesson 7; Unit 5, Lesson 3–Lesson 4; Lesson 6–Lesson 10; Lesson 13; Unit 11, Lesson 10; Lesson 12–Lesson 13; Lesson 17; Lesson 19–Lesson 22; Lesson 24; Unit 13, Lesson 8–Lesson 12

Connections Standard	
• recognize and use connections among mathematical ideas;	Unit 1, Lesson 23; Unit 2, Lesson 1–Lesson 4; Unit 4, Lesson 2–Lesson 3; Unit 6, Lesson 1–Lesson 3; Unit 7, Lesson 9–Lesson 14; Unit 8, Lesson 1–Lesson 3; Unit 9, Lesson 11; Unit 10, Lesson 1; Lesson 5; Unit 12, Lesson 1–Lesson 2; Lesson 4; Lesson 6
• understand how mathematical ideas interconnect and build on one another to produce a coherent whole;	Unit 3, Lesson 14; Unit 7, Lesson 9-Lesson 14; Unit 9, Lesson 11; Unit 12, Lesson 1; Unit 14, Lesson 1–Lesson 2
• recognize and apply mathematics in contexts outside of mathematics.	Unit 1, Lesson 2–Lesson 5; Lesson 7–Lesson 8; Lesson 10–Lesson 15; Lesson 17–Lesson 22; Unit 3, Lesson 2–Lesson 3; Lesson 5–Lesson 13; Unit 5, Lesson 2–Lesson 6; Lesson 10–Lesson 15; Lesson 17; Lesson 19–Lesson 20; Unit 7, Lesson 2–Lesson 14; Unit 9, Lesson 1–Lesson 4; Lesson 6– Lesson 16; Unit 11, Lesson 2–Lesson 9; Lesson 11–Lesson 13; Lesson 15–Lesson 22; Unit 12, Lesson 3–Lesson 5; Unit 7, Lesson 1–Lesson 12

Representation Standard	
• create and use representations to organize, record, and communicate mathematical ideas;	Unit 1, Lesson 2; Lesson 23; Unit 2, Lesson 1–Lesson 3; Unit 4, Lesson 1; Unit 5, Lesson 4–Lesson 6; Lesson 10–Lesson 14; Lesson 15–Lesson 17; Lesson 19; Unit 7, Lesson 9–Lesson 14; Unit 9, Lesson 3–Lesson 4; Lesson 11–Lesson 12; Lesson 14–Lesson 16; Unit 10, Lesson 3; Unit 11, Lesson 2–Lesson 3; Lesson 6–Lesson 8; Lesson 14–Lesson 17; Lesson 22; Lesson 24; Unit 12, Lesson 6; Unit 13, Lesson 1–Lesson 5; Lesson 13
• select, apply, and translate among mathematical representations to solve problems;	Unit 1, Lesson 2; Unit 5, Lesson 4–Lesson 6; Lesson 10–Lesson 13; Lesson 15–Lesson 17; Lesson 19– Lesson 20; Unit 7, Lesson 9–Lesson 14; Unit 9, Lesson 3–Lesson 4; Lesson 11-Lesson 12; Lesson 14–Lesson 17; Unit 11, Lesson 2–Lesson 3; Lesson 6–Lesson 8; Lesson 14–Lesson 17; Lesson 22; Unit 13, Lesson 1–Lesson 5
• use representations to model and interpret physical, social, and mathematical phenomena.	Unit 5, Lesson 4–Lesson 6; Lesson 10–Lesson 13; Lesson 15–Lesson 17; Lesson 19; Unit 7, Lesson 16; Unit 9, Lesson 3–Lesson 4; Unit 11, Lesson 6; Lesson 8; Lesson 14– Lesson 15; Lesson 17; Lesson 22; Unit 12, Lesson 5–Lesson 6; Unit 13, Lesson 1–Lesson 5

Diagonals and Midpoints

UNIT 8 BEGINS WITH a review of naming quadrilaterals. Children are then introduced to drawing diagonals in quadrilaterals. After discussing types of triangles, children describe the shapes resulting from drawing diagonals in quadrilaterals. Children also explore different ways of finding midpoints of line segments and apply these skills to decomposing quadrilaterals by joining midpoints of their opposite sides. Children describe the resulting shapes in several ways, and compare them to the original quadrilaterals.

Skills Trace

Grade 1	Grade 2	Grade 3
• Relate shapes and numbers.	• Describe shapes formed by drawing diagonals in a quadrilateral. • Describe shapes formed by connecting the midpoints of opposite sides of a quadrilateral.	• Identify and classify quadrilaterals. • Label figures with letters and compose and decompose quadrilaterals.

Unit 8 Contents

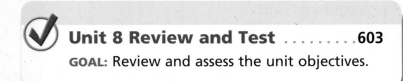

Big Idea **Decomposing Quadrilaterals**

Planning Unit 8

NCTM Curriculum Focal Points and Connections Key: **1.** Number and Operations **2.** Number and Operations and Algebra **3.** Measurement **4.** Number and Operations **5.** Geometry and Measurement **6.** Algebra

Lesson NCTM Focal Points NCTM Standards	Resources	Materials for Lesson Activities	Materials for Going Further
8-1 **Diagonals of Quadrilaterals** NCTM Focal Point: 5.4 NCTM Standards: 3, 4, 8, 9	TE pp. 585–590 SAB pp. 257–260 H&R pp. 171–172 AC 8-1 MCC 29	✓ MathBoard materials ✓ 25-cm rulers	Cut Along Diagonals (TRB M71) Scissors Math Journals
8-2 **Connect Midpoints in Quadrilaterals** NCTM Focal Points: 3.4, 3.6, 5.1, 5.4 NCTM Standards: 3, 4, 8, 9	TE pp. 591–596 SAB pp. 261–262 H&R pp. 173–174 AC 8-2 MCC 30	✓ 25-cm rulers ✓ MathBoard materials ✓ Counters	Quadrilateral Cutouts (TRB M72) Scissors ✓ 25-cm rulers Math Journals
8-3 **Practice with Diagonals and Connecting Midpoints** NCTM Focal Point: 5.4 NCTM Standards: 3, 8, 9	TE pp. 597–602 SAB pp. 263–264 H&R pp. 171–174, 175–176 AG Quick Quiz AC 8-3 MCC 31, 32	✓ 25-cm rulers	Masking tape ✓ MathBoard materials Math Journals
✓ Unit Review and Test	TE pp. 603–606 SAB pp. 265–268 AG Unit 8 Tests		

Resources/Materials Key: TE: Teacher Edition SAB: Student Activity Book H&R: Homework and Remembering AC: Activity Cards MCC: Math Center Challenge AG: Assessment Guide ✓: Grade 2 kits TRB: Teacher's Resource Book

NCTM Standards and Expectations Key: 1. Number and Operations 2. Algebra 3. Geometry 4. Measurement 5. Data Analysis and Probability 6. Problem Solving 7. Reasoning and Proof 8. Communication 9. Connections 10. Representation

Manipulatives and Materials

Essential materials for teaching *Math Expressions* are available in the Grade 2 kits. These materials are indicated by a ✓ in these lists. At the front of this Teacher Edition is more information about kit contents, alternatives for the materials, and use of the materials.

Independent Learning Activities

Ready-Made Math Challenge Centers

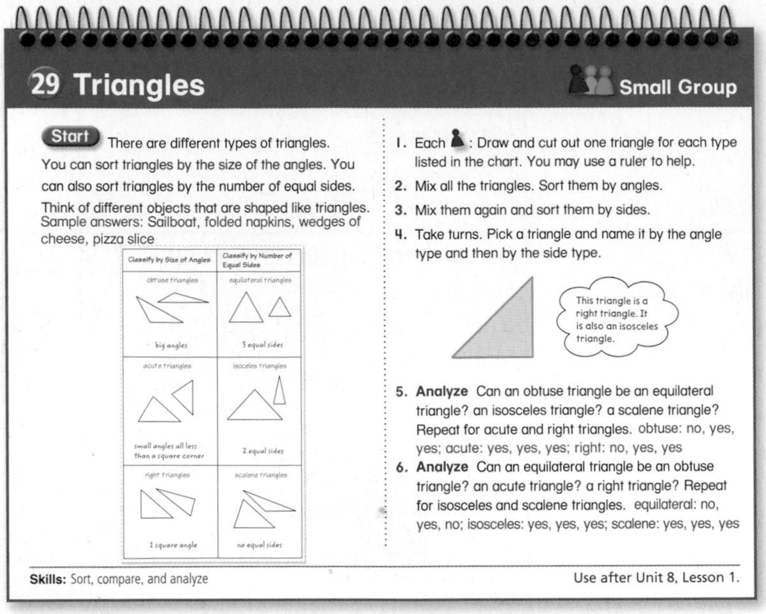

29 Triangles — Small Group

Start There are different types of triangles. You can sort triangles by the size of the angles. You can also sort triangles by the number of equal sides.

Think of different objects that are shaped like triangles. Sample answers: Sailboat, folded napkins, wedges of cheese, pizza slice

Classify by Size of Angles	Classify by Number of Equal Sides
obtuse triangles big angles	equilateral triangles 3 equal sides
acute triangles small angles all less than a square corner	isosceles triangles 2 equal sides
right triangles 1 square angle	scalene triangles no equal sides

1. Each : Draw and cut out one triangle for each type listed in the chart. You may use a ruler to help.
2. Mix all the triangles. Sort them by angles.
3. Mix them again and sort them by sides.
4. Take turns. Pick a triangle and name it by the angle type and then by the side type.

This triangle is a right triangle. It is also an isosceles triangle.

5. **Analyze** Can an obtuse triangle be an equilateral triangle? an isosceles triangle? a scalene triangle? Repeat for acute and right triangles. obtuse: no, yes, yes; acute: yes, yes, yes; right: no, yes, yes
6. **Analyze** Can an equilateral triangle be an obtuse triangle? an acute triangle? a right triangle? Repeat for isosceles and scalene triangles. equilateral: no, yes, no; isosceles: yes, yes, yes; scalene: yes, yes, yes

Skills: Sort, compare, and analyze — Use after Unit 8, Lesson 1.

Grouping Small Group

Materials Scissors

Objective Children identify and sort triangles.

Connections Geometry and Representation

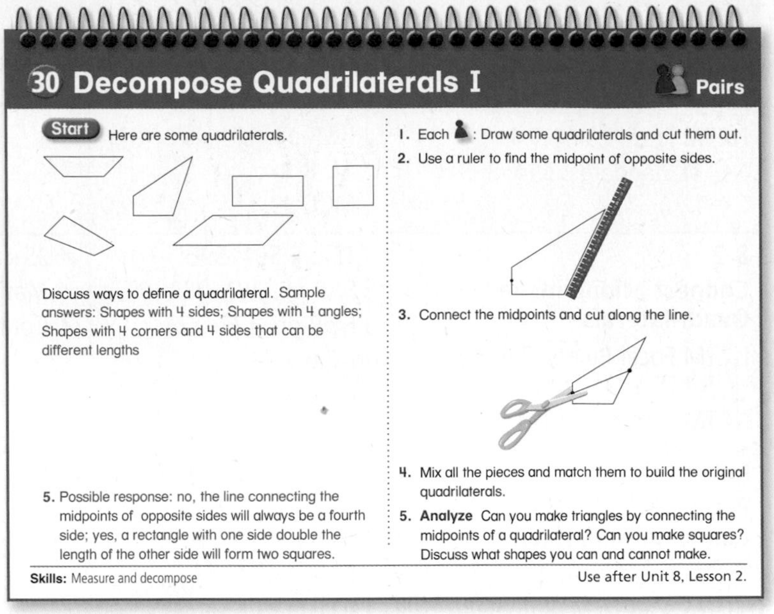

30 Decompose Quadrilaterals I — Pairs

Start Here are some quadrilaterals.

Discuss ways to define a quadrilateral. Sample answers: Shapes with 4 sides; Shapes with 4 angles; Shapes with 4 corners and 4 sides that can be different lengths

1. Each : Draw some quadrilaterals and cut them out.
2. Use a ruler to find the midpoint of opposite sides.
3. Connect the midpoints and cut along the line.
4. Mix all the pieces and match them to build the original quadrilaterals.
5. **Analyze** Can you make triangles by connecting the midpoints of a quadrilateral? Can you make squares? Discuss what shapes you can and cannot make.

5. Possible response: no, the line connecting the midpoints of opposite sides will always be a fourth side; yes, a rectangle with one side double the length of the other side will form two squares.

Skills: Measure and decompose — Use after Unit 8, Lesson 2.

Grouping Pairs

Materials Centimeter rulers, scissors

Objective Children identify midpoints on sides of quadrilaterals and use them to decompose quadrilaterals.

Connections Geometry and Measurement

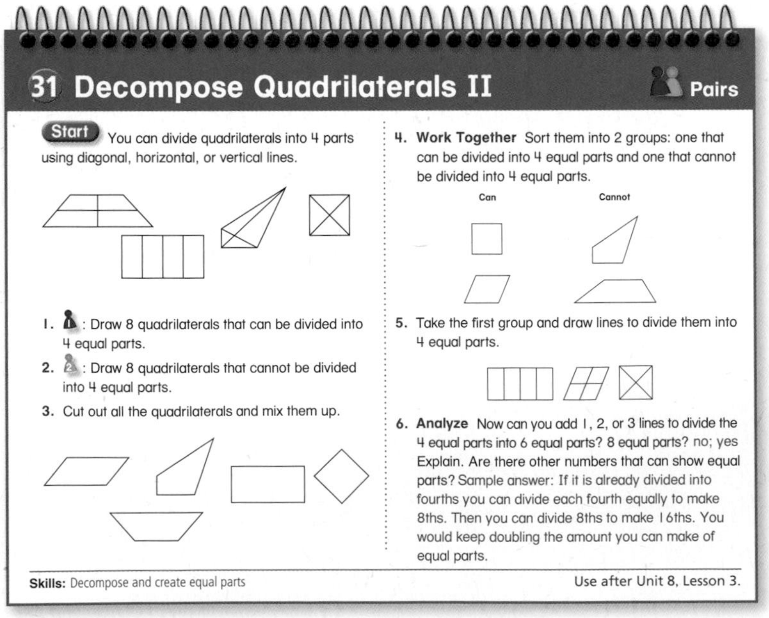

31 Decompose Quadrilaterals II — Pairs

Start You can divide quadrilaterals into 4 parts using diagonal, horizontal, or vertical lines.

1. : Draw 8 quadrilaterals that can be divided into 4 equal parts.
2. : Draw 8 quadrilaterals that cannot be divided into 4 equal parts.
3. Cut out all the quadrilaterals and mix them up.
4. **Work Together** Sort them into 2 groups: one that can be divided into 4 equal parts and one that cannot be divided into 4 equal parts.

5. Take the first group and draw lines to divide them into 4 equal parts.
6. **Analyze** Now can you add 1, 2, or 3 lines to divide the 4 equal parts into 6 equal parts? 8 equal parts? no; yes Explain. Are there other numbers that can show equal parts? Sample answer: If it is already divided into fourths you can divide each fourth equally to make 8ths. Then you can divide 8ths to make 16ths. You would keep doubling the amount you can make of equal parts.

Skills: Decompose and create equal parts — Use after Unit 8, Lesson 3.

Grouping Pairs

Materials Scissors

Objective Children draw and sort quadrilaterals according to whether they can be divided into equal parts or not.

Connections Geometry and Representation

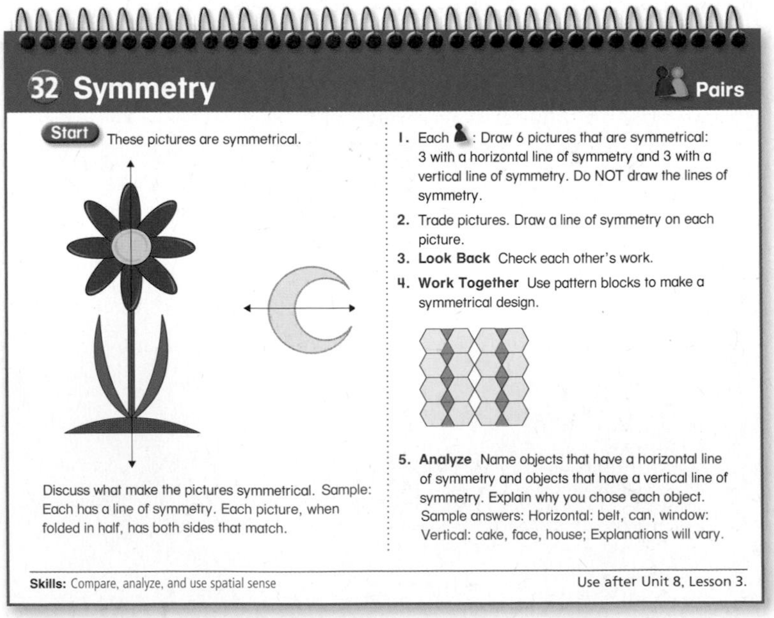

32 Symmetry — Pairs

Start These pictures are symmetrical.

Discuss what make the pictures symmetrical. Sample: Each has a line of symmetry. Each picture, when folded in half, has both sides that match.

1. Each : Draw 6 pictures that are symmetrical: 3 with a horizontal line of symmetry and 3 with a vertical line of symmetry. Do NOT draw the lines of symmetry.
2. Trade pictures. Draw a line of symmetry on each picture.
3. **Look Back** Check each other's work.
4. **Work Together** Use pattern blocks to make a symmetrical design.
5. **Analyze** Name objects that have a horizontal line of symmetry and objects that have a vertical line of symmetry. Explain why you chose each object. Sample answers: Horizontal: belt, can, window: Vertical: cake, face, house; Explanations will vary.

Skills: Compare, analyze, and use spatial sense — Use after Unit 8, Lesson 3.

Grouping Pairs

Materials Crayons or markers, pattern blocks

Objective Children draw symmetrical pictures and lines of symmetry. They also make symmetrical designs.

Connections Geometry and Algebra

Ready-Made Math Resources

Technology — Tutorials, Practice, and Intervention

Go Digital

Soar to Success Math

Use online, individualized intervention and support to bring students to proficiency.

HARCOURT MEGA MATH Grades K-6

Help students practice skills and apply concepts through exciting math adventures.

DESTINATION Math®

Extend and enrich students' understanding of skills and concepts through engaging, interactive lessons and activities.

Visit **Education Place®**
www.eduplace.com

Visit www.eduplace.com/mx2t/ and find family, teacher, and student materials, activities, games, and more.

Literature Links

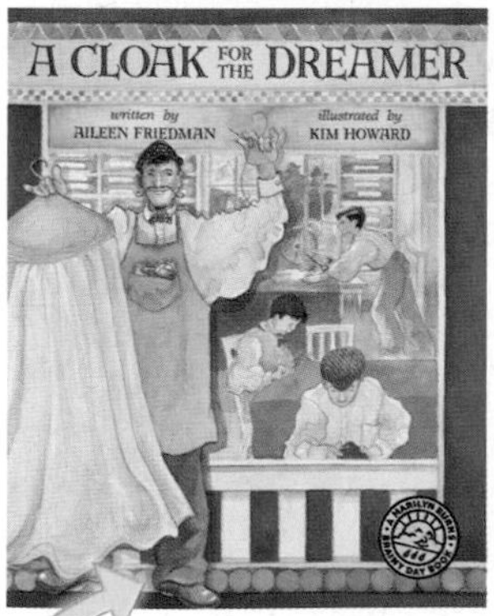

A Cloak for the Dreamer

A Cloak for the Dreamer
For an inspirational look at geometric principals put to use in fabric design, check out this unique story by Aileen Friedman.

Unit 8 Assessment

Unit Objectives Tested	Unit Test Items	Lessons
8.1 Draw diagonals in quadrilaterals.	1–2	1, 3
8.2 Find the midpoint of a line segment.	3, 10	2
8.3 Describe shapes formed by drawing diagonals in a quadrilateral.	4–6	1, 3
8.4 Describe shapes formed by connecting the midpoints of opposite sides of a quadrilateral.	7–9	2, 3

Assessment and Review Resources

Formal Assessment

Student Activity Book

- Unit Review and Test (pp. 265–268)

Assessment Guide

- Quick Quiz (p. A85)
- Test A–Open Response (pp. A86–A88)
- Test B–Multiple Choice (pp. A89–A91)
- Performance Assessment (pp. A92–A94)

Test Generator CD-ROM

- Open Response Test
- Multiple Choice Test
- Test Bank Items

Informal Assessment

Teacher Edition

- Ongoing Assessment (in every lesson)
- Quick Practice (in every lesson)
- Portfolio Suggestions (p. 605)

Math Talk

- Math Talk in Action (p. 593)
- In Activities (pp. 586, 598, 599)

Review Opportunities

Homework and Remembering

- Review of recently taught topics
- Spiral Review

Teacher Edition

- Unit Review and Test (pp. 603–606)

Test Generator CD-ROM

- Custom Review Sheets

Unit 8 Teaching Resources

Differentiated Instruction

Individualizing Instruction		
	Level	Frequency
Activities	• Intervention • On Level • Challenge	All 3 in every lesson
	Level	Frequency
Math Writing Prompts	• Intervention • On Level • Challenge	All 3 in every lesson
Math Center Challenges	For advanced students	
	4 in every unit	

Reaching All Learners		
English Language Learners	Lessons	Pages
	1, 2, 3	585, 591, 597

Strategies for English Language Learners

Present this problem to all students. Offer the different levels of support to meet children's levels of language proficiency.

Objective Children identify quadrilaterals and their properties.

Problem Give children cut outs of a square, rectangle, and parallelogram. Have them hold up each shape and count the sides.

Newcomer

- Hold up each shape. Say: **This is a** <u>square</u>**. It has 4 equal sides. It is a *quadrilateral*.** Have children repeat.

Beginning

- Hold up a square. Ask: **How many sides does it have?** 4 sides **Is it a *quadrilateral*?** yes Continue with other shapes.

Intermediate

- Have children hold up and identify their shapes. Ask: **Is it a *quadrilateral*?**
- Review other properties. Ask: **Are the lengths of the sides equal? Are the opposite sides parallel? Are the corners square?**

Advanced

- Have children work in pairs to tell about each shape. Invite volunteers to share their descriptions.

Connections

Social Studies Connections
Lesson 2, page 596
Lesson 3, page 602

Math Background

Putting Research into Practice for Unit 8

Geometry offers students an aspect of mathematical thinking that is different from, but connected to, the world of numbers. As students become familiar with shape, structure, location, and transformations and as they develop spatial reasoning, they lay the foundation for understanding not only their spatial world but also other topics in mathematics and in art, science, and social studies. Some students' capabilities with geometric and spatial concepts exceed their number skills. Building on these strengths fosters enthusiasm for mathematics and provides a context in which to develop number and other mathematics concepts (Razel and Eylon 1991).

National Council of Teachers of Mathematics. *Principles and Standards for School Mathematics.* Reston, VA: NCTM, 2000. 97.

Developing spatial sense, as well as number sense, as described in NCTM's *Curriculum and Evaluation Standards for School Mathematics* (1989), is a central goal of mathematics instruction that engenders problem solving in particular and doing mathematics in general. A strong spatial sense allows students to formulate image-based solutions to mathematics problems. In geometry, having a mental image of a parallelogram is fundamental. Without spatial sense, a student may only act mechanically with shapes and symbols that have little meaning.

Wheatley, Grayson H., Anne M. Reynolds. "Image Maker: Developing Spatial Sense." *Teaching Children Mathematics* 5.6 (Feb. 1999): 374.

Other Useful References: Spatial Sense

Clements, Douglas H. "Geometric and Spatial Thinking in Young Children." *Mathematics in the Early Years.* Ed. Juanita V. Copley. Reston, VA: NCTM, 1999. Co-published with the National Association for the Education of Young Children. 66–79.

Fuys, David. J., Amy K. Liebov. "Geometry and Spatial Sense." *Research Ideas for the Classroom: Early Childhood Mathematics.* Ed. R.J. Jensen. Old Tappan, NJ: Macmillan, 1993. 195–222.

Handbook of Research on Mathematics Teaching and Learning (Macmillan Library Reference). Ed. Douglas A. Grouws. Reston, VA: NCTM, 1992. 442–444.

Burton, Grace, Douglas Clements, Terrence Coburn, John Del Grande, John Firkins, Jeane Joyner, Miriam A. Leiva, Mary M. Lindquist, Lorna Morrow. *Fourth-Grade Book: Addenda Series,* Grades K–6. Reston, VA: NCTM, 1992. 23, 26–27.

Getting Ready To Teach Unit 8

In Unit 4, children had opportunities to sort, name, and classify quadrilaterals, and to look at the inclusive nature of quadrilateral names. Children begin this unit by consolidating their learning about quadrilaterals as they identify whether each quadrilateral name applies to various shapes, and explaining their reasoning. Later in the unit, children build their spatial sense as they decompose quadrilaterals by adding diagonals and joining midpoints of opposite sides. In these activities, children describe and compare the resulting shapes, an activity which gives them further practice in naming quadrilaterals.

Sort Triangles
Lessons 1 and 3

In Unit 4, children classified triangles using their own language (for example, "three-sides-equal" triangles or "no-big-angle" triangles). In the first lesson of this unit, children review how to classify triangles by sizes of angles and by number of equal sides. Later in the unit, children are required to describe and compare the triangles formed by drawing diagonals in quadrilaterals.

Diagonals in Quadrilaterals
Lessons 1 and 3

In this unit, children are introduced to diagonals of quadrilaterals. At this grade level, it is adequate for them to have a working definition of a diagonal as "a line segment that connects opposite corners of a quadrilateral." In later years, children will be introduced to the formal definition of a diagonal: "a line segment that connects nonconsecutive vertices." The focus of the activities in this unit is on drawing diagonals and then describing and comparing the resulting shapes. For instance, children will identify that two diagonals drawn from corner to corner of a square create four triangles that are the same size and the same shape, and that each triangle has a square corner and two sides of equal length. In subsequent years, children will use formal language to describe and compare the resulting shapes, and they will measure and compare the lengths of the diagonals on different quadrilaterals.

Congruent Figures
Lessons 2 and 3

In this unit, children are required to make comparisons of the shapes they form when they decompose quadrilaterals. They will use language like "same size and same shape" for congruent shapes. In Unit 10, children will learn the term *congruent* and complete activities dedicated to finding congruent shapes.

Decompose Quadrilaterals by Joining Midpoints of Opposite Sides
Lesson 2

Children decompose quadrilaterals by joining midpoints of opposite sides. This provides children with further opportunities to apply the language associated with quadrilaterals, to practice finding midpoints of line segments, and to continue developing their spatial sense.

MINI UNIT 8

LESSON 1

Diagonals of Quadrilaterals

Lesson Objectives

- Review and define quadrilaterals.
- Draw diagonals in quadrilaterals.
- Observe shapes formed by diagonal lines in quadrilaterals.

Vocabulary

quadrilateral
square
rectangle
parallelogram
diagonal

The Day at a Glance

Today's Goals	Materials	
1 Teaching the Lesson **A1:** Define, discuss, and draw quadrilaterals. **A2:** Draw diagonals in quadrilaterals and discuss the shapes they form.	**Lesson Activities** Student Activity Book pp. 257–260 (includes Family Letter) Homework and Remembering pp. 171–172 MathBoard materials 25-cm rulers	**Going Further** Activity Cards 8-1 Cut Along Diagonals (TRB M71) Scissors Math Journals
2 Going Further ▸ Differentiated Instruction		
3 Homework		

Use Math Talk today!

Keeping Skills Sharp

Daily Routines	English Language Learners
Telling Time Naming the Hands, Telling Time on the Time Poster (See pp. xxv–xxvi.) ▸ Led by Student Leaders **Money Routine** Using the 120 Poster, Using the Money Flip Chart, Using the Number Path, Using Secret Code Cards (See pp. xxiii–xxv.) ▸ Led by Student Leaders	Draw and identify a horizontal, vertical, and diagonal line on the board. Hold your arms up. Have children stand up and copy you. Continue with other lines. • **Beginning** Say: **Vertical!** Have children repeat. • **Intermediate** Say: **Our arms are ___.** vertical • **Advanced** Model how to hold your arms for each line then play Simon Says.

1 Teaching the Lesson

Activity 1

Review Quadrilaterals

25 MINUTES

Goal: Define, discuss, and draw quadrilaterals.

Materials: MathBoard materials, 25-cm rulers, Student Activity Book page 257

NCTM Standards:
Geometry
Communication

▶ Define Quadrilaterals SMALL GROUPS

Write the term *Quadrilaterals* on the board.

Ask for Ideas Ask children to work in small groups to define the term; have them draw several examples on their MathBoards using a centimeter ruler.

Invite one member from each group to write his or her definition on the board.

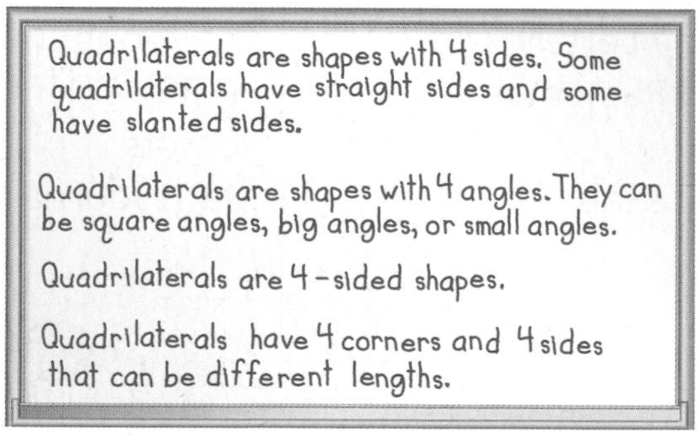

Quadrilaterals are shapes with 4 sides. Some quadrilaterals have straight sides and some have slanted sides.
Quadrilaterals are shapes with 4 angles. They can be square angles, big angles, or small angles.
Quadrilaterals are 4-sided shapes.
Quadrilaterals have 4 corners and 4 sides that can be different lengths.

Help the class choose the best definition. You might also combine several definitions. Explain that a good definition is correct, complete, and easy to remember.

Have another member from each group draw examples of quadrilaterals on the board.

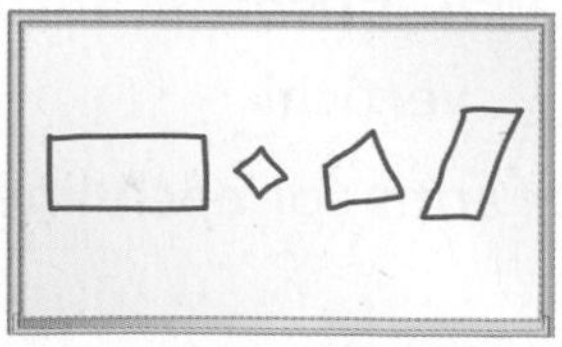

- Are all these shapes quadrilaterals? yes
- How do you know? They all have 4 sides.

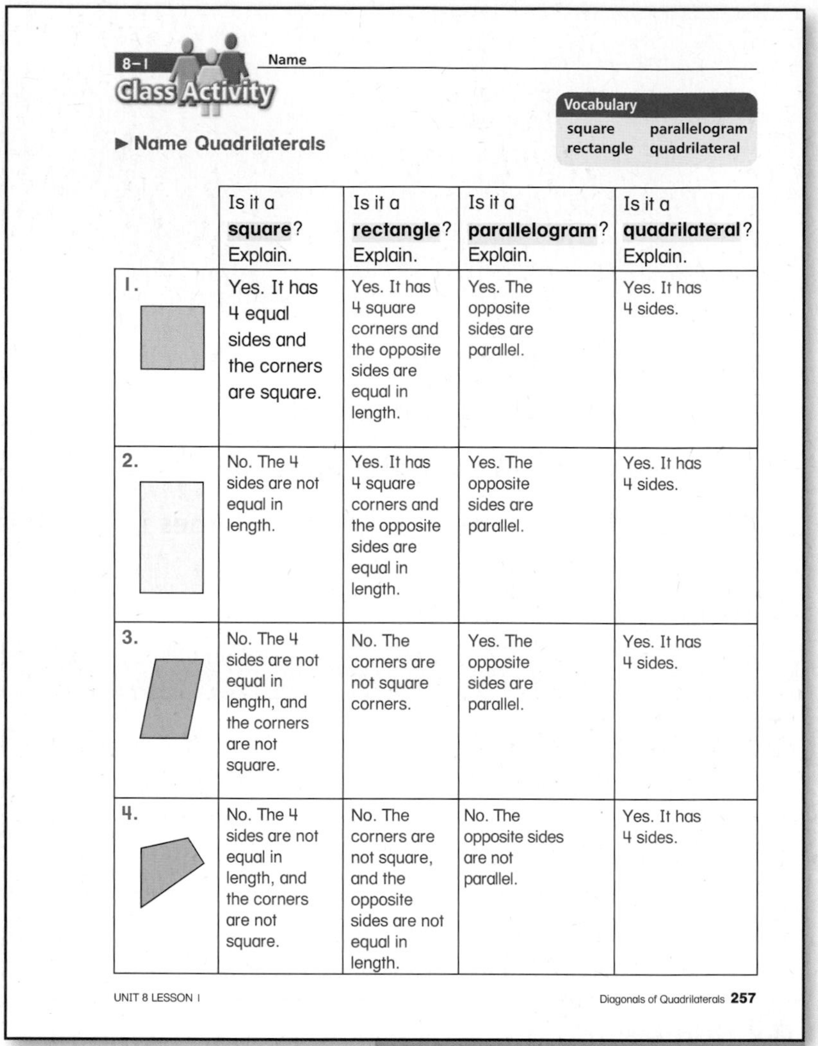

8–1 Class Activity Name

▶ Name Quadrilaterals

Vocabulary
square parallelogram
rectangle quadrilateral

	Is it a **square**? Explain.	Is it a **rectangle**? Explain.	Is it a **parallelogram**? Explain.	Is it a **quadrilateral**? Explain.
1.	Yes. It has 4 equal sides and the corners are square.	Yes. It has 4 square corners and the opposite sides are equal in length.	Yes. The opposite sides are parallel.	Yes. It has 4 sides.
2.	No. The 4 sides are not equal in length.	Yes. It has 4 square corners and the opposite sides are equal in length.	Yes. The opposite sides are parallel.	Yes. It has 4 sides.
3.	No. The 4 sides are not equal in length, and the corners are not square.	No. The corners are not square corners.	Yes. The opposite sides are parallel.	Yes. It has 4 sides.
4.	No. The 4 sides are not equal in length, and the corners are not square.	No. The corners are not square, and the opposite sides are not equal in length.	No. The opposite sides are not parallel.	Yes. It has 4 sides.

UNIT 8 LESSON 1 Diagonals of Quadrilaterals 257

Student Activity Book page 257

▶ Name Quadrilaterals SMALL GROUPS

Math Talk Refer children to Student Activity Book page 257. Work through exercise 1 together.

- Is this shape a square? yes How do you know? It has 4 square corners and 4 sides of equal length.
- Is it a rectangle? yes How do you know? It has 4 square corners and opposite sides are equal length.
- Is it a parallelogram? yes How do you know? The opposite sides are parallel.
- Is it a quadrilateral? yes How do you know? It has 4 sides.

Have children complete exercises 2–4 in small groups. When they are finished, discuss their answers.

Activity 2

Draw Diagonals in Quadrilaterals

35 MINUTES

Goal: Draw diagonals in quadrilaterals and discuss the shapes they form.

Materials: Student Activity Book page 258, 25-cm rulers, MathBoard materials

NCTM Standards:
Geometry
Measurement
Connection

▶ Draw Diagonals PAIRS

Draw a square, a rectangle, a parallelogram, and a quadrilateral (that is not a parallelogram) on the board. Draw a diagonal in each shape.

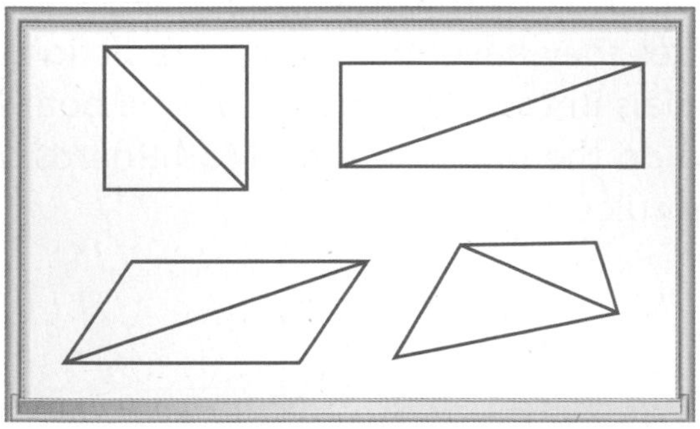

- How can you describe the line segments I just drew? They all go from one corner to another corner. They are all slanted.

Tell children that these line segments are called *diagonals*.

Refer children to Student Activity Book page 258 and have them complete exercises 5–9 in pairs. These exercises are intended to give children an opportunity to decompose shapes by drawing diagonals and to become more comfortable with the language used to describe the new shapes that are formed. Keep in mind, however, that children are not expected to memorize the relationships between the original and the decomposed shapes.

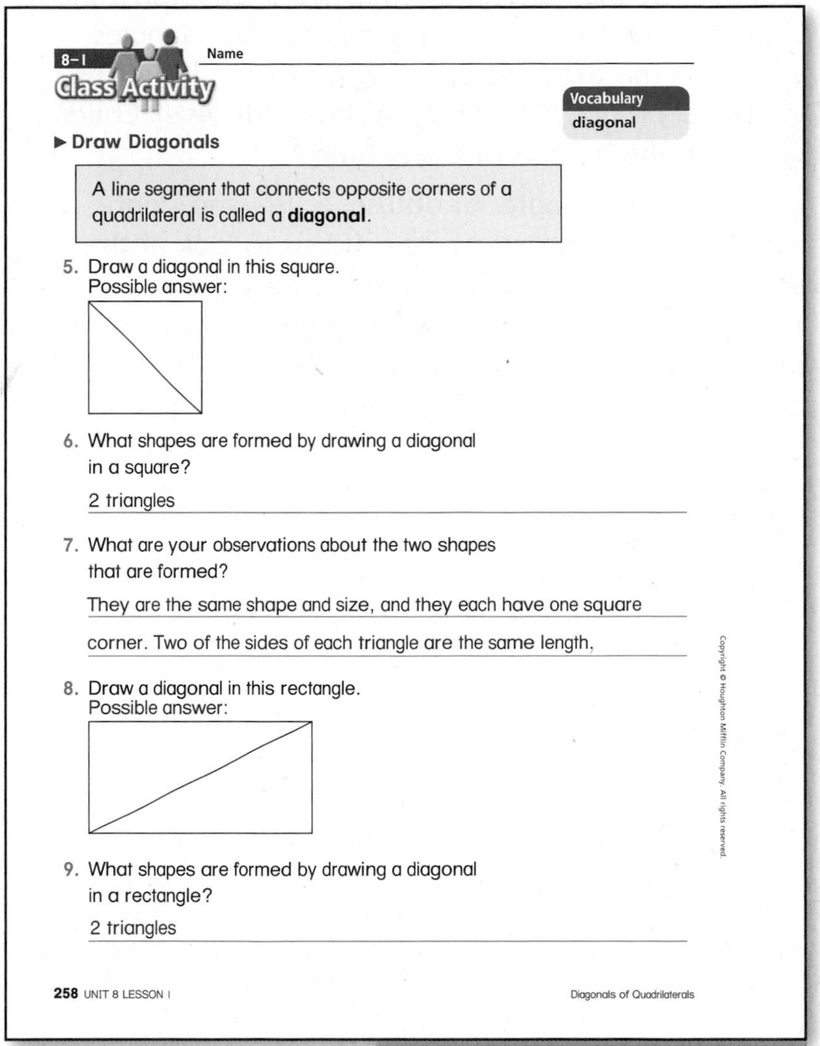

8–1 Class Activity

Name

Vocabulary
diagonal

▶ Draw Diagonals

A line segment that connects opposite corners of a quadrilateral is called a **diagonal**.

5. Draw a diagonal in this square.
Possible answer:

6. What shapes are formed by drawing a diagonal in a square?
2 triangles

7. What are your observations about the two shapes that are formed?
They are the same shape and size, and they each have one square corner. Two of the sides of each triangle are the same length.

8. Draw a diagonal in this rectangle.
Possible answer:

9. What shapes are formed by drawing a diagonal in a rectangle?
2 triangles

258 UNIT 8 LESSON 1 Diagonals of Quadrilaterals

Student Activity Book page 258

When children are finished, have them compare the shapes formed by drawing a diagonal in a square to the shapes formed by drawing a diagonal in a rectangle. Invite them to share their ideas.

Teaching Note

Language and Vocabulary The formal definition of a diagonal of a polygon is "a line segment that connects nonconsecutive vertices." For this grade level, however, you can define a diagonal as a line segment that connects opposite corners of a quadrilateral.

Activity continued ▶

❶ Teaching the Lesson (continued)

▶ Review Types of Triangles WHOLE CLASS

Remind children that they can describe triangles by their angles or by the number of equal sides. Children may choose to use their own words to describe triangles while you use the math terms. Keep in mind that this vocabulary is not mandatory at this grade level. Children will learn the math terms over time.

Draw several examples of obtuse, acute, and right triangles on the board. Invite children to look at the angles and name each group of triangles. Next, draw examples of equilateral, isosceles, and scalene triangles on the board. Ask children to look at the number of equal sides and to name each group of triangles.

Classify by Size of Angles	Classify by Number of Equal Sides
"big-angle" triangles 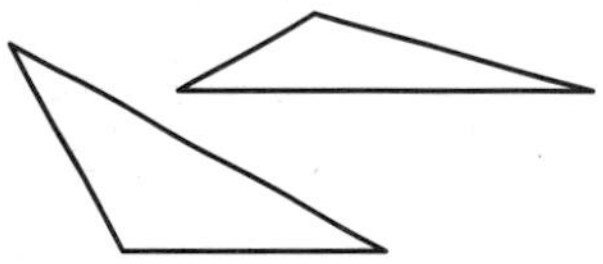 obtuse triangles (measure of 1 angle > 90°)	"equal-sides" triangles  equilateral triangles (three equal sides)
"no-big-angle" triangles  acute triangles (measure of each angle < 90°)	"two-sides-equal" triangles 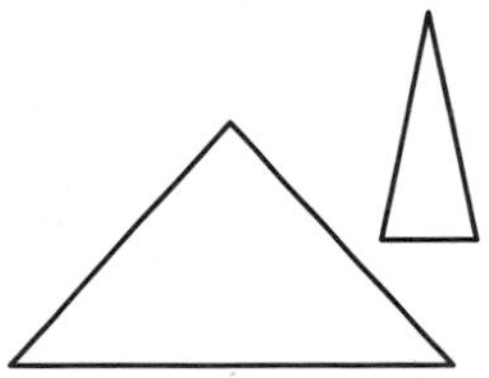 isosceles triangles (two equal sides)
"square-corner" triangles 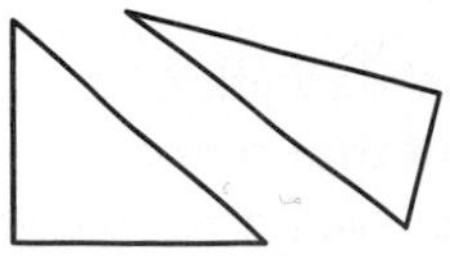 right triangles (measure of 1 angle = 90°, or a right angle)	"all-sides-different" triangles 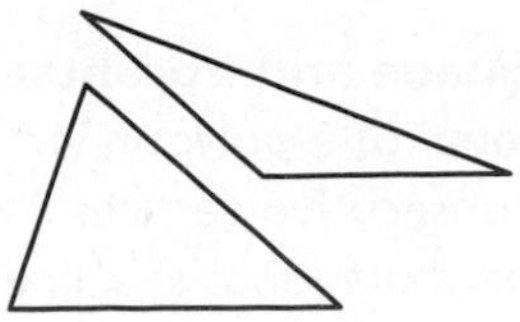 scalene triangles (no equal sides)

▶ Two Diagonals in Quadrilaterals

WHOLE CLASS

Draw three identical squares on the board. Ask children to draw three identical squares on their MathBoards using a centimeter ruler. Draw a different diagonal in each of the first two squares on the board. Have children do the same.

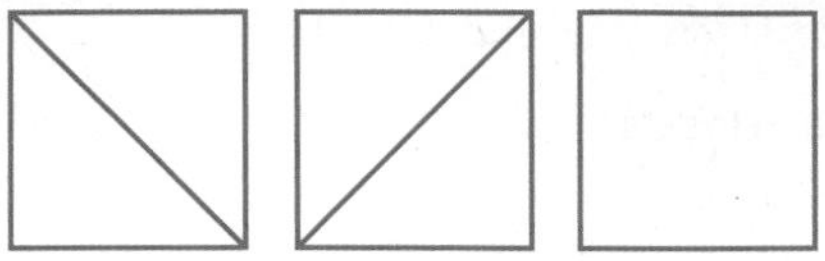

- What shapes are made by these diagonals? triangles, square-corner triangles
- How do the triangles in the first square compare with the triangles in the second square? They look the same, but they are facing in different directions.

Invite children to discuss with a partner what shapes will be formed when they draw two diagonals in a square. After they have made their predictions, draw two diagonals in the third square on the board. Invite children to do the same on their MathBoards using a centimeter ruler.

- Describe the shapes that you see in the third square. I see 4 triangles that look the same. Each triangle has a square corner. Each triangle has 2 sides of equal length.

Ongoing Assessment

Ask children to draw a square, a rectangle, a parallelogram, and a quadrilateral with four unequal sides on their MathBoards and to draw one diagonal in each shape.

2 Going Further

Differentiated Instruction

Intervention — Activity Card 8-1

Cut Along Diagonals — Activity Card 8-1 ●

Work: individual
Use:
- Cut Along Diagonals (TRB M71)
- scissors

1. Cut out each shape on the Cut Along Diagonals page. You should have four shapes.
2. Identify each shape.
3. Cut each shape along the diagonal.

4. Identify the shapes created.
5. Compare the shapes and your names for them with another child.

Unit 8, Lesson 1

Activity Note Each child needs Cut Along Diagonals (TRB M71) and scissors. Check that children identify each quadrilateral and each pair of triangles.

Math Writing Prompt

Explain Your Thinking Anita says that if you cut a quadrilateral along a diagonal, you will always make two triangles. Do you agree? Draw a picture to explain your thinking.

Soar to Success Math **Software Support**

Warm Up 37.04

On Level — Activity Card 8-1

Triangles with Square Corners — Activity Card 8-1 ▲

Work: individual
Use:
- Cut Along Diagonals (TRB M71)
- scissors

1. Cut out each shape on the Cut Along Diagonals page. You should have four shapes.
2. Identify each shape.
3. Cut each shape along the diagonal.
4. Use the square corner of a piece of paper to see which shapes form triangles with square corners.

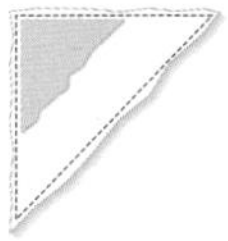

5. Compare the triangles with square corners with the triangles a classmate found.

Unit 8, Lesson 1

Activity Note Each child needs Cut Along Diagonals (TRB M71) and scissors. Help children match the square corners. Some will be a better match than others.

Math Writing Prompt

You Decide Can a quadrilateral have more than two diagonals? Explain why or why not.

Harcourt MegaMath Grades K-6 **Software Support**

Shapes Ahoy: Ship Shapes, Level G

Challenge — Activity Card 8-1

Quadrilaterals From Triangles — Activity Card 8-1 ■

Work: individual
Use:
- Cut Along Diagonals (TRB M71)
- scissors

1. Cut out each shape on the Cut Along Diagonals page. You should have four shapes.
2. Identify each shape.
3. Cut each shape along the diagonal.
4. Mix up the pieces. Try to put the pieces back together.

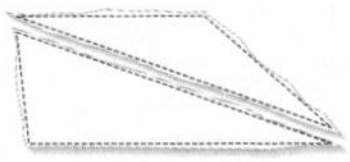

5. Sort the triangles by the lengths of the sides.
6. Sort the triangles by the sizes of the angles.

Unit 8, Lesson 1

Activity Note Each child needs Cut Along Diagonals (TRB M71) and scissors. Help children realize that the two triangles do not have to match.

Math Writing Prompt

Investigate Math How many diagonals does a triangle have? Why?

Destination Math **Software Support**

Course II: Module 3: Unit 1: Area

3 Homework

8–1 Homework **Goal:** Additional Practice

This Homework page provides practice drawing diagonals in different quadrilaterals.

8–1 Homework Name ____________________

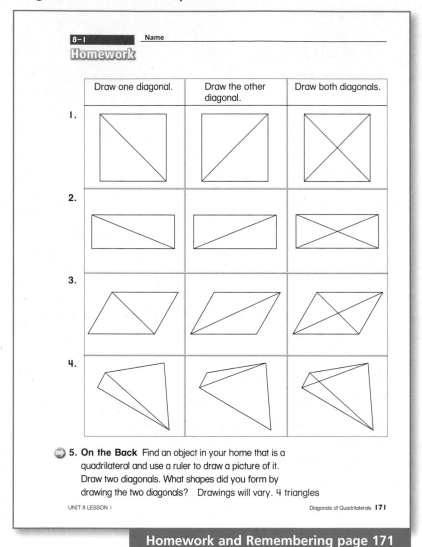

	Draw one diagonal.	Draw the other diagonal.	Draw both diagonals.

1.
2.
3.
4.

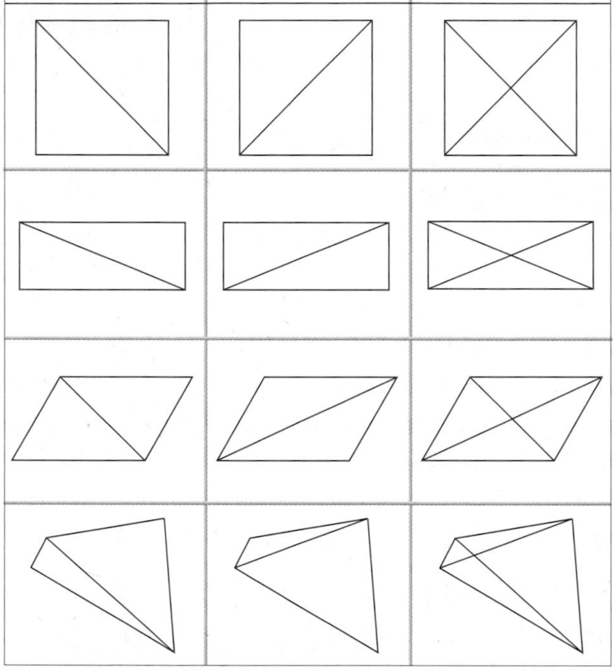

5. **On the Back** Find an object in your home that is a quadrilateral and use a ruler to draw a picture of it. Draw two diagonals. What shapes did you form by drawing the two diagonals? Drawings will vary. 4 triangles

UNIT 8 LESSON 1 Diagonals of Quadrilaterals 171

Homework and Remembering page 171

Class Management

Looking Ahead Children will need their completed Homework page from this lesson in Lesson 3.

Home and School Connection

Family Letter Have children take home the Family Letter on Student Activity Book page 259. This letter explains how the concept of dividing quadrilaterals into smaller shapes is developed in *Math Expressions.* It gives parents and guardians a better understanding of the learning that goes on in math class and creates a bridge between school and home. A Spanish translation of this letter is on the following page in the Student Activity Book.

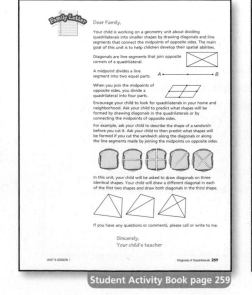

Family Letter

Dear Family,

Your child is working on a geometry unit about dividing quadrilaterals into smaller shapes by drawing diagonals and line segments that connect the midpoints of opposite sides. The main goal of this unit is to help children develop their spatial abilities.

Diagonals are line segments that join opposite corners of a quadrilateral.

A midpoint divides a line segment into two equal parts.

When you join the midpoints of opposite sides, you divide a quadrilateral into four parts.

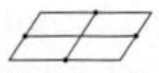

Encourage your child to look for quadrilaterals in your home and neighborhood. Ask your child to predict what shapes will be formed by drawing diagonals in the quadrilaterals or by connecting the midpoints of opposite sides.

For example, ask your child to describe the shape of a sandwich before you cut it. Ask your child to then predict what shapes will be formed if you cut the sandwich along the diagonals or along the line segments made by joining the midpoints on opposite sides.

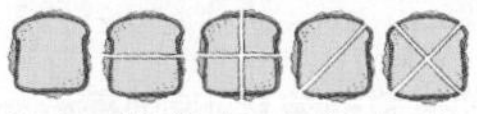

In this unit, your child will be asked to draw diagonals on three identical shapes. Your child will draw a different diagonal in each of the first two shapes and draw both diagonals in the third shape.

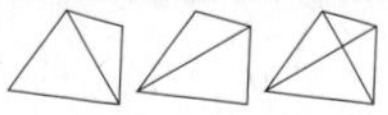

If you have any questions or comments, please call or write to me.

Sincerely,
Your child's teacher

UNIT 8 LESSON 1 Diagonals of Quadrilaterals 259

Student Activity Book page 259

Carta a la familia

Estimada familia:

Su niño está trabajando en una unidad de geometría. Aprenderá a dividir cuadriláteros en figuras más pequeñas dibujando diagonales y segmentos que unen los puntos medios de lados opuestos. El objetivo principal de esta unidad es ayudar a los niños a desarrollar su sentido espacial.

Las diagonales son segmentos que unen vértices opuestos de un cuadrilátero.

Los puntos medios dividen un segmento en dos partes iguales.

Cuando se unen los puntos medios de lados opuestos se divide el cuadrilátero en cuatro partes.

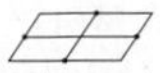

Anime a su niño a buscar cuadriláteros en la casa y en el vecindario. Pídale que prediga qué figuras se formarán al dibujar diagonales en los cuadriláteros o al unir los puntos medios de lados opuestos.

Por ejemplo, pida a su niño que describa la figura de un sándwich antes de cortarlo. Pídale que prediga qué figuras se formarán is corta el sándwich por las diagonales o por los segmentos formados al unir los puntos medios con los lados opuestos.

En esta unidad su niño deberá dibujar diagonales en tres figuras idénticas. Se le pedirá que dibuje una diagonal diferente en cada una de las primeras dos figuras y que dibuje ambas diagonales en la tercera figura.

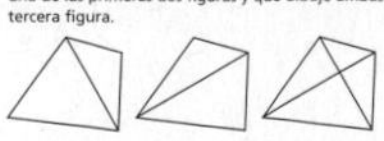

Si tiene alguna pregunta o comentario, por favor comuníquese conmigo.

Atentamente,
El maestro de su niño

260 UNIT 8 LESSON 1 Diagonals of Quadrilaterals

Student Activity Book page 260

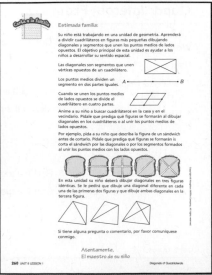

MINI UNIT 8

LESSON 2

Connect Midpoints in Quadrilaterals

Lesson Objectives

- **Define *midpoint.***
- **Explore ways to find the midpoint of a line segment.**
- **Predict the shapes that will be formed by joining midpoints of opposite sides of quadrilaterals.**
- **Join midpoints of opposite sides of quadrilaterals.**

Vocabulary

midpoint
opposite sides

The Day at a Glance

Today's Goals	Materials	
1 Teaching the Lesson **A1:** Explore ways to find the midpoint of a line segment. **A2:** Find and join midpoints of opposite sides of quadrilaterals.	**Lesson Activities** Student Activity Book pp. 261–262 Homework and Remembering pp. 173–174 25-cm rulers MathBoard materials Counters	**Going Further** Activity Cards 8-2 Quadrilateral Cutouts (TRB M72) Scissors 25-cm rulers Math Journals
2 Going Further ▸ Differentiated Instruction		
3 Homework		

Use **Math Talk** today!

Keeping Skills Sharp

Daily Routines	English Language Learners
Telling Time Naming the Hands, Telling Time on the Time Poster (See pp. xxv–xxvi.) ▸ Led by Student Leaders **Money Routine** Using the 120 Poster, Using the Money Flip Chart, Using the Number Path, Using Secret Code Cards (See pp. xxiii–xxv.) ▸ Led by Student Leaders	Have 5 children stand in a line and hold a string. Point to the string then the 5 children. Say: **This is a line. They are the points on the line.** • **Beginning** Gesture to the middle child. Say: **(Name of child) is in the middle. (S/He) is the *midpoint*.** Have children repeat. • **Intermediate** Ask: **Who is in the middle?** name of child **Is** (s/he) **the *midpoint*?** yes • **Advanced** Say: **The point in the middle of the line is the *midpoint*.** Ask: **Who is the *midpoint*?** name of child

Teaching the Lesson

Activity 1

Find Midpoints of Line Segments

30 MINUTES

Goal: Explore ways to find the midpoint of a line segment.

Materials: Student Activity Book page 261, 25-cm rulers, MathBoard materials, counters (8 per small group of children)

NCTM Standards:
Geometry
Measurement
Connections
Communication

▶ Explore Methods of Finding Midpoints SMALL GROUPS

Refer children to Student Activity Book page 261 and read aloud the definition of the midpoint of a line segment.

Ask for Ideas Invite children to work in small groups to brainstorm different ways of finding the midpoint of a line segment. Encourage them to experiment using counters and drawings on their MathBoards. Circulate while they discuss possible strategies, and ask leading questions as necessary.

- How can you use estimation to help you?
- How can you use the 1-cm marks on the ruler to help you?
- What happens if you fold the line segment so the ends match?
- How can you use doubles partners to help you?

Ask children to complete exercises 1–5 in pairs and to share with each other their methods of finding the midpoint.

When children are finished, invite five or six volunteers to the board to present their methods of finding the midpoint of the line segment in exercise 3.

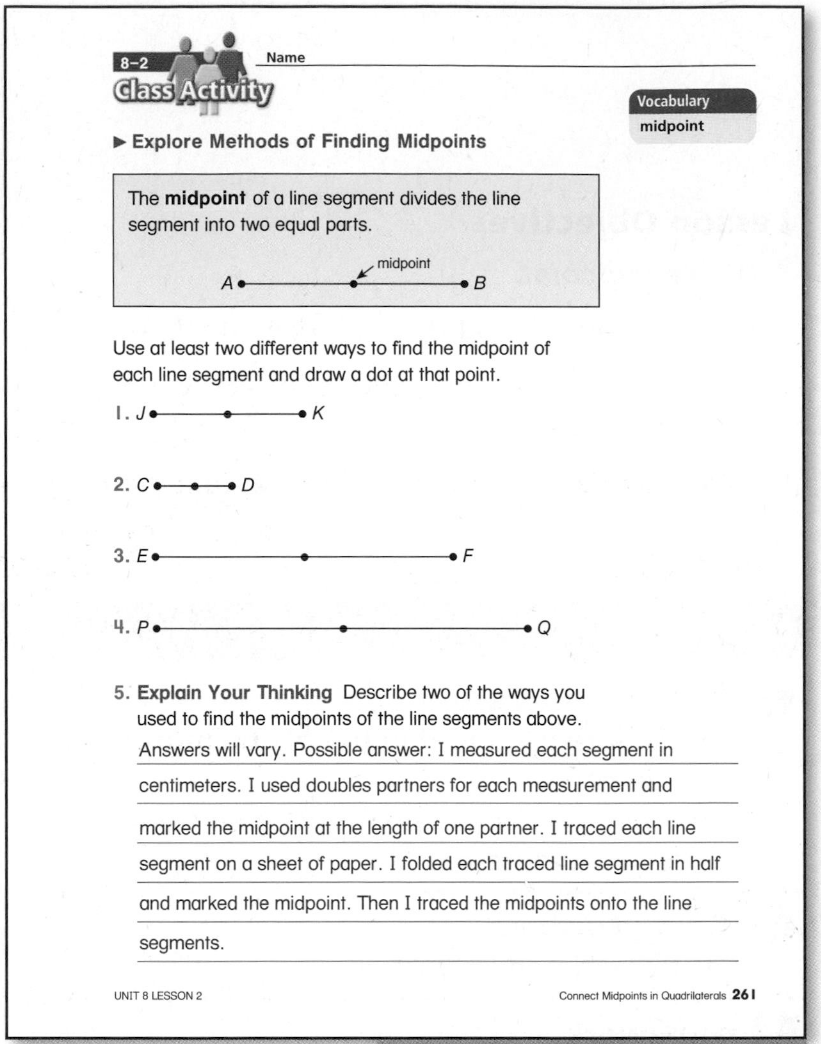
8-2 Class Activity

Name

Vocabulary
midpoint

▶ Explore Methods of Finding Midpoints

The **midpoint** of a line segment divides the line segment into two equal parts.

Use at least two different ways to find the midpoint of each line segment and draw a dot at that point.

1. J K
2. C D
3. E F
4. P Q

5. **Explain Your Thinking** Describe two of the ways you used to find the midpoints of the line segments above.
Answers will vary. Possible answer: I measured each segment in centimeters. I used doubles partners for each measurement and marked the midpoint at the length of one partner. I traced each line segment on a sheet of paper. I folded each traced line segment in half and marked the midpoint. Then I traced the midpoints onto the line segments.

UNIT 8 LESSON 2 Connect Midpoints in Quadrilaterals 261

Student Activity Book page 261

Be sure that you discuss the following four methods: using doubles to compute numerically, marking and counting 1-cm lengths, estimating and checking, and folding. See **Math Talk in Action** on the next page for an example of classroom dialogue.

Ongoing Assessment

Have children draw two line segments with an even number of centimeters on their MathBoards. If children have difficulty choosing even-centimeter measurements on their own, you might specify measurements like 6 cm, 8 cm, or 10 cm. Ask them to mark the midpoint on each line segment.

Math Talk in Action

How did you find the midpoint of the line segment in exercise 3?

Rosa: I guessed the midpoint and put a dot there. Next, I took a piece of paper and marked the distance from one end to the dot.

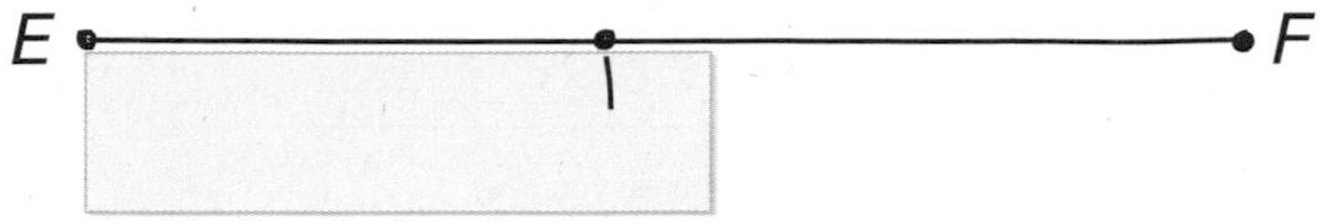

Then I moved the piece of paper over to see if the length of the other side was the same.

I kept moving the dot until both sides were the same.

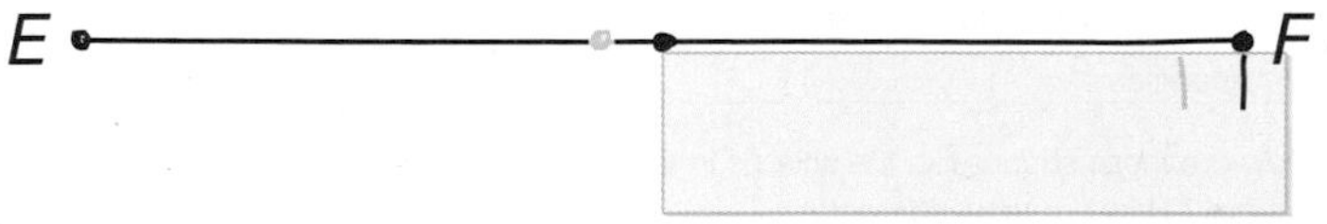

Carlos: How did you know which way to move the dot?

Rosa: If the right side was longer, I moved the dot to the right. If the right side was shorter, I moved the dot to the left.

Patty: I did it differently. I traced the line segment on a sheet of paper and then folded it so the ends matched. When I unfolded it, I had two equal parts. I marked the midpoint with a dot on the fold line.

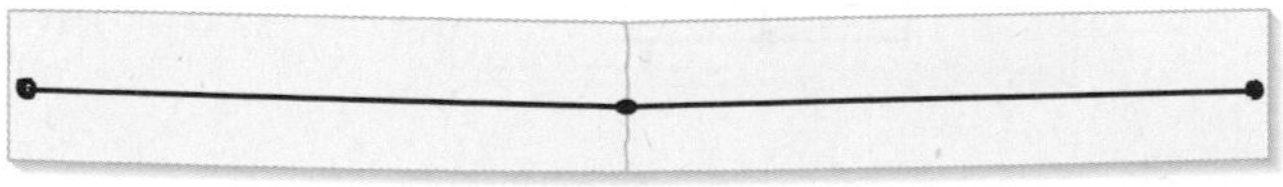

Sue Jung: I marked the line segment with 1-cm lengths to help me find the midpoint. I guessed where the midpoint was and put a dot there. I moved the dot until I had the same number of 1-cm lengths on both sides.

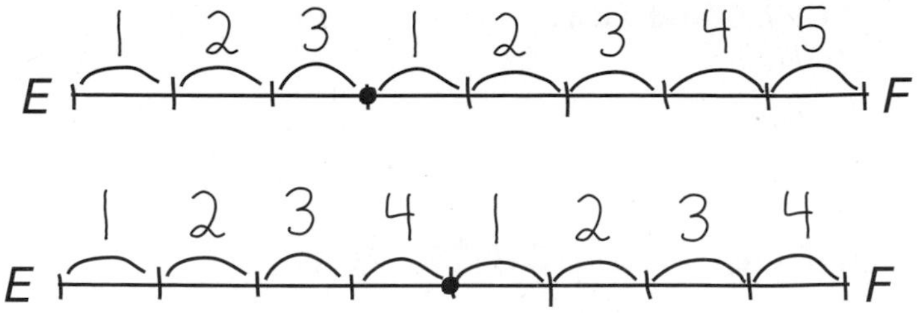

Ben: I measured the line segment and found that it was 8 cm long. I found the doubles partners for 8: 4 and 4. I measured 4 cm from one end and marked the midpoint with a dot.

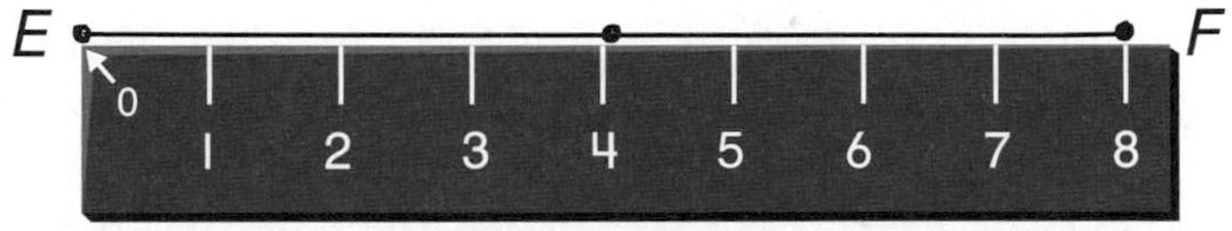

Wenona: I don't know how to find the doubles partners for 8. Can you tell me how?

Ben: Use eight counters and put them into two equal groups. Each group will have four counters. The doubles partners for 8 are 4 and 4.

Activity 2

Connect Midpoints to Decompose Quadrilaterals

30 MINUTES

Goal: Find and join midpoints of opposite sides of quadrilaterals.

Materials: Student Activity Book page 262, 25-cm rulers, MathBoard materials

NCTM Standards:
Geometry
Connections

▶ Connect Midpoints PAIRS

Remind children of the new shapes that form when they draw diagonals in quadrilaterals (triangles). Explain to them that they are now going to make new shapes by finding and joining the midpoints of opposite sides of quadrilaterals.

Refer children to Student Activity Book page 262 and ask them to complete exercises 6–11 in pairs. When they are finished, discuss their answers as a class.

Connecting Two Sets of Midpoints Sketch a square with sides about 10 cm in length on the board. Ask children to draw a square with sides 10 cm in length on their MathBoards.

Demonstrate how to visually approximate the midpoints of all four sides. Ask children to do the same on their MathBoards.

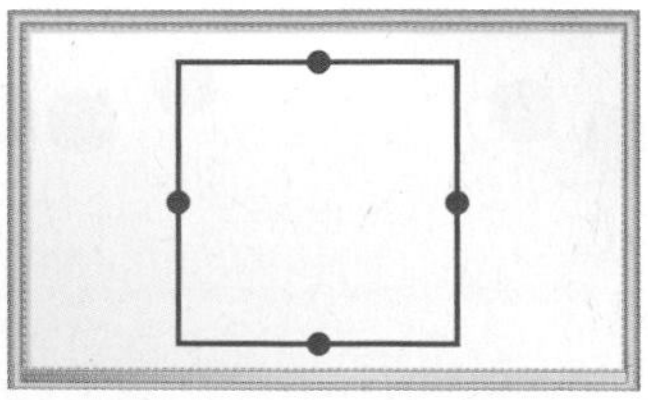

- If I connect the midpoints that are opposite each other, what shapes do you think you will see? squares
- How many squares do you think I will make? 4 squares

Join the midpoints on opposite sides of the square and have children do the same on their MathBoards.

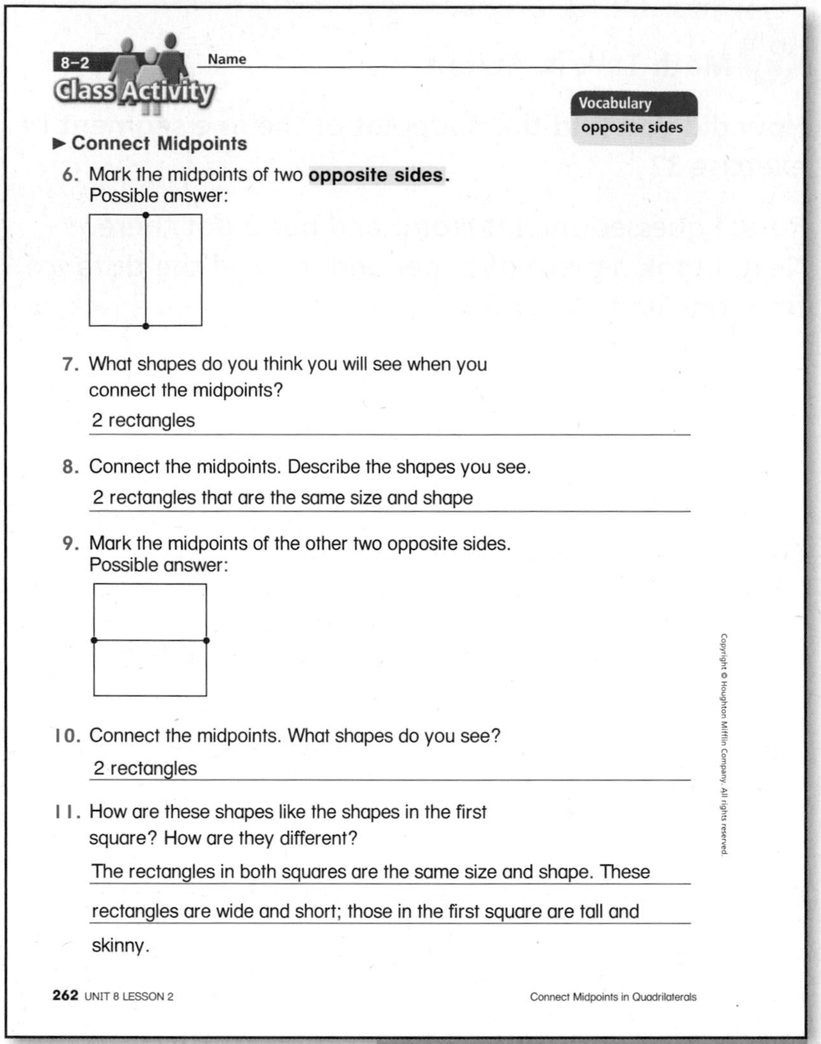

8–2 Class Activity Name

Vocabulary
opposite sides

▶ Connect Midpoints

6. Mark the midpoints of two **opposite sides**.
Possible answer:

7. What shapes do you think you will see when you connect the midpoints?
2 rectangles

8. Connect the midpoints. Describe the shapes you see.
2 rectangles that are the same size and shape

9. Mark the midpoints of the other two opposite sides.
Possible answer:

10. Connect the midpoints. What shapes do you see?
2 rectangles

11. How are these shapes like the shapes in the first square? How are they different?
The rectangles in both squares are the same size and shape. These rectangles are wide and short; those in the first square are tall and skinny.

262 UNIT 8 LESSON 2 Connect Midpoints in Quadrilaterals

Student Activity Book page 262

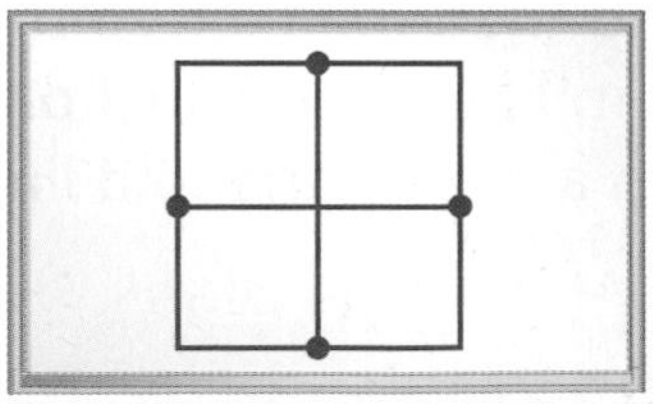

- How are these shapes different from the shapes that are formed by joining only one set of midpoints? These shapes are squares. If I join only 1 pair of midpoints, I make rectangles. These squares are exactly half the size of the rectangles.

2 Going Further

Differentiated Instruction

Intervention — Activity Card 8-2

Cut Out Shapes — Activity Card 8-2 ●

Work: 1 person
Use:
- Quadrilateral Cutouts (TRB M72)
- scissors

1. Cut out each shape on the Quadrilateral Cutouts page. You should have four shapes.
2. Identify each shape.
3. Cut each shape along the line connecting the midpoints of two opposite sides.

4. **Math Talk** Meet with a friend. Discuss the new shapes. Sample answer: When I cut the square, I made rectangles.

Unit 8, Lesson 2

Activity Note Each child needs Quadrilateral Cutouts (TRB M72) and scissors. Help children identify the new shapes.

Math Writing Prompt

Explain a Method Pete found the midpoint of a line segment by folding the sheet of paper on which it was drawn. Explain another method Pete could have used.

Soar to Success Math **Software Support**

Warm Up 37.04

On Level — Activity Card 8-2

Rebuild Quadrilaterals — Activity Card 8-2 ▲

Work: 1 person
Use:
- Quadrilateral Cutouts (TRB M72)
- scissors

1. Cut out each shape on the Quadrilateral Cutouts page. You should have four shapes.
2. Identify each shape.
3. Cut each shape along the line joining the midpoints of two opposite sides.

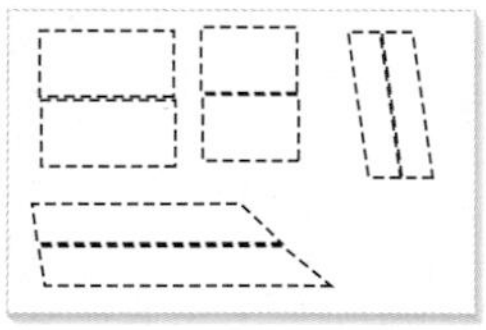

4. Mix up the cutouts.
5. Rebuild the original shapes.

Unit 8, Lesson 2

Activity Note Each child needs Quadrilateral Cutouts (TRB M72) and scissors. Children will take apart and then put together the shapes.

Math Writing Prompt

Show Your Thinking What shapes are formed when the four midpoints on the sides of a parallelogram are connected? Include a drawing in your answer.

Harcourt Mega Math **Software Support**

Shapes Ahoy: Ship Shapes, Level J

Challenge — Activity Card 8-2

Estimate Midpoints — Activity Card 8-2 ■

Work: pairs
Use:
- 25-cm ruler

1. **Work Together** Draw a line segment that is 7 cm long.
2. Find the midpoint of the line. Share with another pair how you found the midpoint. Sample response below.

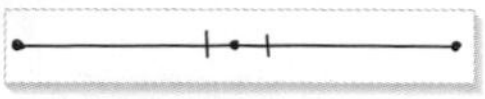

3. Use another method to find the midpoint.
4. **Math Talk** Which method do you think might work best for a stick that is 15 cm long?
   2. Sample answer: We measured 3 cm from each end and then estimated where to put the midpoint between each mark. We folded the piece of paper in half so that the ends matched.

Unit 8, Lesson 2

Activity Note Each pair needs a 25-cm ruler. Discuss the methods children used.

Math Writing Prompt

Predict and Verify A line segment connects the midpoint of opposite sides of a quadrilateral. If you cut along the line segment, will you always make two quadrilaterals? Explain.

Destination Math **Software Support**

Course II: Module 3: Unit 1: Area

3 Homework

8–2 Homework **Goal:** Additional Practice

This Homework page provides practice in connecting the midpoints of opposite sides of quadrilaterals.

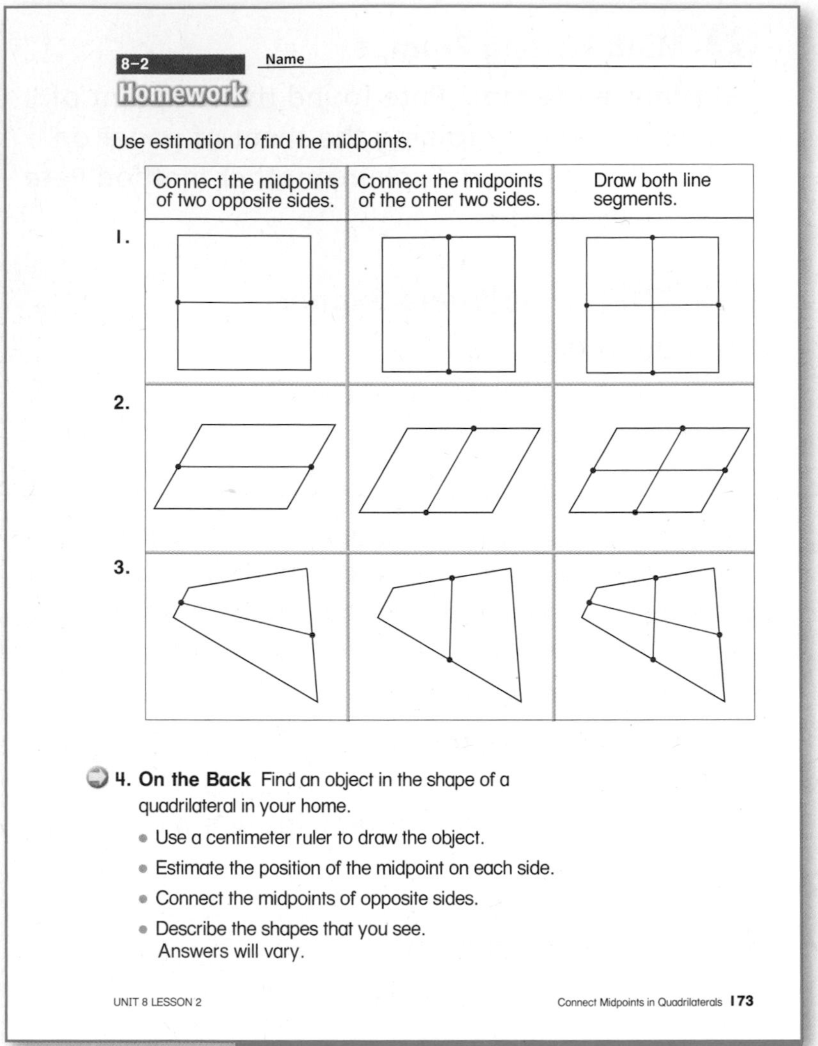

8–2 Homework Name

Use estimation to find the midpoints.

	Connect the midpoints of two opposite sides.	Connect the midpoints of the other two sides.	Draw both line segments.
1.			
2.			
3.			

4. **On the Back** Find an object in the shape of a quadrilateral in your home.
   - Use a centimeter ruler to draw the object.
   - Estimate the position of the midpoint on each side.
   - Connect the midpoints of opposite sides.
   - Describe the shapes that you see.
   Answers will vary.

UNIT 8 LESSON 2 Connect Midpoints in Quadrilaterals 173

Homework and Remembering page 173

Class Management

Looking Ahead Children will need their completed Homework page from this lesson in Lesson 3.

Home or School Activity

Social Studies Connection

Flag Designs Flags have been used for thousands of years to represent places, organizations, and people. Flags are designed to be seen from a distance and to be easily identified and remembered. The design of some flags includes line segments that join the midpoints of opposite sides.

Invite children to design their own flag using one or two line segments that join the midpoints of opposite sides. Encourage them to use color to highlight the shapes that are formed.

MINI UNIT 8
LESSON 3

Practice with Diagonals and Connecting Midpoints

Lesson Objectives

- **Draw diagonals and connect midpoints of opposite sides in quadrilaterals.**
- **Observe shapes formed by decomposing quadrilaterals.**

Vocabulary
diagonal
midpoint

The Day at a Glance

Today's Goals	Materials	
1 Teaching the Lesson **A1:** Discuss the shapes in the homework exercises from Lessons 1 and 2. **A2:** Draw diagonals and line segments that join midpoints of opposite sides in six identical quadrilaterals.	**Lesson Activities** Student Activity Book pp. 263–264 Homework and Remembering pp. 175–176 Homework pages from Lessons 1 and 2 Quick Quiz (Assessment Guide) 25-cm rulers	**Going Further** Activity Cards 8-3 Masking tape MathBoard materials Math Journals
2 Going Further ▸ Differentiated Instruction		
3 Homework		

Use Math Talk today!

Keeping Skills Sharp

Daily Routines	English Language Learners
Telling Time Naming the Hands, Telling Time on the Time Poster (See pp. xxv–xxvi.) ▸ Led by Student Leaders **Money Routine** Using the 120 Poster, Using the Money Flip Chart, Using the Number Path, Using Secret Code Cards (See pp. xxiii–xxv.) ▸ Led by Student Leaders	Draw right, equilateral, acute isosceles, and obtuse isosceles triangles on the board. Say: **These triangles are all a little different.** • **Beginning** Point to and describe the sides and angles of each triangle. Use simple sentences and have children repeat. • **Intermediate** Point to each angle. Ask: **Is this a square angle? Is it a big angle or a small angle?** Point to each triangle and ask: **How many sides are equal?** • **Advanced** Number the triangles. Ask: **Which triangles have 2 equal sides? Which triangle has no big angles?** Continue with other properties.

1 Teaching the Lesson

Activity 1

Observe Homework Shapes

30 MINUTES

Goal: Discuss the shapes in the homework exercises from Lessons 1 and 2.

Materials: Homework pages from Lessons 1 and 2

NCTM Standards:
Geometry
Connections
Communication

▶ Draw Diagonals to Make Shapes

WHOLE CLASS

Draw three enlarged versions of each shape from Homework and Remembering page 171 on the board. Invite four children to the board to draw diagonals as they did for their homework in Lesson 1.

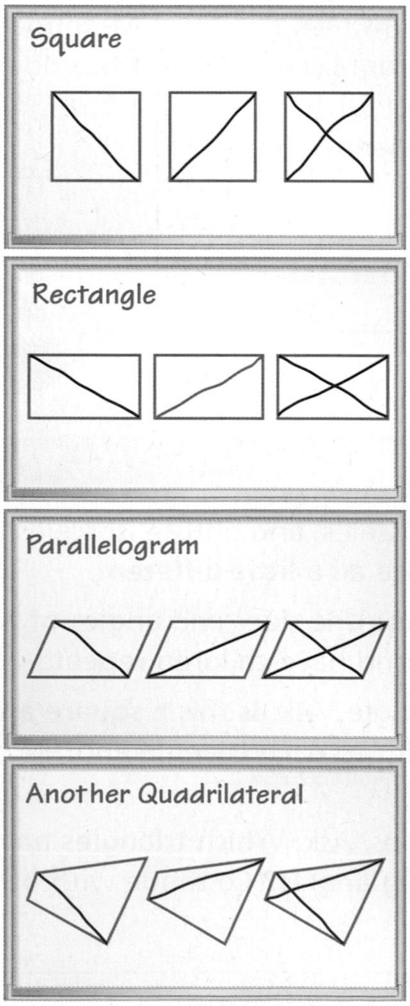

Math Talk Lead a class discussion to elicit observations about the shapes that are formed by drawing diagonals.

- When you drew one diagonal, what shapes did you make? triangles
- How many triangles did you make by drawing one diagonal? 2 triangles
- Did you make triangles with square corners when you drew a diagonal in any of these shapes? yes Which shapes formed triangles with square corners? squares and rectangles
- Did any of the shapes form two different triangles? the shapes in exercise 4
- When you drew two diagonals, what shapes did you make? triangles How many? 4 triangles
- Which shape formed four triangles with square corners when you drew two diagonals? square
- What kinds of triangles did you make when you drew two diagonals on the rectangle? 2 big-angle (obtuse) triangles; 2 no-big-angle (acute) triangles; 4 triangles with 2 equal sides (isosceles)

▶ Connect Midpoints to Make Shapes

WHOLE CLASS

Draw three enlarged versions of each shape from Homework and Remembering page 173 on the board. Invite four children to draw line segments joining the midpoints of opposite sides as they did for their homework in Lesson 2.

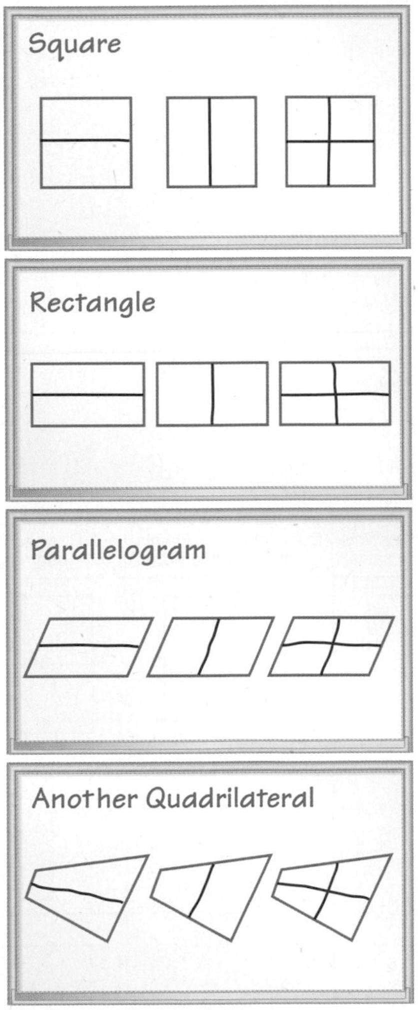

Math Talk Lead a class discussion to elicit observations about the shapes that are formed by drawing these line segments.

- When you connect two midpoints on opposite sides of a square, what shapes do you make? 2 rectangles on a rectangle? 2 rectangles on a parallelogram? 2 parallelograms on any quadrilateral? 2 quadrilaterals
- When you connect both sets of midpoints on a square, what shapes do you make? 4 squares on a rectangle? 4 rectangles on a parallelogram? 4 parallelograms on any quadrilateral? 4 quadrilaterals
- When you connect both sets of midpoints on a square, what do you observe about the four new squares that are formed? They are all the same size.
- When you connect both sets of midpoints on a rectangle, what do you observe about the four new rectangles that are formed? They are all the same size and shape.
- When you connect both sets of midpoints on a parallelogram, what do you observe about the four new parallelograms that are formed? They are all the same size and shape.
- When you connected both sets of midpoints on the quadrilateral in exercise 4, what do you notice about the four new quadrilaterals that were formed? They are not all the same shape.

Ongoing Assessment

Ask children the following questions:

- ▶ When you draw two diagonals in a square, what shapes do you make?
- ▶ When you connect the midpoints on opposite sides of a square, what shapes do you make?

Quick Quiz

See Assessment Guide for Unit 8 Quick Quiz.

Activity 2

Practice Decomposing Shapes

20 MINUTES

Goal: Draw diagonals and line segments that join midpoints of opposite sides in six identical quadrilaterals.

Materials: Student Activity Book pages 263–264, 25-cm rulers (1 ruler per child)

NCTM Standards:
Geometry
Connections

▶ Add Line Segments to Shapes

INDIVIDUALS

Refer children to Student Activity Book pages 263–264.

Have children use their centimeter rulers to draw diagonals and to connect the midpoints on opposite sides in each shape, as they did for homework in Lessons 1 and 2.

Circulate while children are working and assist those who are having difficulty.

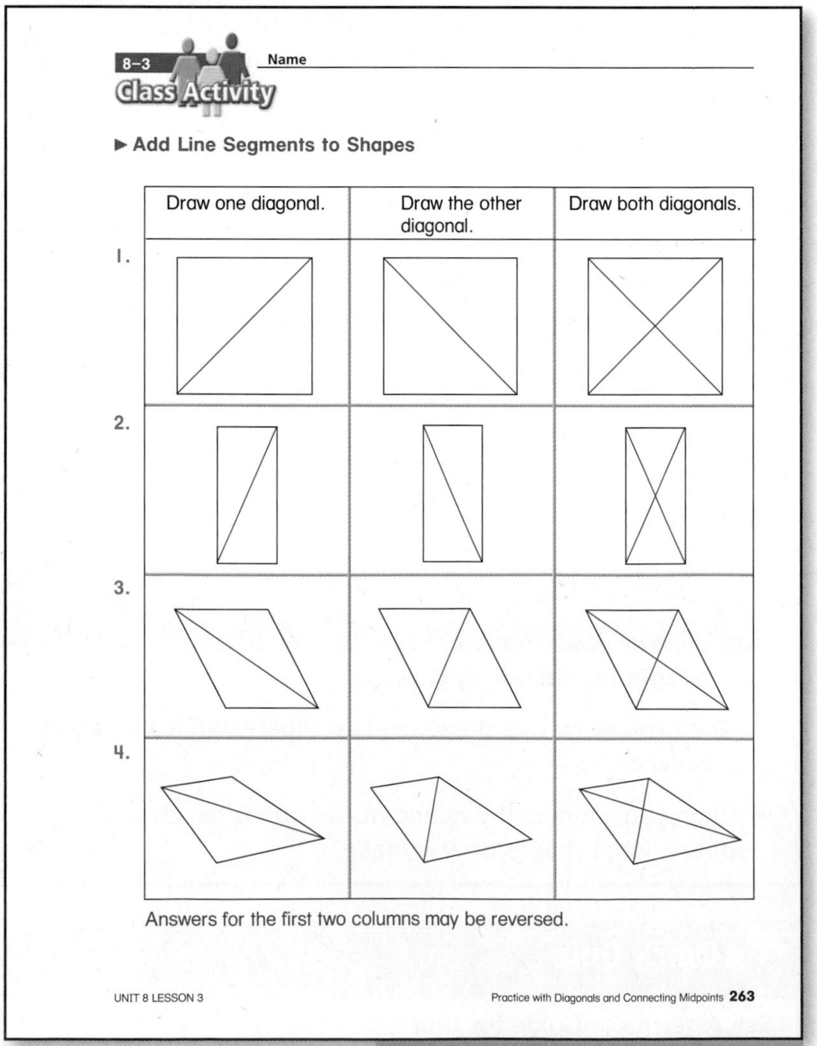
8–3 Class Activity Name

▶ Add Line Segments to Shapes

	Draw one diagonal.	Draw the other diagonal.	Draw both diagonals.
1.			
2.			
3.			
4.			

Answers for the first two columns may be reversed.

UNIT 8 LESSON 3 Practice with Diagonals and Connecting Midpoints 263

Student Activity Book page 263

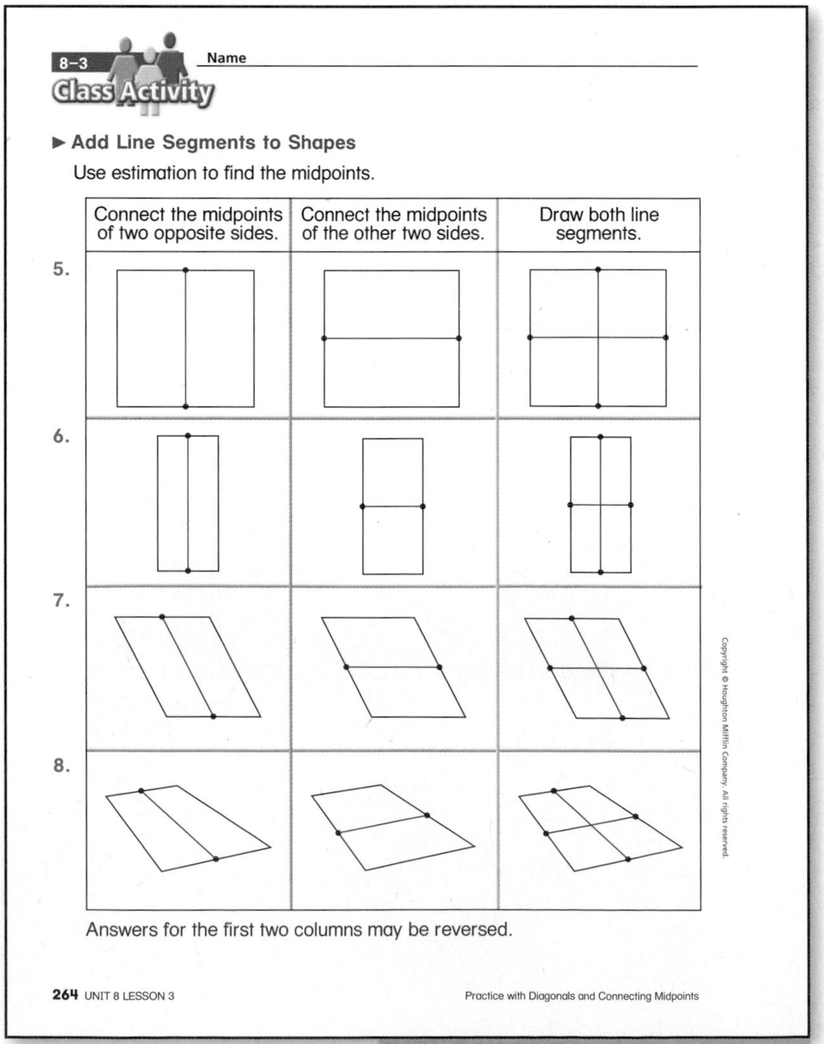
8–3 Class Activity Name

▶ Add Line Segments to Shapes

Use estimation to find the midpoints.

	Connect the midpoints of two opposite sides.	Connect the midpoints of the other two sides.	Draw both line segments.
5.			
6.			
7.			
8.			

Answers for the first two columns may be reversed.

264 UNIT 8 LESSON 3 Practice with Diagonals and Connecting Midpoints

Student Activity Book page 264

Differentiated Instruction

Intervention — Activity Card 8-3

Quadrilaterals in the Classroom

Activity Card 8-3 ●

Work: pairs

Use:

- masking tape

1. **Work Together** Look for quadrilaterals in your classroom. Try to find three or four.
2. Use the masking tape to mark the diagonals in each quadrilateral you found.

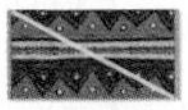

3. Use the masking tape to join the midpoints of opposite sides of each quadrilateral you found.

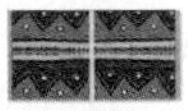

4. **Math Talk** Share observations about the new shapes you made. Sample answers: When we mark a diagonal, we make two triangles that are the same size and shape; When we connect the midpoints, we make two rectangles that are the same size and shape.

Unit 8, Lesson 3

Activity Note Each pair needs a roll of masking tape. You may want to help children tape the diagonals and midpoints.

Math Writing Prompt

Explain a Method Hai wants to divide a rectangle into two smaller rectangles that are the same size and shape. Explain a method Hai can use.

Soar to Success Math Software Support

Warm Up 37.02

On Level — Activity Card 8-3

Quadrilaterals with Square Corners

Activity Card 8-3 ▲

Work: pairs

Use:

- MathBoard materials

When Sofia drew a line segment in a quadrilateral, she made two shapes with square corners. What shapes might Sofia have started with? What kinds of line segments could she have added?

1. **Work Together** Read the story problem above.
2. Show at least 3 possible solutions on your MathBoard.
3. Share your solutions with another pair. Sample drawings show.

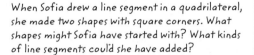

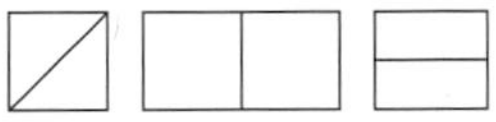

Unit 8, Lesson 3

Activity Note Each pair needs MathBoard materials. Encourage pairs to find at least three possible solutions to the problem.

Math Writing Prompt

Show Your Thinking Pia wants to make two parallelograms that are the same size and shape from a quadrilateral. What type of quadrilateral should she start with? Include a drawing in your answer.

Mega Math Software Support

Shapes Ahoy: Ship Shapes, Level J

Challenge — Activity Card 8-3

Same Size and Shape

Activity Card 8-3 ■

Work: pairs

Use:

- MathBoard materials

Oscar divides a quadrilateral into four parts that are the same size and shape. What shapes might Oscar have started with? What kinds of line segments could he have added?

1. **Work Together** Read the story problem above.
2. Show at least 4 possible solutions on your MathBoard.
3. **Math Talk** Share your solutions with another pair. Talk about how you solved the story problem.

Unit 8, Lesson 3

Activity Note Each pair needs MathBoard materials. Encourage pairs to find at least four possible solutions.

Math Writing Prompt

Predict and Verify Jean wants to make four triangles with square corners from a quadrilateral. What possible shapes can Jean start with? Draw sketches to check your answer.

Destination Math Software Support

Course II: Module 3: Unit 1: Area

3 Homework

8–3 Homework **Goal:** Additional Practice

✓ Include children's completed Homework page as part of their portfolios.

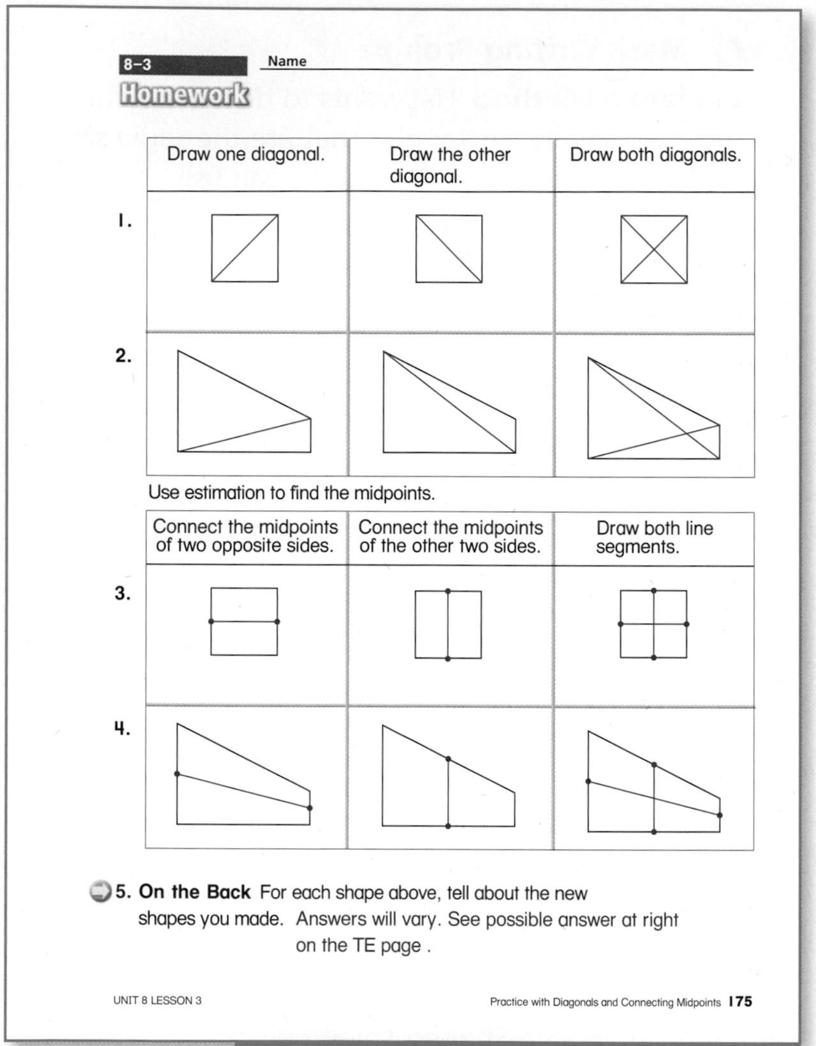

8–3 Homework Name

	Draw one diagonal.	Draw the other diagonal.	Draw both diagonals.
1.			
2.			

Use estimation to find the midpoints.

	Connect the midpoints of two opposite sides.	Connect the midpoints of the other two sides.	Draw both line segments.
3.			
4.			

5. **On the Back** For each shape above, tell about the new shapes you made. Answers will vary. See possible answer at right on the TE page .

UNIT 8 LESSON 3 Practice with Diagonals and Connecting Midpoints **175**

Homework and Remembering page 175

Possible answer for exercise 5:

For the square, drawing 2 diagonals creates 4 equal triangles with 2 equal sides each. Drawing 2 midpoint line segments creates 4 equal squares.

For the quadrilateral in exercises 2 and 4, drawing 2 diagonals creates 4 triangles, all of different size and shape. Drawing 2 midpoint line segments creates 4 smaller quadrilaterals, all of different size and shape.

Home or School Activity

Social Studies Connection

Signal Flags Boats use signal flags to communicate messages while at sea. Each flag represents a letter of the alphabet and a specific meaning like "driver below."

Invite children to make their own alphabet code using squares with diagonal lines and line segments connecting midpoints of opposite sides. Encourage children to write a coded message with their flags.

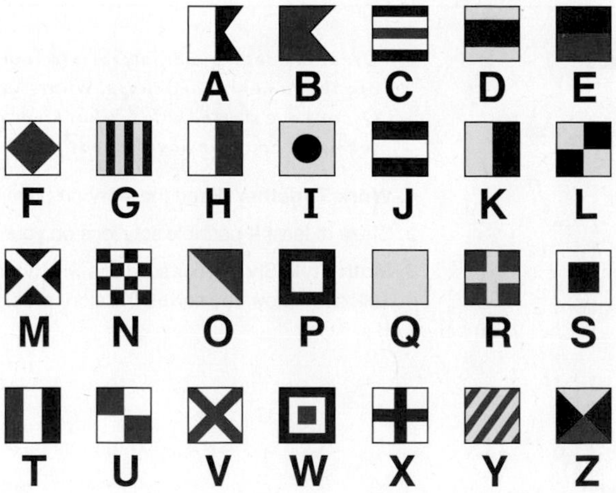

MINI UNIT 8

Unit Review and Test

Lesson Objectives

- Assess children's progress on unit objectives.

The Day at a Glance

Today's Goals	Materials
1 Assessing the Unit ▶ Assess children's progress on unit objectives. ▶ Use activities from unit lessons to reteach content.	Unit 8 Test, Student Activity Book pages 265–268 Unit 8 Test, Form A or B, Assessment Guide (optional) Unit 8 Performance Assessment, Assessment Guide (optional)
2 Extending the Assessment ▶ Use remediation for common errors.	
There is no homework assignment on a test day.	

Keeping Skills Sharp

Quick Practice 5 MINUTES	
If you are doing a unit review day, go over the homework. If this is a test day, omit the homework review.	**Review and Test Day** You may want to choose a quiet game or other activity (reading a book or working on homework for another subject) for children who finish early.

1 Assessing the Unit

Assess Unit Objectives

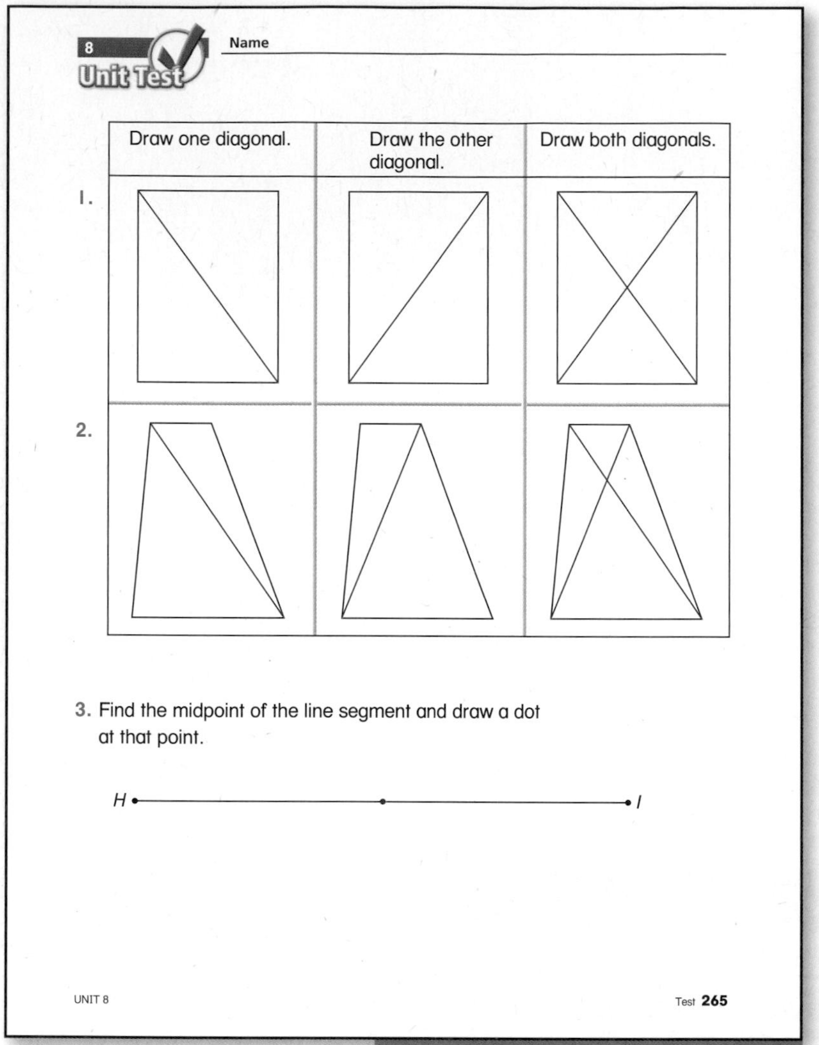
8 Unit Test

Name

	Draw one diagonal.	Draw the other diagonal.	Draw both diagonals.
1.			
2.			

3. Find the midpoint of the line segment and draw a dot at that point.

H I

UNIT 8 Test 265

Student Activity Book page 265

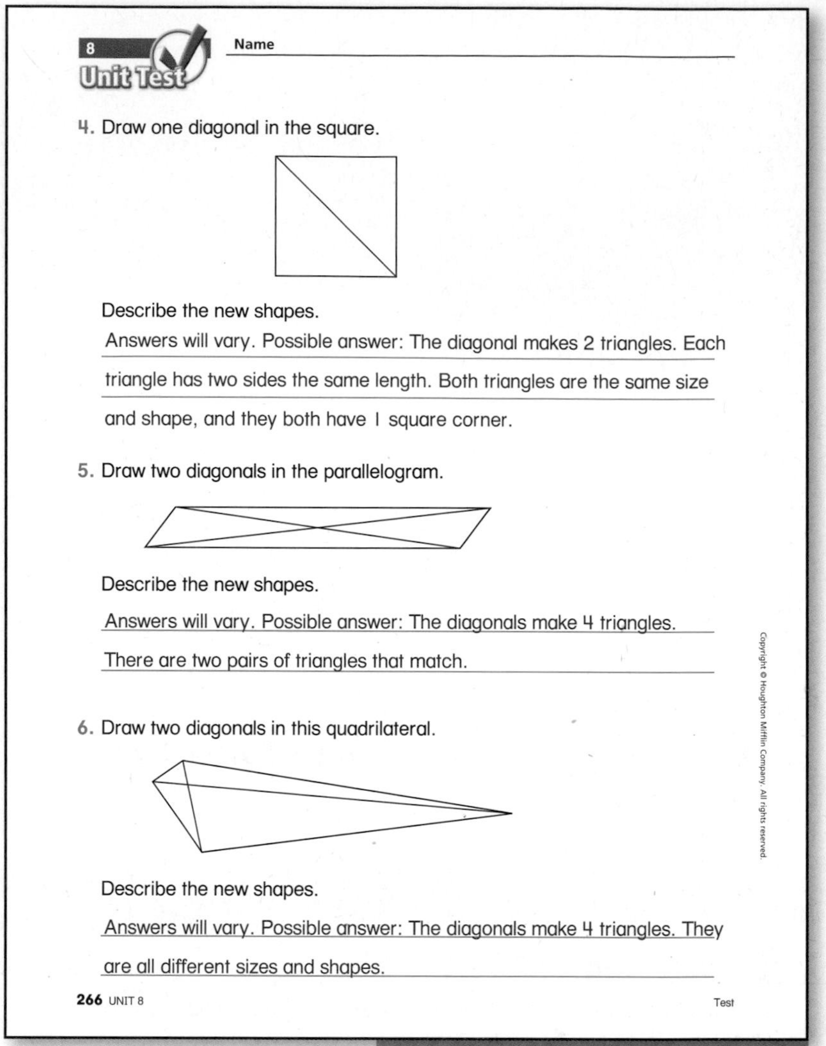
8 Unit Test

Name

4. Draw one diagonal in the square.

Describe the new shapes.

Answers will vary. Possible answer: The diagonal makes 2 triangles. Each triangle has two sides the same length. Both triangles are the same size and shape, and they both have 1 square corner.

5. Draw two diagonals in the parallelogram.

Describe the new shapes.

Answers will vary. Possible answer: The diagonals make 4 triangles. There are two pairs of triangles that match.

6. Draw two diagonals in this quadrilateral.

Describe the new shapes.

Answers will vary. Possible answer: The diagonals make 4 triangles. They are all different sizes and shapes.

266 UNIT 8 Test

Student Activity Book page 266

45 MINUTES (more if schedule permits)

Goal: Assess children's progress on unit objectives.

Materials: Student Activity Book pages 265–268, Assessment Guide (optional)

▶ Review and Assessment

If your students are ready for assessment on the unit objectives, use either the test on the Student Activity Book pages or one of the forms of the Unit 8 Test in the Assessment Guide to assess student progress. To assign a numerical score for all of these test forms, use 10 points for each question.

The chart to the right lists the test items, the unit objectives they cover, and the lesson activities in which the objective is covered in this unit.

▶ Reteaching Resources

Unit Test Items	Unit Objectives Tested	Activities to Use for Reteaching
1, 2	**8.1** Draw diagonals in quadrilaterals.	Lesson 1, Activity 2 Lesson 3, Activity 1 Lesson 3, Activity 2
3, 10	**8.2** Find the midpoint of a line segment.	Lesson 2, Activity 1

8 Unit Test Name

7. Connect the midpoints of two opposite sides.
Possible answer:

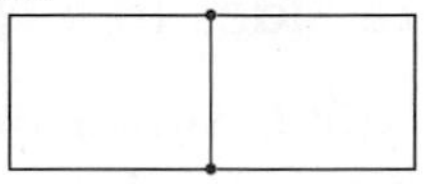

Describe the new shapes.

Answers will vary. Possible answer: The new shapes are 2 rectangles. They are the same size and shape.

8. Connect the midpoints of two opposite sides. Then connect the midpoints of the other two sides.

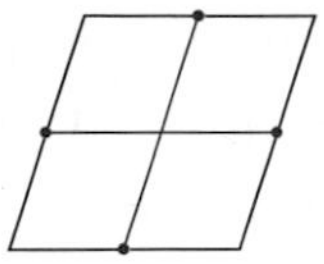

Describe the new shapes.

Answers will vary. Possible answer: The new shapes are all the same size and shape. They are all the same shape as the large shape.

UNIT 8 Test 267

Student Activity Book page 267

8 Unit Test Name

9. Connect the midpoints of two opposite sides. Then connect the midpoints of the other two sides.

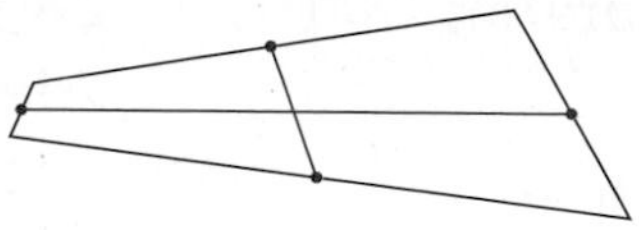

Describe the new shapes.

Answers will vary. Possible answer: The new shapes are 4 quadrilaterals. They are all different sizes and shapes.

10. **Extended Response** Use two different methods to find the midpoint of this line segment.

Describe both methods.

Answers will vary. Possible answer: I measured the line segment. It was 8 cm long. 4 cm and 4 cm are doubles partners, so I marked the midpoint at 4 cm.

I traced the line segment onto a piece of paper. I folded the traced line segment in half and marked the midpoint. Then I traced it onto the line segment above.

268 UNIT 8 Test

Student Activity Book page 268

Unit Test Items	Unit Objectives Tested	Activities to Use for Reteaching
4–6	**8.3** Describe shapes formed by drawing diagonals in a quadrilateral.	Lesson 1, Activity 2 Lesson 3, Activity 1 Lesson 3, Activity 2
7–9	**8.4** Describe shapes formed by connecting the midpoints of opposite sides of a quadrilateral.	Lesson 2, Activity 2 Lesson 3, Activity 1 Lesson 3, Activity 2

▶ Assessment Guide Resources

Form A, Free Response Test (Assessment Guide)
Form B, Multiple-Choice Test (Assessment Guide)
Performance Assessment (Assessment Guide)

▶ Portfolio Assessment

Teacher-selected Items for Student Portfolios:

- Homework, Lesson 3
- Class Activity work, Lessons 1 and 2

Student-selected Items for Student Portfolios:

- Favorite Home or School Activity
- Best Writing Prompt

2 Extending the Assessment

Common Errors

Activities for Remediation

Unit Objective 8.1

Draw diagonals in quadrilaterals.

Common Error: Doesn't Identify Diagonals in Quadrilaterals that Aren't Rectangles

Some students may think diagonals occur only in rectangles and squares.

Remediation Have students use two different colors to mark the two pairs of opposite corners. Then have them draw the diagonals.

Unit Objective 8.2

Find the midpoint of a line segment.

Common Error: Doesn't Use Estimation to Help Find or Check a Midpoint

Some students aren't proficient at using mental imagery to estimate the midpoint of a line segment.

Remediation If students have difficulty estimating the midpoint of a line segment, provide them with a great deal of practice at estimating midpoints of line segments and then folding the line segments in half to confirm the midpoints.

Discuss with students different times when estimating midpoints of line segments is appropriate: it is a good starting point for finding the midpoint with a ruler; it is a good way to verify the location of a midpoint; sometimes a precise midpoint isn't needed.

Unit Objective 8.3

Describe shapes formed by drawing diagonals in a quadrilateral.

Common Error: May Think Triangles Are the Same Shape and Size When They Are Not

Remediation Have children use tracing paper to check if figures are the same shape and size.

Unit Objective 8.4

Describe shapes formed by connecting the midpoints of opposite sides of a quadrilateral.

Common Error: Doesn't Provide Enough Information When Describing Decomposed Shapes

Some students may not include enough detail when describing shapes formed by joining midpoints of opposite sides of quadrilaterals.

Remediation If students don't provide enough detail in their descriptions of the decomposed shapes, ask them leading questions: What shapes are formed by joining one set of opposite side midpoints? How many shapes are formed? Are the shapes the same size and shape? How do the shapes compare to the original quadrilateral? Repeat questions for shapes formed by joining both sets of opposite side midpoints.

Common Error: Doesn't Correctly Name the Quadrilaterals Formed by Joining Midpoints of Opposite Sides of a Quadrilateral

Some students may incorrectly name the quadrilaterals formed by decomposing quadrilaterals.

Remediation Provide students with a great deal of practice naming quadrilaterals. Point out that often more than one name applies but they should use the name that is most specific to the shape. For instance, if a rectangle is formed that is a square, it is more informative to say the shape is a square. In the case of quadrilaterals that aren't parallelograms, students need to include more information than just using the term *quadrilateral.* For instance, they could say a quadrilateral with 4 sides of different measures, a quadrilateral with 4 different size angles, or a quadrilateral that does not have two sets of parallel sides.

Subtracting 2-Digit Numbers

The essential task that children face in multi-digit subtraction is determining whether there are enough ones in the ones place and tens in the tens place to subtract. If not, children must ungroup a hundred into 10 tens and a ten into 10 ones. Children will learn two ungrouping methods, the Expanded Method and the Ungroup First Method, as well as the Adding Up Method for subtraction. They use conceptual tools to understand the concept and develop their own solution methods.

Skills Trace

Grade 1	Grade 2	Grade 3
• Find money amounts. • Solve subtraction equations. • Represent and solve subtraction story problems.	• Count quarters, dimes, nickels, and pennies all together. • Subtract a 2-digit number from a 2- or 3-digit number, with and without regrouping. • Solve addition and subtraction story problems.	• Add and subtract money amounts. • Add and subtract whole numbers. • Write a related subtraction word problem for an addition problem; write an addition word problem for a subtraction problem.

Unit 9 Contents

Big Idea Quarters and Dollars

Big Idea Multi-Digit Subtraction Strategies

Big Idea Relating Addition and Subtraction Strategies

Unit 9 Assessment

Unit Objectives Tested	Unit Test Items	Lessons
9.1 Count quarters, dimes, nickels, and pennies all together.	1–3	1, 2
9.2 Subtract 2-digit numbers with or without ungrouping.	4–7	4–10, 13
9.3 Subtract a 2-digit number from a 3-digit number with two zeros.	8–9	7, 14
9.4 Subtract a 2-digit number from a 3-digit number with or without ungrouping a hundred.	10–11	8, 12, 13
9.5 Subtract a 2-digit number from a 3-digit number with one zero.	12–13	9, 13
9.6 Subtract a 2-digit number from a 3-digit number, ungrouping twice.	14–15, 20	7–10, 13
9.7 Solve addition and subtraction story problems.	16–19	4, 11, 15, 16

Assessment and Review Resources

Formal Assessment

Student Activity Book

- Unit Review and Test (pp. 311–314)

Assessment Guide

- Quick Quizzes (pp. A95–A96)
- Test A–Open Response (pp. A97–A99)
- Test B–Multiple Choice (pp. A100–A102)
- Performance Assessment (pp. A103–A105)

Test Generator CD-ROM

- Open Response Test
- Multiple Choice Test
- Test Bank Items

Informal Assessment

Teacher Edition

- Ongoing Assessment (in every lesson)
- Quick Practice (in every lesson)
- Portfolio Suggestions (p. 717)

Math Talk

- The Learning Classroom (p. 654)
- Math Talk in Action (pp. 671, 692)
- Solve and Discuss (pp. 640, 666)
- In Activities (pp. 608, 614, 620, 630, 636, 639, 644, 645, 650, 652, 658, 659, 670, 676, 683, 688, 700, 704, 710, 711)
- Student Pairs
  Helping Pairs (pp. 693, 699)
- Step-By-Step at the Board (pp. 640, 654, 672)

Review Opportunities

Homework and Remembering

- Review of recently taught topics
- Spiral Review

Teacher Edition

- Unit Review and Test (pp. 715–718)

Test Generator CD-ROM

- Custom Review Sheets

Planning Unit 9

NCTM Curriculum Focal Points and Connections Key: **1.** Number and Operations **2.** Number and Operations and Algebra **3.** Measurement **4.** Number and Operations **5.** Geometry and Measurement **6.** Algebra

Lesson NCTM Focal Points NCTM Standards	Resources	Materials for Lesson Activities	Materials for Going Further
9-1 **Explore Quarters** NCTM Focal Point: 6.1 NCTM Standard: 1	TE pp. 607–612 SAB pp. 269–274 H&R pp. 177–178 AC 9-1	Scissors ✓ Sticky board (optional) ✓ Real or play money Snack bags ✓ MathBoard materials	✓ Real or play money Paper bags Index cards Math Journals
9-2 **Explore Dollars** NCTM Focal Point: 6.1 NCTM Standard: 1	TE pp. 613–618 SAB pp. 275–276 H&R pp. 179–180 AG Quick Quiz 1 AC 9-2 MCC 33	Scissors ✓ Real or play money ✓ Sticky board (optional)	✓ Real or play money Paper bags Number cubes ✓ MathBoard materials Math Journals
9-3 **Partners and Subtraction** NCTM Focal Points: 2.4, 2.7, 2.11, 4.4 NCTM Standards: 1, 8, 10	TE pp. 619–626 SAB pp. 277–278 H&R pp. 181–182 AC 9-3	✓ MathBoard materials ✓ Demonstration Secret Code Cards ✓ Secret Code Cards	✓ MathBoard materials or Number Path and Dot Array Index cards Math Journals
9-4 **Subtraction Story Problems** NCTM Focal Points: 2.4, 2.7, 2.11, 4.4 NCTM Standards: 1, 6, 8, 10	TE pp. 627–632 SAB pp. 279–280 H&R pp. 183–184 AC 9-4	✓ MathBoard materials or Dot Array ✓ Demonstration Secret Code Cards ✓ Secret Code Cards	Index cards ✓ Game Cards (TRB M23) ✓ MathBoard materials Math Journals
9-5 **Two Methods of Subtractions** NCTM Focal Points: 2.4, 2.7, 2.11, 4.4 NCTM Standard: 1	TE pp. 633–642 SAB pp. 281–286 H&R pp. 185–186 AC 9-5	Strips of colored paper or 25-cm rulers ✓ Demonstration Secret Code Cards ✓ Secret Code Cards ✓ Base ten blocks	✓ Base ten blocks Index cards Math Journals
9-6 **Practice and Explain a Method** NCTM Focal Points: 2.4, 2.7, 2.8, 2.11 NCTM Standards: 1, 8	TE pp. 643–648 SAB pp. 287–288 H&R pp. 187–188 AC 9-6	None	✓ Base ten blocks Index cards ✓ MathBoard materials Math Journals
9-7 **Subtract from 200** NCTM Focal Points: 2.7, 2.11 NCTM Standards: 1, 8	TE pp. 649–656 SAB pp. 289–290 H&R pp. 189–190 AC 9-7	✓ MathBoard materials Dollar Equivalents (TRB M75–M76) ✓ Demonstration Secret Code Cards ✓ Secret Code Cards Base ten blocks	Colored pencils Index cards Math Journals
9-8 **Practice with Ungrouping First Method** NCTM Focal Points: 2.7, 2.11 NCTM Standards: 1, 8	TE pp. 657–662 SAB pp. 291–292 H&R pp. 191–192 AC 9-8	✓ MathBoard materials	Colored pencils Index cards Math Journals
9-9 **Zero in the Ones or Tens Place** NCTM Focal Points: 2.7, 2.11 NCTM Standards: 1, 8	TE pp. 663–668 SAB pp. 293–294 H&R pp. 193–194 AC 9-9	✓ MathBoard materials	Base ten blocks Math Journals

Resources/Materials Key: TE: Teacher Edition SAB: Student Activity Book H&R: Homework and Remembering AC: Activity Cards MCC: Math Center Challenge AG: Assessment Guide ✓: Grade 2 kits TRB: Teacher's Resource Book

NCTM Standards and Expectations Key: 1. Number and Operations 2. Algebra 3. Geometry 4. Measurement 5. Data Analysis and Probability 6. Problem Solving 7. Reasoning and Proof 8. Communication 9. Connections 10. Representation

Lesson NCTM Focal Points NCTM Standards	Resources	Materials for Lesson Activities	Materials for Going Further
9-10 **Model Subtraction with Money** NCTM Focal Points: 2.7. 2.11 NCTM Standards: 1, 8	TE pp. 669–674 SAB pp. 295–296 H&R pp. 195–196 AG Quick Quiz 2 AC 9-10 MCC 34	✓ Real or play money Small box labeled *Bank*	✓ Real or play money Small box labeled *Bank* Paper bags, Strips of paper Index cards, Calculators *Tightwad Tod*, by Daphne Skinner Math Journals
9-11 **Story Problems with Addition and Subtraction** NCTM Focal Points: 2.7, 2.8, 2.11 NCTM Standards: 1, 6, 9	TE pp. 675–680 SAB pp. 297–298 H&R pp. 197–198 AC 9-11	✓ MathBoard materials	Index cards ✓ Secret Code Cards Paper bags Math Journals
9-12 **Math Mountain Equations with Larger Numbers** NCTM Focal Points: 2.7, 2.9, 2.11, 4.4 NCTM Standards: 1, 6, 10	TE pp. 681–686 SAB pp. 299–300 H&R pp. 199–200 AC 9-12 MCC 35	Symbol Cards (TRB M45) Index cards ✓ 120 Poster	✓ MathBoard materials *100th Day Worries* Math Journals
9-13 **Practice Addition and Subtraction** NCTM Focal Points: 2.7, 2.11 NCTM Standards: 1, 6, 8	TE pp. 687–690 SAB pp. 301–302 H&R pp. 201–202 AC 9-13	None	✓ 120 Poster (TRB M60) Index cards Math Journals
9-14 **Buy and Sell with Two Dollars** NCTM Focal Points: 2.10, 2.11 NCTM Standards: 1, 6, 10	TE pp. 691–696 SAB pp. 303–304 H&R pp. 203–204 AC 9-14	✓ Real or play money Small classroom objects with price tags	✓ Real or play money Small classroom objects with price tags Index cards, Number cubes *Pigs Will Be Pigs: Fun with Math and Money* Math Journals
9-15 **Story Problems with Unknown Partners** NCTM Focal Points: 2.7, 2.11 NCTM Standards: 1, 6, 10	TE pp. 697–702 SAB pp. 305–306 H&R pp. 205–206 AC 9-15 MCC 36	✓ MathBoard materials	✓ MathBoard materials Index cards Math Journals
9-16 **More Story Problems with Unknown Partners** NCTM Focal Points: 2.10, 2.11 NCTM Standards: 1, 6, 10	TE pp. 703–708 SAB pp. 307–308 H&R pp. 207–208 AG Quick Quiz 3 AC 9-16	None	✓ MathBoard materials Index cards Symbol Cards (TRB M45) ✓ Number cubes Math Journals
9-17 **Use Mathematical Processes** NCTM Standards: 6, 7, 8, 9, 10	TE pp. 709–714 SAB pp. 309–310 AC 9-17 H&R pp. 209–210	10×10 Grid (TRB M62)	✓ Secret Code Cards Index Cards Math Journals
✓ **Unit Review and Test**	TE pp. 715–718 SAB pp. 311–314 AG Unit 9 Tests		

Manipulatives and Materials

Essential materials for teaching *Math Expressions* are available in the Grade 2 kits. These materials are indicated by a ✓ in these lists. At the front of this Teacher Edition is more information about kit contents, alternatives for the materials, and use of the materials.

Independent Learning Activities

Ready-Made Math Challenge Centers

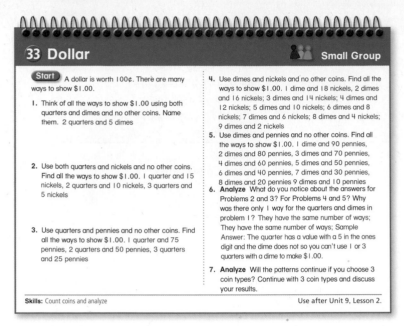

33 Dollar — Small Group

Start A dollar is worth 100¢. There are many ways to show $1.00.

1. Think of all the ways to show $1.00 using both quarters and dimes and no other coins. Name them. 2 quarters and 5 dimes
2. Use both quarters and nickels and no other coins. Find all the ways to show $1.00. 1 quarter and 15 nickels, 2 quarters and 10 nickels, 3 quarters and 5 nickels
3. Use quarters and pennies and no other coins. Find all the ways to show $1.00. 1 quarter and 75 pennies, 2 quarters and 50 pennies, 3 quarters and 25 pennies
4. Use dimes and nickels and no other coins. Find all the ways to show $1.00. 1 dime and 18 nickels, 2 dimes and 16 nickels; 3 dimes and 14 nickels; 4 dimes and 12 nickels; 5 dimes and 10 nickels; 6 dimes and 8 nickels; 7 dimes and 6 nickels; 8 dimes and 4 nickels; 9 dimes and 2 nickels
5. Use dimes and pennies and no other coins. Find all the ways to show $1.00. 1 dime and 90 pennies, 2 dimes and 80 pennies, 3 dimes and 70 pennies, 4 dimes and 60 pennies, 5 dimes and 50 pennies, 6 dimes and 40 pennies, 7 dimes and 30 pennies, 8 dimes and 20 pennies 9 dimes and 10 pennies
6. **Analyze** What do you notice about the answers for Problems 2 and 3? For Problems 4 and 5? Why was there only 1 way for the quarters and dimes in problem 1? They have the same number of ways; They have the same number of ways; Sample Answer: The quarter has a value with a 5 in the ones digit and the dime does not so you can't use 1 or 3 quarters with a dime to make $1.00.
7. **Analyze** Will the patterns continue if you choose 3 coin types? Continue with 3 coin types and discuss your results.

Skills: Count coins and analyze — Use after Unit 9, Lesson 2.

Grouping Small Group

Materials Play coins

Objective Children show a dollar using two coin types and then three coin types.

Connections Measurement and Real World

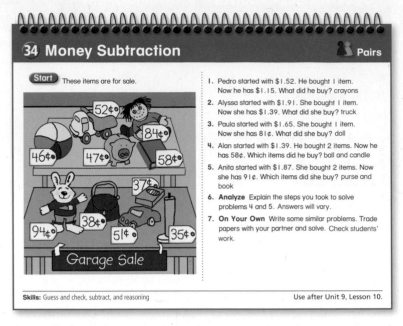

34 Money Subtraction — Pairs

Start These items are for sale.

1. Pedro started with $1.52. He bought 1 item. Now he has $1.15. What did he buy? crayons
2. Alyssa started with $1.91. She bought 1 item. Now she has $1.39. What did she buy? truck
3. Paula started with $1.65. She bought 1 item. Now she has 81¢. What did she buy? doll
4. Alan started with $1.39. He bought 2 items. Now he has 58¢. Which items did he buy? ball and candle
5. Anita started with $1.87. She bought 2 items. Now she has 91¢. Which items did she buy? purse and book
6. **Analyze** Explain the steps you took to solve problems 4 and 5. Answers will vary.
7. **On Your Own** Write some similar problems. Trade papers with your partner and solve. Check students' work.

Skills: Guess and check, subtract, and reasoning — Use after Unit 9, Lesson 10.

Grouping Pairs

Materials None

Objective Children identify which item was bought when given a starting and ending amount.

Connections Measurement and Real World

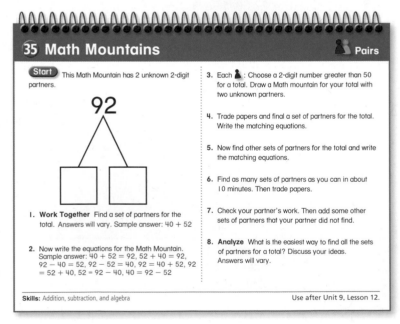

35 Math Mountains — Pairs

Start This Math Mountain has 2 unknown 2-digit partners.

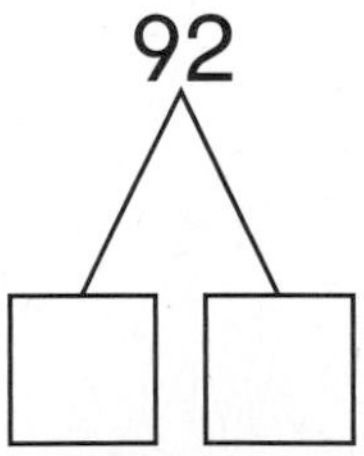

1. **Work Together** Find a set of partners for the total. Answers will vary. Sample answer: 40 + 52
2. Now write the equations for the Math Mountain. Sample answer: 40 + 52 = 92, 52 + 40 = 92, 92 − 40 = 52, 92 − 52 = 40, 92 = 40 + 52, 92 = 52 + 40, 52 = 92 − 40, 40 = 92 − 52
3. Each [partner icon]: Choose a 2-digit number greater than 50 for a total. Draw a Math mountain for your total with two unknown partners.
4. Trade papers and find a set of partners for the total. Write the matching equations.
5. Now find other sets of partners for the total and write the matching equations.
6. Find as many sets of partners as you can in about 10 minutes. Then trade papers.
7. Check your partner's work. Then add some other sets of partners that your partner did not find.
8. **Analyze** What is the easiest way to find all the sets of partners for a total? Discuss your ideas. Answers will vary.

Skills: Addition, subtraction, and algebra — Use after Unit 9, Lesson 12.

Grouping Pairs

Materials None

Objective Children find sets of partners for a given total and write the matching equations.

Connections Computation and Algebra

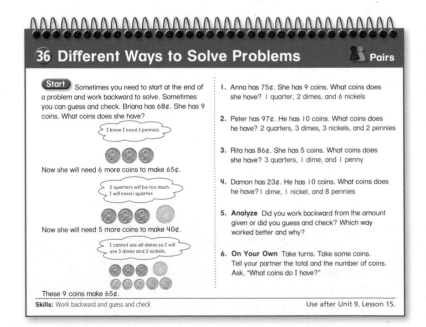

36 Different Ways to Solve Problems — Pairs

Start Sometimes you need to start at the end of a problem and work backward to solve. Sometimes you can guess and check. Briana has 68¢. She has 9 coins. What coins does she have?

I know I need 3 pennies.

Now she will need 6 more coins to make 65¢.

2 quarters will be too much. I will need 1 quarter.

Now she will need 5 more coins to make 40¢.

I cannot use all dimes so I will use 3 dimes and 2 nickels.

These 9 coins make 65¢.

1. Anna has 75¢. She has 9 coins. What coins does she have? 1 quarter, 2 dimes, and 6 nickels
2. Peter has 97¢. He has 10 coins. What coins does he have? 2 quarters, 3 dimes, 3 nickels, and 2 pennies
3. Rita has 86¢. She has 5 coins. What coins does she have? 3 quarters, 1 dime, and 1 penny
4. Damon has 23¢. He has 10 coins. What coins does he have? 1 dime, 1 nickel, and 8 pennies
5. **Analyze** Did you work backward from the amount given or did you guess and check? Which way worked better and why?
6. **On Your Own** Take turns. Take some coins. Tell your partner the total and the number of coins. Ask, "What coins do I have?"

Skills: Work backward and guess and check — Use after Unit 9, Lesson 15.

Grouping Pairs

Materials Play coins

Objective Children determine the coins used when given money amount and the number of coins.

Connections Reasoning and Real World

Ready-Made Math Resources

Go Digital

Technology — Tutorials, Practice, and Intervention

Soar to Success Math

Use online, individualized intervention and support to bring students to proficiency.

HARCOURT MEGA MATH Grades K-6

Help students practice skills and apply concepts through exciting math adventures.

DESTINATION Math®

Extend and enrich students' understanding of skills and concepts through engaging, interactive lessons and activities.

Visit Education Place®
www.eduplace.com

Visit www.eduplace.com/mx2t/ and find family, teacher, and student materials, activities, games, and more.

Literature Links

Henry Hikes to Fitchburg

Henry Hikes to Fitchburg

Using a distance of 30 miles, students can create two-digit subtraction sentences about Henry the Bear's hike to Fitchburg, writen by D.B. Johnson.

Literature Connections

- *Tightwad Tod*, by Daphne Skinner, illustrated by John A. Nez (Disney Press, 2005)
- *100th Day Worries*, by Margery Cuyler, illustrated by Arthur Howard (Simon & Schuster Children's Publishing, 2000)
- *Pigs Will Be Pigs: Fun with Math and Money*, by Amy Axelrod, illustrated by Sharon McGinley-Nally (Aladdin Picture Books, 1997)

Unit 9 Teaching Resources

Differentiated Instruction

Individualizing Instruction		
	Level	**Frequency**
Activities	• Intervention • On Level • Challenge	All 3 in every lesson
	Level	**Frequency**
Math Writing Prompts	• Intervention • On Level • Challenge	All 3 in every lesson
Math Center Challenges	For advanced students	
	4 in every unit	

Reaching All Learners		
	Lessons	**Pages**
English Language Learners	1, 2, 3, 4, 5, 6, 7, 8, 9, 10, 11, 12, 13, 14, 15, 16, 17	609, 615, 620, 628, 634, 644, 650, 658, 664, 670, 676, 682, 688, 692, 698, 704, 711
	Lessons	**Pages**
Extra Help	9, 12, 14, 15	665, 684, 693, 700
	Lesson	**Page**
Advanced Learners	15	698

Strategies for English Language Learners

Present this problem to all children. Offer the different levels of support to meet children's levels of language proficiency.

Objective To model how to *expand* and *ungroup* double digit numbers.

Problem Write *expand* and *ungroup* on the board. Give children 26 cubes. Say: **Let us *expand* 26.** Model how to make two 10 strips and a group of 6 ones. Point and say: **We *expand* 26 into 6 ones and 2 tens.** Have children repeat.

Newcomer

- **Let us *ungroup* 1 ten.** Model how to ungroup. Say: **We ungroup 1 ten. Now we have 16 ones.** Have children repeat.

Beginning

- Say: **Let us *ungroup* a ten.** Model how to ungroup. Ask: **How many ones do we have now?** 16 ones **How many tens?** 1 ten

Intermediate

- Ask: **Does expand mean show the tens and ones?** yes
- Say: **Let us *ungroup* a ten.** Model how to ungroup. Say: ***Ungroup* means break apart 1 ten and add it to the __.** ones

Advanced

- Ask: **What groups do we show when we *expand* a number?** tens, ones
- Say: **Now let us take apart 1 group of ten**. Ask: **Did we *ungroup* a ten?** yes

Connections

Art Connection
Lesson 3, page 626

Multicultural Connection
Lesson 9, page 668

Real-World Connection
Lesson 13, page 690

Science Connections
Lesson 4, page 632
Lesson 6, page 648
Lesson 15, page 702
Lesson 17, page 714

Social Studies Connections
Lesson 2, page 618
Lesson 8, page 662
Lesson 11, page 680

Sport Connection
Lesson 16, page 708

Literature Connections
Lesson 10, page 674
Lesson 12, page 686
Lesson 14, page 696

Technology Connection
Lesson 7, page 656

Math Background

Putting Research into Practice for Unit 9

From Our Curriculum Research Project: Two-Digit Subtraction

The key concept that children need to grasp concerning two-digit subtraction is the making of enough ones in the ones place and enough tens in the tens place to allow for the completion of the subtraction calculation. Fortunately, the concept of ungrouping 1 ten into 10 ones when needed, can be readily shown with 10-sticks and circles and with dollars and cents.

Children are encouraged to develop their own methods of subtracting two-digit numbers before being given any formal instruction. They then explore the Ungroup First and Expanded methods. We found that children can understand ungrouping from the tens and the ones and that this made subtracting 3-digit numbers much easier.

–Karen Fuson, Author
Math Expressions

From Current Research: Subtraction Algorithms

[The left-to-right ungrouping method is] a slight variation of [the common U.S. algorithm] in which Step 1 (regrouping) is done for all columns first...The goal is to fix the top number so that every top digit is larger than the corresponding bottom digit. The second major step is then to subtract in every column. This subtraction can also be done in any direction. [This method] clarif[ies] that the top number is a single number that must be rewritten in a form equivalent in value but ready for subtraction in every column.

National Research Council. "Developing Proficiency with Whole Numbers." *Adding It Up: Helping Students Learn Mathematics.* Washington, D.C.: National Academy Press, 2001. 205–206.

Other Useful References: Subtraction

Carpenter, T.P., M.L. Franke, V.R. Jacobs, E. Fennema, & S.B. Empson. "A Longitudinal Study of Invention and Understanding in Children's Multidigit Addition and Subtraction." *Journal for Research in Mathematics Education* 29 (1998): 3–20.

Hiebert, J., and D. Wearne. "Instruction, Understanding, and Skill in Multidigit Addition and Subtraction." *Cognition and Instruction* 14 (1996): 251–83.

Getting Read to Teach Unit 9

In this unit, children learn to subtract 2-digit numbers from 2- and 3-digit numbers, using various ungrouping methods described below. They build communication skills as they explain and justify their thinking and continue to solve story problems.

Math Expressions Vocabulary

As you teach this unit, emphasize understanding of these terms:

- break apart
- ungroup
- decade partners
- money string
- Math Mountain

See Glossary on pp. T7–T20.

Subtraction Methods

Lessons 3, 4, 5, 6, 7, 8, 9, 11, 12, 13, 14, 15, and 16

The Expanded Method and the Ungroup First Method are research-based, accessible algorithms that children can understand and explain. The steps in these drawings correspond to steps in numerical methods. Children may devise different approaches in which they ungroup or subtract in either direction.

136 - 47 = □

Boxes, Sticks, and Circles Children draw the number that is being subtracted from using boxes, sticks, and circles. They show the ungrouping in their drawings. Then they cross out to subtract. Children relate the drawings to a numerical method. They may do different numerical methods.

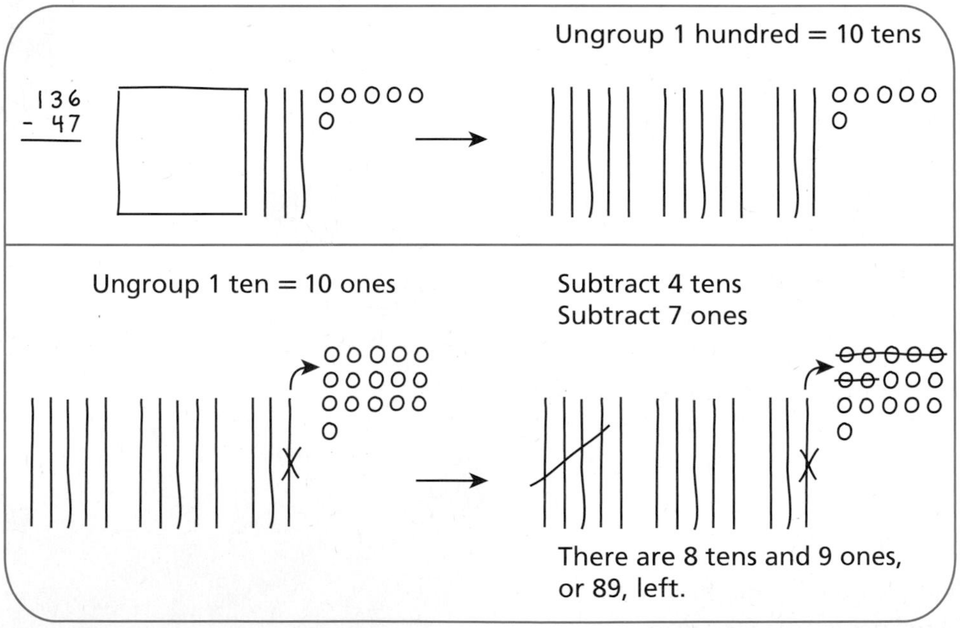

Expanded Method Children break apart the numbers to begin. They break apart 3-digit numbers into hundreds, tens, and ones, and 2-digit numbers into tens and ones. This helps them see the real value of each part of the number as they ungroup and subtract.

Ungrouping Left to Right

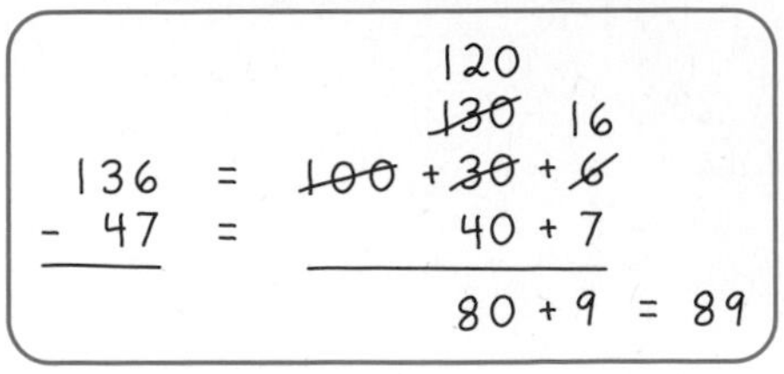

Ungrouping Right to Left

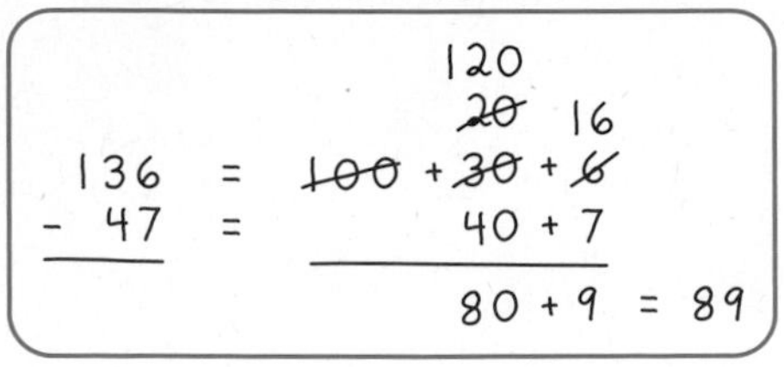

Secret Code Cards These are especially helpful in showing the Expanded Method.

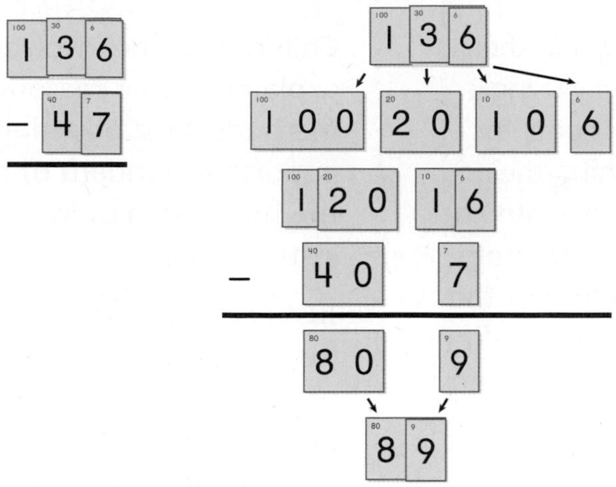

Ungroup First Method Children will continue their understanding of a number and its value as they learn how to work with the number they are subtracting from as a whole. They ungroup everything first to prepare the number for subtraction. A magnifying glass enables children to "look inside" the number and see that they are not changing the number to a new amount, but are, instead, making a new form of the number. For the advantages of this method over the common subtraction method, see Lesson 8.

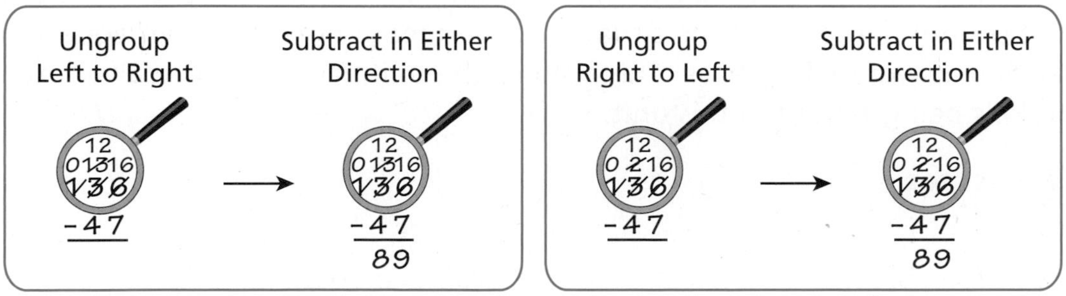

Adding Up Method Children are introduced to finding unknown addends. This strategy is based on Counting On and Making a Ten. The three ways that children can add up to find the unknown partner are shown in these examples.

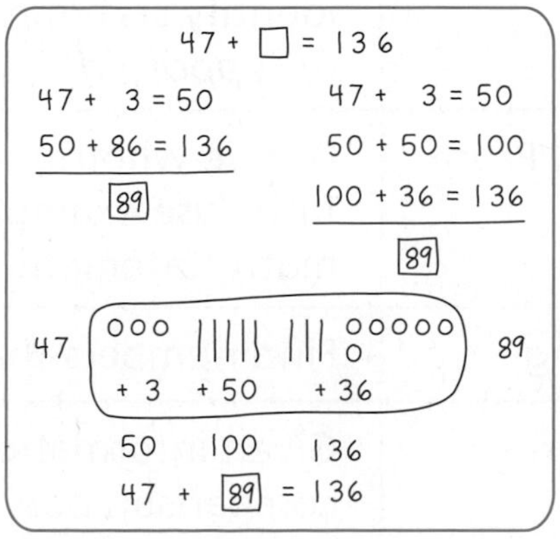

Explaining One Step at a Time
All Lessons

Throughout the unit, children learn to explain their subtraction methods clearly and completely using place value language. This is an important goal for children—to become comfortable explaining their mathematical thinking. Also, examining one step at a time can advance children who need extra help. With time, children build an understanding of the whole process of subtraction. All children benefit in both their communication and process skills when they learn to hear, and then present, a step-by-step explanation of their methods for subtraction and relate the visual proof drawings to each step of a numerical method.

Reasoning
All Lessons

Children will be involved in describing and explaining their reasoning as they share their methods for subtracting. This work is part of the important standard of reasoning, which includes the broad idea of informal explanations and justification.

Justification involves "providing sufficient reason for," according to the standards, and proof is a form of justification. As children are involved in making proof drawings for their subtraction methods, they provide justification of their methods. Also, as they make proof drawings, children confirm for themselves and others that their methods do indeed work. Children can become more confident in their mathematical abilities with this support for their justification work.

Problem Solving
In *Math Expressions* a research-based, algebraic problem-solving approach that focuses on problem types is used: understand the situation, represent the situation with a math drawing or an equation, solve the problem, and see that the answer makes sense. Throughout the unit, children solve a variety of problems using the subtraction skills being taught in this unit.

Use Mathematical Processes
Lesson 17

The NCTM process skills of problem solving, reasoning and proof, communication, connections, and representation are interwoven through all lessons throughout the year. The last lesson of this unit allows children to extend their use of mathematical processes to other situations.

Activity	NCTM Process Skill	Goal
Math and Science	Connections	Identify statements as *true, not true, or unsupported.*
True or False?	Reasoning and Proof	Decide whether a math statement is true or false; use examples as proof; write and test a math statement.
Number Puzzles	Problem Solving	Find numbers that meet given requirements.
Make Comparison Bars	Representation	Given information about a set of data, make comparison bars to show the data.
Be a Helper	Communication	Identify an error and explain how to correct it.

UNIT 9 LESSON 1

Explore Quarters

Lesson Objectives

- Combine pennies, nickels, and dimes to make 25 cents.
- Count by quarters, dimes, nickels, and pennies up to different totals.

Vocabulary

penny	dime
nickel	quarter

The Day at a Glance

Today's Goals	Materials	
1 Teaching the Lesson A1: Discuss quarters and combine pennies, nickels, and dimes to make 25 cents. A2: Count by 25s (quarters) from various starting numbers. Make money strings. A3: Count money–quarters, dimes, nickels, and pennies. **2 Going Further** ▶ Differentiated Instruction **3 Homework and Targeted Practice**	**Lesson Activities** Student Activity Book pp. 269–274 (includes Coin Cards, Quarter Squares, Family Letter) Homework and Remembering pp. 177–178 Scissors Sticky board (optional) Real or play money Snack bags MathBoard materials	**Going Further** Activity Cards 9-1 Real or play money Paper bags Index cards Math Journals

Use Math Talk today!

Keeping Skills Sharp

Quick Practice — 5 MINUTES

Goal: Practice subtraction with teen totals.

Teen Subtraction Flash Have a **Student Leader** call out a teen total and one of its partners. The class flashes the other partner with their fingers. For example: The Student Leader says: "16 take away 7 equals something." The children flash 9 fingers to show the unknown addend. (See Unit 7 Lesson 5.)

Repeated Quick Practice Use this Quick Practice from a previous lesson.

- ▶ **Make-a-Ten Cards: Subtraction** (See Unit 7 Lesson 5.)

Daily Routines

Quarters and Other Coins Making and Counting Coins that Make a Quarter, Counting to 200¢ by 25¢, Making and Counting Dollars and Cents: 3-Digit Numbers as Dollars and Cents (See pp. xxvi–xxvii.)

- ▶ Led by teacher

Money Routine Using the 120 Poster, Using the Money Flip Chart, Using the Number Path, Using Secret Code Cards (See pp. xxiii–xxv.)

- ▶ Led by Student Leaders

1 Teaching the Lesson

Activity 1

Explore and Make Quarters

25 MINUTES

Goals: Discuss quarters and combine pennies, nickels, and dimes to make 25 cents.

Materials: scissors (1 pair per child), Coin Cards and Quarter Squares (Student Activity Book pages 269–272), MathBoard materials

NCTM Standard:
Number and Operations

Class Management

Make sure children cut exactly on the dotted lines, especially when cutting out the Quarter Squares. Have Student Helpers work with children experiencing difficulty.

The Coin Cards on Student Activity Book page 269 and the Quarter Squares on Student Activity Book pages 271–272 are also available on TRB M77 and M73–M74. You can make sturdy coins for classroom use by copying the copymasters onto cardstock.

The Learning Classroom

Building Concepts Children need a great deal of experience with coins in order to understand their different values and which different combinations of coins have the same value as another coin.

It is important to return to the discussion of the value of coins not only today in math class, but whenever the opportunity arises during the year, both in math class and in other classes.

▶ Discuss Quarters and Other Coins WHOLE CLASS

Have children cut out the Coin Cards on Student Activity Book page 269 and the Quarter Squares on page 271. Then tell the children to put the coins from page 269 in one pile and the quarters from page 271 in another pile with the quarter side face up.

Math Talk Have children share what they know about quarters and other coins.

- What coins do you have in your two piles? quarters, dimes, nickels, and pennies
- What can you buy with a quarter? a dime? a nickel? a penny? *Accept children's answers. They may have little idea about the worth of each monetary unit and may not understand the relative value of the coins.*

▶ Combine Different Coins to Make 25 Cents PAIRS

Ask questions to guide children in making 25 cents using different coins.

- How many pennies do we need to make an amount equal to one quarter? 25 pennies
- How many nickels have the same value as one quarter? 5 nickels

Show students how they can place 5 nickel cards on top of the quarter card to check.

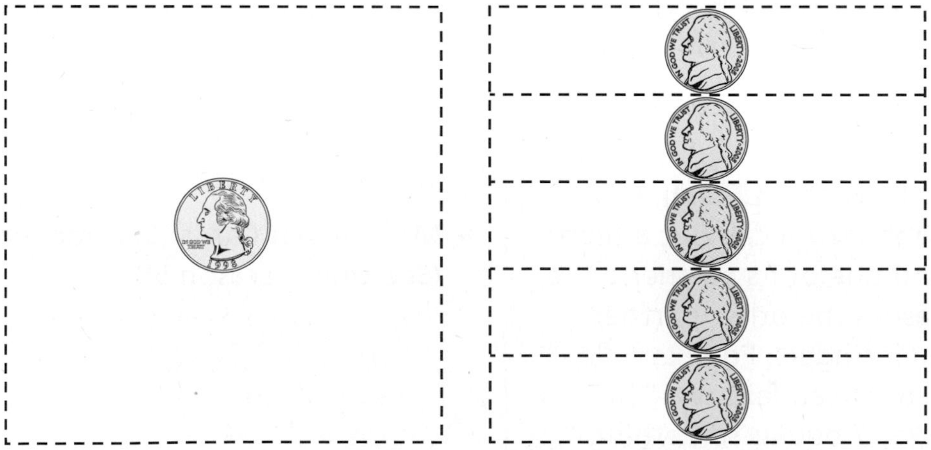

from Student Activity Book page 269

- Now use your coins and try to make 25 cents using just dimes. Remember to count the cents for each coin to see how much you have. Can you make 25 cents with just dimes? no Why not? Two dimes equals 20 cents and that's not enough. Three dimes equals 30 cents and that's too much.

Have **Helping Pairs** combine at least two different kinds of coins such as, dimes and nickels to make 25 cents. They can check by placing the coins of lesser value on top of the Quarter Squares.

Now challenge children to make 25 cents, using any of their coins. Have them record their coin combinations on their MathBoards.

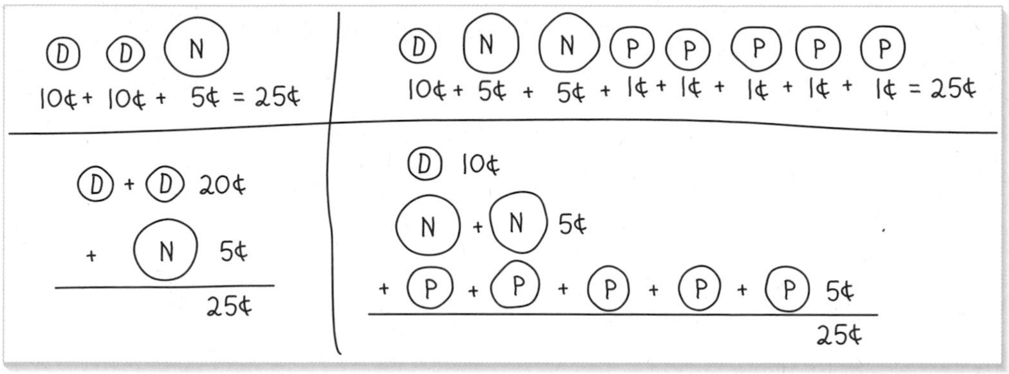

The Learning Classroom

Building Concepts There are many different combinations of coins that equal 25 cents. They are all shown on the backs of the **Quarter Squares** on Student Activity Book page 271.

Have children check whether any of their combinations match the ones shown on the backs of the Quarter Squares. Then have volunteers describe any combinations that have not already been shown.

Activity 2

Count by 25s

▶ Count by 25s from Various Starting Numbers

WHOLE CLASS

Have children count by 25s from various starting numbers up to 200. The starting number should always be a multiple of 25. Begin counting with the number 25 several times so that the children become familiar with the pattern.

Then have children count by quarters. Use cents rather than dollars and cents at this time.

- Let's count by quarters. Start with 25 cents and count with me. 25 cents, 50 cents, 75 cents, 100 cents, 125 cents, and so on
- Now let's start counting at 50 cents. 50 cents, 75 cents, and so on
- Where should we start counting now? (Have a child select a starting number.)

▶ Explore Different Money Equivalencies WHOLE CLASS

Have children identify what different quantities of quarters are worth. For example, 1 quarter is worth 25¢, 2 quarters are worth 50¢, 3 quarters are worth 75¢, and so on.

If time permits, have children make quarter and dollar strings. Write the following two examples on the classroom board. Then have children write their own strings on a piece of paper.

25¢ = 10¢ + 15¢ = 5¢ + 20¢ = 5¢ + 5¢ + 5¢ + 5¢ + 5¢ = . . .

100¢ = 90¢ + 5¢ + 5¢ = 50¢ + 25¢ + 10¢ + 10¢ + 5¢ = . . .

15 MINUTES

Goals: Count by 25s (quarters) from various starting numbers. Make money strings.

NCTM Standard:
Number and Operations

English Language Learners

Draw a row of 4 quarters on the board. Write the cents as you count. Add more rows and continue.

- **Beginning** Say: **1 quarter is 25¢.** Have children repeat.
- **Intermediate** Say: **1 quarter is __.** 25¢ **2 quarters is __.** 50¢
- **Advanced** Ask: **How many cents is 1 quarter?** 25¢ **How many cents is 2 quarters?** 50¢

Activity 3

Coin Shifts

15 MINUTES

Goals: Count money–quarters, dimes, nickels, and pennies.

Materials: sticky board (optional), real or play money, snack bags (1 per child)

✓ **NCTM Standard:**
Number and Operations

Class Management

Looking Ahead In Lesson 2, children will be cutting out paper dollar bills from Student Activity Book pages 275–276. They will also need to use the coins from this lesson. You may wish to have them store the coins in snack bags so they don't get lost.

▶ Count Sequences of Coins WHOLE CLASS

Write the following sequence of coins on the board. (If you have a sticky board, you can show the sequences using real, play, or paper coins.) Then point to the coins, as you and the children count aloud together. Continue to use cents only, rather than dollars and cents.

Each time the coin shifts (for example, from quarter to penny) freeze the counting and have children raise their fingers to show the value of the new coin.

Write:	Q	Q	Q	Q	Q	Q	Q	P	P	P	P
Say:	25¢	50¢	75¢	100¢	125¢	150¢	175¢	176¢	177¢	178¢	179¢

↑ Freeze (show 1) [at 176¢]

Erase some of the coins and write new sequences.

Write:	Q	Q	Q	Q	Q	N	N	N	N	N
Say:	25¢	50¢	75¢	100¢	125¢	130¢	135¢	140¢	145¢	150¢

↑ Freeze (show 5) [at 130¢]

Write:	Q	Q	Q	Q	Q	Q	Q	D	D	D	D	D
Say:	25¢	50¢	75¢	100¢	125¢	150¢	175¢	185¢	195¢	205¢	215¢	225¢

↑ Freeze (show 10) [at 185¢]

Write:	Q	Q	Q	D	D	D	D	N	N	N
Say:	25¢	50¢	75¢	85¢	95¢	105¢	115¢	120¢	125¢	130¢

↑ Freeze (show 10) [at 85¢] ↑ Freeze (show 5) [at 120¢]

Write:	Q	Q	Q	Q	Q	D	D	N	N	N	N	P	P
Say:	25¢	50¢	75¢	100¢	125¢	135¢	145¢	150¢	155¢	160¢	165¢	166¢	167¢

↑ Freeze (show 10) [at 135¢] ↑ Freeze (show 5) [at 150¢] ↑ Freeze (show 1) [at 166¢]

▶ Introduce Dollar and Cent Notation

Introduce how to write and say money amounts over 100¢ as dollars and cents. Some children may be familiar with this way of writing money; others will not be. Write the following on the board.

187¢ = $1.87

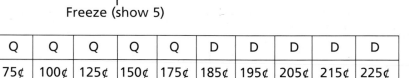

- One hundred eighty-seven cents equals one dollar and eighty-seven cents.
- We will work with this way of writing and saying money later in the year.

Ongoing Assessment

Ask children to tell how much each of these combinations of coins is worth.

1. 3 Dimes + 2 Nickels
2. 2 Dimes + 2 Nickels + 2 Pennies
3. 1 Quarter + 5 Pennies
4. 1 Quarter + 2 Dimes + 1 Nickel
5. 2 Quarters + 2 Dimes + 2 Nickels + 2 Pennies

2 Going Further

Differentiated Instruction

Intervention — Activity Card 9-1

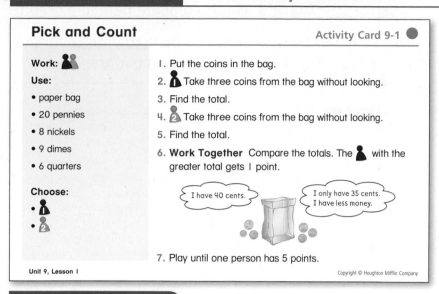

Pick and Count

Activity Card 9-1 ●

Work: pairs

Use:
- paper bag
- 20 pennies
- 8 nickels
- 9 dimes
- 6 quarters

Choose:
- Student 1
- Student 2

1. Put the coins in the bag.
2. Student 1 Take three coins from the bag without looking.
3. Find the total.
4. Student 2 Take three coins from the bag without looking.
5. Find the total.
6. **Work Together** Compare the totals. The student with the greater total gets 1 point.

I have 40 cents.
I only have 35 cents. I have less money.

7. Play until one person has 5 points.

Unit 9, Lesson 1

Activity Note Each pair needs a brown paper bag, 20 pennies, 8 nickels, 9 dimes, and 6 quarters (real or play).

Math Writing Prompt

Draw a Picture What is the total value of 3 quarters and 4 pennies? Draw a picture to help explain your answer.

Soar to Success Math Software Support

Warm Up 3.10

On Level — Activity Card 9-1

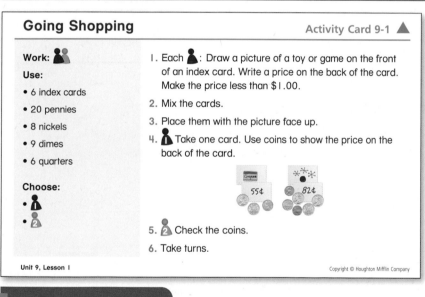

Going Shopping

Activity Card 9-1 ▲

Work: pairs

Use:
- 6 index cards
- 20 pennies
- 8 nickels
- 9 dimes
- 6 quarters

Choose:
- Student 1
- Student 2

1. Each student: Draw a picture of a toy or game on the front of an index card. Write a price on the back of the card. Make the price less than $1.00.
2. Mix the cards.
3. Place them with the picture face up.
4. Student 1 Take one card. Use coins to show the price on the back of the card.

5. Student 2 Check the coins.
6. Take turns.

Unit 9, Lesson 1

Activity Note Each pair needs six index cards, 20 pennies, 8 nickels, 9 dimes, and 6 quarters (real or play) or Coin Card from Student Activity Book p. 269. You may want to prepare index cards for the pairs.

Math Writing Prompt

Explain Your Thinking Do five coins always have a value greater than three coins? Explain why or why not.

Harcourt Mega Math Software Support

Numberopolis: Lulu's Lunch Counter, Level J

Challenge — Activity Card 9-1

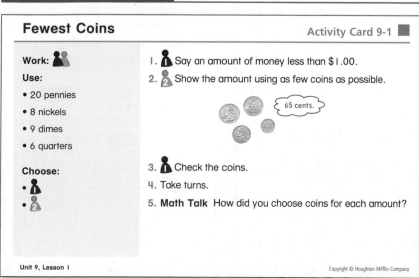

Fewest Coins

Activity Card 9-1 ■

Work: pairs

Use:
- 20 pennies
- 8 nickels
- 9 dimes
- 6 quarters

Choose:
- Student 1
- Student 2

1. Student 1 Say an amount of money less than $1.00.
2. Student 2 Show the amount using as few coins as possible.

3. Student 1 Check the coins.
4. Take turns.
5. **Math Talk** How did you choose coins for each amount?

Unit 9, Lesson 1

Activity Note Each pair needs 20 pennies, 8 nickels, 9 dimes, and 6 quarters (real or play) or Coin Card from Student Activity Book p. 269.

Math Writing Prompt

Make a List How many ways can you make 30 cents using only nickels and dimes?

Destination Math Software Support

Course II: Module 3: Unit 2: Money

3 Homework and Targeted Practice

9–1 Homework **Goal:** Additional Practice

This Homework page provides practice drawing different combinations of coins that have the same value as a quarter.

9–1 Homework Name ______

Draw coins to show 6 different ways to make 25¢ with pennies, nickels, and/or dimes.
Answers will vary. Possible answers given.

1. 25¢ — 10¢ 10¢ 5¢	2. 25¢ — 10¢ 10¢ 1¢ 1¢ 1¢ 1¢ 1¢	3. 25¢ — 10¢ 5¢ 5¢ 1¢ 1¢ 1¢ 1¢ 1¢
4. 25¢ — 5¢ 5¢ 5¢ 5¢ 5¢	5. 25¢ — 10¢ 5¢ 1¢ 1¢ 1¢ 1¢ 1¢ 1¢ 1¢ 1¢ 1¢ 1¢	6. 25¢ — 10¢ 5¢ 5¢ 5¢

Write how to count the money.

7. 

25¢ 50¢ 75¢ 100¢ or $1.00 125¢ or $1.25 150¢ or $1.50 175¢ or $1.75 200¢ or $2.00 225¢ or $2.25

8. 

25¢ 50¢ 75¢ 85¢ 95¢ 96¢ 97¢

UNIT 9 LESSON 1 Explore Quarters 177

Homework and Remembering page 177

9–1 Targeted Practice **Goal:** Compare data in a graph.

This Targeted Practice page can be used with children who need extra practice interpreting bar graphs.

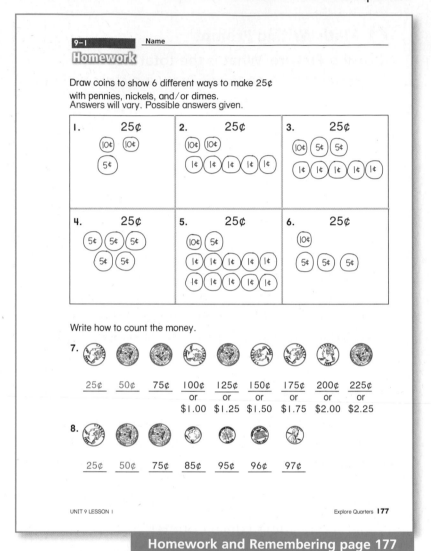

9–1 Targeted Practice Name ______

Use the bar graph to answer the questions below. Write your answers in the boxes. Ring *more* or *fewer.*

Number of Pets in the Pet Store

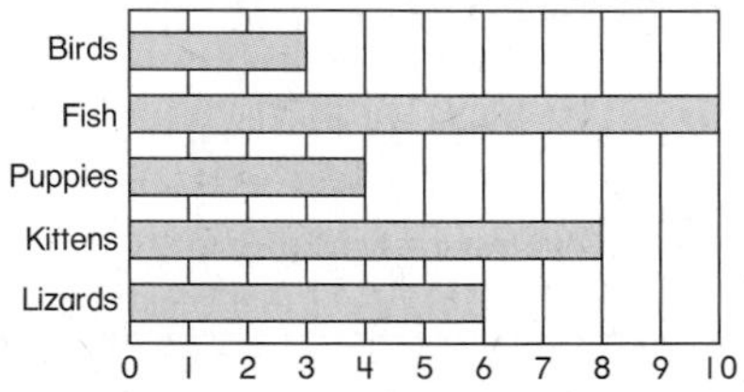

1. There are [3] *more* (*fewer*) birds in the pet store than lizards.
2. There are [4] *more* (*fewer*) puppies in the pet store than kittens.
3. There are [7] (*more*) *fewer* fish in the pet store than birds.
4. There are [2] *more* (*fewer*) lizards in the pet store than kittens.
5. There are [6] *more* (*fewer*) puppies in the pet store than fish.
6. There are (*more*) *fewer* fish than there are birds and lizards combined.
7. There is a total of [12] puppies and kittens.

178 UNIT 9 LESSON 1 Explore Quarters

Homework and Remembering page 178

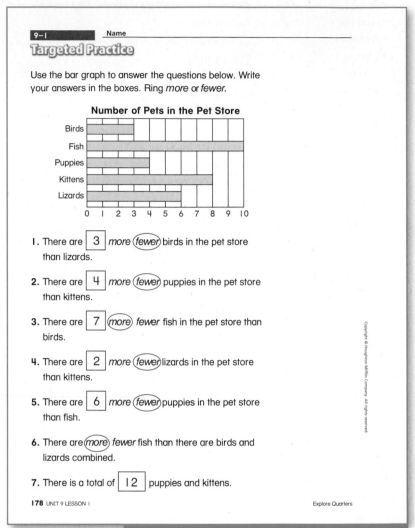

Home and School Connection

Family Letter Have children take home the Family Letter on Student Activity Book page 273. This letter explains how the concept of counting coins is developed in *Math Expressions.* It gives parents and guardians a better understanding of the learning that goes on in math class and creates a bridge between school and home. A Spanish translation of this letter is on the following page in the Student Activity Book.

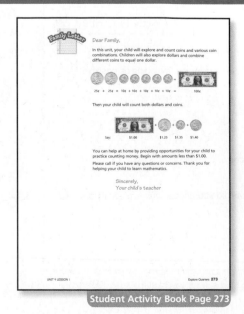

Family Letter

Dear Family,

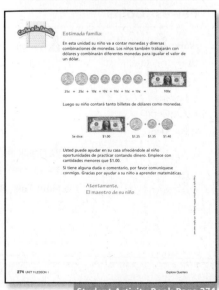

In this unit, your child will explore and count coins and various coin combinations. Children will also explore dollars and combine different coins to equal one dollar.

25¢ + 25¢ + 10¢ + 10¢ + 10¢ + 10¢ + 10¢ = 100¢

Then your child will count both dollars and coins.

Say: $1.00 $1.25 $1.35 $1.40

You can help at home by providing opportunities for your child to practice counting money. Begin with amounts less than $1.00.

Please call if you have any questions or concerns. Thank you for helping your child to learn mathematics.

Sincerely,
Your child's teacher

UNIT 9 LESSON 1 Explore Quarters 273

Student Activity Book Page 273

Carta a la familia

Estimada familia:

En esta unidad su niño va a contar monedas y diversas combinaciones de monedas. Los niños también trabajarán con dólares y combinarán diferentes monedas para igualar el valor de un dólar.

25¢ + 25¢ + 10¢ + 10¢ + 10¢ + 10¢ + 10¢ = 100¢

Luego su niño contará tanto billetes de dólares como monedas.

Se dice: $1.00 $1.25 $1.35 $1.40

Usted puede ayudar en su casa ofreciéndole al niño oportunidades de practicar contando dinero. Empiece con cantidades menores que $1.00.

Si tiene alguna duda o comentario, por favor comuníquese conmigo. Gracias por ayudar a su niño a aprender matemáticas.

Atentamente,
El maestro de su niño

274 UNIT 9 LESSON 1 Explore Quarters

Student Activity Book Page 274

UNIT 9 LESSON 2

Explore Dollars

Lesson Objectives

- State how many pennies, nickels, dimes and quarters equal one dollar.
- Combine quarters, dimes, nickels, and pennies to equal one dollar.
- Count one dollar and coins.

Vocabulary

penny	quarter
nickel	dollar
dime	

The Day at a Glance

Today's Goals	Materials	
1 Teaching the Lesson A1: Explore dollars and the number of different coins that equal a dollar. A2: Count coins and dollars. A3: Make money strings for amounts less than two dollars.	**Lesson Activities** Student Activity Book pp. 275–276 (includes Dollar Equivalents) Homework and Remembering pp. 179–180 Quick Quiz 1 (Assessment Guide) Scissors Real or play money Sticky board (optional)	**Going Further** Activity Cards 9-2 Real or play money Paper bags Number cubes MathBoard materials Math Journals
2 Going Further ► Differentiated Instruction		
3 Homework and Spiral Review		

Use Math Talk today!

Keeping Skills Sharp

Quick Practice — 5 MINUTES

Goal: Write money strings for quarters.

Quarter Strings Have children write money strings for quarters at the board. Some examples of quarter strings are shown below.

25¢ = 5¢ + 5¢ + 5¢ + 5¢ + 5¢

25¢ = 10¢ + 5¢ + 5¢ + 5¢

25¢ = 5¢ + 5¢ + 5¢ + 5¢ + 1¢ + 1¢ + 1¢ + 1¢ + 1¢

Repeated Quick Practice Use this Quick Practice from a previous lesson.

► **Make-a-Ten Cards: Subtraction** (See Unit 7 Lesson 5.)

Daily Routines

Quarters and Other Coins Making and Counting Coins that Make a Quarter, Counting to 200¢ by 25¢, Making and Counting Dollars and Cents: 3-Digit Numbers as Dollars and Cents (See pp. xxvi–xxvii.)

► Led by teacher

Money Routine Using the 120 Poster, Using the Money Flip Chart, Using the Number Path, Using Secret Code Cards (See pp. xxiii–xxv.)

► Led by Student Leaders

1 Teaching the Lesson

Activity 1

Explore Dollars

20 MINUTES

Goal: Explore dollars and the number of different coins that equal a dollar.

Materials: scissors (one pair per child), real or play money (pennies, nickels, dimes, and quarters), Dollar Equivalents (Student Activity Book pages 275–276), sticky board (optional)

NCTM Standard:
Number and Operations

Class Management

Make sure children cut exactly on the dashed lines when cutting out the Dollar Equivalents on Student Activity Book pages 275–276. You might want to have Student Helpers work with children experiencing difficulty so they don't cut off the information shown on the back of each dollar bill. The Dollar Equivalents are also available on TRB M75–M76. You can make sturdy dollar bills for classroom use by copying the copymasters onto cardstock. Be sure to save the Dollar Equivalents. They will be used in the next lesson.

▶ Discuss Dollars WHOLE CLASS

Math Talk

Have children cut out the dollar bills on Student Activity Book page 275. Have them place the dollar bills with the dollar sides facing up.

from Student Activity Book page 275

Ask children what they know about dollars. Accept children's ideas even though they may have little idea about the worth of a dollar and may not understand the value of a dollar relative to different coins. Be sure to return to the discussion of the value of the different monetary units today and in later lessons and other classes.

Discuss the number of cents in a dollar and how that helps us compare the values of different coins and a dollar. Have children use real or play money for this part of the activity.

- Pick up a dollar bill. What else can we call a dollar? 100 cents
- Pick up a quarter. What else can we call a quarter? 25 cents
- Pick up a dime. What else can we call a dime? 10 cents
- Pick up a nickel. What else can we call a nickel? 5 cents
- Pick up a penny. What else can we call a penny? 1 cent
- What do these different names tell us? That each coin and a dollar are worth a different number of cents. We can tell what each one is worth compared to the other coins.
- Which is worth more, a dollar or a penny? a dollar
- Why is a dollar worth more than a penny? Because it takes one hundred pennies to make a dollar.

Continue by comparing other coins to a dollar.

▶ Combine Different Coins that Equal a Dollar PAIRS

Be sure each pair has real, play, or paper money to use for this part of the activity. Then have children find how many pennies, nickels, dimes, and quarters equal one dollar. They can experiment with their coins or they can count or work numerically to find the answers.

- How many pennies equal a dollar? 100 pennies
- How many dimes? 10 dimes
- How many nickels? 20 nickels
- How many quarters? 4 quarters

Have children check their answers by looking at the backs of the dollar bills they cut out.

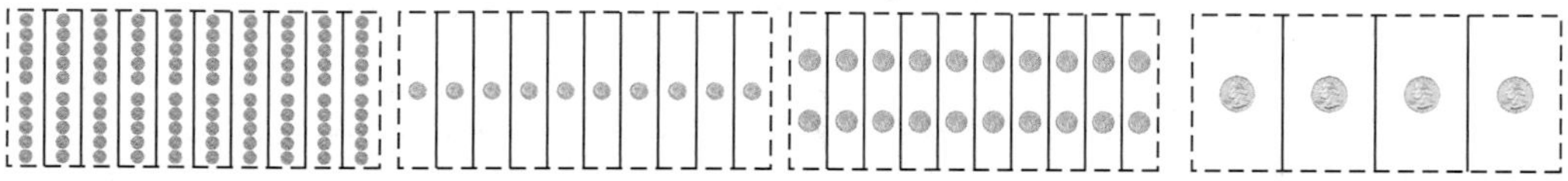

from Student Activity Book page 260 (backs of dollars)

Be sure that children understand that four quarters equal one whole dollar and that one-fourth of a dollar is one quarter.

▶ Other Coin Combinations that Equal a Dollar PAIRS

Give children time to experiment with the coins to find other combinations that equal a dollar. Tell them to put at least two different kinds of coins together. For example, they could use quarters and dimes or quarters and nickels and pennies. Have them record their combinations on a piece of paper.

Then ask several children to share their combinations with the rest of the class. They can write on the board as shown below.

Examples of Ways to Show One Dollar

2 (Q) + 5 (D) = 25¢ + 25¢ + 10¢ + 10¢ + 10¢ + 10¢ + 10¢ = 1 dollar = 100¢	
(Q) (Q) (D) (D) (D) (D) (D) Dollar 25¢ + 25¢ + 10¢ + 10¢ + 10¢ + 10¢ + 10¢ = 100¢	2 (Q) = 50¢ + 5 (D) = 50¢ 1 dollar = 100¢

Have children compare their combinations to the ones shown on the backs of the dollar bills they cut out. Ask if they are the same or different. Explain that there are many other combinations of coins equal to one dollar.

Teaching Note

What to Expect from Students When children turn their dollars over, they may notice that the pennies are small compared to the rest of the coins. Explain that in real life pennies are bigger than dimes and smaller than nickels and quarters. Use actual coins to show the relationships between the different coins. Explain that the pennies are small on the back of the paper dollars because 100 of them had to fit on the back of one of the dollar bills.

Alternate Approach

Sticky Boards and Coins You may wish to have children show their coin combinations by attaching paper or play coins to a sticky board.

English Language Learners

Provide more practice identifying coins and their value. Give students play money.

- **Beginning** Have children hold up a penny. Say: **A penny is 1¢.** Hold up 1 finger. Continue with other coins. Have children flash the values with their hands.
- **Intermediate** Say: **Hold up a penny.** Ask: **How many cents is 1 penny?** 1¢
- **Advanced** Call out different coins. Have children hold them up and say the value. Call out values. Have children hold up the coin and name it.

Activity 2

Count Money Amounts

20 MINUTES

Goal: Count coins and dollars.

NCTM Standard:
Number and Operations

Ongoing Assessment

Ask children to tell how much each of these combinations of bills and coins is worth.

1. 4Ⓠ + 3Ⓓ + 2Ⓝ
2. 10Ⓓ + 2Ⓝ + 2Ⓟ
3. 2Ⓠ + 5Ⓓ + 3Ⓝ + 2Ⓟ
4. 1 Dollar + 2Ⓠ + 2Ⓓ + 1Ⓝ
5. 1 Dollar + 2Ⓓ + 4Ⓝ + 4Ⓟ

Quick Quiz

See Assessment Guide for Unit 9 Quick Quiz 1.

▶ Count Sequences of Coins WHOLE CLASS

Write the three sequences of coins shown below on the board. Point to each dollar and coin and have the class count out loud with you to the total. Remind children that each time the monetary unit shifts (for example, from D to Q or Q to P) you will freeze the counting. Then they should raise their fingers to show the value of the new coin. See Lesson 1 in this unit for examples of freezing and showing fingers.

Tell children that since they can't hold up 25 fingers to show a quarter, they should flash 2 tens and then hold up 5 fingers to show twenty-five.

Write:	$	Q	Q	Q
Say:	100¢	125¢	150¢	175¢

↑ Freeze (show 25)

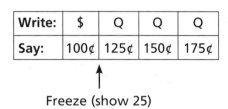

Write:	$	Q	Q	D	D	D
Say:	100¢	125¢	150¢	160¢	170¢	180¢

↑ Freeze (show 25) ↑ Freeze (show 10)

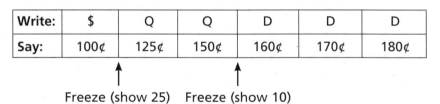

Write:	Q	Q	Q	D	D	D
Say:	25¢	50¢	75¢	85¢	95¢	105¢

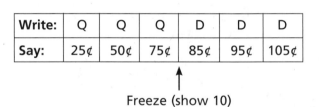

↑ Freeze (show 10)

Activity 3

Make Amounts in Different Ways

15 MINUTES

Goal: Make money strings for amounts less than two dollars.

Materials: real or play money (pennies, nickels, dimes and quarters)

NCTM Standard:
Number and Operations

▶ Make Money Strings for Different Amounts WHOLE CLASS

Have children make two or more money strings for each amount shown below, using different combinations of monetary units. Say and write the coins first using the cent sign and then using the dollar sign and decimal point.

73¢	147¢	182¢	95¢
$0.73	$1.47	$1.82	$0.95

Have several children work at the board while the rest of the children write their money strings at their desk. Have children at the board explain their strings.

2 Going Further

Differentiated Instruction

Intervention

Activity Card 9-2

Find the Total — Activity Card 9-2

Work: pairs

Use:
- paper bag
- 20 pennies
- 5 nickels
- 8 dimes
- 8 quarters

1. Put the coins in the bag.
2. Take six coins from the bag without looking.
3. **Work Together** Find the total.

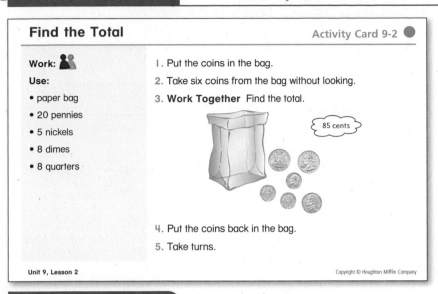

4. Put the coins back in the bag.
5. Take turns.

Unit 9, Lesson 2

Activity Note Each pair needs a paper bag, 20 pennies, 5 nickels, 8 dimes, and 8 quarters.

Math Writing Prompt

Explain Your Thinking Your friend has 2 quarters. You have 5 cents more than your friend. How much money do you have? Explain.

Soar to Success Math **Software Support**

Warm Up 3.10

On Level

Activity Card 9-2

Who Has More Money? — Activity Card 9-2

Work: pairs

Use:
- number cube
- paper bag
- 25 pennies
- 5 nickels
- 8 dimes
- 8 quarters

1. Put the coins in the bag.
2. Each student: Roll the number cube. Take that many coins from the bag without looking.
3. Find the total.
4. **Work Together** Compare the totals. The student with the greater total gets 1 point.

5. Play until one person has 5 points.

Unit 9, Lesson 2

Activity Note Each pair needs a paper bag, a number cube labeled 1 to 6, 25 pennies, 5 nickels, 8 dimes, and 8 quarters.

Math Writing Prompt

Explain Your Thinking You have 1 dollar, 1 quarter, and 2 dimes. Do you have enough money to buy a toy that costs $1.50? Explain your thinking.

Harcourt Mega Math **Software Support**

Numberopolis: Lulu's Lunch Counter, Level J

Challenge

Activity Card 9-2

Equal Amounts — Activity Card 9-2

Work: individual

Use:
- MathBoard materials
- 8 pennies
- 9 nickels
- 7 dimes
- 6 quarters

Group A	Group B	Group C
2 quarters	2 quarters	2 quarters
3 dimes	2 dimes	2 dimes
2 nickels	5 nickels	2 nickels
1 penny	1 penny	6 pennies

1. Find the total of each group of coins.
2. Move coins from group to group. Make all groups have the same total. You can use the coins to help.
3. Make a puzzle like the one above.
4. Trade your puzzle with a partner and solve.

2. Sample answer: Move one nickel from Group B to Group C. Each group has 91¢.

Unit 9, Lesson 2

Activity Note Each child needs MathBoard materials and 8 pennies, 9 nickels, 7 dimes, and 6 quarters, either real or play money.

Math Writing Prompt

Explain Your Thinking You have five coins that are either dimes or nickels and at least one of each coin. What is the greatest amount of money you can have? What is the least amount? Explain.

Destination Math **Software Support**

Course II: Module 3: Unit 2: Money

3 Homework and Spiral Review

9–2 Homework **Goal:** Additional Practice

This Homework page provides practice drawing different combinations of coins that are equivalent to a dollar.

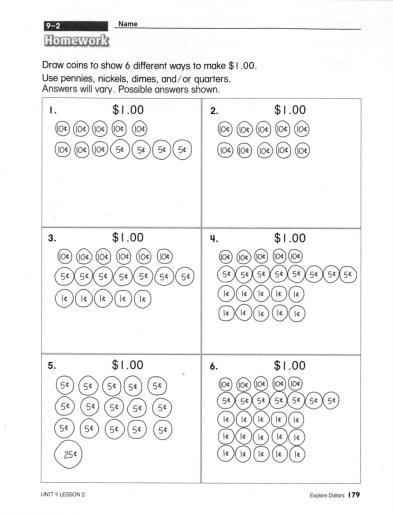

9–2 Homework Name ______

Draw coins to show 6 different ways to make $1.00.
Use pennies, nickels, dimes, and/or quarters.
Answers will vary. Possible answers shown.

1. $1.00 10¢ 10¢ 10¢ 10¢ 10¢ 10¢ 10¢ 10¢ 5¢ 5¢ 5¢ 5¢	2. $1.00 10¢ 10¢ 10¢ 10¢ 10¢ 10¢ 10¢ 10¢ 10¢ 10¢
3. $1.00 10¢ 10¢ 10¢ 10¢ 10¢ 10¢ 5¢ 5¢ 5¢ 5¢ 5¢ 5¢ 5¢ 1¢ 1¢ 1¢ 1¢ 1¢	4. $1.00 10¢ 10¢ 10¢ 10¢ 10¢ 5¢ 5¢ 5¢ 5¢ 5¢ 5¢ 5¢ 5¢ 1¢ 1¢ 1¢ 1¢ 1¢ 1¢ 1¢ 1¢ 1¢ 1¢
5. $1.00 5¢ 5¢ 5¢ 5¢ 5¢ 5¢ 5¢ 5¢ 5¢ 5¢ 5¢ 5¢ 5¢ 5¢ 5¢ 25¢	6. $1.00 10¢ 10¢ 10¢ 10¢ 10¢ 5¢ 5¢ 5¢ 5¢ 5¢ 5¢ 5¢ 1¢ 1¢ 1¢ 1¢ 1¢ 1¢ 1¢ 1¢ 1¢ 1¢ 1¢ 1¢ 1¢ 1¢ 1¢

UNIT 9 LESSON 2 Explore Dollars 179

Homework and Remembering page 179

9–2 Remembering **Goal:** Spiral Review

This Remembering activity would be appropriate anytime after today's lesson.

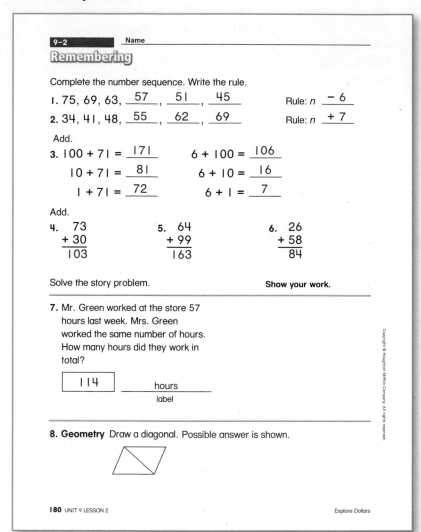

9–2 Remembering Name ______

Complete the number sequence. Write the rule.

1. 75, 69, 63, 57, 51, 45 Rule: n – 6
2. 34, 41, 48, 55, 62, 69 Rule: n + 7

Add.

3. 100 + 71 = 171 6 + 100 = 106
10 + 71 = 81 6 + 10 = 16
1 + 71 = 72 6 + 1 = 7

Add.

4. 73 + 30 = 103
5. 64 + 99 = 163
6. 26 + 58 = 84

Solve the story problem. **Show your work.**

7. Mr. Green worked at the store 57 hours last week. Mrs. Green worked the same number of hours. How many hours did they work in total?

114 hours (label)

8. **Geometry** Draw a diagonal. Possible answer is shown.

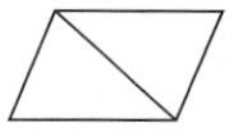

180 UNIT 9 LESSON 2 Explore Dollars

Homework and Remembering page 180

Home or School Activity

Social Studies Connection

Name the President Explain that some United States presidents are shown on U.S. coins and bills. Have children use resources, such as books and computers, to find the names of the presidents shown on several U.S. coins and bills. Children can display the information they find in a chart.

Which President?

Coin	Bill	President
penny		Abraham Lincoln
nickel		Thomas Jefferson
dime		Franklin Roosevelt
quarter		George Washington
	dollar	George Washington
	5 dollar	Abraham Lincoln

UNIT 9 LESSON 3

Partners and Subtraction

REAL WORLD Problem Solving

Lesson Objectives

- Find unknown partners.
- Observe similarities between ten partners and hundred partners.
- Use different methods to find partners of 100.
- Invent different ways to solve 100 – n exercises.

Vocabulary

count on
break apart
decade partners
ungroup
Quick Tens

The Day at a Glance

Today's Goals	Materials	
1 Teaching the Lesson **A1:** Share methods for finding unknown partners. **A2:** Use different methods to find partners of 100. **A3:** Write subtraction exercises, make Proof Drawings, and show solutions with Secret Code Cards.	**Lesson Activities** Student Activity Book pp. 277–278 Homework and Remembering pp. 181–182 MathBoard materials Demonstration Secret Code Cards Secret Code Cards	**Going Further** Activity Cards 9-3 MathBoard materials Index cards Math Journals
2 Going Further ▸ Differentiated Instruction		
3 Homework and Targeted Practice		

Use Math Talk today!

Keeping Skills Sharp

Quick Practice — 5 MINUTES

Goal: Practice subtraction with teen totals.

Teen Subtraction Flash Have a **Student Leader** call out a teen total and one of its partners. The class flashes the other partner with their fingers. Example: The Student Leader says: "18 take away 9 equals something." The children flash nine fingers to show the unknown addend. (See Unit 7 Lesson 5.)

Repeated Quick Practice Use the Quick Practices from previous lesson.

- ▸ **Make-a-Ten Cards: Subtraction** (See Unit 7 Lesson 5.)
- ▸ **Quarter Strings** (See Unit 9 Lesson 2.)

Daily Routines

Quarters and Other Coins
Making and Counting Coins that Make a Quarter, Counting to 200¢ by 25¢, Making and Counting Dollars and Cents: 3-Digit Numbers as Dollars and Cents (See pp. xxvi–xxvii.)

▸ Led by teacher

Money Routine Using the 120 Poster, Using the Money Flip Chart, Using the Number Path, Using Secret Code Cards (See pp. xxiii–xxv.)

▸ Led by Student Leaders

1 Teaching the Lesson

Activity 1

Find Unknown Partners

10 MINUTES

Goal: Share methods for finding unknown partners.

Materials: MathBoards materials

NCTM Standards:
Number and Operations
Representation
Communication

English Language Learners

Review the *count on* and *break apart methods.* Model each method on the board to solve 73 = 34 + □.

- **Beginning** Point and say: **This is the *count on method.* I add sticks and circles to find the partner.** Have children repeat. Point and say: **This is the *break apart method.* I draw tens and ones for 73, then I *break apart* the partners.**
- **Intermediate** Point to each method. Ask: **Did I *break apart* the total or *count on* to find the partner?**
- **Advanced** Label the methods. Ask: **In which method did I add sticks and circles to find the partner?** count on

▶ Share Methods for Finding Unknown Partners

WHOLE CLASS

Math Talk

Draw the following Math Mountain on the board and have children show different methods for finding the unknown partner.

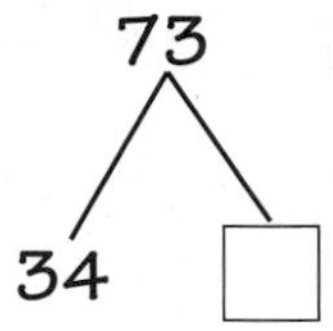

Some methods for solving unknown partner exercises are shown below.

Count on using sticks and circles.	**Break apart 73 into partners.**	**Start at 34 and add up to 73.**
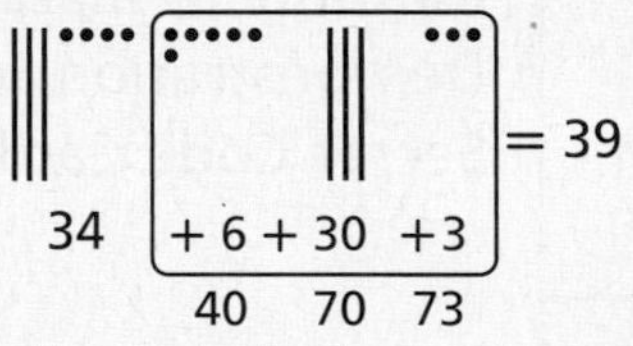	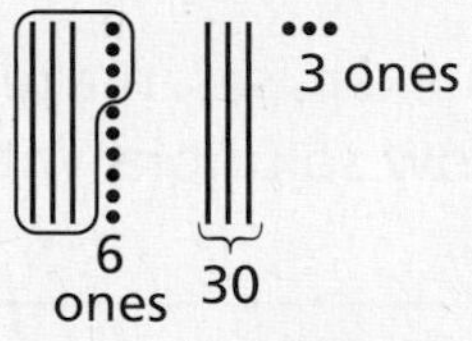	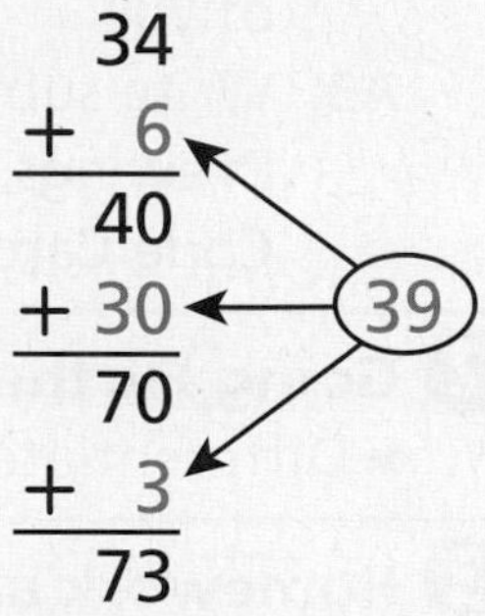
• Already have 34. Count on by ones to 40. (6) • Count on by tens from 40 to 70. (30) • Count on by ones from 70 to 73. (3) • 6 + 30 + 3 = 39, so 39 and 34 are partners of 73.	• Circle 3 tens and 4 ones to show 34, the given partner. • Count the tens and ones left to find the unknown partner. It is 39. • So 34 and 39 are partners of 73.	• Add 6 to get to the next 10. • Add 30 to get to 70. • Add 3 to get to 73. • 6 + 30 + 3 = 39, so 39 and 34 are partners of 73.

After discussing the various methods of finding unknown partners for Math Mountains, help children relate the equation 73 = 34 + □ to break-apart partners and Math Mountains.

Using the Math Mountain, guide children to see that 73 has 34 and 39 hiding inside it.

Activity 2

Explore Hundreds Partners

▶ Relate Partners of 10 to Decade Partners of 100

WHOLE CLASS

Begin by drawing this set of Math Mountains on the board.

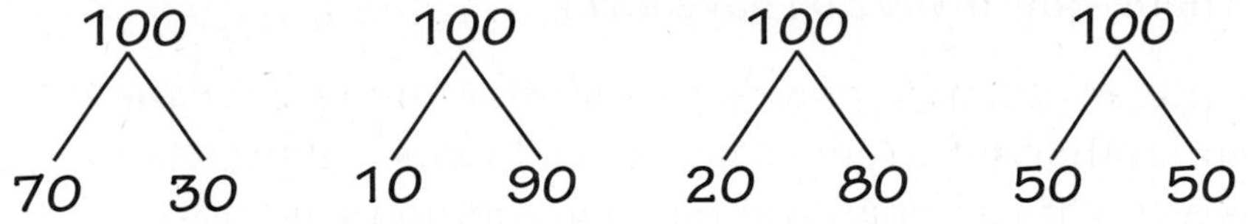

Then have children determine that the smaller numbers are partners of 100. To prove this, ask children to add 7 tens and 3 tens, 1 ten and 9 tens, 2 tens and 8 tens, and 5 tens and 5 tens. Each pair of tens totals 10 tens or 100.

The Tens Total 100

Example:

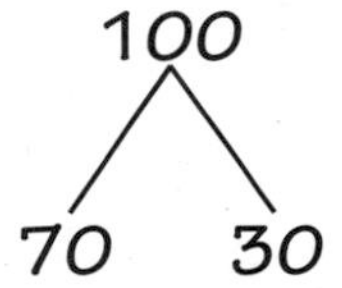

$$\begin{array}{r} 7 \text{ tens} \\ +\ 3 \text{ tens} \\ \hline 10 \text{ tens} \end{array} \qquad \begin{array}{r} 70 \\ +\ 30 \\ \hline 100 \end{array}$$

▶ Find Other Partners of 100

WHOLE CLASS

Now draw this set of Math Mountains on the board.

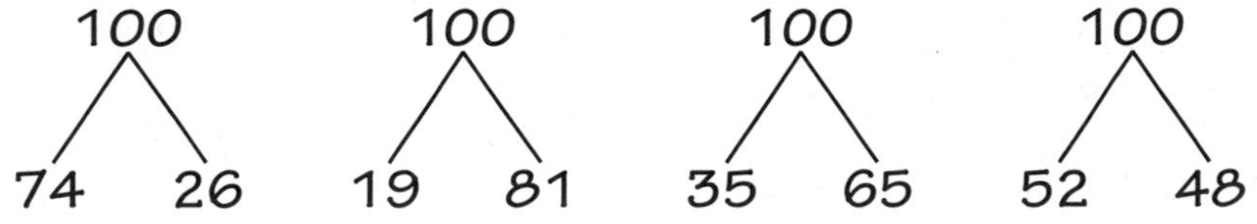

Have children look for patterns in these partners of 100.

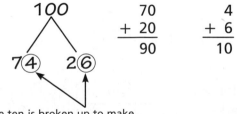

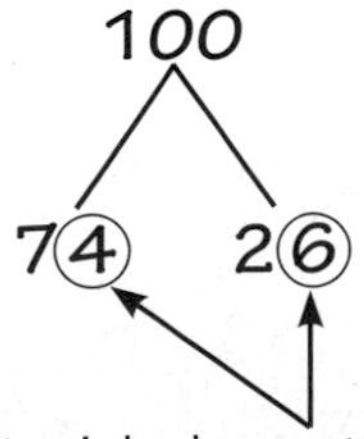

$$\begin{array}{r} 70 \\ +\ 20 \\ \hline 90 \end{array} \qquad \begin{array}{r} 4 \\ +\ 6 \\ \hline 10 \end{array}$$

One ten is broken up to make 10-partners for the ones.

- Do you see a pattern in the partners? Answers will vary.
- What do the tens in each example add up to? 90
- What do the ones in each example add up to? 10

Explain that one of the tens has been broken apart into ones. In this example, 4 ones and 6 ones are "shared" by the two partners. In the previous examples we did, the tens added up to 100 and the ones added up to 0.

15 MINUTES

Goal: Use different methods to find partners of 100.

✔ **NCTM Standard:**
Number and Operations

1 Teaching the Lesson (continued)

Activity 3

Write a Subtraction Story Problem

25 MINUTES

Goal: Write subtraction exercises, make proof drawings, and show solutions with Secret Code Cards.

Materials: MathBoard materials, Student Activity Book pages 277–278, Demonstration Secret Code Cards, Secret Code Cards

NCTM Standards:
Number and Operations
Representation
Communication

▶ Subtract a 2-Digit Number from 100 WHOLE CLASS

Write this problem on the board and have children write a subtraction exercise on their MathBoards showing how to solve the problem.

I have 100 tickets to the ball game.
I sold 68 of them. How many do I have left?

Have children write an equation and draw a Math Mountain for the problem on their MathBoards. Some children will write a subtraction equation. Some will write an unknown partner addition equation.

Have children solve the problem using the dot array on their MathBoards.

Observe children's solution methods. Some children may circle the given partner and then count the dots that are left. They should do whatever they feel is necessary to make the solution clear. Encourage children to use numbers to label the groups they draw. They should also fill in the solution to the equation they wrote.

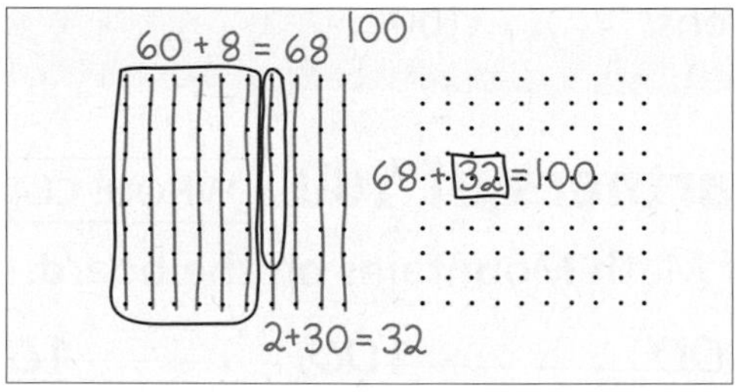

Have several children share their solutions.

▶ Use Dollars to Visualize Ungrouping and Rewriting a Hundred WHOLE CLASS

Discuss two ways to use dollars to ungroup and rewrite a hundred to solve the problem.

- One way is to rewrite or trade 1 dollar for 10 dimes. Then we can rewrite or trade 1 dime for 10 pennies.

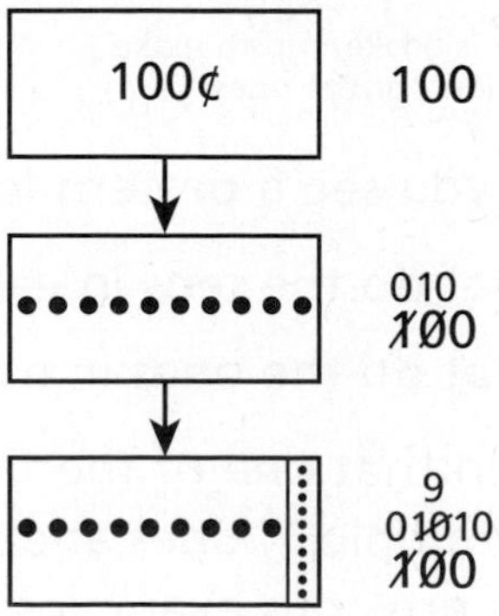

- Another way is to rewrite or trade 1 dollar for 9 dimes and 10 pennies right away, since we know that 1 dime equals 10 pennies.

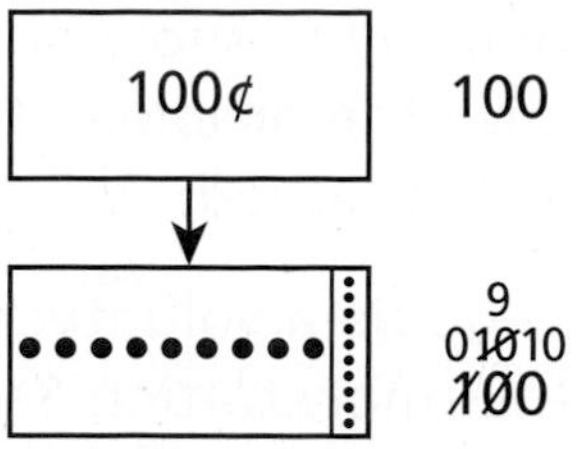

- After we rewrite 1 dollar, we circle 6 tens and 8 ones for the partner we know. Then we see that 3 tens and 2 ones are left. The partner of 68 is 32, so 100 take away 68 is 32.

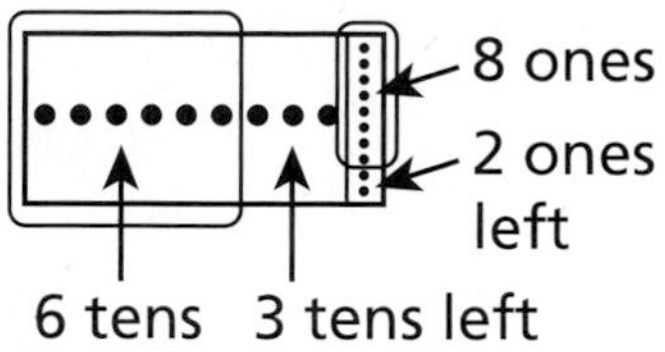

▶ Problems Using 100-Partners WHOLE CLASS

Have children think about dollars to make drawings like the one above to solve the first two problems on Student Activity Book page 277.

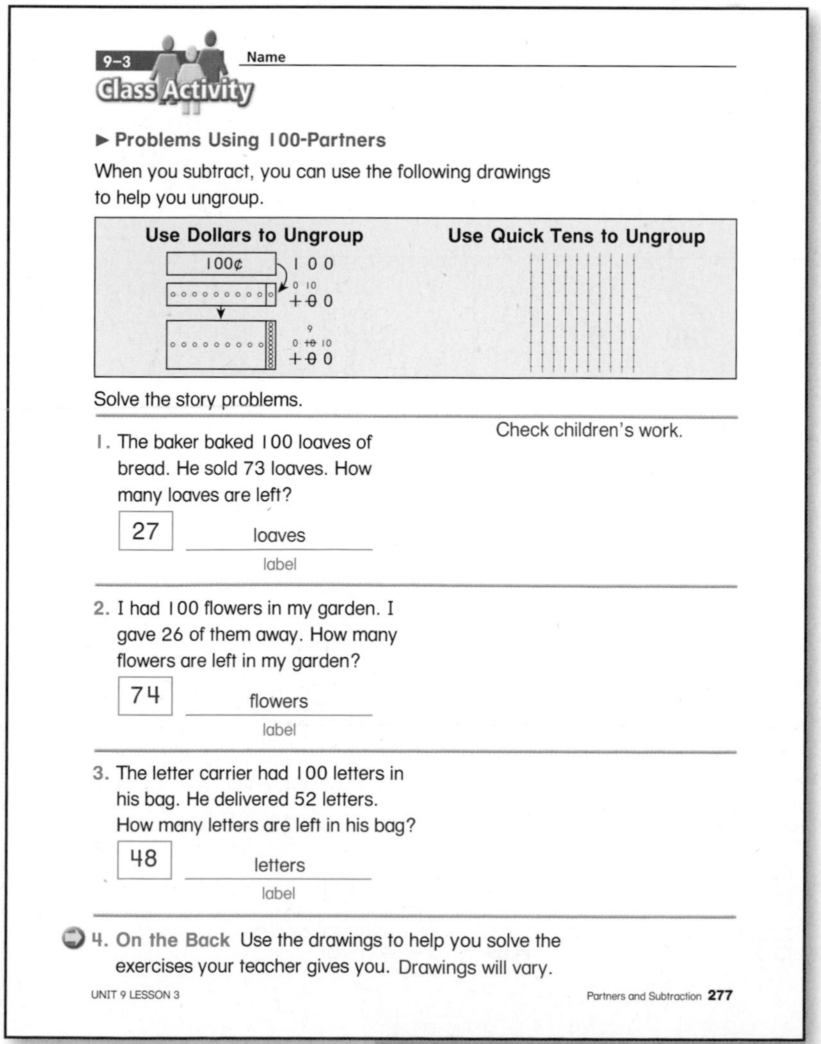
9–3 Class Activity Name

▶ Problems Using 100-Partners

When you subtract, you can use the following drawings to help you ungroup.

Use Dollars to Ungroup | Use Quick Tens to Ungroup

Solve the story problems.

Check children's work.

1. The baker baked 100 loaves of bread. He sold 73 loaves. How many loaves are left?

27 loaves (label)

2. I had 100 flowers in my garden. I gave 26 of them away. How many flowers are left in my garden?

74 flowers (label)

3. The letter carrier had 100 letters in his bag. He delivered 52 letters. How many letters are left in his bag?

48 letters (label)

4. On the Back Use the drawings to help you solve the exercises your teacher gives you. Drawings will vary.

UNIT 9 LESSON 3 Partners and Subtraction 277

Student Activity Book page 277

Activity continued ▶

Teaching Note

What to Expect from Students
Some children may use counting on methods to solve the exercise. Watch for children who are attempting to count down or count back. This is a method that often results in error.

Review partner counting on to make a single digit total if you feel it would be helpful.

❶ Teaching the Lesson (continued)

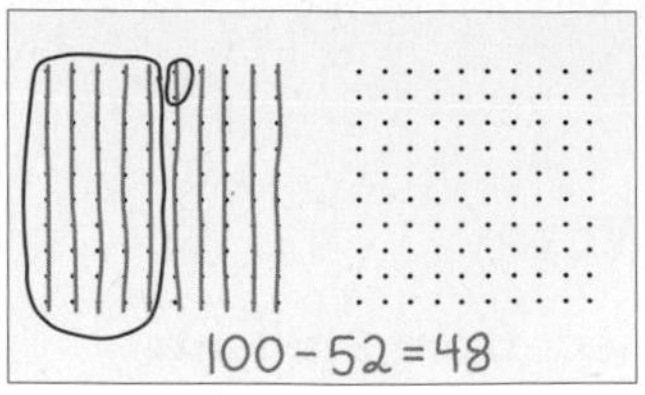

Then have children draw Quick Tens to solve problem 3. (See the side column for a sample.) When children are done, ask them to come up with a way to show how they broke one of the tens into ones in order to solve the problem. Children should check their work using any suitable method.

Then guide a volunteer to construct the solution to the last problem with Demonstration Secret Code Cards. Have the rest of the class work in pairs to construct the solution with their Secret Code Cards.

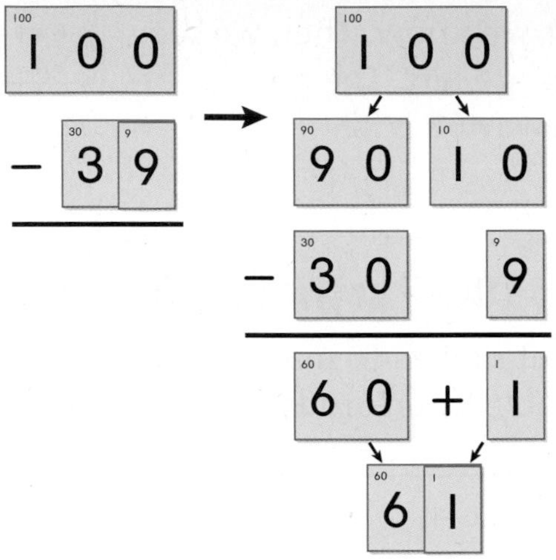

Some children may be able to invent and use methods that do not require pictures or Secret Code Cards. The upcoming lessons will formally introduce ways to show ungrouping.

90 + 10 100 = 1~~00~~ + ~~0~~ − 52 = 50 + 2 40 + 8 = 48	0 9 10 ~~100~~ − 52 48
Ungroup 1 hundred as 10 tens. 10 ~~10~~0 − 52	Ungroup 1 ten as 10 ones. 9 ~~10~~ 10 ~~100~~ − 52 48

On the Back Write the following 4 exercises on the board for children to complete on the back of Student Activity Book page 261.

100 − 62 = 38   100 − 83 = 17

100 − 47 = 53   100 − 54 = 46

Ongoing Assessment

Ask children to solve these exercises using any method they choose.

1. 100 − 25 = ☐
2. 100 − 50 = ☐
3. 100 − 54 = ☐
4. 100 − 73 = ☐
5. 100 − 67 = ☐

Intervention Activity Card 9-3

Subtract on the Number Path

Activity Card 9-3

Work: pairs

Use:

- MathBoard materials or Number Path

Choose:

- 1
- 2

1. (1) Write a subtraction problem. Subtract a two-digit number from 100.
2. Use the Number Path to help you find the answer.

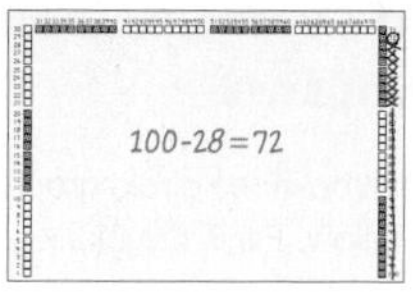

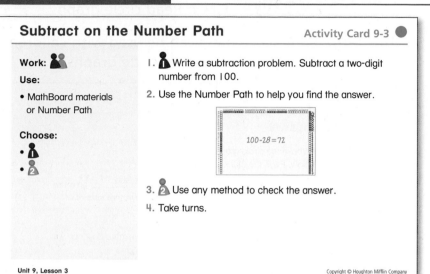

3. (2) Use any method to check the answer.
4. Take turns.

Unit 9, Lesson 3

Activity Note Each pair needs MathBoard materials or a Number Path (TRB M51). Check that children cross out numbers on the Number Path correctly.

Math Writing Prompt

Explain Your Thinking Draw or write to explain how to find 100 − 54.

Soar to Success Math Software Support

Warm Up 11.22

On Level Activity Card 9-3

Make Quick Tens

Activity Card 9-3

Work: pairs

Use:

- 8 index cards
- MathBoard materials or Dot Array

Choose:

- 1
- 2

1. **Work Together** Write a different subtraction problem on each index card. Subtract two-digit numbers from 100.
2. Mix the cards. Place them face down in a pile.
3. (1) Take the top card. Use a Dot Array to find the answer.

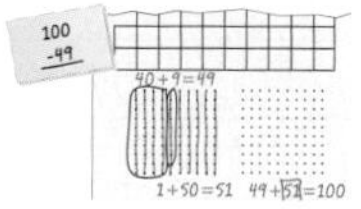

4. (2) Check the answer. If correct, (1) keeps the card. If not correct, the card is put at the bottom of the pile.
5. Take turns. The first person to get four cards wins.

Unit 9, Lesson 3

Activity Note Each pair needs 8 index cards and MathBoard materials or a Dot Array (TRB M63). Have partners check each other's work.

Math Writing Prompt

Two Different Ways Show two different ways to find the unknown partner.

64 + □ = 100

Harcourt Mega Math Software Support

Numberopolis: Carnival Stories, Level Q

Challenge Activity Card 9-3

Number Puzzles

Activity Card 9-3

Work: individual

Use:

- MathBoard materials

Riddle A: I am greater than 100−48.
I am less than 100−38.
I am an odd number.
What number could I be?

Riddle B: I am less than 100−19.
I am greater than 100−26.
I am an even number.
What number could I be?

1. Solve each riddle.
   Sample answers: Riddle A: 53, 55, 57, 59, 61; Riddle B: 76, 78, 80
2. Make a riddle like the ones above.
3. Trade your riddle with a partner and solve.

Unit 9, Lesson 3

Activity Note Each child needs MathBoard materials. You may want to hang the puzzles in the classroom for others to solve.

Math Writing Prompt

Logical Thinking Find a set of three two-digit numbers that have a total of 100. Explain your thinking.

Destination Math Software Support

Course II: Module 1: Unit 1: Comparing and Ordering

3 Homework and Targeted Practice

9–3 Homework **Goal:** Additional Practice

This Homework page provides practice solving problems using hundreds partners.

9–3 **Homework** Name ____________________

Solve the story problems. Rewrite the 100 or make a drawing. Add to check your answer.

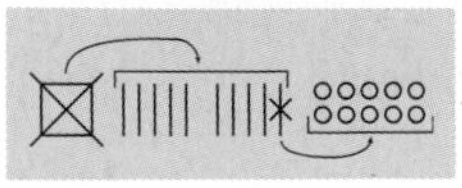

$$\begin{array}{rcl} 100 & = & \overset{90}{\cancel{100}} + \overset{10}{\cancel{0}} \\ -\ 68 & = & 60 + 8 \\ & & 30 + 2 = 32 \end{array}$$

Tens	Ones
9	10
~~10~~	~~0~~
− 6	8
3	2

1. There were 100 rubber ducks in the river race. 19 of them sank. How many ducks are in the race now?

   ☐ ____________ label

2. Ben bought 100 napkins for the picnic. We used 74 of them. How many napkins were left?

   ☐ ____________ label

Find the unknown partner. Check by adding.

3. 100 → 85 and ☐ 100 → 67 and ☐ 100 → 58 and ☐ 100 → 23 and ☐

UNIT 9 LESSON 3 Partners and Subtraction 181

Homework and Remembering page 181

9–3 Targeted Practice **Goal:** Read circle graphs.

This Targeted Practice page can be used with children who need extra practice reading circle graphs.

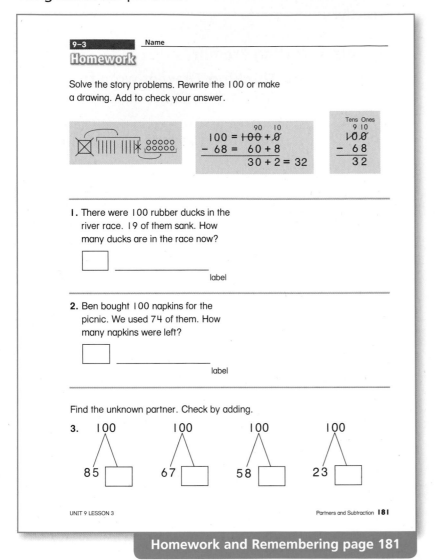

9–3 **Targeted Practice** Name ____________________

Use the information in the circle graph to answer the questions below. Fill in the blanks.

Weather This Month (Number of Days)

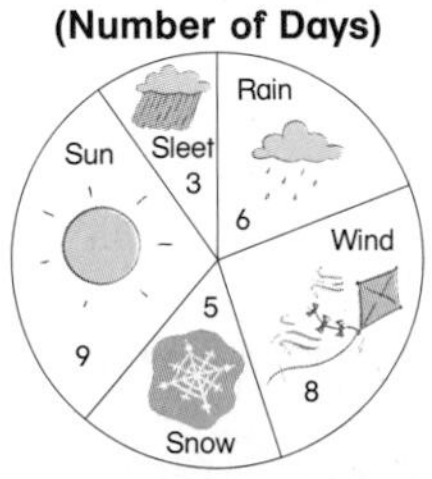

1. We had ___sun___ on more days than any other kind of weather.
2. We had rain 1 more day than we had ___snow___.
3. We had snow 4 fewer days than we had ___sun___.
4. We had wind 5 more days than we had ___sleet___.
5. We had sun and snow for the same total number of days as we had ___rain___ and ___wind___.

Write two other things the circle graph shows.

Check children's work.

182 UNIT 9 LESSON 3 Partners and Subtraction

Homework and Remembering page 182

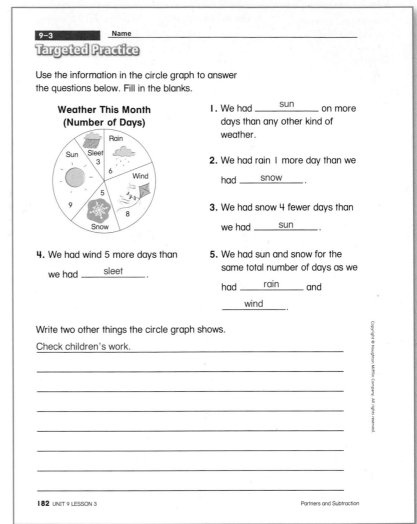

Home or School Activity

Art Connection

Mosaic Design Have children use a 10 × 10 grid to create a mosaic-type design by coloring as many squares as they wish. They must color complete squares.

Have children glue their completed designs on colored construction paper. They should write a subtraction sentence underneath the design indicating how many squares are colored. Display the children's work around the room.

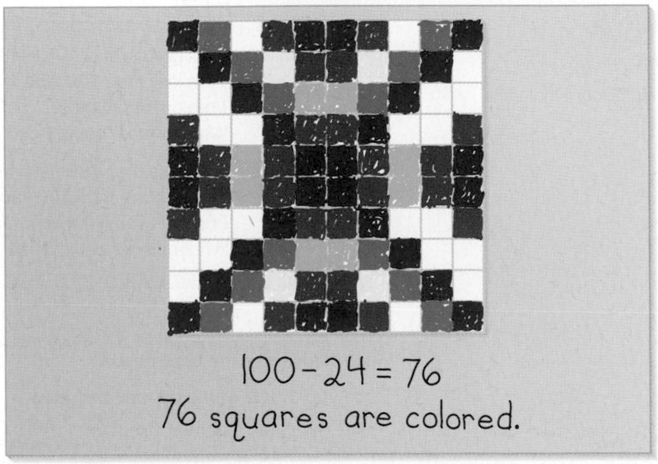

UNIT 9 LESSON 4

Subtraction Story Problems

REAL WORLD Problem Solving

Lesson Objectives

- Ungroup a ten into ten ones in order to subtract.
- Invent ways to solve subtraction story problems. Decide when to ungroup and when not to ungroup.
- Explain subtraction methods for rewriting a top number to show ungrouping.

Vocabulary
ungroup

The Day at a Glance

Today's Goals	Materials	
1 Teaching the Lesson **A1:** Practice subtraction with totals ≤ 18. **A2:** Develop and solve subtraction story problems with 2-digit numbers. **A3:** Decide when to ungroup to solve subtraction problems.	**Lesson Activities** Student Activity Book pp. 279–280 Homework and Remembering pp. 183–184 MathBoard materials or Dot Array Demonstration Secret Code Cards Secret Code Cards	**Going Further** Activity Cards 9-4 Index cards Game Cards (TRB M23) MathBoard materials Math Journals
2 Going Further ▸ Differentiated Instruction		
3 Homework and Spiral Review		

Use Math Talk today!

Keeping Skills Sharp

Quick Practice — 5 MINUTES	Daily Routines
Goal: Practice subtraction with teen totals. **Teen Subtraction Flash** Have a **Student Leader** call out a teen total and one of its partners. The class flashes the other partner with their fingers. For example, the Student Leader says: "17 take away 8 equals something." The children flash 9 fingers to show the unknown addend. (See Unit 7 Lesson 5.)	**Quarters and Other Coins** Making and Counting Coins that Make a Quarter, Counting to 200¢ by 25¢, Making and Counting Dollars and Cents: 3-Digit Numbers as Dollars and Cents (See pp. xxvi – xxvii.) ▸ Led by Student Leaders **Money Routine** Using the 120 Poster, Using the Money Flip Chart, Using the Number Path, Using Secret Code Cards (See pp. xxiii–xxv.) ▸ Led by Student Leaders

1 Teaching the Lesson

Activity 1

Subtraction Sprint

10 MINUTES

Goal: Practice subtraction with totals ≤ 18.

Materials: Student Activity Book pages 279–280

NCTM Standard:
Number and Operations

Class Management

There are many ways to administer the Subtraction Sprint and procedures should vary according to specific classroom needs. You may choose to allow children an unlimited amount of time to complete the activity.

English Language Learners

Write *zip, unzip, group,* and *ungroup* on the board. Act out and say: **I zip my coat. I *unzip* my coat.** Have children copy and repeat the actions.

- **Beginning** Point to the board. Say: ***Unzip* is the opposite of *zip*.** Ask: **Is *ungroup* the opposite of group?** yes
- **Intermediate** Ask: **Is *unzip* the opposite of zip?** yes **What is the opposite of group?** ungroup
- **Advanced** Say: ***Un* means do the opposite. The opposite of zip is __.** unzip **The opposite of group is __.** ungroup

▶ Subtraction Sprint WHOLE CLASS

Direct children's attention to Student Activity Book page 279. Decide how much time to give them to complete the Sprint. Explain the procedure and time limit to them.

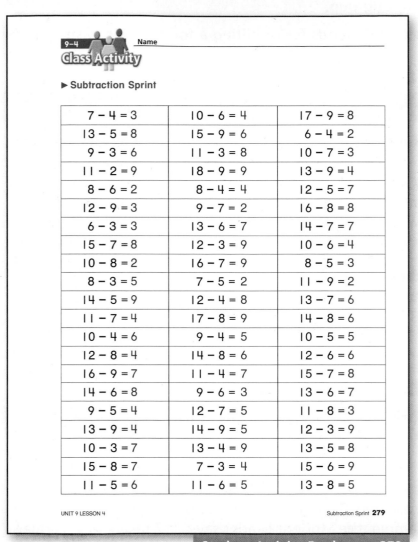

9–4 Class Activity Name ____________

▶ Subtraction Sprint

7 − 4 = 3	10 − 6 = 4	17 − 9 = 8
13 − 5 = 8	15 − 9 = 6	6 − 4 = 2
9 − 3 = 6	11 − 3 = 8	10 − 7 = 3
11 − 2 = 9	18 − 9 = 9	13 − 9 = 4
8 − 6 = 2	8 − 4 = 4	12 − 5 = 7
12 − 9 = 3	9 − 7 = 2	16 − 8 = 8
6 − 3 = 3	13 − 6 = 7	14 − 7 = 7
15 − 7 = 8	12 − 3 = 9	10 − 6 = 4
10 − 8 = 2	16 − 7 = 9	8 − 5 = 3
8 − 3 = 5	7 − 5 = 2	11 − 9 = 2
14 − 5 = 9	12 − 4 = 8	13 − 7 = 6
11 − 7 = 4	17 − 8 = 9	14 − 8 = 6
10 − 4 = 6	9 − 4 = 5	10 − 5 = 5
12 − 8 = 4	14 − 8 = 6	12 − 6 = 6
16 − 9 = 7	11 − 4 = 7	15 − 7 = 8
14 − 6 = 8	9 − 6 = 3	13 − 6 = 7
9 − 5 = 4	12 − 7 = 5	11 − 8 = 3
13 − 9 = 4	14 − 9 = 5	12 − 3 = 9
10 − 3 = 7	13 − 4 = 9	13 − 5 = 8
15 − 8 = 7	7 − 3 = 4	15 − 6 = 9
11 − 5 = 6	11 − 6 = 5	13 − 8 = 5

UNIT 9 LESSON 4 Subtraction Sprint **279**

Student Activity Book page 279

Children will do this Sprint three more times during the year. You may want to have children save their papers and make note of their progress.

For more practice, have children also do the Subtraction Sprint on Student Activity Book page 280.

Activity 2

Find Partners for Numbers Other Than 100

▶ Solve Subtraction Story Problems WHOLE CLASS

Total Is 100 Write the following story problem on the board.

There were 100 puddles on the playground. 27 of them dried up. How many puddles are left on the playground?

Ask children to write the subtraction on their MathBoards to represent the problem. Then have them solve the problem by using the dot array on the MathBoard or by drawing sticks and circles on the plain side of the board. Select a few children to show their MathBoards to the class when they have finished.

Have a few children explain how they ungrouped a ten to get 10 ones so they could subtract. The children should rewrite the 100 to show this.

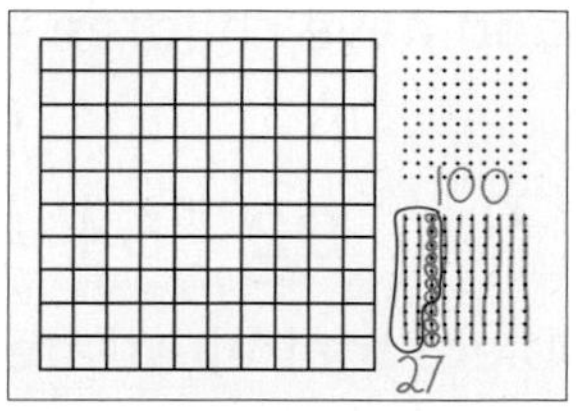

or

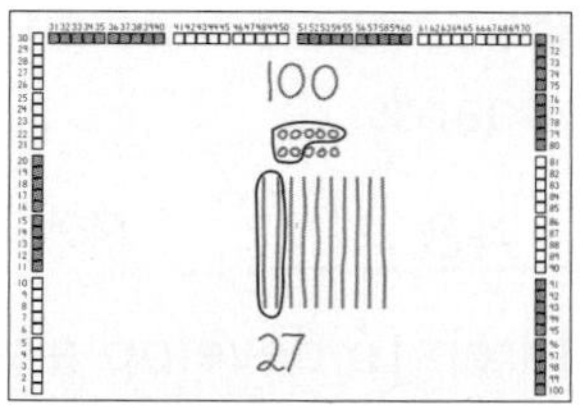

Total Is Not 100 Ask children to use their MathBoards to solve the following problem.

Julia grew 56 roses. She gave 29 of them to her friends. How many roses does Julia have left?

Children may draw lines through 56 dots and then circle 29 dots to find the number of dots that are left (27). The important thing for children to realize is that they had to break a ten into individual ones in order to solve the problem.

Construct or have a child construct the solution to the story problem using Demonstration Secret Code Cards. Have the class work in pairs to construct the solution with their Secret Code Cards at the same time.

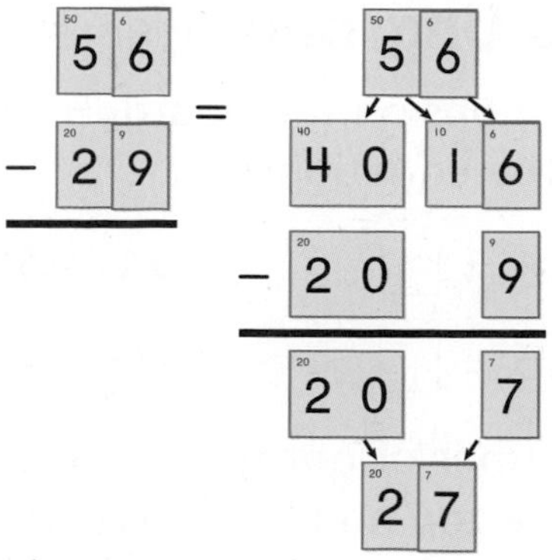

Activity continued ▶

25 MINUTES

Goals: Develop and solve subtraction story problems with 2-digit numbers.

Materials: MathBoard materials or Dot Array, Demonstration Secret Code Cards, Secret Code Cards (1 set per pair)

NCTM Standards:
Number and Operations
Problem Solving
Representation
Communication

Ongoing Assessment

Have children draw a picture or use Secret Code Cards to solve the following story problems.

- ▶ Carmen had 52 marbles. She gave 35 of them to her sister. How many marbles does Carmen have left?
- ▶ Lani had 75 pennies. He put 49 of them in his piggy bank. How many pennies does Lani have left?

Teaching Note

What to Expect from Students
Some children will attempt to draw both of the numbers given in a subtraction problem. This works for addition. However, this only works for subtraction if we match the two sets one-to-one (the comparison method). This method was used for smaller numbers but is too complex for multi-digit numbers. Point out to students that they should draw just the total and take away or circle the known partner.

Too complex; this suggests addition.

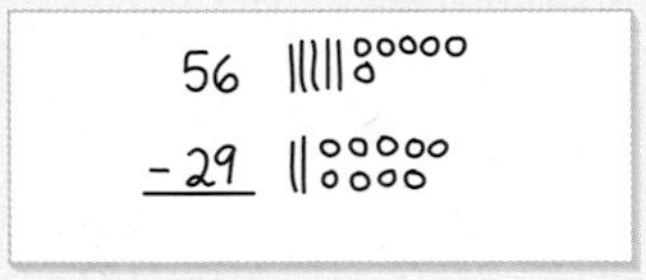

This is easier.

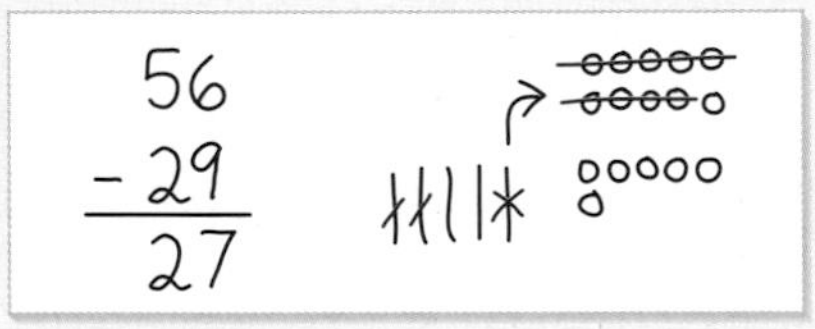

Emphasize that subtraction is finding the unknown partner hiding inside the larger number. We only have the total when we start. We have to look inside it to see the two partners.

Have children devise a way of rewriting the top number to show the ungrouping that was done. Two typical methods are shown below.

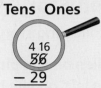

Expanded Method

$$\begin{array}{r} 40 + 16 \\ 56 = \not{5}0 + \not{6} \\ \underline{-\ 29 = 20 + 9} \end{array}$$

Ungroup First Method
Tens Ones

$$\begin{array}{r} 4\ 16 \\ \not{5}\not{6} \\ \underline{-\ 29} \end{array}$$

The magnifying glass shown in the second example helps the children see that they are not changing 56 to a new amount, but are regrouping the tens and ones in 56. They will be less likely to mistakenly subtract the top numbers from the lower numbers. These methods and vocabulary issues are described and discussed more in Lesson 5.

▶ Develop Story Problems for Equations WHOLE CLASS

Write the equations below on the board and have children write them on their MathBoards.

$76 - 48 = \square$ $63 - 35 = \square$ $92 - 54 = \square$

Challenge children to develop a story problem that illustrates each of the equations. Then have them rewrite the numbers to reflect the ungrouping and then check their work. Have children make Proof Drawings for all problems.

Circulate around the room to be sure children are able to represent any ungrouping that they do. From time to time, invite a child to show the class his or her work. Discuss any issues that may arise. Encourage children to use tens and ones language appropriately whenever they explain their work.

Activity 3

Decide When to Ungroup

20 MINUTES

Goals: Decide when to ungroup to solve subtraction problems.

Materials: MathBoard materials

NCTM Standards:
Number and Operations
Problem Solving
Representation
Communication

▶ Discuss When to Ungroup WHOLE CLASS Math Talk

Write the following equations on the board. Have children develop story problems that illustrate the equations.

$56 - 24 = \square$ $81 - 39 = \square$

$67 - 23 = \square$ $76 - 48 = \square$

Discuss with children whether or not they need to ungroup a ten for more ones and rewrite the top number. Have them articulate their reasoning.

Differentiated Instruction

Intervention Activity Card 9-4

Grid Paper Rectangles
Activity Card 9-4

Work: pairs

Use:
- 12 index cards with subtraction problems

Choose:
- 1
- 2

1. (1) Mix the cards.
2. Put subtraction problems that need ungrouping in one pile. Put subtraction problems that do not need ungrouping in another pile.

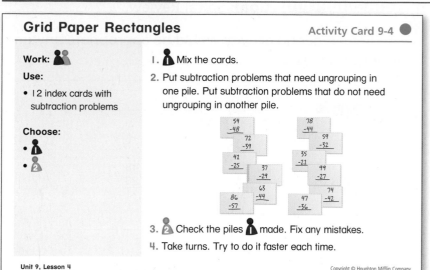

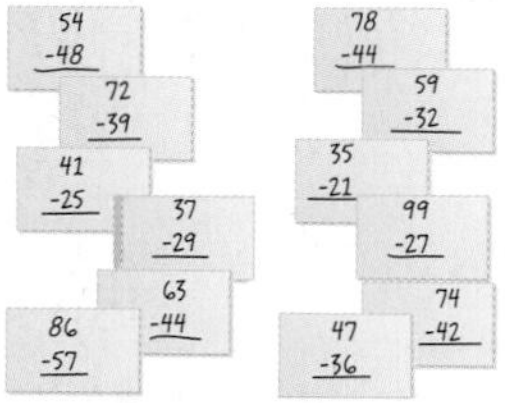

3. (2) Check the piles (1) made. Fix any mistakes.
4. Take turns. Try to do it faster each time.

Unit 9, Lesson 4

Activity Note Each pair needs twelve index cards. Six should have subtraction exercises that require ungrouping. And six should have exercises that do not need ungrouping.

Math Writing Prompt

Make a Drawing Draw a picture to show why 4 tens is the same amount as 3 tens and 10 ones. Explain your drawing.

Soar to Success Math **Software Support**

Warm Up 11.20

On Level Activity Card 9-4

Find the Unknown Partners
Activity Card 9-4

Work: pairs

Use:
- 12 index cards

Choose:
- 1
- 2

1. **Work Together** Use six index cards. On each card, write a subtraction problem that needs ungrouping.
2. **Work Together** Use six index cards. On each card, write a subtraction problem that does not need ungrouping.
3. (1) Mix the cards.
4. (2) Put the cards into two piles. One pile should be exercises that need ungrouping. The other pile should be exercises that do not need ungrouping.

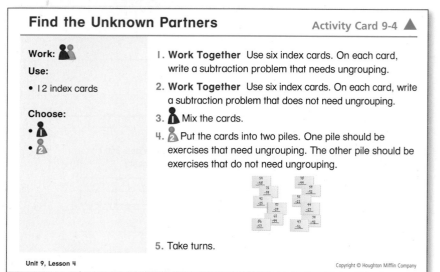

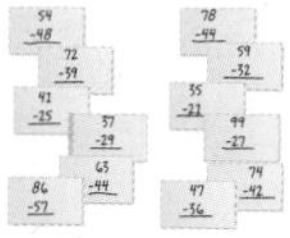

5. Take turns.

Unit 9, Lesson 4

Activity Note Each pair needs 12 index cards. The pair should write six subtraction problems that require ungrouping and six that do not require ungrouping.

Math Writing Prompt

Make a Proof Drawing Make a proof drawing to show how to solve 48 – 29 = ☐. Explain your thinking.

Harcourt Mega Math Grades K-6 **Software Support**

Shapes Ahoy: Sea Cave Sorting, Level H

Challenge Activity Card 9-4

How Many Subtractions?
Activity Card 9-4

Work: individual

Use:
- MathBoard materials
- Game Cards

1. Make a place-value chart on your MathBoard.
2. Mix the Game Cards and choose four cards. Use the cards to make two different two-digit numbers. Solve the subtraction problem.

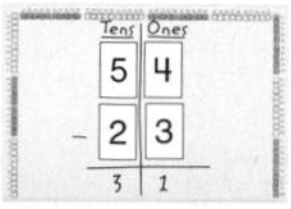

3. Use the same numbers to make as many subtraction exercises as possible. Solve each problem.

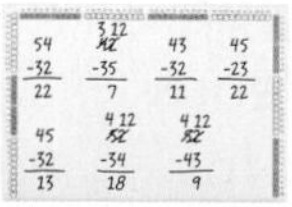

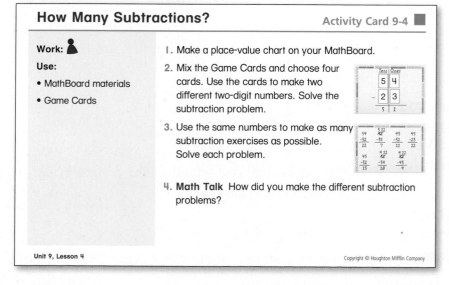

4. **Math Talk** How did you make the different subtraction problems?

Unit 9, Lesson 4

Activity Note Each child needs MathBoard materials and Game Cards (TRB M23). Check that children are subtracting the lesser number from the greater number.

Math Writing Prompt

Write Your Own Write and solve a subtraction story problem that requires ungrouping to solve.

Destination Math® **Software Support**

Course II: Module 2: Unit 1: Differences within 100

3 Homework and Spiral Review

9–4 Homework **Goal:** Additional Practice

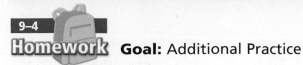

This Homework page provides practice in solving subtraction story problems.

9–4 **Homework** Name ____________

Solve each story problem. Make a proof drawing if you need to. **Show your work.**

1. Amon had 94 tomato seeds. He used 27 of them for a science project. How many seeds did he have left?

   67 seeds (label)

2. Benita made 56 leaf prints. She gave 29 prints to her cousins. How many prints does Benita have now?

   27 prints (label)

3. Denise had 71 straws. She used 33 of them to make a bridge. How many straws does she have left?

   38 straws (label)

4. Cedric had 70 sports cards. He gave away 24 cards to his friends. How many cards does Cedric have now?

   46 cards (label)

UNIT 9 LESSON 4 Subtraction Story Problems 183

Homework and Remembering page 183

9–4 Remembering **Goal:** Spiral Review

This Remembering activity would be appropriate anytime after today's lesson.

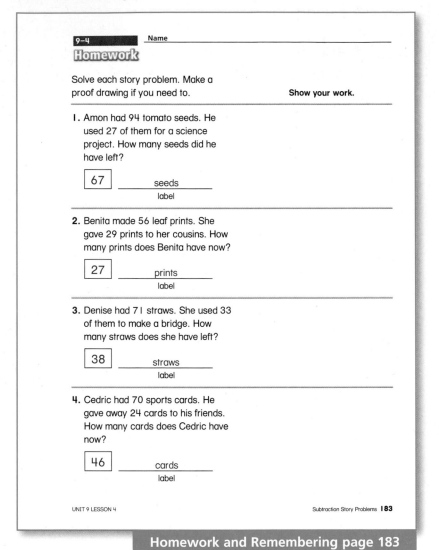

9–4 **Remembering** Name ____________

Add.

1. $45 + 93 = 138$
2. $72 + 59 = 131$
3. $48 + 23 = 71$

4. Draw coins to show two ways to make 25¢.
   Answers will vary. Sample answers shown.

25¢	25¢
10¢ 10¢ 5¢	10¢ 5¢ 5¢ 1¢ 1¢ 1¢ 1¢ 1¢

Solve the story problem. **Show your work.**

5. Josh solved 8 math problems. If he had solved another 7 problems he would have solved as many as Mato. How many problems did Mato solve?

   15 problems (label)

6. **Geometry**

Connect midpoints of two opposite sides.	Connect midpoints of the other two opposite sides.	Draw both line segments.
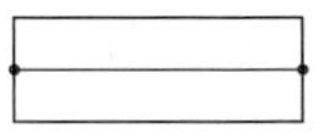	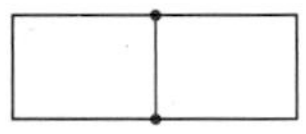	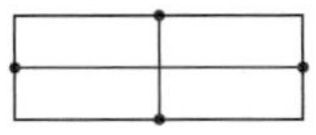

Answers in first two columns may be reversed.

184 UNIT 9 LESSON 4 Subtraction Story Problems

Homework and Remembering page 184

Home or School Activity

Science Connection

Around We Go It takes one year for the Earth to travel around the Sun. Other planets take more or less time depending upon how close they are to the Sun. For example, Mercury and Venus are closer to the Sun than Earth, so it takes less than a year for those planets to travel around the Sun.

Have children use science books or other resources to find out how many years it takes for each planet to travel around the sun. Children can write subtraction story problems using the data.

It takes Jupiter 12 years to go around the sun. It takes Saturn 29 years to go around the sun. How many more years does it take Saturn to go around the sun than Jupiter?

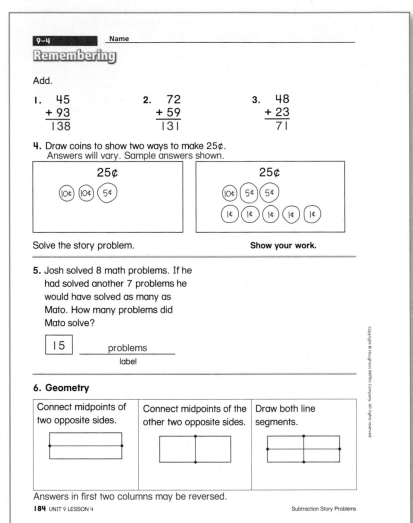

UNIT 9 LESSON 5

Two Methods of Subtraction

Lesson Objective

- **Solve 2-digit subtraction problems using the Expanded Method and the Ungroup First Method.**

Vocabulary

Expanded Method
Ungroup First Method

The Day at a Glance

Today's Goals	Materials	
1 Teaching the Lesson **A1:** Review teen subtraction. **A2:** Discuss and practice the Expanded Method for subtraction. **A3:** Discuss and practice the Ungroup First Method for subtraction.	**Lesson Activities** Student Activity Book pp. 281–286 (includes Family Letter) Homework and Remembering pp. 185–186 Thin strips of colored paper or 25-cm rulers Demonstration Secret Code Cards Secret Code Cards Base ten blocks	**Going Further** Activity Cards 9-5 Base ten blocks Index cards Math Journals
2 Going Further ▸ Differentiated Instruction		
3 Homework and Targeted Practice		

Use Math Talk today!

Keeping Skills Sharp

Quick Practice — 5 MINUTES

Goal: Write money strings for quarters.

Quarter Strings Have 2 or 3 children write money strings for quarters at the board. (See Unit 9 Lesson 2.)

25¢ = 10¢ + 10¢ + 1¢ + 1¢ + 1¢ + 1¢ + 1¢

25¢ = 10¢ + 10¢ + 5¢

25¢ = 10¢ + 5¢ + 5¢ + 1¢ + 1¢ + 1¢ + 1¢ + 1¢

25¢ = 10¢ + 5¢ + 5¢ + 5¢

Daily Routines

Quarters and Other Coins Making and Counting Coins that Make a Quarter, Counting to 200¢ by 25¢, Making and Counting Dollars and Cents: 3-Digit Numbers as Dollars and Cents
(See pp. xxvi – xxvii.)

▸ Led by Student Leaders

Money Routine Using the 120 Poster, Using the Money Flip Chart, Using the Number Path, Using Secret Code Cards
(See pp. xxiii–xxv.)

▸ Led by Student Leaders

1 Teaching the Lesson

Activity 1

Dive the Deep

10 MINUTES

Goal: Review teen subtraction.

Materials: Dive the Deep (Student Activity Book page 281), thin strips of colored paper (1 thin strip per child) or 25-cm ruler

NCTM Standard:
Number and Operations

English Language Learners

On the board, draw a picture of the sea and a fish swimming at the top. Gesture and say: **The sea is *deep*.**

- **Beginning** Point and ask: **Is the fish *deep*?** no Draw an arrow to the bottom. Say: **He *dives* down.** Ask: **Now is he deep?** yes
- **Intermediate** Say: ***Deep* means far down.** Ask: **Is the fish *deep*?** no Draw an arrow to the bottom. Say: **He *dives* down. Now he is ___.** deep
- **Advanced** Ask: **Does *deep* mean far down?** yes Draw an arrow and say: **The fish *dives* down. Now he is ___.** deep

Dive the Deep

11 − 6 = 5	12 − 6 = 6	13 − 8 = 5
12 − 7 = 5	17 − 8 = 9	15 − 6 = 9
12 − 9 = 3	13 − 5 = 8	11 − 9 = 2
13 − 4 = 9	14 − 6 = 8	13 − 9 = 4
11 − 5 = 6	17 − 9 = 8	15 − 7 = 8
14 − 9 = 5	11 − 8 = 3	14 − 8 = 6
14 − 7 = 7	12 − 4 = 8	12 − 5 = 7
16 − 7 = 9	16 − 8 = 8	11 − 3 = 8
11 − 7 = 4	15 − 7 = 8	13 − 6 = 7
12 − 3 = 9	16 − 9 = 7	18 − 9 = 9
13 − 7 = 6	11 − 4 = 7	12 − 8 = 4

UNIT 9 LESSON 5 Dive the Deep 281

Student Activity Book page 281

▶ Introduce Dive the Deep WHOLE CLASS

Have children turn to Student Activity Book page 281. Explain how to do the Dive the Deep activity.

For this activity, have children use a thin strip of paper to cover the answers in a column. You could also have your class use the 25-cm rulers to cover the answers. Today they will cover the answers in the first column. Tell them to start at the top of the first column, saying the answers silently to themselves. As they "dive down" they will uncover the answers to see if they were correct. If they are not correct, they should quietly say the correct equation two times to themselves. Before moving on to the next column, children should "swim" back up to play again.

Children will use Dive the Deep again for Quick Practices. Be sure children keep their pages. If you need to make additional copies, use TRB M78.

Activity 2

The Expanded Method

▶ Introduce the Expanded Method WHOLE CLASS

Explain to children that they will discuss two methods for solving subtraction problems. The first method they'll learn is the Expanded Method. Explain to children that Mr. Green likes this method best. (See Unit 5 Lesson 9.)

- Who remembers Mr. Green? Possible response: We talked about Mr. Green when we added 2-digit numbers.
- Can anyone demonstrate on the board how Mr. Green would add 64 + 28?

$$\begin{array}{r} 64 \\ +\ 28 \\ \hline 80 \\ +\ 12 \\ \hline 92 \end{array}$$

- Mr. Green also has a special method for solving subtraction problems and I'll show you how it works.

Write this story problem on the board:

Mr. Green had 64 tomatoes in a basket. He sold 28. How many tomatoes are left in the basket?

Invite a **Student Leader** to the board and have the child show the class how to write the subtraction for this story problem.

$$\begin{array}{r} 64 \\ -28 \\ \hline \end{array}$$

Activity continued ▶

25 MINUTES

Goal: Discuss and practice the Expanded Method for subtraction.

Materials: Student Activity Book, page 283, Demonstration Secret Code Cards, Secret Code Cards (1 set per pair)

✓ **NCTM Standard:**
Number and Operations

The Learning Classroom

Building Concepts Many children will be successful in inventing their own system of 2-digit subtraction. Others, however, will benefit from seeing methods. The two methods from this lesson incorporate important place value ideas. These methods also work for 3- and 4-digit subtraction. These are the research-based algorithms that children understand and can use.

▶ Explain the Expanded Method WHOLE CLASS

9-5 Class Activity

Name

Vocabulary
Expanded Method

▶ Explain the Expanded Method

Mr. Green likes this method. Explain what he does.

Step 1	Step 2	Step 3
64 = 60 + 4	64 = ~~60~~ (50) + ~~4~~ (14)	64 = ~~60~~ (50) + ~~4~~ (14)
− 28 = 20 + 8	− 28 = 20 + 8	− 28 = 20 + 8
		30 + 6 = 36

▶ Try the Expanded Method

Show your work numerically and with a Proof Drawing.

1. 42 = ~~40~~ (30) + ~~2~~ (12)
 − 19 = 10 + 9
 20 + 3 = 23

2. 75 = ~~70~~ (60) + ~~5~~ (15)
 − 46 = 40 + 6
 20 + 9 = 29

3. 81 = ~~80~~ (70) + ~~1~~ (11)
 − 37 = 30 + 7
 40 + 4 = 44

Check children's work.

UNIT 9 LESSON 5 Two Methods of Subtraction 283

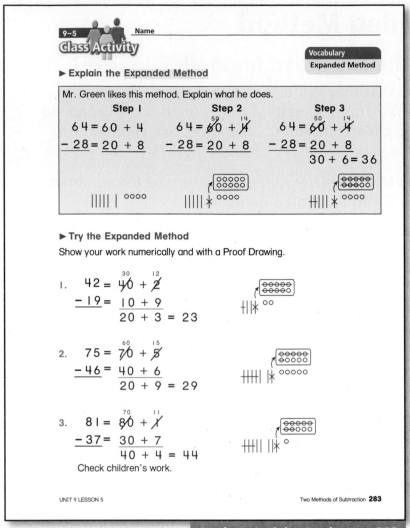

Student Activity Book page 283

Math Talk Have children look at page 283 and direct their attention to the three steps. As you read aloud each step, invite the class to interpret what each step instructs them to do.

Work through each step (shown on page 637) on the board. It is vital that all students initially make a math drawing to show their ungrouping and relate their drawing to their numerical steps. When students can explain their numerical method using tens and ones language, they do not need to continue making drawings.

Step 1: Write out the tens and the ones.

tens ↘ ↙ ones

$$\begin{array}{r} 64 = 60 + 4 \\ -28 = 20 + 8 \\ \hline \end{array}$$

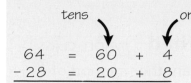

Tens and ones are different. Some children work better when they see the tens and ones separately.

Step 2: Check the tens and ones to see if you can subtract.

$$\begin{array}{r} 64 = 60 + 4 \\ 28 = 20 + 8 \\ \hline \uparrow \quad \uparrow \\ \text{yes} \quad \text{no} \end{array}$$

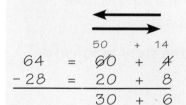

Check the ones and tens place to see if there's enough to subtract from. Writing "yes" and "no" under the numbers may help. If both answers are yes, you don't have to rewrite. I see that I need to get more ones because 4 is less than 8.

If not, ungroup the tens into ones.

$$\begin{array}{r} 50 \quad + \quad 14 \\ 64 = \not{6}\not{0} + \not{4} \\ -28 = 20 + 8 \\ \hline \end{array}$$

Get more ones by taking 1 ten from the tens place. Put those 10 ones in the ones column and rewrite both numbers. I now have 5 tens (50) and 14 ones.

Step 3: Subtract.

← →

$$\begin{array}{r} 50 \quad + \quad 14 \\ 64 = \not{6}\not{0} + \not{4} \\ -28 = 20 + 8 \\ \hline 30 + 6 = 36 \end{array}$$

You can subtract either left to right, or right to left.

Have children brainstorm and explain different ways to check their work. Some children will use addition, and some children will use a Proof Drawing. Both are shown at the top of Student Activity Book page 283.

▶ Try the Expanded Method INDIVIDUALS

Children should complete the page independently to see if they can use the **Expanded Method** to subtract. Have volunteers use the **Step-by-Step at the Board** structure to explain their work.

Alternate Approach

Secret Code Cards Some children may have difficulty understanding the Expanded Method for subtraction. Help them see the connection between the Expanded Method and the use of Secret Code Cards.

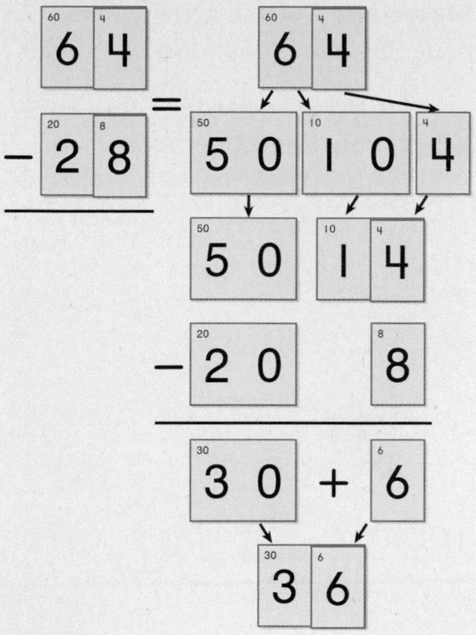

The Learning Classroom

Building Concepts When having volunteers discuss their work, try using the **Step-By-Step at the Board** structure. This is a variation of the **Solve and Discuss** structure, but in this case, a different child performs each step of the problem. It assists the children having the most difficulty, because they only need to describe one step.

Activity 3

The Ungroup First Method

20 MINUTES

Goal: Discuss and practice the Ungroup First Method for subtraction.

Materials: Student Activity Book, page 284, base ten blocks

NCTM Standard:
Number and Operations

▶ Introduce the Ungroup First Method WHOLE CLASS

Explain to children that they are going to learn another method of subtraction. The second way is the Ungroup First Method and Mrs. Green likes this way better. (See Unit 5 Lesson 11.)

- Who remembers Mrs. Green? Possible response: We talked about Mrs. Green when we added double-digit numbers.
- Can anyone show me on the board how Mrs. Green would add 64 and 28?

$$\begin{array}{r} 64 \\ +\ 28 \\ \hline \overset{1}{9}2 \end{array}$$

- Mrs. Green also has a way to subtract 2-digit numbers. You may even like this way better than Mr. Green's way. I'll show you how it works. While I work on the board, you can work on Student Activity Book page 284.

Write this story problem on the board:

Suppose that Mrs. Green had 64 tomatoes in a basket. She sold 28. How many tomatoes are left in the basket?

Have a Student Leader write the subtraction for the story problem on the board.

$$\begin{array}{r} 64 \\ -\ 28 \\ \hline \end{array}$$

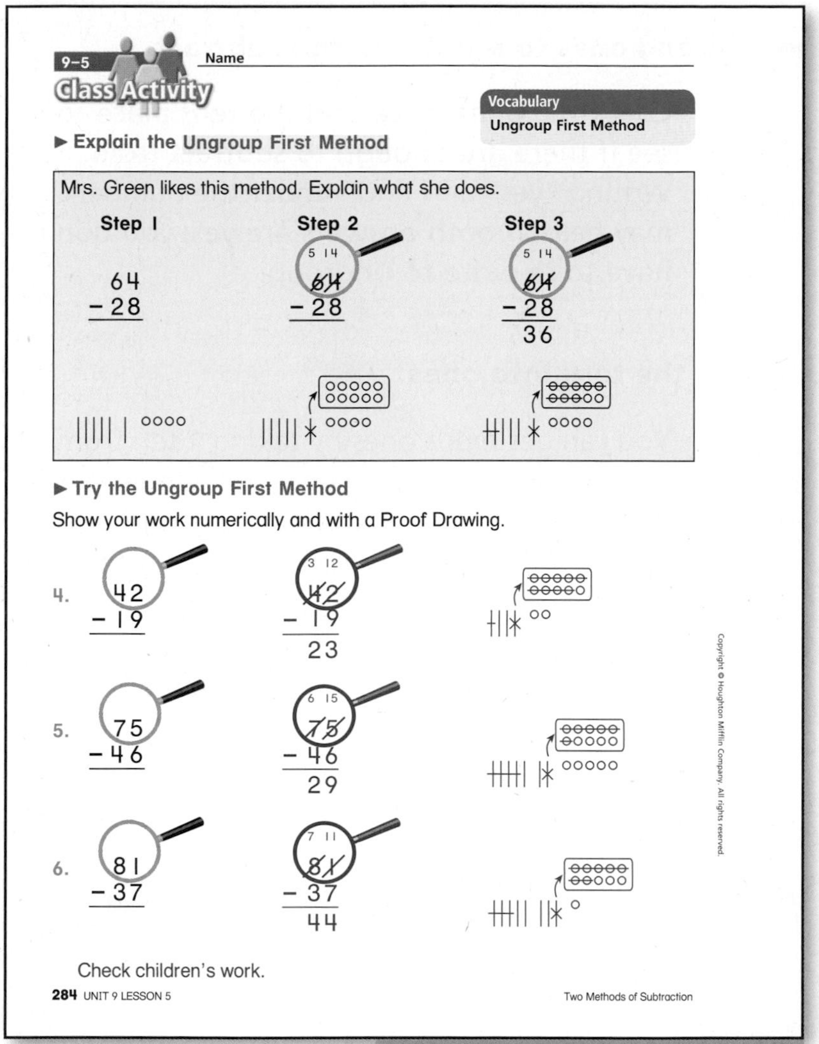
9–5 Class Activity

Name

Vocabulary
Ungroup First Method

▶ Explain the Ungroup First Method

Mrs. Green likes this method. Explain what she does.

Step 1	Step 2	Step 3
64 − 28	5 14 / 64 − 28	5 14 / 64 − 28 = 36

▶ Try the Ungroup First Method

Show your work numerically and with a Proof Drawing.

4. 42 − 19 → 3 12 / 42 − 19 = 23

5. 75 − 46 → 6 15 / 75 − 46 = 29

6. 81 − 37 → 7 11 / 81 − 37 = 44

Check children's work.

284 UNIT 9 LESSON 5 Two Methods of Subtraction

Copyright © Houghton Mifflin Company. All rights reserved.

Student Activity Book page 284

▶ Explain the Ungroup First Method WHOLE CLASS

Math Talk Engage children in a discussion on how to subtract 2-digit numbers using the Ungroup First Method.

Have children look at the top of Student Activity Book page 284 and direct their attention to the three steps. As you read aloud each step with your children, invite the class to try to interpret what each step instructs them to do.

Work through the steps (shown on page 640) on the board.

Activity continued ▶

Teaching Note

Language and Vocabulary Some children may have been exposed to other methods of subtraction. They may use terms like *look inside, open up, trade, borrow,* and so forth to describe the processes of ungrouping a ten to make 10 ones.

If terminology becomes an issue, discuss it with your class, and decide upon a word that everyone understands and will use consistently. *Math Expressions* favors the use of the term *ungroup for subtraction* (and *group* for addition problems) because these terms show how addition and subtraction undo each other. Regrouping is used for both of these processes. Use any terms that you think are clear and conceptual for your students.

It is helpful to discuss all methods as just renaming the top number. Discuss how a person can have different names—some short and some long—that look and sound different. But they are the same person. Similarly *64* and *5 tens and 14 ones* are different names for the same quantity, but the quantity does not change.

Alternate Approach

Base Ten Blocks For children having difficulty with pencil and paper methods, try using base ten blocks. Using base ten blocks helps students see how and why they need to ungroup in subtraction.

$$\begin{array}{r} 64 \\ -\ 28 \\ \hline \end{array}$$

Step 1 Use tens and ones to show 64.

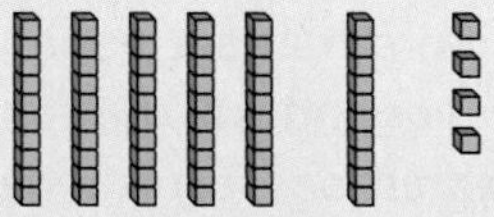

You can't take away 8 ones from 4 ones.

Step 2 Ungroup 1 ten as 10 ones.

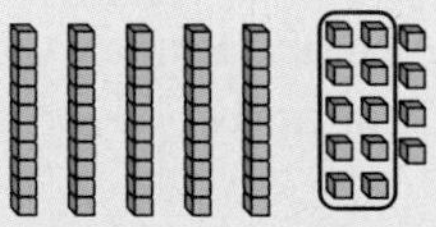

Now there are 5 tens and 14 ones.

Step 3 Take away 2 tens and 8 ones.

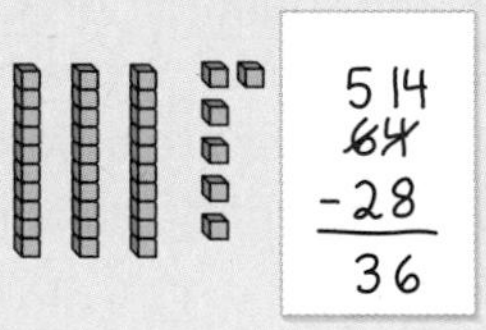

There are 3 tens and 6 ones left over. However, many children prefer math drawings to base-ten blocks, and you can check math drawings made for homework problems. Also, children can see all of the steps at the end in their math drawing.

Ongoing Assessment

- Have children create their own 2-digit subtraction and solve using either method.

As you and your children address each of the steps, make sure the following concepts are included in your discussion.

Step 1: Check the tens and ones to see if you can subtract.

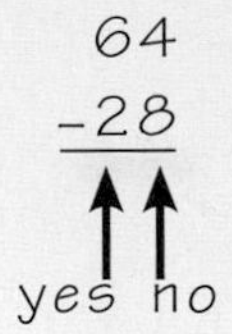

Check the ones place and the tens place to see if there are enough to subtract from. Writing "yes" and "no" under the numbers may help. If both answers are yes, you don't have to re-write to ungroup.

Step 2: If not, ungroup the tens into ones.

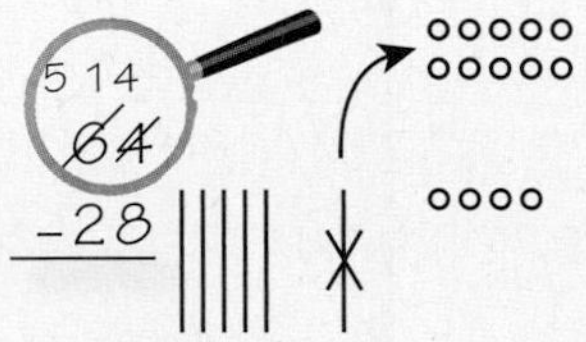

You can get more ones by taking 1 ten from the tens and putting 10 ones in the ones place. Rewrite the numbers to show this ungrouping. A Proof Drawing helps children to make sure they re-wrote the numbers correctly.

Start by drawing a "magnifying glass" to show 64 "opened up" to reveal 5 tens and 14 ones.

Step 3: Subtract.

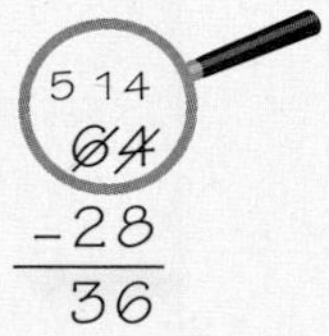

Subtract from either right to left or left to right.

Once you have discussed all three steps, have children brainstorm and explain different ways to check their work.

▶ Try the Ungroup First Method

INDIVIDUALS

Math Talk

Encourage children to complete the page independently using the Ungroup First Method to subtract. Remind children to decide whether or not they need to ungroup and to draw a magnifying glass when they ungroup.

Discuss solution methods and methods of checking with the class using **Solve and Discuss** or **Step-by-Step at the Board.**

2 Going Further

Differentiated Instruction

Intervention — Activity Card 9-5

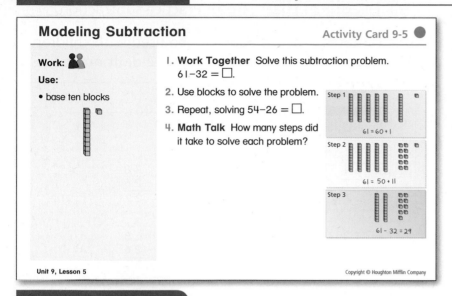

Modeling Subtraction — Activity Card 9-5

Work: pairs

Use:

- base ten blocks

1. **Work Together** Solve this subtraction problem. $61 - 32 = \square$.
2. Use blocks to solve the problem.
3. Repeat, solving $54 - 26 = \square$.
4. **Math Talk** How many steps did it take to solve each problem?

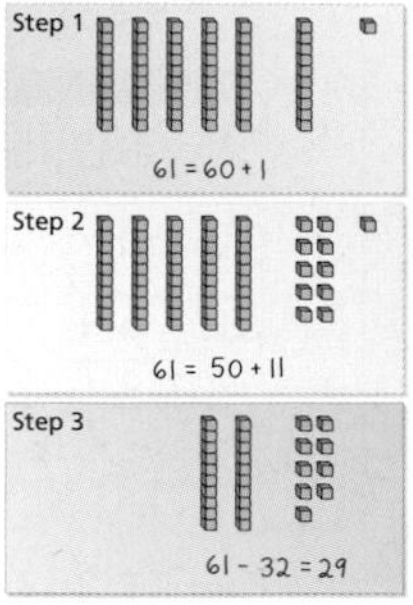

Unit 9, Lesson 5

Activity Note Each pair needs base ten blocks (tens and ones). Help children realize that it may take more than two steps to solve the problem.

Math Writing Prompt

Make a Drawing Use a drawing to show that *5 tens* and *2 ones* is the same as *4 tens* and *12 ones*.

Soar to Success Math Software Support

Warm Up 11.19

On Level — Activity Card 9-5

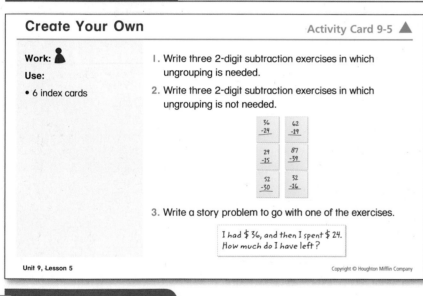

Create Your Own — Activity Card 9-5

Work: individual

Use:

- 6 index cards

1. Write three 2-digit subtraction exercises in which ungrouping is needed.
2. Write three 2-digit subtraction exercises in which ungrouping is not needed.

36 − 24	62 − 19
29 − 15	87 − 39
52 − 30	32 − 16

3. Write a story problem to go with one of the exercises.

I had \$36, and then I spent \$24. How much do I have left?

Unit 9, Lesson 5

Activity Note Each pair needs six index cards. Check that the problems children write are correct and that some require ungrouping and some do not.

Math Writing Prompt

Explain Your Thinking Do you need to ungroup in every subtraction exercise? Explain your answer.

Harcourt MegaMath Software Support

Country Countdown: Block Busters, Level R

Challenge — Activity Card 9-5

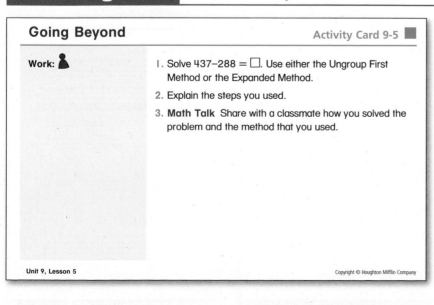

Going Beyond — Activity Card 9-5

Work: individual

1. Solve $437 - 288 = \square$. Use either the Ungroup First Method or the Expanded Method.
2. Explain the steps you used.
3. **Math Talk** Share with a classmate how you solved the problem and the method that you used.

Unit 9, Lesson 5

Activity Note Have children share their work with another child and check that it was done correctly.

Math Writing Prompt

You Decide When Mario was subtracting 57 from 64, he explained that 4 ones take away 7 ones is 3 ones and 6 tens take away 5 tens is 1 ten. Is he correct? Why or why not?

Destination Math Software Support

Course II: Module 1: Unit 1: Expanded Form and Equivalent Representations of a Number

3 Homework and Targeted Practice

9-5 Homework

Goal: Additional Practice

✓ Include students' completed Homework page as part of their portfolios.

9-5 **Homework** Name ____________

The Expanded Method	The Ungrouping First Method	Proof Drawing
80 + 13 93 = 90 + 3 − 57 = 50 + 7 30 + 6 = 36	8 13 93 − 57 36	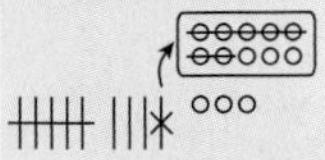

Subtract using any method. Children's methods will vary.

1. 38 − 21 = 17
2. 57 − 39 = 18
3. 95 − 64 = 31
4. 50 − 13 = 37
5. 68 − 15 = 53
6. 77 − 29 = 48
7. 74 − 48 = 26
8. 84 − 49 = 35

UNIT 9 LESSON 5 Two Methods of Subtraction **185**

Homework and Remembering page 185

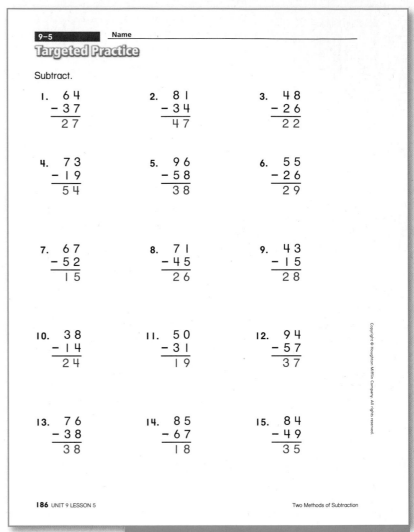

9-5 Targeted Practice

Goal: Practice subtraction.

This Targeted Practice page can be used with children who need extra practice subtracting 2-digit numbers.

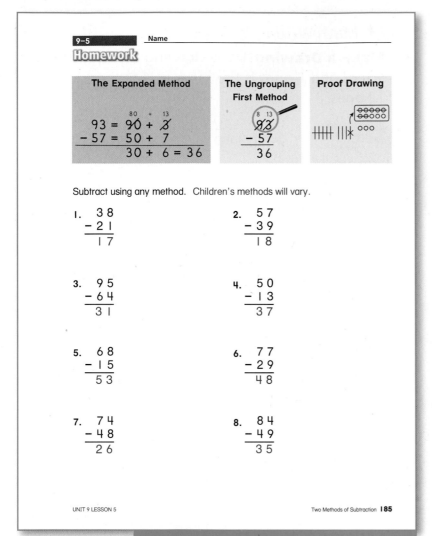

9-5 **Targeted Practice** Name ____________

Subtract.

1. 64 − 37 = 27
2. 81 − 34 = 47
3. 48 − 26 = 22
4. 73 − 19 = 54
5. 96 − 58 = 38
6. 55 − 26 = 29
7. 67 − 52 = 15
8. 71 − 45 = 26
9. 43 − 15 = 28
10. 38 − 14 = 24
11. 50 − 31 = 19
12. 94 − 57 = 37
13. 76 − 38 = 38
14. 85 − 67 = 18
15. 84 − 49 = 35

186 UNIT 9 LESSON 5 Two Methods of Subtraction

Homework and Remembering page 186

Home and School Connection

Family Letter Have children take home the Family Letter on Student Activity Book page 285. This letter explains how the concept of two-digit subtraction is developed in *Math Expressions.* It gives parents and guardians a better understanding of the learning that goes on in math class and creates a bridge between school and home. A Spanish translation of this letter is on the following page in the Student Activity Book.

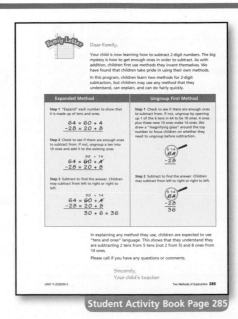

Family Letter

Dear Family,

Your child is now learning how to subtract 2-digit numbers. The big mystery is how to get enough ones in order to subtract. As with addition, children first use methods they invent themselves. We have found that children take pride in using their own methods.

In this program, children learn two methods for 2-digit subtraction, but children may use any method that they understand, can explain, and can do fairly quickly.

Expanded Method	Ungroup First Method
Step 1 "Expand" each number to show that it is made up of tens and ones. 64 = 60 + 4 −28 = 20 + 8	**Step 1** Check to see if there are enough ones to subtract from. If not, ungroup by opening up 1 of the 6 tens in 64 to be 10 ones. 4 ones plus these new 10 ones make 14 ones. We draw a "magnifying glass" around the top number to focus children on whether they need to ungroup before subtraction. 5 14 64 −28
Step 2 Check to see if there are enough ones to subtract from. If not, ungroup a ten into 10 ones and add it to the existing ones. 50 + 14 64 = 60 + 4 −28 = 20 + 8	**Step 2** Subtract to find the answer. Children may subtract from left to right or right to left. 5 14 64 −28 36
Step 3 Subtract to find the answer. Children may subtract from left to right or right to left. 50 + 14 64 = 60 + 4 −28 = 20 + 8 30 + 6 = 36	

In explaining any method they use, children are expected to use "tens and ones" language. This shows that they understand they are subtracting 2 tens from 5 tens (not 2 from 5) and 8 ones from 14 ones.

Please call if you have any questions or comments.

Sincerely,
Your child's teacher

UNIT 9 LESSON 5 Two Methods of Subtraction **285**

Student Activity Book Page 285

Carta a la familia

Estimada familia:

Su niño está aprendiendo a restar números de 2 dígitos. El misterio es cómo obtener suficientes unidades para poder restar. como en la suma, los niños primero usan métodos que ellos mismos inventan. Hemos notado que los niños se sienten orgullosos de usar sus propios métodos.

En este programa, los niños aprenden dos métodos para la resta con números de 2 digitos, pero pueden usar cualquier método que comprendan, puedan explicar y puedan hacer relativamente rápido.

Método extendido	Método de desagrupar primero
Paso 1 "Extender" cada número para mostrar que consta de decenas y unidades. 64 = 60 + 4 −28 = 20 + 8	**Paso 1** Observar si hay suficientes unidades para restar. Si no las hay, entonces desagrupar duna de las 6 decenas en 64 para obtener 10 unidades. 4 unidades más las 10 unidades nuevas hacen 14 unidades. Dibujamos una "lupa" alrededor del número superior para que los niños piensen si necesitan desagrupar antes de restar. 5 14 64 −28
Paso 2 Observar si hay suficientes unidades para restar. Si no las hay, desagrupar una decena para formar 10 unidades y sumarla a las unidades existentes. 50 + 14 64 = 60 + 4 −28 = 20 + 8	**Paso 2** Restar para hallar la respuesta. Los niños pueden restar de izquierda a derecha o de derecha a izquierda. 5 14 64 −28 36
Paso 3 Restar para hallar la respuesta. Los niños pueden restar de izquierda a derecha o de derecha a izquierda. 50 + 14 64 = 60 + 4 −28 = 20 + 8 30 + 6 = 36	

Cuando los niños explican el método que usan, deben usar un lenguaje relacionado con "decenas y unidades". Esto demuestra que comprenden que están restando 2 decenas de 5 decenas (no 2 de 5) y 8 unidades de 14 unidades.

Si tiene alguna duda o comentario, por favor comuniquese conmigo.

Atentamente,
El maestro de su niño

286 UNIT 9 LESSON 5 Two Methods of Subtraction

Student Activity Book Page 286

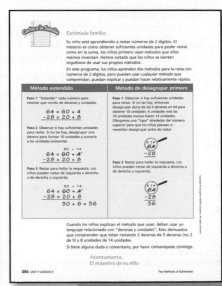

UNIT 9 LESSON 6

Practice and Explain a Method

Lesson Objectives

- Discuss the advantages and disadvantages of two subtraction methods.
- Solve subtraction story problems with a preferred method.
- Explain a 2-digit subtraction method.

Vocabulary

Expanded Method
Ungroup First Method
estimate
difference

The Day at a Glance

Today's Goals	Materials	
1 Teaching the Lesson A: Discuss the advantages and disadvantages of two subtraction methods. Use and explain a preferred method.	**Lesson Activities** Student Activity Book pp. 287–288 Homework and Remembering pp. 187–188	**Going Further** Activity Cards 9-6 Homework and Remembering p. 187 Base ten blocks Index cards MathBoard materials Math Journals
2 Going Further ▸ Math Connection: Round to Estimate Differences ▸ Differentiated Instruction		
3 Homework and Spiral Review		

Use Math Talk today!

Keeping Skills Sharp

Quick Practice — 5 MINUTES

Goals: Write money strings for dollars. Practice subtraction with teen totals.

Materials: Dive the Deep (Student Activity Book page 281 or TRB M78)

Dollar Strings Have two or three children write dollar strings on the board as the other children do the *Dive the Deep* activity.

$1.00 = 25¢ + 25¢ + 10¢ + 10¢ + 5¢ + 5¢ + 5¢ + 5¢ + 5¢ + 5¢
$1.00 = 10¢ + 10¢ + 10¢ + 10¢ + 10¢ + 5¢ + 5¢ + 5¢ + 5¢ + 5¢ + 5¢ + 5¢ + 5¢ + 5¢ + 1¢ + 1¢ + 1¢ + 1¢ + 1¢

Dive the Deep Have children use Student Activity book page 281 or TRB M78 to practice teen subtraction. Remind them to say the whole equation correctly two times if they give a wrong answer. (See Unit 9 Lesson 5.)

Daily Routines

Quarters and Other Coins Making and Counting Coins that Make a Quarter, Counting to 200¢ by 25¢, Making and Counting Dollars and Cents: 3-Digit Numbers as Dollars and Cents (See pp. xxvi–xxvii.)

▸ Led by Student Leaders

Money Routine Using the 120 Poster, Using the Money Flip Chart, Using the Number Path, Using Secret Code Cards (See pp. xxiii–xxv.)

▸ Led by Student Leaders

1 Teaching the Lesson

Activity

Choose a Method

50 MINUTES

Goals: Discuss the advantages and disadvantages of two subtraction methods. Use and explain a preferred method.

Materials: Student Activity Book page 287

NCTM Standards:
Number and Operations
Communication

English Language Learners

Write *advantage* and *disadvantage* on the board. Say each word. Have children repeat. Say: **These words are opposites.**

- **Beginning** Say: An ***advantage* is a good thing. *Disadvantage* means a bad thing.** Have children repeat.
- **Intermediate** Say: **An *advantage* is a good thing. *Disadvantage* means** ___. a bad thing
- **Advanced** Say: **A good thing is an *advantage*. A bad thing is a** ___. disadvantage

Teaching Note

Many students may still need to make math drawings. If students take away from the ungrouped ten, they can see the Make-a-Ten method.

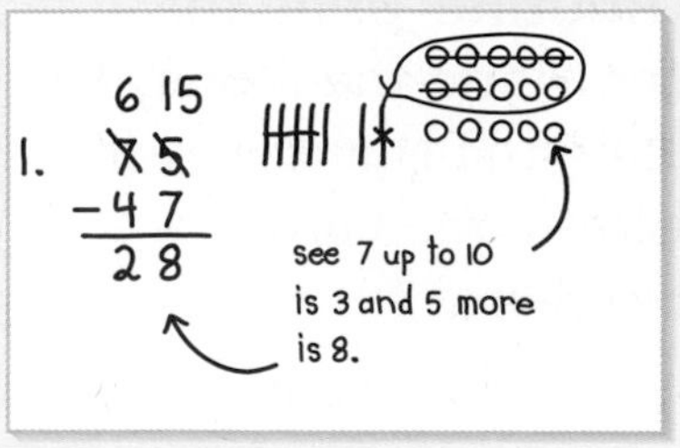

▶ Discuss Two Subtraction Methods

WHOLE CLASS

Math Talk

Ask for Ideas Discuss the advantages and disadvantages of subtraction methods.

- We know how to subtract in a few different ways. Each method has advantages and disadvantages. Advantages are the good things about it.
- Let's look at the Expanded Method first. What are the good things about using it? It is very clear and it is easy to see the ungrouping. You can also clearly see the tens and ones.
- What are the disadvantages of using it? It takes some time to write out the ungrouping.
- Now let's look at the Ungroup First Method. What are the good things about using it? It is faster to use than the Expanded Method.
- What are the disadvantages of using it? You can't see the place values as well; you have to understand the tens and ones that are there.

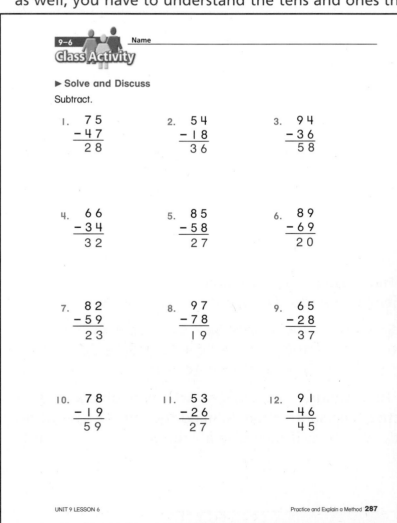

9–6 Class Activity Name ____________

▶ Solve and Discuss

Subtract.

1. 75 − 47 = 28	2. 54 − 18 = 36	3. 94 − 36 = 58
4. 66 − 34 = 32	5. 85 − 58 = 27	6. 89 − 69 = 20
7. 82 − 59 = 23	8. 97 − 78 = 19	9. 65 − 28 = 37
10. 78 − 19 = 59	11. 53 − 26 = 27	12. 91 − 46 = 45

UNIT 9 LESSON 6 Practice and Explain a Method 287

Student Activity Book page 287

▶ Solve and Discuss WHOLE CLASS

Math Talk

Invite four volunteers to come to the board to solve the first four exercises on Student Activity Book page 287. Two children should use the Expanded Method and two should use the Ungroup First Method. The rest of the class should solve the four exercises at their seats, using whichever method they choose.

Before children begin working, remind them of the partners concept.

- Remember that smaller numbers are hiding inside a larger number. That means we can break the larger number into smaller numbers. What happens when we subtract? We find the unknown smaller number hiding inside the larger number.

You may wish to remind children to check their work by adding the two partners together to be sure they get the total. Some children may try other methods to check their work, such as counting on to find the partner.

As children work, circulate around the room and help anyone who is having trouble. You may also wish to have **Student Helpers** provide help as needed. Pay special attention to the issue of whether or not it is necessary to rewrite the tens and ones. Then have one or two children at the board explain their solutions to the class. Be sure children discuss the advantages and disadvantages of each method.

▶ Explain a Solution Method PAIRS

Math Talk

Have children work in pairs to complete the page. Have them take turns explaining the solution method they used to their partner. Remind children to explain the method one step at a time and to use proper tens and ones language.

Then select a pair of children to present a solution using a method they both agree upon. They may also write the solution on the board. If necessary, remind them to use proper tens and ones language. If they forget to use the correct terms, have the rest of the class remind them by waving both hands or using some other prearranged signal.

Finally, have children express the solution in terms of a Math Mountain, showing that the smaller numbers are partners of the larger number. Write in the minus and plus signs if the children find it helpful.

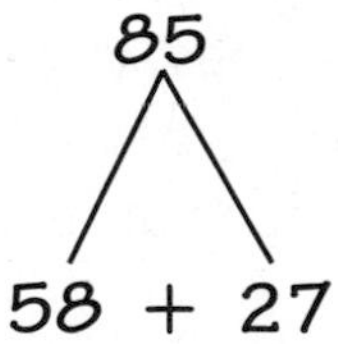

Teaching Note

Watch For! The errors shown below are the most common serious mistakes children make when learning 2-digit subtraction. Address these and any other mistakes you may have noticed. For example, circling the total (the top number) with the magnifying glass should help remind the children that they are subtracting from the number on top.

Subtracting Smaller from Larger
The child does not conceptualize the top number as an entity and simply subtracts the smaller 1-digit number from the larger.

```
  74
– 28
  54 X
```

Failing to Ungroup the Tens
The child ungroups a ten into ten ones and rewrites the number of ones but neglects to rewrite the tens.

```
   14
  7̸4
– 28
  56 X
```

Ungrouping Unnecessarily
The child ungroups a ten into ten ones and rewrites the tens and the ones when it is not necessary.

```
  614
  7̸4̸
–  22
  412 X
```

Ongoing Assessment

Have children subtract using any method of their choice.

1. 78 – 54
2. 63 – 47
3. 94 – 75

2 Going Further

Math Connection: Round to Estimate Differences

Goal: Estimate the difference of 2-digit numbers by rounding to the nearest ten.

Materials: Student Activity Book page 288

✓ **NCTM Standard:**
Number and Operations

Teaching Note

Language and Vocabulary Some children may have previously used the term *difference* to refer to the answer in subtraction. You may choose to begin using this term at this time. Some children may be confused with the multiple meanings that *difference* can have. Explain to children that while *difference* is often used to describe something that is not like something else, in math, the word *difference* is what we call the answer to a subtraction problem.

Teaching Note

Math Background Sometimes it is not necessary to find the exact difference between two numbers. In that case, an estimate can be used. There are several ways to estimate a difference, but the most commonly used way is to round both of the numbers and then subtract the rounded numbers.

Some students may notice that rounding both addends in some cases produces a rounded total that differs from the total you get if you subtract first and then round. For example, 75 – 42 rounded is 80 – 40 = 40, but 75 – 42 = 33 which rounds to 30. You might explain that with such small numbers it often makes sense just to subtract rather than bother with rounding. Some students might want to explore cases and see if they can come up with statements about which cases "don't work" and why. Cases that "don't work" occur when the numbers are rounded in the opposite direction and one or both numbers are far from their rounded number.

▸ Introduce Estimating Differences

WHOLE CLASS

Have children look at Student Activity Book page 288 and discuss the example in the blue box. Use the number lines to briefly review how to round numbers to the nearest ten. Remind children that they must round up if a number is exactly in the middle of two tens.

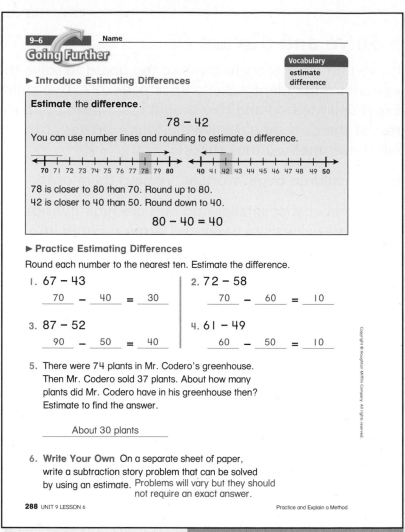

9–6 Going Further Name ______

Vocabulary
estimate
difference

▸ Introduce Estimating Differences

Estimate the **difference**.

78 – 42

You can use number lines and rounding to estimate a difference.

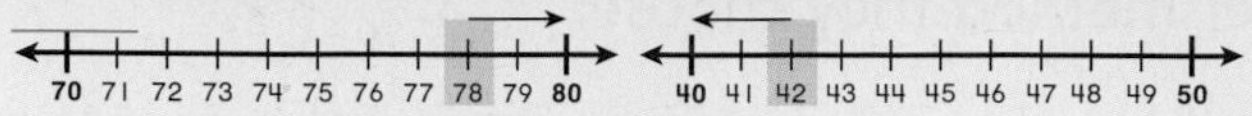

78 is closer to 80 than 70. Round up to 80.
42 is closer to 40 than 50. Round down to 40.

80 – 40 = 40

▸ Practice Estimating Differences

Round each number to the nearest ten. Estimate the difference.

1. 67 – 43
   70 – 40 = 30
2. 72 – 58
   70 – 60 = 10
3. 87 – 52
   90 – 50 = 40
4. 61 – 49
   60 – 50 = 10

5. There were 74 plants in Mr. Codero's greenhouse. Then Mr. Codero sold 37 plants. About how many plants did Mr. Codero have in his greenhouse then? Estimate to find the answer.

   About 30 plants

6. **Write Your Own** On a separate sheet of paper, write a subtraction story problem that can be solved by using an estimate. Problems will vary but they should not require an exact answer.

288 UNIT 9 LESSON 6 Practice and Explain a Method

Student Activity Book page 288

▸ Practice Estimating Differences PAIRS

Have children work individually to find the estimates in exercises 1–4. Have pairs take turns explaining how they found each estimate. Be sure children understand that they are being asked to find an estimate. That means their answer will be a decade number that tells *about* how much the difference is. Then have children complete problems 5 and 6.

▸ Write Your Own WHOLE CLASS

After children have written their story problems, ask volunteers to share their stories with the rest of the class. If a child has written a story problem that requires an exact answer, have another child help them change the question so that it can be answered by estimating.

Intervention — Activity Card 9-6

Base Ten Blocks

Activity Card 9-6

Work: pairs

Use:

- Homework and Remembering page 187
- base ten blocks

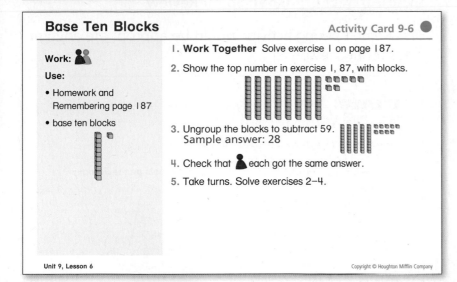

1. **Work Together** Solve exercise 1 on page 187.
2. Show the top number in exercise 1, 87, with blocks.

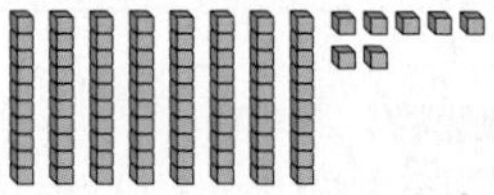

3. Ungroup the blocks to subtract 59. Sample answer: 28

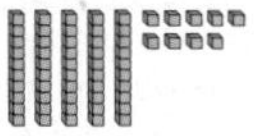

4. Check that each got the same answer.
5. Take turns. Solve exercises 2–4.

Unit 9, Lesson 6

Copyright © Houghton Mifflin Company

Activity Note Each pair needs base ten blocks and Homework and Remembering p. 187. Have children check each other's work.

Math Writing Prompt

Explain Your Thinking Look at the equations below. Which one can be solved without ungrouping? How can you tell?

$46 - 32 = \square$ $\qquad$ $46 - 38 = \square$

Soar to Success Math Software Support

Warm Up 11.19

On Level — Activity Card 9-6

Find and Correct the Errors

Activity Card 9-6

Work: pairs

Use:

- MathBoard materials
- 3 index cards with subtraction exercises

Choose:

- 1
- 2

1. Look at one of the subtraction exercises. Explain what is wrong with the exercise.
2. Solve the problem correctly on your MathBoard.

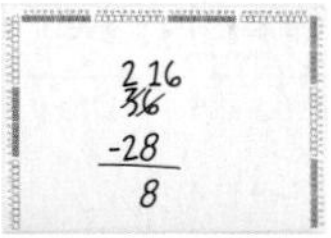

3. Take turns correcting the other exercises.
4. **Math Talk** Explain the errors in the exercises. Make rules for checking subtraction exercises.

Unit 9, Lesson 6

Copyright © Houghton Mifflin Company

Activity Note Each pair needs MathBoard materials and three index cards with these problems: 75 − 13 = 72, 36 − 28 = 7, and 41 − 28 = 23. Pairs need to find the errors.

Math Writing Prompt

Explain Your Thinking Explain how you know whether you need to ungroup in order to subtract.

Harcourt MegaMath Software Support

Numberopolis: Carnival Stories, Level Q

Challenge — Activity Card 9-6

Subtract Across a Zero

Activity Card 9-6

Work: pairs

$$\begin{array}{r} 405 \\ -\ 267 \\ \hline \end{array}$$

1. Each copy the problem above onto a piece of paper.
2. Work to solve the problem.
3. Compare your answers and use addition to check your work.
4. **Math Talk** Take turns explaining the steps that you used to subtract.

Unit 9, Lesson 6

Copyright © Houghton Mifflin Company

Activity Note Each pair needs to use what they know to subtract three-digit numbers. Have pairs talk through the process they used.

Math Writing Prompt

Identify Errors Camilla started to solve the exercise $53 - 32 = \square$ by ungrouping 53 as 4 tens and 13 ones. What did she do wrong?

Destination Math Software Support

Course II: Module 2: Unit 1: Estimating and Finding Differences within 1,000

❸ Homework and Spiral Review

9–6 Homework **Goal:** Additional Practice

This Homework page provides practice subtracting 2-digit numbers with and without ungrouping.

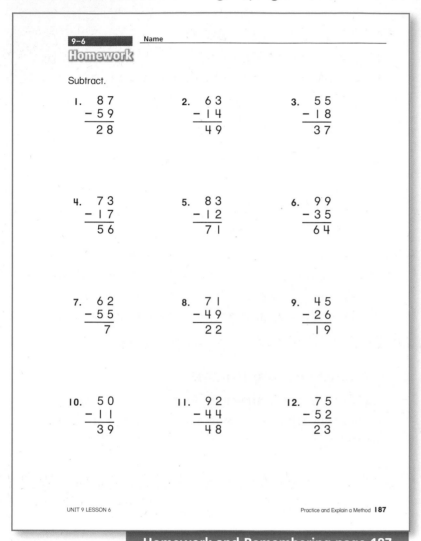

9–6 Homework Name ____________________

Subtract.

1. 87 − 59 = 28
2. 63 − 14 = 49
3. 55 − 18 = 37
4. 73 − 17 = 56
5. 83 − 12 = 71
6. 99 − 35 = 64
7. 62 − 55 = 7
8. 71 − 49 = 22
9. 45 − 26 = 19
10. 50 − 11 = 39
11. 92 − 44 = 48
12. 75 − 52 = 23

UNIT 9 LESSON 6 Practice and Explain a Method 187

Homework and Remembering page 187

9–6 Remembering **Goal:** Spiral Review

This Remembering activity would be appropriate anytime after today's lesson.

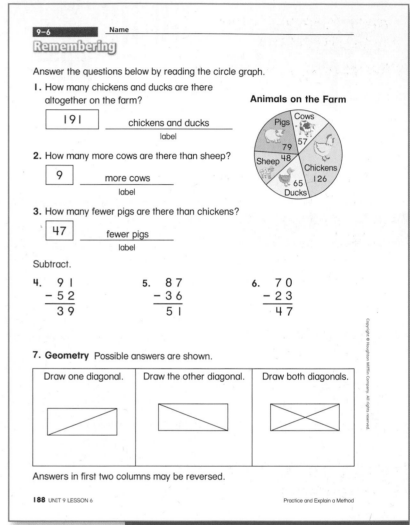

9–6 Remembering Name ____________________

Answer the questions below by reading the circle graph.

Animals on the Farm

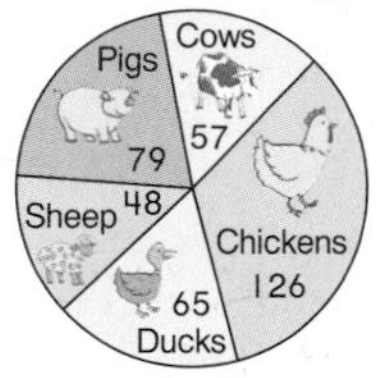

1. How many chickens and ducks are there altogether on the farm?
   191 chickens and ducks (label)
2. How many more cows are there than sheep?
   9 more cows (label)
3. How many fewer pigs are there than chickens?
   47 fewer pigs (label)

Subtract.

4. 91 − 52 = 39
5. 87 − 36 = 51
6. 70 − 23 = 47

7. **Geometry** Possible answers are shown.

Draw one diagonal.	Draw the other diagonal.	Draw both diagonals.

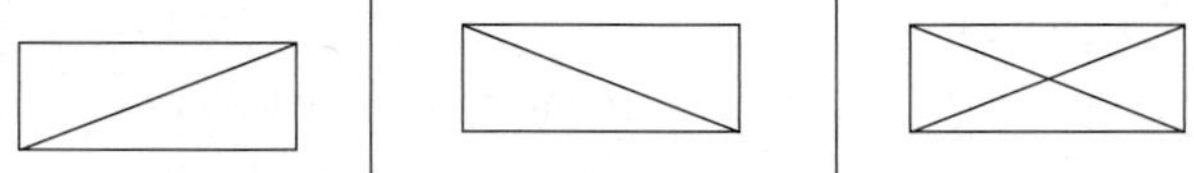

Answers in first two columns may be reversed.

188 UNIT 9 LESSON 6 Practice and Explain a Method

Homework and Remembering page 188

Home or School Activity

Science Connection

Compare Temperatures Have children keep track of the high and low temperature every day for a week by making a table. Then have them find the range in the daily temperatures by subtracting the low temperature from the high temperature. Have students discuss what other comparisons they can make using the data in the table.

Temperature (in degrees Fahrenheit)

Day	High	Low	Range
Sunday	77	68	9
Monday	78	64	14
Tuesday	80	63	17
Wednesday	76	59	17
Thursday	82	64	18
Friday	81	65	16
Saturday	85	67	18

UNIT 9
LESSON 7

Subtract from 200

Lesson Objectives

- Apply methods for solving 2-digit subtraction exercises with totals of 200.
- Explain how to subtract from a total of 200.

Vocabulary
Expanded Method
Ungroup First Method

The Day at a Glance

Today's Goals	Materials	
1 Teaching the Lesson A1: Review the Expanded Method to solve subtraction exercises. A2: Review the Ungroup First Method to solve subtraction exercises. A3: Choose a method to solve subtraction exercises.	**Lesson Activities** Student Activity Book pp. 289–290 Homework and Remembering pp. 189–190 MathBoard materials Dollar Equivalents (TRB M75–M76) Demonstration Secret Code Cards Secret Code Cards Base ten blocks	**Going Further** Activity Cards 9-7 Colored pencils Index cards Math Journals
2 Going Further ▸ Differentiated Instruction		
3 Homework and Targeted Practice		

123 Use Math Talk today!

Keeping Skills Sharp

Quick Practice — 5 MINUTES

Goals: Practice subtraction with teen totals. Write money strings for dollars. Monitor progress in subtracting 2-digit numbers.

Teen Subtraction Flash While some children are preparing for the Quick Check and others are writing dollar strings at the board, have a student leader direct the class in Teen Subtraction Flash. (See Unit 9 Lesson 1.)

Dollar Strings Have two or three children write dollar strings on the board as the other children prepare for the Quick Check. (See Unit 9 Lesson 6.)

Quick Check Monitor children's progress with a brief quick check. Remind children of testing protocols, and then write the exercises shown on the board. One of the problems requires ungrouping, and the other does not.

$$\begin{array}{r} 67 \\ -\ 34 \\ \hline 33 \end{array} \qquad \begin{array}{r} 42 \\ -\ 27 \\ \hline 15 \end{array}$$

Daily Routines

Quarters and Other Coins
Making and Counting Coins that Make a Quarter, Counting to 200¢ by 25¢, Making and Counting Dollars and Cents: 3-Digit Numbers as Dollars and Cents
(See pp. xxvi – xxvii.)

▸ Led by Student Leaders

Money Routine Using the 120 Poster, Using the Money Flip Chart, Using the Number Path, Using Secret Code Cards
(See pp. xxiii–xxv.)

▸ Led by Student Leaders

1 Teaching the Lesson

Activity 1

The Expanded Method

15 MINUTES

Goals: Review the Expanded Method to solve subtraction exercises.

Materials: MathBoard materials, Dollar Equivalents (from Unit 5 Lesson 2 or TRB M75–M76), Demonstration Secret Code Cards, Secret Code Cards

NCTM Standards:
Number and Operations
Communication

English Language Learners

Use a spring and a balloon to model *expand*.

- **Beginning** Stretch the spring. Say: **I am *expanding* the spring.** Blow up the balloon. Say: **I made it bigger.** Ask: **Did I expand it?** yes
- **Intermediate** Stretch the spring. Ask: **Am I *expanding* the spring?** yes Blow up the balloon. Ask: **What am I doing to the balloon?** expanding it
- **Advanced** Say: ***Expand* means make something bigger so it is easier to see.** Have children suggests ways to expand the balloon and spring.

▶ Review the Expanded Method of Subtraction

WHOLE CLASS

Math Talk

Write the following story problem on the board.

There were 200 people on the train. 68 of them got off at the Main Street station. How many people are still on the train?

Use **Solve and Discuss** and have children solve the problem at the board using the Expanded Method. Ask all of the children to make Proof Drawings.

Children who are seated at their desks should solve the problem on their MathBoards. They can use the Number Path side of the board or they can use the Dot Array to help them visualize the problem. Point out to children that the Dot Array contains 200 dots.

Children can also use their dollars to visualize ungrouping in the problem as they did in Lesson 2. (See the illustration below.) Encourage children to check their work by adding.

Ungrouping Dollars

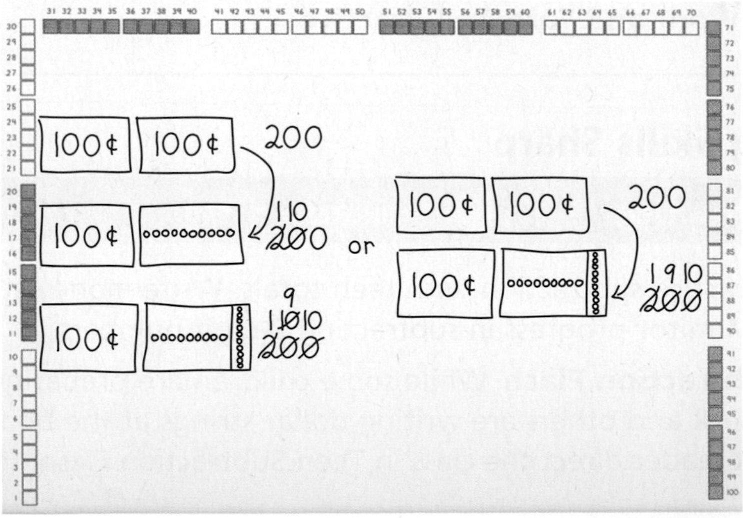

Discuss the Expanded Method Have several children who are at the board explain how they solved the problem. Have the class discuss whether or not the Expanded Method they just learned over the past few days works with larger numbers. If children are not able to apply the method, lead them through it step-by-step.

Expanded Method

Step 1: Write out the hundreds, tens, and ones.

$$\begin{array}{rcl} 200 & = & 200 + 0 + 0 \\ -68 & = & 60 + 8 \\ \hline \end{array}$$

200 is the same as 2 hundreds, 0 tens, and 0 ones or 200 + 0 + 0.

68 is the same as 6 tens and 8 ones or 60 + 8.

Step 2: Check to see if you can subtract.

$$\begin{array}{rcl} 200 & = & 200 + 0 + 0 \\ -68 & = & + 60 + 8 \\ \hline \end{array}$$

↑ yes ↑ no ↑ no

Check the ones, tens and hundreds place to see if there's enough to subtract from. Writing "yes" or 'no" under the numbers may help. If all the answers are yes, you don't have to ungroup.

If not, ungroup.

$$\begin{array}{rcl} & & 90 + 10 \\ & & 100 + \cancel{100} \\ 200 & = & \cancel{200} \\ -68 & = & + 60 + 8 \\ \hline \end{array}$$

Get more tens by taking 10 tens from the hundreds place. 10 tens is the same as 100. Put those 10 tens in the tens column and rewrite 200 as 100.

Then get ones by taking 10 ones from the tens place. 10 ones is the same as 10. Put those 10 ones in the ones column and rewrite 100 as 90.

Step 3: Subtract.

$$\begin{array}{rcl} & & 90 + 10 \\ & & 100 + \cancel{100} \\ 200 & = & \cancel{200} \\ -68 & = & + 60 + 8 \\ \hline & & 100 + 30 + 2 = 132 \end{array}$$

You can subtract either left to right, or right to left.

Add to check the answer. 132 plus 68 should equal 200. It does.

Have children make a proof drawing using Quick Hundreds for each hundred, Quick Tens for each ten, and circles for each one. This drawing is linked step-by-step to the numerical method.

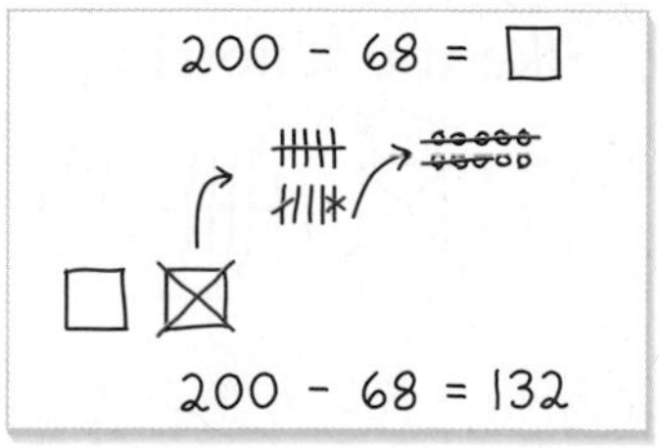

Activity continued ▶

Alternate Approach

Secret Code Cards If some children are having difficulty understanding the Expanded Method, use Demonstration Secret Code Cards to show the subtraction. Have children use their own sets of Secret Code Cards at the same time.

200 − 68 = □

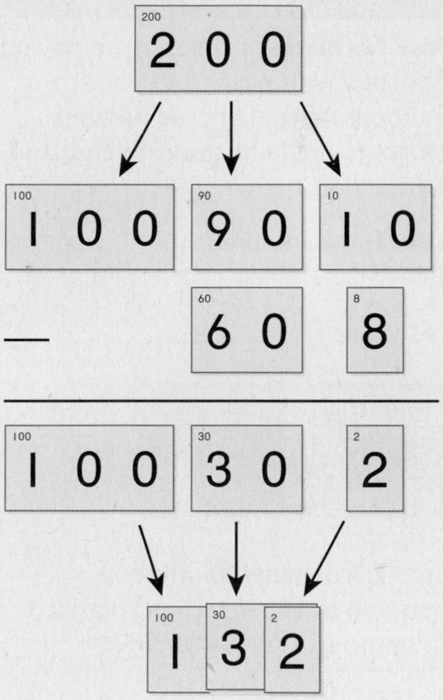

Activity 2

The Ungroup First Method

15 MINUTES

Goal: Review the Ungroup First Method to solve subtraction exercises.

Materials: MathBoard materials, base ten blocks

✓ **NCTM Standards:**
Number and Operations
Communication

Alternate Approach

Base Ten Blocks If children are having difficulty with paper and pencil methods, have them use base ten blocks to model the ungrouping and subtraction.

Step 1: Use hundreds to show 200.

```
 200
− 68
```

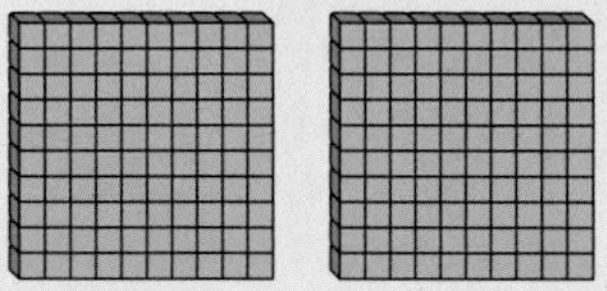

Step 2: You need to ungroup 1 hundred as 10 tens. Then you need to ungroup 1 ten as 10 ones.

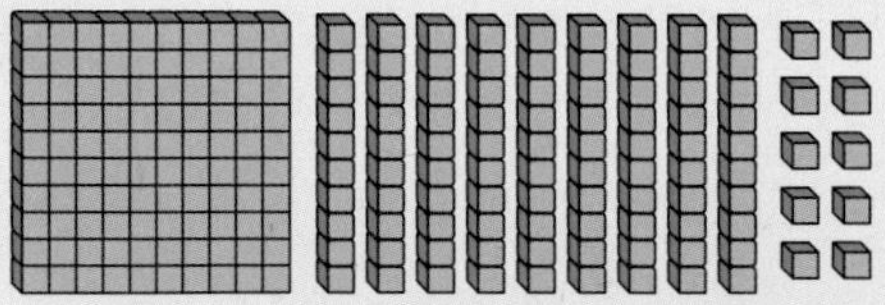

Now there are 1 hundred, 9 tens, and 10 ones.

Step 3: Subtract ones, tens, and hundreds.

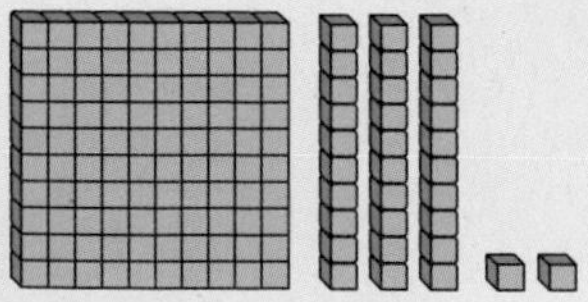

```
    9
 1 1̸0 10
 2̸ 0̸ 0̸
 −  6 8
 1  3 2
```

▸ Review the Ungroup First Method of Subtraction WHOLE CLASS

Math Talk

Write the same story problem that was used for Activity 1 on the board.

There were 200 people on the train. 68 of them got off at the Main Street station. How many people are still on the train?

Invite six or more children to the board to solve the problem using the Ungroup First Method of Subtraction. Children who are seated should solve the problem on their MathBoards. Be sure children use the magnifying glass to show the numbers they are ungrouping. Ask children to make proof drawings and have several children at the board explain how they solved the problem.

Ungroup First Method

Step 1: Check the ones, tens, and hundreds to see if you can subtract.

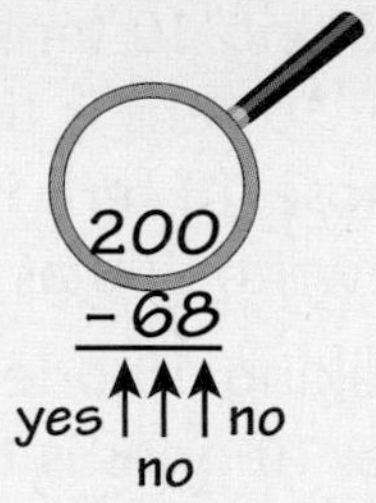

Check the ones, tens and hundreds place to see if there's enough to subtract from. Writing "yes" or "no" under the numbers may help. If all of the answers are yes, you don't have to ungroup.

If not, ungroup.

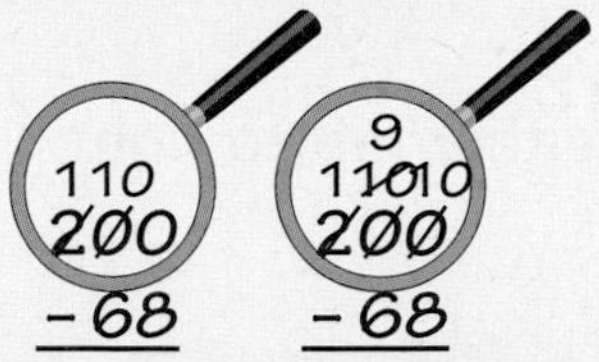

Use two steps. Get tens by taking 10 tens from the hundreds place. Get ones by taking 10 ones from the tens place and putting them in the ones place.

Use one step. Rewrite 2 hundreds as 1 hundred, 9 tens, and 10 ones. Draw a magnifying glass to show the 1 hundred, 9 tens and 10 ones.

Step 2: Subtract.

You may subtract either left to right, or right to left. The proof drawing may look like the following:

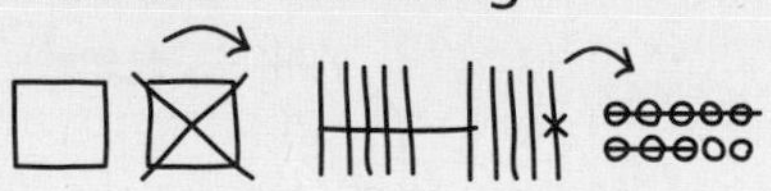

Activity 3

Choose a Method

▶ Review Both Methods WHOLE CLASS

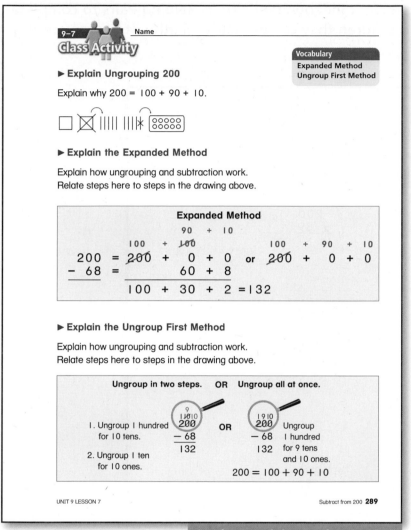

9–7 Class Activity Name ____________

Vocabulary
Expanded Method
Ungroup First Method

▶ Explain Ungrouping 200

Explain why 200 = 100 + 90 + 10.

▶ Explain the Expanded Method

Explain how ungrouping and subtraction work.
Relate steps here to steps in the drawing above.

Expanded Method

$$\begin{array}{rcl} 200 & = & \overset{100 \; + \; \overset{90 \; + \; 10}{\cancel{100}}}{\cancel{200}} + 0 + 0 \\ -\;68 & = & \quad\; 60 + 8 \\ \hline & & 100 + 30 + 2 = 132 \end{array}$$

or

$$\overset{100 \; + \; 90 \; + \; 10}{\cancel{200} + 0 + 0}$$

▶ Explain the Ungroup First Method

Explain how ungrouping and subtraction work.
Relate steps here to steps in the drawing above.

Ungroup in two steps. OR **Ungroup all at once.**

1. Ungroup 1 hundred for 10 tens.
2. Ungroup 1 ten for 10 ones.

$$\begin{array}{r} \overset{1\,\overset{9}{\cancel{10}}\,10}{\cancel{200}} \\ -\;68 \\ \hline 132 \end{array}$$

OR

$$\begin{array}{r} \overset{1\,9\,10}{\cancel{200}} \\ -\;68 \\ \hline 132 \end{array}$$

Ungroup 1 hundred for 9 tens and 10 ones.

200 = 100 + 90 + 10

UNIT 9 LESSON 7 Subtract from 200 **289**

Student Activity Book page 289

Have children review both subtraction methods and use Student Activity Book page 289 to guide them through the exercises on Student Activity Book page 290.

Activity continued ▶

25 MINUTES

Goal: Choose a method to solve subtraction exercises.

Materials: Student Activity Book pages 289–290

NCTM Standards:
Number and Operations

1 Teaching the Lesson (continued)

Class Management

Circulate around the room to see that children are rewriting and subtracting correctly. If possible, have student helpers circulate as well. Pay special attention to how children rewrite the hundreds, tens, and ones. If necessary, remind them to put a magnifying glass around the numbers they are ungrouping. If there are a few children who are experiencing difficulty, you may wish to work with them at the board.

The Learning Classroom

Math Talk When children use the **Step-by-Step at the Board** structure, a different child performs each step of the exercise, describing the step before everyone does it. Then everyone else at the board and at their desks carries out that step. This helps children learn to verbalize their methods more clearly, since they can just focus on describing their own step.

Each step with the proof drawing is related to a step in the numerical method.

Ongoing Assessment

Ask the following questions:

- ▶ Do both subtraction methods give the same answer?
- ▶ Does it matter if you subtract before you ungroup?
- ▶ Does it matter if you subtract from left to right or right to left once the ungrouping and rewriting are done?

▶ Practice Both Methods WHOLE CLASS

Math Talk

Direct children's attention to Student Activity book page 290. Have volunteers use the **Step-By-Step at the Board** structure to do exercise 1. Then have children work independently or in **Helping Pairs** to complete the page. Remind children they can use either method to complete this page.

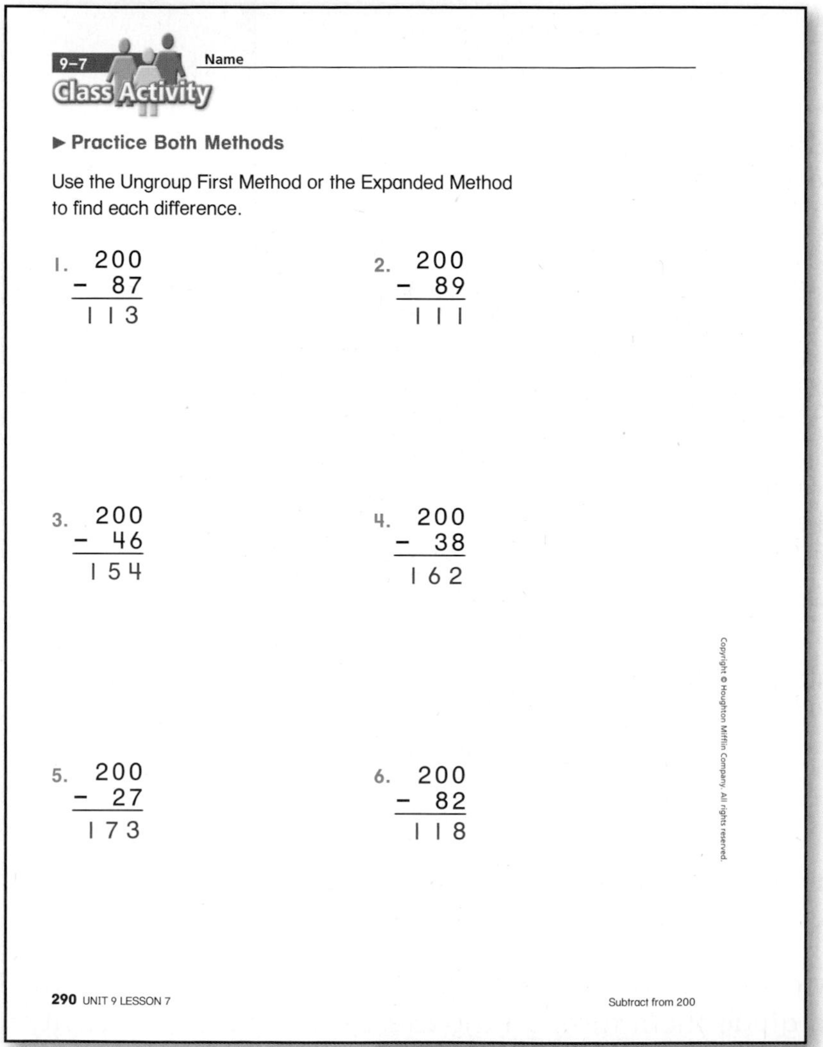
9–7 Class Activity Name

▶ Practice Both Methods

Use the Ungroup First Method or the Expanded Method to find each difference.

1. 200 − 87 = 113
2. 200 − 89 = 111
3. 200 − 46 = 154
4. 200 − 38 = 162
5. 200 − 27 = 173
6. 200 − 82 = 118

Copyright © Houghton Mifflin Company. All rights reserved.

290 UNIT 9 LESSON 7 Subtract from 200

Student Activity Book page 290

Intervention — Activity Card 9-7

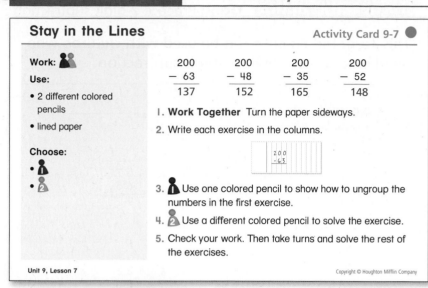

Stay in the Lines
Activity Card 9-7 ●

Work: (pair)

Use:
- 2 different colored pencils
- lined paper

Choose:
- 1
- 2

200	200	200	200
− 63	− 48	− 35	− 52
137	152	165	148

1. **Work Together** Turn the paper sideways.
2. Write each exercise in the columns.

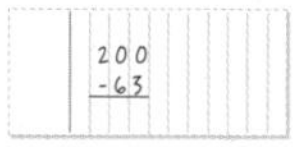

3. (1) Use one colored pencil to show how to ungroup the numbers in the first exercise.
4. (2) Use a different colored pencil to solve the exercise.
5. Check your work. Then take turns and solve the rest of the exercises.

Unit 9, Lesson 7

Activity Note Each pair needs two colored pencils. Show children how to write the problems in columns on lined paper.

Math Writing Prompt
Explain Your Thinking When do you need to ungroup 100 and rewrite it as 10 tens?

Soar to Success Math Software Support
Warm Up 11.23

On Level — Activity Card 9-7

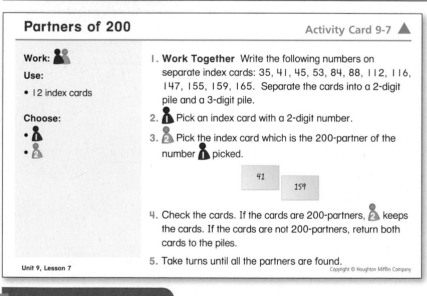

Partners of 200
Activity Card 9-7 ▲

Work: (pair)

Use:
- 12 index cards

Choose:
- 1
- 2

1. **Work Together** Write the following numbers on separate index cards: 35, 41, 45, 53, 84, 88, 112, 116, 147, 155, 159, 165. Separate the cards into a 2-digit pile and a 3-digit pile.
2. (1) Pick an index card with a 2-digit number.
3. (2) Pick the index card which is the 200-partner of the number (1) picked.

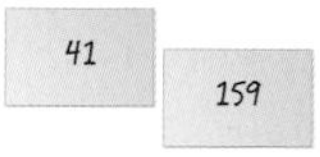

4. Check the cards. If the cards are 200-partners, (2) keeps the cards. If the cards are not 200-partners, return both cards to the piles.
5. Take turns until all the partners are found.

Unit 9, Lesson 7

Activity Note Each pair needs 12 index cards. Have pairs subtract to check that they have the correct 200-partners.

Math Writing Prompt
Explain Your Thinking Describe the steps you need to take to find 200 − 34.

Harcourt Mega Math Software Support
Country Countdown: Block Busters, Level U

Challenge — Activity Card 9-7

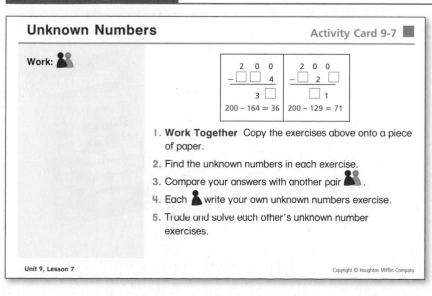

Unknown Numbers
Activity Card 9-7 ■

Work: (pair)

2 0 0	2 0 0
− □ □ 4	− □ 2 □
3 □	□ 1
200 − 164 = 36	200 − 129 = 71

1. **Work Together** Copy the exercises above onto a piece of paper.
2. Find the unknown numbers in each exercise.
3. Compare your answers with another pair.
4. Each (person) write your own unknown numbers exercise.
5. Trade and solve each other's unknown number exercises.

Unit 9, Lesson 7

Activity Note Each pair works together to solve the unknown number exercise. Have pairs use addition to check their work.

Math Writing Prompt
What's Wrong? Sherry solved the subtraction problem 200 − 54 = 156. She ungrouped 200 as 1 hundred, 1 ten, and 10 ones. What did she do wrong?

Destination Math Software Support
Course II: Module 2: Unit 1: Estimating and Finding Differences within 1,000

3 Homework and Targeted Practice

9–7 **Homework** **Goal:** Additional Practice

This Homework page provides practice in subtracting from 200.

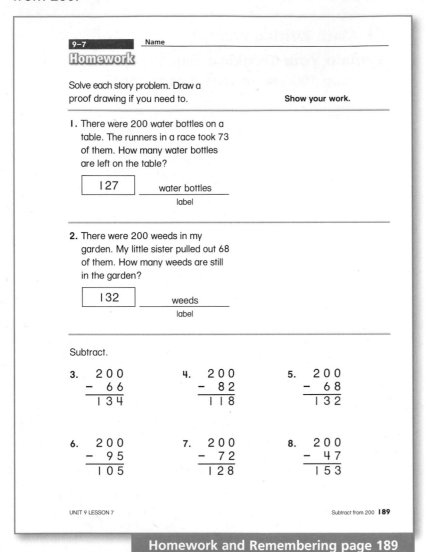

9–7 Homework Name ____________

Solve each story problem. Draw a proof drawing if you need to. **Show your work.**

1. There were 200 water bottles on a table. The runners in a race took 73 of them. How many water bottles are left on the table?

   127 water bottles (label)

2. There were 200 weeds in my garden. My little sister pulled out 68 of them. How many weeds are still in the garden?

   132 weeds (label)

Subtract.

3. $\begin{array}{r}200\\-\ 66\\\hline 134\end{array}$
4. $\begin{array}{r}200\\-\ 82\\\hline 118\end{array}$
5. $\begin{array}{r}200\\-\ 68\\\hline 132\end{array}$
6. $\begin{array}{r}200\\-\ 95\\\hline 105\end{array}$
7. $\begin{array}{r}200\\-\ 72\\\hline 128\end{array}$
8. $\begin{array}{r}200\\-\ 47\\\hline 153\end{array}$

UNIT 9 LESSON 7 Subtract from 200 **189**

Homework and Remembering page 189

9–7 **Targeted Practice** **Goal:** Practice 2-digit subtraction.

This Targeted Practice can be used with children who need extra practice with 2-digit subtraction.

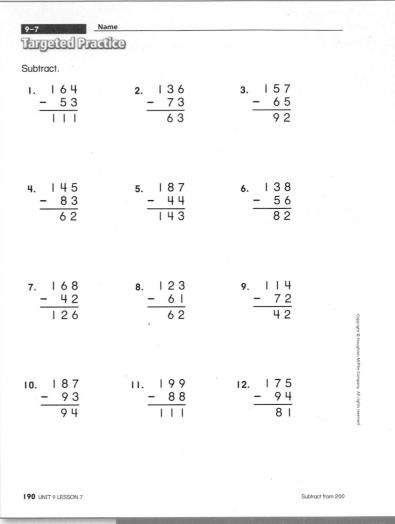

9–7 Targeted Practice Name ____________

Subtract.

1. $\begin{array}{r}164\\-\ 53\\\hline 111\end{array}$
2. $\begin{array}{r}136\\-\ 73\\\hline 63\end{array}$
3. $\begin{array}{r}157\\-\ 65\\\hline 92\end{array}$
4. $\begin{array}{r}145\\-\ 83\\\hline 62\end{array}$
5. $\begin{array}{r}187\\-\ 44\\\hline 143\end{array}$
6. $\begin{array}{r}138\\-\ 56\\\hline 82\end{array}$
7. $\begin{array}{r}168\\-\ 42\\\hline 126\end{array}$
8. $\begin{array}{r}123\\-\ 61\\\hline 62\end{array}$
9. $\begin{array}{r}114\\-\ 72\\\hline 42\end{array}$
10. $\begin{array}{r}187\\-\ 93\\\hline 94\end{array}$
11. $\begin{array}{r}199\\-\ 88\\\hline 111\end{array}$
12. $\begin{array}{r}175\\-\ 94\\\hline 81\end{array}$

190 UNIT 9 LESSON 7 Subtract from 200

Homework and Remembering page 190

Home or School Activity

Technology Connection

Who's Faster? Show children how to use a calculator to subtract. Be sure to remind them to clear the display before starting each new subtraction. Have children work with a partner to solve exercises 3–5 on Homework page 189. One person should use a calculator to solve the exercises while the other person uses mental math or paper and pencil.

Have children discuss which method was the fastest.

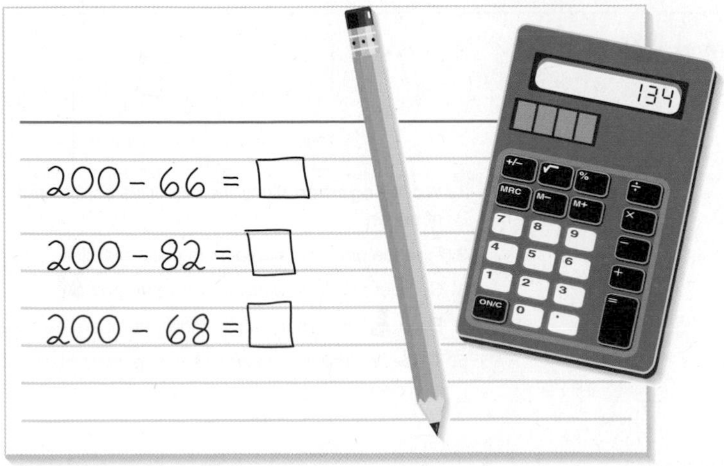

UNIT 9 LESSON 8

Practice with the Ungroup First Method

Lesson Objectives

- Subtract a 2-digit number from any 3-digit number under 200.
- Decide when to ungroup and rewrite in subtraction.

Vocabulary

Expanded Method
Ungroup First Method

The Day at a Glance

Today's Goals	Materials	
1 Teaching the Lesson **A1:** Decide whether ungrouping is necessary. Subtract a 2-digit number from a 3-digit number less than 200. **A2:** Practice deciding whether ungrouping is necessary to solve subtraction exercises.	**Lesson Activities** Student Activity Book pp. 291–292 Homework and Remembering pp. 191–192 MathBoard materials	**Going Further** Activity Cards 9-8 Colored pencils Index cards Math Journals
2 Going Further ▸ Differentiated Instruction		
3 Homework and Spiral Review		

Use Math Talk today!

Keeping Skills Sharp

Quick Practice — 5 MINUTES

Goal: Practice subtraction with totals ≤ 18.

Materials: Student Activity book page 291, thin strips of colored paper

Subtraction Sprint Direct children's attention to Student Activity Book page 291. Decide on a time limit to complete the Sprint. Explain the procedure and time limit to them. (See Unit 9 Lesson 4 Activity 1.)

Repeated Quick Practice Use this Quick Practice from a previous lesson.

▸ **Dive the Deep**
(See Unit 9 Lesson 5.)

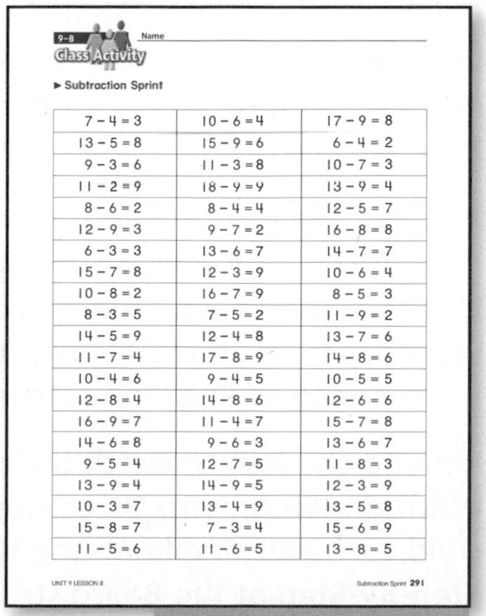

9-8 Class Activity Name

▸ Subtraction Sprint

7 − 4 = 3	10 − 6 = 4	17 − 9 = 8
13 − 5 = 8	15 − 9 = 6	6 − 4 = 2
9 − 3 = 6	11 − 3 = 8	10 − 7 = 3
11 − 2 = 9	18 − 9 = 9	13 − 9 = 4
8 − 6 = 2	8 − 4 = 4	12 − 5 = 7
12 − 9 = 3	9 − 7 = 2	16 − 8 = 8
6 − 3 = 3	13 − 6 = 7	14 − 7 = 7
15 − 7 = 8	12 − 3 = 9	10 − 6 = 4
10 − 8 = 2	16 − 7 = 9	8 − 5 = 3
8 − 3 = 5	7 − 5 = 2	11 − 9 = 2
14 − 5 = 9	12 − 4 = 8	13 − 7 = 6
11 − 7 = 4	17 − 8 = 9	14 − 8 = 6
10 − 4 = 6	9 − 4 = 5	10 − 5 = 5
12 − 8 = 4	14 − 8 = 6	12 − 6 = 6
16 − 9 = 7	11 − 4 = 7	15 − 7 = 8
14 − 6 = 8	9 − 6 = 3	13 − 6 = 7
9 − 5 = 4	12 − 7 = 5	11 − 8 = 3
13 − 9 = 4	14 − 9 = 5	12 − 3 = 9
10 − 3 = 7	13 − 4 = 9	13 − 5 = 8
15 − 8 = 7	7 − 3 = 4	15 − 6 = 9
11 − 5 = 6	11 − 6 = 5	13 − 8 = 5

UNIT 9 LESSON 8 Subtraction Sprint 291

Student Activity Book Page 291

Daily Routines

Quarters and Other Coins Making and Counting Coins that Make a Quarter, Counting to 200¢ by 25¢, Making and Counting Dollars and Cents: 3-Digit Numbers as Dollars and Cents
(See pp. xxvi–xxvii.)

▸ Led by Student Leaders

Money Routine Using the 120 Poster, Using the Money Flip Chart, Using the Number Path, Using Secret Code Cards
(See pp. xxiii–xxv.)

▸ Led by Student Leaders

1 Teaching the Lesson

Activity 1

Decide Whether to Ungroup

25 MINUTES

Goal: Decide whether ungrouping is necessary. Subtract a 2-digit number from a 3-digit number less than 200.

Materials: MathBoard materials

NCTM Standards:
Number and Operations
Communication

English Language Learners

Provide children with practice using *greater than* and *less than* to describe numbers. Draw a number line from 1 to 10 on the board.

- **Beginning** Ask: **Is 5 greater than 4?** yes **Is 4 *less than* 5?** yes **Is 6 *greater than* 8?** no Continue with other numbers.
- **Intermediate** Ask: **Which is *greater*, 4 or 5?** 5 Say: **4 is ___.** less than 5 Continue with other numbers.
- **Advanced** Have students work in pairs. One says 2 numbers, the other makes *greater than* and *less than* sentences.

▶ Determine When and Why to Ungroup WHOLE CLASS

Write these subtraction exercises on the board.

$$\begin{array}{r} 142 \\ -\ 71 \\ \hline 71 \end{array} \qquad \begin{array}{r} 142 \\ -\ 31 \\ \hline 111 \end{array}$$

Math Talk Give the children a few minutes to look at the exercises. Use the following questions to help children explain *when* and *why* they need to ungroup.

- Look at 142 − 71. Are there enough ones to subtract from? Yes, 2 is greater than 1.
- Are there enough tens to subtract from? No, 4 tens is less than 7 tens.
- Do we need to ungroup to solve this exercise? Yes, there are not enough tens to subtract from, so we need to ungroup 1 hundred.
- Look at 142 − 31. Are there enough ones to subtract from? Yes, 2 is greater than 1.
- Are there enough tens to subtract from? Yes, 4 tens is greater than 3 tens.
- Do we need to ungroup to solve this exercise? No, there are enough ones and tens to subtract from, so we don't need to ungroup anything.

Emphasize to children that they must first decide whether or not to ungroup before they begin solving any subtraction exercise. They may enjoy making up a rule for deciding how to do this. You may want to have children demonstrate their rules on the board.

Ask for Ideas Ask volunteers to come to the board and review the steps for solving 3-digit subtraction exercises, using the Ungroup First Method. Then have children use their MathBoards to solve the two exercises from above. Instruct children to use the Ungroup First Method if they need to ungroup rather than the Expanded Method.

Remind children to check their work by either adding or by making proof drawings with Quick Hundreds, Quick Tens, and circles. After children have completed the two exercises, have volunteers use the **Step-By-Step at the Board** structure to explain how they solved each of the exercises.

▶ Continue Discussing Ungrouping WHOLE CLASS

Write these subtraction exercises on the board.

157	133
− 96	− 14
61	119

Math Talk Discuss these exercises with children.

- Look at 157 − 96. Are there enough ones to subtract from? Yes, 7 is greater than 6. Are there enough tens to subtract from? No, 5 tens is less than 9 tens.
- Do we need to ungroup to solve this exercise? Yes, there are not enough tens to subtract from, so we need to ungroup 1 hundred.
- Look at 133 − 14. Are there enough ones to subtract from? No, 3 is less than 4. Are there enough tens to subtract from? Yes, 3 tens is greater than 1 ten.
- Do we need to ungroup to solve this exercise? Yes, there are not enough ones to subtract from, so we need to ungroup 1 ten.

Then give children a few minutes to solve each exercise. After children have finished, have volunteers use the **Step-By-Step at the Board** structure to explain how they solved each of the exercises.

Now provide children with more exercises of this kind to discuss. Encourage them to invent story problems to go with these exercises.

163	163	163
− 62	− 82	− 67
101	81	96

Ask children the following questions to help them with subtraction.

- Look at 163 − 62. Does it require any ungrouping? No, there are enough ones and enough tens to subtract from.
- Look at 163 − 82. Does it require any ungrouping? Yes, there are not enough tens to subtract from, so we need to ungroup 1 hundred.
- Look at 163 − 67. Does it require any ungrouping? Yes, there are not enough ones to subtract from, so we need to ungroup 1 ten. Then there will not be enough tens to subtract from, so we will need to ungroup 1 hundred.

Give children a few minutes to solve each exercise and to check their work by making proof drawings. After children have finished, have volunteers come to the board to explain how to solve each of the exercises.

Teaching Note

Research Research indicates that when children ungroup the top number *before* they do any subtracting, they are less likely to make errors, particularly the *subtraction switch error* where they subtract the top number from the bottom number. This error is even more likely to occur in 3-digit subtraction.

Ungrouping and renaming the top number avoids this tendency because the renamed hundreds, tens, and ones are all there before children do any subtracting. (Be sure, however, that children first determine where ungrouping is needed.)

Ungroup first, beginning at the left

Ungroup first, beginning at the right

In both examples, children ungrouped 163 and rewrote it as 15 tens, and 13 ones.

The common method alternates ungrouping and subtracting, so students are more likely to subtract top from bottom than when they ungroup first.

1 Teaching the Lesson (continued)

Activity 2

Practice Deciding When to Ungroup

25 MINUTES

Goal: Practice deciding whether ungrouping is necessary to solve subtraction exercises.

Materials: Student Activity Book page 292

NCTM Standards:
Number and Operations
Communication

▶ Decide When to Ungroup INDIVIDUALS

Distribute Student Activity Book page 292 and have the children work alone or in **Helping Pairs** to solve the exercises. If the children work in pairs, they should discuss and agree with each other as to when to ungroup and rewrite.

Circulate around the room as the children work. You may wish to work with children having difficulty in small groups at the board. **Student Leaders** can also provide help as needed.

After children have finished the exercises, have volunteers come to the board and explain their work.

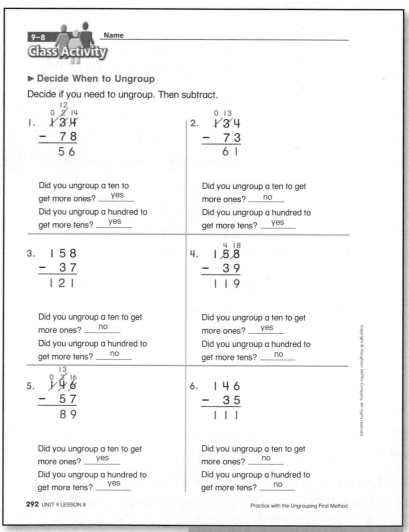

9–8 Class Activity Name ____________

▶ **Decide When to Ungroup**

Decide if you need to ungroup. Then subtract.

1. 134 − 78 = 56 (ungrouped: 0, 12, 14)
Did you ungroup a ten to get more ones? yes
Did you ungroup a hundred to get more tens? yes

2. 134 − 73 = 61 (ungrouped: 0, 13)
Did you ungroup a ten to get more ones? no
Did you ungroup a hundred to get more tens? yes

3. 158 − 37 = 121
Did you ungroup a ten to get more ones? no
Did you ungroup a hundred to get more tens? no

4. 158 − 39 = 119 (ungrouped: 4, 18)
Did you ungroup a ten to get more ones? yes
Did you ungroup a hundred to get more tens? no

5. 146 − 57 = 89 (ungrouped: 0, 13, 16)
Did you ungroup a ten to get more ones? yes
Did you ungroup a hundred to get more tens? yes

6. 146 − 35 = 111
Did you ungroup a ten to get more ones? no
Did you ungroup a hundred to get more tens? no

292 UNIT 9 LESSON 8 Practice with the Ungrouping First Method

Student Activity Book page 292

Ongoing Assessment

Ask children to look at the following exercises and explain whether or not ungrouping is necessary.

1. 159 − 43
2. 158 − 75
3. 141 − 25
4. 131 − 35

Intervention — Activity Card 9-8

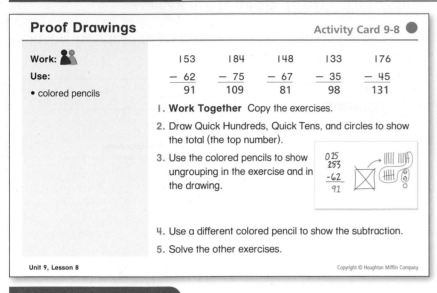

Proof Drawings
Activity Card 9-8 ●

Work: pairs
Use:
- colored pencils

153	184	148	133	176
− 62	− 75	− 67	− 35	− 45
91	109	81	98	131

1. **Work Together** Copy the exercises.
2. Draw Quick Hundreds, Quick Tens, and circles to show the total (the top number).
3. Use the colored pencils to show ungrouping in the exercise and in the drawing.

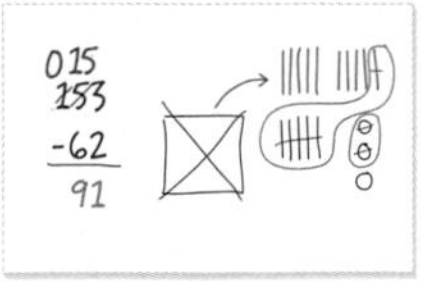

4. Use a different colored pencil to show the subtraction.
5. Solve the other exercises.

Unit 9, Lesson 8

Activity Note Each pair needs two different colored pencils. Check children's drawings as they ungroup the numbers.

Math Writing Prompt

How Do You Know? Make a drawing to show that the amounts below are the same
1 hundred, 4 tens, and 8 ones.
14 tens and 8 ones.

Soar to Success Math Software Support

Warm Up 11.24

On Level — Activity Card 9-8

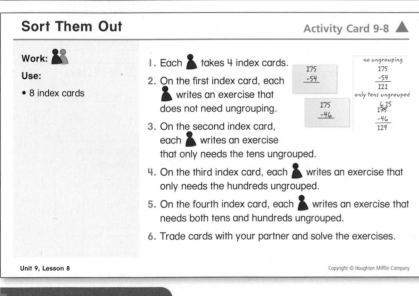

Sort Them Out
Activity Card 9-8 ▲

Work: pairs
Use:
- 8 index cards

1. Each takes 4 index cards.
2. On the first index card, each writes an exercise that does not need ungrouping.
3. On the second index card, each writes an exercise that only needs the tens ungrouped.
4. On the third index card, each writes an exercise that only needs the hundreds ungrouped.
5. On the fourth index card, each writes an exercise that needs both tens and hundreds ungrouped.
6. Trade cards with your partner and solve the exercises.

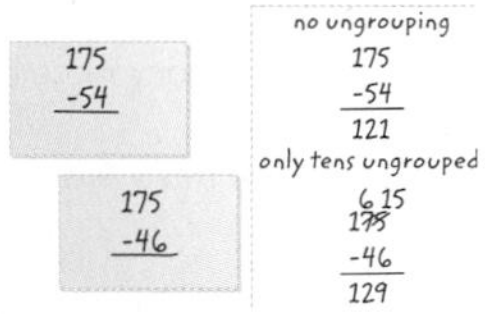

Unit 9, Lesson 8

Activity Note Each pair needs eight index cards. Have children check each other's work.

Math Writing Prompt

Explain Your Thinking In which exercise do you have to ungroup twice. Explain.

138	138
− 46	− 39

Harcourt MegaMath Software Support

Country Countdown: Block Busters, Level X

Challenge — Activity Card 9-8

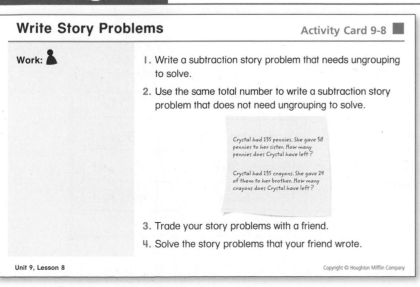

Write Story Problems
Activity Card 9-8 ■

Work: individual

1. Write a subtraction story problem that needs ungrouping to solve.
2. Use the same total number to write a subtraction story problem that does not need ungrouping to solve.

Crystal had 135 pennies. She gave 38 pennies to her sister. How many pennies does Crystal have left?

Crystal had 135 crayons. She gave 24 of them to her brother. How many crayons does Crystal have left?

3. Trade your story problems with a friend.
4. Solve the story problems that your friend wrote.

Unit 9, Lesson 8

Activity Note Ask children to explain how they decided what numbers to use to write each story problem.

Math Writing Prompt

What's Wrong? Look how Remah subtracted. What did she do wrong?

```
  18
 148
− 49
 109
```

(the 8 in 148 is crossed out)

Destination Math Software Support

Course II: Module 2: Unit 1: Estimating and Finding Differences within 1,000

3 Homework and Spiral Review

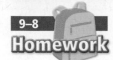

9–8 Homework **Goal:** Additional Practice

This Homework page provides practice deciding whether ungrouping is necessary to subtract.

9–8 Homework Name ____________________

Decide if you need to ungroup. Then subtract.

1. 147 − 32 = 115	2. 147 − 38 = 109	3. 147 − 48 = 99
4. 126 − 54 = 72	5. 126 − 57 = 69	6. 126 − 97 = 29
7. 187 − 46 = 141	8. 187 − 49 = 138	9. 187 − 99 = 88
10. 172 − 35 = 137	11. 172 − 85 = 87	12. 172 − 31 = 141

UNIT 9 LESSON 8 Practice with the Ungrouping First Method 191

Homework and Remembering page 191

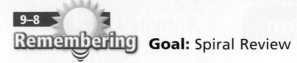

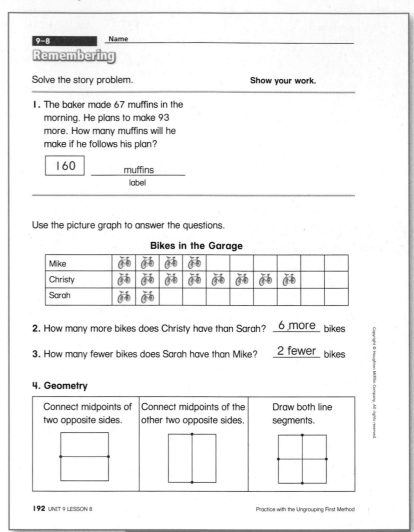

9–8 Remembering **Goal:** Spiral Review

This Remembering activity would be appropriate anytime after today's lesson.

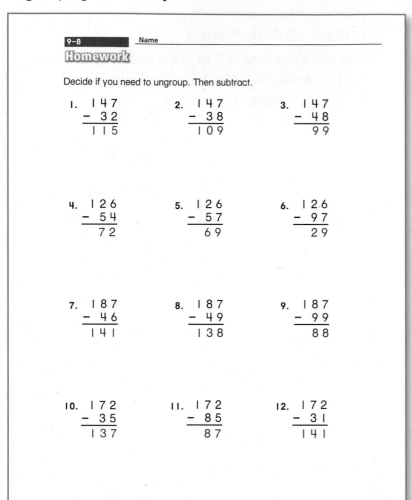

9–8 Remembering Name ____________________

Solve the story problem. **Show your work.**

1. The baker made 67 muffins in the morning. He plans to make 93 more. How many muffins will he make if he follows his plan?

160 muffins (label)

Use the picture graph to answer the questions.

Bikes in the Garage

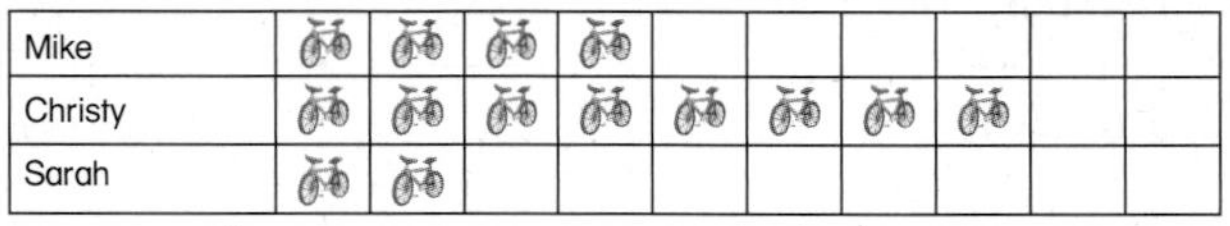

2. How many more bikes does Christy have than Sarah? 6 more bikes

3. How many fewer bikes does Sarah have than Mike? 2 fewer bikes

4. **Geometry**

Connect midpoints of two opposite sides.	Connect midpoints of the other two opposite sides.	Draw both line segments.
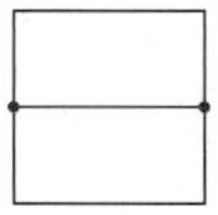		

192 UNIT 9 LESSON 8 Practice with the Ungrouping First Method

Homework and Remembering page 192

Home or School Activity

Social Studies Connection

Famous Landmarks Display pictures of several landmarks. Have children discuss what they know about any of the landmarks.

Have children find the actual height of four landmarks and make a chart to display the information. Then have them write three subtraction questions comparing the heights of the different landmarks. When they have finished, have them give their problems to a friend to solve.

White House	70 feet
Washington Monument	555 feet
Golden Gate Bridge	746 feet
Eiffel Tower	986 feet

UNIT 9 LESSON 9

Zero in the Ones or Tens Place

Lesson Objective

- Subtract 2-digit numbers from numbers with a zero in the tens or ones place (totals to 200).

Vocabulary

hundreds	ones
tens	ungrouping

The Day at a Glance

Today's Goals	Materials: Lesson Activities	Materials: Going Further
1 Teaching the Lesson A1: Learn to solve subtraction exercises with a zero in the total. A2: Practice solving subtraction exercises and story problems with zeros in the total.	**Lesson Activities** Student Activity Book pp. 293–294 Homework and Remembering pp. 193–194 MathBoard materials	**Going Further** Activity Cards 9-9 Base ten blocks Math Journals
2 Going Further ▸ Differentiated Instruction		
3 Homework and Targeted Practice		

Use Math Talk today!

Keeping Skills Sharp

Quick Practice — 5 MINUTES

Goal: Write money strings for dollars. Monitor progress in subtracting 3-digit numbers.

Dollar Strings Have two or three children write dollar strings at the board as the other children prepare for the Quick Check. (See Unit 9 Lesson 6.)

Quick Check Monitor children's progress with a brief quick check. Write these exercises on the board. One of them requires ungrouping, and the other does not.

$$\begin{array}{r} 187 \\ -\ 55 \\ \hline 132 \end{array} \qquad \begin{array}{r} 200 \\ -\ 93 \\ \hline 107 \end{array}$$

Repeated Quick Practice Use this Quick Practice from a previous lesson.

▸ **Teen Subtraction Flash**
(See Unit 9 Lesson 1.)

Daily Routines

Quarters and Other Coins
Making and Counting Coins that Make a Quarter, Counting to 200¢ by 25¢, Making and Counting Dollars and Cents: 3-Digit Numbers as Dollars and Cents
(See pp. xxvi–xxvii.)

▸ Led by Student Leaders

Money Routine Using the 120 Poster, Using the Money Flip Chart, Using the Number Path, Using Secret Code Cards
(See pp. xxiii–xxv.)

▸ Led by Student Leaders

1 Teaching the Lesson

Activity 1

Subtract with a Zero

25 MINUTES

Goal: Learn to solve subtraction exercises with a zero in the total.

Materials: Student Activity Book page 293, MathBoard materials

NCTM Standards:
Number and Operations
Communication

English Language Learners

Draw proof drawings for 101 and 110. Have children identify the circles, Quick Tens, and Quick Hundreds.

- **Beginning** Point and ask: **How many ones circles are there?** 1 one circle **How many Quick Tens are there?** zero Quick Tens **How many Quick Hundreds are there?** 1 Quick Hundred Write 101.
- **Intermediate** Point to the proof for 101 as children identify each part. Ask: **How many do I put in the ones/tens/hundreds column?** Write 101. Continue with 110.
- **Advanced** Have children tell about the proof drawings and say what numbers they represent.

▶ Subtract with Zeroes WHOLE CLASS

Ask for Ideas Direct children's attention to Student Activity Book page 293. Write the first exercise on the board. Then ask a volunteer to create a story problem that goes with the exercise.

$$\begin{array}{r} 108 \\ -\ 46 \\ \hline \end{array}$$

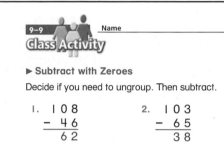

9–9 Class Activity

Name ____________________

▶ Subtract with Zeroes

Decide if you need to ungroup. Then subtract.

1. 108 − 46 = 62	2. 103 − 65 = 38	3. 150 − 79 = 71
4. 102 − 83 = 19	5. 160 − 92 = 68	6. 107 − 61 = 46
7. 106 − 38 = 68	8. 170 − 40 = 130	9. 180 − 93 = 87
10. 140 − 57 = 83	11. 150 − 84 = 66	12. 106 − 43 = 63

UNIT 9 LESSON 9 Zero in the Ones or Tens Place 293

Student Activity Book page 293

Next have a volunteer go to the board and represent the top number, using Quick Hundreds, Quick Tens, and circles. The remaining children should work at their MathBoards at their seats.

Then have children determine if there are enough tens and ones to subtract the bottom number from the top number. Remind children that they may need to go to the tens to get 10 ones or to the hundreds to get 10 tens.

The proof drawing below shows the ungrouping for the first exercise.

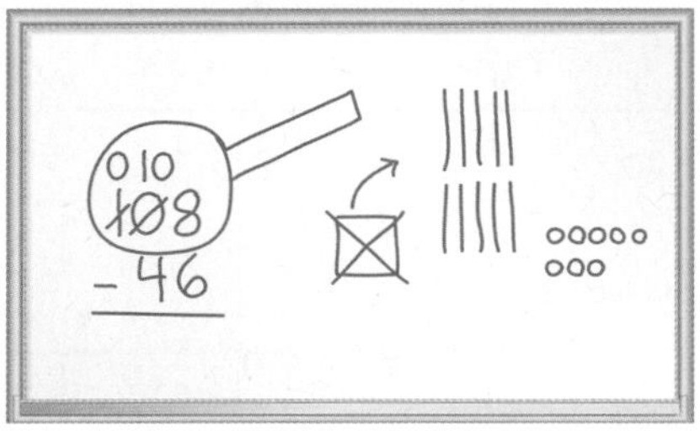

Children should now ungroup the top number in the numerical exercise so that it matches their drawing. Be sure they draw the magnifying glass to help them visually and conceptually hold the 108 together.

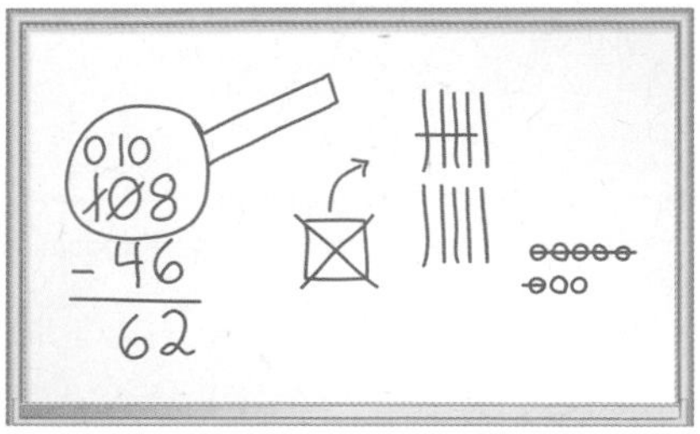

Have children review their drawing and the top number in the exercise to determine whether the value of the number has changed. They should realize that although the number is expressed in a different way, its value is the same.

Have children subtract to solve the exercise. Review the procedures as necessary and address any errors or misconceptions you may notice. Be sure to use hundreds, tens, and ones language.

Use the **Solve and Discuss** structure with the rest of the exercises on the page. Have some of the children work at the board and explain their solutions. Encourage the other children to ask questions and make comments.

Differentiated Instruction

Extra Help For some children 12 subtraction exercises may be overwhelming. You may want to have some children complete only the odd or even exercises. Or, you could have children select any 6 exercises they would like to complete.

Activity 2

Practice Subtracting with a Zero

25 MINUTES

Goal: Practice solving subtraction exercises and story problems with zeros in the total.

Materials: Student Activity Book page 294

NCTM Standards:
Number and Operations
Communication

Ongoing Assessment

Have children write a subtraction exercise that requires ungrouping. Have them use a 3-digit total that has a zero in the ones or tens place. Then have them find the answers, using the Ungrouping First Method.

Teaching Note

Making math drawings is very helpful for these problems.

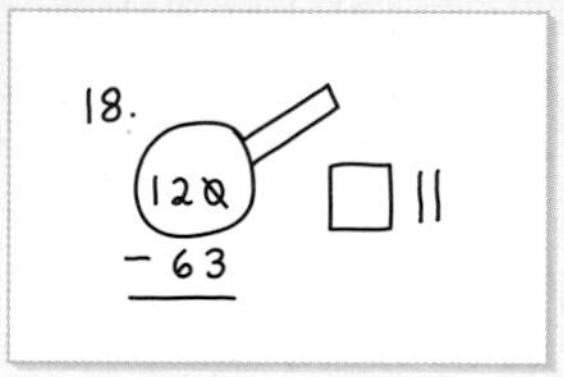

Ungroup from the right or the left

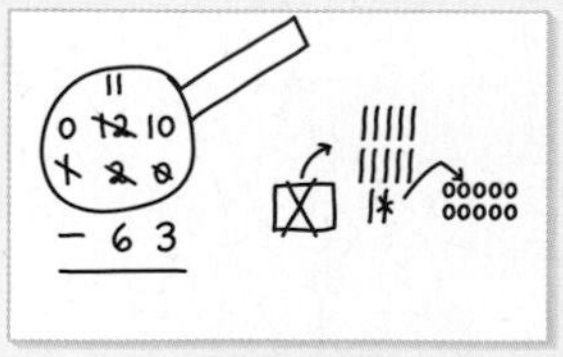

Subtract

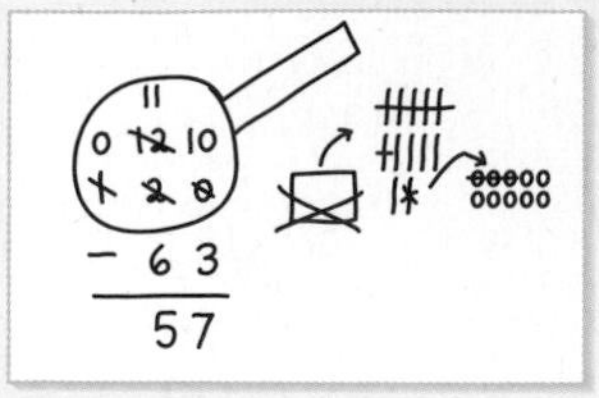

▶ Solve and Discuss INDIVIDUALS

Math Talk

Have children work alone or in Helping Pairs to complete Student Activity Book page 294. If children work in pairs, they should come to an agreement about when to ungroup and rewrite numbers when subtracting.

Circulate around the room as children work. Encourage children to make drawings and show the ungrouping in the drawings as well as in the numeric exercises.

After children have completed the page, have volunteers come to the board and explain their work. Encourage the other children to ask questions and make comments.

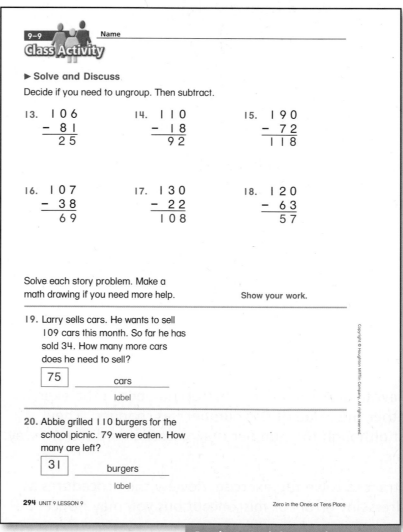

9–9 Class Activity

Name

▶ Solve and Discuss

Decide if you need to ungroup. Then subtract.

13. $106 - 81 = 25$

14. $110 - 18 = 92$

15. $190 - 72 = 118$

16. $107 - 38 = 69$

17. $130 - 22 = 108$

18. $120 - 63 = 57$

Solve each story problem. Make a math drawing if you need more help.

Show your work.

19. Larry sells cars. He wants to sell 109 cars this month. So far he has sold 34. How many more cars does he need to sell?

75 cars (label)

20. Abbie grilled 110 burgers for the school picnic. 79 were eaten. How many are left?

31 burgers (label)

294 UNIT 9 LESSON 9 Zero in the Ones or Tens Place

Student Activity Book page 294

2 Going Further

Differentiated Instruction

Intervention — Activity Card 9-9

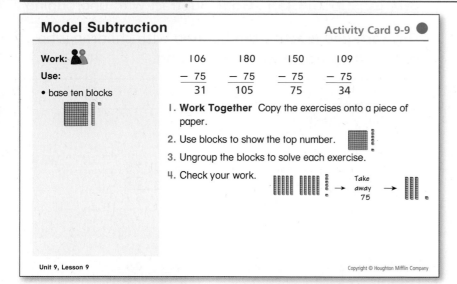

Model Subtraction — Activity Card 9-9

Work: pairs

Use:
- base ten blocks

106	180	150	109
− 75	− 75	− 75	− 75
31	105	75	34

1. **Work Together** Copy the exercises onto a piece of paper.
2. Use blocks to show the top number.
3. Ungroup the blocks to solve each exercise.
4. Check your work.

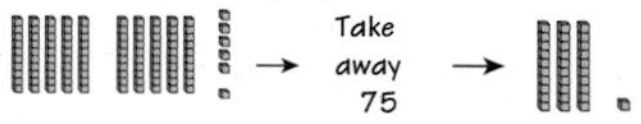

Unit 9, Lesson 9

Activity Note Each pair needs hundreds, tens, and ones base ten blocks. Have children explain the steps as they ungroup.

Math Writing Prompt

Make a Proof Drawing Tell how making a proof drawing can help you solve this exercise.

$$\begin{array}{r} 104 \\ -\ 75 \\ \hline \end{array}$$

Soar to Success Math Software Support

Warm Up 11.25

On Level — Activity Card 9-9

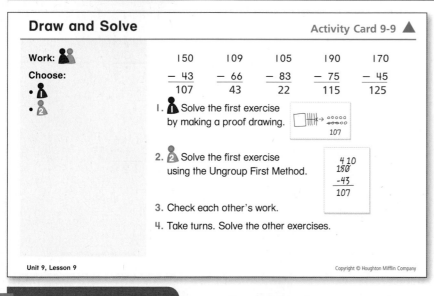

Draw and Solve — Activity Card 9-9

Work: pairs

Choose:
- 1
- 2

150	109	105	190	170
− 43	− 66	− 83	− 75	− 45
107	43	22	115	125

1. (1) Solve the first exercise by making a proof drawing.

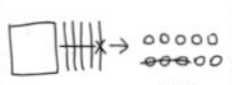

2. (2) Solve the first exercise using the Ungroup First Method.

$$\begin{array}{r} 4\,10 \\ 150 \\ -43 \\ \hline 107 \end{array}$$

3. Check each other's work.
4. Take turns. Solve the other exercises.

Unit 9, Lesson 9

Activity Note Each pair needs to solve each exercise two different ways. Remind children to check that each partner got the same answer.

Math Writing Prompt

Write About It Explain how to ungroup 102 in order to solve this exercise.

$$\begin{array}{r} 102 \\ -\ 58 \\ \hline \end{array}$$

Harcourt Mega Math Software Support

Country Countdown: Block Busters, Level X

Challenge — Activity Card 9-9

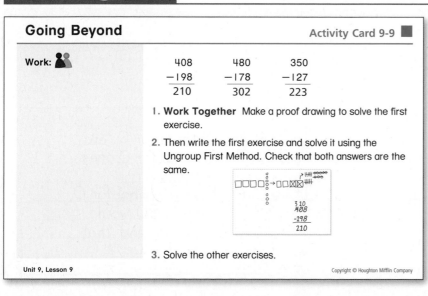

Going Beyond — Activity Card 9-9

Work: pairs

408	480	350
−198	−178	−127
210	302	223

1. **Work Together** Make a proof drawing to solve the first exercise.
2. Then write the first exercise and solve it using the Ungroup First Method. Check that both answers are the same.

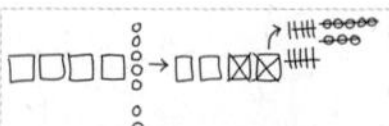

$$\begin{array}{r} 3\,10 \\ 408 \\ -198 \\ \hline 210 \end{array}$$

3. Solve the other exercises.

Unit 9, Lesson 9

Activity Note Each pair will use both methods to solve the exercises. If necessary, have pairs compare their solutions.

Math Writing Prompt

Explain Your Thinking When you subtract, do you always need to ungroup if there is a zero in the ones or tens place? Give examples.

Destination Math Software Support

Course II: Module 2: Unit 1: Estimating and Finding Differences within 1,000

3 Homework and Targeted Practice

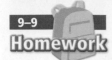

9–9 Homework **Goal:** Additional Practice

This Homework page provides practice subtracting with zeros in the ones or tens place.

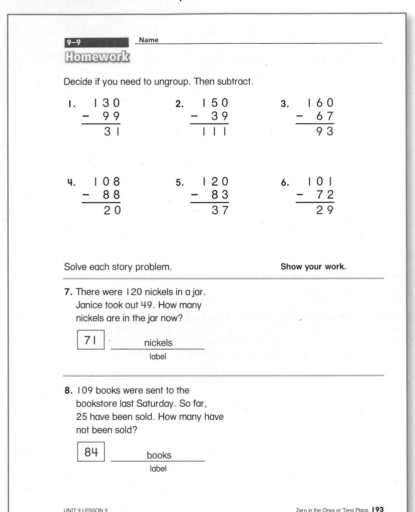

9–9 Homework Name ______

Decide if you need to ungroup. Then subtract.

1. $130 - 99 = 31$
2. $150 - 39 = 111$
3. $160 - 67 = 93$
4. $108 - 88 = 20$
5. $120 - 83 = 37$
6. $101 - 72 = 29$

Solve each story problem. **Show your work.**

7. There were 120 nickels in a jar. Janice took out 49. How many nickels are in the jar now?

   71 nickels (label)

8. 109 books were sent to the bookstore last Saturday. So far, 25 have been sold. How many have not been sold?

   84 books (label)

UNIT 9 LESSON 9 Zero in the Ones or Tens Place 193

Homework and Remembering page 193

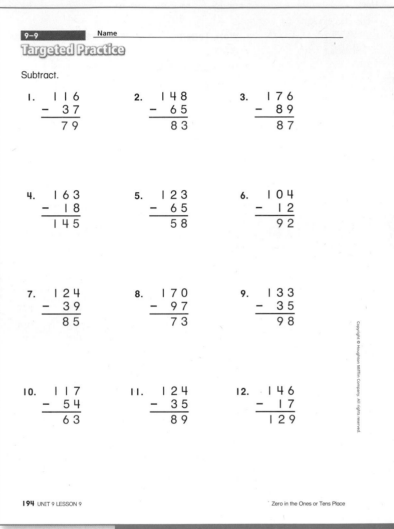

9–9 Targeted Practice **Goal:** Subtract with ungrouping.

This Targeted Practice can be used with children who need extra practice with ungrouping.

9–9 Targeted Practice Name ______

Subtract.

1. $116 - 37 = 79$
2. $148 - 65 = 83$
3. $176 - 89 = 87$
4. $163 - 18 = 145$
5. $123 - 65 = 58$
6. $104 - 12 = 92$
7. $124 - 39 = 85$
8. $170 - 97 = 73$
9. $133 - 35 = 98$
10. $117 - 54 = 63$
11. $124 - 35 = 89$
12. $146 - 17 = 129$

194 UNIT 9 LESSON 9 Zero in the Ones or Tens Place

Homework and Remembering page 194

Home or School Activity

Multicultural Connection

Who Invented Zero? Explain to children that the invention of zero is often credited to the Hindu mathematician Aryabhata (476–550 A.D.) The original symbol for zero was a small dot. Later the small dot became a circle, now called zero.

Have children discuss the number zero. Ask them to describe what zero means in the numbers 308 and 380. Then tell them to write about what problems might occur if we didn't have a symbol for zero or "nothing."

In 308, the 0 stands for 0 tens.
In 380, the 0 stands for 0 ones.

If we didn't have a symbol for 0, then 38, 308, and 380 would all be written as 38, and that would be very confusing.

UNIT 9 LESSON 10

Model Subtraction with Money

REAL WORLD Problem Solving

Lesson Objectives

- Make change for a dollar in dimes and pennies.
- Use exact change.

Vocabulary

dollar
dime
penny
exact change
decimal notation

The Day at a Glance

Today's Goals	Materials	
1 Teaching the Lesson A: Change money amounts in order to make purchases.	**Lesson Activities** Student Activity Book pp. 295–296 Homework and Remembering pp. 195–196 Quick Quiz 2 (Assessment Guide) Real or play money Small box labeled *Bank*	**Going Further** Activity Cards 9-10 Real or play money Small box labeled *Bank* Paper bags Strips of paper Index cards Calculators *Tightwad Tod* by Daphne Skinner Math Journals
2 Going Further ▸ Extension: Use Decimal Notation for Dollars and Cents ▸ Differentiated Instruction		
3 Homework and Spiral Review		

Use Math Talk today!

Keeping Skills Sharp

Quick Practice — 5 MINUTES

Goals: Practice subtraction with teen totals. Write money strings for dollars.

Teen Subtraction Flash Have a **Student Leader** direct the class in Teen Subtraction Flash while some of the children write dollar strings. (See Unit 9 Lesson 1.)

Dollar Strings Have two or three children write dollar strings at the board. (See Unit 9 Lesson 6.)

Daily Routines

Quarters and Other Coins
Making and Counting Coins that Make a Quarter, Counting to 200¢ by 25¢, Making and Counting Dollars and Cents: 3-Digit Numbers as Dollars and Cents
(See pp. xxvi–xxvii.)

▸ Led by Student Leaders

Money Routine Using the 120 Poster, Using the Money Flip Chart, Using the Number Path, Using Secret Code Cards
(See pp. xxiii–xxv.)

▸ Led by Student Leaders

1 Teaching the Lesson

Activity

The Yard Sale

25 MINUTES

Goal: Change money amounts in order to make purchases.

Materials: Student Activity Book page 295, real or play money (1 dollar, 20 dimes, 20 pennies per pair), small box labeled *Bank.*

NCTM Standards:
Number and Operations
Communication

The Learning Classroom

Building Concepts In this scenario, children use only pennies, dimes, and dollars. This is to help them practice the same ungrouping that they use when they subtract 3-digit numbers. Some children may suggest exchanging a dollar for 4 quarters or a dime for 2 nickels. Tell children that this is also correct, but in this activity we will be focusing only on pennies, dimes, and dollars.

English Language Learners

Say: **A group of coins is *change*.** Jingle some change in your pocket.

- **Beginning** Say: **I have *change* in my pocket.** Show the coins. Name them and count the cents. Have children repeat.
- **Intermediate** Ask: **Do I have *change* in my pocket?** yes Show the coins and guide children to count the change.
- **Advanced** Ask: **What do I have in my pocket?** change Show the coins and have children count the change.

▶ Use Exact Change PAIRS

Math Talk

In this scenario, children use dollars, dimes, and pennies to model hundreds, tens and ones in subtraction.

Refer children to Student Activity book page 295. Be sure pairs have a dollar bill, 20 dimes, and 20 pennies in their "bank." Explain to children that they will work in **Helping Pairs** to act out a yard sale scenario using the items shown at the top of the page. One child will play the part of the *customer* and the other the part of the *banker.* After each exercise, children will switch roles.

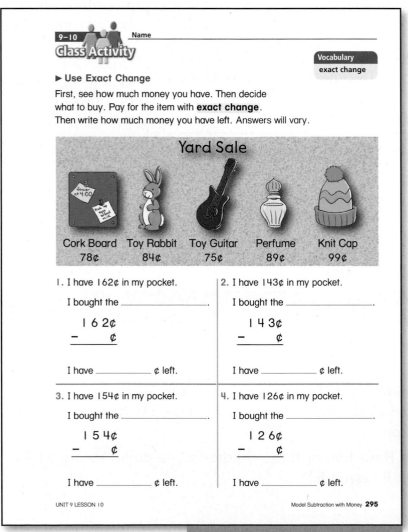

9–10 Class Activity

Name ________________

Vocabulary
exact change

▶ **Use Exact Change**

First, see how much money you have. Then decide what to buy. Pay for the item with **exact change**.
Then write how much money you have left. Answers will vary.

1. I have 162¢ in my pocket.
   I bought the ________________.
   162¢
   − ¢
   I have ________ ¢ left.

2. I have 143¢ in my pocket.
   I bought the ________________.
   143¢
   − ¢
   I have ________ ¢ left.

3. I have 154¢ in my pocket.
   I bought the ________________.
   154¢
   − ¢
   I have ________ ¢ left.

4. I have 126¢ in my pocket.
   I bought the ________________.
   126¢
   − ¢
   I have ________ ¢ left.

UNIT 9 LESSON 10 Model Subtraction with Money 295

Student Activity Book page 295

Direct children's attention to the first exercise on Student Activity Book page 295. The banker should give the customer the exact amount of money shown in the first box (162¢) in the form of 1 dollar, 6 dimes, and 2 pennies. Be sure children see the relationship between hundreds, tens, and ones, and dollars, dimes, and pennies. The customer then decides what he or she wants to buy and writes the name of the item on the line provided. The child also enters the price on the line next to the minus sign.

Next, the customer pays the banker for the item using exact change. To do this, the child must ask the banker for change for a dollar (10 dimes), change for a dime (10 pennies), or both as needed. The banker provides the correct change to the customer. The customer then gives the banker the money for the item using exact change. See **Math Talk in Action** for possible classroom dialogue.

After making the payment, the customer counts the money he or she has left. For example, if the customer bought the toy rabbit, the customer will have 7 dimes and 8 pennies or 78¢ left. The child writes that amount on the line at the bottom of the first box.

Have the pair check the exchange by subtracting the cost of the toy rabbit from the amount the customer started out with.

$$\begin{array}{r} 162¢ \\ -\ 84¢ \\ \hline 78¢ \end{array} \quad \text{or} \quad \begin{array}{rcl} & & \qquad 150 \\ & & \qquad \cancel{50} + 12 \\ 162¢ & = & \cancel{100} + \cancel{60} + \cancel{2} \\ -\ 84 & = & \quad 80 + 4 \\ \hline & & \quad 70 + 8 = 78¢ \end{array}$$

Children should see that the answer matches the amount of money the customer had left after the purchase. They should also see that when subtracting, they make the same exchanges that the customer made in order to pay for the items.

If necessary, demonstrate a sample transaction in front of the class. Then allow the class to continue in their Helping Pairs.

When children have finished the page, ask volunteers to come to the board and show how they completed each of the exercises. Encourage other children to comment and ask questions.

Math Talk in Action

Nina (customer): I want to buy the toy rabbit, which costs 84 cents. That means I need 8 dimes and 4 pennies. I have 1 dollar, 6 dimes, and 2 pennies. So I need to get more dimes and more pennies.

Diego (banker): So which do you want to exchange first, a dime or a dollar?

Nina (customer): I think I'll start by exchanging a dime to get enough pennies. Here's a dime.

Diego (banker): One dime equals 10 pennies. Here are 10 pennies.

Nina (customer): OK, now I have 12 pennies, which is more than enough since I only need 4 pennies. But I still need to exchange a dollar to get enough dimes. So here's a dollar.

Diego (banker): One dollar equals 10 dimes. So here are 10 dimes.

Nina (customer): Now I have 15 dimes which is more than enough since I only need 8 dimes. So now I have enough dimes and pennies to buy the toy rabbit with exact change.

Ongoing Assessment

Have children use dollars, dimes, and pennies to find each difference.

1. $\begin{array}{r} 158¢ \\ -\ 85¢ \end{array}$ **2.** $\begin{array}{r} 126¢ \\ -\ 87¢ \end{array}$

Quick Quiz

See Assessment Guide for Unit 9 Quick Quiz 2.

2 Going Further

Extension: Use Decimal Notation for Dollars and Cents

Goal: Use decimal notation for dollars and cents.

Materials: Student Activity Book page 296, real or play money (1 dollar bill, 20 dimes, 20 pennies per pair)

✓ **NCTM Standard:**
Number and Operations

▶ Introduce Decimal Notation for Money WHOLE CLASS

Decimal notation for dollars and cents will be formally taught in Unit 6, but, you can use this activity with children who are ready to use decimal notation now.

Write 100¢ on the board and ask children to describe what it means? 100 cents or 100 pennies or 1 dollar Ask children if there is another way to write the same amount. Write the following on the board if no one suggests it.

100¢ = $1.00

Explain that 100¢ is read as "one hundred cents" and $1.00 is read as "one dollar." Point out the dollar sign symbol and the decimal point. Tell children that the decimal point separates the number of dollars from the number of cents. Then ask children to discuss the two different ways of writing the same amount of money.

- How are the two ways alike? They both use the same three digits.
- How are the two ways different? The first way uses a ¢ sign. The second way uses a dollar sign and a decimal point.
- What does the 1 in $1.00 mean? one dollar
- What do the zeros mean? 0 dimes and 0 pennies

Now write 165¢ and 65¢ on the board. Have volunteers use their money to show how many dollars, dimes, and pennies are in each amount. Explain to children that they should use a dollar if they can and then as many dimes as possible. Show children how to write the amounts, using decimal notation.

165¢ = 1 dollar 6 dimes 5 pennies = $1.65
65¢ = 0 dollars 6 dimes 5 pennies = $0.65

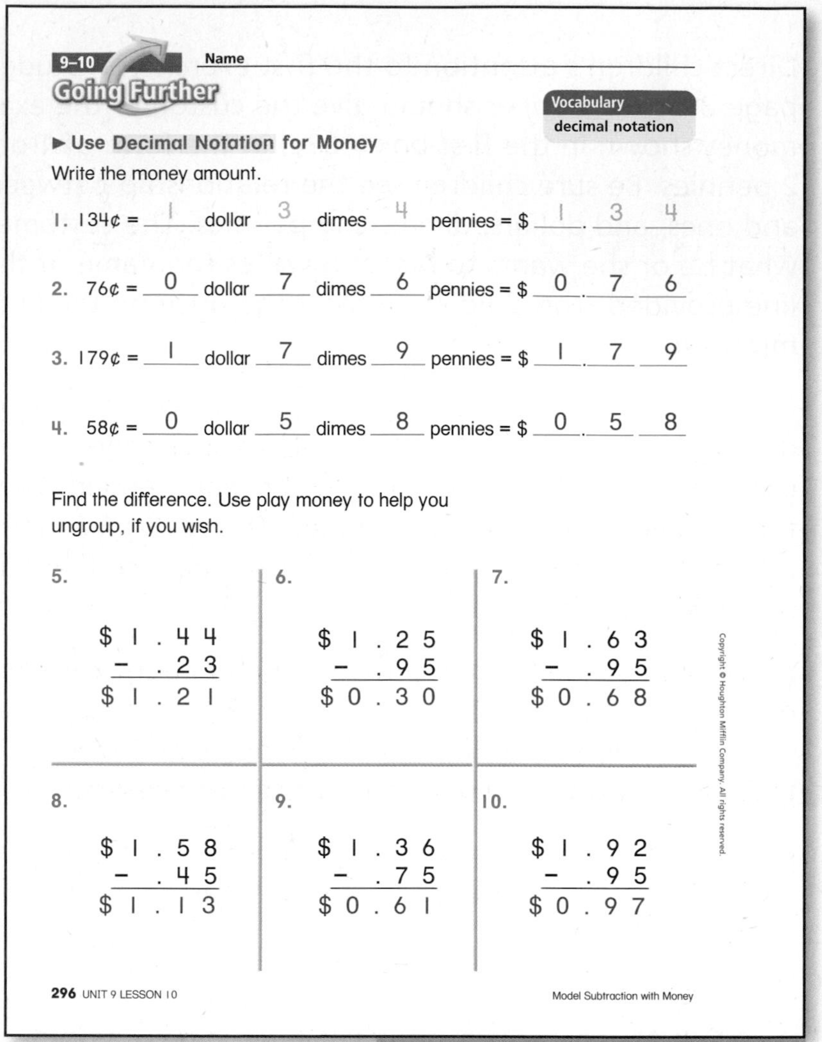
9–10 Going Further   Name

Vocabulary
decimal notation

▶ Use Decimal Notation for Money

Write the money amount.

1. 134¢ = 1 dollar 3 dimes 4 pennies = $ 1 . 3 4
2. 76¢ = 0 dollar 7 dimes 6 pennies = $ 0 . 7 6
3. 179¢ = 1 dollar 7 dimes 9 pennies = $ 1 . 7 9
4. 58¢ = 0 dollar 5 dimes 8 pennies = $ 0 . 5 8

Find the difference. Use play money to help you ungroup, if you wish.

5. $1.44 − .23 = $1.21
6. $1.25 − .95 = $0.30
7. $1.63 − .95 = $0.68
8. $1.58 − .45 = $1.13
9. $1.36 − .75 = $0.61
10. $1.92 − .95 = $0.97

Student Activity Book page 296

▶ Use Decimal Notation for Money PAIRS

Math Talk

Have children work in Helping Pairs to complete the top half of Student Activity Book page 296. When they have finished ask children to share and discuss their work.

Use the **Step-By-Step at the Board** structure and have volunteers show how to solve exercises 5–7. If they wish, allow children to use their money to show the ungrouping. Exercise 5 does not require any ungrouping, exercise 6 requires children to ungroup once, and exercise 7 requires children to ungroup twice. Then have children complete exercises 8–10.

Differentiated Instruction

Intervention — Activity Card 9-10

Ungroup Dollars and Dimes
Activity Card 9-10

Work: pairs

Use:
- 2 dollars
- 20 dimes
- 20 pennies
- paper bag
- box labeled *Bank*

Choose:
- 1
- 2

1. **Work Together** Put 9 dimes and 9 pennies in the bag. Put the other dimes and pennies in the *Bank*. Each child keeps one dollar. Make a chart with the heads *Dollars*, *Dimes*, and *Pennies*.
2. Take money from the bag. Write on the chart how many dollars, dimes, and pennies you have.
3. Use the money in the *Bank* to ungroup the dollar. Write how many dimes and pennies you have.

Dollars	Dimes	Pennies
1	5	6
0	15	6
0	14	16

4. Next ungroup 1 dime and add the amounts to the chart.
5. Change roles and repeat.

Unit 9, Lesson 10

Activity Note Each pair needs two dollars, 20 dimes, and 20 pennies (real or play), a paper bag, and a box labeled *Bank*. Pairs need to ungroup the money two times.

Math Writing Prompt

Draw a Picture Sam has 172¢. He has only dimes and pennies. Draw the coins he has.

Soar to Success Math **Software Support**

Warm Up 3.15

On Level — Activity Card 9-10

What's the Change?
Activity Card 9-10

Work: pairs

Use:
- 6 strips of paper
- paper bag

Choose:
- 1
- 2

Arts and Crafts Supplies

Crayons	74¢	Sketch paper	19¢
Yarn	53¢	Water color paint	26¢
Glue	85¢	Paintbrushes	91¢

1. **Work Together** Write these amounts on the strips of paper: 154¢, 116¢, 122¢, 178¢, 193¢, and 149¢. Each strip should have one amount on it. Put the strips in the bag.
2. Take one strip from the bag. Then choose an item to buy from the chart.
3. Subtract to see how much money is left over after buying the item.
4. Take turns until all of the strips are used.

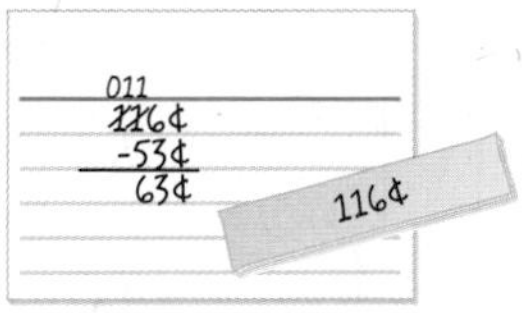

Unit 9, Lesson 10

Activity Note Each pair needs six strips of paper and a paper bag. Have children check their work with their partner.

Math Writing Prompt

Connect How does knowing how to find 154 − 64 help you find 154¢ − 64¢

Harcourt Mega Math Grades K-6 **Software Support**

Numberopolis: Lulu's Lunch Counter, Level Q

Challenge — Activity Card 9-10

Mental Math Match
Activity Card 9-10

Work: pairs

Use:
- 16 index cards
- calculator

Choose:
- 1
- 2

1. Write these amounts on the index cards:

$1.20	$0.80	$0.84	$1.16
$1.55	$0.45	$1.37	$0.63
$1.49	$0.51	$1.74	$0.26
$0.33	$1.67	$0.72	$1.28

2. Mix up the cards. Choose one card.
3. Use mental math to choose another card that will make the total of the two cards equal $2.00.
4. Take turns until all of the matches have been made.
5. **Work Together** Use the calculator to check that each match is correct.

Unit 9, Lesson 10

Activity Note Each pair needs 16 index cards and a calculator. You may want to prepare the index cards for pairs.

Math Writing Prompt

Crete Your Own Write a story problem that can be solved by subtracting money amounts. Then give your problem to a friend to solve.

Destination Math **Software Support**

Course II: Module 3: Unit 2: Money

3 Homework and Spiral Review

9–10 Homework **Goal:** Additional Practice

This Homework page provides practice subtracting money amounts.

9–10 **Homework** Name ______________________

What would you like to buy? First, see how much money you have. Pay for the item. How much money will you have left?

Yard Sale

Globe	Ring	Sports Bag	Eraser	Colored Pencils
85¢	67¢	98¢	79¢	66¢

Answers will vary.

1. I have 124¢ in my pocket.
I bought the ____________.

  124¢
– ___¢

I have ____________ ¢ left.

2. I have 152¢ in my pocket.
I bought the ____________.

  152¢
– ___¢

I have ____________ ¢ left.

3. I have 145¢ in my pocket.
I bought the ____________.

  145¢
– ___¢

I have ____________ ¢ left.

4. I have 131¢ in my pocket.
I bought the ____________.

  131¢
– ___¢

I have ____________ ¢ left.

UNIT 9 LESSON 10 Model Subtraction with Money **195**

Homework and Remembering page 195

9–10 Remembering **Goal:** Spiral Review

This Remembering activity would be appropriate anytime after today's lesson.

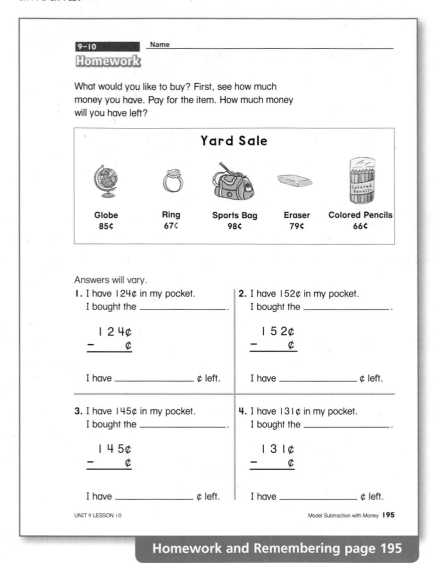

9–10 **Remembering** Name ______________________

Subtract.

1. 103 – 55 = 48
2. 150 – 91 = 59
3. 170 – 93 = 77
4. 140 – 54 = 86
5. 109 – 22 = 87
6. 108 – 49 = 59

Write the time on the digital clock.

7.

2:45

8.

1:30

9.

4:55

10.

2:25

11. Geometry

Draw one diagonal.	Draw the other diagonal.	Draw both diagonals.

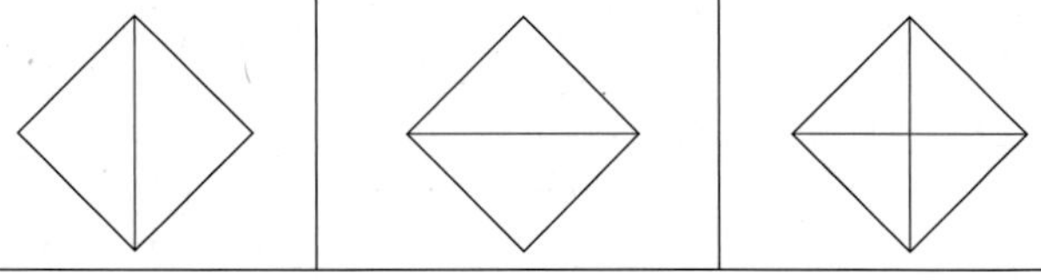

Answers in first two columns may be reversed.

196 UNIT 9 LESSON 10 Model Subtraction with Money

Homework and Remembering page 196

Home or School Activity

Literature Connection

Make Purchases Use the book *Tightwad Tod* by Daphne Skinner and John Nez (Disney Press, 2005) as a read-aloud, covering up the math information at the bottom of each page. When Tod and his brother start to buy items at the mall, encourage children to discuss how Tod might pay for each item and what change he might receive.

After children have finished making their predictions, display the information at the bottom of each page which shows the running tally of remaining cash, how Tod pays for each item, and the change he receives.

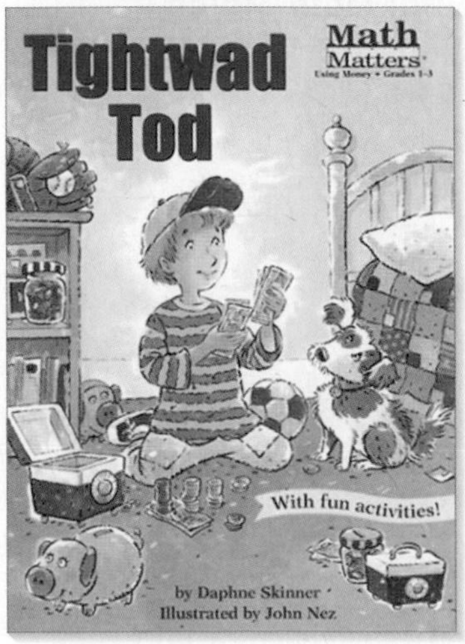

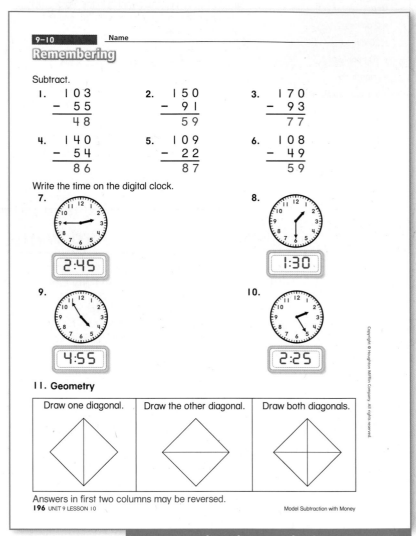

UNIT 9 LESSON 11

Story Problems with Addition and Subtraction

REAL WORLD Problem Solving

Vocabulary

money string
group
ungroup
Expanded Method

Lesson Objective

- Compare addition and subtraction methods.

The Day at a Glance

Today's Goals	Materials	
1 Teaching the Lesson **A1:** Compare grouping in addition and ungrouping in subtraction. **A2:** Solve addition and subtraction story problems.	**Lesson Activities** Student Activity Book pp. 297–298 Homework and Remembering pp. 197–198 MathBoard materials	**Going Further** Activity Cards 9-11 Index cards Secret Code Cards Paper bags Math Journals
2 Going Further ▸ Math Connection: Estimation ▸ Differentiated Instruction		
3 Homework and Targeted Practice		

Use Math Talk today!

Keeping Skills Sharp

Quick Practice — 5 MINUTES

Goals: Show ways to make money amounts between one and two dollars.

Money Strings Have the class choose two money amounts between one and two dollars. Have two to four **Student Leaders** work at the board and the rest of the children work at their seats. Children should write combinations of dollars and/or coins that equal the amounts they chose. Children can check each other's money strings for correctness.

Money String Examples:

\$1.29 = \$1 + 25¢ + 1¢ + 1¢ + 1¢ + 1¢ = 25¢ + 25¢ + 25¢ + 10¢ + 10¢ + 10¢ + 5¢ + 5¢ + 5¢ + 5¢ + 1¢ + 1¢ + 1¢ + 1¢ and so on.

\$1.62 = 25¢ + 25¢ + 25¢ + 25¢ + 25¢ + 25¢ + 10¢ + 1¢ + 1¢ = \$1 + 25¢ + 5¢ + 5¢ + 5¢ + 5¢ + 5¢ + 5¢ + 5¢ + 1¢ + 1¢ and so on.

Daily Routines

Quarters and Other Coins
Making and Counting Coins that Make a Quarter, Counting to 200¢ by 25¢, Making and Counting Dollars and Cents: 3-Digit Numbers as Dollars and Cents
(See pp. xxvi–xxvii.)

▸ Led by Student Leaders

Money Routine Using the 120 Poster, Using the Money Flip Chart, Using the Number Path, Using Secret Code Cards
(See pp. xxiii–xxv.)

▸ Led by Student Leaders

1 Teaching the Lesson

Activity 1

Compare Addition and Subtraction Methods

25 MINUTES

Goal: Compare grouping in addition and ungrouping in subtraction.

Materials: MathBoard materials

NCTM Standards:
Number and Operations
Problem Solving
Connections

The Learning Classroom

Building Concepts Making Proof Drawings with sticks and circles may help children see the relationship between grouping for addition and ungrouping for subtraction.

Math Mountain diagrams, like the ones below, reinforce the concept that larger numbers can be broken down into smaller numbers. The smaller numbers are partners. You may wish to draw in the minus or plus signs, as shown.

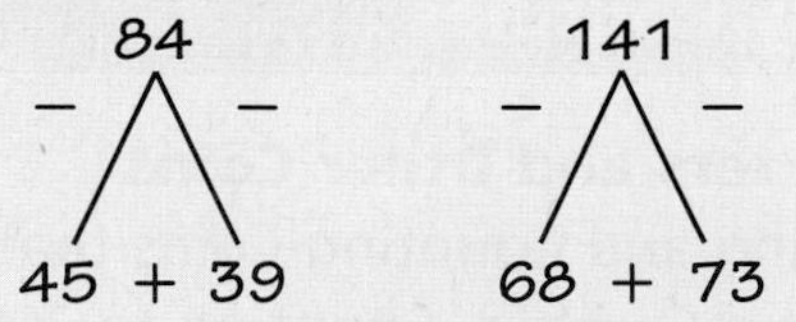

English Language Learners

Review *group* and *ungroup*. Model an addition and a subtraction problem on the board.

- **Beginning** Point and ask: **Did I *group* or *ungroup* here?**
- **Intermediate and Advanced** Ask: **Did I *group* in the addition or subtraction problem?** addition problem **When did I *ungroup*?** subtraction problem

▶ Tell Story Problems WHOLE CLASS

Math Talk

Addition Present children with an addition problem, such as 79 + 84. Have children make up a story problem for it, such as:

Mr. Jones baked 79 muffins in the morning. He baked 84 muffins in the afternoon. How many muffins did he bake altogether?

Have children divide the Number Path side of their MathBoards or a piece of paper into two sections by drawing a vertical line down the middle. They should solve the addition problem on the left side.

Subtraction When children have finished the addition problem, give them a numeric subtraction problem to solve, such as 141 − 68. Have children make up a story problem for it; then have them solve it on the right side of their MathBoards or papers.

Compare Addition and Subtraction When children are finished solving both problems, discuss how the numeric problems are similar and how they are different.

- How are these problems alike? In each problem, there is a total, and there are two partners.
- How are the problems different? In the addition problem, we know the two partners, but not the total. In the subtraction problem, we know the total and one partner.

Ask for Ideas Elicit from children that when adding, if the total in the ones column is 10 or more ones, 10 ones are grouped as a new ten with the tens. If the total in the tens column is 10 or more tens, 10 tens are grouped as a new hundred with the hundreds.

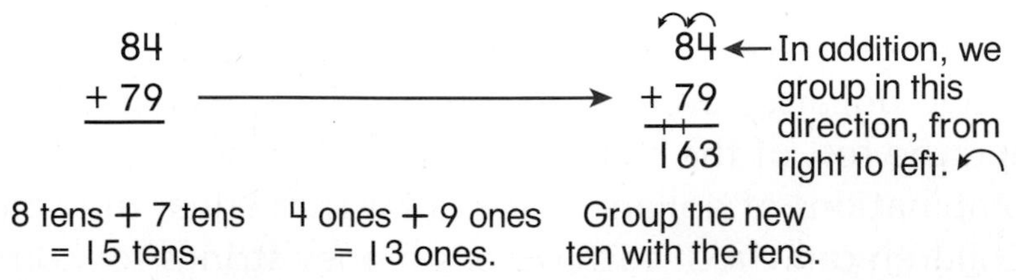

Ask for Ideas Elicit from children that when subtracting, if there are not enough ones, one 10 is ungrouped as ten ones. If there are not enough tens, one hundred is ungrouped as 10 tens. Ungrouping can be from right to left or from left to right, or can be done using the Expanded Method.

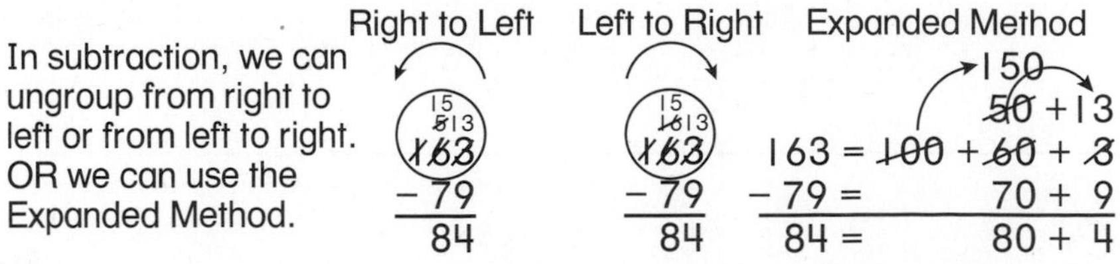

Activity 2

Practice Addition and Subtraction

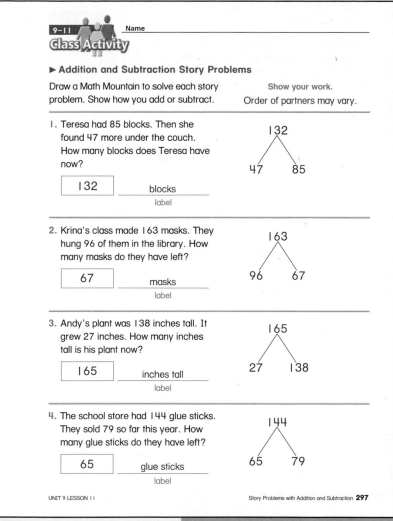

9–11 **Class Activity** Name ____________________

▶ **Addition and Subtraction Story Problems**

Draw a Math Mountain to solve each story problem. Show how you add or subtract.

Show your work. Order of partners may vary.

1. Teresa had 85 blocks. Then she found 47 more under the couch. How many blocks does Teresa have now?

   132 blocks (label)

   132 / 47 85

2. Krina's class made 163 masks. They hung 96 of them in the library. How many masks do they have left?

   67 masks (label)

   163 / 96 67

3. Andy's plant was 138 inches tall. It grew 27 inches. How many inches tall is his plant now?

   165 inches tall (label)

   165 / 27 138

4. The school store had 144 glue sticks. They sold 79 so far this year. How many glue sticks do they have left?

   65 glue sticks (label)

   144 / 65 79

UNIT 9 LESSON 11 Story Problems with Addition and Subtraction **297**

Student Activity Book page 297

▶ Addition and Subtraction Story Problems PAIRS

Have children work in Helping Pairs to solve the problems on Student Activity Book page 297.

As you circulate around the room, watch for children who are using different strategies. Have them explain their solutions to the class. They should use hundreds, tens, and ones language.

You may want to work at the board with children who are experiencing difficulty, or have **Student Helpers** work with them.

Children who finish early may write two more story problems on a separate piece of paper.

30 MINUTES

Goal: Solve addition and subtraction story problems.

Materials: Student Activity Book page 297

NCTM Standards:
Number and Operations
Problem Solving
Representation

Teaching Note

Watch For! Be alert to children who show only the answer on the Student Activity Book page and omit the details of the solution, such as the Math Mountain or the grouping or ungrouping. Review the directions for the page in detail; ask children to restate the information they need to include in a complete answer.

Ongoing Assessment

Have each child write and solve a story problem for each exercise below. Ask children to explain their solutions.

▶ $63 + 78 = \square$

▶ $94 - 57 = \square$

2 Going Further

Math Connection: Estimation

Goal: Estimate solutions to addition and subtraction problems.

Materials: Student Activity Book page 298

✓ **NCTM Standard:**
Number and Operations

▶ Estimate to Find the Answer

WHOLE CLASS

Ask for Ideas Elicit from children what estimation is and when it is useful. Review with children different strategies for estimating, such as rounding. (See Going Further, Unit 5 Lesson 5.)

Review the directions for the Student Activity Book page. For exercises 1–4, children should use any method to estimate the answer. They should then use the estimate to find the match to the correct answer. Discuss why the estimate and exact answers need not be the same numbers.

▶ Review Estimation

WHOLE CLASS

Ask children to tell everyday examples where they might use an estimate rather than an exact answer. For example:

- Estimating if they have enough money to buy all the items they want in a store.
- Estimating the number of weeks or days before a special date, such as a birthday.
- Estimating the number of people that might come to a soccer game.

Have children analyze why an estimate is appropriate in each situation. Ask if there is anything the situations have in common.

Have children use estimation to solve problems 5 and 6. When discussing children's answers, point out that both numbers (38 and 19) were rounded up, so the estimate can be used to answer question 6. If one or both of the numbers had been rounded down, an estimate might not have been sufficient to answer question 6.

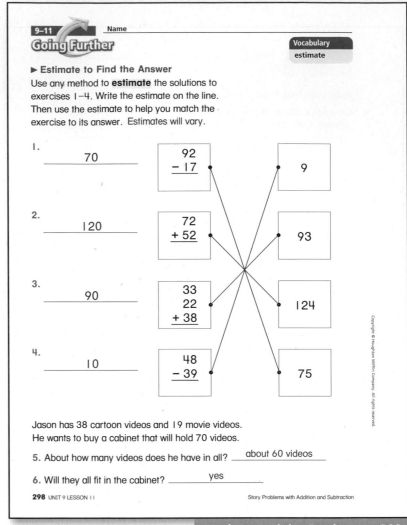

9–11 Going Further Name

Vocabulary
estimate

▶ Estimate to Find the Answer

Use any method to **estimate** the solutions to exercises 1–4. Write the estimate on the line. Then use the estimate to help you match the exercise to its answer. Estimates will vary.

	Estimate	Exercise	Answer
1.	70	92 − 17	9
2.	120	72 + 52	93
3.	90	33 + 22 + 38	124
4.	10	48 − 39	75

Jason has 38 cartoon videos and 19 movie videos. He wants to buy a cabinet that will hold 70 videos.

5. About how many videos does he have in all? about 60 videos

6. Will they all fit in the cabinet? yes

298 UNIT 9 LESSON 11 Story Problems with Addition and Subtraction

Student Activity Book page 298

Teaching Note

Watch For! Some children may think that an estimate can be *any* number because it is only an approximate solution. Point out that an estimate should be close to the exact answer and give a guide to the exact solution. Give the addition example $19 + 22 = 41$. Show how the estimate $20 + 20 = 40$ is a reasonable estimate of the solution. Ask children to give examples of unreasonable estimates. Discuss how close an estimate should be to the exact number before either the estimate or the exact answer is considered incorrect.

Intervention — Activity Card 9-11

Group to Win
Activity Card 9-11 ●

Work: pairs
Use:
- 10 index cards

Choose:
- 1
- 2

1. Write the following numbers on 10 separate index cards: 14, 22, 29, 35, 43, 57, 60, 75, 86, 91. Mix the cards and place them face down.
2. 1 Choose two cards.

57
86

3. If grouping is needed to find the total, keep the cards and score 1 point.
4. If grouping is not needed to find the total, turn the cards back over.
5. Take turns. When all of the cards are taken, the person with the most points wins.

Unit 9, Lesson 11

Activity Note Each pair needs 10 index cards. Both children should agree if grouping is needed or not.

Math Writing Prompt
Addition Story Problem Write an addition story problem so that the answer is *58 purple balloons*.

Soar to Success Math Software Support
Warm Up 10.27

On Level — Activity Card 9-11

Story Problems
Activity Card 9-11 ▲

Work: pairs
Use:
- Secret Code Cards
- 2 paper bags

Choose:
- 1
- 2

1. **Work Together** Put the 10s Secret Code Cards in one bag and the 1s Secret Code Cards in the other bag. Mix up the cards in the bags.
2. Each 1 takes one Secret Code Card from each bag to make a two-digit number.
3. 1 Use the numbers to write an addition story problem.
4. 2 Use the numbers to write a subtraction story problem.
5. Take turns with other numbers.

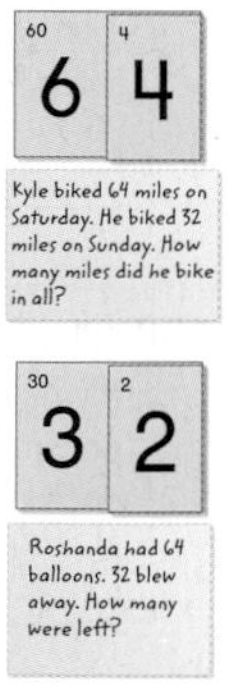
60 4
6 4
Kyle biked 64 miles on Saturday. He biked 32 miles on Sunday. How many miles did he bike in all?
30 2
3 2
Roshanda had 64 balloons. 32 blew away. How many were left?

Unit 9, Lesson 11

Activity Note Each pair needs Secret Code Cards (TRB M3–M4) (10s and 1s, 1 set per pair) and two paper bags. Have pairs solve the story problems that they write.

Math Writing Prompt
Subtraction Story Problem Write a subtraction story problem so that the answer is *42 kangaroos*.

Harcourt Mega Math Software Support
Numberopolis: Carnival Stories, Level R

Challenge — Activity Card 9-11

Start with the Answer
Activity Card 9-11 ■

Work: pairs
Use:
- Secret Code Cards
- 2 paper bags

Choose:
- 1
- 2

1. **Work Together** Put the 10s Secret Code Cards in one bag and the 1s Secret Code Cards in the other bag. Mix up the cards in the bags.
2. 1 Choose one card from each bag and make a two-digit number. Write a subtraction story problem that has the number you made with the cards as the answer.

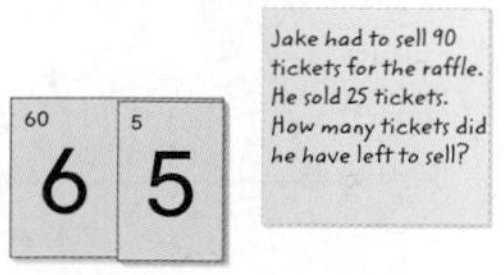
Jake had to sell 90 tickets for the raffle. He sold 25 tickets. How many tickets did he have left to sell?
60 5
6 5

3. 2 Write an addition story that uses the same number as the answer.
4. Trade problems and solve. Take turns.

Unit 9, Lesson 11

Activity Note Each pair needs Secret Code Cards (TRB M3–M4) (10s and 1s, 1 set per pair) and two paper bags. Have children trade roles with a new number.

Math Writing Prompt
Make a List List three words or phrases you might include in an addition story problem. List three words or phrases you might include in a subtraction story problem.

Destination Math Software Support
Course II: Module 2: Unit 1: Differences within 100

3 Homework and Targeted Practice

9–11 **Homework** **Goal:** Additional Practice

✓ Include children's completed Homework page as part of their portfolios.

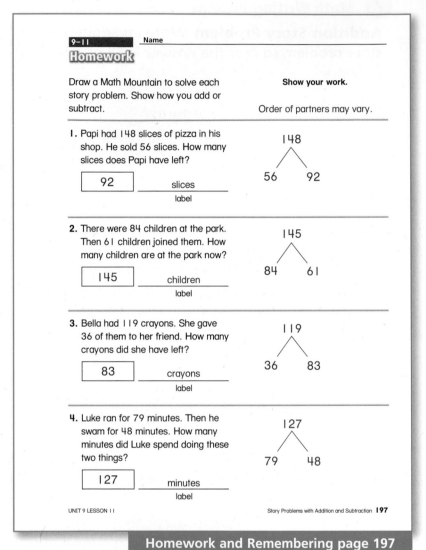

9–11 **Homework** Name ____________

Draw a Math Mountain to solve each story problem. Show how you add or subtract.

Show your work.

Order of partners may vary.

1. Papi had 148 slices of pizza in his shop. He sold 56 slices. How many slices does Papi have left?

   92 slices (label)

   148 → 56, 92

2. There were 84 children at the park. Then 61 children joined them. How many children are at the park now?

   145 children (label)

   145 → 84, 61

3. Bella had 119 crayons. She gave 36 of them to her friend. How many crayons did she have left?

   83 crayons (label)

   119 → 36, 83

4. Luke ran for 79 minutes. Then he swam for 48 minutes. How many minutes did Luke spend doing these two things?

   127 minutes (label)

   127 → 79, 48

UNIT 9 LESSON 11 Story Problems with Addition and Subtraction 197

Homework and Remembering page 197

9–11 **Targeted Practice** **Goal:** Solve story problems.

This page can be used with children who need extra practice solving story problems.

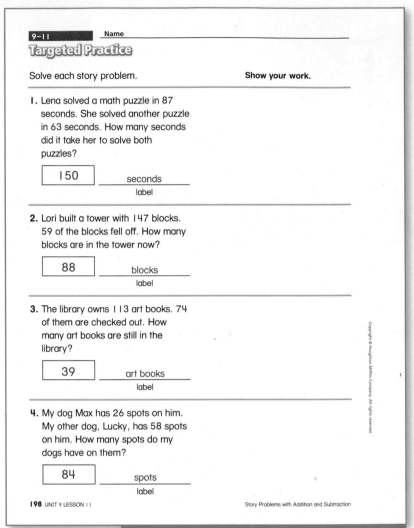

9–11 **Targeted Practice** Name ____________

Solve each story problem. **Show your work.**

1. Lena solved a math puzzle in 87 seconds. She solved another puzzle in 63 seconds. How many seconds did it take her to solve both puzzles?

   150 seconds (label)

2. Lori built a tower with 147 blocks. 59 of the blocks fell off. How many blocks are in the tower now?

   88 blocks (label)

3. The library owns 113 art books. 74 of them are checked out. How many art books are still in the library?

   39 art books (label)

4. My dog Max has 26 spots on him. My other dog, Lucky, has 58 spots on him. How many spots do my dogs have on them?

   84 spots (label)

198 UNIT 9 LESSON 11 Story Problems with Addition and Subtraction

Homework and Remembering page 198

Home or School Activity

Social Studies Connection

Distance on a Map Make a simple map like the one shown on the right. Have children find the total distance between several places on the map. Then have them write and solve an addition and subtraction story problem using the information in the map.

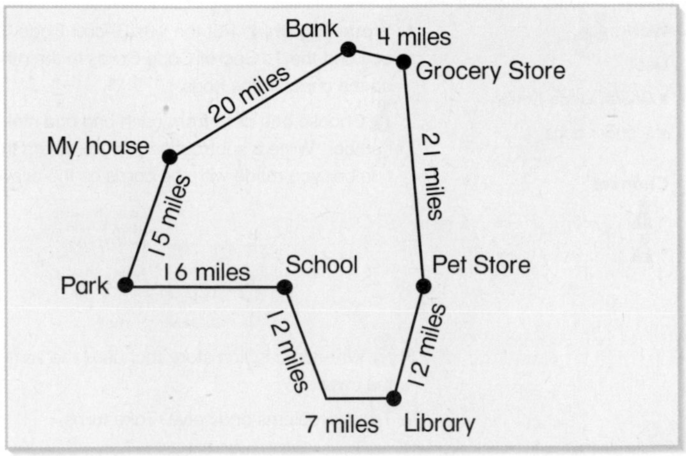

UNIT 9 LESSON 12

Math Mountain Equations with Larger Numbers

Lesson Objectives

- Identify partners in numbers to 200.
- Subtract and count on to find unknown partners.
- Generate eight equations from a Math Mountain.

Vocabulary

money string	partner
Math Mountain	unknown partner
equation	

The Day at a Glance

Today's Goals	Materials	
1 Teaching the Lesson **A1:** Generate equations from Math Mountains with 2- and 3-digit totals. **A2:** Find unknown partners by subtracting and by counting on.	**Lesson Activities** Student Activity Book pp. 299–300 Homework and Remembering pp. 199–200 Symbol Cards (TRB M45) Index cards 120 Poster	**Going Further** Activity Cards 9-12 MathBoard materials *100th Day Worries* by Margery Cuyler and Arthur Howard Math Journals
2 Going Further ▸ Differentiated Instruction		
3 Homework and Spiral Review		

Use Math Talk today!

Keeping Skills Sharp

Quick Practice — 5 MINUTES

Goals: Show ways to make money amounts between one and two dollars.

Money Strings Have the class choose two money amounts between one and two dollars. Have two to four **Student Leaders** work at the board while the rest of the children work at their seats. Children should write combinations of dollars and/or coins that equal the amounts they choose. (See Unit 9 Lesson 11.)

$1.49 = $1 + 25¢ + 10¢ + 10¢ + 1¢ + 1¢ + 1¢ + 1¢ = 25¢ + 25¢ + 25¢ + 25¢ + 10¢ + 10¢ + 10¢ + 5¢ + 5¢ + 5¢ + 1¢ + 1¢ + 1¢ + 1¢ and so on.

Repeated Quick Practice
Use these Quick Practices from previous lessons.

- **Teen Subtraction Flash** (See Unit 9 Lesson 1.)
- **Make-a-Ten Cards: Subtraction** (See Unit 7 Lesson 5.)

Daily Routines

Quarters and Other Coins
Making and Counting Coins that Make a Quarter, Counting to 200¢ by 25¢, Making and Counting Dollars and Cents: 3-Digit Numbers as Dollars and Cents
(See pp. xxvi–xxvii.)

▸ Led by Student Leaders

Money Routine Using the 120 Poster, Using the Money Flip Chart, Using the Number Path, Using Secret Code Cards
(See pp. xxiii–xxv.)

▸ Led by Student Leaders

1 Teaching the Lesson

Activity 1

Math Mountain Equations

30 MINUTES

Goal: Generate equations from Math Mountains with 2- and 3-digit totals.

Materials: Student Activity Book page 299, Symbol Cards (from Unit 1 Lesson 18 or TRB M45), index cards (3 per child)

NCTM Standards:
Number and Operations
Problem Solving
Representation

Alternate Approach

Symbol Cards If children have difficulty recognizing how the equations relate to the Math Mountain, have them write 14, 8, and 6 on separate index cards. They can use the +, −, and = symbol cards to rearrange different equations. Challenge children to manipulate the cards to find all 8 equations for the teen number 14 on their own.

English Language Learners

Make sure children can identify the *total* and *partners* in the 14, 8, 6 Math Mountain.

- **Beginning** Point to 6. Ask: **Is 6 a *partner* or the *total*?** partner Continue with 14 and 8.
- **Intermediate** Say: **The *partners* are 8 and __.** 6 **14 is the __.** total
- **Advanced** Ask: **Which number is the *total*?** 14 **What do we call 8 and 6?** partners

▶ Review Teen Math Mountains WHOLE CLASS

Draw a 14, 8, 6, Math Mountain on the board.

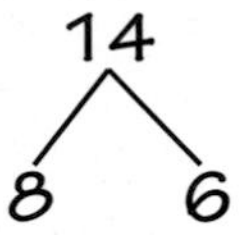

Ask for Ideas Use it as an example to review equations from Math Mountains. Elicit as much from the children as possible.

$14 = 8 + 6$	$8 + 6 = 14$
$14 = 6 + 8$	$6 + 8 = 14$
$14 - 8 = 6$	$6 = 14 - 8$
$14 - 6 = 8$	$8 = 14 - 6$

The equations in the second column are the same as those in the first column, but with the sides of the equation reversed. Emphasize that 8 and 6 are *partners* of 14 and 14 is the *total.*

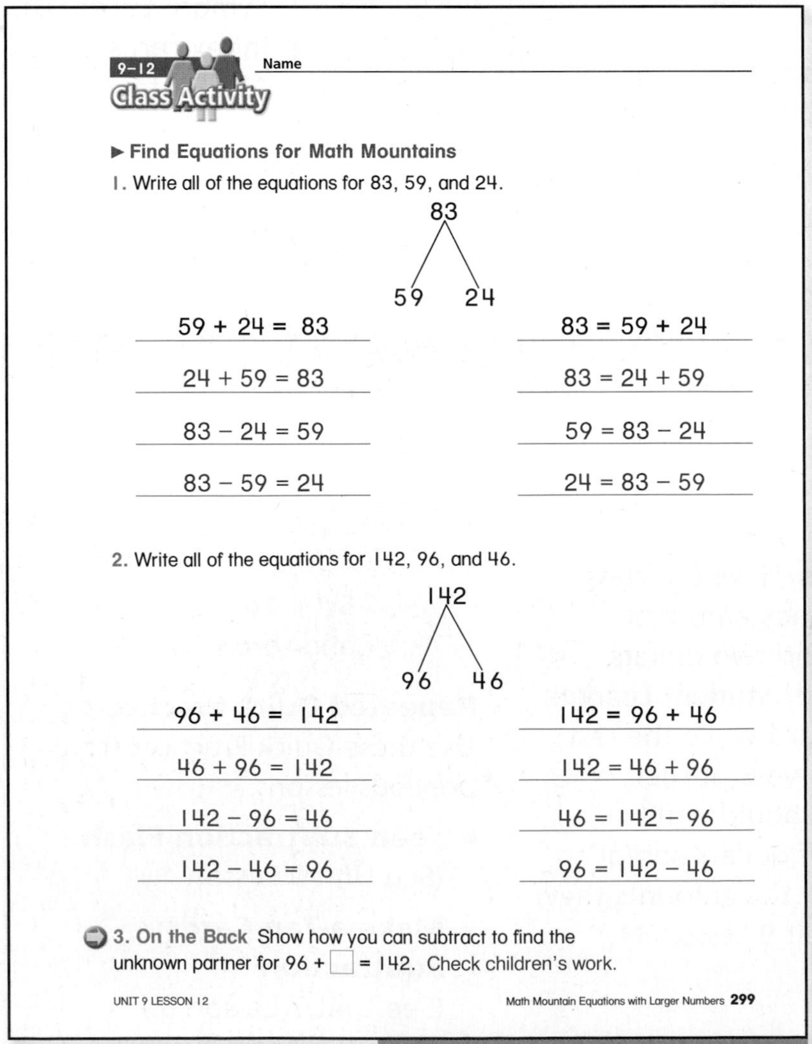
9-12 Class Activity
Name

▶ Find Equations for Math Mountains

1. Write all of the equations for 83, 59, and 24.

83
59 24

59 + 24 = 83	83 = 59 + 24
24 + 59 = 83	83 = 24 + 59
83 − 24 = 59	59 = 83 − 24
83 − 59 = 24	24 = 83 − 59

2. Write all of the equations for 142, 96, and 46.

142
96 46

96 + 46 = 142	142 = 96 + 46
46 + 96 = 142	142 = 46 + 96
142 − 96 = 46	46 = 142 − 96
142 − 46 = 96	96 = 142 − 46

3. On the Back Show how you can subtract to find the unknown partner for 96 + ☐ = 142. Check children's work.

UNIT 9 LESSON 12 Math Mountain Equations with Larger Numbers 299

Student Activity Book page 299

▶ Find Equations for Math Mountains WHOLE CLASS

Erase the numbers in the Math Mountain and replace them with 83, 59, and 24.

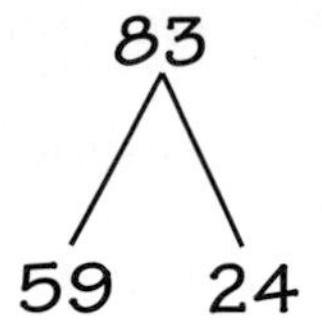

Math Talk Have children discuss whether or not these larger numbers will work the same way as the smaller numbers did on the teen Math Mountain. For example, will the two bottom numbers added together equal the top number (the total)? Emphasize that 59 and 24 are partners of 83.

Direct children's attention to Student Activity Book page 299. Work as a class to find all the equations that can be generated from the three numbers. Write them on the board as children write them on the page.

$59 + 24 = 83 \qquad 83 = 59 + 24$

$24 + 59 = 83 \qquad 83 = 24 + 59$

$83 - 24 = 59 \qquad 59 = 83 - 24$

$83 - 59 = 24 \qquad 24 = 83 - 59$

Refer children to the 142, 96, and 46 Math Mountain on Student Activity Book page 299. Have them work individually to generate all eight equations for the numbers in the Math Mountain.

When the majority of the class has finished, invite various children to create a story problem for one of the equations they wrote. They should use a sketch of a Math Mountain with one of the numbers erased to illustrate their problem.

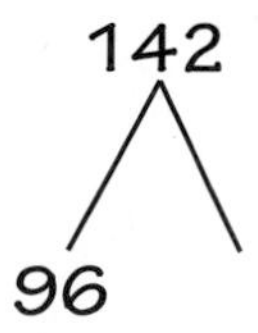

Teaching Note

What to Expect from Students Children may have an easier time writing equations for larger numbers if they recognize that the patterns for writing the equations for 2-digit and 3-digit numbers are the same as for teen numbers. After children write the eight equations for the 83, 59, and 24 Math Mountain, have them compare the equations to the set for 14, 8, and 6. Ask them how the equations are alike and different. See if they can pair the equations that have the same order and structure, but different numbers (example: $14 = 8 + 6$ and $83 = 59 + 24$).

The Learning Classroom

Building Concepts Note that the sample problem for the Math Mountain shown might be expressed as subtraction ($142 - 96 = ?$) or as unknown partner addition ($96 + ? = 142$). These two ways of showing the problem will set up the strategies of *subtracting* and *counting on* to unknown partners. Exercise 3 will help children make the connection between unknown partner (or mystery) addition and subtraction. Both ways of showing the problem emphasize that the smaller numbers are partners of the larger number, which is the total.

1 Teaching the Lesson (continued)

Activity 2

Two Ways to Find Unknown Partners

20 MINUTES

Goal: Find unknown partners by subtracting and by counting on.

NCTM Standards:
Number and Operations
Problem Solving
Representation

▶ Subtract to Find the Unknown Partner

WHOLE CLASS

Write 96 + ☐ = 142 on the board.

Have several children work at the board to subtract and find the unknown partner. The rest of the class may work at their seats.

- What is one way to find a unknown partner? subtract
- Summarize how you subtract to find a unknown partner. Subtract the smaller number (the partner) from the total.

Possible subtraction method:

```
                13
               1̶4̶12
  142          1̶4̶2̶
 - 96         - 96
 ----         ----
                46
```

▶ Count On to Find the Unknown Partner

WHOLE CLASS

Now have children count on to find the unknown partner. Ask volunteers to demonstrate.

- We can start at 96 and count on. We could count on by ones: Put 96 in our heads, 97, 98, 99, 100, 101, … 142. Is this a good way to count on? No. It takes a long time to count by ones.
- Can we count on using a shorter way?
- We can count up to the next ten and count by tens until we get close to 142: 96, 106, 116, 126, 136, (now we shift!) 137, 138, 139, 140, 141, 142.

Discuss the advantages of each method for finding an unknown partner.

Differentiated Instruction

Extra Help You may want to display the front side of the 120 Poster for 1 to 120 and the back side of the 120 Poster for the numbers 121 to 240 to help children count on by tens and ones when they find unknown partners.

Ongoing Assessment

Write the Math Mountain for 78, 36, and 42 on the board. Have children write the eight equations for this Math Mountain.

Differentiated Instruction

Intervention — Activity Card 9-12

From Equations to a Math Mountain

Activity Card 9-12 ●

Work: (one child)
Use:
- MathBoard materials

48 + 26 = 74	74 = 48 + 26
26 + 48 = 74	74 = 26 + 48
74 − 48 = 26	26 = 74 − 48
74 − 26 = 48	48 = 74 − 26

1. Look at the eight equations above.
2. Draw a Math Mountain for the equations. Include the + and − signs.
3. Create other equations and Math Mountains.

Unit 9, Lesson 12

Activity Note Each child needs MathBoard materials. Have children share their Math Mountains with others and explain their work.

Math Writing Prompt

Unknown Partner Show how you can subtract to find the unknown partner for 68 + □ = 112.

Software Support

Warm Up 10.13

On Level — Activity Card 9-12

Fill in the Equations

Activity Card 9-12 ▲

Work: (one child)
Use:
- MathBoard materials

85 = 46 + 39	85 − 46 = 39
85 = 39 + 46	85 − 39 = 46

1. Look at the four equations above.
2. Draw the Math Mountain for these equations. Include the + and − signs.
3. Write the four other equations for this Math Mountain.
   Sample answer: 46 + 39 = 85, 39 + 46 = 85, 39 = 85 − 46, 46 = 85 − 39
4. **Math Talk** Share with a friend how you decided what the Math Mountain should be.

Unit 9, Lesson 12

Activity Note Each child needs MathBoard materials. Make sure children realize they need to find the missing equations.

Math Writing Prompt

Count On Show how you can count on to find the unknown partner for 65 + □ = 123.

Software Support

Country Countdown: Block Busters, Level R

Challenge — Activity Card 9-12

Mental Math Match

Activity Card 9-12 ■

Work: (pairs)
Use:
- MathBoard materials

Choose:
- 1
- 2

1. (1) Create a Math Mountain with an unknown partner.
2. (2) Create a Math Mountain with an unknown partner.
3. Trade Math Mountains with your partner. Each finds the unknown partner.
4. Write all the possible equations for each Math Mountain.

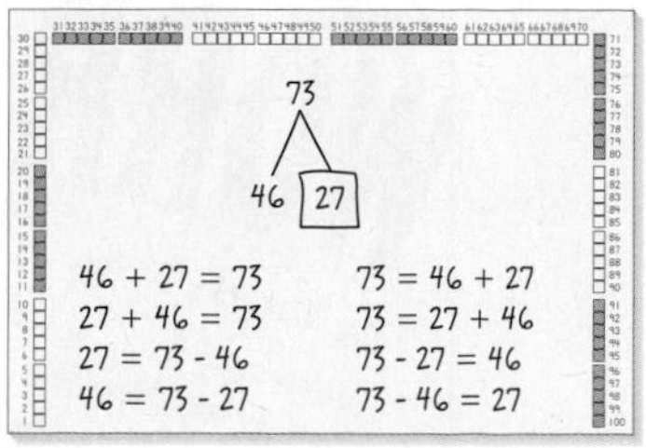

73
46
27
46 + 27 = 73
27 + 46 = 73
27 = 73 - 46
46 = 73 - 27
73 = 46 + 27
73 = 27 + 46
73 - 27 = 46
73 - 46 = 27

Unit 9, Lesson 12

Activity Note Each pair needs MathBoard materials. Children should not use one-digit numbers in their Math Mountains.

Math Writing Prompt

Multiple Answers Draw two different Math Mountains that have a total of 92.

Software Support

Course II: Module 2: Unit 1: Differences within 100

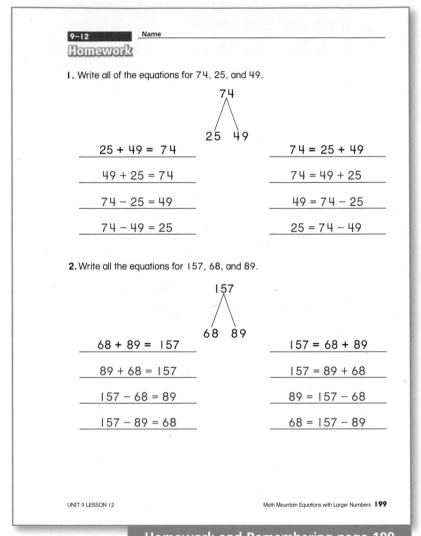

3 Homework and Spiral Review

9–12 Homework Goal: Additional Practice

This Homework page provides practice generating equations from Math Mountains.

9–12 **Homework** Name ______

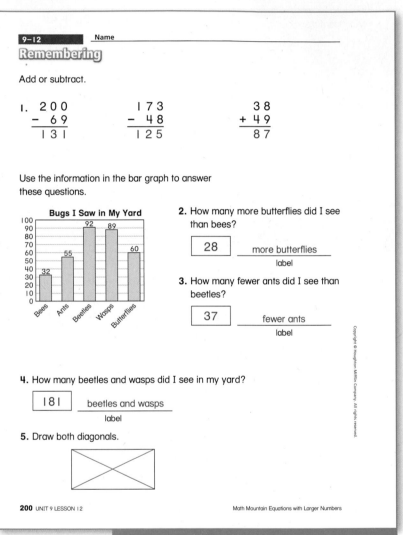

1. Write all of the equations for 74, 25, and 49.

74
25 49

25 + 49 = 74	74 = 25 + 49
49 + 25 = 74	74 = 49 + 25
74 − 25 = 49	49 = 74 − 25
74 − 49 = 25	25 = 74 − 49

2. Write all the equations for 157, 68, and 89.

157
68 89

68 + 89 = 157	157 = 68 + 89
89 + 68 = 157	157 = 89 + 68
157 − 68 = 89	89 = 157 − 68
157 − 89 = 68	68 = 157 − 89

UNIT 9 LESSON 12 Math Mountain Equations with Larger Numbers **199**

Homework and Remembering page 199

9–12 Remembering Goal: Spiral Review

This Remembering activity would be appropriate anytime after today's lesson.

9–12 **Remembering** Name ______

Add or subtract.

1. 200 − 69 = 131 173 − 48 = 125 38 + 49 = 87

Use the information in the bar graph to answer these questions.

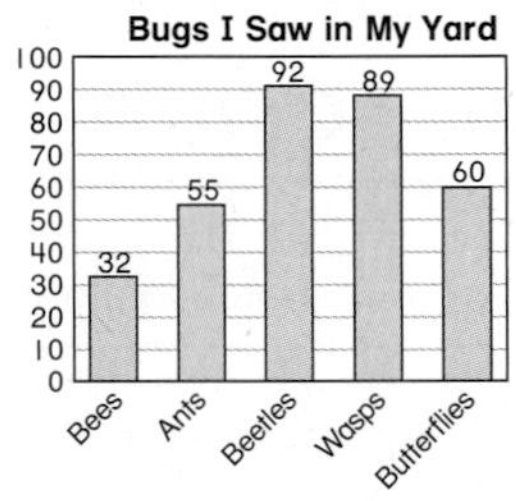

2. How many more butterflies did I see than bees?

28 more butterflies (label)

3. How many fewer ants did I see than beetles?

37 fewer ants (label)

4. How many beetles and wasps did I see in my yard?

181 beetles and wasps (label)

5. Draw both diagonals.

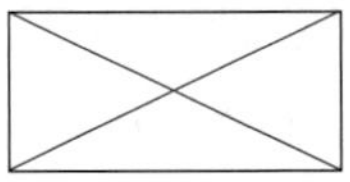

200 UNIT 9 LESSON 12 Math Mountain Equations with Larger Numbers

Homework and Remembering page 200

Home or School Activity

Literature Connection

100th Day Worries Read aloud or have children read *100th Day Worries* by Margery Cuyler and Arthur Howard (Simon & Schuster Children's Publishing, 2000). Then have them identify any partners of 100 and write the numbers as Math Mountains. Children then write the eight equations for the numbers in each Math Mountain.

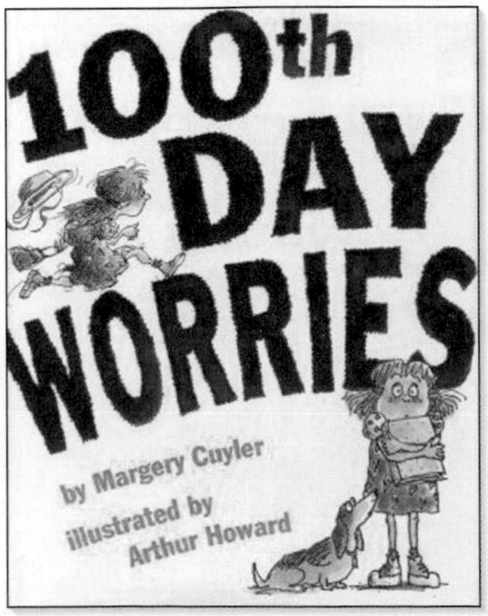

UNIT 9 LESSON 13

Practice Addition and Subtraction

Lesson Objectives

- Use a preferred method to solve addition and subtraction problems.
- Explain a method for solving 2-digit addition and subtraction problems.

Vocabulary

dollar	total
money string	group
partner	ungroup

The Day at a Glance

Today's Goals	Materials	
1 Teaching the Lesson A: Solve 2-digit addition and subtraction problems, and explain the method for solving them.	**Lesson Activities** Student Activity Book pp. 301–302 Homework and Remembering pp. 201–202	**Going Further** Activity Cards 9-13 120 Poster (TRB M60) Index cards Math Journals
2 Going Further ▸ Differentiated Instruction		
3 Homework and Targeted Practice		

Use Math Talk today!

Keeping Skills Sharp

Quick Practice — 5 MINUTES

Goals: Monitor progress in subtracting 2-digit numbers.

Quick Check: Monitor children's progress with a brief Quick Check. Remind children of testing protocols, and then write the following exercises on the board.

$$\begin{array}{r} 64 \\ +\ 97 \\ \hline \end{array} \qquad \begin{array}{r} 132 \\ -\ 78 \\ \hline \end{array}$$

Repeated Quick Practice Use these Quick Practices from previous lessons.

- ▸ **Teen Subtraction Flash** (See Unit 9 Lesson 1.)
- ▸ **Money Strings** (See Unit 9 Lesson 11.)

Daily Routines

Quarters and Other Coins Making and Counting Coins that Make a Quarter, Counting to 200¢ by 25¢, Making and Counting Dollars and Cents: 3-Digit Numbers as Dollars and Cents (See pp. xxvi–xxvii.)

▸ Led by Student Leaders

Money Routine Using the 120 Poster, Using the Money Flip Chart, Using the Number Path, Using Secret Code Cards (See pp. xxiii–xxv.)

▸ Led by Student Leaders

1 Teaching the Lesson

Activity

Solve and Explain

50 MINUTES

Goal: Solve 2-digit addition and subtraction problems, and explain the method for solving them.

Materials: Student Activity Book page 301

NCTM Standards:
Number and Operations
Problem Solving
Communication

The Learning Classroom

Building Concepts Explaining solutions one step at a time helps children experiencing some difficulty to examine each aspect of the addition or subtraction process.

Ongoing Assessment

Write four different 2-digit numbers on separate index cards, such as 46, 38, 91, and 65. Have each child select two cards, then add the numbers and explain the solution. Have children subtract the smaller number from the larger number and explain that solution.

English Language Learners

Write 100 − 25 = 75 on the board. Ask: **Is 100 *larger* or *smaller* than 25?** larger Continue with 75.

- **Beginning** Point and say: **The *larger* number is the *total*. The *smaller* numbers are *partners*.** Have children repeat.
- **Intermediate and Advanced** Ask: **Is the *larger* number the *total*?** yes Say: **The *smaller* numbers are the __.** partners

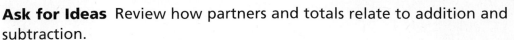

▶ Practice Preferred Methods WHOLE CLASS Math Talk

Ask for Ideas Review how partners and totals relate to addition and subtraction.

- What happens when we solve a subtraction problem? We find one of the smaller numbers (the partners) hiding inside the larger one (the total).
- What happens when we solve an addition problem? We add two partners and find the total.

Have each child choose a suitable method for solving additions and subtractions on Student Activity Book page 301.

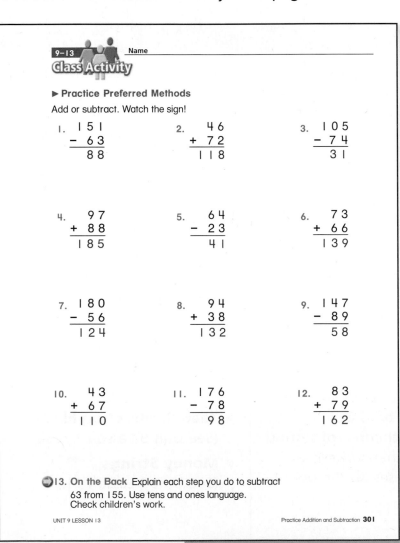

9–13 Class Activity Name ____________

▶ Practice Preferred Methods

Add or subtract. Watch the sign!

1. 151 − 63 = 88
2. 46 + 72 = 118
3. 105 − 74 = 31
4. 97 + 88 = 185
5. 64 − 23 = 41
6. 73 + 66 = 139
7. 180 − 56 = 124
8. 94 + 38 = 132
9. 147 − 89 = 58
10. 43 + 67 = 110
11. 176 − 78 = 98
12. 83 + 79 = 162

13. **On the Back** Explain each step you do to subtract 63 from 155. Use tens and ones language.
Check children's work.

UNIT 9 LESSON 13 Practice Addition and Subtraction 301

Student Activity Book page 301

▶ Explain Your Method PAIRS Math Talk

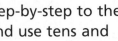

Select several pairs of children to present a solution step-by-step to the class. They should use one method they agree upon and use tens and ones language.

2 Going Further

Differentiated Instruction

Intervention

Activity Card 9-13

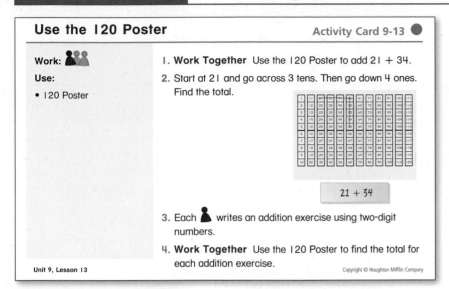

Use the 120 Poster — Activity Card 9-13 ●

Work:

Use:

- 120 Poster

1. **Work Together** Use the 120 Poster to add 21 + 34.
2. Start at 21 and go across 3 tens. Then go down 4 ones. Find the total.

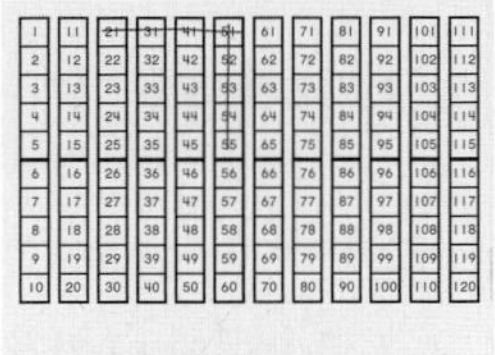

21 + 34

3. Each writes an addition exercise using two-digit numbers.
4. **Work Together** Use the 120 Poster to find the total for each addition exercise.

Unit 9, Lesson 13

Activity Note Each group needs 120 Poster (TRB M60). You may want to check the exercises children write to make sure the totals are less than 120.

Math Writing Prompt

To Group or Not to Group Explain how you know if this exercise needs regrouping.

44 + 34 = ☐

Soar to Success Math Software Support

Warm Up 10.24

On Level

Activity Card 9-13

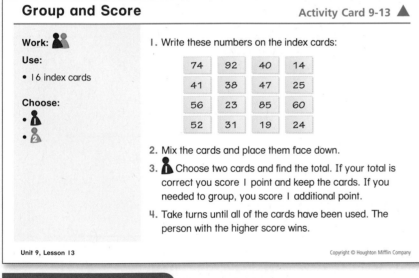

Group and Score — Activity Card 9-13 ▲

Work:

Use:

- 16 index cards

Choose:

- 1
- 2

1. Write these numbers on the index cards:

74	92	40	14
41	38	47	25
56	23	85	60
52	31	19	24

2. Mix the cards and place them face down.
3. Choose two cards and find the total. If your total is correct you score 1 point and keep the cards. If you needed to group, you score 1 additional point.
4. Take turns until all of the cards have been used. The person with the higher score wins.

Unit 9, Lesson 13

Activity Note Each pair needs 16 index cards. You can have pairs repeat the activity by subtracting the lesser number from the greater number. They score an extra point if they need to ungroup.

Math Writing Prompt

Compare and Contrast How is adding 63 + 32 like adding 63 + 38? How is it different?

Harcourt MegaMath Software Support

Country Countdown: Block Busters, Level L

Challenge

Activity Card 9-13

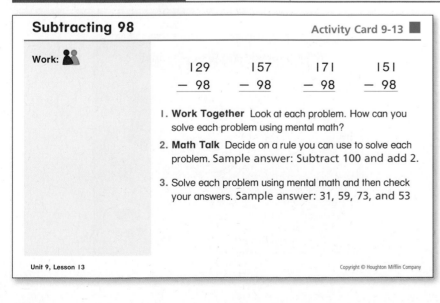

Subtracting 98 — Activity Card 9-13 ■

Work:

$129 - 98$ $\quad$ $157 - 98$ $\quad$ $171 - 98$ $\quad$ $151 - 98$

1. **Work Together** Look at each problem. How can you solve each problem using mental math?
2. **Math Talk** Decide on a rule you can use to solve each problem. Sample answer: Subtract 100 and add 2.
3. Solve each problem using mental math and then check your answers. Sample answer: 31, 59, 73, and 53

Unit 9, Lesson 13

Activity Note Each pair needs to come up with a rule to use mental math to solve the problems. You may want to have pairs share their solutions.

Math Writing Prompt

Use Logical Reasoning Without solving, explain how you know that the sum of 56 + 49 is greater than 100.

Destination Math Software Support

Course II: Module 2: Unit 1: Estimating and Finding Differences within 1,000

3 Homework and Targeted Practice

9–13 Homework **Goal:** Additional Practice

This Homework page provides practice in addition and subtraction.

9–13 Homework Name ____________

Add or subtract. Watch the sign!

1. $75 + 28 = 103$
2. $133 - 85 = 48$
3. $47 + 98 = 145$
4. $87 - 48 = 39$
5. $34 + 18 = 52$
6. $162 - 84 = 78$
7. $76 + 93 = 169$
8. $156 - 29 = 127$
9. $58 + 95 = 153$
10. $121 - 53 = 68$
11. $96 + 37 = 133$
12. $101 - 39 = 62$

UNIT 9 LESSON 13 Practice Addition and Subtraction **201**

Homework and Remembering page 201

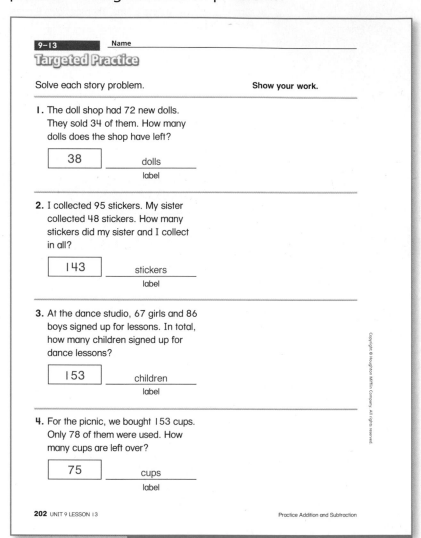

9–13 Targeted Practice **Goal:** Solve story problems.

This page can be used with children who need extra practice solving subtraction problems.

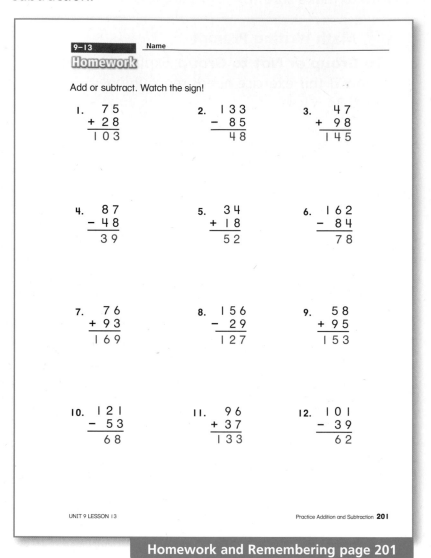

9–13 Targeted Practice Name ____________

Solve each story problem. **Show your work.**

1. The doll shop had 72 new dolls. They sold 34 of them. How many dolls does the shop have left?

38 dolls (label)

2. I collected 95 stickers. My sister collected 48 stickers. How many stickers did my sister and I collect in all?

143 stickers (label)

3. At the dance studio, 67 girls and 86 boys signed up for lessons. In total, how many children signed up for dance lessons?

153 children (label)

4. For the picnic, we bought 153 cups. Only 78 of them were used. How many cups are left over?

75 cups (label)

202 UNIT 9 LESSON 13 Practice Addition and Subtraction

Homework and Remembering page 202

Home or School Activity

Real-World Connection

At the Supermarket Display real flyers or supermarket circulars that advertise fresh produce or other products with 2-digit prices. Have children make a list of items they want to purchase and find the total cost.

UNIT 9 LESSON 14

Buy and Sell with Two Dollars

REAL WORLD Problem Solving

Lesson Objectives

- Add up to find unknown partners.
- Add up to calculate change from two dollars.
- Add money amounts and subtract the total from two dollars numerically or by adding up.

Vocabulary
Adding Up Method
money string
Math Mountain
unknown partner

The Day at a Glance

Today's Goals	Materials	
1 Teaching the Lesson **A1:** Add up to find unknown partners. **A2:** Determine the total cost of two items and make change from $2.00. **2 Going Further** ▸ Differentiated Instruction **3 Homework and Spiral Review**	**Lesson Activities** Student Activity Book pp. 303–304 Homework and Remembering pp. 203–204 Real or play money Small classroom objects with price tags	**Going Further** Activity Cards 9-14 Real or play money Small classroom objects with price tags Index cards Number cubes *Pigs Will Be Pigs: Fun with Math and Money* by Amy Axelrod and Sharon McGinley-Nally Math Journals

Use Math Talk today!

Keeping Skills Sharp

Quick Practice (5 MINUTES)

Goals: Show ways to make money amounts between one and two dollars.

Money Strings Have the class choose two money amounts between one and two dollars. Have two to four **Student Leaders** work at the board while the rest of the children work at their seats, writing combinations of dollars and/or coins that equal the amounts they chose. (See Unit 9 Lesson 11.)

$1.05 = $1 + 1¢ + 1¢ + 1¢ + 1¢ + 1¢ = 25¢ + 25¢ + 25¢ + 10¢ + 10¢ + 5¢ + 5¢ and so on.

$1.56 = 25¢ + 25¢ + 25¢ + 25¢ + 25¢ + 25¢ + 5¢ + 1¢ = $1 + 25¢ + 5¢ + 5¢ + 5¢ + 5¢ + 5¢ + 5¢ + 1¢ and so on.

Repeated Quick Practice Use this Quick Practice from a previous lesson.

▸ **Teen Subtraction Flash** (See Unit 9 Lesson 1.)

Daily Routines

Quarters and Other Coins Making and Counting Coins that Make a Quarter, Counting to 200¢ by 25¢, Making and Counting Dollars and Cents: 3-Digit Numbers as Dollars and Cents (See pp. xxvi–xxvii.)

▸ Led by Student Leaders

Money Routine Using the 120 Poster, Using the Money Flip Chart, Using the Number Path, Using Secret Code Cards (See pp. xxiii–xxv.)

▸ Led by Student Leaders

1 Teaching the Lesson

Activity 1

Introduce the Adding Up Method

10 MINUTES

Goal: Add up to find unknown partners.

NCTM Standards:
Number and Operations
Problem Solving
Representation

English Language Learners

Write 151 and 84 on the board. Point to each digit in 151. Invite children to identify the *ones*, *tens*, and *hundreds*. Continue with 84.

- **Beginning** Say: **This is the *ones* column. There is 1 *one*.** Have children repeat. Continue with the other digits.
- **Intermediate** Ask: **Is this the *ones* column?** yes **How many *ones* in 151?** 1 one Continue with the other digits.
- **Advanced** Ask: **What column is this?** ones **How many *ones* are there?** 1 one Continue with the other digits.

▶ Add Up from a Partner WHOLE CLASS

In this activity, children will explore the Adding Up Method to find an unknown partner. The Adding Up Method is based on the Counting On strategy. Draw this Math Mountain with an unknown partner on the board.

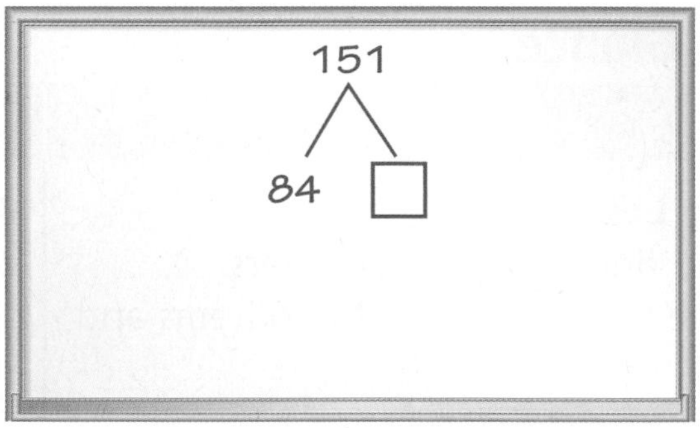

Have children explore and share different ways to add up from 84 to get to 151.

Math Talk in Action

How can we add up from 84 to 151?

James: We start at 84 and add to the next 10: 84 + 6 = 90. Then we count by tens to 150: 100, 110, 120, 130, 140, 150. Then we count one more to 151. That's 6 tens and 7 ones, or 67.

Is there another way to add up from 84 to 151?

Elisha: We could also count by tens from 84 until we get close to 151, then count by ones: 94, 104, 114, 124, 134, 144, and switch, 145, 146, 147, 148, 149, 150, 151. That's also 6 tens and 7 ones, or 67.

Anyone else?

Pamela: We could add 6 to 84 to get to 90. Then we need 61 more to get to 151. That's 6 + 61, or 67.

84 + 6 = 90
+61 = 151
[67]

Sean: I'd add 6 to 84 to get 90. Then I'd add 10 to 90 to get 100. Then I'd add 51 to get to 151. 6 + 10 + 51 = 67.

84 + 6 = 90
+10 = 100
+51 = 151
[67]

Activity 2

The Juice Bar

▶ Introduce the Juice Bar PAIRS Math Talk

9–14 Class Activity Name

▶ Introduce the Juice Bar

Grapefruit Juice 68¢	Red Apple Juice 59¢	Lemon Juice 77¢	Pear Juice 78¢
Green Apple Juice 89¢	Peach Juice 88¢	Orange Juice 97¢	Cantaloupe Juice 87¢
Pineapple Juice 98¢	Raspberry Juice 65¢	Banana Juice 76¢	Watermelon Juice 56¢
Grape Juice 67¢	Celery Juice 58¢	Tomato Juice 96¢	Carrot Juice 79¢

UNIT 9 LESSON 14 Buy and Sell with Two Dollars 303

Student Activity Book page 303

Be sure children have the real or play money they will need for this activity. Children should work in **Helping Pairs.** One will be the customer (or buyer) and the other will be the seller. They will switch roles after each complete transaction.

The customer first reviews the selections from the Juice Bar on Student Activity Book page 303 and chooses two fruit or vegetable juices to mix into a drink. The customer then announces his or her choices to the seller, who adds the two prices together.

The seller announces the total cost of the drink. The customer gives the seller two dollars. The seller then gives the customer the correct amount of change.

The seller can calculate the amount of change numerically or by adding up to find the unknown partner.

Activity continued ▶

30 MINUTES

Goal: Determine the total cost of two items and make change from $2.00.

Materials: Real or play money (dollars, pennies, nickels, dimes, and quarters), small classroom objects with price tags, Student Activity Book pages 303–304

NCTM Standards:
Number and Operations
Problem Solving
Representation

Differentiated Instruction

Extra Help To involve both children throughout the activity, challenge the buyer to also find the sum and change. He or she can check the seller's calculations. Point out that when children shop in real life they should check that they receive the proper change.

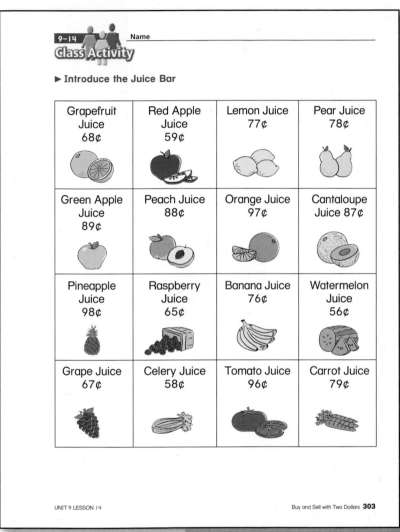

❶ Teaching the Lesson (continued)

The Learning Classroom

Building Concepts Most cash registers today calculate the amount of change a customer will receive. In the past, cashiers would use the Adding Up Method to give change. This method can be used today in situations in which a cash register is not available, for example, at a bake sale, a garage sale, or a school event.

Encourage children to use the Adding Up Method in this activity. Using the method in conjunction with coins provides them with a valuable concrete model for this method.

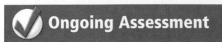

Ongoing Assessment

Circulate around the room. Ask individual students to show you how to use the Adding Up Method to find the change.

▶ Continue Buying and Selling PAIRS

9–14 Class Activity   Name ______

▶ **Continue Buying and Selling**

Choose two juices from the Juice Bar you would like to mix together. Find the total cost. Then find the change from two dollars. Answers will vary.

1. I pick ______
and ______.
Juice #1 price: ______¢
Juice #2 price: + ______¢
Total: ______
200¢ − ______ = ______
My change is ______¢.

2. I pick ______
and ______.
Juice #1 price: ______¢
Juice #2 price: + ______¢
Total: ______
200¢ − ______ = ______
My change is ______¢.

3. I pick ______
and ______.
Juice #1 price: ______¢
Juice #2 price: + ______¢
Total: ______
200¢ − ______ = ______
My change is ______¢.

4. I pick ______
and ______.
Juice #1 price: ______¢
Juice #2 price: + ______¢
Total: ______
200¢ − ______ = ______
My change is ______¢.

304 UNIT 9 LESSON 14   Buy and Sell with Two Dollars

Student Activity Book page 304

Have children fill in the first box on Student Activity Book page 304 to show the transaction they just completed.

This Math Mountain diagram summarizes the relationship between the elements of any transaction.

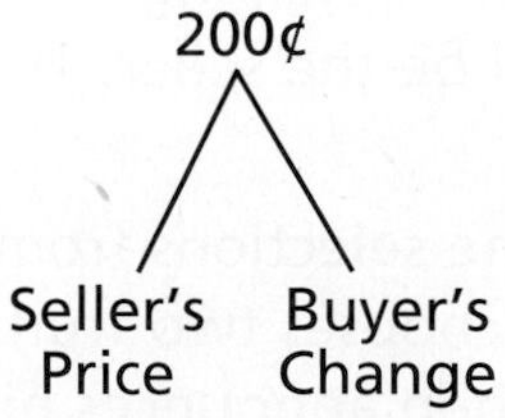

If time allows, demonstrate buying and selling in front of the class with a volunteer. When everyone understands what to do, allow the class to continue in Helping Pairs.

Circulate around the room as children work, answering questions and checking progress. Be sure they are filling in Student Activity Book page 304 correctly.

Intervention Activity Card 9-14

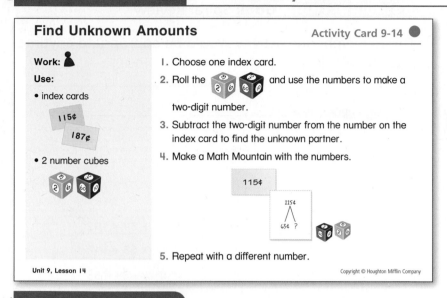

Find Unknown Amounts
Activity Card 9-14

Work: 1 child

Use:
- index cards

- 2 number cubes

1. Choose one index card.
2. Roll the number cubes and use the numbers to make a two-digit number.
3. Subtract the two-digit number from the number on the index card to find the unknown partner.
4. Make a Math Mountain with the numbers.

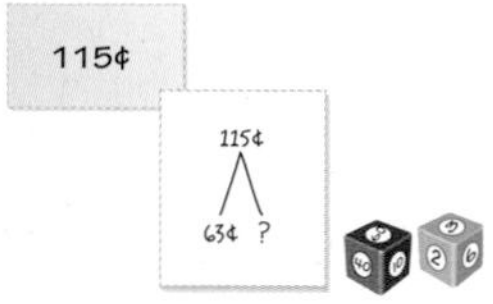

5. Repeat with a different number.

Unit 9, Lesson 14

Activity Note Each child needs two index cards with 115¢ and 187¢ and two number cubes (1–6 and 10–60). Have children check their work with each other.

Math Writing Prompt
Explain Explain how you can add up to find the unknown partner for 69 + ☐ = 132.

Soar to Success Math Software Support
Warm Up 11.22

On Level Activity Card 9-14

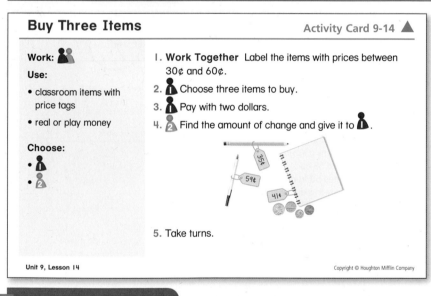

Buy Three Items
Activity Card 9-14

Work: pairs

Use:
- classroom items with price tags
- real or play money

Choose:
- 1
- 2

1. **Work Together** Label the items with prices between 30¢ and 60¢.
2. 1 Choose three items to buy.
3. 1 Pay with two dollars.
4. 2 Find the amount of change and give it to 1.

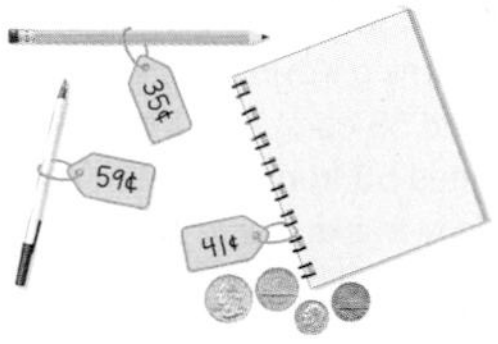

5. Take turns.

Unit 9, Lesson 14

Activity Note Each pair needs 6–7 small classroom items like pencils or pads with price tags and $2.00 in real or play money. Children take turns buying and selling the items.

Math Writing Prompt
Show Your Work You buy items that cost 45¢ and 69¢. How much change will you receive from two dollars? Show your work.

MegaMath Software Support
Numberopolis: Lulu's Lunch Counter, Level Q

Challenge Activity Card 9-14

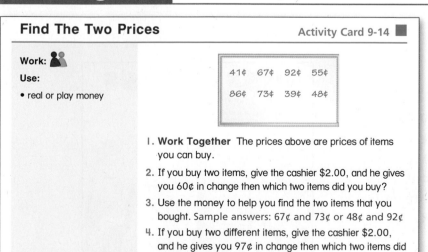

Find The Two Prices
Activity Card 9-14

Work: pairs

Use:
- real or play money

41¢	67¢	92¢	55¢
86¢	73¢	39¢	48¢

1. **Work Together** The prices above are prices of items you can buy.
2. If you buy two items, give the cashier $2.00, and he gives you 60¢ in change then which two items did you buy?
3. Use the money to help you find the two items that you bought. Sample answers: 67¢ and 73¢ or 48¢ and 92¢
4. If you buy two different items, give the cashier $2.00, and he gives you 97¢ in change then which two items did you buy? Sample answer: 55¢ and 48¢

Unit 9, Lesson 14

Activity Note Each pair needs real or play dollars, quarters, dimes, nickels, and pennies. You may want to have children make a list of combinations of items.

Math Writing Prompt
Name Your Price Identify two prices that when added together get 58¢ change from two dollars.

Destination Math Software Support
Course II: Module 3: Unit 2: Money

3 Homework and Spiral Review

9–14 Homework **Goal:** Additional Practice

This Homework page provides practice in making change from two dollars.

9–14 Homework Name ______

Mr. Green wants to buy some things at a flea market.
He will pay for the items with two dollars (200 cents).
How much change will he get back?

Mittens	Toy Binoculars	Toy Camera	Toy Lamb	Plant
57¢	89¢	96¢	78¢	65¢

1. Mr. Green buys the mittens and the plant.
   57 ¢
   \+ 65 ¢
   Total: 122¢
   200¢ − 122¢ = 78¢
   His change will be 78 ¢.

2. Mr. Green buys the toy lamb and the toy camera.
   78 ¢
   \+ 96 ¢
   Total: 174¢
   200¢ − 174¢ = 26¢
   His change will be 26 ¢.

3. Mr. Green buys the toy binoculars and the toy lamb.
   89 ¢
   \+ 78 ¢
   Total: 167¢
   200¢ − 167¢ = 33¢
   His change will be 33 ¢.

4. Mr. Green buys the toy camera and the plant.
   96 ¢
   \+ 65 ¢
   Total: 161¢
   200¢ − 161¢ = 39¢
   His change will be 39 ¢.

UNIT 9 LESSON 14 Buy and Sell with Two Dollars 203

Homework and Remembering page 203

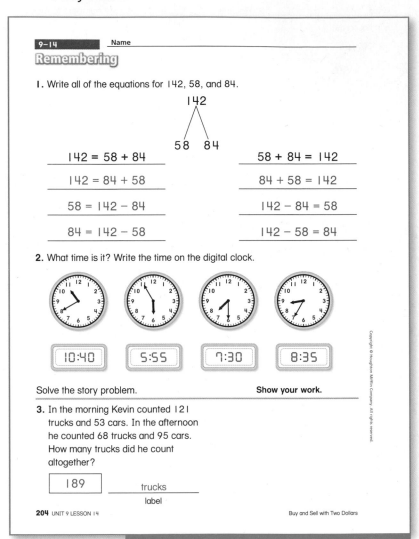

9–14 Remembering **Goal:** Spiral Review

This Remembering activity would be appropriate anytime after today's lesson.

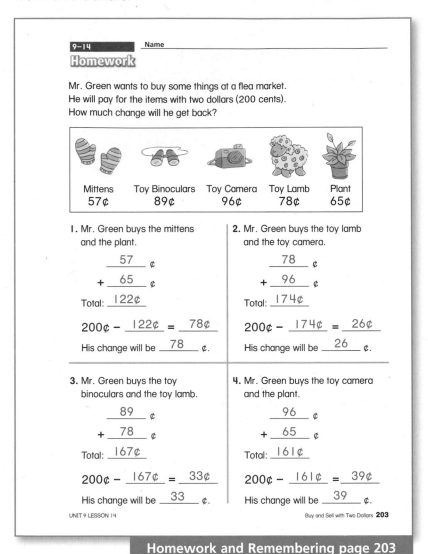

9–14 Remembering Name ______

1. Write all of the equations for 142, 58, and 84.

142
58 84

142 = 58 + 84	58 + 84 = 142
142 = 84 + 58	84 + 58 = 142
58 = 142 − 84	142 − 84 = 58
84 = 142 − 58	142 − 58 = 84

2. What time is it? Write the time on the digital clock.

10:40	5:55	7:30	8:35

Solve the story problem. **Show your work.**

3. In the morning Kevin counted 121 trucks and 53 cars. In the afternoon he counted 68 trucks and 95 cars. How many trucks did he count altogether?

189 trucks
label

204 UNIT 9 LESSON 14 Buy and Sell with Two Dollars

Homework and Remembering page 204

Home or School Activity

Literature Connection

Pigs Will Be Pigs: Fun with Math and Money by Amy Axelrod and Sharon McGinley-Nally (Illustrator) (Aladdin Picture Books, 1997) Read aloud *Pigs Will Be Pigs* to your class. As the pigs search for and find money throughout their home, have the children add up the money amounts and estimate how much the pigs will need for a feast at the Enchanted Enchilada.

UNIT 9 LESSON 15

Story Problems with Unknown Partners

Vocabulary

Adding Up Method
Math Mountain
unknown partner
unknown addend
total

Lesson Objective

- Add up to solve unknown partner story problems.

The Day at a Glance

Today's Goals	Materials: Lesson Activities	Materials: Going Further
1 Teaching the Lesson **A1:** Discover and create ways to solve unknown addend problems. **A2:** Practice adding up to solve unknown addend story problems. **2 Going Further** ► Problem-Solving Strategy: Reasonable Answers ► Differentiated Instruction **3 Homework and Spiral Review**	Student Activity Book pp. 305–306 Homework and Remembering pp. 205–206 MathBoard materials	Activity Cards 9-15 MathBoard materials Index cards Math Journals

Use Math Talk today!

Keeping Skills Sharp

Quick Practice — 5 MINUTES

Goals: Add up to find unknown partners.

Add Up from a Partner Draw the Math Mountain with an unknown partner on the board. Then have one child lead the class in adding up to get from the partner to the total. (See Unit 9 Lesson 14 Activity 1.) One **Student Leader** writes what the class says:

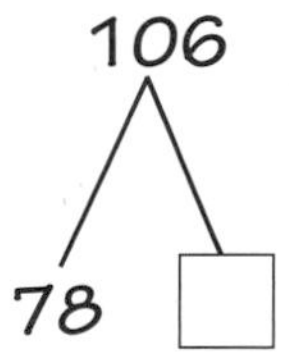

78 + 2 = 80
+26 = 106
[28]

OR

78 + 2 = 80
+20 = 100
+ 6 = 106
[28]

A second Student Leader completes the Math Mountain.

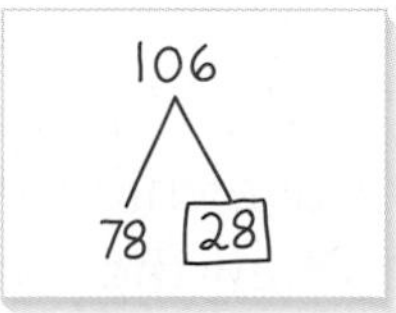

Daily Routines

Quarters and Other Coins Making and Counting Coins that Make a Quarter, Counting to 200¢ by 25¢, Making and Counting Dollars and Cents: 3-Digit Numbers as Dollars and Cents (See pp. xxvi–xxvii.)

► Led by Student Leaders

Money Routine Using the 120 Poster, Using the Money Flip Chart, Using the Number Path, Using Secret Code Cards (See pp. xxiii–xxv.)

► Led by Student Leaders

1 Teaching the Lesson

Activity 1

Find Unknown Addends

25 MINUTES

Goal: Discover and create ways to solve unknown addend problems.

Materials: MathBoard materials

NCTM Standards:
Number and Operations
Problem Solving
Representation

Differentiated Instruction

Advanced Learners Challenge children to find the unknown partner in 78 + □ = 146 two different ways. They might, for example, add up and use the subtraction method. Ask them to compare and contrast the two methods.

English Language Learners

Write 78 + □ = 146, *addend*, and *unknown addend* on the board.

- **Beginning** Say: **78 is an *addend*.** Point to the □. Say: **This is an *unknown addend*.** Have children repeat.
- **Intermediate** Ask: **Is 76 an *addend* or the total?** addend Point to the □. Say: **This is an *unknown* __.** addend
- **Advanced** Have children identify the total and known *addend*. Point to the □. Ask: **What is this?** unknown addend

▶ Try Different Strategies PAIRS

You may want to have children work in pairs for this activity.

Present children with the equation given below and discuss what kind of an equation it is.

78 + □ = 146

- What do we know in this equation? The total is one hundred forty-six. One partner is seventy-eight.
- What don't we know? the other partner
- So what do we need to find out? the second partner

Ask for Ideas Have children make up a story problem for the equation. Be sure it is an unknown addend problem. Accept several suggestions and have the class decide which ones fit the problem.

Write the following example on the board:

Eric had seventy-eight coins in his collection. His uncle gave him some more. Now he has one hundred forty-six coins. How many coins did his uncle give him?

Have children solve the problem on their MathBoards. Observe children as they work. Select several children who used different strategies to hold up their MathBoards to show their solutions. You may want to have one or two children use a pointer to explain their solutions.

This example shows different ways to add up to solve the problem.

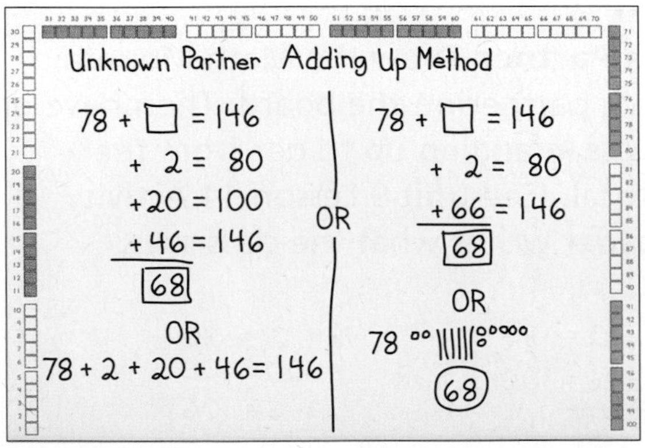

Have children copy the various methods. They can refer to these notes when they solve the problems on Student Activity Book page 305.

Activity 2

Solve Unknown Addend Story Problems

▶ Practice the Adding Up Method PAIRS Math Talk

Direct children's attention to Student Activity Book page 305. You may want to have the children work in **Helping Pairs** to solve the problems.

If children finish early, have them create more unknown addend story problems.

9–15 Class Activity

Name ____________

▶ **Practice the Adding Up Method**

Add up to solve each story problem. **Show your work.**

1. Doug has 92 baseball cards. After he goes shopping today, he will have 175 baseball cards. How many baseball cards is Doug going to buy?

   83 cards (label)

2. Myra had 87 dollars. After she bought some gifts, she had 68 dollars. How much money did Myra spend on gifts?

   19 dollars (label)

3. There were 151 tons of corn in a silo in May. In June there were 213 tons of corn. How many tons of corn were added to the silo?

   62 tons (label)

4. Azim found 113 golf balls. After he gave some of them to Max, he had 54 golf balls left. How many golf balls did Azim give to Max?

   59 golf balls (label)

UNIT 9 LESSON 15 Story Problems with Unknown Partners 305

Student Activity Book page 305

25 MINUTES

Goal: Practice adding up to solve unknown addend story problems.

Materials: Student Activity Book page 305

NCTM Standards:
Number and Operations
Problem Solving
Representation

Class Management

Circulate around the room to help children who are having difficulty. It is helpful to work with them at the board so they can draw and explain the strategies.

Ongoing Assessment

Ask individual children to explain their solution methods.

2 Going Further

Problem-Solving Strategy: Reasonable Answers

Goal: Choose reasonable answers and estimates.

Materials: Student Activity Book page 306

NCTM Standards:
Number and Operations
Problem Solving

Teaching Note

Math Background Being able to determine if an answer is reasonable can help children check an answer or eliminate incorrect answer choices in multiple-choice questions.

An answer is reasonable if it is close to an estimate, is within the right order of magnitude, or makes sense within the context of the problem. If, for example, the problem requires addition to solve, then the answer should be larger than either addend. Rounding and other strategies can be used to pick reasonable answers.

▶ Choose a Reasonable Answer

WHOLE CLASS

Math Talk

Review the directions on Student Activity Book page 306. Be sure children understand that the priced item, coins, and answer choices in each box make up a single exercise.

Direct children's attention to exercise 1. Explain that Ella is going shopping with the coins shown and wants to buy the item pictured. There is not enough money to buy the pencil. Discuss ways to find how much more money Ella needs. Encourage children to use rounding or logical reasoning to select the most reasonable answer. Point out that the best answer choice need not be the exact answer.

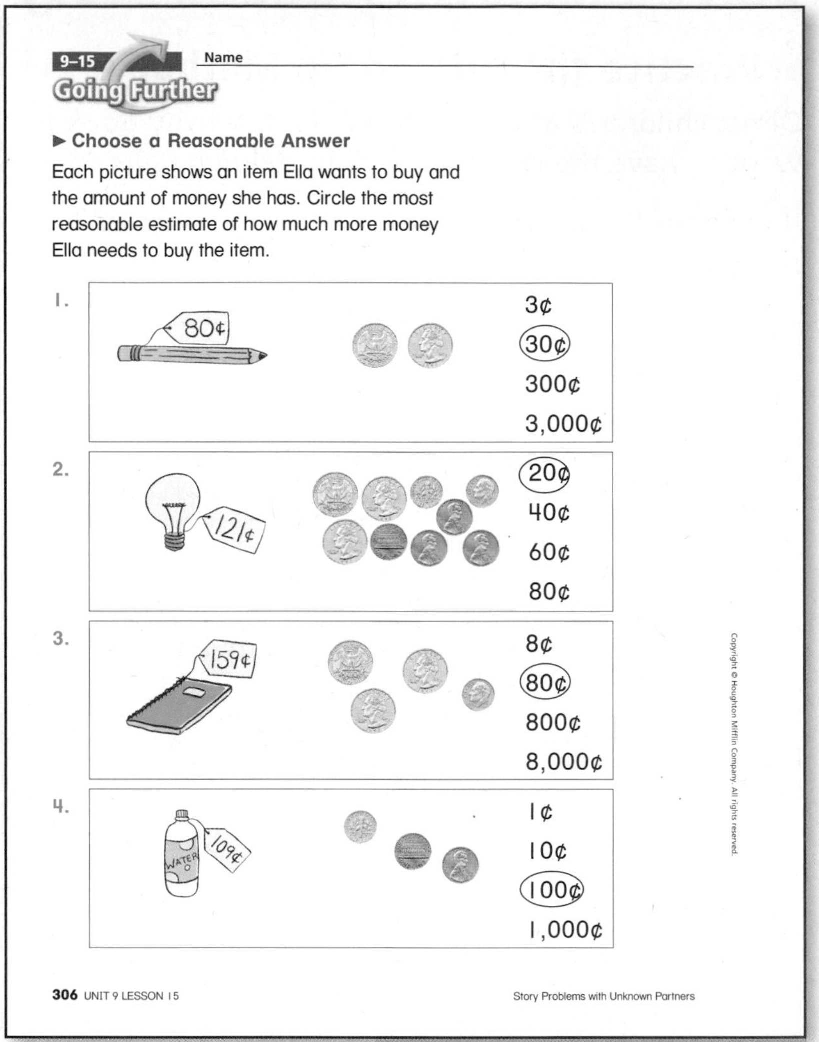
9–15 Going Further Name

▶ Choose a Reasonable Answer

Each picture shows an item Ella wants to buy and the amount of money she has. Circle the most reasonable estimate of how much more money Ella needs to buy the item.

1. 80¢ — 3¢, (30¢), 300¢, 3,000¢

2. 121¢ — (20¢), 40¢, 60¢, 80¢

3. 159¢ — 8¢, (80¢), 800¢, 8,000¢

4. 109¢ WATER — 1¢, 10¢, (100¢), 1,000¢

306 UNIT 9 LESSON 15 Story Problems with Unknown Partners

Student Activity Book page 306

Differentiated Instruction

Extra Help You may want to review the value and features of the quarter, dime, nickel, and penny before children complete this page. If children need practice finding money amounts, pairs can make each other coin combinations and find the value.

Intervention — Activity Card 9-15

Add Up to Find an Unknown Partner
Activity Card 9-15

Work: (pairs)

Use:
- 2 index cards
- MathBoard materials

Choose:
- Student 1
- Student 2

1. Student 1: Write a three-digit number between 100 and 200 on one index card.
2. Student 2: Write a two-digit number on one index card.
3. **Work Together** The sum of the two-digit number and an unknown addend is the three-digit number. Find the unknown addend.
4. Record your steps on the MathBoard.

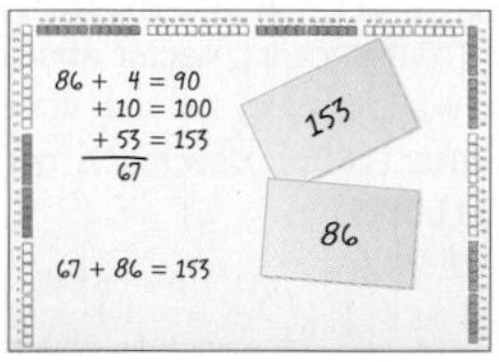

Unit 9, Lesson 15

Activity Note Each pair needs two index cards and MathBoard materials. Have pairs add up to find the unknown addend.

Math Writing Prompt

Add Up Show how you add up to find the unknown partner in
69 + □ = 112.

Soar to Success Math Software Support

Warm Up 11.22

On Level — Activity Card 9-15

Make a Math Mountain
Activity Card 9-15

Work: (pairs)

Use:
- 9 index cards
- MathBoard materials

1. **Work Together** Write the following numbers on the index cards: 132, 72, 68, 35, 64, 119, 56, 84, and 128.
2. Sort the cards into sets of three, so that in each set two of the cards are partners for the third card.
3. Record each set as a Math Mountain on the MathBoard.

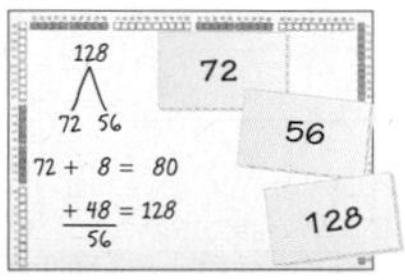

4. To make the total, add up from one partner. Show your work on your MathBoard.

Unit 9, Lesson 15

Activity Note Each pair needs nine index cards and MathBoard materials. Challenge children to make a Math Mountain with different numbers.

Math Writing Prompt

Unknown Addend Story Problem Write an unknown addend story problem about red balloons. The known partner is 47 and the total is 105.

Harcourt Mega Math Software Support

Country Countdown: Block Busters, Level M

Challenge — Activity Card 9-15

Work Backward
Activity Card 9-15

Work: (individual)

? + □ = 118
+ 3 = 60
+ 40 = 100
+ 18 = 118
□

1. Look at the adding up problem above. There are two unknown addends.
2. Use the steps to identify each partner. Sample answer: 57 + 61 = 118
3. Create an adding up problem. Trade with a friend and solve.

Unit 9, Lesson 15

Activity Note Point out that one unknown addend is represented by a question mark (?) and the other one by a box (□).

Math Writing Prompt

Guess and Check The total of two partners is 126. One partner is 38 more than the other partner. What are the two partners? Explain how you found your answer.

Destination Math Software Support

Course II: Module 2: Unit 1: Estimating and Finding Sums less than 1,000

3 Homework and Targeted Practice

9–15 Homework **Goal:** Additional Practice

✓ Include children's completed Homework page as part of their portfolios.

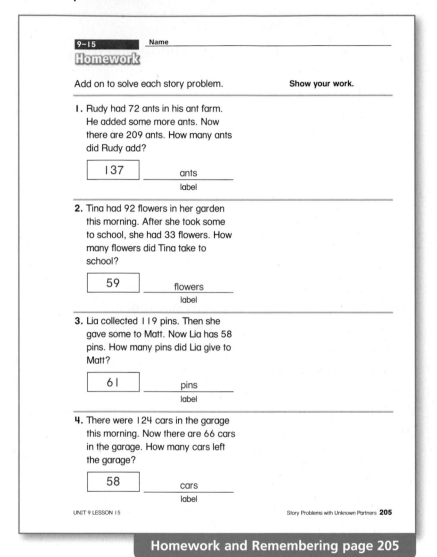

9–15 Homework Name ______

Add on to solve each story problem. **Show your work.**

1. Rudy had 72 ants in his ant farm. He added some more ants. Now there are 209 ants. How many ants did Rudy add?

   137 ants (label)

2. Tina had 92 flowers in her garden this morning. After she took some to school, she had 33 flowers. How many flowers did Tina take to school?

   59 flowers (label)

3. Lia collected 119 pins. Then she gave some to Matt. Now Lia has 58 pins. How many pins did Lia give to Matt?

   61 pins (label)

4. There were 124 cars in the garage this morning. Now there are 66 cars in the garage. How many cars left the garage?

   58 cars (label)

UNIT 9 LESSON 15 Story Problems with Unknown Partners **205**

Homework and Remembering page 205

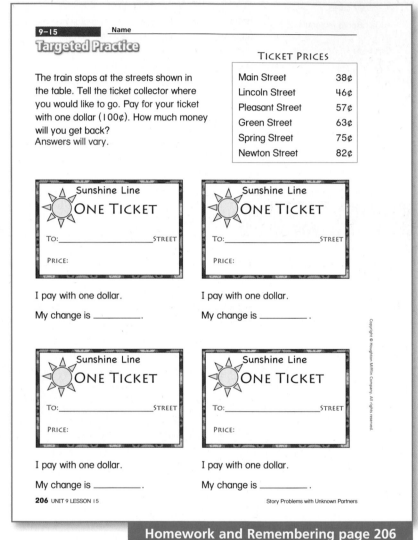

9–15 Targeted Practice **Goal:** Practice buying and making change.

This Targeted Practice page can be used with children who need extra practice buying and making change.

9–15 Targeted Practice Name ______

The train stops at the streets shown in the table. Tell the ticket collector where you would like to go. Pay for your ticket with one dollar (100¢). How much money will you get back?
Answers will vary.

TICKET PRICES

Main Street	38¢
Lincoln Street	46¢
Pleasant Street	57¢
Green Street	63¢
Spring Street	75¢
Newton Street	82¢

Sunshine Line ONE TICKET
To: ______ STREET
PRICE:

I pay with one dollar.
My change is ______.

Sunshine Line ONE TICKET
To: ______ STREET
PRICE:

I pay with one dollar.
My change is ______.

Sunshine Line ONE TICKET
To: ______ STREET
PRICE:

I pay with one dollar.
My change is ______.

Sunshine Line ONE TICKET
To: ______ STREET
PRICE:

I pay with one dollar.
My change is ______.

206 UNIT 9 LESSON 15 Story Problems with Unknown Partners

Homework and Remembering page 206

Home or School Activity

Science Connection

Temperature Changes Explain that on a Fahrenheit thermometer, the numbers tell us how hot or cold something is. As the number increases, the warmer the temperature gets. For example, 96° temperature is warmer than 46° temperature. Discuss the different types of activities and clothing that are appropriate for different temperatures.

Have children write and solve an unknown addend story problem about an increase in temperature.

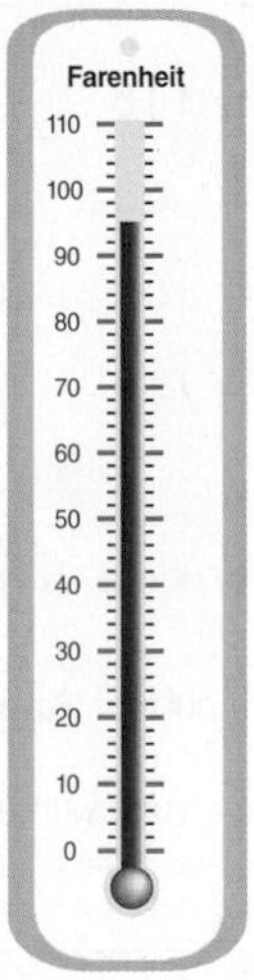

The water temperature was 95°F. Then Julia heated it to 160°F. How much did the temperature of the water increase?

65°F

UNIT 9 LESSON 16

More Story Problems with Unknown Partners

REAL WORLD Problem Solving

Vocabulary

Math Mountain
unknown partner
Adding Up Method
partner
total

Lesson Objective

- Add up to solve unknown partner story problems.

The Day at a Glance

Today's Goals	Materials	
1 Teaching the Lesson **A1:** Review adding up to solve unknown partner problems. **A2:** Practice adding up to solve unknown partner story problems.	**Lesson Activities** Student Activity Book pp. 307–308 Homework and Remembering pp. 207–208 Quick Quiz 3 (Assessment Guide)	**Going Further** Activity Cards 9-16 MathBoard materials Index cards Symbol Cards (TRB M45) Number cubes Math Journals
2 Going Further ▸ Extra Practice ▸ Differentiated Instruction		
3 Homework and Spiral Review		

Use Math Talk today!

Keeping Skills Sharp

Quick Practice — 5 MINUTES

Goals: Add up to find unknown partners.

Add Up from a Partner Draw the Math Mountain with an unknown partner on the board. Then have one child lead the class in adding up to get from the partner to the total. (See Unit 9 Lesson 14 Activity 1.) One **Student Leader** writes what the class says:

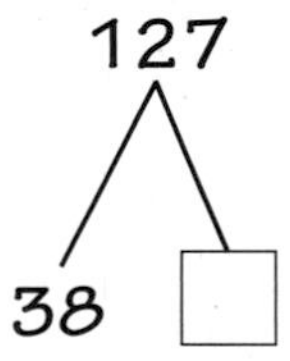

$$\begin{array}{r} 38 + 2 = 40 \\ +87 = 127 \\ \hline \boxed{89} \end{array} \quad \text{OR} \quad \begin{array}{r} 38 + 2 = 40 \\ +80 = 120 \\ +\ 7 = 127 \\ \hline \boxed{89} \end{array}$$

A second Student Leader completes the Math Mountain.

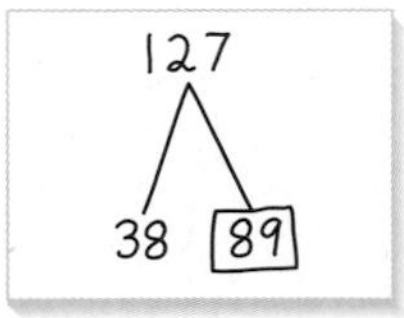

Daily Routines

Quarters and Other Coins Making and Counting Coins that Make a Quarter, Counting to 200¢ by 25¢, Making and Counting Dollars and Cents: 3-Digit Numbers as Dollars and Cents
(See pp. xxvi–xxvii.)

▸ Led by Student Leaders

Money Routine Using the 120 Poster, Using the Money Flip Chart, Using the Number Path, Using Secret Code Cards
(See pp. xxiii–xxv.)

▸ Led by Student Leaders

1 Teaching the Lesson

Activity 1

Review the Adding Up Method

25 MINUTES

Goal: Review adding up to solve unknown partner problems.

NCTM Standards:
Number and Operations
Problem Solving
Representation

Teaching Note

What to Expect from Students By now, children should be skilled at adding up to find an unknown partner. If they are not, try to pinpoint the source of the difficulty. Carefully watch them solve a problem and listen as they talk out the solution. Are they having trouble deciding what information they need to find? Are they making numerical errors when they add up? Do they add up correctly but misunderstand how to use the information to solve the problem?

English Language Learners

Provide support to help children write or tell their own *unknown partner* story problems. Write the example story problem on the board.

- **Beginning** Model how to change the activities and numbers. Have children read the new story problem aloud.
- **Intermediate** Provide children with options for changing the story. For example, say: **Tom and Emma can watch TV, write letters, or draw pictures.**
- **Advanced** Have children work in pairs to change the story problem then tell the new one before they write it.

▶ Find Unknown Addends WHOLE CLASS Math Talk

Have children refer to the notes they took in the last lesson on the Adding Up Method. Present this equation and review the strategy.

$$67 + \square = 165$$

- What do we call this kind of equation? unknown partner
- Why do we call it that? We don't know what the partner is.
- What do we know? What do we want to find out? We know the total and one partner. We have to find the other partner.

Ask for Ideas Have children make up a story problem for the equation. Be sure it is an unknown partner problem. You can accept several suggestions and have the class choose the one they want to solve, or you may want to write the following example problem on the board.

Tom read one hundred sixty-five pages in his book this week. Emma read sixty-seven pages. How many more pages did Tom read than Emma?

Have several children use the **Solve and Discuss** structure at the board while the rest of the children solve the problem at their desks. Remind children that they can use their notes about the Adding Up Method as they work.

You may want to circulate around the room to help children who are having difficulty.

When the class has finished, have the children at the board explain the strategies they used to solve the problem. Have the class discuss the solutions on the board.

Activity 2

Solve Story Problems

▶ Practice the Adding Up Method PAIRS

Refer children to Student Activity Book page 307. You may want to have children work in Helping Pairs to solve the problems.

If children finish early, have them create more unknown partner story problems.

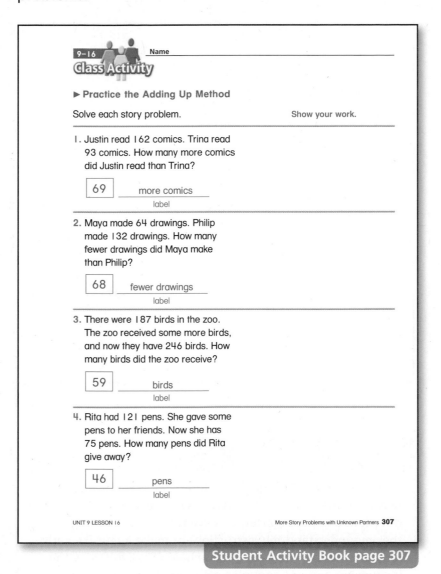

9–16 Class Activity Name ______

▶ Practice the Adding Up Method

Solve each story problem. Show your work.

1. Justin read 162 comics. Trina read 93 comics. How many more comics did Justin read than Trina?

69 more comics
label

2. Maya made 64 drawings. Philip made 132 drawings. How many fewer drawings did Maya make than Philip?

68 fewer drawings
label

3. There were 187 birds in the zoo. The zoo received some more birds, and now they have 246 birds. How many birds did the zoo receive?

59 birds
label

4. Rita had 121 pens. She gave some pens to her friends. Now she has 75 pens. How many pens did Rita give away?

46 pens
label

UNIT 9 LESSON 16 More Story Problems with Unknown Partners 307

Student Activity Book page 307

25 MINUTES

Goal: Practice adding up to solve unknown partner story problems.

Materials: Student Activity Book page 307

NCTM Standards:
Number and Operations
Problem Solving
Representation

Class Management

You may want to circulate around the room to help children who are having difficulty. It is helpful to work with them at the board so they can draw and explain the strategies.

Ongoing Assessment

Have children solve and explain how they find the unknown partner in 59 + □ = 132. Be sure they use the Adding Up Method.

2 Going Further

Extra Practice

Goal: Practice addition and subtraction.

Materials: Student Activity Book page 308

✓ **NCTM Standard:**
Number and Operations

▶ Alphabet Math Puzzle INDIVIDUALS

Have children complete Student Activity Book page 308. Explain that the goal is to discover which letter belongs on each line of the message at the bottom of the page.

▶ Critical Thinking

Challenge children who finish early to create their own alphabet puzzles in the same format as the Extra Practice page. They can then trade and solve each other's puzzles.

9–16 Name ______________________

Extra Practice

▶ Alphabet Math Puzzle

Add or subtract. Then, solve the alphabet puzzle by using the answer for the exercise to find the next letter in the puzzle.

A = $42 + 79 = 121$

O = $142 - 17 = 125$

H = $137 - 76 = 61$

M = $125 + 38 = 163$

C = $126 - 84 = 42$

N = $121 - 37 = 84$

D = $84 + 58 = 142$

A = $163 - 75 = 88$

T = $88 + 49 = 137$

I	C	A	N	D	O	M	A	T	H !
	42	121	84	142	125	163	88	137	61

Student Activity Book page 308

Class Management

Circulate around the room as children begin to solve the puzzle on their own. Check that they understand the directions and have started to solve the puzzle correctly. If they misunderstand the instructions or make a mistake early on, they will spend too much time being challenged by the instructions and not enough time practicing addition and subtraction.

Quick Quiz

See Assessment Guide for Unit 9 Quick Quiz 3.

Intervention — Activity Card 9-16

Make and Solve Unknown Partner Problems
Activity Card 9-16 ●

Work: pairs

Use:
- MathBoard materials
- 5 index cards
- Symbol Cards (TRB M45)

Choose:
- Student 1
- Student 2

1. (Student 2) Write a three-digit number between 100 and 200 on an index card.
2. (Student 1) Write a two-digit number on another index card.
3. Arrange the cards so that they show an unknown partner.

65 + □ = 147

4. Find the unknown partner.
5. Repeat with different numbers.

Unit 9, Lesson 16

Activity Note Each pair needs + and = Symbol Cards (TRB M45), five index cards, and MathBoard materials. On a card draw a □.

Math Writing Prompt

Two Way Explain two ways you might solve the equation 84 + □ = 173.

Soar to Success Math Software Support

Warm Up 10.32

On Level — Activity Card 9-16

Find the Unknown Partners
Activity Card 9-16 ▲

Work: individual

Use:
- MathBoard materials

□ + □ = 136

1. Find at least three different ways to solve the equation above.
2. Show each solution on your MathBoard.

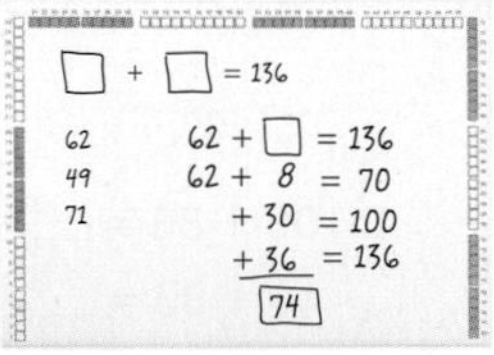

3. For each number you choose, find the unknown partner that will make the equation correct.

Unit 9, Lesson 16

Activity Note Each pair needs MathBoard materials. Suggest that pairs select one number that is less than 100 as the first addend and then find the unknown addend.

Math Writing Prompt

You Decide Is the unknown partner for 59 + □ = 143 the number 74? Explain.

Harcourt MegaMath Software Support

Numberopolis: Carnival Stories, Level R

Challenge — Activity Card 9-16

Number Cube Unknown Partners
Activity Card 9-16 ■

Work: individual

Use:
- 2 number cubes

- MathBoard materials

1. Toss the number cubes to make a two-digit number.
2. Toss the number cubes to make another two-digit number.
3. Add the second number to the first number. Continue until the total is greater than 150.

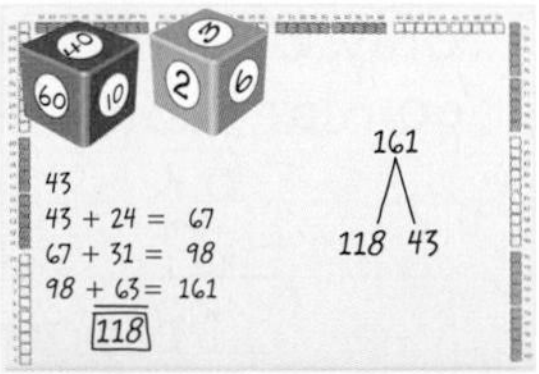

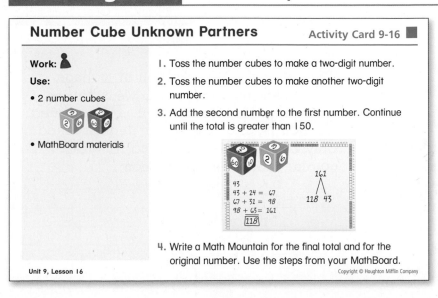

4. Write a Math Mountain for the final total and for the original number. Use the steps from your MathBoard.

Unit 9, Lesson 16

Activity Note Each pair needs two number cubes, one labeled 1–6 and the other one labeled 10–60 and MathBoard materials.

Math Writing Prompt

Write Your Own Write an unknown partner addend story problem about picking blueberries. Use this equation.
58 + □ = 144

Destination Math Software Support

Course II: Module 2: Unit 1: Estimating and Finding Sums less than 1,000

3 Homework and Spiral Review

9–16 Homework **Goal:** Additional Practice

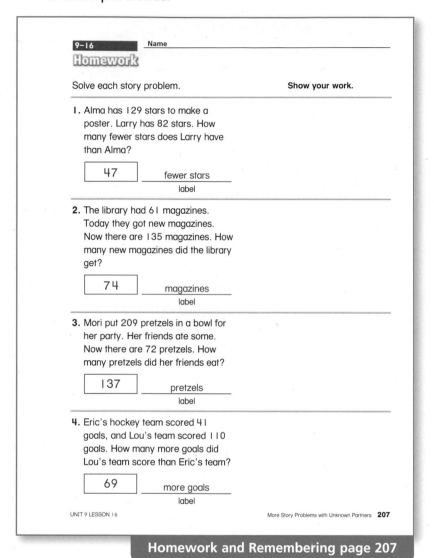

Include children's completed Homework page as part of their portfolios.

9–16 Homework Name ____

Solve each story problem. **Show your work.**

1. Alma has 129 stars to make a poster. Larry has 82 stars. How many fewer stars does Larry have than Alma?

   47 fewer stars (label)

2. The library had 61 magazines. Today they got new magazines. Now there are 135 magazines. How many new magazines did the library get?

   74 magazines (label)

3. Mori put 209 pretzels in a bowl for her party. Her friends ate some. Now there are 72 pretzels. How many pretzels did her friends eat?

   137 pretzels (label)

4. Eric's hockey team scored 41 goals, and Lou's team scored 110 goals. How many more goals did Lou's team score than Eric's team?

   69 more goals (label)

UNIT 9 LESSON 16 — More Story Problems with Unknown Partners 207

Homework and Remembering page 207

9–16 Remembering **Goal:** Spiral Review

This Remembering activity would be appropriate anytime after today's lesson.

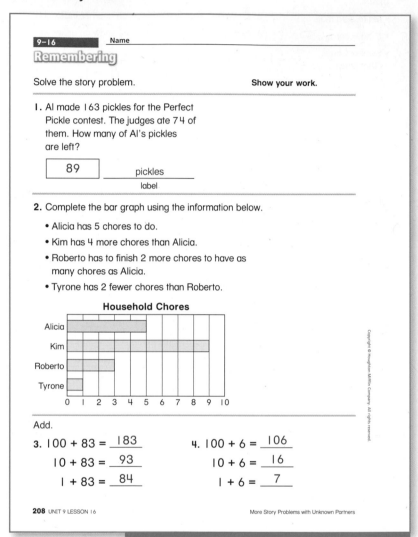

9–16 Remembering Name ____

Solve the story problem. **Show your work.**

1. Al made 163 pickles for the Perfect Pickle contest. The judges ate 74 of them. How many of Al's pickles are left?

   89 pickles (label)

2. Complete the bar graph using the information below.
   - Alicia has 5 chores to do.
   - Kim has 4 more chores than Alicia.
   - Roberto has to finish 2 more chores to have as many chores as Alicia.
   - Tyrone has 2 fewer chores than Roberto.

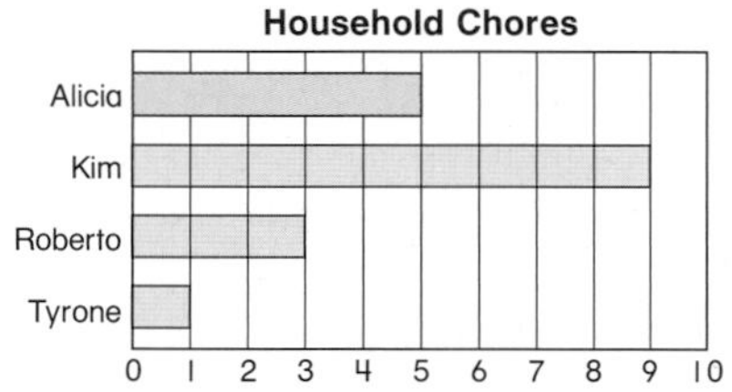

Add.

3. 100 + 83 = 183
   10 + 83 = 93
   1 + 83 = 84

4. 100 + 6 = 106
   10 + 6 = 16
   1 + 6 = 7

208 UNIT 9 LESSON 16 — More Story Problems with Unknown Partners

Homework and Remembering page 208

Home or School Activity

Sports Connection

How Many More Points? Ask children what they know about basketball. Help them research scores of their favorite or local teams. Children will find that the scores for most basketball games are 2-digit, and sometimes 3-digit, numbers. Have children use the actual scores from a basketball game and subtract to find out how many more points one team made than the other. Children could also write a story about a basketball game they saw or played in.

My sister plays basketball at college. Last week my dad and I went to see her play. Her team won! They scored 87 points, and the other team scored only 69. Her team scored 18 more points than the other team.

$$\begin{array}{r} 87 \\ -69 \\ \hline 18 \end{array}$$ points

UNIT 9 LESSON 17

Use Mathematical Processes

REAL WORLD Problem Solving

Lesson Objectives

- Apply mathematical concepts and skills in meaningful contexts.
- Reinforce the NCTM process skills embedded in this unit, and in previous units, with a variety of problem-solving situations.

The Day at a Glance

Today's Goals	Materials	
1 Teaching the Lesson **A1: Science Connection** Identify statements as true, not true, or unsupported. **A2: Reasoning and Proof** Decide whether a math statement is true or false; use examples as proof; write and test a math statement. **A3: Problem Solving** Find numbers that meet given requirements. **A4: Representation** Given information about a set of data, make comparison bars to show the data. **A5: Communication** Identify an error and explain how to correct it.	**Lesson Activities** Student Activity Book pp. 309–310 Homework and Remembering pp. 209–210 10×10 Grid (TRB M62)	**Going Further** Activity Cards 9-17 Secret Code Cards (TRB M3–M4) Index cards Math Journals
2 Going Further Differentiated Instruction		
3 Homework and Spiral Review		

Use Math Talk today!

Keeping Skills Sharp

Quick Practice/Daily Routines	
If you wish to include Quick Practice or a Daily Routine, choose content based on the needs of your class.	**Class Management** Select activities from this lesson that support important goals and objectives, or that help children prepare for state or district tests.

1 Teaching the Lesson

Activity 1

Connections

Math and Science

45 MINUTES

Goals: Identify statements as true, not true, or unsupported.

Materials: Student Activity Book page 309

NCTM Standards:
Reasoning and Proof
Connections

9–17 Class Activity Name ____________

▶ **Math and Science**

Dr. Grant is a zoologist who studies how animals move. She collects data to use in her reports.

One data table tells how far some animals can move in 1 second.

Distance Moved in 1 Second

Animal	Cheetah	Chicken	Elephant	Lion	Spider
Distance	103 feet	13 feet	37 feet	73 feet	1 foot

Dr. Grant wants to compare these distances in a report.
Decide whether a statement is *true* or *not true* or has *no data.*
Ring your answer.

1. An elephant goes farther in 1 second than a lion.
   True (Not True) No Data
2. A cheetah goes farther in 1 second than a spider.
   (True) Not True No Data
3. A chicken and a cheetah travel the same distance in 1 second.
   True (Not True) No Data
4. A spider goes farther in 1 second than a snail.
   True Not True (No Data)
5. Use the data. Write 2 true statements for the report.
   Answers may vary. Possible answer: The cheetah went farther in 1 second than the elephant or the lion. The spider traveled a shorter distance in 1 second than any other animal in the list.

UNIT 9 LESSON 17 Use Mathematical Processes 309

Student Activity Book page 309

Teaching Note

Math Background The first two activities in this lesson provide an informal introduction to the concepts of truth and proof of statements. In the first activity, children decide on the validity of statements based on whether the given data support the statements. In the second activity, children use examples to support assertions about the truth or falsity of statements.

▶ What Is Science?

Ask for Ideas Elicit from children what they know about science and what scientists do.

▶ What is a scientist? What do scientists study? Who can be a scientist? Allow children to share their ideas.

Tell children that a zoologist is a scientist who studies and works with animals. The table contains data that Dr. Grant collected about how far some animals can move in 1 second. Have children explore this data and comment on what they see.

▶ Review Statements — Math Talk

Tasks 1–4 Ask children to read the statements in items 1–4, decide whether the data shows that the statements are true, not true, or if there is no data to use, and to ring the answer. When children finish, ask questions like these to check on children's thinking.

▶ Can the elephant go farther in 1 second than a lion? No. How do you know? 37 feet, the distance the elephant went, is not greater than 73 feet, the distance the lion went.

▶ Can the spider go farther in 1 second than a snail? The question cannot be answered because snails are not listed in the data table, so the statement has no data to support it. What other information would you need to be able to decide about the truth of this statement? the distance a snail can move in 1 second

Task 5 Tell children that Dr. Grant needs more true statements about the data to use in her report, so they will help her by writing some. After they complete the statements, have volunteers read theirs and let others tell what data support the statements.

Activity 2 **Reasoning and Proof**

True or False

45 MINUTES

Goals: Decide whether a math statement is true or false; use examples as proof; write and test a math statement.

Materials: Student Activity Book page 310

NCTM Standards:

Problem Solving | Communication
Reasoning and Proof | Representation

9–17 Class Activity Name ____ Date ____

▶ True or False?

Mathematicians must support their statements with proof. One example can prove that a statement is false. It is harder to show that a statement is true.

Decide whether each statement is true or false. Then show why. Find 3 examples to support true statements. Find one example to show that a statement is false.

1. If you double any number, the answer is always even.
True. Possible examples: $3 + 3 = 6$; $8 + 8 = 16$; $22 + 22 = 44$

2. You can always divide a rectangle into 4 triangles with 1 straight line.
False. Possible examples shown: 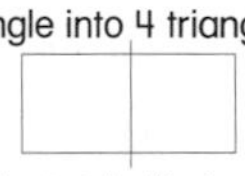 or 

3. If you add two odd numbers, the total will always be an odd number.
False. Possible example: $3 + 9 = 12$. 12 is an even number.

4. There are many different ways to make 50¢ with nickels, dimes, and quarters.
True. Possible examples: 2 quarters; 3 dimes and 4 nickels; 1 quarter, 2 dimes, and 1 nickel.

5. Write a math statement. It can be true or false. Tell whether it is true or false. Use examples.
Answers may vary. Possible answer: If you add 2 to a number and then subtract 2 from the total, the answer is 2. False. $4 + 2 = 6$, $6 - 2 = 4$, 4 is not 2.

310 UNIT 9 LESSON 17 Use Mathematical Processes

Student Activity Book page 310

English Language Learners

Write *proof* on the board. Draw a group of 2 trees and 3 trees.

- **Beginning** Say: **This is a *proof*. It shows that $2 + 3 = 5$ is true.** Have children repeat.
- **Intermediate and Advanced** Ask: **Does the drawing show that $2 + 3 = 5$ is true?** yes **Is this a *proof*?** yes

▶ What Is Proof?

Tell children that mathematicians think about different kinds of mathematics and then make a statement about their ideas. Then they must prove, following very detailed rules, whether the statement is true or false. Often the proof consists of examples. To prove that a statement is false, only one example is needed that does not go along with the statement. To prove a statement is true is much harder, and needs examples that cover every possibility.

Tasks 1–4 Point out the four mathematical statements on the student page. Explain that the children's job will be to use words and/or drawings to show why each statement is true or false.

▶ Discuss the Reasoning Math Talk

Use questions like the following to have volunteers tell whether the statements are true or false and to give their examples. Allow others to present different examples.

- ▶ Is the first statement true or false? True. What are some examples that show the statement is true? Write the examples the children give on the board.
- ▶ Is the second statement true or false? False. What example did you find to show the statement is false? Write the examples the children give on the board.

Task 5 Now have children write a math statement and label it as true or false. Ask them to exchange statements with a partner, so the partner can give an example to support whether the statement is true or false. Afterwards let partners share statements and examples with the class.

- ▶ What math statement did you write? Is your statement true or false? What example did your partner use? Write statements, true or false labels, and examples on the board.

Discuss whether the examples support the statements and the true or false labels.

Activity 3

Problem Solving

Number Puzzles

15 MINUTES

Goal: Find numbers that meet given requirements.

NCTM Standards:
Problem Solving
Reasoning and Proof

Write this puzzle on the board.

I am thinking of a number. It is greater than 100 − 30. It is less than 100 − 24. It is an odd number. What number am I thinking of? Three numbers are possible answers: 71, 73, 75

Encourage children to offer different ideas as you discuss the problem.

- ► How did you figure out what my number might be? Answers may vary. Possible answer: 100 − 30 is 70 and 100 − 24 is 76. So the number has to be greater than 70 but less than 76. It is an odd number so the only numbers it can be are 71, 73, and 75.
- ► How can the puzzle be changed so only one number is the answer? Answers may vary. Possible answer: Change "It is greater than 100 − 30" to "It is greater than 103 − 30" and the answer will be 75.

Activity 4

Representation

Make Comparison Bars

15 MINUTES

Goal: Given information about a set of data, make comparison bars to show the data.

Materials: 10 × 10 Grid (TRB M62)

NCTM Standards:
Problem Solving
Connections
Representation

At the zoo are 6 elephants. The number of zebras is 1 more than the number of elephants. There are 3 fewer lions than zebras. How many lions are there? Use comparison bars to represent the situation. Then find the answer. There are 4 lions.

Have children share their comparison-bar diagrams. Ask questions to show how the diagrams were set up.
Answers may vary. Possible diagram:

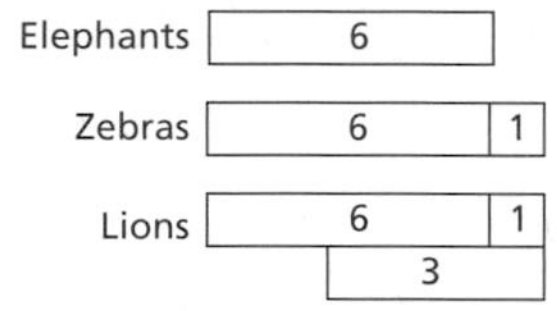

- ► What bar did you draw first? Answers may vary. Possible answer: A bar with 6 for the elephants.
- ► What bar did you draw next? Answers may vary. Possible answer: The bar for the zebras.

Continue in this way to study as many different diagrams as children have made.

Activity 5

Communication

Be a Helper

15 MINUTES

Goal: Identify an error and explain how to correct it.

NCTM Standards:
Problem Solving
Communication

Jason subtracted 39 from 65. His answer was 34. Explain his error. Answers may vary.

Use a **Scenario** structure. Ask one volunteer to describe Jason's error and another to tell how he can correct it. Let several pairs describe possible errors and show ways to correct them.

- ► Explain the mistake you think Jason made. He didn't regroup to get enough ones to subtract 9 from.
- ► Help Jason understand how to do the subtraction. Children work at the board, with the first child carrying out the instructions from the helper.

2 Going Further

Differentiated Instruction

Intervention

Activity Card 9-17

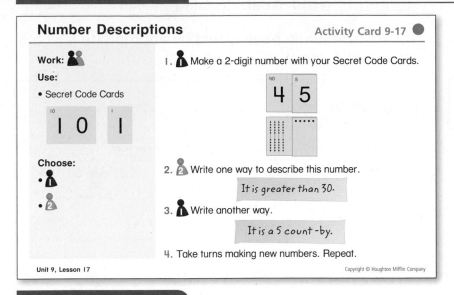

Number Descriptions — Activity Card 9-17 ●

Work: (pairs)

Use:

- Secret Code Cards

10 1

Choose:

- Student 1
- Student 2

1. Student 1: Make a 2-digit number with your Secret Code Cards.

   4 5

2. Student 2: Write one way to describe this number.

   It is greater than 30.

3. Student 1: Write another way.

   It is a 5 count-by.

4. Take turns making new numbers. Repeat.

Unit 9, Lesson 17

Activity Note Children need Secret Code Cards (TRB M3-M4). If children easily make description statements about the number, have them repeat steps 2 and 3 several times for each number.

Math Writing Prompt

Describe a Number Choose a number. Write two ways to describe the number.

Soar to Success Math Software Support

Warm Up 2.12

On Level

Activity Card 9-17

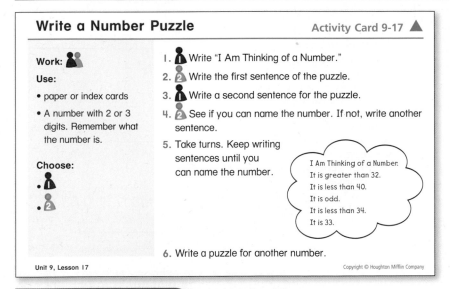

Write a Number Puzzle — Activity Card 9-17 ▲

Work: (pairs)

Use:

- paper or index cards
- A number with 2 or 3 digits. Remember what the number is.

Choose:

- Student 1
- Student 2

1. Student 1: Write "I Am Thinking of a Number."
2. Student 2: Write the first sentence of the puzzle.
3. Student 1: Write a second sentence for the puzzle.
4. Student 2: See if you can name the number. If not, write another sentence.
5. Take turns. Keep writing sentences until you can name the number.

   I Am Thinking of a Number.
   It is greater than 32.
   It is less than 40.
   It is odd.
   It is less than 34.
   It is 33.

6. Write a puzzle for another number.

Unit 9, Lesson 17

Activity Note To extend this activity, suggest to children that they try to write puzzles that identify the number in 3 steps. You might encourage pairs to trade puzzles with other pairs.

Math Writing Prompt

I Am Thinking of a Shape Write an "I Am Thinking of a Shape" puzzle.

Harcourt MegaMath Software Support

Numberopolis: Cross Town Number Line, Level N

Challenge

Activity Card 9-17

Round Table Puzzles — Activity Card 9-17 ■

Work:

Use:

- sheets of paper or large index cards

1. Sit around the table. Each student writes an "I Am Thinking of a Number" puzzle.
2. Pass your puzzle to the person on your right. Get a puzzle from the person on your left.
3. Solve the new puzzle. Write the answer.
4. Pass the new puzzle to the person on your right. Get a new puzzle from the person on your left.
5. Check the answer. Write Agree or Disagree.
6. Pass the puzzles again. You should now have your puzzle back.
7. Discuss the puzzles. Did the group find all the right numbers?

Unit 9, Lesson 17

Activity Note Be sure that the groups of three sit so that they can easily pass the puzzles to each other three times. Explain how to write an "I Am Thinking of a Number" puzzle.

Math Writing Prompt

How to Write a Number Puzzle Describe three things a person needs to think about when writing a number puzzle.

Destination Math Software Support

Course II: Module 1: Unit 1: Place Value: Tens and Ones

3 Homework and Spiral Review

9–17 **Homework** **Goal:** Additional Practice

✓ Include children's completed Homework page as part of their portfolios.

9–17 **Remembering** **Goal:** Spiral Review

This Remembering page would be appropriate anytime after today's lesson.

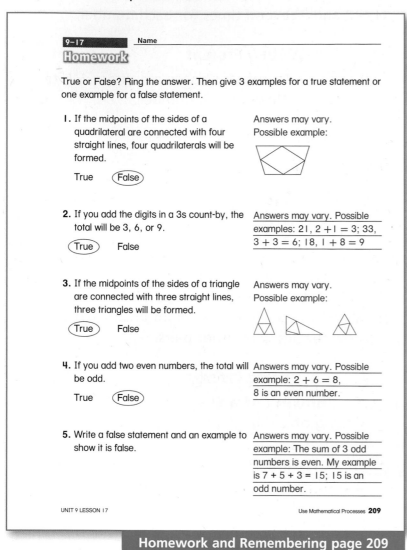

9–17 Name

Homework

True or False? Ring the answer. Then give 3 examples for a true statement or one example for a false statement.

1. If the midpoints of the sides of a quadrilateral are connected with four straight lines, four quadrilaterals will be formed.

True (False)

Answers may vary. Possible example:

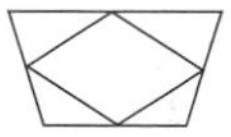

2. If you add the digits in a 3s count-by, the total will be 3, 6, or 9.

(True) False

Answers may vary. Possible examples: 21, 2 + 1 = 3; 33, 3 + 3 = 6; 18, 1 + 8 = 9

3. If the midpoints of the sides of a triangle are connected with three straight lines, three triangles will be formed.

(True) False

Answers may vary. Possible example:

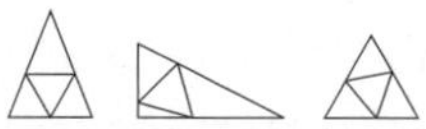

4. If you add two even numbers, the total will be odd.

True (False)

Answers may vary. Possible example: 2 + 6 = 8, 8 is an even number.

5. Write a false statement and an example to show it is false.

Answers may vary. Possible example: The sum of 3 odd numbers is even. My example is 7 + 5 + 3 = 15; 15 is an odd number.

UNIT 9 LESSON 17 Use Mathematical Processes 209

Homework and Remembering page 209

9–17 Name Date

Remembering

Solve each story problem. **Show your work.**

1. Mr. Lopez had 135 puppets in his toy store. He sold 48 puppets. How many puppets does he have left?

puppets

87 puppets (label)

2. Mary has 36 dog stamps and 47 cat stamps. Tam has 142 dog stamps and 56 cat stamps. How many dog stamps do they have all together?

dog stamps

178 dog stamps (label)

Find all possible answers.

3. Pedro is thinking of a number. The number has 3 digits. The digit in the hundreds place is 6 more than the digit in the tens place. The digit in the ones place is 4. What number could Pedro be thinking of? 934, 824, 714, or 604

4. Ming-Na is thinking of a number. The number is between 30 and 40. It is an even number. The digit in the tens place is less than the digit in the ones place. What number could Ming-Na be thinking of? 34, 36, or 38

210 UNIT 9 LESSON 17 Use Mathematical Processes

Homework and Remembering page 210

Home or School Activity

Science Connection

Animal Facts Have children decide what kind of animal facts they would like to write a report about (weight, size, foods, speeds, sounds, and so on). Suggest that they use the library or Internet to find information. Then ask them to use the information they find to write a short report or make a display.

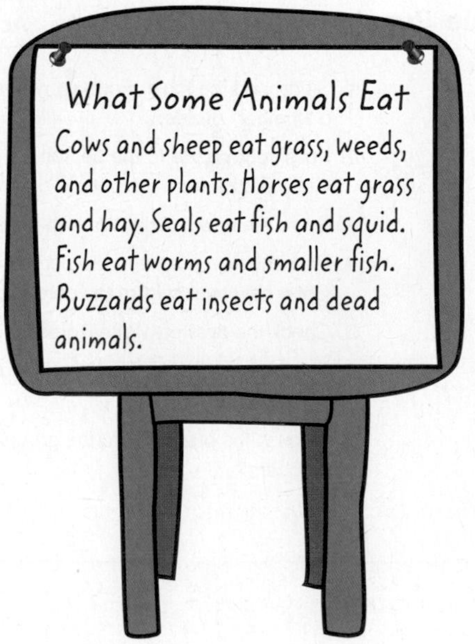

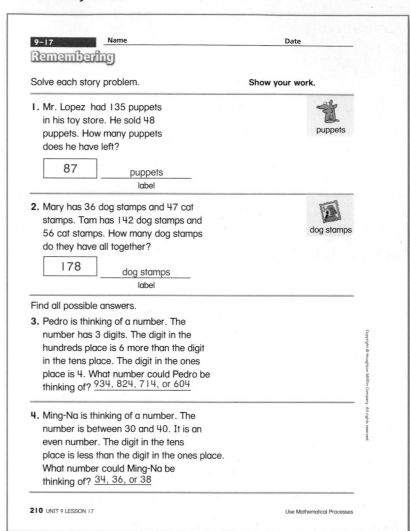

UNIT 9

Unit Review and Test

Lesson Objectives

- Assess children's progress on unit objectives.

The Day at a Glance

Today's Goals	Materials
1 Assessing the Unit ▶ Assess children's progress on unit objectives. ▶ Use activities from unit lessons to reteach content.	Unit 9 Test, Student Activity Book pages 311–314 Unit 9 Test, Form A or B, Assessment Guide (optional) Unit 9 Performance Assessment, Assessment Guide (optional)
2 Extending the Assessment ▶ Use remediation for common errors.	
There is no homework assignment on a test day.	

Keeping Skills Sharp

Quick Practice — 5 MINUTES

Goal: Review any skills you choose to meet the needs of your class.

If you are doing a unit review day, use any of the Quick Practice activities that provide support for your class. If this is a test day, omit Quick Practice.

Review and Test Day You may want to choose a quiet game or other activity (reading a book or working on homework for another subject) for children who finish early.

1 Assessing the Unit

Assess Unit Objectives

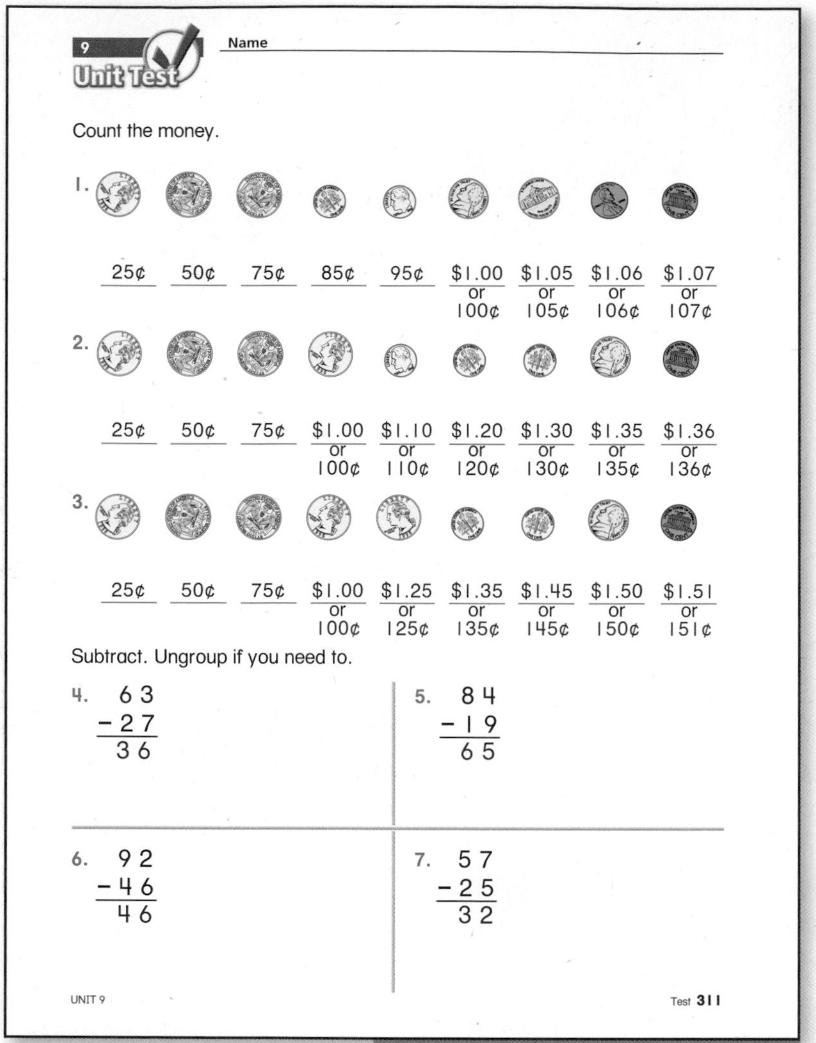
9 Unit Test

Name

Count the money.

1. 25¢ 50¢ 75¢ 85¢ 95¢ $1.00 or 100¢ $1.05 or 105¢ $1.06 or 106¢ $1.07 or 107¢

2. 25¢ 50¢ 75¢ $1.00 or 100¢ $1.10 or 110¢ $1.20 or 120¢ $1.30 or 130¢ $1.35 or 135¢ $1.36 or 136¢

3. 25¢ 50¢ 75¢ $1.00 or 100¢ $1.25 or 125¢ $1.35 or 135¢ $1.45 or 145¢ $1.50 or 150¢ $1.51 or 151¢

Subtract. Ungroup if you need to.

4. 63 − 27 = 36

5. 84 − 19 = 65

6. 92 − 46 = 46

7. 57 − 25 = 32

UNIT 9 Test 311

Student Activity Book page 311

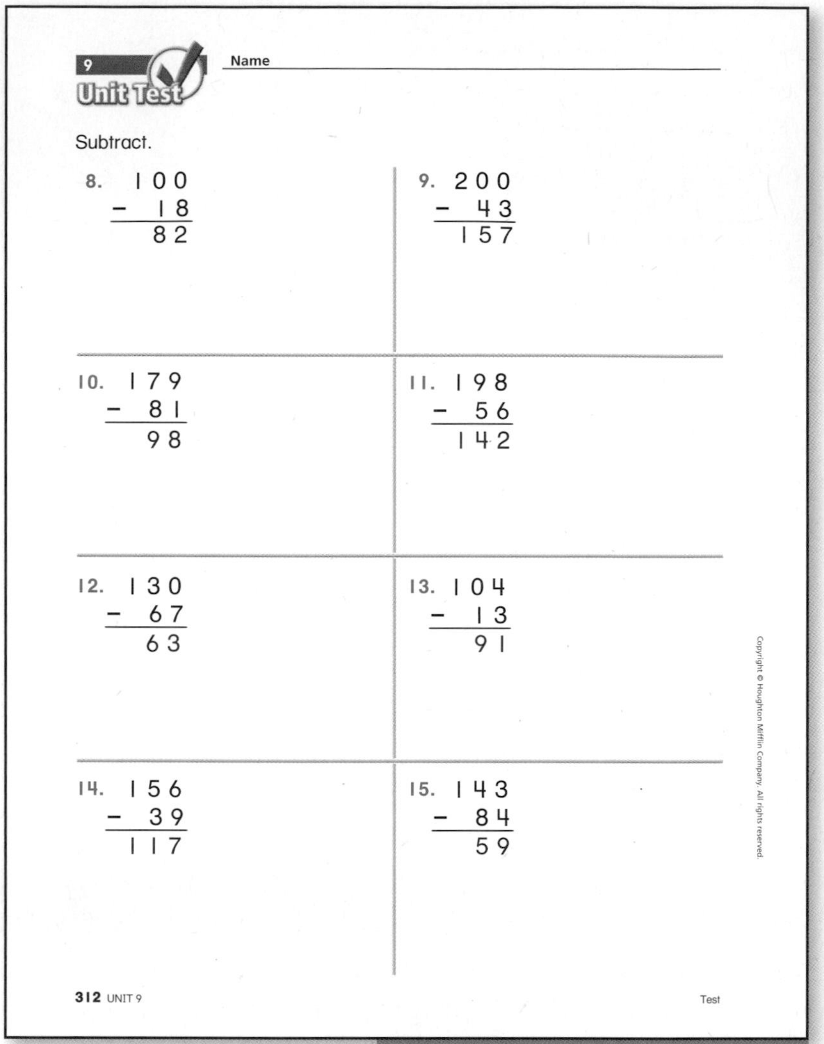
9 Unit Test

Name

Subtract.

8. 100 − 18 = 82

9. 200 − 43 = 157

10. 179 − 81 = 98

11. 198 − 56 = 142

12. 130 − 67 = 63

13. 104 − 13 = 91

14. 156 − 39 = 117

15. 143 − 84 = 59

Copyright © Houghton Mifflin Company. All rights reserved.

312 UNIT 9 Test

Student Activity Book page 312

45 MINUTES (more if schedule permits)

Goal: Assess children's progress on unit objectives.

Materials: Student Activity Book pages 311–314, Assessment Guide (optional)

▶ Review and Assessment

If your students are ready for assessment on the unit objectives, use either the test on the Student Activity Book pages or one of the forms of the Unit 9 Test in the Assessment Guide to assess student progress. To assign a numerical score for all of these test forms, use 5 points for each question.

The chart to the right lists the test items, the unit objectives they cover, and the lesson activities in which the objective is covered in this unit.

▶ Reteaching Resources

Test Items	Unit Objectives Tested	Activities to Use for Reteaching
1–3	**9.1** Count quarters, dimes, nickels, and pennies all together.	Lesson 1, Activity 3
4–7	**9.2** Subtract 2-digit numbers with or without ungrouping.	Lesson 4, Activity 2 Lesson 4, Activity 3
8–9	**9.3** Subtract a 2-digit number from a 3-digit number with two zeros.	Lesson 7, Activity 1 Lesson 7, Activity 2

9 Unit Test Name

Solve the story problems. Show your work.

16. Vince has 89 purple bicycles and 47 red bicycles in his store. How many bicycles does he have altogether?

Check children's work.

136 bicycles
label

17. Bonita had 97 raisins. She ate 58 of them. How many raisins are left?

39 raisins
label

18. There are 42 birds at the feeder in our tree. There are 35 more at the feeder on the fence. How many birds are at both feeders in all?

77 birds
label

19. Jeffrey bought 200 paper cups for his party. 79 cups were used. How many paper cups does Jeffrey have left?

121 paper cups
label

UNIT 9 Test 313

Student Activity Book page 313

9 Unit Test Name

20. **Extended Response** Explain all the steps you do to subtract 59 from 148. Check children's work.

*Item 20 also assesses the Process Skills of Communication and Reasoning.

314 UNIT 9 Test

Student Activity Book page 314

Test Items	Unit Objectives Tested	Activities to Use for Reteaching
10–11	**9.4** Subtract a 2-digit number from a 3-digit number with or without ungrouping a hundred.	Lesson 8, Activity 1
12–13	**9.5** Subtract a 2-digit number from a 3-digit number with one zero.	Lesson 9, Activity 1
14–15, 20	**9.6** Subtract a 2-digit number from a 3-digit number, ungrouping twice.	Lesson 11, Activity 1
16–19	**9.7** Solve addition and subtraction story problems.	Lesson 4, Activity 2 Lesson 11, Activity 2 Lesson 15, Activity 2

► Assessment Resources

Form A, Free Response Test (Assessment Guide)
Form B, Multiple-Choice Test (Assessment Guide)
Performance Assessment (Assessment Guide)

► Portfolio Assessment

Teacher-selected Items for Student Portfolios:

- Homework, Lessons 5, 11, 15, 16, and 17
- Class Activity work, Lessons 3, 6, 9, and 10

Student-selected Items for Student Portfolios:

- Favorite Home or School Activity
- Best Writing Prompt

2 Extending the Assessment

Common Errors

Activities for Remediation

Unit Objective 9.1

Count quarters, dimes, nickels, and pennies all together.

Common Error: Counts Coins Incorrectly

Students must be proficient in skip counting by fives, tens, and twenty-fives to be successful with counting coins.

Remediation Have a group of students take turns saying the next number when counting by fives, tens, or twenty-fives Then switch counting rules while students are counting. For example, when 4 students have counted by tens, say to the next student, "switch to fives." Remind students always to count coins starting with the coins that have the greatest value.

Unit Objective 9.2

Subtract 2-digit numbers with or without ungrouping.

Common Error: Does Not Ungroup Correctly

Some students make errors when ungrouping in subtraction.

Remediation Distribute base ten blocks and have students act out the ungrouping in each place. Working in pairs, have one student manipulate the materials while the other student records the subtraction.

Unit Objective 9.3

Subtract a 2-digit number from a 3-digit number with two zeros.

Common Error: Doesn't Subtract in Tens and Ones Places

When subtracting from a hundreds number, children may not subtract in the tens and ones places. They may write either a zero or the digits to be subtracted in the tens and ones places in the answer.

Remediation Have children model the subtraction using play money. Explain how they can exchange $1.00 for 10 dimes, and 1 dime for 10 pennies.

Unit Objective 9.4

Subtract a 2-digit number from a 3-digit number with or without ungrouping a hundred.

Common Error: Makes Errors in Subtracting Ones, Tens, or Hundreds

Children may include the given partner when they count on to find how many more they need to reach the total.

Remediation Before beginning counting on from a partner, have them use a gesture (putting the partner on their shoulder or in a pocket) to emphasize the number that is "already counted," and to be sure they do not count it again.

Unit Objective 9.5

Subtract a 2-digit number from a 3-digit number with one zero.

Common Error: Does Not Ungroup When Subtracting From Zero

When subtracting from a zero, children may record a zero in the difference instead of ungrouping.

Remediation Have children model the subtraction using base ten blocks. Help children model with the blocks and record the action as the child ungroups the blocks.

Unit Objective 9.6

Subtract a 2-digit number from a 3-digit number, ungrouping twice.

Common Error: Difficulty Ungrouping Twice

Children may forget to ungroup the second time when more than one ungrouping is needed.

Remediation Remind children that they need to ungroup when there are not enough tens or ones to subtract. Review the "Ungrouping First" method with these children, having them ungroup both hundreds and tens and then subtract.

Shapes and Patterns

IN THIS UNIT, children continue to develop their knowledge of 2-dimensional shapes. Activities include identifying congruent shapes and similar shapes, composing and decomposing shapes, and grouping shapes according to sorting rules. Children are introduced to slides, flips, and turns of geometric figures and they use these transformations to extend geometric patterns. The unit concludes with an introduction to finding area.

Skills Trace

Grade 1	Grade 2	Grade 3
• Relate shapes and numbers. • Estimate and measure length in centimeters.	• Identify congruent and similar figures. • Identify slides, flips, and turns. • Calculate area by counting square centimeters.	• Identify figures that are congruent. • Recognize slides, flips, and turns in geometric patterns. • Use formulas for the area and perimeter of squares and rectangles.

Unit 10 Contents

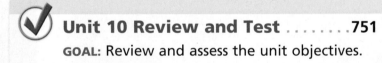

Big Idea Patterns

Unit 10 Assessment

Unit Objectives Tested	Unit Test Items	Lessons
10.1 Identify congruent figures.	1	1
10.2 Identify similar figures.	2	1
10.3 Sort 2-D figures using a sorting rule.	3, 10	1
10.4 Identify slides.	4	2
10.5 Identify flips.	5	2
10.6 Identify turns.	6	2
10.7 Use slides, flips, and turns to draw the next figure in a pattern.	7	2
10.8 Calculate area by counting square centimeters.	8, 9	4

Assessment and Review Resources

Formal Assessment

Student Activity Book
- Unit Review and Test (pp. 335–338)

Assessment Guide
- Quick Quiz (p. A106)
- Test A–Open Response (pp. A107–A109)
- Test B–Multiple Choice (pp. A110–A112)
- Performance Assessment (pp. A113–A115)

Test Generator CD-ROM
- Open Response Test
- Multiple Choice Test
- Test Bank Items

Informal Assessment

Teacher Edition
- Ongoing Assessment (in every lesson)
- Quick Practice (in every lesson)
- Portfolio Suggestions (p. 753)

Math Talk
- In Activities (pp. 721, 732, 733, 741, 748)

Review Opportunities

Homework and Remembering
- Review of recently taught topics
- Spiral Review

Teacher Edition
- Unit Review and Test (pp. 751–754)

Test Generator CD-ROM
- Custom Review Sheets

Planning Unit 10

NCTM Curriculum Focal Points and Connections Key: **1.** Number and Operations **2.** Number and Operations and Algebra **3.** Measurement **4.** Number and Operations **5.** Geometry and Measurement **6.** Algebra

Lesson NCTM Focal Points NCTM Standards	Resources	Materials for Lesson Activities	Materials for Going Further
10-1 **Compare Shapes** NCTM Focal Point: 5.4 NCTM Standards: 3, 4, 7, 9	TE pp. 719–724 SAB pp. 315–320 H&R pp. 211–212 AC 10-1 MCC 37	✓ 25-cm rulers Tangrams or Tangrams (TRB M59) Scissor	Figure Match (TRB M79) Scissors Index Cards Math Journals
10-2 **Combine and Cut Shapes** NCTM Focal Point: 5.4 NCTM Standards: 3, 4, 7, 10	TE pp. 725–730 SAB pp. 321–324 H&R pp. 213–214 AC 10-2	Paper shapes Scissors Pattern Blocks (TRB M58)	Paper shapes Scissors Glue Math Journals
10-3 **Motion Geometry** NCTM Focal Point: 5.4 NCTM Standards: 3, 9, 10	TE pp. 731–738 SAB pp. 325–330 H&R pp. 215–216 AC 10-3	✓ Pattern Blocks ✓ MathBoard materials Tracing paper Scissors ✓ 25-cm rulers Transparent plastic mirrors	Large construction paper Plastic mirrors *The M.C. Escher Coloring Book*, by M.C. Escher Math Journals
10-4 **Patterns with Shapes** NCTM Standards: 2, 3, 7, 8	TE pp. 739–744 SAB pp. 331–332 H&R pp. 217–218 AC 10-4 MCC 38, 39	Markers or crayons ✓ Connecting cubes Cardstock Scissors Squares and triangles for tracing Centimeter Dot Paper (TRB M49)	Cubes Centimeter Dot Paper (TRB M49) Cardstock Scissors Math Journals
10-5 **Count Square Units** NCTM Focal Points: 4.5, 4.6 NCTM Standards: 4, 9	TE pp. 745–750 SAB pp. 333–334 H&R pp. 219–220 AG Quick Quiz AC 10-5 MCC 40	✓ MathBoard materials ✓ 25-cm rulers ✓ Square Tiles (TRB M82) Cardstock Scissors Centimeter Grid Paper (TRB M50)	✓ Pattern blocks ✓ Square Tiles (TRB M82) Cardstock Scissors Math Journals
✓ Unit Review and Test	TE pp. 751–754 SAB pp. 335–338 AG Unit 10 Tests		

Resources/Materials Key: TE: Teacher Edition SAB: Student Activity Book H&R: Homework and Remembering AC: Activity Cards MCC: Math Center Challenge AG: Assessment Guide ✓: Grade 2 kits TRB: Teacher's Resource Book

NCTM Standards and Expectations Key: 1. Number and Operations 2. Algebra 3. Geometry 4. Measurement 5. Data Analysis and Probability 6. Problem Solving 7. Reasoning and Proof 8. Communication 9. Connections 10. Representation

Manipulatives and Materials

Essential materials for teaching *Math Expressions* are available in the Grade 2 kits. These materials are indicated by a ✓ in these lists. At the front of this Teacher Edition is more information about kit contents, alternatives for the materials, and use of the materials.

Unit 10 Teaching Resources

Differentiated Instruction

Individualizing Instruction		
	Level	**Frequency**
Activities	• Intervention • On Level • Challenge	All 3 in every lesson
	Level	**Frequency**
Math Writing Prompts	• Intervention • On Level • Challenge	All 3 in every lesson
Math Center Challenges	**For advanced students**	
	4 in every unit	

Reaching All Learners		
English Language Learners	**Lessons**	**Pages**
	1, 2, 3, 4, 5	719, 725, 731, 739, 745
Extra Help	**Lessons**	**Pages**
	1, 3	720, 732, 734

Strategies for English Language Learners

Present this problem to all children. Offer the different levels of support to meet children's levels of language proficiency.

Objective To help children describe the properties of different shapes.

Problem Draw the following shapes on the board and help children describe them.

Newcomer

- Point to and describe each shape. Have children trace the shape in the air as they repeat.
- For example, say: **Shape *a* has 4 sides. It has 4 straight lines. It has 4 angles. The angles are equal.**

Beginning

- Point to shape *a*. Ask: **How many sides are there?** 4 sides **How many angles?** 4 angles **Are the lines straight?** yes Continue with other shapes.

Intermediate

- Ask questions to help children describe the shapes. For example, ask: **Which shapes have 4 sides?** a, b, g

Advanced

- Have children work in pairs to tell about the shapes.
- Invite volunteers to tell the class what they said.

Connections

Art Connections
Lesson 2, page 730
Lesson 3, page 738

Real-World Connection
Lesson 4, page 744

Science Connection
Lesson 5, page 750

Independent Learning Activities

Ready-Made Math Challenge Centers

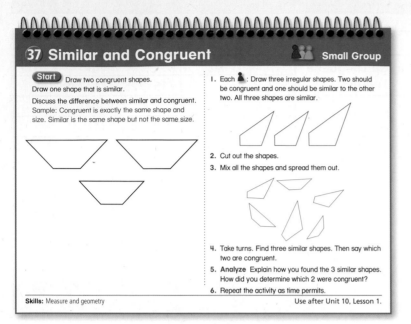

37 Similar and Congruent — Small Group

Start Draw two congruent shapes. Draw one shape that is similar.

Discuss the difference between similar and congruent. Sample: Congruent is exactly the same shape and size. Similar is the same shape but not the same size.

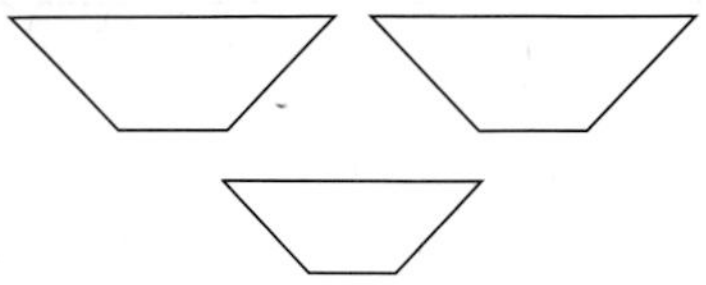

1. Each: Draw three irregular shapes. Two should be congruent and one should be similar to the other two. All three shapes are similar.

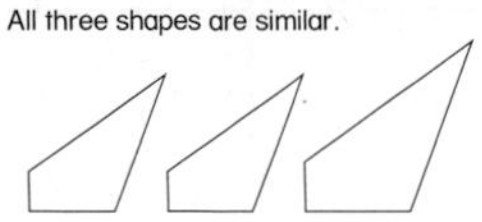

2. Cut out the shapes.
3. Mix all the shapes and spread them out.

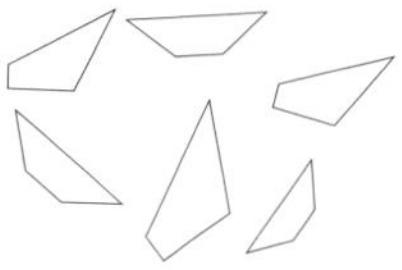

4. Take turns. Find three similar shapes. Then say which two are congruent.
5. **Analyze** Explain how you found the 3 similar shapes. How did you determine which 2 were congruent?
6. Repeat the activity as time permits.

Skills: Measure and geometry — Use after Unit 10, Lesson 1.

Grouping Small Groups

Materials Scissors

Objective Children create and identify similar and congruent shapes.

Connections Measurement and Geometry

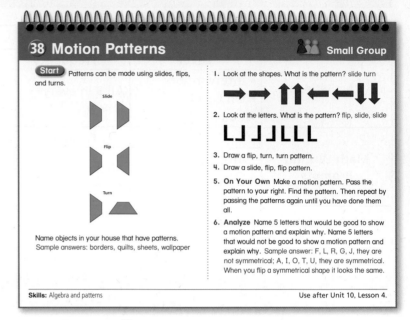

38 Motion Patterns — Small Group

Start Patterns can be made using slides, flips, and turns.

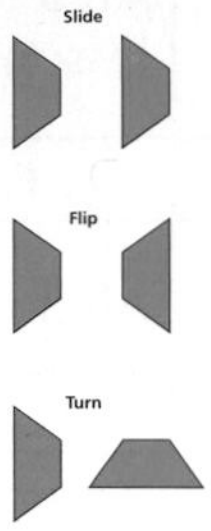

Name objects in your house that have patterns. Sample answers: borders, quilts, sheets, wallpaper

1. Look at the shapes. What is the pattern? slide turn

→→↑↑←←↓↓

2. Look at the letters. What is the pattern? flip, slide, slide

LJ J J LLL

3. Draw a flip, turn, turn pattern.
4. Draw a slide, flip, flip pattern.
5. **On Your Own** Make a motion pattern. Pass the pattern to your right. Find the pattern. Then repeat by passing the patterns again until you have done them all.
6. **Analyze** Name 5 letters that would be good to show a motion pattern and explain why. Name 5 letters that would not be good to show a motion pattern and explain why. Sample answer: F, L, R, G, J, they are not symmetrical; A, I, O, T, U, they are symmetrical. When you flip a symmetrical shape it looks the same.

Skills: Algebra and patterns — Use after Unit 10, Lesson 4.

Grouping Small Groups

Materials None

Objective Children create motion patterns (slide, flip, turn) with at least 2 motions.

Connections Algebra and Representation

39 Show Patterns — Small Group

Start You can show the same repeating pattern many different ways.

You can use letters.

ABBABBABB

You can use numbers.

122122122

You can use shapes.

You can use motions.

LJ J J LLL

You can use sounds.

1. Name a repeating number pattern. Sample answer: 1233, 1233
2. Each: Take turns. Name the same pattern using different numbers. Sample answer: 4566, 4566
3. Each: Take turns. Name the same pattern using shapes. Sample answer: triangle, square, circle, circle
4. Each: Take turns. Name the same pattern using motions. Sample answer: flip, slide, turn, turn
5. Each: Take turns. Name the same pattern using sounds. Sample answer: snap, clap, stomp, stomp
6. **Analyze** Think of other ways to show patterns and share them with the group.

Skills: Algebra and representation — Use after Unit 10, Lesson 4.

Grouping Small Groups

Materials None

Objective Children represent patterns 5 different ways.

Connections Algebra and Representation

40 Square Units — Small Group

Start Count the squares in a shape to find how many square units it covers.

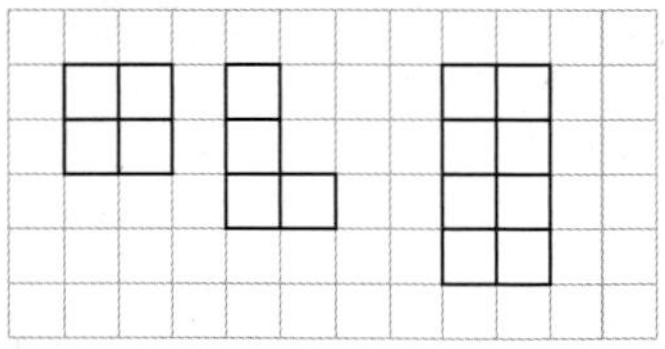

Discuss which objects in the class have a large area and which objects have a small area.

1. Look at the shapes. How many square units are in the square? L shape? rectangle? 4, 4, 8
2. Each: Draw shapes on grid paper. Estimate the area. Then check.
3. Trade papers. Estimate and check the areas. Pass the papers again. Continue until you have done them all.
4. Each: Draw a shape that has an area of 11 square units.
5. Each: Draw a shape that is 17 square units.
6. **Look Back** Check each other's work.
7. **Analyze** Did you all draw the same shapes for 4 and 5? How can you have the same area for different shapes?
8. Name other areas and draw shapes with those areas.

Skills: Measure and estimate — Use after Unit 10, Lesson 5.

Grouping Small Groups

Materials 10 × 10 Grid (TRB M62)

Objective Children estimate and determine the area of shapes and create shapes for given areas.

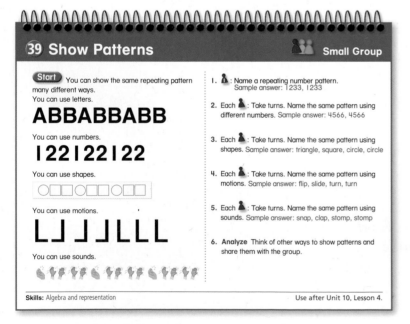

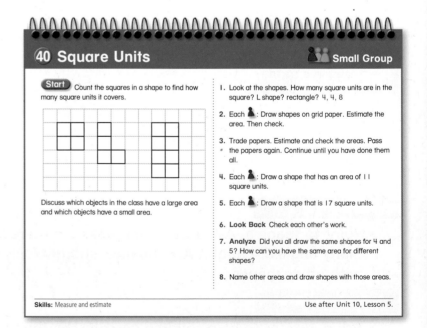

Connections Measure and Estimate

Ready-Made Math Resources

Technology — Tutorials, Practice, and Intervention

Go Digital

Soar to Success Math

Use online, individualized intervention and support to bring students to proficiency.

Harcourt Mega Math Grades K-6

Help students practice skills and apply concepts through exciting math adventures.

Destination Math®

Extend and enrich students' understanding of skills and concepts through engaging, interactive lessons and activities.

Visit **Education Place®**
www.eduplace.com

Visit www.eduplace.com/mx2t/ and find family, teacher, and student materials, activities, games, and more.

Literature Links

Patterns in Nature

Patterns in Nature
Children will discover that there are repeated patterns in the natural world. Rozines and Roy's clever use of photography can be the focus for discussion. They will also inspire children to look around them for more examples of natural patterning.

Math Background

Putting Research into Practice for Unit 10

Transformations

Children come to school with many intuitive notions of space because their early experiences in the environment have been mostly spatial. The behavior of very young children is essentially spatial because it is prelinguistic. A child's first encounter with, and exploration of, the world are undertaken without the benefit of language. Children are naturally attuned to spatial tasks and benefit both psychologically and mathematically from activities involving manipulatives and objects from the space in which they live. The fundamental ideas of sliding and turning are basic to every child's spatial explorations, and putting these notions into a geometric context should be the starting point for a child's mathematical development in the earliest grades.

Del Grande, John, Lorna J. Morrow. *Geometry and Spatial Sense: Addenda Series, Grades K–6.* Reston: NCTM, 1993. 1.

Patterns

Working with patterns is an exciting and motivating experience for children and a significant form of problem solving. Understanding and using patterns and relationships lead students towards algebraic thinking. Recording and analyzing data to discover patterns build students' confidence in their ability to do mathematics independently, without the need for constant confirmation from the teacher. At each repetition of a simple pattern, children are validating for themselves, the pattern that they discovered.

Burton, Grace, Douglas Clements, Terrence Coburn, John Del Grande, John Firkins, Jeane Joyner, Miriam A. Leiva, Mary M. Lindquist, Lorna Morrow. *Third-Grade Book: Addenda Series, Grades K–6.* Reston: NCTM, 1992.

Classifying Figures

Young children should explore geometric concepts informally and intuitively. The use of manipulatives is crucial. Sorting and classifying geometric figures in many ways provides children with informal analysis of the properties of these figures before the more formal work in later grades.

Del Grande, John, Lorna J. Morrow. *Geometry and Spatial Sense: Addenda Series, Grades K–6.* Reston: NCTM, 1993. 17.

Other Useful References: Spatial Sense

Clements, Douglas H. "Geometric and Spatial Thinking in Young Children." *Mathematics in the Early Years*. Ed. Juanita V. Copley. Co-published with the National Association for the Education of Young Children. Reston: NCTM, 1999. 22–79.

Del Grande, John, Lorna J. Morrow. *Geometry and Spatial Sense: Addenda Series, Grades K–6.* Reston: NCTM, 1993.

Findell, Carol R., Marian Small, Mary Cavanagh, Linda Dacey, Carole E. Greenes, Linda Jensen Sheffield. *Navigating through Geometry in Prekindergarten–Grade 2 (with CD-ROM).* Reston: NCTM, 2001.

Jacobson, Cathy, Richard Lehrer. "Teacher Appropriation and Student Learning of Geometry Through Design." *Journal for Research in Mathematics Education* 31.1 (Jan. 2000): 71–88.

National Council of Teachers of Mathematics. "Geometry and Geometric Thinking" (Focus Issue). *Teaching Children Mathematics* 5.6 (Feb. 1999).

National Council of Teachers of Mathematics. *Principles and Standards for School Mathematics.* Reston: NCTM, 2000. 97, 99, 100.

National Council of Teachers of Mathematics. "Virtual Tile Turning." *On-Math: Online Journal of Mathematics* 1.3 (Spring, 2003).

Getting Ready to Teach Unit 10

In this unit, children explore ideas about plane shapes, from analyzing and classifying them to composing and decomposing them. They identify transformations, use them to extend geometric patterns, work with a variety of patterns, and begin to develop ideas about area.

Congruent and Similar Figures
Lesson 1

In Unit 8, children identified figures that were the "same size and the same shape" while decomposing quadrilaterals. In this unit, children are formally introduced to the terms congruent and similar; they learn that all congruent figures are also similar figures. The activities on congruency prepare children for the transformation work later in the unit.

Classify 2-D Shapes
Lesson 1

In this unit, children classify figures according to sorting rules like polygons/not polygons, quadrilaterals/not quadrilaterals, and regular/not regular, thus developing their ability to think analytically and observe similarities in structures of 2-dimensional figures.

Compose and Decompose 2-D Shapes
Lesson 2

Children cut apart and put together plane shapes to explore how shapes can be composed and decomposed.

Transformations
Lesson 3

Children identify slides, flips, and turns of geometric figures and identify which of these transformations are used to create geometric patterns. Students also apply these transformations to extend geometric patterns.

Patterns
Lesson 4

In this lesson, children create and extend repeating patterns, extend growing patterns, and create motion and rhythm patterns. These activities begin the important process of developing children's ability to form generalizations. In subsequent years, children's experiences with patterning will be extended to developing pattern rules that describe how patterns begin and how they continue.

Area
Lesson 5

In the final lesson of this unit, children find area by counting square units (non-standard units) and then by counting square centimeters (standard units). Activities include finding areas of rectangles, areas of shapes composed of square units, and areas of unusual 2-dimensional shapes. These activities provide opportunities for children to develop their measurement and estimation skills further.

MINI UNIT 10

LESSON 1

Compare Shapes

Vocabulary
congruent
similar
polygon
quadrilateral
regular polygon
irregular polygon

Lesson Objectives

- Identify congruent figures.
- Identify similar figures.
- Use a sorting rule to group 2-D figures.

The Day at a Glance

Today's Goals	Materials	
1 Teaching the Lesson **A1:** Identify figures that have the same shape and are the same size. **A2:** Identify figures that have the same shape but are not necessarily the same size. **A3:** Group 2-D figures using a sorting rule.	**Lesson Activities** Student Activity Book pp. 315–320 (includes Family Letter) Homework and Remembering pp. 211–212 25-cm rulers Tangrams (TRB M59) Scissors	**Going Further** Activity Cards 10-1 Figure Match (TRB M79) Scissors Index cards Math Journals
2 Going Further ▸ Differentiated Instruction		
3 Homework		

Use Math Talk today!

Keeping Skills Sharp

Daily Routines	English Language Learners
Quarters and Other Coins Making and Counting Coins that Make a Quarter, Counting to 200¢ by 25¢, Making and Counting Dollars and Cents: 3-Digit Numbers as Dollars and Cents (See pp. xxvi–xxvii.) ▸ Led by Student Leaders **Money Routine** Using the 120 Poster, Using the Money Flip Chart, Using the Number Path, Using Secret Code Cards (See pp. xxiii–xxv.) ▸ Led by Student Leaders	Write *size* and *shape* on the board. Give children cut outs of small and large triangles, squares, rectangles, and circles. • **Beginning** Have children hold up the circles. Ask: **Are these the same *shape*?** yes **Are these the same *size*?** no Continue with other shapes. • **Intermediate** Hold up a large triangle. Ask: **What *shape* is this?** triangle Say: **Hold up the other triangle.** Ask: **Are they the same *size*?** no Continue with other shapes. • **Advanced** Have children sort the cut outs by shape then size. Have them name each shape and compare the sizes.

1 Teaching the Lesson

Activity 1

Same Shape, Same Size (Congruence)

20 MINUTES

Goal: Identify figures that have the same shape and are the same size.

Materials: Student Activity Book page 315, 25-cm rulers (1 ruler per child)

NCTM Standards:
Geometry
Measurement
Reasoning and Proof

▶ Congruent Figures WHOLE CLASS

On the board, draw two triangles that have the same shape and are the same size.

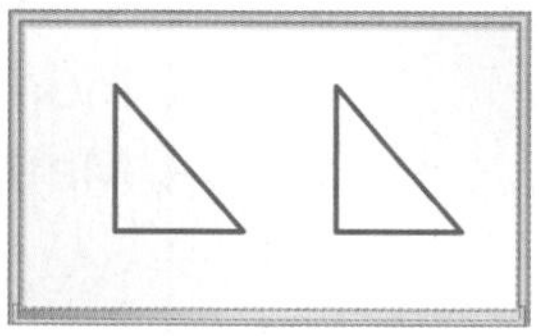

- Do these triangles have the same shape? yes
- Are these triangles the same size? yes

Explain to children that these figures are *congruent:* they have the same shape and are the same size.

Draw a rectangle and a square on the board. Explain that both figures are called *quadrilaterals,* meaning that they have four sides and four angles.

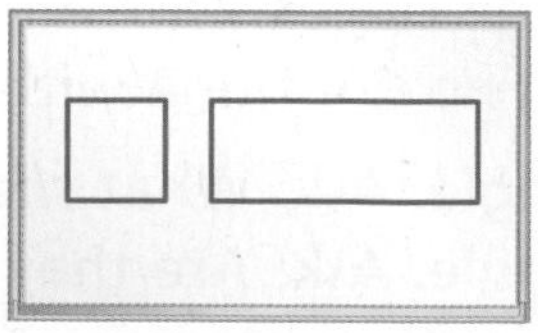

- Do these two quadrilaterals have the same shape? no
- Are they the same size? no
- Are they congruent? no

Refer children to Student Activity Book page 315 and ask them to look at the example of congruent figures.

- Why are these two figures congruent? They are the same size and shape.

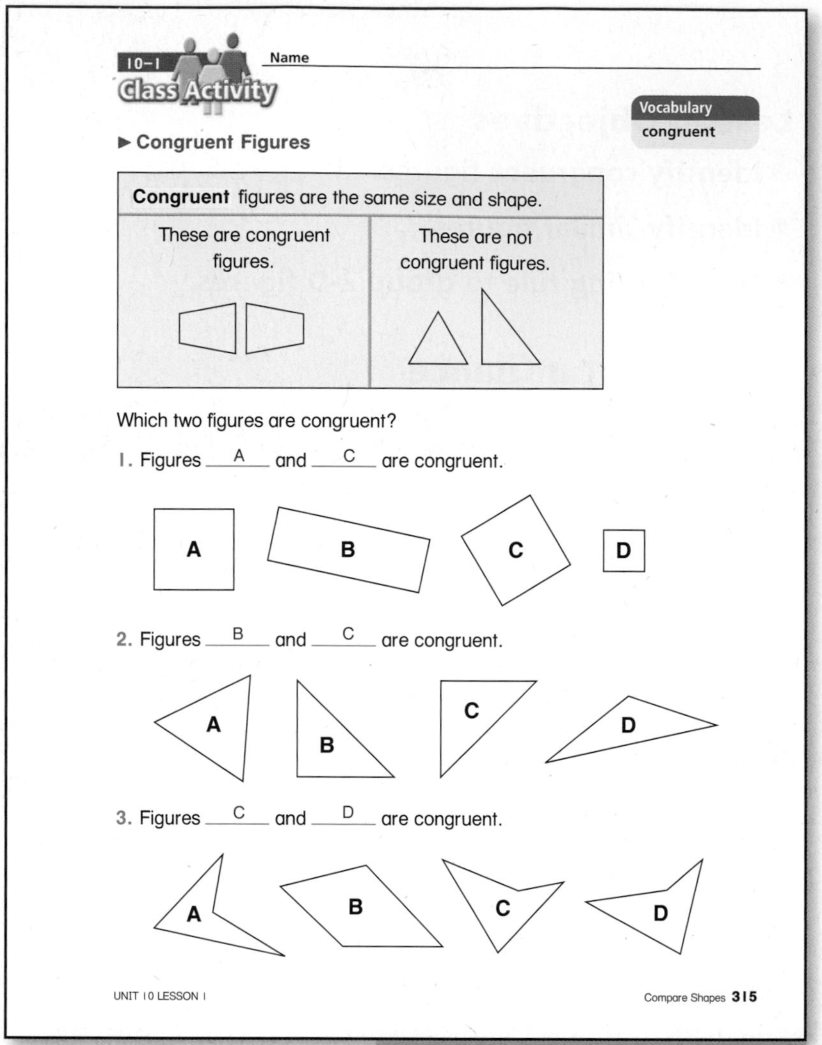

10–1 Class Activity Name

Vocabulary
congruent

▶ Congruent Figures

Congruent figures are the same size and shape.	
These are congruent figures.	These are not congruent figures.

Which two figures are congruent?

1. Figures A and C are congruent.

2. Figures B and C are congruent.

3. Figures C and D are congruent.

UNIT 10 LESSON 1 Compare Shapes 315

Student Activity Book page 315

- What is different about these two figures? They are facing in different directions.

Explain to children that congruent figures can be in different positions.

Have children complete exercises 1–3 individually. Suggest that they can use their centimeter rulers to check if the side lengths of different figures are equal.

Differentiated Instruction

Extra Help Some children will benefit from tracing figures and placing their tracings on top of other figures to check for congruency. Explain to children that if the tracing fits exactly on top of the other figure, the two are congruent. Point out that they can slide, flip, or turn the tracings as they check for congruency.

Activity 2

Same Shape (Similarity)

20 MINUTES

Goal: Identify figures that have the same shape but are not necessarily the same size.

Materials: Student Activity Book page 316, tangrams or Tangrams (TRB M59)

NCTM Standards:
Geometry
Reasoning and Proof

▶ Similar Figures WHOLE CLASS Math Talk

Draw two squares of different sizes on the board.

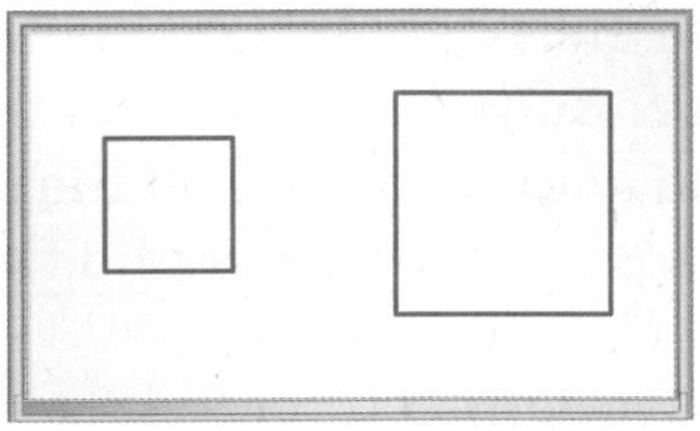

- Do these two quadrilaterals have the same shape? yes
- Are they the same size? no

Explain to children that we describe figures that have the same shape as *similar.* The shapes may be the same size but they don't have to be.

Refer children to Student Activity Book page 316 and have them look at the first example.

- Why are these two figures similar? They have the same shape.

Ask children to look at the second example.

- Why are these two figures similar? They have the same shape.

Point out to children that similar figures can also be congruent figures. Reinforce that figures do not have to be different sizes in order to be similar.

Have children look at the third example.

- Why aren't these two figures similar? They are different shapes.

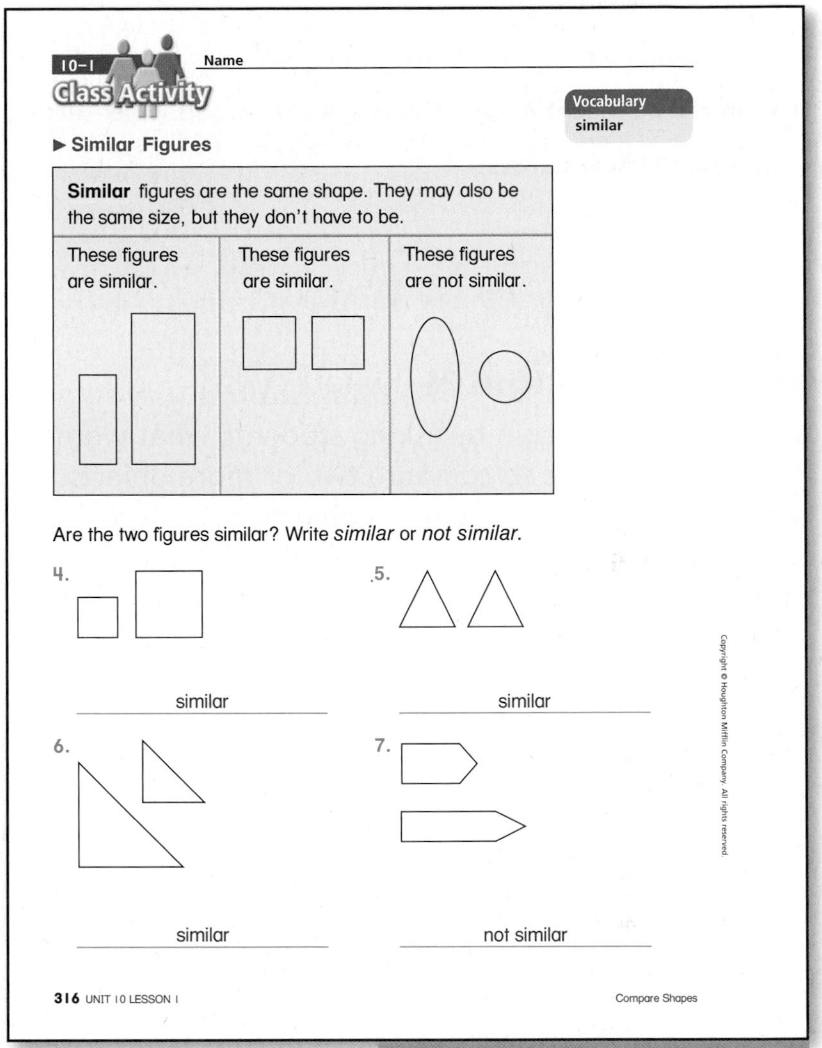

10-1 Class Activity

Name

Vocabulary
similar

▶ Similar Figures

Similar figures are the same shape. They may also be the same size, but they don't have to be.		
These figures are similar.	These figures are similar.	These figures are not similar.

Are the two figures similar? Write *similar* or *not similar.*

4. similar

5. similar

6. similar

7. not similar

Student Activity Book page 316

Ask children to complete exercises 4–7 individually. When they are finished, discuss their answers as a class.

Ongoing Assessment

Provide children with a set of tangrams or cutouts from TRB M59. Ask the following questions:

▶ Which figures are congruent?

▶ Which figures are similar?

Activity 3

Sort and Classify 2-D Figures

20 MINUTES

Goal: Group 2-D figures using a sorting rule.

Materials: Student Activity Book page 317, scissors (1 per child)

NCTM Standards:
Geometry
Measurement
Connections

▶ Compare Figures WHOLE CLASS

Ask for Ideas Begin by asking students what words we sometimes use to compare two or more objects. Take some common classroom objects, such as a piece of paper, an eraser, pencils, crayons, books. Ask children to compare these objects by describing their relative shapes and sizes using the following words:

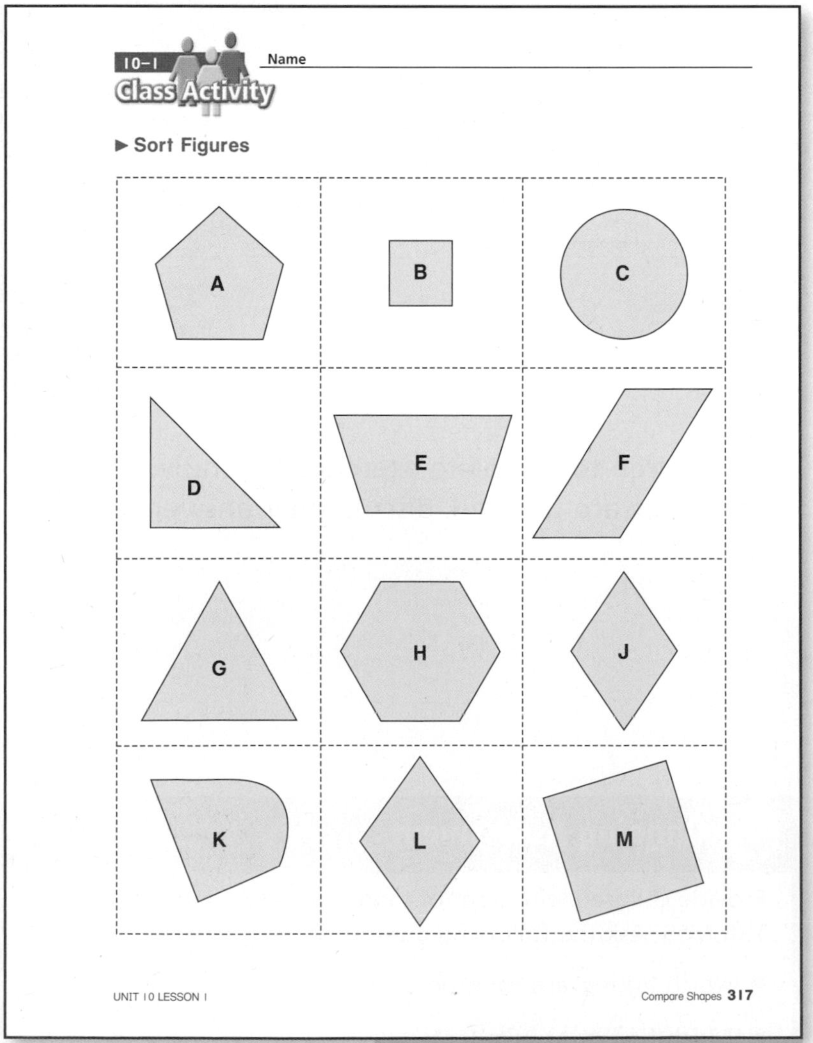
10-1
Class Activity
Name

▶ Sort Figures

UNIT 10 LESSON 1 Compare Shapes 317

Student Activity Book page 317

smaller/larger/same size, wider/narrower, or longer/shorter. Tell children that they will now compare various geometrical figures to explore their different characteristics.

Have children cut out the shapes on Student Activity Book page 317. Have them compare these shapes using the terms above.

▶ Sort Figures WHOLE CLASS

Tell children that you can use a sorting rule to separate shapes into different groups. Explain to them that polygons are closed shapes made of three or more straight-line segments. Have children sort them into two groups: polygons and not polygons. (C and K are not polygons. All the other figures are polygons.)

Explain the difference between regular and irregular polygons. *Regular polygons* have sides that are all the same length and angles that are all the same size. *Irregular polygons* can have sides of different lengths and angles of different sizes.

Ask children to now sort the polygons from Student Activity Book page 317 according to this sorting rule: regular polygons and irregular polygons.

- Which polygons are regular polygons? B, G, H, M
- Which polygons are irregular polygons? A, D, E, F, J, L

Discuss other ways you could sort the shapes from Student Activity Book page 317. Some examples are shown below.

- quadrilaterals/not quadrilaterals
- triangles/not triangles

Have children sort the figures according to these rules.

Alternate Approach

If computers and appropriate geometry software is available, encourage children to use this technology to further explore, make, and verify their conjectures about geometric objects.

2 Going Further

Differentiated Instruction

Intervention — Activity Card 10-1

Congruent Shapes
Activity Card 10-1

Work: (pair)
Use:
- Figure Match (TRB M79)
- scissors

Choose:
- 1
- 2

1. **Work Together** Cut apart the shapes on Figure Match.
2. Mix up the cards. Place them face down in rows of four.
3. (1) Turn over two cards.
   - If the cards are congruent, keep the cards.
   - If the cards are not congruent, put them back in the rows face down.

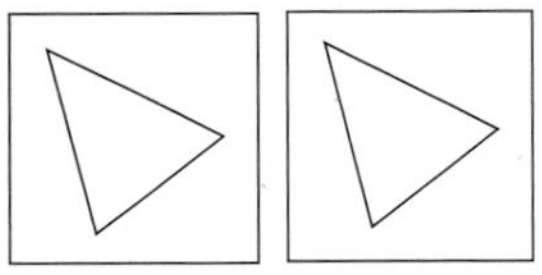

4. Take turns. Play until all the cards have been matched.

Unit 10, Lesson 1

Activity Note Each pair needs Figure Match (TRB M79) and scissors. Both children need to agree that the figures are congruent.

Math Writing Prompt

Draw a Picture How do you know if two figures are congruent? Draw a picture of two congruent figures.

Soar to Success Math Software Support

Warm Up 37.04

On Level — Activity Card 10-1

Similar Shapes
Activity Card 10-1

Work: (pair)
Use:
- Figure Match (TRB M79)
- scissors

Choose:
- 1
- 2

1. **Work Together** Cut apart the shapes on Figure Match.
2. Mix up the cards. Place them face down in rows of four.
3. (2) Turn over two cards.
   - If the cards are similar, keep the cards.
   - If the cards are not similar, put them back in the rows face down.

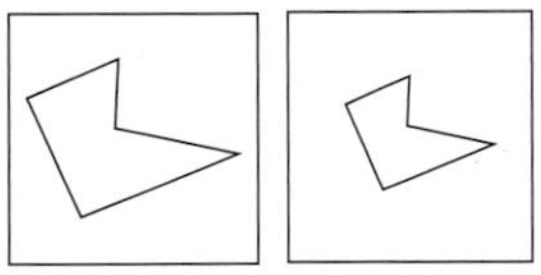

4. Take turns. Play until all the cards have been matched.

Unit 10, Lesson 1

Activity Note Each pair needs Figure Match (TRB M79) and scissors. Ask pairs to also state if their match is congruent.

Math Writing Prompt

You Decide Robert says that all squares are congruent. Tina says that all squares are similar. Who is correct? Explain.

Harcourt Mega Math Software Support

Shapes Ahoy: Ship Shapes, Level I

Challenge — Activity Card 10-1

Make Your Own
Activity Card 10-1

Work: (pair)
Use:
- Figure Match (TRB M79)
- scissors
- index cards

Choose:
- 1
- 2

1. **Work Together** Cut apart the shapes on Figure Match. Mix up the cards. Place them face down in rows of four.
2. (1) Turn over two cards.
   - If the cards are similar, keep the cards.
   - If the cards are not similar, put them back in the rows face down.
3. Take turns.
4. Make additional similar shapes. Add your cards to the others and play the game again.

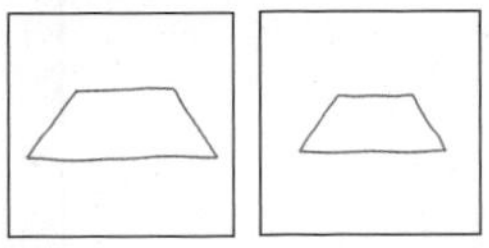

Unit 10, Lesson 1

Activity Note Each pair needs Figure Match (TRB M79), scissors, and index cards that are cut to the same size square as the Figure Match cards.

Math Writing Prompt

Explain Your Thinking Can two figures be both congruent and similar? Explain your thinking.

Destination Math Software Support

Course II: Module 3: Unit 1: Area

3 Homework

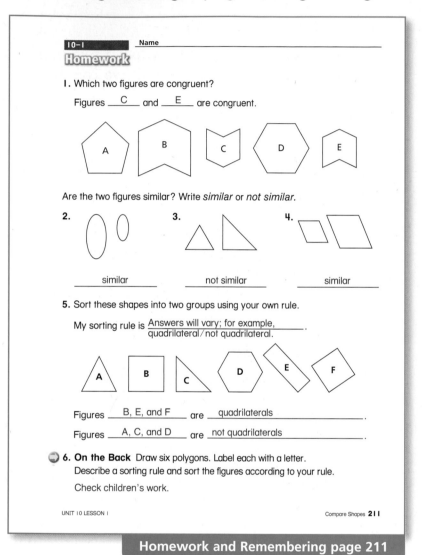

10–1 Homework **Goal:** Additional Practice

This Homework page provides practice in identifying congruent and similar figures and group figures, using a sorting rule.

10–1 Homework Name ____________

1. Which two figures are congruent?

Figures C and E are congruent.

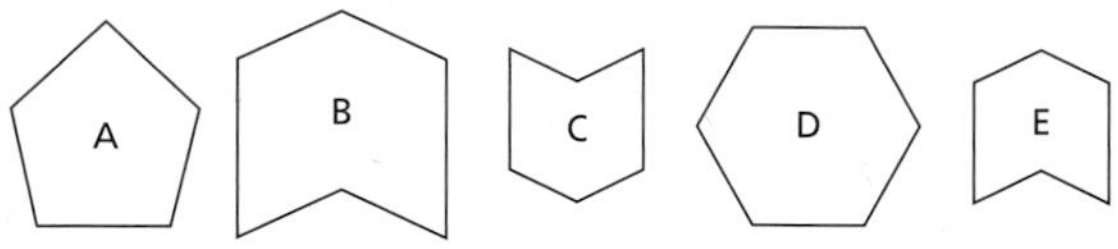

Are the two figures similar? Write *similar* or *not similar*.

2. similar

3. not similar

4. similar

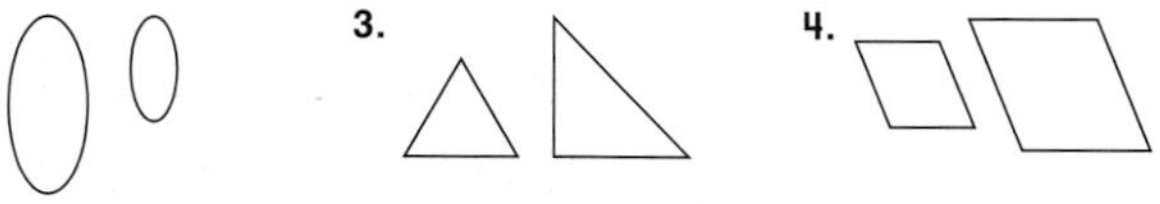

5. Sort these shapes into two groups using your own rule.

My sorting rule is Answers will vary; for example, quadrilateral/not quadrilateral.

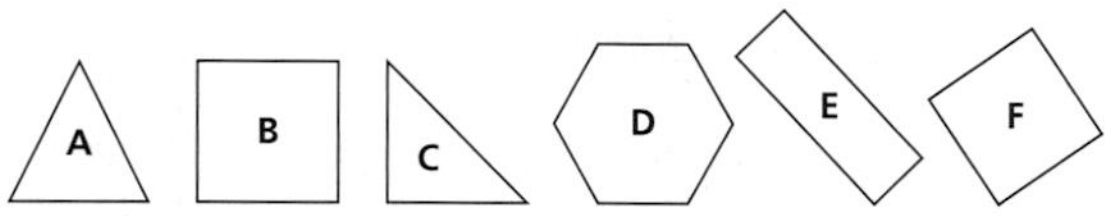

Figures B, E, and F are quadrilaterals.

Figures A, C, and D are not quadrilaterals.

6. On the Back Draw six polygons. Label each with a letter. Describe a sorting rule and sort the figures according to your rule.

Check children's work.

UNIT 10 LESSON 1 Compare Shapes 211

Homework and Remembering page 211

Home and School Connection

Family Letter Have children take home the Family Letter on Student Activity Book page 319. This letter explains how the concept of congruent figures is developed in *Math Expressions.* It gives parents and guardians a better understanding of the learning that goes on in math class and creates a bridge between school and home. A Spanish translation of this letter is on the following page in the Student Activity Book.

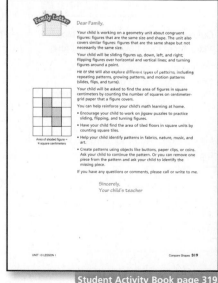

Family Letter

Dear Family,

Your child is working on a geometry unit about congruent figures: figures that are the same size and shape. The unit also covers similar figures: figures that are the same shape but not necessarily the same size.

Your child will be sliding figures up, down, left, and right; flipping figures over horizontal and vertical lines; and turning figures around a point.

He or she will also explore different types of patterns, including repeating patterns, growing patterns, and motion patterns (slides, flips, and turns).

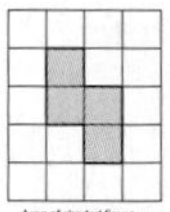

Area of shaded figure = 4 square centimeters

Your child will be asked to find the area of figures in square centimeters by counting the number of squares on centimeter-grid paper that a figure covers.

You can help reinforce your child's math learning at home.

- Encourage your child to work on jigsaw puzzles to practice sliding, flipping, and turning figures.
- Have your child find the area of tiled floors in square units by counting square tiles.
- Help your child identify patterns in fabrics, nature, music, and art.
- Create patterns using objects like buttons, paper clips, or coins. Ask your child to continue the pattern. Or you can remove one piece from the pattern and ask your child to identify the missing piece.

If you have any questions or comments, please call or write to me.

Sincerely,
Your child's teacher

UNIT 10 LESSON 1 Compare Shapes 319

Student Activity Book page 319

Carta a la familia

Estimada familia:

Su niño está trabajando en una unidad de geometría sobre figuras congruentes: figuras que tienen el mismo tamaño y forma. La unidad también incluye figuras semejantes: figuras que tienen la misma forma pero no necesariamente el mismo tamaño.

Su niño trasladará figuras hacia arriba, hacia abajo, hacia la izquierda y hacia la derecha; invertirá figuras sobre rectas horizontales y verticales y hará girar figuras alrededor de un punto.

También explorará diferentes tipos de patrones, incluidos patrones que se repiten, patrones que aumentan y patrones de movimiento (traslaciones, inversiones y giros).

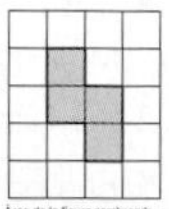

Área de la figura sombreada = 4 centímetros cuadrados

Se le pedirá a su niño que halle el área de figuras en centímetros cuadrados contando el número de cuadrados de un papel cuadriculado que están cubiertos por una figura.

Usted puede ayudar a que su niño refuerce el aprendizaje de matemáticas en casa.

- Anime a su niño a trabajar con rompecabezas para practicar la traslación, la inversión y el giro de figuras.
- Pídale a su niño que halle el área de pisos de baldosas en unidades cuadradas, contando baldosas cuadradas.
- Ayude a su niño a identificar patrones en las telas, la naturaleza, la música y el arte.
- Haga patrones utilizando objetos como botones, sujetapapeles o monedas. Pida a su niño que continúe el patrón. También, puede quitar una pieza del patrón y pedirle al niño que identifique la pieza que falta.

Si tiene alguna pregunta o comentario, por favor comuníquese conmigo.

Atentamente,
El maestro de su niño

320 UNIT 10 LESSON 1 Compare Shapes

Student Activity Book page 320

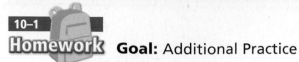

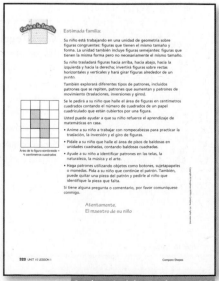

UNIT 10 LESSON 2

Combine and Cut Shapes

Lesson Objectives

- Combine two-dimensional shapes to make new shapes.
- Predict the results of combining two-dimensional shapes.
- Predict the results of cutting apart two-dimensional shapes.

Vocabulary
combine

The Day at a Glance

Today's Goals	Materials	
1 Teaching the Lesson **A1:** Investigate and predict the results of combining two-dimensional shapes. **A2:** Predict what new shapes will be formed by cutting apart shapes.	**Lesson Activities** Student Activity Book pp. 321–324 Homework and Remembering pp. 213–214 Paper shapes Scissors Pattern Blocks (TRB M58)	**Going Further** Activity Cards 10-2 Paper shapes Scissors Glue Math Journals
2 Going Further ▶ Differentiated Instruction		
3 Homework		

Use Math Talk today!

Keeping Skills Sharp

Daily Routines	English Language Learners
Quarters and Other Coins Making and Counting Coins that Make a Quarter, Counting to 200¢ by 25¢, Making and Counting Dollars and Cents: 3-Digit Numbers as Dollars and Cents (See pp. xxvi–xxvii.) ▶ Led by Student Leaders **Money Routine** Using the 120 Poster, Using the Money Flip Chart, Using the Number Path, Using Secret Code Cards (See pp. xxiii–xxv.) ▶ Led by Student Leaders	Write *semi-circle* and *trapezoid* on the board. Draw then point to each shape. • **Beginning** Ask: **Is this a *circle*?** no **Is it a *half* circle?** yes Say: **This is a *semi-circle*.** Ask: **Is this a *rectangle*?** no **Is this a *trapezoid*?** yes • **Intermediate** Say: **This is a half __.** circle **It is a *semi-*__.** circle **This is a __.** trapezoid • **Advanced** Have children identify each shape and tell about its properties.

1 Teaching the Lesson

Activity 1

Combine Shapes

30 MINUTES

Goal: Investigate and predict the results of combining two-dimensional shapes.

Materials: paper shapes, Student Activity Book page 321, scissors

NCTM Standards:
Geometry
Representation

▶ Build It SMALL GROUPS

Prepare 2 right triangles (by cutting diagonally across a square), 2 semicircles (by cutting across a circle), and 2 right triangles (by cutting down the middle of a equilateral triangle) for each small group.

- Find 2 shapes that you think you can combine to make a circle.

Explain that combine means to put together.

- Put the 2 shapes together to check if they make a circle.
- Which shapes did you use? semicircles
- Can you use the same 2 shapes to make a butterfly? If yes, make the butterfly.

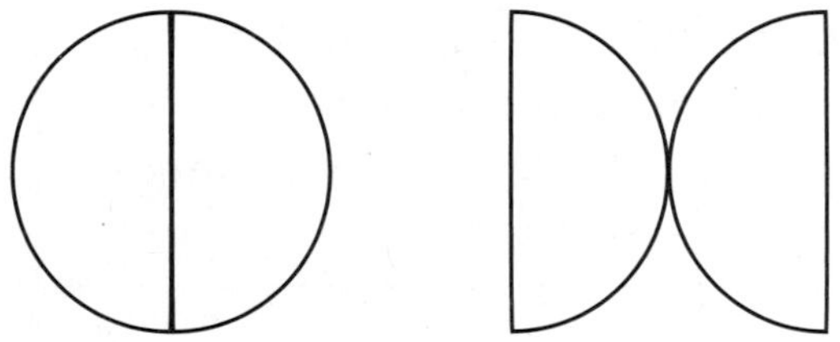

- Find 2 shapes that will make a square. Which shapes did you use? triangles
- Can you use the same 2 shapes to make a bowtie? If yes, make the bowtie.

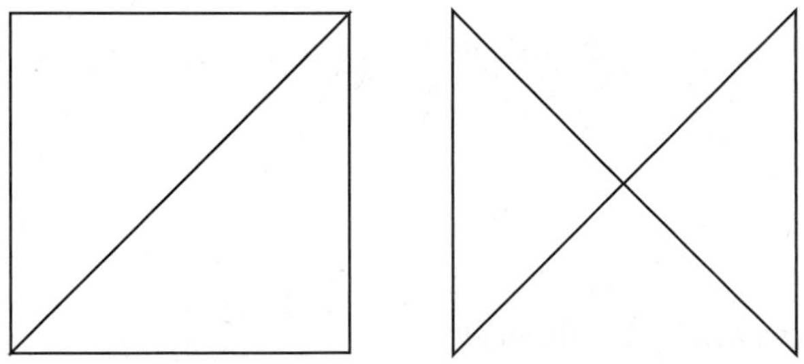

- Find 2 shapes that will make a triangle. Which shapes did you use? triangles
- Can you use the triangles that made the square to make a triangle? yes

Math Talk Have children take the 2 triangles that make the equilateral triangle and try to make a square with those 2 triangles. Discuss how these triangles are different than the ones that made the square. Explain that the type of triangles will depend on what shape can or cannot be made when combined with other triangles or shapes.

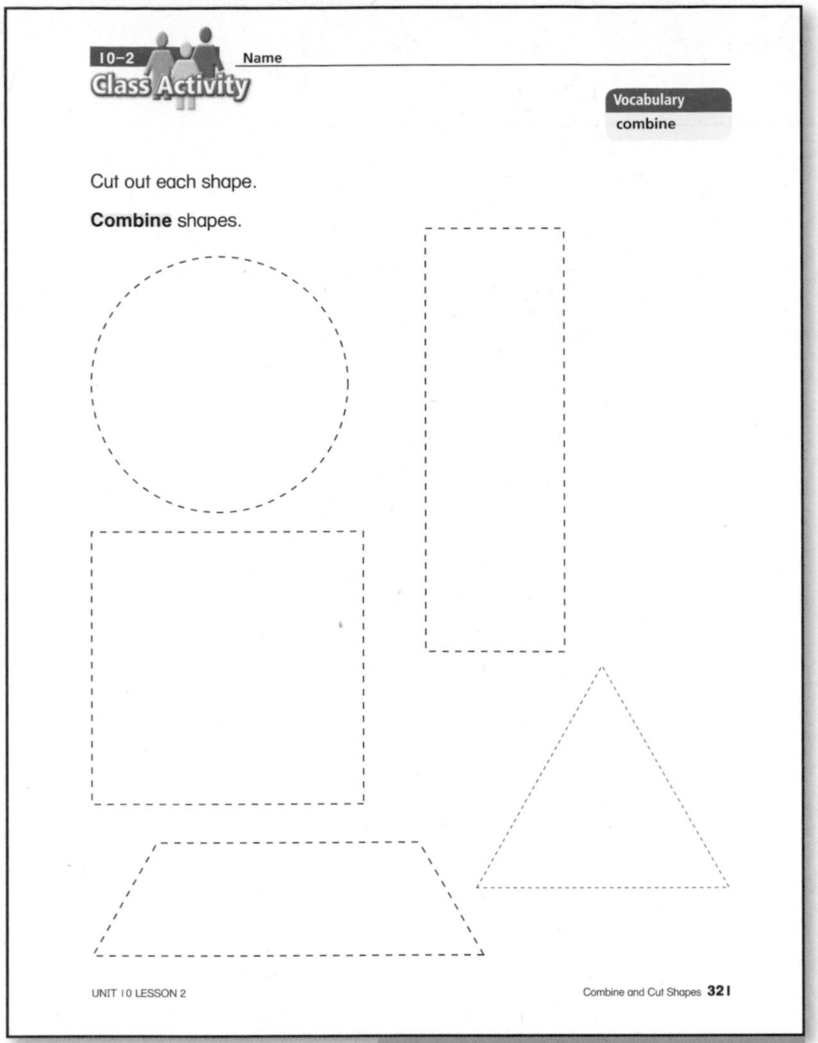
10-2
Class Activity
Name
Vocabulary
combine

Cut out each shape.

Combine shapes.

UNIT 10 LESSON 2
Combine and Cut Shapes 321

Student Activity Book page 321

▶ Predict Shapes or Objects

WHOLE CLASS

Direct children's attention to Student Activity Book page 321. Review the names of each shape: circle, square, rectangle, triangle, trapezoid.

- What shape or object do you think you will get if you combine the circle and triangle together? Possible answers: ice cream cone, head with party hat, head Combine the shapes to see if you were correct.
- What shape or object do you think you will get if you combine the square and triangle? Sample answer: house Combine the shapes to see if you were correct.
- What shape or object do you think you will get if you combine the rectangle and triangle? Sample answers: tree, arrow Combine the shapes to see if you were correct.
- What shape do you think you will get if you combine the rectangle and circle? Sample answers: tree, lollipop Combine the shapes to see if you were correct.

Continue with similar questioning for other shape combinations.

Alternate Approach

Make the Shape Have children use the shapes from the Student Activity Book page 321. Name a shape and have children name the shapes they would use to make the shape. Example: a pyramid (trapezoid and triangle) Then have children combine the shapes to check.

Teaching Note

Cut Shapes Carefully cut out each shape. Cut right along the lines. (Tell children to begin on the outside and cut toward the shapes rather than try to punch into the middle of the page.)

Activity 2

Decompose Shapes

20 MINUTES

Goal: Predict what new shapes will be formed by cutting apart shapes.

Materials: Student Activity Book page 323, scissors

NCTM Standards:
Geometry
Reasoning and Proof
Representation

Ongoing Assessment

Ask the following questions:

- What shape will you make by combining 2 squares? rectangle
- What shape or object will you make by combining a rectangle and a triangle? Sample answers: tree, arrow

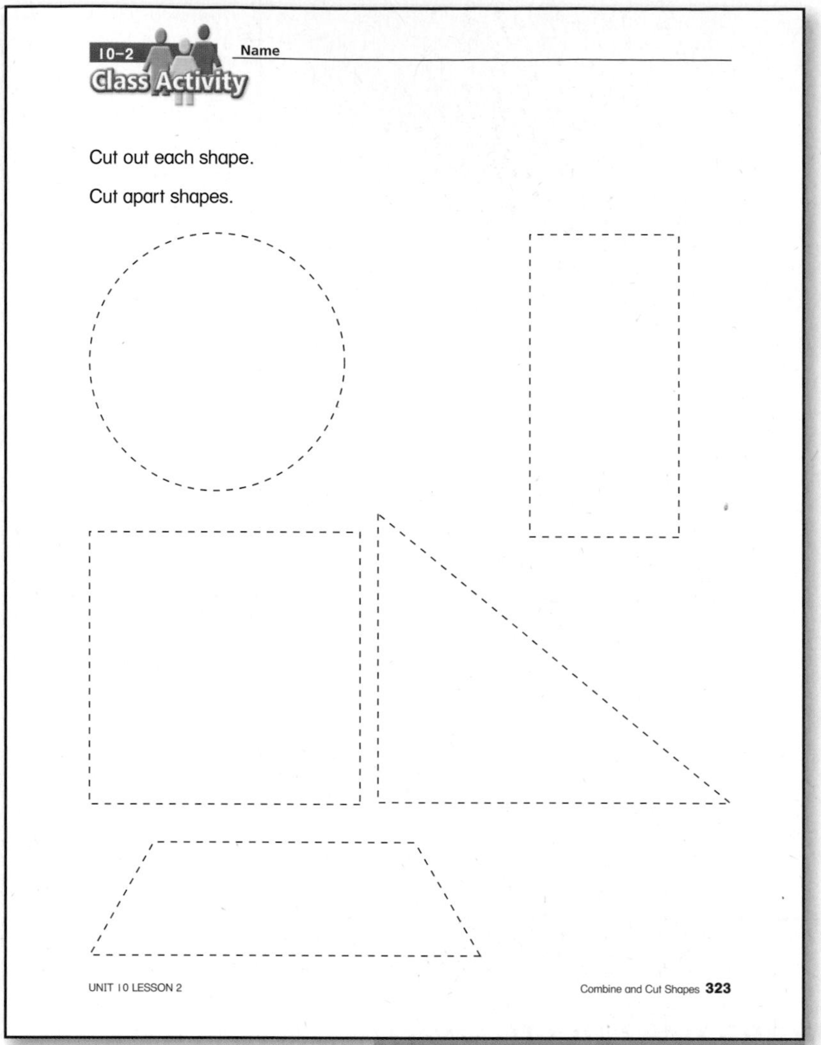
10-2 Class Activity
Name

Cut out each shape.

Cut apart shapes.

UNIT 10 LESSON 2

Combine and Cut Shapes 323

Student Activity Book page 323

► What Shapes Will It Make? WHOLE CLASS

Have children find Student Activity Book page 323.

- Look at the square. What shapes can you make if you cut it into 2 pieces? Cut it to see if you were correct.
- What shapes did you make? Possible answers: 2 triangles, 2 rectangles
- Look at the rectangle or triangle. What shapes can you make if you cut it into 2 pieces? Cut it to see if you were correct.
- What shapes did you make? Sample answers: 2 squares, 2 triangles

Continue the same line of questioning with the remaining shapes.

Intervention

Activity Card 10-2

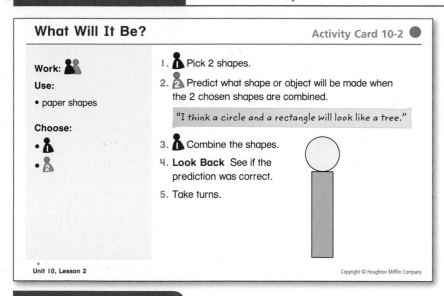

What Will It Be? Activity Card 10-2

Work:
Use:
- paper shapes

Choose:
- 1
- 2

1. Pick 2 shapes.
2. Predict what shape or object will be made when the 2 chosen shapes are combined.

"I think a circle and a rectangle will look like a tree."

3. Combine the shapes.
4. **Look Back** See if the prediction was correct.
5. Take turns.

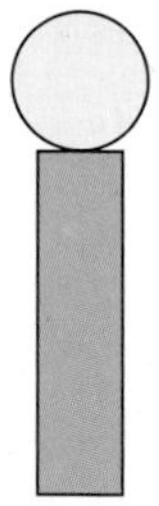

Unit 10, Lesson 2

Activity Note Prepare cut-out paper shapes for each pair (circles, squares, rectangles, triangles, trapezoids, and hexagons). Explain that the 2 chosen shapes may make more than one shape or object depending on their placement.

Math Writing Prompt

Explain Your Thinking Explain how you can tell what shape will be made by combining 2 or more shapes.

Soar to Success Math **Software Support**

Warm Up 35.15

On Level

Activity Card 10-2

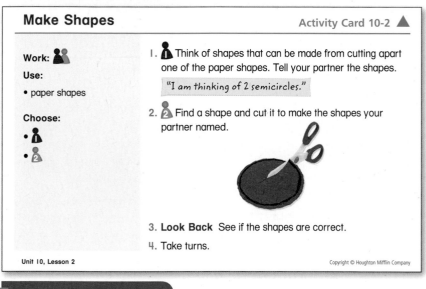

Make Shapes Activity Card 10-2

Work:
Use:
- paper shapes

Choose:
- 1
- 2

1. Think of shapes that can be made from cutting apart one of the paper shapes. Tell your partner the shapes.

"I am thinking of 2 semicircles."

2. Find a shape and cut it to make the shapes your partner named.

3. **Look Back** See if the shapes are correct.
4. Take turns.

Unit 10, Lesson 2

Activity Note Prepare cut-out paper shapes for each pair (circles, squares, rectangles, triangles, trapezoids, and hexagons). Tell children that a shape can be cut into more than 2 shapes. For example, a square can be cut to make 4 squares.

Math Writing Prompt

Explain Write how you would cut a trapezoid to make a square and 2 triangles.

Harcourt Mega Math **Software Support**

Shapes Ahoy: Ship Shapes, Level K

Challenge

Activity Card 10-2

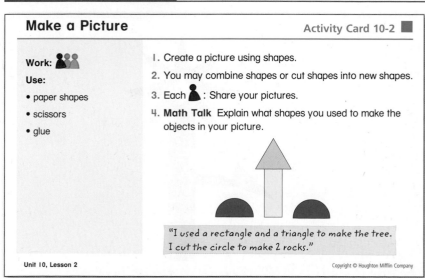

Make a Picture Activity Card 10-2

Work:
Use:
- paper shapes
- scissors
- glue

1. Create a picture using shapes.
2. You may combine shapes or cut shapes into new shapes.
3. Each: Share your pictures.
4. **Math Talk** Explain what shapes you used to make the objects in your picture.

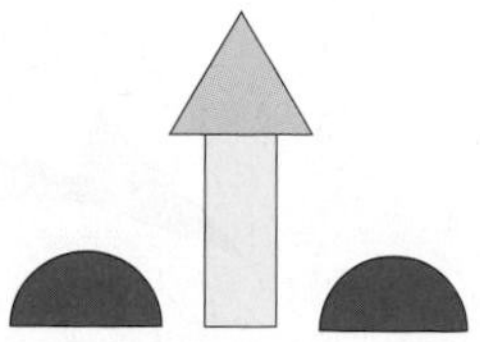

"I used a rectangle and a triangle to make the tree. I cut the circle to make 2 rocks."

Unit 10, Lesson 2

Activity Note Prepare cut-out paper shapes for each group.

Math Writing Prompt

Investigate Math Describe the ways you can cut a square to get different shapes. How many of each shape would you have?

Destination Math **Software Support**

Course II: Module 3: Unit 1: Area

3 Homework

10–2 Homework **Goal:** Additional Practice

Provide each student with a copy of the pattern blocks page (TRB M58). Use this homework activity to provide children more practice with combining and cutting shapes.

10–2 Homework Name ______________________

Cut out the pattern blocks from page M58.
Use them to complete the exercises.

1. Combine shapes to show 2 ways to make a trapezoid.
   List the shapes you used and how many.
   Possible answer: 3 triangles
   Possible answer: rhombus and 1 triangle

2. Combine shapes to show 3 ways to make a hexagon.
   List the shapes you used and how many.
   Possible answer: 6 triangles
   Possible answer: 2 trapezoids
   Possible answer: 1 trapezoid and 3 triangles

Ring the shapes you can cut to make the named shapes.
Cut them to check.

3. 2 triangles

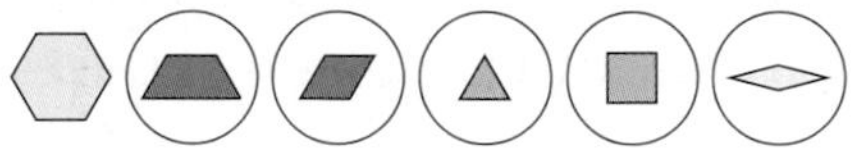

4. 4 squares

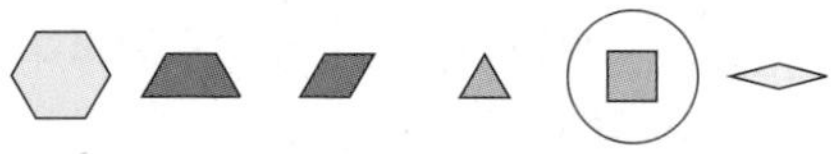

5. **On the Back** Draw 3 different shapes. Draw a shape you can make by combining the 3 shapes. Check children's work.

UNIT 10 LESSON 2 Combine and Cut Shapes **213**

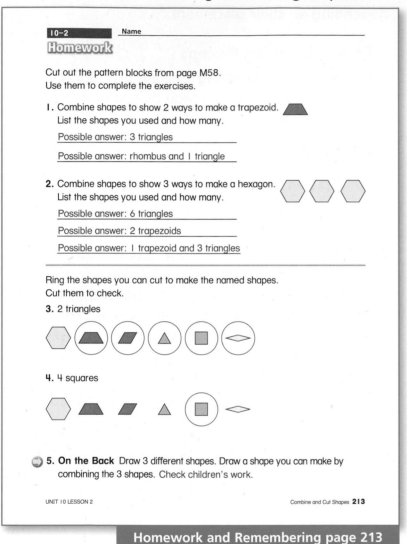

Homework and Remembering page 213

Home or School Activity

Art Connection

Mosaics Mosaic is the art of decorating with small pieces to make a design or picture. Mosaics can be done with glass, stone, tile, paper, or other materials. Look around when you are out to see if you see any examples of mosaic art. Have children take different colored papers and cut them into small shapes such as squares and triangles. Then have children use them to make a picture.

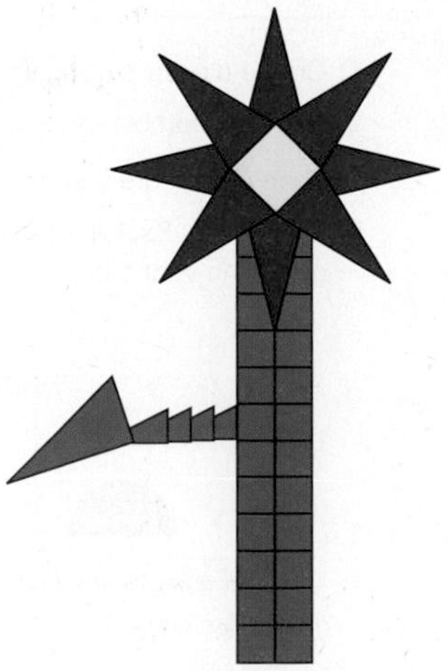

MINI UNIT 10

LESSON 3

Motion Geometry

Vocabulary	
slide	rotation
flip	rotate
horizontal	turn
vertical	

Lesson Objectives

- Recognize transformations: slides, flips, and turns.
- Extend geometric patterns that use transformations.

The Day at a Glance

Today's Goals	Materials	
1 Teaching the Lesson **A1:** Recognize and describe slides of geometric figures. **A2:** Identify and describe flips of geometric figures. **A3:** Recognize turns of geometric figures. **A4:** Extend geometric patterns that use slides, flips, and turns.	**Lesson Activities** Student Activity Book pp. 325–330 Homework and Remembering pp. 215–216 Pattern blocks MathBoard materials Tracing paper Scissors 25-cm rulers Transparent plastic mirrors	**Going Further** Activity Cards 10-3 Large construction paper Plastic mirrors *The M.C. Escher Coloring Book*, by M.C. Escher Math Journals
2 Going Further ▸ Extension: Tessellations ▸ Differentiated Instruction		
3 Homework		

Use Math Talk today!

Keeping Skills Sharp

Daily Routines	English Language Learners
Quarters and Other Coins Making and Counting Coins that Make a Quarter, Counting to 200¢ by 25¢, Making and Counting Dollars and Cents: 3-Digit Numbers as Dollars and Cents (See pp. xxvi–xxvii.) ▸ Led by Student Leaders **Money Routine** Using the 120 Poster, Using the Money Flip Chart, Using the Number Path, Using Secret Code Cards (See pp. xxiii–xxv.) ▸ Led by Student Leaders	Write *slide, flip,* and *rotate* on the board. Give each child a cut out of an arrow • **Beginning** Model as you say: ***Slide* the arrow.** Have children copy and repeat the action. Continue with *flip* and *rotate.* • **Intermediate** Model each action and have children repeat. Call out each action and have children move their arrows. • **Advanced** Model each action. Have children work in pairs. One says an action, the other moves the arrow. Then they switch.

1 Teaching the Lesson

Activity 1

Explore Slides

15 MINUTES

Goal: Recognize and describe slides of geometric figures.

Materials: pattern blocks, MathBoard materials, Student Activity Book page 325, tracing paper, scissors

NCTM Standards:
Geometry
Representation

▶ Draw Slides WHOLE CLASS

Math Talk

Have children select a pattern block and trace it on the left side of their MathBoards. Ask them to then slide the block to the right and trace it again.

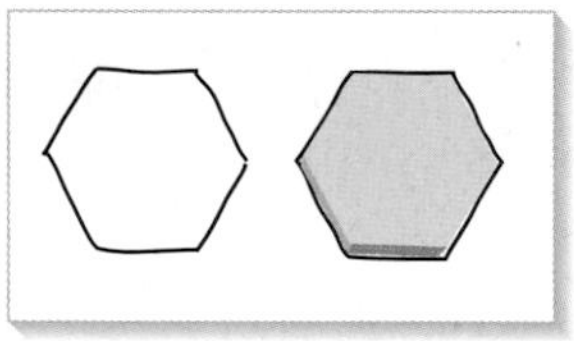

- Are your two tracings the same size? yes Are they the same shape? yes

Explain to children that the second tracing is called a *slide* of the first one.

Invite children to select a second pattern block and to trace it in the middle of their MathBoards. Ask them to then slide the block down and trace it again.

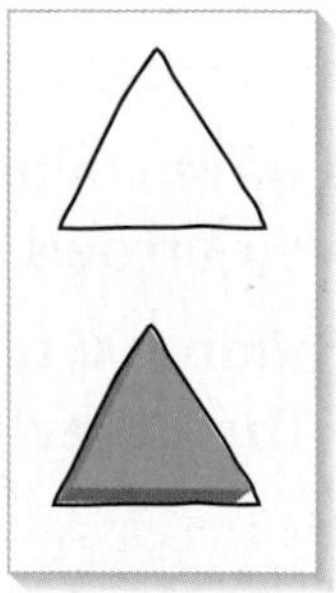

- Are your two tracings the same size? yes
- Are they the same shape? yes

Point out for children that this example is also a slide.

▶ Identify Slides INDIVIDUALS

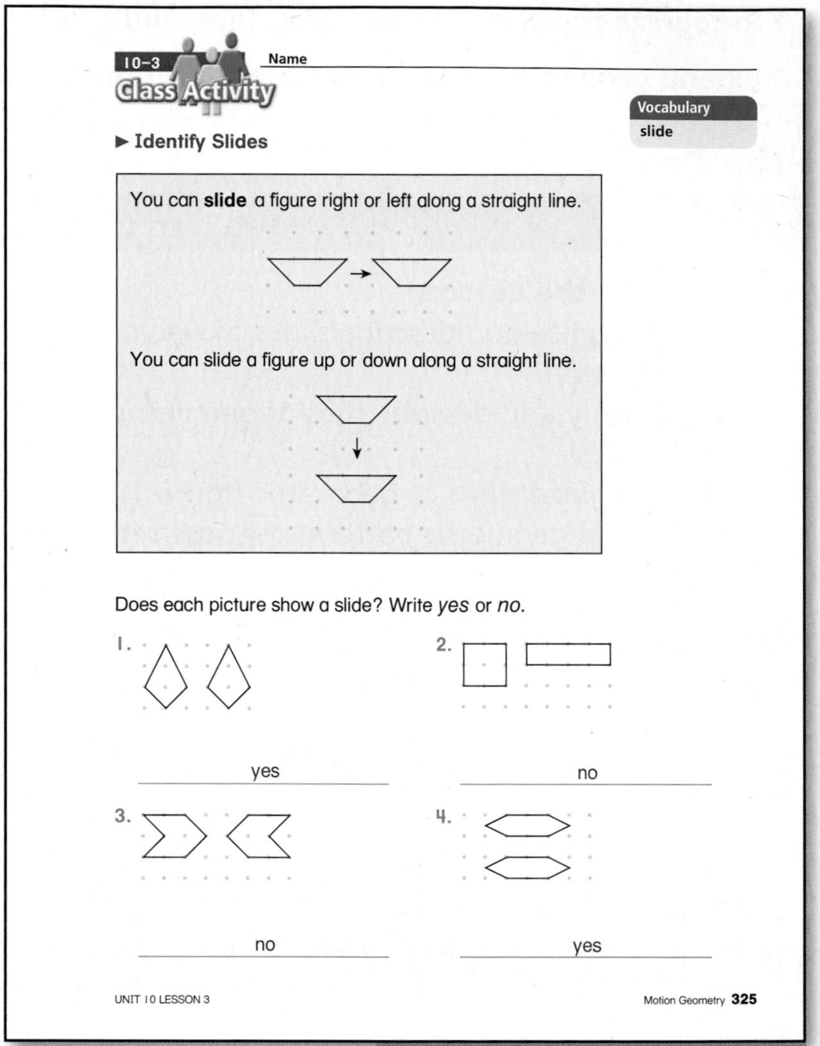
10-3 Class Activity

Name

Vocabulary
slide

▶ Identify Slides

You can **slide** a figure right or left along a straight line.

You can slide a figure up or down along a straight line.

Does each picture show a slide? Write *yes* or *no*.

1. yes

2. no

3. no

4. yes

UNIT 10 LESSON 3

Motion Geometry **325**

Student Activity Book page 325

Refer children to Student Activity Book page 325. Read aloud the first two sentences in order to emphasize that you can slide a figure up, down, right, or left, in a straight line.

Ask children to complete exercises 1–4 individually. When they are finished, discuss their answers as a class.

Differentiated Instruction

Extra Help To identify slides, some children may benefit from tracing the first figure, cutting it out, and trying to slide it to fit exactly on top of the second figure.

Activity 2

Explore Flips

15 MINUTES

Goal: Identify and describe flips of geometric figures.

Materials: pattern blocks, MathBoard materials, 25-cm rulers, Student Activity Book page 326, transparent plastic mirrors

NCTM Standards:
Geometry
Connections

▶ Draw Flips WHOLE CLASS

Math Talk

Invite children to each select a blue parallelogram pattern block and trace it on the lower part of their MathBoards. Ask them to use their rulers to draw a horizontal dotted line above the pattern block and then to flip the pattern block over the horizontal line. Have them trace the block again. If necessary, demonstrate this process on the board.

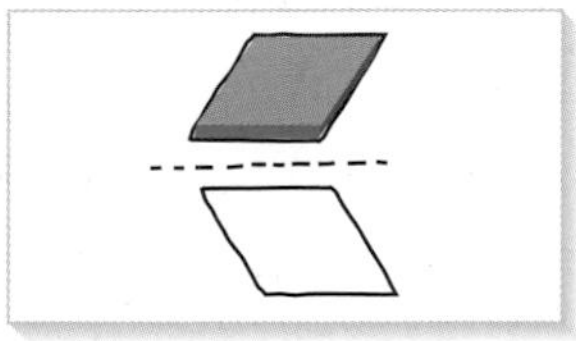

- Are your two tracings the same size and shape? yes
- How is the top figure different from the bottom one? The top figure is upside down.

Explain that one tracing is a flip of the other.

Have children trace the same pattern block on the left side of their MathBoards. Ask them to draw a vertical dotted line and flip the figure over the vertical line.

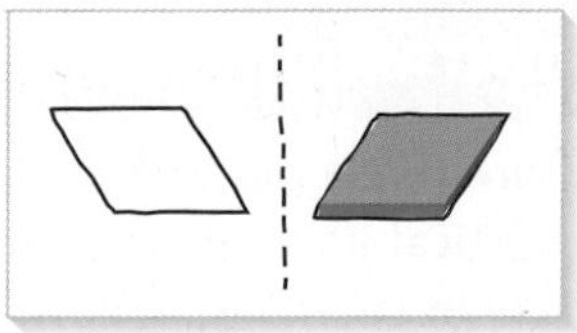

- Are your two tracings the same size and shape? yes
- How are the figures different? One has been flipped; it looks likethe image you see in a mirror.

▶ Identify Flips INDIVIDUALS

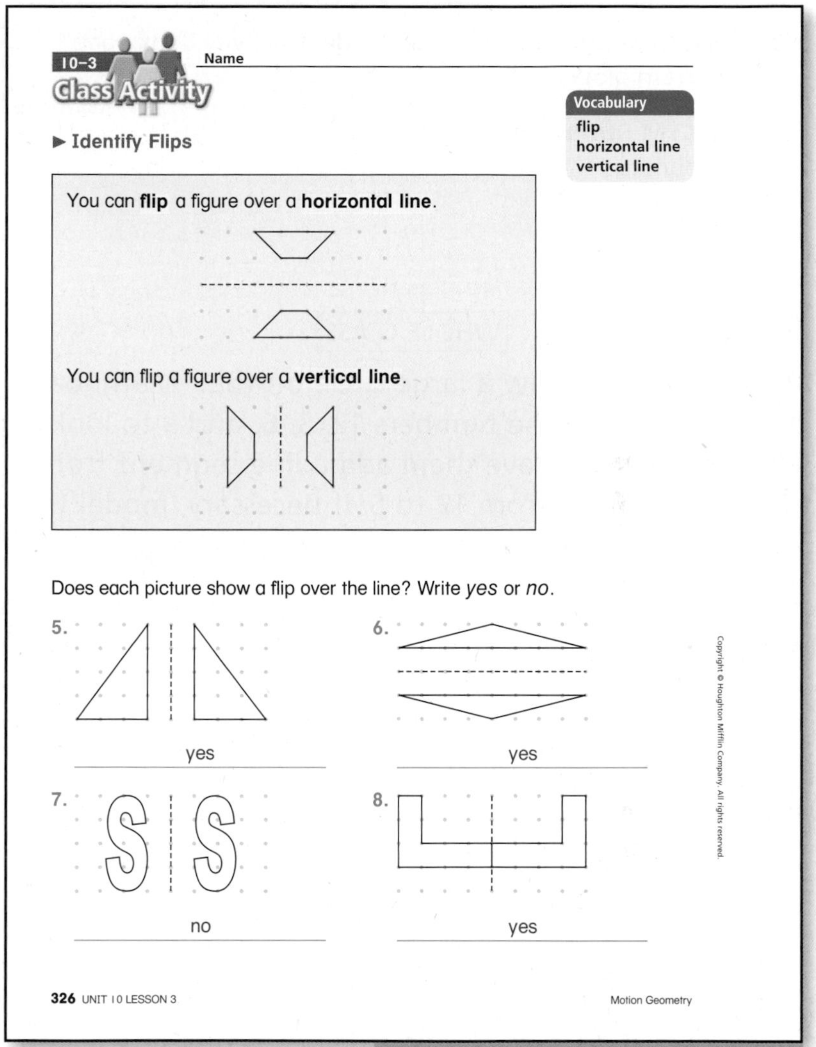

10–3 Class Activity Name

Vocabulary
flip
horizontal line
vertical line

▶ Identify Flips

You can **flip** a figure over a **horizontal line**.

You can flip a figure over a **vertical line**.

Does each picture show a flip over the line? Write *yes* or *no*.

5. yes

6. yes

7. no

8. yes

Student Activity Book page 326

Refer children to Student Activity Book page 326. Ask children to complete exercises 5–8 individually. Some children may not recognize that exercise 8 shows a flip since the figure lies on the flip line.

Alternate Approach

Transparent Plastic Mirror A transparent plastic mirror can be used to help children draw a flip. Have the children look through the mirror from the same side as the figure they want to flip. Then have them trace the image they see.

1 Teaching the Lesson (continued)

Activity 3

Explore Turns

15 MINUTES

Goal: Recognize turns of geometric figures.

Materials: MathBoard materials, Student Activity Book page 327, pattern blocks

NCTM Standards:
Geometry
Representation

▶ Draw Turns WHOLE CLASS

Ask children to draw a large circle on their MathBoards and label it with the numbers 12, 3, 6, and 9 to look like a clock face. Have them add a line segment from 9 to 3 and another from 12 to 6. If necessary, model the drawing on the board.

Hold up the trapezoid pattern block. Have children each select a trapezoid pattern block and place it with its longest edge along the line segment from the center of the circle to 12. Ask children to then trace the pattern block.

Next, have them turn the trapezoid so that its longest side is along the line segment from the center of the circle to 3. Have them trace the figure in its new position.

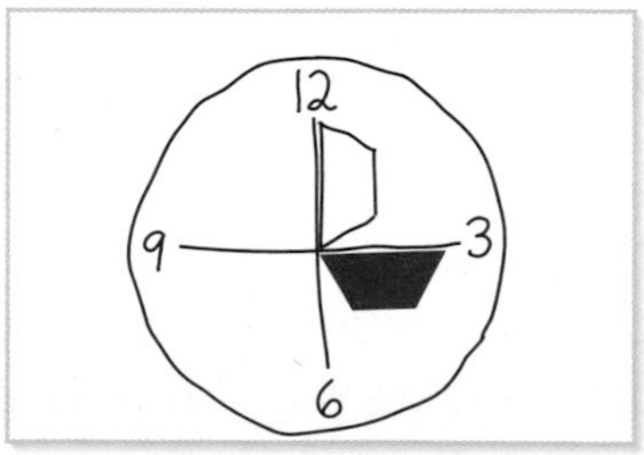

- Are your two tracings the same size and shape? yes
- How has the figure changed in the second tracing? It is in a new position.

Explain to children that the second tracing is a rotation, or turn, of the first one.

Encourage children to continue to turn their block and make more tracings. Invite them to then experiment with rotations in the opposite direction around the circle.

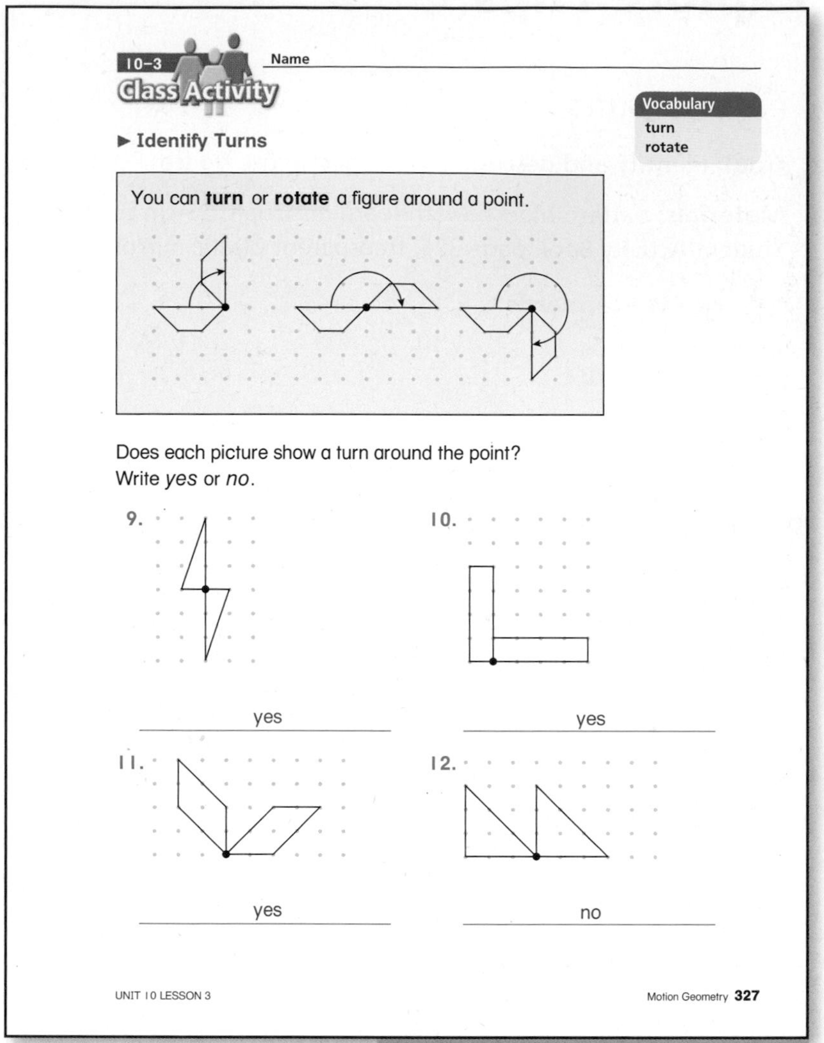
10–3 Class Activity Name

Vocabulary
turn
rotate

▶ Identify Turns

You can **turn** or **rotate** a figure around a point.

Does each picture show a turn around the point?
Write *yes* or *no*.

9. yes

10. yes

11. yes

12. no

UNIT 10 LESSON 3 Motion Geometry 327

Student Activity Book page 327

▶ Identify Turns INDIVIDUALS

Refer children to Student Activity Book page 327 and ask them to complete exercises 9–12 individually. When they are finished, discuss their answers as a class.

Differentiated Instruction

Extra Help Some children may benefit from using a ruler to add horizontal and vertical lines through the point of rotation in these exercises, to help them visualize the rotation. They can then trace the first shape on a separate sheet of paper, place a pencil on the point of rotation, and turn the tracing paper. If they can rotate the tracing of the first shape to exactly fit on top of the second shape, they can identify the example as a rotation.

Activity 4

Patterns with Slides, Flips, and Turns

15 MINUTES

Goal: Extend geometric patterns that use slides, flips, and turns.

Materials: Student Activity Book pages 328–329

NCTM Standards:
Geometry
Connections

▶ Identify Slides, Flips, and Turns PAIRS

Explain to children that you can create patterns with slides, flips, and turns. Ask children to look at the patterns in exercises 13–18 on Student Activity Book page 328 and to work in pairs to decide whether each pattern uses a slide, a flip, or a turn.

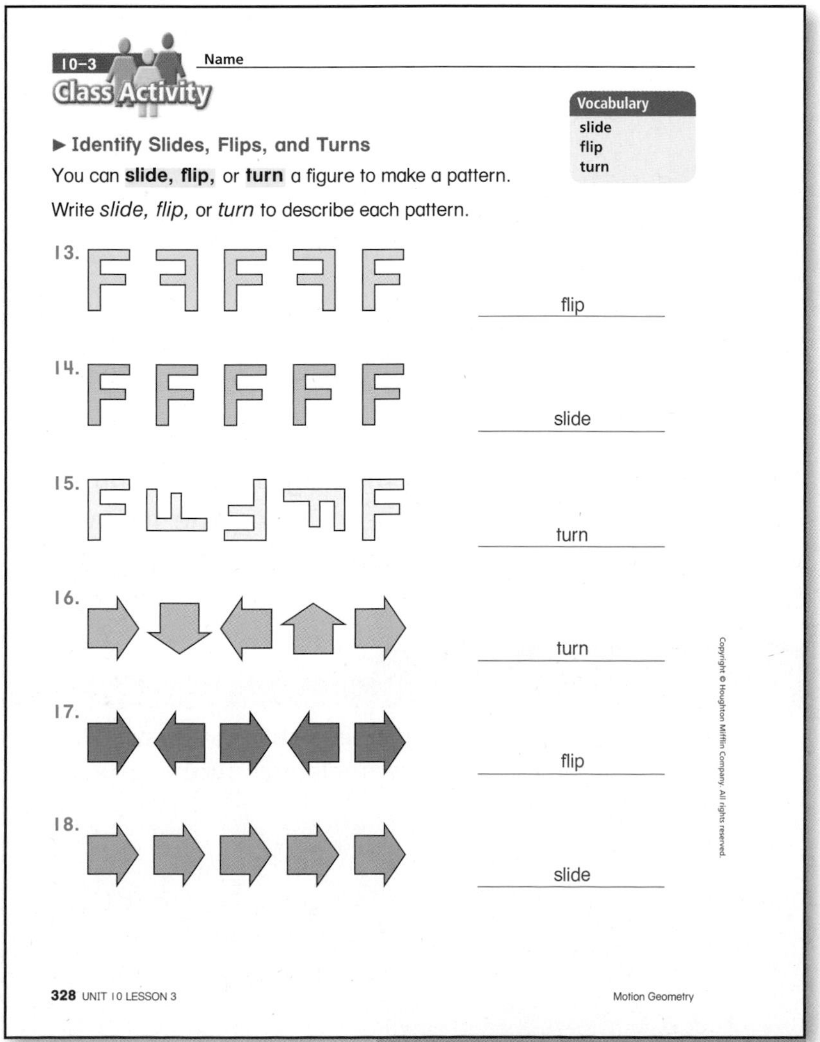

10–3 Class Activity Name

Vocabulary
slide
flip
turn

▶ Identify Slides, Flips, and Turns

You can **slide**, **flip**, or **turn** a figure to make a pattern.

Write *slide*, *flip*, or *turn* to describe each pattern.

13. flip

14. slide

15. turn

16. turn

17. flip

18. slide

Student Activity Book page 328

▶ Extend Patterns INDIVIDUALS

Refer children to Student Activity Book page 329 and ask them to complete exercises 19–23 on their own.

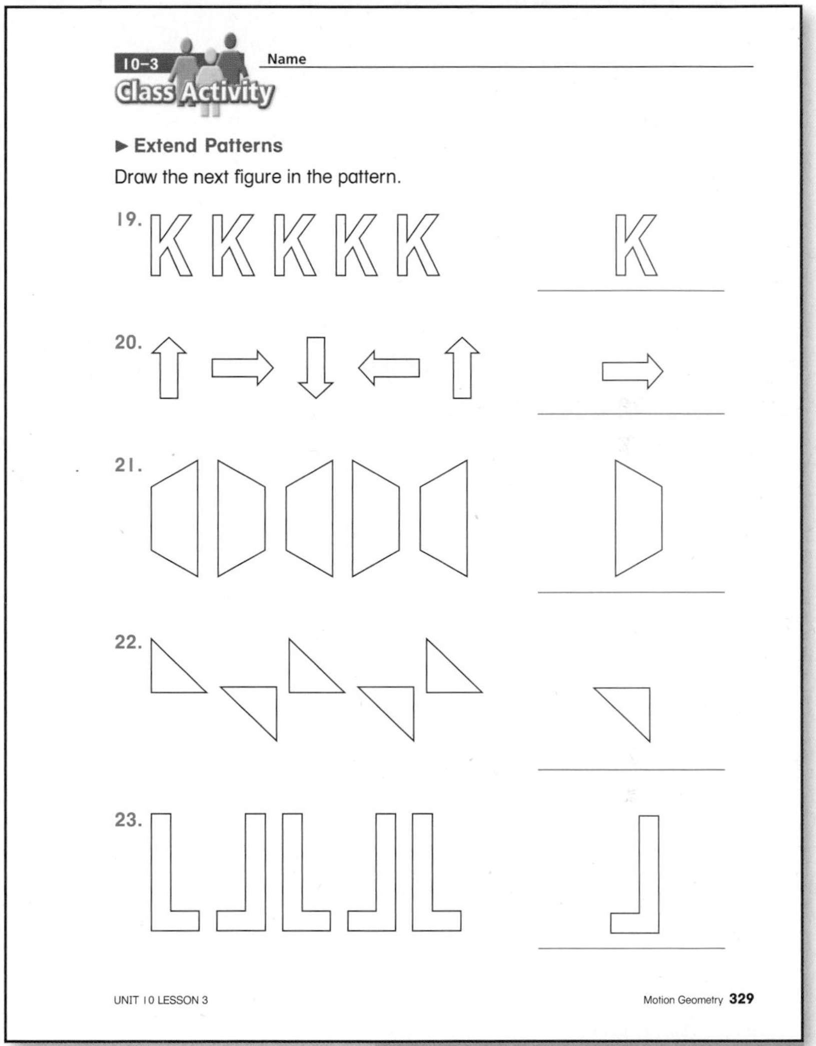

10–3 Class Activity Name

▶ Extend Patterns

Draw the next figure in the pattern.

19.

20.

21.

22.

23.

Student Activity Book page 329

Ongoing Assessment

As children work independently, circulate around the room and ask questions such as these:

- ▶ How do you know that this figure was flipped?
- ▶ How do you know that this figure was turned?

2 Extending the Lesson

Extension: Tessellations

Goal: Explore tessellations of plane figures.

Materials: Student Activity Book page 330

✓ **NCTM Standard:**
Geometry

▶ Explore Tessellations WHOLE CLASS

Discuss tiling of patios, floors, or bathroom walls.

- Suppose you had to design a patio tile. Could you use a square? yes
- Why? because squares will fit together without any gaps to cover the patio
- Could you use a circle? no
- Why not? because circles won't fit together; there will be gaps between the circles

If some students are not convinced, use models or cutouts of circles and squares to have them try to cover a surface without gaps or overlapping.

Explain that the pattern made by repeating a single figure to cover a surface without gaps or overlapping is called a *tessellation.* Turn to the example in the Student Activity Book and have the children complete exercises 1 and 2.

Teaching Note

Math Background To make a tessellation, the angles of a regular polygon must be a factor of 360° for copies of the polygon to fit around a point without overlapping. For this reason, the only regular polygons that will tessellate are the equilateral triangle, square, and regular hexagon.

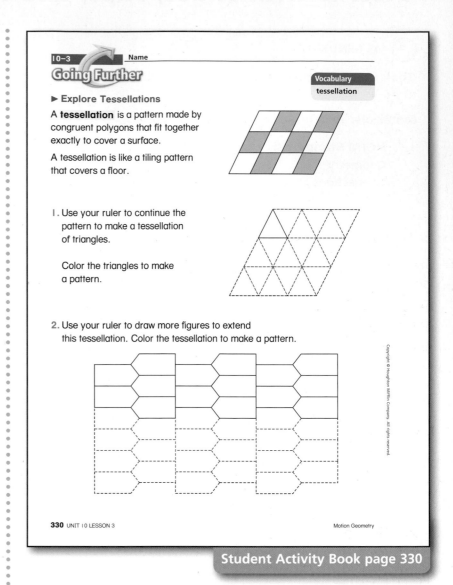

10–3 Name

Going Further

Vocabulary
tessellation

▶ Explore Tessellations

A **tessellation** is a pattern made by congruent polygons that fit together exactly to cover a surface.

A tessellation is like a tiling pattern that covers a floor.

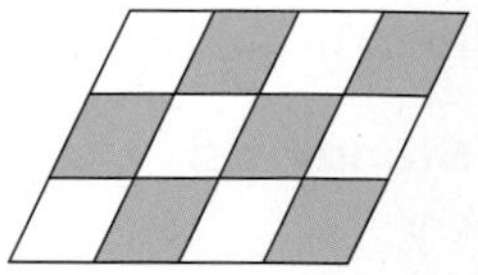

1. Use your ruler to continue the pattern to make a tessellation of triangles.

   Color the triangles to make a pattern.

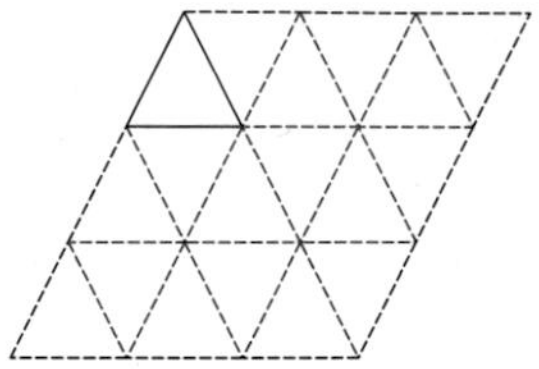

2. Use your ruler to draw more figures to extend this tessellation. Color the tessellation to make a pattern.

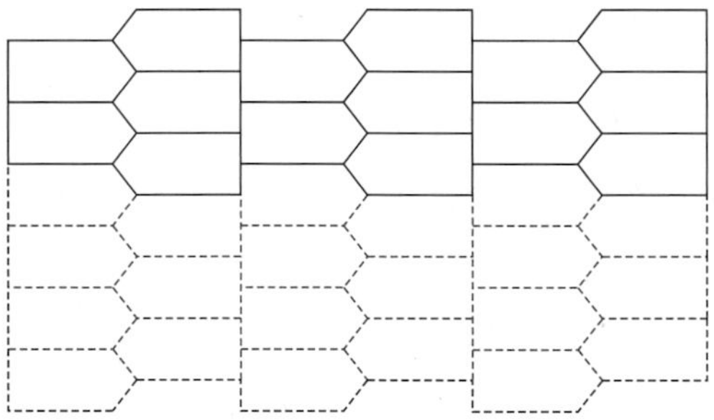

330 UNIT 10 LESSON 3 Motion Geometry

Student Activity Book page 330

After children have finished making their tessellations, have them describe their patterns using the following words: inside, outside, left, right, above, below, between.

Alternate Approach

If computers and appropriate geometry software is available, encourage children to use this technology to further explore and make tessellations.

2 Going Further

Differentiated Instruction

Intervention — Activity Card 10-3

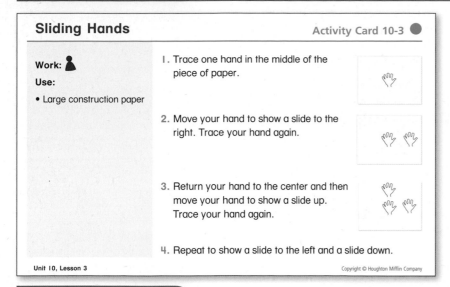

Sliding Hands

Activity Card 10-3 ●

Work: individual

Use:

- Large construction paper

1. Trace one hand in the middle of the piece of paper.

2. Move your hand to show a slide to the right. Trace your hand again.

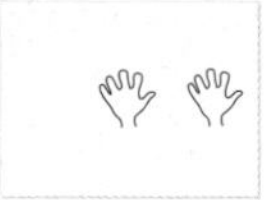

3. Return your hand to the center and then move your hand to show a slide up. Trace your hand again.

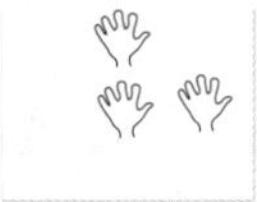

4. Repeat to show a slide to the left and a slide down.

Unit 10, Lesson 3

Activity Note Each child needs a large piece of construction paper. You may want to have each child trace a partner's hand.

Math Writing Prompt

Same or Different? When you slide a figure, does the size of the figure change? Explain.

Soar to Success Math **Software Support**

Warm Up 35.15

On Level — Activity Card 10-3

Secret Message

Activity Card 10-3 ▲

Work: pairs

Use:

- plastic mirrors

1. Each: Use a mirror to help you write a secret message that you need to flip to read.

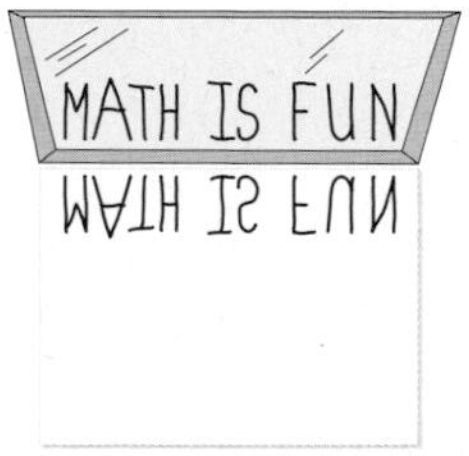

2. Each: Use a mirror to read each other's secret message.
3. Write and read more messages.

Unit 10, Lesson 3

Activity Note Each child needs a plastic mirror. Show pairs how to use the mirrors to write a message and then how to read the message.

Math Writing Prompt

Explain Your Thinking Mike drew a slide of the letter R. He says the flip of the letter R will look the same. Do you agree with Mike? Explain your thinking. Include a drawing in your answer.

Harcourt MegaMath Grades K-6 **Software Support**

Shapes Ahoy: Ship Shapes, Level K

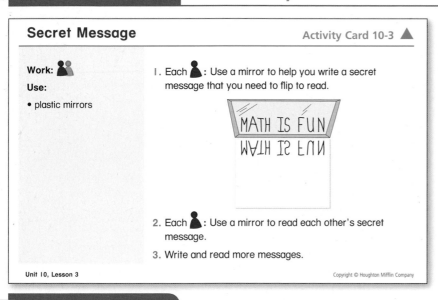

Challenge — Activity Card 10-3

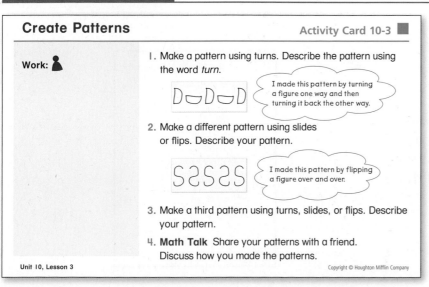

Create Patterns

Activity Card 10-3 ■

Work: individual

1. Make a pattern using turns. Describe the pattern using the word *turn*.

I made this pattern by turning a figure one way and then turning it back the other way.

2. Make a different pattern using slides or flips. Describe your pattern.

I made this pattern by flipping a figure over and over.

3. Make a third pattern using turns, slides, or flips. Describe your pattern.
4. **Math Talk** Share your patterns with a friend. Discuss how you made the patterns.

Unit 10, Lesson 3

Activity Note Each child makes repeating patterns using slides, flips, and turns.

Math Writing Prompt

You Decide Hoon drew these two figures.

Does his drawing show a slide or a flip? Explain.

DESTINATION Math® **Software Support**

Course II: Module 3: Unit 1: Area

3 Homework

10–3 Homework **Goal:** Additional Practice

✓ Include children's completed work for page 215 as part of their portfolios.

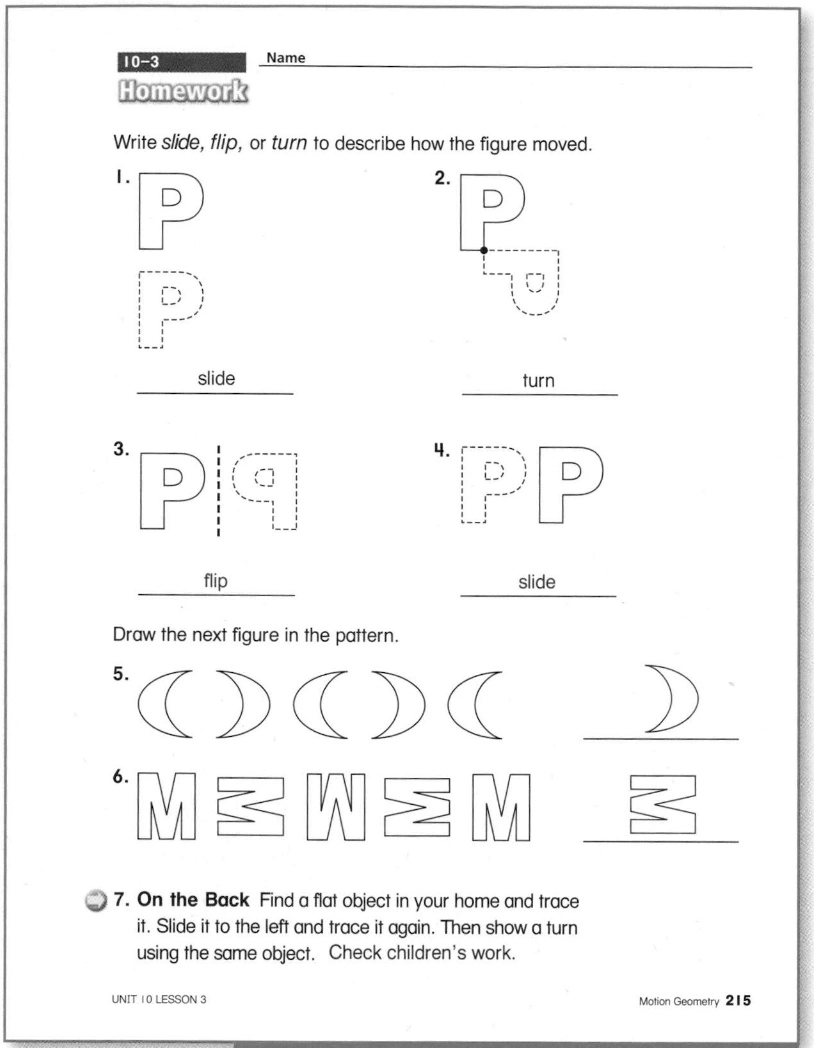
10–3 Homework Name

Write *slide*, *flip*, or *turn* to describe how the figure moved.

1. slide

2. turn

3. flip

4. slide

Draw the next figure in the pattern.

5.

6.

7. **On the Back** Find a flat object in your home and trace it. Slide it to the left and trace it again. Then show a turn using the same object. Check children's work.

UNIT 10 LESSON 3 Motion Geometry **215**

Homework and Remembering page 215

Home or School Activity

Art Connection

Explore Tessellations Complex tessellations can be created to make unusual designs and artwork. Artist M.C. Escher is famous for his works that use tessellations of real objects such as fish and birds. Have children explore tessellations and the work of Escher by using *The M.C. Escher Coloring Book* (Abrams, 1995).

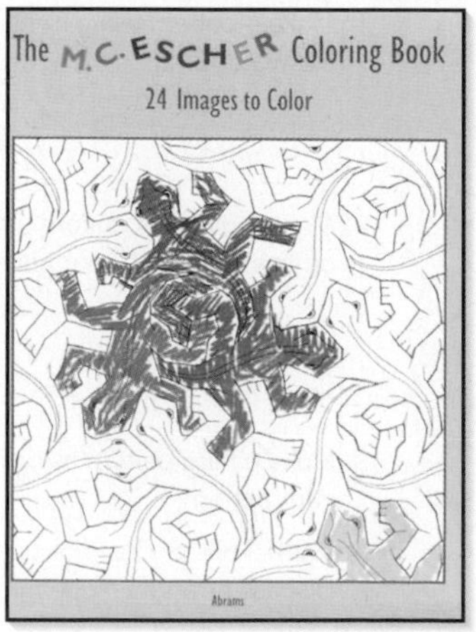

UNIT 10 LESSON 4

Patterns with Shapes

Lesson Objectives

- Represent and analyze patterns.
- Create and extend growing and motion patterns.

Vocabulary
growing pattern
motion pattern

The Day at a Glance

Today's Goals	Materials	
1 Teaching the Lesson **A1:** Identify and extend shape patterns. **A2:** Create and extend growing patterns. **A3:** Extend patterns including growing patterns. **A4:** Create and extend motion pattern.	**Lesson Activities** Student Activity Book pp. 331–332 Homework and Remembering pp. 217–218 Markers or crayons Connecting cubes Cardstock Scissors Squares and triangles for tracing Centimeter Dot Paper (TRB M49)	**Going Further** Activity Cards 10–4 Cubes Centimeter Dot Paper (TRB M49) Cardstock Scissors Math Journals
2 Going Further ▸ Differentiated Instruction		
3 Homework		

Use Math Talk today!

Keeping Skills Sharp

Daily Routines

Quarters and Other Coins Making and Counting Coins that Make a Quarter, Counting to 200¢ by 25¢, Making and Counting Dollars and Cents: 3-Digit Numbers as Dollars and Cents (See pp. xxvi–xxvii.)

▸ Led by Student Leaders

Money Routine Using the 120 Poster, Using the Money Flip Chart, Using the Number Path, Using Secret Code Cards (See pp. xxiii–xxv.)

▸ Led by Student Leaders

English Language Learners

Write *repeating pattern* on the board. Draw:

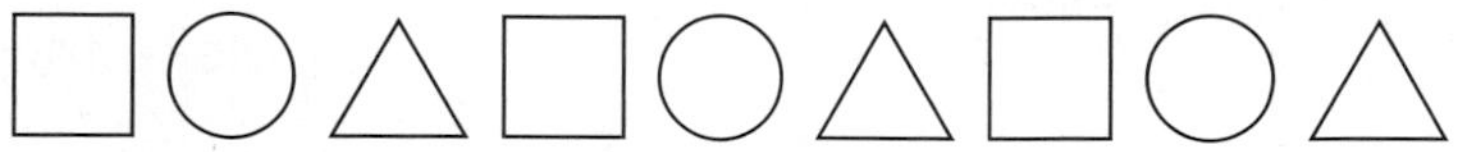

- **Beginning** Have children read the pattern aloud. Ask: **Is this a *pattern*?** yes **How many times does it repeat?** 3 times
- **Intermediate** Ask: **Is this a *growing* or *repeating pattern*?** repeating pattern Have children tell how the shapes repeat.
- **Advanced** Have children describe the pattern and identify the type of pattern.

1 Teaching the Lesson

Activity 1

Shape Patterns

10 MINUTES

Goal: Identify and extend shape patterns.

Materials: paper, markers or crayons

NCTM Standards:
Algebra
Geometry
Communication

▶ Shape Patterns PAIRS

Write ABCABCABC on the board. Tell children that each letter stands for a different shape, for example, *A* could be triangle, *B* could be circle, and *C* could be a rectangle. Have pairs create a repeating pattern using 3 different shapes. Explain that the pattern should repeat at least 3 times. Tell children to trade with other pairs and then draw the next 2 shapes of the pattern.

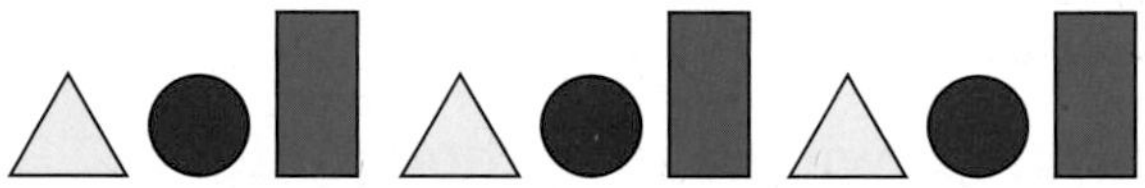

- Then have children repeat the above activity with the pattern AABAABAAB.

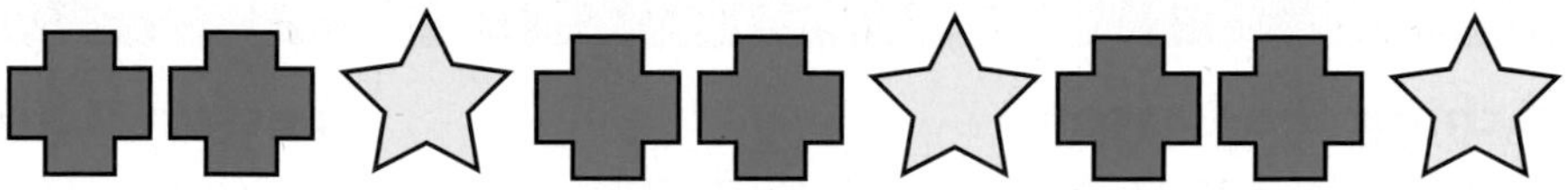

Activity 2

Growing Patterns

10 MINUTES

Goal: Create and extend growing patterns.

Materials: connecting cubes

NCTM Standards:
Algebra
Geometry
Reasoning and Proof

▶ Extend the Pattern SMALL GROUPS

Provide connecting cubes to each group. Build a staircase pattern as shown below.

- What pattern do you notice about the cubes? Sample answers: There are more each time; They make steps.

Introduce the term growing pattern. Explain that a growing pattern is a pattern that gets bigger or grows with each new piece.

- Make the next 2 steps of the pattern.
- Now make a new growing pattern.

Then have children move to a different group and extend the new pattern.

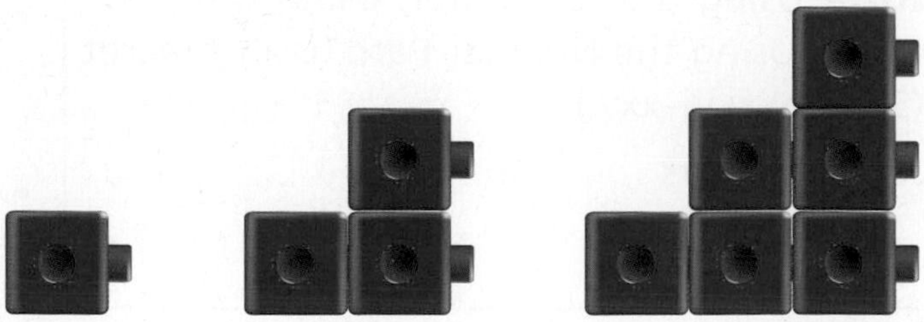

Activity 3

Extend Patterns

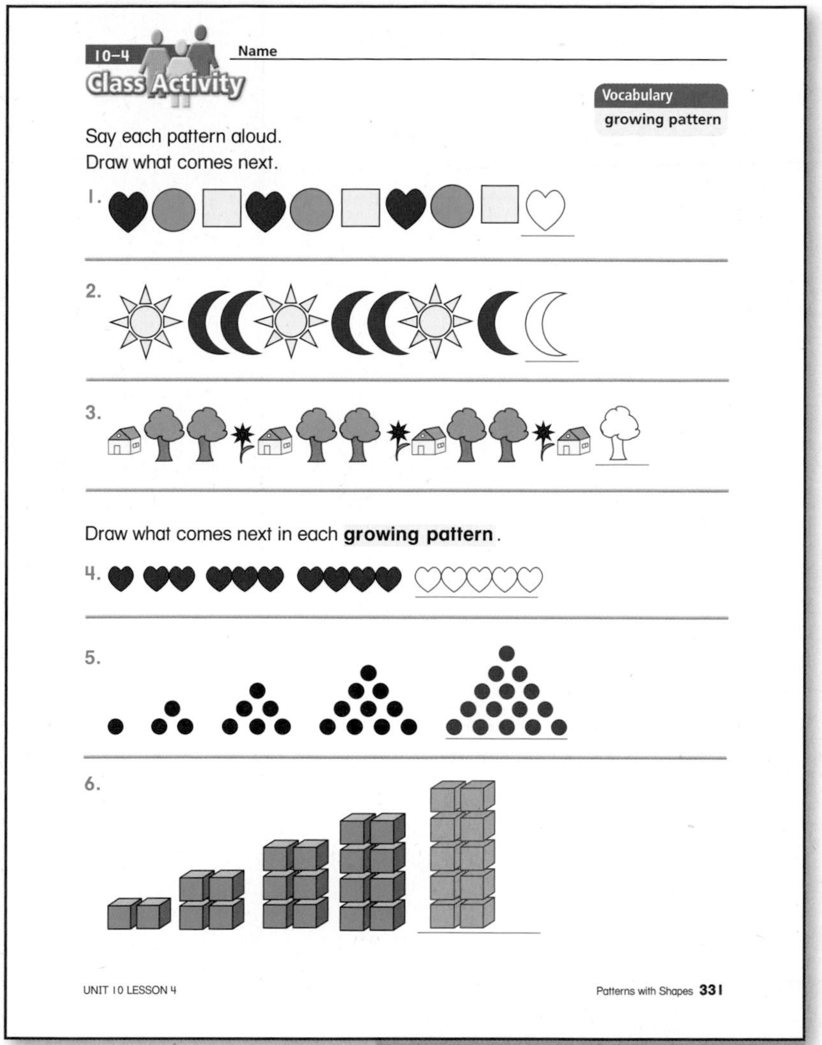
10-4 Class Activity

Name

Vocabulary
growing pattern

Say each pattern aloud.
Draw what comes next.

1.

2.

3.

Draw what comes next in each **growing pattern**.

4.

5.

6.

UNIT 10 LESSON 4

Patterns with Shapes 331

Student Activity Book page 331

15 MINUTES

Goal: Extend patterns including growing patterns.

Materials: Student Activity Book page 331

NCTM Standards:
Algebra
Reasoning and Proof

Teaching Note

Pattern Unit You may wish to have children determine the rule of the pattern, such as repeating, growing by 2 ... before drawing the next piece.

► Extend Repeating and Growing Patterns

WHOLE CLASS

Math Talk 123

Direct children's attention to Student Activity Book page 331, Exercise 1.

- What is the pattern? heart, circle, square, heart, circle, square What part keeps repeating? heart, circle, square

Use similar questioning for Exercises 2 and 3.

Explain that some patterns grow, as in Exercise 4.

- What is the pattern? 1 heart, 2 hearts, 3 hearts, 4 hearts. What is happening in the pattern? There is 1 more heart each time.

Use similar questioning for Exercises 5 and 6.

Have children discuss different ways they could make a growing pattern using coins. Sample responses: 2 pennies, 3 pennies, 4 pennies...; 1 dime, 3 dimes, 5 dimes...; 1 penny, 2 nickels, 3 dimes...

Activity 4

Motion Patterns

15 MINUTES

Goal: Create and extend motion patterns.

Materials: Student Activity Book page 332, cardstock, scissors, 2 × 2 centimeter squares for tracing (for each child), one 3 × 3 × 3 centimeter triangle for tracing, Centimeter Dot Paper (TRB M49)

NCTM Standards:
Algebra
Geometry

Ongoing Assessment

Assess children's understanding of growing patterns. Draw 1 star, 2 stars, 3 stars, and 4 stars.

- ▶ What is next in this pattern? 5 stars
- ▶ How do you know? the stars are increasing by 1 each time

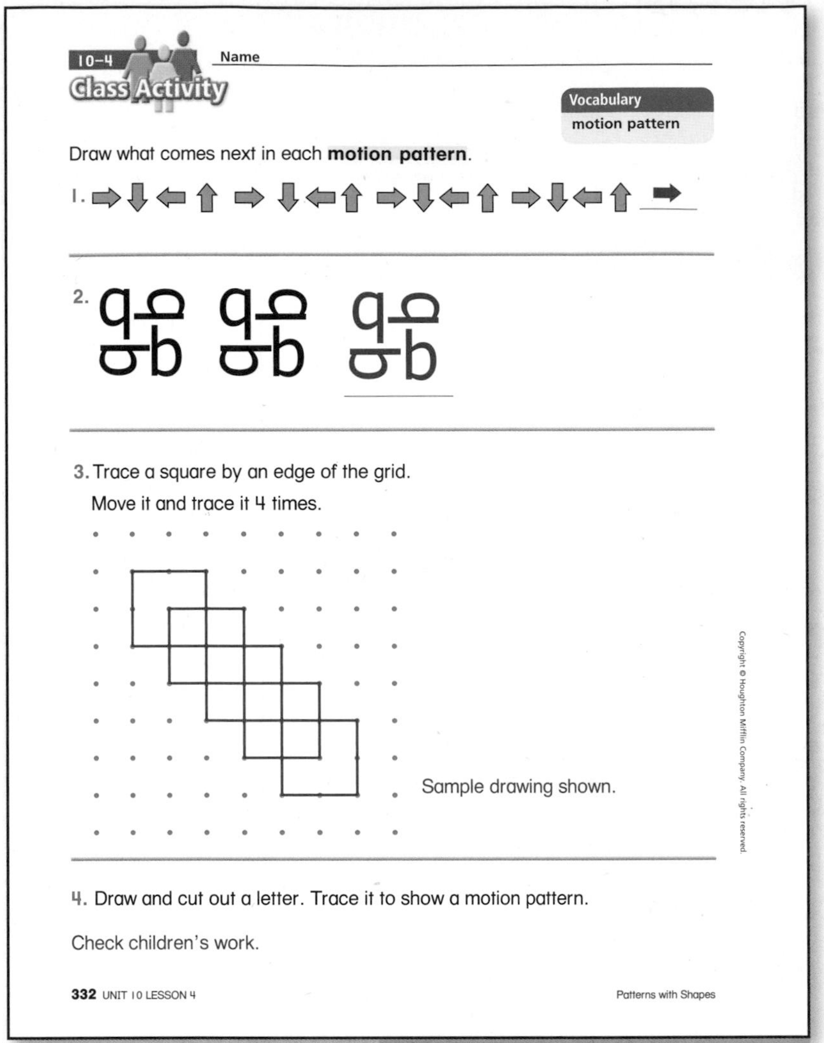

10–4 Class Activity

Name

Vocabulary
motion pattern

Draw what comes next in each **motion pattern**.

1.

2.

3. Trace a square by an edge of the grid. Move it and trace it 4 times.

Sample drawing shown.

4. Draw and cut out a letter. Trace it to show a motion pattern.

Check children's work.

332 UNIT 10 LESSON 4 Patterns with Shapes

Student Activity Book page 332

▶ Motion Patterns WHOLE CLASS

Show a motion pattern on the board by tracing your hand up, then to the right, down, and to the left. Discuss how the pattern moves. Instruct children to look at the pattern for Exercise 1 on Student Activity Book page 332.

- What is happening to the arrow? it keeps turning What comes after the up arrow? right arrow

For Exercise 2, explain that the letter b is being used to make a pattern.

- What is happening to the letter? it keeps turning

Tape a sheet of cm dot paper to the board. Demonstrate a moving pattern by tracing a triangle and moving it diagonally down the paper as you continue tracing it each time. Pass out the tracing squares and have children make a motion pattern for Exercise 3.

For Exercise 4 pass out cardstock and scissors. Have children make a letter pattern similar to the one in Exercise 2.

Intervention Activity Card 10-4

Make It Grow

Activity Card 10-4

Work:
Use:
- cubes

Choose:
-
-

1. Make a growing pattern.
2. Describe the pattern.
3. Continue the pattern.
4. **Look Back** Check your work.
5. Repeat. Take turns.

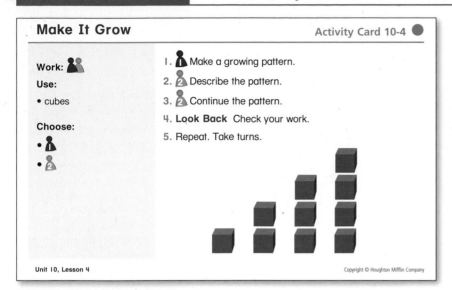

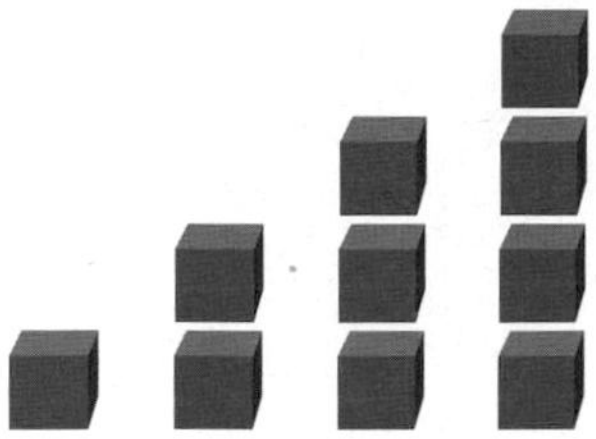

Unit 10, Lesson 4

Activity Note Give each pair about 50 cubes. Remind children to think of the pattern rule first and use it to build their pattern.

Math Writing Prompt

Explain A pattern has 5 squares in the first part, 10 in the second, 15 in the third, and 20 in the fourth. Explain how can you find what comes next.

Software Support

Warm Up 25.12

On Level Activity Card 10-4

Watch It Move

Activity Card 10-4

Work:
Use:
- Centimeter Dot Paper (TRB M49)
- scissors
- cardstock

1. Each : Use cardstock. Cut out a simple shape.
2. Each : Use the shape. Make a motion pattern on the dot paper.
3. Trade papers. Add the next shape.

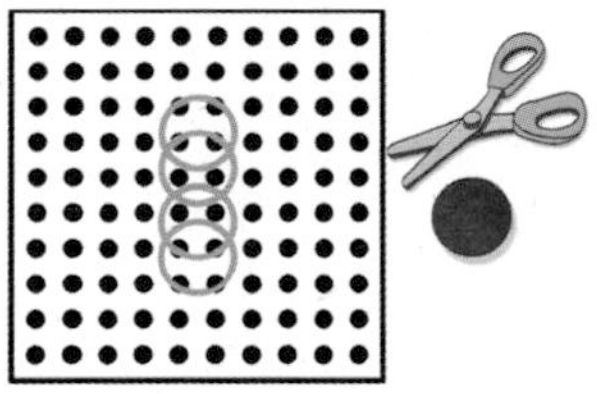

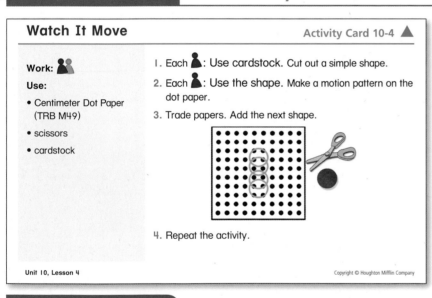

4. Repeat the activity.

Unit 10, Lesson 4

Activity Note Make sure children do not make the shapes too large. Remind them that at least 5 should fit. Instruct children to keep moving the shape in the same direction.

Math Writing Prompt

Explain Your Thinking Write about a time when a motion pattern would be helpful to explain something.

Software Support

Shapes Ahoy: Ship Shapes, Level O

Challenge Activity Card 10-4

Motion Designs

Activity Card 10-4

Work:
Use:
- scissors
- cardstock

1. Use cardstock. Cut out a shape.
2. Trace the shape several times to make a motion pattern.

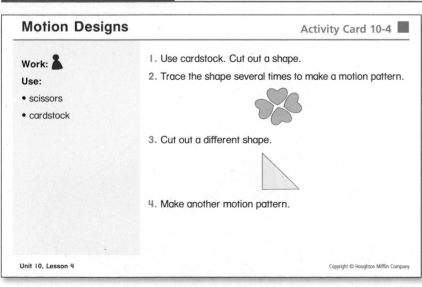

3. Cut out a different shape.

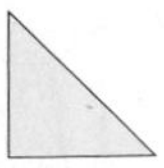

4. Make another motion pattern.

Unit 10, Lesson 4

Activity Note Remind children that to make a motion pattern they must keep moving a shape in the same direction. Tell children that they can use different shapes and motions for their designs.

Math Writing Prompt

Investigate Math Where might you see motion patterns? How can they be helpful?

Software Support

Course II: Module 3: Unit 1: Area

3 Homework

10–4 **Homework** **Goal:** Additional Practice

Use this homework activity to provide children more practice with growing and motion patterns.

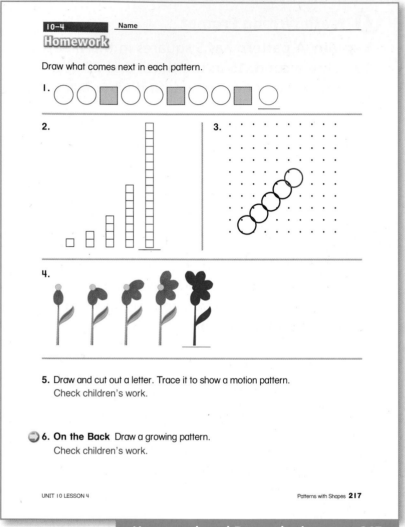

10–4 **Homework** Name ______________________

Draw what comes next in each pattern.

1. 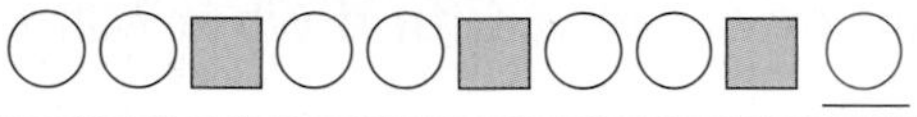

2. 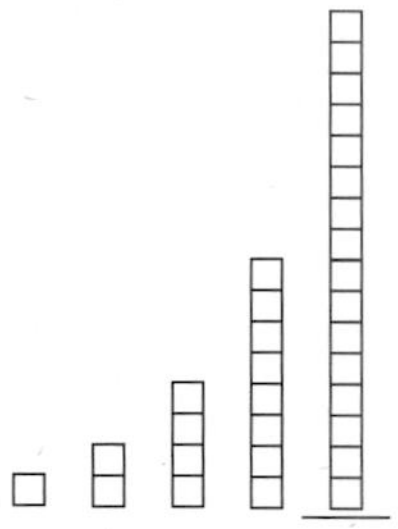

3. 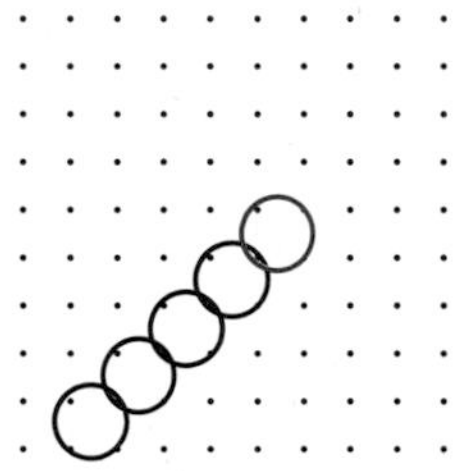

4. 

5. Draw and cut out a letter. Trace it to show a motion pattern.
Check children's work.

6. **On the Back** Draw a growing pattern.
Check children's work.

UNIT 10 LESSON 4 — Patterns with Shapes **217**

Homework and Remembering page 217

Home or School Activity

Real-World Connection

Find Patterns Have children look around the school or their homes for things with patterns. Have them draw or write about the patterns they find.

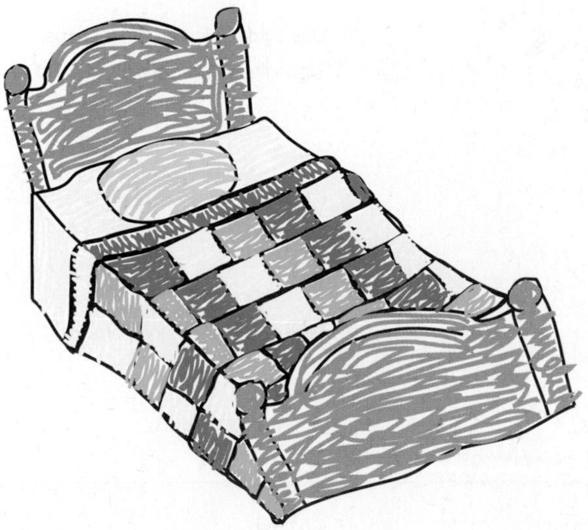

MINI UNIT 10

LESSON 5

Count Square Units

Lesson Objectives

- Find area by covering and counting non-standard square units.
- Calculate area by counting square centimeters.
- Estimate the area of figures on centimeter grid paper.

Vocabulary

area
square unit
standard unit
square centimeter

The Day at a Glance

Today's Goals	Materials	
1 Teaching the Lesson **A1:** Find area by counting square units. **A2:** Find area by counting square centimeters. **A3:** Estimate the area of figures on grid paper. **2 Going Further** ▸ Differentiated Instruction **3 Homework**	**Lesson Activities** Student Activity Book pp. 333–334 Homework and Remembering pp. 219–220 Quick Quiz (Assessment Guide) MathBoard materials 25-cm rulers Square Tiles (TRB M82) Centimeter Grid Paper (TRB M50) Cardstock Scissors	**Going Further** Activity Cards 10-5 Pattern blocks Square Tiles (TRB M82) Cardstock Scissors Math Journals

Use Math Talk today!

Keeping Skills Sharp

Daily Routines

Quarters and Other Coins Making and Counting Coins that Make a Quarter, Counting to 200¢ by 25¢, Making and Counting Dollars and Cents: 3-Digit Numbers as Dollars and Cents
(See pp. xxvi–xxvii.)

▸ Led by Student Leaders

Money Routine Using the 120 Poster, Using the Money Flip Chart, Using the Number Path, Using Secret Code Cards
(See pp. xxiii–xxv.)

▸ Led by Student Leaders

English Language Learners

Draw a rectangle on the board. Point and say: **We can find the area of this rectangle in square units.** Model finding the area of the rectangle using square untis.

- **Beginning** Ask: **How many *square units* did I use?** Say: **That is the *area* of the rectangle.**
- **Intermediate** Say: **We measure *area* in *square units*.** Ask: **What is the *area* of the rectangle?**
- **Advanced** Have children find the area of different large flat objects in the classroom using square units.

1 Teaching the Lesson

Activity 1

Area in Square Units

20 MINUTES

Goal: Find area by counting square units.

Materials: MathBoard materials, 25-cm rulers (1 per child), Square Tiles (TRB M82) printed on cardstock, Student Activity Book page 333, scissors (1 per child)

NCTM Standards:
Measurement
Connections

▶ Cover Areas WHOLE CLASS

Ask children to use their centimeter rulers to draw a square with sides that are 9 cm in length on their MathBoards.

Distribute 10 square tiles from TRB M82 printed on cardstock to each child.

Explain to children that they can find the area of a figure by covering it with equal-sized squares and counting the number of squares they used. Tell them that the area will be in square units.

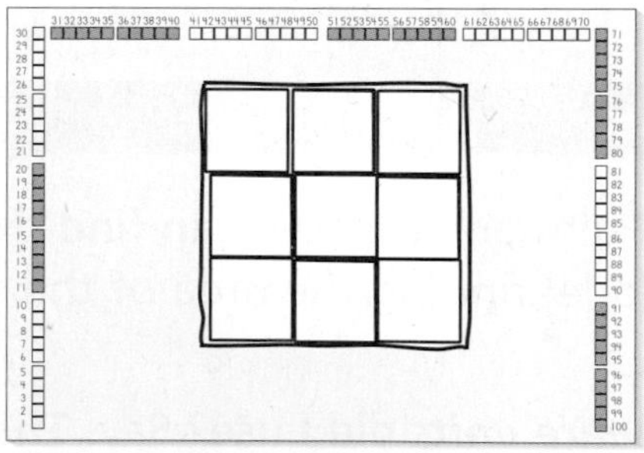

Invite children to use the cardstock squares to find the area of the square on their MathBoard. As children are working, remind them to align the sides of the card-stock squares without overlapping.

- How many square units is the square on your MathBoard? 9 square units

Next, ask children to draw a rectangle with a longer side that is 9 cm in length and a shorter side that is 6 cm in length. Have them use their cardstock squares to find its area. 6 square units

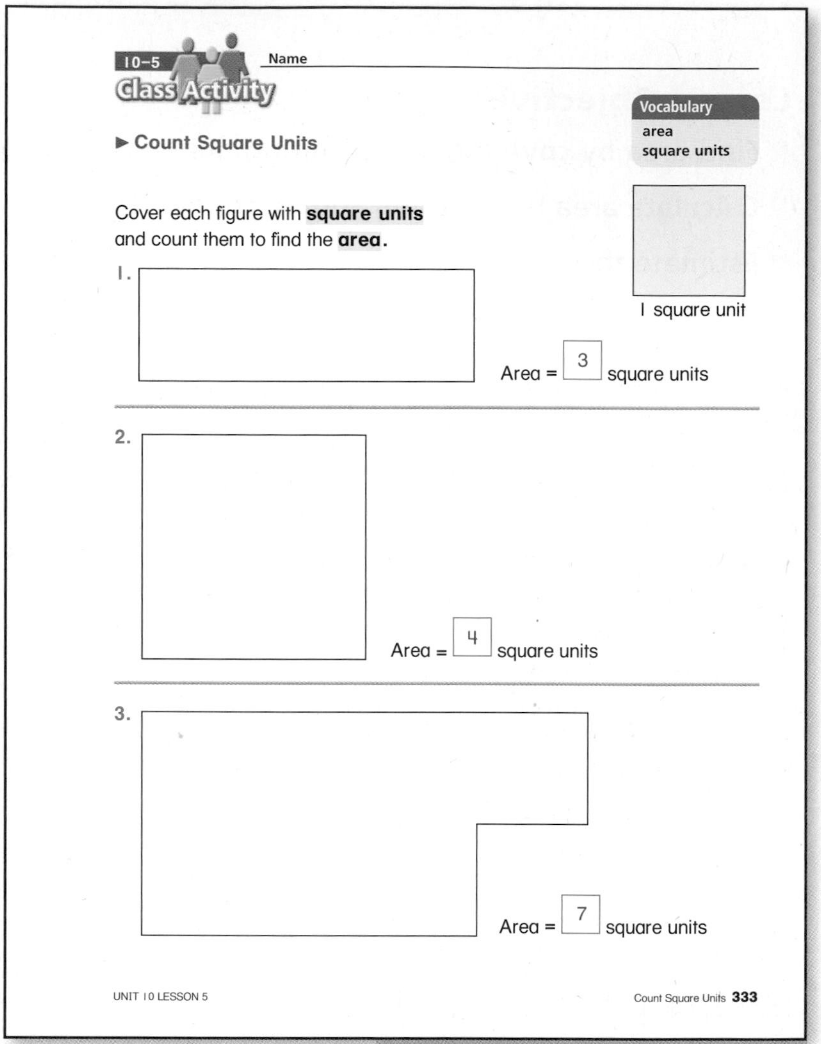

10-5 Class Activity

Name

Vocabulary
area
square units

▶ Count Square Units

Cover each figure with **square units** and count them to find the **area**.

1 square unit

1. Area = 3 square units

2. Area = 4 square units

3. Area = 7 square units

UNIT 10 LESSON 5 Count Square Units 333

Student Activity Book page 333

▶ Count Square Units INDIVIDUALS

Refer children to Student Activity Book page 333. Ask children to use the cardstock squares to find the area of the shapes in exercises 1–3.

When they are finished, hold up one of the cardstock squares and cut it into four smaller squares.

- If you measure area using these smaller squares, will you get the same number of squares? no

Ask children to cut several cardstock squares into four smaller squares. Invite them to then measure the figure in exercise 1 using these smaller squares. Help children to see that the amount of area does not change, but if a smaller unit is used, the number of units will be larger.

Activity 2

Area in Square Centimeters

20 MINUTES

Goal: Find area by counting square centimeters.

Materials: Student Activity Book page 334, Centimeter Grid Paper (TRB M50)

NCTM Standards:
Measurement
Connections

▶ Count Square Centimeters WHOLE CLASS

Discuss the purpose of standard units with the class.

- Why do people measure length in centimeters instead of paper clips? Possible answer: If you measure length in centimeters, you can tell other people the measurement and they will know what it means.

Explain to children that centimeters are a *standard unit* used to measure length.

- Do you think square units are a standard unit of area measure? no Why not? If you measure with square units of different sizes, the measurements will be different.

Refer children to Student Activity Book page 334. Point out that the square unit shown at the top of the page is 1 square centimeter, which is a standard unit of measure for area.

Explain to children that when they see a figure on centimeter grid paper, they can count the number of squares inside the figure to find its area in square centimeters.

Have children complete exercises 4–7 individually.

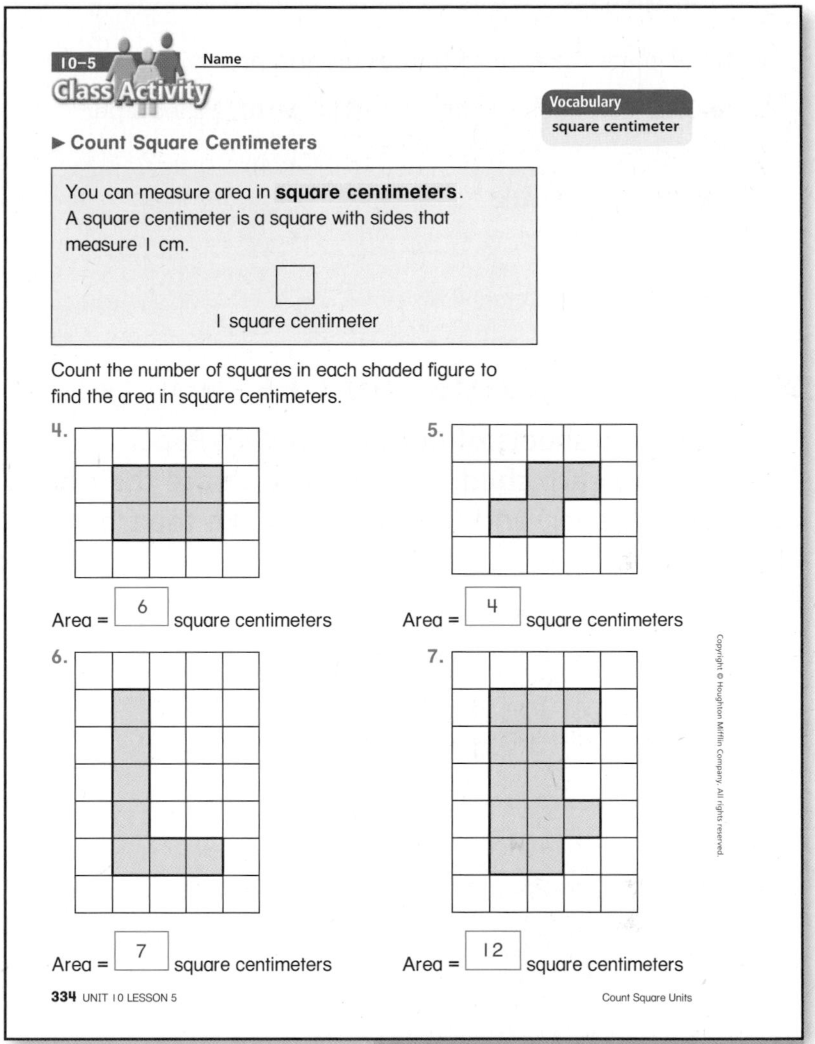
10–5 Class Activity Name

Vocabulary
square centimeter

▶ Count Square Centimeters

You can measure area in **square centimeters**.
A square centimeter is a square with sides that measure 1 cm.

1 square centimeter

Count the number of squares in each shaded figure to find the area in square centimeters.

4. Area = 6 square centimeters

5. Area = 4 square centimeters

6. Area = 7 square centimeters

7. Area = 12 square centimeters

Copyright © Houghton Mifflin Company. All rights reserved.

334 UNIT 10 LESSON 5 Count Square Units

Student Activity Book page 334

▶ Draw Figures and Find Areas PAIRS

Distribute a sheet of Centimeter Grid Paper (TRB M50) to each child. Invite children to draw different figures using the grid lines and then to challenge a partner to find the area of each figure.

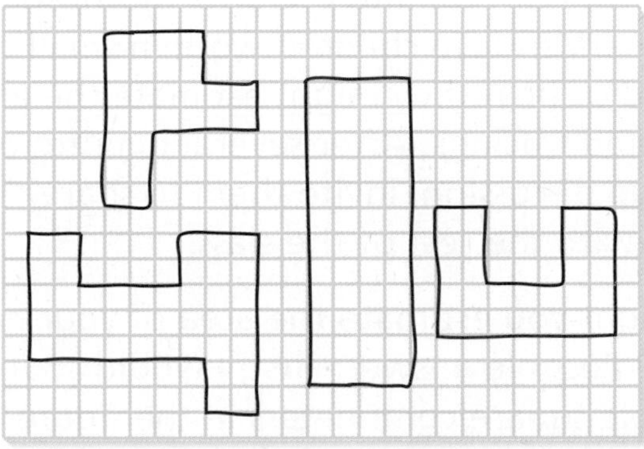

Activity 3

Estimate Area of Unusual Figures

20 MINUTES

Goal: Estimate the area of figures on grid paper.

Materials: Centimeter Grid Paper (TRB M50) (2 sheets per child)

NCTM Standards:
Measurement
Connections

▶ Areas of Unusual Figures SMALL GROUPS

Distribute two sheets of Centimeter Grid Paper (TRB M50) to each child. Have children trace their hand on the grid paper, and tell them to make the tracing a closed figure.

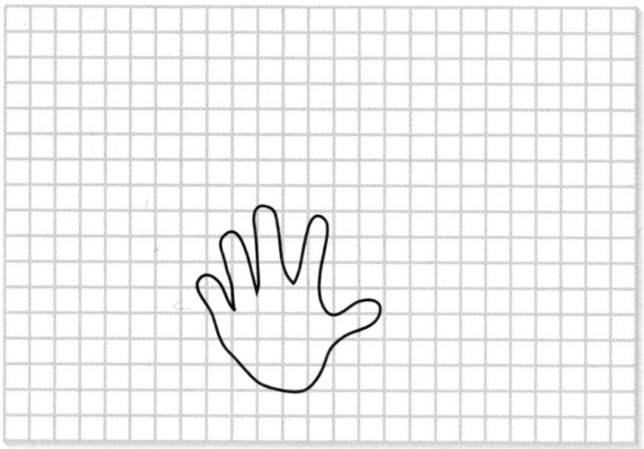

- Do you think you can find the exact area of your hand by counting the whole square centimeters inside the tracing? no
- What is the word for finding a measurement that is close to the exact one? estimating

Math Talk Explain to children that there are different ways to estimate the area of unusual figures, like their hands. Have children work in small groups to share ideas of how they might estimate the area of their hand tracings. After several minutes of small-group discussion, invite them to share their strategies with the rest of the class.

- How might you estimate the area of your hand tracing? Possible answer: First, I would count all of the whole square centimeters in the figure. Then I would count the squares that are more than half covered. I wouldn't count the squares that are less than half covered.
- Can anyone suggest a different way to count the parts of squares? Possible answer: I would look at the squares that are partly covered and add the pieces together in my mind to make whole squares.

Encourage children to share all of their ideas and reinforce that there are many ways to estimate.

After your discussion, ask children to work on their own to estimate the area of their hand tracing.

Invite children to draw other unusual figures on grid paper and to estimate their areas.

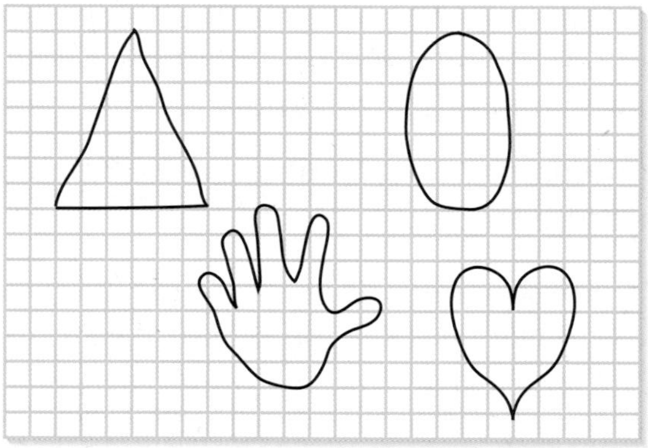

Ongoing Assessment

Ask children to draw a figure on Centimeter Grid Paper (TRB M50).

▶ What is the area of your figure?

▶ Explain how you found the area.

Next, ask children to draw an unusual figure that does not follow the lines on the grid paper.

▶ Estimate the area of your figure.

▶ Explain how you estimated the area.

Quick Quiz

See Assessment Guide for Unit 10 Quick Quiz.

2 Going Further

Differentiated Instruction

Intervention — Activity Card 10-5

Measure with Pattern Blocks — Activity Card 10-5

Work: (1 child)

Use:
- pattern blocks

1. Measure the area of a piece of paper by tracing a pattern block.
2. You can slide, turn, or flip your pattern block.

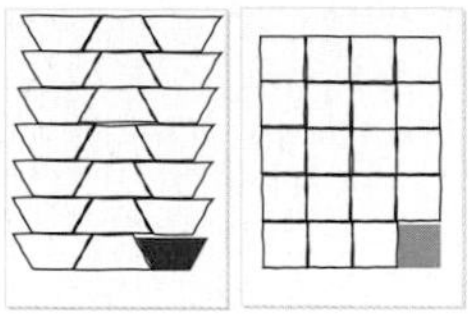

3. Measure the area of a piece of paper of the same size by tracing a different shape.
4. **Math Talk** Share your papers with a friend. Explain which method you like better and why you like it better.

Unit 10, Lesson 5

Activity Note Each child needs pattern blocks. Help children trace the pattern blocks to cover the entire page.

Math Writing Prompt

Draw a Picture Stacie wants to find the area of the front cover of her favorite book. Write instructions on how to find the area in square units. Include a drawing.

Software Support

Warm Up 37.20

On Level — Activity Card 10-5

Area of Different Figures — Activity Card 10-5

Work: (1 child)

Use:
- Square Tiles on cardstock
- scissors

1. Cut the squares out of the paper.
2. Use eight squares. Make a figure with the squares.
3. Make 4 other figures using eight squares.

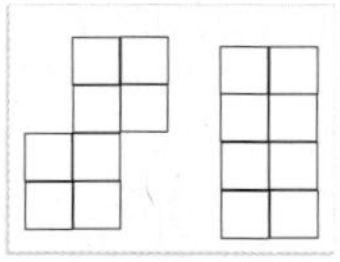

4. Check the area of each figure.
5. Repeat using more squares. Is the area always the same?
6. **Math Talk** Share what you learned with a friend. Did you find the same areas?

Unit 10, Lesson 5

Activity Note Each child needs Square Tiles (TRB M82) on cardstock and scissors. Have children record the area of each figure.

Math Writing Prompt

Explain a Method Yoon Ki wants to find the area of a rectangle in square centimeters. Explain a method he can use to find the area.

Software Support

Shapes Ahoy: Ship Shapes, Level X

Challenge — Activity Card 10-5

Area of a Rug — Activity Card 10-5

Work: (pairs)

Ishana made a rug in the shape of a rectangle using equal-sized squares. The rug was 5 feet long and 3 feet wide. What is the area of the rug? 15 square feet

1. **Work Together** Solve the story problem.
2. **Math Talk** Does the picture match the problem? yes
3. Each (child): Write a problem like the one above.
4. Trade problems with your partner. Draw a picture to solve.

Unit 10, Lesson 5

Activity Note Explain that you can measure an area in square feet. A square foot is a square with sides that measure 1 foot.

Math Writing Prompt

Predict and Verify Lola's figure has an area of 9 square units. Otis' figure has an area of 9 square units. Could they have different figures? Use a drawing in your answer.

DESTINATION Math Software Support

Course II: Module 3: Unit 1: Area

3 Homework

10–5 Homework **Goal:** Additional Practice

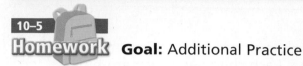

This Homework page provides practice in estimating and finding the area of different figures in square centimeters.

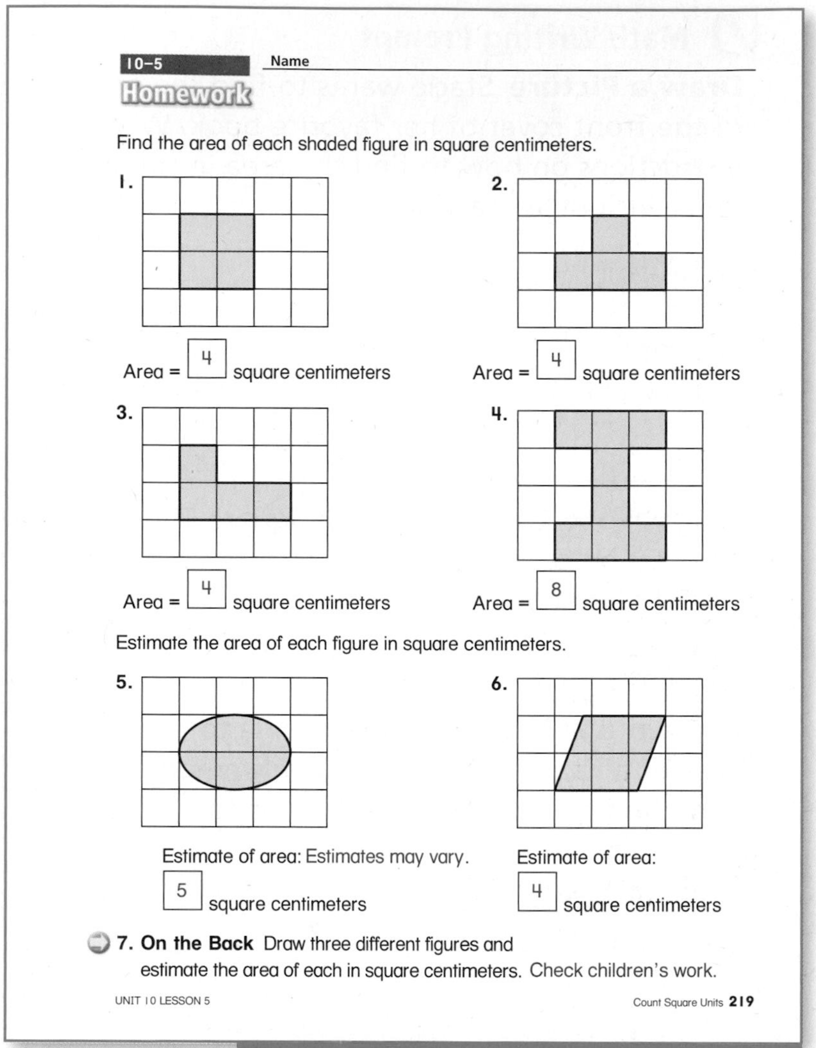
10–5 Homework Name

Find the area of each shaded figure in square centimeters.

1. Area = 4 square centimeters

2. Area = 4 square centimeters

3. Area = 4 square centimeters

4. Area = 8 square centimeters

Estimate the area of each figure in square centimeters.

5. Estimate of area: Estimates may vary. 5 square centimeters

6. Estimate of area: 4 square centimeters

7. **On the Back** Draw three different figures and estimate the area of each in square centimeters. Check children's work.

UNIT 10 LESSON 5 Count Square Units **219**

Homework and Remembering page 219

Home or School Activity

Science Connection

Area of Leaves Plants use sunlight to turn water and carbon dioxide into sugar. Leaves with a greater surface area receive more sunlight and can make more food.

Invite children to collect leaves from different plants and trees, trace them on centimeter grid paper, and estimate the area of each leaf in square centimeters.

MINI UNIT 10

Unit Review and Test

Lesson Objectives

- Assess children's progress on unit objectives.

The Day at a Glance

Today's Goals	Materials
1 Assessing the Unit ▶ Assess children's progress on unit objectives. ▶ Use activities from unit lessons to reteach content. **2 Extending the Assessment** ▶ Use remediation for common errors. There is no homework assignment on a test day.	Unit 10 Test, Student Activity Book pages 335–338 Unit 10 Test, Form A or B, Assessment Guide (optional) Unit 10 Performance Assessment, Assessment Guide (optional)

Keeping Skills Sharp

Quick Practice 5 MINUTES	
If you are doing a unit review day, go over the homework. If this is a test day, omit the homework review.	**Review and Test Day** You may want to choose a quiet game or other activity (reading a book or working on homework for another subject) for children who finish early.

Assessing the Unit

Assess Unit Objectives

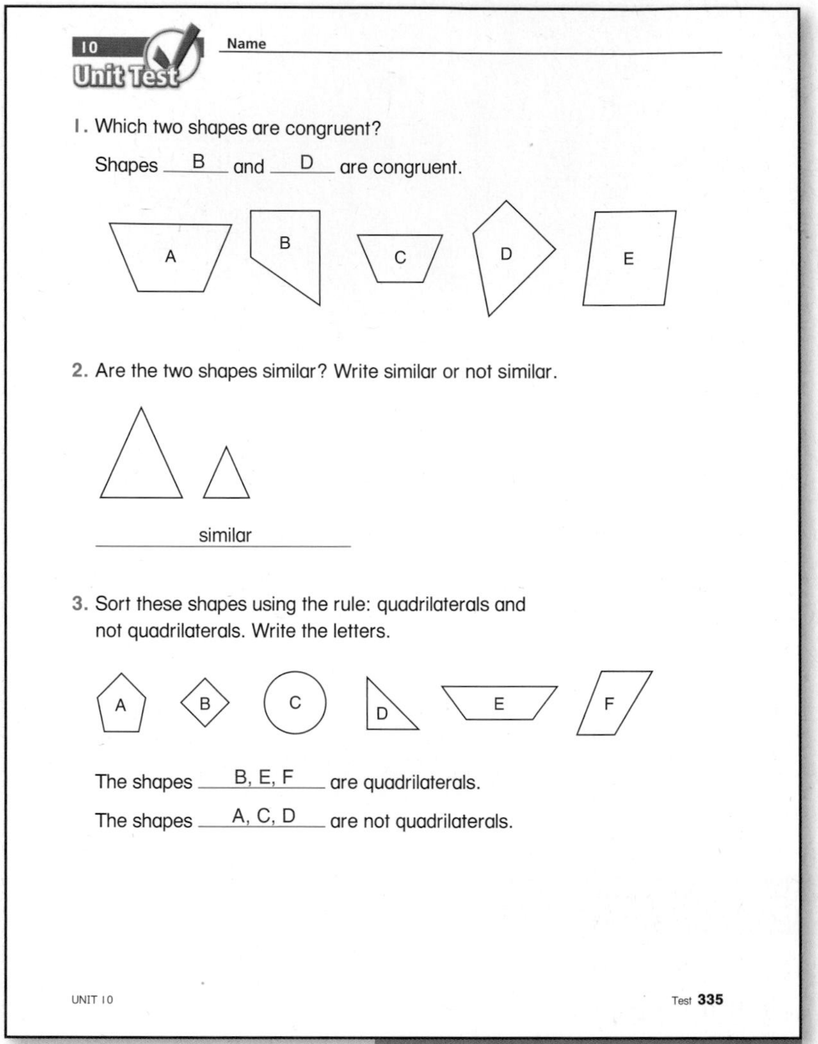
10 Unit Test

Name ______

1. Which two shapes are congruent?

Shapes __B__ and __D__ are congruent.

2. Are the two shapes similar? Write similar or not similar.

__similar__

3. Sort these shapes using the rule: quadrilaterals and not quadrilaterals. Write the letters.

The shapes __B, E, F__ are quadrilaterals.

The shapes __A, C, D__ are not quadrilaterals.

UNIT 10 Test 335

Student Activity Book page 335

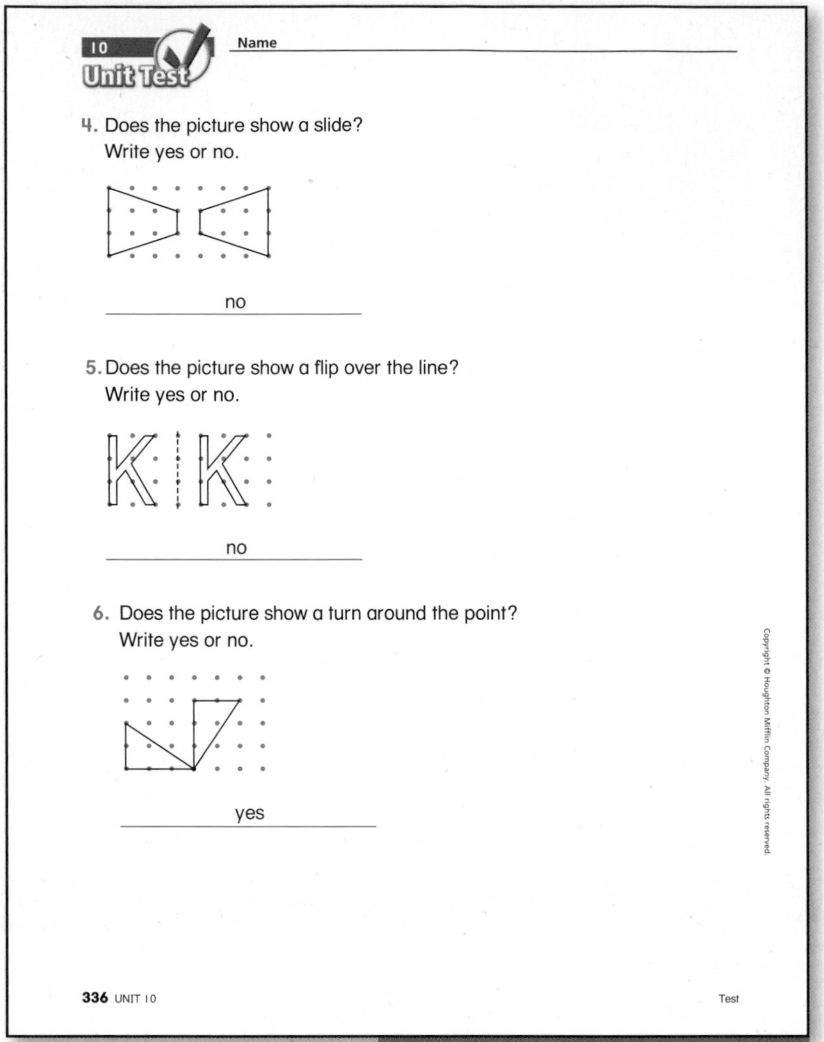
10 Unit Test

Name ______

4. Does the picture show a slide? Write yes or no.

__no__

5. Does the picture show a flip over the line? Write yes or no.

__no__

6. Does the picture show a turn around the point? Write yes or no.

__yes__

336 UNIT 10 Test

Student Activity Book page 336

45 MINUTES (more if schedule permits)

Goal: Assess student progress on unit objectives.

Materials: Student Activity Book pages 335–338; Assessment Guide (optional)

▸ Review and Assessment

If your students are ready for assessment on the unit objectives, use either the test on the Student Activity Book pages or one of the forms of the Unit 10 Test in the Assessment Guide to assess student progress. To assign a numerical score for all of these test forms, use 10 points for each question.

The chart to the right lists the test items, the unit objectives they cover, and the lesson activities in which the objective is covered in this unit.

▸ Reteaching Resources

Unit Test Items	Unit Objectives Tested	Activities to Use for Reteaching
1	**10.1** Identify congruent figures.	Lesson 1, Activity 1
2	**10.2** Identify similar figures.	Lesson 1, Activity 2
3, 10	**10.3** Sort 2-D figures using a sorting rule.	Lesson 1, Activity 3
4	**10.4** Identify slides.	Lesson 2, Activity 1
5	**10.5** Identify flips.	Lesson 2, Activity 2

10 Unit Test

Name ________________

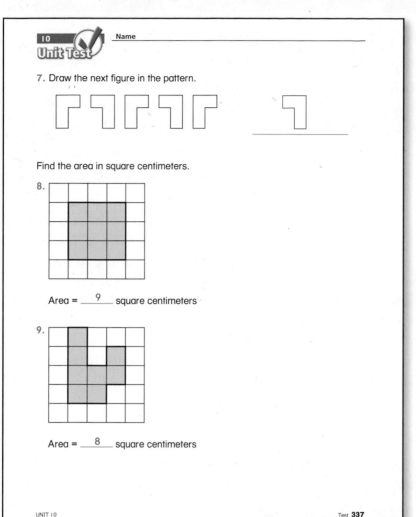

7. Draw the next figure in the pattern.

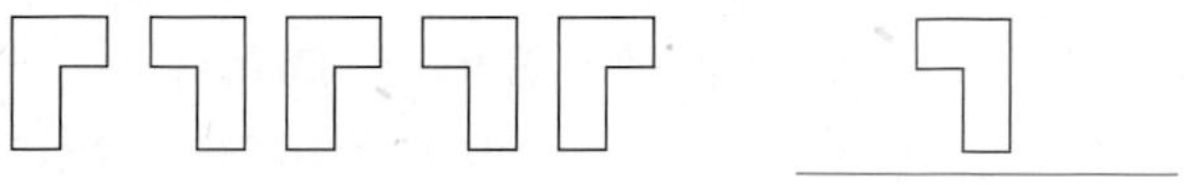

Find the area in square centimeters.

8.

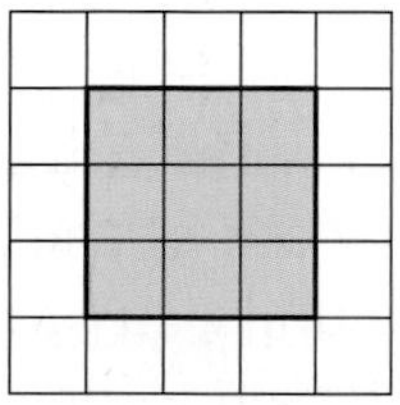

Area = 9 square centimeters

9.

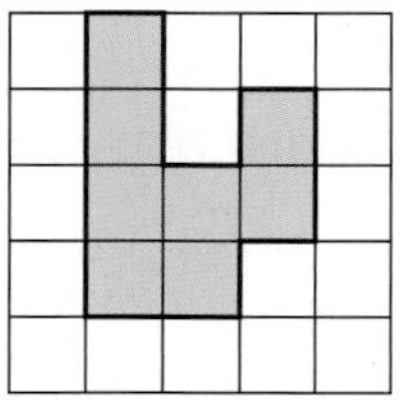

Area = 8 square centimeters

Student Activity Book page 337

10 Unit Test

Name ________________

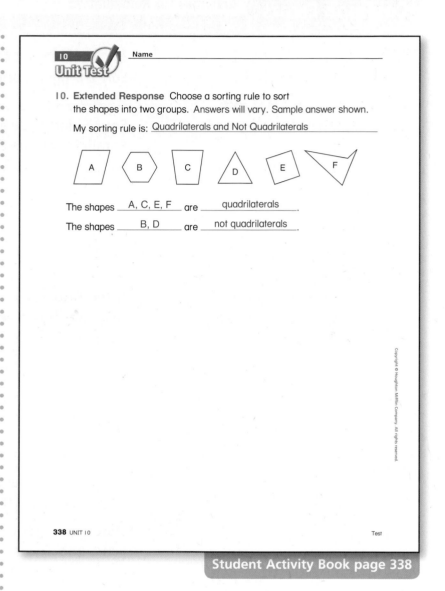

10. **Extended Response** Choose a sorting rule to sort the shapes into two groups. Answers will vary. Sample answer shown.

My sorting rule is: Quadrilaterals and Not Quadrilaterals

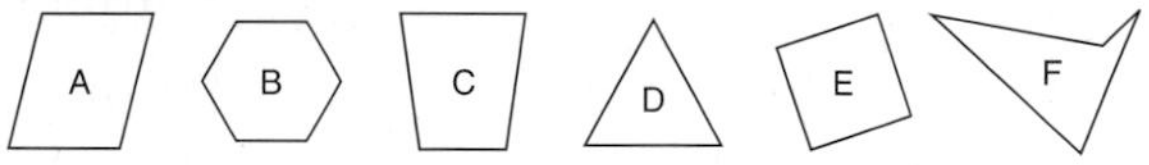

The shapes A, C, E, F are quadrilaterals.

The shapes B, D are not quadrilaterals.

Student Activity Book page 338

Unit Test Items	Unit Objectives Tested	Activities to Use for Reteaching
6	**10.6** Identify turns.	Lesson 2, Activity 3
7	**10.7** Use slides, flips, and turns to draw the next figure in a pattern.	Lesson 2, Activity 4
8, 9	**10.8** Calculate area by counting square centimeters.	Lesson 4, Activity 2

▶ Assessment Resources

Form A, Free Response Test (Assessment Guide)
Form B, Multiple-Choice Test (Assessment Guide)
Performance Assessment (Assessment Guide)

▶ Portfolio Assessment

Teacher-selected Items for Student Portfolios:

- Homework, Lesson 3
- Class Activity work, Lesson 1

Student-selected Items for Student Portfolios:

- Favorite Home or School Activity
- Best Writing Prompt

2 Extending the Assessment

Common Errors

Activities for Remediation

Unit Objective 10.1

Identify congruent figures.

Common Error: Doesn't Correctly Identify Congruent Figures

When first introduced to the concept of congruency, some children may not readily identify congruent figures.

Remediation Children can use tracing paper to verify congruency. If the traced figure fits exactly on top of the second figure, the figures are congruent.

Unit Objective 10.2

Identify similar figures.

Common Error: Doesn't Identify Congruent Figures as Similar Figures

Some children may not identify congruent figures as similar figures.

Remediation Remind children that similar figures are the same shape and they can be the same size or they can be a different size. The identifying attribute with similar figures is that they are the same shape. Provide children with plenty of opportunities to classify figures as congruent and not congruent and as similar and not similar. Include congruent figures when asking children to identify similarity.

Unit Objective 10.3

Sort 2-D figures using a sorting rule.

Common Error: Doesn't Identify Four-Sided Figures Without Parallel Sides as Quadrilaterals

Some children may routinely see such four-sided figures as squares, rectangles, and parallelograms as quadrilaterals but not recognize other four-sided figures as quadrilaterals.

Remediation Have children sort polygons based solely on the number of sides. Include triangles, quadrilaterals, pentagons, and hexagons. Include regular (all sides equal and all angles equal) and irregular polygons.

Unit Objective 10.7

Use slides, flips, and turns to draw the next figure in a pattern.

Common Error: Confuses Slides, Flips, and Turns

Some children may confuse slides, flips, and turns.

Remediation Have children make cutouts of the shapes they are working with and add a dot in one corner of each one. Children can then note the position of the dot to help them determine if the transformation was a slide, flip, or turn.

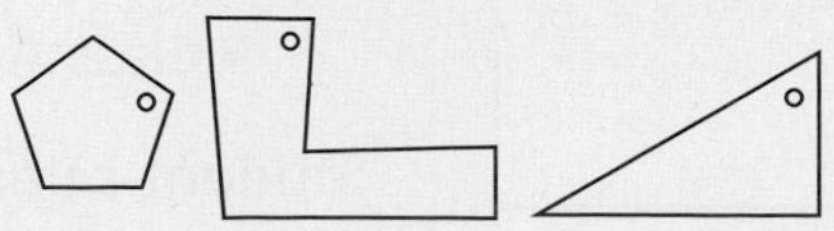

Unit Objective 10.8

Calculate area by counting square centimeters.

Common Error: Doesn't Correctly Count Square Units

Some children may miscount the square units while measuring area.

Remediation If children have difficulty keeping track of the number of square units, suggest they work out a system to help them. They might count the squares row by row, tick off each square as they count it, or place a marker on each square after they count it.

3-Digit Addition and Subtraction

IN THIS UNIT, children will extend their understanding of addition and subtraction to three-digit numbers. They will continue to group and ungroup as necessary. Good explanations and good questions using hundreds, tens, and ones language are emphasized as much as finding solutions to problems. Children will use Secret Code Cards and Proof Drawings as aids for addition and subtraction.

Skills Trace

Grade 1	Grade 2	Grade 3
• Represent two-digit numbers. • Add a 2-digit number and a 1-digit number. • Solve story problems.	• Add, making a new ten, a new hundred, or both. • Subtract, ungrouping a hundred, a ten, or both. • Solve story problems with multi-digit addition or subtraction.	• Add and subtract whole numbers. • Solve a variety of word problems involving addition and subtraction.

Unit 11 Contents

Big Idea Understanding Numbers to 1,000

Big Idea Money Through $10.00

Big Idea Adding to 1,000

Big Idea 3-Digit Subtraction

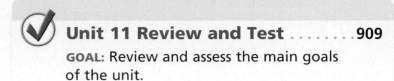

Big Idea 3-Digit Addition and Subtraction

REAL WORLD Problem Solving

Planning Unit 11

NCTM Curriculum Focal Points and Connections Key: 1. Number and Operations 2. Number and Operations and Algebra 3. Measurement 4. Number and Operations 5. Geometry and Measurement 6. Algebra

Lesson NCTM Focal Points NCTM Standards	Resources	Materials for Lesson Activities	Materials for Going Further
11-1 **Count Numbers to 1,000** NCTM Focal Points: 1.1, 1.2, 4.1 NCTM Standards: 1	TE pp. 755–762 SAB pp. 339–342 H&R pp. 221–222 AC 11-1	Dollars with Penny Array ✓ MathBoard materials	✓ Base ten blocks ✓ Real or play money Index cards Math Journals
11-2 **Place Value** NCTM Focal Points: 1.4, 1.5, 2.4, 4.1, 4.2 NCTM Standards: 1, 10	TE pp. 763–770 SAB pp. 343–344 H&R pp. 223–224 AC 11-2	✓ MathBoard materials ✓ Demonstration Secret Code Cards ✓ Secret Code Cards	✓ Secret Code Cards ✓ Base ten blocks *Earth Day–Hooray!* by Stuart J. Murphy Math Journals
11-3 **Count by Ones and by Tens** NCTM Focal Points: 1.1, 1.2, 6.1 NCTM Standards: 1, 10	TE pp. 771–776 SAB pp. 345–346 H&R pp. 225–226 AC 11-3	✓ MathBoard materials	✓ Base ten blocks Math Journals
11-4 **Group into Hundreds** NCTM Focal Points: 1.4, 2.4, 2.8 NCTM Standard: 1	TE pp. 777–782 SAB pp. 347–348 H&R pp. 227–228 AC 11-4	Beans or other countable objects Transparent containers	Beans or other countable objects Transparent containers ✓ Base ten blocks Paper bags Index cards Ant Colony (TRB M83) Math Journals
11-5 **Add Ones, Tens, and Hundreds** NCTM Focal Point: 2.4 NCTM Standard: 1	TE pp. 783–790 SAB pp. 349–352 H&R pp. 229–230 AC 11-5 MCC 41 AG Quick Quiz 1	✓ Demonstration Secret Code Cards (optional) ✓ Secret Code Cards Transparent container Beans or other countable objects ✓ MathBoard materials	✓ Base ten blocks Lined paper Math Journals
11-6 **Review Quarters** NCTM Focal Point: 4.8 NCTM Standards: 1, 4, 6, 10	TE pp. 791–796 SAB pp. 353–354 H&R pp. 231–232 AC 11-6	Coin Strips ✓ Real or play money	✓ Real or play money ✓ MathBoard materials Spinners (TRB M27) Paper clips Math Journals
11-7 **Buy with Dollars and Cents** NCTM Focal Point: 4.8 NCTM Standards: 1, 4, 6, 10	TE pp. 797–802 SAB pp. 355–356 H&R pp. 233–234 AC 11-7	✓ Real or play money ✓ MathBoard materials	✓ Real or play money Objects with price tags ✓ MathBoard materials Math Journals
11-8 **Change from $5.00** NCTM Focal Point: 4.8 NCTM Standards: 1, 4, 6, 10	TE pp. 803–808 SAB pp. 357–358 H&R pp. 235–236 AC 11-8 MCC 42 AG Quick Quiz 2	Five-Dollar Bills (TRB M84) ✓ Dollar Bills ✓ Real or play money ✓ Secret Code Cards	✓ Real or play money Five-Dollar Bills (TRB M84) ✓ Dollar Bills Chart Paper Magazines and shopping circulars Index cards Scissors Tape Poster board Spinners (TRB M27) Paper clips Math Journals

Resources/Materials Key: TE: Teacher Edition SAB: Student Activity Book H&R: Homework and Remembering AC: Activity Cards MCC: Math Center Challenge AG: Assessment Guide ✓: Grade 2 kits TRB: Teacher's Resource Book

Lesson NCTM Focal Points NCTM Standards	Resources	Materials for Lesson Activities	Materials for Going Further
11-9 **Add Over the Hundred** NCTM Focal Points: 2.6, 2.10 NCTM Standard: 1	TE pp. 809–814 H&R pp. 237–238 AC 11-9	✓ Secret Code Cards ✓ MathBoard materials	✓ Base ten blocks ✓ MathBoard materials Math Journals
11-10 **Solve and Discuss** NCTM Focal Points: 2.6, 2.10 NCTM Standards: 1, 8	TE pp. 815–824 SAB pp. 359–364 H&R pp. 239–240 AC 11-10 MCC 43	✓ MathBoard materials	The Muffin Stand (TRB M85) Math Journals
11-11 **Add Money Amounts** NCTM Focal Points: 2.6, 11.11 NCTM Standard: 1	TE pp. 825–830 SAB pp. 365–366 H&R pp. 241–242 AC 11-11	✓ MathBoard materials	✓ MathBoard materials ✓ Secret Code Cards (1–300) Math Journals
11-12 **Discuss 3-Digit Addition** NCTM Focal Points: 2.6, 2.10 NCTM Standards: 1, 8	TE pp. 831–836 SAB pp. 367–370 H&R pp. 243–244 AC 11-12	✓ MathBoard materials Crayons or markers	✓ MathBoard materials ✓ Secret Code Cards Math Journals
11-13 **Story Problems: Unknown Addends** NCTM Focal Points: 2.10, 4.8 NCTM Standards: 1, 8	TE pp. 837–842 SAB pp. 371–372 H&R pp. 245–246 AC 11-13 AG Quick Quiz 3	✓ MathBoard materials Five-Dollar Bills ✓ Dollar Bills ✓ Real or play money Small box labeled *Cash Register* ✓ Sticky board (optional)	✓ MathBoard materials Five-Dollar Bills ✓ Dollar Bills ✓ Real or play money Index cards Math Journals
11-14 **Story Problems with Hundreds Numbers** NCTM Focal Points: 2.7, 2.11, 4.8 NCTM Standards: 1, 2, 6, 10	TE pp. 843–852 SAB pp. 373–376 H&R pp. 247–248 AC 11-14	✓ MathBoard materials ✓ Base ten blocks	✓ Base ten blocks ✓ Secret Code Cards Symbol Cards (TRB M45) Math Journals
11-15 **Subtract from Numbers with Zeros** NCTM Focal Points: 2.7, 2.11 NCTM Standards: 1, 10	TE pp. 853–858 SAB pp. 377–378 H&R pp. 249–250 AC 11-15	✓ Secret Code Cards ✓ MathBoard materials	✓ Secret Code Cards ✓ Base ten blocks Game Cards (TRB M23) Paper bags Markers or crayons Math Journals
11-16 **Subtract Money Amounts** NCTM Focal Points: 2.7, 2.11 NCTM Standards: 1, 10	TE pp. 859–864 H&R pp. 251–252 AC 11-16	✓ MathBoard materials ✓ Secret Code Cards	✓ Real or play money Dollar Bills (TRB M67–M68) ✓ Secret Code Cards Index cards Grocery store flyers Math Journals

Manipulatives and Materials

Essential materials for teaching *Math Expressions* are available in the Grade 2 kits. These materials are indicated by a ✓ in these lists. At the front of this Teacher Edition is more information about kit contents, alternatives for the materials, and use of the materials.

Lesson NCTM Focal Points NCTM Standards	Resources	Materials for Lesson Activities	Materials for Going Further
11-17 **Subtract from Any 3-Digit Number** NCTM Focal Points: 2.7, 2.11 NCTM Standard: 1, 10	TE pp. 865–872 H&R pp. 253–254 AC 11-17	✓ MathBoard materials ✓ Secret Code Cards	✓ Base ten blocks ✓ Real or play money ✓ Dollar Bills Five-Dollar Bills Classroom items Index cards, Paper bags *The 329th Friend* by Marjorie Weinman Sharmat Math Journals
11-18 **Practice Ungrouping** NCTM Focal Points: 2.7, 2.11 NCTM Standard: 1	TE pp. 873–878 H&R pp. 255–256 AC 11-18 MCC 44 AG Quick Quiz 4	✓ Secret Code Cards ✓ MathBoard materials	✓ Secret Code Cards ✓ MathBoard materials Practice Ungrouping (TRB M86) Multiple-Step Story Problems (TRB M87) Math Journals
11-19 **Relationships between Addition and Subtraction Methods** NCTM Focal Points: 2.6, 2.7, 2.10, 2.11 NCTM Standards: 1, 8	TE pp. 879–884 SAB pp. 379–380 H&R pp. 257–258 AC 11-19	✓ Secret Code Cards ✓ MathBoard materials	✓ Base ten blocks Index cards Math Journals
11-20 **Unknown Start and Comparison Problems** NCTM Focal Points: 2.7, 2.11 NCTM Standards: 1, 8	TE pp. 885–890 SAB pp. 381–382 H&R pp. 259–260 AC 11-20	✓ MathBoard materials	*Hannah's Collections* by Marthe Jocelyn Math Journals
11-21 **Mixed Addition and Subtraction Story Problems** NCTM Focal Points: 2.6, 2.7, 2.10, 2.11 NCTM Standards: 1, 8	TE pp. 891–896 SAB pp. 383–384 H&R pp. 261–262 AC 11-21	✓ MathBoard materials	Buy or Sell? (TRB M88) ✓ Base ten blocks Math Journals
11-22 **Spend Money** NCTM Focal Point: 2.8 NCTM Standards: 1, 8, 10	TE pp. 897–902 SAB pp. 385–388 H&R pp. 263–264 AC 11-22 AG Quick Quiz 5	✓ MathBoard materials ✓ Secret Code Cards Real or play money	✓ Real or play money Index cards Ten-Dollar Bills (TRB M89) ✓ Dollar Bills Newspaper ads Math Journals
11-23 **Use Mathematical Processes** NCTM Focal Point: 5.4 NCTM Standards: 6, 7, 8, 9, 10	TE pp. 903–908 SAB pp. 389–390 H&R pp. 265–266 AC 11-23	✓ Pattern Blocks Crayons Centimeter Grid Paper (TRB M50)	10 × 10 Grid (TRB M62) Math Journals
✓ **Unit Review and Test**	TE pp. 909–912 SAB pp. 391–394 AG Unit 11 Tests		

Resources/Materials Key: TE: Teacher Edition SAB: Student Activity Book H&R: Homework and Remembering AC: Activity Cards MCC: Math Center Challenge AG: Assessment Guide ✓: Grade 2 kits TRB: Teacher's Resource Book

Unit 11 Assessment

Unit Objectives Tested	Unit Test Items	Lessons
11.1 Recognize and draw boxes, sticks, and circles for numbers through 999.	1, 2	1–3
11.2 Write 3-digit numbers in expanded form.	3, 4	2
11.3 Count by 1s and 10s through 999.	5, 6	3
11.4 Write the value of a group of dollars and coins using decimal notation.	7, 8	7
11.5 Add, making a new ten, a new hundred, or both.	9–12	9–13
11.6 Add money amounts to $9.99.	13, 14	11
11.7 Subtract, ungrouping a ten, hundred, or both.	15–17	14–18
11.8 Subtract from a number with one or two zeros.	18, 19	15–18, 22
11.9 Subtract money amounts from $10.00.	20, 21	16, 22
11.10 Solve story problems with multi-digit addition or subtraction.	22–25	5, 10, 13, 14, 20, 21

Assessment and Review Resources

Formal Assessment

Student Activity Book
- Unit Review and Test (pp. 391–394)

Assessment Guide
- Quick Quizzes (pp. A116–A119)
- Test A–Open Response (pp. A120–A123)
- Test B–Multiple Choice (pp. A124–A127)
- Performance Assessment (pp. A128–A130)

Test Generator CD-ROM
- Open Response Test
- Multiple Choice Test
- Test Bank Items

Informal Assessment

Teacher Edition
- Ongoing Assessment (in every lesson)
- Quick Practice (in every lesson)
- Portfolio Suggestions (p. 911)

Math Talk
- The Learning Classroom (pp. 832, 848, 860, 874)
- Math Talk in Action (pp. 805, 847, 855, 866)
- Solve and Discuss (pp. 786, 816, 822, 849, 860, 881, 888, 892, 893, 894)
- In Activities (pp. 757, 758, 765, 772, 778, 793, 794, 798, 799, 806, 810, 818, 819, 832, 838, 850, 868, 870, 875, 880, 886, 892, 894, 900, 904, 905)
- Student Pairs
  Helping Pairs (pp. 768, 784, 827, 832, 839, 876, 882, 888, 892)
- Step-By-Step at the Board (pp. 876, 850)

Review Opportunities

Homework and Remembering
- Review of recently taught topics
- Spiral Review

Teacher Edition
- Unit Review and Test (pp. 909–912)

Test Generator CD-ROM
- Custom Review Sheets

Independent Learning Activities

Ready-Made Math Challenge Centers

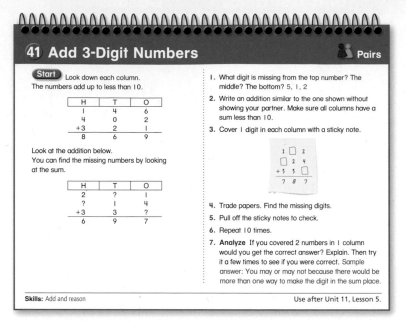

41 Add 3-Digit Numbers — Pairs

Start Look down each column.
The numbers add up to less than 10.

H	T	O
1	4	6
4	0	2
+3	2	1
8	6	9

Look at the addition below.
You can find the missing numbers by looking at the sum.

H	T	O
2	?	1
?	1	4
+3	3	?
6	9	7

1. What digit is missing from the top number? The middle? The bottom? 5, 1, 2
2. Write an addition similar to the one shown without showing your partner. Make sure all columns have a sum less than 10.
3. Cover 1 digit in each column with a sticky note.

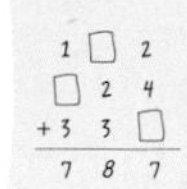

4. Trade papers. Find the missing digits.
5. Pull off the sticky notes to check.
6. Repeat 10 times.
7. **Analyze** If you covered 2 numbers in 1 column would you get the correct answer? Explain. Then try it a few times to see if you were correct. Sample answer: You may or may not because there would be more than one way to make the digit in the sum place.

Skills: Add and reason — Use after Unit 11, Lesson 5.

Grouping Pairs

Materials Sticky notes

Objective Children find missing digits in 3-digit addition problems.

Connections Computation and Algebra

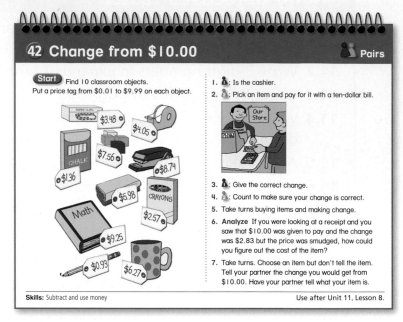

42 Change from $10.00 — Pairs

Start Find 10 classroom objects.
Put a price tag from $0.01 to $9.99 on each object.

1. (player 1): Is the cashier.
2. (player 2): Pick an item and pay for it with a ten-dollar bill.

3. (player 1): Give the correct change.
4. (player 2): Count to make sure your change is correct.
5. Take turns buying items and making change.
6. **Analyze** If you were looking at a receipt and you saw that $10.00 was given to pay and the change was $2.83 but the price was smudged, how could you figure out the cost of the item?
7. Take turns. Choose an item but don't tell the item. Tell your partner the change you would get from $10.00. Have your partner tell what your item is.

Skills: Subtract and use money — Use after Unit 11, Lesson 8.

Grouping Pairs

Materials Classroom objects, play money

Objective Children make change from $10.00 by purchasing classroom objects.

Connections Measurement and Real World

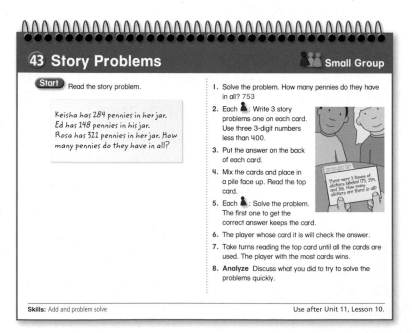

43 Story Problems — Small Group

Start Read the story problem.

Keisha has 284 pennies in her jar. Ed has 148 pennies in his jar. Rosa has 321 pennies in her jar. How many pennies do they have in all?

1. Solve the problem. How many pennies do they have in all? 753
2. Each (player): Write 3 story problems one on each card. Use three 3-digit numbers less than 400.

3. Put the answer on the back of each card.
4. Mix the cards and place in a pile face up. Read the top card.
5. Each (player): Solve the problem. The first one to get the correct answer keeps the card.
6. The player whose card it is will check the answer.
7. Take turns reading the top card until all the cards are used. The player with the most cards wins.
8. **Analyze** Discuss what you did to try to solve the problems quickly.

Skills: Add and problem solve — Use after Unit 11, Lesson 10.

Grouping Small Group

Materials Index cards

Objective Children write story problems adding three 3-digit numbers.

Connections Computation and Problem Solving

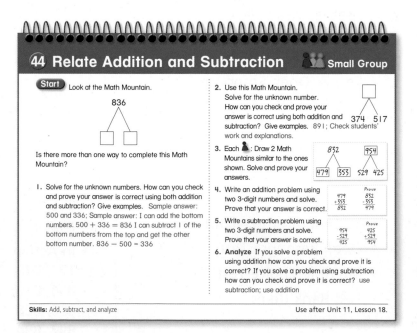

44 Relate Addition and Subtraction — Small Group

Start Look at the Math Mountain.

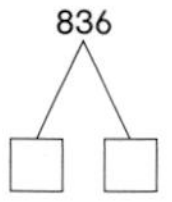

Is there more than one way to complete this Math Mountain?

1. Solve for the unknown numbers. How can you check and prove your answer is correct using both addition and subtraction? Give examples. Sample answer: 500 and 336; Sample answer: I can add the bottom numbers. 500 + 336 = 836 I can subtract 1 of the bottom numbers from the top and get the other bottom number. 836 − 500 = 336
2. Use this Math Mountain. Solve for the unknown number. How can you check and prove your answer is correct using both addition and subtraction? Give examples. 891; Check students' work and explanations.

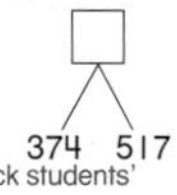

3. Each (player): Draw 2 Math Mountains similar to the ones shown. Solve and prove your answers.

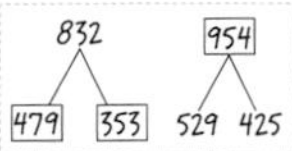

4. Write an addition problem using two 3-digit numbers and solve. Prove that your answer is correct.
   479 + 353 = 832; Prove: 832 − 353 = 479
5. Write a subtraction problem using two 3-digit numbers and solve. Prove that your answer is correct.
   954 − 529 = 425; Prove: 425 + 529 = 954
6. **Analyze** If you solve a problem using addition how can you check and prove it is correct? If you solve a problem using subtraction how can you check and prove it is correct? use subtraction; use addition

Skills: Add, subtract, and analyze — Use after Unit 11, Lesson 18.

Grouping Small Group

Materials None

Objective Children use opposite operations to check and prove addition and subtraction problems.

Connections Computation and Reasoning

Ready-Made Math Resources

Technology — Tutorials, Practice, and Intervention

Go Digital

Soar to Success Math

Use online, individualized intervention and support to bring students to proficiency.

Harcourt Mega Math Grades K-6

Help students practice skills and apply concepts through exciting math adventures.

DESTINATION Math®

Extend and enrich students' understanding of skills and concepts through engaging, interactive lessons and activities.

Visit **Education Place®**
www.eduplace.com

Visit www.eduplace.com/mx2t/ and find family, teacher, and student materials, activities, games, and more.

Literature Links

One Grain of Rice

One Grain of Rice

In this beautiful book written and illustrated by Demi, children learn how knowledge of math permitted the main character to accumulate over a billion grains of rice in just 30 days. The story is based upon the principle of doubling a number. Children can use their 2- and 3-digit addition skills to track Rani's accumulations early in the story.

Literature Connections

Earth Day—Hooray!, by Stuart J. Murphy and Renee Andriani (HarperTrophy, 2004)

The 329th Friend, by Marjorie Weinman Sharmat and Cyndy Szekeres (Four Winds Press, 1979)

Hannah's Collections, by Marthe Jocelyn (Dutton Children's Books, 2000)

Unit 11 Teaching Resources

Differentiated Instruction

Individualizing Instruction		
	Level	Frequency
Activities	• Intervention • On Level • Challenge	All 3 in every lesson
	Level	Frequency
Math Writing Prompts	• Intervention • On Level • Challenge	All 3 in every lesson
Math Center Challenges	For advanced students	
	4 in every unit	

Reaching All Learners		
	Lessons	Pages
English Language Learners	1, 2, 3, 4, 5, 6, 7, 8, 9, 10, 11, 12, 13, 14, 15, 16, 17, 18, 19, 20, 21, 22, 23	756, 764, 772, 778, 785, 793, 799, 804, 811, 816, 827, 833, 838, 844, 855, 862, 867, 875, 880, 887, 892, 899, 905
	Lessons	Pages
Extra Help	7, 8, 11, 13, 14, 17	798, 799, 804, 826, 840, 844, 868
	Lesson	Page
Special Needs	18	875
	Lessons	Pages
Advanced Learners	11, 12, 13	828, 833, 840

Strategies for English Language Learners

Present this problem to all children. Offer the different levels of support to meet children's levels of language proficiency.

Objective To review place value in 3-digit numbers and introduce 1,000.

Problem Write the numbers 1,000 and 324 on the board. Have children identify the numbers and the place value for each digit in 324.

Newcomer

- Point and say: **This is 1,000.** Have children repeat.
- Point and say: **324.** Have children repeat. Say: **4 is in the *ones* place.** Have children repeat. Continue with other digits.

Beginning

- Point and ask: **Is this 1,000?** yes **How many zeroes are in the number 1,000?** 3 zeroes
- Point to 324. Have children read it aloud. Point and ask: **Is the 4 in the *ones* or *tens* place?** ones place Continue with other digits.

Intermediate

- Point and ask: **Is this 100 or 1,000?** 1,000 **What number is this?** 324
- Point and ask: **What is the place value of the digit 4?** ones Continue with other digits.

Advanced

- Point and ask: **Is this 100 or 1,000?** 1,000
- Have children identify 324 and tell the place value for each digit.

Connections

Art Connections
Lesson 8, page 808
Lesson 23, page 908

Language Arts Connection
Lesson 16, page 864

Real-World Connection
Lesson 13, page 842

Science Connections
Lesson 4, page 782
Lesson 5, page 790
Lesson 9, page 814
Lesson 11, page 830
Lesson 18, page 878
Lesson 21, page 896

Social Studies Connections
Lesson 6, page 796
Lesson 12, page 836
Lesson 19, page 884

Technology Connections
Lesson 3, page 776
Lesson 7, page 802
Lesson 15, page 858
Lesson 22, page 902

Literature Connections
Lesson 2, page 770
Lesson 17, page 872
Lesson 20, page 890

Math Background

Putting Research into Practice for Unit 11

From Our Curriculum Research Project: Three-Digit Addition and Subtraction

In this unit, children will learn different ways to add and subtract three-digit numbers. For three-digit addition, the important concept that children need to grasp is that one new hundred is made when there are 10 or more tens. For three-digit subtraction, children will be extending their knowledge of subtracting two-digit numbers from three-digit numbers to subtracting three-digit numbers from three-digit numbers. They continue to make enough ones in the ones place and enough tens in the tens place to allow for the completion of the subtraction calculation. Now they will need to subtract in the hundreds place, as well.

Children are encouraged to continue to invent their own methods or extend the use of methods they have learned for addition and subtraction. Children will continue applying, understanding, and explaining the New Groups Below and Show All Totals Methods of addition, and the Ungrouping First and Expanded Method of subtraction.

–Karen Fuson, Author
Math Expressions

From Current Research: Addition Algorithms

In the New Groups Below method, the new 1 or regrouped 10 (or new hundred) is recorded on the line separating the problem from the answer. This arrangement makes it easier to see the 14 that generated the regrouped 10 than when the 1 is written above the problem. Because the new 1 sits below in the answer space, it does not change the top number. Adding is easy: You just add the two numbers you see and then increase that total by one.

This method requires that children understand what to do when they get 10 or more in a given column. Because they can only write 9 or less of a given grouping in a column, they must make a group of 10 ones (or tens or hundreds, etc.) and give that group to the next left place. This conceptual trouble spot for students is called carrying or regrouping or trading.

National Research Council. "Developing Proficiency with Whole Numbers." Adding It Up: Helping Students Learn Mathematics. Washington, D.C.: National Academy Press, 2001. 203.

Other Useful References: Addition and Subtraction

Bowers, J., P. Cobb, and K. McClain. "The Evolution of Mathematical Practices: A Case Study." Cognition and Instruction 17 (1999): 25–64.

Carpenter, T.P., M.L. Franke, V.R. Jacobs, E. Fennema, and S.B. Empson. "A Longitudinal Study of Invention and Understanding in Children's Multidigit Addition and Subtraction." Journal for Research in Mathematics Education 29 (1998): 3–20.

Hiebert, J., and D. Wearne. "Instruction, Understanding, and Skill in Multidigit Addition and Subtraction." Cognition and Instruction 14 (1996): 251–83.

Kamii, C. Young Children Continue to Reinvent Arithmetic—2nd grade: Implications of Piaget's Theory. New York: Teachers College Press, 1989.

Getting Ready to Teach Unit 11

In this unit, children extend their understanding of place value through 1,000, learn several methods for adding and subtracting 3-digit numbers, and continue to develop problem solving and reasoning skills as they discuss and support their thinking about these operations and using them to solve problems.

Math Expressions Vocabulary

As you teach this unit, emphasize understanding of these terms:

- decade number
- Adding up Method
- ungrouping
- New Groups Below
- New Groups Above

See Glossary on pp. T7–T20.

Understanding Numbers to 1,000

Lessons 1, 2, 3, 4, and 5

In the first part of this unit, children are involved in meaningful exercises and activities that will help them truly understand numbers to 1,000. They will recognize the meaning of hundreds through counting exercises, and further their understanding of place value as they represent numbers using drawings.

After drawing a box, sticks, and circles to represent 190, and then more circles as we count to 200, we discuss the new ten and new hundred.

- We just made a ten and now we have 9 tens (sticks) and 10 ones (circles).

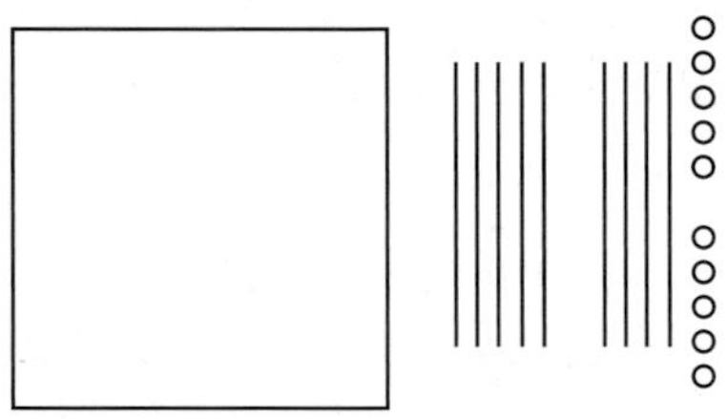

190, 191, 192, 193, 194,195, 196, 197, 198, 199, **200**

- We draw a line through the 10 circles or ones to show that there are 10 ones. 9 tens and 10 ones means that we have made a new hundred. We draw a box around the 9 sticks and 10 circles.

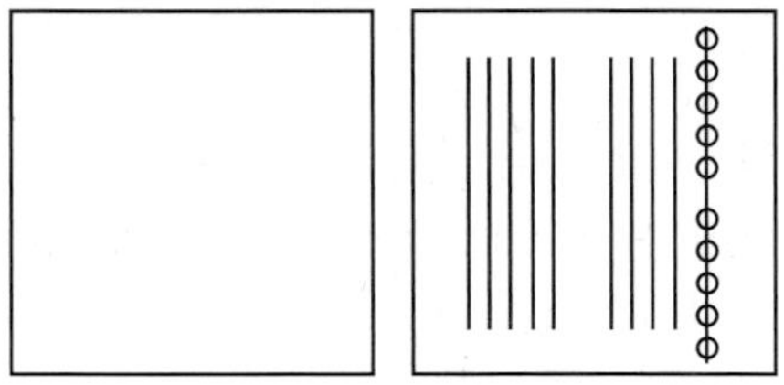

200

This process continues for other hundreds. Children also use Secret Code Cards to see the numerical structure of numbers through 1,000.

Strategies for Adding 3-Digit Numbers

Lessons 6, 7, 8, 9, 10, 11, 12, 13, 19, 20, 21, and 22

Proof Drawings Children use Proof Drawings to help add. They record the final answer they find. Initially, each step in the drawing is related to a step in the numerical method (see next page) to give the numbers correct, quantitative meanings. Eventually, when children understand and can explain their numerical method, they do not make a drawing.

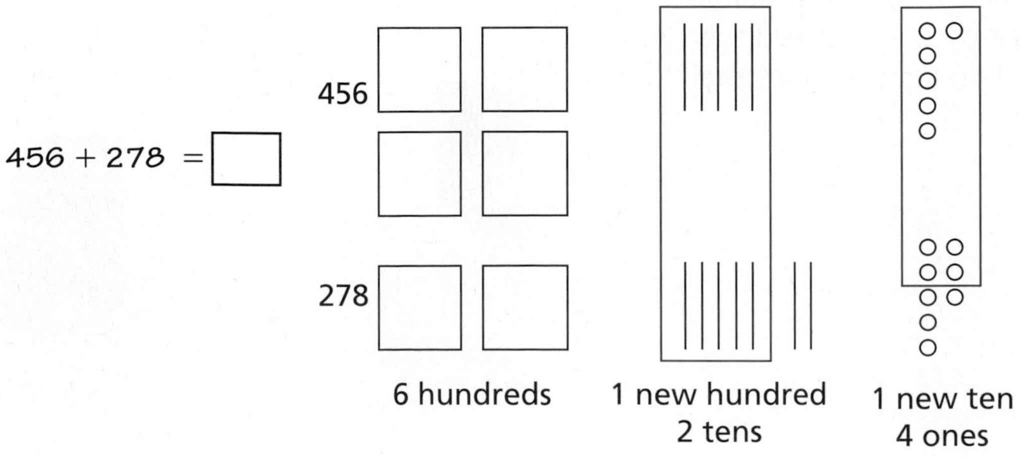

7 hundreds, 3 tens, 4 ones = 734

Methods for Adding 3-Digit Numbers Three numeric methods of addition, shown below, that we have used originally with 2-digit addition are reviewed in this unit. Children discuss these and their own methods to see how each method addresses what happens when there is a new ten or new hundred.

Show All Totals	New Groups Below	New Groups Above
$\begin{array}{r} 456 \\ +\ 278 \\ \hline 600 \\ 120 \\ 14 \\ \hline 734 \end{array}$	$\begin{array}{r} 456 \\ +\ 278 \\ \hline {}^{1\,1} \\ 734 \end{array}$	$\begin{array}{r} {}^{1\,1} \\ 456 \\ +\ 278 \\ \hline 734 \end{array}$

More-advanced and on-level children may enjoy using and explaining different methods and less-advanced children will usually choose and use one method.

Strategies for Subtracting 3-Digit Numbers
Lessons 14, 15, 16, 17, 18, 19, 20, 21, and 22

Proof Drawings Children can also combine proof drawings with their numerical methods. See pages 847 and 855 for examples. They can ungroup first from either direction and then subtract in either direction.

Methods for Subtracting 3-Digit Numbers Two numeric methods of subtraction, shown below, that we have used originally with 2-digit subtraction are reviewed in this unit.

Ungroup First Method Children will continue their understanding of a whole as they prepare a 3-digit number for subtraction by doing all necessary ungrouping first.

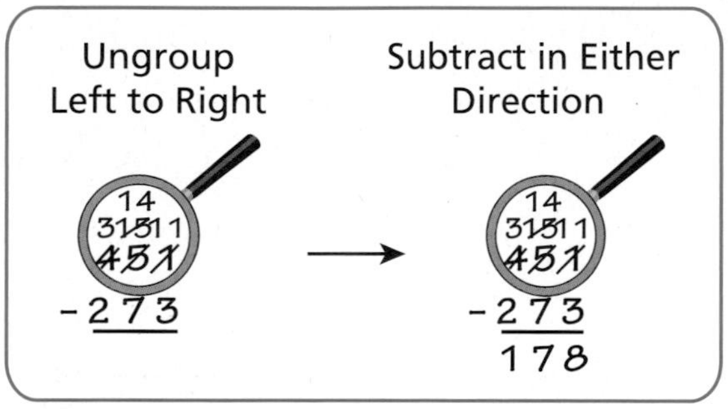

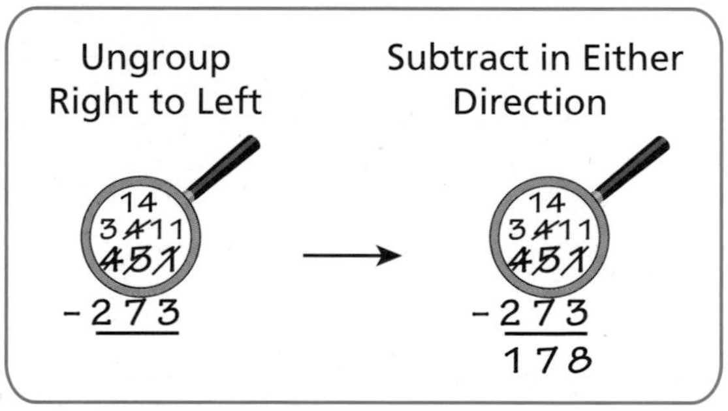

Expanded Method Children break apart both of the 3-digit numbers into hundreds, tens, and ones. This helps them see the real value of each digit as they ungroup and subtract. They do all necessary ungrouping first, and then subtract.

$$\begin{array}{rcl} & & 140 \\ & & 300 + \cancel{40} + 11 \\ 451 & = & \cancel{400} + \cancel{50} + \cancel{1} \\ -\ 273 & = & 200 + 70 + 3 \\ \hline & & 100 + 70 + 8 \quad = 178 \end{array}$$

Problem Solving

In *Math Expressions,* a research-based, algebraic problem-solving approach that focuses on problem types is used: understanding the situation; representing the situation with a math drawing or an equation; solving the problem; and see that the answer makes sense. Throughout the unit, children solve a variety of problems using the concepts and skills taught in this unit.

Reasoning Children will show their ability to reason as they share their methods for adding and subtracting 3-digit numbers. Throughout this unit, good explanations and good questions using hundreds, tens, and ones language are emphasized as much as finding answers. (See examples on pages 758 to 760.)

Proof Drawings Children provide justification of their methods as they are involved in making Proof Drawings and in explaining the methods they used for their addition and subtraction. In the first phase, children look back and forth between their Proof Drawing and numerical work. They relate each step in their Proof Drawing to each step in their numerical work. In the second phase, children can show and explain each step in the numerical solution without making a Proof Drawing. They are able to use ones, tens, and hundreds language proficiently and carry out their numerical method. In the third, long-delayed phase, children sometimes think about or make a Proof Drawing to keep their numerical method meaningful or to self-correct as errors creep in.

Use Mathematical Processes
Lesson 23

The NCTM process skills of problem solving, reasoning and proof, communication, connections, and representation are interwoven through all lessons throughout the year. The last lesson of this unit allows children to extend their use of mathematical processes to other situations.

Activity	NCTM Process Skill	Goal
Math and Art	Connections	Transfer a repeating pattern from one medium to another.
Following Directions	Communication	Follow, write, and give directions.
True or False?	Reasoning and Proof	Decide whether a math statement is true or false and use examples as support.
Same Perimeter, Different Area	Representation	Draw 2 different rectangles with the same perimeter; find the area of a rectangle.
Making Change	Problem Solving	Explain why the change in a buying situation will not be more than a given amount.

UNIT 11 LESSON 1

Count Numbers to 1,000

Lesson Objectives

- Count to 1,000 by hundreds.
- Represent 3-digit numbers with boxes, sticks, and circles.
- Count from a 3-digit number into the next hundred.

Vocabulary
ones
tens
hundreds
one thousand

The Day at a Glance

Today's Goals	Materials	
1 Teaching the Lesson A1: Count to 1,000 by hundreds. A2: Represent 3-digit numbers with boxes, sticks, and circles. A3: Use boxes, sticks, and circles to count from a 3-digit number into the next hundred.	**Lesson Activities** Student Activity Book pp. 339–342 (includes Dollars with Penny Array, Family Letter) Homework and Remembering pp. 221–222 Dollars with Penny Array MathBoard materials	**Going Further** Activity Cards 11-1 Base ten blocks Real or play money Index cards Math Journals
2 Going Further ▶ Differentiated Instruction		
3 Homework and and Targeted Practice		

Use Math Talk today!

Keeping Skills Sharp

Quick Practice — 5 MINUTES	Daily Routines
Goal: Write money strings for specific money amounts. **Money Strings** Have the class choose two money amounts between one and two dollars. Have two to four **Student Leaders** work at the board and the rest of the children work at their seats. Children should write combinations of dollars and/or coins that equal the amounts they chose. (See Unit 9 Lesson 11.)	**Making Change and Counting Coins** Making Change from $5.00, Combining Coins and Counting Money (See pp. xxvii–xxviii.) ▶ Led by teacher **Money Routine** Using the 120 Poster, Using the Money Flip Chart, Using the Number Path, Using Secret Code Cards (See pp. xxiii–xxv.) ▶ Led by **Student Leaders**

1 Teaching the Lesson

Activity 1

Count to 1,000

10 MINUTES

Goal: Count to 1,000 by hundreds.

Materials: Dollars with Penny Array (Student Activity Book pages 339–340)

NCTM Standard:
Number and Operations

The Learning Classroom

Building Concepts Decimal and cent notation was introduced informally in previous lessons in Unit 9. In addition, some children may already be very familiar with this topic from everyday experiences while other children may not. However, decimal notation for money will be a focus of this unit as children pretend to buy items, add money amounts, and make change.

English Language Learners

Write 549 on the board and have children say it aloud. Write *digit*. Say: **This number has 3 *digits*.**

- **Beginning** Point to and count the digits. Ask: **Is 9 a *digit*?** yes **Is 49?** no **Is 4 a digit?** yes **Is 5 a digit?** yes
- **Intermediate** Ask: **What are the *digits*?** 5, 4, 9 **Is the digit 9 in the ones place?** yes
- **Advanced** Ask: **Which *digit* is in the ones place?** 9 **Which digit is in the tens place?** 4 **Which digit is in the hundreds place?** 5

11–1 Class Activity

Name ____________________

► Count to 1,000 by Hundreds

Cut on dashed lines.

UNIT 11 LESSON 1 Dollars with Penny Array (front) 339

Student Activity Book page 339

► Count to 1,000 by Hundreds WHOLE CLASS

Invite children to look at the Dollars with Penny Array on Student Activity Book pages 339–340. Point out that each dollar bill has pennies on the back. Have children cut out the dollar bills. Remind children to cut carefully on the dashed lines.

Ask children to recall how many pennies are in one dollar. 100 pennies Have children check to see that there are 100 hundred pennies on the back of each dollar bill. Some children may notice that the pennies are arranged in columns of ten and that they can quickly check how many pennies are on the back of each bill by counting by tens.

Have children place the dollar bills in a stack on their desk with the dollar side up. As a class, count the dollar bills, taking the top dollar off the stack and saying *one dollar*. Continue counting and taking dollars off the stack one by one.

- How many one dollar bills are there in your stack? 10 one-dollar bills

Explain to children that they will now count the pennies on the backs of the dollars. Be sure children make the connection between counting one dollar and counting 100 pennies or 100 cents.

- Since there are 100 pennies on the back of each dollar, we can count the number of pennies in ten dollars by counting by hundreds.

Have children turn the stack of dollar bills over so that the penny side is up. As a class, count the pennies by taking the top bill off the stack and say *one hundred* aloud. Continue with each dollar bill and saying each hundred.

When children reach the last bill, some of them may call it *ten hundreds*, which is correct. Tell them that *ten hundreds* is called *one thousand* and it is written like this: 1,000.

Be sure children understand that the value of one dollar is the same as 100 pennies and that the value of ten dollars is the same as 1,000 pennies.

- How many cents are in one dollar? 100 cents or 100 pennies
- How many cents are in ten dollars? 1,000 cents or 1,000 pennies

Ask children to put their dollar bills, penny-side up, back in a stack and count by hundreds again in unison. This time write the numbers 100, 200, and so on to 1,000 on the board as children count.

If time permits, have the class count by hundreds again, but this time have a **Student Leader** write the numbers on the board.

Teaching Note

Math Background Some children may ask why 1,000 is written with a comma between the thousands and hundreds place. Explain to children that in the United States a comma is used after every third digit, from right to left, in whole numbers of more than three digits. This makes large numbers easier to read. However, not all countries follow this convention. For example, in some European countries, periods or blank spaces are used to separate every third digit.

Activity 2

Represent 3-Digit Numbers

▶ Review the Hundred-Box WHOLE CLASS — Math Talk

Remind children that they can use a box that is shaped roughly like a dollar bill to represent one hundred. Demonstrate by drawing a rectangle around 10 sticks.

- What do we use to show that we have 1? a circle
- What do we use to show that we have 10? a stick
- What do we use to show that we have 100? 10 sticks
- Here are 10 sticks.
  (Draw 10 sticks on the board.)

Draw a box around the sticks so that they look like a dollar bill. The box means 100.

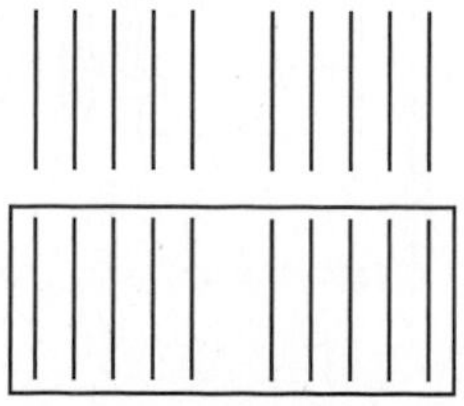

Activity continued ▶

15 MINUTES

Goal: Represent 3-digit numbers with boxes, sticks, and circles.

Materials: MathBoard materials

NCTM Standard:
Number and Operations

❶ Teaching the Lesson (continued)

Class Management

Every day in this unit several different children will go to the board and write money strings. They will check each other's strings while the rest of the class does another Quick Practice. Then they will write their strings on cling paper or chart paper. Each day the class will quickly look at the money strings to notice different things. If you wish, you can keep some of the sheets and discuss them during or at the end of this unit.

▶ Represent 3-Digit Numbers WHOLE CLASS

Draw 1 box, 8 sticks, and 3 circles on the board and have children do the same on their MathBoards. Then ask children to identify what number they are drawing. 183

Have children write the number for the boxes, sticks, and circles somewhere near their drawings, as you model how to write the number near your drawing.

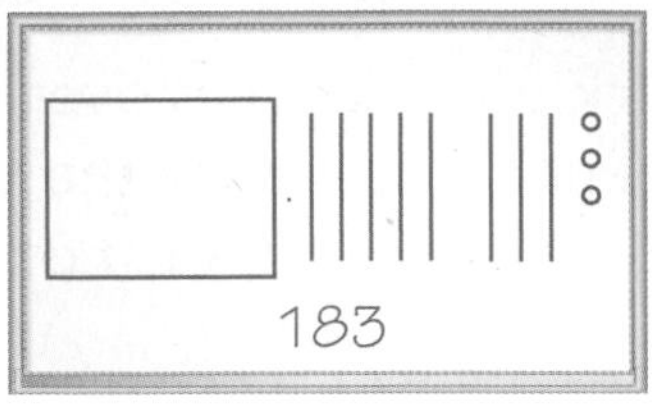

Send a few children to the board to work while the rest of the class works at their seats. Suggest another 3-digit number for children to represent.

- How can we draw 427 with boxes, sticks, and circles? 4 boxes, 2 sticks, and 7 circles

Ask volunteers to suggest other numbers up to 999 that the class can represent by drawing boxes, sticks, and circles. Reverse the process and have volunteers make drawings of boxes, sticks, and circles for the class to decipher and label. Continue as time permits.

Activity 3

Count Over the Hundreds

25 MINUTES

Goal: Use boxes, sticks, and circles to count from a 3-digit number into the next hundred.

Materials: MathBoard materials

NCTM Standards:
Number and Operations

▶ Represent Counting over the Hundreds

WHOLE CLASS

Math Talk

Tell children that they will be counting by ones from a number that begins with one hundred to a number that begins with two hundred.

Write 190 on the board. Have children discuss how to represent 190 by drawing boxes, sticks, and circles. Have them draw on their MathBoards while you demonstrate on the board.

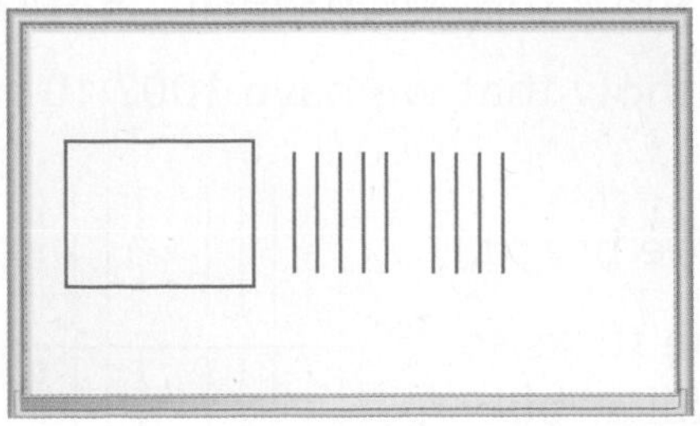

Have children count from 190 to 200. As they count, have children write a number beside each circle that is counted. Have children at their seats do the same on their MathBoards. Be sure children draw and label one circle at a time.

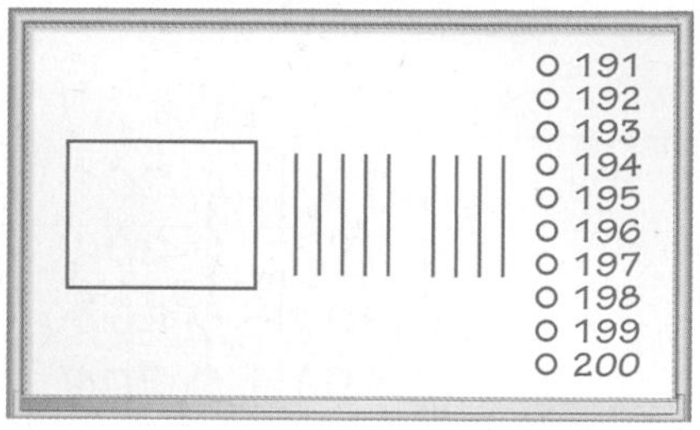

- We just made a ten and now we have 9 tens (sticks) and 10 ones (circles).

Draw a line through the 10 circles or ones to show that there are 10 ones while children do the same on their MathBoards.

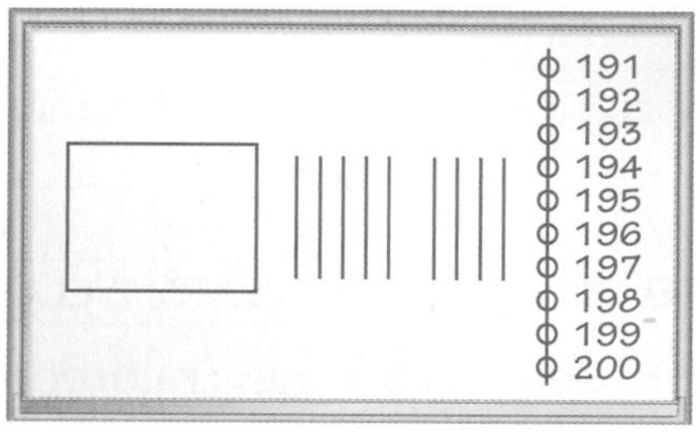

- 9 tens and 10 ones means that we have made a new hundred.

Draw a box around the 9 sticks and 10 circles on the board while children do the same on their Mathboards.

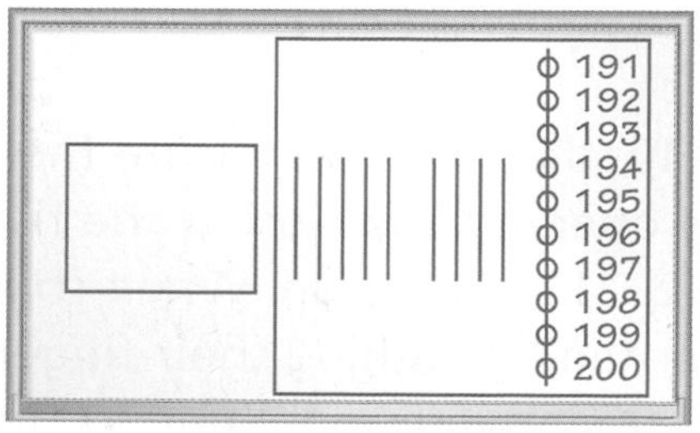

Activity continued ▶

Alternate Approach

Base Ten Blocks If some children are experiencing difficulty representing 3-digit numbers using boxes, sticks, and circles, have them use base ten blocks. Tactile learners are often more comfortable first using manipulatives to represent numbers and then drawing visual representations of the numbers.

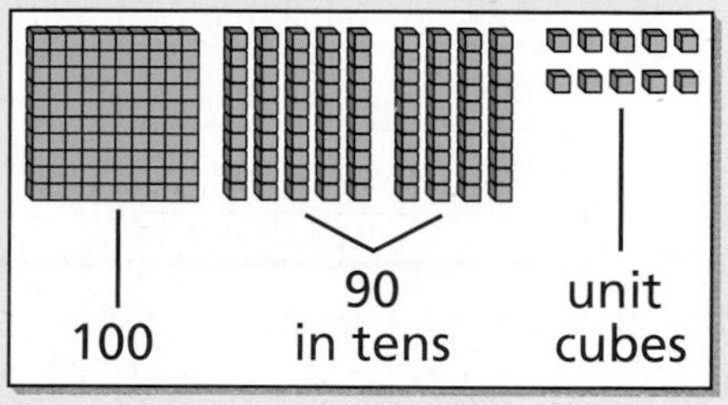

❶ Teaching the Lesson (continued)

Ongoing Assessment

Ask children to use gestures to indicate ones, tens, and hundreds as they count aloud from the starting numbers to the ending numbers shown below.

Starting Number	Ending Number
380	410
490	520
595	610

Continue counting by ones from 200 to 210, drawing a stick through the 10 circles to indicate *ten.* Then count to 220 and mark the ten with a stick. Finally, count to 230 and mark the ten with a stick.

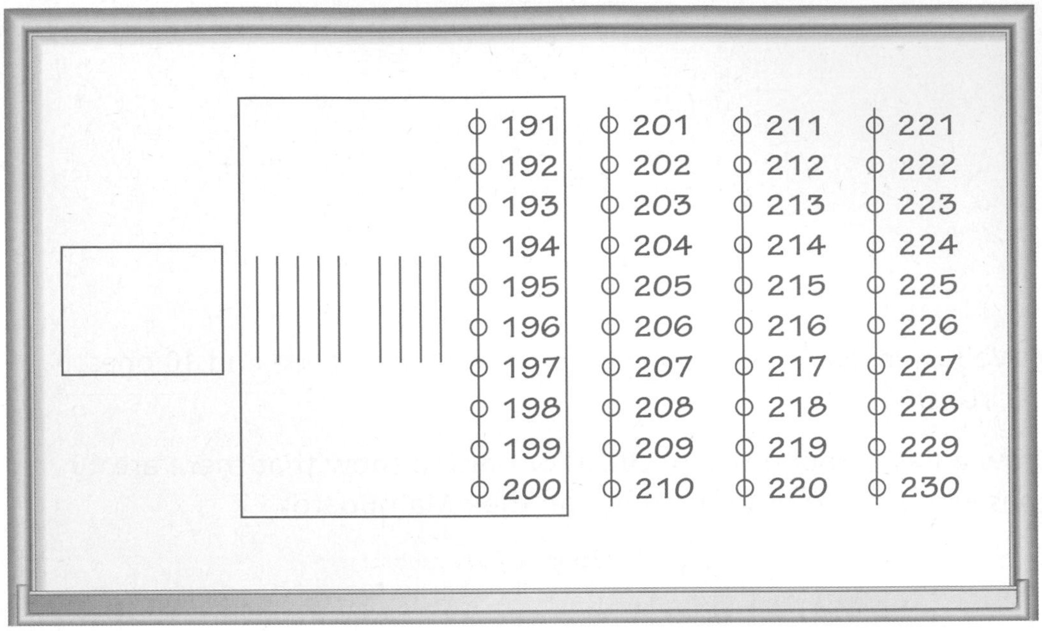

▶ Count Over the Hundred WHOLE CLASS

Count Orally and with Gestures Have children start at 190 and count aloud to 230, using gestures to indicate each number, each ten, and each hundred.

Tell children to start counting at 190 and as they count forward to raise a finger for each number mentioned. When children reach 200, have them draw an imaginary box in the air to indicate a new hundred. They should then resume counting, raising individual fingers for each new number (201, 202, 203, . . .).

When children reach 210, they should indicate the ten by flashing 10 fingers. This is done by opening and closing the fists one time. Counting continues with 211, 212, 213, and so on. When children reach 220, they should indicate another ten by flashing their fingers once. They should continue counting and raising individual fingers until they reach 230. They should once again indicate the new ten by flashing their fingers.

If time permits, repeat the activity beginning with 290 and ending with 320.

Intervention — Activity Card 11-1

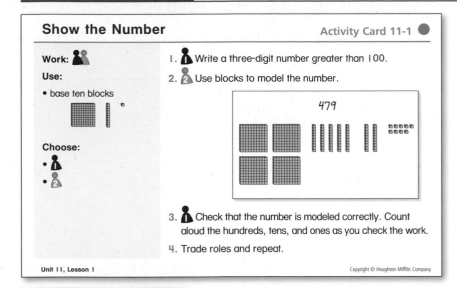

Show the Number
Activity Card 11-1

Work: pairs

Use:
- base ten blocks

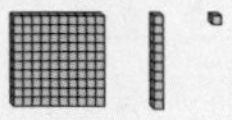

Choose:
- 1
- 2

1. 1 Write a three-digit number greater than 100.
2. 2 Use blocks to model the number.

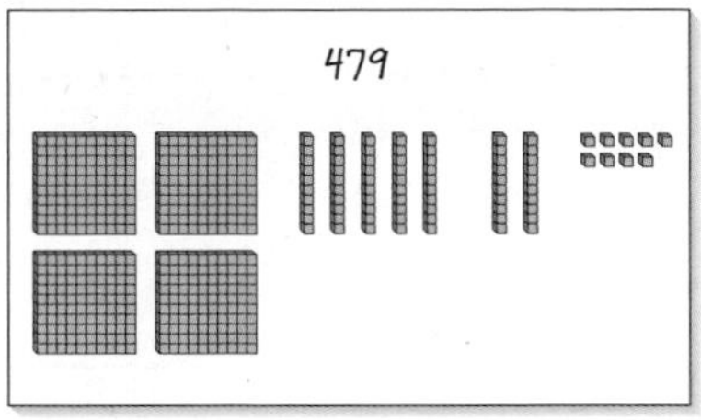

3. 1 Check that the number is modeled correctly. Count aloud the hundreds, tens, and ones as you check the work.
4. Trade roles and repeat.

Unit 11, Lesson 1

Activity Note Each pair needs hundreds, tens, or ones base ten blocks. You may want to have children draw the same number with blocks, sticks, and circles.

Math Writing Prompt

Make a Drawing Use two drawings to show the numbers 374 and 347. How are the drawings the same? How are they different?

Soar to Success Math **Software Support**

Warm Up 2.13

On Level — Activity Card 11-1

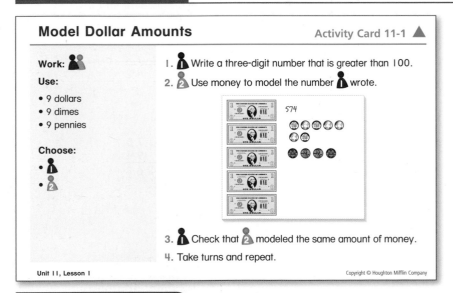

Model Dollar Amounts
Activity Card 11-1

Work: pairs

Use:
- 9 dollars
- 9 dimes
- 9 pennies

Choose:
- 1
- 2

1. 1 Write a three-digit number that is greater than 100.
2. 2 Use money to model the number 1 wrote.

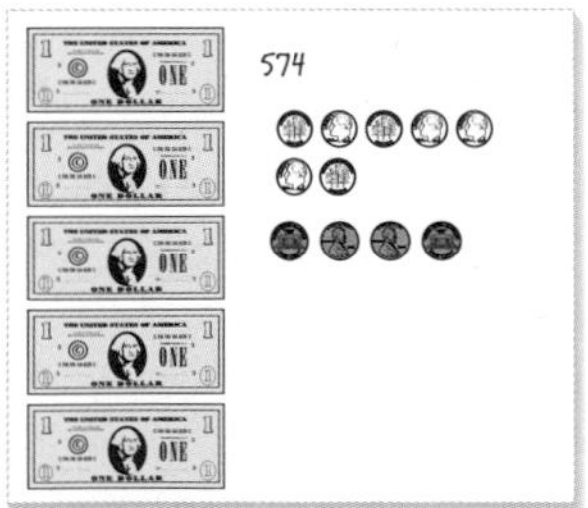

3. 1 Check that 2 modeled the same amount of money.
4. Take turns and repeat.

Unit 11, Lesson 1

Activity Note Each pair needs 9 dollars, 9 dimes, and 9 pennies (real or play). Extend the activity by having one child make a number using the money and the other write the three-digit number shown.

Math Writing Prompt

Explain Your Thinking Is the value of 5 in 451 the same as the value of 5 in 541? Explain why or why not.

Harcourt Mega Math Grades K-6 **Software Support**

Numberopolis: Lulu's Lunch Counter, Level L

Challenge — Activity Card 11-1

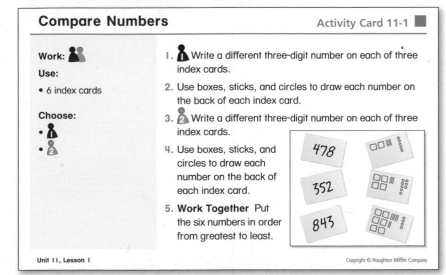

Compare Numbers
Activity Card 11-1

Work: pairs

Use:
- 6 index cards

Choose:
- 1
- 2

1. 1 Write a different three-digit number on each of three index cards.
2. Use boxes, sticks, and circles to draw each number on the back of each index card.
3. 2 Write a different three-digit number on each of three index cards.
4. Use boxes, sticks, and circles to draw each number on the back of each index card.
5. **Work Together** Put the six numbers in order from greatest to least.

Unit 11, Lesson 1

Activity Note Each pair needs six index cards. Have children check that they drew the number correctly on the back of each card.

Math Writing Prompt

Write About It What is the greatest three-digit number you can write? What is the smallest three-digit number you can write? Explain your thinking.

DESTINATION Math® **Software Support**

Course II: Module 1: Unit 1: Place Value: Hundreds, Tens and Ones

3 Homework and Targeted Practice

11–1 Homework **Goal:** Additional Practice

This Homework page provides practice in writing and drawing 3-digit numbers.

11–1 Homework Name

Count the hundreds, tens, and ones.
Write the totals.

1. 

1	9	8	Total 198
Hundreds	Tens	Ones	

2. 

4	5	9	Total 459
Hundreds	Tens	Ones	

Draw the hundreds, tens, and ones for the numbers below. Use boxes, sticks, and circles.

3. 2 Hundreds 4 Tens 3 Ones

4. 5 Hundreds 6 Tens 8 Ones

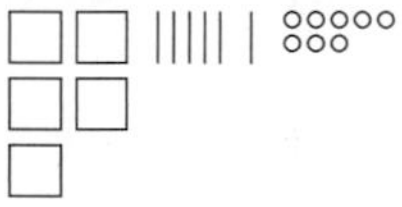

5. 3 Hundreds 8 Tens 2 Ones

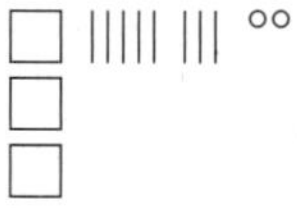

6. 1 Hundreds 7 Tens 7 Ones

UNIT 11 LESSON 1 Count Numbers to 1,000 221

Homework and Remembering page 221

11–1 Targeted Practice **Goal:** Multi-digit Subtraction

This Targeted Practice page can be used with children who need extra practice subtracting.

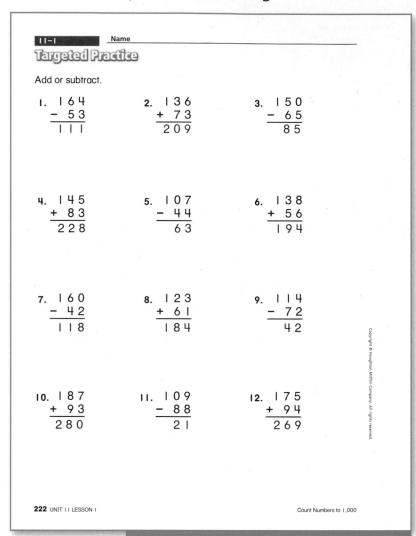

11–1 Targeted Practice Name

Add or subtract.

1. $164 - 53 = 111$
2. $136 + 73 = 209$
3. $150 - 65 = 85$
4. $145 + 83 = 228$
5. $107 - 44 = 63$
6. $138 + 56 = 194$
7. $160 - 42 = 118$
8. $123 + 61 = 184$
9. $114 - 72 = 42$
10. $187 + 93 = 280$
11. $109 - 88 = 21$
12. $175 + 94 = 269$

222 UNIT 11 LESSON 1 Count Numbers to 1,000

Homework and Remembering page 222

Home and School Connection

Family Letter Have children take home the Family Letter on Student Activity Book page 341. This letter explains how the concepts of counting and writing numbers to 1,000 are developed in *Math Expressions.* It gives parents and guardians a better understanding of the learning that goes on in math class and creates a bridge between school and home. A Spanish translation of this letter is on the following page in the Student Activity Book.

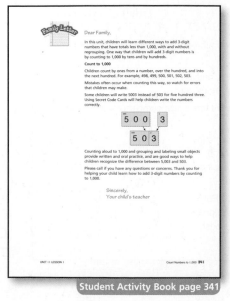

Family Letter

Dear Family,

In this unit, children will learn different ways to add 3-digit numbers that have totals less than 1,000, with and without regrouping. One way that children will add 3-digit numbers is by counting to 1,000 by tens and by hundreds.

Count to 1,000

Children count by ones from a number, over the hundred, and into the next hundred. For example, 498, 499, 500, 501, 502, 503.

Mistakes often occur when counting this way, so watch for errors that children may make.

Some children will write 5003 instead of 503 for five hundred three. Using Secret Code Cards will help children write the numbers correctly.

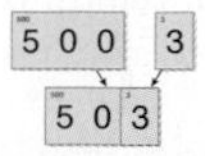

Counting aloud to 1,000 and grouping and labeling small objects provide written and oral practice, and are good ways to help children recognize the difference between 5,003 and 503.

Please call if you have any questions or concerns. Thank you for helping your child learn how to add 3-digit numbers by counting to 1,000.

Sincerely,
Your child's teacher

UNIT 11 LESSON 1 Count Numbers to 1,000 341

Student Activity Book page 341

Carta a la familia

Estimada familia:

En esta unidad los niños están aprendiendo diferentes maneras de sumar números de 3 dígitos con totales de menos de 1,000, reagrupando y sin reagrupar. Una manera en que los niños sumarán números de 3 dígitos es contando hasta 1,000 de diez en diez y de cien en cien.

Contar hasta 1,000

Los niños cuentan de uno en uno a partir de un número, llegan a la centena y comienzan con la siguiente centena.

Por ejemplo, 498, 499, 500, 501, 502, 503.

Cuando se cuenta de esta manera los niños suelen cometer errores. Por lo tanto, preste atención a errores que los niños puedan cometer.

Algunos niños podrian escribir 5003 en vez de 503 al intentar escribir quinientos tres. Usar las Tarjetas de código secreto ayudará a los niños a escribir correctamente los números.

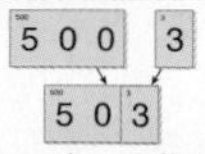

Contar hasta 1,000 en voz alta y poner objectos pequeños en grupos y rotularlos proporcionan práctica oral y escrita, y ayudan a los niños a reconocer la diferencia entre 5,003 y 503.

Si tiene alguna duda o pregunta, por favor comuníquese conmigo. Gracias por ayudar a su niño a aprender a sumar números de 3 digitos contando hasta 1,000.

Atentamente,
El maestro de su niño

342 UNIT 11 LESSON 1 Count Numbers to 1,000

Student Activity Book page 342

UNIT 11 LESSON 2

Place Value

Vocabulary

hundreds
tens
ones
one thousand
expanded numbers

Lesson Objective

- **Differentiate between hundreds, tens, and ones and place them in the correct order.**

The Day at a Glance

Today's Goals	Materials	
1 Teaching the Lesson **A1:** Count over 1,000. Count and add over a hundred. **A2:** Review how to represent 3-digit numbers with boxes, sticks, and circles. **A3:** Take apart and put together 3-digit numbers by using Secret Code Cards and by writing expanded numbers.	**Lesson Activities** Student Activity Book pp. 343–344 Homework and Remembering pp. 223–224 MathBoard materials Demonstration Secret Code Cards Secret Code Cards	**Going Further** Activity Cards 11-2 Secret Code Cards Base ten blocks *Earth Day—Hooray!* by Stuart J. Murphy Math Journals
2 Going Further ▸ Differentiated Instruction		
3 Homework and Spiral Review		

Use Math Talk today!

Keeping Skills Sharp

Quick Practice 5 MINUTES	Daily Routines
Goal: Write money strings for specific money amounts. **Money Strings** Have children discuss the money strings by asking questions like the following: • What amounts will always have pennies in their strings? amounts that don't end in 5 pennies or 0 pennies • How can you make a long string shorter? by trading lesser coins for greater coins or a dollar (See Unit 9 Lesson 11.)	**Making Change and Counting Coins** Making Change from \$5.00, Combining Coins and Counting Money (See pp. xxvii–xxviii.) ▸ Led by teacher **Money Routine** Using the 120 Poster, Using the Money Flip Chart, Using the Number Path, Using Secret Code Cards (See pp. xxiii–xxv.) ▸ Led by Student Leaders

1 Teaching the Lesson

Activity 1

Introduce Quick Practices

10 MINUTES

Goal: Count over 1,000. Count and add over a hundred.

Materials: MathBoard materials, Demonstration Secret Code Cards

NCTM Standards:
Number and Operations
Representation

Class Management

These activities will be used as Quick Practices in future lessons.

English Language Learners

Write 10, 100, and 1,000 on the board. Have children read each number aloud.

- **Beginning** Point and say: **There are 2 digits in 10. There is a zero and a one**. Have children repeat. Continue with 100 and 1,000.
- **Intermediate** Ask: **Which number has 3 digits – 100 or 1,000?** 100 **How many zeroes are in 100?** 2 zeroes **How many zeroes are in 1,000?** 3 zeroes
- **Advanced** Have children describe the digits in the numbers. 10,100, and 1,000.

▶ Count Over 1,000

Have children count from 990 to 1,004. Write each number on the board as children say the numbers. Pause when they reach 1,000. Then discuss what the one and the zeros mean. 1 thousand, 0 hundreds, 0 tens, and 0 ones

Have two **Student Leaders** show 1,000 to 1,004 with the Demonstration Secret Code Cards as the rest of the class continues to count and write 1,001, 1,002, 1,003, and 1,004. Then have children discuss the number 1,004 in terms of place value. Ask how many thousands there are. 1 How many hundreds? 0 How many tens? 0 How many ones? 4 Be aware that some children may write 10,004 for the number 1,004. This is a common error, but using Secret Code Cards will help children write numbers correctly.

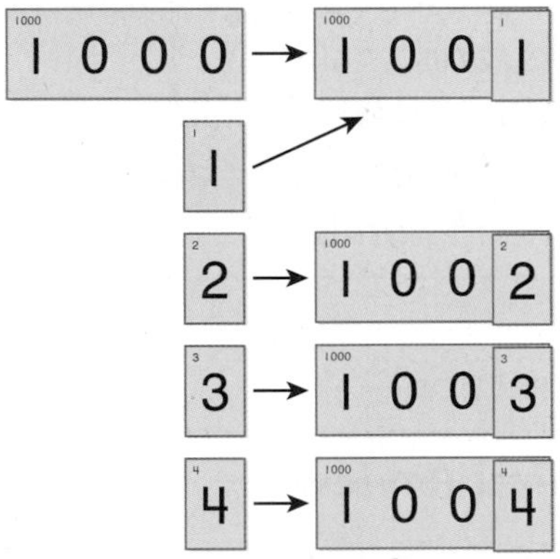

If children need more visual support, have a child draw boxes, sticks, and circles on the board for the class to see while they are counting.

▶ Count Over a Hundred from 190 to 222

Have children show 190 by drawing an imaginary box in the air to represent 100 and then flashing 10 fingers nine times to represent 90. From there, they should count to 222 by raising one finger at a time. When they reach 200, they should draw two imaginary boxes in the air to show 200. When they reach 10 and 20, they should flash all 10 fingers. (See Unit 11 Lesson 1 Activity 3.)

If children need more visual support, have a child draw boxes, sticks, and circles on the board for the class to see while they count with their fingers.

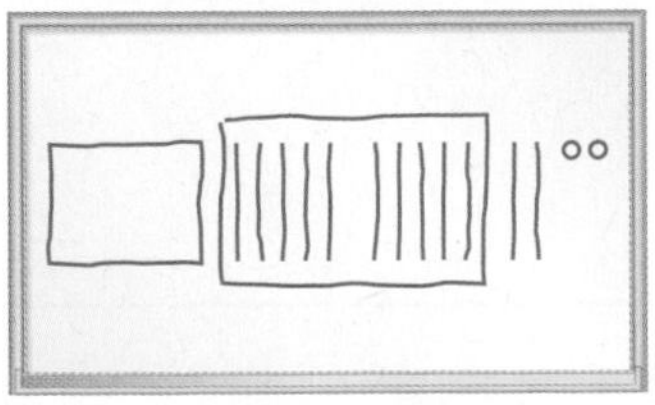

▶ Add Over the Hundred

Write the exercises shown below on the board. Have children say the answers at your class signal. Most of the children will count on to go over the hundred and that is fine.

297 + 6 = ☐ 303

495 + 7 = ☐ 502

698 + 5 = ☐ 703

Activity 2

Review Boxes, Sticks, and Circles

▶ Review the Use of Boxes, Sticks and Circles to Represent Numbers

WHOLE CLASS

Math Talk

Name some 3-digit numbers and have children represent the numbers by drawing boxes, sticks, and circles on their MathBoards. Ask volunteers to suggest other 3-digit numbers up to 999 that the class can represent.

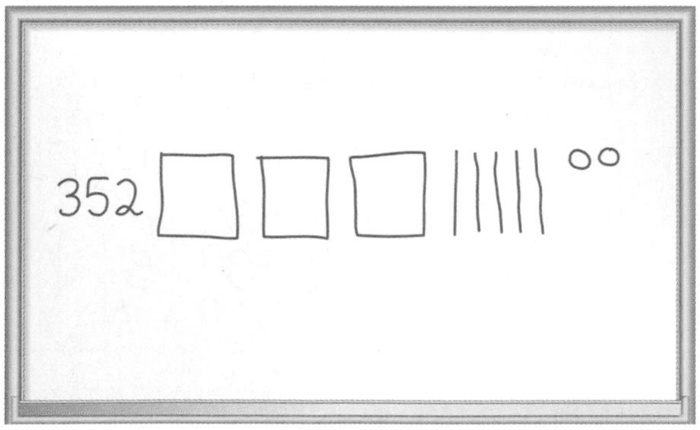

Then reverse the process and have children come to the board and draw boxes, sticks, and circles for the class to decipher and label. Continue as time permits.

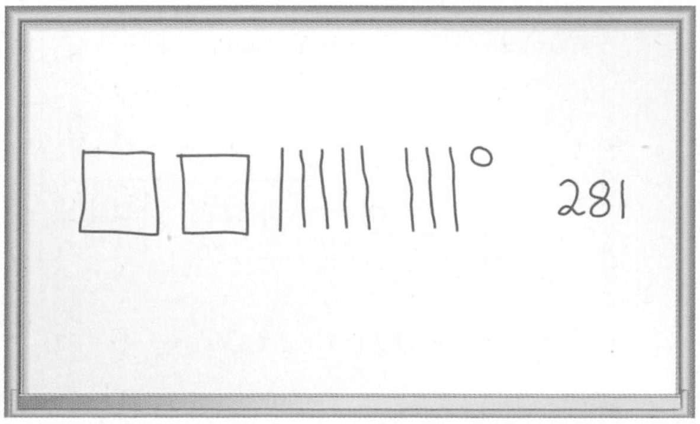

10 MINUTES

Goal: Review how to represent 3-digit numbers with boxes, sticks, and circles.

Materials: MathBoard materials

NCTM Standards:
Number and Operations
Representation

Activity 3

Find Hidden Numbers

35 MINUTES

Goal: Take apart and put together 3-digit numbers by using Secret Code Cards and by writing expanded numbers.

Materials: Demonstration Secret Code Cards, Secret Code Cards (1 set per child), MathBoard materials, Student Activity Book page 343

NCTM Standards:
Number and Operations
Representation

▶ Represent 3-Digit Numbers in Various Ways

WHOLE CLASS

Ask for Ideas Draw the number 265 on the board using boxes, sticks, and circles. Have children describe what they see in terms of hundreds, tens, and ones. Then have one child represent the number using Demonstration Secret Code Cards, while the rest of the class represents the number using their Secret Code Cards. Children should assemble the cards on the Number Path side of their MathBoards.

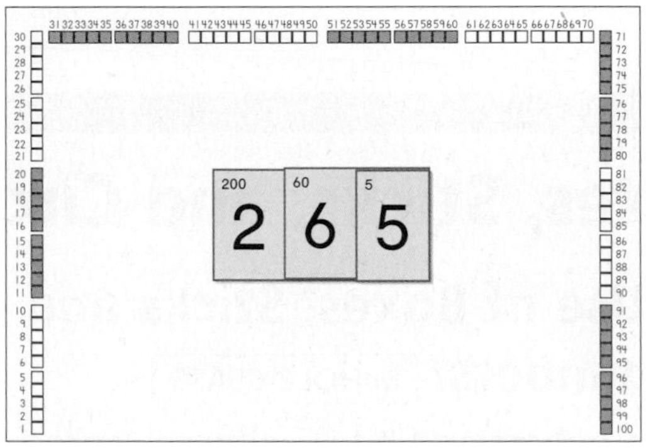

Have children spread out the individual Secret Code Cards to show the hundreds, tens, and ones.

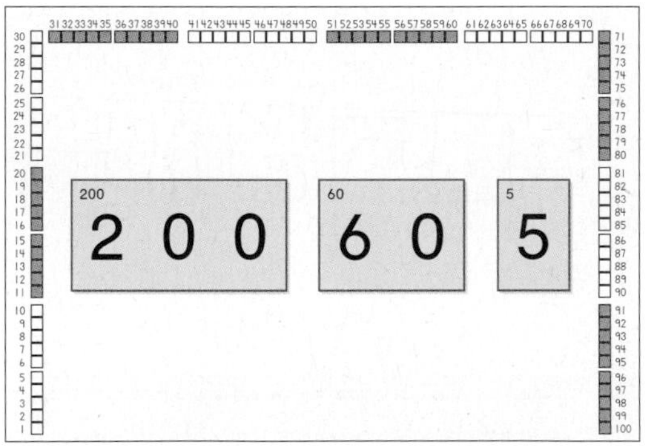

When children have spread out the cards, have them use the Secret Code Cards to write the number in expanded form.

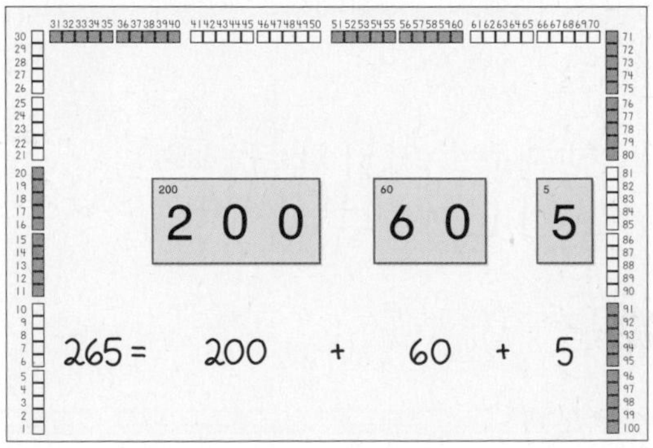

Write 400 + 70 + 3 on the board. Have children find the appropriate Secret Code Cards. Everyone should then assemble the cards to form the 3-digit number. Have one child show the number using Demonstration Secret Code Cards.

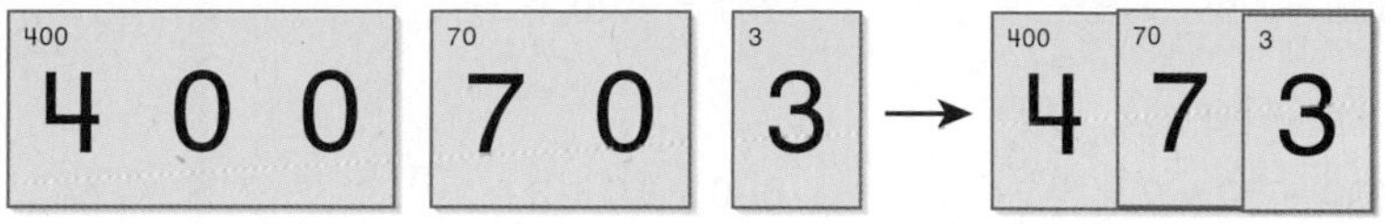

Have children reinforce their understanding by representing 473 by drawing boxes, sticks, and circles.

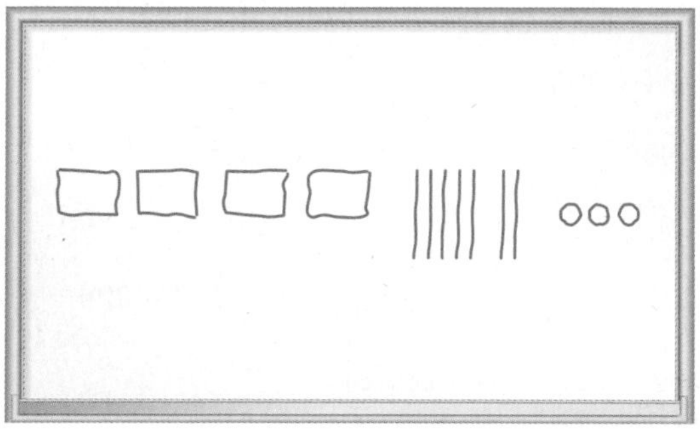

Repeat the process with two different expanded numbers. Have children represent each number with Secret Code Cards and then boxes, sticks, and circles.

Discuss Place Value Have children explain what each of the digits in a 3-digit number represents. For example, because of its place, the 4 in 473 represents 4 hundreds, not 4 ones or 4 tens. Repeat with other numbers as time permits.

▶ Scrambled 3-Digit Numbers WHOLE CLASS

Present children with another number, but this time mix the order of the hundreds, tens, and ones. For example write the following on the board:

$$20 + 500 + 8$$

Have children determine what the number is. 528 Then have them use their Secret Code Cards to represent the number.

Present other scrambled 3-digit numbers for children to represent and identify. Then have volunteers create their own scrambled 3-digit numbers for the rest of the class to represent and identify.

Activity continued ▶

Teaching Note

Language and Vocabulary In this lesson, children learn to take apart and write 3-digit numbers in *expanded form*. Expanded form, often called *expanded notation*, refers to numbers written in a form that shows the place value of the digits. For example, 254 = 2 hundreds + 5 tens + 4 ones or 200 + 50 + 4.

Ongoing Assessment

Have children identify these expanded numbers.

- ▶ 200 + 50 + 4
- ▶ 800 + 2
- ▶ 30 + 400 + 5

Then have children write these numbers as expanded numbers.

- ▶ 459
- ▶ 237
- ▶ 305

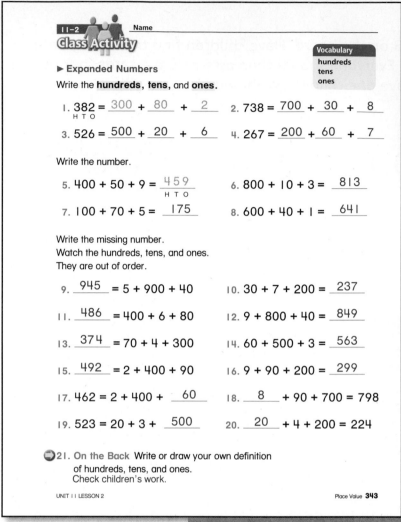

11-2 Class Activity

Name

Vocabulary
hundreds
tens
ones

▶ Expanded Numbers

Write the **hundreds**, **tens**, and **ones**.

1. 382 = 300 + 80 + 2 (H T O)
2. 738 = 700 + 30 + 8
3. 526 = 500 + 20 + 6
4. 267 = 200 + 60 + 7

Write the number.

5. 400 + 50 + 9 = 459 (H T O)
6. 800 + 10 + 3 = 813
7. 100 + 70 + 5 = 175
8. 600 + 40 + 1 = 641

Write the missing number.
Watch the hundreds, tens, and ones.
They are out of order.

9. 945 = 5 + 900 + 40
10. 30 + 7 + 200 = 237
11. 486 = 400 + 6 + 80
12. 9 + 800 + 40 = 849
13. 374 = 70 + 4 + 300
14. 60 + 500 + 3 = 563
15. 492 = 2 + 400 + 90
16. 9 + 90 + 200 = 299
17. 462 = 2 + 400 + 60
18. 8 + 90 + 700 = 798
19. 523 = 20 + 3 + 500
20. 20 + 4 + 200 = 224

21. On the Back Write or draw your own definition of hundreds, tens, and ones.
Check children's work.

UNIT 11 LESSON 2 Place Value 343

Student Activity Book page 343

▶ Expanded Numbers PAIRS

Math Talk

Have children work in **Helping Pairs** to complete the top half of Student Activity Book page 343. Explain that they should write the hundreds, tens, and ones for each of the numbers in exercises 1–4 and that they should write the 3-digit numbers that are being described in exercises 5–8. Before children start exercises 9–20, point out that they need to be extra careful as the hundreds, tens, and ones places are scrambled.

While children are completing the page, invite a few volunteers to go to the board to solve the problems. The children who are seated at their desks can check their answers by consulting the board as they work.

Encourage volunteers to share their answers to exercise 21.

Intervention — Activity Card 11-2

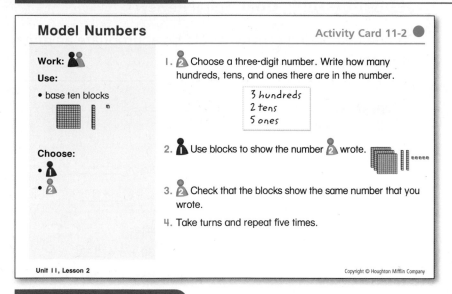

Model Numbers
Activity Card 11-2

Work: (pairs)
Use:
- base ten blocks

Choose:
- 1
- 2

1. (2) Choose a three-digit number. Write how many hundreds, tens, and ones there are in the number.

   3 hundreds
   2 tens
   5 ones

2. (1) Use blocks to show the number (2) wrote.
3. (2) Check that the blocks show the same number that you wrote.
4. Take turns and repeat five times.

Unit 11, Lesson 2 — Copyright © Houghton Mifflin Company

Activity Note Each pair needs hundreds, tens, and ones base ten blocks. After children have completed their turns, encourage them to mix up the order of the hundreds, tens, and ones when describing the number.

Math Writing Prompt

Make a Drawing Use boxes, sticks, and circles to show the number below. Write the expanded number below the drawing.
4 hundreds, 5 tens, and 3 ones

Soar to Success Math **Software Support**

Warm Up 2.13

On Level — Activity Card 11-2

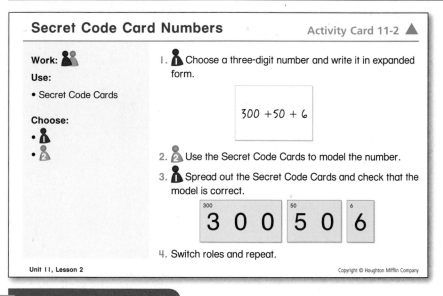

Secret Code Card Numbers
Activity Card 11-2

Work: (pairs)
Use:
- Secret Code Cards

Choose:
- 1
- 2

1. (1) Choose a three-digit number and write it in expanded form.

   300 + 50 + 6

2. (2) Use the Secret Code Cards to model the number.
3. (1) Spread out the Secret Code Cards and check that the model is correct.

300	50	6
3 0 0	5 0	6

4. Switch roles and repeat.

Unit 11, Lesson 2 — Copyright © Houghton Mifflin Company

Activity Note Each pair needs Secret Code Cards (TRB M3-M6). Have pairs explain what they are doing in each step.

Math Writing Prompt

Write About It Describe the number 658 in two different ways.

Harcourt MegaMath Grades K-6 **Software Support**

Country Countdown: Block Busters, Level S

Challenge — Activity Card 11-2

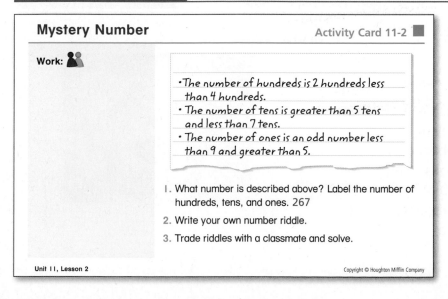

Mystery Number
Activity Card 11-2

Work: (pairs)

- The number of hundreds is 2 hundreds less than 4 hundreds.
- The number of tens is greater than 5 tens and less than 7 tens.
- The number of ones is an odd number less than 9 and greater than 5.

1. What number is described above? Label the number of hundreds, tens, and ones. 267
2. Write your own number riddle.
3. Trade riddles with a classmate and solve.

Unit 11, Lesson 2 — Copyright © Houghton Mifflin Company

Activity Note Have children explain how they used the clues to find the mystery number. Share children's riddles with the class.

Math Writing Prompt

Write About It What is the greatest number you can make using the digits 3, 0, and 4? Explain your thinking.

DESTINATION Math **Software Support**

Course II: Module 1: Unit 1: Expanded Form and Equivalent Representations of a Number

3 Homework and Spiral Review

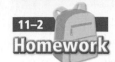

11–2 Homework **Goal:** Additional Practice

This Homework page provides practice in writing expanded 3-digit numbers.

11–2 Homework Name ____________

Write the hundreds, tens, and ones.

1. 675 = 600 + 70 + 5 (H T O)
2. 519 = 500 + 10 + 9
3. 831 = 800 + 30 + 1
4. 487 = 400 + 80 + 7
5. 222 = 200 + 20 + 2
6. 765 = 700 + 60 + 5

Write the number.

7. 300 + 40 + 6 = 346 (H T O)
8. 100 + 60 + 2 = 162
9. 700 + 20 + 4 = 724
10. 200 + 50 + 3 = 253
11. 400 + 70 + 1 = 471
12. 800 + 80 + 8 = 888

Write the missing number. Watch the hundreds, tens, and ones. They are out of order.

13. 435 = 30 + 5 + 400
14. 2 + 80 + 600 = 682
15. 863 = 60 + 800 + 3
16. 900 + 7 + 40 = 947
17. 354 = 300 + 4 + 50
18. 1 + 500 + 70 = 571
19. 729 = 20 + 9 + 700
20. 90 + 6 + 200 = 296

UNIT 11 LESSON 2 Place Value 223

Homework and Remembering page 223

11–2 Remembering **Goal:** Spiral Review

This Remembering activity would be appropriate anytime after today's lesson.

11–2 Remembering Name ____________

Complete the number sequence. Write the rule.

1. 43, 39, 35, 31, 27, 23 Rule: n − 4
2. 66, 69, 72, 75, 78, 81 Rule: n + 3

Write the hundreds, tens, and ones.

3. 695 = 600 + 90 + 5
4. 547 = 500 + 40 + 7

Write the number.

5. 400 + 30 + 6 = 436
6. 700 + 80 + 1 = 781

Add ones, tens, or a hundred.

7. 100 + 58 = 158
   10 + 58 = 68
   1 + 58 = 59
8. 3 + 100 = 103
   3 + 10 = 13
   3 + 1 = 4

Add or subtract.

9. 126 − 59 = 67
10. 93 − 45 = 48
11. 78 + 67 = 145

12. **Time** On a separate sheet of paper, draw what you do at 8 o'clock in the morning. Show the time on a digital clock. Check children's work.

224 UNIT 11 LESSON 2 Place Value

Homework and Remembering page 224

Home or School Activity

Literature Connection

Earth Day—Hooray! Extend children's knowledge of place value by reading aloud *Earth Day—Hooray!*, by Stuart J. Murphy and Renee Andriani (HarperTrophy, 2004). In this book, members of the Save-the-Planet Club prepare for Earth Day celebrations. They collect cans and bag them in groups of 1,000, 100, and 10. As you read the book, invite children to share what they know about place value. This book can also serve as an introduction to multi-digit addition.

UNIT 11 LESSON 3

Count by Ones and by Tens

Lesson Objective

- Count by ones and tens over a hundred, from a number more than 100 to a number less than 1,000.

Vocabulary

one thousand
hundreds
tens
ones
decade number

The Day at a Glance

Today's Goals	Materials	
1 Teaching the Lesson Count by ones and tens over a hundred and write number sequences.	**Lesson Activities** Student Activity Book p. 345 Homework and Remembering pp. 225–226 MathBoard materials	**Going Further** Activity Cards 11-3 Student Activity Book p. 346 Base ten blocks Math Journals
2 Going Further ▸ Extension: Write Word Names for 100 to 1,000 ▸ Differentiated Instruction		
3 Homework and Targeted Practice		

Use Math Talk today!

Keeping Skills Sharp

Quick Practice — 5 MINUTES

Goal: Write money strings for specific money amounts. Count over 1,000. Count and add over a hundred.

Materials: Demonstration Secret Code Cards

Money Strings As children are doing the Quick Practice activities below, have two or three children write money strings for amounts between one and two dollars on the board. At the end of Quick Practice, have the class quickly check that the money strings are correct. (See Unit 9 Lesson 11.)

Count Over 1,000 From 993 to 1,009. (See Unit 11 Lesson 2 Activity 1.)

Count Over a Hundred from 290 to 325 (See Unit 11 Lesson 2 Activity 1.)

Add Over the Hundred Use these equations: $396 + 8 = 404$, $794 + 7 = 801$, $597 + 9 = 606$ (See Unit 11 Lesson 2 Activity 1.)

Daily Routines

Making Change and Counting Coins Making Change from $5.00, Combining Coins and Counting Money (See pp. xxvii–xxviii.)

▸ Led by teacher

Money Routine Using the 120 Poster, Using the Money Flip Chart, Using the Number Path, Using Secret Code Cards (See pp. xxiii–xxv.)

▸ Led by Student Leaders

1 Teaching the Lesson

Activity

Count by Ones and by Tens

45 MINUTES

Goals: Count by ones and tens over a hundred and write number sequences.

Materials: Mathboard materials, Student Activity Book page 345

NCTM Standards:
Number and Operations
Representation

English Language Learners

Write the *decade numbers* from 10 to 90 on the board. Have children count.

- **Beginning** Ask: **Did we count the *decade numbers*?** yes Say: **We counted from 10 to 90 by *tens*.**
- **Intermediate** Ask: **Are these *decade numbers*?** yes **Are they tens numbers?** yes **Did we count by *tens*?** yes
- **Advanced** Ask: **What kind of numbers are these?** decade numbers **Are they made up of tens?** yes Say: **We counted by __.** tens

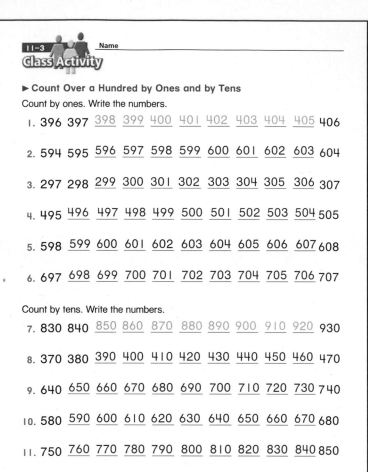

11-3 Class Activity Name ____________

▶ Count Over a Hundred by Ones and by Tens

Count by ones. Write the numbers.

1. 396 397 398 399 400 401 402 403 404 405 406
2. 594 595 596 597 598 599 600 601 602 603 604
3. 297 298 299 300 301 302 303 304 305 306 307
4. 495 496 497 498 499 500 501 502 503 504 505
5. 598 599 600 601 602 603 604 605 606 607 608
6. 697 698 699 700 701 702 703 704 705 706 707

Count by tens. Write the numbers.

7. 830 840 850 860 870 880 890 900 910 920 930
8. 370 380 390 400 410 420 430 440 450 460 470
9. 640 650 660 670 680 690 700 710 720 730 740
10. 580 590 600 610 620 630 640 650 660 670 680
11. 750 760 770 780 790 800 810 820 830 840 850
12. 460 470 480 490 500 510 520 530 540 550 560

UNIT 11 LESSON 3 Count by Ones and by Tens 345

Student Activity Book page 345

▶ Count Over a Hundred by Ones and by Tens

WHOLE CLASS Math Talk

Direct children's attention to the top of Student Activity Book page 345. Explain to children that they will count by ones and write the numbers. At the bottom of the page they will count by tens and write the numbers.

Count by Ones Review counting over a hundred by ones, if necessary. (See Unit 11 Lesson 1 Activity 3.)

Give children a few minutes to complete exercises 1–6. When they are finished, go over a few of the exercises with the class. Have children count with their fingers and draw an imaginary box in the air when they reach a new hundred. If you wish, have one of the children lead the class in doing this.

Count by Tens Explain to children that they will count by tens from a number that begins with eight hundred to a number that begins with nine hundred. Write the number 830 on the board.

Have children explain how to represent 830 with boxes and sticks. Have them draw on their MathBoards while you draw on the board.

Have children begin counting from 830 to 930, writing a number as each stick is drawn and counted. Model at the board while children write on their MathBoards. Stop when you reach 900.

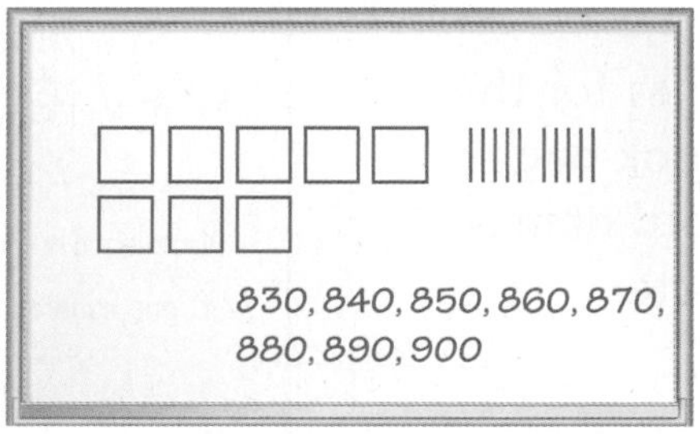

Draw a box around the ten sticks when you reach a hundred to indicate that a hundred has been made. Discuss this with children and have them draw a box around ten sticks on their MathBoards as well. Then continue counting by tens from 900 to 930. Draw a stick for each ten you count.

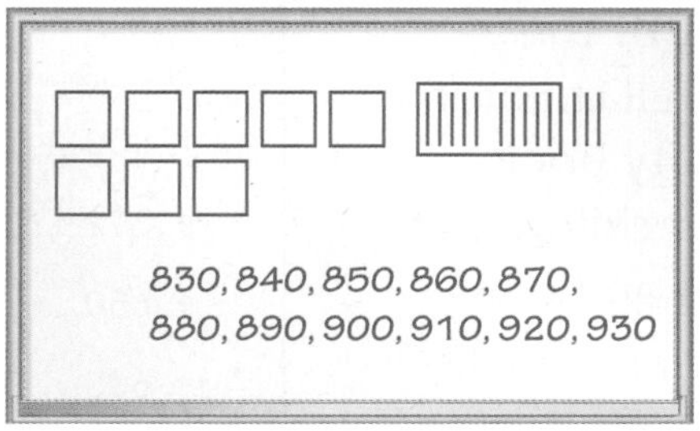

Count by Tens Orally and with Gestures Review what children have just done by having them begin at 830 and count forward by tens. They should start by drawing eight imaginary boxes in the air to represent 800, flashing their fingers three times to represent 30, and flashing ten fingers at every decade number. When they reach 900, have them draw an imaginary box in the air to indicate a new hundred. They should then resume counting, flashing their fingers once each, when they say the ten in 910, the twenty in 920, and the thirty in 930.

Have children take a few minutes to complete exercises 7–12 on Student Activity Book page 345. When they are finished, go over a few of the exercises with the class, having children count with their fingers and draw an imaginary box in the air when they reach a new hundred.

Ongoing Assessment

Have children count by ones using gestures, from the starting numbers to the ending numbers shown below. Then have them repeat the activity, counting by tens.

Starting Number	Ending Number
380	410
490	520
540	610

2 Going Further

Extension: Write Word Names for 100 to 1,000

Goal: Read and write word names for numbers 100 to 1,000.

Materials: Student Activity Book page 346

NCTM Standard:
Number and Operations

▶ Introduce Word Names for Greater Numbers WHOLE CLASS

As a class, have children read the word names for the numbers in the chart on Student Activity Book page 346. Then explain to children that these word names can be combined to spell the names of greater numbers.

Ask volunteers to write the word names for the following numbers on the board as the rest of the children write them on their MathBoards. Tell children to use the chart at the top of Student Activity Book page 346 to help them. If necessary, remind children to write a hyphen between the words for tens and ones.

6 six
506 five hundred six

30 thirty
530 five hundred thirty

47 forty-seven
547 five hundred forty-seven

After children have written the word names for the numbers, ask them to discuss how the numbers in each pair are the same and how they are different. Each pair of numbers has the same number of tens and ones. But the second number in each pair is 500 more than the first number.

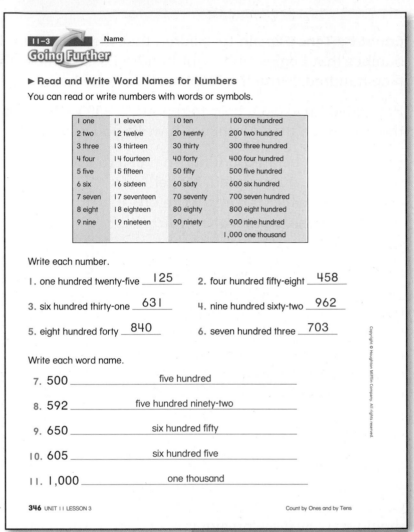

11-3 Going Further Name

▶ **Read and Write Word Names for Numbers**

You can read or write numbers with words or symbols.

1 one	11 eleven	10 ten	100 one hundred
2 two	12 twelve	20 twenty	200 two hundred
3 three	13 thirteen	30 thirty	300 three hundred
4 four	14 fourteen	40 forty	400 four hundred
5 five	15 fifteen	50 fifty	500 five hundred
6 six	16 sixteen	60 sixty	600 six hundred
7 seven	17 seventeen	70 seventy	700 seven hundred
8 eight	18 eighteen	80 eighty	800 eight hundred
9 nine	19 nineteen	90 ninety	900 nine hundred
			1,000 one thousand

Write each number.

1. one hundred twenty-five 125
2. four hundred fifty-eight 458
3. six hundred thirty-one 631
4. nine hundred sixty-two 962
5. eight hundred forty 840
6. seven hundred three 703

Write each word name.

7. 500 five hundred
8. 592 five hundred ninety-two
9. 650 six hundred fifty
10. 605 six hundred five
11. 1,000 one thousand

Student Activity Book page 346

▶ Read and Write Word Names for Numbers INDIVIDUALS

Have children complete Student Activity Book page 346 independently. Circulate around the room looking for children who are forgetting to use hyphens to separate the tens and ones. Also check to be sure children are not using the word *and* between the hundreds and the tens. (The word *and* is used to separate whole numbers and decimals, for example, three and two tenths.)

Intervention — Activity Card 11-3

Say and Show

Activity Card 11-3

Work:

Use:

- base ten blocks

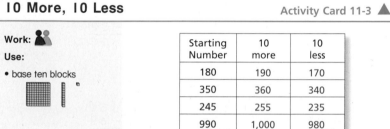

Starting Number	Ending Number
180	210
390	420
670	710
890	930

1. **Work Together** Start with the first number in the chart. Count by ones and then tens to the ending number. Use gestures to show ones, tens, and hundreds.
2. If you disagree or are unsure, use the blocks to model the numbers.
3. Repeat with the other numbers in the table.

Unit 11, Lesson 3

Activity Note Each pair needs base ten blocks. Suggest that each pair create gestures for showing hundred, ten, and one and use the gestures to count from the starting number.

Math Writing Prompt

Make a Drawing Use boxes, sticks, and circles to show the number that comes just after 910.

Soar to Success Math Software Support

Warm Up 2.15

On Level — Activity Card 11-3

10 More, 10 Less

Activity Card 11-3

Work:

Use:

- base ten blocks

Starting Number	10 more	10 less
180	190	170
350	360	340
245	255	235
990	1,000	980

1. **Work Together** Copy the table above onto a piece of paper.
2. Complete the table. Model the numbers using base ten blocks.
3. **Math Talk** What do you notice about the numbers that are 10 more and 10 less?

Unit 11, Lesson 3

Activity Note Each pair needs base ten blocks. Have both members of the pair agree to each answer.

Math Writing Prompt

Patterns Write the unknown numbers. Then explain how you knew which number to write.

280, 290, ____, ____, 320

697, 698, ____, ____, 701

Harcourt Mega Math Software Support

Numberopolis: Cross Town Number Line, Level P

Challenge — Activity Card 11-3

Skip Counting

Activity Card 11-3

Work:

Work Together Find the unknown numbers in each pattern below. Use boxes, sticks, and circles if needed. Describe how to skip count to find the unknown numbers in each pattern.

1. 450, 500, 550 ____, ____, ____ Answer: 600, 650, 700; skip count by 50
2. 492, 494, 496, ____, ____, ____ Answer: 498, 500, 502; skip count by 2
3. 643, 653, 663, ____, ____, ____ Answer: 673, 683, 693; skip count by 10
4. 980, 985, 990, ____, ____, ____ Answer: 995, 1,000, 1005; skip count by 5

Unit 11, Lesson 3

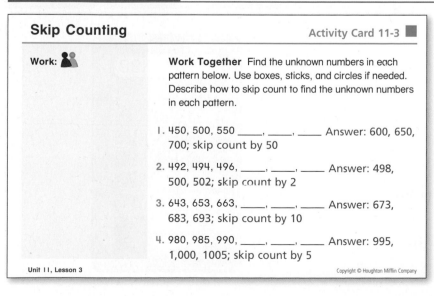

Activity Note Each pair needs to complete each pattern. Challenge pairs to write a unknown number pattern and share it with the class.

Math Writing Prompt

Representation Show the number 453 by making a drawing, using addition, and writing the words.

Destination Math Software Support

Course II: Module 1: Unit 1: Comparing and Ordering

3 Homework and Targeted Practice

11-3 Homework **Goal:** Additional Practice

This Homework page provides practice counting by ones and by tens.

11-3 Homework Name ____________________

Count by ones. Write the numbers.

1. 396 397 398 399 400 401 402 403 404 405 406
2. 695 696 697 698 699 700 701 702 703 704 705
3. 498 499 500 501 502 503 504 505 506 507 508
4. 894 895 896 897 898 899 900 901 902 903 904
5. 796 797 798 799 800 801 802 803 804 805 806
6. 597 598 599 600 601 602 603 604 605 606 607

Count by tens. Write the numbers.

7. 830 840 850 860 870 880 890 900 910 920 930
8. 470 480 490 500 510 520 530 540 550 560 570
9. 740 750 760 770 780 790 800 810 820 830 840
10. 380 390 400 410 420 430 440 450 460 470 480
11. 560 570 580 590 600 610 620 630 640 650 660
12. 690 700 710 720 730 740 750 760 770 780 790

UNIT 11 LESSON 3 Count by Ones and by Tens **225**

Homework and Remembering page 225

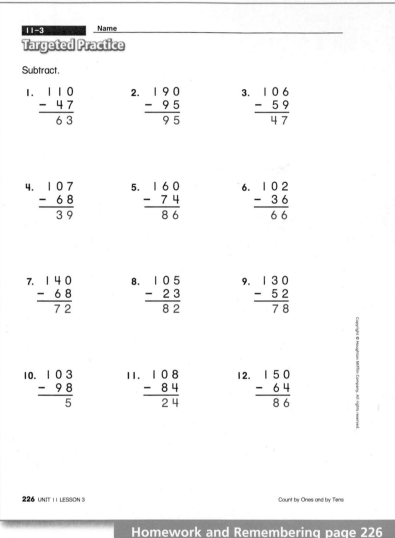

11-3 Targeted Practice **Goal:** Subtracting with zero

This page can be used with children who need practice subtracting from a number with a zero.

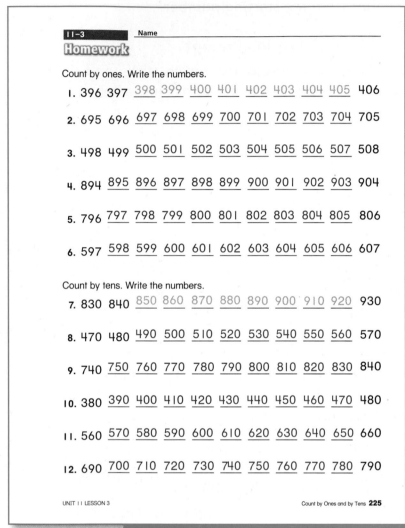

11-3 Targeted Practice Name ____________________

Subtract.

1. $110 - 47 = 63$
2. $190 - 95 = 95$
3. $106 - 59 = 47$
4. $107 - 68 = 39$
5. $160 - 74 = 86$
6. $102 - 36 = 66$
7. $140 - 68 = 72$
8. $105 - 23 = 82$
9. $130 - 52 = 78$
10. $103 - 98 = 5$
11. $108 - 84 = 24$
12. $150 - 64 = 86$

226 UNIT 11 LESSON 3 Count by Ones and by Tens

Homework and Remembering page 226

Home or School Activity

Technology Connection

Calculator Skip Counting Show children how to use a calculator to count by tens.

- Enter the number 10 into the calculator.
- Then press + 1 0 =. The display should now show 20.
- Continue pressing the = button. Each time you press the button, the calculator will add another 10 to the total.

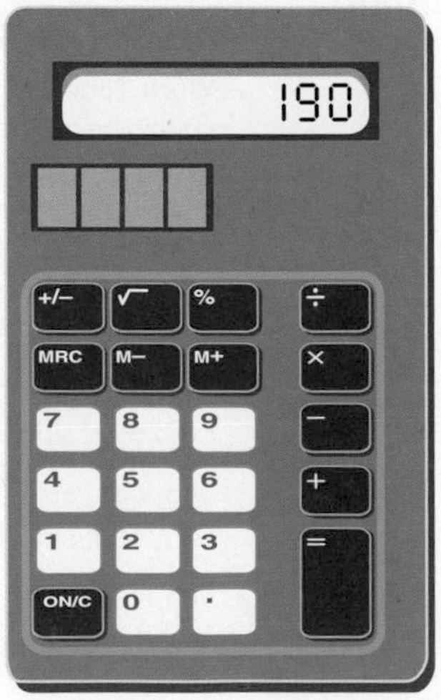

UNIT 11 LESSON 4

Group into Hundreds

Lesson Objectives

- Estimate quantities (up to 1,000).
- Group objects into tens and hundreds.
- Recognize that 10 ones are equal to a ten and that 10 tens are equal to a hundred.

Vocabulary
estimate
actual amount

The Day at a Glance

Today's Goals	Materials	
1 Teaching the Lesson Estimate the number of objects in a container. Then count the objects by hundreds, tens, and ones to determine the actual amount.	**Lesson Activities** Student Activity Book pp. 347–348; Homework and Remembering pp. 227–228; Beans or other countable objects; Transparent containers	**Going Further** Activity Cards 11-4; Beans or other countable objects; Transparent containers; Base ten blocks; Paper bags; Index cards; Ant Colony (TRB M83); Math Journals
2 Going Further ▸ Differentiated Instruction		
3 Homework and Spiral Review		

Use Math Talk today!

Keeping Skills Sharp

Quick Practice — 5 MINUTES

Goals: Count over 1,000. Count and add over a hundred.

Materials: Demonstration Secret Code Cards (TRB M7–M22)

Count Over 1,000 Have the children count from 993 to 1,009. (See Unit 11 Lesson 2 Activity 1.)

Count Over a Hundred from 390 to 427 (See Unit 11 Lesson 2 Activity 1.)

Add Over the Hundred Use these equations: $498 + 5 = 503$, $899 + 8 = 907$, $797 + 9 = 806$ (See Unit 11 Lesson 2 Activity 1.)

Repeated Quick Practice Use this Quick Practice from a previous lesson.

- ▸ **Money Strings** (See Unit 9 Lesson 11.)

Daily Routines

Making Change and Counting Coins Making Change from $5.00, Combining Coins and Counting Money (See pp. xxvii–xxviii.)

- ▸ Led by Student Leaders

Money Routine Using the 120 Poster, Using the Money Flip Chart, Using the Number Path, Using Secret Code Cards (See pp. xxiii–xxv.)

- ▸ Led by Student Leaders

1 Teaching the Lesson

Activity

Estimate and Group

40 MINUTES

Goals: Estimate the number of objects in a container. Then count the objects by hundreds, tens, and ones to determine the actual amount.

Materials: Beans or other countable objects (600 to 1,000), transparent container, Student Activity Book pages 347–348

NCTM Standard:
Number and Operations

The Learning Classroom

Building Concepts You may want to review the meaning of "one hundred" by asking children how many tens there are in one hundred.

English Language Learners

Write *estimate* on the board. Hold up a handful of pennies. Ask: **Do you know exactly how many pennies I have?** no Write 2, 10, and 50.

- **Beginning** Ask: **Is 2 a good guess?** no **Is 50 a good guess?** no **Is 10 a good guess?** yes Say: **10 is an *estimate*.**
- **Intermediate** Ask: **Which number is a good guess?** 10 **Is a good guess an *estimate*?** yes Say: **10 is an __.** estimate
- **Advanced** Ask: **Is an *estimate* a good guess?** yes **Which number is an *estimate*?** 10

▶ Estimate the Number of Objects in a Container

WHOLE CLASS

Math Talk

Fill a transparent container with 600 to 1,000 beans or other countable objects and place the container in plain view for children to see.

- What do we do when we estimate? We make a thoughtful guess about some number amount.

Refer children to Student Activity Book page 347 and work with children to help them estimate the number of objects in the container.

- How many beans do you think are in this container? Answers will vary.
- How many hundreds do you think we can make? Answers will vary.
- How many tens do you think we can make. Answers will vary.
- Write down your estimate at the top of Student Activity Book page 347 underneath the word *Estimate.*

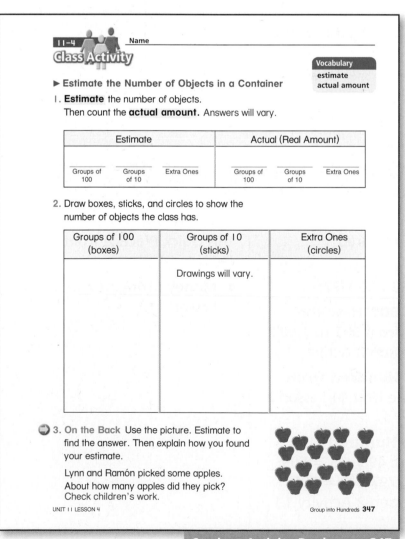

11-4 Class Activity

Name __________

Vocabulary
estimate
actual amount

▶ Estimate the Number of Objects in a Container

1. **Estimate** the number of objects.
Then count the **actual amount.** Answers will vary.

Estimate			Actual (Real Amount)		
Groups of 100	Groups of 10	Extra Ones	Groups of 100	Groups of 10	Extra Ones

2. Draw boxes, sticks, and circles to show the number of objects the class has.

Groups of 100 (boxes)	Groups of 10 (sticks)	Extra Ones (circles)
	Drawings will vary.	

3. **On the Back** Use the picture. Estimate to find the answer. Then explain how you found your estimate.

Lynn and Ramón picked some apples.
About how many apples did they pick?
Check children's work.

UNIT 11 LESSON 4

Group into Hundreds 347

Student Activity Book page 347

▶ Count the Objects in a Container SMALL GROUPS

After children have written their estimates, tell them that they will be counting the objects in the container as a class. Give each child between 20 and 60 objects from the container. Have each child count and make groups of ten and extra ones from their objects.

Then organize the class into groups. Each child in the group contributes his or her beans to the group's total. Group members should put their extra ones together to form more tens. They should then determine the number of hundreds, tens, and extra ones that they have. See below for an example of what four groups might do.

Group 1

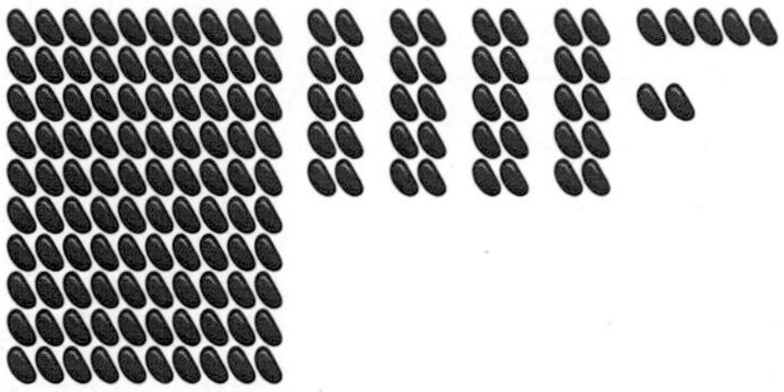

1 hundred 4 tens 7 ones

Group 2

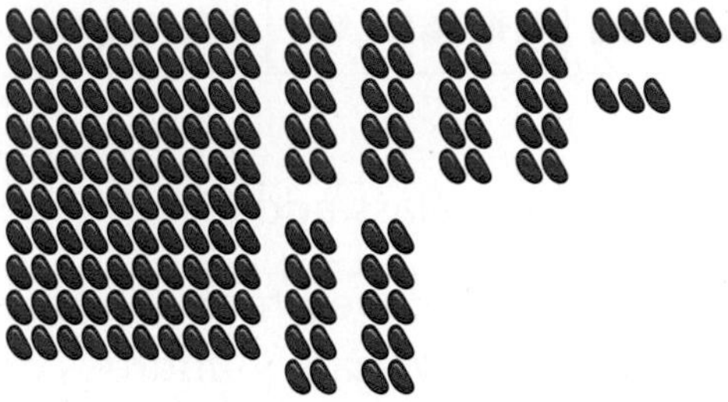

1 hundred 6 tens 8 ones

Group 3

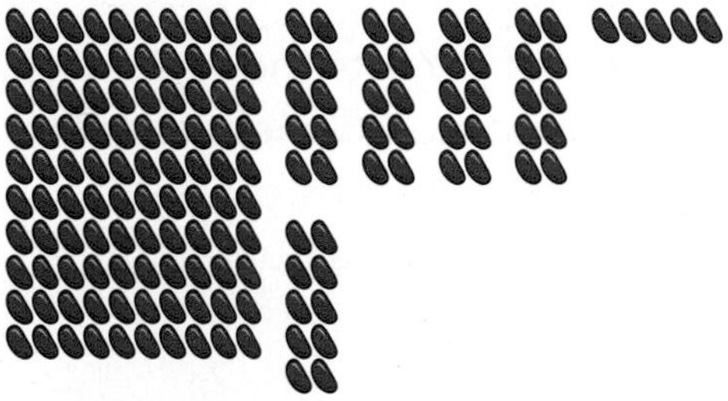

1 hundred 5 tens 5 ones

Group 4

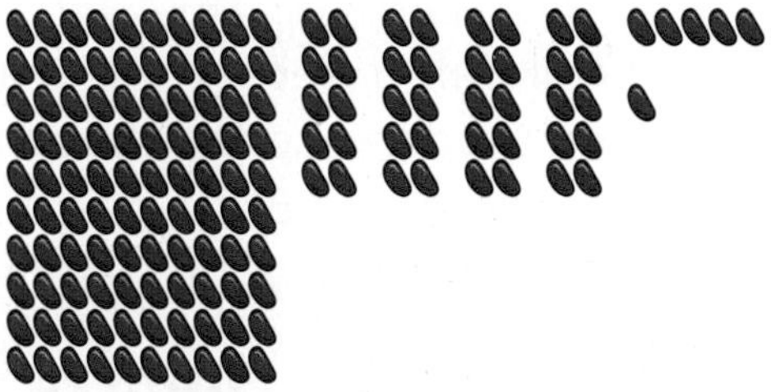

1 hundred 4 tens 6 ones

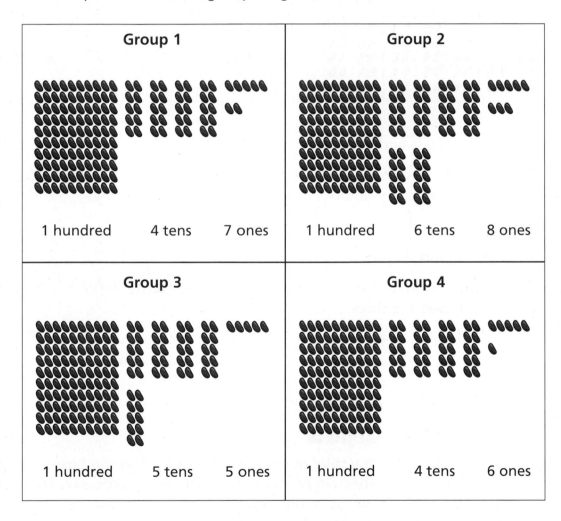

Have the class come together and make tens out of each group's extra ones. See below for an example of how this might look for the four groups.

Group 1		Group 2		Group 3		Group 4		
7 ones	+	8 ones	+	5 ones	+	6 ones	=	2 tens 6 ones

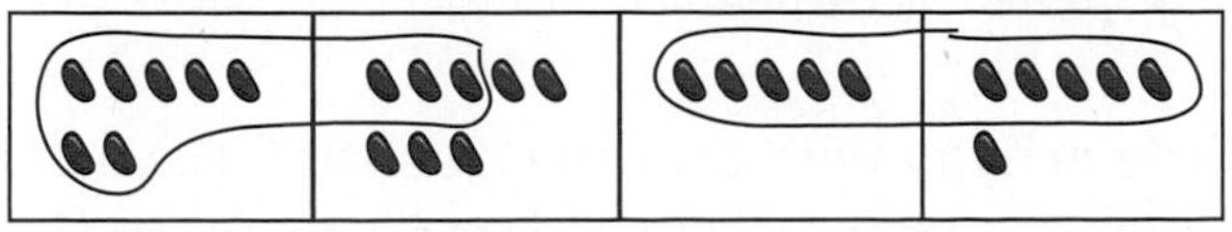

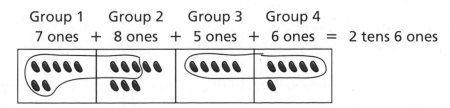

Activity continued ▶

Class Management

This hands-on counting and grouping may seem chaotic at times, but it is a highly valuable activity that helps children understand the meaning of hundreds, tens, and ones. Encourage children to talk about what they are doing when they group so that everyone can understand what is happening.

❶ Teaching the Lesson (continued)

Have the class make hundreds out of each group's extra tens.

- How many tens make a hundred? 10 tens
- How many hundreds can you make? Answer will vary.

See below for an example of how this might look for the four groups.

Group 1 4 tens + Group 2 6 tens + Group 3 5 tens + Group 4 4 tens + 2 Extra Tens = 2 hundreds 1 ten

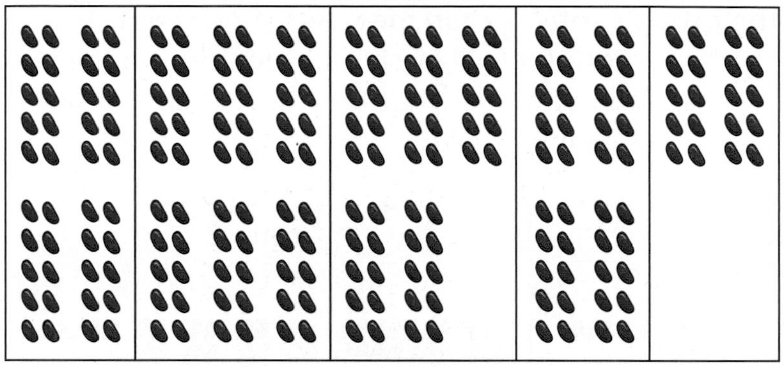

Then have the class add all their objects together.

- Now that we have grouped all our objects, let's add all of our hundreds together. How many hundreds do we have? Answers will vary.
- How many tens do we have left? Answers will vary.
- How many ones do we have? Answers will vary.
- How many hundreds, tens, and ones do we have? (Write the number on the board as the class responds.)

Then tell children to record the actual number of objects they counted as a class on Student Activity Book page 347 underneath the words *Actual (Real Amount).* Explain that the word *actual* means the real number. Then ask if anyone's estimate was close to the actual number.

▶ Represent the Objects WHOLE GROUP

Have children represent the total number of objects by drawing boxes, sticks, and circles, on the bottom of Student Activity Book page 347. The example below shows how this might look for the four groups.

6 hundreds + 1 ten + 6 ones = 616

If time permits, repeat the activity with another quantity. Have children work individually on exercise 3. Encourage volunteers to share their answers.

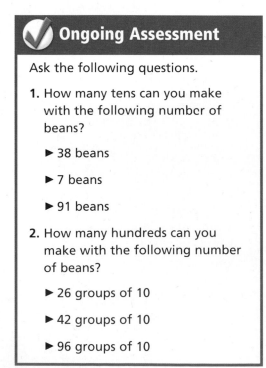

Ongoing Assessment

Ask the following questions.

1. How many tens can you make with the following number of beans?
   - ▶ 38 beans
   - ▶ 7 beans
   - ▶ 91 beans
2. How many hundreds can you make with the following number of beans?
   - ▶ 26 groups of 10
   - ▶ 42 groups of 10
   - ▶ 96 groups of 10

2 Going Further

Differentiated Instruction

Intervention

Activity Card 11-4

Estimate Number of Cubes — Activity Card 11-4

Work: pairs

Use:
- base ten blocks

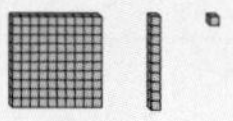

- 4 index cards
- paper bag

1. **Work Together** Grab a big handful of ones cubes.
2. Place the ones cubes in front of you.
3. Each child estimates how many ones cubes there are. Record your estimate.
4. **Work Together** Group the ones into tens. Trade the 10 ones for a ten. Then trade 10 tens for a hundred. The child closest to the actual number wins.

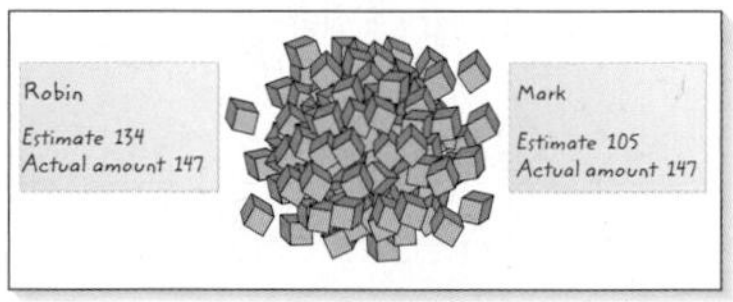

5. Put the ones cubes back in the bag and repeat.

Unit 11, Lesson 4

Activity Note Each pair needs at least 130 ones blocks and some tens and hundreds blocks, index cards, and a paper bag.

Math Writing Prompt

What's Wrong? Miki made this drawing to show 191 beans in a jar. What does Miki need to do to fix her drawing?

Soar to Success Math Software Support

Warm Up 15.11

On Level

Activity Card 11-4

Use Ten to Estimate — Activity Card 11-4

Work: pairs

1. Each child draws 30 to 100 circles on a piece of paper. Place the circles randomly on the paper.
2. Trade papers.
3. Ring a group of 10 circles on the paper. Use that group to estimate how many tens there are in all.
4. Write your estimate on the paper.

5. Compare your estimates. Who do you think came closer?
6. Repeat the activity with a new drawing.

Unit 11, Lesson 4

Activity Note Remind children to place their circles randomly on the page. You may want pairs to count to find the actual number of circles.

Math Writing Prompt

Make an Estimate Explain how you might estimate the number of children in your class today.

Harcourt MegaMath Software Support

Numberopolis: Block Busters, Level J

Challenge

Activity Card 11-4

Use a Benchmark — Activity Card 11-4

Work: individual

Use:
- clear jars with items inside

1. Look at the jar with 100 on it.
2. Use the 100-jar to help you estimate the number of items in each of the other jars.

3. Record your estimates.
4. Compare your estimates with a classmate. Share how you used the 100-jar to help you.

Unit 11, Lesson 4

Activity Note Prepare four transparent jars with small items. One jar, labeled 100, should have 100 items. The other jars have 50, 200, and 300 items.

Math Writing Prompt

Explain Your Thinking There are 520 beans in a jar. Sue estimates 550 beans, Bob 500 beans. Explain which is better.

Destination Math Software Support

Course II: Module 1: Unit 1: Counting by Grouping

3 Homework and Spiral Review

11–4 Homework **Goal:** Additional Practice

This Homework page provides practice solving problems and identifying and representing numbers.

11–4 **Homework** Name

Add or subtract.

1. 46 + 97 = 143

2. 154 − 83 = 71

3. 74 + 58 = 132

Solve each story problem. **Show your work.**

4. You have 100¢ to buy a necklace. The necklace costs 67¢. How much change should you get back?

33 ¢

5. Joy caught 47 insects. Ben caught 56. How many insects did the two children catch altogether?

103 insects
label

6. What number is shown?

467

7. Draw boxes, sticks, and circles to show the number 348.

UNIT 11 LESSON 4 Group into Hundreds 227

Homework and Remembering page 227

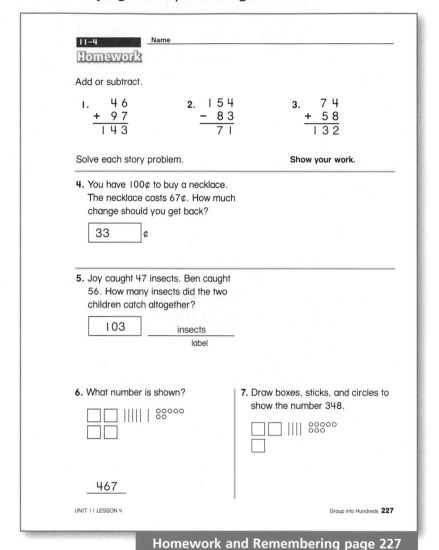

11–4 Remembering **Goal:** Spiral Review

This Remembering activity would be appropriate anytime after today's lesson.

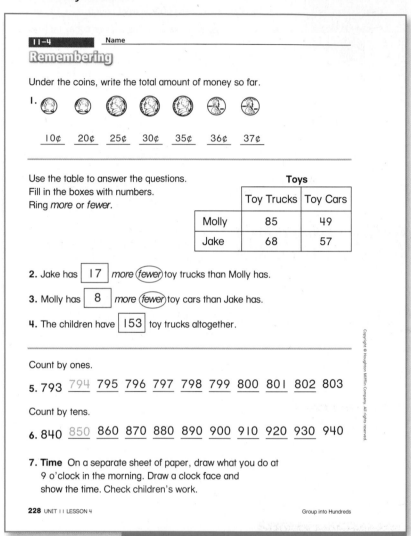

11–4 **Remembering** Name

Under the coins, write the total amount of money so far.

1.

10¢ 20¢ 25¢ 30¢ 35¢ 36¢ 37¢

Use the table to answer the questions.
Fill in the boxes with numbers.
Ring *more* or *fewer*.

Toys

	Toy Trucks	Toy Cars
Molly	85	49
Jake	68	57

2. Jake has 17 *more* (*fewer*) toy trucks than Molly has.

3. Molly has 8 *more* (*fewer*) toy cars than Jake has.

4. The children have 153 toy trucks altogether.

Count by ones.

5. 793 794 795 796 797 798 799 800 801 802 803

Count by tens.

6. 840 850 860 870 880 890 900 910 920 930 940

7. Time On a separate sheet of paper, draw what you do at 9 o'clock in the morning. Draw a clock face and show the time. Check children's work.

228 UNIT 11 LESSON 4 Group into Hundreds

Homework and Remembering page 228

Home or School Activity

Science Connection

Sampling Explain that scientists often keep track of how many animals live in a given area through sampling. Since it is not possible to count every animal, they sometimes estimate how many animals live in an area. Have children pretend to be scientists who want to estimate how many ants live in an ant colony, using Ant Colony (TRB M83). Have children estimate how many ants live in the colony, using any strategy. Then have children discuss and compare results.

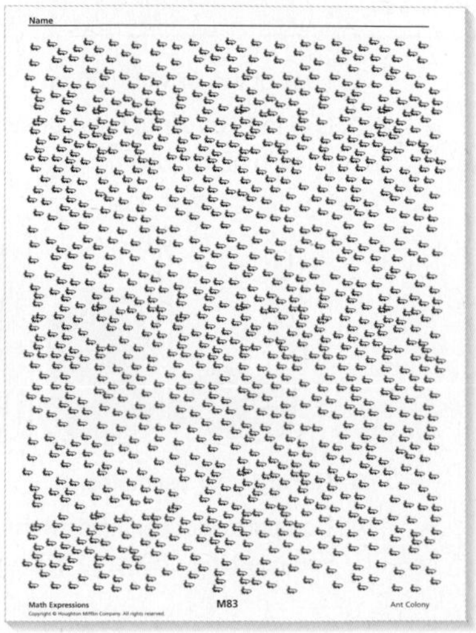

UNIT 11 LESSON 5

Add Ones, Tens, and Hundreds

REAL WORLD Problem Solving

Lesson Objectives

- Represent addition exercises to show place value.
- Apply knowledge of place value to story problems with groups of ten and a hundred and leftover ones.

Vocabulary
hundreds
tens
ones

The Day at a Glance

Today's Goals	Materials	
1 Teaching the Lesson **A1:** Add hundreds, tens, and ones, using Secret Code Cards and Proof Drawings. **A2:** Solve story problems with groups of hundreds, tens, and ones. **A3:** Estimate the number of objects in a container, then determine the exact number in two ways: grouping by hundreds, tens, and ones; and grouping by 25s. **A4:** Round numbers.	**Lesson Activities** Student Activity Book pp. 349–352 Homework and Remembering pp. 229–230 Quick Quiz 1 (Assessment Guide) Demonstration Secret Code Cards (optional) Secret Code Cards Transparent container Beans or other countable objects MathBoard materials	**Going Further** Activity Cards 11-5 Student Activity Book p. 350 Base ten blocks Lined paper Math Journals
2 Going Further ▸ Differentiated Instruction		
3 Homework and Targeted Practice		

Use Math Talk today!

Keeping Skills Sharp

Quick Practice — 5 MINUTES

Goal: Find partners of 100.

Partners of One Hundred Draw an unknown partner Math Mountain for 100 on the board. At the **Student Leader's** signal, children say the unknown partner as the Student Leader writes it in the box. Another Student Leader writes the eight addition and subtraction equations as quickly as possible as the class says them. (The order of equations does not matter.)

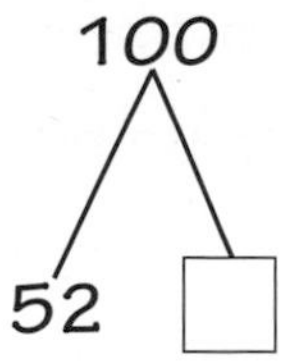

Repeated Quick Practice Use this Quick Practice from a previous lesson.

- ▸ **Money Strings** (See Unit 9 Lesson 11.)

Daily Routines

Making Change and Counting Coins Making Change from $5.00, Combining Coins and Counting Money (See pp. xxvii–xxviii.)

- ▸ Led by Student Leaders

Money Routine Using the 120 Poster, Using the Money Flip Chart, Using the Number Path, Using Secret Code Cards (See pp. xxiii–xxv.)

- ▸ Led by Student Leaders

1 Teaching the Lesson

Activity 1

Add Numbers with 1, 2, and 3 Digits

15 MINUTES

Goal: Add hundreds, tens, and ones, using Secret Code Cards and proof drawings.

Materials: Demonstration Secret Code Cards, Secret Code Cards (1 set per child), Student Activity Book page 349

NCTM Standard:
Number and Operations

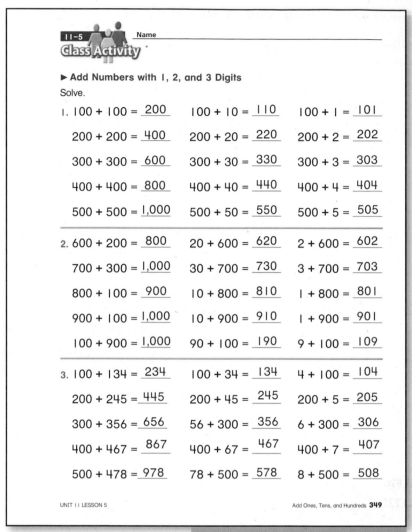

11–5 Class Activity

Name ________________

► Add Numbers with 1, 2, and 3 Digits

Solve.

1. 100 + 100 = 200	100 + 10 = 110	100 + 1 = 101
200 + 200 = 400	200 + 20 = 220	200 + 2 = 202
300 + 300 = 600	300 + 30 = 330	300 + 3 = 303
400 + 400 = 800	400 + 40 = 440	400 + 4 = 404
500 + 500 = 1,000	500 + 50 = 550	500 + 5 = 505
2. 600 + 200 = 800	20 + 600 = 620	2 + 600 = 602
700 + 300 = 1,000	30 + 700 = 730	3 + 700 = 703
800 + 100 = 900	10 + 800 = 810	1 + 800 = 801
900 + 100 = 1,000	10 + 900 = 910	1 + 900 = 901
100 + 900 = 1,000	90 + 100 = 190	9 + 100 = 109
3. 100 + 134 = 234	100 + 34 = 134	4 + 100 = 104
200 + 245 = 445	200 + 45 = 245	200 + 5 = 205
300 + 356 = 656	56 + 300 = 356	6 + 300 = 306
400 + 467 = 867	400 + 67 = 467	400 + 7 = 407
500 + 478 = 978	78 + 500 = 578	8 + 500 = 508

UNIT 11 LESSON 5 Add Ones, Tens, and Hundreds 349

Student Activity Book page 349

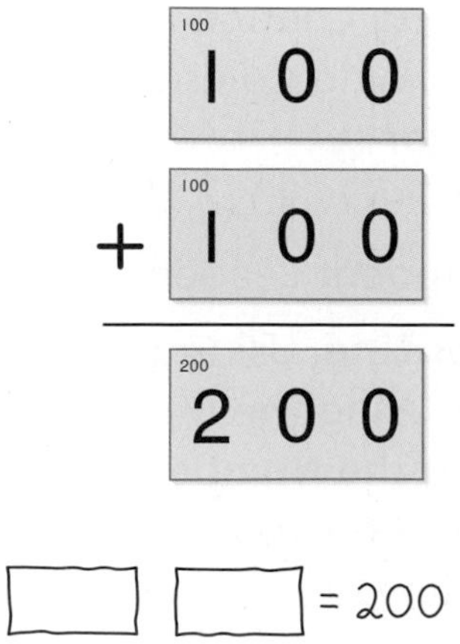

► Add Numbers with 1, 2, and 3 Digits

PAIRS

Math Talk

Have children work in **Helping Pairs**, and use Secret Code Cards to complete Student Activity Book page 349.

Add Hundreds Work together as a class to solve the first equation in exercise 1.

- The first equation on the page is 100 + 100 = ______.
- How can you show the exercise with Secret Code Cards? *Draw the cards on the board or use the Demonstration Secret Code Cards.*

Then have children solve the same exercise by drawing boxes, sticks, and circles.

- How many boxes do you need? 2
- How many sticks? 0
- How many circles? 0

Add Tens and Hundreds Work together as a class to solve the second equation in exercise 1 on Student Activity Book page 349.

- Now let's solve this exercise: 100 + 10 = ______.
- Who can show me how to add these two numbers using Secret Code Cards?

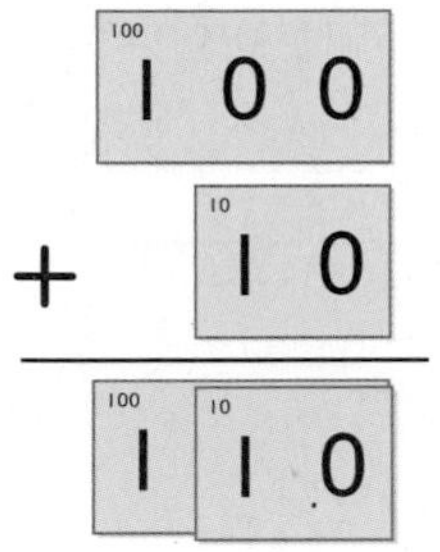

Have the children solve the same exercise by drawing boxes, sticks, and circles.

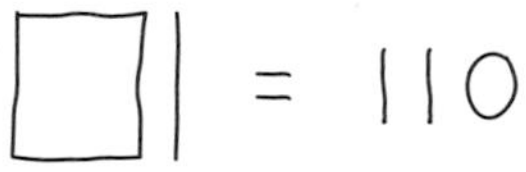

- How many boxes do you need? 1
- How many sticks? 1
- How many circles? 0

Draw a diagram on the classroom board for the children to see.

Add Ones and Hundreds Now work together as a class to solve the third equation in exercise 1 on Student Activity Book page 349. First have children solve the exercise by using Secret Code Cards and then by drawing boxes, sticks, and circles.

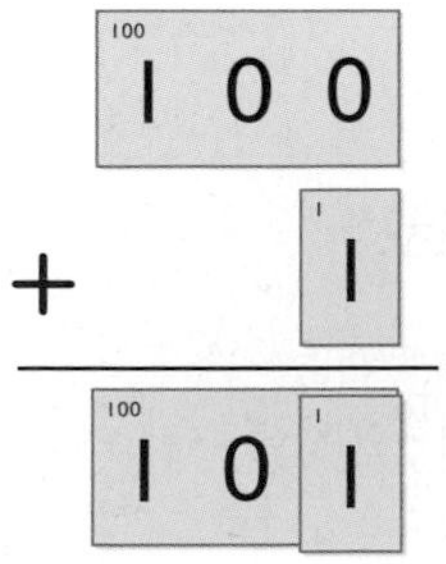

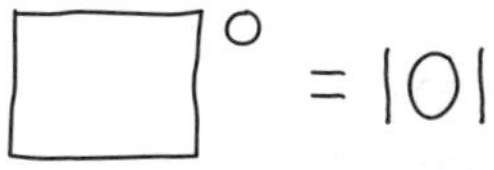

Have children work in Helping Pairs to solve the remainder of the equations on the page. When everyone is finished, invite volunteers to come to the board to show and discuss some of the answers.

Alternate Approach

Line Up the Digits If children get confused as to whether they are adding tens or ones, suggest that they rewrite the exercises vertically on a separate piece of paper in order to help them line up the digits properly.

English Language Learners

Model more 3-digit numbers with the Secret Code Cards. Have children read the numbers aloud.

- **Beginning** Point to each digit, say its place value, and have children repeat.
- **Intermediate** Ask: **What digit is in the ones/tens/hundreds place?**
- **Advanced** Have children work in pairs to make 3-digit numbers. One partner reads the number aloud, the other tells the place value for each digit. Then they switch.

Ongoing Assessment

Circulate around the room as children are completing the page. Ask pairs to explain how they found each answer. Ask one child to use the Secret Code Cards and the other to make a drawing.

Activity 2

Story Problems with Ones, Tens, and Hundreds

20 MINUTES

Goal: Solve story problems with groups of hundreds, tens, and ones.

Materials: Secret Code Cards (1 set per child), Student Activity Book pages 350–351

NCTM Standard:
Number and Operations

11-5 Class Activity Name ______

▶ **Solve and Discuss**

Solve each story problem. Use your Secret Code Cards or Proof Drawings if you wish.

4. A camping club bought some raisins. They bought 3 cartons that had 100 bags each. They had 24 bags left from their last trip. How many bags of raisins does the club have?

324 bags of raisins (label)

5. Two friends want to make necklaces. They buy 1 package of a hundred red beads, 1 package of a hundred blue beads, and 1 package of a hundred green beads. They already have 12 loose beads. How many beads do they have altogether?

312 beads (label)

6. Mia and Bo want to advertise their yard sale. They decide to make flyers. They buy 2 packs of paper. Each pack has 200 sheets in it. They have 32 sheets in their art box. How many sheets of paper do they have?

432 sheets of paper (label)

7. All of the students at a school went out on the playground. They formed 8 groups of one hundred students and 6 groups of ten. There were 5 students left. How many students go to this school?

865 students (label)

Student Activity Book page 350

▶ Solve and Discuss

WHOLE CLASS

Math Talk

Using the **Solve and Discuss** structure, have three to five children solve problem 4 on Student Activity Book page 350. Tell children that they can make proof drawings or use their Secret Code Cards if they find them helpful.

Encourage children at their seats to ask questions or offer suggestions. Be sure that someone shows the solution with Secret Code Cards. Then continue in this way with problems 5–7.

Class Management

You may wish to have children who finish early help any children who are experiencing difficulty, or you may wish to encourage them to write their own story problems to share with the class.

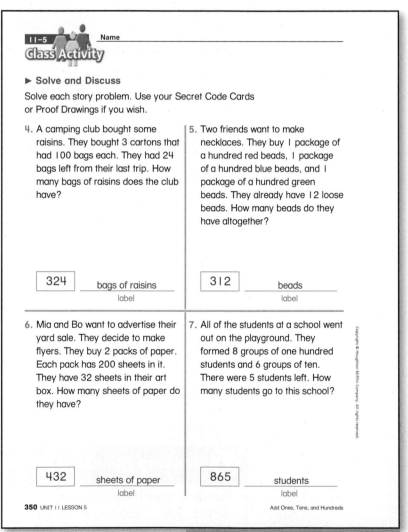

11-5 Class Activity Name ______

▶ **More Story Problems**

Solve each story problem.

8. The scout troop collected aluminum cans to recycle. They counted 2 groups of one hundred cans and 5 groups of ten. They had 7 more cans. How many cans did the troop collect?

257 cans (label)

9. Angelica bought some toothpicks. She bought 8 packets of one hundred and 4 packets of ten. She already had 3 toothpicks. How many toothpicks does Angelica have in all?

843 toothpicks (label)

10. Dawn put up strings of lights in the yard. She used 4 strings that had one hundred lights on them. She also used 8 strings that had ten lights on them. How many lights did she use?

480 lights (label)

11. Neil works at a newspaper stand. He counted 5 groups of one hundred newspapers and 3 groups of ten. He also counted 6 more loose newspapers. How many newspapers were at the stand?

536 newspapers (label)

12. **On the Back** Write ten 3-digit numbers. Round each one to the nearest hundred. Tell whether you round up or down. Check children's work

Student Activity Book page 351

▶ More Story Problems

INDIVIDUALS

You can have children complete Student Activity Book page 351 now or at a later time. This page provides children with more practice solving problems involving hundreds, tens, and ones. You should not expect mastery by all children at this time.

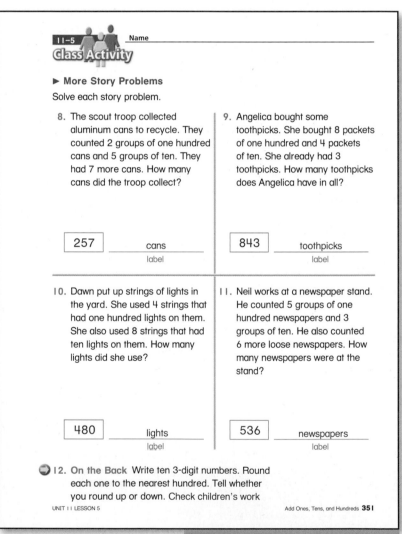

Activity 3

Grouping by 25s

20 MINUTES

Goal: Estimate the number of objects in a container. Then determine the exact number in two ways: grouping by hundreds, tens, and ones; and grouping by 25s.

Materials: transparent container, beans or other countable objects (600–1,000), MathBoard materials

NCTM Standard:
Number and Operations

▶ Estimate and Group Objects WHOLE CLASS

This activity is similar to Activity 1 done in Lesson 4. Children will estimate the number of objects in a container and then determine the actual number by grouping them into tens and then hundreds. (See pages 778–780.)

Children represent the total by writing a 3-digit number and by drawing boxes, sticks, and circles. Have children write on their MathBoards and display their findings to the class. The grand total should be written on the board.

The children will then count the objects again using groups of 25. Remind children that they counted by 25 when they found the total amount of money for a set of quarters.

After children have determined the total number of objects in the container, have them sort the objects into groups of 25. They should then count the objects by 25s to determine the total number of objects.

- How many groups of 25 do we have? Answers will vary.
- How many objects is that? Answers will vary.
- How many objects are left over? Answers will vary.
- How many objects do we have altogether? Answers will vary.
- Is this the same total that we got before? Both counting methods should produce the same result.

Quick Quiz

See Assessment Guide for Unit 11 Quick Quiz 1.

Activity 4

Round Numbers

20 MINUTES

Goal: Round numbers.

Materials: MathBoard materials, Secret Code Cards

NCTM Standard:
Number and Operations

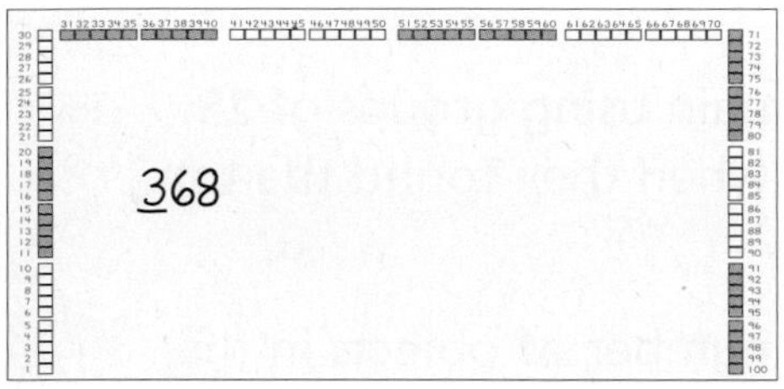

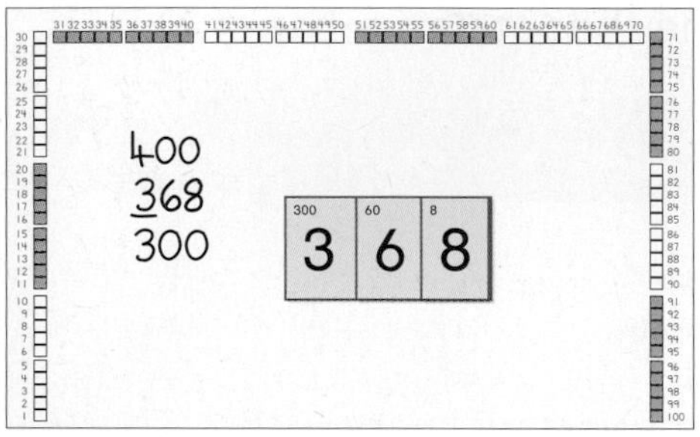

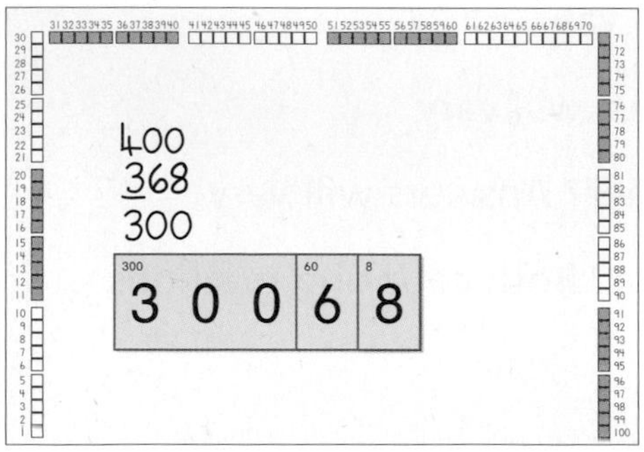

▶ Use Secret Code Cards

Discuss rounding numbers in mathematics.

- Knowing how to round helps you estimate. In math, there are rules that tell you when to round up and when to round down. In this lesson, we'll look at the rules for rounding to the hundreds place.

Write 368 on the left side of the board, leaving enough room above and below the number. Ask children to do the same on their MathBoards.

- We are going to round 368 to the hundreds place. What digit is in the hundreds place? 3 Let's underline the 3 so we remember the place we are rounding to.
- We want to round to the nearest hundred. First, let's find the two hundred numbers that 368 is between. Which hundred number is right below 368? 300 Which hundred number is right above 368? 400

Have children write 300 below 368 and 400 above it.

- Ask children which Secret Code Cards are needed to build 368. Have a volunteer build the number.
- Tell children that to figure out how to round to the hundreds place, they should "open up" the Secret Code Cards, separating 3 hundreds from the rest of the number.

Explain that to determine whether to round up or down, they should look at the 68.

- Does 68 have more than 5 tens or fewer than 5 tens? more than 5 tens
- So, the 68 is closer to 100 than to 0 and is rounded up to the next hundred. *Draw an arrow from 368 to 400.*

Now discuss rounding down.

- When rounding 368 to the nearest hundred, it is rounded *up* to 400. Can anyone think of a number that would be rounded *down* to 300? Possible answer: 345

Erase 368 and replace it with the number suggested. Choose a volunteer to use place-value drawings to explain why we round down. Have a second volunteer explain the rounding, using the Demonstration Secret Code Cards.

Next, erase everything except 300 and 400. Draw a line across the board between the two numbers. Ask students to suggest several numbers that would round up to 400, and write those numbers above the line. Then ask for numbers that would round down to 300, and write them below the line.

Intervention — Activity Card 11-5

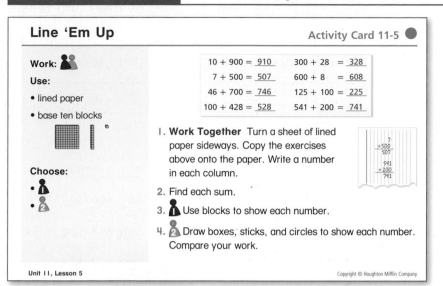

Line 'Em Up

Activity Card 11-5

Work: pairs

Use:
- lined paper
- base ten blocks

Choose:
- 1
- 2

10 + 900 = 910	300 + 28 = 328
7 + 500 = 507	600 + 8 = 608
46 + 700 = 746	125 + 100 = 225
100 + 428 = 528	541 + 200 = 741

1. **Work Together** Turn a sheet of lined paper sideways. Copy the exercises above onto the paper. Write a number in each column.
2. Find each sum.
3. 1 Use blocks to show each number.
4. 2 Draw boxes, sticks, and circles to show each number. Compare your work.

Unit 11, Lesson 5

Activity Note Each pair needs lined notebook paper and base ten blocks. Help children set up the exercises on the paper.

Math Writing Prompt

Explain Your Thinking Is Tanya's answer correct? Explain how you know.

$$\begin{array}{r} 300 \\ +\ 6 \\ \hline 900 \end{array}$$

Soar to Success Math Software Support

Warm Up 10.09

On Level — Activity Card 11-5

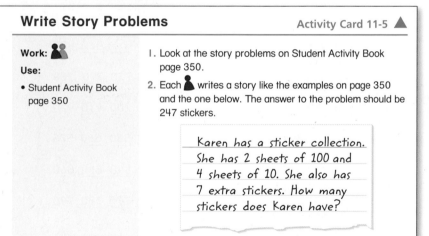

Write Story Problems

Activity Card 11-5

Work: pairs

Use:
- Student Activity Book page 350

1. Look at the story problems on Student Activity Book page 350.
2. Each child writes a story like the examples on page 350 and the one below. The answer to the problem should be 247 stickers.

> Karen has a sticker collection. She has 2 sheets of 100 and 4 sheets of 10. She also has 7 extra stickers. How many stickers does Karen have?

3. Give your story problem to your partner to solve.

Unit 11, Lesson 5

Activity Note Each child writes a story problem for his or her partner. Have pairs write a second story problem for other pairs.

Math Writing Prompt

Explain Your Thinking Sami said 485 is 4 hundreds, 8 tens, and 5 ones. Kim said 485 is 3 hundreds, 18 tens, and 5 ones. Luis said 485 is 4 hundreds, 7 tens, and 15 ones. Who is correct? Explain.

Harcourt Mega Math Software Support

Numberopolis: Carnival Stories, Level R

Challenge — Activity Card 11-5

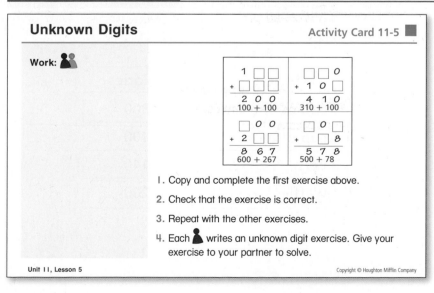

Unknown Digits

Activity Card 11-5

Work: pairs

1 □ □ + □ □ □ 2 0 0 100 + 100	□ □ 0 + 1 0 □ 4 1 0 310 + 100
□ 0 0 + 2 □ □ 8 6 7 600 + 267	□ 0 □ + □ 8 5 7 8 500 + 78

1. Copy and complete the first exercise above.
2. Check that the exercise is correct.
3. Repeat with the other exercises.
4. Each child writes an unknown digit exercise. Give your exercise to your partner to solve.

Unit 11, Lesson 5

Activity Note Each pair needs to copy and solve the unknown digits problems.

Math Writing Prompt

Patterns Find the unknown numbers. Explain.

900, 925, 950, ____, ____

375, 350, 325, ____, ____

Destination Math Software Support

Course II: Module 2: Unit 1: Estimating and Finding Sums less than 1,000

3 Homework and Targeted Practice

11–5 **Homework** **Goal:** Additional Practice

This Homework page provides practice in adding hundreds, tens, and ones.

11–5 Name ____________

Homework

Solve each story problem.

1. Maria blew up some balloons for a party. She divided them into 4 groups of one hundred and 7 groups of ten. 6 balloons were left over. How many balloons did Maria blow up for the party?

   476 balloons (label)

2. Roger has 5 erasers. He bought 6 packages of one hundred and 2 packages of ten. How many erasers does Roger have altogether?

   625 erasers (label)

3. Add.

400 + 200 = 600	440 + 7 = 447	16 + 700 = 716
40 + 50 = 90	84 + 10 = 94	70 + 7 = 77
8 + 460 = 468	200 + 9 = 209	53 + 500 = 553
30 + 10 = 40	60 + 40 = 100	60 + 4 = 64
380 + 10 = 390	900 + 80 = 980	800 + 200 = 1,000

UNIT 11 LESSON 5 Add Ones, Tens, and Hundreds 229

Homework and Remembering page 229

11–5 **Targeted Practice** **Goal:** Count by ones and tens.

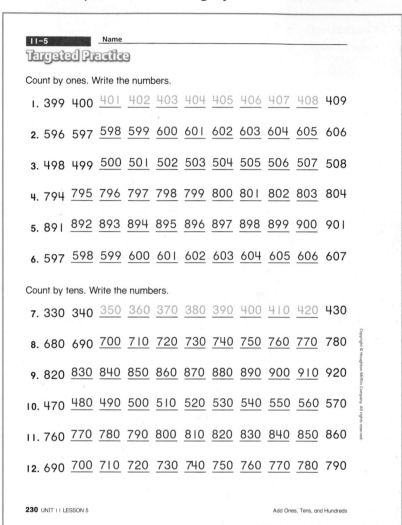

This Targeted Practice can be used with children who need extra practice counting by ones and tens.

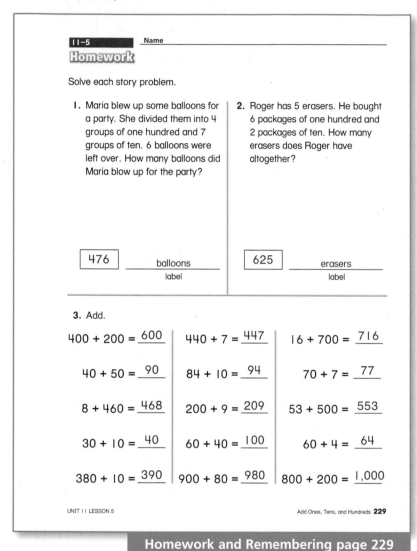

11–5 Name ____________

Targeted Practice

Count by ones. Write the numbers.

1. 399 400 401 402 403 404 405 406 407 408 409
2. 596 597 598 599 600 601 602 603 604 605 606
3. 498 499 500 501 502 503 504 505 506 507 508
4. 794 795 796 797 798 799 800 801 802 803 804
5. 891 892 893 894 895 896 897 898 899 900 901
6. 597 598 599 600 601 602 603 604 605 606 607

Count by tens. Write the numbers.

7. 330 340 350 360 370 380 390 400 410 420 430
8. 680 690 700 710 720 730 740 750 760 770 780
9. 820 830 840 850 860 870 880 890 900 910 920
10. 470 480 490 500 510 520 530 540 550 560 570
11. 760 770 780 790 800 810 820 830 840 850 860
12. 690 700 710 720 730 740 750 760 770 780 790

230 UNIT 11 LESSON 5 Add Ones, Tens, and Hundreds

Homework and Remembering page 230

Home or School Activity

Science Connection

Count Calories Display the table of calorie counts for the breakfast foods shown at the right. Explain to children that calories are used to measure the amount of energy made by food.

Ask children to choose what they would like to eat for breakfast. Tell them to list each food and the number of calories for that food. Then have them find the total number of calories for the breakfast they chose.

Breakfast Foods

Food	Calories
1 cup of oatmeal	300
1 cup of milk	100
2 eggs	140
1 waffle	200

UNIT 11 LESSON 6

Review Quarters

Lesson Objective

- Make twenty-five cents with combinations of dimes, nickels, and pennies.

Vocabulary

quarter **penny**
dime **cent**
nickel

The Day at a Glance

Today's Goals	Materials	
1 Teaching the Lesson Combine dimes, nickels, and pennies in different ways to make twenty-five cents.	**Lesson Activities** Student Activity Book p. 353 Homework and Remembering pp. 231–232 Coin Strips Real or play money	**Going Further** Activity Cards 11-6 Student Activity Book p. 354 Real or play money MathBoard materials Spinners (TRB M27) Paper clips Math Journals
2 Going Further ▸ Problem-Solving Strategy: Guess and Check ▸ Differentiated Instruction		
3 Homework and Spiral Review		

Use **Math Talk** today!

Keeping Skills Sharp

Quick Practice — 5 MINUTES

Goals: Identify a 3-digit number from the values of its digits.

Unscramble the Hundreds, Tens, and Ones Write a problem such as 70 + 400 + 2 = ☐ on the board. The hundreds, tens, and ones should not be in order. Children should then determine the number presented (472). A **Student Leader** then writes two more scrambled numbers and the class unscrambles them.

Repeated Quick Practice Use these Quick Practices from previous lessons.

- ▸ **Money Strings** (See Unit 9 Lesson 11.)
- ▸ **Partners of One Hundred** (See Unit 11 Lesson 5.)

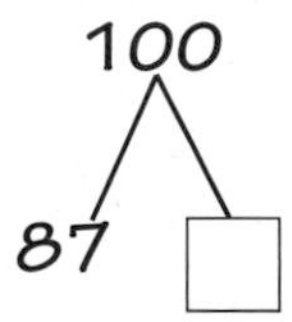

Daily Routines

Making Change and Counting Coins Making Change from $5.00, Combining Coins and Counting Money (See pp. xxvii–xxviii.)

- ▸ Led by Student Leaders

Money Routine Using the 120 Poster, Using the Money Flip Chart, Using the Number Path, Using Secret Code Cards (See pp. xxiii–xxv.)

- ▸ Led by Student Leaders

1 Teaching the Lesson

Activity

The Quarter Machine

45 MINUTES

Goals: Combine dimes, nickels, and pennies in different ways to make twenty-five cents.

Materials: Student Activity Book page 353, Coin Strips (TRB M1), real or play money

NCTM Standards:
Number and Operations
Measurement
Problem Solving
Representation

Teaching Note

What to Expect from Students In Unit 9, children put together coins to make twenty-five cents. Finding coins that have a value of twenty-five cents will be a review for many of them. The challenge for these children will be to find all of the different combinations or to find combinations with specific requirements.

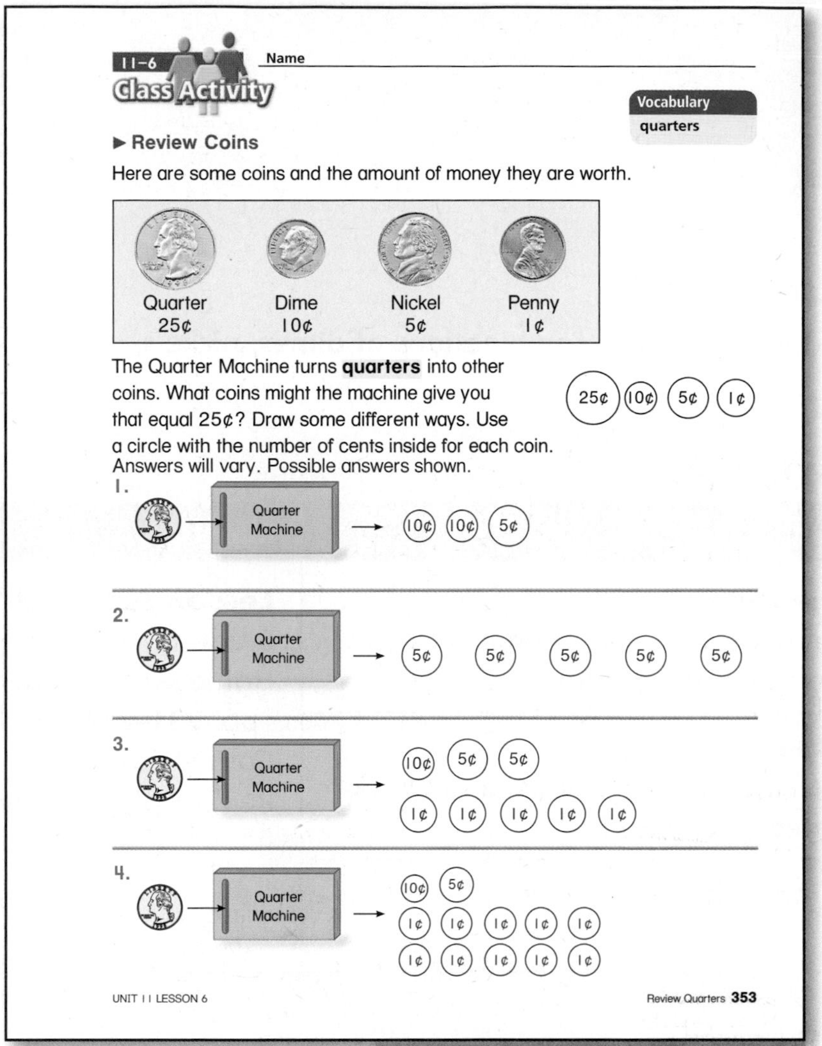
11–6 Class Activity

Name

Vocabulary
quarters

▶ Review Coins

Here are some coins and the amount of money they are worth.

Quarter	Dime	Nickel	Penny
25¢	10¢	5¢	1¢

The Quarter Machine turns **quarters** into other coins. What coins might the machine give you that equal 25¢? Draw some different ways. Use a circle with the number of cents inside for each coin.

25¢ 10¢ 5¢ 1¢

Answers will vary. Possible answers shown.

1. Quarter Machine → 10¢ 10¢ 5¢

2. Quarter Machine → 5¢ 5¢ 5¢ 5¢ 5¢

3. Quarter Machine → 10¢ 5¢ 5¢ 1¢ 1¢ 1¢ 1¢ 1¢

4. Quarter Machine → 10¢ 5¢ 1¢ 1¢ 1¢ 1¢ 1¢ 1¢ 1¢ 1¢ 1¢ 1¢

UNIT 11 LESSON 6 Review Quarters 353

Student Activity Book page 353

▶ Review Coins WHOLE CLASS

Direct the children's attention to the top of Student Activity Book page 353, which shows a quarter, dime, nickel, and penny. Discuss the various coins and the number of cents each one is worth.

Review the number of pennies in a nickel, pennies in a dime, and nickels in a dime. Some children may benefit from looking at Coin Strips.

▶ Ways to Make 25¢ WHOLE CLASS

Math Talk

Introduce the Quarter Machine described on Student Activity Book page 353. Explain that if the children put a quarter into the machine, it will give them back some coins. The coins will always equal exactly twenty-five cents. Invite children to sketch different ways the machine could give them back twenty-five cents.

Ask for Ideas Discuss the various ways children found to make twenty-five cents. Record them in a table. The table below shows all twelve combinations of coins that will make exactly twenty-five cents.

Quarter = 25¢		
D	N	P
2	1	0
2	0	5
1	0	15
1	1	10
1	2	5
1	3	0
0	5	0
0	4	5
0	3	10
0	2	15
0	1	20
0	0	25

Have children create puzzles for each other with the combinations they found. For example, someone might ask:

- What is the smallest number of coins, other than one quarter, that makes twenty-five cents? Three: two dimes and one nickel
- Can you make twenty-five cents using no nickels and no dimes? Yes: twenty-five pennies
- Can you make twenty-five cents with exactly ten coins? No

Alternate Approach

Real or Play Money Have students use real or play money to model the coin combinations for making 25¢.

English Language Learners

Review coins and their values. Give children play money. Write 25¢, 10¢, 5¢, and 1¢ on the board.

- **Beginning** Point to 25¢. Say: **25¢ is a *quarter*.** Have children hold up a quarter. Continue with other coins.
- **Intermediate** Ask: **Is 25¢ a *quarter* or a *dime*?** quarter Have children hold up a quarter.
- **Advanced** Have children identify and hold up the coin for each value.

Ongoing Assessment

Observe children as they work. Circulate around the room and ask individual children to explain their thinking. Ask how they found the different combinations and ask them to show you how they count the coins in a particular combination.

2 Going Further

Problem-Solving Strategy: Guess and Check

Goal: Make twenty-five cents with a specific number of coins.

Materials: Student Activity Book page 354, real or play money (dimes, nickels, and pennies)

NCTM Standards:
Number and Operations
Problem Solving

▶ Coin Combinations WHOLE CLASS

Direct children's attention to Student Activity Book page 354. Tell children that the Quarter Machines on this page are special. Each machine gives out a certain number of coins at a time. That number is on the front of the machine. In this activity, children must identify ways to make twenty-five cents with a specific number of coins. You may want to distribute dimes, nickels, and pennies for children to use to model their answers.

▶ Discuss Coin Combinations WHOLE CLASS

Math Talk After children have completed Student Activity Book page 354, have them discuss their answers.

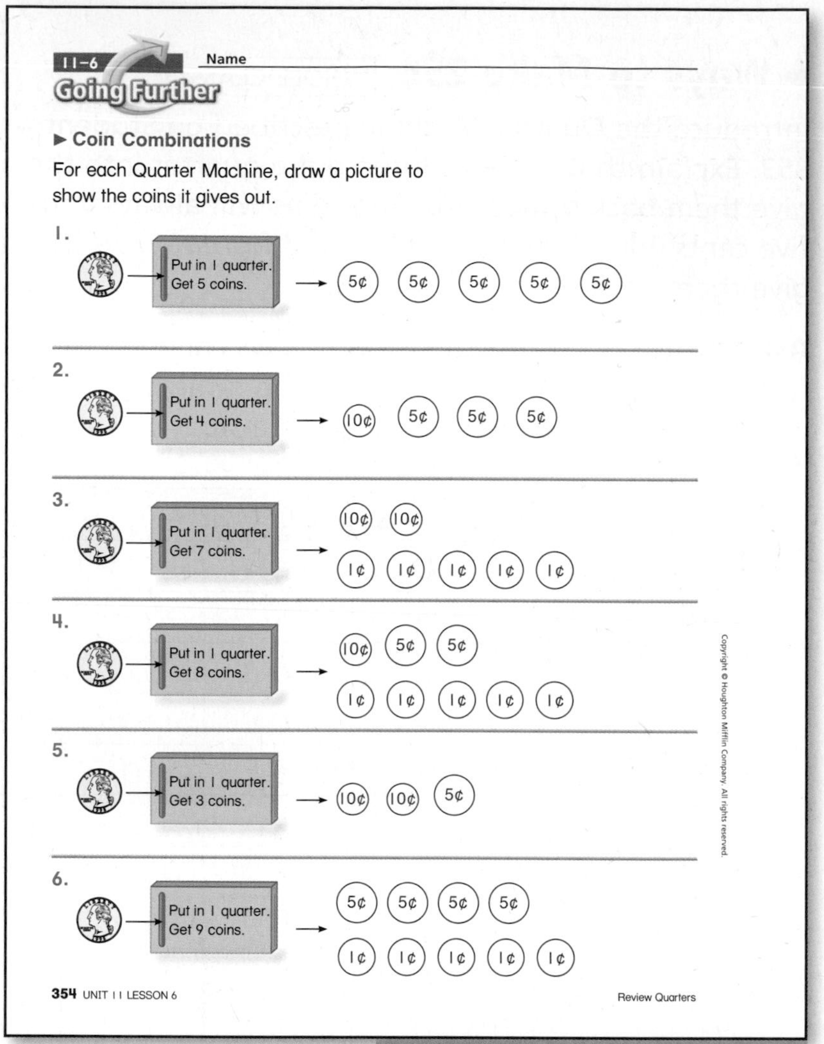
11-6 Going Further Name

▶ Coin Combinations

For each Quarter Machine, draw a picture to show the coins it gives out.

1. Put in 1 quarter. Get 5 coins. → 5¢ 5¢ 5¢ 5¢ 5¢

2. Put in 1 quarter. Get 4 coins. → 10¢ 5¢ 5¢ 5¢

3. Put in 1 quarter. Get 7 coins. → 10¢ 10¢ 1¢ 1¢ 1¢ 1¢ 1¢

4. Put in 1 quarter. Get 8 coins. → 10¢ 5¢ 5¢ 1¢ 1¢ 1¢ 1¢ 1¢

5. Put in 1 quarter. Get 3 coins. → 10¢ 10¢ 5¢

6. Put in 1 quarter. Get 9 coins. → 5¢ 5¢ 5¢ 5¢ 1¢ 1¢ 1¢ 1¢ 1¢

354 UNIT 11 LESSON 6 Review Quarters

Student Activity Book page 354

Class Management

You may want to circulate around the classroom to check that children complete the first exercise correctly. Check that they draw exactly five coins worth a total of twenty-five cents. You may also want to have children stop after they complete the first exercise and go over the answer with the group.

2 Going Further

Differentiated Instruction

Intervention

Activity Card 11-6

Make a List — Activity Card 11-6

Work:

Use:

- 1 dime
- 3 nickels
- 15 pennies
- MathBoard materials

1. **Work Together** Make a three-column chart on the MathBoard. The heads are *Dimes, Nickels,* and *Pennies.*

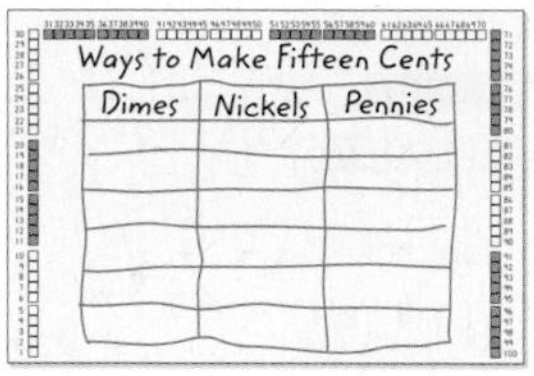

2. Find six different ways to make fifteen cents using dimes, nickels, and pennies.
3. Write each way to make fifteen cents on the MathBoard.
4. **Math Talk** Share how you found all the different ways to make fifteen cents.

Unit 11, Lesson 6

Activity Note Each pair needs MathBoard materials and 1 dime, 3 nickels, and 15 pennies (real or play). Check that pairs make six unique combinations.

Math Writing Prompt

Explain Your Thinking Can you make twenty-five cents with just dimes? Explain your thinking.

Soar to Success Math Software Support

Warm Up 3.10.

On Level

Activity Card 11-6

Make Twenty-five Cents — Activity Card 11-6

Work:

Use:

- 4 dimes
- 10 nickels
- 50 pennies

Choose:

- 1
- 2

1. 1 You want to buy something that costs 25¢. Use the coins to show an amount less than 25¢. Place the coins on the desk.
2. 2 Add coins to 1 coins until you make twenty-five cents.

3. Trade roles and repeat the activity.
4. **Math Talk** How did you know how many coins to add to the first group of coins?

Unit 11, Lesson 6

Activity Note Each pair needs 4 dimes, 10 nickels, and 50 pennies (real or play). Have pairs count the money aloud each round.

Math Writing Prompt

Coin Combinations What is the greatest number of coins you can use to make 25¢? What is the least number of coins you can use to make 25¢? Draw to explain your answers.

Harcourt Mega Math Software Support

Numberopolis: Lulu's Lunch Counter, Level K

Challenge

Activity Card 11-6

Different Combinations — Activity Card 11-6

Work:

Use:

- spinner
- paper clip
- 4 dimes
- 10 nickels
- 20 pennies

Choose:

- 1
- 2

1. 2 Use the paper clip to spin the spinner.

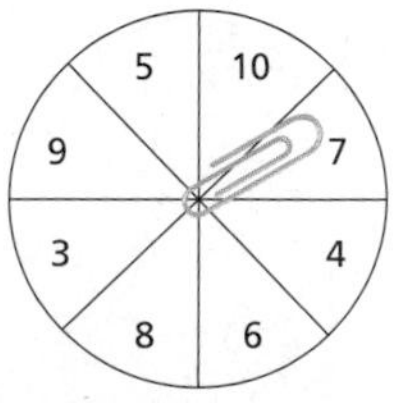

2. Look at the number on the spinner and choose that number of coins to make twenty-five cents. If you cannot make twenty-five cents with that number of coins, explain why.
3. 1 Check the coin combination that 2 used.
4. Trade roles and repeat the activity.

Unit 11, Lesson 6

Activity Note Each pair needs an eight-section spinner (TRB M27) with the numbers 3–10, 4 dimes, 10 nickels, and 20 pennies.

Math Writing Prompt

Guess and Check Suppose you make 25¢ with eight coins (dimes, nickels, and pennies). There are twice as many nickels as dimes. How many of each kind are there? Explain.

Destination Math Software Support

Course II: Module 3: Unit 1: Money

3 Homework and Spiral Review

11-6 Homework **Goal:** Additional Practice

This Homework page provides practice in making twenty-five cents with different coin combinations.

11-6 Name

Homework

The quarter machine is broken today. Sometimes it works. Sometimes it doesn't. Write "Yes" if it gave you 25¢. Write "No" if it didn't.

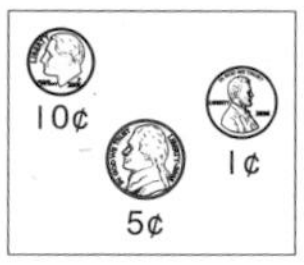

1.
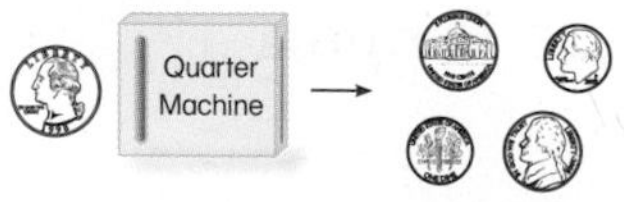

25¢? No

2.
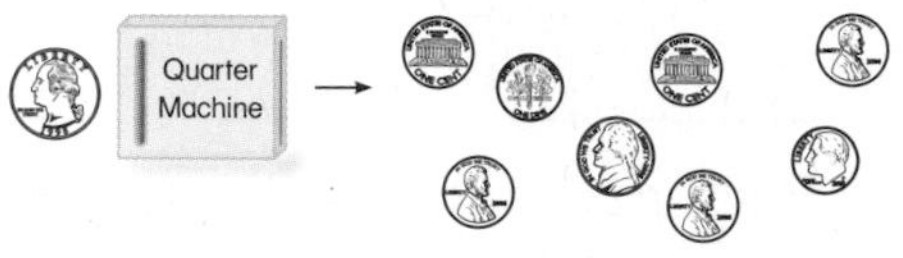

25¢? No

3.
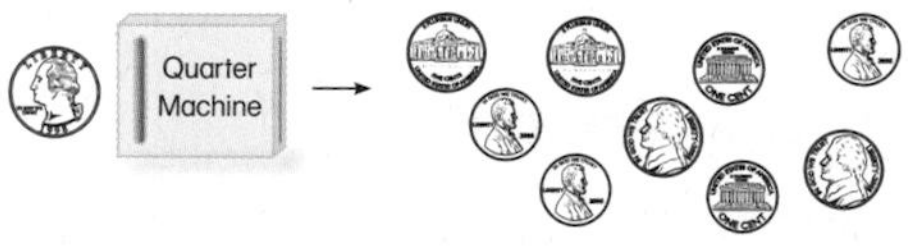

25¢? Yes

4.

25¢? Yes

UNIT 11 LESSON 6 Review Quarters 231

Homework and Remembering page 231

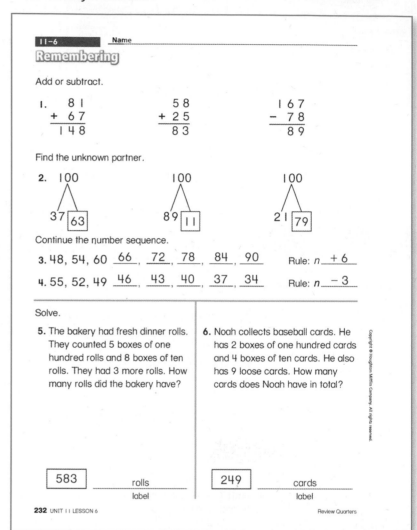

11-6 Remembering **Goal:** Spiral Review

This Remembering activity would be appropriate anytime after today's lesson.

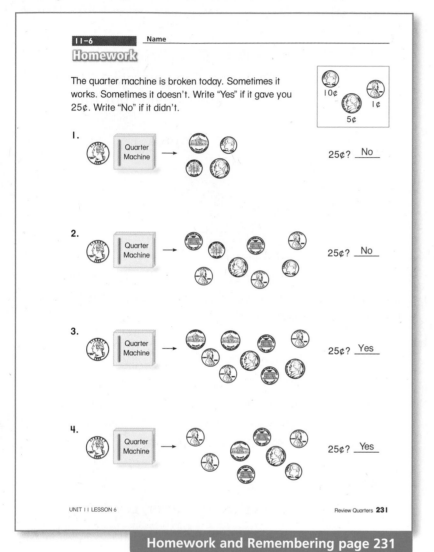

11-6 Name

Remembering

Add or subtract.

1. $81 + 67 = 148$ $58 + 25 = 83$ $167 - 78 = 89$

Find the unknown partner.

2. 100: 37 and 63 100: 89 and 11 100: 21 and 79

Continue the number sequence.

3. 48, 54, 60 66, 72, 78, 84, 90 Rule: n + 6

4. 55, 52, 49 46, 43, 40, 37, 34 Rule: n − 3

Solve.

5. The bakery had fresh dinner rolls. They counted 5 boxes of one hundred rolls and 8 boxes of ten rolls. They had 3 more rolls. How many rolls did the bakery have?

583 rolls
label

6. Noah collects baseball cards. He has 2 boxes of one hundred cards and 4 boxes of ten cards. He also has 9 loose cards. How many cards does Noah have in total?

249 cards
label

232 UNIT 11 LESSON 6 Review Quarters

Homework and Remembering page 232

Home or School Activity

Social Studies Connection

State Quarters Tell children that the U.S. Mint produces special quarters for each state. Starting in 1999, the Mint began releasing 5 quarters each year. They will continue until 2008, when all 50 states will be represented. Have children collect these kinds of quarters and identify the state on each one. Ask them to describe the features of each quarter and use the features to learn more about the state.

UNIT 11 LESSON 7

Buy with Dollars and Cents

REAL WORLD Problem Solving

Lesson Objectives

- Use the dollar sign and decimal point to write dollar amounts.
- Buy and sell goods using exact money amounts.

Vocabulary

cent	dollar
dime	dollar notation
penny	dollar sign ($)

The Day at a Glance

Today's Goals	Materials	
1 Teaching the Lesson A1: Practice writing money amounts using dollar notation. A2: Buy and sell items using exact money amounts.	**Lesson Activities** Student Activity Book pp. 355–356 Homework and Remembering pp. 233–234 Real or play money MathBoard materials	**Going Further** Activity Cards 11-7 Real or play money MathBoard materials Objects with price tags Math Journals
2 Going Further ▸ Differentiated Instruction		
3 Homework and Targeted Practice		

123 Use Math Talk today!

Keeping Skills Sharp

Quick Practice — 5 MINUTES

Goal: Identify a 3-digit number from the value of its digits.

Unscramble the Hundreds, Tens, and Ones Write a problem such as 70 + 400 + 2 = ☐ on the board. The hundreds, tens, and ones should not be in order. Children should then determine the number presented (472). A **Student Leader** then writes two more scrambled numbers and the class unscrambles them.

Repeated Quick Practice Use these Quick Practices from previous lessons.

- ▸ **Money Strings** (See Unit 9 Lesson 11.)
- ▸ **Partners of One Hundred** (See Unit 11 Lesson 5.)

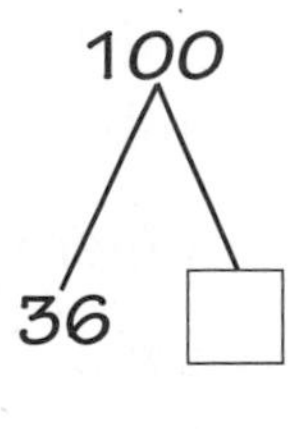

Daily Routines

Making Change and Counting Coins Making Change from $5.00, Combining Coins and Counting Money (See pp. xxvii–xxviii.)

▸ Led by Student Leaders

Money Routine Using the 120 Poster, Using the Money Flip Chart, Using the Number Path, Using Secret Code Cards (See pp. xxiii–xxv.)

▸ Led by Student Leaders

1 Teaching the Lesson

Activity 1

Dollar Notation

25 MINUTES

Goals: Practice writing money amounts using dollar notation.

Materials: Real or play money (dollars, dimes, and pennies)

NCTM Standards:
Number and Operations
Measurement
Problem Solving
Representation

Teaching Note

Language and Vocabulary Mention that the *dot* or *period* in dollar notation has a special name. It is called a *decimal point.*

Differentiated Instruction

Extra Help Have pairs practice dollar notation using play dollar bills, dimes, and pennies. Each child presents his or her partner with three or fewer bills, five or fewer dimes, and five or fewer pennies to count and write the amount in dollar notation. Pairs then help each other check the notation for accuracy.

▶ Review Decimal Notation for Money Amounts

WHOLE CLASS

Math Talk 123

Write symbols and examples on the board as you review money concepts with children. ¢ 42¢ 100¢ $ $1.00

- We have been using a cent sign, ¢, to show how many pennies, or cents, we have. Forty-two cents looks like this: 42¢—with a cent sign. One hundred cents looks like this: 100¢. *Point to each symbol as it comes up in the discussion.*
- Who remembers another way to write amounts of money? What other sign can we use besides the cent sign? a dollar sign
- Write 42¢ and 100¢ using a dollar sign. $0.42, $1.00

Have children discuss how the ¢ and $ notations relate to each other.

- How is this new way of writing one dollar like the way we have been writing money amounts? The numbers are the same; there are three numbers.
- How is it different from the way we have been writing money amounts? There is a dollar sign at the beginning of the number instead of a cents sign at the end, and there is a period or dot between the dollars and the cents.
- Why do we write a 0 to the left of the dot in $0.42? We write a zero to the left of the dot because the dot is very small and without the 0 some people may not see the dot and think it is forty-two dollars ($42).

▶ Place Value in Dollar Amounts

WHOLE CLASS

Present the following problem to children.

- In my pocket I have three pennies, one dollar, and five dimes. I want to write the amount of money I have. Where do these numbers go?

Draw the example below on the board. Have children decide which money amount belongs in each position of the number. Fill in the numbers as they are discussed. Do other examples as necessary.

- Where does the number of pennies go? in the ones place
- Where does the number of dollars go? in the hundreds place
- Where does the number of dimes go? in the tens place

1 5 3 ¢ = $ 1 . 5 3

Math Talk Have children use the new system to rewrite a money amount over one dollar and discuss what they have done. Then have them draw the money for that amount or vice versa. Do this with a few different amounts.

- How can we write one hundred thirty-four cents with this new method? $1.34
- What does the four mean? four pennies
- What does the three mean? three dimes
- What does the one mean? one dollar or one hundred pennies
- Let's draw one dollar and thirty-four cents. How can we do this?

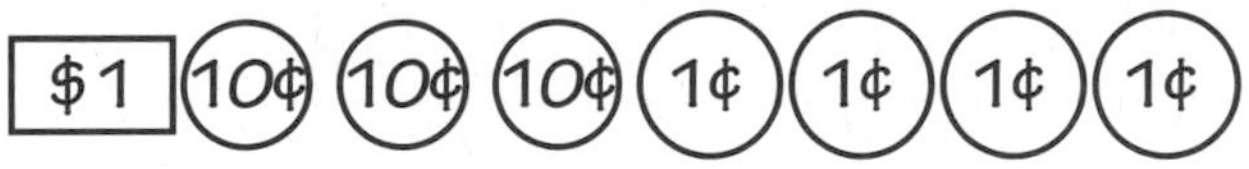

Continue with amounts such as 128¢, 152¢, and 245¢.

▶ Write Money Amounts Less than One Dollar

WHOLE CLASS

Have children make a simple table in their Math Journals to show amounts in cents and in dollar notation.

¢	$
86¢	$0.86
78¢	$0.78

- How can we write eighty-six cents? 86¢ or $0.86
- What does the zero mean? no dollars

- Let's make a table and write these amounts using the dollar sign and the period: seventy-eight cents, ninety-nine cents, sixty-five cents, and fifty-three cents.

Remind children to use zero as a place-holder for dimes or pennies.

- How could we write seven cents and seventy cents using a $? $0.07 and $0.70
- What does the zero mean in each number? no dimes, no pennies

Have children enter these amounts: thirteen cents, five cents, sixty-seven cents, eight cents, fifty cents, eighty cents, one hundred eighty-six cents, and two hundred fifty-six cents.

Differentiated Instruction

Extra Help Children may have an easier time relating dollars, dimes, and pennies to hundreds, tens, and ones if they draw bills and coins in order from left to right. Encourage them to draw the bills together on the left to align with the "dollar" digit on the left of the number. Dimes should be drawn in the middle and pennies on the right.

Teaching Note

Watch For! Children might draw thirteen dimes and four pennies instead of a dollar, 3 dimes, and 4 pennies. If they do, have them draw a box around ten dimes to show that ten dimes have the same value as one dollar.

English Language Learners

Write $0.50 and *decimal point* on the board. Ask: **Is this 50¢?** yes

- **Beginning** Point and say: **This is a *decimal point*.** Have children repeat.
- **Intermediate** Point and say: **This is 0 dollars and 50 __.** cents **This is a *decimal* __.** point
- **Advanced** Ask: **Did I write 50 before or after the *decimal point*?** after Say: **This means it is 50 __.** cents

Activity 2

The Garage Sale

25 MINUTES

Goal: Buy and sell items using exact money amounts.

Materials: Student Activity Book pages 355–356

NCTM Standards:
Number and Operations
Measurement
Problem Solving
Representation

Class Management

Looking Ahead In the next lesson, children will use Dollar Bills and Five-Dollar Bills. Dollar Bills are on Student Activity Book pages 339–340 and TRB pages M67–M68. They are also available in the *Math Expressions* materials kits. Five-Dollar Bills are on TRB page M84. You may want to copy the copymaster onto green paper for classroom use.

Ongoing Assessment

Ask children to identify the bills and coins they could use to buy a magazine that costs $2.59.

Dimes	Nickels
7	2
6	4
5	6
4	8
3	10
2	12
1	14

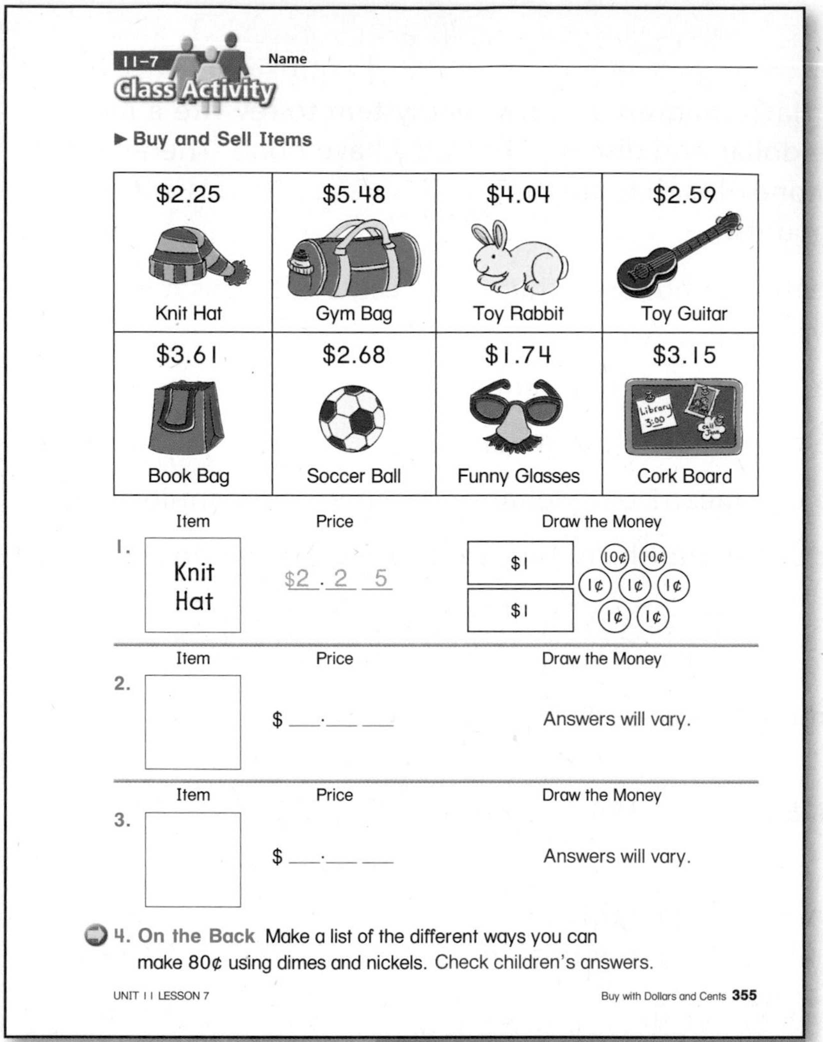

11-7 Class Activity Name

► Buy and Sell Items

$2.25 Knit Hat	$5.48 Gym Bag	$4.04 Toy Rabbit	$2.59 Toy Guitar
$3.61 Book Bag	$2.68 Soccer Ball	$1.74 Funny Glasses	$3.15 Cork Board

	Item	Price	Draw the Money
1.	Knit Hat	$2.25	$1, $1, 10¢, 10¢, 1¢, 1¢, 1¢, 1¢, 1¢
2.		$ ___.___ ___	Answers will vary.
3.		$ ___.___ ___	Answers will vary.

4. On the Back Make a list of the different ways you can make 80¢ using dimes and nickels. Check children's answers.

UNIT 11 LESSON 7 Buy with Dollars and Cents 355

Student Activity Book page 355

► Buy and Sell Items PAIRS

Refer children to Student Activity Book page 355. They will work in pairs to buy and sell items at a garage sale with exact amounts of money.

The buyer picks something to buy, writes the name in the box, writes the price, and gives the exact amount of money to the seller. The seller draws the money to check if the amount is correct.

Then the buyer and seller switch roles. Pairs continue until each has bought 3 items.

► Make 80¢

After children have had time to work on the **On the Back** problem, compile a class list of all possible ways. (See side column.) Help children see how recognizing patterns can help in making the list.

Intervention — Activity Card 11-7

Money Tables

Activity Card 11-7

Work: pairs

Use:

- 4 quarters
- 10 dimes
- 5 nickels
- 25 pennies

100¢			100¢			100¢		
Q	3	=75¢	Q	3	=75¢	Q	2	= 50¢
D	1	=10¢	D	1	=10¢	D	0	= 0¢
N	2	=10¢	N	2	=10¢	N	5	=25¢
P	5	= 5¢	P	5	= 5¢	P	25	=25¢
Total		100¢	Total		100¢	Total		100¢

1. **Work Together** Look at the money tables above. Use coins to check the numbers in the first table.
2. Copy the second table. Use coins to find the unknown numbers. Record the numbers in the table.
3. Copy the third table. Use coins to find the unknown numbers and amounts. Record the numbers and the unknown amounts.
4. Check the amounts in each money table.

Unit 11, Lesson 7

Activity Note Each pair needs 4 quarters, 10 dimes, 5 nickels, and 25 pennies. Explain that a money table is a way to record combinations of coins.

Math Writing Prompt

Represent Coins What bills and coins could you use to buy a toy that costs $2.89? Draw a picture if it helps.

Soar to Success Math Software Support

Warm Up 3.10

On Level — Activity Card 11-7

The Money Table

Activity Card 11-7

Work: pairs

Use:

- MathBoard materials
- quarters, dimes, nickels, and pennies

Choose:

- 1
- 2

1. Each makes a Money Table like this one on their MathBoard.

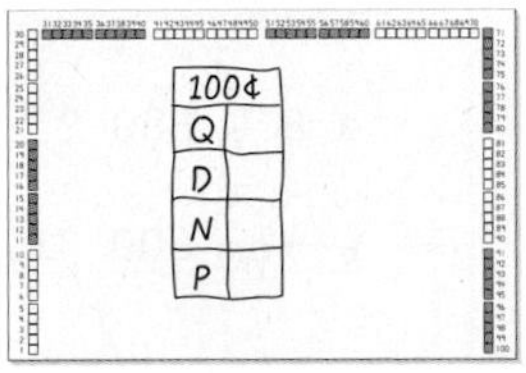

2. 1 Fill in three pieces of information in your Money Table. For example you might fill in the number of dimes and the value of the pennies.
3. 2 Fill in three pieces of information in your Money Table. For example you might fill in the number of nickels and the value of the quarters.
4. Give your Money Table to your partner to find the unknown numbers and amounts.

Unit 11, Lesson 7

Activity Note Each pair needs MathBoard materials and real or play money available. Have children check each other's work.

Math Writing Prompt

Make a Purchase Draw or list the bills you would use to purchase a frozen yogurt for $2.95 and extra granola for $0.08.

Harcourt Mega Math Software Support

Numberopolis: Lulu's Lunch Counter, Level K

Challenge — Activity Card 11-7

The Flea Market

Activity Card 11-7

Work: individual

Use:

- 4 quarters
- 10 dimes
- 5 nickels
- 25 pennies
- objects with price tags

1. Choose an item you would like to buy.
2. Draw two money tables on a piece of paper. Each money table should have space at the top to show the price of the item and rows to show how many quarters (Q), dimes (D), nickels (N), and pennies (P) you use.
3. Use the money tables to show two ways to represent the price of the item you would like to buy. Use the coins to help if you want.

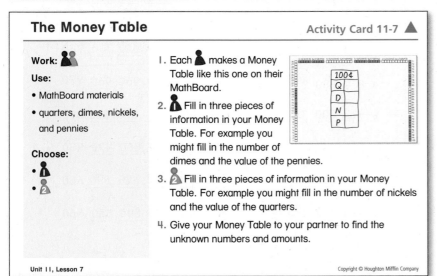

54¢			54¢		
Q	1	=25¢	Q	0	= 0¢
D	2	=20¢	D	5	=50¢
N	1	= 5¢	N	0	= 0¢
P	4	= 4¢	P	4	= 4¢
Total		54¢	Total		54¢

Unit 11, Lesson 7

Activity Note Place price tags on several small classroom items. The prices should be 25¢–90¢. Have real or play coins available.

Math Writing Prompt

Guess and Check A pile of coins is worth $1.00. There are 5 pennies. There are an equal number of dimes and nickels. How many of each coin are there? Explain how you found the answer.

Destination Math Software Support

Course II: Module 3: Unit 1: Money

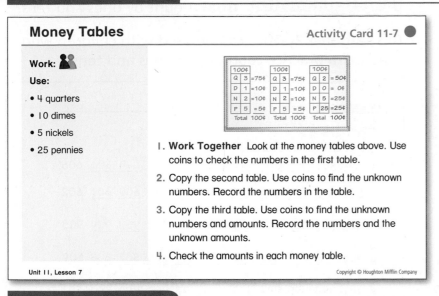

❸ Homework and Targeted Practice

11-7 **Homework** **Goal:** Additional Practice

This Homework page provides practice in writing and adding money amounts.

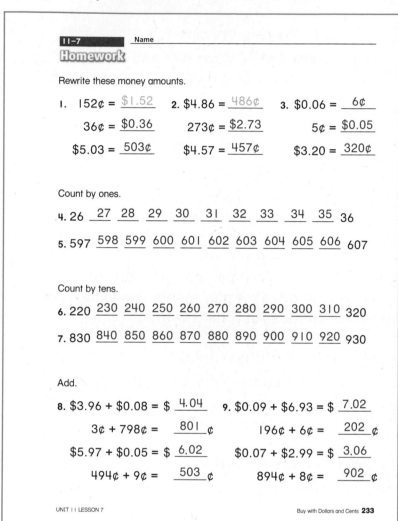

11-7 Name ____________
Homework

Rewrite these money amounts.

1. 152¢ = $1.52 36¢ = $0.36 $5.03 = 503¢
2. $4.86 = 486¢ 273¢ = $2.73 $4.57 = 457¢
3. $0.06 = 6¢ 5¢ = $0.05 $3.20 = 320¢

Count by ones.

4. 26 27 28 29 30 31 32 33 34 35 36
5. 597 598 599 600 601 602 603 604 605 606 607

Count by tens.

6. 220 230 240 250 260 270 280 290 300 310 320
7. 830 840 850 860 870 880 890 900 910 920 930

Add.

8. $3.96 + $0.08 = $ 4.04
   3¢ + 798¢ = 801 ¢
   $5.97 + $0.05 = $ 6.02
   494¢ + 9¢ = 503 ¢
9. $0.09 + $6.93 = $ 7.02
   196¢ + 6¢ = 202 ¢
   $0.07 + $2.99 = $ 3.06
   894¢ + 8¢ = 902 ¢

UNIT 11 LESSON 7 Buy with Dollars and Cents 233

Homework and Remembering page 233

11-7 **Targeted Practice** **Goal:** Count by ones and tens.

This Targeted Practice can be used with children who need extra practice counting by ones and tens.

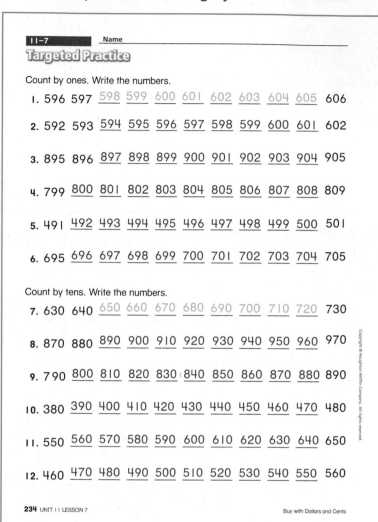

11-7 Name ____________
Targeted Practice

Count by ones. Write the numbers.

1. 596 597 598 599 600 601 602 603 604 605 606
2. 592 593 594 595 596 597 598 599 600 601 602
3. 895 896 897 898 899 900 901 902 903 904 905
4. 799 800 801 802 803 804 805 806 807 808 809
5. 491 492 493 494 495 496 497 498 499 500 501
6. 695 696 697 698 699 700 701 702 703 704 705

Count by tens. Write the numbers.

7. 630 640 650 660 670 680 690 700 710 720 730
8. 870 880 890 900 910 920 930 940 950 960 970
9. 790 800 810 820 830 840 850 860 870 880 890
10. 380 390 400 410 420 430 440 450 460 470 480
11. 550 560 570 580 590 600 610 620 630 640 650
12. 460 470 480 490 500 510 520 530 540 550 560

234 UNIT 11 LESSON 7 Buy with Dollars and Cents

Homework and Remembering page 234

Home or School Activity

Technology Connection

Cents of Color Have children go to www.usmint.gov and click on the H.I.P. pocket change icon. Next have them play the *Cents of Color* game. First they should pick a state from the map provided. Then, they should read the background information given about the state quarter they chose. Next, they should use the palate to color their quarter however they want. Finally they should present their colored quarter and one fact they learned about the state to the class.

UNIT 11 LESSON 8

Change from $5.00

REAL WORLD Problem Solving

Lesson Objectives

- Buy and sell goods using a five-dollar bill, and make change.
- Explain how to make change from a five-dollar bill.

Vocabulary

dollar
five dollars
Adding up Method
ungrouping

The Day at a Glance

Today's Goals	Materials	
1 Teaching the Lesson A1: Buy goods and use various strategies to make change from a five-dollar bill. A2: Explain strategies for making change from a five-dollar bill.	**Lesson Activities** Student Activity Book pp. 357–358 Homework and Remembering pp. 235–236 Quick Quiz 2 (Assessment Guide) Five-Dollar Bills (TRB M84) Dollar Bills Real or play money Secret Code Cards	**Going Further** Activity Cards 11-8 Real or play money Five-Dollar Bills Dollar Bills Magazines and shopping circulars Index cards Scissors Tape Poster board Spinners (TRB M27) Paper clips Math Journals
2 Going Further ► Differentiated Instruction		
3 Homework and Spiral Review		

Use Math Talk today!

Keeping Skills Sharp

Quick Practice — 5 MINUTES

Goal: Make money strings for specific money amounts.

Money Strings Have two or three children write money strings for amounts between one and two dollars on the board. Have the class check that the money strings are correct. (See Unit 9 Lesson 11.)

Repeated Quick Practice Use this Quick Practice from a previous lesson.

► **Blue Math Mountain Cards** (See Unit 7 Lesson 13.)

Daily Routines

Making Change and Counting Coins Making Change from $5.00, Combining Coins and Counting Money (See pp. xxvii–xxviii.)

► Led by Student Leaders

Money Routine Using the 120 Poster, Using the Money Flip Chart, Using the Number Path, Using Secret Code Cards (See pp. xxiii–xxv.)

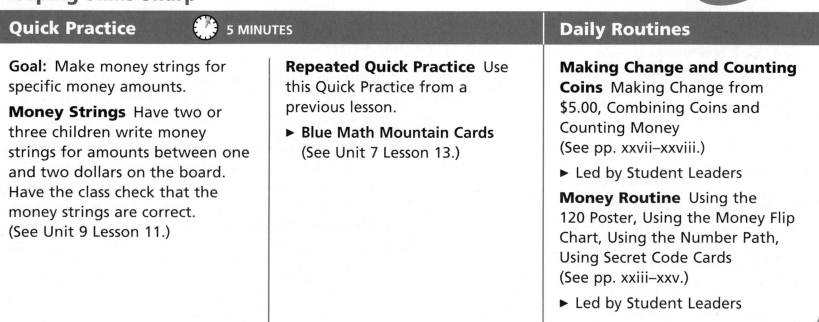

► Led by Student Leaders

1 Teaching the Lesson

Activity 1

Change from a Five-Dollar Bill

40 MINUTES

Goals: Buy goods and use various strategies to make change from a five-dollar bill.

Materials: Five-Dollar Bills (TRB M84), Dollar Bills, real or play money, Secret Code Cards, Student Activity Book pages 357–358

NCTM Standards:
Number and Operations
Measurement
Problem Solving
Representation

Teaching Note

Math Background This lesson does not teach children the traditional method of counting up to make change. It allows children to use a variety of methods, including adding up, to find out how much change to give.

Differentiated Instruction

Extra Help Remind children that they already know how to make change from one dollar and two dollars. It may help to review and practice those skills before extending them to five dollars.

English Language Learners

Provide support with grocery vocabulary and prices. Point and ask: **How much do the *muffins* cost?** 99¢ Continue with other items.

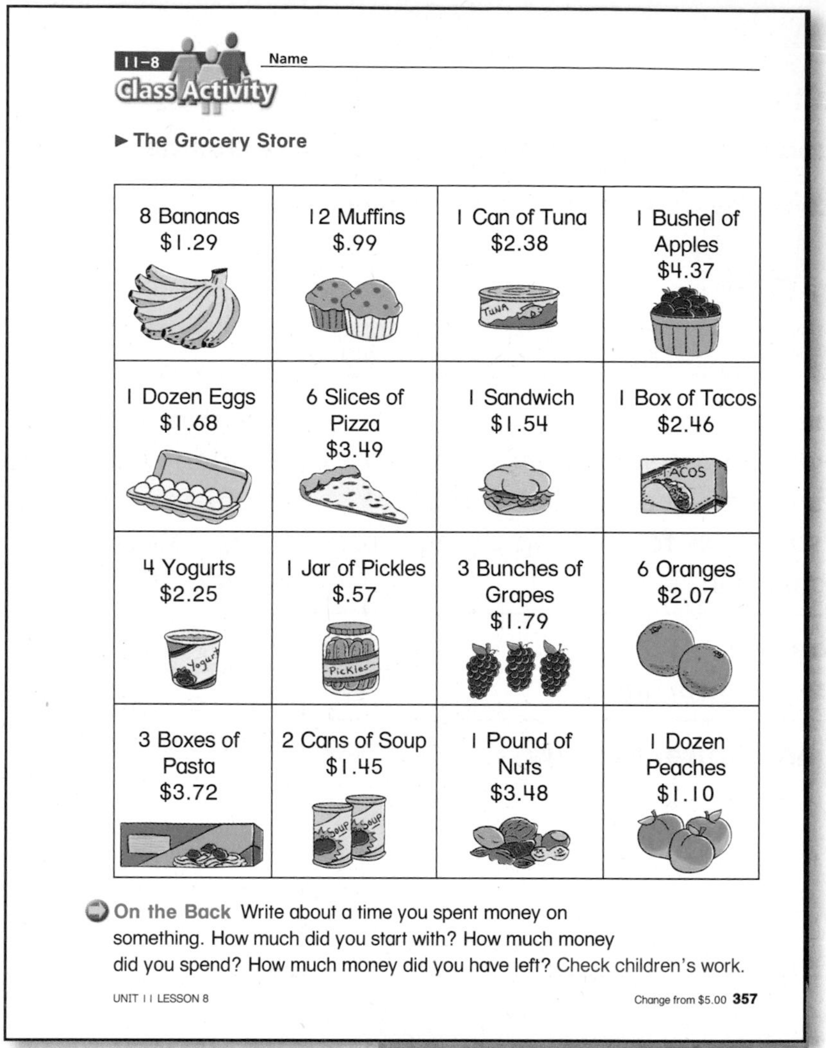

11-8 Class Activity Name

▶ The Grocery Store

8 Bananas $1.29	12 Muffins $.99	1 Can of Tuna $2.38	1 Bushel of Apples $4.37
1 Dozen Eggs $1.68	6 Slices of Pizza $3.49	1 Sandwich $1.54	1 Box of Tacos $2.46
4 Yogurts $2.25	1 Jar of Pickles $.57	3 Bunches of Grapes $1.79	6 Oranges $2.07
3 Boxes of Pasta $3.72	2 Cans of Soup $1.45	1 Pound of Nuts $3.48	1 Dozen Peaches $1.10

On the Back Write about a time you spent money on something. How much did you start with? How much money did you spend? How much money did you have left? Check children's work.

UNIT 11 LESSON 8 Change from $5.00 357

Student Activity Book page 357

▶ The Grocery Store PAIRS

Ask for Ideas To begin this activity, ask children to share real-life shopping experiences. Have them name items they have bought with a five-dollar bill, such as a sandwich or a magazine.

Direct children's attention to the items they can buy from a grocery store on Student Activity Book page 357. Explain the activity to children. One child will be the buyer and one will be the seller. Buyers purchase items from the store using the five-dollar bill. The seller makes change, draws the coins on a separate piece of paper, and gives that amount of money to the buyer. The buyer also determines how much change is due from the seller.

The buyer chooses something to buy, writes the price on a separate piece of paper, and gives the seller a five-dollar bill. The seller then draws the change for the item as dollars and coins. Then the seller counts the amount of change owed to the buyer.

To make sure children understand the process, guide them through a sample purchase. You may want to work with a child to demonstrate this transaction and have two or three children work at the board to figure out the change. See the **Math Talk in Action** in the side column for a sample classroom dialogue. Possible methods children might use are shown below.

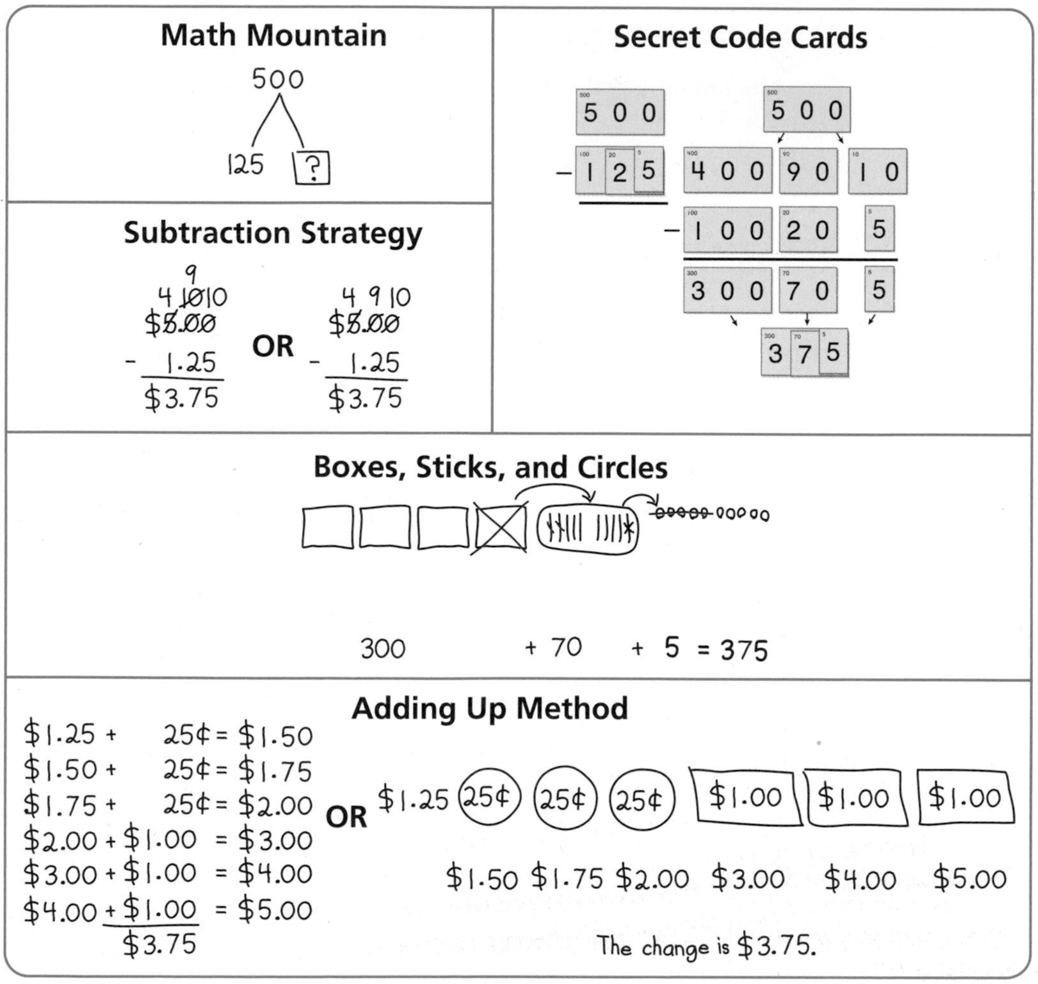

Have children begin buying and making change. Remind them to keep a record of what they do. They should use extra paper if they need more room to record their transactions. After about fifteen minutes, have the buyer and seller reverse roles.

Math Talk in Action

Suppose I am the buyer and I want to buy eight bananas. How much is that?

Andrew: $1.29

I'll give Andrew a five-dollar bill. Andrew has to figure how much change I should get and give it to me. While he does that, I also figure out how much change I should receive so I'll know if he is correct.

Let's help Andrew. How can Andrew solve the problem?

Luisa: Andrew could subtract $5.00 − $1.29.

Kayla: I think he could use a Proof Drawing.

Richie: And I think he could use Secret Code Cards!

Any of those methods would be fine. Richie, please explain how to use Secret Code Cards to find how much change he should give me.

Richie: First, I change the 500 into 400, 90 and 10. Then I separate 129 into 100, 20, and 9. Then I can subtract,
400 − 100 = 300,
90 − 20 = 70, and
10 − 9 = 1.

Irini: Andrew has to give you $3.71 in change!

Activity 2

Strategies for Making Change

15 MINUTES

Goal: Explain strategies for making change from a five-dollar bill.

NCTM Standards:
Number and Operations
Measurement
Problem Solving
Representation

Class Management

Sharing Children's Methods You may want to have children demonstrate and explain their strategies on chart paper or poster board. You can then display the different strategies for an extended period of time.

Ongoing Assessment

Have children make change from five dollars for a sandwich that costs \$3.65. They can show the bills and coins using real or play money or draw the change on a piece of paper.

Quick Quiz

See Assessment Guide for Unit 11 Quick Quiz 2.

▶ Explain Strategies WHOLE CLASS

Math Talk

Ask children who used different strategies to make change to explain their work at the board. Look for children who used the following strategies:

Ungrouping in subtraction
Adding Up Method
Model with real or play money
Proof Drawings with Numeric Methods
Represent with Secret Code Cards
Draw Math Mountains in order to see the unknown partner

▶ Ask Questions WHOLE CLASS

Encourage the class to ask each other questions about the strategies. You may want to guide children to ask questions that focus on interesting aspects of their strategies.

- Why did you ungroup when you subtracted?
- Why did you add up by dollars first, then quarters? Is there another way you could have added up?
- How did using Secret Code Cards make it easier to solve the problem?

Remind children that they can use more than one strategy to solve problems and suggest that they use the examples to learn new ways to solve these kinds of problems.

2 Going Further

Differentiated Instruction

Intervention

Activity Card 11-8

Make Change from Five Dollars Activity Card 11-8 ●

Work: (pair)

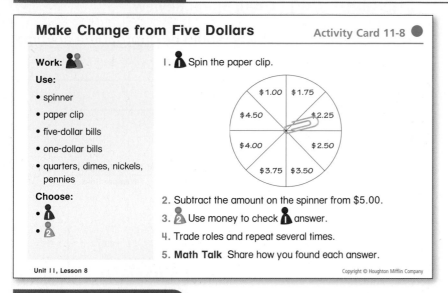

Use:
- spinner
- paper clip
- five-dollar bills
- one-dollar bills
- quarters, dimes, nickels, pennies

Choose:
- 1
- 2

1. (1) Spin the paper clip.

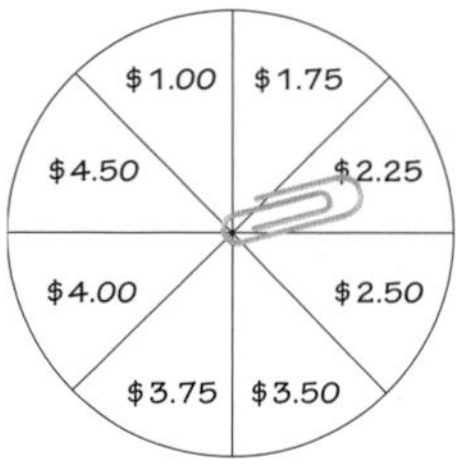

2. Subtract the amount on the spinner from $5.00.
3. (2) Use money to check (1) answer.
4. Trade roles and repeat several times.
5. **Math Talk** Share how you found each answer.

Unit 11, Lesson 8

Activity Note Each pair needs an eight-section spinner (TRB M27) with $1.00, $1.75, $2.25, $2.50, $3.50, $3.75, $4.00, and $4.50 in the sections.

Math Writing Prompt

Work Backward Suppose you buy a toy and pay with a five-dollar bill. You get $1.06 in change. How much did the toy cost?

Soar to Success Math **Software Support**

Warm Up 3.16

On Level

Activity Card 11-8

Change from Five Dollars Poster Activity Card 11-8 ▲

Work: (group)

Use:
- magazine
- shopping circulars
- scissors
- tape
- poster board

1. **Work Together** Cut out pictures from the magazines and shopping circulars that cost less than five dollars.
2. Tape the pictures and their prices onto the poster board.
3. Write the change you would receive from a five-dollar bill for each item.

4. Check that the amount of change is correct for each item.

Unit 11, Lesson 8

Activity Note Each group needs magazines and store circulars that have pictures of items. Have children assign a price to each item and then find the change from $5.00.

Math Writing Prompt

Getting Change Story Problems Write and solve a story problem about buying something with a five-dollar bill and getting $2.71 back in change.

Harcourt Mega Math Grades K-6 **Software Support**

Numberopolis: Lulu's Lunch Counter, Level O

Challenge

Activity Card 11-8

Work Back to the Beginning Activity Card 11-8 ■

Work: (pair)

Use:
- spinner
- paper clip
- 8 index cards

1. **Work Together** Write one of these amounts on each index card: $4.08, $4.17, $4.24, $4.25, $4.36, $4.45, $4.57, and $4.71.
2. Mix the cards up and deal them out.
3. Take turns spinning the spinner.

$5.00 - $0.92 = $4.08. I have the card with $4.08.

4. The person holding the card that shows the spinner amount subtracted from $5.00 places the card down.
5. The game ends when one partner has no more cards.

Unit 11, Lesson 8

Activity Note Each pair needs a spinner (TRB M27) with $0.43, $0.76, $0.92, $0.83, $0.55, $0.29, $0.75, and $0.64 in the sections.

Math Writing Prompt

Correct Change Molly bought a bracelet for $3.57. She paid $5.00 and received $1.43 in change. Did she get the right change? Explain.

DESTINATION Math® **Software Support**

Course II: Module 3: Unit 1: Money

3 Homework and Spiral Review

11–8 **Homework** **Goal:** Additional Practice

This Homework page provides practice in making change from $5.00.

11–8 Name ______________________

Homework

Here are some foods from the Grocery Store. The prices are shown too. Answer the questions below.

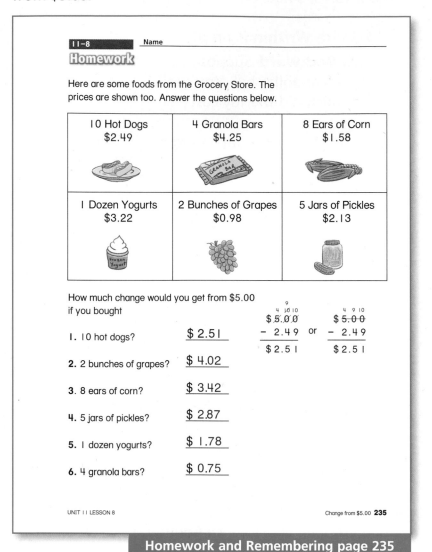

10 Hot Dogs $2.49 	4 Granola Bars $4.25 	8 Ears of Corn $1.58 
1 Dozen Yogurts $3.22 	2 Bunches of Grapes $0.98 	5 Jars of Pickles $2.13 

How much change would you get from $5.00 if you bought

1. 10 hot dogs? $ 2.51
2. 2 bunches of grapes? $ 4.02
3. 8 ears of corn? $ 3.42
4. 5 jars of pickles? $ 2.87
5. 1 dozen yogurts? $ 1.78
6. 4 granola bars? $ 0.75

$$\begin{array}{r} \overset{4\ \overset{9}{10}\ 10}{\$\cancel{5}.\cancel{0}\cancel{0}} \\ -\ 2.49 \\ \hline \$2.51 \end{array} \quad \text{or} \quad \begin{array}{r} \overset{4\ 9\ 10}{\$\cancel{5.00}} \\ -\ 2.49 \\ \hline \$2.51 \end{array}$$

UNIT 11 LESSON 8 Change from $5.00 235

Homework and Remembering page 235

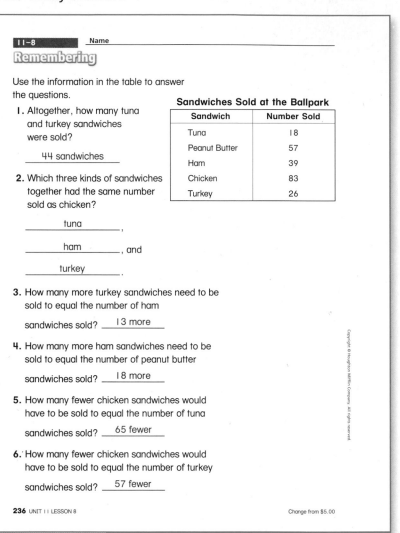

11–8 **Remembering** **Goal:** Spiral Review

This Remembering activity would be appropriate anytime after today's lesson.

11–8 Name ______________________

Remembering

Use the information in the table to answer the questions.

Sandwiches Sold at the Ballpark

Sandwich	Number Sold
Tuna	18
Peanut Butter	57
Ham	39
Chicken	83
Turkey	26

1. Altogether, how many tuna and turkey sandwiches were sold?
   44 sandwiches
2. Which three kinds of sandwiches together had the same number sold as chicken?
   tuna,
   ham, and
   turkey.
3. How many more turkey sandwiches need to be sold to equal the number of ham sandwiches sold? 13 more
4. How many more ham sandwiches need to be sold to equal the number of peanut butter sandwiches sold? 18 more
5. How many fewer chicken sandwiches would have to be sold to equal the number of tuna sandwiches sold? 65 fewer
6. How many fewer chicken sandwiches would have to be sold to equal the number of turkey sandwiches sold? 57 fewer

236 UNIT 11 LESSON 8 Change from $5.00

Homework and Remembering page 236

Home or School Activity

Art Connection

Design Money Discuss with children the different design elements on $1, $5, and $10 bills. Point out elements such as monuments, historical figures, and symbols. Then have children design a bill of their own. They can choose any value (not just $1, $5, or $10) for the bill and make up designs for the front and the back. Display children's work.

UNIT 11 LESSON 9

Add Over the Hundred

Lesson Objective

- Group numbers when adding over a hundred.

Vocabulary

hundreds
ones
tens

The Day at a Glance

Today's Goals	Materials	
1 Teaching the Lesson Add single-digit numbers to 3-digit numbers where the answer goes over the next hundred.	**Lesson Activities** Homework and Remembering pp. 237–238; Secret Code Cards; MathBoard materials	**Going Further** Activity Cards 11-9; Homework and Remembering p. 237; Base ten blocks; MathBoard materials; Math Journals
2 Going Further ▸ Differentiated Instruction		
3 Homework and Targeted Practice		

Use Math Talk today!

Keeping Skills Sharp

Quick Practice — 5 MINUTES

Goals: Write money strings for specific money amounts. Practice teen addition and subtraction.

Materials: Math Mountain Cards

Money Strings As children are doing the Quick Practice activity below, have two or three children write money strings for amounts between two and five dollars on the board. At the end of Quick Practice, have the class quickly check that the money strings are correct. (See Unit 9 Lesson 11.)

Blue Math Mountain Cards Have children practice addition and subtraction with Math Mountain Cards. Remind them that there are four equations on each card. (See Unit 7 Lesson 13.)

Daily Routines

Making Change and Counting Coins Making Change from $5.00, Combining Coins and Counting Money (See pp. xxvii–xxviii.)

▸ Led by Student Leaders

Money Routine Using the 120 Poster, Using the Money Flip Chart, Using the Number Path, Using Secret Code Cards (See pp. xxiii–xxv.)

▸ Led by Student Leaders

1 Teaching the Lesson

Activity

Making a New Hundred

30 MINUTES

Goals: Add single digit numbers to 3-digit numbers where the answer goes over the next hundred.

Materials: Secret Code Cards (1 set per child), MathBoard materials

NCTM Standard:
Number and Operations

The Learning Classroom

Building Concepts These exercises help children see 3-digit numbers as hundreds, tens, and ones. Many children think 200 + 2 is written as 2002. They just add 2 onto the 200. The Secret Code Cards will help them see what happens when they put the 2 on top of the 0 in the ones place. It is very important that children use their Secret Code Cards for this activity.

▶ Add 3-Digit and 1-Digit Numbers

WHOLE CLASS

Math Talk

Tell children that in this activity they will add 3- and 1-digit numbers. Point out that these exercises will help them see 3-digit numbers as hundreds, tens, and ones. For example, two hundred two is 202, not 2002.

Write 199 + 4 = ☐ on the board and have children represent the equation with Secret Code Cards. Then have them work together as a class to solve the exercise.

- What is 199 and 4? 203

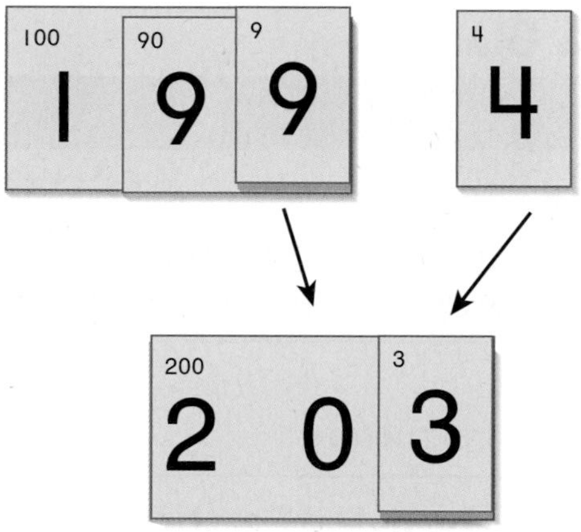

- Let's prove that this is the correct answer by drawing boxes, sticks, and circles on our MathBoards.

Ask a volunteer to show his or her drawing on the board while the rest of the class makes their drawings on their MathBoards.

Be sure children see how the 1 one can be grouped with the 9 ones to make a new ten and how the 9 tens and 10 ones make a new hundred. Have children draw a box around the tens and ones to represent a hundred.

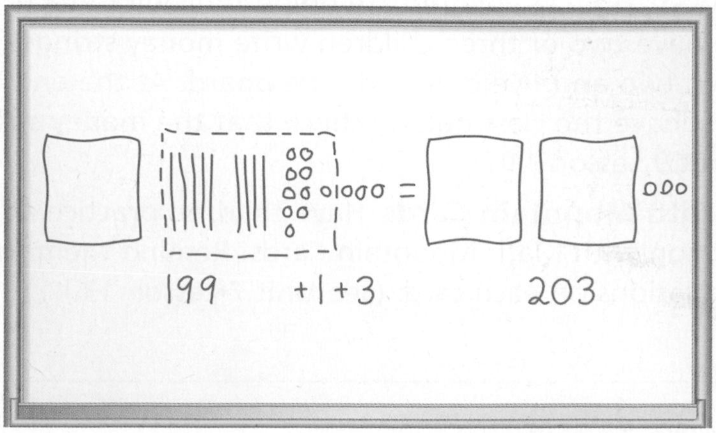

Now write the exercise 391 + 9 = ☐ on the board. Once again have children represent the equation with Secret Code Cards and then work together as a class to find the sum.

- How can we solve this problem? Use Secret Code Cards, make drawings, use fingers, use mental math, and so on.
- What is the answer? 400

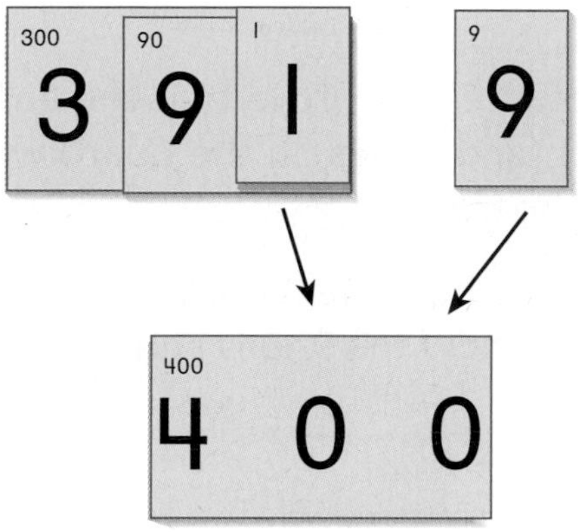

Ask a volunteer to prove that the answer is correct by drawing boxes, sticks, and circles on the board while the rest of the class draws on their MathBoards.

Again, be sure that children see how the 9 ones can be grouped with the 1 one to make a new ten and how the 9 tens and 10 ones make a new hundred.

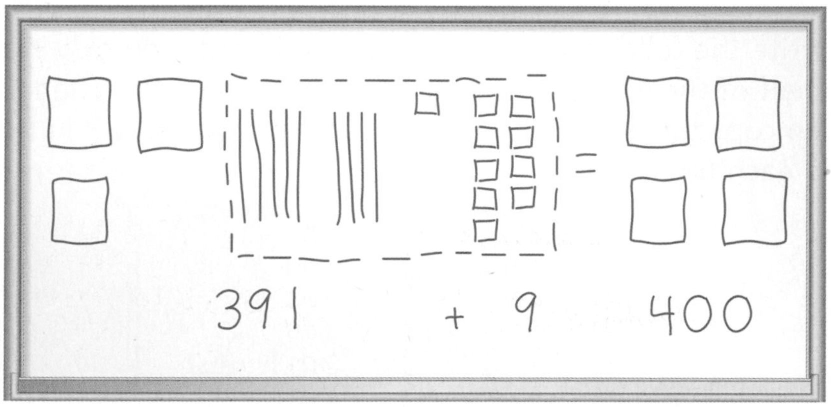

Now write 2 + 598 = ☐ on the board and work together as a class to solve it.

- This next problem is a little different. How is it different from the problems we just solved? The smaller number comes first.

Activity continued ▶

Teaching Note

What to Expect from Students
Some children may suggest that they can solve these exercises by counting on from the larger number. Tell them that counting on is a good method, but today they should just use that method to check their answers. Today everyone should make drawings and show the numbers with Secret Code Cards so that they see these large numbers.

English Language Learners

Write *group* and a proof drawing for 57 + 33 on the board. Circle the ones.

- **Beginning** Say: **We can *group* the ones.** Ask: **Did I put all the ones together?** yes
- **Intermediate** Ask: **Did I *group* the ones?** yes **What did I make?** a new ten
- **Advanced** Have children tell how to *group* the ones to make a new ten.

❶ Teaching the Lesson (continued)

- Does it matter which number is first? No, except it is easier to start with the larger number Why or why not? When you add, you can start with either number and find the same answer.
- What is the answer? 600

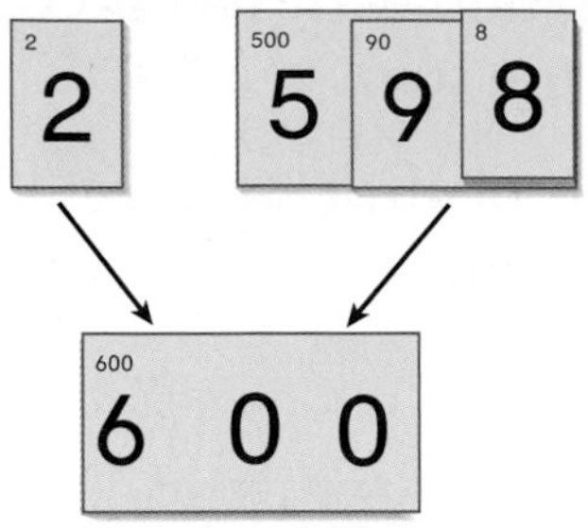

Once again, ask a volunteer to prove that the answer is correct by drawing boxes, sticks, and circles on the board while the rest of the class draws on their MathBoards.

Be sure that children see how the 8 ones can be grouped with the 2 ones to make a new ten and how the 9 tens and 10 ones make a new hundred.

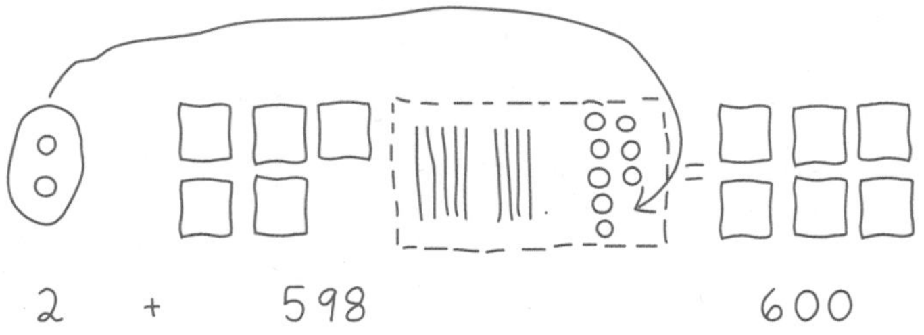

Switch the numbers in the exercise around and write 598 + 2 = ☐ on the board. Ask children if the answer is still the same. yes

Now write the following equations on the board. You may wish to write up to half of the exercises with the lesser number first. Then have the children copy the exercises on a piece of paper and work in Helping Pairs to find each total.

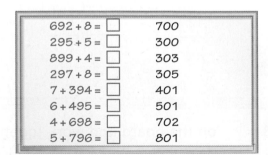

692 + 8 = ☐	700
295 + 5 = ☐	300
899 + 4 = ☐	303
297 + 8 = ☐	305
7 + 394 = ☐	401
6 + 495 = ☐	501
4 + 698 = ☐	702
5 + 796 = ☐	801

Encourage children to use the Secret Code Cards and to make drawings of boxes, sticks, and circles to solve each exercise.

Once children have finished the exercises, have volunteers come to the board and show their work. Encourage the other children to ask questions and make comments.

Ongoing Assessment

Circulate around the room as children are solving the exercises. Ask the pairs to explain how they found each answer. Have one child use Secret Code Cards while the other child makes a drawing.

2 Going Further

Differentiated Instruction

Intervention Activity Card 11-9

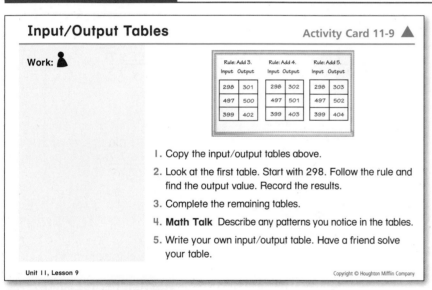

Use Base Ten Blocks

Activity Card 11-9

Work: pairs

Use:

- MathBoard materials
- base ten blocks

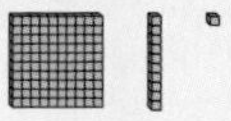

- Homework and Remembering page 237

Choose:

- 1
- 2

1. Use blocks to find the total of each exercise in number 3 on Homework and Remembering page 237.
2. Make a proof drawing to find the total for each exercise in number 3 on Homework and Remembering page 237.

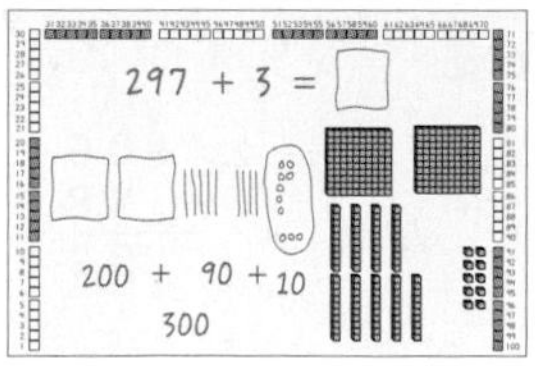

3. Compare your totals.
4. Take turns and solve exercise 4–6.

Unit 11, Lesson 9

Activity Note Each pair needs base ten blocks, MathBoard materials, and Homework and Remembering p. 237. Ask pairs to share how they solved each exercise.

Math Writing Prompt

Make a Drawing Draw boxes, sticks, and circles to show how to add 198 + 3.

Soar to Success Math **Software Support**

Warm Up 10.29

On Level Activity Card 11-9

Input/Output Tables

Activity Card 11-9

Work: individual

Rule: Add 3.

Input	Output
298	301
497	500
399	402

Rule: Add 4.

Input	Output
298	302
497	501
399	403

Rule: Add 5.

Input	Output
298	303
497	502
399	404

1. Copy the input/output tables above.
2. Look at the first table. Start with 298. Follow the rule and find the output value. Record the results.
3. Complete the remaining tables.
4. **Math Talk** Describe any patterns you notice in the tables.
5. Write your own input/output table. Have a friend solve your table.

Unit 11, Lesson 9

Activity Note Each child needs to follow the rules and complete the tables. Share the input/output tables children create with the class.

Math Writing Prompt

Explain Your Thinking Explain how you would group two numbers whose ones add up to 17.

Harcourt MegaMath **Software Support**

Numberopolis: Cross Town Number Line, Level R

Challenge Activity Card 11-9

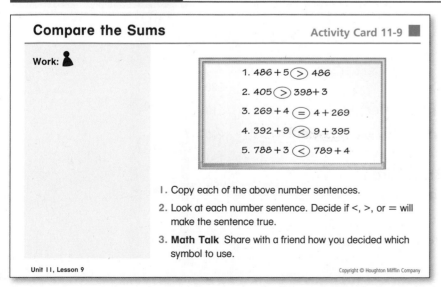

Compare the Sums

Activity Card 11-9

Work: individual

1. 486 + 5 (>) 486
2. 405 (>) 398 + 3
3. 269 + 4 (=) 4 + 269
4. 392 + 9 (<) 9 + 395
5. 788 + 3 (<) 789 + 4

1. Copy each of the above number sentences.
2. Look at each number sentence. Decide if <, >, or = will make the sentence true.
3. **Math Talk** Share with a friend how you decided which symbol to use.

Unit 11, Lesson 9

Activity Note Review the meaning of the < and > symbols with children. Have children compare their answers.

Math Writing Prompt

Find the Error Look at how Carl added 598 and 2. Explain what Carl did wrong.

$$\begin{array}{r} 598 \\ +\ \ 2 \\ \hline 5{,}910 \end{array}$$

Destination Math **Software Support**

Course II: Module 4: Unit 1: Number Patterns and Properties

3 Homework and Targeted Practice

11–9 Homework **Goal:** Additional Practice

✓ Include children's completed Homework page as part of their portfolios.

11–9 Homework Name ______

Solve each story problem.

1. Rita counts the visitors to the museum. She counted 5 groups of one hundred and 2 groups of ten. She also counted a small group of 7. How many visitors did Rita count?

527 visitors (label)

2. Kay packs buttons at the button factory. She packed 7 boxes of one hundred buttons and 5 boxes of ten. She packed one box of 9 buttons. How many buttons did Kay pack?

759 buttons (label)

Add.

3. 297 + 3 = 300
7 + 285 = 292
5 + 143 = 148
100 + 200 = 300

4. 98 + 9 = 107
6 + 97 = 103
45 + 3 = 48
40 + 30 = 70

5. 38 + 500 = 538
9 + 300 = 309
295 + 9 = 304
50 + 500 = 550

6. 200 + 200 = 400
11 + 80 = 91
30 + 410 = 440
20 + 380 = 400

UNIT 11 LESSON 9 Add Over the Hundred **237**

Homework and Remembering page 237

11–9 Targeted Practice **Goal:** Practice subtraction

This page can be used with children who need practice subtracting from numbers with two zeros.

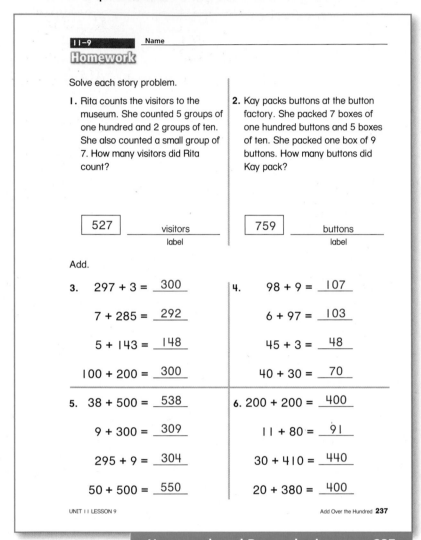

11–9 Targeted Practice Name ______

Add or subtract.

1. 200 − 79 = 121
2. 100 − 48 = 52
3. 200 − 87 = 113
4. 100 − 35 = 65
5. 200 − 51 = 149
6. 100 − 62 = 38
7. 200 + 116 = 316
8. 100 + 324 = 424
9. 200 + 597 = 797
10. 100 + 243 = 343
11. 200 + 458 = 658
12. 100 + 677 = 777

238 UNIT 11 LESSON 9 Add Over the Hundred

Homework and Remembering page 238

Home or School Activity

Science Connection

Compare Fahrenheit and Celsius Display a dual scale thermometer and explain that it can be used to measure temperature in both customary units and metric units.

Tell children that water boils at 212° Fahrenheit. Then ask children to look at the thermometer to find what that temperature is on the Celsius side of the thermometer. 100° Celsius

Provide children with problems about temperature in which they need to add over the hundred.

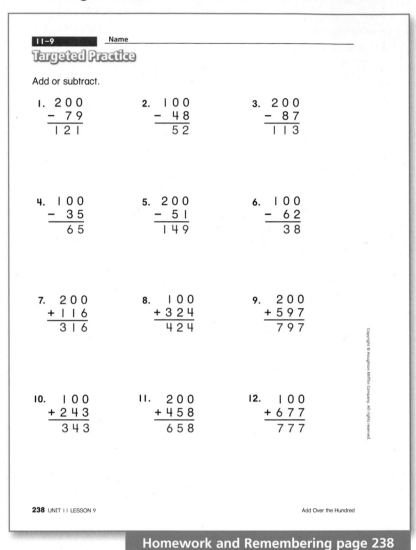

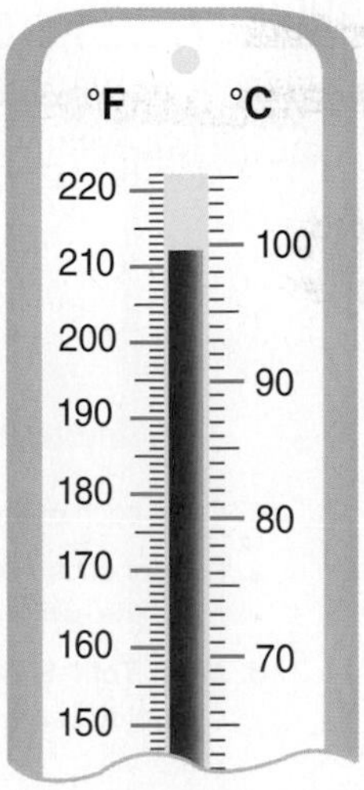

UNIT 11 LESSON 10

Solve and Discuss

REAL WORLD Problem Solving

Lesson Objectives

- Explain the methods used to solve addition story problems.
- Discuss good explanations and good questions.
- Invent ways to solve addition problems in which both numbers have three digits.

Vocabulary

Show All Totals
New Groups Below
New Groups Above

The Day at a Glance

Today's Goals	Materials	
1 Teaching the Lesson **A1:** Find totals for 1-digit partners. **A2:** Discuss the methods used to solve addition story problems. Discuss good explanations and good questions. Invent ways to add two 3-digit numbers. **2 Going Further** ▶ Extra Practice ▶ Differentiated Instruction **3 Homework and Spiral Review**	**Lesson Activities** Student Activity Book pp. 359–360, 363–364 (includes Addition Sprint, Family Letter) Homework and Remembering pp. 239–240 MathBoard materials	**Going Further** Activity Cards 11-10 Student Activity Book pp. 361–362 The Muffin Stand (TRB M85) Math Journals

Use Math Talk today!

Keeping Skills Sharp

Quick Practice — 5 MINUTES

Goal: Monitor progress in addition of 2-digit numbers.

Quick Check Monitor children's progress with a brief quick check. Write these exercises on the board. One of them requires ungrouping, and the other does not.

$42 + 27 = \square$ 69

$84 + 39 = \square$ 123

Repeated Quick Practice
Use this Quick Practice from a previous lesson.

▶ **Money Strings** (See Unit 9 Lesson 11.)

Daily Routines

Making Change and Counting Coins Making Change from $5.00, Combining Coins and Counting Money (See pp. xxvii–xxviii.)

▶ Led by Student Leaders

Money Routine Using the 120 Poster, Using the Money Flip Chart, Using the Number Path, Using Secret Code Cards (See pp. xxiii–xxv.)

▶ Led by Student Leaders

1 Teaching the Lesson

Activity 1

Addition Sprint

10 MINUTES

Goal: Find totals for 1-digit partners.

Materials: Student Activity Book page 359

NCTM Standard:
Number and Operations

Class Management

This is the fifth time children do this Addition Sprint. You may wish to impose a short time limit (for example, 2 minutes) and challenge chiildren to see how many correct answers they can get in that time.

English Language Learners

Write *sprint* and *mental math* on the board. Model Student Activity Book page 359. Ask: **Is the Addition *sprint* fast or slow?** fast

- **Beginning** Point and say: ***Mental math* means add in your head.** Ask: **Is *mental math* fast?** yes
- **Intermediate** Ask: **Does *mental math* mean add on paper or in your head?** in your head
- **Advanced** Ask: **Which is faster – *mental math* or adding on paper?** mental math

▶ Addition Sprint INDIVIDUALS

Direct children's attention to Student Activity Book page 359. Decide how much time to give them to complete the Sprint. Explain the procedure and time limit to them.

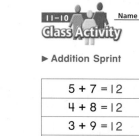

11–10 Class Activity Name ______

▶ Addition Sprint

5 + 7 = 12	9 + 6 = 15	7 + 6 = 13
4 + 8 = 12	7 + 8 = 15	4 + 6 = 10
3 + 9 = 12	9 + 7 = 16	0 + 7 = 7
7 + 5 = 12	9 + 2 = 11	4 + 9 = 13
4 + 5 = 9	5 + 2 = 7	6 + 8 = 14
8 + 4 = 12	6 + 4 = 10	8 + 5 = 13
8 + 6 = 14	8 + 7 = 15	6 + 1 = 7
6 + 9 = 15	5 + 5 = 10	5 + 4 = 9
9 + 9 = 18	1 + 9 = 10	7 + 4 = 11
6 + 3 = 9	7 + 9 = 16	3 + 6 = 9
9 + 0 = 9	4 + 7 = 11	9 + 4 = 13
7 + 7 = 14	8 + 8 = 16	5 + 8 = 13
9 + 1 = 10	6 + 6 = 12	3 + 4 = 7
8 + 9 = 17	3 + 5 = 8	6 + 7 = 13
2 + 5 = 7	9 + 3 = 12	1 + 6 = 7
3 + 9 = 12	2 + 9 = 11	5 + 6 = 11
2 + 7 = 9	2 + 6 = 8	5 + 5 = 10
9 + 4 = 13	5 + 9 = 14	6 + 8 = 14
2 + 8 = 10	8 + 2 = 10	4 + 4 = 8
0 + 8 = 8	9 + 8 = 17	1 + 8 = 9
8 + 3 = 11	6 + 5 = 11	6 + 7 = 13

UNIT 11 LESSON 10 Addition Sprint **359**

Student Activity Book page 359

Activity 2

Solve and Explain Story Problems

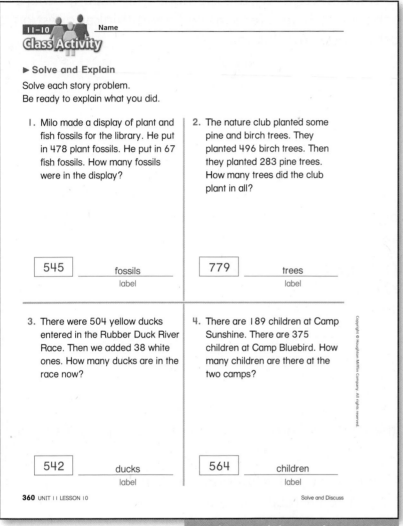

11-10 Class Activity Name ____________

▶ Solve and Explain

Solve each story problem.
Be ready to explain what you did.

1. Milo made a display of plant and fish fossils for the library. He put in 478 plant fossils. He put in 67 fish fossils. How many fossils were in the display?

545 fossils
label

2. The nature club planted some pine and birch trees. They planted 496 birch trees. Then they planted 283 pine trees. How many trees did the club plant in all?

779 trees
label

3. There were 504 yellow ducks entered in the Rubber Duck River Race. Then we added 38 white ones. How many ducks are in the race now?

542 ducks
label

4. There are 189 children at Camp Sunshine. There are 375 children at Camp Bluebird. How many children are there at the two camps?

564 children
label

Student Activity Book page 360

▶ Solve and Discuss WHOLE CLASS

Math Talk

Direct children's attention to Student Activity Book page 360. Using the **Solve and Discuss** structure, have four to five children solve the first problem at the board while the rest of the class works at their seats. They may use any method they choose.

When children have completed the first problem, select two or three children who used different methods to explain what they did, at the board. Have the rest of the class comment and ask questions.

Use this lesson as an opportunity to help children learn to ask good questions and give thoughtful answers that show their understanding of math concepts.

Activity continued ▶

40 MINUTES

Goal: Discuss the methods used to solve addition story problems. Discuss good explanations and good questions. Invent ways to add two 3-digit numbers.

Materials: MathBoard materials, Student Activity Book page 360

NCTM Standards:
Number and Operations
Communication

The Learning Classroom

Building Concepts The purpose of this lesson is to help children focus their attention on good questions and good explanations as they use what they already know about addition to add larger numbers.

Teaching Note

Watch For! Listen for children who are not using hundreds, tens, and ones language. Encourage them to use proper math language to ask their questions and justify their methods. Explain that using the proper math terms makes it easier for everyone to understand what they mean.

▶ Discuss Good Questions

Math Talk

Be sure children understand what a "good" question might be. Ask them to suggest sample "good" questions. Encourage any children who are explaining their solution to justify the methods they used if other children challenge them. See below for sample "good thinker questions" and appropriate justifications for this solution.

$$\begin{array}{r} 478 \\ +\ \ 67 \\ \hline {}_{1}\,{}_{1}\quad \\ 545 \end{array}$$

Good Thinker Questions and Justifications

Q: How did you know you were supposed to add?
A: I read the story problem. It was about a collection of plant fossils and fish fossils. To find the total number of fossils, I had to add.

Q: Why did you put the 7 under the 8?
A: I put it there because it is 7 ones and the 8 is really 8 ones so they should be in the same place.

Q: 7 + 8 is 15. What happened to the 10 in 15? I see only 5.
A: I had 7 ones plus 8 ones which made 15 ones, which is 10 ones and 5 ones. I wrote the new ten in the tens column.

Q: What do the 1s on the line mean?
A: That means there's 1 new group of ten and 1 new group of a hundred.

Q: Where did the new group of a hundred come from?
A: 7 tens + 6 tens + 1 ten is really 14 tens, or 1 hundred and 4 tens.

Q: Where did you write your new hundred?
A: I wrote it on the line in the hundreds place.

▶ Discuss Good Explanations

Math Talk

Have children discuss how a good explanation uses hundreds, tens, and ones language and addresses the problem with both numbers and a proof drawing.

Be sure that your more-advanced children are modeling good explanations such as the ones below and on the next page. Expand children's explanations as necessary and have children help other children make full explanations.

Good Explanation for Show All Totals Method

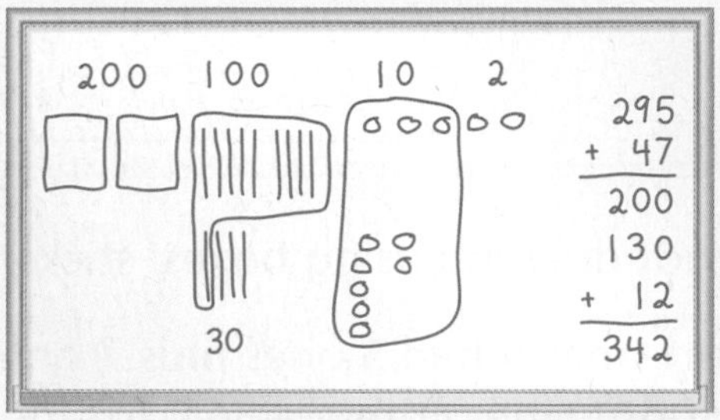

1. First, I made a proof drawing, using boxes, sticks, and circles.
2. Then I counted my hundreds. I had 2 hundreds plus 0 hundred, which made 2 hundreds. So I wrote 200 above the boxes and I wrote 200 in my problem.
3. Next, I counted my tens. I had 9 tens plus 4 tens (or 90 plus 40), which made 13 tens (or 130). I saw that I had more than 10 tens, so I drew a line around ten of the sticks in my proof drawing to show the new hundred. Then I wrote 100 above the 10 sticks and 30 below the 3 extra sticks. Then in my problem, I added 9 tens (or 90) plus 4 tens (or 40), which gave me 13 tens or 130. So I wrote 130 under the 200.
4. Then I counted my ones. I had 5 ones plus 7 ones, which made 12 ones. I drew a line around 10 circles in my proof drawing to show the new ten. Then I wrote 10 above the 10 circles and 2 above the 2 extra circles. Then I did the ones in my problem. I added 5 ones and 7 ones, which gave me 12 ones. So I wrote 12 under the 130.
5. Then I added 200 + 130 + 12 = 342.
6. Finally, I checked to see that my proof drawing showed 3 hundreds, 4 tens, and 2 ones just like the numbers did. The two answers from the two methods were the same.

Activity continued ▶

Teaching Note

Watch For! Look for children who do not align the ones properly when they write the total for the ones. Look at the proof drawing to see that they need to add ones to ones.

Teaching Note

Remember! Some children may prefer to do Show All Totals starting from the ones, though more students start from the left.

$$\begin{array}{r} 295 \\ +\ 47 \\ \hline 12 \\ 130 \\ \underline{200} \\ 342 \end{array}$$

Make a Ten methods help students see how the drawings show make-a-ten methods: 9 tens + 4 tens became 10 tens + 3 tens = 130. 7 ones + 5 ones became 10 ones + 2 ones (7 + 3 + 2).

More students may use mental make-a-ten methods now because they need the answer in the numerical problem as 1 ten + some ones.

Teaching Note

What to Expect from Students The explanations given here represent exemplary explanations. Do not expect all second graders to be able to explain with this level of sophistication. However, it is important that children use hundreds, tens, and ones language and use both numbers and drawings to explain their work. With continued modeling from more-advanced students and from you, many students will learn to give full explanations. It is helpful for students to practice explaining in Helping Partners later on after they have seen full explanations at the board.

Good Explanation for New Groups Below or New Groups Above Methods

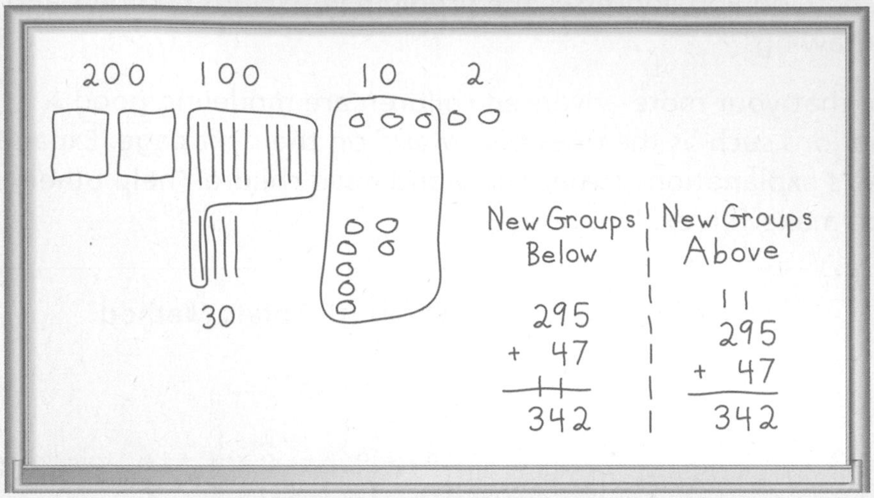

1. First I made a proof drawing using boxes, sticks, and circles.
2. Then I counted my ones. I had 5 ones plus 7 ones, which made 12 ones. In my proof drawing, I drew a line around 10 circles. Then in the numbers I wrote 1 on the line in the tens column (or above the tens). I had 2 extra ones so I wrote 2 in the ones place. I can see that 5 ones plus 7 ones make twelve—1 ten and 2 ones.
3. Next, I counted my tens. I had 9 tens plus 4 tens, which made 13 tens and a new ten from adding the ones. I added 9 tens, 4 tens, and 1 ten which made 14 tens. In my proof drawing, I made a group around 10 of the tens to show the new hundred and labeled it 100. Then I wrote 30 next to the 3 extra tens. In the numbers, I wrote the number 4 for 4 tens. On the line in the hundreds column (or above the hundreds), I wrote a 1 for the new hundred. I can see that 9 tens plus 4 tens is 13 tens plus 1 more ten is 14 tens or 90 + 40 is 130.
4. Then I counted my hundreds. I had 2 hundreds plus 1 new hundred, which made 3 hundreds. I wrote 3 in the hundreds column.
5. Finally, I checked to see that my proof drawing showed 3 hundreds, 4 tens, and 2 ones just like the numbers did. The two answers from the two methods were the same. I can see my new hundred in my drawing (point to new circled 10 tens) and in my problem (point to the new 1 written in the hundreds column) and my new ten in my drawing (point to the circled ten ones circles) and in my problem (point to the new 1 ten in the tens column).

▶ Add 3-Digit Numbers WHOLE CLASS

Before moving on to exercise 2, guide children to extend the addition methods they have already learned to add two 3-digit numbers. Write 152 + 283 = □ on the board and ask children to find the total. Tell them to make a proof drawing and to try to find a way to show the new hundred in addition to the existing hundreds.

Invite volunteers to the board to solve this exercise while the rest of the class solves it on their MathBoards. Try to send children to the board who use different methods. Then discuss the methods that the children used.

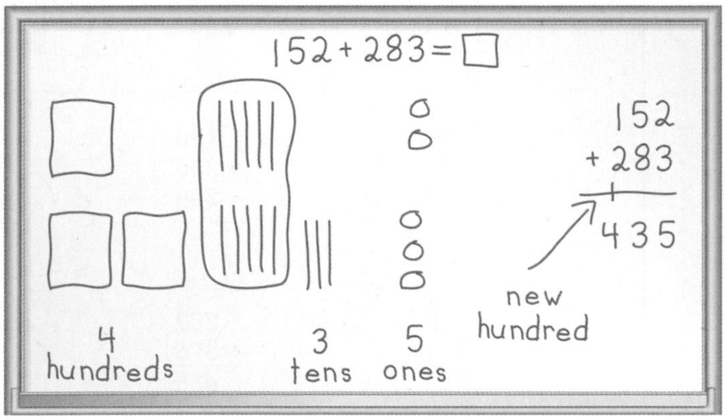

Try to relate different methods to each other.

- Let's look at the proof drawing and count the boxes, sticks, and circles. How many boxes, or hundreds, do we have? 3 boxes
- Did we make a new hundred? yes How did we show it? We looped the 10 tens. Now how many hundreds do we have? 4 hundreds
- How many sticks, or tens, do we have? 3
- How many circles, or ones, do we have? 5
- What is the total? 435
- *Point to the example that uses New Groups Below.* How did we show the new hundred using this method? We put a small 1 on the line in the hundreds place.

Repeat the process with the numbers 174 and 352. Write 174 + 352 = □ on the board and ask volunteers to solve it. Some possible solution methods are shown at the right.

Then, using the **Solve and Discuss** structure, have children solve problems 2–4 on Student Activity Book page 360. Point out that to solve some of these problems, children will need to add two 3-digit numbers.

Show All Totals

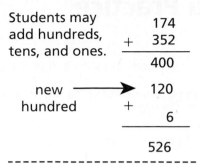

Students may add hundreds, tens, and ones.

```
   174
 + 352
 -----
   400
   120   ← new hundred
 +   6
 -----
   526
```

New Groups Below

```
   174
 + 352
   1
 -----
   526
```

new hundred (the 1 on the line)

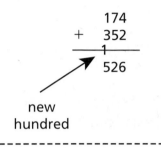

New Groups Above

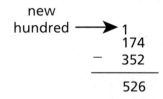

```
new hundred → 1
              174
            − 352
            -----
              526
```

Proof Drawing

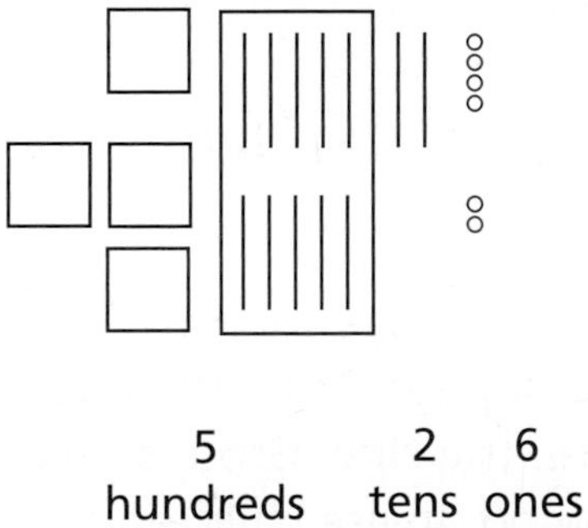

Ongoing Assessment

Circulate around the room as children are solving the problems on the page. Note how they are writing the exercises. If they write the numbers vertically, be sure they are aligning the digits correctly.

2 Going Further

Extra Practice

Goal: Practice addition with 3-digit numbers.

Materials: Student Activity Book pages 361–362

▶ Number Sense WHOLE CLASS

Before beginning this page, you may wish to provide some opportunities for children to use their number sense. Refer children to Student Activity Book page 361. Ask questions, such as those given below. Encourage children to give good explanations for their answers.

- Look at the first row of exercises. Which exercise will have the least total? exercise 2
- Look at exercise 4. Will the total be more than 700? yes More than 800? yes
- Look at exercise 8. Will the total be more than 600? yes More than 700? no
- In exercise 9 will you need to make a new ten? yes a new hundred? no

Invite volunteers to then ask others questions about the exercises.

▶ Solve and Discuss

WHOLE CLASS **Math Talk**

Direct children's attention to the top of Student Activity Book page 361. Two addition methods are shown here: the New Groups Below Method and a proof drawing. Invite children to use these or any other addition method they choose for the exercises on this page

Use the **Solve and Discuss** structure for exercises 1 and 2. Then have students finish the rest of the page independently.

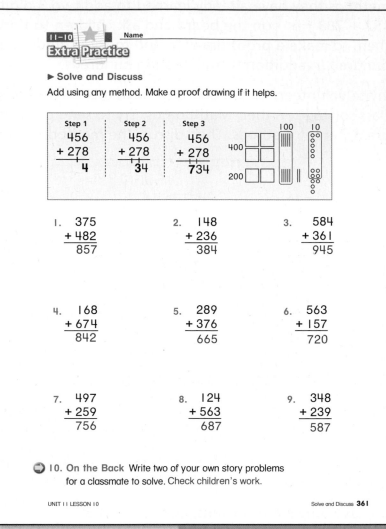

11-10 Extra Practice Name

▶ Solve and Discuss

Add using any method. Make a proof drawing if it helps.

Step 1	Step 2	Step 3
456 + 278 4	456 + 278 34	456 + 278 734

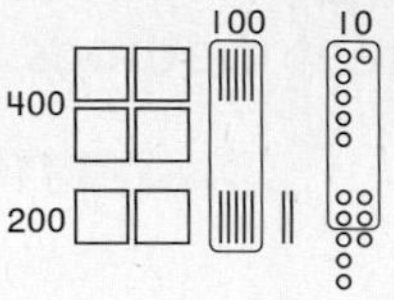

1. 375 + 482 = 857	2. 148 + 236 = 384	3. 584 + 361 = 945
4. 168 + 674 = 842	5. 289 + 376 = 665	6. 563 + 157 = 720
7. 497 + 259 = 756	8. 124 + 563 = 687	9. 348 + 239 = 587

10. **On the Back** Write two of your own story problems for a classmate to solve. Check children's work.

UNIT 11 LESSON 10 Solve and Discuss 361

Student Activity Book page 361

Intervention Activity Card 11-10

Review Single-Digit Addition
Activity Card 11-10

Work: pairs

9 + 4 = ____	90 + 40 = ____
8 + 3 = ____	80 + 30 = ____
5 + 7 = ____	50 + 70 = ____
9 + 5 = ____	90 + 50 = ____

Choose:
- 1
- 2

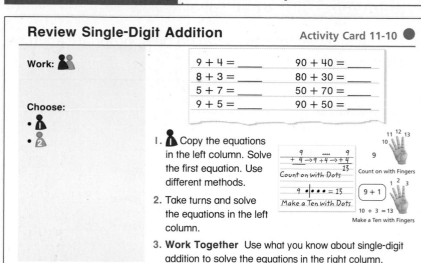

1. Copy the equations in the left column. Solve the first equation. Use different methods.
2. Take turns and solve the equations in the left column.
3. **Work Together** Use what you know about single-digit addition to solve the equations in the right column.

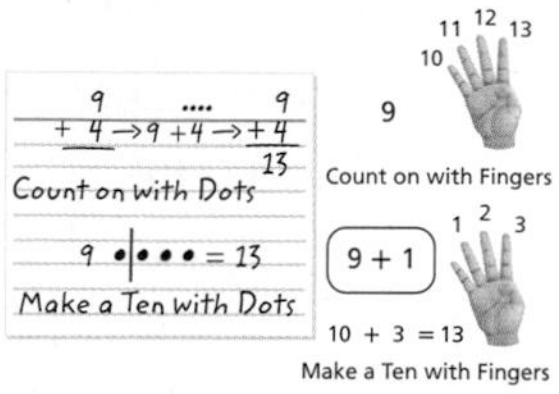

Activity Note Have children explain how to solve each single-digit equation. Then have them use what they know to solve the decade numbers equations.

Math Writing Prompt

Draw a Picture Make a proof drawing to show how to solve 450 + 250.

Soar to Success Math Software Support

Warm Up 10.18

On Level Activity Card 11-10

Muffins for Sale
Activity Card 11-10

Work: pairs

Use:
- The Muffin Stand (TRB M85)

1. **Work Together** Look at problem 1 on The Muffin Stand. Discuss how to find the answer. Write your answer in the box.
2. Make a proof drawing to check your work.
3. Solve the rest of the problems. Make a proof drawing for each problem.
4. Write a story problem using The Muffin Stand page. Trade story problems with another pair. Solve their story problem.

Activity Note Each pair needs The Muffin Stand (TRB M85). Encourage pairs to explain how they solved each problem.

Math Writing Prompt

Use Pictures and Numbers Make a proof drawing and use numbers to show how to solve 454 + 257.

Harcourt Mega Math Software Support

Numberopolis: Carnival stories, Level R

Challenge Activity Card 11-10

Extend the Muffin Activity
Activity Card 11-10

Work: pairs

Use:
- The Muffin Stand (TRB M85)

1. **Work Together** Solve the problems on The Muffin Stand. Check your work.
2. The baker wants to make some new kinds of muffins. She wants to mix two kinds of muffins into one muffin. Banana Blueberry will be one kind.
3. List all of the different combinations if you mix two muffin flavors together. Sample answers: banana orange, banana apple, banana lemon, blueberry orange, blueberry apple, blueberry lemon, orange apple, orange lemon, apple lemon
4. **Math Talk** Discuss how you found all of the different combinations.

Activity Note Each pair needs The Muffin Stand (TRB M85). Have pairs check their lists with other pairs.

Math Writing Prompt

Show Two Ways Show two different methods to solve 175 + 358.

Destination Math Software Support

Course II: Module 4: Unit 1: Number Patterns and Properties

3 Homework and Spiral Review

11–10 Homework **Goal:** Additional Practice

This Homework page provides practice with multi-digit addition.

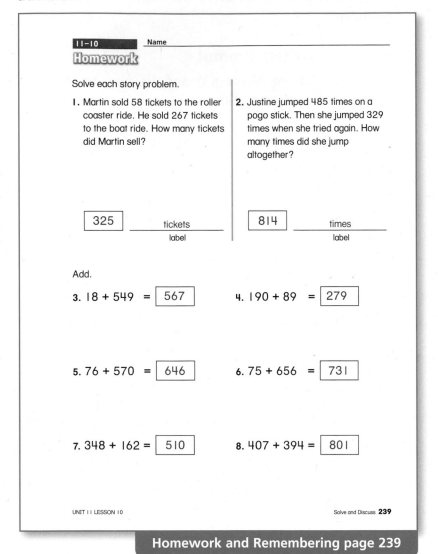

11-10 Name

Homework

Solve each story problem.

1. Martin sold 58 tickets to the roller coaster ride. He sold 267 tickets to the boat ride. How many tickets did Martin sell?

325 tickets
label

2. Justine jumped 485 times on a pogo stick. Then she jumped 329 times when she tried again. How many times did she jump altogether?

814 times
label

Add.

3. 18 + 549 = 567

4. 190 + 89 = 279

5. 76 + 570 = 646

6. 75 + 656 = 731

7. 348 + 162 = 510

8. 407 + 394 = 801

UNIT 11 LESSON 10 Solve and Discuss 239

Homework and Remembering page 239

11–10 Remembering **Goal:** Spiral Review

This Remembering activity would be appropriate anytime after today's lesson.

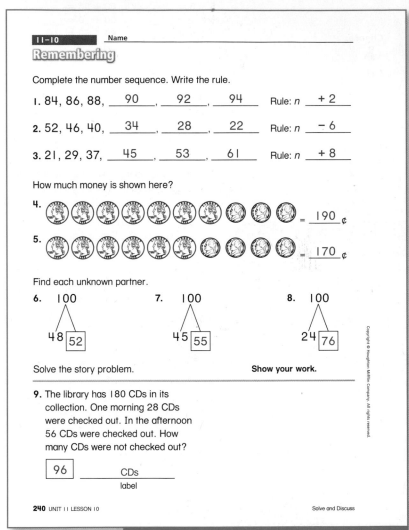

11-10 Name

Remembering

Complete the number sequence. Write the rule.

1. 84, 86, 88, 90, 92, 94 Rule: n + 2

2. 52, 46, 40, 34, 28, 22 Rule: n − 6

3. 21, 29, 37, 45, 53, 61 Rule: n + 8

How much money is shown here?

4.  = 190¢

5.  = 170¢

Find each unknown partner.

6. 100: 48 and 52

7. 100: 45 and 55

8. 100: 24 and 76

Solve the story problem. **Show your work.**

9. The library has 180 CDs in its collection. One morning 28 CDs were checked out. In the afternoon 56 CDs were checked out. How many CDs were not checked out?

96 CDs
label

240 UNIT 11 LESSON 10 Solve and Discuss

Homework and Remembering page 240

Home and School Connection

Family Letter Have children take home the Family Letter on Student Activity Book page 363. This letter explains how the concepts of 3-digit addition are developed in *Math Expressions.* It gives parents and guardians a better understanding of the learning that goes on in math class and creates a bridge between school and home. A Spanish translation of this letter is on the following page in the Student Activity Book.

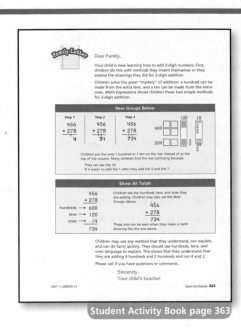

Family Letter

Dear Family,

Your child is now learning how to add 3-digit numbers. First, children do this with methods they invent themselves or they extend the drawings they did for 2-digit addition.

Children solve the great "mystery" of addition: a hundred can be made from the extra tens, and a ten can be made from the extra ones. *Math Expressions* shows children these two simple methods for 3-digit addition.

New Groups Below

Step 1	Step 2	Step 3
456 + 278 = 4	456 + 278 = 34	456 + 278 = 734

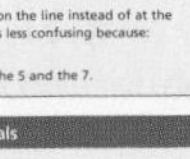

Children put the new 1 hundred or 1 ten on the line instead of at the top of the column. Many children find this less confusing because:

They can see the 14.
It is easier to add the 1 after they add the 5 and the 7.

Show All Totals

456
+ 278
hundreds → 600
tens → 120
ones → 14
734

Children see the hundreds, tens, and ones they are adding. Children may also use the New Groups Above.

456 + 278 = 734

These also can be seen when they make a math drawing like the one above.

Children may use any method that they understand, can explain, and can do fairly quickly. They should use hundreds, tens, and ones language to explain. This shows that they understand that they are adding 4 hundreds and 2 hundreds and not 4 and 2.

Please call if you have questions or comments.

Sincerely,
Your child's teacher

UNIT 11 LESSON 10 Solve and Discuss 363

Student Activity Book page 363

Carta a la familia

Estimada familia:

Ahora su niño está aprendiendo a sumar números de 3 digitos. Primero, los niños hacen esto con métodos que ellos mismos inventan, o amplilan los dibujos que hicieron para la suma de números de dos digitos.

Los niños resuelven el "misterio" de la suma: se puede formar una centena a partir de las decenas que sobran y se puede formar una decena a partir de las unidades que sobran. *Math Expressions* les muestra a los niños estos dos métodos simples de suma de números de tres digitos.

Grupos nuevos abajo

Paso 1	Paso 2	Paso 3
456 + 278 = 4	456 + 278 = 34	456 + 278 = 734

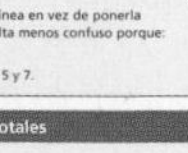

Los niños ponen la nueva centena o decena en la línea en vez de ponerla arriba de la columna. A muchos niños esto les resulta menos confuso porque:

Pueden ver el 14.
Es más fácil sumar el 1 después de que sumaron 5 y 7.

Mostrar todos los totales

456
+ 278
centenas → 600
decenas → 120
unidades → 14
734

Los niños ven las centenas, las decenas y las unidades que están sumando. Los niños también pueden usar los Grupos nuevos arriba.

456 + 278 = 734

Esto también se puede observar cuando hacen un dibujo matemático como el de arriba.

Los niños pueden usar cualquier método que comprendan, puedan explicar y puedan hacer relativamente rápido. Para explicar deben usar un lenguaje relacionado con centenas, decenas y unidades. Esto demuestra que entienden que están sumando 4 centenas y 2 centenas, y no 4 y 2.

Si tiene alguna duda o pregunta, por favor comuníquese conmigo.

Atentamente,
El maestro de su niño

364 UNIT 11 LESSON 10 Solve and Discuss

Student Activity Book page 364

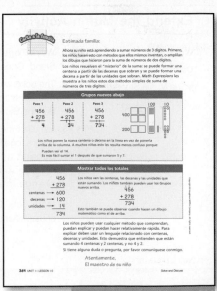

UNIT 11 LESSON 11

Add Money Amounts

Lesson Objectives

- Organize data in a table.
- Use information from a table to solve problems.
- Add 3-digit money amounts.

Vocabulary
table
dollar sign
decimal point
function table

The Day at a Glance

Today's Goals	Materials	
1 Teaching the Lesson Create a data table from information. Use the information in the table to solve addition problems with 3-digit money amounts.	**Lesson Activities** Student Activity Book pp. 365–366; Homework and Remembering pp. 241–242; MathBoard materials	**Going Further** Activity Cards 11-11; Student Activity Book p. 365; MathBoard materials; Secret Code Cards (1–300); Math Journals
2 Going Further ▶ Differentiated Instruction		
3 Homework and Targeted Practice		

Use Math Talk today!

Keeping Skills Sharp

Quick Practice — 5 MINUTES

Goal: Find the addition rule for a function table.

What's My Rule? Have a **Student Leader** draw the table shown at the right on the board. Then have children figure out the rule for the function table. $n + 4$ The Student Leader then completes the rule by writing the number 4 in the mystery box. Have children say the numbers that will complete the table as another Student Leader writes them in the function table.

n	$n + \square$
7	11
34	38
67	71
55	59
83	87
88	92

Repeated Quick Practice
Use this Quick Practice from a previous lesson.

- ▶ **Money Strings** As children are doing the Quick Practice activity What's My Rule?, have two or three children write money strings for amounts between five and ten dollars on the board. At the end of Quick Practice, have the class quickly check that the money strings are correct. (See Unit 9 Lesson 11.)

Daily Routines

Making Change and Counting Coins Making Change from $5.00, Combining Coins and Counting Money (See pp. xxvii–xxviii.)

- ▶ Led by Student Leaders

Money Routine Using the 120 Poster, Using the Money Flip Chart, Using the Number Path, Using Secret Code Cards (See pp. xxiii–xxv.)

- ▶ Led by Student Leaders

1 Teaching the Lesson

Activity

Animal Club Collection

40 MINUTES

Goals: Create a data table from information. Use the information in the table to solve addition problems with 3-digit money amounts.

Materials: Student Activity Book pages 365–366, MathBoard materials

NCTM Standard:
Number and Operations

Differentiated Instruction

Extra Help Each animal name starts with a different letter to help facilitate alphabetization. If children still have difficulty putting the animals in alphabetical order, have them list all the letters of the alphabet and cross out each letter as they use it.

Toy	Price
Bear	$4.96
Chimpanzee	$4.94
Elephant	$3.79
Giraffe	$3.57
Kangaroo	$3.79
Leopard	$4.67
Owl	$1.55
Penguin	$2.81
Raccoon	$2.68
Swan	$1.86
Turtle	$1.58
Zebra	$2.93

11-11 Class Activity Name

▶ Make a Table

$1.86 Swan	$2.93 Zebra	$4.67 Leopard
$4.96 Bear	$2.68 Raccoon	$3.79 Elephant
$3.79 Kangaroo	$1.55 Owl	$1.58 Turtle
$4.94 Monkey	$2.81 Penguin	$3.57 Giraffe

UNIT 11 LESSON 11 Add Money Amounts 365

Student Activity Book page 365

▶ Make a Table WHOLE CLASS

Ask for Ideas Refer children to Student Activity Book page 365. Explain to children that they need to organize the stuffed animal collection at the zoo's gift shop into an organized table.

Help children arrange the information into a table.

- What information should go in the table? the name of the animal and the money amount
- How should we set up the information? The table could be set up alphabetically by animal or by the amount of money a stuffed animal costs.

Work with the class and help children set up the first two or three entries of the table on a separate sheet of paper. Then have the children work in **Helping Pairs** to complete the table. A sample table is shown to the left.

11-11 Class Activity

Name ______________________

▶ Add 3-Digit Money Amounts
Answers will vary.

1. Animals: ______________________

$.
+ $.

Make a new ten? ______
Make a new hundred? ______

2. Animals: ______________________

$.
+ $.

Make a new ten? ______
Make a new hundred? ______

3. Animals: ______________________

$.
+ $.

Make a new ten? ______
Make a new hundred? ______

4. Animals: ______________________

$.
+ $.

Make a new ten? ______
Make a new hundred? ______

5. Animals: ______________________

$.
+ $.

Make a new ten? ______
Make a new hundred? ______

6. Animals: ______________________

$.
+ $.

Make a new ten? ______
Make a new hundred? ______

366 UNIT 11 LESSON 11 Add Money Amounts

Student Activity Book page 366

▶ Add 3-Digit Money Amounts PAIRS **Math Talk**

Direct children's attention to Student Activity Book page 366. Have children pretend the cash register is broken at the zoo's gift shop and they need to use this page to record stuffed animal purchases. Work together as a class to solve the first exercise.

- We will work in **Helping Pairs** today and practice adding 3-digit money amounts. This time, we are going to fill out Student Activity Book page 366 to record what we did. We will do an example together to help us get started.

Activity continued ▶

The Learning Classroom

Building Concepts Before beginning the first exercise, you may wish to review the meaning of the dollar sign and decimal point in money notation to be sure that children understand the money amounts that they are writing.

English Language Learners

Make sure children can identify the animals on Student Activity Book page 365.

- **Beginning** Point to the swan. Ask: **What animal is this?** swan Say: **The swan costs $1.86.** Have children repeat. Continue with other animals.
- **Intermediate** Ask: **How much does the swan cost?** $1.86 Continue with other animals.
- **Advanced** Ask: **Which stuffed animal costs $3.79?** kangaroo

❶ Teaching the Lesson (continued)

Differentiated Instruction

Advanced Learners Have children who finish early choose three stuffed animals to buy that cost less than $10.00.

Ongoing Assessment

As children complete Student Activity Book page 366, ask them to explain how they solved each exercise. As they explain, look to see if children remembered to:

- show a new ten or new hundred
- add a new ten or new hundred
- place a dollar sign and decimal point in their answer.

Invite two children to each select a stuffed animal to buy from the gift shop. Then have the class write the names of the animals on the lines on Student Activity Book page 366, as you write them on the board.

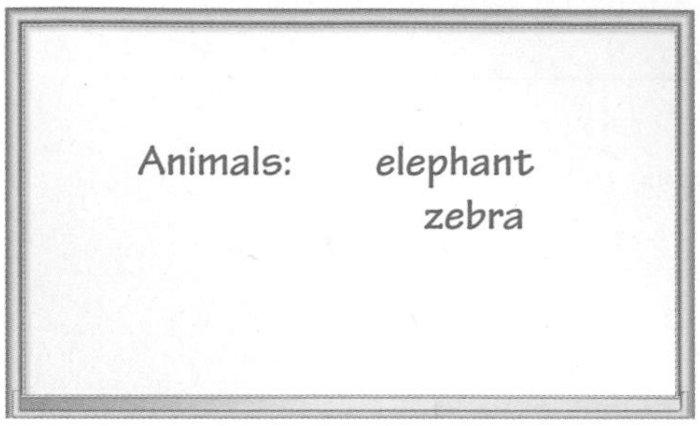

Then ask the questions below to help children complete the exercise.

- How much money does it cost to buy the stuffed elephant? $3.79
- How much does it cost to buy the stuffed zebra? $2.93

Have children write those amounts on their page as you demonstrate by writing the amounts on the board. Then ask a volunteer to come to the board and demonstrate how to add the two numbers as the rest of the children add them at their seats. Encourage children to use their MathBoards to make a proof drawing. They should record any extra tens or extra hundreds in the picture and in the numerical example.

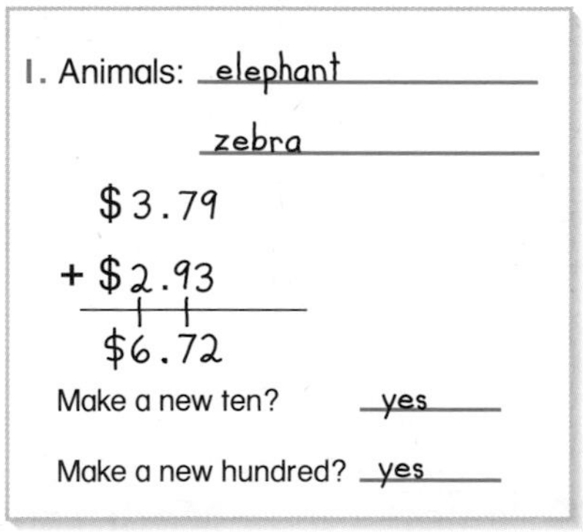
1. Animals: elephant
zebra

$3.79
+ $2.93
$6.72

Make a new ten? yes

Make a new hundred? yes

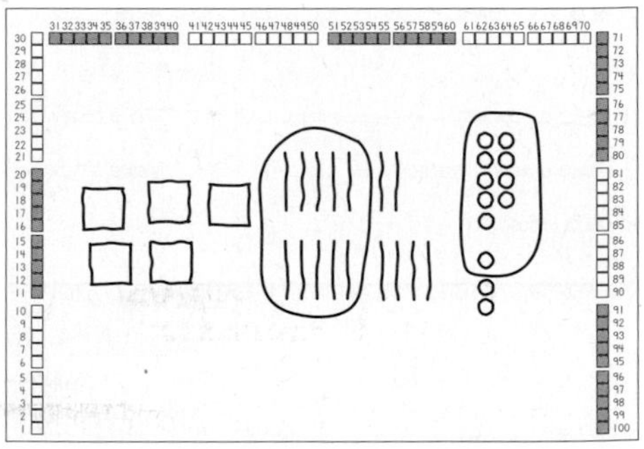

- Did you have to make a new ten? yes
- Did you have to make a new hundred? yes

After children have completed exercise 1, have children work in pairs to complete the page. Remind them to make a proof drawing and to show any new tens or hundreds in both the picture and in the numerical example.

As the class completes the activity, you may wish to work with small groups of children who are having difficulty. Have them come to the board and take turns describing the next step in solving each of the exercises.

2 Going Further

Differentiated Instruction

Intervention — Activity Card 11-11

Make the Greater Total

Activity Card 11-11

Work: pairs
Use:
- Secret Code Cards

1. **Work Together** Sort the Secret Code Cards into three piles: hundreds, tens, and ones.
2. Take turns picking cards from each pile until each person has six cards.
3. Each uses the cards to make two three-digit numbers.

   3 5 7

   2 4 5

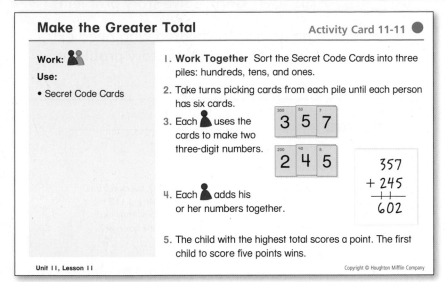

   $$\begin{array}{r} 357 \\ +\ 245 \\ \hline 602 \end{array}$$
4. Each adds his or her numbers together.
5. The child with the highest total scores a point. The first child to score five points wins.

Unit 11, Lesson 11

Activity Note Each pair needs Secret Code Cards 1–300 (TRB M3-M6). Have children check their addition and explain how they know which total is greater.

Math Writing Prompt

Write About It How does knowing how to find 455 + 346 help you find \$4.55 + \$3.46?

Soar to Success Math Software Support

Warm Up 10.31

On Level — Activity Card 11-11

Guess and Check

Activity Card 11-11

Work: pairs
Use:
- Student Activity Book page 365

Choose:
- 1
- 2

1. Choose two toy animals from Student Activity Book page 365. Don't tell 2 which toys you chose.
2. Find the total cost of the two toys.

   \$4.67

   Leopard

   \$1.58

   Turtle
3. Tell 2 the cost of the two toys.
4. 2 Guess the two toys 1 chose.
5. Switch roles and repeat.
6. **Math Talk** Share how you guessed the two toys chosen by your partner.

Unit 11, Lesson 11

Activity Note Each pair needs Student Activity Book p. 365. Remind children not to tell their partner which toys they selected. Have pairs check their partner's addition.

Math Writing Prompt

Compare and Contrast What is the same about adding 568 and \$5.68? What is different? Explain your thinking.

Harcourt Mega Math Software Support

Numberopolis: Lulu's Lunch Counter, Level S

Challenge — Activity Card 11-11

Magic Square

Activity Card 11-11

Work: pairs
Use:
- MathBoard materials

\$1.33	\$1.56	\$1.46
\$1.58	\$1.45	\$1.32
\$1.44	\$1.34	\$1.57

1. **Work Together** Copy the magic square above onto your MathBoard.
2. The total for every row, column, and diagonal is \$4.35. Find the unknown numbers in the magic square.
3. Share your completed magic square with another pair.
4. **Math Talk** Share how you found the unknown numbers.

Unit 11, Lesson 11

Activity Note Each pair needs Math Board materials. Have children check their math to be sure all rows, columns, and diagonals equal \$4.35.

Math Writing Prompt

Create Your Own Write and solve a story problem about adding money amounts.

Destination Math Software Support

Course II: Module 3: Unit 1: Money

3 Homework and Targeted Practice

11–11 Homework **Goal:** Additional Practice

This Homework page provides practice in adding money amounts.

11–11 **Homework** Name ______

Add. Use any method.

1. $2.67 + $1.56 = $4.23
   Make a new ten? Yes
   Make a new hundred? Yes

2. $4.82 + $3.43 = $8.25
   Make a new ten? No
   Make a new hundred? Yes

3. $2.75 + $5.39 = $8.14
   Make a new ten? Yes
   Make a new hundred? Yes

4. $6.09 + $1.88 = $7.97
   Make a new ten? Yes
   Make a new hundred? No

5. $2.94 + $4.12 = $7.06
   Make a new ten? No
   Make a new hundred? Yes

6. $3.07 + $3.66 = $6.73
   Make a new ten? Yes
   Make a new hundred? No

UNIT 11 LESSON 11 Add Money Amounts 241

Homework and Remembering page 241

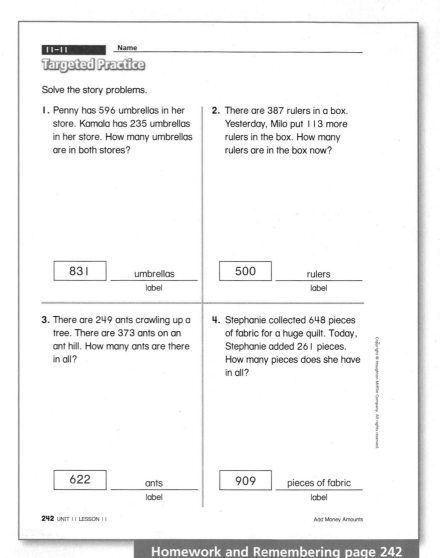

11–11 Targeted Practice **Goal:** Solve story problems.

This page can be used with children who need extra practice in solving 3-digit addition story problems.

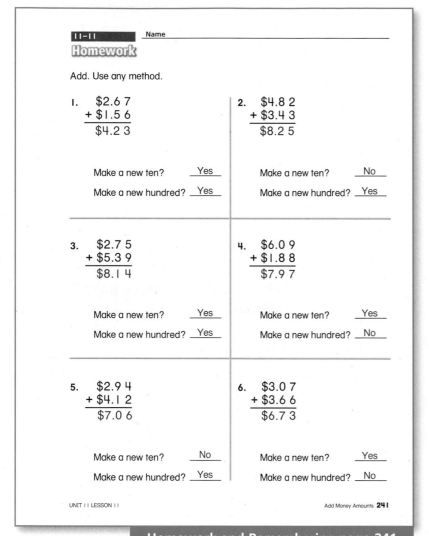

11–11 **Targeted Practice** Name ______

Solve the story problems.

1. Penny has 596 umbrellas in her store. Kamala has 235 umbrellas in her store. How many umbrellas are in both stores?
   831 umbrellas (label)

2. There are 387 rulers in a box. Yesterday, Milo put 113 more rulers in the box. How many rulers are in the box now?
   500 rulers (label)

3. There are 249 ants crawling up a tree. There are 373 ants on an ant hill. How many ants are there in all?
   622 ants (label)

4. Stephanie collected 648 pieces of fabric for a huge quilt. Today, Stephanie added 261 pieces. How many pieces does she have in all?
   909 pieces of fabric (label)

242 UNIT 11 LESSON 11 Add Money Amounts

Homework and Remembering page 242

Home or School Activity

Science Connection

Endangered Animals Have children research several endangered animals such as the Asian Elephant, American Black Bear, Bengal Tiger, Giant Panda, Manatee, and Arctic Wolf. Have them research what the animals look like, where they live, and what they eat. Then have them organize the information in a table.

Animal	Habitat	Food
Asian Elephant	Tropical forests in India	grass leaves fruit bark
Giant Panda	Damp forests in China	Bamboo
Bengal Tiger	Grassy areas by rivers in India	deer wild pigs small buffalo small elephants

UNIT 11 LESSON 12

Discuss 3-Digit Addition

Lesson Objectives

- Present good explanations of methods used to solve numeric addition exercises.
- Practice solving 2- and 3-digit addition exercises.

Vocabulary
hundreds
tens
ones

The Day at a Glance

Today's Goals	Materials	
1 Teaching the Lesson A1: Solve and explain the methods used in 3-digit addition. A2: Solve 2- and 3-digit addition exercises to solve a math puzzle.	**Lesson Activities** Student Activity Book pp. 367–370 Homework and Remembering pp. 243–244 MathBoard materials Crayons or markers	**Going Further** Activity Cards 11-12 Student Activity Book p. 369 MathBoard materials Secret Code Cards Math Journals
2 Going Further ▶ Differentiated Instruction		
3 Homework and Spiral Review		

Use Math Talk today!

Keeping Skills Sharp

Quick Practice — 5 MINUTES

Goal: Monitor progress on addition with 3-digit numbers.

Quick Check Monitor children's progress on 3-digit addition with a brief Quick Check. Write these exercises on the board.

$$\begin{array}{r} 332 \\ +477 \\ \hline 809 \end{array} \qquad \begin{array}{r} 129 \\ +786 \\ \hline 915 \end{array}$$

Repeated Quick Practice Use this Quick Practice from a previous lesson.

- ▶ **Money String** (See Unit 9 Lesson 11.)

Daily Routines

Making Change and Counting Coins Making Change from \$5.00, Combining Coins and Counting Money (See pp. xxvii–xxviii.)

- ▶ Led by Student Leaders

Money Routine Using the 120 Poster, Using the Money Flip Chart, Using the Number Path, Using Secret Code Cards (See pp. xxiii–xxv.)

- ▶ Led by Student Leaders

1 Teaching the Lesson

Activity 1

Explain Addition Methods

35 MINUTES

Goal: Solve and explain the methods used in 3-digit addition.

Materials: Student Activity Book page 367, MathBoard materials

NCTM Standards:
Number and Operations
Communication

The Learning Classroom

Math Talk This activity emphasizes good explanations. Refer to Lesson 10 for examples of "Good Thinker Questions." Have a Student Leader give the first explanation. Some children will be quite proficient at this by now. Others may still benefit from exposure to modeling by more skillful children. The goal of this activity is that everyone eventually be able to present a competent explanation of a solution.

Student Helpers can assist children who are experiencing difficulty both with explaining and finding the totals.

▶ Discuss Good Explanations WHOLE CLASS Math Talk

Lead a discussion on the characteristics of a good, clear explanation. Be sure children understand that when explaining their math work, they should:

- use hundreds, tens, and ones language
- show the solution numerically
- be able to show the solution with a proof drawing
- explain step-by-step what they did to get the answer.

▶ Solve and Discuss PAIRS Math Talk

Have children work in **Helping Pairs** on the exercises on Student Activity Book page 367.

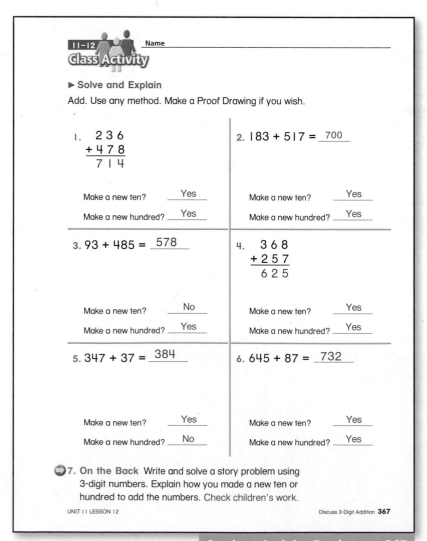

11–12 Class Activity Name ____________

▶ **Solve and Explain**

Add. Use any method. Make a Proof Drawing if you wish.

1. $\begin{array}{r} 236 \\ +\,478 \\ \hline 714 \end{array}$

Make a new ten? Yes
Make a new hundred? Yes

2. 183 + 517 = 700

Make a new ten? Yes
Make a new hundred? Yes

3. 93 + 485 = 578

Make a new ten? No
Make a new hundred? Yes

4. $\begin{array}{r} 368 \\ +\,257 \\ \hline 625 \end{array}$

Make a new ten? Yes
Make a new hundred? Yes

5. 347 + 37 = 384

Make a new ten? Yes
Make a new hundred? No

6. 645 + 87 = 732

Make a new ten? Yes
Make a new hundred? Yes

7. **On the Back** Write and solve a story problem using 3-digit numbers. Explain how you made a new ten or hundred to add the numbers. Check children's work.

UNIT 11 LESSON 12 Discuss 3-Digit Addition 367

Student Activity Book page 367

Have **Helping Pairs** take turns explaining their solution methods using hundreds, tens, and ones language. Children should show any new tens and new hundreds with numerical methods, but encourage children to make a proof drawing for at least one of the exercises on the page.

Point out to children that four of the exercises on the page are shown horizontally. Remind them to rewrite the exercises vertically and to properly align the numbers before adding them. Encourage children to discuss how they did this as part of their explanation.

▶ Present Good Explanations WHOLE CLASS

When the children have completed the page, select a few of them to show their solutions at the classroom board. Tell the children to make a proof drawing to check their numerical solution. Be sure at least one or two of these children are advanced in giving explanations. If you have children who are having difficulty solving these exercises, have them write the procedure on a piece of paper as it is explained.

▶ Provide More Practice INDIVIDUALS

If you have children who need more practice with these types of exercises, use the exercises shown below.

195 + 172 = 367	95 + 863 = 958
85 + 98 = 183	325 + 596 = 921
486 + 347 = 833	264 + 85 = 349
213 + 587 = 800	842 + 58 = 900

Differentiated Instruction

Advanced Learners Challenge children who finish early to solve exercises such as the one shown below.

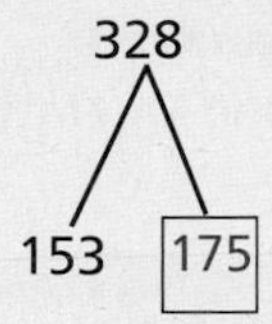

English Language Learners

Write *numerical method* and *proof drawing* on the board. Model both ways of showing the solution for 247 + 156.

- **Beginning** Point to and identify each method. Have children point and repeat. Ask: **Does the *numerical method* have numbers?** yes
- **Intermediate** Ask: **Does the *numerical method* use numbers or drawings?** numbers
- **Advanced** Have children identify each method.

Activity 2

Hidden Picture Puzzle

20 MINUTES

Goal: Solve 2- and 3-digit addition exercises to solve a math puzzle.

Materials: Student Activity Book pages 369–370, crayons or markers

NCTM Standard:
Number and Operations

Class Management

If time is limited, you may wish to have children work in pairs or small groups, so that all children do not need to do every exercise.

Ongoing Assessment

Circulate around the room as children are solving the exercises on Student Activity Book page 369. Ask individual children to explain the method they are using to solve specific exercises on the page.

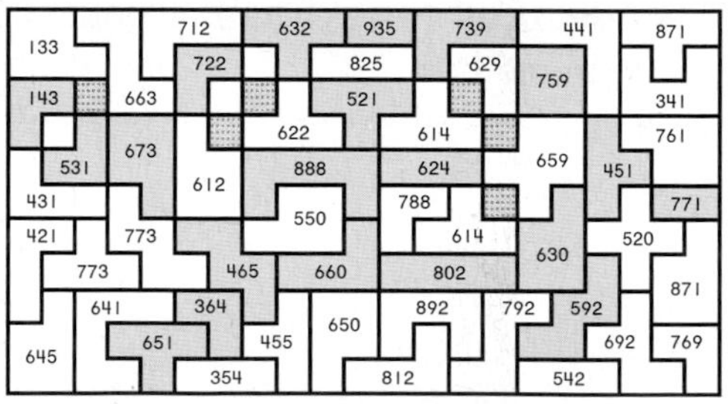

From Student Activity Book page 370

11-12 Class Activity

Name

▶ **Find the Hidden Animal**

Directions for the puzzle appearing on page 370.

1. Start by coloring in the six dotted squares. These are "free" squares. They are part of the puzzle solution.
2. Solve a problem below. Then look for the answer in the puzzle grid. Color it in.
3. Solve all 20 questions correctly. Color in all 20 correct answers.
4. Name the hidden picture. It is a(n) turtle.

524 + 247 = 771	287 + 164 = 451	384 + 375 = 759	456 + 174 = 630	327 + 265 = 592
207 + 595 = 802	248 + 376 = 624	282 + 457 = 739	548 + 387 = 935	233 + 288 = 521
367 + 265 = 632	293 + 595 = 888	284 + 376 = 660	295 + 463 = 758	138 + 327 = 465
286 + 78 = 364	407 + 266 = 673	503 + 148 = 651	78 + 65 = 143	192 + 339 = 531

UNIT 11 LESSON 12 Discuss 3-Digit Addition 369

Student Activity Book page 369

▶ Find the Hidden Animal INDIVIDUALS

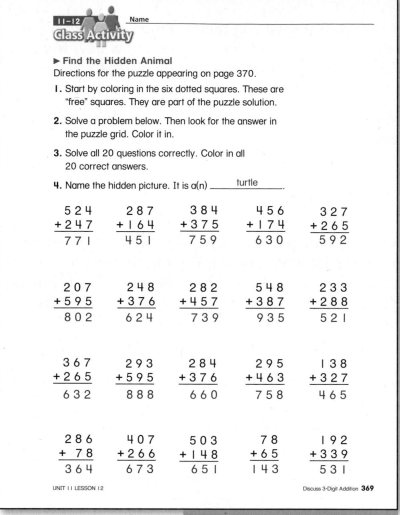

Refer children to Student Activity Book pages 369 and 370. Explain how to find the hidden animal in the puzzle.

- First solve the addition exercises on Student Activity Book page 369.
- Then find each answer on the puzzle on Student Activity Book page 370 and color in the puzzle piece.
- If you have colored in all the puzzle pieces correctly, you will see a picture of an animal.
- If you have trouble recognizing the animal, hold the picture a short distance away from you.

Once all children have completed the page, ask them to share what the animal is. a turtle

2 Going Further

Differentiated Instruction

Intervention — Activity Card 11-12

Solve and Draw

Activity Card 11-12

Work:

Use:

- MathBoard materials
- Student Activity Book page 369

1. Each chooses an exercise from Student Activity Book page 369. Don't tell anyone else in your group your exercise.
2. Make a proof drawing for the exercise you chose on your MathBoard.

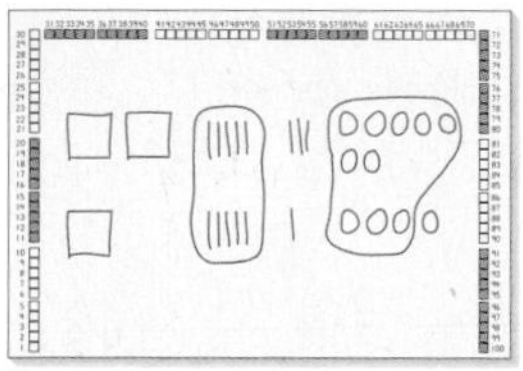

3. Trade MathBoards with your group members.
4. Identify which exercise your group member chose.

Unit 11, Lesson 12

Activity Note Each group needs MathBoard materials and Student Activity Book p. 369.

Math Writing Prompt

Find the Error
Look at how Keisha solved the exercise. What does she need to do to fix her work?

$$\begin{array}{r} 458 \\ +28 \\ \hline 738 \end{array}$$

Soar to Success Math Software Support

Warm Up 10.30

On Level — Activity Card 11-12

Who's Closer?

Activity Card 11-12

Work:

Use:

- Secret Code Cards

1. **Work Together** Sort the Secret Code Cards into three piles: hundreds, tens, and ones. Take turns picking cards from each pile until each person has six cards.
2. Each uses the cards to make two three-digit numbers. Make the sum of the two numbers as close to 999 as possible without going over 999.

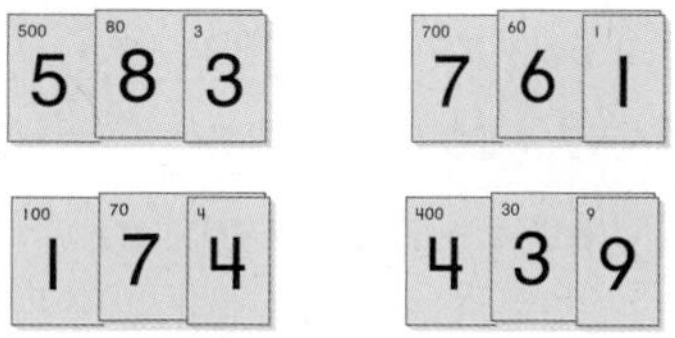

3. The child with the total closest to 999 wins a point. Repeat. The first child to get five points wins.

Unit 11, Lesson 12

Activity Note Each pair needs Secret Code Cards 1-900 (TRB M3-M6). Have pairs check their sums carefully.

Math Writing Prompt

Guess and Check Dawn needs to find the two greatest equal partners that have a total closest to 999. What are her numbers? Explain how you find your answer.

Harcourt Mega Math Software Support

Country Countdown: Block Busters, Level U

Challenge — Activity Card 11-12

What's My Rule?

Activity Card 11-12

Work:

Use:

- MathBoard materials

Table 1

n	$n + 25$
125	150
378	403
487	512

Table 2

n	$n + 236$
154	390
573	809
249	485

1. Copy each input/output table on to your MathBoard.
2. Find the rule for each table.
3. Fill in the unknown numbers.
4. Share the rule and unknown numbers with a classmate.
5. **Math Talk** Discuss how you found the rule and the unknown numbers.

Unit 11, Lesson 12

Activity Note Have children explain what the rule is for each input/output table.

Math Writing Prompt

Explain Your Thinking Each shape stands for a different number. Find the value of each shape.

$\triangle + \triangle = 230$

$\square + \square + 30 = 130$

$\triangle + \square + \bigcirc = 175$

Destination Math Software Support

Course II: Module 4: Unit 1: Number Patterns and Properties

3 Homework and Spiral Review

11–12 Homework **Goal:** Additional Practice

This Homework page provides practice in 3-digit addition.

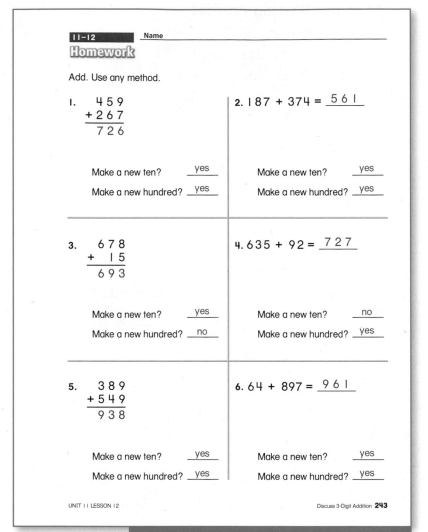

11–12 Homework Name ____________

Add. Use any method.

1. 459 + 267 = 726

Make a new ten? yes
Make a new hundred? yes

2. 187 + 374 = 561

Make a new ten? yes
Make a new hundred? yes

3. 678 + 15 = 693

Make a new ten? yes
Make a new hundred? no

4. 635 + 92 = 727

Make a new ten? no
Make a new hundred? yes

5. 389 + 549 = 938

Make a new ten? yes
Make a new hundred? yes

6. 64 + 897 = 961

Make a new ten? yes
Make a new hundred? yes

UNIT 11 LESSON 12 Discuss 3-Digit Addition 243

Homework and Remembering page 243

11–12 Remembering **Goal:** Spiral Review

This Remembering activity would be appropriate anytime after today's lesson.

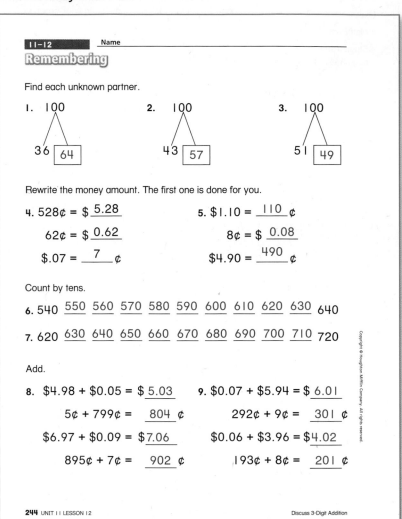

11–12 Remembering Name ____________

Find each unknown partner.

1. 100: 36 and 64
2. 100: 43 and 57
3. 100: 51 and 49

Rewrite the money amount. The first one is done for you.

4. 528¢ = $5.28
62¢ = $0.62
$.07 = 7¢

5. $1.10 = 110¢
8¢ = $0.08
$4.90 = 490¢

Count by tens.

6. 540 550 560 570 580 590 600 610 620 630 640

7. 620 630 640 650 660 670 680 690 700 710 720

Add.

8. $4.98 + $0.05 = $5.03
5¢ + 799¢ = 804¢
$6.97 + $0.09 = $7.06
895¢ + 7¢ = 902¢

9. $0.07 + $5.94 = $6.01
292¢ + 9¢ = 301¢
$0.06 + $3.96 = $4.02
193¢ + 8¢ = 201¢

244 UNIT 11 LESSON 12 Discuss 3-Digit Addition

Homework and Remembering page 244

Home or School Activity

Social Studies Connection

Round Trip Travel Discuss what is meant by the term *round trip.* Have students choose a city they would like to visit and locate it on a map. Students should research the distance between their hometown and the city they would like to visit. Then, have students calculate the total number of miles they would travel round trip from their hometown to their city of choice and back.

Boston to New York City
190 Miles

Round Trip

190 miles
+ 190 miles
380 miles

UNIT 11 LESSON 13

Story Problems: Unknown Addends

REAL WORLD Problem Solving

Lesson Objectives

- **Use the Adding Up Method to solve unknown partner exercises containing 3-digit numbers.**
- **Use the Adding Up Method to make change.**

Vocabulary

Adding Up Method
unknown partner

The Day at a Glance

Today's Goals	Materials	
1 Teaching the Lesson **A1:** Apply the Adding Up Method to exercises with 3-digit numbers. **A2:** Use the Adding Up Method to solve story problems containing 3-digit numbers. **A3:** Use the Adding Up Method to make change from five dollars. **2 Going Further** ▸ Differentiated Instruction **3 Homework and Targeted Practice**	**Lesson Activities** Student Activity Book pp. 371–372 Homework and Remembering pp. 245–246 MathBoard materials Five-Dollar Bills Dollar Bills Real or play money Small box labeled *Cash Register* Sticky board (optional) Quick Quiz 3 (Assessment Guide)	**Going Further** Activity Cards 11-13 MathBoard materials Five-Dollar Bills Dollar Bills Real or play money Index cards Math Journals

123 Use Math Talk today!

Keeping Skills Sharp

Quick Practice — 5 MINUTES

Goal: Find the addition rule for a function table.

What's My Rule? Have a **Student Leader** draw the table shown at the right, on the board. Then have children use the filled-in numbers to figure out the rule. $n + 6$ The Student Leader then completes the rule by writing the number 6 in the mystery box. Have children say the numbers that will complete the table as another Student Leader writes them in the function table. (See Unit 11 Lesson 11.)

n	*n* + ☐
8	14
15	21
9	15
72	78
78	84
47	53

Repeated Quick Practice
Use this Quick Practice from a previous lesson.

▸ **Money Strings** (See Unit 9 Lesson 11.)

Daily Routines

Making Change and Counting Coins Making Change from $5.00, Combining Coins and Counting Money (See pp. xxvii–xxviii.)

▸ Led by Student Leaders

Money Routine Using the 120 Poster, Using the Money Flip Chart, Using the Number Path, Using Secret Code Cards (See pp. xxiii–xxv.)

▸ Led by Student Leaders

1 Teaching the Lesson

Activity 1

Add Up to Find Unknown Partners

20 MINUTES

Goal: Apply the Adding Up Method to exercises with 3-digit numbers.

Materials: MathBoard materials

NCTM Standards:
Number and Operations
Communication

Class Management

Have children take notes on the different ways to apply the Adding Up Method to exercises where both numbers are three digits. They can choose the method they like best or take notes about all of the methods.

English Language Learners

Write 812 + 188 = 1,000 on the board. Ask: **Is 1,000 a partner?** no **Are 812 and 188 partners?** yes Replace 188 with □.

- **Beginning** Say: **Now one partner is *unknown*.** Have children point to the □ and repeat.
- **Intermediate** Say: **Now we do not know one partner.** Ask: **Is it an *unknown partner*?** yes
- **Advanced** Say: **Now we only know one partner.** Point and say: **The other partner is __.** unknown

▶ Adding Up Method WHOLE CLASS

Math Talk

Write the problem shown below, on the board. Have a volunteer read it aloud to the class.

Main School has 734 children.
156 children walk to school.
The rest take the bus.
How many children take the bus?

- What kind of problem is this? unknown partner problem
- What's a way to show this problem? write an equation, draw a Math Mountain

Ask children to come to the board to show the problem.

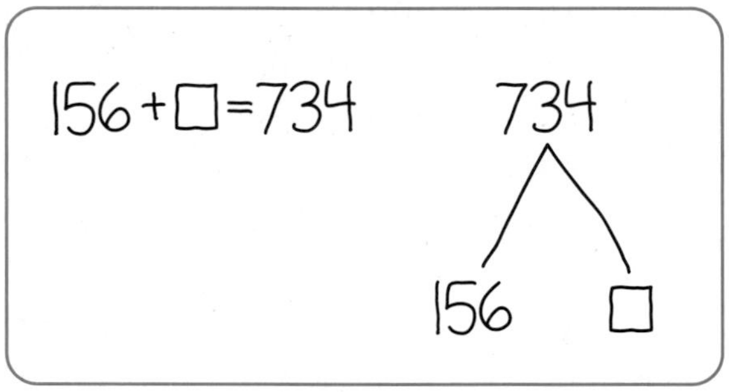

Review the Adding Up Method for finding unknown partners that children learned in Unit 9, Lessons 15 and 16.

- Who can tell me how we add up to find an unknown partner? We add to the next ten, then add to the total. Or, we add to the next ten, then add to the next hundred, and then add to the total.

Have several children work at the board to find the unknown partner using the Adding Up Method, while the rest of the children work at their seats. Have children share their solutions.

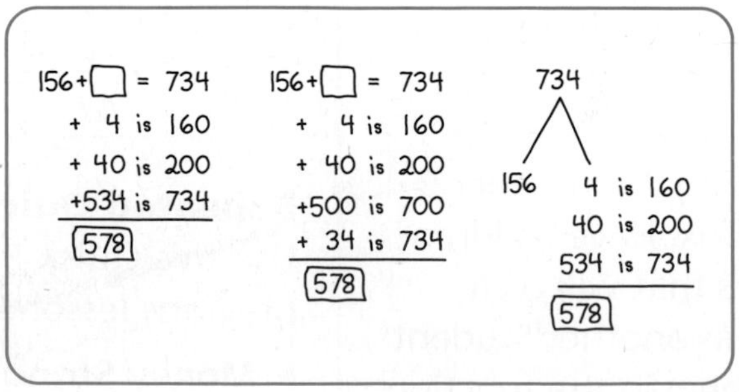

Activity 2

Story Problems with Unknown Partners

11–13
Class Activity

Name ____________________

▶ **Adding Up to Solve Story Problems**

Solve each story problem. **Show your work.**

1. Mr. Cruz planted 750 yams to sell. After he sold some, he had 278 yams left. How many yams did he sell?

   472 yams (label)

2. Last year there were 692 houses in our town. This year some new houses were built. Now there are 976 houses. How many new houses were built this year?

   284 houses (label)

3. Delia had 524 rocks in her collection. She gave some to her sister. Then she had 462 rocks. How many rocks did she give away?

   62 rocks (label)

4. On Saturday, 703 people went to a movie. 194 went in the afternoon. The rest went in the evening. How many people went in the evening?

   509 people (label)

5. **On the Back** Write a story problem with the answer **235 seashells.**
   Check children's work.

UNIT 11 LESSON 13 — Story Problems: Unknown Addends **371**

Student Activity Book page 371

▶ Adding Up to Solve Story Problems

PAIRS

Math Talk 123

Have children work in **Helping Pairs** to solve the story problems on Student Activity Book page 371.

Invite volunteers to share the story problems they wrote for exercise 5.

20 MINUTES

Goal: Use the Adding Up Method to solve story problems containing 3-digit numbers.

Materials: Student Activity Book pages 371–372

✓ **NCTM Standard:**
Number and Operations

The Learning Classroom

Helping Community As the class completes the page, work at the board with children who are having difficulty. You may also wish to have Student Helpers help children as well.

Ongoing Assessment

Have the children show how to use the Adding Up Method to find the following unknown addends.

- ▶ 358 + ☐ = 405
- ▶ 435 + ☐ = 558
- ▶ 124 + ☐ = 353

1 Teaching the Lesson (continued)

Activity 3

Connect to Making Change

15 MINUTES

Goal: Use the Adding Up Method to make change from five dollars.

Materials: Five-Dollar Bill, Dollar Bills, real or play money (4 quarters, 10 dimes, 10 nickels, 10 pennies), small box labeled *Cash Register*, sticky board (optional)

NCTM Standard:
Number and Operations

Differentiated Instruction

Extra Help If you find that some children have difficulty with counting up to $5.00, modify the activity using a one-dollar bill.

Advanced Learners On the other hand, if you find that some children finish quickly and need more of a challenge, modify the activity using a ten-dollar bill.

Quick Quiz

See Assessment Guide for Unit 11 Quick Quiz 3.

▶ Make Change WHOLE CLASS

Place 5 one-dollar bills, 4 quarters, 10 dimes, 10 nickels, and 10 pennies in a small box labeled *Cash Register.* Then ask for two volunteers to come to the front of the class to show how to make change from $5.00.

If you have a Sticky Board, the Seller can use it to display each coin or bill as it is counted.

Give one child, the *Buyer,* a $5 bill and have that child pretend that he or she is buying something that costs $2.37. (Write this amount on the board.) Have the other child, the *Seller,* give back the correct change to the Buyer. Have the Seller count out the change by adding up from the purchase price of $2.37 to get to $5.00.

The Seller gives: 

The Seller says: $2.38 $2.39 $2.40 $2.50 $2.75 $3.00 $4.00 $5.00

After the change has been given, children should count the change and add the purchase price to the change to check that the total is $5.00.

Then ask two more volunteers to come to the front of the class to repeat the activity. This time have the purchase price be $3.58. (Write this amount on the board.) Remind the Seller to add up from the purchase price in order to count out the change. Once again encourage children to count the change and add the purchase price and the change to check that it totals $5.00.

The Seller gives: 

The Seller says: $3.59 $3.60 $3.70 $3.75 $4.00 $5.00

Have different volunteers repeat the activity using different purchase prices, as time permits. You could also have children work in pairs and act out their own shopping situation.

2 Going Further

Differentiated Instruction

Intervention

Activity Card 11-13

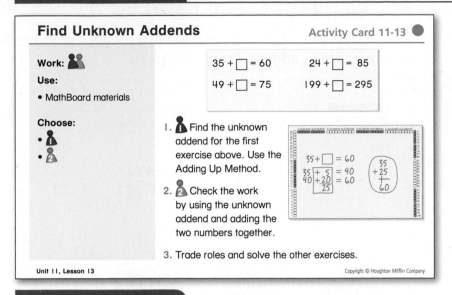

Find Unknown Addends

Activity Card 11-13

Work: (pairs)

Use:

- MathBoard materials

Choose:

- 1
- 2

35 + □ = 60	24 + □ = 85
49 + □ = 75	199 + □ = 295

1. (1) Find the unknown addend for the first exercise above. Use the Adding Up Method.
2. (2) Check the work by using the unknown addend and adding the two numbers together.

35 + □ = 60
35 + 5 = 40
40 + 20 = 60
25

35
+25
60

3. Trade roles and solve the other exercises.

Unit 11, Lesson 13

Activity Note Each pair needs MathBoard materials. Have children check each other's work.

Math Writing Prompt

Number Sense Suppose you have a five-dollar bill. Will you get more change if you buy something for $1.75 or $1.25? Explain your thinking.

Soar to Success Math **Software Support**

Warm Up 10.34

On Level

Activity Card 11-13

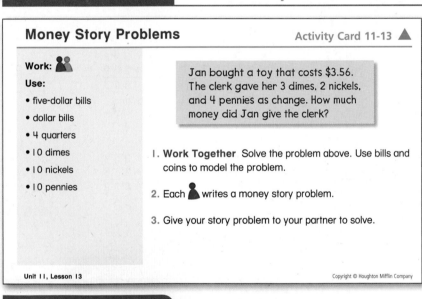

Money Story Problems

Activity Card 11-13

Work: (pairs)

Use:

- five-dollar bills
- dollar bills
- 4 quarters
- 10 dimes
- 10 nickels
- 10 pennies

Jan bought a toy that costs $3.56. The clerk gave her 3 dimes, 2 nickels, and 4 pennies as change. How much money did Jan give the clerk?

1. **Work Together** Solve the problem above. Use bills and coins to model the problem.
2. Each (person) writes a money story problem.
3. Give your story problem to your partner to solve.

Unit 11, Lesson 13

Activity Note Each pair needs five-dollar bills, dollar bills, and real or play quarters, dimes, nickels, and pennies.

Math Writing Prompt

Write About It Carla bought a toy with a five-dollar bill. The toy cost $4.74. What is the least number of coins Carla could get back as change?

HARCOURT MEGA MATH Grades K-6 **Software Support**

Numberopolis: Lulu's Lunch Counter, Level Q

Challenge

Activity Card 11-13

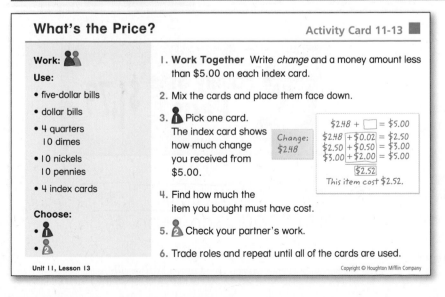

What's the Price?

Activity Card 11-13

Work: (pairs)

Use:

- five-dollar bills
- dollar bills
- 4 quarters
  10 dimes
- 10 nickels
  10 pennies
- 4 index cards

Choose:

- 1
- 2

1. **Work Together** Write *change* and a money amount less than $5.00 on each index card.
2. Mix the cards and place them face down.
3. (1) Pick one card. The index card shows how much change you received from $5.00.

Change: $2.48

$2.48 + □ = $5.00
$2.48 + $0.02 = $2.50
$2.50 + $0.50 = $3.00
$3.00 + $2.00 = $5.00
$2.52
This item cost $2.52.

4. Find how much the item you bought must have cost.
5. (2) Check your partner's work.
6. Trade roles and repeat until all of the cards are used.

Unit 11, Lesson 13

Activity Note Each pair needs five-dollar bills, dollar bills, real or play money, and index cards.

Math Writing Prompt

Explain Your Thinking Al bought a game that costs $3.68. He gave the clerk $4.00. The clerk gave him 4 coins back as change. What coins did Al get back? Explain.

DESTINATION Math **Software Support**

Course II: Module 3: Unit 1: Money

3 Homework and Targeted Practice

11–13 Homework **Goal:** Additional Practice

This Homework page provides practice adding 2-digit and 3-digit numbers.

11–13 Homework Name ____________

Add. Use any method.

1. 114 + 286 = 400
   Make a new ten? Yes
   Make a new hundred? Yes

2. 207 + 595 = 802
   Make a new ten? Yes
   Make a new hundred? Yes

3. 68 + 393 = 461
   Make a new ten? Yes
   Make a new hundred? Yes

4. 457 + 72 = 529
   Make a new ten? No
   Make a new hundred? Yes

5. 328 + 235 = 563
   Make a new ten? Yes
   Make a new hundred? No

6. 549 + 326 = 875
   Make a new ten? Yes
   Make a new hundred? No

UNIT 11 LESSON 13 Story Problems: Unknown Addends 245

Homework and Remembering page 245

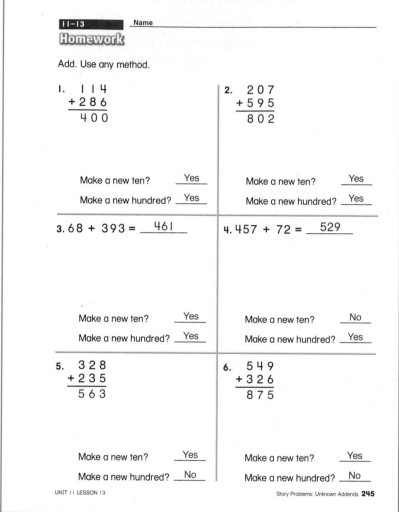

11–13 Targeted Practice **Goal:** Practice addition.

This Targeted Practice can be used with children who need extra practice in adding 3-digit numbers.

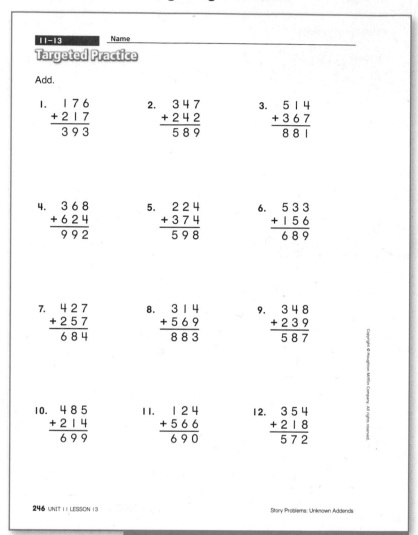

11–13 Targeted Practice Name ____________

Add.

1. 176 + 217 = 393
2. 347 + 242 = 589
3. 514 + 367 = 881
4. 368 + 624 = 992
5. 224 + 374 = 598
6. 533 + 156 = 689
7. 427 + 257 = 684
8. 314 + 569 = 883
9. 348 + 239 = 587
10. 485 + 214 = 699
11. 124 + 566 = 690
12. 354 + 218 = 572

246 UNIT 11 LESSON 13 Story Problems: Unknown Addends

Homework and Remembering page 246

Home or School Activity

Real-World Connection

Buying Groceries Have children look through grocery store ads and find three items that each cost less than $5.00. Tell them to cut out each ad and glue it on a piece of paper.

Have children find the change they would receive if they bought each item with a five-dollar bill. Have them draw a picture of the coins they would get back from the clerk and to write money amounts under the coins to show how to add up from the purchase price to find the correct change.

(P) (D) (D) [$1] [$1] [$1] = $3.21

$1.80 $1.90 $2.00 $3.00 $4.00 $5.00

UNIT 11 LESSON 14

Story Problems with Hundreds Numbers

REAL WORLD Problem Solving

Vocabulary

ungroup
situation equation
solution equation

Lesson Objective

- Create and solve story problems involving 3-digit subtraction.

The Day at a Glance

Today's Goals	Materials	
1 Teaching the Lesson **A1:** Practice subtraction (totals ≤ 18). **A2:** Solve story problems involving 3-digit subtraction. **A3:** Create story problems to match 3-digit subtraction exercises.	**Lesson Activities** Student Activity Book pp. 373–376 (includes Family Letter) Homework and Remembering pp. 247–248 MathBoard materials Base ten blocks	**Going Further** Activity Cards 11-14 Base ten blocks Secret Code Cards Symbol Cards (TRB M45) Math Journals
2 Going Further ▸ Differentiated Instruction		
3 Homework and Spiral Review		

Use Math Talk today!

Keeping Skills Sharp

Quick Practice — 5 MINUTES

Goals: Write money strings for specific money amounts. Find the addition rule for a function table.

Money Strings As children are doing the Quick Practice activity below, have two or three children write money strings for amounts between five and ten dollars on the board. At the end of Quick Practice, have the class quickly check that the money strings are correct. (See Unit 9 Lesson 11.)

What's My Rule? Have a **Student Leader** draw the table shown at the right, on the board. Then have children figure out the rule for the function table. *n* − 12 The Student Leader then completes the rule by writing the number 12 in the mystery box. Have children say the numbers that will complete the table as another Student Leader writes them in the function table. (See Unit 11 Lesson 11.)

n	$n - \square$
30	18
15	3
74	62
301	289
91	79
211	199

Daily Routines

Making Change and Counting Coins Making Change from $5.00, Combining Coins and Counting Money (See pp. xxvii–xxviii.)

▸ Led by Student Leaders

Money Routine Using the 120 Poster, Using the Money Flip Chart, Using the Number Path, Using Secret Code Cards (See pp. xxiii–xxv.)

▸ Led by Student Leaders

1 Teaching the Lesson

Activity 1

Subtraction Sprint

10 MINUTES

Goal: Practice subtraction (totals ≤ 18).

Materials: Student Activity Book page 373

NCTM Standard:
Number and Operations

Differentiated Instruction

Extra Help Some children may have difficulty finding the differences. Remind children to use strategies such as counting on and making a ten.

English Language Learners

Write *solution equation, situation equation*, 137 + 273 = ☐, and 137 + ☐ = 400 on the board.

- **Beginning** Point and say: **This tells us what to do.** Ask: **Is this a *solution equation*.** yes Continue with *situation equation*.
- **Intermediate** Have children point to the correct equation. Ask: **Which equation tells us what to do? Is that a *solution* equation or *situation* equation?** solution
- **Advanced** Have children identify each equation and tell the difference.

11–14 Class Activity Name ______________________

► Subtraction Sprint

7 − 4 = 3	10 − 6 = 4	17 − 9 = 8
13 − 5 = 8	15 − 9 = 6	6 − 4 = 2
9 − 3 = 6	11 − 3 = 8	10 − 7 = 3
11 − 2 = 9	18 − 9 = 9	13 − 9 = 4
8 − 6 = 2	8 − 4 = 4	12 − 5 = 7
12 − 9 = 3	9 − 7 = 2	16 − 8 = 8
6 − 3 = 3	13 − 6 = 7	14 − 7 = 7
15 − 7 = 8	12 − 3 = 9	10 − 6 = 4
10 − 8 = 2	16 − 7 = 9	8 − 5 = 3
8 − 3 = 5	7 − 5 = 2	11 − 9 = 2
14 − 5 = 9	12 − 4 = 8	13 − 7 = 6
11 − 7 = 4	17 − 8 = 9	14 − 8 = 6
10 − 4 = 6	9 − 4 = 5	10 − 5 = 5
12 − 8 = 4	14 − 8 = 6	12 − 6 = 6
16 − 9 = 7	11 − 4 = 7	15 − 7 = 8
14 − 6 = 8	9 − 6 = 3	13 − 6 = 7
9 − 5 = 4	12 − 7 = 5	11 − 8 = 3
13 − 9 = 4	14 − 9 = 5	12 − 3 = 9
10 − 3 = 7	13 − 4 = 9	13 − 5 = 8
15 − 8 = 7	7 − 3 = 4	15 − 6 = 9
11 − 5 = 6	11 − 6 = 5	13 − 8 = 5

UNIT 11 LESSON 14 Subtraction Sprint 373

Student Activity Book page 373

► Subtraction Sprint INDIVIDUALS

Direct children's attention to Student Activity Book page 373. Decide how much time to give them to complete the Sprint. Explain the procedure and time limit to them.

Activity 2

Solve Subtraction Problems

▶ Discuss Subtraction Problems WHOLE CLASS

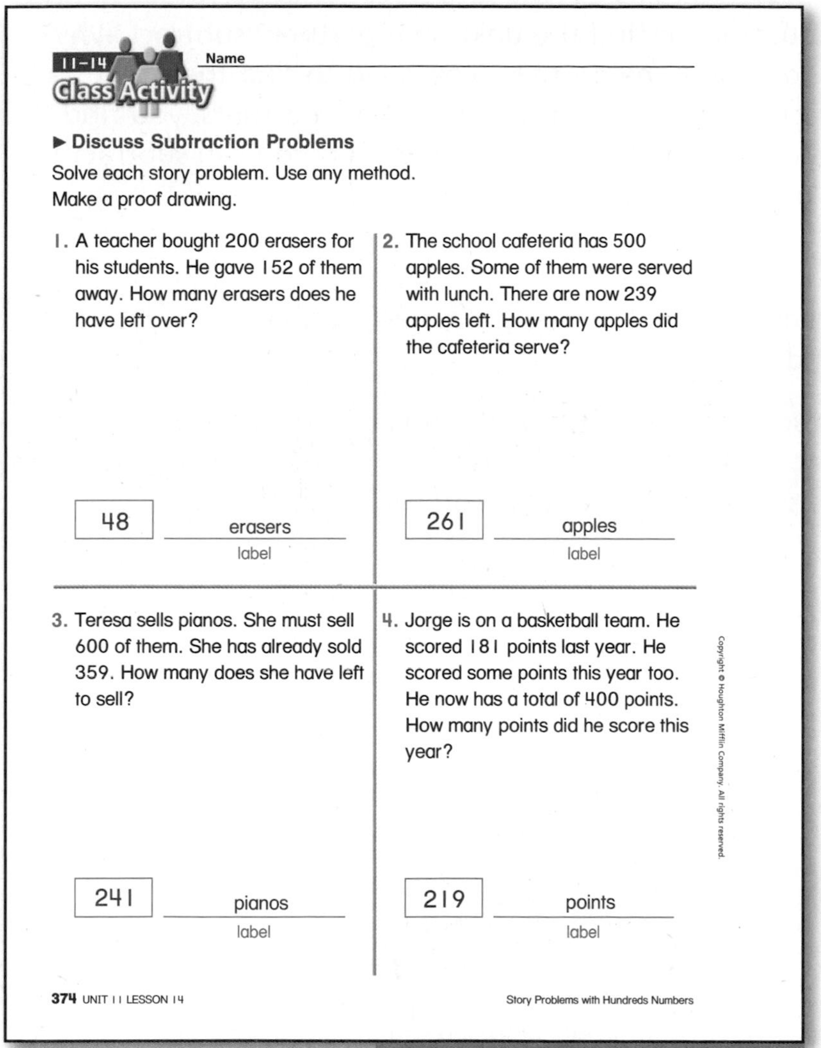
11–14 Class Activity

Name ______________________

▶ Discuss Subtraction Problems

Solve each story problem. Use any method.
Make a proof drawing.

1. A teacher bought 200 erasers for his students. He gave 152 of them away. How many erasers does he have left over?

48 erasers (label)

2. The school cafeteria has 500 apples. Some of them were served with lunch. There are now 239 apples left. How many apples did the cafeteria serve?

261 apples (label)

3. Teresa sells pianos. She must sell 600 of them. She has already sold 359. How many does she have left to sell?

241 pianos (label)

4. Jorge is on a basketball team. He scored 181 points last year. He scored some points this year too. He now has a total of 400 points. How many points did he score this year?

219 points (label)

Copyright © Houghton Mifflin Company. All rights reserved.

374 UNIT 11 LESSON 14 Story Problems with Hundreds Numbers

Student Activity Book page 374

Read aloud, or ask a volunteer to read aloud, the first problem on Student Activity Book page 374. Ask volunteers to write an equation that shows the problem situation and draw a Math Mountain that shows the situation. Be sure they draw the plus and minus signs.

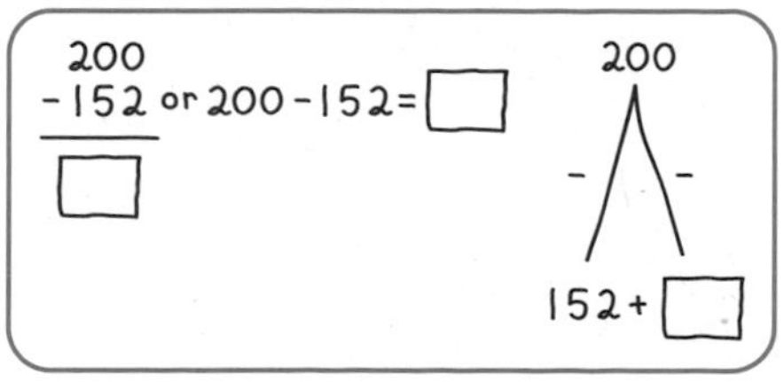

Activity continued ▶

🕒 **30 MINUTES**

Goal: Solve story problems involving 3-digit subtraction.

Materials: Student Activity Book page 374, MathBoard materials, base ten blocks

✔ **NCTM Standards:**
Number and Operations
Algebra
Problem Solving
Representation

The Learning Classroom

Building Concepts Experimenting with various methods for subtracting 3-digit numbers helps children to build skills by using ideas that make sense to them. Children are already familiar with Math Mountains and finding unknown partners. They may use what they know about addends and sums to understand the numbers they are finding in subtraction.

Class Management

Children will not be required to use only one formal method of subtracting 3-digit numbers. Encourage children to use and adapt all workable methods that consistently result in a correct answer.

Alternate Approach

Base Ten Blocks Children who have difficulty with visual-motor ability may have difficulty with ungrouping a number and maintaining the equivalent hundreds, tens, and ones. Have the children use base ten blocks to do the ungrouping. When children have finished ungrouping, encourage them to double-check that their hundreds, tens, and ones are still equal to the original number.

Math Talk Discuss the problem with the class.

- What are you looking for in the problem? an unknown partner
- How do you know that's what you need to find? The Math Mountain shows us; the problem tells us.
- Do you add or subtract to find the unknown partner? subtract Why? You know the total and one partner. You need to find the other partner. You subtract to find it. When you add the 2 partners, you find the total. When you know the total and one partner, you can subtract to find the other partner.
- What are some ways you subtract?

Encourage children to suggest as many ways as possible. See next page for sample methods.

Invite children to solve the problem at the board while the rest of the children solve it at their seats. Tell children they can use any of the strategies, but be sure each strategy is represented at the board.

Boxes, Sticks, and Circles

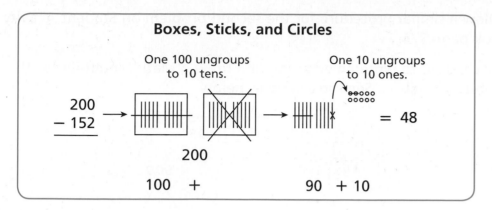

One 100 ungroups to 10 tens.

One 10 ungroups to 10 ones.

$$\begin{array}{r} 200 \\ -\ 152 \\ \hline \end{array}$$

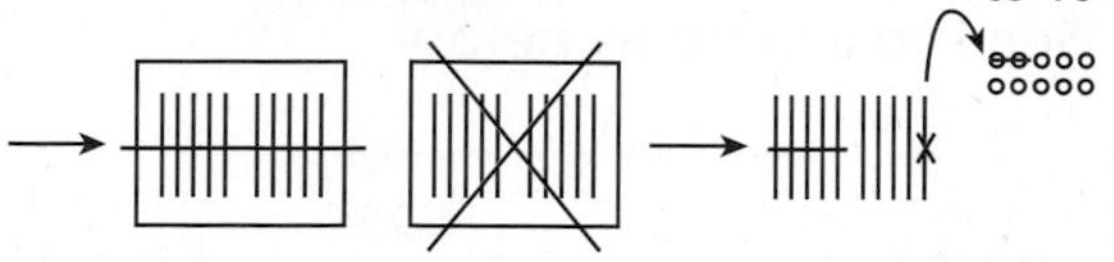

= 48

200

100 + 90 + 10

Ungroup First Method

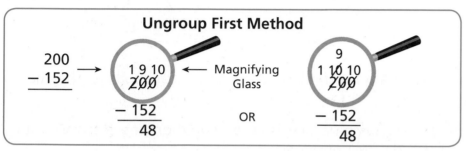

$$\begin{array}{r} 200 \\ -\ 152 \\ \hline \end{array}$$

1 9 10
~~200~~
− 152
48

← Magnifying Glass

OR

9
1 ~~10~~ 10
~~200~~
− 152
48

Expanded Method

$$\begin{array}{rcl} & & \quad\ \ 100 \quad \overset{90}{\cancel{100}} \quad 10 \\ 200 = 200 + 0 + 0 & = & \cancel{200} + 0 + \cancel{0} \\ -\ 152 = 100 + 50 + 2 & = & 100 + 50 + 2 \\ \hline & & 40 + 8 = 48 \end{array}$$

Adding Up Method

$152 + 8 = 160$

$160 + 40 = 200$

48

Secret Code Cards

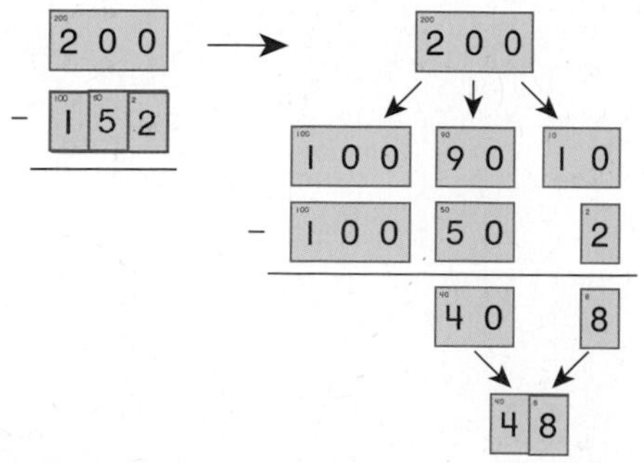

Have the children at the board explain their work. See **Math Talk in Action** for possible classroom dialogue.

Activity continued ▶

Teaching Note

Language and Vocabulary The word *ungroup* is helpful to children for subtraction by giving them a visual of the concept that a number is being "unwrapped." Children may encounter the word *regroup* since some programs use the term *regroup* for both addition and subtraction. Let them know that *regroup* means *ungroup,* and it can also mean *group* in addition.

Math Talk in Action

Lilia, can you explain how you used boxes, sticks, and circles to ungroup 200 in order to subtract 152?

Lilia: I took one hundred and ungrouped it to 10 tens. Then I took one ten and ungrouped it to 10 ones. And I did the same in my problem.

Please show us your ungrouping in your problem.

Lilia: Here I crossed out the 2 hundreds and wrote 1 hundred. I knew 1 hundred is 9 tens and 10 ones so I crossed out the 0 tens and 0 ones. Then I wrote above the 9 tens and 10 ones I have now.

Very good. Does the value of the number change when you ungroup?

Lilia: No. It's the same number.

Yes. Now how did you subtract 152?

Lilia: I crossed out 1 hundred. I crossed out 5 tens. I crossed out 2 ones. That leaves 4 tens and 8 ones. I did it in my drawing and in my problem. I like to subtract left to right like reading.

❶ Teaching the Lesson (continued)

Follow a similar procedure for the second problem on Student Activity Book page 374.

Ask children to write an equation and draw a Math Mountain for the problem situation. See the examples below.

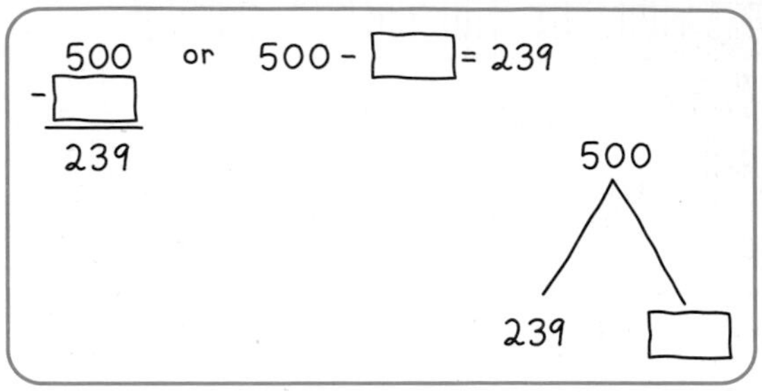

Draw your equation and Math Mountain on the board if they have been erased.

Ask children to compare this situation equation and Math Mountain to the ones for the first problem.

Be sure children understand that these problems are both solved by subtracting.

- Do the situation equations look the same for the first 2 problems? no
- What is different in each one? The unknown number is in a different place for each one.
- Do the Math Mountains look the same? yes, except for the numbers
- How can you solve this problem? the same way you solved the first problem, by subtracting to find an unknown addend

Teaching Note

Math Background If a word problem is directly translated into an equation, that equation is called a **situation equation.** For example, $500 - \square = 239$ is a situation equation for problem 2. A **solution equation** reflects the operation that can be used to solve a problem. For example, $500 - 239 = \square$ is the solution equation for problem 2.

Situation equations are vital to problem solving. Children naturally write situation equations for addition and subtraction problems with unknown partners or totals. For small numbers, this is all they need. For these larger multi-digit numbers, many will need to rewrite their situation equation or Math Mountain as a vertical subtraction example.

The Learning Classroom

Math Talk Children can work in pairs to role-play the problem situations on Student Activity Book page 374. Children can model the action in the story as they try to find the appropriate operation and solution to the problem.

▶ Solve and Discuss WHOLE CLASS

Math Talk

Have several children solve the remaining problems on Student Activity Book page 374 on the board while the class solves them at their seats.

When the answers are determined, children compare the solutions on the board and ask questions of the solvers.

Using the **Solve and Discuss** structure, invite one or two children to the board to explain their solution methods. As always, explanations need to include hundreds, tens, and ones language. Children match their drawings (made with boxes, sticks, and circles) to the numeric problem. Encourage the class to compare the solution methods and ask questions.

Children can point out how the different solutions lead to the same answer. For the Expanded and Ungrouping First methods, the top number is rewritten because it does not have enough of either tens or ones. For the Adding Up method, the top number does not need to be rewritten, but new tens and ones are made when they are added up.

Remind children to draw a "magnifying glass" around the top number to show how it can be opened up to reveal the hundreds, tens, and ones.

The Learning Classroom

Building Concepts *Math Expressions* did subtraction to 200 earlier, and not just to 100 as many programs do, to give children experience with ungrouping 100 to make 10 tens as well as ungrouping 1 ten to make 10 ones. This makes the step to 3-digit subtraction much simpler for children. The only new thing they need to learn is subtracting the hundreds, which is easy.

Ongoing Assessment

Ask questions such as the following:

- ▶ When you ungroup a number, what are you preparing the number for?
- ▶ When you are adding up, what do you do to make sure you have the correct unknown partner?

Activity 3

Tell and Solve Story Problems

15 MINUTES

Goal: Create story problems to match 3-digit subtraction exercises.

Materials: MathBoard materials

NCTM Standards:
Number and Operations
Problem Solving

► Create Story Problems from Subtraction Exercises INDIVIDUALS

Math Talk

Ask for Ideas Be sure children have their MathBoards. They may work individually or in **Helping Pairs** to create story problems from the subtraction exercises shown below. Ask children to turn these numeric exercises into story problems. An example is shown.

$$\begin{array}{r} 500 \\ -\,347 \\ \hline 153 \end{array}$$

Alisha makes deep-dish and thin-crust pizzas. She made 500 pizzas last week. 347 of them were thin crust. The rest were deep dish. How many were deep dish?

$$\begin{array}{r} 600 \\ -\,259 \\ \hline 341 \end{array}$$

$$\begin{array}{r} 800 \\ -\,673 \\ \hline 127 \end{array}$$

$$\begin{array}{r} 700 \\ -\,418 \\ \hline 282 \end{array}$$

$$\begin{array}{r} 600 \\ -\,165 \\ \hline 435 \end{array}$$

You may wish to work with small groups of children who are having difficulty. Invite these children to create a problem in which the action involves separating a part from a whole. Then have the children find the answers by using the **Step-By-Step at the Board** structure, in which children take turns determining and describing each step needed in a process.

2 Going Further

Differentiated Instruction

Intervention — Activity Card 11-14

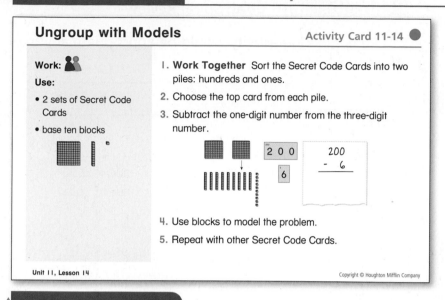

Ungroup with Models — Activity Card 11-14

Work: (pairs)

Use:
- 2 sets of Secret Code Cards
- base ten blocks

1. **Work Together** Sort the Secret Code Cards into two piles: hundreds and ones.
2. Choose the top card from each pile.
3. Subtract the one-digit number from the three-digit number.

200
\- 6

4. Use blocks to model the problem.
5. Repeat with other Secret Code Cards.

Unit 11, Lesson 14

Activity Note Each pair needs base ten blocks (9 hundreds, 9 tens, and 10 ones) and Secret Code Cards 1-9 and 100-900 (TRB M3-M6).

Math Writing Prompt

Draw a Picture Jen drew boxes, sticks, and circles to find the answer for 200 − 140 and 200 − 143. For which exercise did Jen use more steps to find the answer? Draw a picture to explain.

Soar to Success Math **Software Support**

Warm Up 11.27

On Level — Activity Card 11-14

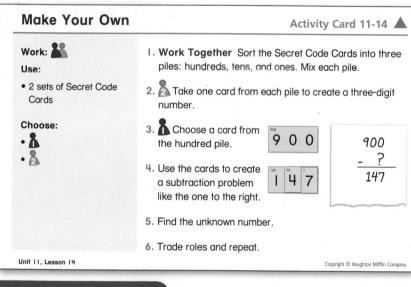

Make Your Own — Activity Card 11-14

Work: (pairs)

Use:
- 2 sets of Secret Code Cards

Choose:
- 1
- 2

1. **Work Together** Sort the Secret Code Cards into three piles: hundreds, tens, and ones. Mix each pile.
2. (2) Take one card from each pile to create a three-digit number.
3. (1) Choose a card from the hundred pile.
4. Use the cards to create a subtraction problem like the one to the right.

900
\- ?
147

5. Find the unknown number.
6. Trade roles and repeat.

Unit 11, Lesson 14

Activity Note Each pair needs two sets of Secret Code Cards 1-900 (TRB M3-M6). Point out that the three-digit number is the answer.

Math Writing Prompt

Use Two Strategies Solve 400 − 253 = ___. Use two different methods and show your work. Which method do you like better? Tell why.

Harcourt Mega Math Grades K-6 **Software Support**

Country Countdown: Block Busters, Level X

Challenge — Activity Card 11-14

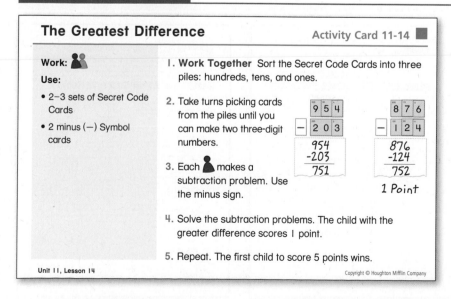

The Greatest Difference — Activity Card 11-14

Work: (pairs)

Use:
- 2–3 sets of Secret Code Cards
- 2 minus (−) Symbol cards

1. **Work Together** Sort the Secret Code Cards into three piles: hundreds, tens, and ones.
2. Take turns picking cards from the piles until you can make two three-digit numbers.
3. Each (child) makes a subtraction problem. Use the minus sign.

954 − 203 = 751

876 − 124 = 752 — 1 Point

4. Solve the subtraction problems. The child with the greater difference scores 1 point.
5. Repeat. The first child to score 5 points wins.

Unit 11, Lesson 14

Activity Note Each pair needs three sets of Secret Code Cards 1-900 (TRB M3-M6) and two minus signs (TRB M45).

Math Writing Prompt

Compare and Contrast Explain how ungrouping with hundreds, tens, and ones, is like making change with dollar bills, dimes, and pennies. How are the amounts different?

Destination Math **Software Support**

Course II: Module 2: Unit 1: Estimating and Finding Differences within 1,000

3 Homework and Spiral Review

11–14 Homework **Goal:** Additional Practice

This Homework page provides practice in solving 3-digit subtraction story problems..

11–14 Homework   Name ____________

Solve the story problems. Use your favorite method.
Make a Proof Drawing if it helps.

1. Ricardo likes olives. He had 100 olives. He ate 43 of them. How many olives does he have left?

   57 olives (label)

2. Dawn has 300 pennies in her piggy bank. She gave some to her sister. Now she has 147 left. How many pennies did Dawn give to her sister?

   153 pennies (label)

3. Tory sells hockey sticks to teams in her city. She had 500 and sold 353 to one team. How many hockey sticks does she have left to sell?

   147 hockey sticks (label)

4. Randy collects magnets. Over two years he collected 400 magnets. He collected 125 magnets the first year. How many did he collect the second year?

   275 magnets (label)

UNIT 11 LESSON 14   Story Problems with Hundreds Numbers **247**

Homework and Remembering page 247

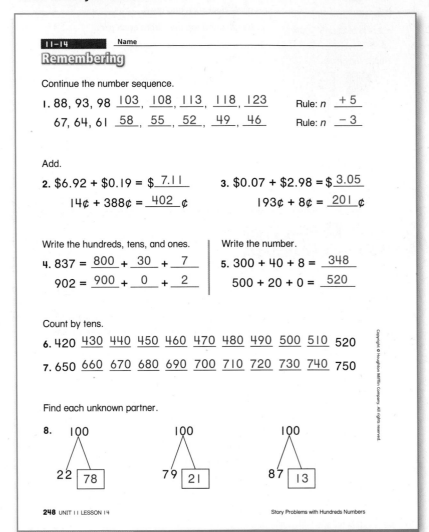

11–14 Remembering **Goal:** Spiral Review

This Remembering activity would be appropriate anytime after today's lesson.

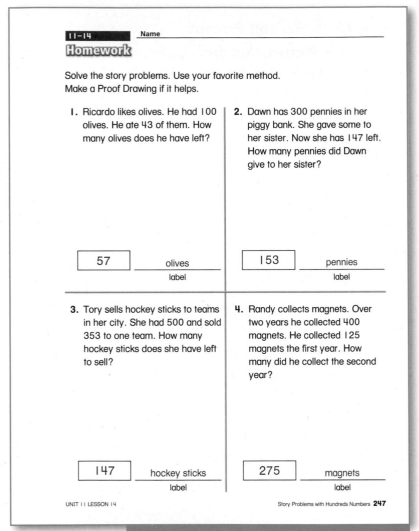

11–14 Remembering   Name ____________

Continue the number sequence.

1. 88, 93, 98, 103, 108, 113, 118, 123   Rule: n + 5
   67, 64, 61, 58, 55, 52, 49, 46   Rule: n − 3

Add.

2. \$6.92 + \$0.19 = \$7.11
   14¢ + 388¢ = 402¢
3. \$0.07 + \$2.98 = \$3.05
   193¢ + 8¢ = 201¢

Write the hundreds, tens, and ones.

4. 837 = 800 + 30 + 7
   902 = 900 + 0 + 2

Write the number.

5. 300 + 40 + 8 = 348
   500 + 20 + 0 = 520

Count by tens.

6. 420 430 440 450 460 470 480 490 500 510 520
7. 650 660 670 680 690 700 710 720 730 740 750

Find each unknown partner.

8. 100 → 22 and 78;   100 → 79 and 21;   100 → 87 and 13

248 UNIT 11 LESSON 14   Story Problems with Hundreds Numbers

Homework and Remembering page 248

Home and School Connection

Family Letter Have children take home the Family Letter on Student Activity Book page 375. This letter explains how the concept of subtracting 3-digit numbers is developed in *Math Expressions.* It gives parents and guardians a better understanding of the learning that goes on in math class and creates a bridge between school and home. A Spanish translation of this letter is on the following page in the Student Activity Book.

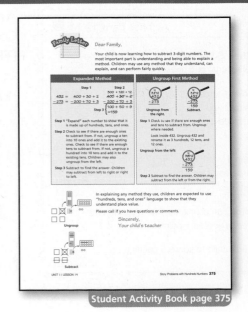

Family Letter

Dear Family,

Your child is now learning how to subtract 3-digit numbers. The most important part is understanding and being able to explain a method. Children may use any method that they understand, can explain, and can perform fairly quickly.

Expanded Method

Step 1: 432 = 400 + 30 + 2; −273 = −200 + 70 + 3
Step 2: 300 + 120 + 12
Step 3: 100 + 50 + 9 = 159

Step 1 "Expand" each number to show that it is made up of hundreds, tens, and ones.
Step 2 Check to see if there are enough ones to subtract from. If not, ungroup a ten into 10 ones and add it to the existing ones. Check to see if there are enough tens to subtract from. If not, ungroup a hundred into 10 tens and add it to the existing tens. Children may also ungroup from the left.
Step 3 Subtract to find the answer. Children may subtract from left to right or right to left.

Ungroup First Method

432 − 273: Ungroup from the right. / 432 − 273 = 159 Subtract.

Step 1 Check to see if there are enough ones and tens to subtract from. Ungroup where needed.
Look inside 432. Ungroup 432 and rename it as 3 hundreds, 12 tens, and 12 ones.
Ungroup from the left: 432 − 273 = 159
Step 2 Subtract to find the answer. Children may subtract from the left or from the right.

Ungroup / Subtract

In explaining any method they use, children are expected to use "hundreds, tens, and ones" language to show that they understand place value.

Please call if you have questions or comments.

Sincerely,
Your child's teacher

UNIT 11 LESSON 14   Story Problems with Hundreds Numbers 375

Student Activity Book page 375

Carta a la familia

Estimada familia:

Su niño está aprendiendo a restar números de 3 dígitos. Lo más importante es comprender y saber explicar un método. Los niños pueden usar cualquier método que comprendan, puedan explicar y puedan hacer relativamente rápido.

Método extendido

Paso 1: 432 = 400 + 30 + 2; −273 = −200 + 70 + 3
Paso 2: 300 + 120 + 12
Paso 3: 100 + 50 + 9 = 159

Paso 1 "Extender" cada número para mostrar que consta de centenas, decenas y unidades.
Paso 2 Observar si hay suficientes unidades para restar. Si no, desagrupar una decena para formar 10 unidades y sumarlas a las unidades existentes. Observar si hay suficientes decenas para restar. Si no, desagrupar una centena para formar 10 decenas y sumarlas a las decenas existentes. Los niños también pueden desagrupar por la izquierda.
Paso 3 Restar para hallar la respuesta. Los niños pueden restar de izquierda a derecha o de derecha a izquierda.

Método de desagrupar primero

432 − 273: Desagrupar por la derecha / 432 − 273 = 159 Restar

Paso 1 Observar si hay suficientes unidades y decenas para restar. Desagrupar cuando haga falta.
Mirar dentro de 432. Desagrupar 432 y volver a nombrarlo como 3 centenas, 12 decenas y 12 unidades.
Desagrupar por la izquierda: 432 − 273 = 159
Paso 2 Restar para hallar la respuesta. Los niños pueden restar empezando por la izquierda o por la derecha.

Desagrupar / Restar

Para explicar cualquier método que usen, los niños deben usar un lenguaje relacionado con centenas, decenas y unidades para demostrar que comprenden el valor posicional.

Si tiene alguna duda o comentario, por favor comuníquese conmigo.

Atentamente,
El maestro de su niño

376 UNIT 11 LESSON 14   Story Problems with Hundreds Numbers

Student Activity Book page 376

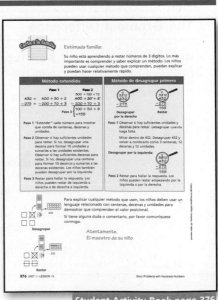

UNIT 11
LESSON 15

Subtract from Numbers with Zeros

Lesson Objectives

- Subtract 3-digit numbers with a zero in the ones or tens place of the top number.
- Create story problems involving 3-digit subtraction.

Vocabulary
ungroup

The Day at a Glance

Today's Goals	Materials	
1 Teaching the Lesson Represent, find the difference, and check subtraction exercises with zeros in the tens or ones place of the top number.	**Lesson Activities** Student Activity Book pp. 377–378 Homework and Remembering pp. 249–250 Secret Code Cards MathBoard materials	**Going Further** Activity Cards 11-15 Secret Code Cards Base ten blocks Game Cards Paper bags Markers or crayons Math Journals
2 Going Further ▶ Differentiated Instruction		
3 Homework and Targeted Practice		

Use Math Talk today!

Keeping Skills Sharp

Quick Practice — 5 MINUTES

Goal: Count a sequence of coins.

Materials: real or play money (quarters, dimes and pennies), sticky board (optional)

Count Coins Write a sequence of quarters, dimes, and pennies (Q, D, P) on the board or place coins on a sticky board.

Q Q D D P P P P P P

Point to each letter or coin and begin counting the money. Have the class count along with you. When you have finished, recount the money.

Add or erase some Qs, Ds, and Ps and repeat the activity.

Repeated Quick Practice
Use this Quick Practice from a previous lesson.

▶ **What's My Rule?** (See Unit 11 Lesson 13.)

n	$n - \boxed{3}$
7	4
16	13
92	89
338	335
104	101
102	99

Daily Routines

Making Change and Counting Coins Making Change from $5.00, Combining Coins and Counting Money
(See pp. xxvii–xxviii.)

▶ Led by Student Leaders

Money Routine Using the 120 Poster, Using the Money Flip Chart, Using the Number Path, Using Secret Code Cards
(See pp. xxiii–xxv.)

▶ Led by Student Leaders

1 Teaching the Lesson

Activity

Subtraction with One or More Zeros

55 MINUTES

Goal: Represent, find the difference, and check subtraction exercises with zeros in the tens or ones place of the top number.

Materials: Secret Code Cards 1–900, Student Activity Book page 377

NCTM Standards:
Number and Operations
Representation

Teaching Note

What to Expect from Students
Some children may have learned the traditional method of subtracting: ungroup the tens, rewrite the ones, and subtract the ones; then ungroup the hundreds and subtract the tens; and finally, subtract the hundreds. This method of ungrouping one place at a time is similar to our Ungroup First Method; however, it is more prone to error, partly because children forget where they are in the process. If children insist on subtracting in this more traditional way, permit them to do so, but ask them to try the other methods so they can compare which works best. Now that children are subtracting 3-digit numbers, the advantages of ungrouping everything first should be more evident than it was when they were doing 2-digit subtraction.

Ungroup first.

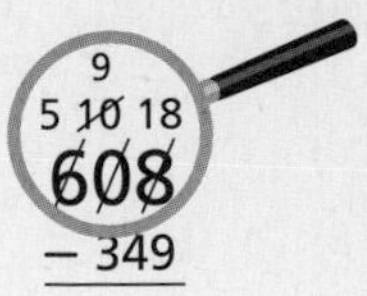

Then subtract.

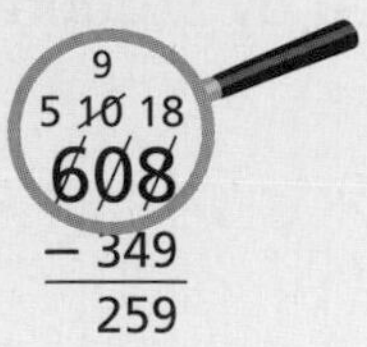

► Represent a Subtraction Exercise WHOLE CLASS

Note that each exercise on Student Activity Book page 377 has a zero in either the ones place, the tens place, or both, so children must ungroup once or twice. Write the first exercise on the board. Let children draw a Math Mountain to show the exercise.

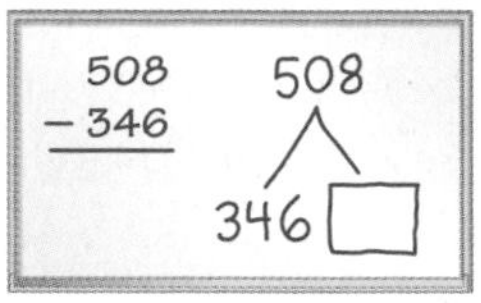

Have a volunteer draw the top number on the board with boxes, sticks, and circles.

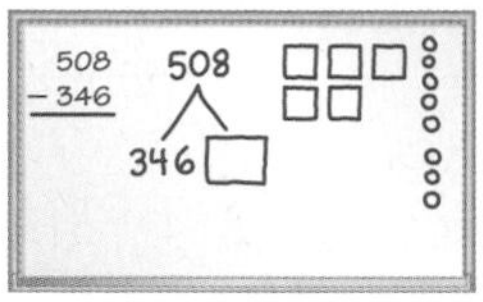

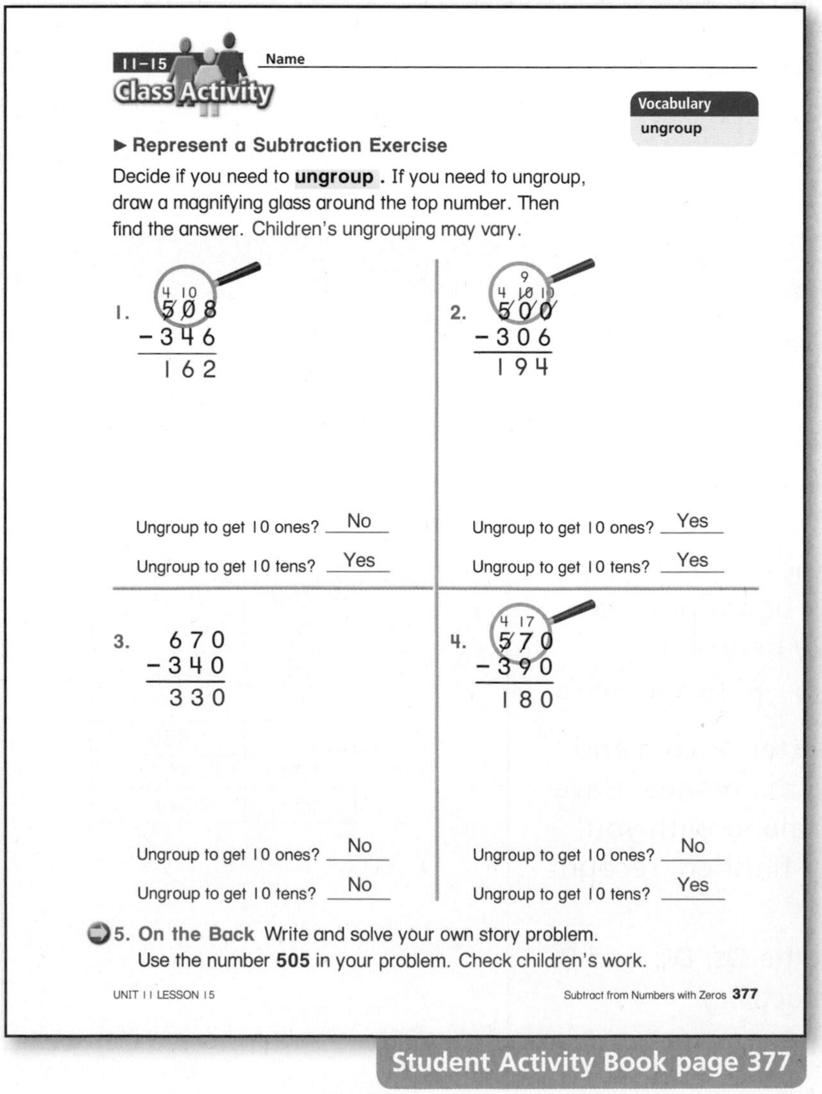

11-15 Class Activity   Name

Vocabulary
ungroup

► Represent a Subtraction Exercise

Decide if you need to **ungroup**. If you need to ungroup, draw a magnifying glass around the top number. Then find the answer. Children's ungrouping may vary.

1. 508 − 346 = 162 (4 10)
Ungroup to get 10 ones? No
Ungroup to get 10 tens? Yes

2. 500 − 306 = 194 (4 10 10, 9)
Ungroup to get 10 ones? Yes
Ungroup to get 10 tens? Yes

3. 670 − 340 = 330
Ungroup to get 10 ones? No
Ungroup to get 10 tens? No

4. 570 − 390 = 180 (4 17)
Ungroup to get 10 ones? No
Ungroup to get 10 tens? Yes

5. **On the Back** Write and solve your own story problem. Use the number **505** in your problem. Check children's work.

UNIT 11 LESSON 15   Subtract from Numbers with Zeros 377

Student Activity Book page 377

Have children determine if there are enough tens and ones to subtract the bottom number from the top number. Children may need to go to the hundreds to get 10 tens or to the tens to get 10 ones. For some of the exercises, they will need to do both. The questions on Student Activity Book page 377—Ungroup to get 10 ones? and Ungroup to get 10 tens?—accompanying each exercise help children focus on this concept. The diagram below shows how the first exercise would look.

Write problem and draw 508

In drawing and in problem ungroup 1 hundred to make 10 tens.

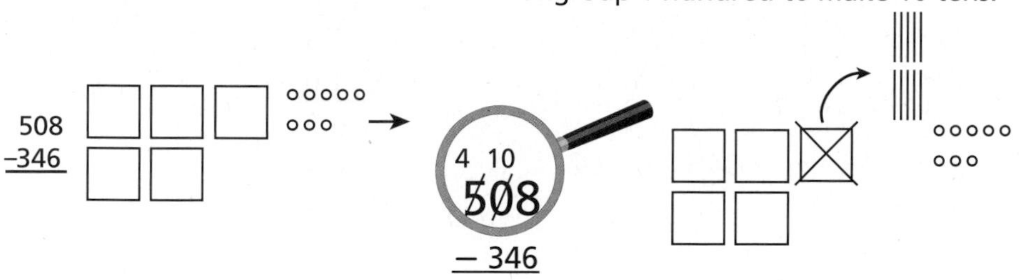

Subtract left to right or right to left.

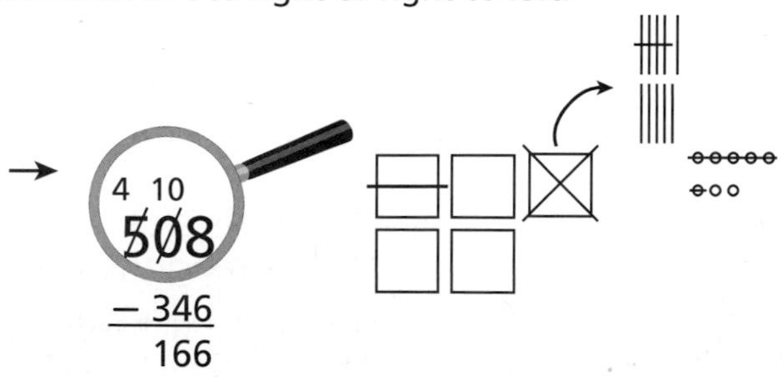

I can see that
4 H 10 T, 8 ones
5 H 8 ones
is the same as 508.

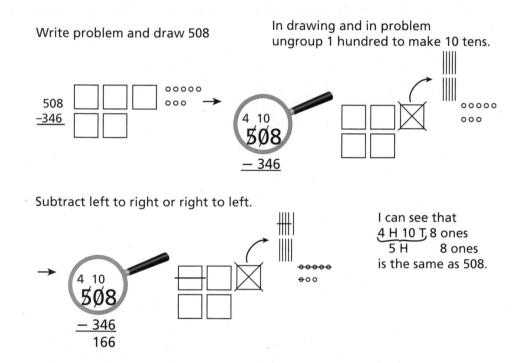

Have children review the drawing and the top number to determine whether the value of the number has changed. It has not changed. The value of 4 hundreds, 10 tens, and 8 ones is the same as the value of 5 hundreds, 0 tens, 8 ones. For a sample of classroom dialogue, see **Math Talk in Action** in the side column.

Have children represent the regrouping with Secret Code Cards to show that the quantity of the top number does not change.

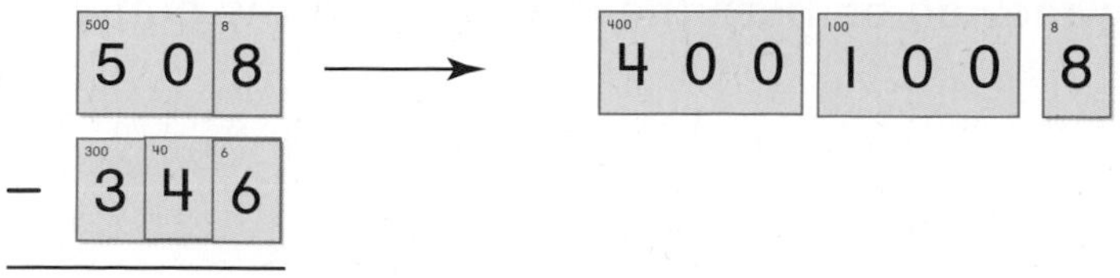

Activity continued ▶

Teaching Note

For problems with zeros, you must do all ungrouping first, so children see this is a natural process that can be done for any problem.

Math Talk in Action

We need to subtract the 3 hundreds, 4 tens and 6 ones in 346 from 5 hundreds and 8 ones. Are there enough tens and ones in 5 hundreds and 8 ones?

Saria: There are enough ones but not enough tens.

How do we get enough tens?

Alisa: Get some from the 5 hundreds.

Yes. How do we ungroup 5 hundreds and 8 ones?

Alisa: Take 1 of the hundreds and ungroup it to 10 tens.

Good. How many hundreds, tens, and ones do we have now?

Alisa: 4 hundreds, 10 tens, 8 ones

Very good. Does the value of the number change when we ungroup?

Trent: No. We just changed how many hundreds, tens, and ones.

English Language Learners

Write *ungroup* on the board. Model 10 red and 5 green cubes mixed together.

- **Beginning** Divide the cubes by color. Ask: **Did I *ungroup* the cubes?** yes
- **Intermediate** Divide the cubes by color. Ask: **What did I do to the cubes?** ungroup
- **Advanced** Have children tell how to *ungroup* the cubes.

❶ Teaching the Lesson (continued)

Class Management

You may want to circulate around the room to find out if children are having difficulty. Encourage individual children to describe aloud, the steps they are using. This will help you to evaluate their methods and correct any errors.

Alternate Approach

Base Ten Blocks Children can use base ten blocks to model subtraction and ungrouping.

Instead of drawing boxes, sticks, and circles, using models may be helpful for some children.

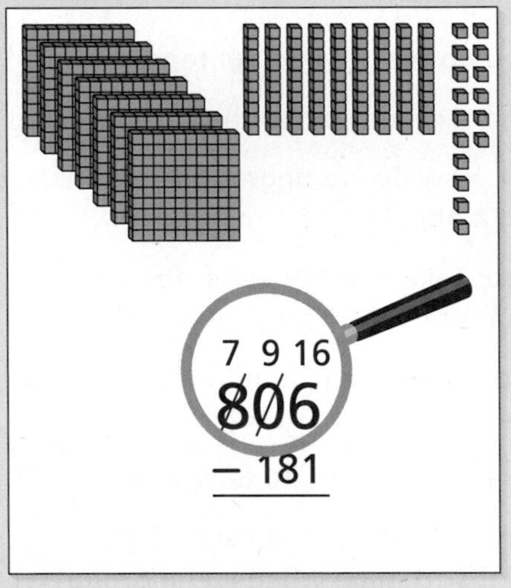

Ongoing Assessment

Ask questions such as the following:

- ▶ How do you know when to ungroup a number?
- ▶ How can you check to make sure your ungrouping is correct?

Invite children to subtract to find the answer. 162 Discuss the procedure as necessary and address any children's errors or misconceptions you or the class notice.

▶ Check a Subtraction Answer WHOLE CLASS

Add the Two Partners Discuss with children how they can check their work. If no one suggests it, encourage children to check by adding up from the bottom, one place at a time. They may work right to left or left to right. In this example (working left to right), children would add 1 + 3 to equal 4, 6 + 4 to equal 10, and 2 + 6 to equal 8. They should notice that 4, 10, and 8 are the numbers they started with and are equivalent to 508. This system works as long as the ungrouping is done correctly.

508
346 162

4 10
~~5~~ ~~0~~ 8
− 3 4 6
1 6 2
add up ↑↑↑

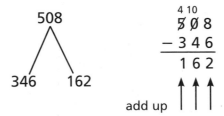

Finish the Examples Repeat the procedure with the rest of the examples on the page. If you feel that it would be beneficial, let some children work at the board and explain their methods and answers.

▶ Subtract 3-Digit Numbers with Zeros SMALL GROUPS

Write the subtraction exercises below on the board. Children should copy them onto their MathBoards. Be sure they draw a magnifying glass around the top number of each exercise if ungrouping is necessary.

806	790	840	507	900	500
− 181	− 272	− 618	− 438	− 563	− 234
625	518	222	69	337	266

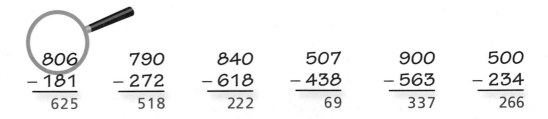

Children may work alone, in **Helping Pairs**, or in small groups to solve the subtraction exercises using drawings and numbers. Children should show any ungrouping they do on both the drawing and the numbers.

2 Going Further

Differentiated Instruction

Intervention

Activity Card 11-15

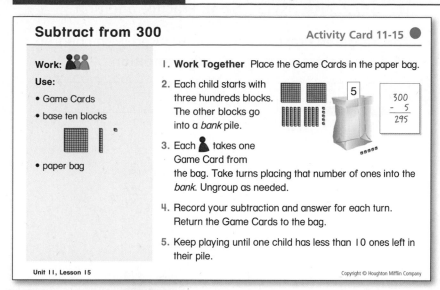

Subtract from 300 — Activity Card 11-15 ●

Work:
Use:
- Game Cards
- base ten blocks

- paper bag

1. **Work Together** Place the Game Cards in the paper bag.
2. Each child starts with three hundreds blocks. The other blocks go into a *bank* pile.

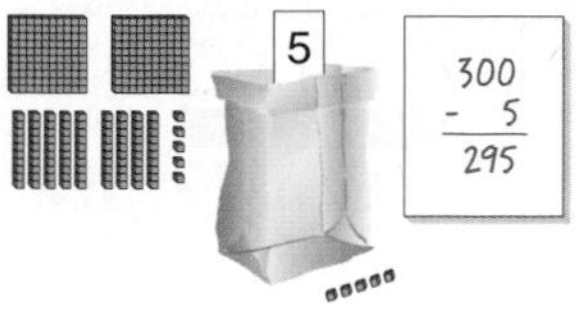

3. Each takes one Game Card from the bag. Take turns placing that number of ones into the *bank*. Ungroup as needed.
4. Record your subtraction and answer for each turn. Return the Game Cards to the bag.
5. Keep playing until one child has less than 10 ones left in their pile.

Unit 11, Lesson 15

Activity Note Each group needs Game Cards (TRB M23), base ten blocks, and a paper bag. Have the group members check their work.

Math Writing Prompt

Explain Your Thinking Explain all the steps you take to subtract 5 from 300.

Soar to Success Math **Software Support**

Warm Up 11.23

On Level

Activity Card 11-15

Subtract 155 — Activity Card 11-15 ▲

Work:
Use:
- 2 sets of Secret Code Cards

1. **Work Together** Sort the Secret Code Cards into two piles: hundreds and ones. Mix up the cards in each pile.
2. Each takes one card from each pile to make a three-digit number.

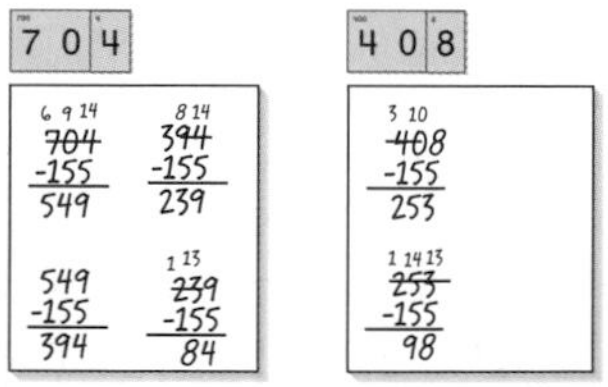

3. Subtract 155 from each number as many times as possible.
4. When neither child can subtract 155 again, compare the final answers. The child with the smaller answer scores 1 point. Repeat. The first child to score 5 points wins.

Unit 11, Lesson 15

Activity Note Each pair needs two sets of Secret Code Cards 1-9 and 200-900 (TRB M3-M6). Have children check their math.

Math Writing Prompt

Write a Story Write a story about someone who always loses things. They start out with 300 things in a collection. Include a problem in your story that can be solved by using subtraction.

Harcourt MegaMath **Software Support**

Country Countdown: Block Busters, Level X

Challenge

Activity Card 11-15

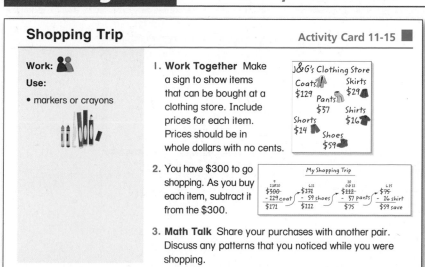

Shopping Trip — Activity Card 11-15 ■

Work:
Use:
- markers or crayons

1. **Work Together** Make a sign to show items that can be bought at a clothing store. Include prices for each item. Prices should be in whole dollars with no cents.

2. You have $300 to go shopping. As you buy each item, subtract it from the $300.

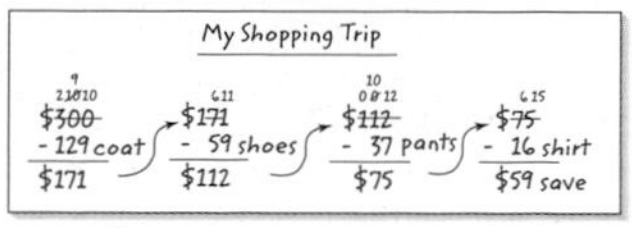

3. **Math Talk** Share your purchases with another pair. Discuss any patterns that you noticed while you were shopping.

Unit 11, Lesson 15

Activity Note Each pair makes a sign for items from a clothing store. You may want to provide clothing magazines for children.

Math Writing Prompt

Step-by-Step Explain all the steps you take to subtract 413 from 600.

DESTINATION Math® **Software Support**

Course II: Module 3: Unit 1: Money

3 Homework and Targeted Practice

11–15 **Homework** **Goal:** Additional Practice

This Homework page provides practice in solving 3-digit subtraction.

11–15 Name ______

Homework

Children's ungrouping may vary.

Decide if you need to ungroup. If you need to ungroup, draw a magnifying glass around the top number. Then find the answer.

1. 730 − 499 = 231
   Ungroup to get 10 ones? Yes
   Ungroup to get 10 tens? Yes

2. 950 − 639 = 311
   Ungroup to get 10 ones? Yes
   Ungroup to get 10 tens? No

3. 300 − 167 = 133
   Ungroup to get 10 ones? Yes
   Ungroup to get 10 tens? Yes

4. 404 − 188 = 216
   Ungroup to get 10 ones? Yes
   Ungroup to get 10 tens? Yes

5. 420 − 183 = 237
   Ungroup to get 10 ones? Yes
   Ungroup to get 10 tens? Yes

6. 502 − 149 = 353
   Ungroup to get 10 ones? Yes
   Ungroup to get 10 tens? Yes

UNIT 11 LESSON 15 Subtract from Numbers with Zeros **249**

Homework and Remembering page 249

11–15 **Targeted Practice** **Goal:** Practice addition

This Targeted Practice page can be used with children who need extra practice in 3-digit addition.

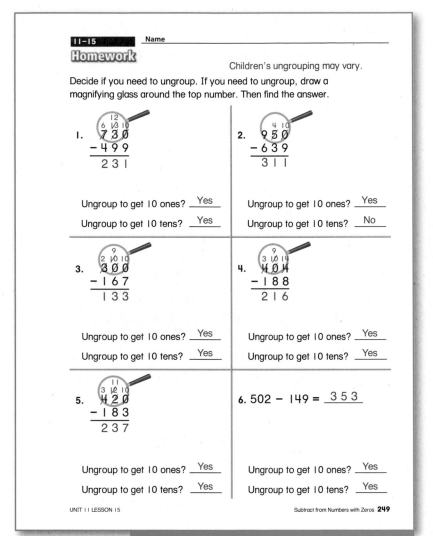

11–15 Name ______

Targeted Practice

Add.

1. 226 + 457 = 683
2. 547 + 332 = 879
3. 424 + 357 = 781
4. 458 + 214 = 672
5. 114 + 874 = 988
6. 623 + 256 = 879
7. 537 + 457 = 994
8. 424 + 269 = 693
9. 458 + 439 = 897
10. 575 + 324 = 899
11. 234 + 456 = 690
12. 438 + 329 = 767

250 UNIT 11 LESSON 15 Subtract from Numbers with Zeros

Homework and Remembering page 250

Home or School Activity

Technology Connection

Number Puzzle Invite children to solve a number puzzle using a calculator. Write the following six numbers randomly on the board: 462, 134, 328, 329, 500 and 171. Have children write two subtraction equations using these numbers. Then have them use a calculator to check their work.

462 329 134 500 171 328

500 − 171 = 329

462 − 134 = 328

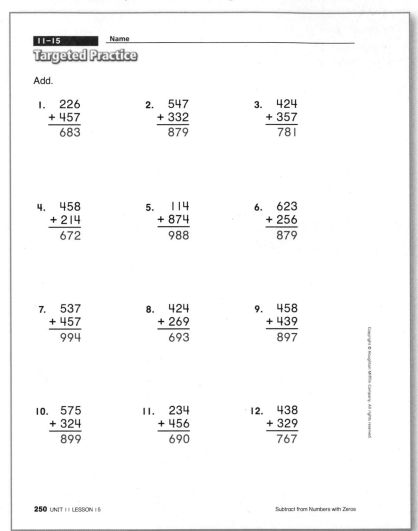

UNIT 11 LESSON 16

Subtract Money Amounts

Lesson Objectives

- Subtract 3-digit numbers using ungrouping.
- Subtract money amounts.
- Solve story problems involving money amounts.

Vocabulary
ungroup
decimal point

The Day at a Glance

Today's Goals	Materials	
1 Teaching the Lesson A1: Practice 3-digit subtraction with zeros in the top number. A2: Solve subtraction story problems involving money amounts.	**Lesson Activities** Homework and Remembering pp. 251–252 MathBoard materials Secret Code Cards	**Going Further** Activity Cards 11-16 Real or play money Dollar Bills (TRB M67–M68) Secret Code Cards Index cards Grocery store flyers Math Journals
2 Going Further ▸ Differentiated Instruction		
3 Homework and Spiral Review		

Use Math Talk today!

Keeping Skills Sharp

Quick Practice — 5 MINUTES

Goal: Count a sequence of coins.

Materials: real or play money (quarters, dimes, and pennies), sticky board (optional)

Count Coins Write a sequence of quarters, dimes, and pennies (Q, D, P) on the board or place coins on a sticky board.

Q Q Q Q Q D D D P P P

Point to each letter or coin and begin counting the money. Invite the class to count along with you. When you have finished, recount the money to check your total. (See Unit 11 Lesson 15.)

Repeated Quick Practice
Use this Quick Practice from a previous lesson.

▸ **What's My Rule?** (See Unit 11 Lesson 11.)

n	n + 8
102	110
504	512
920	928
7	15
52	60
91	99

Daily Routines

Making Change and Counting Coins Making Change from $5.00, Combining Coins and Counting Money (See pp. xxvii–xxviii.)

▸ Led by Student Leaders

Money Routine Using the 120 Poster, Using the Money Flip Chart, Using the Number Path, Using Secret Code Cards (See pp. xxiii–xxv.)

▸ Led by Student Leaders

1 Teaching the Lesson

Activity 1

Practice Subtracting 3-Digit Numbers

🕒 25 MINUTES

Goal: Practice 3-digit subtraction with zeros in the top number.

Materials: MathBoard materials

✓ **NCTM Standard:**
Number and Operations

The Learning Classroom

Math Talk As children are sharing their methods for finding the answers to these subtraction examples, help them to find some patterns in subtracting.

- Ungrouping helps if there are not enough ones or tens.
- You do not need to ungroup if the number of ones or tens you are taking away is not greater than the ones or tens you have.
- If there is a zero in the top number and no zero in the bottom number, you need to ungroup.

Teaching Note

Watch For! Some children may automatically ungroup everything above for all examples, even when ungrouping may not be necessary. Encourage them to always compare before they begin ungrouping because they may not need to ungroup in every case.

▶ Practice 3-Digit Subtraction WHOLE CLASS

Write some or all of the following exercises on the board for children to copy onto their Mathboards. For each exercise, children should decide first whether they need more ones, tens, or both to find the answer. Ask them to draw a magnifying glass around the top number in each exercise if ungrouping is necessary.

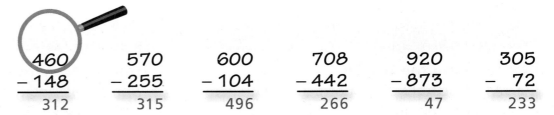

(more 1s)	(more 1s)	(both)	(more 10s)	(both)	(more 10s)
460	570	600	708	920	305
− 148	− 255	− 104	− 442	− 873	− 72
312	315	496	266	47	233

Math Talk Solve and Discuss Have a few children use the **Solve and Discuss** structure at the board, while the rest of the class works at their seats to find the answers.

Have the children at the board explain how they found the answers. If another child found the answer in a different way, ask that child to explain. Invite the class to ask questions or offer suggestions.

Check Work Tell children to check their work by adding up each column of numbers. (They may do this right to left or left to right.) Other children may prefer to draw a Math Mountain and add the partners to confirm the total.

460
148 312

Activity 2

Solve Money Problems

▶ Apply Subtraction Strategies to Story Problems About Money SMALL GROUPS

Present children with the following story problem that they can solve on their MathBoards:

Jessica had $5.00. She paid $2.13 for her lunch at school. How much money does she have left?

$$\begin{array}{r} \$5.00 \\ -\ \ 2.13 \\ \hline \$2.87 \end{array}$$

Review money notation with children as necessary.

As with any subtraction exercise, children should first determine whether they need to do any ungrouping. Then they ungroup the top number as necessary.

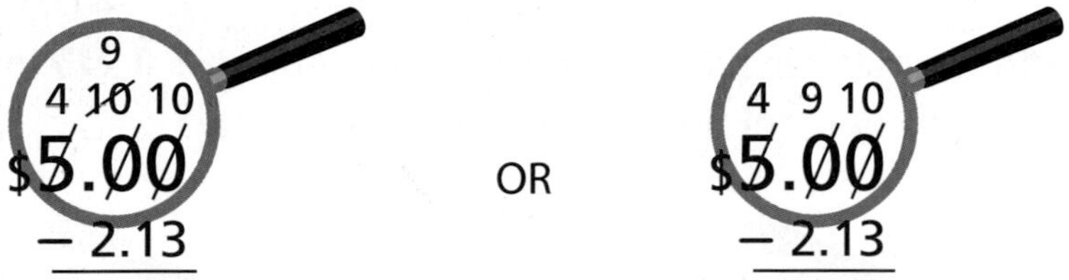

Invite children to make a Proof Drawing with boxes, sticks, and circles. Be sure they understand that the quantity in the drawing (500 cents, or $5.00) has not changed.

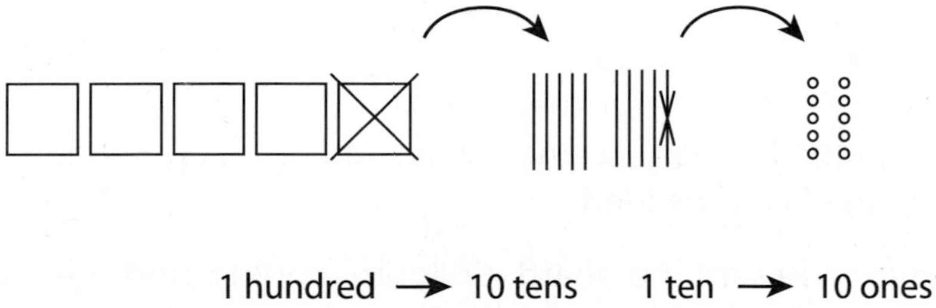

Activity continued ▶

25 MINUTES

Goal: Solve subtraction story problems involving money amounts.

Materials: Secret Code Cards 1–900, MathBoard materials

NCTM Standards:
Number and Operations
Representation

Alternate Approach

Play Money Children can use real or play money to model subtraction of money amounts and ungrouping.

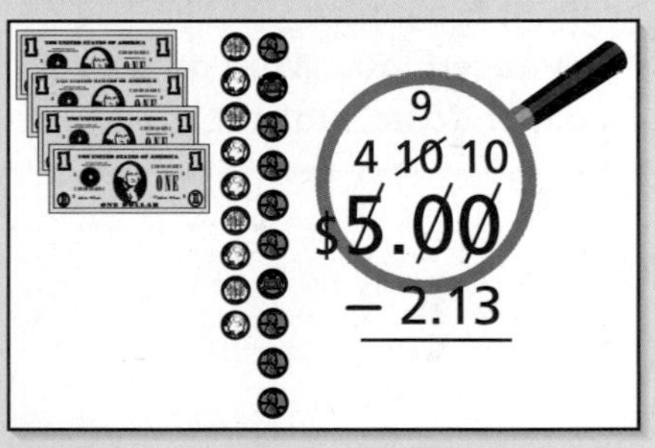

Teaching Note

Math Symbols In this activity, children will not be expected to master decimal numbers in terms of values of less than one (wholes, tenths, hundredths). Money amounts are presented here as an extension of subtracting 3-digit whole numbers. Children should, for example, think about $5.00 as 500 cents.

❶ Teaching the Lesson (continued)

The Learning Classroom

Student Leaders Children may work individually, in Helping Pairs, or in small groups to find the answers. You may wish to work with a small group of children and invite Student Leaders to circulate, offering help to those who need it.

English Language Learners

Write *dollar bill* on the board. Hold up a coin. Ask: **Is this a coin?** yes Hold up a dollar bill.

- **Beginning** Ask: **Is this a coin?** no Say: **This is a *dollar bill*.** Have children repeat.
- **Intermediate** Say: **This is not a coin. It is a *dollar* __.** bill
- **Advanced** Ask: **What do we call a paper dollar?** dollar bill

Ongoing Assessment

Ask questions such as the following:

- ► Between which places do you put the decimal point? Is it important how you line up the numbers?
- ► When you ungroup 1 hundred, how many tens do you get? When you ungroup 1 ten, how many ones do you get?

Have children show the exercise using Secret Code Cards to help them see that the quantity of the top number has not changed; it has been ungrouped to make enough tens and ones to be able to subtract.

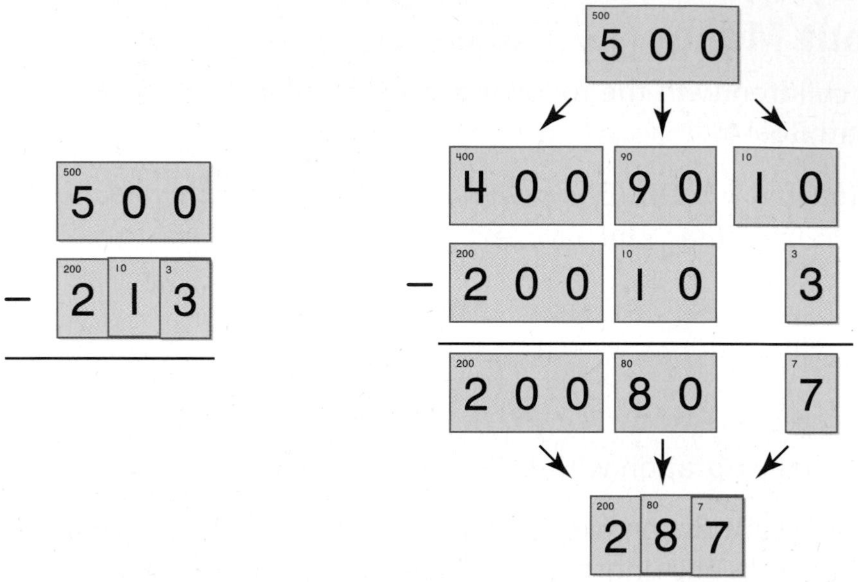

Repeat the process with a second story problem:

Carlos found four dollar bills in his room. He spent $ 1.87 on games at the fun fair. How much money does he have now?

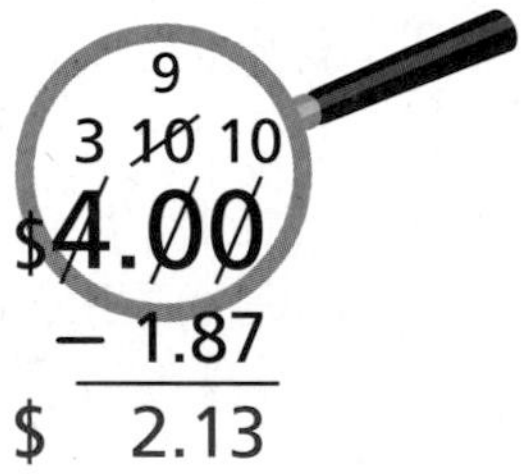

OR

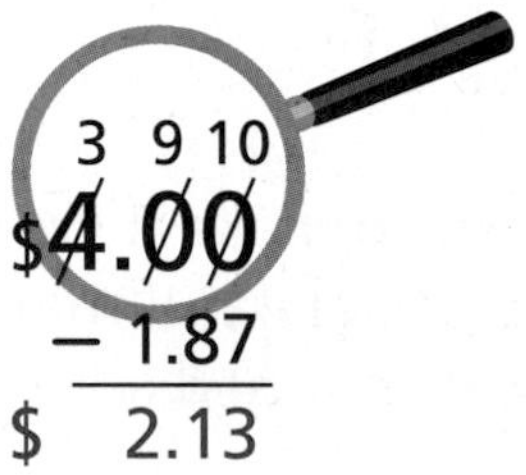

Be sure that children are keeping the numbers and the decimal point aligned. This will be easier for them to do if they notice that the decimal point comes between the tens and the hundreds place. Remind them of the magnifying glass if needed.

Write these exercises on the board. Children work to find the answers and record their work on their MathBoards.

$8.00	$4.03	$3.83
− 6.23	− 1.26	− 0.67
$1.77	$2.77	$3.13

Intervention Activity Card 11-16

Show Money Amounts
Activity Card 11-16

Work: pairs
Use:
- 10 dimes
- 5 nickels
- 10 pennies
- dollar bills
- Secret Code Cards

Choose:
- Student 1
- Student 2

1. **Work Together** Sort the Secret Code Cards into three piles: hundreds, tens, and ones.
2. Student 1 Take one card from each pile and make a money amount.
3. Subtract the money amount that you made from $5.00.
4. Student 2 Check the subtraction.
5. Show the answer by using the fewest number of coins.
6. Then show the answer another way.
7. Trade roles and repeat.

Secret Code Cards: 200 | 70 | 3 → 2 7 3

$$\begin{array}{r} \$5.00 \\ -\ 2.73 \\ \hline \$2.27 \end{array}$$

Unit 11, Lesson 16

Copyright © Houghton Mifflin Company

Activity Note Each pair needs 10 dimes, 5 nickels, 10 pennies (real or play), Dollar Bills (TRB M67-M68), and Secret Code Cards 1-400 (TRB M3-M6).

Math Writing Prompt
Write a Story Suppose you had $5.00 to spend at a grocery store. Write a subtraction story problem about buying an item and getting change.

Soar to Success Math Software Support
Warm Up 3.17

On Level Activity Card 11-16

Shopping Trip
Activity Card 11-16

Work: pairs
Use:
- grocery store flyers

1. **Work Together** Choose the same three items from both store flyers. The items are: Milk, one half gallon; Eggs, large, 1 dozen; Bananas, 1 pound.
2. Write down the price of each item.
3. Find the total of all three items at both stores.
4. Find out how much change you would get if you paid $8.00.
5. **Math Talk** At which store would you have spent less money?

Martin's Grocery Store		Shop Town	
Milk $2.79	$2.79 + 1.29 + 0.49 = $4.57	Milk $2.89	$2.89 + 1.49 + 0.59 = $4.97
Eggs $1.29		Eggs $1.49	
Bananas $0.49	$8.00 − 4.57 = $3.43	Bananas $0.59	$8.00 − 4.97 = $3.03

Unit 11, Lesson 16

Copyright © Houghton Mifflin Company

Activity Note Provide several grocery flyers for pairs. Help pairs select similar items to purchase. Remind children to check their work.

Math Writing Prompt
Explain Your Thinking Explain why you can add up to check you answer in subtraction. How is making change like adding up?

Harcourt MegaMath Software Support
Numberopolis: Lulu's Lunch Counter, Level T

Challenge Activity Card 11-16

Money Clues
Activity Card 11-16

Work: pairs
Use:
- index cards

1. Each student writes a money amount less than $5.00 on the back of an index card. Don't show your amount to your partner.
2. On the other side of the index card, write clues to help your partner guess the unknown amount. At least one clue should involve subtracting a three-digit amount.
3. **Math Talk** Share your clues with another pair. Which clues are most helpful?

Unknown Amount: $1.22

The unknown amount is less than $3.00. It is greater than $1.00. If you start with $5.00 and buy a toy that costs $3.69, your change is 9 cents away from the unknown amount. All you need to do is buy another toy that costs 9 cents. The amount you have left is the unknown amount.

Unit 11, Lesson 16

Copyright © Houghton Mifflin Company

Activity Note Each pair needs two index cards. If necessary, help children write their clues.

Math Writing Prompt
Work Backward You pay for a sandwich with a five-dollar bill. With your change, you buy a juice for $1.29. You have $1.52 left. How much was the sandwich? Explain your steps.

Destination Math Software Support
Course II: Module 3: Unit 1: Money

3 Homework and Spiral Review

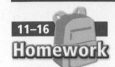

11–16 Homework **Goal:** Additional Practice

This Homework page provides practice in subtracting money amounts.

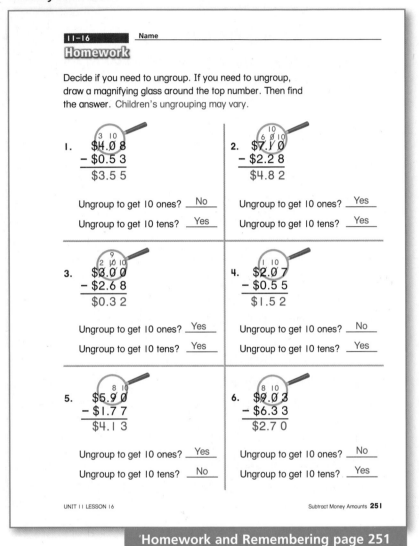

11–16 Name ______

Homework

Decide if you need to ungroup. If you need to ungroup, draw a magnifying glass around the top number. Then find the answer. Children's ungrouping may vary.

1. $4.08 − $0.53 = $3.55
Ungroup to get 10 ones? No
Ungroup to get 10 tens? Yes

2. $7.10 − $2.28 = $4.82
Ungroup to get 10 ones? Yes
Ungroup to get 10 tens? Yes

3. $3.00 − $2.68 = $0.32
Ungroup to get 10 ones? Yes
Ungroup to get 10 tens? Yes

4. $2.07 − $0.55 = $1.52
Ungroup to get 10 ones? No
Ungroup to get 10 tens? Yes

5. $5.90 − $1.77 = $4.13
Ungroup to get 10 ones? Yes
Ungroup to get 10 tens? No

6. $9.03 − $6.33 = $2.70
Ungroup to get 10 ones? No
Ungroup to get 10 tens? Yes

UNIT 11 LESSON 16 Subtract Money Amounts **251**

Homework and Remembering page 251

11–16 Remembering **Goal:** Spiral Review

This Remembering activity would be appropriate anytime after today's lesson.

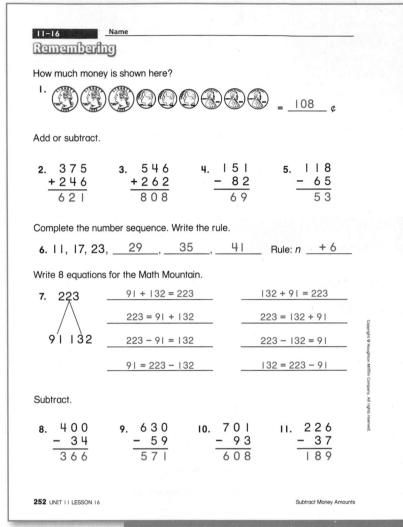

11–16 Name ______

Remembering

How much money is shown here?

1.  = 108 ¢

Add or subtract.

2. 375 + 246 = 621
3. 546 + 262 = 808
4. 151 − 82 = 69
5. 118 − 65 = 53

Complete the number sequence. Write the rule.

6. 11, 17, 23, 29, 35, 41 Rule: n + 6

Write 8 equations for the Math Mountain.

7. 223 (91, 132)

91 + 132 = 223	132 + 91 = 223
223 = 91 + 132	223 = 132 + 91
223 − 91 = 132	223 − 132 = 91
91 = 223 − 132	132 = 223 − 91

Subtract.

8. 400 − 34 = 366
9. 630 − 59 = 571
10. 701 − 93 = 608
11. 226 − 37 = 189

252 UNIT 11 LESSON 16 Subtract Money Amounts

Homework and Remembering page 252

Home or School Activity

Language Arts Connection

A Penny Saved Is a Penny Earned Explain that a proverb is a wise saying. Tell children that there are many proverbs about money—saving money, spending money, and how to use money wisely. Share these examples:

- A penny saved is a penny earned.
- Beware of little expenses; a small leak will sink a great ship.
- A penny in time is as good as a dollar.

Have children discuss the meaning of the proverbs, then make up a proverb of their own about money.

Don't spend a dollar, except if you know you have a few more.

Save a penny, and then soon you will have more to spend.

UNIT 11
LESSON 17

Subtract from Any 3-Digit Number

Lesson Objectives

- Subtract from any 3-digit number, with or without ungrouping.
- Represent subtraction of any 3-digit number.

Vocabulary
ungroup
difference

The Day at a Glance

Today's Goals	Materials	
1 Teaching the Lesson A1: Represent 3-digit subtraction with boxes, sticks, and circles and Secret Code Cards. Practice ungrouping. A2: Find and correct errors in 3-digit subtraction.	**Lesson Activities** Homework and Remembering pp. 253–254 MathBoard materials Secret Code Cards	**Going Further** Activity Cards 11-17 Base ten blocks Real or play money Dollar Bills Five-Dollar Bils Classroom items Index cards Paper bags *The 329th Friend* by Marjorie Weinman Sharmat Math Journals
2 Going Further ▸ Differentiated Instruction		
3 Homework and Targeted Practice		

Use Math Talk today!

Keeping Skills Sharp

Quick Practice — 5 MINUTES

Goal: Count a sequence of coins.

Materials: real or play money (quarters, dimes, and pennies), sticky board (optional)

Count Coins Write a sequence of quarters, dimes, and pennies (Q, D, P) on the board or place coins on a sticky board to represent a number of quarters, dimes, and pennies:

Q Q Q D D P P P P

Point to each letter or coin and begin counting the money. Invite the class to count along with you. When you have finished, recount the money to check your total. (See Unit 11 Lesson 15.)

Repeated Quick Practice
Use this Quick Practice from a previous lesson.

▸ **What's My Rule?** (See Unit 11 Lesson 11.)

n	*n* − 5
606	601
27	22
90	85
432	427
325	320
31	26

Daily Routines

Making Change and Counting Coins Making Change from $5.00, Combining Coins and Counting Money
(See pp. xxvii–xxviii.)

▸ Led by Student Leaders

Money Routine Using the 120 Poster, Using the Money Flip Chart, Using the Number Path, Using Secret Code Cards
(See pp. xxiii–xxv.)

▸ Led by Student Leaders

1 Teaching the Lesson

Activity 1

Ungroup the Top Number and Subtract

30 MINUTES

Goal: Represent 3-digit subtraction with boxes, sticks, and circles and Secret Code Cards. Practice ungrouping.

Materials: MathBoard materials, Secret Code Cards 1–900

NCTM Standards:
Number and Operations
Representation

Math Talk in Action

We need to subtract 273 from 432. Are there enough ones and tens in 432 to subtract?

Serg: No. We need to subtract 3 ones and there are only 2 ones, and we need to subtract 7 tens and there are only 3 tens.

Yes. So how do we get enough ones and tens?

Katy: To get enough ones, we need to ungroup 1 ten. To get enough tens, we need to ungroup 1 hundred.

Good. Let's be sure to draw the ungrouping with boxes, sticks, and circles. Then in our problem, we do the ungrouping in each place.

▶ Represent 3-Digit Subtraction WHOLE CLASS

Ask for Ideas Write this exercise on the board. Ask a volunteer to make up a story problem to go with the numeric exercise.

$$\begin{array}{r} 432 \\ -\ 273 \\ \hline \end{array}$$

Use boxes, sticks, and circles Children draw the top number (432) on their MathBoards using boxes, sticks, and circles. This will help prevent confusion later when any necessary ungrouping is done. Draw this on the classroom board, too.

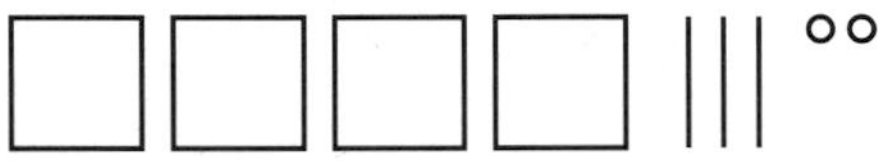

Have children determine whether they need more ones, tens, or both to subtract. If they do, they draw a magnifying glass around the top number. A volunteer at the board ungroups as necessary while the rest of the class works on their MathBoards. For a sample of classroom dialogue, see **Math Talk in Action** in the side column. Be sure to facilitate direct student-to-student talk during **Solve and Discuss**.

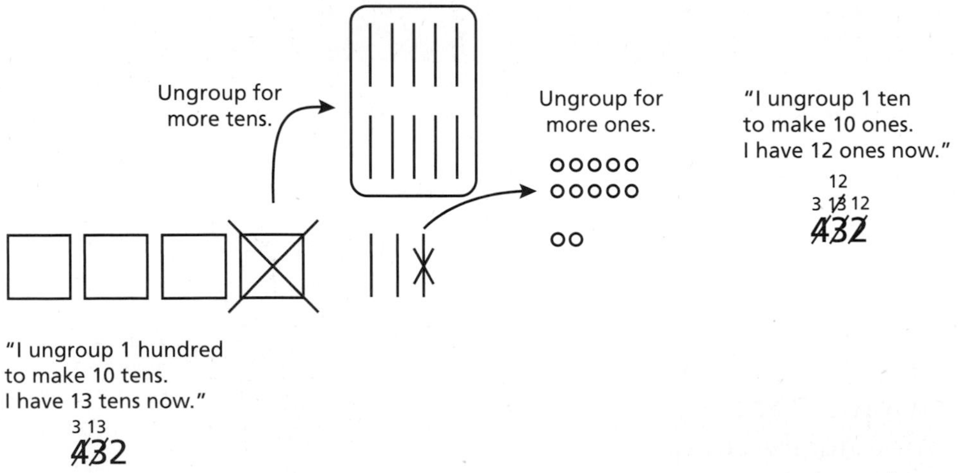

This ungrouping was done left to right. Some children may ungroup right to left (see numeric example on 867).

Children check their drawings to be sure that they have not changed the amount represented. The amount will be the same if the ungrouping was done correctly.

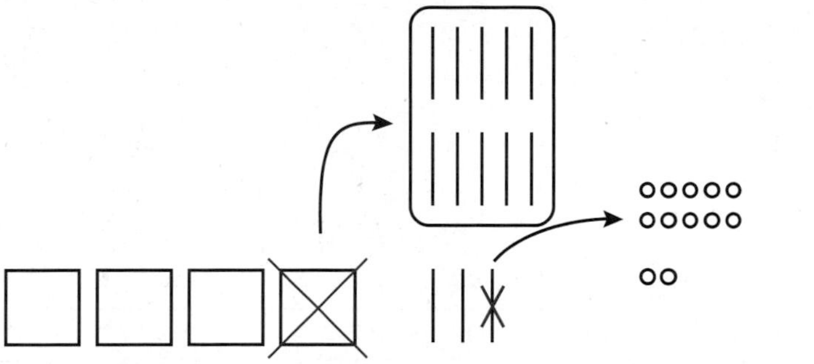

300 + 100 + 20 + 12 = 432

Then have children show the subtraction by drawing a line through boxes, sticks, and circles for 273.

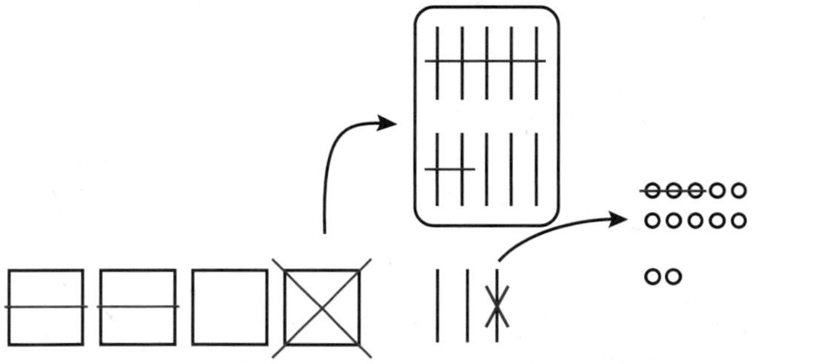

1 hundred, 5 tens, 9 ones remain.
432 − 273 = 159

Use numeric methods Children ungroup the top number to reflect the changes that they made in their drawing. This may be done in either of the ways shown here. They draw a "magnifying glass" view of the ungrouped top number. A volunteer explains why the ungrouped amount in the magnifying glass is the same amount they started with. (If you regroup the numbers, you will have 432, the number you are subtracting from.)

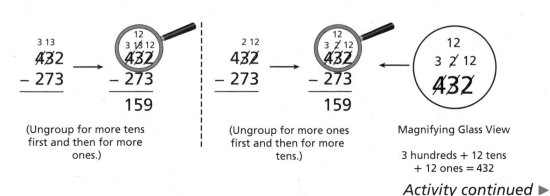

Left to Right Ungrouping | Right to Left Ungrouping

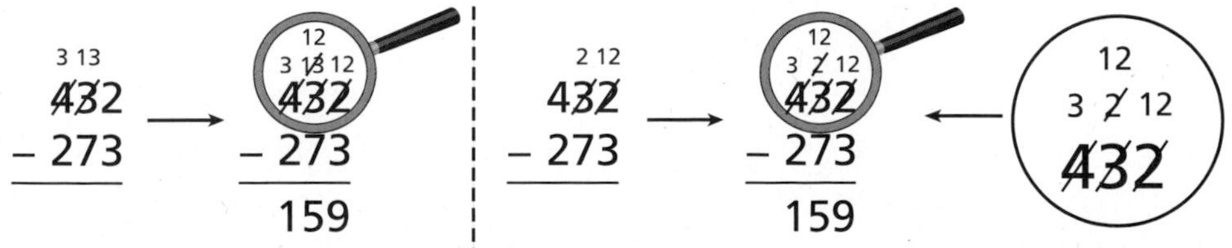

(Ungroup for more tens first and then for more ones.)

(Ungroup for more ones first and then for more tens.)

Magnifying Glass View

3 hundreds + 12 tens + 12 ones = 432

Activity continued ▶

The Learning Classroom

Building Concepts The magnifying glass is a visual support to make the top number a conceptual whole (many children view multi-digit problems primarily as columns). It is also a reminder to look and see if you need to ungroup.

English Language Learners

Write *left* and *right* on the board. Point and say: **Left starts with the letter L.** Hold your hands in front of you, palms out, and thumbs perpendicular. Have children copy you.

- **Beginning** Say: **Our *left* hands makes an L.** Have children trace the L with their right hand.
- **Intermediate** Ask: **Does your left hand make an L?** yes **Does your right hand?** no
- **Advanced** Ask: **Which hand makes an L?** left hand

❶ Teaching the Lesson (continued)

Differentiated Instruction

Extra Help Some children may have difficulty representing the ungrouped top number correctly with the Secret Code Cards. Tell children that after they have made their ungrouping drawing, they need to find a card that shows the new number of boxes, and the new number of sticks, and the new number of circles. Tell children to check that their ungrouping drawing matches the original top number in value. Then they should make sure they have chosen the correct Secret Code Card for each group by recounting the boxes, sticks, and circles.

Use Secret Code Cards Have children represent the exercise with their Secret Code Cards.

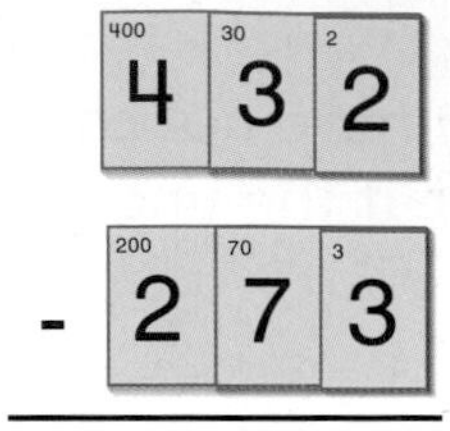

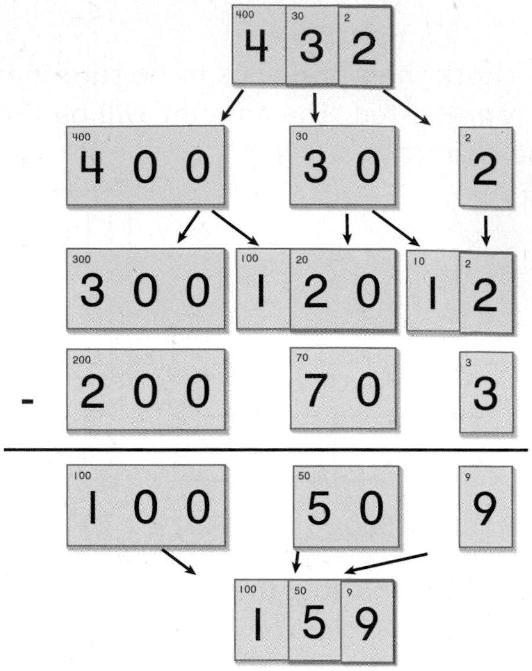

Math Talk Discuss the top number in the subtraction and how the Secret Code Cards show the number ungrouped. You may ask:

- ▶ Why do we show 300, 120, and 12 for 432? We ungrouped 1 of the hundreds from 400 to 10 tens, so we got 300 and 130. Then we ungrouped 1 ten from 130, so we got 120 and 12.

Direct children's attention to the top number they are working on in this example. Ask them to compare this top number with the other top numbers they have been subtracting from in earlier lessons. Help children notice that each top number in earlier lessons had zeros in it. You may ask:

- ▶ If we subtract from a number such as 432, instead of from a number such as 508, how is the subtraction different? Answers will vary. Possible response: With 508, there are no tens to start. With 432, there are some tens to start.

▶ Checking the Answer

Children may check their work by adding the partners to find the total.

432

273 159

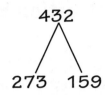

▶ Practice Subtraction with Ungrouping

Write the following exercises on the board for children to solve. Remind them to draw a magnifying glass around each top number if ungrouping is necessary.

625	\$5.48	473	224	\$6.86
– 317	– 3.72	– 354	– 169	– 2.59
308	\$1.76	119	55	\$4.27

Explain Answers Invite some children to the board to work while the rest of the class works on their MathBoards at their seats. Ask a few children to explain their methods and answers to the class. Encourage them to use hundreds, tens, and ones (or dollars, dimes, and pennies) language as the exercise requires.

Teaching Note

Language and Vocabulary You may wish to present or have children recall the term *difference*. The difference is the answer in a subtraction problem. You find the difference between two numbers when you subtract.

Class Management

Walk around the room and observe children as they subtract. If you notice any child who has invented a method that works, keep the child in mind to show the method at the board when it is time to share.

Ongoing Assessment

Ask questions such as the following:

- ▶ How does ungrouping help you when you subtract?
- ▶ How can you check your answer in a subtraction example?

Activity 2

Find and Correct Errors

20 MINUTES

Goal: Find and correct errors in 3-digit subtraction.

Materials: MathBoard materials

NCTM Standard:
Number and Operations

Teaching Note

What to Expect from Students
Some children may be embarrassed about making errors and mistakes. Tell children it is okay to make mistakes. Tell them that we can learn from our mistakes and work toward getting the correct answer in the future.

▶ Model Common Subtraction Errors for Correcting

WHOLE CLASS

Math Talk

Assume the role of the Amazing Ms. (or Mr. or Mrs.) Mistake, and try to solve a few subtraction exercises on the board. Make some of the errors you have observed, and invite the children to show you how to correct them. (See examples below.) Whenever possible, ask children to explain how to avoid the error.

$$\begin{array}{r} 903 \\ -\ 647 \\ \hline 344 \end{array}$$

Error: Subtracted top ones and tens from bottom ones and tens.

$$\begin{array}{r} {\scriptstyle 9} \\ {\scriptstyle 1\not{0}\,13} \\ 9\not{0}\not{3} \\ -\ 647 \\ \hline 356 \end{array}$$

Error: Did not record the ungrouping in the hundreds place.

$$\begin{array}{r} {\scriptstyle 10\,13} \\ 9\not{0}\not{3} \\ -\ 647 \\ \hline 366 \end{array}$$

Error: Did not correctly record the ungrouping in the tens and hundreds place.

$$\begin{array}{r} {\scriptstyle 9} \\ {\scriptstyle 8\,1\not{0}\,13} \\ \not{9}\not{0}\not{3} \\ -\ 647 \\ \hline 256 \end{array}$$

Correct solution

Give interested children a turn at playing the role of Ms. or Mr. Mistake.

2 Going Further

Differentiated Instruction

Intervention — Activity Card 11-17

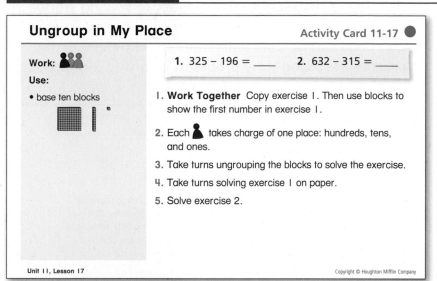

Ungroup in My Place

Activity Card 11-17 ●

Work:

Use:

- base ten blocks

1. 325 − 196 = ____   2. 632 − 315 = ____

1. **Work Together** Copy exercise 1. Then use blocks to show the first number in exercise 1.
2. Each takes charge of one place: hundreds, tens, and ones.
3. Take turns ungrouping the blocks to solve the exercise.
4. Take turns solving exercise 1 on paper.
5. Solve exercise 2.

Unit 11, Lesson 17

Activity Note Each group needs hundreds, tens, and ones blocks. Each child in the group takes charge of one place; hundreds, tens, or ones.

Math Writing Prompt

Draw a Picture Draw boxes, sticks, and circles to show how to subtract 315 − 128. Include an explanation with your picture.

Soar to Success Math Software Support

Warm Up 11.23

On Level — Activity Card 11-17

Shop Owners

Activity Card 11-17 ▲

Work:

Use:

- quarters, dimes, nickels, and pennies
- dollar bills
- five-dollar bills
- 4 index cards
- classroom items

Choose:

- 1
- 2

1. **Work Together** Choose four items from the classroom to sell in your store. Give each item a price less than $5.00.

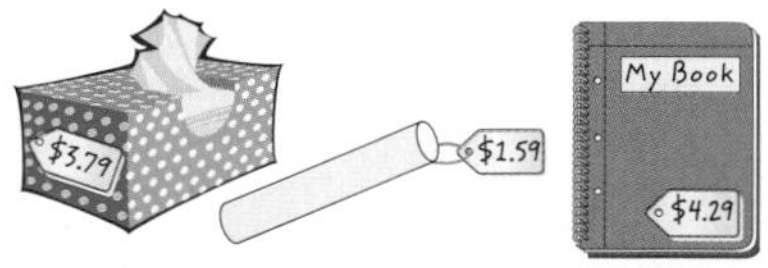

2. 1 Choose one item to buy. Pay with a five-dollar bill.
3. 2 Take the role of the shop owner. Give 1 the change for the item. Show how you ungrouped to find the correct amount.
4. Trade roles and repeat.

Unit 11, Lesson 17

Activity Note Each pair needs real or play quarters, dimes, nickels, pennies, dollar bills, and five-dollar bills.

Math Writing Prompt

Compare and Contrast How is subtracting from a three-digit number without zeros different from subtracting from three-digit number with zeros? How is the subtraction alike? Explain.

Harcourt MegaMath Grades K-6 Software Support

Numberopolis: Lulu's Lunch Counter, Level Q

Challenge — Activity Card 11-17

What Is the Change?

Activity Card 11-17 ■

Work:

Use:

- 10 index cards
- paper bag

Choose:

- 1
- 2

Arts and Crafts Supplies	
Watercolor paints	$4.65
Set of paintbrushes	$3.84
Drawing paper	$5.79
Crayons	$2.58
Chalk	$1.90

1. **Work Together** Write amounts between $2.00 and $7.00 on index cards. Put the cards in the bag.
2. 2 Take an index card from the bag. Choose an item from the list above that you can buy.
3. 1 Subtract to find out how much change 2 should get. Both children should check the math.
4. Trade roles and repeat.

Unit 11, Lesson 17

Activity Note Each pair needs a paper bag and index cards. Ask each pair to explain how they subtracted the money amounts.

Math Writing Prompt

Investigate Math How do you think subtracting from a four-digit number might be like subtracting from a three-digit number? How might it be different? Explain.

Destination Math Software Support

Course II: Module 3: Unit 1: Money

3 Homework and Targeted Practice

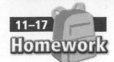

11–17 Homework **Goal:** Additional Practice

This Homework page provides practice in subtraction and solving subtraction story problems.

11–17 Targeted Practice **Goal:** Practice solving story problems.

This page can be used with children who need extra practice in solving story problems involving 3-digits.

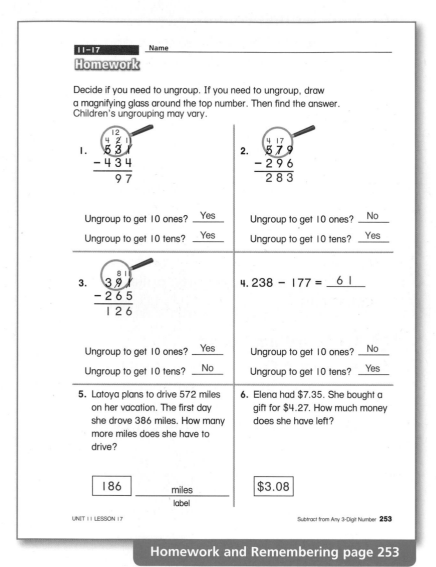

11–17 Name ____________

Homework

Decide if you need to ungroup. If you need to ungroup, draw a magnifying glass around the top number. Then find the answer.

Children's ungrouping may vary.

1. 531 − 434 = 97

Ungroup to get 10 ones? Yes

Ungroup to get 10 tens? Yes

2. 579 − 296 = 283

Ungroup to get 10 ones? No

Ungroup to get 10 tens? Yes

3. 391 − 265 = 126

Ungroup to get 10 ones? Yes

Ungroup to get 10 tens? No

4. 238 − 177 = 61

Ungroup to get 10 ones? No

Ungroup to get 10 tens? Yes

5. Latoya plans to drive 572 miles on her vacation. The first day she drove 386 miles. How many more miles does she have to drive?

186 miles (label)

6. Elena had $7.35. She bought a gift for $4.27. How much money does she have left?

$3.08

UNIT 11 LESSON 17 — Subtract from Any 3-Digit Number **253**

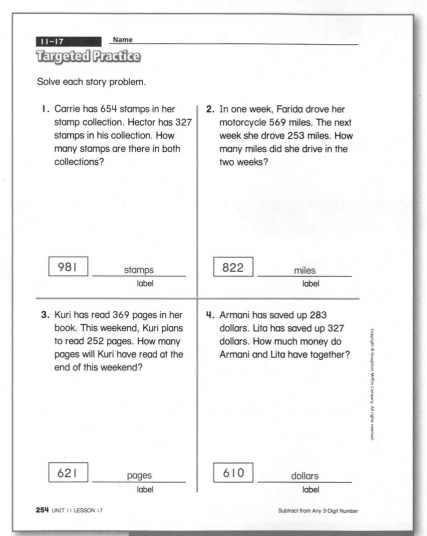

Homework and Remembering page 253

11–17 Name ____________

Targeted Practice

Solve each story problem.

1. Carrie has 654 stamps in her stamp collection. Hector has 327 stamps in his collection. How many stamps are there in both collections?

981 stamps (label)

2. In one week, Farida drove her motorcycle 569 miles. The next week she drove 253 miles. How many miles did she drive in the two weeks?

822 miles (label)

3. Kuri has read 369 pages in her book. This weekend, Kuri plans to read 252 pages. How many pages will Kuri have read at the end of this weekend?

621 pages (label)

4. Armani has saved up 283 dollars. Lita has saved up 327 dollars. How much money do Armani and Lita have together?

610 dollars (label)

254 UNIT 11 LESSON 17 — Subtract from Any 3-Digit Number

Homework and Remembering page 254

Home or School Activity

Literature Connection

Subtract with *The 329th Friend* Read or have children read the book *The 329th Friend* by Marjorie Weinman Sharmat and Cyndy Szekeres (Four Winds Press, 1979). Children can describe how Emery Raccoon used numbers when he prepared for the lunch, for example, the number of potatoes he peeled and tarts he baked. Then have children write a story problem about the book that uses subtraction to solve.

Children can share and solve each other's story problems.

UNIT 11 LESSON 18

Practice Ungrouping

Lesson Objectives

- **Recognize whether or not ungrouping is necessary to subtract 3-digit numbers.**
- **Practice ungrouping.**

Vocabulary
ungroup

The Day at a Glance

Today's Goals	Materials	
1 Teaching the Lesson A: Determine when and when not to ungroup in 3-digit subtraction. Practice 3-digit subtraction, with and without ungrouping.	**Lesson Activities** Homework and Remembering pp. 255–256 Quick Quiz 4 (Assessment Guide) Secret Code Cards MathBoard materials	**Going Further** Activity Cards 11-18 Secret Code Cards MathBoard materials Practice Ungrouping (TRB M86) Multiple-Step Story Problems (TRB M87) Math Journals
2 Going Further ▸ Differentiated Instruction		
3 Homework and Spiral Review		

Use Math Talk today!

Keeping Skills Sharp

Quick Practice — 5 MINUTES

Goal: Monitor children's progress adding and subtracting 3-digit numbers.

Quick Check Monitor children's progress adding and subtracting 3-digit numbers. Write these exercises on the board. One of them requires a new ten, and the other requires ungrouping.

$$\begin{array}{r} 443 \\ +\ 272 \\ \hline 715 \end{array} \qquad \begin{array}{r} 800 \\ -\ 174 \\ \hline 626 \end{array}$$

Daily Routines

Making Change and Counting Coins Making Change from $5.00, Combining Coins and Counting Money
(See pp. xxvii–xxviii.)

▸ Led by Student Leaders

Money Routine Using the 120 Poster, Using the Money Flip Chart, Using the Number Path, Using Secret Code Cards
(See pp. xxiii–xxv.)

▸ Led by Student Leaders

1 Teaching the Lesson

Activity

When Must I Ungroup?

25 MINUTES

Goal: Determine when and when not to ungroup in 3-digit subtraction. Practice 3-digit subtraction, with and without ungrouping.

Materials: Secret Code Cards, 1–900 (from Unit 1 Lesson 5 or TRB M3–M4), MathBoard materials

NCTM Standard:
Number and Operations

The Learning Classroom

Math Talk As you discuss whether ungrouping is needed in these subtraction examples, help children to express some patterns:

- Ungrouping is needed if you need to subtract a number of ones and there are not enough ones in the top number.
- Ungrouping is needed if you need to subtract a number of tens and there are not enough tens in the top number.
- You do not need to ungroup if you have enough ones or tens in the top number to subtract from.

▶ Decide When to Ungroup in 3-Digit Subtraction

WHOLE CLASS

Guide children to distinguish exercises that require ungrouping from those that do not. Write the following four examples on the board:

$$\begin{array}{r}427\\-\ 165\\\hline\end{array}\qquad\begin{array}{r}423\\-\ 165\\\hline\end{array}\qquad\begin{array}{r}483\\-\ 165\\\hline\end{array}\qquad\begin{array}{r}487\\-\ 165\\\hline\end{array}$$

Ask for Ideas Ask children to look at each exercise carefully. Invite them to think about which of the exercises they can solve without having to ungroup the tens or the ones or both the tens and ones. After a few moments, have a child select the exercise that needs no ungrouping and explain why it does not. Circle that exercise. (487 – 165) Encourage the child to explain that the top number has enough ones and tens from which to subtract the ones and tens in the lower number.

Next, children look at the exercises that are left and think about which exercises they need to ungroup only once (either for more ones or for more tens) in order to subtract. Children may represent exercises with their Secret Code Cards to help them decide. After a few moments, a child identifies those exercises and explains how he or she can tell. Circle those exercises. (427 – 165 and 483 – 165)

Ask children to look at the exercise that is left uncircled. (423 – 165) Encourage them to think about how it is different from the others. Allow time for children to consider their answers. (The exercise requires them to ungroup twice.) Invite children to respond and to explain their reasoning.

Write the exercises shown below on the board. Children do not need to find the answers for now, just determine the number of times they must ungroup, if any, before they subtract.

Math Talk When children finish studying the examples, have them describe their strategies for deciding how many times ungrouping is needed in each example. Have children tell why they need to consider each example individually. Each example is different and has a different number of ones and tens in the top number and the bottom number.

The last exercise (570 − 176) poses a special problem. Ask children to explain why it requires them to ungroup twice and not just once. Let a volunteer draw a "magnifying glass" showing how the number should be ungrouped before subtracting.

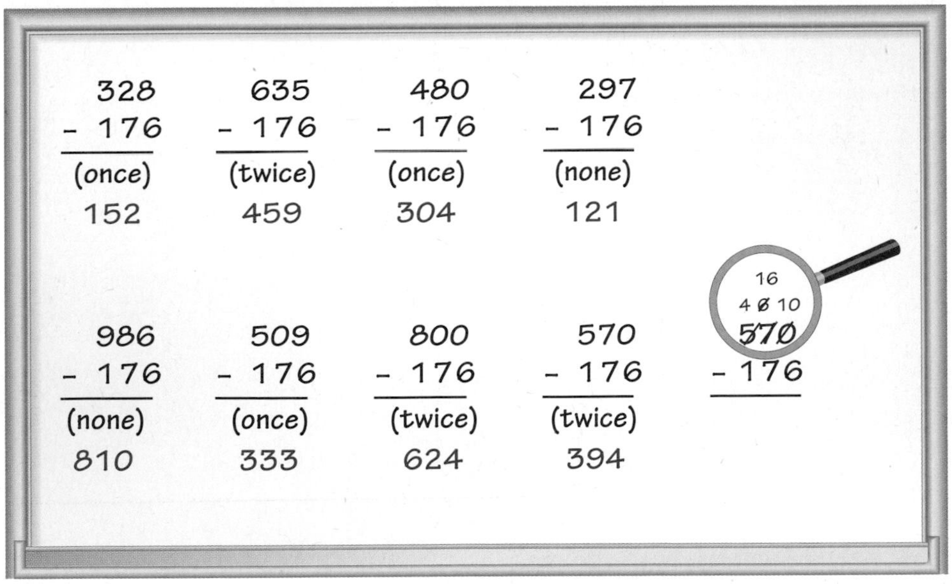

Leave the exercises on the board. Children will find the answers in the next part of this activity.

Differentiated Instruction

Special Needs Some children may have difficulty focusing on exercises with many variations, at once. To reduce the number of variations, you may wish to present examples that all have the same top number. For example:

$$\begin{array}{r}457\\-126\\\hline\end{array}\quad\begin{array}{r}457\\-128\\\hline\end{array}\quad\begin{array}{r}457\\-198\\\hline\end{array}$$

Work with children to compare how the bottom numbers are different. Then have them compare the ones and the tens between the numbers being subtracted and the top number.

English Language Learners

Write *once* and *twice* on the board. Say: ***Once* means do something one time.** Have children repeat.

- **Beginning** Turn around once. Say: **I turned around *once*.** Continue with *twice*.
- **Intermediate** Ask: **Does *twice* mean do something 2 times?** yes
- **Advanced** Turn around 2 times. Ask: **How many times did I turn around?** twice

Activity continued ▶

Teaching Note

What to Expect from Students Children who are having difficulty often lose track of what to do next when subtracting multi-digit numbers. The step-by-step format is helpful because it allows children to take turns choosing and explaining discrete steps in order. If anyone does not know what to do, the other children can offer help.

Ongoing Assessment

Ask questions such as the following:

- What are the steps you used to subtract?
- Why do you need to ungroup?
- How many tens are there now, after you have ungrouped a hundred? How many ones are there now, after you ungrouped a ten?

Quick Quiz

See Assessment Guide for Unit 11 Quick Quiz 4.

▶ Practice with Ungrouping WHOLE CLASS Math Talk

Some children can work to find the answers to the examples at the board. Children working at their seats copy the exercises onto their MathBoards. They may work in **Helping Pairs.** They discuss and agree with each other to decide when to ungroup and when not to. Student Leaders may circulate through the class, helping those who need it.

As the rest of the class finds the answers, work with a small group of children who are having difficulty. Let them explain their methods for finding the answers using the **Step-By-Step at the Board** structure. They may also use their Secret Code Cards to explain.

2 Going Further

Differentiated Instruction

Intervention — Activity Card 11-18

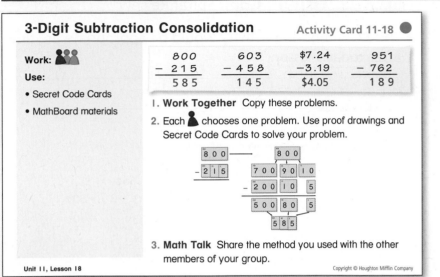

3-Digit Subtraction Consolidation — Activity Card 11-18

Work:

Use:

- Secret Code Cards
- MathBoard materials

800	603	$7.24	951
− 215	− 458	−3.19	− 762
585	145	$4.05	189

1. **Work Together** Copy these problems.
2. Each chooses one problem. Use proof drawings and Secret Code Cards to solve your problem.

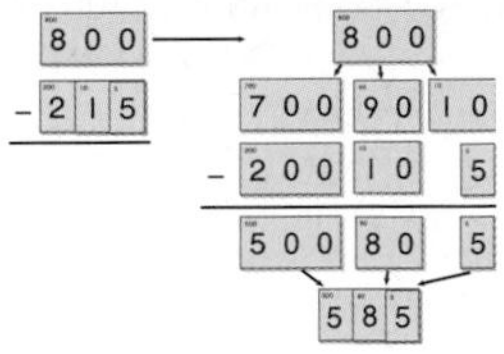

3. **Math Talk** Share the method you used with the other members of your group.

Unit 11, Lesson 18

Activity Note Each group needs Secret Code Cards 1-900 (TRB M3-M6) and MathBoard materials.

Math Writing Prompt

Write a Story You have $3.75. Write a story about two things you would buy. Tell how much each item costs and write the amount of change you should get back after buying each item.

Soar to Success Math Software Support

Warm Up 11.24

On Level — Activity Card 11-18

Subtraction Consolidation — Activity Card 11-18

Work:

Use:

- Practice Ungrouping (TRB M86)

Choose:

- 1
- 2

1. **Work Together** Look at problem 1 on Practice Ungrouping.
2. Decide if you need to ungroup. Follow the directions.
3. 1 Solve the problem. Explain to 2 the method you used to solve the problem.
4. Trade roles and solve the other problems.

Unit 11, Lesson 18

Activity Note Each pair needs Practice Ungrouping (TRB M86). Have children explain the steps they used to subtract.

Math Writing Prompt

Explain Your Thinking Give two examples of how you might use three-digit subtraction in your daily life. Explain why subtraction is used in each situation.

Harcourt Mega Math Software Support

Country Countdown: Block Busters, Level Y

Challenge — Activity Card 11-18

Story Problem Consolidation — Activity Card 11-18

Work:

Use:

- Multiple-Step Story Problems (TRB M87)

Choose:

- 1
- 2

1. 1 Look at problem 1 on Multiple-Step Story Problems.
2. Solve the problem on a separate sheet of paper.
3. Explain the steps you used to 2.
4. Trade roles and solve the other problems.
5. **Math Talk** Think about the steps you used to solve each problem. Discuss any patterns you might see.

Unit 11, Lesson 18

Activity Note Each pair needs Multiple-Step Story Problems (TRB M87). Have children explain how to solve each problem.

Math Writing Prompt

Write and Solve a Story Problem Write and solve a multi-step story problem that involves ungrouping, about the number of students in your school.

Destination Math Software Support

Course II: Module 2: Unit 1: Estimating and Finding Differences within 1,000

3 Homework and Spiral Review

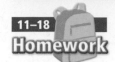

11–18 Homework **Goal:** Additional Practice

✓ Include children's completed Homework page as part of their portfolios.

11–18 Homework Name ______

Decide if you need to ungroup. If you need to ungroup, draw a magnifying glass around the top number. Then find the answer. Children's ungrouping may vary.

1.
```
    2 10
   6 3 0
 - 3 1 8
   3 1 2
```
Ungroup to get 10 ones? Yes
Ungroup to get 10 tens? No

2.
```
     12
   8 2 11
   9 3 1
 - 8 4 5
     8 6
```
Ungroup to get 10 ones? Yes
Ungroup to get 10 tens? Yes

3.
```
   3 10
   4 0 7
 - 2 7 4
   1 3 3
```
Ungroup to get 10 ones? No
Ungroup to get 10 tens? Yes

4.
```
   4 9 8
 - 2 7 6
   2 2 2
```
Ungroup to get 10 ones? No
Ungroup to get 10 tens? No

5. Jamal had 590 craft sticks. He used 413 craft sticks to make a building. How many craft sticks does he have left?

177 craft sticks (label)

6. Clare and her family are driving to Blue Valley Mountains. Blue Valley Mountains is 290 miles from their home. They drove 184 miles. How many more miles do they have to go?

106 miles (label)

UNIT 11 LESSON 18 Practice Ungrouping 255

Homework and Remembering page 255

11–18 Remembering **Goal:** Spiral Review

This Remembering activity would be appropriate anytime after today's lesson.

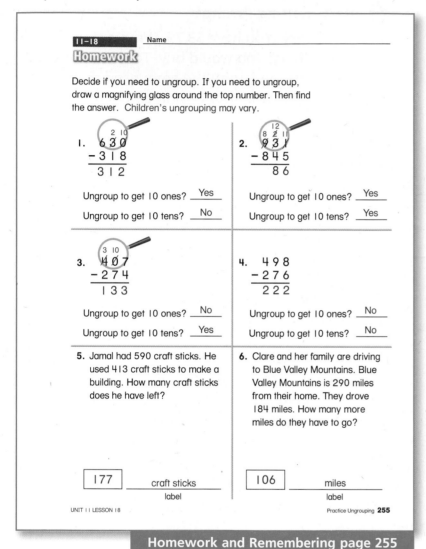

11–18 Remembering Name ______

Complete the money tables. Answers will vary. Sample answers shown.

1. 49¢

Q	1	= 25¢
D	1	= 10¢
N	2	= 10¢
P	4	= 4¢
		49¢

2. 72¢

Q	2	= 50¢
D	2	= 20¢
N	0	= 0¢
P	2	= 2¢
		72¢

3. 65¢

Q	2	= 50¢
D	1	= 10¢
N	1	= 5¢
P	0	= 0¢
		65¢

The market sells fresh fruit. The table shows how much fruit they sold this week.

Fresh Fruit Sold This Week

Lemons	200
Apples	680
Bananas	450

4. How many fewer lemons did the market sell than bananas?

250 fewer lemons

5. How many more apples did the market sell than bananas?

230 more apples

6. How many fewer lemons did the market sell than apples?

480 fewer lemons

7. **Time** On a separate piece of paper, draw what you do at 10 o'clock P.M. Show the time on a digital clock. Check children's work.

256 UNIT 11 LESSON 18 Practice Ungrouping

Homework and Remembering page 256

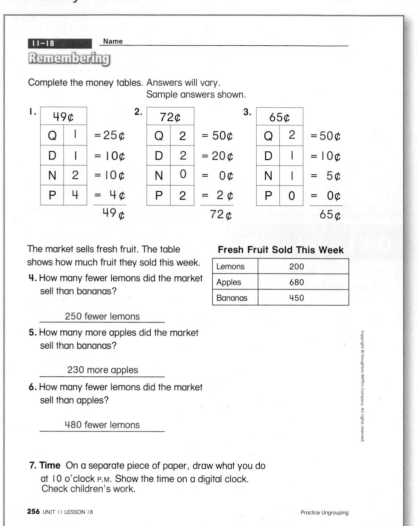

Home or School Activity

Science Connection

Animal Lengths Have children research the length or height, in inches, of different animals. Tell them to look for lengths that are 3-digit numbers. Have them use subtraction to write statements comparing the lengths or heights of the animals.

An Anaconda snake is 141 inches longer than a crocodile.

```
  2 13
  3 3 3  Anaconda snake
- 1 9 2  Crocodile
  1 4 1  inches
```

A giraffe is 72 inches taller than an African elephant.

```
  1 12
  2 2 8  Giraffe
- 1 5 6  African elephant
    7 2  inches
```

UNIT 11 LESSON 19

Relationships Between Addition and Subtraction Methods

Lesson Objectives

- Discriminate between addition and subtraction situations and apply the appropriate operation.
- Use addition to check subtraction and subtraction to check addition.

Vocabulary
grouping
ungrouping

The Day at a Glance

Today's Goals	Materials	
1 Teaching the Lesson A1: Make grouping and ungrouping decisions about addition and subtraction exercises. A2: Solve addition and subtraction exercises.	**Lesson Activities** Student Activity Book pp. 379–380 Homework and Remembering pp. 257–258 Secret Code Cards MathBoard materials	**Going Further** Activity Cards 11-19 Base ten blocks Index cards Math Journals
2 Going Further ► Differentiated Instruction		
3 Homework and Targeted Practice		

Use Math Talk today!

Keeping Skills Sharp

Quick Practice — 5 MINUTES

Goal: Find partners of 3-digit numbers.

Partners of 3-Digit Numbers Draw these two Math Mountains on the board. Have two **Student Leaders** write and check the unknown partners.

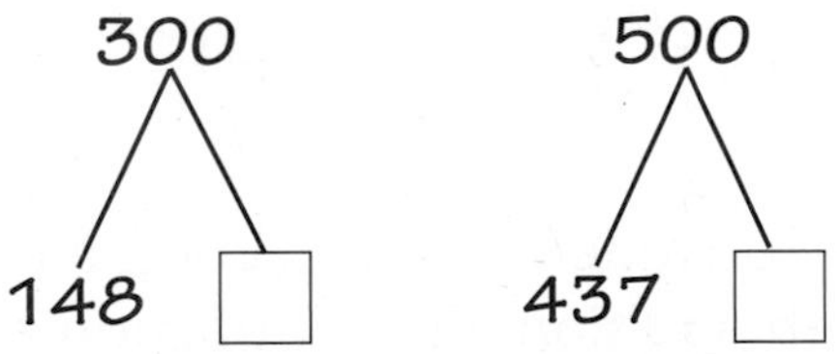

Then have a third Student Leader lead the class in saying the four addition and four subtraction equations as two other Student Leaders write them as quickly as possible on the board. (The order of the equations does not matter.)

148 + 152 = 300	300 − 148 = 152	437 + 63 = 500	500 − 437 = 63
152 + 148 = 300	300 − 152 = 148	63 + 437 = 500	500 − 63 = 437
300 = 148 + 152	152 = 300 − 148	500 = 437 + 63	63 = 500 − 437
300 = 152 + 148	148 = 300 − 152	500 = 63 + 437	437 = 500 − 63

Daily Routines

Making Change and Counting Coins Making Change from $5.00, Combining Coins and Counting Money (See pp. xxvii–xxviii.)

► Led by Student Leaders

Money Routine Using the 120 Poster, Using the Money Flip Chart, Using the Number Path, Using Secret Code Cards (See pp. xxiii–xxv.)

► Led by Student Leaders

1 Teaching the Lesson

Activity 1

Decide Whether to Add or Subtract

25 MINUTES

Goal: Make grouping and ungrouping decisions about addition and subtraction exercises.

Materials: Student Activity Book page 379, Secret Code Cards, 1–900 (1 set per child; optional)

NCTM Standards:
Number and Operations
Communication

English Language Learners

Write 15 – 4, 15 – 7, and *enough* on the board. Point to 15 – 4. Say: **5 ones minus 4 ones. We have *enough* ones to subtract.**

- **Beginning** Say: **Enough means all the ones we need.** Point to 15 – 7. Say: 5 ones minus 7 ones. **We do not have *enough* ones.**
- **Intermediate** Point to 15 – 7. Ask: **Are there *enough* ones to subtract?** no
- **Advanced** Have children tell whether there are *enough* ones in 15 – 7 to subtract.

11–19 Class Activity

Name

► Review Addition and Subtraction

Ring *add* or *subtract*. Check if you need to ungroup or make a new ten or hundred. Then find the answer.

1. 762 − 395 = 367
   (Subtract) ✓ Ungroup to get 10 ones; ✓ Ungroup to get 10 tens
   Add ☐ Make 1 new ten; ☐ Make 1 new hundred

2. 395 + 367 = 762
   Subtract ☐ Ungroup to get 10 ones; ☐ Ungroup to get 10 tens
   (Add) ✓ Make 1 new ten; ✓ Make 1 new hundred

3. 287 − 193 = 94
   (Subtract) ☐ Ungroup to get 10 ones; ✓ Ungroup to get 10 tens
   Add ☐ Make 1 new ten; ☐ Make 1 new hundred

4. 437 + 324 = 761
   Subtract ☐ Ungroup to get 10 ones; ☐ Ungroup to get 10 tens
   (Add) ✓ Make 1 new ten; ☐ Make 1 new hundred

5. **On the Back** Explain how you know when to ungroup in subtraction. Use the words *ones, tens,* and *hundreds.* Check children's work.

UNIT 11 LESSON 19 — Relationships between Addition and Subtraction Methods 379

Student Activity Book page 379

► Review Addition and Subtraction

WHOLE CLASS

Math Talk

Direct children's attention to Student Activity Book page 379. Explain to children that there are both addition and subtraction exercises on the page and that they will need to decide which operation to use to solve each exercise.

Review the addition operation with children.

- What is the most important thing to decide in addition? whether you will make a new ten, a new hundred, or both
- What do you do when you make a new ten? If there are enough extra ones to make a new ten, you add the new ten to the tens already there.
- What do you do when you make a new hundred? If there are enough extra tens to make a new hundred, you add the new hundred to the hundreds already there.

Review the subtraction operation with the children.

- What is the most important thing to decide in subtraction? if you need to ungroup for more ones, for more tens, or both
- What do you do when you ungroup to get more ones? If there are not enough ones to subtract, you ungroup 1 ten for 10 ones.
- What do you do when you ungroup to get more tens? If there are not enough tens to subtract, you ungroup 1 hundred for 10 tens.

Math Talk Solve and Discuss After reviewing the operations of addition and subtraction, have children solve the exercises on Student Activity Book page 379. Have a few children work at the board while the rest of the class works at their seats. Using the **Solve and Discuss** structure, have one child at the board explain how he or she solved the first exercise and have another child explain the second exercise. Tell the child who explains the subtraction exercise to draw a "magnifying glass" view of the ungrouped and rewritten top number.

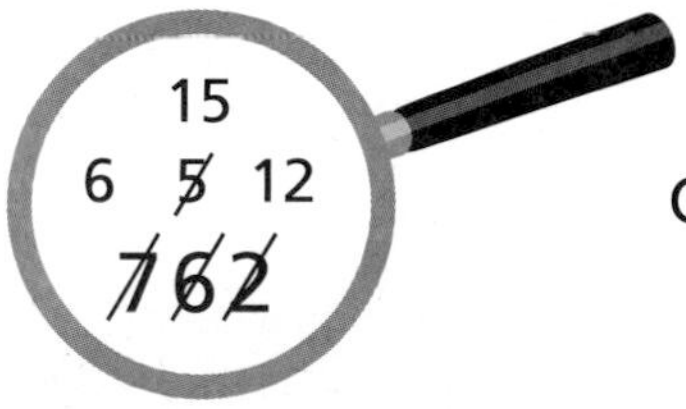

OR

Check the Answer Have children describe how they should check their work. Some children may realize that they can add to check their answer in subtraction and they can subtract to check their answer in addition.

The concept of partners will help make clear to children why this works.

762

– /\ –

395 + 367

Others may draw a proof drawing or use base ten blocks. More advanced children can discuss in detail how grouping in addition and ungrouping in subtraction are opposite regroupings: they undo each other (we call such operations *inverse operations*).

Ongoing Assessment

As children solve and discuss the exercises on Student Activity Book page 379, look for children who make any of the following errors.

- Start to add or subtract without first checking the operation sign. Remind them to look at the sign before starting each exercise.
- Forget to add the grouped numbers when adding. Encourage them to write the grouped numbers on the line so they are easier to see.
- Neglect to use the correct ungrouped numbers when they subtract. Remind them to draw a magnifying glass around the ungrouped and rewritten top number to help them stop just subtracting the top from the bottom.

Activity 2

Add and Subtract

20 MINUTES

Goal: Solve addition and subtraction exercises.

Materials: MathBoard materials

NCTM Standard:
Number and Operations

▶ Practice Adding and Subtracting

WHOLE CLASS

Math Talk

Write the exercises below on the board and have children copy them onto their MathBoards.

476	873	643	333	461	564
+ 272	− 496	− 458	+ 578	− 352	− 266
748	377	185	911	109	298

Then have children work individually, in **Helping Pairs**, or in small groups to solve the exercises. If they work with other children, encourage them to spend some time explaining to each other how they solved each exercise. Remind them to draw magnifying glasses for the subtraction problems and to check their work by doing the opposite operation.

After children have completed the exercises, ask volunteers to come to the board to discuss their work. Encourage other children to ask questions and make suggestions.

2 Going Further

Differentiated Instruction

Intervention — Activity Card 11-19

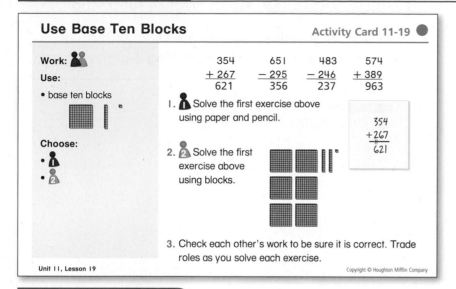

Use Base Ten Blocks

Activity Card 11-19

Work: pairs
Use:
- base ten blocks

Choose:
- 1
- 2

354	651	483	574
+ 267	− 295	− 246	+ 389
621	356	237	963

1. Solve the first exercise above using paper and pencil.

$354 + 267 = 621$

2. Solve the first exercise above using blocks.

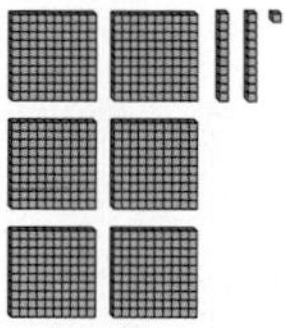

3. Check each other's work to be sure it is correct. Trade roles as you solve each exercise.

Unit 11, Lesson 19

Activity Note Each pair needs base ten blocks; 9 hundreds, 19 tens, and 19 ones. Have pairs explain how they solved each problem.

Math Writing Prompt

Write About It Solve this equation:

$587 + 247 = \square$.

How can you check that the answer is correct?

Soar to Success Math Software Support

Warm Up 27.11

On Level — Activity Card 11-19

Math Mountains

Activity Card 11-19

Work: pairs

Math Mountains: 723 (□, □) and 967 (□, □)

1. **Work Together** Talk about how to find the unknown partners for the Math Mountains.
2. Find at least two addition equations for each Math Mountain. Sample answer: 1. 485 + 238 = 723, 341 + 382 = 723; 2. 579 + 388 = 967, 627 + 340 = 967
3. Find at least two subtraction equations for each Math Mountain. Sample answer: 1. 723 − 485 = 238, 723 − 341 = 382; 2. 967 − 579 = 388, 967 − 627 = 340
4. Share your answers with another pair. How are your answers different?

Unit 11, Lesson 19

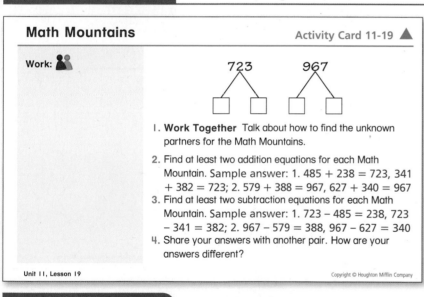

Activity Note Each pair needs to find the unknown partners for two Math Mountains.

Math Writing Prompt

Find the Error Derek used addition to check his subtraction answer. Explain what he needs to do differently.

$367 - 189 = 178$

$367 + 178 = 545$

Harcourt Mega Math Software Support

Country Countdown: Block Busters, Level W

Challenge — Activity Card 11-19

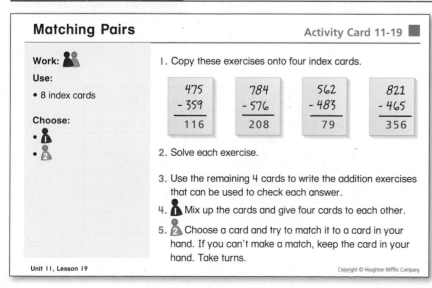

Matching Pairs

Activity Card 11-19

Work: pairs
Use:
- 8 index cards

Choose:
- 1
- 2

1. Copy these exercises onto four index cards.

475	784	562	821
− 359	− 576	− 483	− 465
116	208	79	356

2. Solve each exercise.
3. Use the remaining 4 cards to write the addition exercises that can be used to check each answer.
4. Mix up the cards and give four cards to each other.
5. Choose a card and try to match it to a card in your hand. If you can't make a match, keep the card in your hand. Take turns.

Unit 11, Lesson 19

Activity Note Each pair needs eight index cards. Pairs copy the subtraction problems on to 4 cards and then write the addition problems used to check the answers on the other 4 cards.

Math Writing Prompt

Write About It Write a rule to describe how to use subtraction to check an answer in addition.

Destination Math Software Support

Course II: Module 2: Unit 1: Estimating and Finding Differences within 1,000

3 Homework and Targeted Practice

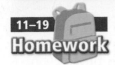

11–19
Homework **Goal:** Additional Practice

This Homework page provides practice adding and subtracting 3-digit numbers.

11–19 **Homework** Name ____________________

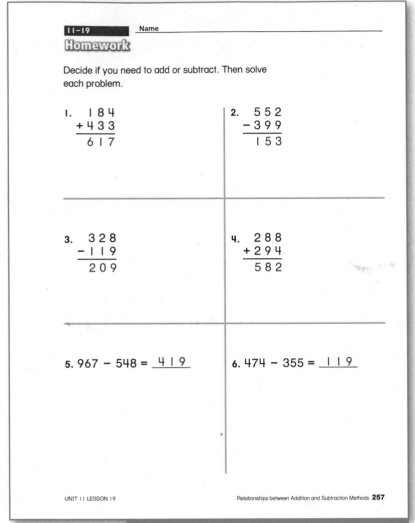

Decide if you need to add or subtract. Then solve each problem.

1. 184 + 433 = 617
2. 552 − 399 = 153
3. 328 − 119 = 209
4. 288 + 294 = 582
5. 967 − 548 = 419
6. 474 − 355 = 119

UNIT 11 LESSON 19 Relationships between Addition and Subtraction Methods **257**

Homework and Remembering page 257

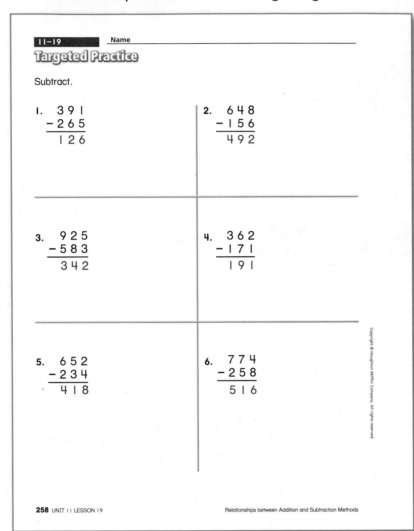

11–19
Targeted Practice **Goal:** Practice subtraction.

This Targeted Practice page can be used with children who need extra practice in subtracting 3-digit numbers.

11–19 **Targeted Practice** Name ____________________

Subtract.

1. 391 − 265 = 126
2. 648 − 156 = 492
3. 925 − 583 = 342
4. 362 − 171 = 191
5. 652 − 234 = 418
6. 774 − 258 = 516

258 UNIT 11 LESSON 19 Relationships between Addition and Subtraction Methods

Homework and Remembering page 258

Home or School Activity

Social Studies Connection

The Great Lakes Explain to children that the five lakes between Canada and the United States are called the Great Lakes. If possible, use a map to show them where the Great Lakes are located. Draw the table at the right that shows the average depth of each lake. Then challenge children to write and solve an addition or subtraction problem using the information in the table.

Depth of the Great Lakes

Name of Lake	Average Depth
Lake Erie	62 feet
Lake Huron	195 feet
Lake Michigan	279 feet
Lake Ontario	283 feet
Lake Superior	500 feet

UNIT 11 LESSON 20

Unknown Start and Comparison Problems

REAL WORLD Problem Solving

Vocabulary
situation equation
solution equation
unknown start
comparison problem

Lesson Objective

- **Solve complex story problems containing 3-digit numbers.**

The Day at a Glance

Today's Goals	Materials	
1 Teaching the Lesson Solve story problems where the starting number is unknown. Solve comparison story problems that contain misleading language.	**Lesson Activities** Student Activity Book pp. 381–382 (includes Subtraction Sprint) Homework and Remembering pp. 259–260 MathBoard materials	**Going Further** Activity Cards 11-20 *Hannah's Collections,* by Marthe Jocelyn Math Journals
2 Going Further ▶ Differentiated Instruction		
3 Homework and Spiral Review		

Use Math Talk today!

Keeping Skills Sharp

Quick Practice — 5 MINUTES

Goal: Practice subtraction (totals $\leq$ 18).

Materials: Student Activity Book page 381

Subtraction Sprint Direct children's attention to Student Activity Book page 381. Decide how much time to give them to complete the Sprint. Explain the procedure and time limit to them. (This is the same Subtraction Sprint students did in previous lessons.)

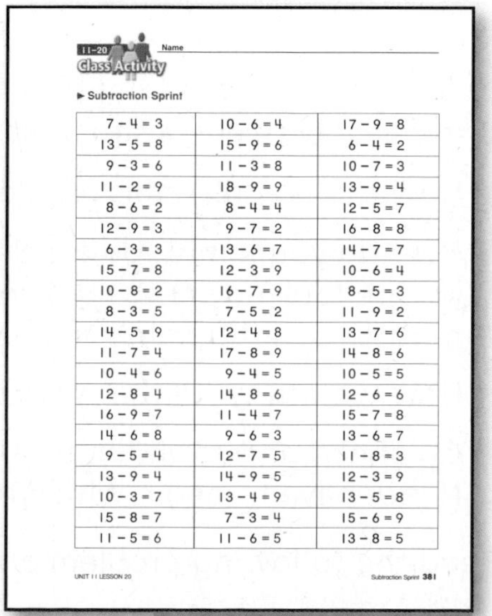

11-20 Class Activity Name

▶ Subtraction Sprint

7 − 4 = 3	10 − 6 = 4	17 − 9 = 8
13 − 5 = 8	15 − 9 = 6	6 − 4 = 2
9 − 3 = 6	11 − 3 = 8	10 − 7 = 3
11 − 2 = 9	18 − 9 = 9	13 − 9 = 4
8 − 6 = 2	8 − 4 = 4	12 − 5 = 7
12 − 9 = 3	9 − 7 = 2	16 − 8 = 8
6 − 3 = 3	13 − 6 = 7	14 − 7 = 7
15 − 7 = 8	12 − 3 = 9	10 − 6 = 4
10 − 8 = 2	16 − 7 = 9	8 − 5 = 3
8 − 3 = 5	7 − 5 = 2	11 − 9 = 2
14 − 5 = 9	12 − 4 = 8	13 − 7 = 6
11 − 7 = 4	17 − 8 = 9	14 − 8 = 6
10 − 4 = 6	9 − 4 = 5	10 − 5 = 5
12 − 8 = 4	14 − 8 = 6	12 − 6 = 6
16 − 9 = 7	11 − 4 = 7	15 − 7 = 8
14 − 6 = 8	9 − 6 = 3	13 − 6 = 7
9 − 5 = 4	12 − 7 = 5	11 − 8 = 3
13 − 9 = 4	14 − 9 = 5	12 − 3 = 9
10 − 3 = 7	13 − 4 = 9	13 − 5 = 8
15 − 8 = 7	7 − 3 = 4	15 − 6 = 9
11 − 5 = 6	11 − 6 = 5	13 − 8 = 5

UNIT 11 LESSON 20 Subtraction Sprint 381

Student Activity Book Page 381

Daily Routines

Making Change and Counting Coins Making Change from $5.00, Combining Coins and Counting Money (See pp. xxvii–xxviii.)

▶ Led by Student Leaders

Money Routine Using the 120 Poster, Using the Money Flip Chart, Using the Number Path, Using Secret Code Cards (See pp. xxiii–xxv.)

▶ Led by Student Leaders

1 Teaching the Lesson

Activity

Complex Story Problems

50 MINUTES

Goals: Solve story problems where the starting number is unknown. Solve comparison story problems that contain misleading language.

Materials: MathBoard materials, Student Activity Book page 382

NCTM Standards:
Number and Operations
Communication

Teaching Note

Math Background A *situation equation* is a direct translation of a story problem. In this example, ☐ + 135 = 576 is the situation equation.

A *solution equation* reflects the operation that can be used to solve the problem. 576 − ☐ = 135 is the solution equation for this example.

Sometimes the situation and solution equations are the same. However, story problems where the starting number is unknown can be confusing to children because the situation equation does not always match the solution equation. Math Mountains are particularly helpful at illustrating this difference.

▶ Solve Complex Story Problems

WHOLE CLASS

Math Talk 123

Story Problems with Unknown Starting Numbers Read the following problem aloud to children.

Jim and Nancy collect postcards.
They just added 135 postcards to their collection.
Now they have 576 postcards.
How many postcards did they have to begin with?

Invite children to write an equation that shows the situation on their MathBoards as you write it on the board. Doing so will help them see that the number they must find is the starting number.

Situation Equation:

☐ + 135 = 576

Have children discuss the meaning of each part of the situation equation. The unknown number is the number of postcards Jim and Nancy had before they added 135 to their collection. 576 is the total number of postcards they have now. It is the total of how many they had at the beginning plus the 135 they added.

Then have children draw a Math Mountain on their MathBoards to show the situation while you draw one on the board.

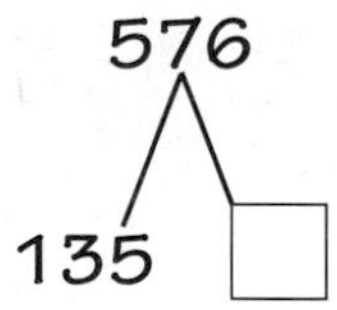

Help children understand how to solve the problem and to see the difference between a situation equation and a solution equation.

- How can we solve this problem? Subtract 135 from 576.
- How do you know you can subtract? The Math Mountain shows that we are looking for a unknown partner. We can find the unknown partner by subtracting the partner we know from the total.
- Now we can write the *solution equation*: 576 − 135 = ☐
- Go ahead and solve the problem. How many postcards did Jim and Nancy have to begin with? 441 postcards

Read the following problem aloud to children.

Luke's hobby is raising tropical fish. His adult guppies just had babies. There were so many babies that Luke gave 279 of them to his friends. Now Luke has 154 baby guppies. How many baby guppies did he have to start with?

Using the same procedure as before, have children draw a situation equation, discuss the situation, draw a Math Mountain, discuss a solution procedure, write a solution equation, and solve the problem.

In their discussion, children should note that the unknown number is the total baby guppies Luke had at the start. Children should know this because Luke gave some away. This situation is clearly shown in the Math Mountain. To find a total, children need to add the two partners.

Situation Equation:

$\square - 279 = 154$

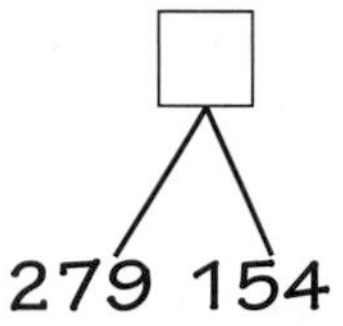

Solution Equation:

$279 + 154 = \square$

11–20 **Class Activity** Name ______

Vocabulary
unknown start problem
comparison problem

▶ **Solve Complex Story Problems**

Solve the **unknown start** and **comparison problems.**

1. Marian had a collection of miniature cars. Then she gave 465 cars to her brother Simon. Now Marian has 288 cars. How many cars did she have to begin with?

753 cars (label)

2. In September the Shaws planted some bulbs. In October they planted 178 more bulbs. Altogether they planted 510 bulbs. How many bulbs did they plant in September?

332 bulbs (label)

3. Lila has 288 mugs in her collection, which is 158 fewer than her friend Letty has. How many mugs does Letty have in her collection?

446 mugs (label)

4. One year the Ricos planted 640 flowers. This was 243 more than the Smiths planted. How many flowers did the Smiths plant?

397 flowers (label)

382 UNIT 11 LESSON 20 Unknown Start and Comparison Problems

Student Activity Book page 382

Ongoing Assessment

Have children write a situation equation and draw a Math Mountain to represent each of the following story problems.

▶ Justin had a bank full of pennies. He spent 175 of the pennies. He still has 265 pennies left. How many pennies were in the box to start?

▶ Ms. Bennett keeps pencils in a box. Today she put 164 pencils in the box. Now there are 255 pencils in the box. How many pencils were in the box to start?

English Language Learners

Have children underline *more than* and *fewer than* in the problems on Student Activity Book page 382.

- **Beginning** Say: **These are comparing words.** Ask: **Are these *comparison problems*?** yes
- **Intermediate** Ask: **Do these words tell us to *compare*?** yes **What kind of problems are these?** comparison problems
- **Advanced** Have children tell what kind of problems use the terms *more than* and *fewer than*.

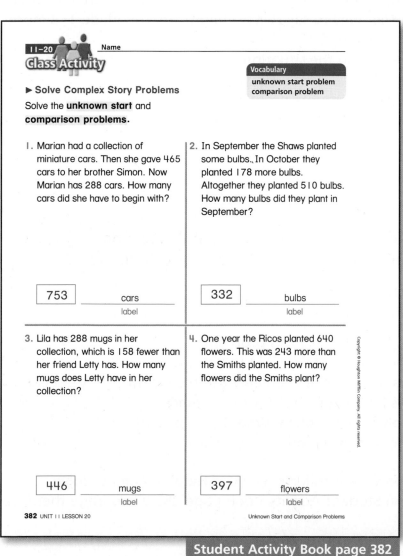

Activity continued ▶

Math Talk Have children solve the first two problems on Student Activity Book page 382. Use the **Solve and Discuss** structure.

When children have finished, select one or two of the children at the board to explain how they solved each problem.

Comparison Story Problems Read the following problem aloud.

> **Laura made 354 sandwiches for the school picnic. This was 132 fewer sandwiches than George made. How many sandwiches did George make?**

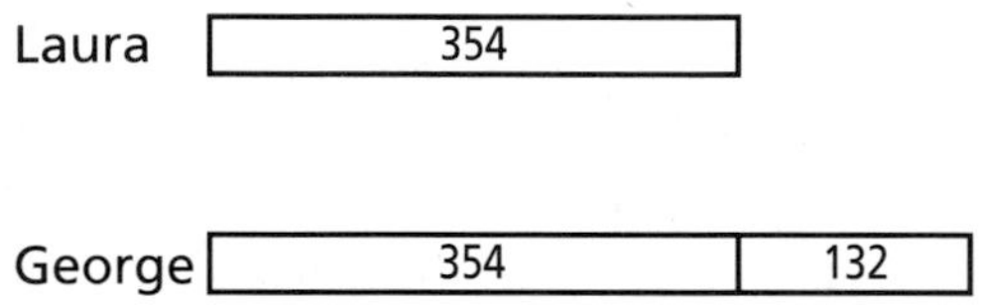

You may wish to have children draw comparison bars. Then explain that saying the problem in two ways often helps to see how to solve the problem.

- The problem says that Laura made 132 fewer sandwiches than George did. What is another way to say this problem? George made 132 more sandwiches than Laura did.
- Which way of describing the situation helps us solve the problem more easily? George made 132 more sandwiches than Laura did.
- Why is this easier? Because the problem asks how many sandwiches George made. Saying that George made 132 more tells you to add 132 to 354 to find how many he made.
- Go ahead and solve the problem. What is the answer? 132 + 354 = 486; so, George made 486 sandwiches.

Read the following problem aloud to children.

> **Tanya made 538 muffins for the school picnic. This was 212 more muffins than Annie made. How many muffins did Annie make?**

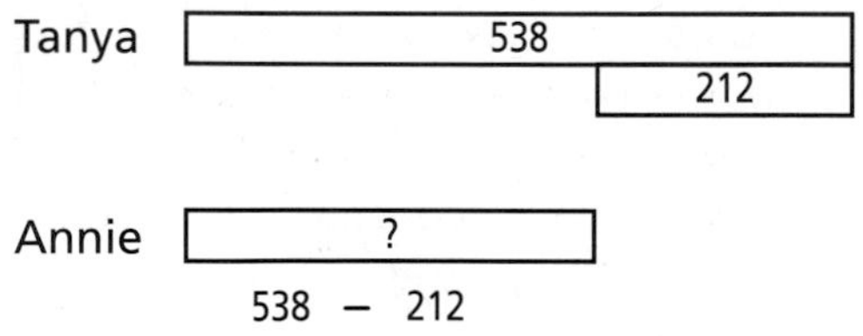

Once again have children make drawings to show the problem. Then ask the questions below to help them understand and solve it.

- What are the two ways to say this problem? Tanya made 212 more muffins than Annie. Annie made 212 fewer muffins than Tanya.
- Which way helps us solve the problem? the second way Why? because the problem asks how many muffins Annie made
- Go ahead and solve the problem. What is the answer? 538 − 212 = 326; so Annie made 326 muffins.

Math Talk Now have children work in **Helping Pairs** to solve exercises 3 and 4 on Student Activity Book page 382. Encourage them to check their work.

2 Going Further

Differentiated Instruction

Intervention — Activity Card 11-20

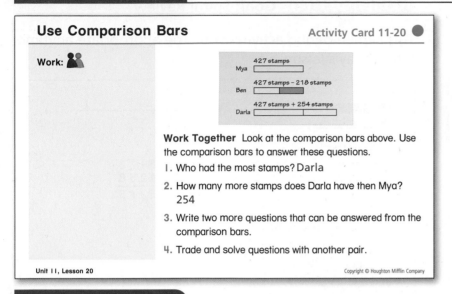

Use Comparison Bars — Activity Card 11-20

Work: (pairs)

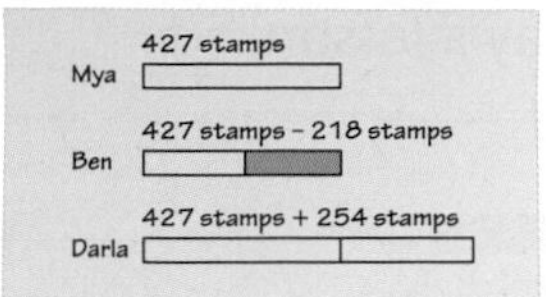

Work Together Look at the comparison bars above. Use the comparison bars to answer these questions.

1. Who had the most stamps? Darla
2. How many more stamps does Darla have then Mya? 254
3. Write two more questions that can be answered from the comparison bars.
4. Trade and solve questions with another pair.

Unit 11, Lesson 20

Activity Note Review how to read the comparison bars. Have children explain the bars to each other.

Math Writing Prompt

Representation Karen and Uju have sticker collections. Karen has 248 stickers. She has 154 less than Uju. Draw and label comparison bars to show this.

Soar to Success Math Software Support

Warm Up 27.9

On Level — Activity Card 11-20

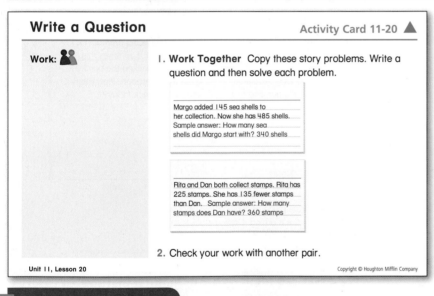

Write a Question — Activity Card 11-20

Work: (pairs)

1. **Work Together** Copy these story problems. Write a question and then solve each problem.

   Margo added 145 sea shells to her collection. Now she has 485 shells. Sample answer: How many sea shells did Margo start with? 340 shells

   Rita and Dan both collect stamps. Rita has 225 stamps. She has 135 fewer stamps than Dan. Sample answer: How many stamps does Dan have? 360 stamps

2. Check your work with another pair.

Unit 11, Lesson 20

Activity Note Each pair needs to write a question for each story problem and then find the answer to the problem.

Math Writing Prompt

Write Your Own Write a story problem about a marble collection in which the starting number is unknown.

Harcourt MegaMath Grades K-6 Software Support

Country Countdown: Block Busters, Level W

Challenge — Activity Card 11-20

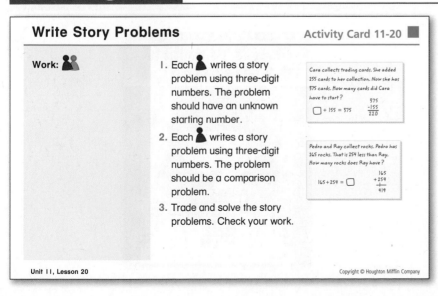

Write Story Problems — Activity Card 11-20

Work: (pairs)

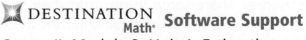

1. Each (child) writes a story problem using three-digit numbers. The problem should have an unknown starting number.
2. Each (child) writes a story problem using three-digit numbers. The problem should be a comparison problem.
3. Trade and solve the story problems. Check your work.

Cara collects trading cards. She added 155 cards to her collection. Now she has 375 cards. How many cards did Cara have to start?

$\square + 155 = 375$
$375 - 155 = 220$

Pedro and Ray collect rocks. Pedro has 165 rocks. That is 254 less than Ray. How many rocks does Ray have?

$165 + 254 = \square$
$165 + 254 = 419$

Unit 11, Lesson 20

Activity Note Each child writes two story problems and then gives their problems to their partner to solve.

Math Writing Prompt

Work Backward Write a comparison problem that has the answer *25 beavers*.

Destination Math Software Support

Course II: Module 2: Unit 1: Estimating and Finding Differences within 1,000

3 Homework and Spiral Review

11–20 Homework **Goal:** Additional Practice

This Homework page provides practice in solving unknown start and comparison story problems.

11–20 **Homework** Name ____________

Solve each story problem.

1. Abigail's mother gave her some carrots to sell at the state fair. Then Abigail picked 367 more from the garden. Now Abigail has 825 carrots to sell. How many did her mother give her?

   [458] carrots (label)

2. Stanley the grocer had lots of mushrooms. He sold 679 in the morning. Now he has 244 left to sell. How many mushrooms did Stanley have at the beginning?

   [923] mushrooms (label)

3. Carmen has 347 guppies in her fish tank. Peter must give away 156 of his guppies to have the same number as Carmen. How many guppies does Peter have in his tank?

   [503] guppies (label)

4. Stanley bought 283 bags of flour for his store. Ted needs 148 bags of flour to have as many as Stanley. How many bags of flour does Ted have?

   [135] bags of flour (label)

UNIT 11 LESSON 20 Unknown Start and Comparison Problems **259**

Homework and Remembering page 259

11–20 Remembering **Goal:** Spiral Review

This Remembering activity would be appropriate anytime after today's lesson.

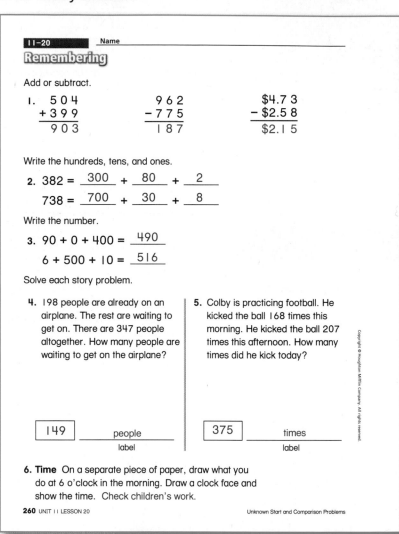

11–20 **Remembering** Name ____________

Add or subtract.

1. 504 + 399 = 903 962 − 775 = 187 \$4.73 − \$2.58 = \$2.15

Write the hundreds, tens, and ones.

2. 382 = 300 + 80 + 2
   738 = 700 + 30 + 8

Write the number.

3. 90 + 0 + 400 = 490
   6 + 500 + 10 = 516

Solve each story problem.

4. 198 people are already on an airplane. The rest are waiting to get on. There are 347 people altogether. How many people are waiting to get on the airplane?

   [149] people (label)

5. Colby is practicing football. He kicked the ball 168 times this morning. He kicked the ball 207 times this afternoon. How many times did he kick today?

   [375] times (label)

6. **Time** On a separate piece of paper, draw what you do at 6 o'clock in the morning. Draw a clock face and show the time. Check children's work.

260 UNIT 11 LESSON 20 Unknown Start and Comparison Problems

Homework and Remembering page 260

Home or School Activity

Literature Connection

Collections Read aloud or have children read *Hannah's Collections,* by Marthe Jocelyn (Dutton Children's Books, 2000). Explain that some people collect things as a hobby. Have children share some things that they or someone they know collects. Then have children write and solve unknown start and comparison story problems about a collection of items.

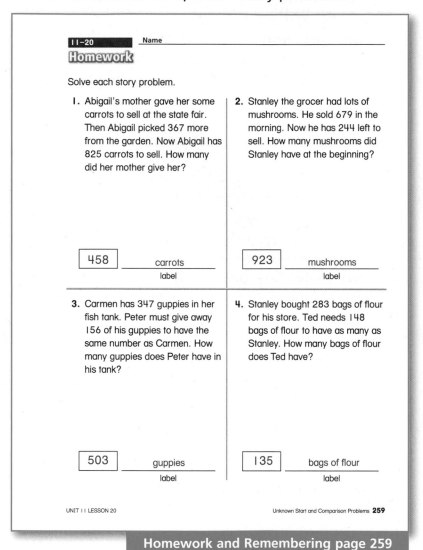

UNIT 11 LESSON 21

Mixed Addition and Subtraction Story Problems

REAL WORLD Problem Solving

Lesson Objective

- **Discriminate between addition and subtraction situations and apply the appropriate operation.**

Vocabulary
unknown addends
group
ungroup

The Day at a Glance

Today's Goals	Materials	
1 Teaching the Lesson **A1:** Solve addition and subtraction exercises. **A2:** Solve addition and subtraction story problems.	**Lesson Activities** Student Activity Book p. 383 Homework and Remembering pp. 261–262 MathBoard materials	**Going Further** Activity Cards 11-21 Student Activity Book p. 384 Buy or Sell? (TRB M88) Base ten blocks Math Journals
2 Going Further ► Extra Practice ► Differentiated Instruction		
3 Homework and Targeted Practice		

Use Math Talk today!

Keeping Skills Sharp

Quick Practice — 5 MINUTES

Goal: Find partners of 3-digit numbers.

Partners of 3-Digit Numbers Draw the two Math Mountains below on the board and have two **Student Leaders** write the unknown partners. Have them check that the unknown partners are correct.

Then have a third Student Leader lead the class in saying the four addition and four subtraction equations as two other Student Leaders write them as quickly as possible on the board. (See Unit 11 Lesson 19.)

482
348 | 134

$348 + 134 = 482$ $482 - 348 = 134$
$134 + 348 = 482$ $482 - 134 = 348$
$482 = 348 + 134$ $134 = 482 - 348$
$482 = 134 + 348$ $348 = 482 - 134$

918
259 | 659

$259 + 659 = 918$ $918 - 259 = 659$
$659 + 259 = 918$ $918 - 659 = 259$
$918 = 259 + 659$ $659 = 918 - 259$
$918 = 659 + 259$ $259 = 918 - 659$

Daily Routines

Making Change and Counting Coins Making Change from $5.00, Combining Coins and Counting Money (See pp. xxvii–xxviii.)

► Led by Student Leaders

Money Routine Using the 120 Poster, Using the Money Flip Chart, Using the Number Path, Using Secret Code Cards (See pp. xxiii–xxv.)

► Led by Student Leaders

1 Teaching the Lesson

Activity 1

Solve Addition and Subtraction Exercises

25 MINUTES

Goal: Solve addition and subtraction exercises.

Materials: MathBoard materials

NCTM Standards:
Number and Operations
Communication

English Language Learners

Write *partner* and *addend* on the board. Say: **Another word for *partner* is *addend*.** Write 538 + 311 = 849.

- **Beginning** Ask: **Are 538 and 311 *partners*?** yes **Are they *addends*?** yes
- **Intermediate** Say: **538 and 311 are *partners* or __.** addends
- **Advanced** Ask: **Which numbers are *partners*?** 538, 311 Say: **We also call them __.** addends

▶ Addition and Subtraction Exercises WHOLE CLASS

Write the exercises below on the board. Have children copy them onto their MathBoards.

176	502	486	845	411
+ 589	− 108	+ 324	− 228	− 267
765	394	810	617	144

Math Talk Use the questions from Lesson 19 to review addition and subtraction operations.

- What is the most important thing to decide in addition? if you need to make a new ten, a new hundred, or both
- What do you do when you make a new ten? You put the new ten with the tens that were in the problem.
- What do you do when you make a new hundred? You put the new hundred with the hundreds that were in the problem.
- What is the most important thing to decide in subtraction? if you need to ungroup to get more ones, to get more tens, or both
- What do you do when you ungroup to get more ones? You ungroup 1 ten for 10 ones and add the 10 ones to the ones you have.
- What do you do when you ungroup to get more tens? You ungroup 1 hundred for 10 tens and add the 10 tens to the tens you have.

Then have a few volunteers work at the board to complete the exercises while the rest of the class works at their seats. Children may work individually, in **Helping Pairs**, or in small groups. If they work in pairs or small groups, have children explain to each other how they solved the exercises.

When children have completed the exercises, use the **Solve and Discuss** structure to review their work. Select one or two children at the board to explain what they did. Encourage the other children to ask questions and make comments. If children solved an exercise in different ways, encourage them to share their methods with the class.

Activity 2

Practice Solving Complex Story Problems

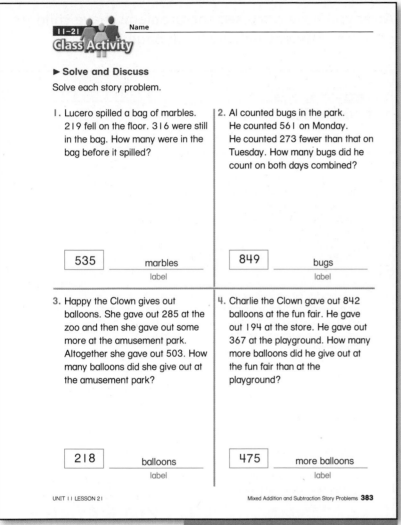

11–21 **Class Activity** Name ______________________

► Solve and Discuss

Solve each story problem.

1. Lucero spilled a bag of marbles. 219 fell on the floor. 316 were still in the bag. How many were in the bag before it spilled?

   535 marbles (label)

2. Al counted bugs in the park. He counted 561 on Monday. He counted 273 fewer than that on Tuesday. How many bugs did he count on both days combined?

   849 bugs (label)

3. Happy the Clown gives out balloons. She gave out 285 at the zoo and then she gave out some more at the amusement park. Altogether she gave out 503. How many balloons did she give out at the amusement park?

   218 balloons (label)

4. Charlie the Clown gave out 842 balloons at the fun fair. He gave out 194 at the store. He gave out 367 at the playground. How many more balloons did he give out at the fun fair than at the playground?

   475 more balloons (label)

UNIT 11 LESSON 21 — Mixed Addition and Subtraction Story Problems 383

Student Activity Book page 383

► Solve and Discuss WHOLE CLASS

Math Talk

Refer children to Student Activity Book page 383. Explain to children that sometimes they will need to add and sometimes they will need to subtract to solve the problems on the page. Also point out the fact that some of the problems may contain extra information and some may require more than one step to solve.

Allow children to work individually, in Helping Pairs, or in small groups to complete the page. Tell them that they may use any method to solve the problems but they must show their work. Encourage children to check their work by doing the opposite operation.

Near the end of the activity, invite children to come to the board to explain their work. Discuss the solution with the class and also discuss any errors that come to light. Repeat as time and interest permit.

25 MINUTES

Goal: Solve addition and subtraction story problems.

Materials: Student Activity Book page 383

NCTM Standards:
Number and Operations
Communication

Ongoing Assessment

As children are working, circulate around the room. Engage individual children by asking questions such as the following:

- ► Do you need to add or subtract to solve this problem? How do you know?
- ► What method (or strategy) will you use to solve this problem? Why?

2 Going Further

Extra Practice

Goal: Solve addition and subtraction story problems.

Materials: Student Activity Book page 384

▶ Solve and Discuss WHOLE CLASS

If children have difficulties, you can use these questions to help them think about how to solve the problems. Also suggest that they draw a situation equation and a Math Mountain and comparison bars for any comparison problems.

- Read problem 1. Will the answer be more or less than 383 stamps? How do you know? It will be more than 383 stamps because Damon bought more stamps at the yard sale.
- So which operation should you use to solve problem 1? Addition How do you know? I need to find how many stamps Damon has after he bought the stamps at the yard sale.
- Will you need to group ones or tens when you add? I will need to group tens How do you know? 8 tens and 2 tens is 10 tens or 1 hundred.
- Read problem 5. Should you add or subtract to find out how many more fliers Pawel passed out at the grocery store than at the bakery? Subtract How do you know? I have to find the difference. But Jo Ann might add on to 194 to get 358.
- Will you need to ungroup when you subtract? Yes How do you know? 5 tens is less than 9 tens.
- Read problem 6. Which operation will you use to find how many cards Cora collected this year? Subtraction How do you know? Cora collected fewer cards this year than last year.
- What operation will you use to find how many cards Cora collected altogether? Addition How do you know? I need to find the total number of cards that Cora has.

▶ Practice Story Problems

After you have discussed the problems, have children complete Student Activity Book page 384.

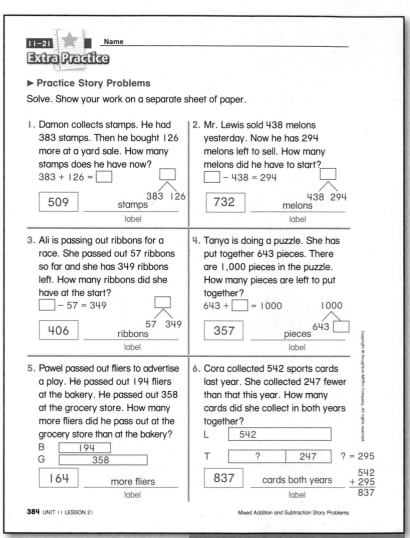

11-21 Extra Practice Name ________

▶ Practice Story Problems

Solve. Show your work on a separate sheet of paper.

1. Damon collects stamps. He had 383 stamps. Then he bought 126 more at a yard sale. How many stamps does he have now?
383 + 126 = ☐ (Math Mountain: ☐; 383, 126)
509 stamps (label)

2. Mr. Lewis sold 438 melons yesterday. Now he has 294 melons left to sell. How many melons did he have to start?
☐ − 438 = 294 (Math Mountain: ☐; 438, 294)
732 melons (label)

3. Ali is passing out ribbons for a race. She passed out 57 ribbons so far and she has 349 ribbons left. How many ribbons did she have at the start?
☐ − 57 = 349 (Math Mountain: ☐; 57, 349)
406 ribbons (label)

4. Tanya is doing a puzzle. She has put together 643 pieces. There are 1,000 pieces in the puzzle. How many pieces are left to put together?
643 + ☐ = 1000 (Math Mountain: 1000; 643, ☐)
357 pieces (label)

5. Pawel passed out fliers to advertise a play. He passed out 194 fliers at the bakery. He passed out 358 at the grocery store. How many more fliers did he pass out at the grocery store than at the bakery?
B 194
G 358
164 more fliers (label)

6. Cora collected 542 sports cards last year. She collected 247 fewer than that this year. How many cards did she collect in both years together?
L 542
T ? 247 ? = 295
$542 + 295 = 837$
837 cards both years (label)

384 UNIT 11 LESSON 21 Mixed Addition and Subtraction Story Problems

Student Activity Book page 384

Math Talk After children have finished solving the problems, use the **Solve and Discuss** structure and invite volunteers to the board to explain how they solved each problem. If other children in the class solved the problems using a different method, encourage them to share their methods as well.

Intervention — Activity Card 11-21

Use Base Ten Blocks

Activity Card 11-21

Work: pairs

Use:
- Buy or Sell? (TRB M88)
- base ten blocks

Choose:
- 1
- 2

1. Look at the first row of boxes on "Buy or Sell?".
2. 1 Be the buyer for this turn. Pay 2 $236 for the bicycle. Find out how much money you have left.
3. 2 Be the seller for this turn. Receive $236 from 1 for the bicycle. Find out how much money you have now.
4. Take turns until all of the items have been bought and sold.

Unit 11, Lesson 21

Activity Note Each pair needs Buy and Sell? (TRB M88) and base ten blocks. Help pairs with the first problem.

Math Writing Prompt

Explain Your Thinking
Explain why the 6 was changed to 5 and the 3 was changed to 13.

$$\begin{array}{r} {\scriptstyle 5\ 13} \\ \not{5}\not{6}\not{3} \\ -\ 236 \\ \hline \end{array}$$

Soar to Success Math Software Support

Warm Up 27.11

On Level — Activity Card 11-21

Buy or Sell?

Activity Card 11-21

Work: pairs

Use:
- Buy or Sell? (TRB M88)

Choose:
- 1
- 2

1. Look at the first row of boxes on "Buy or Sell?".
2. 2 Be the buyer. Pay 1 $236 for the bicycle. Find out how much money you have left.
3. 1 Be the seller. Receive $236 from 2 for the bicycle. Find out how much money you have now.
4. Take turns being the buyer and the seller. Find out how much money you have after each round.

Unit 11, Lesson 21

Activity Note Each pair needs Buy or Sell? (TRB M88). Review with children the first exercise.

Math Writing Prompt

Write Your Own Write an addition story problem and a subtraction story problem that both have an answer of $463.

Harcourt Mega Math Software Support

Country Countdown: Block Busters, Level Y

Challenge — Activity Card 11-21

Check the Totals

Activity Card 11-21

Work: pairs

Use:
- Buy or Sell? (TRB M88)

Choose:
- 1
- 2

1. 2 Be the buyer for the first exercise. Pay 1 $236 for the bicycle. Find how much money you have left.
2. 1 Be the seller. Receive $236 from 2. Find out how much money you have now.
3. Take turns being the buyer and the seller. Find out how much money you have after each round.
4. **Math Talk** Discuss how you can check your work. Compare the beginning total and the final total.

Unit 11, Lesson 21

Activity Note Each pair needs Buy or Sell? (TRB M88)

Math Writing Prompt

Analyze Which of the examples below do you need to ungroup? Explain.

$472 - 138 =$ ____ $677 - 354 =$ ____

Destination Math Software Support

Course II: Module 2: Unit 1: Estimating and Finding Differences within 1,000

3 Homework and Targeted Practice

11–21
Homework **Goal:** Additional Practice

✓ Include children's completed Homework page as part of their portfolios.

11–21
Targeted Practice **Goal:** Solve story problems.

This page can be used with children who need extra practice solving story problems with 3-digit numbers.

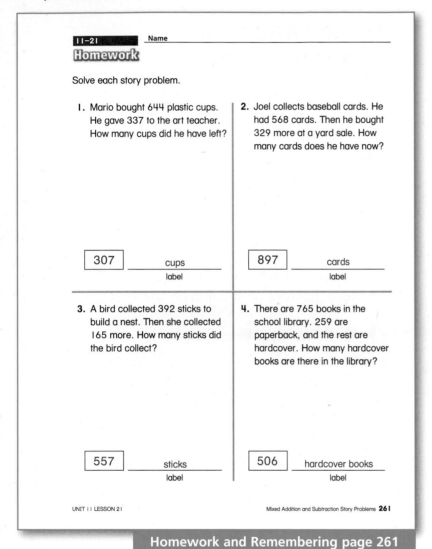

11–21
Homework
Name ______

Solve each story problem.

1. Mario bought 644 plastic cups. He gave 337 to the art teacher. How many cups did he have left?

307 cups
label

2. Joel collects baseball cards. He had 568 cards. Then he bought 329 more at a yard sale. How many cards does he have now?

897 cards
label

3. A bird collected 392 sticks to build a nest. Then she collected 165 more. How many sticks did the bird collect?

557 sticks
label

4. There are 765 books in the school library. 259 are paperback, and the rest are hardcover. How many hardcover books are there in the library?

506 hardcover books
label

UNIT 11 LESSON 21 Mixed Addition and Subtraction Story Problems 261

Homework and Remembering page 261

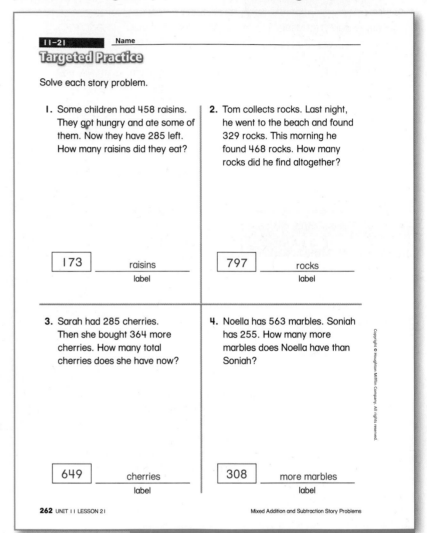

11–21
Targeted Practice
Name ______

Solve each story problem.

1. Some children had 458 raisins. They got hungry and ate some of them. Now they have 285 left. How many raisins did they eat?

173 raisins
label

2. Tom collects rocks. Last night, he went to the beach and found 329 rocks. This morning he found 468 rocks. How many rocks did he find altogether?

797 rocks
label

3. Sarah had 285 cherries. Then she bought 364 more cherries. How many total cherries does she have now?

649 cherries
label

4. Noella has 563 marbles. Soniah has 255. How many more marbles does Noella have than Soniah?

308 more marbles
label

262 UNIT 11 LESSON 21 Mixed Addition and Subtraction Story Problems

Homework and Remembering page 262

Home or School Activity

Science Connection

Animal Weights Draw the table at the right. Point out that the numbers in the table show the least and the most each animal usually weighs.

Invite children to write comparison story problems using the information in the table. Tell them to decide on a weight for each of the animals they want to include in their problems. When they are finished, have them give their problems to a partner to solve.

Name of Animal	Weight Range (in pounds)
African lion	264 to 550
brown bear	209 to 800
gorilla	150 to 600
tiger	143 to 670

The lion at the zoo weighs 454 pounds. The brown bear at the zoo would need to lose 163 pounds to weigh as much as the lion. How much does the bear at the zoo weigh?

UNIT 11 LESSON 22

Spend Money

REAL WORLD Problem Solving

Lesson Objectives

- Subtract money amounts from $10.
- Buy and sell goods.

Vocabulary
ungrouping
making change
counting on
front-end estimation

The Day at a Glance

Today's Goals	Materials	
1 Teaching the Lesson **A1:** Practice ungrouping $10.00 in order to subtract. **A2:** Buy pretend items with $10.00 and make change.	**Lesson Activities** Student Activity Book pp. 385–386 Homework and Remembering pp. 263–264 Quick Quiz 5 (Assessment Guide) MathBoard materials Secret Code Cards Real or play money	**Going Further** Activity Cards 11-22 Student Activity Book pp. 387–388 Real or play money Index cards Ten-Dollar Bills (TRB M89) Dollar Bills Newspaper ads Math Journals
2 Going Further ▶ Math Connection: Use Front-End Estimation ▶ Differentiated Instruction		
3 Homework		

Use Math Talk today!

Keeping Skills Sharp

Quick Practice — 5 MINUTES

Goal: Identify a 3-digit number from the values of its digits.

Unscramble the Hundreds, Tens, and Ones Write an exercise, or have a **Student Leader** write an exercise, such as 5 + 800 + 40 = ☐ on the board. The hundreds, tens, and ones should not be in order. Children should then determine the number presented (845). The Student Leader then quickly writes two more such scrambled numbers for the class to solve. (See Unit 11 Lesson 6.)

Repeated Quick Practice Use this Quick Practice from a previous lesson.

▶ **Blue Math Mountain Cards** (See Unit 7 Lesson 13.)

Daily Routines

Making Change and Counting Coins Making Change from $5.00, Combining Coins and Counting Money (See pp. xxvii–xxviii.)

▶ Led by Student Leaders

Money Routine Using the 120 Poster, Using the Money Flip Chart, Using the Number Path, Using Secret Code Cards (See pp. xxiii–xxv.)

▶ Led by Student Leaders

1 Teaching the Lesson

Activity 1

Subtract from $10.00

15 MINUTES

Goal: Practice ungrouping $10.00 in order to subtract.

Materials: MathBoard materials, Secret Code Cards, 1–900 (optional)

NCTM Standards:
Number and Operations
Representation
Communication

Teaching Note

Watch For! Some children may ungroup the 1 in one thousand as 10 ones. If they do make that error, point out that their trade is not an even trade. Emphasize that the 1 in one thousand is equal to 10 hundreds not 10 ones.

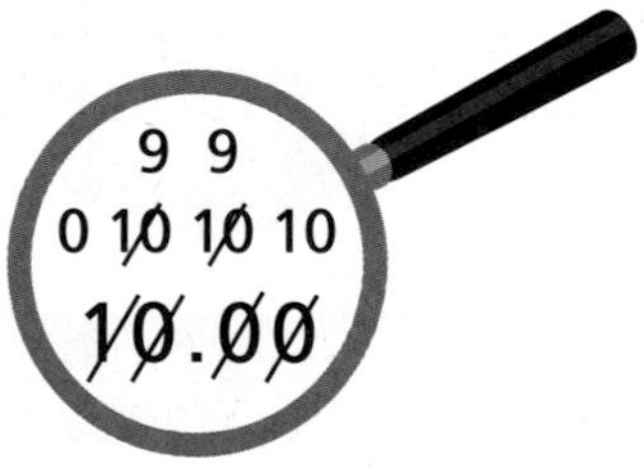

▶ Subtract a Money Amount from $10.00 WHOLE CLASS

Explain to children that they will be subtracting from $10.00 in the next activity. Write $10.00 on the board. Point to each digit, beginning at the right, and elicit from children what each digit represents in terms of money: 0 pennies, 0 dimes, 0 one-dollar bills, and 1 ten-dollar bill. Be sure children understand that 10 dollars is the same as 1000 pennies.

$ 10.00
↑ ↑ ↑ ↑

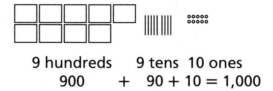

Have children solve the exercises below. Building on what they already know about subtraction, have them discuss how they might do this. Encourage children to add up to $10.00 as one method of solving the exercises.

$10.00	$10.00
– 7.52	– 4.87
$ 2.4 8	$ 5.1 3

Invite a child to draw a "magnifying glass" view of the ungrouped top number. Have the class confirm that 9 hundreds, 9 tens, and 10 ones are equal to 1 thousand by drawing boxes, sticks, and circles.

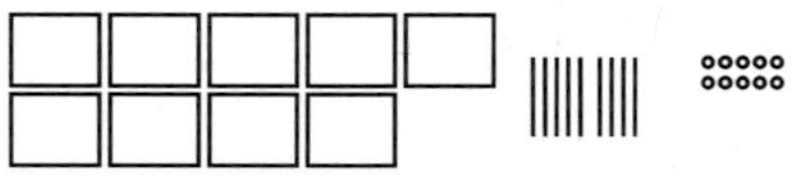

9 hundreds 9 tens 10 ones
900 + 90 + 10 = 1,000

When children have finished subtracting, have them confirm their answers by making Proof Drawings and by using addition to check the answers. They may also show the solutions with Secret Code Cards.

Activity 2

The Yard Sale

30 MINUTES

Goal: Buy pretend items with $10.00 and make change.

Materials: real or play money, Student Activity Book pages 385–386

NCTM Standards:
Number and Operations
Communication

▶ Introduce the Ten-Dollar Bill

Refer children to Student Activity Book pages 385 and 386. Point out the ten-dollar bill on the bottom of the page.

The back of the ten-dollar bill shows the number of pennies in $10.00. Have students use the back to answer these questions:

- How many one-dollars are in a ten-dollar bill? 10 one-dollars
- How many pennies are in a one-dollar bill? 100 pennies
- How many pennies are in a ten-dollar bill? 1,000 pennies

11–22 Class Activity

Name ____________________

▶ The Yard Sale

Choose any two toys to buy. Pay for them with $10.00.

$4.87 Baseball Glove	$3.49 Globe	$2.59 Perfume	$1.64 Funny Glasses
$1.55 Toy Binoculars	$2.48 Toy Lamb	$4.86 Ring	$3.97 Toy Guitar

UNIT 11 LESSON 22 Spend Money **385**

Student Activity Book page 385

▶ The Yard Sale PAIRS

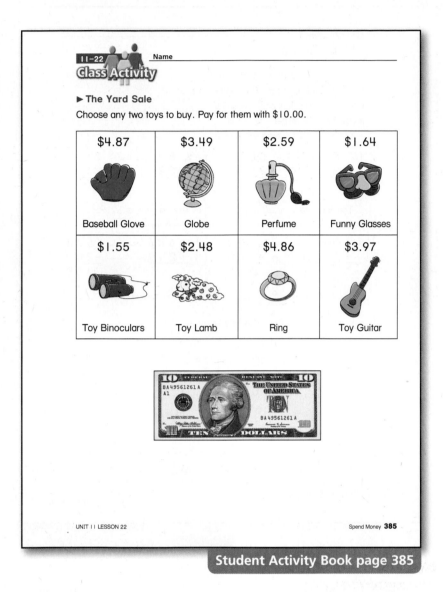

The top of Student Activity Book page 385 shows items at a yard sale that children can pretend to buy with the ten-dollar bill. Explain to children how to do the activity.

- You will be working with a partner to buy and sell items from the yard sale. One of you will be the buyer. One of you will be the seller.
- The buyer picks two items to buy and the seller finds the total cost.
- The buyer checks that the total cost is correct. If it is, he or she gives the seller a ten-dollar bill.
- The seller gives the change to the buyer by counting on.
- The buyer checks the amount of change by subtracting with numbers. If there is a mistake, both buyer and seller try to find it and correct it.
- The buyer and seller switch roles and play again.

Work through a few transactions with a child so the class understands how the activity works.

English Language Learners

Write *change* on the board. Draw a football priced $5. Hold up a $10 bill. Say: **I give the seller my $10 bill. He gives me the football.**

- **Beginning** Say: **$10 – $5 = $5. He gives me $5 *change*.**
- **Intermediate** Ask: **Does the seller keep *all* my money?** no **Does he give me $5 *change*?** yes
- **Advanced** Ask: **How much money do I get back?** $5 **Is that *change*?** yes

Ongoing Assessment

Circulate around the room as the children do the activity. Watch for children who are misaligning digits and the decimal point when they are subtracting with numbers. Also watch for children who have difficulty ungrouping $10.00 correctly.

2 Going Further

Math Connection: Use Front-End Estimation

Goal: Estimate sums and differences, using front-end estimation.

Materials: Student Activity Book pages 387–388.

▶ Introduce Front-End Estimation

WHOLE CLASS — Math Talk

Before beginning this activity, you may wish to briefly review estimating by rounding. (See Unit 9 Lesson 6.) Then explain to children that there is another way to estimate. You can also only use the front digits of a number. Tell children that this is called *front-end estimation*. Be sure they understand that the front end of a number is the digit in the greatest place value.

Have children look at the top of Student Activity Book page 387. Discuss the steps they should follow to estimate using front-end estimation. Then work together as a class to complete exercises 1–4.

Have children compare estimating by rounding with front-end estimation.

- Which is easier, estimating by rounding or using front-end estimation? using front-end estimation Why? Possible response: You do not change the numbers very much.
- Why is front-end estimation less exact than estimating by rounding? It ignores all the digits except for the one in the greatest place value.

▶ Practice Using Front-End Estimation

PAIRS

Have children work individually to complete exercises 5 and 6. Then have pairs take turns explaining to each other how they found each estimate.

▶ Number Sense

INDIVIDUALS

Have children answer exercise 7 independently. Then ask volunteers to share their thinking with the class. Encourage other children to ask questions and offer comments.

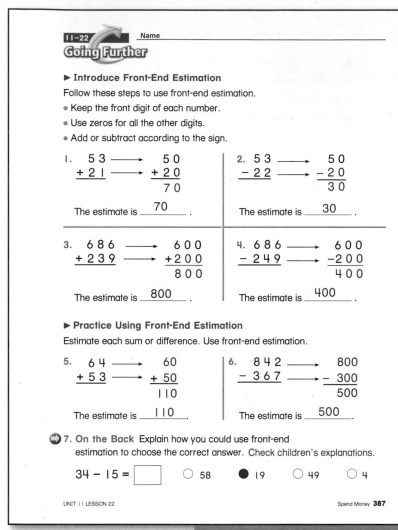

11–22 Going Further Name

▶ Introduce Front-End Estimation

Follow these steps to use front-end estimation.

- Keep the front digit of each number.
- Use zeros for all the other digits.
- Add or subtract according to the sign.

1. 53 + 21 → 50 + 20 = 70. The estimate is 70.

2. 53 − 22 → 50 − 20 = 30. The estimate is 30.

3. 686 + 239 → 600 + 200 = 800. The estimate is 800.

4. 686 − 249 → 600 − 200 = 400. The estimate is 400.

▶ Practice Using Front-End Estimation

Estimate each sum or difference. Use front-end estimation.

5. 64 + 53 → 60 + 50 = 110. The estimate is 110.

6. 842 − 367 → 800 − 300 = 500. The estimate is 500.

7. **On the Back** Explain how you could use front-end estimation to choose the correct answer. Check children's explanations.

34 − 15 = ☐ ○ 58 ● 19 ○ 49 ○ 4

UNIT 11 LESSON 22 — Spend Money 387

Student Activity Book page 387

Teaching Note

Math Background Be sure children understand that although front-end estimation is a fast, easy way to estimate, it often provides a less accurate estimate than they would get if they used rounding.

If you wish, challenge children to suggest ways to make front-end estimation more accurate. For example, when you use front-end estimation for addition, you could adjust the estimated answer up to account for the other digits in the number.

Quick Quiz

See Assessment Guide for Unit 11, Quick Quiz 5.

2 Going Further

Differentiated Instruction

Intervention — Activity Card 11-22

Sets of Three — Activity Card 11-22

Work: (pair)

Use:

- 9 index cards

Choose:

- (student 1)
- (student 2)

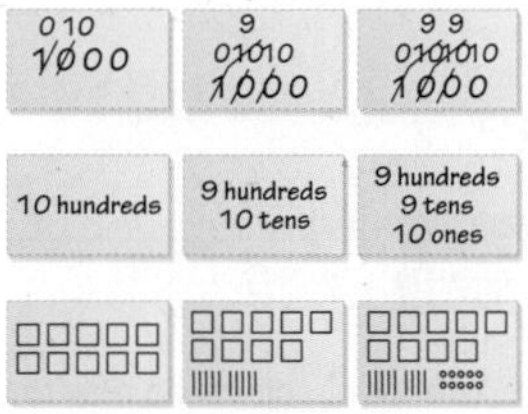

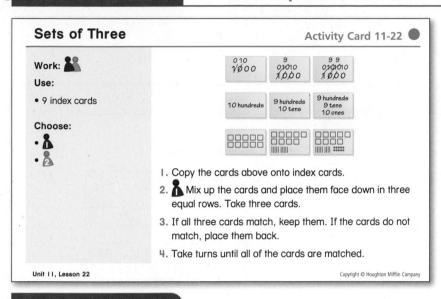

1. Copy the cards above onto index cards.
2. Mix up the cards and place them face down in three equal rows. Take three cards.
3. If all three cards match, keep them. If the cards do not match, place them back.
4. Take turns until all of the cards are matched.

Unit 11, Lesson 22

Activity Note Each pair needs nine index cards. Help children copy the images onto the index cards. Have children check the matches.

Math Writing Prompt

Explain Tell how you could explain to a friend that 1,000 pennies and $10.00 are the same amount.

Soar to Success Math **Software Support**

Warm Up 2.13

On Level — Activity Card 11-22

Classroom Items for Sale — Activity Card 11-22

Work: (pair)

Use:

- 6 index cards
- quarters, dimes, nickels, pennies
- dollar bills
- ten-dollar bills

Choose:

- (student 1)
- (student 2)

1. **Work Together** Make price tags for six items in the classroom. All prices should be less than $10.00.
2. (student 1) Chose one item to buy. Give (student 2) $10.00.
3. (student 2) Count on to make change. Write a subtraction problem to show how much money (student 1) has left.

4. Trade roles and repeat until all of the items have been bought.

Unit 11, Lesson 22

Activity Note Each pair needs 6 index cards, real or play quarters, dimes, nickels, pennies, dollar bills (TRB M67-M68), and ten-dollar bills (TRB M89).

Math Writing Prompt

Explain Your Thinking Explain how you would ungroup 1,000 to find 1,000 – 378.

Harcourt MegaMath Grades K-6 **Software Support**

Numberopolis: Lulu's Lunch Counter, Level Q

Challenge — Activity Card 11-22

Newspaper Shopping — Activity Card 11-22

Work: (individual)

Use:

- newspaper ads
- ten-dollar bills

1. Look through the newspaper ads. Find two items you would like to buy. The two items must cost less than $20.00.
2. Write about the items you would like to buy.
3. Find out how much money you will spend and how much money you will have left.
4. **Math Talk** Share your purchases with a friend. Talk about what you each wanted to buy.

I have $20.00 to spend. I would like to buy a baseball for $8.99 and a baseball bat for $6.98. I will have $4.03 left after I buy the items.
$8.99 + 6.98 = $15.97
$20.00 – 15.97 = $4.03
On Sale!
$6.98
$8.99

Unit 11, Lesson 22

Activity Note Each child needs newspaper ads and two ten-dollar bills (TRB M89). Have children check their work with a friend.

Math Writing Prompt

Write Your Own Write and solve a story problem about buying something with $10.00.

Destination Math **Software Support**

Course II: Module 3: Unit 1: Money

3 Homework

11–22 Homework **Goal:** Additional Practice

This Homework activity is similar to the puzzle in Unit 11 Lesson 12 Activity 2. (See page 834.)

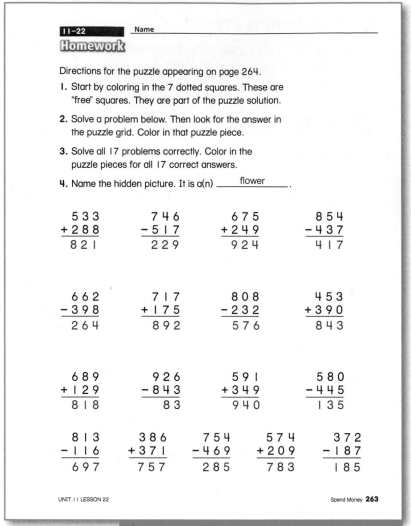

11–22 Homework Name

Directions for the puzzle appearing on page 264.

1. Start by coloring in the 7 dotted squares. These are "free" squares. They are part of the puzzle solution.
2. Solve a problem below. Then look for the answer in the puzzle grid. Color in that puzzle piece.
3. Solve all 17 problems correctly. Color in the puzzle pieces for all 17 correct answers.
4. Name the hidden picture. It is a(n) flower.

$533 + 288 = 821$ $\quad$ $746 - 517 = 229$ $\quad$ $675 + 249 = 924$ $\quad$ $854 - 437 = 417$

$662 - 398 = 264$ $\quad$ $717 + 175 = 892$ $\quad$ $808 - 232 = 576$ $\quad$ $453 + 390 = 843$

$689 + 129 = 818$ $\quad$ $926 - 843 = 83$ $\quad$ $591 + 349 = 940$ $\quad$ $580 - 445 = 135$

$813 - 116 = 697$ $\quad$ $386 + 371 = 757$ $\quad$ $754 - 469 = 285$ $\quad$ $574 + 209 = 783$ $\quad$ $372 - 187 = 185$

Homework and Remembering page 263

11–22 Homework Name

See page 263 for directions on how to solve the puzzle.

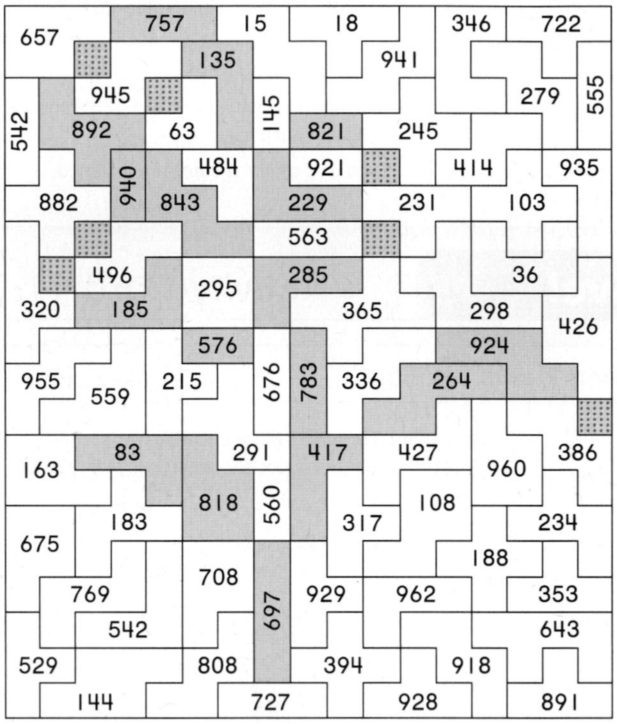

Homework and Remembering page 264

Home or School Activity

Technology Connection

Subtract Money on a Calculator Show children how to enter money amounts on a calculator. Point out that there is no dollar sign on a calculator but there is a decimal key. Emphasize the importance of using the decimal key to separate dollars from cents.

Have children use a calculator to find the answers to the exercises shown on the right. You may also wish to challenge the children to check that their answers are reasonable by using front-end estimation.

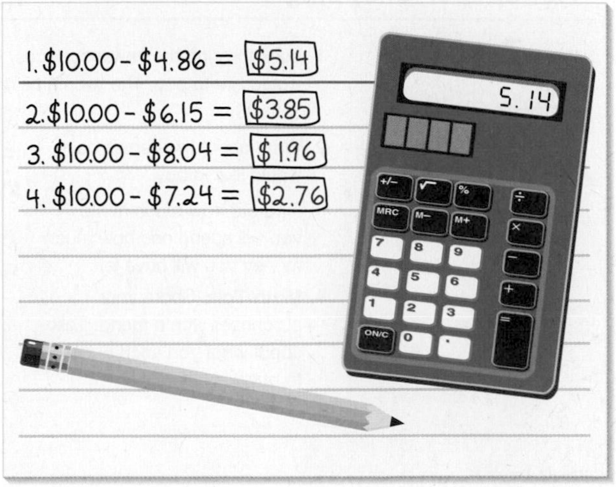

UNIT 11 LESSON 23

Use Mathematical Processes

REAL WORLD Problem Solving

Lesson Objectives

- Apply mathematical concepts and skills in meaningful contexts.
- Reinforce the NCTM process skills embedded in this unit, and previous units, with a variety of problem-solving situations.

The Day at a Glance

Today's Goals	Materials	
1 Teaching the Lesson **A1: Art Connection** Transfer a repeating pattern from one medium to another. **A2: Communication** Follow, write, and give directions. **A3: Reasoning and Proof** Decide whether a math statement is true or false and use examples as support. **A4: Representation** Draw 2 different rectangles with the same perimeter; find the area of a rectangle. **A5: Problem Solving** Explain why the change in a buying situation will not be more than a given amount.	**Lesson Activities** Student Activity Book pp. 389–390 Homework and Remembering pp. 265–266 Pattern blocks Crayons Centimeter Grid Paper (TRB M50)	**Going Further** Activity Cards 11–23 10 × 10 Grid (TRB M62) Math Journals
2 Going Further Differentiated Instruction		
3 Homework and Spiral Review		

Use Math Talk today!

Keeping Skills Sharp

Quick Practice/Daily Routines	
If you wish to include Quick Practice or a Daily Routine, choose content based on the needs of your class.	**Class Management** Select activities from this lesson that support important goals and objectives, or that help children prepare for state or district tests.

1 Teaching the Lesson

Activity 1

Connections

Math and Art

45 MINUTES

Goals: Transfer a repeating pattern from one medium to another.

Materials: Student Activity Book page 389, crayons

NCTM Standards:
Problem Solving
Connections
Representation

11-23 Class Activity

Name ____________________

►Math and Art

In many cultures beads are woven in geometric patterns to make hatbands, belts, necklaces, and other items.
Find the shapes in these beadwork items.

You have learned to describe a pattern using letters.
The pattern below is an ABB pattern.

1. Make a hatband design with shapes.
   Use an ABAB pattern. Draw your design here.

   Answers will vary. Check children's work.

2. Make a belt designs with shapes.
   Make an AAB pattern. Draw your design here.

   Answers will vary. Check children's work.

3. Make a design with shapes for another item.
   Use any pattern you like.
   Describe your pattern with letters. ____________________

   Answers will vary. Check children's work.

UNIT 11 LESSON 23 Use Mathematical Processes **389**

Student Activity Book page 389

Alternate Approach

Using More than One Medium Continue this activity as an art project and let children produce their patterns using various materials, such as construction paper, clay, foam shapes, fabric, foil, and so on.

► Make Designs

Ask children whether they have any things that are made with beads. You might gather beaded items or strings of beads to use in this discussion.

Have children look at the picture with beadwork on the student page.

► What kind of patterns do you see? Allow children to talk about the patterns they see in the beadwork.

Then remind children that they have learned how to describe patterns using letters.

► Why is the pattern of triangles and squares called an ABBABB pattern? Answers may vary. Possible answer: Because in ABB, 1 A is followed by 2 Bs. In the triangle and square pattern, 1 triangle is followed by 2 squares.

Tasks 1–3 Ask children to make designs as described in the instructions for items 1–3. Encourage them to be creative, especially for their work on item 3.

► Analyze Designs

Math Talk

Have children share ideas about making patterns.

► How did you decide what shapes to use? How did you decide what colors to use? Answers may vary. Let children tell their reasons and allow others to ask questions.

► Let's look at our ABAB patterns. Who wants to tell about theirs? Have children show their patterns to the class. Have others look at each pattern and tell why a pattern is or is not an ABAB pattern.

Do the same for the AABAAB patterns and the original patterns. You might ask the class to describe the original patterns with letters as children show their work.

Activity 2

Communication

Following Directions

45 MINUTES

Goals: Follow, write, and give directions.

Materials: Student Activity Book page 390, Pattern Blocks

NCTM Standards:
Problem Solving
Communication
Representation

11–23 Name ________________

Class Activity

▶ **Following Directions**

1. Follow the directions. Use pattern blocks.
   A. Put the yellow hexagon on the line. Place one of its sides on the line.
   B. Put green triangles to the right and left of the hexagon. Place one side of each triangle on the line. Let another side of each triangle touch the side of the hexagon.
   C. Put an orange square on top of the hexagon. Place one side of the square on one side of the hexagon.

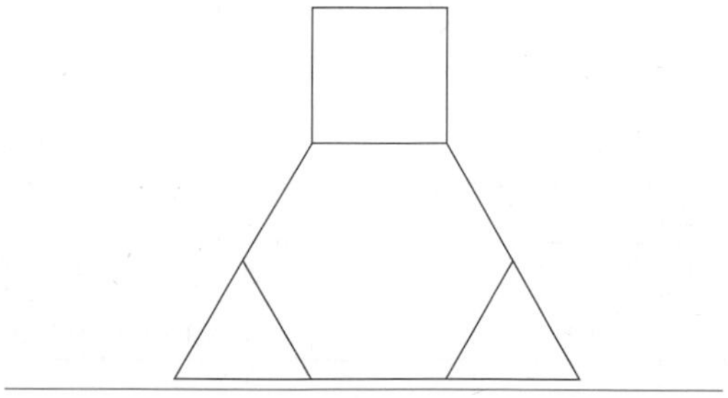

2. Trace the pattern blocks to show your work.
3. Use pattern blocks to make a design.
   A. Write directions for making your design on a separate sheet of paper.
   B. Give the directions to your partner to follow.
   C. Did your partner make your design? Explain.
   Answers may vary. Possible answer: My partner's design was very close to my design but the square was not in the right place.

Student Activity Book page 390

English Language Learners

Write *directions, first, next, then,* and *finally* on the board. Act out making a sandwich as you give directions. Have children copy and repeat.

- **Beginning** Say: ***Directions* are steps to do something.** Have children repeat.
- **Intermediate and Advanced** Have children give *directions* on how to write their names.

▶ Follow Directions

Ask for Ideas Ask children to tell about any experiences they have with following directions (instances they may mention include driving to a new place, putting together a kit, or trying a new recipe). Encourage discussion of times that directions were not clear or complete.

Task 1 Tell children they are going to follow directions to make a design out of pattern blocks. They will trace the pattern blocks to show their work on the design. Start by asking:

▶ What things are important when you give directions to someone? Answers will vary. Elicit the idea that directions need to be clear and exact.

Depending on the children's reading level, you may want to read the directions on the student page to them. When children finish tracing their designs, draw the design on the board. Read the directions for the design again so that children can see that the design meets all the requirements of the directions.

▶ Write Directions

Math Talk

Task 2 Explain that children will now create their own pattern-block designs, write directions for making the designs, and give the directions to a partner to follow.

When children complete this task, discuss what it was like to write the directions for their own designs and to follow their partner's directions.

▶ Who found it easy (hard) to write directions? Explain why. Answers may vary. Possible answer: It was hard because I made a complicated design.

▶ Who found it easy (hard) to follow their partner's directions? Explain why. Answers may vary. Possible answer: It was easy because there were only three parts to the design.

Activity 3

Reasoning and Proof

True or False?

15 MINUTES

Goal: Decide whether a math statement is true or false and use examples as support.

NCTM Standards:
Problem Solving
Reasoning and Proof

True or False? If the midpoints of a square are connected with straight lines, a square is formed. Give an example to support your answer.

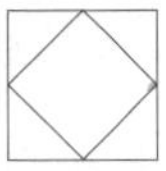

True is the most likely response.

Ask children to think again about the problem.

- Suppose the midpoint on one side is connected to the midpoint on the other side with a straight line, and then the other two midpoints are connected the same way. Could this be what the statement means? yes What was formed? 4 squares
- Now, can you tell whether the statement is true or false? No.

Discuss how the statement could be made clearer. If the four midpoints of a square are connected from side to side with four straight lines, another square is formed. Caution children to think carefully about true-false statements to be sure that they cover all possible meanings.

Activity 4

Representation

Same Perimeter, Different Area

15 MINUTES

Goal: Draw 2 different rectangles with the same perimeter; find the area of a rectangle.

Materials: Centimeter Grid Paper (TRB M50)

NCTM Standards:
Problem Solving
Representation

A rectangle has a perimeter of 12 centimeters. Draw the rectangle. Label the drawing. Tell the area of each rectangle. Answers may vary. Possible answer: a drawing of a 2 cm by 4 cm rectangle. Area: 8 square centimeters

Use the **Solve and Discuss** structure for this problem. When children complete work at the board, point out that several such rectangles can be drawn.

What are some different rectangles that have a perimeter of 12 centimeters? What is the area of each? Make a table on the board.

Rectangle	Area
5 cm by 1 cm	5 square centimeters
4 cm by 2 cm	8 square centimeters
3 cm by 3 cm	9 square centimeters

- Do rectangles with the same perimeter always have the same area? No.

Activity 5

Problem Solving

Making Change

15 MINUTES

Goal: Explain why the change in a buying situation will not be more than a given amount.

NCTM Standards:
Problem Solving
Communication

Jason bought a book for $5.34 and paid with a $10 bill. Explain why his change will not be more than $5.00. Answers may vary. Possible answer: $5 + $5 is $10. If the cost is over $5, then the change has to be under $5.

Discuss and extend the activity.

- How did you explain why Jason's change will not be more than $5? Allow children to share their explanations.
- If the book had cost less than $5, what could you say about the change from a $10 bill? It would be more than $5.

2 Going Further

Differentiated Instruction

Intervention — Activity Card 11-23

Match the Perimeter
Activity Card 11-23

Work: (pair)
Use:
- 10 × 10 Grid

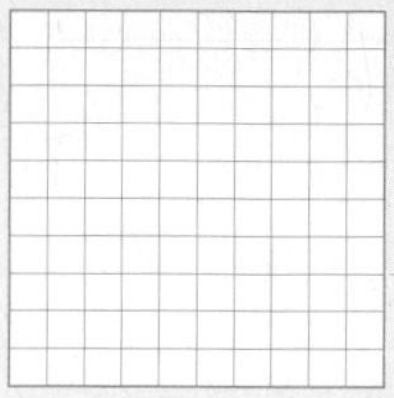

1. **Work Together** Choose a number between 8 and 24.

2. Each (child) draws a shape on grid paper with a perimeter that is the same as the chosen number.

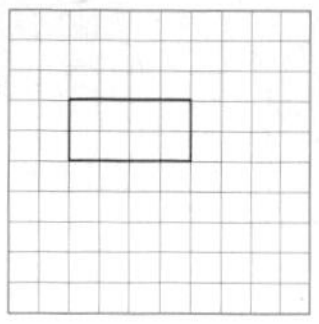

3. Compare the shapes you drew. Check that they have the same perimeter.
4. Choose another number and repeat.

Unit 11, Lesson 23

Activity Note Children need 10 × 10 Grid (TRB M62). To extend the activity, have children count the squares to find the areas of their shapes and then compare the areas.

Math Writing Prompt

Explain Is there more than 1 way to draw a shape with a perimeter of 16? Explain.

Software Support

Warm Up 44.28

On Level — Activity Card 11-23

Target Area: 20–50 Square Units
Activity Card 11-23

Work: (pair)
Use:
- 10 × 10 Grid

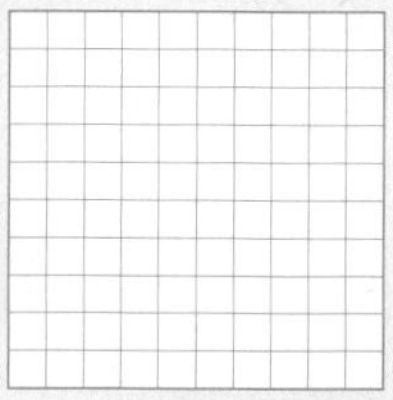

1. **Work Together** Choose a number between 20 and 50.

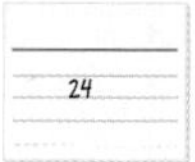

2. Each (child) draws a shape that has the same number of square units of area as the number chosen.

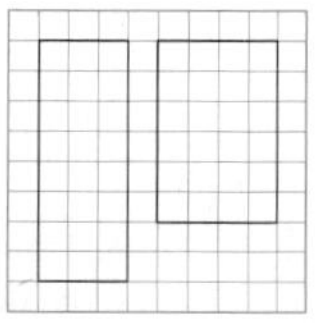

3. Compare shapes with your partner. Are the areas the same? Are the shapes the same? Are the perimeters the same?
4. Choose another number and repeat.

Unit 11, Lesson 23

Activity Note Children need 10 × 10 Grid (TRB M62). To increase the challenge of this activity, have children draw the shapes without counting the squares as they go along. This helps them estimate area.

Math Writing Prompt

Explain What helps you draw a shape when you know how many square units of area it has?

Software Support

Shapes Ahoy: Ship Shapes, Level X

Challenge — Activity Card 11-23

Greater and Lesser Area
Activity Card 11-23

Work: (pair)
Use:
- 10 × 10 Grid

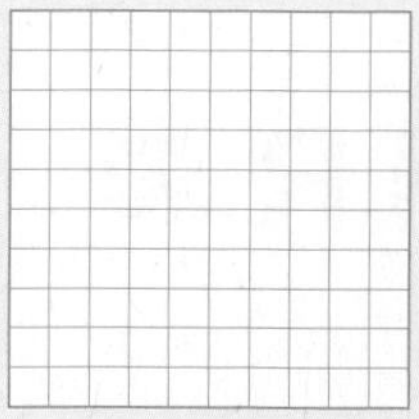

1. **Work Together** Choose a number between 20 and 40.

2. Each (child) draws 2 shapes: one with an area greater than the chosen number of square units and one with a lesser area than the chosen number of square units. Make the perimeters as close to 24 units as you can.

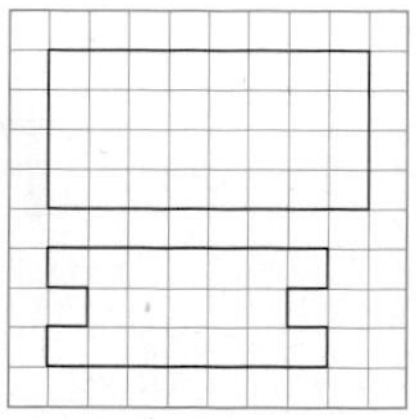

3. Compare shapes with your partner. Discuss any differences.
4. Choose another number and repeat.

Unit 11, Lesson 23

Activity Note Children need 10 × 10 Grid (TRB M62). If children have difficulty drawing shapes with the given perimeter, point out that one of the shapes on the card is an irregular shape. Explain that they do not have to draw rectangles.

Math Writing Prompt

Explain Your Thinking What did you do to make shapes whose perimeters were exactly 24 units?

Software Support

Course II: Module 3: Unit 1: Area

3 Homework and Spiral Review

11–23 Homework **Goal:** Additional Practice

✓ Include children's completed Homework page as part of their portfolios.

11–23 Name ______

Homework

1. Use shapes to make a pattern. Draw your pattern here.
   Answers may vary. Possible answer:

2. Use letters to describe your pattern.
   Possible answer: ABCABCABC

3. Ella bought a toy for \$4.32. She paid with a \$10 bill. Explain why her change will be greater than \$5.
   Answers may vary. Possible answer: Since \$5 + \$5 is \$10, if one amount is less than \$5, then the other amount has to be greater than \$5 to make \$10. So since the price of the toy is less than \$5, Ella's change has to be greater than \$5.

4. Yoshiro has \$6. He wants to buy one toy that costs \$1.98 and another toy that costs \$3.75. Explain how Yoshiro can tell whether he has enough money without adding \$1.98 and \$3.75.
   Answers may vary. Possible answer: \$2 + \$4 is \$6. \$1.98 is less than \$2. \$3.75 is less than \$4. So \$1.98 + \$3.75 is less than \$6. Yoshiro has enough money to buy both toys.

5. True or False? Similar shapes are also congruent.
   Ring the answer. True (False)
   Give an example to support your answer.
   Possible answer:

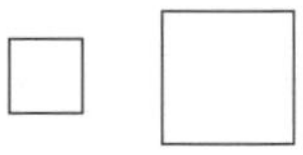

UNIT 11 LESSON 23 Use Mathematical Processes 265

Homework and Remembering page 265

11–23 Remembering **Goal:** Spiral Review

This Remembering page would be appropriate anytime after today's lesson.

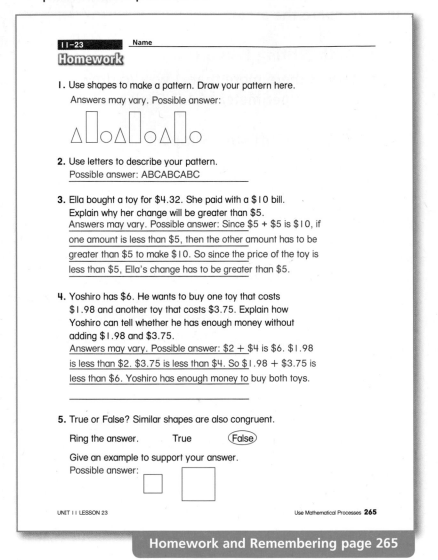

11–23 Name ______

Remembering

Add or subtract.

1.
$$\begin{array}{r} 306 \\ +\,499 \\ \hline 805 \end{array} \qquad \begin{array}{r} 731 \\ -\,264 \\ \hline 467 \end{array} \qquad \begin{array}{r} \$5.64 \\ -\,\$2.38 \\ \hline \$3.26 \end{array}$$

Write the hundreds, tens, and ones.

2. 471 = 400 + 70 + 1
   569 = 500 + 60 + 9

The table shows the number of days until each child's birthday. Use the table to answer exercises 3–5.

Days Until My Birthday

Name	Number of Days
Linda	200
Lupe	176
Chung	302

3. Who has to wait the longest for their birthday? Chung

4. How many more days does Chung have to wait than Linda? 102 more days

5. How many fewer days does Lupe have to wait than Linda? 24 fewer days

6. **Time** On a separate piece of paper, draw what you do at 3 o'clock in the afternoon. Draw a clock face and show the time. Check children's work.

266 UNIT 11 LESSON 23 Use Mathematical Processes

Homework and Remembering page 266

Home or School Activity

Art Connection

Initials and Patterns Have children make a pattern with slides, flips, and/or turns of the initial of their first name. Encourage them to make another pattern that uses the initials for their first and last names. Some children may want to make initial patterns for the members of their families.

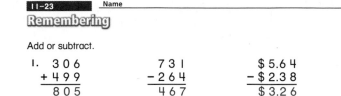

11 Unit Test

Name

Subtract.

18. 505 − 371 = 134

19. 300 − 239 = 61

20. \$10.00 − \$4.81 = \$5.19

21. \$10.00 − \$2.72 = \$7.28

Solve. Show your work.

22. Dena picked 472 apples. She sold 187 at the Farmers Market. How many apples did she have left?

285 apples (label)

23. This morning 256 books were returned to the library. 596 more were returned this afternoon. How many books were returned altogether?

852 books (label)

UNIT 11 Test 393

Student Activity Book page 393

11 Unit Test

Name

Solve. Show your work.

24. Ada read 124 pages in a book. The book has 300 pages. How many more pages does she still have to read to finish the book?

176 more pages (label)

25. **Extended Response** Write and solve an addition or subtraction story problem using the numbers 458 and 279. Check children's work.

*Item 25 also assesses the Process Skills of Problem Solving and Reasoning.

394 UNIT 11 Test

Student Activity Book page 394

Test Items	Unit Objectives Tested	Activities to Use for Reteaching
13, 14	**11.6** Add money amounts to \$9.99.	Lesson 11, Activity 1
15–17	**11.7** Subtract ungrouping a ten, hundred, or both.	Lesson 17, Activity 1 Lesson 18, Activity 1
18, 19	**11.8** Subtract from a number with one or two zeros.	Lesson 15, Activity 1 Lesson 16, Activity 1
20, 21	**11.9** Subtract money amounts from \$10.00.	Lesson 22, Activity 1
22–25	**11.10** Solve story problems with multi-digit addition or subtraction.	Lesson 5, Activity 2 Lesson 13, Activity 2 Lesson 21, Activity 2

▶ Assessment Resources

Form A, Free Response Test (Assessment Guide)
Form B, Multiple-Choice Test (Assessment Guide)
Performance Assessment (Assessment Guide)

▶ Portfolio Assessment

Teacher-selected Items for Student Portfolios:

- Homework, Lessons 9, 18, 21, and 23
- Class Activity work, Lessons 2, 5, 12, 15, and 20

Student-selected Items for Student Portfolios:

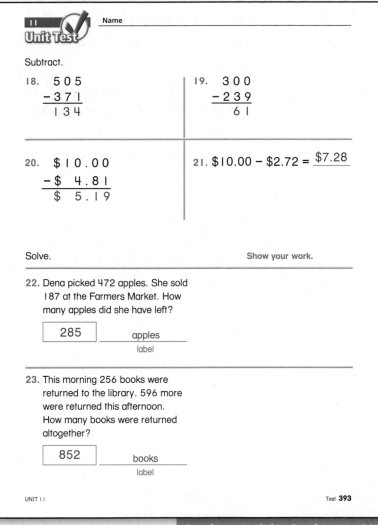

- Favorite Home or School Activity
- Best Writing Prompt

2 Extending the Assessment

Common Errors

Activities for Remediation

Unit Objective 11.1

Recognize and draw boxes, sticks, and circles for numbers through 999.

Common Error: Draws Incorrect Numbers of Boxes, Sticks, and Circles for Numbers

Children's drawings showing boxes, sticks, and circles may not match the given number.

Remediation Have children use base ten blocks to show numbers. Help children make the connection to boxes, sticks, and circles.

Unit Objective 11.2

Write 3-digit numbers in expanded form.

Common Error: Writes Incorrect Values for Parts of the Expanded Form of a Number

Children may write incorrect values for the different digits in a number.

Remediation Have children use base ten blocks to show the number. Then have them isolate the hundreds and write the number, isolate the tens and write the number, and finally write the number of ones.

Unit Objective 11.3

Count by 1s and 10s through 999.

Common Error: Counts Incorrectly by Tens when Counting over a Hundred

Children may have difficulty with counting by tens over a hundred.

Remediation Remind children of how to use gestures, beginning at 340 to count forward by tens. Draw three imaginary boxes in the air, flash ten fingers four times for 40, and flash ten fingers at every decade number: 350, 360, 370, 380, 390. At 400, stop and draw an imaginary box to indicate a new hundred. Resume counting and flashing fingers for 410, 420, 430.

Unit Objective 11.4

Write the value of a group of dollars and coins using decimal notation.

Common Error: Finds Incorrect Values for Coin Combinations

Children may find incorrect values for given coin combinations.

Remediation Have children identify each coin and find and record the value of each one. Then have them count again, using their recorded values to help. When recording the total value, have students show the amount using a dollar sign and decimal point.

Unit Objective 11.5

Add making a new ten, a new hundred, or both.

Common Error: Forgets to Add the New Ten or New Hundred

Children may forget to add the new ten made from adding the ones, or the new hundred made from adding the tens.

Remediation Remind children to write the newly made ten or hundred on the line below the addition or above the column. Have them make sure to write it in the correct place-value column. Remind them to add the numbers in each column, along with any new ten or hundred.

Unit Objective 11.7

Subtract ungrouping a ten, hundred, or both.

Common Error: Incorrectly Ungroups to Prepare a Number for Subtracting

Children may incorrectly ungroup to prepare a number for subtracting.

Remediation Have children use base ten blocks to model the ungrouping. Then ask them to make sure that their final ungrouped number has the same value as the original number. For example, 200 is ungrouped to 1 hundred, 9 tens, 10 ones. Tell them to check the value of each form of the number—1 hundred, 9 tens, 10 ones is equal to 200.

Metric Measurement and 3-D Shapes

IN THIS UNIT, children continue to develop their measurement skills and learn to convert between metric units of length. Activities with 3-dimensional figures include identifying faces, edges, and vertices of rectangular prisms, and sorting shapes according to attributes. Children continue to develop their spatial sense as they sketch faces of solid figures, build rectangular prisms from nets, draw rectangular prisms from different viewpoints and find volume by counting cubic units.

Skills Trace

Grade 1	Grade 2	Grade 3
• Write the value of a group of dimes and pennies. • Estimate and measure length in centimeters. • Relate shapes and numbers.	• Connect place value, money, and metric units of length. • Convert measures in centimeters to a combination of meters, decimeters, and centimeters. • Count cubic units to find volume.	• Convert measurements within the customary and metric system. • Solve problems involving customary or metric units. • Identify and describe cubes, prisms, cones, pyramids, cylinders, and spheres.

Unit 12 Contents

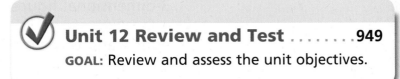

Big Idea Patterns in Measurement and Geometry

Planning Unit 12

NCTM Curriculum Focal Points and Connections Key: **1.** Number and Operations **2.** Number and Operations and Algebra **3.** Measurement **4.** Number and Operations **5.** Geometry and Measurement **6.** Algebra

Lesson NCTM Focal Points NCTM Standards	Resources	Materials for Lesson Activities	Materials for Going Further
12-1 **Meters and Decimeters** NCTM Focal Points: 3.1, 3.3, 3.4, 3.5, 3.6, 4.5, 4.6 NCTM Standards: 4, 5, 8, 9	TE pp. 913–918 SAB pp. 395–400 H&R pp. 267–268 AC 12-1 MCC 45	Meter stick or Meter Stick (TRB M90) Yardstick Scissors Tape or glue Colored pencils Cardstock (optional)	Meter sticks ✓ Base ten blocks Index cards Math Journals
12-2 **Fun with Measuring** NCTM Focal Points: 3.4, 3.6, 3.7, 5.1 NCTM Standards: 4, 9	TE pp. 919–924 SAB pp. 401–404 H&R pp. 269–270 AC 12-2	Paper meter sticks from Lesson 1 Masking tape Index cards Pennies	Meter sticks Toy cars Ramp *Tell Me How Far It Is* by Shirley Willis Math Journals
12-3 **Meter, Decimeter, and Centimeter Equivalencies** NCTM Focal Points: 3.2, 3.4, 3.6, 4.5 NCTM Standards: 4, 8, 9	TE pp. 925–930 H&R pp. 269, 271–272 AC 12-3	Paper meter sticks from Lesson 1 ✓ MathBoard materials	Index cards Math Journals
12-4 **Practice with Meters and Money** NCTM Focal Point: 4.5 NCTM Standards: 4, 6, 9	TE pp. 931–934 SAB pp. 405–406 H&R pp. 273–274 AC 12-4 MCC 46	Paper meter sticks from Lesson 1	Place value charts ✓ Base ten blocks Index cards *Millions to Measure* by David M. Schwartz Math Journals
12-5 **3-Dimensional Shapes** NCTM Focal Point: 3.6 NCTM Standard: 3, 4, 9, 10	TE pp. 935–942 SAB pp. 407–410 H&R pp. 275–276 AC 12-5 MCC 47	✓ 25-cm rulers Stack of paper bound by rubber bands Scissors Tape Empty non-food packages in the shape of rectangular prisms ✓ MathBoard materials ✓ Connecting cubes	Clay Straws Unit cubes Empty non-food packages in the shape of rectangular prisms Containers with curved sides Math Journals
12-6 **Analyze 3-Dimensional Shapes** NCTM Standards: 3, 9, 10	TE pp. 943–948 SAB pp. 411–414 H&R pp. 277–278 AC 12-6 MCC 48 AG Quick Quiz	Objects in the shape of cones, cubes, rectangular prisms, spheres, square pyramids, and cylinders Square Pyramid (TRB M91) Cone (TRB M92) ✓ Commercial sets of 3-dimensional shapes	✓ Commercial sets of 3-dimensional shapes Paper bags Math Journals
✓ Unit Review and Test	TE pp. 949–952 SAB pp. 415–416 AG Unit 12 Tests		

Resources/Materials Key: TE: Teacher Edition SAB: Student Activity Book H&R: Homework and Remembering AC: Activity Cards MCC: Math Center Challenge AG: Assessment Guide ✓: Grade 2 kits TRB: Teacher's Resource Book

Manipulatives and Materials

Essential materials for teaching *Math Expressions* are available in the Grade 2 kits. These materials are indicated by a ✓ in these lists. At the front of this Teacher Edition is more information about kit contents, alternatives for the materials, and use of the materials.

Unit 12 Assessment

Unit Objectives Tested	Unit Test Items	Lessons
12.1 Connect place value, money, and metric units of length.	10	3, 4
12.2 Convert measures in centimeters to a combination of meters, decimeters, and centimeters.	1, 2, 3	2, 3
12.3 Distinguish between two-dimensional (2-D) and three-dimensional (3-D) shapes.	4, 5	5
12.4 Draw a front, side, and top view of a rectangular prism.	6	5
12.5 Count cubic units to find volume.	7, 8	5
12.6 Sort three-dimensional shapes using a Venn diagram.	9	6

Assessment and Review Resources

Formal Assessment

Student Activity Book

- Unit Review and Test (pp. 415–416)

Assessment Guide

- Quick Quiz (p. A131)
- Test A–Open Response (pp. A132–A133)
- Test B–Multiple Choice (pp. A134–A135)
- Performance Assessment (pp. A136–A138)

Test Generator CD-ROM

- Open Response Test
- Multiple Choice Test
- Test Bank Items

Informal Assessment

Teacher Edition

- Ongoing Assessment (in every lesson)
- Quick Practice (in every lesson)
- Portfolio Suggestions (p. 951)

Math Talk

- Math Talk in Action (p. 945)
- Small Groups (p. 922)
- In Activities (pp. 914, 926, 937, 946)
- Student Pairs (p. 932)

Review Opportunities

Homework and Remembering

- Review of recently taught topics
- Spiral Review

Teacher Edition

- Unit Review and Test (pp. 949–952)

Test Generator CD-ROM

- Custom Review Sheets

Unit 12 Teaching Resources

Differentiated Instruction

Individualizing Instruction		
	Level	Frequency
Activities	• Intervention • On Level • Challenge	All 3 in every lesson
	Level	Frequency
Math Writing Prompts	• Intervention • On Level • Challenge	All 3 in every lesson
Math Center Challenges	For advanced students	
	4 in every unit	

Reaching All Learners		
English Language Learners	Lessons	Pages
	1, 2, 3, 4, 5, 6	913, 919, 925, 931, 935, 943
Special Needs	Lessons	Pages
	1, 2	916, 922

Strategies for English Language Learners

Present this problem to all children. Offer the different levels of support to meet children's levels of language proficiency.

Objective To measure the length of an object.

Problem Write *length* and *long* on the board. Say: **Let's measure the *length* across the tops of our desks with a pencil.** Have children measure the tops of their desks using their pencils.

Newcomer

- Model how to measure across the top of a desk. Have children count the pencil lengths. Say: **The *length* of the desk is ___ pencils. The desk is ___ pencils *long*.** Have children repeat.

Beginning

- Ask: **How many pencils in length was the top of your desk?** Say: **It is ___ pencils *long*.** Have children repeat.

Intermediate

- Ask: **What unit did you use to measure *length*?** pencils Have volunteers tell how *long* their desks are. Ask: **Is everyone's measurement the same?** no

Advanced

- Have volunteers tell the *length* of their desks in pencils. Have children tell why other children's measurements are different.

Connections

Language Arts Connections
Lesson 5, page 942
Lesson 6, page 948

Sports Connection
Lesson 3, page 930

Literature Connections
Lesson 2, page 924
Lesson 4, page 934

Independent Learning Activities

Ready-Made Math Challenge Centers

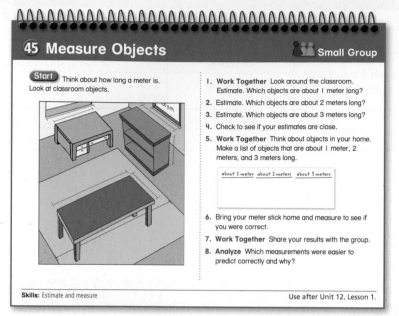

45 Measure Objects — Small Group

Start Think about how long a meter is. Look at classroom objects.

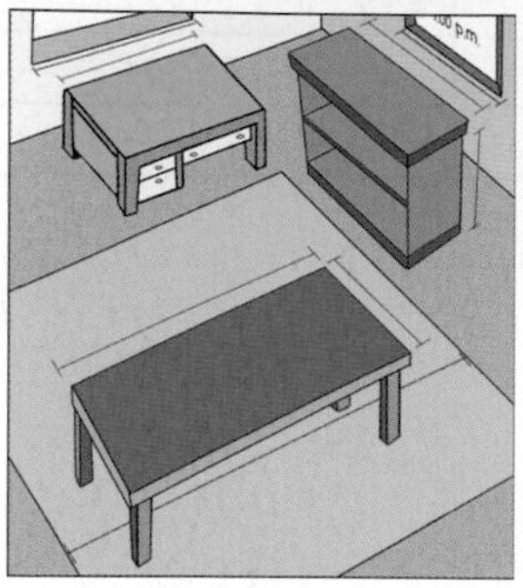

1. **Work Together** Look around the classroom. Estimate. Which objects are about 1 meter long?
2. Estimate. Which objects are about 2 meters long?
3. Estimate. Which objects are about 3 meters long?
4. Check to see if your estimates are close.
5. **Work Together** Think about objects in your home. Make a list of objects that are about 1 meter, 2 meters, and 3 meters long.

about 1 meter	about 2 meters	about 3 meters

6. Bring your meter stick home and measure to see if you were correct.
7. **Work Together** Share your results with the group.
8. **Analyze** Which measurements were easier to predict correctly and why?

Skills: Estimate and measure — Use after Unit 12, Lesson 1.

Grouping Small Group

Materials Meter sticks, classroom objects

Objective Children estimate and measure objects in meters.

Connections Measurement and Estimation

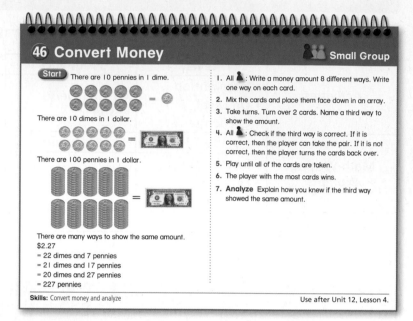

46 Convert Money — Small Group

Start There are 10 pennies in 1 dime.

There are 10 dimes in 1 dollar.

There are 100 pennies in 1 dollar.

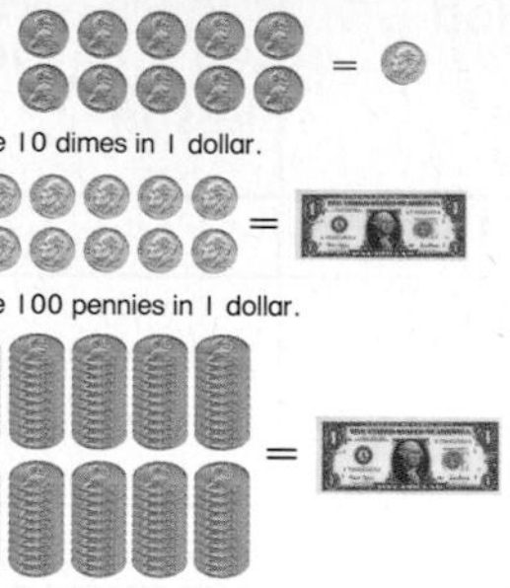

There are many ways to show the same amount.
$2.27
= 22 dimes and 7 pennies
= 21 dimes and 17 pennies
= 20 dimes and 27 pennies
= 227 pennies

1. All: Write a money amount 8 different ways. Write one way on each card.
2. Mix the cards and place them face down in an array.
3. Take turns. Turn over 2 cards. Name a third way to show the amount.
4. All: Check if the third way is correct. If it is correct, then the player can take the pair. If it is not correct, then the player turns the cards back over.
5. Play until all of the cards are taken.
6. The player with the most cards wins.
7. **Analyze** Explain how you knew if the third way showed the same amount.

Skills: Convert money and analyze — Use after Unit 12, Lesson 4.

Grouping Small Group

Materials Index cards

Objective Children write equal money amounts different ways.

Connections Measurement and Real World

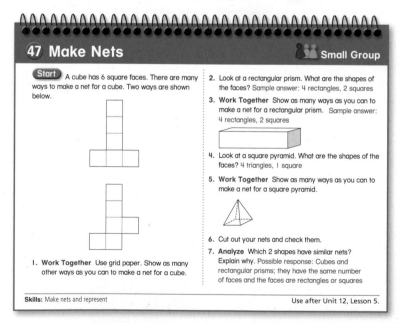

47 Make Nets — Small Group

Start A cube has 6 square faces. There are many ways to make a net for a cube. Two ways are shown below.

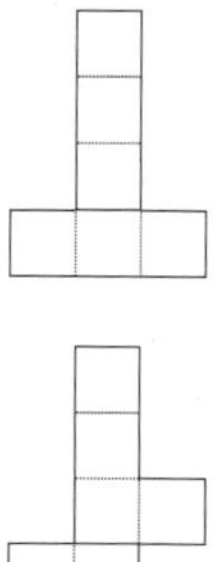

1. **Work Together** Use grid paper. Show as many other ways as you can to make a net for a cube.
2. Look at a rectangular prism. What are the shapes of the faces? Sample answer: 4 rectangles, 2 squares
3. **Work Together** Show as many ways as you can to make a net for a rectangular prism. Sample answer: 4 rectangles, 2 squares

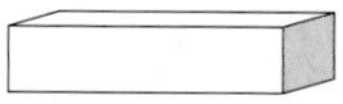

4. Look at a square pyramid. What are the shapes of the faces? 4 triangles, 1 square
5. **Work Together** Show as many ways as you can to make a net for a square pyramid.

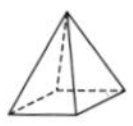

6. Cut out your nets and check them.
7. **Analyze** Which 2 shapes have similar nets? Explain why. Possible response: Cubes and rectangular prisms; they have the same number of faces and the faces are rectangles or squares

Skills: Make nets and represent — Use after Unit 12, Lesson 5.

Grouping Small Group

Materials Scissors, Inch Grid Paper (TRB M70)

Objective Children create nets for solids.

Connections Geometry and Problem Solving

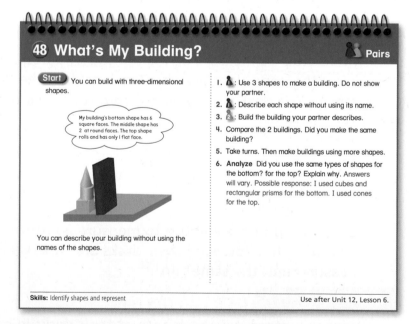

48 What's My Building? — Pairs

Start You can build with three-dimensional shapes.

My building's bottom shape has 6 square faces. The middle shape has 2 flat round faces. The top shape rolls and has only 1 flat face.

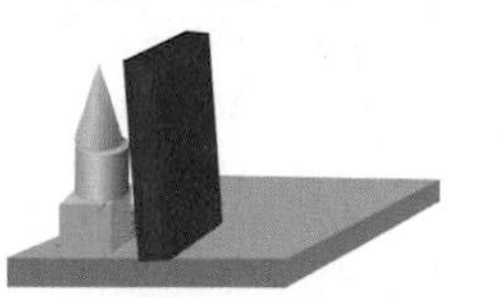

You can describe your building without using the names of the shapes.

1. Use 3 shapes to make a building. Do not show your partner.
2. Describe each shape without using its name.
3. Build the building your partner describes.
4. Compare the 2 buildings. Did you make the same building?
5. Take turns. Then make buildings using more shapes.
6. **Analyze** Did you use the same types of shapes for the bottom? for the top? Explain why. Answers will vary. Possible response: I used cubes and rectangular prisms for the bottom. I used cones for the top.

Skills: Identify shapes and represent — Use after Unit 12, Lesson 6.

Grouping Pairs

Materials Three-dimensional shapes

Objective Children use three-dimensional shapes to build and then describe the shapes they used.

Connections Geometry and Representation

Ready-Made Math Resources

Technology — Tutorial, Practice, and Intervention

Go Digital

Soar to Success Math

Use online, individualized intervention and support to bring students to proficiency.

HARCOURT MEGA MATH Grades K-6

Help students practice skills and apply concepts through exciting math adventures.

DESTINATION Math®

Extend and enrich students' understanding of skills and concepts through engaging, interactive lessons and activities.

Visit Education Place®
www.eduplace.com

Visit www.eduplace.com/mx2t/ and find family, teacher, and student materials, activities, games, and more.

Literature Links

Measuring Penny

Measuring Penny
Why on earth is Lisa measuring her dog's head with a tape measure? Find out in Loreen Leedy's great book on measurement.

Literature Connections

- *Tell Me How Far It Is,* by Shirley Willis (Gardners Books, 2005)
- *Millions to Measure,* by David M. Schwartz, illustrated by Steven Kellogg (Harper Collins, 2003)

Math Background

Putting Research into Practice for Unit 12

From Current Research:

Metrication

The National Council of Teachers of Mathematics recommends the use of the metric system as the primary measurement system in mathematics instruction.

Measurement is a common daily activity performed throughout the world and in all sectors of society. As a well-conceived, logical system of units, the metric system provides models that reinforce concepts and skills involving numeration, decimal relationships, and estimation, connecting mathematics to the rest of the pre-K–12 curriculum. For example:

- Conversion between metric units is facilitated by the decimal nature and consistent prefixes of the system, which leads to a high degree of accuracy in measurements.
- Units for volume, capacity, and mass are interrelated (for example, one cubic decimeter of water, which is one liter, has a mass of one kilogram).

On an international level in the scientific and industrial worlds, the metric system is the standard system of measurement. Canada adopted the metric system long ago and immediately mandated that all school curricula use the metric system exclusively. To compete in a world that already functions with this system, our students also need to be competent with the metric system.

National Council of Teachers of Mathematics. Metrication. March 2000. Path: NCTM: About; Position Statements; Metrication.

Spatial Sense

Drawing changed radically when someone discovered that three-dimensional objects could be made to look real on a two-dimensional canvas. The ability to work with perspective is critical in many fields, including engineering, architecture, and construction. Most of us use perspective skills almost daily, for example, when interpreting pictures of three-dimensional objects.

In our work with students, we have discovered that their background experiences have been insufficient. Their perception of the appearance of a block construction when pictured on a two-dimensional plane was often incorrect. They failed to change their beliefs until they actually assumed a position where their eye level was even with the object and then compared their expectation of its appearance with what they really saw. For these students, seeing was believing, and with practice, they were able to better understand what happens when a three-dimensional object is represented on a two-dimensional surface.

Kelly, Gwen, Tim Ewers, Lanna Proctor. "Developing Spatial Sense: Comparing Appearance with Reality." *Mathematics Teacher* 95.9 (Dec. 2002): 702.

Other Useful References:

Metric System

Taylor, P. Mark, Ken Simms, Ok-Kyeong Kim, Robert E. Reys. "Do Your Students Measure up Metrically?" *Teaching Children Mathematics* 7.5 (Jan. 2001): 282.

Three-Dimensional Geometry

Findell, Carol R., Marian Small, Mary Cavanagh, Linda Dacey, Carole E. Greenes, Linda Jensen Sheffield. *Navigating through Geometry in Prekindergarten–Grade 2* (with CD-ROM). Reston: NCTM, 2001.

Jacobs, Anne, Sharon Rak. *"Geometry." Teaching Children Mathematics* 5.6 (Feb. 1999): 346.

Place Value

Ross, Sharon R. "Place Value: Problem Solving and Written Assessment." *Teaching Children Mathematics* 8.7 (Mar. 2002): 419.

Getting Ready to Teach Unit 12

In this unit, relating linear measurement in the metric system to our base-ten numeration system and our decimal monetary system leads into exploratory work with solid figures and volume.

Linear Measurement
Lessons 1, 2, 3, and 4

In previous units, children estimated and measured lengths in centimeters. In Unit 12, children continue to develop and practice their estimating and measuring skills by making and using a meter stick. By connecting the metric system with the monetary and base ten systems, children learn to convert centimeters to meters and decimeters. In Unit 14, children will explore customary units of measurement.

Solid Figures
Lessons 5 and 6

Earlier in the year, children identified characteristics of two-dimensional figures. In this unit, children learn to distinguish between two-dimensional and three-dimensional figures. In the activities, children name and describe cubes, rectangular prisms, cylinders, cones, square pyramids, and spheres. They trace the faces of these solid figures, count edges, vertices, and faces, and observe if they stack, roll, or slide to help identify, sort, and classify these solid figures. Observing the attributes of stacking, rolling, or sliding prepares children for identifying if solid figures have parallel bases (stack), flat surfaces (slide), or curved surfaces (roll) in subsequent years.

Spatial Sense
Lessons 5 and 6

In Unit 12, children develop their spatial sense through observations of the relationships between two-dimensional faces, views, and nets and three-dimensional objects. They observe the faces of three-dimensional solids, identifying their two-dimensional shapes and counting them, and they build rectangular prisms from nets. Activities also include building rectangular prisms from cubes and drawing them from the front, side, and top views.

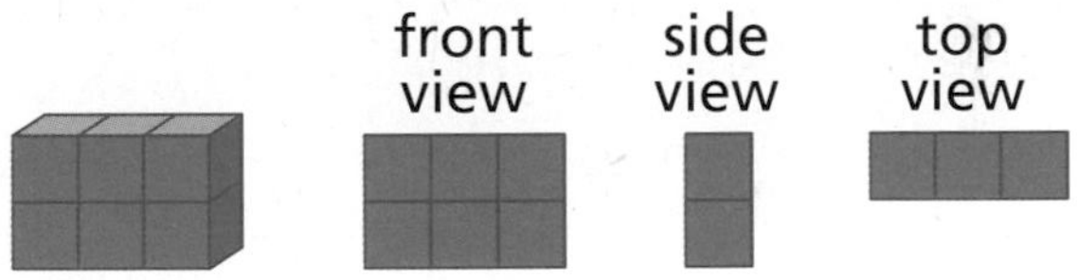

Volume
Lesson 5

In this unit, children are introduced to finding volume by counting cubic units. Activities include finding the volume of rectangular prisms and three-dimensional buildings made from cubic units. For the three-dimensional buildings, children model them and then count the number of cubes they used. These activities prepare children for finding the volume of cube buildings by counting hidden cubes in drawings in subsequent years.

MINI UNIT 12

LESSON 1

Meters and Decimeters

Lesson Objectives

- Make a meter stick.
- Compare metric and monetary systems.
- Measure the length and height of objects and people.
- Enter data in a table.
- Create and answer questions about data.
- Define meter, centimeter, and decimeter.

Vocabulary

meter
centimeter
decimeter

The Day at a Glance

Today's Goals	Materials	
1 Teaching the Lesson **A1:** Make and use a meter stick. **A2:** Estimate and measure height and create questions based on collected data.	**Lesson Activities** Student Activity Book pp. 395–400 (includes Meter Stick, Family Letter) Homework and Remembering pp. 267–268 Meter stick or Meter Stick (TRB M90) Yardstick Scissors Tape or glue Colored pencils Cardstock (optional)	**Going Further** Activity Cards 12-1 Meter sticks Base ten blocks Index cards Math Journals
2 Going Further ▸ Differentiated Instruction		
3 Homework		

Use Math Talk today!

Keeping Skills Sharp

Daily Routines	English Language Learners
Making Change and Counting Coins Making Change from \$5.00, Combining Coins and Counting Money (See pp. xxvii–xxviii.) ▸ Led by Student Leaders **Money Routine** Using the 120 Poster, Using the Money Flip Chart, Using the Number Path, Using Secret Code Cards (See pp. xxiii–xxv.) ▸ Led by Student Leaders	Draw a line segment about $1\frac{1}{2}$ meters long on the board. Write *estimate* and *measure*. Model a meter stick, but don't measure the line. Say: **I *think* the line is about $1\frac{1}{2}$ meters.** • **Beginning** Ask: **Did I measure the line?** no Say: **I *estimated*.** Ask: **Is an estimate a good guess?** yes • **Intermediate** Ask: **Did I *estimate* or *measure* the length?** estimate Measure the line. Write the length on the board. Say: **An *estimate* is a good guess. A *measurement* is __.** exact • **Advanced** Ask: **When I make a good guess am I *estimating* or *measuring*?** estimating Have children tell how to get an exact measurement.

Teaching the Lesson

Activity 1

Become Familiar With Meter Sticks

30 MINUTES

Goal: Make and use a meter stick.

Materials: meter stick or Meter Stick (TRB M90), yardstick, Student Activity Book pages 395–396, scissors (1 pair per child), tape or glue, colored pencils, cardstock (optional)

NCTM Standards:
Measurement
Connections

▶ Make a Meter Stick WHOLE CLASS

Hold up a meter stick and ask children to tell what it is. If a child calls it a yardstick, show the class a yardstick and point out that a meter stick is a bit longer and that it has centimeter units instead of inch units on it.

- Where else have you heard the word *meter?* Possible answers: water meter, gas meter, electric meter, parking meter, thermometer, speedometer, centimeter

Explain that *meter* means "to measure" and that the metric system uses meters as a unit of measurement for length.

Tell children that they are going to make their own meter sticks. Refer them to Student Activity Book page 395 and have them follow the instructions. (If you want to make sturdy meter sticks, you can copy TRB M90 onto cardstock.) Have children add the numbers 25, 50, and 75 to their meter sticks.

When children are finished, hold up one of the paper meter sticks and point to the numbers 1–100 on it.

- What unit do these numbers show? centimeters

To help children visualize centimeters as lengths, they can color the lengths of the first ten centimeters on their meter sticks using two alternating colored pencils.

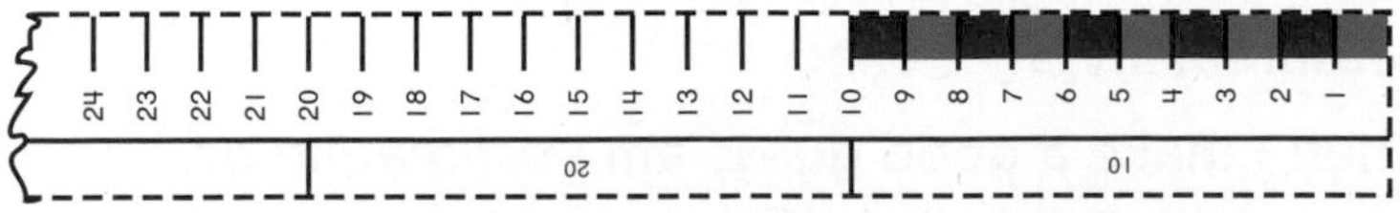

From Student Activity Book page 395.

- How many centimeters are in one meter? 100 centimeters

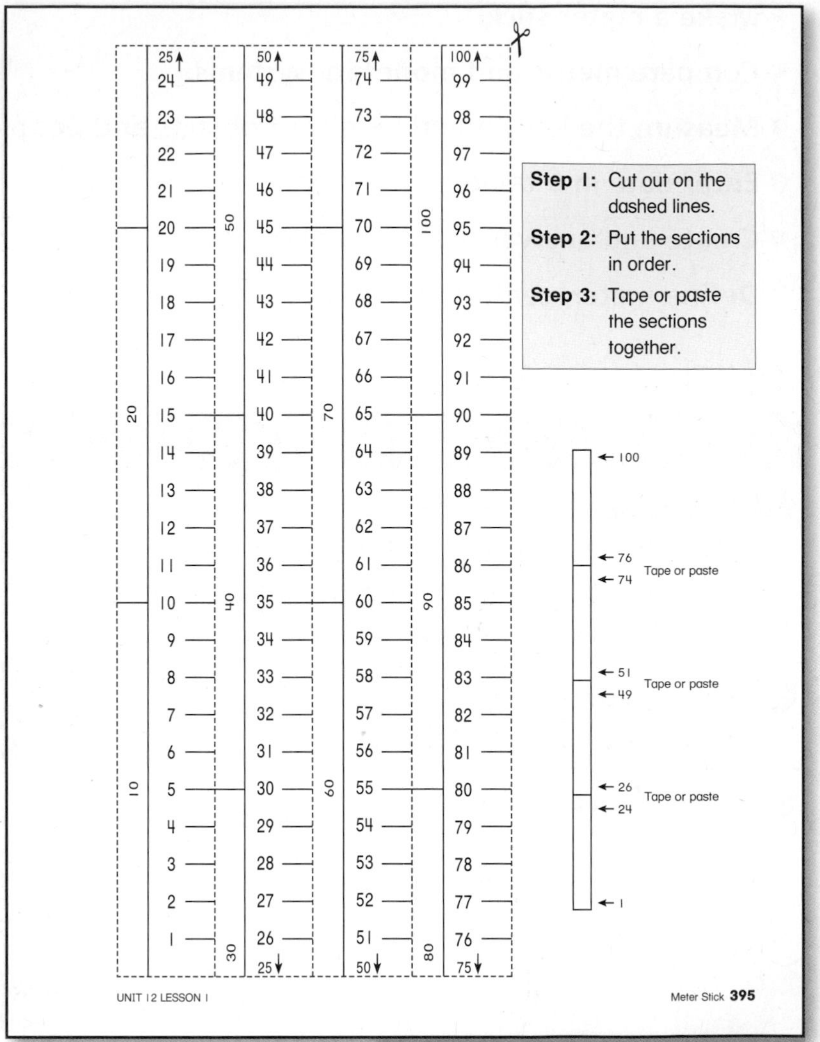

Student Activity Book page 395

Math Talk Ask children to look at the numbers on the left side of their meter sticks. Tell them that 10 centimeters is equal to 1 decimeter.

Have children mark the length of each decimeter on their meter sticks using alternating colored pencils.

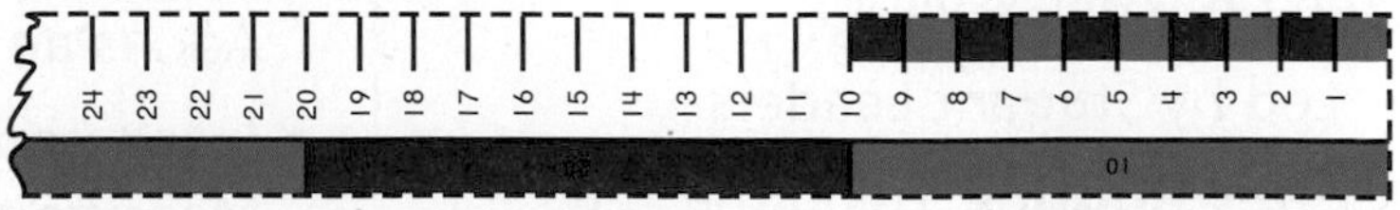

- How many decimeters are in one meter? 10 decimeters
- How many centimeters are in one decimeter? 10 centimeters

Summarize the relationship among the metric units for length on the board.

Length
1 meter = 100 centimeters
1 meter = 10 decimeters
1 decimeter = 10 centimeters

Compare Metric and Monetary Systems Explain to children that the metric system of measurement is based on the number 10. Point out that they are already familiar with another system based on the number 10.

- When you talk about money, what does the word *cent* mean? 1 penny
- How many cents are in one dollar? 100 cents
- How many dimes are in one dollar? 10 dimes
- How many cents are in one dime? 10 cents

Summarize the relationship among the units of money on the board.

Money
1 dollar = 100 cents
1 dollar = 10 dimes
1 dime = 10 cents

Point out for children that the words *cents* and *centimeters* both have *cent* in them and that the words *decimeters* and *dimes* both begin with the letter "d."

▶ Estimate and Measure PAIRS

Explain to children that we can use an abbreviation (a short way) when we write a metric unit with a number. Write the metric units and their symbols on the board.

Unit	Short Way
meter	m
centimeter	cm
decimeter	dm

Refer children to Student Activity Book page 397 and have them complete exercises 1–3, which help them become more familiar with the abbreviations for metric units. When children are finished, discuss their findings.

12–1 Class Activity Name ______

▶ **Estimate and Measure**

Find a part of your hand that is about the length of each measure.

1. 1 cm Possible answer: width of thumbnail
2. 1 dm Possible answer: length of hand

Find a part of your body that is about 1 meter long.

3. 1 m Possible answer: arm span

Find the real object. Estimate and measure its length. Round if necessary. Answers will vary.

4.

Estimate: about ____ cm
Measure: ____ cm

5.
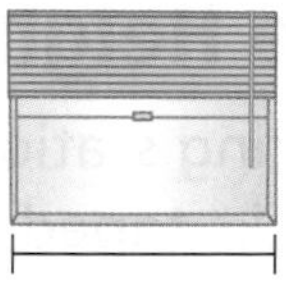
Estimate: about ____ cm
Measure: ____ cm

6.
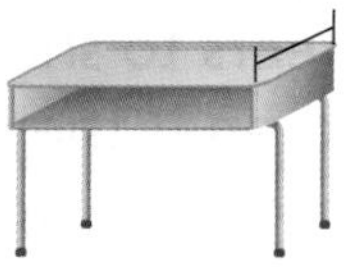
Estimate: about ____ dm
Measure: ____ dm

7.
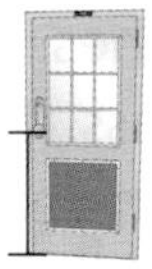
Estimate: about ____ m
Measure: ____ m

Draw a line segment to show each length.

8. 1 cm ——
9. 1 dm ————————————

UNIT 12 LESSON 1 Meters and Decimeters **397**

Student Activity Book page 397

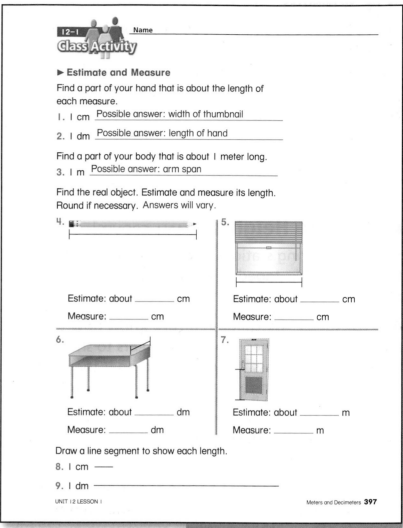

Next, ask children to complete exercises 4–7, using their meter sticks to measure several objects. Encourage different ways of estimating, such as using the personal referents from exercises 1–3. Have children then complete exercises 8 and 9. When they are finished, invite them to take turns drawing one-meter lengths on the board.

Ongoing Assessment

Ask children to explain how their meter sticks show that there are 100 centimeters in a meter, 10 centimeters in a decimeter, and 10 decimeters in a meter.

1 Teaching the Lesson

Activity 1

Use Metric Units

20 MINUTES

Goal: Use metric units and find equivalent metric lengths.

Materials: Student Activity Book page 401, paper meter sticks from Lesson 1 or Meter Stick (TRB M90)

NCTM Standards:
Measurement
Connections

▶ Metric Units WHOLE CLASS

Write the abbreviations cm, dm, and m on the board and ask children the meaning of each. centimeter, decimeter, meter

▶ Equivalent Metric Lengths WHOLE CLASS

Ask children to show you the following measurements on their paper meter sticks.

- Show me 10 centimeters.
- Show me 100 centimeters.
- Show me 50 centimeters.
- Show me 1 meter.
- Show me 2 decimeters.
- Show me 7 decimeters.

Next, ask children to show you estimations of the following measurements using personal referents.

- Show me about 1 centimeter.
- Show me about 10 centimeters.
- Show me about 1 decimeter.
- Show me about 100 centimeters.
- Show me about 1 meter.

Have children complete exercises 1–4 independently to reinforce that one decimeter equals ten centimeters.

Then ask children to complete exercises 5–10 in pairs to see that 1 meter equals 10 decimeters and 1 meter equals 100 centimeters.

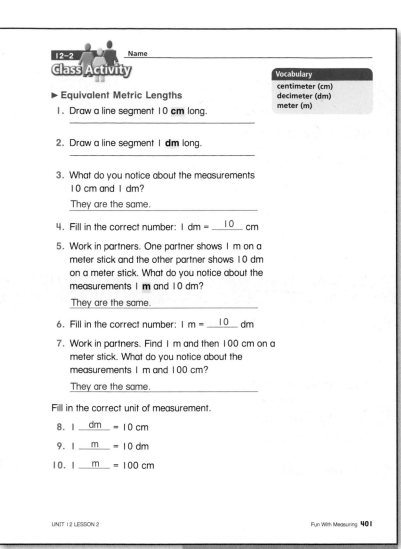

12–2 Class Activity

Name ____________

Vocabulary
centimeter (cm)
decimeter (dm)
meter (m)

▶ **Equivalent Metric Lengths**

1. Draw a line segment 10 **cm** long.

2. Draw a line segment 1 **dm** long.

3. What do you notice about the measurements 10 cm and 1 dm?
They are the same.

4. Fill in the correct number: 1 dm = 10 cm

5. Work in partners. One partner shows 1 m on a meter stick and the other partner shows 10 dm on a meter stick. What do you notice about the measurements 1 **m** and 10 dm?
They are the same.

6. Fill in the correct number: 1 m = 10 dm

7. Work in partners. Find 1 m and then 100 cm on a meter stick. What do you notice about the measurements 1 m and 100 cm?
They are the same.

Fill in the correct unit of measurement.

8. 1 dm = 10 cm
9. 1 m = 10 dm
10. 1 m = 100 cm

UNIT 12 LESSON 2 Fun With Measuring 401

Student Activity Book page 401

Ongoing Assessment

Ask children to show you an estimation of each of the following lengths. Then have them show each length on their paper meter sticks.

▶ 40 cm
▶ 1 m
▶ 3 dm

Activity 2

Measurement Games

40 MINUTES

Goal: Practice measuring by playing games.

Materials: meter sticks, masking tape, index cards (3 per pair of children), pennies, Student Activity Book pages 402–404

NCTM Standards:
Measurement
Connections

▶ Introduce Games SMALL GROUPS

Tell the class that today they will play a jumping game, a guessing game, and a penny toss game. Use the guidelines below to set up game stations.

Jumping Game

For the jumping game, tape two meter sticks to the floor (end to end) and mark a start line with tape.

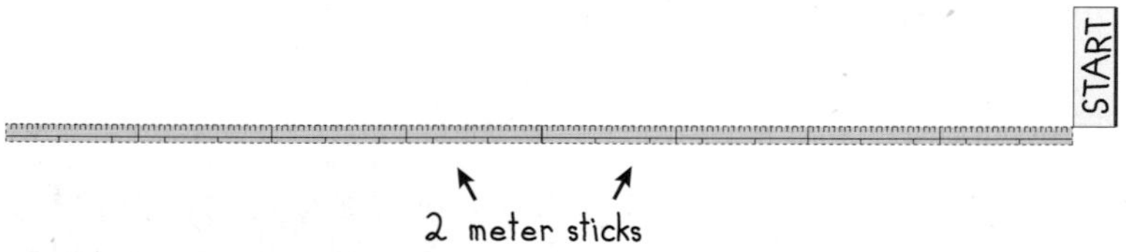

Guessing Game

For the guessing game, set aside three index cards for each pair of children.

Penny Toss Game

For the penny toss game, tape meter sticks to the floor about 1 meter apart. Make a start line and a goal line with tape. Set aside one penny for each child.

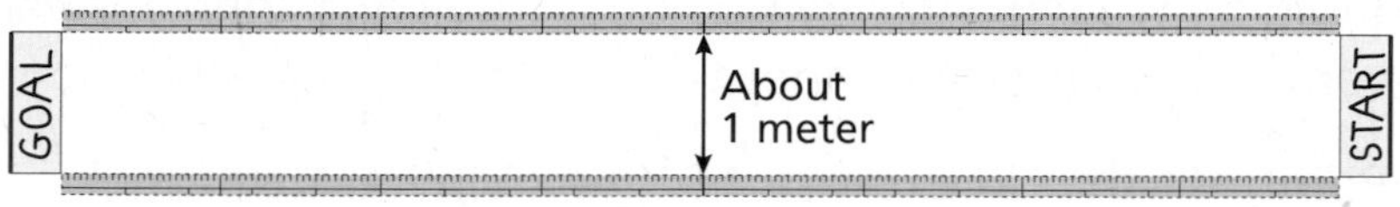

Demonstrate how to play each game as described in the next three sections. Then divide the class into three groups. Once children are in groups, refer them to Student Activity Book pages 402–404. Have them follow the instructions for each game and complete all of the related exercises.

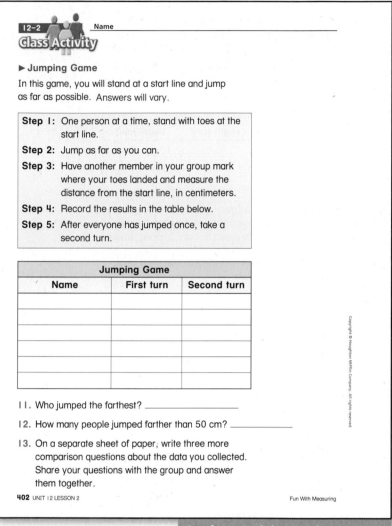

12–2 Class Activity Name ____________________

▶ **Jumping Game**

In this game, you will stand at a start line and jump as far as possible. Answers will vary.

Step 1: One person at a time, stand with toes at the start line.
Step 2: Jump as far as you can.
Step 3: Have another member in your group mark where your toes landed and measure the distance from the start line, in centimeters.
Step 4: Record the results in the table below.
Step 5: After everyone has jumped once, take a second turn.

Jumping Game		
Name	**First turn**	**Second turn**

11. Who jumped the farthest? ____________
12. How many people jumped farther than 50 cm? ____________
13. On a separate sheet of paper, write three more comparison questions about the data you collected. Share your questions with the group and answer them together.

402 UNIT 12 LESSON 2 Fun With Measuring

Student Activity Book page 402

▶ Jumping Game SMALL GROUPS

Demonstrate how to play. Stand with both feet together with toes at the start line. Jump as far as you can. Invite a volunteer to mark where your toes land and measure the distance of your jump.

Tell children to record the results in the table on Student Activity Book page 402 and then answer and write several comparison questions about the data.

Activity continued ▶

12-2 Class Activity

Name ____________________

▶ Guessing Game

In this game, you and a partner will write clues that describe rectangular objects in the classroom. You will trade clues with another pair and try to find their objects.

Step 1: Measure the length and width of 3 objects. Record your measurements in the table below.

Answers will vary.

Object Dimensions		
Object	**Length (cm)**	**Width (cm)**

Step 2: Write 2 clues that describe each object.
Clue 1: Write the object's length and width.
Clue 2: Describe the object by color, location, shape, or use.

Step 3: Write the name of the object on the back of the index card.

What Am I?
Clue 1: I am 67 cm long and 44 cm wide.
Clue 2: I usually hang on the wall at the front of the classroom.

Answer
bulletin board

Step 4: Read your clues to another pair. Ask them to guess each of your objects by first estimating and then measuring to check.

UNIT 12 LESSON 2 Fun With Measuring 403

Student Activity Book page 403

12-2 Class Activity

Name ____________________

▶ Penny Toss Game

In this game, you will stand at the start line and toss a penny as close as possible to the goal line. Answers will vary.

Step 1: Take turns tossing a penny as close as possible to the goal line.

Step 2: Measure the distance of your toss in centimeters from the goal line.

Step 3: Complete the table below.

Penny Toss Game	
Name	**Distance from the goal line (cm)**

14. Whose penny landed closest to the goal line? ____________

15. How many children's pennies landed less than 10 cm from the goal line? ____________

16. On a separate sheet of paper, write three more comparison questions about the data you collected. Share your questions with the group and answer them together.

404 UNIT 12 LESSON 2 Fun With Measuring

Student Activity Book page 404

▶ Guessing Game

SMALL GROUPS

Math Talk

Demonstrate how to play the guessing game by selecting a rectangular object in the classroom and measuring its length and width. Next, write two clues about the object on an index card. In the first clue, record its length and width and in the second clue, describe its color, location, shape, or use. Write the name of the object on the back of the index card.

Explain to children that they will be working in pairs and writing clues for three different objects. After writing their clues, they will trade with another pair in their group and try to guess each other's objects. Tell children to first estimate measurements to help them name the objects, and then measure to check their guesses.

▶ Penny Toss Game

SMALL GROUPS

Math Talk

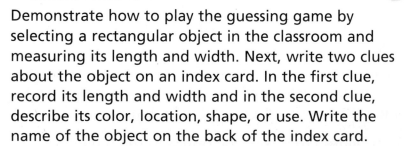

Demonstrate how to play the penny toss game. Stand at the start line and try to toss a penny as close as possible to the goal line. Measure the distance of your toss from the goal line.

Explain to children that they will record the results in the table on Student Activity Book page 404 and then answer comparison questions about the data they collected.

Point out that in exercise 16, they will have an opportunity to write three comparison questions of their own for the rest of their group to answer.

Differentiated Instruction

Special Needs You might adapt these games to accommodate children with special needs, or choose to use only those games that are appropriate for all of your students.

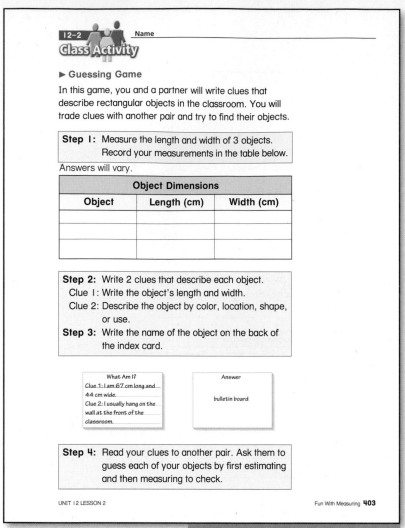

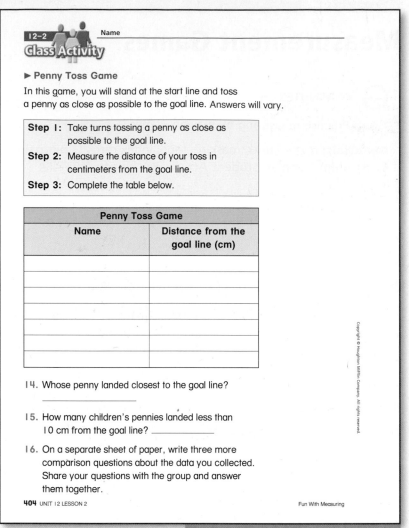

2 Going Further

Differentiated Instruction

Intervention — Activity Card 12-2

Estimate and Measure Distance — Activity Card 12-2 ●

Work: (pairs)

Use:
- toy cars
- ramp
- meter stick

1. Release a toy car down the ramp.
2. Estimate, in centimeters, how far the car went from the bottom of the ramp to its stopping point. Record your estimate.
3. Then measure the actual distance. Round to the nearest centimeter. Record.

I estimated that my car went 60 cm. I measured the distance and found that it went 68 cm.

4. Take turns. Repeat four times.
5. **Math Talk** Which estimate was the closest? What are some ways to make good estimates?

Unit 12, Lesson 2

Activity Note Each pair needs toy cars, a ramp made from cardstock or wood, and a meter stick.

Math Writing Prompt

Explain Your Thinking Mischa drew a line segment 30 cm in length. Ryan drew a line segment 3 dm in length. Are the lines the same length? Explain.

Soar to Success Math **Software Support**

Warm Up 38.14

On Level — Activity Card 12-2

Measure in Different Units — Activity Card 12-2 ▲

Work: (pairs)

Use:
- toy cars
- ramp
- meter stick

1. Release a toy car down the ramp.
2. Measure the distance from the bottom of the ramp to the stopping point. Round to the nearest centimeter. Record.
3. Then measure the distance, rounding to the nearest decimeter. Record.
4. Take turns. Repeat four times.
5. **Math Talk** Compare the measurements for each turn. Explain which you think is more accurate and why.

My car went 84 cm or 8 dm. The measurement in centimeters is more exact. When I measured to the nearest decimeter, I lost 4 cm from the distance.

Unit 12, Lesson 2

Activity Note Each pair needs toy cars, a ramp made from cardstock or wood, and a meter stick.

Math Writing Prompt

Explain a Method When Sami spreads her fingers apart, the distance between the tip of her pinky and the tip of her index finger is 10 cm. How can she use this distance to estimate length?

Harcourt MegaMath Grades K-6 **Software Support**

Shapes Ahoy: Made to Measure, Level I

Challenge — Activity Card 12-2

What Do I See? — Activity Card 12-2 ■

Work: (pairs)

Choose:
- 1
- 2

1. (1) Choose an object in the classroom. Do not tell what it is.

   "I spy an object that is longer than a pencil but shorter than the board."

2. Play *What Do I See?* Give comparison clues. Use words like *longer, taller, shorter, wider, thinner, greater than,* and *less than.*
3. (2) Use the clues. Try to guess the object. Ask for more clues if you need them.

   "Is the object longer or shorter than Mrs. Trettola's desk?"

4. Switch roles. Repeat.

Unit 12, Lesson 2

Activity Note Discuss the directions for the game and practice making up clues.

Math Writing Prompt

You Decide Mark measures a table to the nearest meter. Devon measures the table to the nearest decimeter. Andie measures the table to the nearest centimeter. Explain which measurement is the most exact.

Destination Math **Software Support**

Course II: Module 3: Unit 1: Area

3 Homework

12–2 Homework **Goal:** Additional Practice

Children measure four objects at home, write descriptive clues for each, and have a Homework Helper guess the objects.

12–2 Homework Name ____________________

Measure four rectangular objects using your paper meter stick. Include at least two objects that have measurements greater than 100 cm. Write a clue for each object about its color, shape, location, or use. Ask your Homework Helper to guess each of your objects.
Answers will vary.

1. The length of the object is __________ cm.
   The width of the object is __________ cm.
   Clue: ______________________________

2. The length of the object is __________ cm.
   The width of the object is __________ cm.
   Clue: ______________________________

3. The length of the object is __________ cm.
   The width of the object is __________ cm.
   Clue: ______________________________

4. The length of the object is __________ cm.
   The width of the object is __________ cm.
   Clue: ______________________________

5. **On the Back** Use your paper meter stick to measure the height of one or more people in your family. Make a list with the name of each family member and his or her height. Answers will vary.

UNIT 12 LESSON 2 Fun With Measuring **269**

Homework and Remembering page 269

Class Management

Looking Ahead This homework page will be used in the next lesson.

Home or School Activity

Literature Connection

Tell Me How Far It Is Read aloud *Tell Me How Far It Is* by Shirley Willis (Gardners Books, 2005). This book explores the concepts of distance and length. It also discusses units of measure, how various measurements are made and why measuring is important. Use this book to extend children's understanding of measurement and to spur class discussion.

MINI UNIT 12

LESSON 3

Meter, Decimeter, and Centimeter Equivalencies

REAL WORLD Problem Solving

Lesson Objectives

- Convert measures in centimeters to a combination of meters, decimeters, and centimeters.
- Solve story problems requiring metric conversion.
- Understand the base ten system in metric measurement and numbers.

Vocabulary

centimeter
decimeter
meter

The Day at a Glance

Today's Goals	Materials	
1 Teaching the Lesson **A1:** Convert measures in centimeters to a combination of meters, decimeters, and centimeters. **A2:** Solve measurement story problems and relate the base ten system to metric measurements of length.	**Lesson Activities** Homework and Remembering pp. 271–272 Paper meter sticks from Lesson 1 Completed Homework and Remembering page 269 (from Lesson 2) MathBoard materials	**Going Further** Activity Cards 12-3 Index cards Math Journals
2 Going Further ▸ Differentiated Instruction		
3 Homework		

Use Math Talk today!

Keeping Skills Sharp

Daily Routines

Making Change and Counting Coins Making Change from $5.00, Combining Coins and Counting Money (See pp. xxvii–xxviii.)

▸ Led by Student Leaders

Money Routine Using the 120 Poster, Using the Money Flip Chart, Using the Number Path, Using Secret Code Cards (See pp. xxiii–xxv.)

▸ Led by Student Leaders

English Language Learners

Write 300 cm, 3 m, *equivalent,* and *measurement equivalencies* on the board. Ask: **Do 300 cm *equal* 3 m?** yes Say: **They are *equivalent*.**

- **Beginning** Say: ***Measurement equivalencies* are measurements that are equal.** Have children repeat.
- **Intermediate** Write 30 dm. Ask: **Are 3 m equivalent to 30 dm?** yes Write 3 m = 30 dm = 300 cm. Say: **These are *measurement equivalencies*.**
- **Advanced** Ask: **How many dm are *equivalent* to 3 m?** 30 dm Write 3 m = 30 dm = 300 cm. Ask: **Are these *measurement equivalencies*?** yes

1 Teaching the Lesson

Activity 1

Measurement Equivalencies

25 MINUTES

Goal: Convert measures in centimeters to a combination of meters, decimeters, and centimeters.

Materials: paper meter sticks from Lesson 1, completed Homework and Remembering page 269

NCTM Standards:
Measurement
Connections

▶ Convert Metric Length Measurements WHOLE CLASS Math Talk

Ask for Ideas Begin by asking children to approximate different lengths using their fingers or hands. If necessary, they can mention personal referents or use meter sticks. Make sure that children keep their hands in about the same position for equivalent measurements, such as 9 decimeters and 90 centimeters.

- Show me 4 centimeters.
- Show me 4 decimeters.
- Show me 40 centimeters.
- Show me 1 meter.
- Show me 90 centimeters.
- Show me 9 decimeters.

Demonstrate how to show 60 centimeters on a meter stick by placing one hand at the 0 end and the other hand at the 60-centimeter mark. Have children do the same on their paper meter sticks, and then ask them to hold up their hands to show this length.

- What is another way to say this length? 6 dm

Have children hold up both hands to show 6 decimeters. Be sure that they have their hands in about the same position as they did for 60 centimeters.

Next, ask children to measure the length of their Student Activity Book. Have them sketch their book and write the length above it. 28 cm

Ask children to tell how you can write 28 cm in a different way. Encourage them to use their meter sticks to determine that 28 cm is equal to 2 dm 8 cm. Have them write this equation:

28 cm = 2 dm 8 cm

Ask children to measure the width of their Student Activity Book (or a page from the book), round the measurement to the nearest centimeter, and label their drawing. Challenge them to find another way to write 22 cm and use their meter stick to check their answer. 2 dm 2 cm

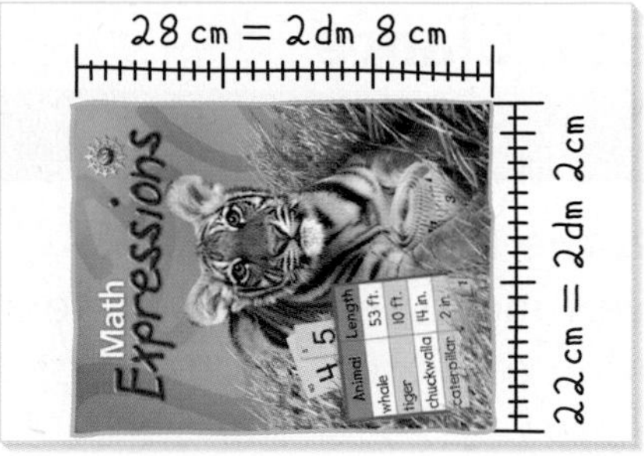

You might also have children measure the length and width of their desks to the nearest centimeter. They can sketch their desk, write labels in centimeters, and convert their measurements to decimeters and centimeters. For example, a desk with a length of 52 centimeters will have labels *52 cm* and *5 dm 2 cm.*

▶ Convert Height Measurements

INDIVIDUALS

Ask children to convert their own height measurement from centimeters to meters, decimeters, and centimeters. If they cannot remember their height in centimeters, they can refer to Student Activity Book page 398 (from Lesson 1), where children measured and recorded each other's heights in small groups.

Have children sketch themselves on a separate sheet of paper, draw a line indicating their height, and write their height in centimeters. Ask them to then convert the measurement to meters, decimeters, and centimeters.

Have children refer to their Homework page from Lesson 2. Ask them to select one of the objects they found at home with a measure greater than 100 centimeters (1 meter) and repeat the exercise above. The artwork below shows the example of a refrigerator.

You may want to encourage children to look at their meter sticks so they can see the measurement.

equivalencies. They can write centimeter equivalencies to check their meter measures.

1 m 5 dm 3 cm = 100 cm 50 cm 3 cm = 153 cm

You might also suggest that children write the various combinations of meters, decimeters, and centimeters for each measurement.

Ongoing Assessment

Ask children to fill in each blank.

- 30 cm = ________ dm
- 200 cm = ________ m
- 175 cm = ________ m ________ dm ________ cm

Activity 2

Story Problems

35 MINUTES

Goal: Solve measurement story problems and relate the base ten system to metric measurements of length.

Materials: MathBoard materials, paper meter sticks from Lesson 1 or Meter Stick (TRB M90)

NCTM Standards:
Measurement
Connections
Communication

▶ Metric Story Problems SMALL GROUPS

Have children work in small groups to solve story problems on their MathBoards. Make sure children use their meter sticks to draw pictures to help them find the answers.

Write this story problem on the board and read it aloud.

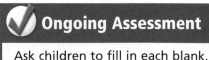

Austin can jump 19 dm.
Is that more or less than
2 m?

Invite several groups to present their answer and explain how they solved the problem. It's less. 19 dm is less than 2 m because 2 m is 20 dm.

Write another story problem on the board and read it aloud.

Tamara can jump 205 cm.
Is that more or less than
2 m?

Ask children to solve the problem and then invite groups to share their answers. It's more. 205 cm is more than 2 m because 2 m is 200 cm.

Activity continued ▶

1 Teaching the Lesson (continued)

Write a third story problem on the board and read it aloud.

> Theo and Lucy want to make a border out of yarn for the top of the bulletin board. The bulletin board is 3 m 2 dm long. Theo has a piece of yarn 186 cm long. Lucy has a piece of yarn 138 cm long. Together, do they have enough yarn to make the border?

When groups are finished, ask them to share their answers. Invite several groups to show their work on the board.

▶ Metric Conversions Using Place Value

WHOLE CLASS

If no group solved the yarn story problem by first converting each length into meters, decimeters, and centimeters, write the solution on the board.

186 cm = 1 m 8 dm 6 cm
138 cm = 1 m 3 dm 8 cm

$$\begin{array}{r} \;1\quad 1\phantom{\text{ dm }8\text{ cm}} \\ 1\text{ m }8\text{ dm }6\text{ cm} \\ +\;1\text{ m }3\text{ dm }8\text{ cm} \\ \hline 3\text{ m }2\text{ dm }4\text{ cm} \end{array}$$

- When you convert 324 cm to meters, decimeters, and centimeters, what do you get? 3 m 2 dm 4 cm
- If I call this *(point to the ones place in 324)* the centimeters place, can I call this *(point to the tens place)* the decimeters place? yes Why? 10 cm is the same as 1 dm, just like 10 ones is the same as 1 ten.
- What can I call this place *(point to the hundreds place)*? You can call it the meters place because 10 dm is the same as 1 m, just like 10 tens is the same as 1 hundred.

▶ Comparison Stories

Write this story problem on the board and read it aloud.

> Mateo, Gracia, and Cora all have different lengths of colored yarn. Mateo's blue yarn is 186 cm long. Let's call his Yarn A. Gracia's red yarn is 153 cm long. We will call hers Yarn B. Cora has a yellow piece of yarn that is 127 cm long. Her yarn will be called Yarn C.

It might be helpful if you can have actual pieces of this yarn on hand, cut to the stated lengths.

Now ask the children:

- Which child has the longest yarn? Mateo What do we call his yarn? Yarn A
- How long is Gracia's yarn? 153 cm Using the yarns' names, compare Mateo's yarn to Gracia's yarn. Yarn A is longer than Yarn B
- Who has the shortest piece of yarn? Cora How might you compare her yarn's length to the other two? Possible answer: Cora's yarn is shorter than both Mateo's yarn and Gracia's yarn.
- Using their names, compare Gracia's yarn to Cora's yarn. Yarn B is longer than Yarn C.
- We already know that Yarn A, Mateo's yarn, is longer than Yarn B, Gracia's yarn. We also know that Gracia's yarn, Yarn B, is longer than Cora's yarn, Yarn C. What can you say about Mateo's yarn in comparison to Cora's? Yarn A is longer than Yarn C.

Elicit from the children the idea of the Transitive Property when comparing lengths of objects. Help the children to realize and explain comfortably that if A is longer than B, and B is longer than C, then A is longer than C.

2 Going Further

Differentiated Instruction

Intervention — Activity Card 12-3

Metric Measure with Centimeters — Activity Card 12-3

Work: pairs
Use:
- 16 index cards

1. **Work Together** Take eight index cards. Write a measure greater than 10 cm and less than 100 cm on each card.
2. Write the same measures in decimeters and centimeters on the other eight cards.

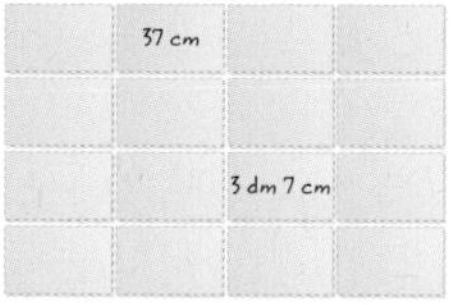

3. Mix up the cards. Place them face down in four rows.
4. Take turns turning over two cards. If the cards show the same measure, keep them. If the cards do not show the same measure, put them back.

Unit 12, Lesson 3

Activity Note Each pair needs 16 index cards. Pairs need to write the same measure in centimeters and in centimeters and decimeters on two separate cards.

Math Writing Prompt

Explain a Method Lorenzo wants to write 60 cm as decimeters. Explain how to do this.

Soar to Success Math Software Support

Warm Up 41.18

On Level — Activity Card 12-3

Metric Match with Meters — Activity Card 12-3

Work: pairs
Use:
- 16 index cards

1. **Work Together** Take eight index cards. Write a measure greater than 100 cm and less than 500 cm on each card.
2. Write the same measures in meters, decimeters, and centimeters on the other eight cards.

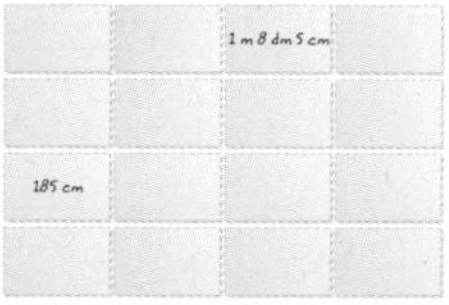

3. Mix up the cards and place them face down in four rows.
4. Take turns turning over two cards. If the cards show the same measure, keep them. If the cards do not show the same measure, put them back.

Unit 12, Lesson 3

Activity Note Each pair needs 16 index cards. Pairs need to write the same measure in centimeters and in centimeters, decimeters, and meters on two separate cards.

Math Writing Prompt

Summarize Daphne wants to write 295 cm as meters, decimeters, and centimeters. Explain how to do this.

Harcourt Mega Math Software Support

Shapes Ahoy: Made to Measure, Level I

Challenge — Activity Card 12-3

Solve Problems — Activity Card 12-3

Work: pairs

1. Each child: Write a story problem with metric conversions.
2. Solve the story problem. Write the solution on the bottom of the page. Fold the paper to hide the solution.

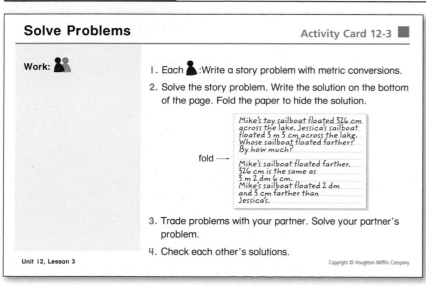

Mike's toy sailboat floated 326 cm across the lake. Jessica's sailboat floated 3 m 3 cm across the lake. Whose sailboat floated farther? By how much?

fold →

Mike's sailboat floated farther. 326 cm is the same as 3 m 2 dm 6 cm. Mike's sailboat floated 2 dm and 3 cm farther than Jessica's.

3. Trade problems with your partner. Solve your partner's problem.
4. Check each other's solutions.

Unit 12, Lesson 3

Activity Note Each child writes two story problems that involve metric conversions. Have children explain how they solved the problems.

Math Writing Prompt

You Decide Malcolm wrote 368 cm as 3 m 68 cm. Tony wrote 368 as 3 m 6 dm 8 cm. Are they both correct? Explain why or why not.

Destination Math Software Support

Course II: Module 3: Unit 1: Area

3 Homework

12–3 Homework **Goal:** Additional Practice

✓ Include children's work on page 271 as part of their portfolios.

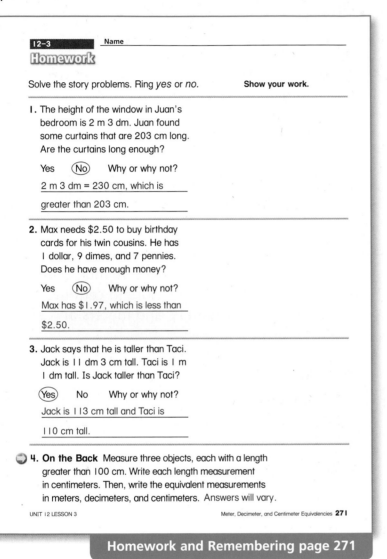

12–3 Homework — Name ______________________

Solve the story problems. Ring *yes* or *no*. **Show your work.**

1. The height of the window in Juan's bedroom is 2 m 3 dm. Juan found some curtains that are 203 cm long. Are the curtains long enough?

Yes (No) Why or why not?

2 m 3 dm = 230 cm, which is greater than 203 cm.

2. Max needs $2.50 to buy birthday cards for his twin cousins. He has 1 dollar, 9 dimes, and 7 pennies. Does he have enough money?

Yes (No) Why or why not?

Max has $1.97, which is less than $2.50.

3. Jack says that he is taller than Taci. Jack is 11 dm 3 cm tall. Taci is 1 m 1 dm tall. Is Jack taller than Taci?

(Yes) No Why or why not?

Jack is 113 cm tall and Taci is 110 cm tall.

4. On the Back Measure three objects, each with a length greater than 100 cm. Write each length measurement in centimeters. Then, write the equivalent measurements in meters, decimeters, and centimeters. Answers will vary.

UNIT 12 LESSON 3 — Meter, Decimeter, and Centimeter Equivalencies **271**

Homework and Remembering page 271

Home or School Activity

Sports Connection

Olympic Measurements Invite children to investigate the types of measurement units used in different Olympic events. They can create a list or draw pictures to show their findings.

Olympic running races are measured in meters.

MINI UNIT 12

LESSON 4

Practice With Meters and Money

REAL WORLD Problem Solving

Lesson Objectives

- Recognize the base ten system in metric and monetary systems.
- Solve story problems involving metric and monetary systems.

Vocabulary

meter
decimeter
centimeter

The Day at a Glance

Today's Goals	Materials	
1 Teaching the Lesson A: Translate measurements and monetary amounts into place value notation. Solve addition problems and write answers in place value notation. **2 Going Further** ▸ Differentiated Instruction **3 Homework**	**Lesson Activities** Student Activity Book pp. 405–406 Homework and Remembering pp. 273–274 Paper meter sticks from Lesson 1	**Going Further** Activity Cards 12-4 Place value charts Base ten blocks Index cards *Millions to Measure* by David M. Schwartz Math Journals

Use Math Talk today!

Keeping Skills Sharp

Daily Routines	English Language Learners
Making Change and Counting Coins Making Change from $5.00, Combining Coins and Counting Money (See pp. xxvii–xxviii.) ▸ Led by Student Leaders **Money Routine** Using the 120 Poster, Using the Money Flip Chart, Using the Number Path, Using Secret Code Cards (See pp. xxiii–xxv.) ▸ Led by Student Leaders	Write 1 dollar = 10 dimes = 100 pennies on the board. Write *equivalent* and *money equivalencies*. • **Beginning** Say: **Money equivalencies are money amounts that are equal.** Have children repeat. • **Intermediate** Ask: **Is 1 dollar *equivalent* to 10 dimes?** yes **Is 10 dimes *equivalent* to 100 pennies?** yes **Are these *money equivalencies*?** yes • **Advanced** Say: **These amounts of money are *equal* or __.** equivalent **This is an example of *money* __.** equivalencies

1 Teaching the Lesson

Activity

Meters and Money

55 MINUTES

Goal: Translate measurements and monetary amounts into place value notation. Solve addition problems and write answers in place value notation.

Materials: Student Activity Book page 405, paper meter sticks from Lesson 1

NCTM Standards:
Measurement
Connections
Problem Solving

▶ Money and Length Equivalencies

WHOLE CLASS

Refer children to Student Activity Book page 405. Work through exercises 1–9 together or have children complete the exercises in pairs. Encourage children to confirm their answers using their meter sticks.

Have several children share the drawings they made for exercise 10.

▶ Money and Measurement Story Problems

PAIRS

Math Talk

Write these story problems on the board and invite a volunteer to read aloud each problem. Ask children to work in pairs to solve the problems using a method of their choice. When they are finished, share answers as a class.

Erik has 423 pennies in his bank. Luz has 289 pennies in her bank. How much money do they have together?

_7_ dollars _1_ dimes _2_ pennies

The children at Central School moved two lunch tables together. One table was 423 cm long and the other table was 289 cm long. How long are the tables together?

_7_ meters _1_ decimeters _2_ centimeters

12–4 **Class Activity** Name ________

▶ **Money and Length Equivalencies**

Answer each question. Draw a picture if you need to.

1. How many ones in 1 ten? _10_
2. How many dimes in 1 dollar? _10_
3. How many pennies in 1 dime? _10_
4. How many tens in 1 hundred? _10_
5. How many centimeters in 1 dm? _10_
6. How many cents in 1 dime? _10_
7. How many pennies in 1 dollar? _100_
8. How many ones in 1 hundred? _100_
9. Write the numbers.

5 m 8 dm 4 cm = _58_ dm 4 cm = _584_ cm	_4_ m _1_ dm _2_ cm = 41 dm 2 cm = _412_ cm
\$3.18 = _31_ dimes _8_ pennies = _318_ pennies	\$ _4.12_ = _41_ dimes _2_ pennies = 412 pennies

10. **On the Back** Draw a picture to show the relationship between metric lengths (meters, decimeters, centimeters) and money (dollars, dimes, pennies).
Check children's drawings.

UNIT 12 LESSON 4 Practice with Meters and Money **405**

Student Activity Book page 405

Ongoing Assessment

Check that children understand that the relationship between meters, decimeters, and centimeters is the same as the relationship between dollars, dimes, and pennies.

Intervention — Activity Card 12-4

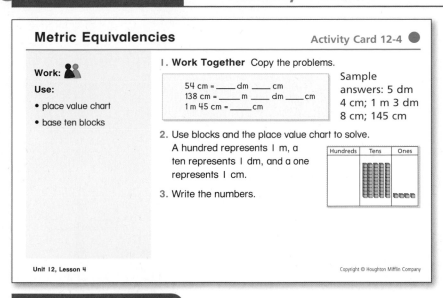

Metric Equivalencies

Activity Card 12-4

Work: pairs
Use:
- place value chart
- base ten blocks

1. **Work Together** Copy the problems.

54 cm = ____ dm ____ cm
138 cm = ____ m ____ dm ____ cm
1 m 45 cm = ____ cm

Sample answers: 5 dm 4 cm; 1 m 3 dm 8 cm; 145 cm

2. Use blocks and the place value chart to solve. A hundred represents 1 m, a ten represents 1 dm, and a one represents 1 cm.
3. Write the numbers.

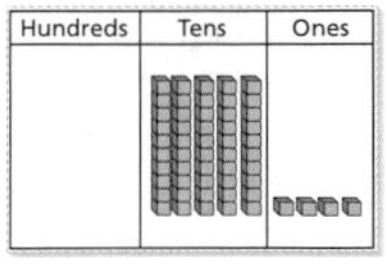

Unit 12, Lesson 4

Activity Note Each pair needs hundreds, tens, and ones base ten blocks, and a large place value chart (see activity card). Explain that a hundred represents 1 m, a ten represents 1 dm, and a one represents 1 cm.

Math Writing Prompt

Connections How does knowing about ones and tens help you understand centimeters and decimeters?

Soar to Success Math Software Support

Warm Up 41.18

On Level — Activity Card 12-4

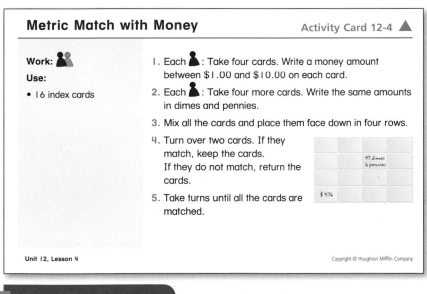

Metric Match with Money

Activity Card 12-4

Work: pairs
Use:
- 16 index cards

1. Each student: Take four cards. Write a money amount between \$1.00 and \$10.00 on each card.
2. Each student: Take four more cards. Write the same amounts in dimes and pennies.
3. Mix all the cards and place them face down in four rows.
4. Turn over two cards. If they match, keep the cards. If they do not match, return the cards.
5. Take turns until all the cards are matched.

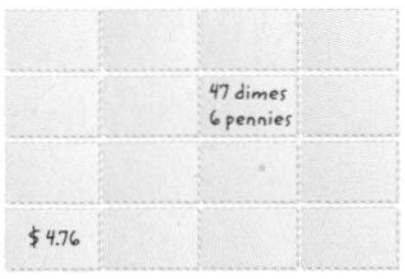

Unit 12, Lesson 4

Activity Note Each pair needs 16 index cards. Eight cards will show dollar amounts greater than \$1.00 and less than \$10.00. The other cards will show the equivalent amounts in dimes and pennies.

Math Writing Prompt

Pennies and Dollars How does knowing about pennies and dollars help you with centimeters and meters?

Harcourt Mega Math Software Support

Numberopolis: Lulu's Lunch Counter, Level U

Challenge — Activity Card 12-4

Explore Equivalent Measures

Activity Card 12-4

Work: pairs
Use:
- base ten blocks

1. **Work Together** Make a list of all the ways you can show 232 cm. Use base ten blocks to help you find the different combinations.
2. Compare your list with other pairs.
3. **Math Talk** How many combinations did each pair find? Share how you found the different combinations.

Unit 12, Lesson 4

Activity Note Each pair needs base ten blocks (hundreds, tens, and ones). Have pairs show each combination using the blocks.

Math Writing Prompt

Pennies, Dimes, and Dollars How does knowing about pennies, dimes, and dollars help you with metric units of lengths?

Destination Math Software Support

Course II: Module 3: Unit 1: Area

3 Homework

12–4 Homework **Goal:** Additional Practice

This Homework page provides practice finding equivalencies in metric, monetary, and number systems.

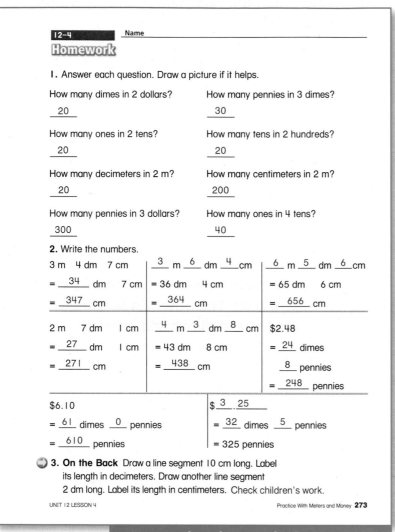

12–4 Homework Name ______________________

1. Answer each question. Draw a picture if it helps.

How many dimes in 2 dollars? 20

How many pennies in 3 dimes? 30

How many ones in 2 tens? 20

How many tens in 2 hundreds? 20

How many decimeters in 2 m? 20

How many centimeters in 2 m? 200

How many pennies in 3 dollars? 300

How many ones in 4 tens? 40

2. Write the numbers.

3 m 4 dm 7 cm = 34 dm 7 cm = 347 cm	3 m 6 dm 4 cm = 36 dm 4 cm = 364 cm	6 m 5 dm 6 cm = 65 dm 6 cm = 656 cm
2 m 7 dm 1 cm = 27 dm 1 cm = 271 cm	4 m 3 dm 8 cm = 43 dm 8 cm = 438 cm	$2.48 = 24 dimes 8 pennies = 248 pennies

$6.10 = 61 dimes 0 pennies = 610 pennies	$ 3 . 25 = 32 dimes 5 pennies = 325 pennies

3. On the Back Draw a line segment 10 cm long. Label its length in decimeters. Draw another line segment 2 dm long. Label its length in centimeters. Check children's work.

UNIT 12 LESSON 4 Practice With Meters and Money **273**

Homework and Remembering page 273

Home or School Activity

Literature Connection

Millions to Measure Read *Millions to Measure* by David M. Schwartz, illustrated by Steven Kellogg (HarperCollins, 2003) with your class. In this book, four children and a dog learn about measurement, including distance, volume, and weight.

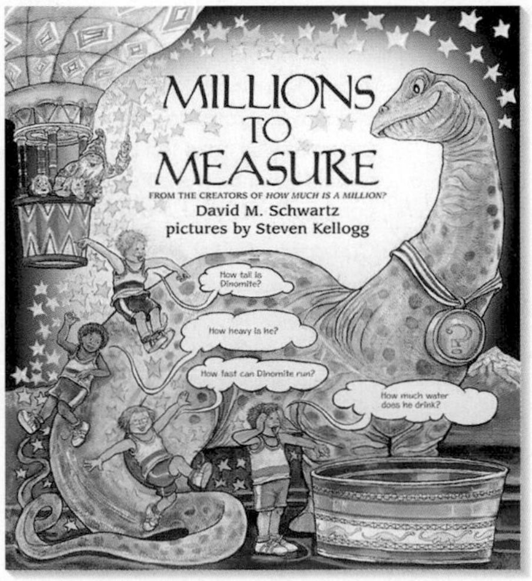

MINI UNIT 12 LESSON 5

3-Dimensional Shapes

Vocabulary	
length	rectangular prism
width	face
height	edge
two-dimensional (2-D)	vertex
	view
three-dimensional (3-D)	volume
	cubic unit

Lesson Objectives

- Distinguish between 2- and 3-dimensional shapes.
- Measure the length, width, and height of a rectangular prism.
- Identify faces, edges, and vertices of a rectangular prism.
- Count cubic units to find volume.

The Day at a Glance

Today's Goals	Materials	
1 Teaching the Lesson **A1:** Observe 3-dimensional shapes. Identify faces, edges, and vertices of a rectangular prism. **A2:** See relationships between 3-dimensional shapes and sketches of their faces. **A3:** Find the volume of 3-dimensional shapes by counting cubic units.	**Lesson Activities** Student Activity Book pp. 407–410 (Includes Rectangular Prisms) Homework and Remembering pp. 275–276 25-cm Rulers Stack of paper bound by rubber bands Scissors Tape Empty non-food packages in the shape of rectangular prisms MathBoard materials Connecting cubes	**Going Further** Activity Cards 12-5 Clay Straws Unit cubes Empty non-food packages in the shape of rectangular prisms Containers with curved sides Math Journals
2 Going Further ▸ Differentiated Instruction		
3 Homework		

Use Math Talk today!

Keeping Skills Sharp

Daily Routines	English Language Learners
Making Change and Counting Coins Making Change from $5.00, Combining Coins and Counting Money (See pp. xxvii–xxviii.) ▸ Led by Student Leaders **Money Routine** Using the 120 Poster, Using the Money Flip Chart, Using the Number Path, Using Secret Code Cards (See pp. xxiii–xxv.) ▸ Led by Student Leaders	Draw a rectangle and a rectangular prism on the board. Have children say how the shapes are different. Write *two-dimensional* and *three-dimensional*. • **Beginning** Point to the square. Say: **Two-dimensional shapes are flat.** Point to the cube. Say: **Three-dimensional shapes have space inside.** • **Intermediate** Ask: **Is the rectangle flat?** yes **Is the rectangle two-dimensional?** yes **Is the prism flat?** no **Is the prism two-dimensional?** no **Is the prism three-dimensional?** yes • **Advanced** Have children tell how two-dimensional shapes and three-dimensional shapes are alike and different.

Activity 2

Build and Draw 3-Dimensional Shapes

20 MINUTES

Goal: See relationships between 3-dimensional shapes and sketches of their faces.

Materials: paper unit cubes from Activity 1, MathBoard materials, Student Activity Book page 409, connecting cubes

NCTM Standards:
Geometry
Representation
Connections

▶ Build and Draw Rectangular Prisms

SMALL GROUPS

Have children work together in groups of three so that each group has six paper unit cubes from Activity 1.

Ask children to line up their six cubes in a row to form a rectangular prism. Explain that three-dimensional shapes often look different from different viewpoints.

Have children look at the front of their rectangular prism from eye level, and then sketch a two-dimensional drawing of the front face on their MathBoards.

Invite children to then predict what the top face of their prism will look like. Have them stand over the rectangular prism one at a time and draw what they see. Repeat with the side view.

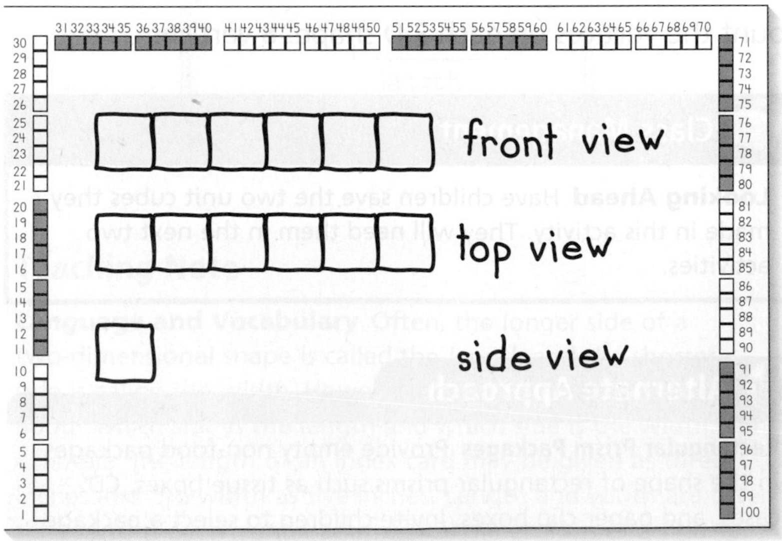

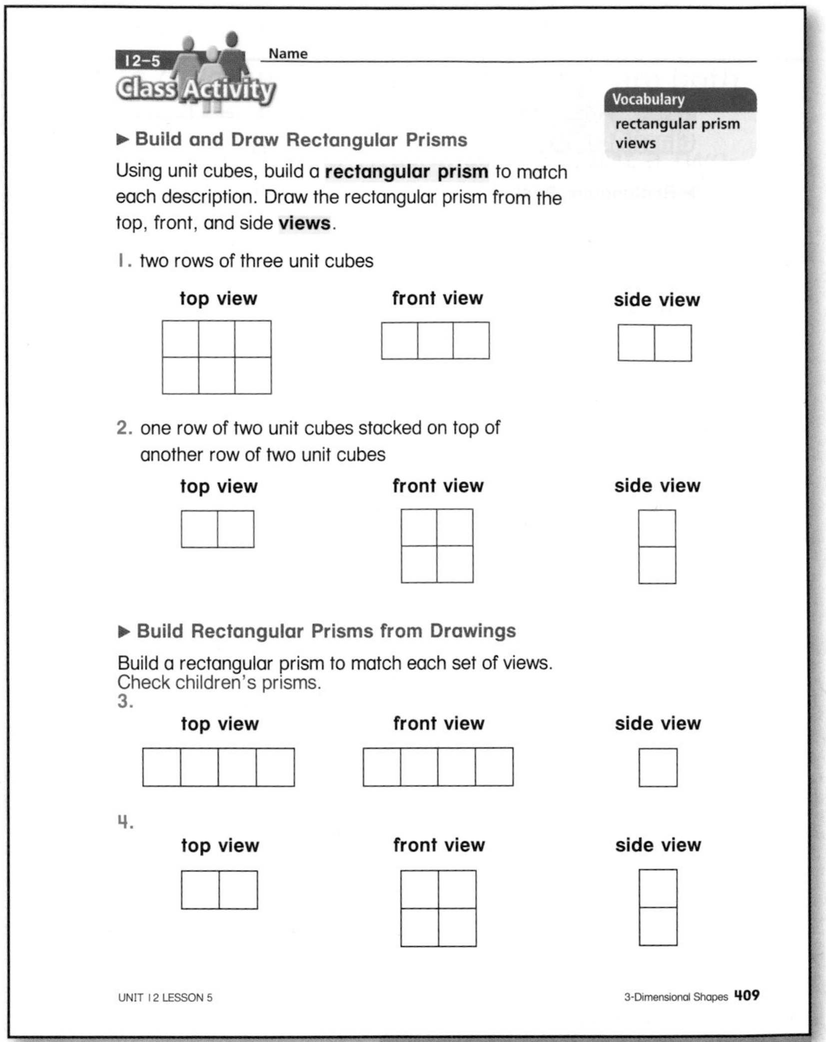
12-5 Class Activity

Name

Vocabulary
rectangular prism
views

▶ Build and Draw Rectangular Prisms

Using unit cubes, build a **rectangular prism** to match each description. Draw the rectangular prism from the top, front, and side **views**.

1. two rows of three unit cubes

top view | front view | side view

2. one row of two unit cubes stacked on top of another row of two unit cubes

top view | front view | side view

▶ Build Rectangular Prisms from Drawings

Build a rectangular prism to match each set of views.
Check children's prisms.

3. top view | front view | side view

4. top view | front view | side view

UNIT 12 LESSON 5 — 3-Dimensional Shapes 409

Student Activity Book page 409

Refer children to Student Activity Book page 409 and have them complete exercises 1–2 in small groups.

Ongoing Assessment

As children are working, circulate throughout the room and ask questions such as the following:

- How many rows does this rectangular prism have?
- How many cubes are in each row?
- Show me the front face of this rectangular prism.
- How can you draw the front view?

▶ Build Rectangular Prisms from Drawings SMALL GROUPS

On the board, draw these three views of a rectangular prism made from unit cubes.

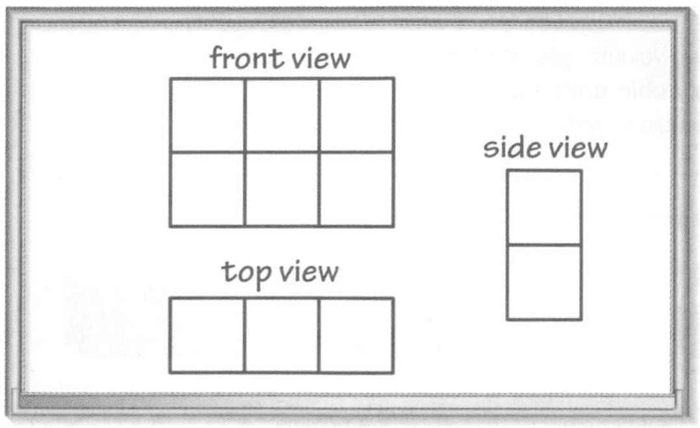

Explain to children that they will build a three-dimensional shape using your drawings as a guide.

- How many unit cubes will be in your rectangular prism? 6
- How many rows high will it be? 2 How do you know? The front and side views show two rows.
- How many rows deep will it be? 1 How do you know? The top view shows only one row.

Have children work in groups of three to build the corresponding rectangular prism with unit cubes.

When they are finished, children can complete exercises 3–4 in their small groups. Circulate while they are working to check that they have built a correct rectangular prism and to assist those who are having difficulty.

Alternate Approach

Connecting Cubes Children can use connecting cubes or other commercial cubes rather than paper cubes.

3 Homework

12-5 Homework **Goal:** Additional Practice

This Homework page provides practice identifying 3-dimensional shapes and counting cubic units to find volume.

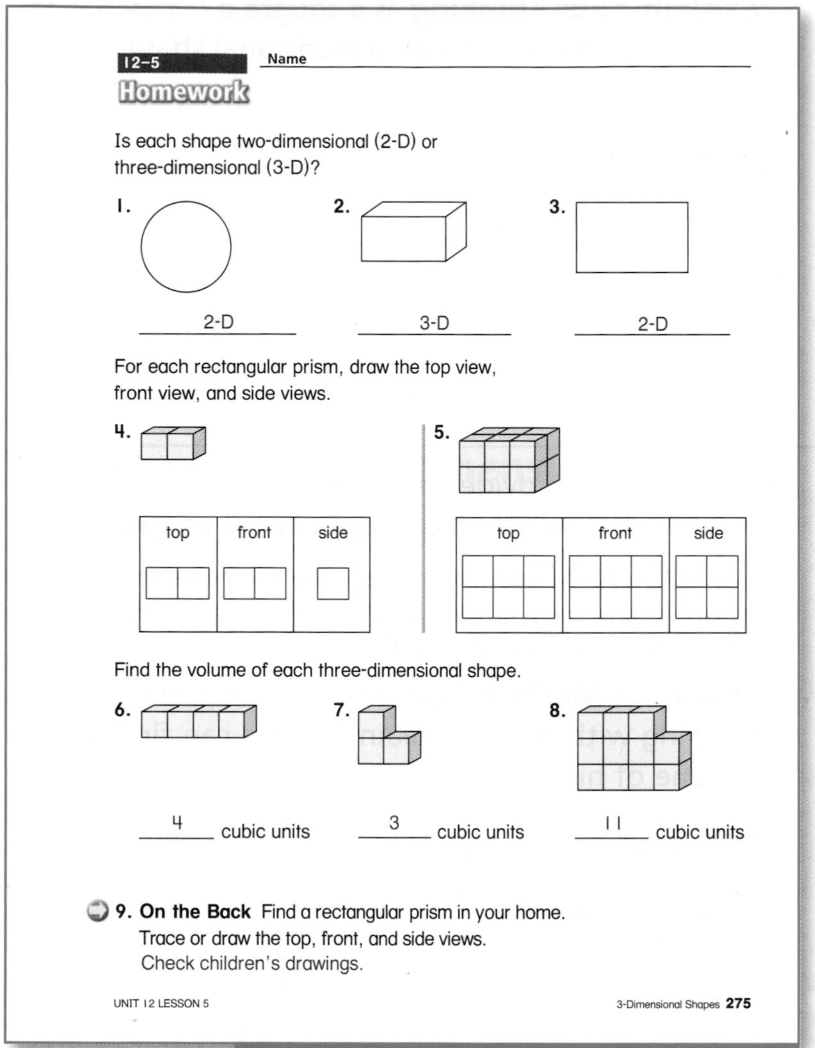

12-5 Homework Name

Is each shape two-dimensional (2-D) or three-dimensional (3-D)?

1. 2-D
2. 3-D
3. 2-D

For each rectangular prism, draw the top view, front view, and side views.

4.

top	front	side

5.

top	front	side

Find the volume of each three-dimensional shape.

6. 4 cubic units
7. 3 cubic units
8. 11 cubic units

9. **On the Back** Find a rectangular prism in your home. Trace or draw the top, front, and side views.
Check children's drawings.

UNIT 12 LESSON 5 3-Dimensional Shapes 275

Homework and Remembering page 275

Home or School Activity

Language Arts Connection

Same Word, Different Meaning Ask children to look up the definition of the word *volume* in a dictionary. Invite them to write sentences with the word *volume* using the definitions they find.

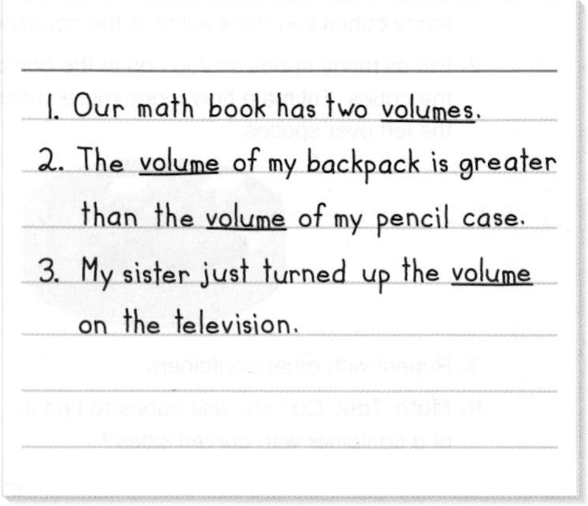

1. Our math book has two volumes.
2. The volume of my backpack is greater than the volume of my pencil case.
3. My sister just turned up the volume on the television.

MINI UNIT 12
LESSON 6

Analyze 3-Dimensional Shapes

Lesson Objectives

- Identify and name 3-dimensional shapes.
- Determine if a solid stacks, rolls, and/or slides.
- Compare 3-dimensional shapes.
- Sort 3-dimensional shapes using a Venn diagram.

Vocabulary	
cone	slide
sphere	roll
square pyramid	Venn diagram
cylinder	sort
stack	attribute

The Day at a Glance

Today's Goals	Materials	
1 Teaching the Lesson **A1:** Investigate attributes of 3-dimensional shapes and use these attributes to compare the shapes. **A2:** Sort and classify 3-dimensional shapes using a sorting rule and a Venn diagram.	**Lesson Activities** Student Activity Book pp. 411–414 Homework and Remembering pp. 277–278 Quick Quiz (Assessment Guide) Objects in the shape of cones, cubes, rectangular prisms, spheres, square pyramids, and cylinders Square Pyramid (TRB M91) Cone (TRB M92) Commercial sets of 3-dimensional shapes	**Going Further** Activity Cards 12-6 Commercial sets of 3-dimensional shapes Paper bags Math Journals
2 Going Further ▶ Differentiated Instruction		
3 Homework		

123 Use Math Talk today!

Keeping Skills Sharp

Daily Routines	English Language Learners
Making Change and Counting Coins Making Change from $5.00, Combining Coins and Counting Money (See pp. xxvii–xxviii.) ▶ Led by Student Leaders **Money Routine** Using the 120 Poster, Using the Money Flip Chart, Using the Number Path, Using Secret Code Cards (See pp. xxiii–xxv.) ▶ Led by Student Leaders	Draw a triangle and a triangular prism on the board. Write *solid shapes*. • **Beginning** Point to the prism. Say: **This is a *solid shape*. It has space inside. It is *three-dimensional*.** Have children repeat. • **Intermediate** **Is the triangle a *solid shape*?** no **Is the prism a *solid shape*?** yes **Are *solid shapes three-dimensional*?** yes • **Advanced** Ask: **Which one is a solid shape?** the prism Have children state the attributes of a *solid shape*.

1 Teaching the Lesson

Activity 1

Compare 3-Dimensional Shapes

40 MINUTES

Goal: Investigate attributes of 3-dimensional shapes and use these attributes to compare the shapes.

Materials: objects in the shape of cones, cubes, rectangular prisms, spheres, square pyramids, and cylinders, Square Pyramid (TRB M91), Cone (TRB M92), Student Activity Book pages 411–413, 3-D shapes

NCTM Standards:
Geometry
Connections

▶ Identify Solid Shapes INDIVIDUALS

Set up a collection of objects that are in the shape of cones, cubes, rectangular prisms, spheres, square pyramids, and cylinders for children to examine. Label each group of objects with the name of the shape. If you have trouble finding objects in the shape of a square pyramid and/or a cone, you can use the nets on Square Pyramid and Cone (TRB M91–M92) to make these shapes.

Refer children to Student Activity Book page 411 and ask them to name the shapes shown in exercises 1–6. Point out that they should choose the names from the names given in the table for exercise 7. Discuss their answers. Then invite children to hunt for objects in the classroom and write the names of the objects in the table in exercise 7.

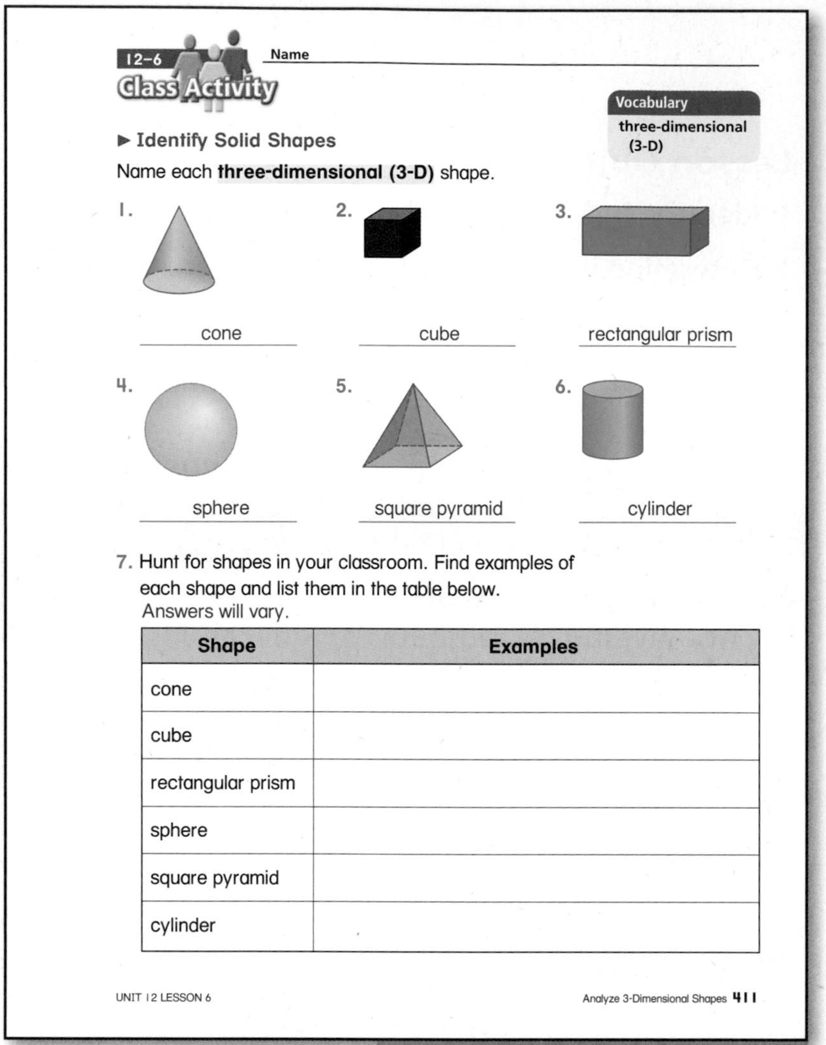

12-6 Class Activity Name

Vocabulary
three-dimensional (3-D)

▶ Identify Solid Shapes

Name each **three-dimensional (3-D)** shape.

1. cone
2. cube
3. rectangular prism
4. sphere
5. square pyramid
6. cylinder

7. Hunt for shapes in your classroom. Find examples of each shape and list them in the table below.
Answers will vary.

Shape	Examples
cone	
cube	
rectangular prism	
sphere	
square pyramid	
cylinder	

UNIT 12 LESSON 6 Analyze 3-Dimensional Shapes 411

Student Activity Book page 411

Differentiated Instruction

Extra Help This lesson has many vocabulary words in it. Using flash cards can help children organize these new words into a meaningful context.

Sample flashcard:

Word picture	definition real-world use

Alternate Approach

Commercial Shape Sets If available, provide commercial sets of solid three-dimensional shapes for children to examine and identify. If geometry software is available, have children use it to explore relationships in shapes.

Ongoing Assessment

Circulate around the room to check that children are matching the classroom objects to the correct shapes.

▶ Stack, Slide, and Roll SMALL GROUPS

Provide small groups of children with at least two objects for each 3-dimensional shape.

Demonstrate that you can stack cubes, but not square pyramids.

Show that a cylinder can slide along its face and roll along its curved surface.

Refer children to Student Activity Book page 412 and have them complete the table in exercise 8. Encourage them to experiment with the objects to determine if each shape slides, rolls, and/or stacks.

▶ Alike and Different SMALL GROUPS

Invite children to look closely at a cube and a cylinder. Guide a discussion comparing these two shapes.

Math Talk in Action

How are these two shapes alike?

Danielle: They are both three-dimensional shapes.

Carla: You can stack both shapes.

Emmett: You can slide both shapes.

How are these two shapes different?

Sharon: A cylinder can roll but a cube cannot.

Yazed: A cylinder has two flat surfaces and one curved surface. All of the surfaces on a cube are flat.

Have children work in small groups to complete exercises 9–12 on Student Activity Book page 413.

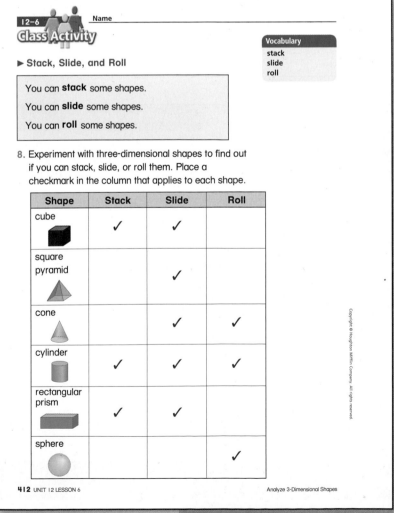

12-6 Class Activity Name

Vocabulary
stack
slide
roll

▶ Stack, Slide, and Roll

You can **stack** some shapes.
You can **slide** some shapes.
You can **roll** some shapes.

8. Experiment with three-dimensional shapes to find out if you can stack, slide, or roll them. Place a checkmark in the column that applies to each shape.

Shape	Stack	Slide	Roll
cube 	✓	✓	
square pyramid 		✓	
cone 		✓	✓
cylinder 	✓	✓	✓
rectangular prism 	✓	✓	
sphere 			✓

Student Activity Book page 412

12-6 Class Activity Name

▶ Alike and Different

Describe how each pair of shapes is alike and different.

Shapes	How these shapes are alike	How these shapes are different
9. 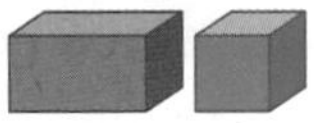	They both stack and slide, they are both three-dimensional, and they both have six flat faces.	The faces of a cube are all the same size and the faces of a rectangular prism are not.
10. 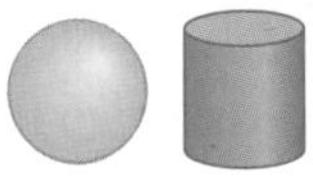	They are both three-dimensional, they both roll, and they both have a curved surface.	A cylinder has two flat faces and a sphere has none. A cylinder can stack and slide. A sphere can only roll.
11. 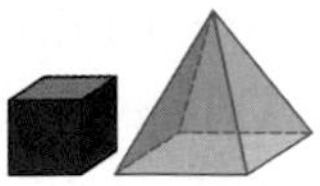	They are both three-dimensional, they both slide, and all faces on both are flat.	All the faces of a cube are square and only one face on a square pyramid is square. A cube can stack.
12. 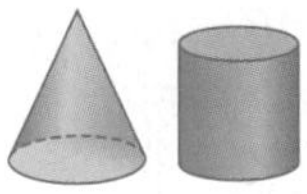	They are both three-dimensional, they both slide and roll, and they both have a curved surface.	A cylinder can stack. A cone has one flat face and a cylinder has two flat faces. A cone has a vertex and a cylinder has no vertices.

Student Activity Book page 413

Activity 2

Sort and Classify 3-Dimensional Shapes

20 MINUTES

Goal: Sort and classify 3-dimensional shapes using a sorting rule and a Venn diagram.

Materials: objects in the shape of cones, cubes, rectangular prisms, spheres, square pyramids, and cylinders, Student Activity Book page 414

NCTM Standards:
Geometry
Representation

▶ Sort Three-Dimensional Shapes

WHOLE CLASS

Ask for Ideas Display a set of objects in the shape of a cube, square pyramid, rectangular prism, cone, cylinder, and sphere. Explain to children that you can separate these shapes into groups using a sorting rule. Invite them to help you sort the objects into two groups: shapes that roll and shapes that don't roll.

- Which of these shapes roll? sphere, cylinder, cone
- Which of these shapes don't roll? cube, square pyramid, rectangular prism
- What are some other attributes that we can use to sort these shapes? Possible answers: size, color, shapes that stack, two-dimensional shape of faces

Ask children to complete exercise 13 on Student Activity Book page 414. When they are finished, invite several children to present their sorting rules and groups to the rest of the class.

▶ Venn Diagram

WHOLE CLASS Math Talk

Explain to children that you would like to sort the 3-dimensional shapes according to the attributes rectangular face and circle face. Draw an empty Venn diagram on the board and ask questions to encourage children to help you sort the shapes. Write the names of the shapes in the diagram as you sort. Have children complete exercise 14 on Student Activity Book page 414 as you complete the Venn diagram on the board.

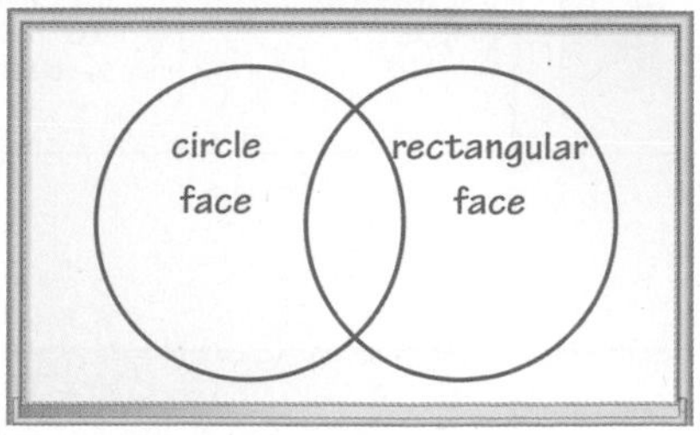

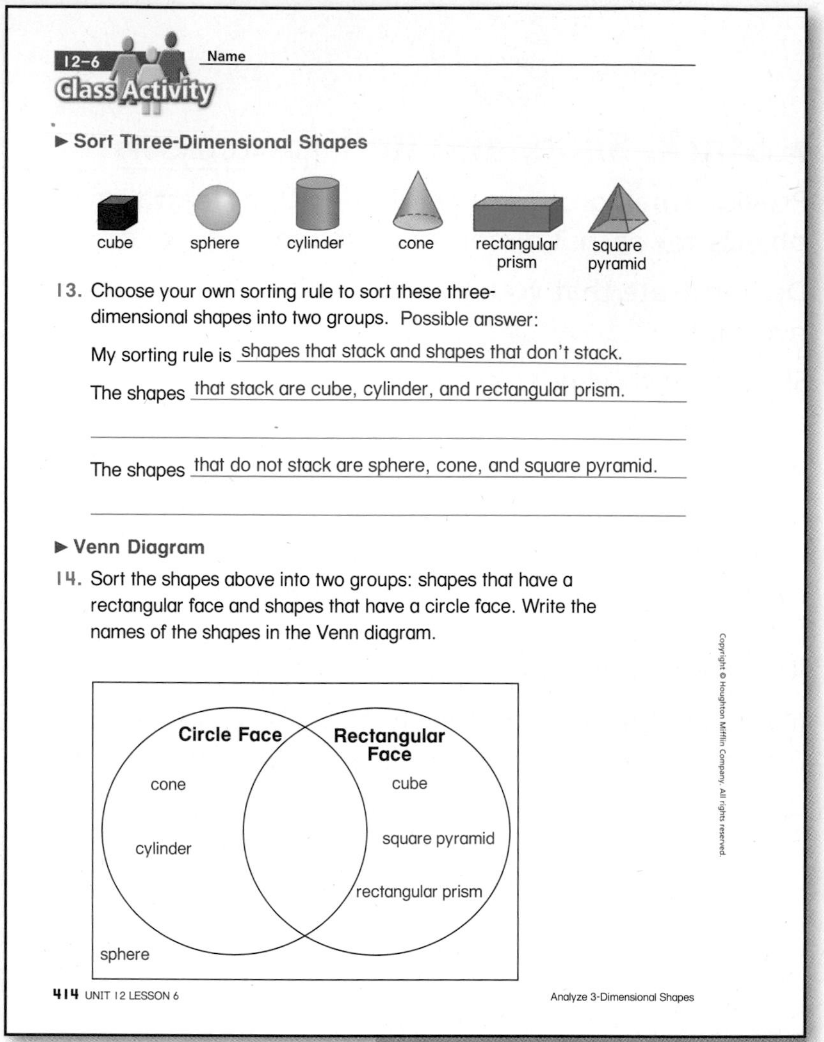
12-6 Class Activity

Name

▶ Sort Three-Dimensional Shapes

cube sphere cylinder cone rectangular prism square pyramid

13. Choose your own sorting rule to sort these three-dimensional shapes into two groups. Possible answer:

My sorting rule is shapes that stack and shapes that don't stack.

The shapes that stack are cube, cylinder, and rectangular prism.

The shapes that do not stack are sphere, cone, and square pyramid.

▶ Venn Diagram

14. Sort the shapes above into two groups: shapes that have a rectangular face and shapes that have a circle face. Write the names of the shapes in the Venn diagram.

Circle Face: cone, cylinder
Rectangular Face: cube, square pyramid, rectangular prism
sphere

Student Activity Book page 414

You can also create a Venn diagram using string or tape on the floor and actual objects. See page 913A.

- Which of these shapes have a rectangular face? cube, rectangular prism, square pyramid
- Where should I place the cube, square pyramid, and rectangular prism on the Venn diagram? in the section labeled "rectangular face"
- Which of these shapes have a circle face? cylinder
- Where should I place the cylinder and cone on the Venn diagram? in the section labeled "circle face"
- Which of these shapes doesn't belong in either category sphere
- Where should I place the sphere on the Venn diagram? outside the two sections

Quick Quiz

See Assessment Guide for Unit 12 Quick Quiz.

Intervention Activity Card 12-6

Hidden Shapes

Activity Card 12-6 ●

Work: pairs

Use:

- paper bag
- set of three-dimensional shapes

Choose:

- 1
- 2

1. Put the shapes into the bag.
2. 1 Reach into the bag. Choose a shape. Do not take the shape out of the bag.
3. 1 Give clues to describe the shape.

This shape has 6 faces that are all the same size.

4. 2 Use the clues to guess the shape.

I think it is a cube.

5. Trade roles and repeat three times.

Unit 12, Lesson 6

Activity Note Each pair needs a paper bag and a set of three-dimensional shapes. Review the attributes of the shapes with pairs.

Math Writing Prompt

Summarize Describe a square pyramid.

Soar to Success Math **Software Support**

Warm Up 36.21

On Level Activity Card 12-6

Build Structures

Activity Card 12-6 ▲

Work: pairs

Use:

- set of three-dimensional shapes

1. **Work Together** Choose three or four shapes.
2. Use the shapes to build a structure.

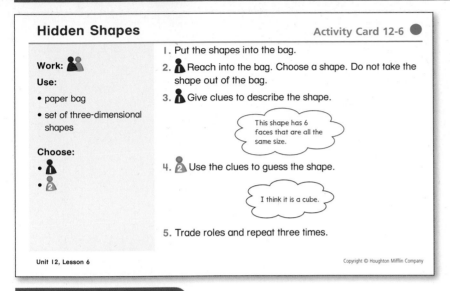

3. Choose different shapes and build another structure.
4. **Math Talk** What shapes work best for the bottom of the structure?

Unit 12, Lesson 6

Activity Note Each pair needs a set of three-dimensional shapes. Have children use the lesson vocabulary as they analyze their structures.

Math Writing Prompt

Make a Comparison How are a cone and a square pyramid alike? How are they different?

Harcourt Mega Math Grades K-6 **Software Support**

Shapes Ahoy: Undersea 3D, Level E

Challenge Activity Card 12-6

Guess Two Shapes

Activity Card 12-6 ■

Work: pairs

Choose:

- 1
- 2

1. 1 Think of two three-dimensional shapes. Don't tell your partner what shapes you are thinking about. Think about the attributes of the shapes.
2. 1 Give clues about the two shapes.

Both shapes have faces that are circles. Both shapes slide and roll. One shape has one face and the other shape has two faces. One shape has a vertex and the other one has no vertices. Neither shape has edges.

3. 2 Use the clues to guess the two shapes.
4. Switch roles and repeat.

Unit 12, Lesson 6

Activity Note Pairs take turns describing two three-dimensional shapes. You may want to have a set of shapes available for children to check the clues.

Math Writing Prompt

Draw a Picture Choose two three-dimensional objects you use every day. Sketch each object and describe how the objects are alike and different.

Destination Math **Software Support**

Course II: Module 3: Unit 1: Volume

3 Homework

12–6 Homework **Goal:** Additional Practice

✓ Include children's completed Homework page as part of their portfolios.

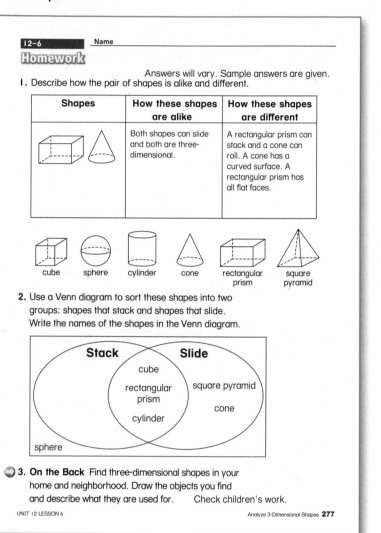

12–6 Homework Name ______

Answers will vary. Sample answers are given.

1. Describe how the pair of shapes is alike and different.

Shapes	How these shapes are alike	How these shapes are different
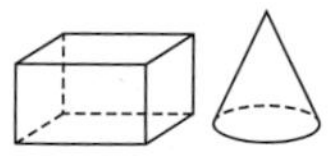	Both shapes can slide and both are three-dimensional.	A rectangular prism can stack and a cone can roll. A cone has a curved surface. A rectangular prism has all flat faces.

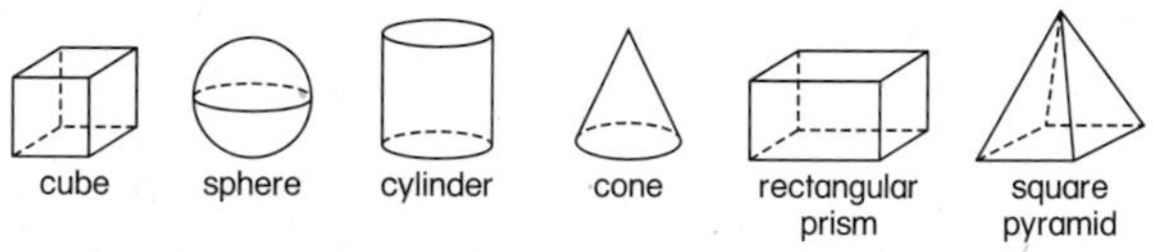

2. Use a Venn diagram to sort these shapes into two groups: shapes that stack and shapes that slide. Write the names of the shapes in the Venn diagram.

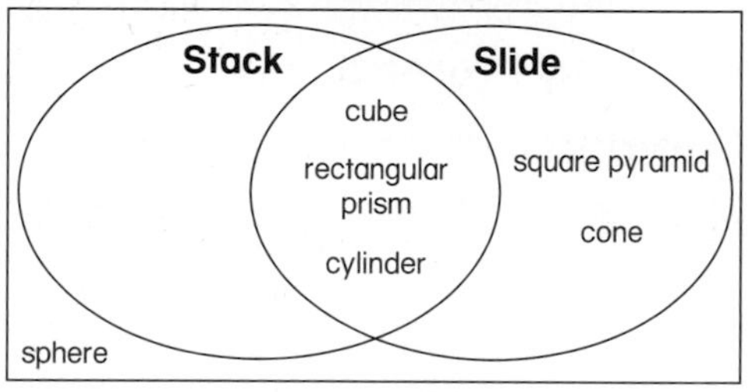

3. On the Back Find three-dimensional shapes in your home and neighborhood. Draw the objects you find and describe what they are used for. Check children's work.

UNIT 12 LESSON 6 Analyze 3-Dimensional Shapes **277**

Homework and Remembering page 277

Home or School Activity

Language Arts Connection

Shape Poems Invite children to write a poem about a 3-dimensional shape using these guidelines.

Line 1: Name the shape.
Line 2: Describe the shape.
Line 3: Describe how the shape stacks and/or moves.
Line 4: Describe a real-world purpose for which we use the shape.
Line 5: Name the shape.

Rectangular Prisms

Rectangular prisms
Each with six rectangular faces
They stack and they don't roll
The bricks that build a house
Rectangular prisms

Spheres

Spheres
No edges, no corners
They roll and bounce so high
The shape of a baseball, soccer ball, and basketball
Spheres

MINI UNIT 12

Unit Review and Test

Lesson Objectives

- **Assess children's progress on unit objectives.**

The Day at a Glance

Today's Goals	Materials
1 Assessing the Unit ▶ Assess children's progress on unit objectives. ▶ Use activities from unit lessons to reteach content.	Unit 12 Test, Student Activity Book pages 415–416 Unit 12 Test, Form A or B, Assessment Guide (optional) Unit 12 Performance Assessment, Assessment Guide (optional)
2 Extending the Assessment ▶ Use remediation for common errors.	
There is no homework assignment on a test day.	

Keeping Skills Sharp

Quick Practice 5 MINUTES	
If you are doing a unit review day, go over the homework. If this is a test day, omit the homework review.	**Review and Test Day** You may want to choose a quiet game or other activity (reading a book or working on homework for another subject) for children who finish early.

1 Assessing the Unit

Assess Unit Objectives

45 MINUTES (more if schedule permits)

Goal: Assess student progress on unit objectives.

Materials: Student Activity Book pages 415–416; Assessment Guide (optional)

▶ Review and Assessment

If your children are ready for assessment on the unit objectives, you may use either the test on the Student Activity Book pages or one of the forms of the Unit 12 Test in the Assessment Guide to assess children's progress.

If you feel that children need some review first, you may use the test on the Student Activity Book pages as a review of unit content, and then use one of the forms of the Unit 12 Test in the Assessment Guide to assess children's progress.

To assign a numerical score for all of these test forms, use 10 points for each question.

You may also choose to use the Unit 12 Performance Assessment. Scoring for that assessment can be found in its rubric in the Assessment Guide.

▶ Reteaching Resources

The chart lists the test items, the unit objectives they cover, and the lesson activities in which the objective is covered in this unit. You may revisit these activities with students who do not show mastery of the objectives.

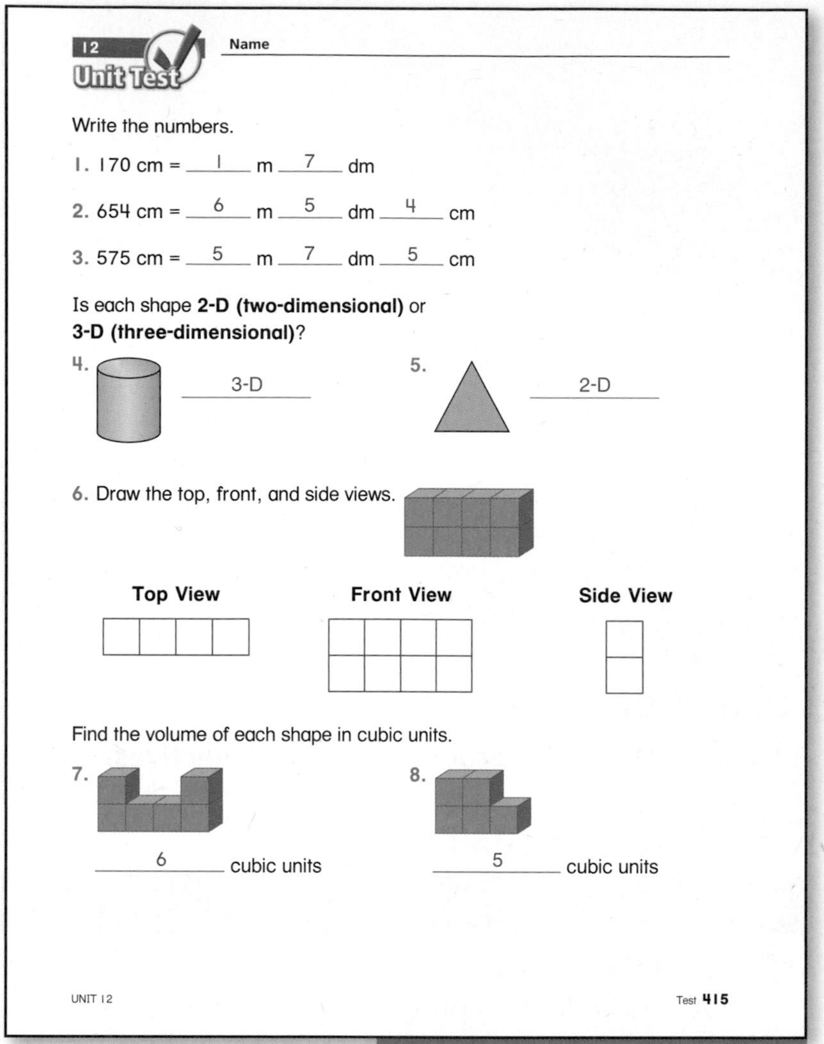

12 Unit Test

Name

Write the numbers.

1. 170 cm = 1 m 7 dm

2. 654 cm = 6 m 5 dm 4 cm

3. 575 cm = 5 m 7 dm 5 cm

Is each shape **2-D (two-dimensional)** or **3-D (three-dimensional)**?

4. 3-D

5. 2-D

6. Draw the top, front, and side views.

Top View | Front View | Side View

Find the volume of each shape in cubic units.

7. 6 cubic units

8. 5 cubic units

UNIT 12 | Test 415

Student Activity Book page 415

Unit Test Items	Unit Objectives Tested	Activities to Use for Reteaching
10	**12.1** Connect place value, money, and metric units of length.	Lesson 3, Activity 2 Lesson 4, Activity 1 Lesson 4, Activity 2
1, 2, 3	**12.2** Convert measures in centimeters to a combination of meters, decimeters, and centimeters.	Lesson 2, Activity 1 Lesson 3, Activity 1
4, 5	**12.3** Distinguish between two-dimensional (2-D) and three-dimensional (3-D) shapes.	Lesson 5, Activity 1

12 Unit Test Name

9. Sort the shapes. Write the names of the shapes in the Venn diagram.

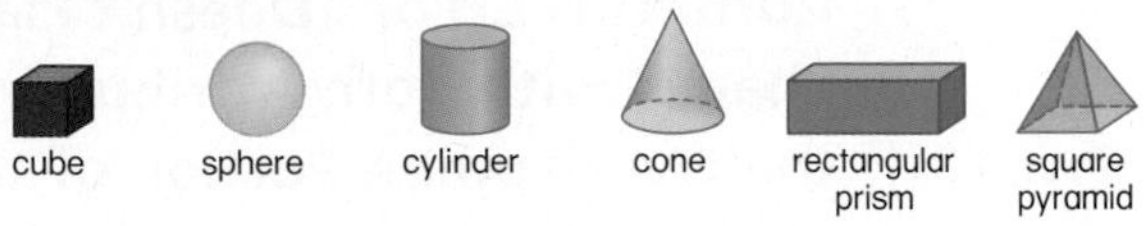

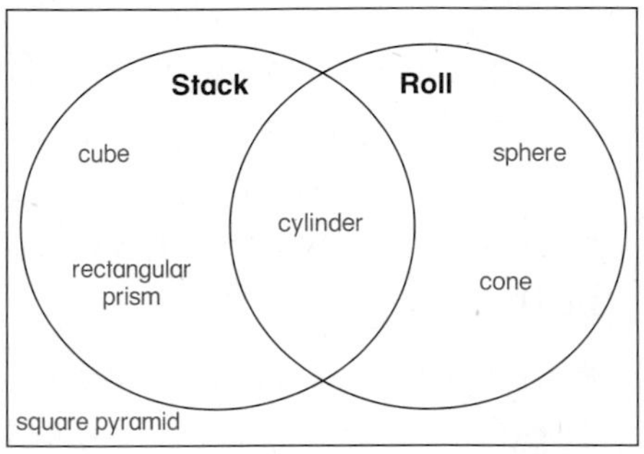

10. **Extended Response** Explain how knowing about ones, tens, and hundreds can help you write 138 centimeters as meters, decimeters, and centimeters.

Possible answer: There are 100 cm in 1 m and 10 cm in 1 dm.

Knowing about ones, tens, and hundreds can help you write 138 cm as

100 cm + 30 cm + 8 cm, which is equal to 1 m 3 dm 8 cm.

416 UNIT 12 Test

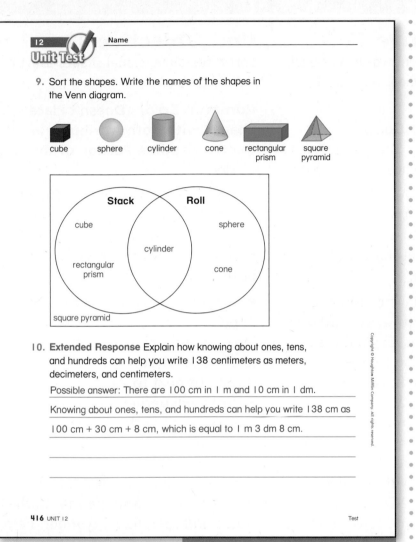

Student Activity Book page 416

Unit Test Items	Unit Objectives Tested	Activities to Use for Reteaching
6	**12.4** Draw a front, side, and top view of a rectangular prism.	Lesson 5, Activity 2
7, 8	**12.5** Count cubic units to find volume.	Lesson 5, Activity 3
9	**12.6** Sort three-dimensional shapes using a Venn diagram.	Lesson 6, Activity 2

▶ Assessment Resources

Free Response Tests

Unit 12 Test, Student Activity Book pages 415–416

Unit 12 Test, Form A, Assessment Guide

Extended Response Item

The last item in the Student Activity Book test and in the Form A test will require an extended response as an answer.

Multiple-Choice Test

Unit 12 Test, Form B, Assessment Guide

Performance Assessment

Unit 12 Performance Assessment, Assessment Guide

Unit 12 Performance Assessment Rubric, Assessment Guide

▶ Portfolio Assessment

Teacher-selected Items for Student Portfolios:

- Homework, Lessons 3, 6
- Class Activity work, Lessons 1, 2, 4, 5

Student-selected Items for Student Portfolios:

- Favorite Home or School Activity
- Best Writing Prompt

2 Extending the Assessment

Common Errors

Activities for Remediation

Unit Objective 12.1

Connect place value, money, and metric units of length.

Common Error: Doesn't Identify the Relationship Between Place Value, Metric Units of Length, and Money

Some children may have difficulty seeing the connection between place value, metric units of length, and money.

Remediation Provide children with strips of paper over a meter long, with exact measurements written in centimeters, for example, 132 centimeters. Have children cut the strips by first cutting as many meter strips as possible, then cutting as many decimeter strips as possible, and then cutting centimeter strips. So, for 132 centimeters, children would cut 1 meter strip, 3 decimeter strips, and 2 centimeter strips.

Next, provide 132 cents using dime strips and pennies. Have children make piles of 10 dime strips to represent dollars, then lay out individual dime and penny strips.

Help children see that 132 cents is the same as 1 dollar, 3 dimes, and 2 pennies.

Unit Objective 12.3

Distinguish between two-dimensional (2-D) and three-dimensional (3-D) shapes.

Common Error: Doesn't Correctly Identify Shapes as Two-Dimensional or Three-Dimensional

Some children may identify a two-dimensional shape as three-dimensional or a three-dimensional shape as two-dimensional.

Remediation Have children measure the length and width of various rectangles. Explain that they are measuring two dimensions. Then have them measure the length, width, and height of various rectangular prisms. Ask them how many dimensions they measured. Provide children with a collection of 3-D solids and 2-D shapes drawn on paper and have children sort the shapes into 2-D and 3-D shapes.

Unit Objective 12.6

Sort three-dimensional shapes using a Venn diagram.

Common Error: Doesn't Place Shapes with Both Attributes in the Overlapping Portion of the Circles

Some children may have difficulty recognizing when shapes go into the overlapping portion of the circles or when they go outside both circles.

Remediation Have children work in pairs to sort a set of 3-D objects into two groups: shapes that stack and shapes that roll. Partners should sit next to each other. One partner will gather all the shapes that stack; the other partner will gather all the shapes that roll. Children should place the shapes in their group in front of them. When the pair gets to a shape that both stacks and rolls, like a cylinder, help children identify that it belongs in both groups. Have children place this shape between them. When the pair gets to a shape that neither stacks nor rolls, like a square pyramid, help them identify that it does not belong in either group. Have them place this shape behind them.

Multiplication and Fractions

UNIT 13 ADDRESSES a variety of mathematical concepts that allow children to explore multiplication and fractions. Children solve multiplication problems first with repeated addition and familiar count-bys, then with arrays, and finally with the standard multiplication equation. Children expand their understanding of comparison language by applying terms such as *half, double, twice,* and *equal shares*. They explore shares, the concept of division, symmetry, fractions, and basic probability concepts.

Skills Trace

Grade 1	Grade 2	Grade 3
• Find doubles of numbers 1 through 10. • Find one half and one fourth of a geometric figure and of a set.	• Count by 2, 3, 4, or 5 to solve simple multiplication problems. • Write multiplication expressions for an array. • Identify and indicate single and multiple fractional parts.	• Recall basic multiplications and divisions with 0, 1, 2, 3, 4, 5, 9, and 10. • Write multiplication equations to represent repeated groups, arrays and area models. • Compare fractions.

Unit 13 Contents

Big Idea Groups and Arrays

Big Idea Shares, Symmetry, and Fractions

Big Idea The Nature of Chance

Unit 13 Assessment

Unit Objectives Tested	Unit Test Items	Lessons
13.1 Count by 2, 3, 4, or 5 to solve simple multiplication problems.	1–4	1–4
13.2 Write multiplication expressions for an array.	5–8	4–5
13.3 Use vocabulary (half, double, twice, equal shares).	9–12	6
13.4 Recognize lines of symmetry.	13–16	7
13.5 Identify and indicate single fractional parts ($\frac{1}{2}, \frac{1}{3}, \frac{1}{4}$).	17–19	8, 9
13.6 Identify and indicate multiple fractional parts ($\frac{2}{3}, \frac{3}{4}$).	20, 25	8, 9
13.7 Determine whether an outcome is possible, impossible, or certain.	21, 22	10, 11
13.8 Determine whether an outcome is more likely or less likely.	23, 24	10, 11

Assessment and Review Resources

Formal Assessment

Student Activity Book
- Unit Review and Test (pp. 549–462)

Assessment Guide
- Quick Quizzes (pp. A139–A143)
- Test A–Open Response (pp. A144–A148)
- Test B–Multiple Choice (pp. A149–A153)
- Performance Assessment (pp. A154–A156)

Test Generator CD-ROM
- Open Response Test
- Multiple Choice Test
- Test Bank Items

Informal Assessment

Teacher Edition
- Ongoing Assessment (in every lesson)
- Quick Practice (in every lesson)
- Portfolio Suggestions (p. 1039)

Math Talk
- Math Talk in Action (pp. 955, 992)
- Solve and Discuss (pp. 964, 1008)
- In Activities (pp. 954, 958, 986, 987, 988, 999, 1004, 1012, 1013, 1014, 1016, 1022, 1026, 1027, 1028, 1033)
- Student Pairs
  Helping Pairs (pp. 955, 957, 969, 981, 999, 1005)

Review Opportunities

Homework and Remembering
- Review of recently taught topics
- Spiral Review

Teacher Edition
- Unit Review and Test (pp. 1037–1040)

Test Generator CD-ROM
- Custom Review Sheets

Planning Unit 13

NCTM Curriculum Focal Points and Connections Key: **1.** Number and Operations **2.** Number and Operations and Algebra **3.** Measurement **4.** Number and Operations **5.** Geometry and Measurement **6.** Algebra

Lesson NCTM Focal Points NCTM Standards	Resources	Materials for Lesson Activities	Materials for Going Further
13-1 **Introduction to Multiplication** NCTM Focal Points: 4.9, 4.10, 6.1 NCTM Standards: 1, 6, 10	TE pp. 953–960 SAB pp. 417–422 H&R pp. 279–280 AC 13-1	✓ MathBoard materials	Paper clips Hole punch Calculators Math Journals
13-2 **Groups of Three** NCTM Focal Points: 4.9, 6.1 NCTM Standards: 1, 6, 10	TE pp. 961–966 SAB pp. 423–426 H&R pp. 281–282 AC 13-2	None	✓ Connecting cubes Rubber bands Beans Cups ✓ Counters ✓ 120 Poster (TRB M60) Math Journals
13-3 **Groups of Four** NCTM Focal Points: 4.9, 6.1 NCTM Standards: 1, 6, 10	TE pp. 967–972 SAB pp. 427–430 H&R pp. 283–284 AC 13-3	None	Index cards ✓ 120 Poster (TRB M60) ✓ MathBoard materials *Each Orange Had 8 Slices: A Counting Book* by Paul Giganti, Jr. Math Journals
13-4 **Groups of Five and Arrays** NCTM Focal Points: 4.9, 6.1 NCTM Standards: 1, 6, 10	TE pp. 973–978 SAB pp. 431–432 H&R pp. 285–286 AC 13-4	Beans or other countable objects	Crayons Inch Grid Paper (TRB M70) ✓ MathBoard materials or Number Path Beans or other countable objects Math Journals
13-5 **Work with Arrays** NCTM Focal Points: 4.9, 6.1 NCTM Standards: 1, 6, 10	TE pp. 979–984 SAB pp. 433–434 H&R pp. 287–288 AC 13-5 MCC 49 AG Quick Quiz 1	Beans or other countable objects ✓ MathBoard materials or 10 × 10 Grid	Beans or other countable objects ✓ MathBoard materials Math Journals
13-6 **The Language of Shares** NCTM Standards: 1, 5, 8	TE pp. 985–990 SAB pp. 435–436 H&R pp. 289–290 AC 13-6	✓ Counters	✓ Counters Index cards Calculators *The Doorbell Rang* by Pat Hutchins Math Journals
13-7 **Model Division** NCTM Focal Points: 2.7, 2.11 NCTM Standards: 1, 10	TE pp. 991–996 SAB pp. 437–438 H&R pp. 291–292 AC 13-7 MCC 50	✓ Counters	✓ Counters Index cards Number cube Math Journals

Resources/Materials Key: TE: Teacher Edition SAB: Student Activity Book H&R: Homework and Remembering AC: Activity Cards MCC: Math Center Challenge AG: Assessment Guide ✓: Grade 2 kits TRB: Teacher's Resource Book

NCTM Standards and Expectations Key: **1.** Number and Operations **2.** Algebra **3.** Geometry **4.** Measurement **5.** Data Analysis and Probability **6.** Problem Solving **7.** Reasoning and Proof **8.** Communication **9.** Connections **10.** Representation

Lesson NCTM Focal Points NCTM Standards	Resources	Materials for Lesson Activities	Materials for Going Further
13-8 **Symmetry** NCTM Standards: 3, 8	TE pp. 997–1002 SAB pp. 439–442 H&R pp. 293–294 AC 13-8	Scissors Colored pencils, crayons, or markers ✓ Rulers or straight edges Classroom objects	Finger paints Newsprint or other plain paper Hole punches Colored pencils or crayons Magazines Glue sticks Scissors *Let's Fly a Kite* by Stuart J. Murphy Math Journals
13-9 **Fractions** NCTM Standards: 1, 8	TE pp. 1003–1010 SAB pp. 443–446 H&R pp. 295–296 AC 13-9 MCC 51	Colored pencils, crayons, or markers	Colored pencils, crayons, or markers Fraction Match Up 1 (TRB M94) Fraction Match Up 2 (TRB M95) Scissors Math Journals
13-10 **More on Fractions** NCTM Standards: 1, 8	TE pp. 1011–1018 SAB pp. 447–452 H&R pp. 297–298 AC 13-10 AG Quick Quiz 2	Crayons or colored pencils Scissors	Fraction Strips Index cards Number Lines (TRB M93) Math Journals
13-11 **Explore Probability** NCTM Standards: 5, 8	TE pp. 1019–1024 SAB pp. 453–454 H&R pp. 299–300 AC 13-11 MCC 52	Small brown paper bag ✓ Connecting cubes Crayons or colored pencils Paper clips ✓ Number cubes	Crayons or colored pencils Spinners (TRB M27) ✓ Real or play money (pennies) Math Journals
13-12 **Possible Outcomes** NCTM Focal Point: 4.10 NCTM Standards: 5, 6, 8	TE pp. 1025–1030 SAB pp. 455–456 H&R pp. 301–302 AC 13-12 AG Quick Quiz 3	Small brown paper bags ✓ Connecting cubes ✓ MathBoard materials	Small brown paper bags ✓ Connecting cubes Math Journals
13-13 **Use Mathematical Processes** NCTM Focal Point: 4.7 NCTM Standards: 6, 7, 8, 9, 10	TE pp. 1031–1036 SAB pp. 457–458 H&R pp. 303–304 AC 13-13	Crayons	✓ Counters Grid paper ✓ Connecting cubes Index cards Math Journals
✓ Unit Review and Test	TE pp. 1037–1040 SAB pp. 459–462 AG Unit 13 Tests		

Manipulatives and Materials

Essential materials for teaching *Math Expressions* are available in the Grade 2 kits. These materials are indicated by a ✓ in these lists. At the front of this Teacher Edition is more information about kit contents, alternatives for the materials, and use of the materials.

Independent Learning Activities

Ready-Made Math Challenge Centers

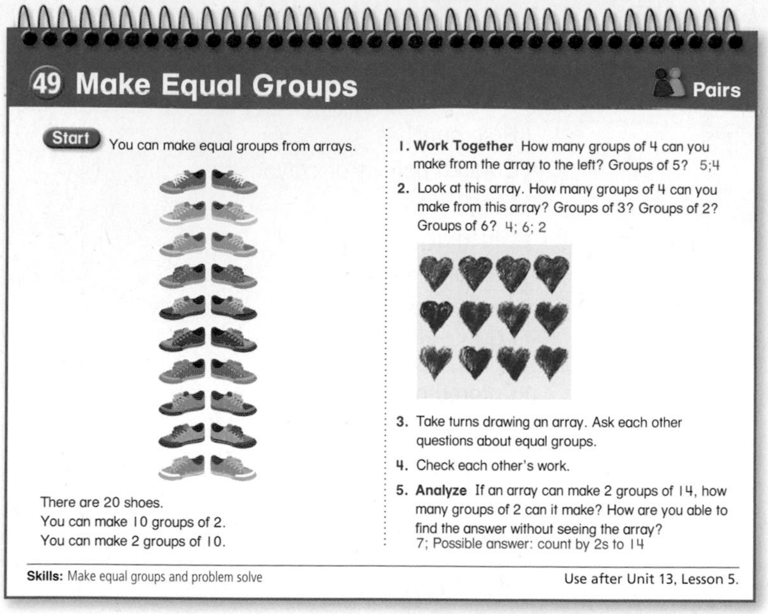

49 Make Equal Groups

Pairs

Start You can make equal groups from arrays.

There are 20 shoes.
You can make 10 groups of 2.
You can make 2 groups of 10.

1. **Work Together** How many groups of 4 can you make from the array to the left? Groups of 5? 5; 4
2. Look at this array. How many groups of 4 can you make from this array? Groups of 3? Groups of 2? Groups of 6? 4; 6; 2
3. Take turns drawing an array. Ask each other questions about equal groups.
4. Check each other's work.
5. **Analyze** If an array can make 2 groups of 14, how many groups of 2 can it make? How are you able to find the answer without seeing the array? 7; Possible answer: count by 2s to 14

Skills: Make equal groups and problem solve

Use after Unit 13, Lesson 5.

Grouping Pairs

Materials None

Objective Children make equal groups from arrays.

Connections Number and Reasoning

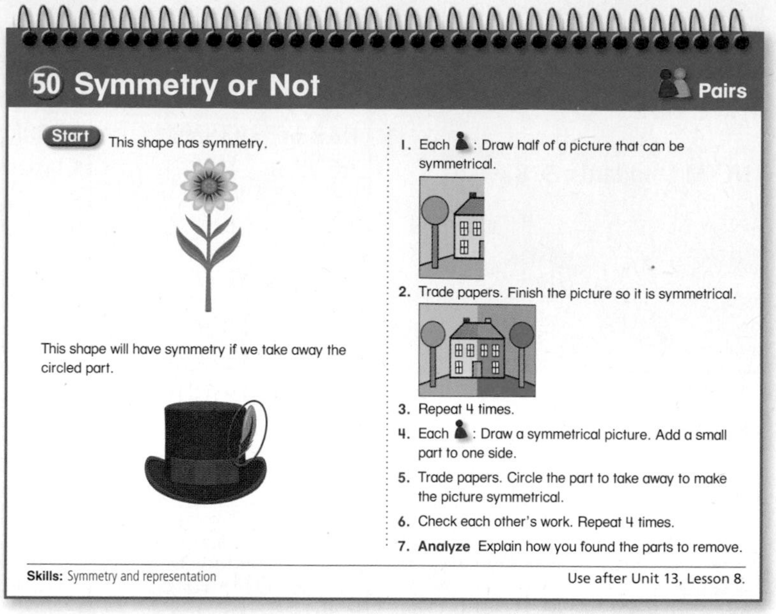

50 Symmetry or Not

Pairs

Start This shape has symmetry.

This shape will have symmetry if we take away the circled part.

1. Each: Draw half of a picture that can be symmetrical.
2. Trade papers. Finish the picture so it is symmetrical.
3. Repeat 4 times.
4. Each: Draw a symmetrical picture. Add a small part to one side.
5. Trade papers. Circle the part to take away to make the picture symmetrical.
6. Check each other's work. Repeat 4 times.
7. **Analyze** Explain how you found the parts to remove.

Skills: Symmetry and representation

Use after Unit 13, Lesson 8.

Grouping Pairs

Materials Crayons or markers

Objective Children create symmetrical drawings and identify parts that do not belong in a symmetrical drawing.

Connections Representation and Problem Solving

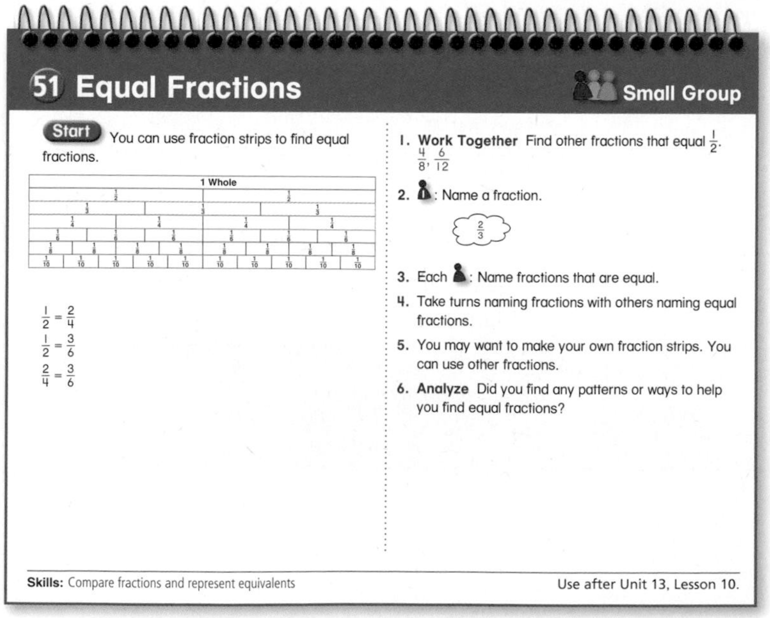

51 Equal Fractions

Small Group

Start You can use fraction strips to find equal fractions.

1 Whole

$\frac{1}{2} = \frac{2}{4}$

$\frac{1}{2} = \frac{3}{6}$

$\frac{2}{4} = \frac{3}{6}$

1. **Work Together** Find other fractions that equal $\frac{1}{2}$. $\frac{4}{8}, \frac{6}{12}$
2. Name a fraction. $\frac{2}{3}$
3. Each: Name fractions that are equal.
4. Take turns naming fractions with others naming equal fractions.
5. You may want to make your own fraction strips. You can use other fractions.
6. **Analyze** Did you find any patterns or ways to help you find equal fractions?

Skills: Compare fractions and represent equivalents

Use after Unit 13, Lesson 10.

Grouping Small Group

Materials Fraction Strips (Student Activity Book page 451)

Objective Children identify equal fractions.

Connections Number and Representation

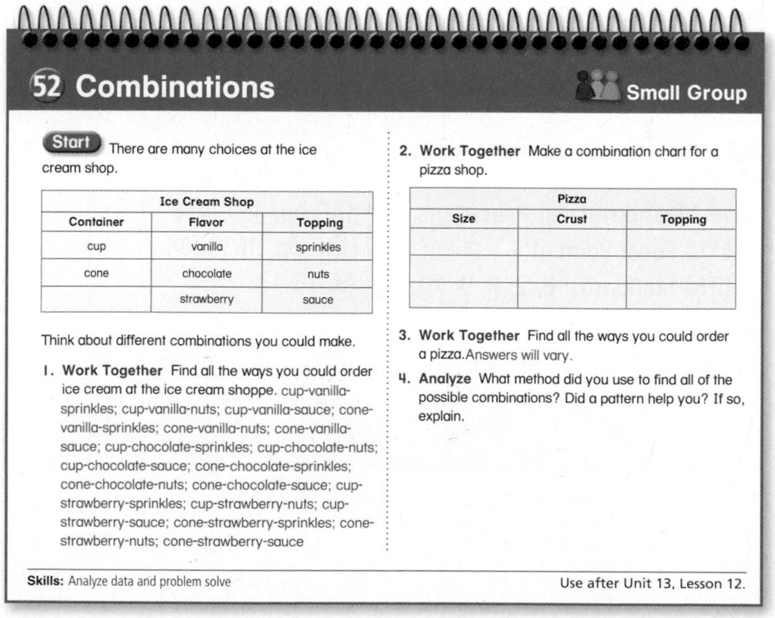

52 Combinations

Small Group

Start There are many choices at the ice cream shop.

Ice Cream Shop		
Container	Flavor	Topping
cup	vanilla	sprinkles
cone	chocolate	nuts
	strawberry	sauce

Think about different combinations you could make.

1. **Work Together** Find all the ways you could order ice cream at the ice cream shoppe. cup-vanilla-sprinkles; cup-vanilla-nuts; cup-vanilla-sauce; cone-vanilla-sprinkles; cone-vanilla-nuts; cone-vanilla-sauce; cup-chocolate-sprinkles; cup-chocolate-nuts; cup-chocolate-sauce; cone-chocolate-sprinkles; cone-chocolate-nuts; cone-chocolate-sauce; cup-strawberry-sprinkles; cup-strawberry-nuts; cup-strawberry-sauce; cone-strawberry-sprinkles; cone-strawberry-nuts; cone-strawberry-sauce
2. **Work Together** Make a combination chart for a pizza shop.

Pizza		
Size	Crust	Topping

3. **Work Together** Find all the ways you could order a pizza. Answers will vary.
4. **Analyze** What method did you use to find all of the possible combinations? Did a pattern help you? If so, explain.

Skills: Analyze data and problem solve

Use after Unit 13, Lesson 12.

Grouping Small Group

Materials None

Objective Children find all possible combinations given 3 groups of data.

Connections Problem Solving and Real World

Ready-Made Math Resources

Technology — Tutorials, Practice, and Intervention

Go Digital

Soar to Success Math

Use online, individualized intervention and support to bring students to proficiency.

HARCOURT MEGA MATH Grades K-6

Help students practice skills and apply concepts through exciting math adventures.

DESTINATION Math®

Extend and enrich students' understanding of skills and concepts through engaging, interactive lessons and activities.

Visit Education Place®
www.eduplace.com

Visit www.eduplace.com/mx2t/ and find family, teacher, and student materials, activities, games, and more.

Literature Links

The Grapes of Math

The Grapes of Math
Greg Tang has a knack for making math seem relevant and understandable. This book contains 16 riddles children can solve. Each riddle will stretch their creative thinking skills.

Literature Connections

Each Orange Had 8 Slices: A Counting Book, by Paul Giganti, Jr. and Donald Crews (HarperTrophy, 1999)

The Doorbell Rang, by Pat Hutchins (HarperTrophy, 1989)

Let's Fly a Kite, by Stuart J. Murphy and Brian Floca (HarperTrophy, 2000)

Unit 13 Teaching Resources

Differentiated Instruction

Individualizing Instruction		
	Level	**Frequency**
Activities	• Intervention • On Level • Challenge	All 3 in every lesson
	Level	**Frequency**
Math Writing Prompts	• Intervention • On Level • Challenge	All 3 in every lesson
Math Center Challenges	**For advanced students**	
	4 in every unit	

Reaching All Learners		
	Lessons	**Pages**
English Learners	1, 2, 3, 4, 5, 6, 7, 8, 9, 10, 11, 12, 13	954, 963, 969, 976, 980, 986, 992, 999, 1005, 1013, 1020, 1027, 1033
	Lessons	**Pages**
Extra Help	1, 2, 3, 4	956, 957, 962, 968, 974
	Lesson	**Page**
Advanced Learners	4, 5	974, 982

Strategies for English Language Learners

Present this problem to all children. Offer the different levels of support to meet children's levels of language proficiency.

Objective To identify equal groups and relate to multiplication

Problem Give children 12 cubes. Say: **Let us put the cubes in equal groups of 3.** Guide them to put the cubes into equal groups of 3.

Newcomer

- Say: **There are 4 groups. There are 3 cubes in each group.** Have children repeat.

Beginning

- Ask: **Are there 4 groups?** yes **Are there 3 cubes in each group?** yes
- Count the cubes by 3s. Have children repeat.

Intermediate

- Ask: **How many groups are there?** 4 groups **How many cubes in each group?** 3 cubes
- Help children count the cubes by 3s. Say: **1 group is 3 cubes. 2 groups is __.** 6 cubes **3 groups is __.** 9 cubes **4 groups is __.** 12 cubes

Advanced

- Have children identify the number of groups and cubes in each group. Guide them to count the cubes by 3s.
- Write $4 \times 3 = 12$. Point to each part. Say: **This means 4 groups times 3 cubes in each group is 12 cubes.** Have children repeat.

Connections

Art Connections
Lesson 2, page 966
Lesson 4, page 978
Lesson 12, page 1030
Lesson 13, page 1036

Math-to-Math Connection
Lesson 11, page 1024

Multicultural Connection
Lesson 9, page 1010

Real-World Connections
Lesson 5, page 984
Lesson 7, page 996
Lesson 10, page 1018

Literature Connections
Lesson 3, page 972
Lesson 6, page 990
Lesson 8, page 1002

Math Background

Putting Research into Practice for Unit 13

From Our Curriculum Research Project: Multiplication and Fractional Parts

In this unit, children will learn about multiplication and fractions. The key ideas that children need to grasp are that for multiplication we are putting together equal groups and for fractions, we have a whole group or a whole figure that is separated into equal groups or equal parts.

As an introduction to multiplication, children will skip count and use these count-bys to help them understand multiplication and to find products. Then children will be involved in making arrays and in looking at real-life situations for multiplication.

For fractions, children find halves, thirds, and fourths of simple geometric shapes shown in equal parts. From there, children write the appropriate fraction and learn the meaning of the numerator and denominator in a fraction. Children will also explore symmetry of simple geometric figures and probability concepts to build on and extend children's understanding of equal parts and fractions.

–Karen Fuson, Author
Math Expressions

From Current Research: Multiplication and Fractions

U.S. children progress through a sequence of multiplication procedures that are somewhat similar to those for addition. They make equal groups and count them all. They learn skip-count lists for different multipliers (e.g., they count 4, 8, 12, 16, 20, … to multiply by four). They then count on and count down these lists using their fingers to keep track of different products. They invent thinking strategies in which they derive related products from products they know.

Soon after entering school, many students can partition quantities into equal shares corresponding to halves, fourths, and eighths. These fractions can be generated by successively partitioning by half, which is an especially fruitful procedure since one half can play a useful role in learning about other fractions. Accompanying their actions of partitioning in half, many students develop the language of "one half" to describe the actions.

National Research Council. "Developing Proficiency with Whole Numbers." *Adding It Up: Helping Students Learn Mathematics.* Washington, D.C.: National Academy Press, 2001. 191, 232.

Other Useful References: Multiplication and Fractions

Lemaire, P., and R.S. Siegler. "Four Aspects of Strategic Change: Contributions to Children's Learning of Multiplication." *Journal of Experimental Psychology: General* 124 (1995): 83–97.

Mulligan, J., and M. Mitchelmore. "Young Children's Intuitive Models of Multiplication and Division." *Journal for Research in Mathematics Education,* 28 (1997): 309–330.

Pothier, Y., and D. Sawada. "Children's Interpretation of Equality in Early Fraction Activities." *Focus on Learning Problems in Mathematics* 11(3) (1989): 27–38.

Steffe, L. "Children's Multiplying Schemes." *The Development of Multiplicative Reasoning in the Learning of Mathematics.* Eds. G. Harel and J. Confrey. Albany: State University of New York Press, 1994. 3–39.

Getting Ready to Teach Unit 13

In this program, making connections between mathematical topics is a central goal. Many connections can be made between concepts in addition and multiplication. In this unit, we build on what children already know about counting and skip-counting to introduce the concept of multiplication. Children are able to see yet another connection when they find they can also use repeated addition to help find products in multiplication.

Once children have grasped the idea of equal groups in multiplication, we have them further explore ideas about equal parts or equal shares division in fractions. Children develop an understanding that fractions mean equal parts of a figure, and that fractions can mean equal parts of a set.

Math Expressions Vocabulary

As you teach this unit, emphasize understanding of these terms:

- count-bys
- Grouping Drawing
- Equal Shares Drawing

See Glossary on pp. T7–T20.

When children are able to apply what they already know to new topics, they become more confident in their mathematical abilities.

Strategies for Multiplying

Lessons 1, 2, 3, 4, and 5

Use Fingers to Show Each Multiplier of an Equal Group Children raise fingers to show each multiplier as they say the multiplication. Children practice count-bys for each number. For example, the 4s count-bys are 4, 8, 12, 16, 20, 24, 28, 32, 36, 40. Each count-by has a pattern. Children explore and describe these patterns.

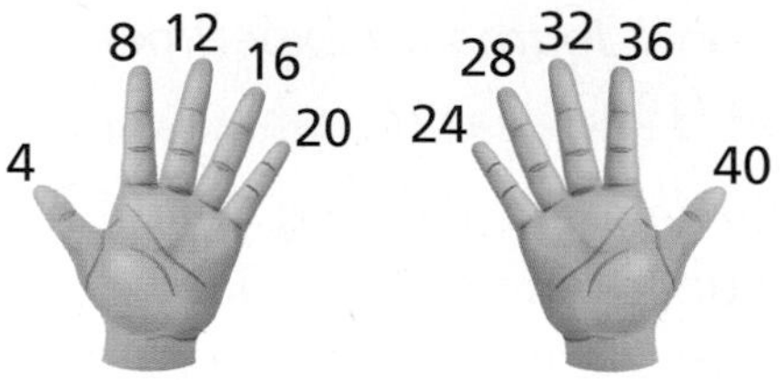

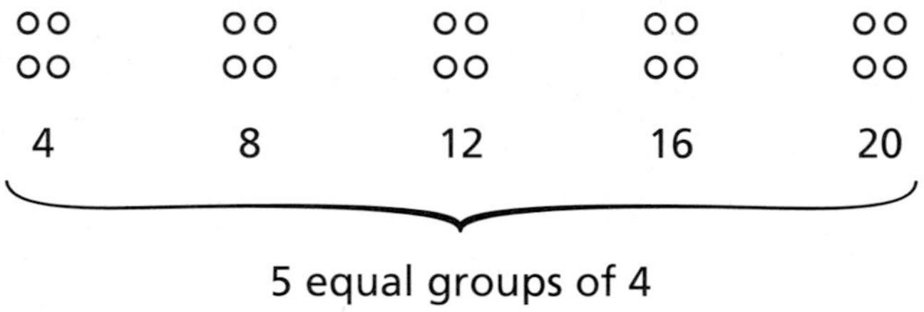

Use Arrays to Show Multiplication Arrays are introduced as another way to show what multiplication means. When presented with an array, children learn to see the equal groups in the rows or columns. They practice using repeated addition or count-bys to help find the product.

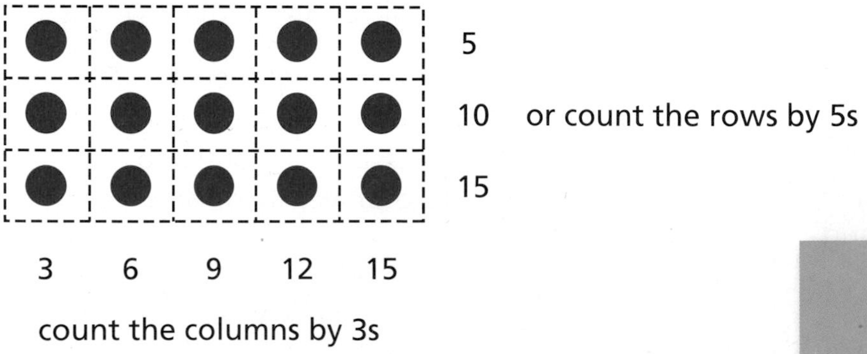

Understanding Fractions and Probability
Lessons 6, 7, 8, 9, 10, 11, and 12

Fractions Children will shade halves, thirds, and fourths of simple geometric shapes that have been divided into the corresponding number of equal parts. From there, children write the appropriate fraction and learn what each part (top and bottom) of the fraction means.

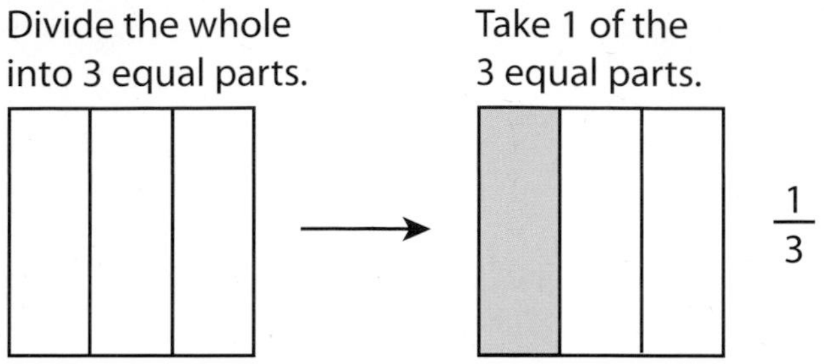
Divide the whole
into 3 equal parts.
Take 1 of the
3 equal parts.
1
3

Children will also solve problems using simple fractions of a set. For example: Kathy has half as many marbles as Yao. Kathy has 6. Yao has 12. In addition, children will explore equal shares division and symmetry.

Probability Children will continue their understanding of fractions of a figure as they color in the parts of a spinner and play a spinner game. They describe the outcome using simple probability language: *more likely, less likely, fair, unfair.*

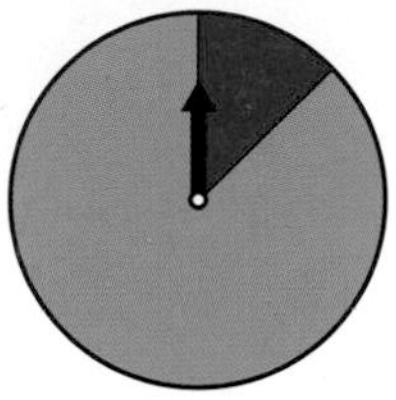

Problem Solving

In *Math Expressions* a research-based, algebraic problem-solving approach that focuses on problem types is used: understand the situation, represent the situation with a math drawing or an equation, solve the problem, and see that the answer makes sense. Throughout the unit, children solve a variety of problems using the concepts and skills being taught in this unit.

Use Mathematical Processes
Lesson 13

The NCTM process skills of problem solving, reasoning and proof, communication, connections, and representation are interwoven through all lessons throughout the year. The last lesson of this unit allows children to extend their use of mathematical processes to other situations.

Activity	NCTM Process Skill	Goal
Math and Science	Connections	Use addition and subtraction to create tables and bar graphs.
Support Math Statements	Reasoning and Proof	Write a paragraph and make drawings to support a math statement.
Mato's Games	Problem Solving	Use multiplying and halving to solve a word problem.
A Spinner	Representation	Draw a spinner to represent a likely given outcome.
Choose a Spinner	Communication	Explain a choice.

UNIT 13 LESSON 1

Introduction to Multiplication

Lesson Objectives

- Recognize that multiplication is counting by a number.
- Relate repeated addition and multiplication.
- Solve multiplication problems.
- Count by 2s.

Vocabulary

multiplication
count by
count-bys
Grouping Drawing
Equal Shares Drawing

The Day at a Glance

Today's Goals	Materials	
1 Teaching the Lesson **A1:** Relate repeated addition and multiplication. **A2:** Write the 2s count-bys and use count-bys to solve simple multiplication problems.	**Lesson Activities** Student Activity Book pp. 417–419, 421–422 (includes Family Letter) Homework and Remembering pp. 279–280 MathBoard materials	**Going Further** Activity Cards 13-1 Student Activity Book page 420 Paper clips Hole punch Calculators Math Journals
2 Going Further ► Math Connection: Multiplication with One ► Differentiated Instruction		
3 Homework and Targeted Practice		

Use Math Talk today!

Keeping Skills Sharp

Quick Practice — 5 MINUTES

Goal: Count by 5s.

Count By 5s Divide the class into two groups. You can appoint a **Student Leader** for each group or ask for volunteers. Have the class count by 5s. The first group starts by saying the number 5. The second group responds with "10." The first group replies with "15," and so on until they have reached at least 50. You may wish to repeat the exercise, asking the second group to begin this time.

Daily Routines

2s, 3s, and 4s Count-Bys Draw Arrays, Draw Groups on the 120 Poster, Draw Groups on the Number Path
(See pp. xxviii–xix.)

► Led by teacher

Money Routine Using the 120 Poster, Using the Money Flip Chart, Using the Number Path, Using Secret Code Cards
(See pp. xxiii–xxv.)

► Led by Student Leaders

1 Teaching the Lesson

Activity 1

What Is Multiplication?

20 MINUTES

Goal: Relate repeated addition and multiplication.

Materials: MathBoard materials, Student Activity Book page 417

NCTM Standards:
Number and Operations
Problem Solving
Representation

Teaching Note

Language and Vocabulary Since this is the first time children have encountered multiplication, emphasize that 5 × 2, five times two, 5 groups of 2, and 5 sets of 2 all mean the same thing. Be sure children are becoming familiar with this vocabulary when explaining their work during **Solve and Discuss.**

English Language Learners

Draw 3 groups of 2 cookies on the board. Write *equal shares.*

- **Beginning** Say: ***Equal shares* means groups that are equal.** Have children repeat.
- **Intermediate** Ask: **How many cookies in each group?** 2 cookies **Are they *equal shares*?** yes
- **Advanced** Have children make a drawing showing *equal shares.*

▶ Introduce Multiplication WHOLE CLASS

Math Talk

Present this problem to children.

- You have 5 vases. There are 2 flowers in each vase. How many flowers do you have in all?

Some children can work at the board to solve the problem while the others work on their MathBoards. Children should make a labeled math drawing to solve the problem.

Ask for Ideas Ask children how they solved the problem. Children may have counted each flower, counted by 2s, or added 2 + 2 + 2 + 2 + 2.

The following drawings represent the situation in the problem. If children did not come up with these on their own, present them to the class.

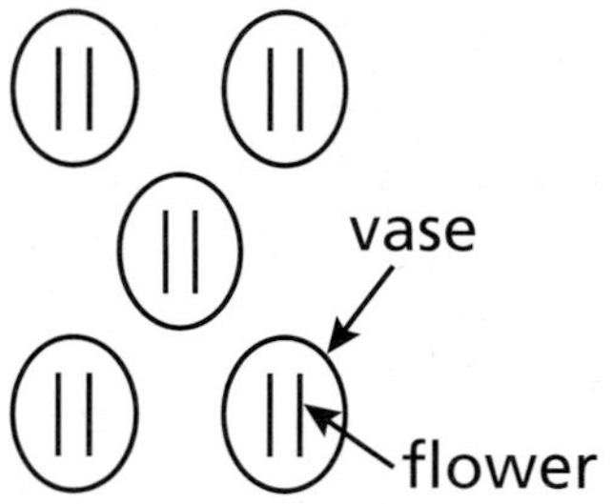

Grouping Drawing

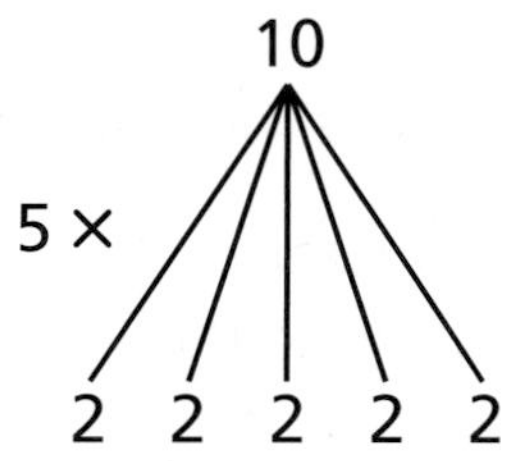

Equal Shares Drawing

Write the equation 5 × 2 = ☐ on the board. Ask children if they know what this equation means. Explain that the "×" is a multiplication sign and that "5 × 2" is read as "five times two." This means 5 groups of 2 or 5 sets of 2. Point out how each of the pictures above shows 5 groups of 2. Help children complete the equation: 5 × 2 = 10. Next, write the following problems on the board.

If a bicycle has 2 tires and there are 3 bicycles, how many tires are there in all?

If a camel has 2 humps, how many humps do 4 camels have?

For each problem, have children make a drawing and write an equation. Use the **Solve and Discuss** structure for class discussion.

▶ Practice Multiplication PAIRS

Math Talk

Have children work in **Helping Pairs** to complete Student Activity Book page 417. The multiplication problem about flowers in a vase is shown as an example at the top of the page. If necessary, work through the first exercise as a class. Encourage children to make either Grouping Drawings or Equal Shares Drawings. See **Math Talk in Action** in the side column for possible classroom dialogue.

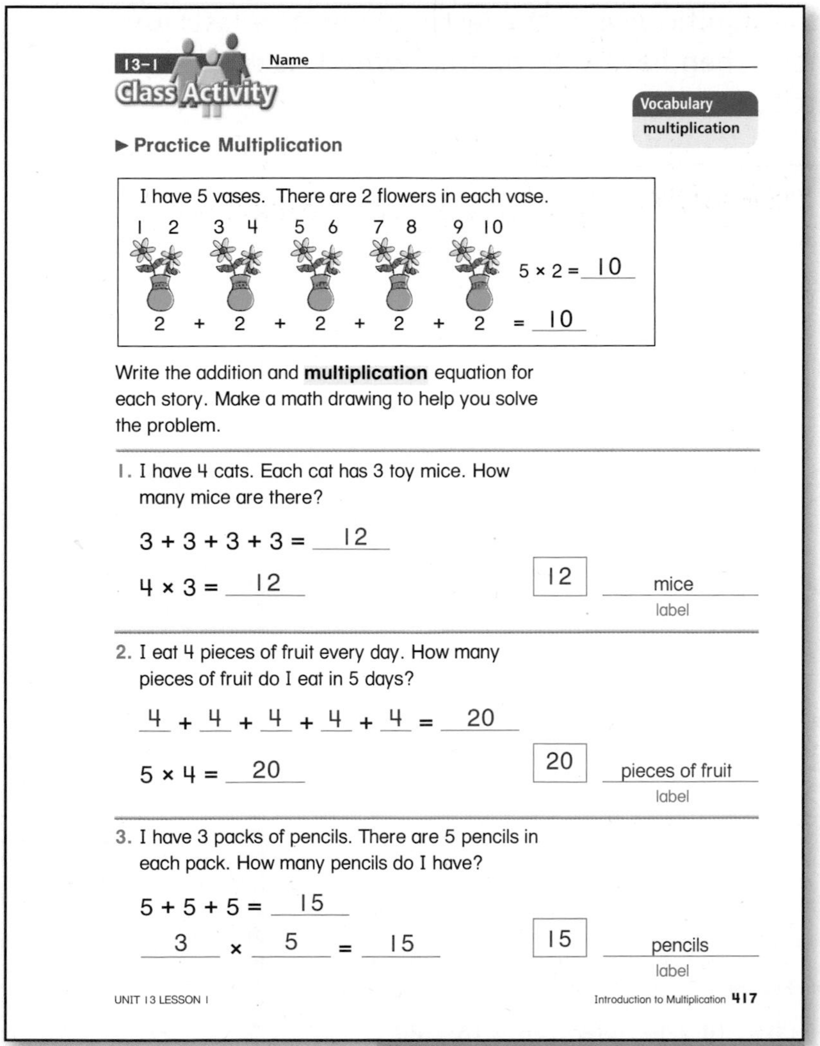

13–1 Class Activity Name ______

Vocabulary: multiplication

▶ Practice Multiplication

I have 5 vases. There are 2 flowers in each vase.

1 2 3 4 5 6 7 8 9 10

5 × 2 = 10

2 + 2 + 2 + 2 + 2 = 10

Write the addition and **multiplication** equation for each story. Make a math drawing to help you solve the problem.

1. I have 4 cats. Each cat has 3 toy mice. How many mice are there?

3 + 3 + 3 + 3 = 12

4 × 3 = 12

12 mice (label)

2. I eat 4 pieces of fruit every day. How many pieces of fruit do I eat in 5 days?

4 + 4 + 4 + 4 + 4 = 20

5 × 4 = 20

20 pieces of fruit (label)

3. I have 3 packs of pencils. There are 5 pencils in each pack. How many pencils do I have?

5 + 5 + 5 = 15

3 × 5 = 15

15 pencils (label)

UNIT 13 LESSON 1 Introduction to Multiplication 417

Student Activity Book page 417

Math Talk in Action

Karen: Exercise 1 says that there are 4 cats and each cat has 3 toy mice. We have to find how many mice there are in all.

Doug: Let's make a drawing to help us. I'll make a Grouping Drawing. Each cat has 3 toy mice, so there are 3 in each group. There are 4 cats, so there are 4 groups.

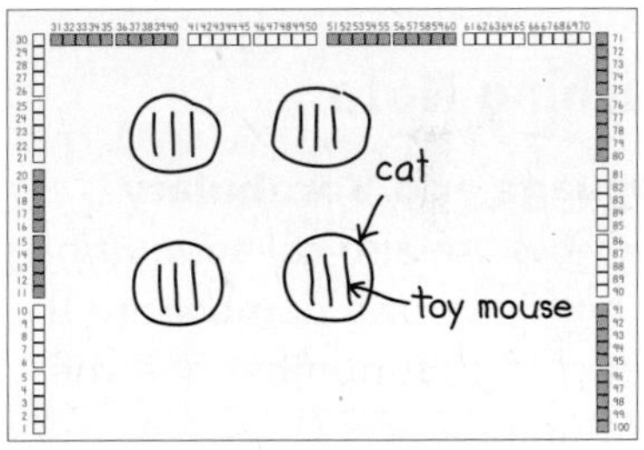

T.J.: I'll make an Equal Shares Drawing that shows the same thing.

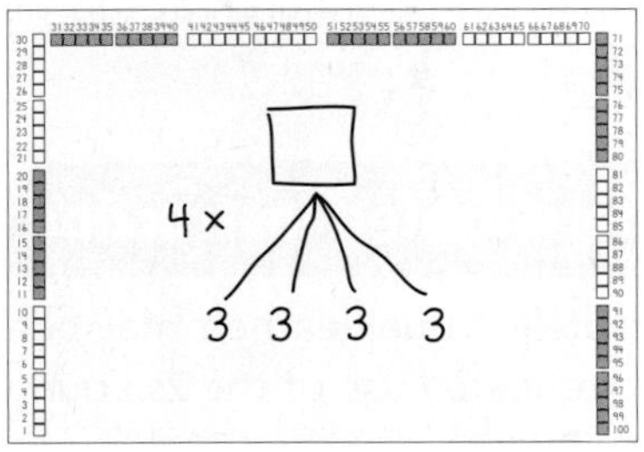

I can count by 3s to find the answer. 3, 6, 9, 12. There are 12 toy mice.

Adele: We can add 3 + 3 + 3 + 3. That's 12!

Karen: So, we can write the multiplication 4 × 3 = 12!

Activity 2

Multiply by 2

30 MINUTES

Goal: Write the 2s count-bys and use count-bys to solve simple multiplication problems.

Materials: Student Activity Book pages 418–419

NCTM Standards:
Number and Operations
Problem Solving
Representation

Teaching Note

Language and Vocabulary
Count-bys are also called *multiples.* The multiples of a number are the product of that number and the counting numbers (1, 2, 3, 4...). The multiples of 2, therefore, are the even counting numbers (2, 4, 6, 8...). It is not necessary to introduce the word *multiples* to the children at this time.

Differentiated Instruction

Extra Help Visual learners may benefit from repeated use of the 2s Count-Bys chart. Provide them with additional copies to complete. Encourage them to emphasize the 2s count-bys in the chart by circling or highlighting those numbers with a marker. It may also help some children to see the chart in a horizontal format rather than a vertical one. You can prepare, or have them create, a 2 by 10 table to complete.

▶ 2s Count-Bys INDIVIDUALS

Refer children to Student Activity Book page 418. Explain to children that working with count-bys will help them understand and solve multiplication problems. Have children fill in the count-by chart for the number 2. The white area contains all of the numbers that are count-bys (multiples) of 2. The shaded area shows the numbers that are not count-bys.

Have the children focus on the groups of 2 that make up this array. Have them ring each pair of numbers in the array (see the first pair below). Elicit from them the significance of the last number (the last number tells the total so far). Then have the children write this count-by list on the blanks in Exercise 5.

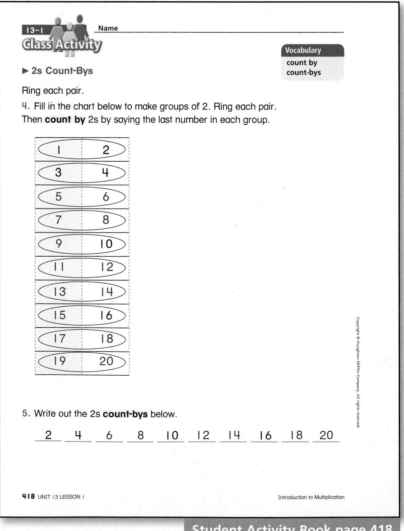

13–1 Class Activity

Name ______

Vocabulary
count by
count-bys

▶ 2s Count-Bys

Ring each pair.

4. Fill in the chart below to make groups of 2. Ring each pair. Then **count by** 2s by saying the last number in each group.

1	2
3	4
5	6
7	8
9	10
11	12
13	14
15	16
17	18
19	20

5. Write out the 2s **count-bys** below.

2 4 6 8 10 12 14 16 18 20

418 UNIT 13 LESSON 1 Introduction to Multiplication

Student Activity Book page 418

► Count By 2s to Multiply INDIVIDUALS

Math Talk

Refer children to Student Activity Book page 419. They should fill in the count-bys and solve the multiplication problems on the page.

Children may work individually or in **Helping Pairs**. You can offer assistance as necessary.

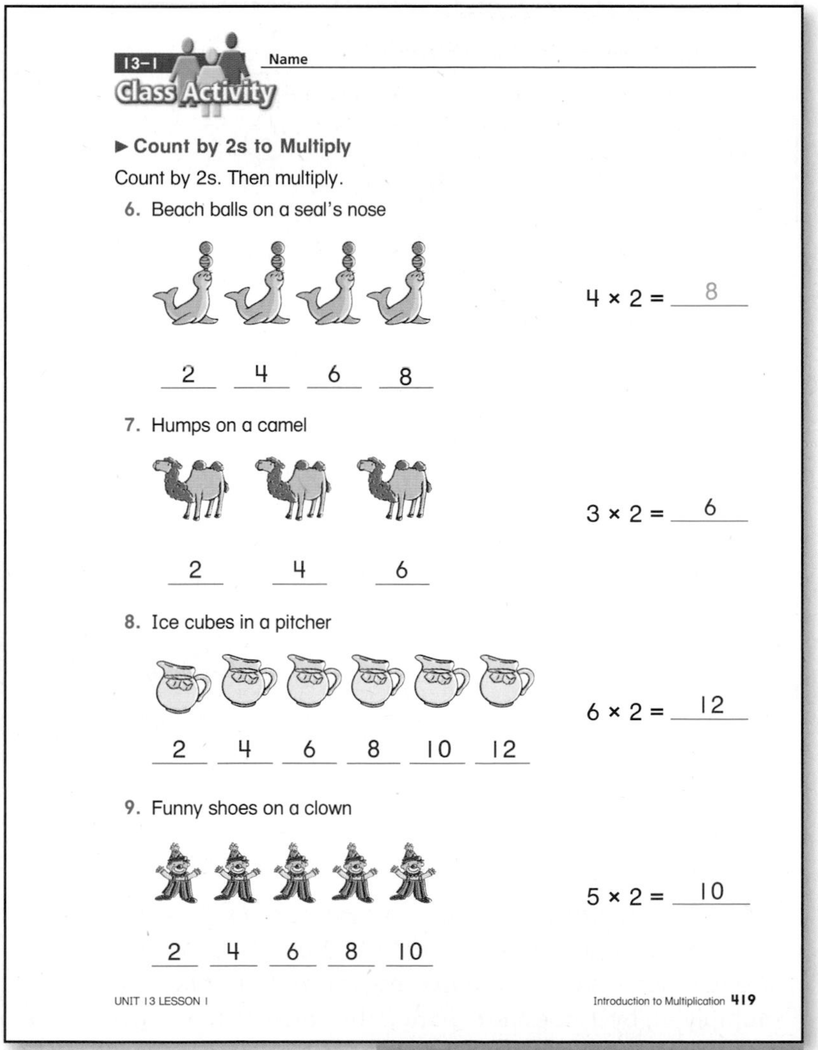

13–1 Class Activity

Name ______

► Count by 2s to Multiply

Count by 2s. Then multiply.

6. Beach balls on a seal's nose

2 4 6 8

$4 \times 2 =$ 8

7. Humps on a camel

2 4 6

$3 \times 2 =$ 6

8. Ice cubes in a pitcher

2 4 6 8 10 12

$6 \times 2 =$ 12

9. Funny shoes on a clown

2 4 6 8 10

$5 \times 2 =$ 10

UNIT 13 LESSON 1

Introduction to Multiplication 419

Student Activity Book page 419

Class Management

Before children complete the page, you might want to review the pictures for each exercise. Have children read each exercise and identify the object being counted. Check that they can find that detail of the picture.

Differentiated Instruction

Extra Help Children often make better learning connections when they can relate a new topic with their everyday lives. Have children make a collage of things that come in twos.

Ongoing Assessment

Circulate around the room as children are working. Encourage them to share their thinking.

- ► Show me how you counted by 2s to find the answer.
- ► Point to a multiplication sign on the page.
- ► Tell me what the numbers in the multiplication sentence mean.

2 Going Further

Math Connection: Multiplication with One

Goal: To multiply 1 by a number or to multiply a number by 1.

Materials: Student Activity Book page 420

▶ Draw Pictures and Write Equations

SMALL GROUPS

Have children complete exercises 1–6 in small groups. Encourage them to discuss the patterns they see with other members of their groups.

▶ Discuss the Pattern

Math Talk

Invite volunteers to describe the pattern. Children should see that when they multiply any number by 1, they get that same number. Also, when they multiply 1 by any number, they get that same number. Have children complete exercise 7 individually.

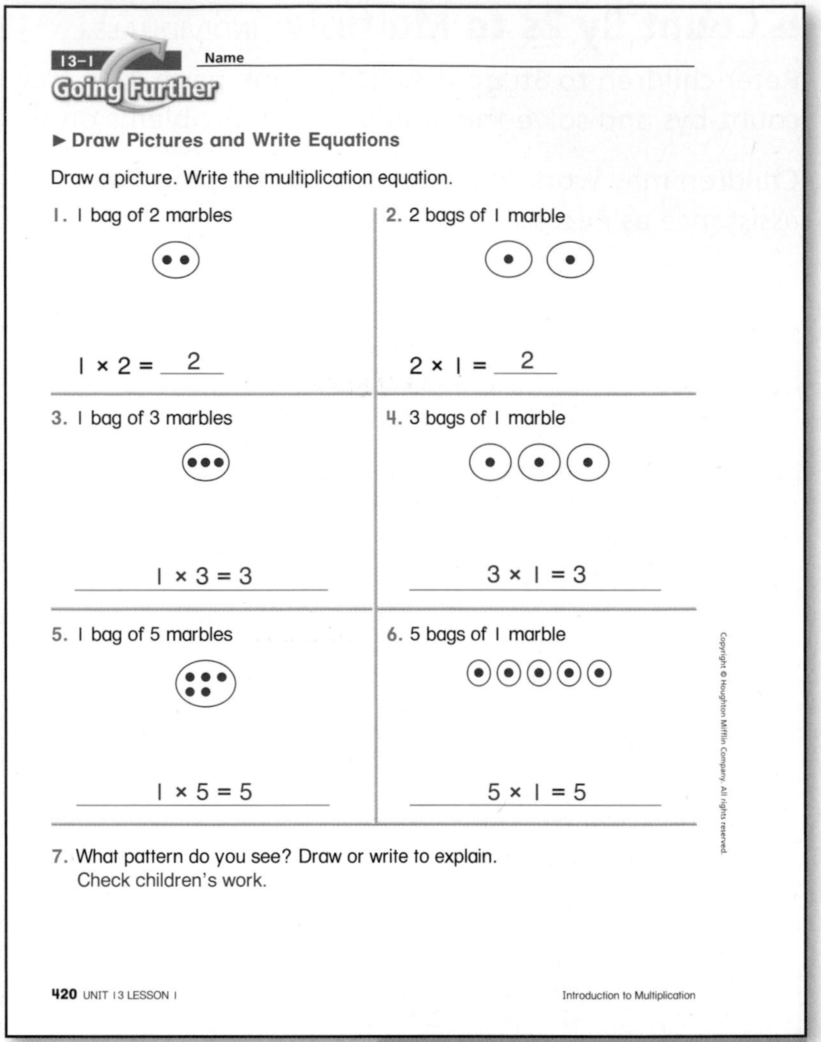

13–1 Going Further

Name

▶ Draw Pictures and Write Equations

Draw a picture. Write the multiplication equation.

1. 1 bag of 2 marbles

$1 \times 2 = 2$

2. 2 bags of 1 marble

$2 \times 1 = 2$

3. 1 bag of 3 marbles

$1 \times 3 = 3$

4. 3 bags of 1 marble

$3 \times 1 = 3$

5. 1 bag of 5 marbles

$1 \times 5 = 5$

6. 5 bags of 1 marble

$5 \times 1 = 5$

7. What pattern do you see? Draw or write to explain.
Check children's work.

Student Activity Book page 420

Teaching Note

Math Background This lesson provides students with an informal introduction to the Identity Property of Multiplication. The number 1 is called the *identity for multiplication* because multiplying by 1 does not change the value of a number. Children will not use this formal vocabulary at this time.

Intervention — Activity Card 13-1

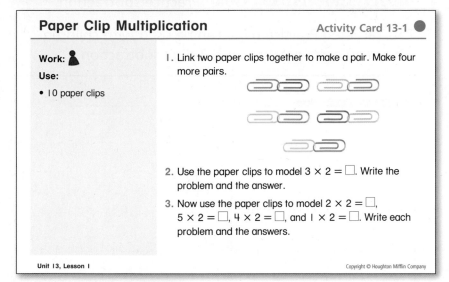

Paper Clip Multiplication

Activity Card 13-1

Work:
Use:
- 10 paper clips

1. Link two paper clips together to make a pair. Make four more pairs.

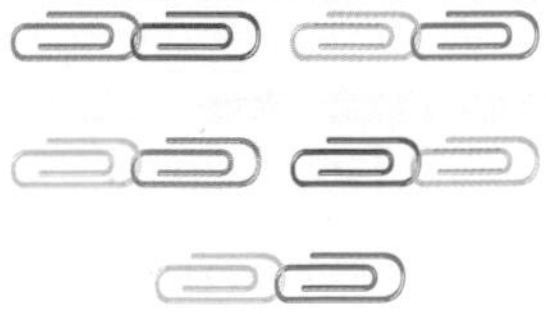

2. Use the paper clips to model 3 × 2 = ☐. Write the problem and the answer.
3. Now use the paper clips to model 2 × 2 = ☐, 5 × 2 = ☐, 4 × 2 = ☐, and 1 × 2 = ☐. Write each problem and the answers.

Unit 13, Lesson 1

Activity Note Each child needs 10 paper clips. Check how children model the problems and each answer.

Math Writing Prompt

Model Multiplication Draw a picture to show 4 × 2. What is the answer?

Soar to Success Math Software Support

Warm Up 12.17

On Level — Activity Card 13-1

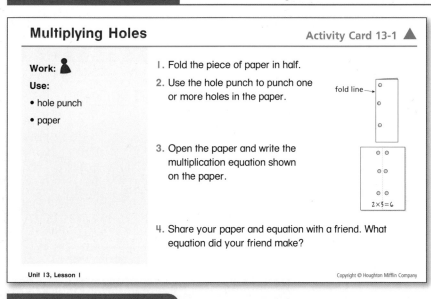

Multiplying Holes

Activity Card 13-1

Work:
Use:
- hole punch
- paper

1. Fold the piece of paper in half.
2. Use the hole punch to punch one or more holes in the paper.

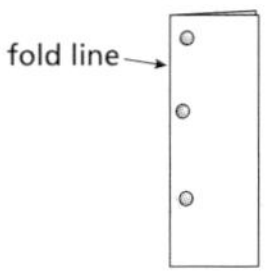

3. Open the paper and write the multiplication equation shown on the paper.

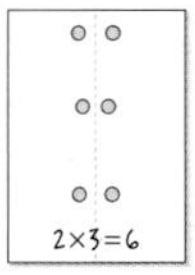

4. Share your paper and equation with a friend. What equation did your friend make?

Unit 13, Lesson 1

Activity Note Have a hole punch available for children to use. Have children check their equation with a friend.

Math Writing Prompt

Draw or Write How is multiplying by 2 like adding doubles? Draw or write to explain.

Harcourt Mega Math Software Support

Country Countdown: Counting Critters, Level V

Challenge — Activity Card 13-1

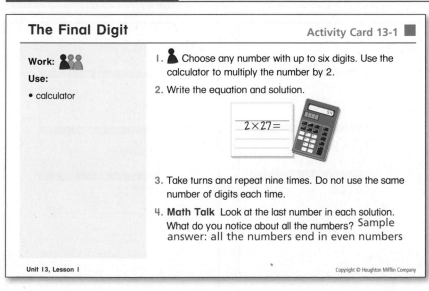

The Final Digit

Activity Card 13-1

Work:
Use:
- calculator

1. Choose any number with up to six digits. Use the calculator to multiply the number by 2.
2. Write the equation and solution.

3. Take turns and repeat nine times. Do not use the same number of digits each time.
4. **Math Talk** Look at the last number in each solution. What do you notice about all the numbers? Sample answer: all the numbers end in even numbers

Unit 13, Lesson 1

Activity Note Each group needs a calculator. Have each group use different numbers. If necessary, have pairs list all the last digits and then prompt with questions.

Math Writing Prompt

Investigate Math How are 5 × 2 and 2 × 5 alike? How are they different?

Destination Math Software Support

Course II: Module 2: Unit 2: Repeated Addition and Arrays

3 Homework and Targeted Practice

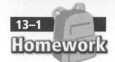

13–1 **Homework** **Goal:** Additional Practice

This Homework page provides practice in multiplication and writing 2s count-bys.

13–1 Name ______________________

Homework

Count by 2s. Then multiply.

1. Horns on a bull

2 4 6 8 $4 \times 2 = 8$

2. Eyes on a teddy bear

2 4 $2 \times 2 = 4$

3. Hearts on a valentine

2 4 6 8 10 12 $6 \times 2 = 12$

4. Leaves on a holly branch

2 4 6 8 10 12 14 16 18 $9 \times 2 = 18$

5. Wheels on a bicycle

2 4 6 8 10 $5 \times 2 = 10$

UNIT 13 LESSON 1 Introduction to Multiplication 279

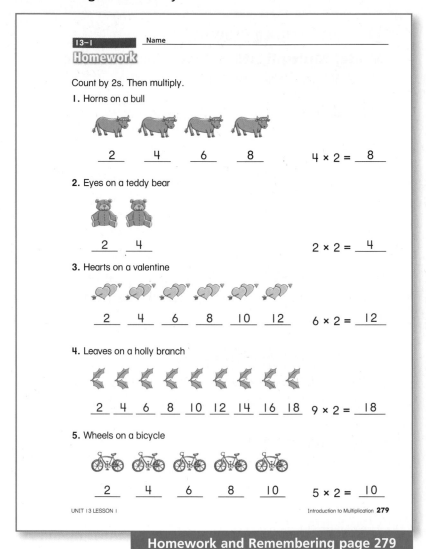

Homework and Remembering page 279

13–1 **Targeted Practice** **Goal:** Practice subtraction.

This Targeted Practice page can be used with children who need extra practice with 3-digit subtraction.

13–1 Name ______________________

Targeted Practice

Subtract. Ungroup if you need to.

1. $592 - 475 = 117$

2. $635 - 464 = 171$

3. $417 - 246 = 171$

4. $773 - 527 = 246$

5. $846 - 584 = 262$

6. $934 - 417 = 517$

280 UNIT 13 LESSON 1 Introduction to Multiplication

Homework and Remembering page 280

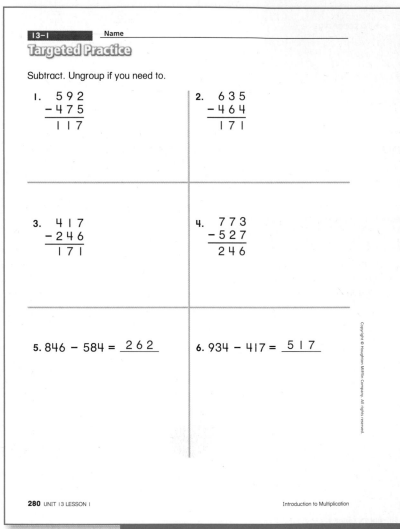

Home and School Connection

Family Letter Have children take home the Family Letter on Student Activity Book page 421. This letter explains how the concept of multiplication is developed in *Math Expressions.* It gives parents and guardians a better understanding of the learning that goes on in math class and creates a bridge between school and home. A Spanish translation of this letter is on the following page in the Student Activity Book.

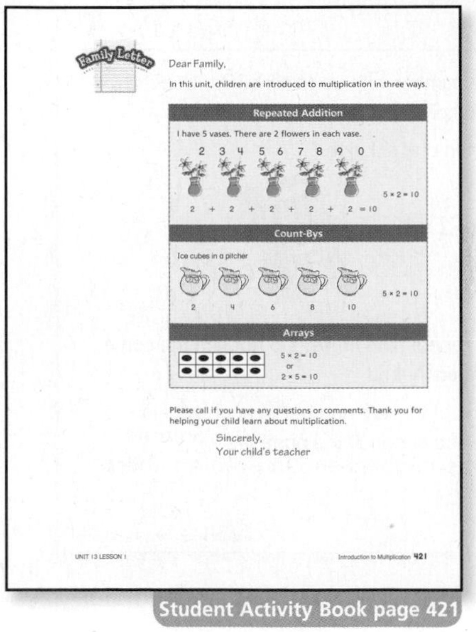

Student Activity Book page 421

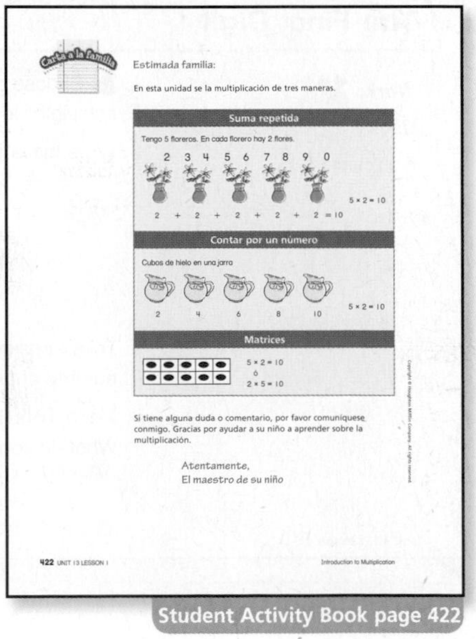

Student Activity Book page 422

UNIT 13 LESSON 2

Groups of Three

Lesson Objectives

- Recognize that multiplication is counting by a number.
- Count by 3s.

Vocabulary
multiply
multiplication
count by/count-bys

The Day at a Glance

Today's Goals	Materials	
1 Teaching the Lesson **A1:** Say and write the 3s count-bys. **A2:** Identify things that come in threes and solve simple multiplication problems.	**Lesson Activities** Student Activity Book pp. 423–424 Homework and Remembering pp. 281–282	**Going Further** Activity Cards 13-2 Student Activity Book pp. 425–426 120 Poster (TRB M60) Connecting cubes Rubber bands Beans Cups Counters Math Journals
2 Going Further ▶ Problem-Solving Strategy: Pictographs ▶ Differentiated Instruction		
3 Homework and Spiral Review		

Use Math Talk today!

Keeping Skills Sharp

Quick Practice — 5 MINUTES

Goal: Count by 2s.

Count By 2s Divide the class into two groups. You can appoint a **Student Leader** for each group or take volunteers. Have the class count by 2s. The first group starts by saying the number 2. The second group responds with "4." The first group replies with "6," and so on until they have reached at least 20. You may wish to repeat the exercise, asking the second group to begin this time.

Have children count by 2s to determine the number of shoes in the classroom.

Repeated Quick Practice
Use this Quick Practice from a previous lesson.

- ▶ **Count By 5s** (See Unit 13 Lesson 1.)

Daily Routines

2s, 3s, and 4s Count-Bys Draw Arrays, Draw Groups on the 120 Poster, Draw Groups on the Number Path (See pp. xxviii–xix.)

- ▶ Led by teacher

Money Routine Using the 120 Poster, Using the Money Flip Chart, Using the Number Path, Using Secret Code Cards (See pp. xxiii–xxv.)

- ▶ Led by Student Leaders

1 Teaching the Lesson

Activity 1

Count By 3s

20 MINUTES

Goal: Say and write the 3s count-bys.

Materials: Student Activity Book page 423

NCTM Standards:
Number and Operations
Problem Solving
Representations

Differentiated Instruction

Extra Help To help children learn the less familiar 3s count-bys, have them write a beat, song, or rhythm to accompany the sequence to 30. They might use a drum or other instruments to help them keep the beat.

The Learning Classroom

Building Concepts Children may use the count-by chart on Student Activity Book page 423 to help them count at first, but encourage them to count by memory as soon as possible. It is important, however, that children commit the correct numbers to memory from the beginning.

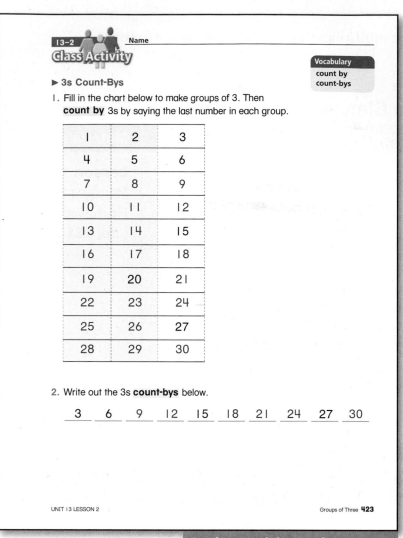

13–2 Class Activity

Name ____________________

Vocabulary
count by
count-bys

► 3s Count-Bys

1. Fill in the chart below to make groups of 3. Then **count by** 3s by saying the last number in each group.

1	2	3
4	5	6
7	8	9
10	11	12
13	14	15
16	17	18
19	20	21
22	23	24
25	26	27
28	29	30

2. Write out the 3s **count-bys** below.

3 6 9 12 15 18 21 24 27 30

UNIT 13 LESSON 2 Groups of Three **423**

Student Activity Book page 423

► 3s Count-Bys INDIVIDUALS

Remind children that working with count-bys will help them solve multiplication problems. Ask them to fill in the count-by chart on Student Activity Book page 423. The white area contains all of the numbers that are count-bys of 3. The shaded area shows the numbers that are not. Then have children write the count-bys on the lines across the bottom of the page.

► Practice Counting By 3s WHOLE CLASS

Have children raise one finger as they count each three. When the class has reached 30, everyone should have all 10 fingers raised.

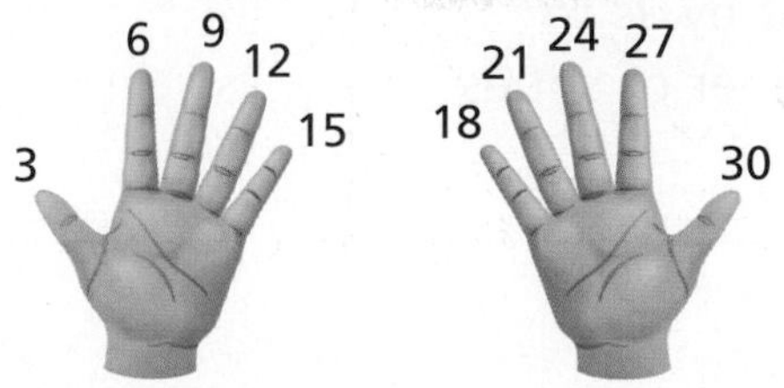

Activity 2

Work with Multiples of 3

▶ Things That Come in 3s WHOLE CLASS

Ask for Ideas Ask children to mention some things that might come in 3s. Examples include cloverleaves, lights on a stoplight, characters in stories (such as *The Three Little Pigs, The Three Bears*).

▶ Count By 3s to Multiply INDIVIDUALS

Have children work individually or in Helping Pairs to complete Student Activity Book page 424. You can offer assistance as necessary. Review the language used to describe multiplication: 4 times 3, 4 × 3, and 4 groups of 3. Children who finish early can make up more problems like the ones on the page to help them practice counting by 3s.

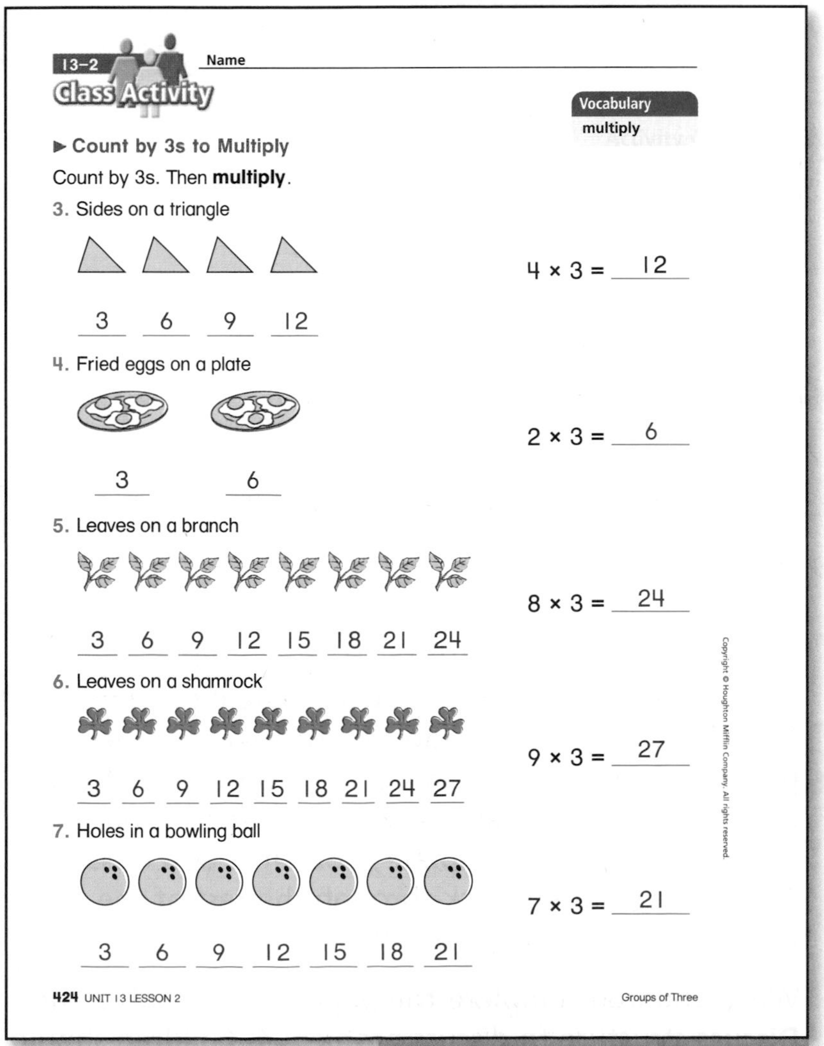

13–2 Class Activity Name

Vocabulary
multiply

▶ Count by 3s to Multiply

Count by 3s. Then **multiply**.

3. Sides on a triangle

3 6 9 12

4 × 3 = 12

4. Fried eggs on a plate

3 6

2 × 3 = 6

5. Leaves on a branch

3 6 9 12 15 18 21 24

8 × 3 = 24

6. Leaves on a shamrock

3 6 9 12 15 18 21 24 27

9 × 3 = 27

7. Holes in a bowling ball

3 6 9 12 15 18 21

7 × 3 = 21

424 UNIT 13 LESSON 2 Groups of Three

Student Activity Book page 424

25 MINUTES

Goal: Identify things that come in 3s and solve simple multiplication problems.

Materials: Student Activity Book page 424

NCTM Standards:
Number and Operations
Problem Solving
Representation

English Language Learners

Write 3, 6, 9, 12, 15 on the board. Write *Counting by 3s*.

- **Beginning** Say: **Counting by 3s means skip count by 3 each time.** Have children repeat.
- **Intermediate** Ask: **Did I skip count by 3 each time?** yes Say: **Is this counting by 3s?** yes
- **Advanced** Have children draw 5 groups of 3 and demonstrate how to *count by 3s*.

Ongoing Assessment

As children complete Student Activity Book page 424, circulate and ask children to explain their thinking aloud as they solve the exercises.

3 Homework and Spiral Review

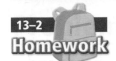

13-2 Homework **Goal:** Additional Practice

This Homework page provides practice in counting by 3s.

13-2 Name ____________
Homework

Count by 3s. Then multiply.

1. Flowers on a stem

3 6 9 12 $4 \times 3 =$ 12

2. Strawberries on a plate

3 6 9 $3 \times 3 =$ 9

3. Sides in triangles

3 6 9 12 15 18 $6 \times 3 =$ 18

4. Crayons in a group

3 6 9 12 15 $5 \times 3 =$ 15

5. Toys in a sandbox play set

3 6 9 12 15 18 21 $7 \times 3 =$ 21

UNIT 13 LESSON 2 Groups of Three **281**

Homework and Remembering page 281

13-2 Remembering **Goal:** Spiral Review

This Remembering activity would be appropriate anytime after today's lesson.

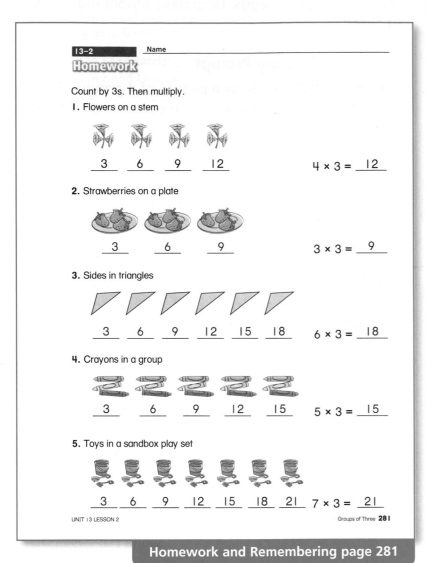

13-2 Name ____________
Remembering

Add or subtract.

1. $415 + 191 = 606$
2. $754 + 187 = 941$
3. $501 - 48 = 453$

Solve the story problems. **Show your work.**

4. There are 5 trucks. Each truck has 2 logs in it. How many logs are there altogether?

$2 + 2 + 2 + 2 + 2 =$ 10

$5 \times 2 =$ 10

10 logs
label

The Mason School spring garden has 10 tulips, 8 daffodils, 11 crocuses, and 6 snowdrops. Make a table to show this. Then answer the questions. Ring *more* or *fewer*. Put a title at the top of your table.

Flowers in the Garden

	Number of Flowers
Tulips	10
Daffodils	8
Crocuses	11
Snowdrops	6

5. There are 3 *more* (*fewer*) daffodils than crocuses in the Mason School garden.
6. There are 2 (*more*) *fewer* tulips than daffodils in the Mason School garden.
7. The school needs to plant 4 more snowdrops to have as many as there are tulips.

282 UNIT 13 LESSON 2 Groups of Three

Homework and Remembering page 282

Home or School Activity

Art Connection

Groups of 3 Have children make a list of objects that come in groups of three, such as wheels on a tricycle and triplets. Then have them work together to make a poster. Children may draw or use pictures from magazines and newspapers.

Children can choose an item from their poster to write and solve a multiplication story problem.

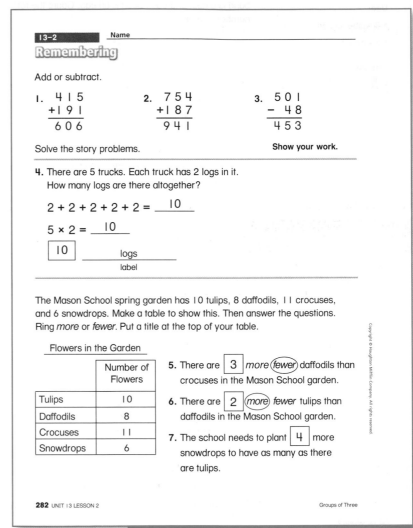

UNIT 13 LESSON 3

Groups of Four

Lesson Objectives

- Recognize that multiplication is counting by a number.
- Count by 4s.

Vocabulary

addition
subtraction
multiplication
count by/count-bys

The Day at a Glance

Today's Goals	Materials	
1 Teaching the Lesson **A1:** Say and write the 4s count-bys. **A2:** Identify things that come in fours and solve simple multiplication problems.	**Lesson Activities** Student Activity Book pp. 427–428 Homework and Remembering pp. 283–284	**Going Further** Activity Cards 13-3 Student Activity Book pp. 429–430 Index cards 120 Poster (TRB M60) MathBoard materials *Each Orange Had 8 Slices: A Counting Book* by Paul Giganti, Jr. Math Journals
2 Going Further ► Problem-Solving Strategy: Pictographs ► Differentiated Instruction		
3 Homework and Targeted Practice		

Use Math Talk today!

Keeping Skills Sharp

Quick Practice — 5 MINUTES

Goal: Monitor children's progress adding and subtracting 3-digit numbers. Count by 3s.

Quick Check Monitor children's progress with a brief quick check. Write these exercises on the board.

$$\begin{array}{r} 643 \\ +\,272 \\ \hline 915 \end{array} \qquad \begin{array}{r} 801 \\ -\,174 \\ \hline 627 \end{array}$$

Count By 3s Divide the class into two groups. You can appoint a **Student Leader** for each group or take volunteers. Have the class count by 3s. The first group starts by saying the number 3. The second group responds with "6." The first group replies with "9," and so on until they have reached 30. It may be helpful to have children use their fingers to mark off each multiple of 3 that they count.

Daily Routines

2s, 3s, and 4s Count-Bys Draw Arrays, Draw Groups on the 120 Poster, Draw Groups on the Number Path
(See pp. xxviii–xix.)

► Led by teacher

Money Routine Using the 120 Poster, Using the Money Flip Chart, Using the Number Path, Using Secret Code Cards
(See pp. xxiii–xxv.)

► Led by Student Leaders

1 Teaching the Lesson

Activity 1

Count By 4s

20 MINUTES

Goal: Say and write the 4s count-bys.

Materials: Student Activity Book page 427

NCTM Standards:
Number and Operations
Problem Solving
Representation

Differentiated Instruction

Extra Help Children who have difficulty memorizing the unfamiliar sequence of 4s count-bys may benefit from a rhyming poem. Have children write a poem with these (or other) rhyming pairs. They can continue with their own rhymes for the other numbers in the sequence to 40.

four ⟶ more, score, floor
eight ⟶ great, weight, fate
twelve ⟶ shelve, delve
sixteen ⟶ seen, between, green
twenty ⟶ plenty

Class Management

Children may use the count-bys chart to help them count at first, but encourage them to count by memory as soon as possible. It is important, however, that children commit the correct numbers to memory from the beginning.

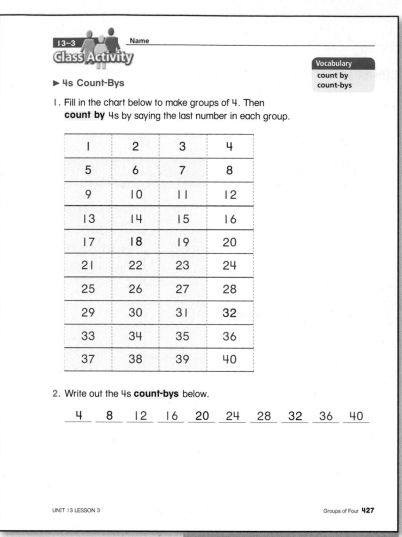

13-3 Class Activity Name ____________

Vocabulary
count by
count-bys

▶ 4s Count-Bys

1. Fill in the chart below to make groups of 4. Then **count by** 4s by saying the last number in each group.

1	2	3	4
5	6	7	8
9	10	11	12
13	14	15	16
17	18	19	20
21	22	23	24
25	26	27	28
29	30	31	32
33	34	35	36
37	38	39	40

2. Write out the 4s **count-bys** below.

4 8 12 16 20 24 28 32 36 40

UNIT 13 LESSON 3 Groups of Four 427

Student Activity Book page 427

▶ 4s Count-Bys WHOLE CLASS

Remind children that working with count-bys will help them solve multiplication problems. Have them fill in the count-by chart on Student Activity Book page 427. The white area contains all of the numbers that are count-bys of 4. The shaded area shows the numbers that are not. Children should then write the count-bys on the lines across the bottom of the page.

Practice Counting By 4s Have children raise one finger as they count each four. Observe that children do this correctly. When the class has reached 40, everyone should have all 10 fingers raised.

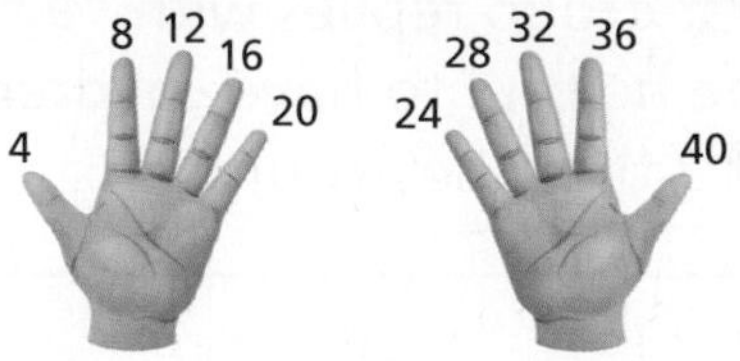

Activity 2

Work with Multiples of 4

▶ Count By 4s to Multiply WHOLE CLASS — Math Talk

Ask for Ideas Ask children to name some things that might come in 4s. Examples include tires on a car, legs on a chair, and corners on a table.

Have children work individually or in **Helping Pairs** to complete Student Activity Book page 428. You can offer assistance as necessary. Children who finish early can make up more problems like the ones on the page to help them practice counting by 4s.

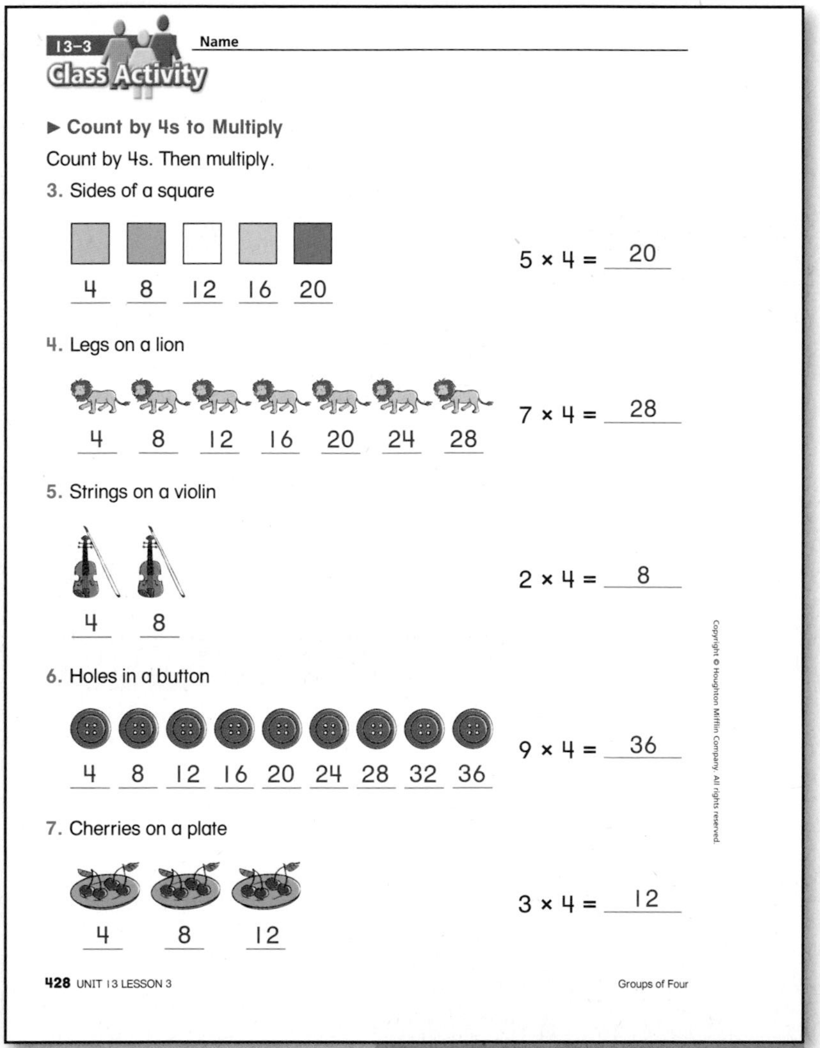
13-3 Class Activity Name ______

▶ Count by 4s to Multiply

Count by 4s. Then multiply.

3. Sides of a square

4 8 12 16 20 — 5 × 4 = 20

4. Legs on a lion

4 8 12 16 20 24 28 — 7 × 4 = 28

5. Strings on a violin

4 8 — 2 × 4 = 8

6. Holes in a button

4 8 12 16 20 24 28 32 36 — 9 × 4 = 36

7. Cherries on a plate

4 8 12 — 3 × 4 = 12

Student Activity Book page 428

25 MINUTES

Goal: Identify things that come in 4s and solve simple multiplication problems.

Materials: Student Activity Book page 428

NCTM Standards:
Number and Operations
Problem Solving
Representation

English Language Learners

Draw 5 groups of 4 apples on the board. Write 5 × 4.

- **Beginning** Say: **5 × 4 means 5 groups of 4 apples.** Have children repeat.
- **Intermediate** Ask: **How many groups?** 5 groups **How many apples in each group?** 4 apples **Does 5 × 4 mean 5 groups of 4?** yes
- **Advanced** Have children tell how 5 × 4 relates to the drawing.

Ongoing Assessment

Ask children to solve 2 × 4 and 5 × 4. Have them explain their thinking aloud as they solve the problems.

2 Going Further

Problem-Solving Strategy: Pictographs

Goal: Read and make a pictograph.

Materials: Student Activity Book pages 429–430

✓ **NCTM Standards:**
Number and Operations
Problem Solving

Teaching Note

Language and Vocabulary *Pictographs* differ from *picture graphs* in that a symbol or picture in a pictograph usually stands for more than 1.

▶ Using Pictographs WHOLE CLASS

You may wish to review pictographs with children. (See Going Further Unit 7 Lesson 2 and Unit 13 Lesson 2.)

Highlight the following:

- A pictograph uses symbols to show information.
- Each symbol in a pictograph represents a certain number.
- The key in a pictograph tells the number each symbol represents.

Direct children's attention to the pictograph on Student Activity Book page 429. Emphasize that the star stands for 4 objects. Have children work individually or in Helping Pairs to complete the page. You may wish to discuss exercise 1 as a class.

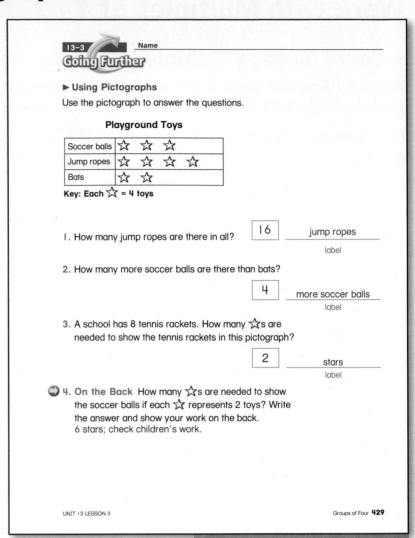

13–3 Going Further Name ____________

▶ Using Pictographs

Use the pictograph to answer the questions.

Playground Toys

Soccer balls	☆ ☆ ☆
Jump ropes	☆ ☆ ☆ ☆
Bats	☆ ☆

Key: Each ☆ = 4 toys

1. How many jump ropes are there in all? 16 jump ropes (label)

2. How many more soccer balls are there than bats? 4 more soccer balls (label)

3. A school has 8 tennis rackets. How many ☆s are needed to show the tennis rackets in this pictograph? 2 stars (label)

4. **On the Back** How many ☆s are needed to show the soccer balls if each ☆ represents 2 toys? Write the answer and show your work on the back.
6 stars; check children's work.

UNIT 13 LESSON 3 Groups of Four **429**

Student Activity Book page 429

Intervention — Activity Card 13-3

Counting Corners
Activity Card 13-3

Work: pairs
Use:
- 10 index cards

1. **Work Together** Draw dots in each corner of the index cards.

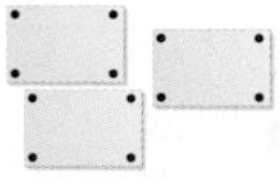

2. Look at three cards. There are four dots on each card. Count by fours to find the total number of dots. Sample answer: 4 + 4 + 4 = 12
3. Write a multiplication sentence to match. Sample answer: 3 × 4 = 12
4. Use the index cards to help you solve these exercises:

2 × 4 = 8	4 × 4 = 16	10 × 4 = 40
1 × 4 = 4	5 × 4 = 20	7 × 4 = 28
8 × 4 = 32	6 × 4 = 24	9 × 4 = 36

Unit 13, Lesson 3

Activity Note Each pair needs ten index cards. Show children how to use the corners on the cards to multiply by four.

Math Writing Prompt
Draw a Picture Draw a picture that shows 5 × 4.

Soar to Success Math Software Support
Warm Up 12.18

On Level — Activity Card 13-3

Repeating Patterns
Activity Card 13-3

Work: pairs
Use:
- 120 Poster (TRB M60)

1. **Work Together** Start at 1 on the 120 Poster and count by 4s.

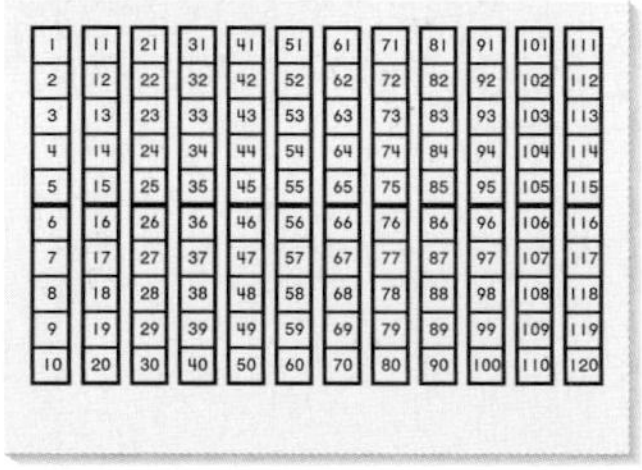

2. Shade the 4s count-bys.
3. **Math Talk** Look at the numbers you shaded. Discuss any patterns you see. Sample answer: the final digits repeat in the pattern 0, 4, 8, 2, 6.

Unit 13, Lesson 3

Activity Note Each pair needs a 120 Poster (TRB M60). Have both children in each pair agree on the numbers they are shading.

Math Writing Prompt
Multiply by 4 Draw a picture for 3 × 4 = ____. Write the 4s count-bys and solve the equation.

Harcourt Mega Math Software Support
Numberopolis: Cross Town Number Line, Level R

Challenge — Activity Card 13-3

Number Puzzles
Activity Card 13-3

Work: individual
Use:
- MathBoard materials

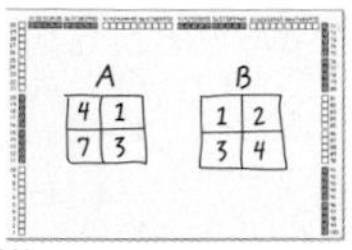

1. Copy each square onto your MathBoard.
2. Use addition, subtraction, and multiplication and the four numbers in problem A to get a final answer of 24. You must use all four numbers.
   For example: 7 × 4 = 28
   28 − 3 = 25
   25 − 1 = 24
   Sample answer: 7 × 3 = 21; 21 + 4 = 25; 25 − 1 = 24
3. Repeat with problem B. Sample answer: 4 × 2 = 8; 8 × 1 = 8; 8 × 3 = 24
4. **Math Talk** Share what you did to find each answer.

Unit 13, Lesson 3

Activity Note Each child needs MathBoard materials. You may want to work through the first problem with children. Challenge children to find other combinations.

Math Writing Prompt
Write Your Own Write a story problem about tires on a car that can be solved with multiplication.

Destination Math Software Support
Course II: Module 2: Unit 2: Skip-Counting to Show Multiplication

3 Homework and Targeted Practice

13–3
Homework **Goal:** Additional Practice

This Homework page provides practice in multiplication and writing 4s count-bys.

13–3 **Homework** Name ____________

Count by 4s. Then multiply.

1. Wings on a dragonfly

4 8 12 16 20 $5 \times 4 =$ 20

2. Sides on a rectangle

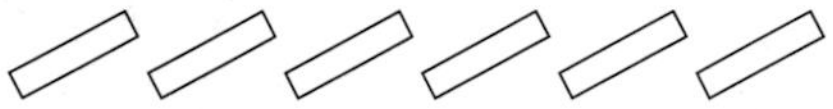

4 8 12 16 20 24 $6 \times 4 =$ 24

3. Legs on a giraffe

4 8 12 16 $4 \times 4 =$ 16

4. Fish in a frying pan

4 8 12 16 20 $5 \times 4 =$ 20

5. Apples on a plate

4 8 12 16 20 24 28 32 $8 \times 4 =$ 32

UNIT 13 LESSON 3 Groups of Four **283**

Homework and Remembering page 283

13–3
Targeted Practice **Goal:** Practice subtraction.

This Targeted Practice page can be used with children who need extra practice with 3-digit subtraction.

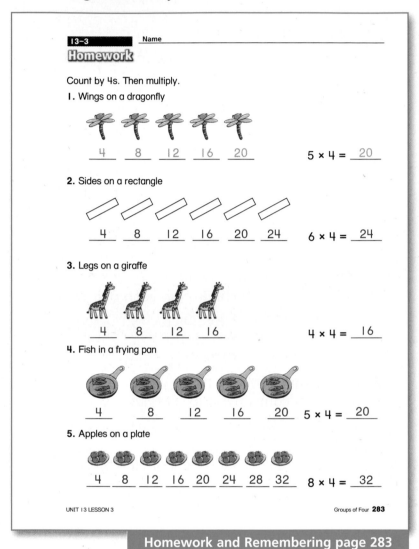

13–3 **Targeted Practice** Name ____________

Subtract.

1. $724 - 358 = 366$

2. $642 - 293 = 349$

3. $663 - 474 = 189$

4. $972 - 389 = 583$

5. $842 - 567 = 275$

6. $\$5.25 - \$2.38 = \$2.87$

284 UNIT 13 LESSON 3 Groups of Four

Homework and Remembering page 284

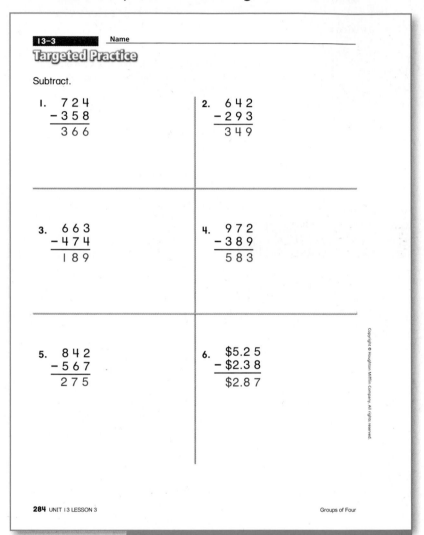

Home or School Activity

Literature Connection

Each Orange Had 8 Slices: A Counting Book Read and discuss *Each Orange Had 8 Slices: A Counting Book* by Paul Giganti, Jr. and Donald Crews (HarperTrophy, 1999). Through illustration and simple text, this book offers a useful introduction to multiplication. Use this book as a visual aid for children to "see" multiplication as repeated addition and groups.

UNIT 13 LESSON 4

Groups of Five and Arrays

REAL WORLD Problem Solving

Lesson Objectives

- Recognize that multiplication is counting by a number.
- Count by 5s.
- Use the array model for multiplication.

Vocabulary
multiplication
count by/count-bys
array

The Day at a Glance

Today's Goals	Materials	
1 Teaching the Lesson **A1:** Say and write the 5s count-bys. **A2:** Explore and make arrays.	**Lesson Activities** Student Activity Book pp. 431–432 Homework and Remembering pp. 285–286 Beans or other countable objects	**Going Further** Activity Cards 13-4 Crayons Inch Grid Paper (TRB M70) MathBoard materials or Number Path Beans or other countable objects Math Journals
2 Going Further ▶ Differentiated Instruction		
3 Homework and Spiral Review		

Use Math Talk today!

Keeping Skills Sharp

Quick Practice — 5 MINUTES

Goal: Count by 4s.

Count By 4s Children can practice the 4s count-bys in the same fashion as the 3s count-bys. Note that another way for children to count by 4s is to have them count by 2s quietly in between every 4. Children often feel secure with the 2s count-bys and can use this knowledge to support their learning of the 4s count-bys. Again, it is important that children commit the correct numbers to memory from the beginning.

Repeated Quick Practice
Use this Quick Practice from a previous lesson.

- ▶ **Count By 3s** (See Unit 13 Lesson 3.)

Daily Routines

2s, 3s, and 4s Count-Bys Draw Arrays, Draw Groups on the 120 Poster, Draw Groups on the Number Path
(See pp. xxviii–xix.)

- ▶ Led by Student Leaders

Money Routine Using the 120 Poster, Using the Money Flip Chart, Using the Number Path, Using Secret Code Cards
(See pp. xxiii–xxv.)

- ▶ Led by Student Leaders

1 Teaching the Lesson

Activity 1

Count By 5s

20 MINUTES

Goal: Say and write the 5s count-bys.

Materials: Student Activity Book page 431

NCTM Standards:
Number and Operations
Problem Solving
Representation

Differentiated Instruction

Extra Help Have a pair of children take turns counting by 5s to find their total number of fingers or toes. Repeat for groups of 3, 4, and 5 children.

Advanced Learners Children who quickly master counting by 5s to 50 can practice counting to 100. They will need 20 fingers to count off the sequence, so they can work with a partner or use their own fingers and toes.

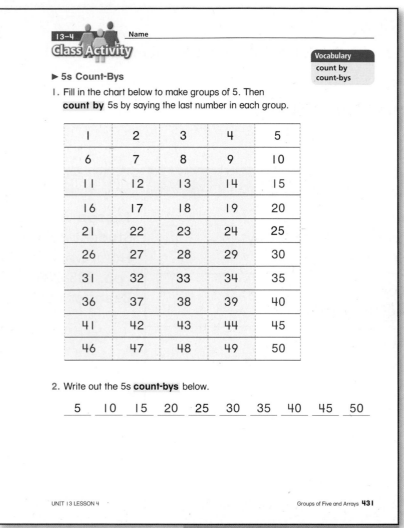

13-4 Class Activity

Name ____________

Vocabulary
count by
count-bys

► 5s Count-Bys

1. Fill in the chart below to make groups of 5. Then **count by** 5s by saying the last number in each group.

1	2	3	4	5
6	7	8	9	10
11	12	13	14	15
16	17	18	19	20
21	22	23	24	25
26	27	28	29	30
31	32	33	34	35
36	37	38	39	40
41	42	43	44	45
46	47	48	49	50

2. Write out the 5s **count-bys** below.

5 10 15 20 25 30 35 40 45 50

UNIT 13 LESSON 4 Groups of Five and Arrays 431

Student Activity Book page 431

► 5s Count-Bys INDIVIDUALS

Remind children that working with count-bys will help them solve multiplication problems. Have children fill in the count-by chart on Student Activity Book page 431. The white area contains all of the numbers that are 5s count-bys. The shaded area shows the numbers that are not. Children should then write the count-bys on the lines across the bottom of the page.

► Practice Counting By 5s WHOLE CLASS

Have children practice counting by 5s. They raise one finger as they count each five. Observe that they count correctly. When the class has reached 50, everyone should have all 10 fingers raised.

Children may use the count-bys chart to help them count at first, but encourage them to count by memory as soon as possible.

Activity 2

My Garden

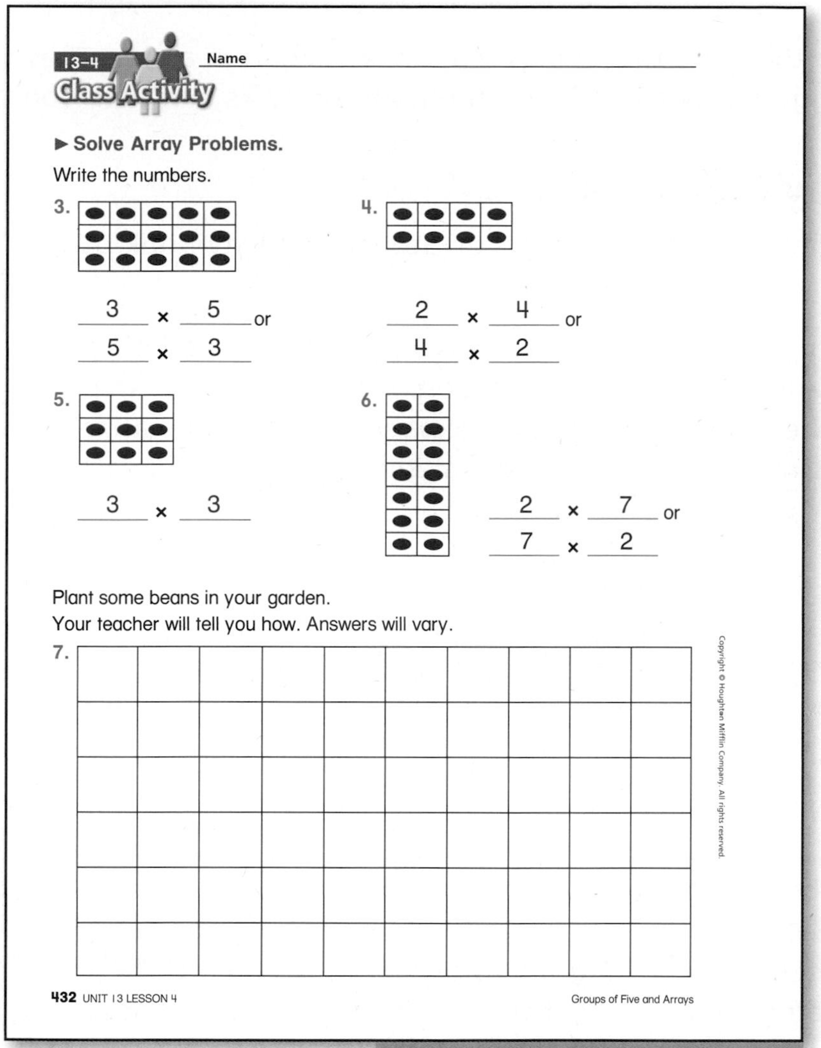

13–4 Class Activity

Name ______________________

► **Solve Array Problems.**

Write the numbers.

3. 3 × 5 or 5 × 3

4. 2 × 4 or 4 × 2

5. 3 × 3

6. 2 × 7 or 7 × 2

Plant some beans in your garden.
Your teacher will tell you how. Answers will vary.

7.

Copyright © Houghton Mifflin Company. All rights reserved.

432 UNIT 13 LESSON 4 Groups of Five and Arrays

Student Activity Book page 432

⏱ **30 MINUTES**

Goal: Explore and make arrays.

Materials: beans (20 per child), Student Activity Book page 432

✔ **NCTM Standards:**
Number and Operations
Problem Solving
Representation

► Introduce Arrays WHOLE CLASS

Explain to children that they will now look at multiplication in a different way, using *arrays.* Explain that an array is an arrangement of objects in rows and columns. Draw a common muffin pan on the board to illustrate an array.

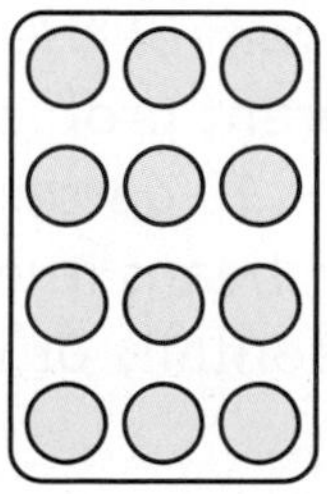

Teaching Note

Language and Vocabulary An *array* is any regular arrangement of objects into rows and columns. Since multiplication combines equal groups, arrays are used in mathematics to represent this operation. The rows show the number in each group and the columns show the number of groups (or vice versa—the columns show the number in each group and the rows show the number of groups). Arrays can also represent division by showing how a number is divided into equal groups.

Activity continued ►

❶ Teaching the Lesson (continued)

Teaching Note

Watch For! Children may not understand why an array with the same number of rows as columns has only one multiplication expression. Have children count the number of rows and columns in a 3 by 3 array, and then write the multiplication expression two times—with the number of rows first and then the number of columns first. Point out that the number expressions are the same, so it is only necessary to write one expression.

English Language Learners

Draw a 3 row × 4 column array on the board. Write *rows* and *columns*. Say: **Arrays have *rows* and *columns*.**

- **Beginning** Say: ***Rows* go across. *Columns* go down.** Have children repeat.
- **Intermediate** Ask: **Do rows go across?** yes **Do columns go across?** no **Do columns go down?** yes
- **Advanced** Have children tell how many rows and columns are in the array.

Ongoing Assessment

Ask children to count by 5s to 50. Have children draw or model a 3 by 4 array, write two different multiplication sentences to show the array, and find the total number.

Have children discuss the properties of this array. They should observe, for example, that there are 3 cups across (3 columns) and 4 cups down (4 rows). There are no cups left over. The array forms a rectangular shape.

Invite children to think of other things that are arranged in arrays. They might suggest eggs in a carton, tiles on the floor, or desks in a classroom.

▶ Solve Array Problems WHOLE CLASS

Direct children's attention to the arrays on Student Activity Book page 432.

Explain that each picture on the page shows a garden marked off into sections. One bean is planted in each section. Ask children how they would describe the arrays of beans. If necessary, you can summarize how many beans go across each row and how many beans go down each column.

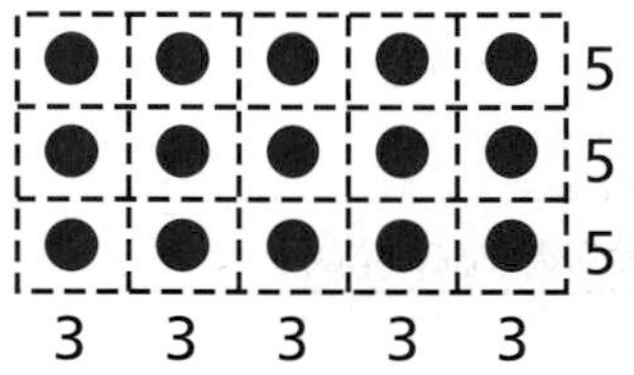

Ask children how they can figure out the total number of beans planted in the first array. Children may call it a 3 × 5 or a 5 × 3 array. Children may count each bean, use count-bys, break the larger array into groups of 5 + 5 + 5 or 3 + 3 + 3 + 3 + 3 and add the numbers together, or devise other strategies for finding the total number of beans. They can use the same strategy or a different strategy to work with the other arrays on the page.

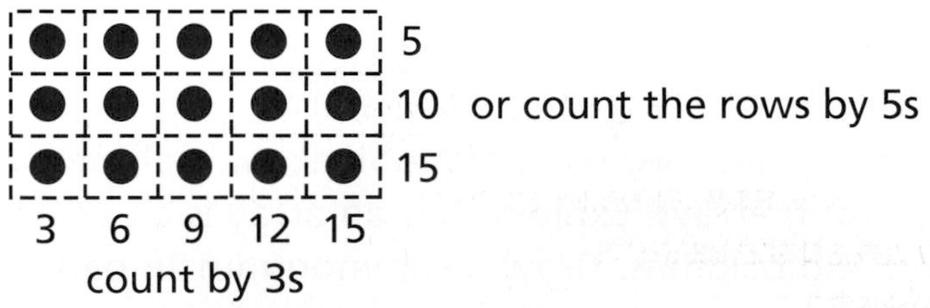

In the larger garden at the bottom of the page, direct children to place beans to illustrate several different problems. Begin with a 3 × 6 garden, then a 4 × 3 garden, then a 2 × 10 garden, and a 5 × 4 garden. Have them determine the number of beans in each one. It does not matter if the gardens are arranged horizontally or vertically, as long as the dimensions are correct.

As time permits, have children make up other garden arrays and discuss their strategies for solving the multiplication problems they represent. Encourage children to explain their thinking and ask questions.

2 Going Further

Differentiated Instruction

Intervention — Activity Card 13-4

Colorful Array — Activity Card 13-4

Work: (group)
Use:
- crayons
- Inch Grid Paper (TRB M70)

Choose:
- 1
- 2
- 3

1. (1) Choose a crayon and draw five circles in a row on the inch grid paper.
2. (2) Choose another crayon color and draw five circles under the first circles.
3. Repeat for each child in the group.
4. **Work Together** Write the multiplication expression for the array.

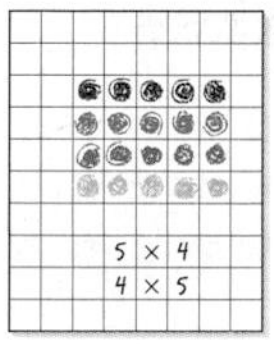

5. Repeat with a different number of circles.

Unit 13, Lesson 4 —

Activity Note Each child needs a different color crayon and the group needs Inch Grid Paper (TRB M70).

Math Writing Prompt

Explain Your Thinking An array of beans has 3 rows and 2 columns. How many beans are in the array? Explain how you found your answer.

Soar to Success Math **Software Support**

Warm Up 12.20

On Level — Activity Card 13-4

5s on the Number Path — Activity Card 13-4

Work: (pair)
Use:
- MathBoard materials or Number Path

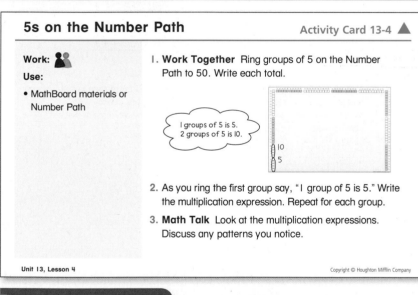

1. **Work Together** Ring groups of 5 on the Number Path to 50. Write each total.

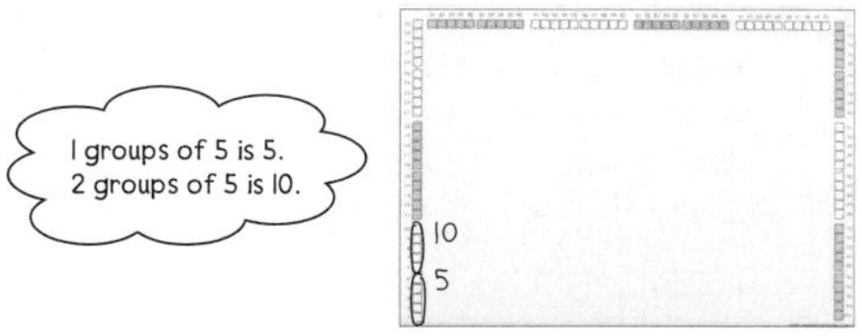

2. As you ring the first group say, "1 group of 5 is 5." Write the multiplication expression. Repeat for each group.
3. **Math Talk** Look at the multiplication expressions. Discuss any patterns you notice.

Unit 13, Lesson 4 —

Activity Note Each pair needs MathBoard materials or Number Path (TRB M51). Have pairs compare their multiplication expressions.

Math Writing Prompt

Draw an Array Write a problem about planting beans in a garden that can be solved using an array. Draw the array.

Harcourt MegaMath Grades K-6 **Software Support**

Numberopolis: Cross Town Number Line, Level Q

Challenge — Activity Card 13-4

The Different Ways of Arrays — Activity Card 13-4

Work: (group)
Use:
- 80 beans or other countable objects

1. Each (child): Take 12 beans.
2. Each (child): Use the beans to make an array.

$12 \times 1 = 12$

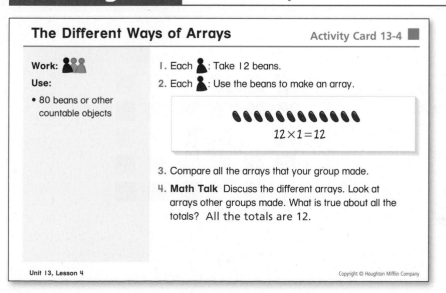

3. Compare all the arrays that your group made.
4. **Math Talk** Discuss the different arrays. Look at arrays other groups made. What is true about all the totals? All the totals are 12.

Unit 13, Lesson 4 —

Activity Note Each group member needs 12 beans or other countable objects. Suggest any arrays the groups may not have made.

Math Writing Prompt

Another Array An array of buttons is arranged in 4 rows and 4 columns. Draw a picture to show an array with the same number of buttons but a different number of rows and columns.

Destination Math **Software Support**

Course II: Module 2: Unit 2: Repeated Addition and Arrays

3 Homework and Spiral Review

13–4 Homework **Goal:** Additional Practice

This Homework page provides practice in 5s count-bys and multiplication.

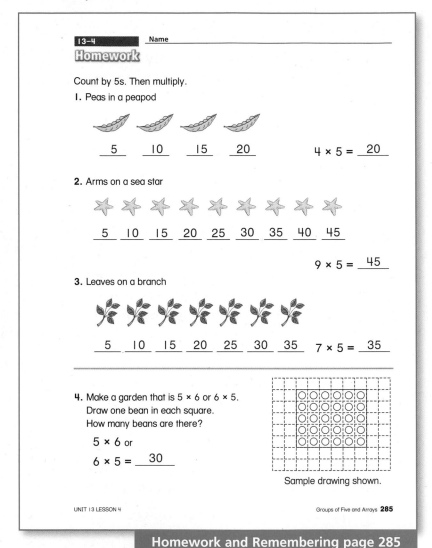

13–4 **Homework** Name ______

Count by 5s. Then multiply.

1. Peas in a peapod

5 10 15 20 $4 \times 5 = 20$

2. Arms on a sea star

5 10 15 20 25 30 35 40 45

$9 \times 5 = 45$

3. Leaves on a branch

5 10 15 20 25 30 35 $7 \times 5 = 35$

4. Make a garden that is 5×6 or 6×5. Draw one bean in each square. How many beans are there?

5×6 or

$6 \times 5 = 30$

Sample drawing shown.

UNIT 13 LESSON 4 Groups of Five and Arrays **285**

Homework and Remembering page 285

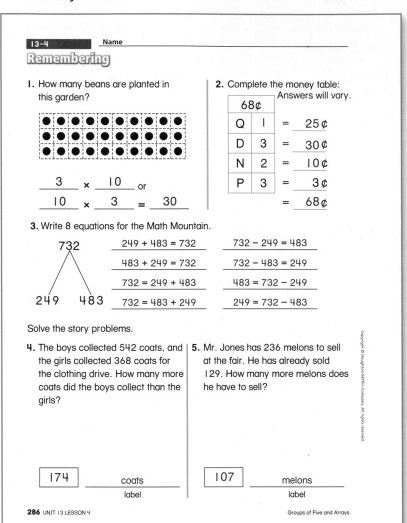

13–4 Remembering **Goal:** Spiral Review

This Remembering activity would be appropriate anytime after today's lesson.

13–4 **Remembering** Name ______

1. How many beans are planted in this garden?

3×10 or

$10 \times 3 = 30$

2. Complete the money table: Answers will vary.

68¢			
Q	1	=	25¢
D	3	=	30¢
N	2	=	10¢
P	3	=	3¢
		=	68¢

3. Write 8 equations for the Math Mountain.

732; 249, 483

$249 + 483 = 732$ $732 - 249 = 483$

$483 + 249 = 732$ $732 - 483 = 249$

$732 = 249 + 483$ $483 = 732 - 249$

$732 = 483 + 249$ $249 = 732 - 483$

Solve the story problems.

4. The boys collected 542 coats, and the girls collected 368 coats for the clothing drive. How many more coats did the boys collect than the girls?

174 coats (label)

5. Mr. Jones has 236 melons to sell at the fair. He has already sold 129. How many more melons does he have to sell?

107 melons (label)

286 UNIT 13 LESSON 4 Groups of Five and Arrays

Homework and Remembering page 286

Home or School Activity

Art Connection

Mosaic Arrays Explain that a mosaic is a type of art made by attaching small pieces of colored glass or tile to a larger surface. Have children cut out 1-inch paper squares in different colors and arrange them in an array on a sheet of paper to create a mosaic. Then have them write a multiplication sentence to match their picture.

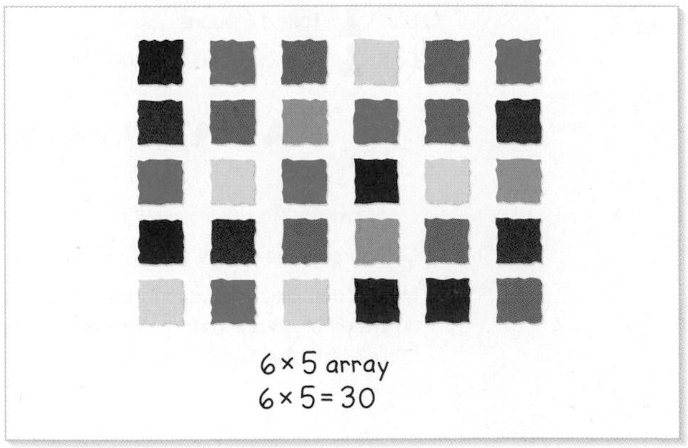

UNIT 13 LESSON 5

Work with Arrays

REAL WORLD Problem Solving

Vocabulary
array
count by/count-bys
multiplication

Lesson Objective

- Use count-bys and arrays to solve multiplication problems.

The Day at a Glance

Today's Goals	Materials	
1 Teaching the Lesson **A:** Use and make arrays to solve problems. Relate arrays to multiplication.	**Lesson Activities** Student Activity Book p. 433 Homework and Remembering pp. 287–288 Quick Quiz 1 (Assessment Guide) Beans or other countable objects MathBoard materials or 10 × 10 Grid	**Going Further** Activity Cards 13-5 Student Activity Book p. 434 Beans or other countable objects MathBoard materials Math Journals
2 Going Further ▶ Extension: Mystery Multiplication ▶ Differentiated Instruction		
3 Homework and Targeted Practice		

Use Math Talk today!

Keeping Skills Sharp

Quick Practice — 5 MINUTES

Goal: Count by 3s.

Count By 3s Divide the class into two groups. You can appoint a **Student Leader** for each group or take volunteers. Have the class count by 3s. The first group starts by saying the number 3. The second group responds with "6." The first group replies with "9," and so on until they have reached 30. You may wish to repeat the exercise, asking the second group to begin this time. (See Unit 13 Lesson 3.)

It may be helpful to have children use their fingers to mark off each multiple of 3 that they count.

Repeated Quick Practice
Use this Quick Practice from a previous lesson.

- ▶ Count By 4s (See Unit 13 Lesson 4.)

Daily Routines

2s, 3s, and 4s Count-Bys Draw Arrays, Draw Groups on the 120 Poster, Draw Groups on the Number Path (See pp. xxviii–xix.)

- ▶ Led by Student Leaders

Money Routine Using the 120 Poster, Using the Money Flip Chart, Using the Number Path, Using Secret Code Cards (See pp. xxiii–xxv.)

- ▶ Led by Student Leaders

Teaching the Lesson

Activity

The Apple Orchard

50 MINUTES

Goal: Use and make arrays to solve problems. Relate arrays to multiplication.

Materials: beans or other small countable objects, MathBoard materials or 10 × 10 Grid, Student Activity Book page 433

NCTM Standards:
Number and Operations
Problem Solving
Representation

Teaching Note

Watch For! Be alert to children who want to count every tree in the picture to find the total number. This strategy may be useful at first to see patterns in the numbers or to check an answer, but children should very quickly begin to use count-bys, repeated addition, or patterns in the array to find the answers in a more systematic (and more rapid) way.

English Language Learners

Draw a 6 row × 3 column array, Write *array*.

- **Beginning** Say: **An *array* shows items in rows and columns.** Have children repeat.
- **Intermediate** Ask: **Does an array show items in rows and columns?** yes **Is this an *array*?** yes
- **Advanced** Have children tell how an array shows items.

► Use Arrays to Solve Problems WHOLE CLASS

Review Arrays Ask children to describe an array. an arrangement of items in rows and columns Have a child draw a simple array on th board and name it according to its dimensions (for example, a 3 × 5 array).

Solve Problems Refer children to Student Activity Book page 433. Explain that the array shows Mr. and Mrs. Green's apple orchard. Ask children how they could find the total number of apple trees in the orchard without counting each one. Some children will add 5 + 5 + 5 + 5 + 5 + 5 + 5 + 5. Others will count by 5s. Some will add 8 + 8 + 8 + 8 + 8 or count by 8s. Space is provided for children to show the count-bys for both 5 and 8 and the corresponding multiplication equations. Children should realize that no matter how they solve the problem the answer will be *40 apple trees.*

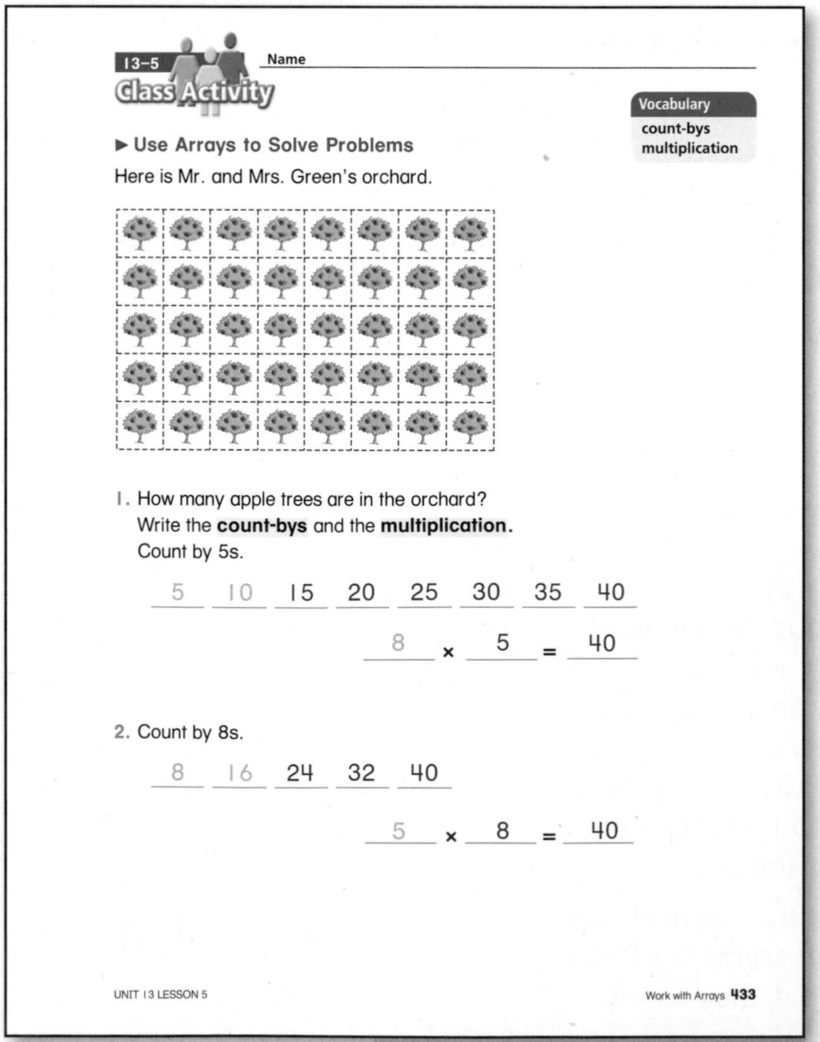
13–5 Class Activity Name

Vocabulary
count-bys
multiplication

► Use Arrays to Solve Problems

Here is Mr. and Mrs. Green's orchard.

1. How many apple trees are in the orchard?
Write the **count-bys** and the **multiplication**.
Count by 5s.

5 10 15 20 25 30 35 40

8 × 5 = 40

2. Count by 8s.

8 16 24 32 40

5 × 8 = 40

UNIT 13 LESSON 5 Work with Arrays 433

Student Activity Book page 433

▶ Make Arrays on MathBoards PAIRS Math Talk

Have children form **Helping Pairs**. They will need their MathBoards and a supply of beans or other small countable objects.

Tell children that Mr. and Mrs. Green have 36 more trees that they want to plant in a new array. They want the class to help them figure out some ways that they can arrange the trees with none left over.

Children should begin by counting out exactly 36 beans. They should then place the beans on the inch-grid portion of their MathBoards in any array that uses all of the beans in even rows and columns.

Children should write the count-bys and a multiplication equation that shows the arrangement of trees in their array. This illustration shows a 4 × 9 (or 9 × 4) array.

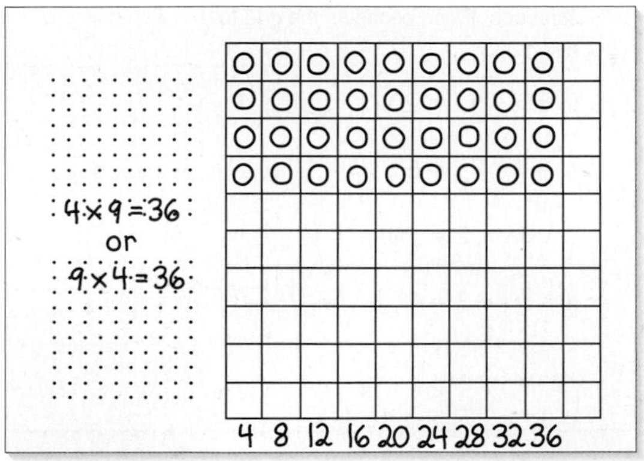

Ask volunteers to explain to the class how they solved the problem. Once children have discovered a suitable array, they may mark the position of each bean on their MathBoards with a marker. This way, they can pick up their Mathboards to show their classmates.

You can repeat the exercise with other numbers of "trees" (up to 50) for Mr. and Mrs. Green to plant in their orchard.

Teaching Note

Language and Vocabulary It might help children to know the names for the numbers in a multiplication equation. The numbers multiplied together are called *factors* and the result of multiplying factors is called the *product*. In the example 2 × 3 = 6, 2 and 3 are factors and 6 is the product. Children need not use these terms, but may find them useful when they describe how their arrays relate to multiplication equations.

Ongoing Assessment

Ask children to use beans to make an array on their MathBoards. Have them write an appropriate multiplication sentence and find the total number. Have children explain their thinking aloud as they use the array to find the total number.

Quick Quiz

See Assessment Guide for Unit 13 Quick Quiz 1.

2 Going Further

Extension: Mystery Multiplication

Goal: Use arrays to solve equations.

Materials: beans or other countable objects, Student Activity Book page 434

✓ **NCTM Standards:**
Number and Operations
Problem Solving
Representation

Differentiated Instruction

Advanced Learners Finding unknown numbers in multiplication sentences develops algebraic thinking. It can also be used to introduce the concept of division and division notation. If children are ready for these concepts, use the example on Student Activity Book page 408 to show how the grid also represents a group of 12 objects split into 3 equal groups (columns). Write 12 ÷ 3 = ☐. Relate the array to the division equation. Explain that the number of rows in the array shows how many objects are in each group and write 12 ÷ 3 = 4.

▶ Introduce Mystery Multiplication

WHOLE CLASS

Direct children's attention to Student Activity Book page 434. Work through exercises 1–4 together as a class. Have children work individually or in Helping Pairs to complete the rest of the page. Children should use the beans and the grid at the bottom of the page to help them solve exercises 5–8.

Be sure children understand that in exercises 5–8, they are not looking for the total number of beans, but rather the number of beans in one row or column.

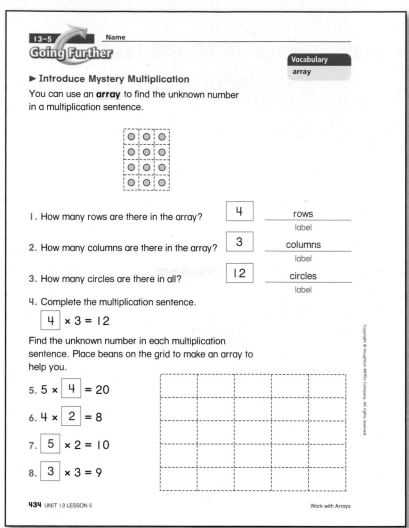

13-5 Going Further Name

Vocabulary
array

▶ Introduce Mystery Multiplication

You can use an **array** to find the unknown number in a multiplication sentence.

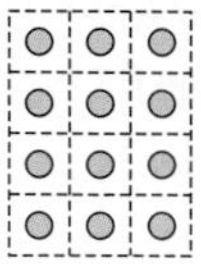

1. How many rows are there in the array? 4 rows (label)
2. How many columns are there in the array? 3 columns (label)
3. How many circles are there in all? 12 circles (label)
4. Complete the multiplication sentence.
   4 × 3 = 12

Find the unknown number in each multiplication sentence. Place beans on the grid to make an array to help you.

5. 5 × 4 = 20
6. 4 × 2 = 8
7. 5 × 2 = 10
8. 3 × 3 = 9

434 UNIT 13 LESSON 5 Work with Arrays

Student Activity Book page 434

Intervention Activity Card 13-5

Quick Arrays

Activity Card 13-5

Work:

Use:

- MathBoard materials or lined paper

1. **Work Together** Make three horizontal line segments.
2. Make four vertical line segments that cross the horizontal line segments. Place a dot at each point where the lines intersect.

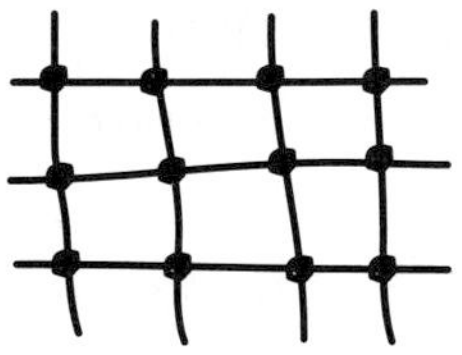

3. Use the array of dots to solve 3×4. Count the number of dots.
4. Draw dot arrays to solve 3×2, 2×5, 4×2, and 3×3.

Unit 13, Lesson 5

Activity Note Each pair needs MathBoard materials or lined paper. Help children draw the first dot array.

Math Writing Prompt

Show Your Work Mrs. Green planted apple trees in an array with 4 rows and 5 columns. How many trees did she plant in all? Draw a picture and explain how you found the answer.

Soar to Success Math **Software Support**

Warm Up 12.23

On Level Activity Card 13-5

12 Beans

Activity Card 13-5

Work:

Use:

- 12 dried beans
- MathBoard materials

1. **Work Together** Find three different arrays. Use all 12 beans in each array.
2. Write two different multiplication sentences for each array.
3. Each : Write a story problem that can be solved using one of the arrays.
4. Trade story problems and solve.

Unit 13, Lesson 5

Activity Note Each pair needs 12 dried beans and MathBoard materials. Challenge other children to solve the story problems that children create.

Math Writing Prompt

Correct the Error Dan says that 4×6 is 25. Draw a picture and use words to explain how you know Dan is incorrect.

Harcourt MegaMath Grades K-6 **Software Support**

Country Countdown: Counting Critters, Level W

Challenge Activity Card 13-5

Square Arrays

Activity Card 13-5

Work:

1. **Work Together** Draw an array for 1×1. Write the equation for the array.
2. Draw an array for 2×2 and write the equation.

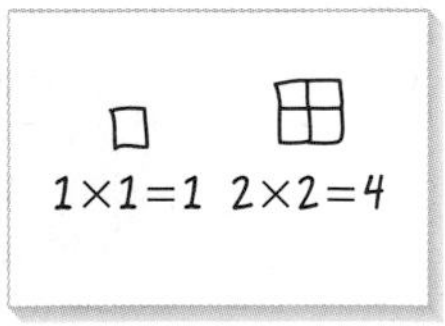

3. Draw arrays for 3×3 and 4×4. What do you notice about all these arrays? Why do you think these numbers are called square numbers?
4. Draw the next three square numbers. 25, 36, and 49

Unit 13, Lesson 5

Activity Note Check that children draw arrays in squares. Discuss what square numbers are and why they are called square numbers.

Math Writing Prompt

Investigate Math Explain how you could use an array to solve 15×4.

DESTINATION Math **Software Support**

Course II: Module 2: Unit 2: Repeated Addition and Arrays

1 Teaching the Lesson

Activity 1

Explore the Language of Comparison

30 MINUTES

Goal: Ask comparison questions based on a picture graph using familiar and new terms such as *half, double, twice,* and *equal shares.*

NCTM Standards:
Data Analysis and Probability
Number and Operations
Communication

English Language Learners

Draw a group of 8 squares and a group of 3 squares. Write *comparison*.

- **Beginning** Say: ***Comparison* means how things are alike or different.** Have children repeat.
- **Intermediate** Ask: **Can we make a *comparison* of how the groups are alike?** yes **Can we make a *comparison* of how the groups are different?** yes
- **Advanced** Have children make a *comparison* between the groups.

▶ Ask Comparison Questions About a Graph

WHOLE CLASS

Math Talk

A picture graph provides a clear visual representation of a comparison situation. Explain to children that graphs are good for comparing things and that in this activity they will talk about graphs and make some comparisons similar to the comparisons they made in previous lessons. Point out that they will also practice some special words that are often used to compare things.

Draw the graph below on the board. Then have children make up a comparison problem based on it.

Maria	★	★	★	★						
Carlos	★	★	★	★	★	★	★	★		

- Who would like to make up a story problem about the graph I just drew? Possible response: Carlos has 8 stars. Maria has 4. How many more stars does Carlos have than Maria?
- Who would like to circle the extra stars that Carlos has? (The volunteer should circle the 4 extra stars.)

Review with children the different ways to ask comparison questions.

- There are many ways we can ask questions. We can ask who has more or we can ask who has fewer.
- We can also ask how many more one person needs in order to have as many as the other person. Another way to say that is to ask how many one person would have to lose to have as many as the other person.
- Who would like to ask one of these questions? Remember that Maria has 4 stars and Carlos has 8 stars. Responses will vary.

Remind children that they can say each comparing sentence in two different ways. Use these questions to help children generate pairs of statements.

How many more stars does Carlos have than Maria?
How many fewer stars does Maria have than Carlos?

How many stars does Maria have to get to have as many as Carlos?
How many stars does Carlos have to lose to have as many as Maria?

▶ Introduce New Comparison Language

WHOLE CLASS

Math Talk

Introduce the term *twice.*

- Here's a word we haven't used before. The word is *twice.* Carlos has *twice* as many stars as Maria. What do you think the word *twice* means? Maria has 4 stars. Carlos has 4 stars like Maria. Then he has the same amount again. 4 + 4 = 8. He has two times as many.
- Who would like to draw a picture on the board to show the meaning of *twice*?

Change the number of stars that Maria has to allow children to demonstrate their understanding of the concept *twice.*

- This time, let's say that Maria has 5 stars. If Carlos has *twice* as many stars as Maria, how many stars does Carlos have? 10 stars
- Who would like to make up another problem using the word *twice*? (As you work through other examples with the class, alter the graph to match their examples.)

Ask for Ideas Introduce the term *double.* Allow children to define *double* in their own words and to draw a diagram on the board. Then have children generate new problems using the word *double.* Children should realize that *twice* and *double* have the same meaning.

Repeat the above process, introducing the term *half.*

- Here's the situation again. Carlos has 8 stars and Maria has 4 stars. We can say the problem another way. Let's use the word *half* this time. Maria has *half* as many stars as Carlos. What does the word *half* mean? If we take Carlos's stars and put them into two equal groups, one of those groups is called *half.*
- Who would like to draw a picture on the board to show the meaning of *half*?
- Who would like to make up another problem using the word *half*?

Finally, draw a picture on the board to show equal shares. Then repeat the above process to introduce the term *equal shares.*

- This time Carlos and Maria have equal shares. What do you think the term *equal shares* means? Carlos and Maria both have the same amount.
- How many stars will Maria have if Carlos has 8 stars? 8 stars
- How many stars will Carlos have if Maria has 10 stars? 10 stars

Teaching Note

Language and Vocabulary
Comparison problems are often difficult for children because they do not clearly understand the situation or the language. To minimize the difficulty, use a wide variety of phrases that children may encounter in such problems in order to help them become more familiar with various ways of describing comparison situations.

Ongoing Assessment

Present the following situation and ask children to answer each of the questions below.

Raymond has 6 pencils.

- ▶ If Tanya has half as many pencils, how many does she have?
- ▶ If Ling has twice as many pencils, how many does he have?
- ▶ If Raymond and Maru have equal shares of pencils, how many does Maru have?

3 Homework and Spiral Review

13–6 Homework **Goal:** Additional Practice

This Homework page provides practice solving comparison problems containing the terms *half, double, twice,* and *equal shares.*

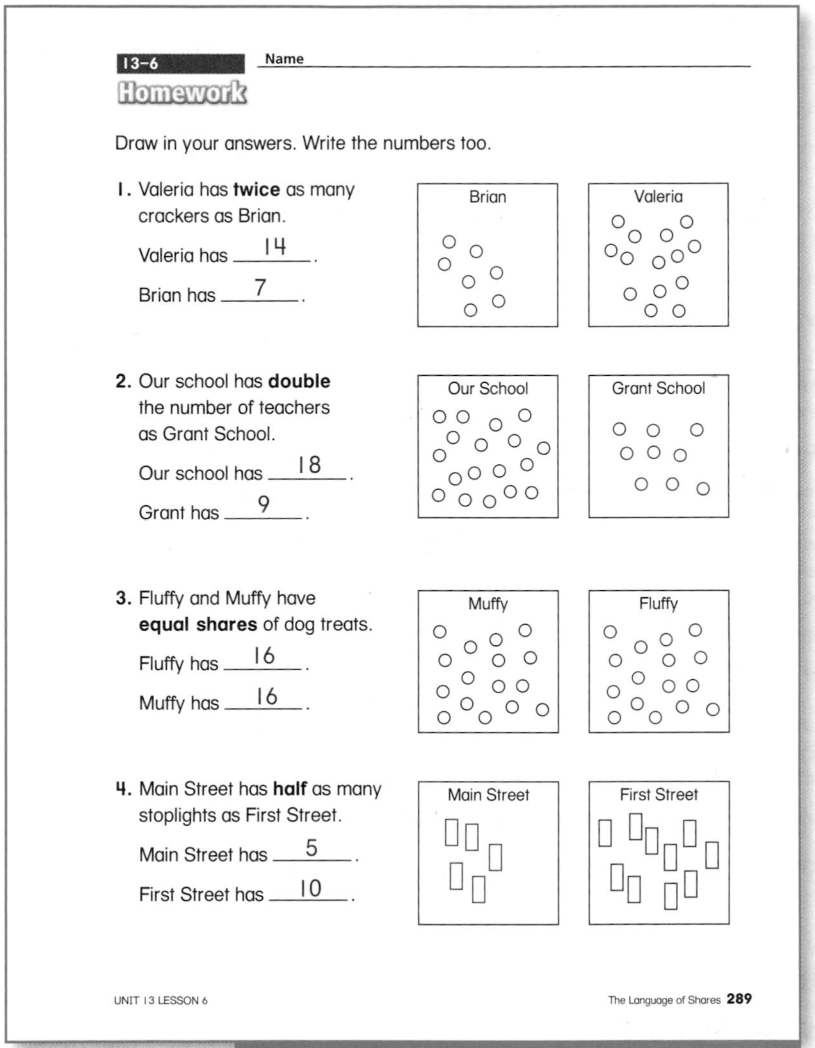

13–6 Name ____

Homework

Draw in your answers. Write the numbers too.

1. Valeria has **twice** as many crackers as Brian.
   Valeria has 14.
   Brian has 7.
   (Brian | Valeria)

2. Our school has **double** the number of teachers as Grant School.
   Our school has 18.
   Grant has 9.
   (Our School | Grant School)

3. Fluffy and Muffy have **equal shares** of dog treats.
   Fluffy has 16.
   Muffy has 16.
   (Muffy | Fluffy)

4. Main Street has **half** as many stoplights as First Street.
   Main Street has 5.
   First Street has 10.
   (Main Street | First Street)

UNIT 13 LESSON 6 The Language of Shares **289**

Homework and Remembering page 289

13–6 Remembering **Goal:** Spiral Review

This Remembering activity would be appropriate anytime after today's lesson.

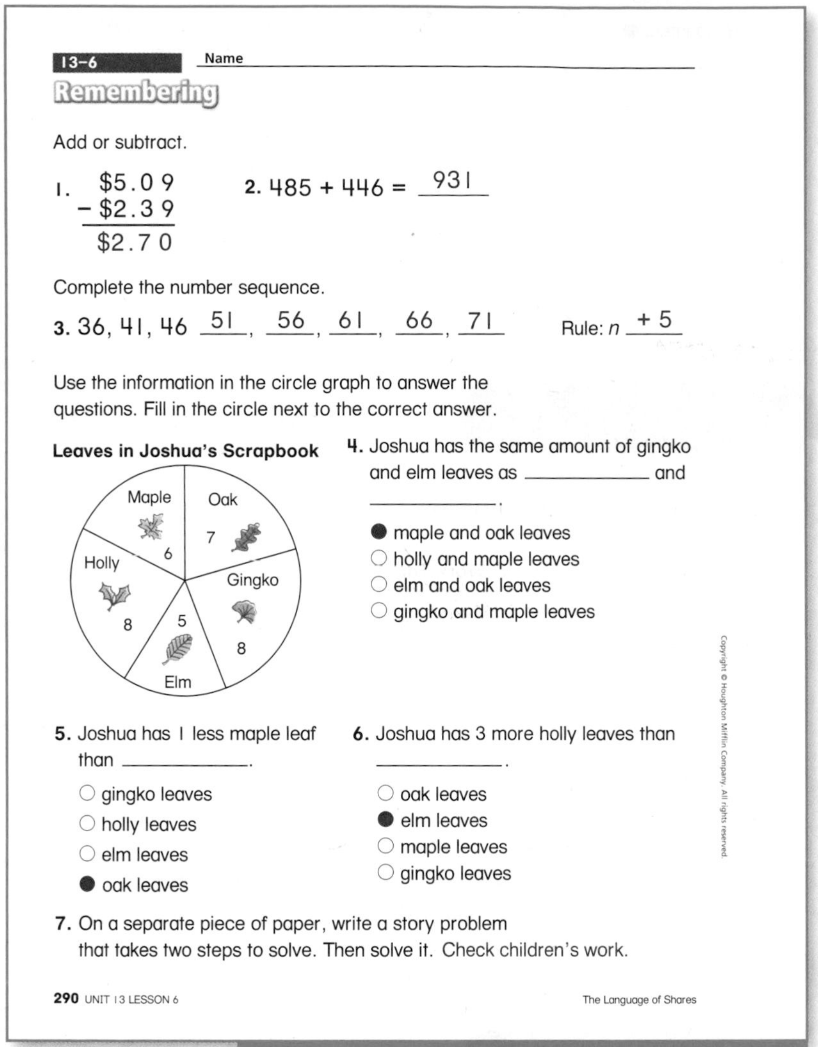

13–6 Name ____

Remembering

Add or subtract.

1. $5.09 − $2.39 = $2.70

2. 485 + 446 = 931

Complete the number sequence.

3. 36, 41, 46, 51, 56, 61, 66, 71 Rule: *n* + 5

Use the information in the circle graph to answer the questions. Fill in the circle next to the correct answer.

Leaves in Joshua's Scrapbook

4. Joshua has the same amount of gingko and elm leaves as ____ and ____.
   - ● maple and oak leaves
   - ○ holly and maple leaves
   - ○ elm and oak leaves
   - ○ gingko and maple leaves

5. Joshua has 1 less maple leaf than ____.
   - ○ gingko leaves
   - ○ holly leaves
   - ○ elm leaves
   - ● oak leaves

6. Joshua has 3 more holly leaves than ____.
   - ○ oak leaves
   - ● elm leaves
   - ○ maple leaves
   - ○ gingko leaves

7. On a separate piece of paper, write a story problem that takes two steps to solve. Then solve it. Check children's work.

290 UNIT 13 LESSON 6 The Language of Shares

Homework and Remembering page 290

Home or School Activity

Literature Connection

Sharing Cookies *The Doorbell Rang* by Pat Hutchins (HarperTrophy, 1989) can be used as an effective way to extend the topic of equal shares.

Read or have a child read this book aloud. As the book is being read, have children use counters to show how many cookies each child in the story can have. This number will change each time the doorbell rings.

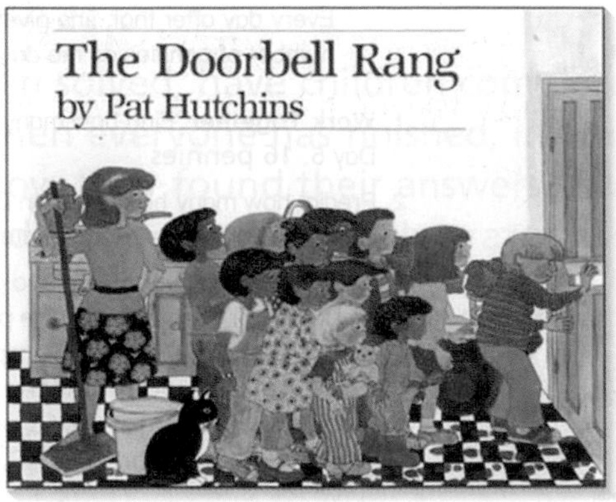

UNIT 13 LESSON 7

Model Division

Lesson Objectives

- **Understand the meaning of division as equal shares and as repeated subtraction.**
- **Use models to solve simple division problems.**

Vocabulary
divide

The Day at a Glance

Today's Goals	Materials	
1 Teaching the Lesson **A1:** Model division as equal shares **A2:** Model division as equal groups. **A3:** Model division with repeated subtraction.	**Lesson Activities** Student Activity Book pp. 437–438 Homework and Remembering pp. 291–292 Counters	**Going Further** Activity Cards 13-7 Counters Index cards Number cubes Math Journals
2 Going Further ▶ Differentiated Instruction		
3 Homework and Spiral Review		

Use Math Talk today!

Keeping Skills Sharp

Quick Practice 5 MINUTES

Goal: Monitor children's progress in addition and subtraction with 3-digit numbers.

Quick Check Monitor children's progress with a brief quick check. Write these exercises on the board.

$$\begin{array}{r} 106 \\ +578 \\ \hline 684 \end{array} \qquad \begin{array}{r} 732 \\ -\ 69 \\ \hline 663 \end{array}$$

Daily Routines

2s, 3s, and 4s Count-Bys Draw Arrays, Draw Groups on the 120 Poster, Draw Groups on the Number Path
(See pp. xxviii–xxix.)

▶ Led by Student Leaders

Money Routine Using the 120 Poster, Using the Money Flip Chart, Using the Number Path, Using Secret Code Cards
(See pp. xxiii–xxv.)

▶ Led by Student Leaders

1 Teaching the Lesson

Activity 1

Equal Shares

15 MINUTES

Goal: Model division as equal shares.

Materials: counters

NCTM Standards:
Number Sense
Representation

English Language Learners

Write *fair shares* on the board. Draw 1 child with 4 cookies and 1 child with 2 cookies.

- **Beginning** Ask: **Do they have the same number of cookies?** no **Is this *fair*?** no
- **Intermediate** Ask: **Is this an example of *fair shares*?** no **What is *fair*?** 3 cookies each
- **Advanced** Have children tell what would be a *fair share*.

Math Talk in Action

Tell about a time you used fair or equal shares.

Kishore: My friends and I took baseball cards and just kept passing them around in a circle so we would all have the same.

Alisha: My family all took some cookies. Then we each counted and gave some away to someone who had less until we all had the same.

Brian: There were only 2 slices of pizza so my brother and I each took 1 slice.

▶ What Is Division? WHOLE CLASS / SMALL GROUPS

Begin by asking children what they know about dividing or division. They may mention sharing food or toys. Explain that in math, division is the opposite of multiplication, and guide them through this example.

Provide each group with 15 counters.

- You know that 5 groups of 3 make 15. How many groups of 3 pencils can you make from 15 pencils? 5 groups of 3 pencils

Have children show how 15 counters can be divided into 5 groups of 3.

▶ Equal Shares SMALL GROUPS

Provide 25 counters to each group.

Tell students to make a pile of 20 counters.

- Select 4 people in your group.
- Make fair shares with the counters.
- How many counters did each person get? 5

Tell students to make a pile of 12 counters.

- Select 3 people in your group.
- Make fair shares with the counters.
- How many counters did each person get? 4

Tell students to make a pile of 24 counters.

- Select 4 people in your group.
- Make fair shares with the counters.
- How many counters did each person get? 6

Activity 2

Equal Groups

13-7 Class Activity Name ____________

Vocabulary
divide

Use counters to model each problem.

1. Pedro has 16 cards. How can he share the cards equally with Erik, Dana, and Audrey? Draw a picture.

   Drawings will vary but should show 4 groups of 4.

You can **divide** 16 cards into 4 groups of 4.

2. There are 20 markers. There are 5 friends. How can they share the markers equally?

   5 groups of 4

3. There are 16 marbles in a jar. How can Nick and Warrick share the marbles equally?

   2 groups of 8

4. There are 24 stickers. There are 3 children. How can they share the stickers equally?

   3 groups of 8

5. Use 12 counters. Show different ways you can make equal groups.

   Check children's work.

UNIT 13 LESSON 7 Model Division 437

Student Activity Book page 437

15 MINUTES

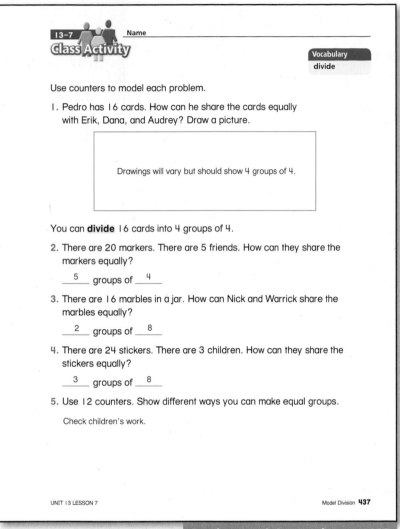

Goal: Model division as equal groups.

Materials: counters, Student Activity Book page 437

NCTM Standards:
Number Sense
Representation

▶ Make Equal Groups PAIRS

Direct children's attention to Student Activity Book page 437, Exercise 1. Instruct children to take 16 counters for the 16 cards.

- How many children are there? 4 children
- How many groups do they need? 4 groups
- Make 4 equal groups.
- How many cards are in each group? 4 cards
- Draw a picture to show what you did.

For Exercise 2 have children use 20 counters to represent the markers.

- How many groups do they need? 5 groups
- How many markers are in each group? 4 markers

Use similar questioning for Exercises 3 and 4.

Teaching Note

Have children look at Exercises 1 and 3. Explain that sometimes there is more than one way to make equal shares from a number. For Exercise 5 explain that they should draw as many different ways to make equal groups of 12 as they can.

Activity 3

Introduce Repeated Subtraction

15 MINUTES

Goal: Model division with repeated subtraction.

Materials: Student Activity Book page 438, scrap paper, counters (optional)

NCTM Standard:
Number Sense

Alternate Approach

Use Counters Children can use counters to model repeated subtraction. Have them start with a group of 15. Have them subtract 3 at a time. Have children count how many times they could subtract 3.

Ongoing Assessment

Assess children's understanding of division. Ask questions such as:

- How can Sarah and Frank share 12 stickers equally? 6 each
- How can Bill, Cindy and Jeff share 15 crackers equally? 5 each

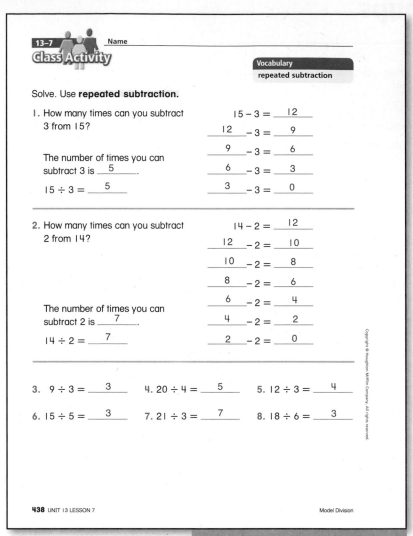

13–7 Class Activity Name ____________

Vocabulary
repeated subtraction

Solve. Use **repeated subtraction.**

1. How many times can you subtract 3 from 15?

15 − 3 = 12
12 − 3 = 9
9 − 3 = 6
6 − 3 = 3
3 − 3 = 0

The number of times you can subtract 3 is 5.

15 ÷ 3 = 5

2. How many times can you subtract 2 from 14?

14 − 2 = 12
12 − 2 = 10
10 − 2 = 8
8 − 2 = 6
6 − 2 = 4
4 − 2 = 2
2 − 2 = 0

The number of times you can subtract 2 is 7.

14 ÷ 2 = 7

3. 9 ÷ 3 = 3 4. 20 ÷ 4 = 5 5. 12 ÷ 3 = 4

6. 15 ÷ 5 = 3 7. 21 ÷ 3 = 7 8. 18 ÷ 6 = 3

Student Activity Book page 438

▶ Repeated Subtraction WHOLE CLASS

Have children find Student Activity Book page 438. Explain that to find how many groups of 3 are in the number 15 you can find the number of times you can subtract 3. Work the subtractions for Exercise 1.

- How many times did you subtract 3? 5
- What is 15 divided by 3? 5

Repeat questioning for Exercise 2.

Provide scrap paper for Exercises 3–8.

For Exercise 3, explain to children that they should begin with the first number shown (9) and then keep subtracting the second number (3) from the answer until they get to 0.

- How many times did you subtract 3? 3

Continue for Exercises 4–8.

Differentiated Instruction

Intervention — Activity Card 13-7

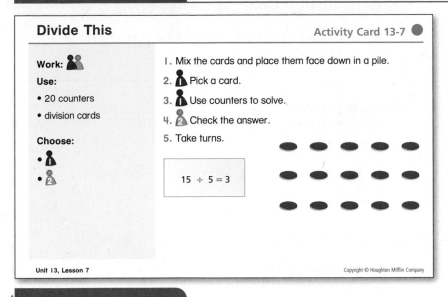

Divide This

Activity Card 13-7

Work: pairs

Use:
- 20 counters
- division cards

Choose:
- 1
- 2

1. Mix the cards and place them face down in a pile.
2. 1 Pick a card.
3. 1 Use counters to solve.
4. 2 Check the answer.
5. Take turns.

15 ÷ 5 = 3

Unit 13, Lesson 7

Activity Note Write simple division problems on index cards, 10 per pair (24 ÷ 6 = □, 12 ÷ 3 = □). To determine the number in each group, tell children to keep passing out the counters to the groups until there are no more left.

Math Writing Prompt

Explain Milo missed school yesterday. Tell him how to divide 20 counters into groups of 4.

Soar to Success Math **Software Support**

Warm Up 13.07

On Level — Activity Card 13-7

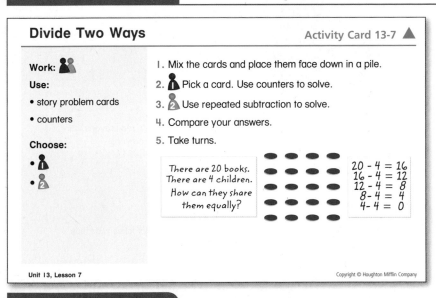

Divide Two Ways

Activity Card 13-7

Work: pairs

Use:
- story problem cards
- counters

Choose:
- 1
- 2

1. Mix the cards and place them face down in a pile.
2. 1 Pick a card. Use counters to solve.
3. 2 Use repeated subtraction to solve.
4. Compare your answers.
5. Take turns.

There are 20 books.
There are 4 children.
How can they share them equally?

20 - 4 = 16
16 - 4 = 12
12 - 4 = 8
8 - 4 = 4
4 - 4 = 0

Unit 13, Lesson 7

Activity Note Write simple division story problems on index cards, 10 per pair. See the activity card for a sample.

Math Writing Prompt

Explain Your Thinking Explain how to solve 28 ÷ 7 using repeated subtraction.

Harcourt Mega Math Grades K-6 **Software Support**

Country Countdown: Counting Critters, Level A

Challenge — Activity Card 13-7

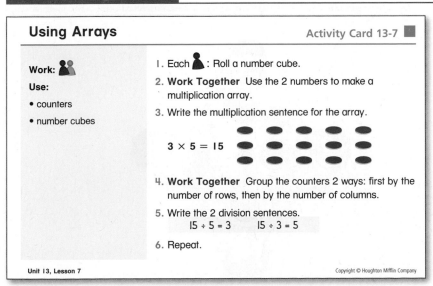

Using Arrays

Activity Card 13-7

Work: pairs

Use:
- counters
- number cubes

1. Each 1: Roll a number cube.
2. **Work Together** Use the 2 numbers to make a multiplication array.
3. Write the multiplication sentence for the array.

   3 × 5 = 15

4. **Work Together** Group the counters 2 ways: first by the number of rows, then by the number of columns.
5. Write the 2 division sentences.

   15 ÷ 5 = 3 15 ÷ 3 = 5

6. Repeat.

Unit 13, Lesson 7

Activity Note Remind children how to make an array using rows and columns. Explain that rows go across and columns go up and down.

Math Writing Prompt

Explain Explain how division is the opposite of multiplication. Use an array drawing to help.

Destination Math **Software Support**

Course II: Module 2: Unit 2: Repeated Addition and Arrays

3 Homework and Spiral Review

13-7 Homework **Goal:** Additional Practice

✓ Use this homework activity to provide children more practice with division.

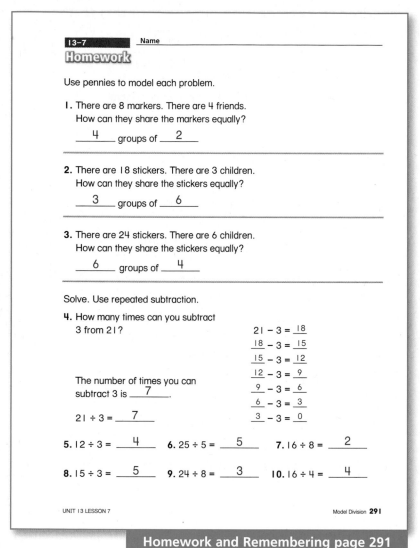

13-7 Homework Name ____________

Use pennies to model each problem.

1. There are 8 markers. There are 4 friends. How can they share the markers equally?
   __4__ groups of __2__

2. There are 18 stickers. There are 3 children. How can they share the stickers equally?
   __3__ groups of __6__

3. There are 24 stickers. There are 6 children. How can they share the stickers equally?
   __6__ groups of __4__

Solve. Use repeated subtraction.

4. How many times can you subtract 3 from 21?

   21 − 3 = 18
   18 − 3 = 15
   15 − 3 = 12
   12 − 3 = 9
   9 − 3 = 6
   6 − 3 = 3
   3 − 3 = 0

   The number of times you can subtract 3 is __7__.

   21 ÷ 3 = __7__

5. 12 ÷ 3 = __4__
6. 25 ÷ 5 = __5__
7. 16 ÷ 8 = __2__
8. 15 ÷ 3 = __5__
9. 24 ÷ 8 = __3__
10. 16 ÷ 4 = __4__

UNIT 13 LESSON 7 Model Division 291

Homework and Remembering page 291

13-7 Remembering **Goal:** Spiral Review

This Remembering activity would be appropriate anytime after today's lesson.

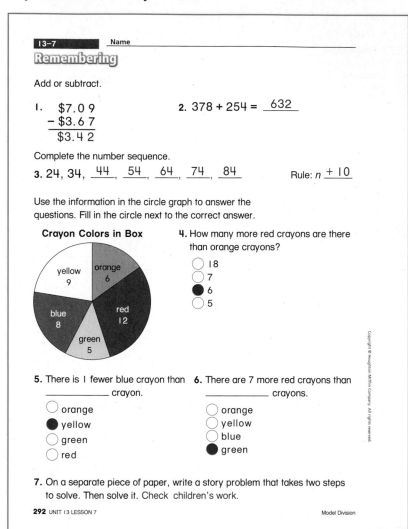

13-7 Remembering Name ____________

Add or subtract.

1. $7.09 − $3.67 = $3.42
2. 378 + 254 = __632__

Complete the number sequence.

3. 24, 34, __44__, __54__, __64__, __74__, __84__ Rule: n __+ 10__

Use the information in the circle graph to answer the questions. Fill in the circle next to the correct answer.

Crayon Colors in Box

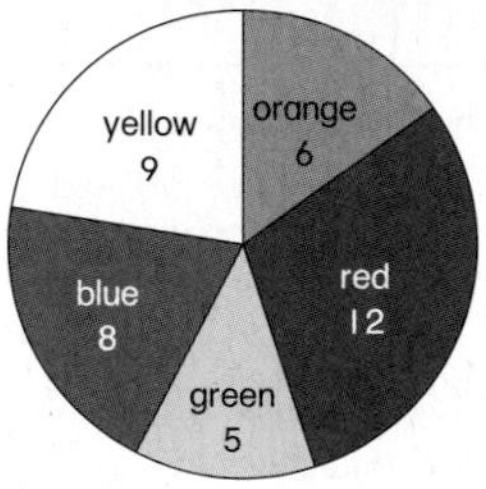

4. How many more red crayons are there than orange crayons?
   ○ 18
   ○ 7
   ● 6
   ○ 5

5. There is 1 fewer blue crayon than ________ crayon.
   ○ orange
   ● yellow
   ○ green
   ○ red

6. There are 7 more red crayons than ________ crayons.
   ○ orange
   ○ yellow
   ○ blue
   ● green

7. On a separate piece of paper, write a story problem that takes two steps to solve. Then solve it. Check children's work.

292 UNIT 13 LESSON 7 Model Division

Homework and Remembering page 292

Home or School Activity

Real-World Connection

Fair Shares Have children make fair shares with their friends or family. Explain that they may do fair shares of a type of food during dinner with their family or fair shares of classroom objects with friends.

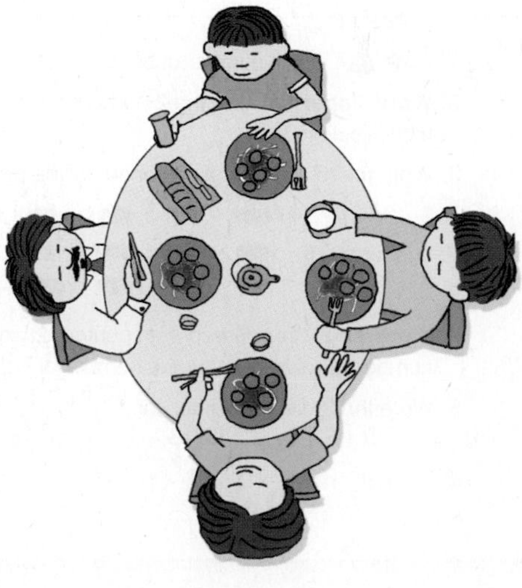

UNIT 13 LESSON 8

Symmetry

Lesson Objectives

- Find lines of symmetry.
- Recognize and draw symmetrical shapes.
- Find symmetry in everyday objects.

Vocabulary
lines of symmetry
symmetrical
symmetry

The Day at a Glance

Today's Goals	Materials	
1 Teaching the Lesson **A1:** Experiment with finding lines of symmetry and then define symmetry. **A2:** Finish drawing symmetrical shapes and create symmetrical shapes. **A3:** Find symmetrical objects in the classroom and play the *Symmetrical Student* game.	**Lesson Activities** Student Activity Book pp. 439–442 Homework and Remembering pp. 293–294 Scissors Colored pencils, crayons, or markers Rulers or straight edges Classroom objects	**Going Further** Activity Cards 13-8 Finger paints Newsprint or other plain paper Hole punches Colored pencils or crayons Magazines Scissors Glue sticks *Let's Fly a Kite* by Stuart J. Murphy Math Journals
2 Going Further ► Differentiated Instruction		
3 Homework and Targeted Practice		

Use Math Talk today!

Keeping Skills Sharp

Quick Practice — 5 MINUTES

Goal: Count by 3s.

Count By 3s Divide the class into two groups. Have the class count by 3s. The first group starts by saying the number 3. The second group responds with "6." The first group replies with "9," and so on until they have reached 30. (See Unit 13 Lesson 3.)

Repeated Quick Practice
Use this Quick Practice from a previous lesson.

- ► **Count By 4s** (See Unit 13 Lesson 4.)

Daily Routines

2s, 3s, and 4s Count-Bys Draw Arrays, Draw Groups on the 120 Poster, Draw Groups on the Number Path
(See pp. xxviii–xix.)

- ► Led by Student Leaders

Money Routine Using the 120 Poster, Using the Money Flip Chart, Using the Number Path, Using Secret Code Cards
(See pp. xxiii–xxv.)

- ► Led by Student Leaders

1 Teaching the Lesson

Activity 1

Explore Symmetry

20 MINUTES

Goals: Experiment with finding lines of symmetry and then define symmetry.

Materials: scissors (1 pair per child), colored pencils, crayons or markers, Student Activity Book page 439

NCTM Standard:
Geometry

The Learning Classroom

Building Concepts Before the children begin experimenting with the shapes on Student Activity Book page 439 point out the fact that not every shape will have a line of symmetry. You may also want to point out that some shapes may have only one line of symmetry and others may have more than one line of symmetry. As children work, look for children who draw different lines of symmetry for the same figure. Have those children share their work with the class.

Both parts match.

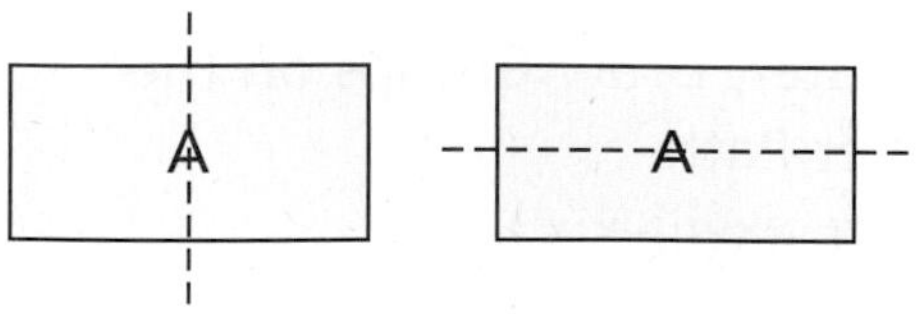

Both parts do not match.

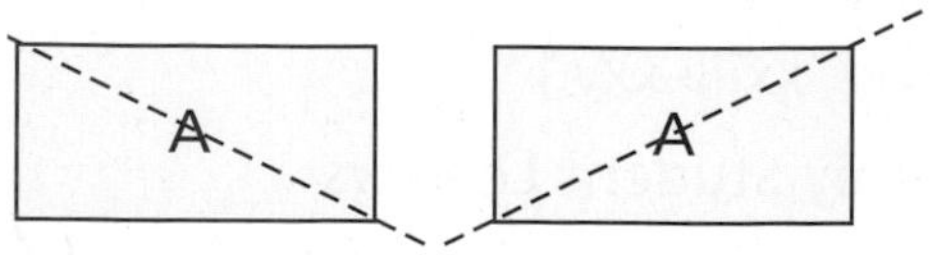

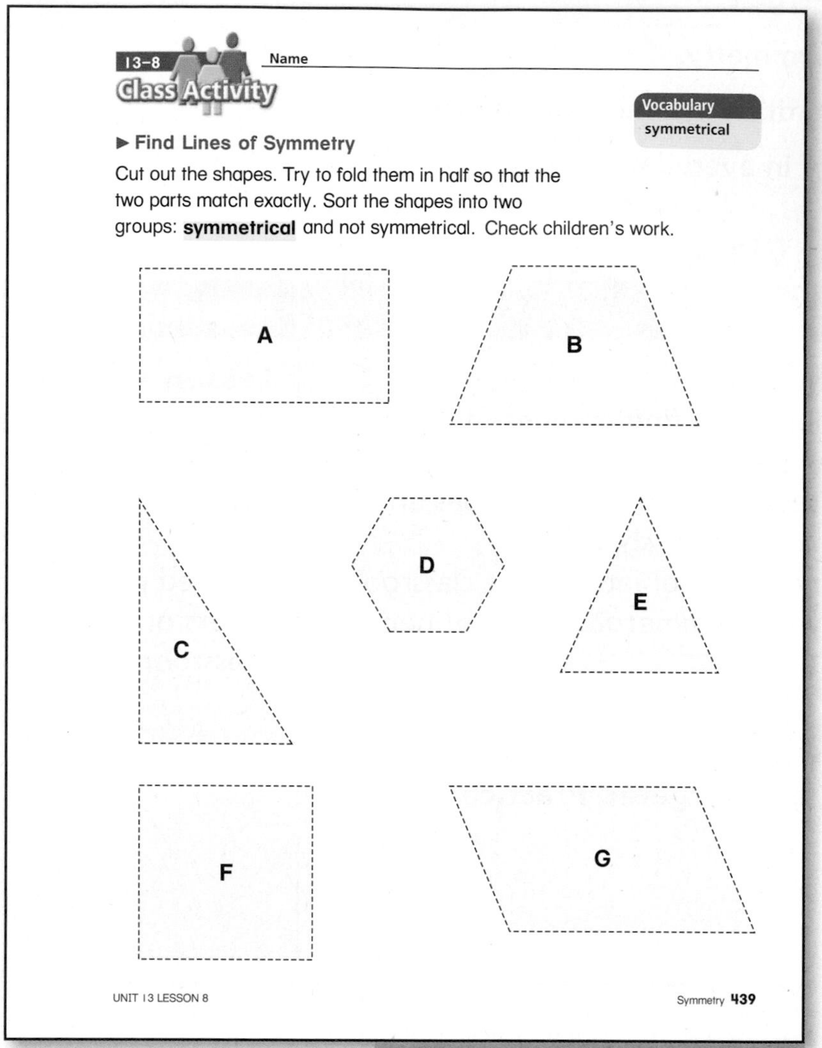
13-8 Class Activity Name

Vocabulary
symmetrical

► Find Lines of Symmetry

Cut out the shapes. Try to fold them in half so that the two parts match exactly. Sort the shapes into two groups: **symmetrical** and not symmetrical. Check children's work.

A B C D E F G

UNIT 13 LESSON 8 Symmetry 439

Student Activity Book page 439

► Find Lines of Symmetry INDIVIDUALS

Have children cut out the rectangle at the top of Student Activity Book page 439. Ask them to fold the rectangle in half so that both halves match exactly. Explain that if both halves match exactly, the fold line is a *line of symmetry.* Then have children experiment to find other ways to fold the rectangle in half symmetrically. (See side column.) They should go over any lines of symmetry that they find with a crayon or marker.

Children should continue experimenting with the other shapes on the page.

You may wish to have children check each line of symmetry by placing a mirror along it. If the mirror is placed along a line of symmetry, the image will restore the original figure.

Children can tape or glue the shapes to another piece of paper so they can save their work.

Activity 2

Create Symmetrical Shapes

13–8 Class Activity

Name ____________________

Vocabulary
line of symmetry

► Complete Drawings of Symmetrical Shapes

Finish drawing the shapes. Check children's work.

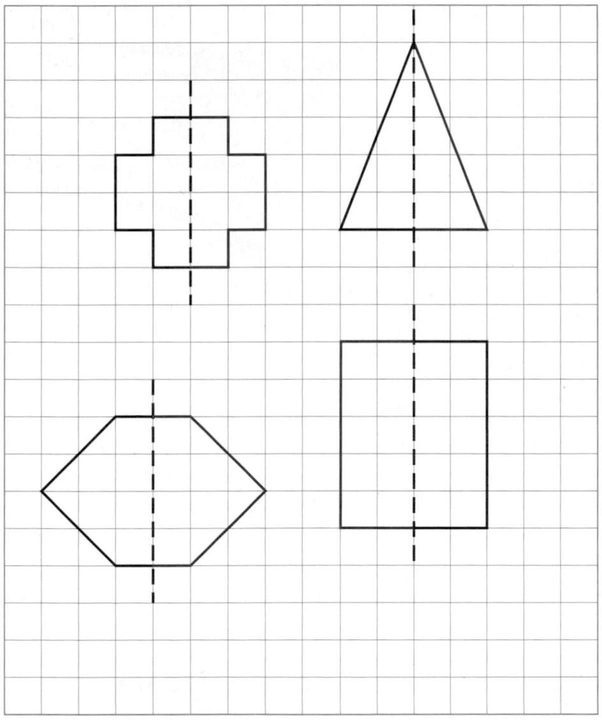

On the Back Draw some symmetrical shapes of your own. Draw a **line of symmetry** for each shape. Check children's work.

UNIT 13 LESSON 8 Symmetry 441

Student Activity Book page 441

► Complete Drawings of Symmetrical Shapes

INDIVIDUALS

Math Talk

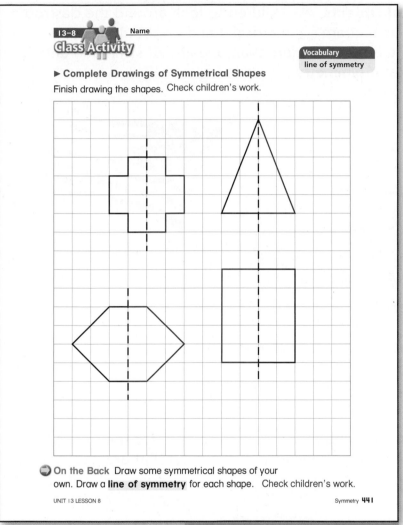

Have children work individually or in **Helping Pairs** to complete the drawings of the symmetrical shapes on Student Activity Book page 441. Suggest that the children use a ruler or straightedge to help them draw straight lines. If they wish, allow them to color the completed shapes. Then have children draw other symmetrical shapes on the back. Tell them to draw two lines of symmetry for these shapes.

Math Talk Invite children to show their classmates the shapes that they made. Children should help each other determine if each shape is truly symmetrical and, if so, how many lines of symmetry it has.

20 MINUTES

Goal: Finish drawing symmetrical shapes and create symmetrical shapes

Materials: rulers or straightedges (1 per child), colored pencils, crayons or markers (optional), Student Activity Book pages 441–442

NCTM Standard:
Geometry
Communication

Teaching Note

Math Background There are two kinds of symmetry for 2-dimensional figures: line symmetry (also called reflectional symmetry) and point symmetry (also called rotational symmetry). This lesson covers line symmetry only. For a definition of point symmetry, see the Teacher Glossary in the back of this book.

English Language Learners

Draw a heart and its line of symmetry. Write *symmetrical*.

- **Beginning** Say: ***Symmetrical* means having the same size and shape.** Have children repeat.
- **Intermediate** Ask: **Are the two parts of the heart the same size and shape?** yes Say: **The parts are *symmetrical*.**
- **Advanced** Have children identify the *symmetrical* parts of the drawing.

Alternate Approach

If computers and appropriate software are available, encourage children to explore the concepts of symmetry with the software.

❶ Teaching the Lesson (continued)

Activity 3

Recognize Symmetry

15 MINUTES

Goals: Find symmetrical objects in the classroom and play the *Symmetrical Student* game.

Materials: classroom objects

NCTM Standards:
Geometry
Communication

Teaching Note

Language and Vocabulary Some children may notice that you can't count the number of lines of symmetry in a circle. You may wish to tell the children that we say that there are an *infinite* number of lines of symmetry in a circle. However, it is not necessary for children to know this term at this time.

Ongoing Assessment

Check children's understanding of symmetry by observing the objects they classify as symmetrical.

▶ Identify Symmetrical Objects WHOLE CLASS

Find Symmetrical Objects Ask children to look around the classroom and identify objects that are symmetrical. Children should discuss whether or not the object has more than one line of symmetry and, if so, how many lines of symmetry.

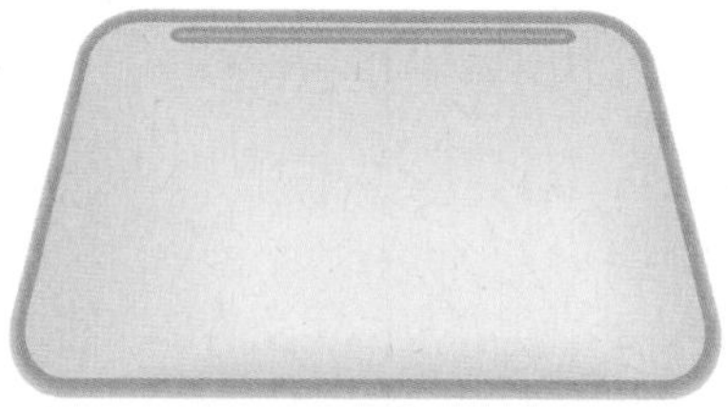

Symmetrical

Not Symmetrical

Play the *Symmetrical Student* Game Invite a volunteer to be the "symmetrical student." Tell the child to strike a pose (arms straight out to the sides, feet apart, for example). Then have the rest of the children in the class decide whether the body position is symmetrical or not.

Repeat the activity allowing other children to pose for the class. Some examples of poses that are symmetrical and poses that are not symmetrical are shown below.

This pose is symmetrical.

This pose is not symmetrical.

Intervention

Activity Card 13-8

Paint Blots Activity Card 13-8

Work:
Use:
- finger paint
- paper

1. Fold the paper in half.
2. Open the paper. Put some paint on one side of the paper.
3. Refold the paper and press the two halves together.
4. Open the paper. Compare the two sides.

5. **Math Talk** Discuss what happened when you folded and unfolded the paper.

Unit 13, Lesson 8

Activity Note Each child needs finger paints and newsprint or other plain paper. Have children dab the paint on one half of the paper.

Math Writing Prompt

Draw a Picture Draw a shape that is symmetrical and draw a line of symmetry. Tell how you know the shape is symmetrical.

Soar to Success Math **Software Support**

Warm Up 37.05

On Level

Activity Card 13-8

Unfold Symmetry Activity Card 13-8

Work:
Use:
- 2 scissors
- 1 hole punch
- paper

1. Each : fold your piece of paper in half.
2. Cut through the paper layers using any shape you want. Keep the paper folded.
3. Open the paper. Discuss the results with your partner.
4. Refold the paper and punch 3–4 holes through both layers. Predict how many holes there will be.

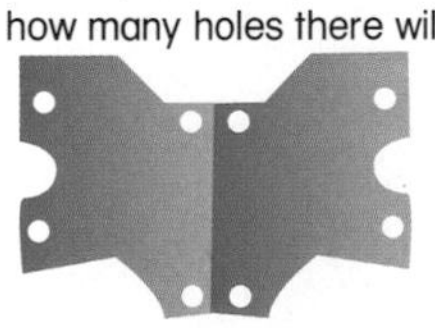

5. **Look Back** Check your prediction about the holes. Discuss the results with your partner.

Unit 13, Lesson 8

Activity Note Each child needs a piece of paper and a pair of scissors. Provide a hole punch for each pair. Explain that children should cut any shape they want.

Math Writing Prompt

Make a Drawing Draw a rectangle with two lines of symmetry, a triangle with no lines of symmetry, and any shape you wish with one line of symmetry.

Harcourt Mega Math Grades K-6 **Software Support**

Shapes Ahoy: Ship Shapes, Level N

Challenge

Activity Card 13-8

Symmetry in the Real World Activity Card 13-8

Work:
Use:
- colored pencils or crayons
- magazines
- scissors
- glue stick

1. Each : Look through the magazines and find two or three pictures that show symmetry.
2. Cut the pictures in half.
3. Glue one half of the picture on to half a sheet of paper.

4. Trade pictures with your partner. Draw the missing part of the picture using the line of symmetry.
5. **Math Talk** Discuss your drawings and how you used the line of symmetry.

Unit 13, Lesson 8

Activity Note Each pair needs magazines with lots of photographs, scissors, a glue stick, and colored pencils or crayons.

Math Writing Prompt

Write About It Write about two ways that you can check that a shape has a line of symmetry.

DESTINATION Math **Software Support**

Course II: Module 3: Unit 1: Area

3 Homework and Targeted Practice

13-8 Homework **Goal:** Additional Practice

✓ Include children's completed Homework page as part of their portfolios.

13-8 Targeted Practice **Goal:** Multiplication Practice

This page can be used with children who need extra practice in 2s count-bys and multiplication.

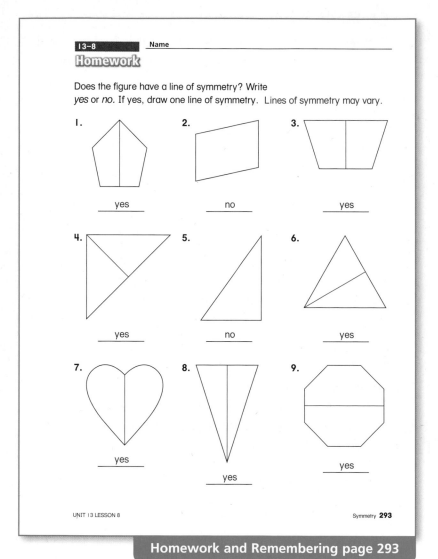

13-8 Name ______

Homework

Does the figure have a line of symmetry? Write *yes* or *no*. If yes, draw one line of symmetry. Lines of symmetry may vary.

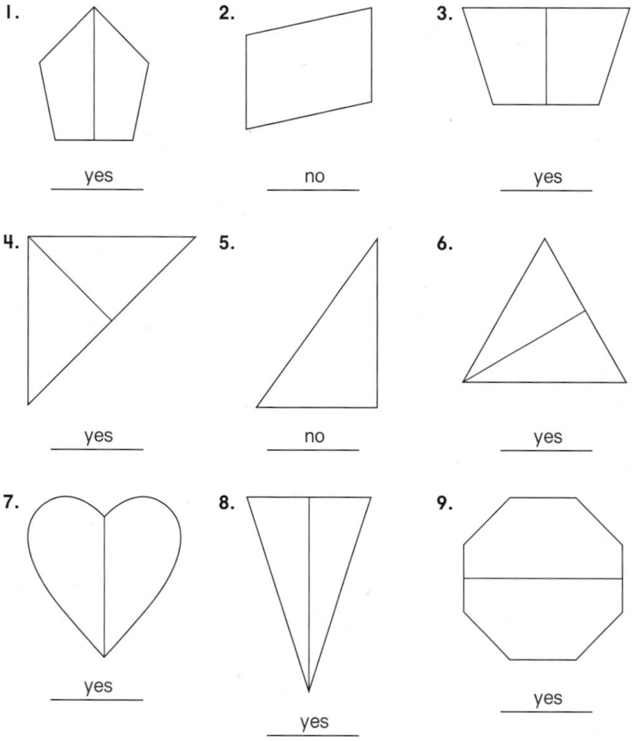

1. yes
2. no
3. yes
4. yes
5. no
6. yes
7. yes
8. yes
9. yes

UNIT 13 LESSON 8 Symmetry **293**

Homework and Remembering page 293

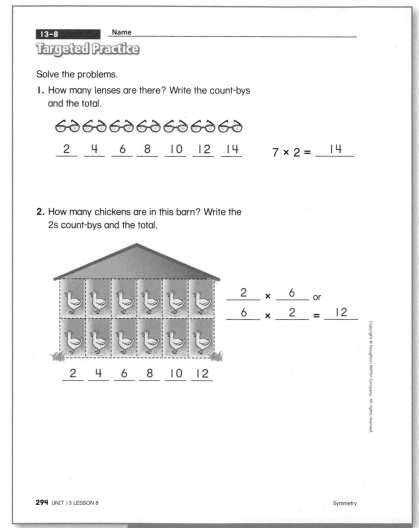

13-8 Name ______

Targeted Practice

Solve the problems.

1. How many lenses are there? Write the count-bys and the total.

2 4 6 8 10 12 14 $7 \times 2 =$ 14

2. How many chickens are in this barn? Write the 2s count-bys and the total.

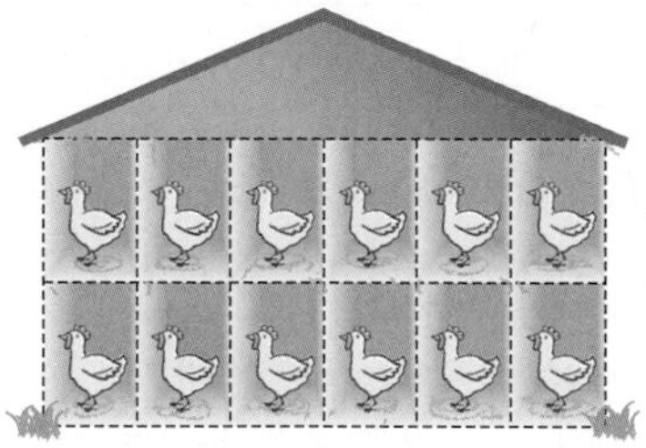

2 × 6 or

6 × 2 = 12

2 4 6 8 10 12

294 UNIT 13 LESSON 8 Symmetry

Homework and Remembering page 294

Home or School Activity

Literature Connection

Let's Fly a Kite Read or have a child read *Let's Fly a Kite* by Stuart J. Murphy and Brian Floca (HarperTrophy, 2000). Tell children that they are going to help Bob and Hannah make a new kite that has two matching parts and a line of symmetry. Have children draw their new kites.

UNIT 13 LESSON 9

Fractions

Lesson Objectives

- Identify and represent one half, one third, one fourth, two thirds, and three fourths in geometrical shapes.
- Understand what numerator and denominator signify.

Vocabulary
fractions
unit fraction
numerator
denominator

The Day at a Glance

Today's Goals	Materials	
1 Teaching the Lesson **A1:** Identify and represent unit fractions. **A2:** Identify and represent non-unit fractions.	**Lesson Activities** Student Activity Book pp. 443–445 Homework and Remembering pp. 295–296 Colored pencils, crayons, or markers	**Going Further** Activity Cards 13-9 Student Activity Book p. 446 Colored pencils, crayons, or markers Fraction Match Up 1 (TRB M94) Fraction Match Up 2 (TRB M95) Scissors Math Journals
2 Going Further ► Math Connection: Five or More Equal Parts ► Differentiated Instruction		
3 Homework and Spiral Review		

Use Math Talk today!

Keeping Skills Sharp

Quick Practice — 5 MINUTES

Goal: Count by 3s and 4s.

Count By 3s Divide the class into two groups. You can appoint a **Student Leader** for each group or take volunteers. Have the class count by 3s. The first group starts by saying the number 3. The second group responds with "6." The first group replies with "9," and so on until they have reached 30. You may wish to repeat the exercise, asking the second group to begin this time. (See Unit 13 Lesson 3.)

It may be helpful to have children use their fingers to mark off each multiple of 3 that they count.

Count By 4s Have children practice the 4 count-bys in the same fashion. (See Unit 13 Lesson 4.)

Daily Routines

2s, 3s, and 4s Count-Bys Draw Arrays, Draw Groups on the 120 Poster, Draw Groups on the Number Path
(See pp. xxviii–xix.)

► Led by Student Leaders

Money Routine Using the 120 Poster, Using the Money Flip Chart, Using the Number Path, Using Secret Code Cards
(See pp. xxiii–xxv.)

► Led by Student Leaders

1 Teaching the Lesson

Activity 1

Unit Fractions

20 MINUTES

Goals: Identify and represent unit fractions.

Materials: colored pencils, crayons or markers (1 per child), Student Activity Book page 443

NCTM Standards:
Number and Operations
Communication

Teaching Note

Language and Vocabulary At the end of this lesson, children should know the term *fraction* and understand that a fraction is used to name equal parts of a whole. They should also know that the top number in a fraction names the part of the whole that we are concerned with (for example, the shaded part) and that the bottom number tells how many equal parts there are in the whole. It is not important for children to know the terms *numerator* and *denominator* at this point. However, if they express an interest in knowing the specific math terms for the numbers in a fraction, you may wish to share the terms with them.

▶ Introduce Halves, Thirds, and Fourths

INDIVIDUALS

Math Talk

If children are already familiar with one half, one third, and one fourth, you may wish to abbreviate this lesson as necessary.

Begin by drawing a rectangle on the board and then dividing it into two equal parts by drawing a vertical line through its center.

- Here is a rectangle. I'll divide it into two equal parts. Now I have two parts.

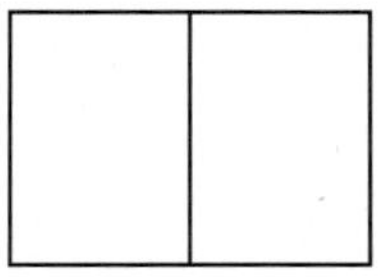

Shade or invite a volunteer to shade one of the parts.

- Now one part of the rectangle is shaded. Remember that the rectangle is divided into two equal parts. How can we write this? $\frac{1}{2}$
- What does the 1 mean? the number of parts that are shaded
- What does the 2 mean? the total number of equal parts
- We have shaded 1 part out of 2. So we shaded $\frac{1}{2}$ of the rectangle.

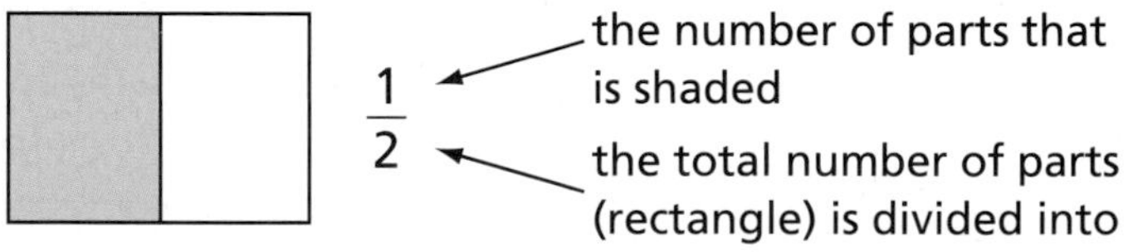

Repeat the process with $\frac{1}{3}$ using a triangle as the whole.

- Here is a triangle. I'll divide this one into three equal parts. Now I have three parts.

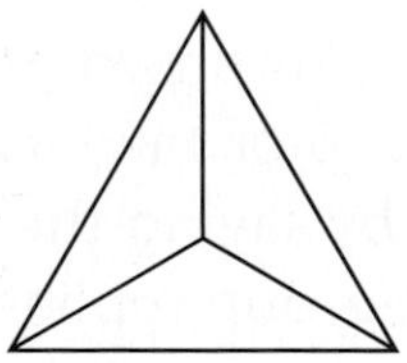

Shade or invite a volunteer to shade one of the parts.

- Now one part of the triangle is shaded. Remember that the triangle is divided into three equal parts. How can we write this? $\frac{1}{3}$
- What does the 1 mean? the number of parts that are shaded
- What does the 3 mean? the total number of equal parts
- We have shaded 1 part out of 3. So we have shaded $\frac{1}{3}$ of the triangle.

Repeat the process for $\frac{1}{3}$, using a square.

After the child has shaded $\frac{1}{4}$ of the square, ask the class if it matters which portion of the square gets shaded. They should realize that if they shade only one portion, whichever one that is, the fraction that describes the figure is still $\frac{1}{4}$.

Have children suggest other ways to divide the square into four equal parts. Then have volunteers shade $\frac{1}{4}$ of each square.

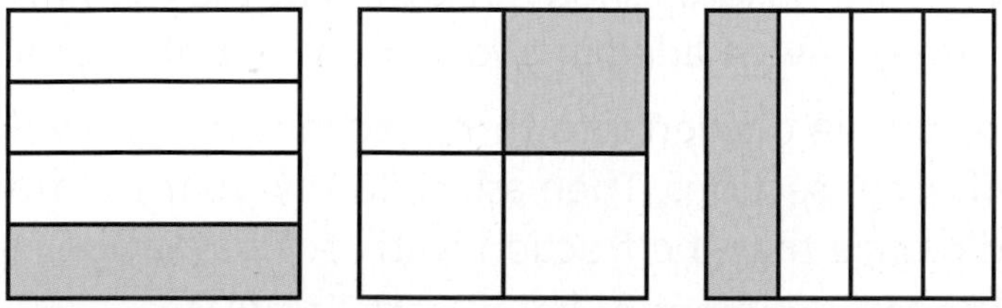

▶ Shade Unit Fractions INDIVIDUALS

Math Talk

Have children work individually or in **Helping Pairs** to color in the shapes on Student Activity Book page 443. When children have completed the page, ask if there are any other ways that a figure on the page could be divided into the same number of equal parts.

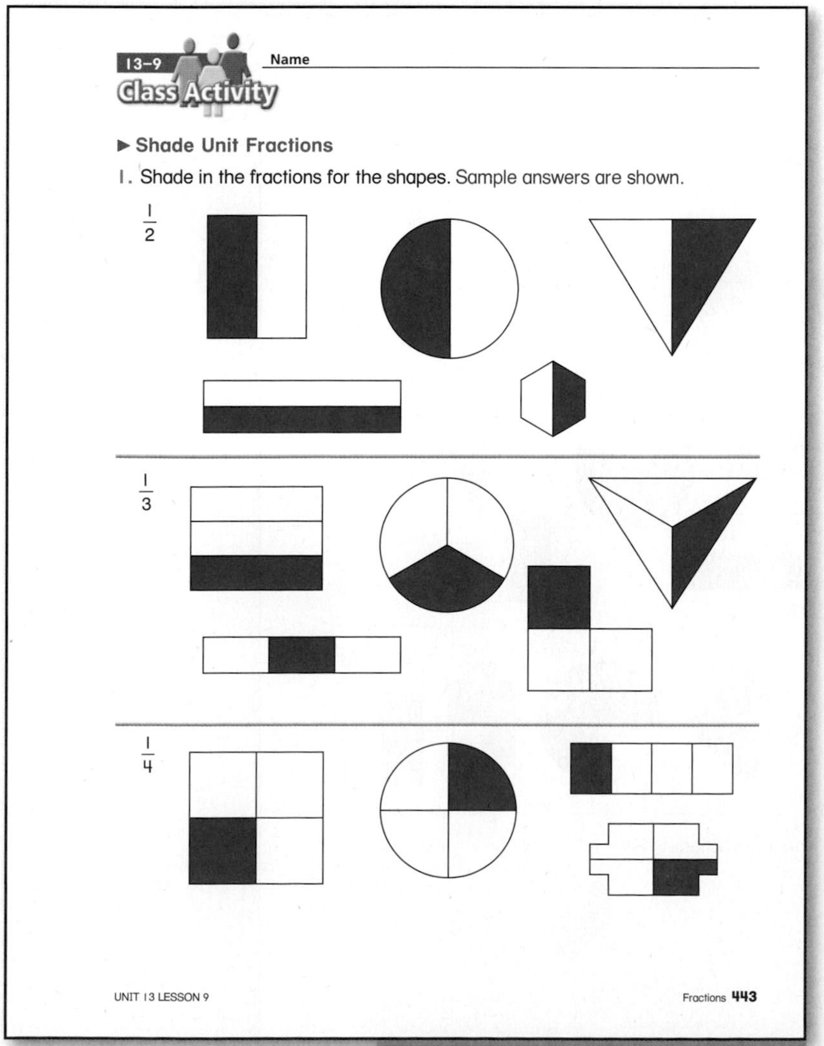
13–9 Class Activity Name

▶ Shade Unit Fractions

1. Shade in the fractions for the shapes. Sample answers are shown.

$\frac{1}{2}$

$\frac{1}{3}$

$\frac{1}{4}$

UNIT 13 LESSON 9 Fractions 443

Student Activity Book page 443

English Language Learners

Draw a square. Shade $\frac{1}{2}$ of it. Write *fractions*. Say: ***Fractions* are equal parts of a whole.**

- **Beginning** Point and say: **This is a *fraction* of the square.** Have children repeat.
- **Intermediate** Ask: **Are the 2 parts of the square equal?** yes **Are they *fractions*?** yes
- **Advanced** Ask: **How many parts are there?** 2 parts **Are they equal?** yes Say: **Each part is a __.** fraction

1 Teaching the Lesson (continued)

Activity 2

Fractional Parts: Non-Unit Fractions

15 MINUTES

Goals: Identify and represent non-unit fractions.

Materials: colored pencils, crayons or markers (1 per child), Student Activity Book pages 444–445

NCTM Standards:
Number and Operations
Communication

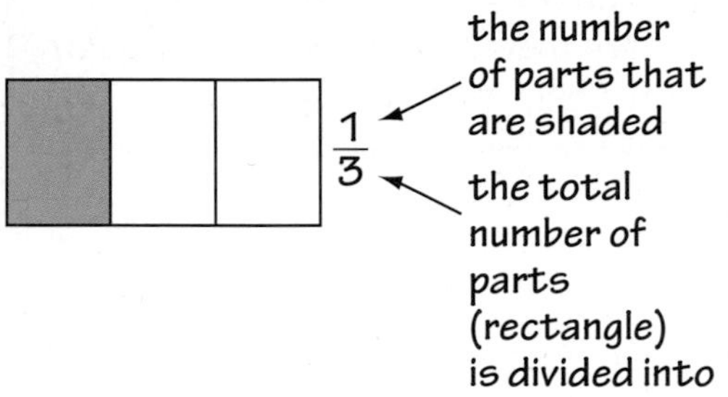

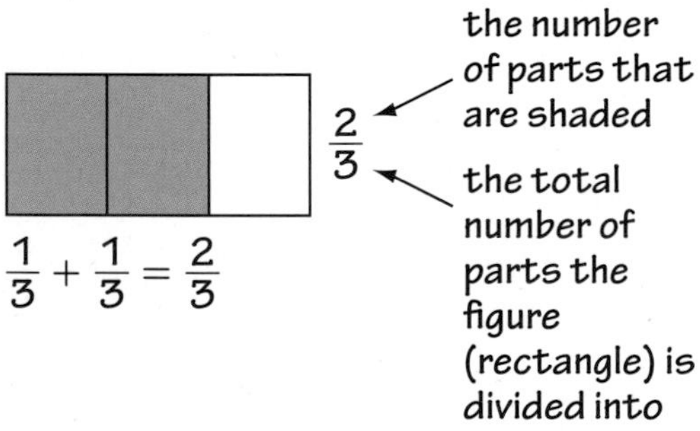

Two thirds of each figure is shaded.

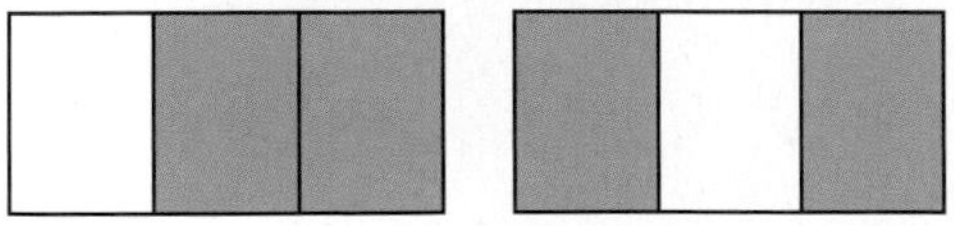

Teaching Note

Language and Vocabulary In *Math Expressions,* a fraction is represented as the sum of the unit fractions. For example, the fraction $\frac{2}{3}$ is the sum of $\frac{1}{3}$ and $\frac{1}{3}$, the unit fractions.

▶ Introduce Two Thirds WHOLE CLASS

Draw a rectangle divided into thirds on the board. As a review, ask a volunteer to shade in one portion of the figure and write the fraction that names the shaded part. Have the child explain the meaning of both the top and bottom number. (See side column.)

Then ask a different child to shade in another section of the rectangle so that two of the three sections are shaded. Have children write the fraction that names the shaded part. Children should realize that the top number must now be a 2 since they have shaded in two sections out of a total of three.

Draw another rectangle divided into three sections. Have a volunteer shade in two different sections. Then ask children what the fraction is now. Children should realize that the fraction is still $\frac{2}{3}$. The number of shaded parts is still 2. The total number of equal parts is still 3.

▶ Shade and Write Fractions INDIVIDUALS

Have children complete Student Activity Book page 444 independently or in Helping Pairs. Point out that at the bottom of the page children will need to write fractions to represent what is shown in the drawing.

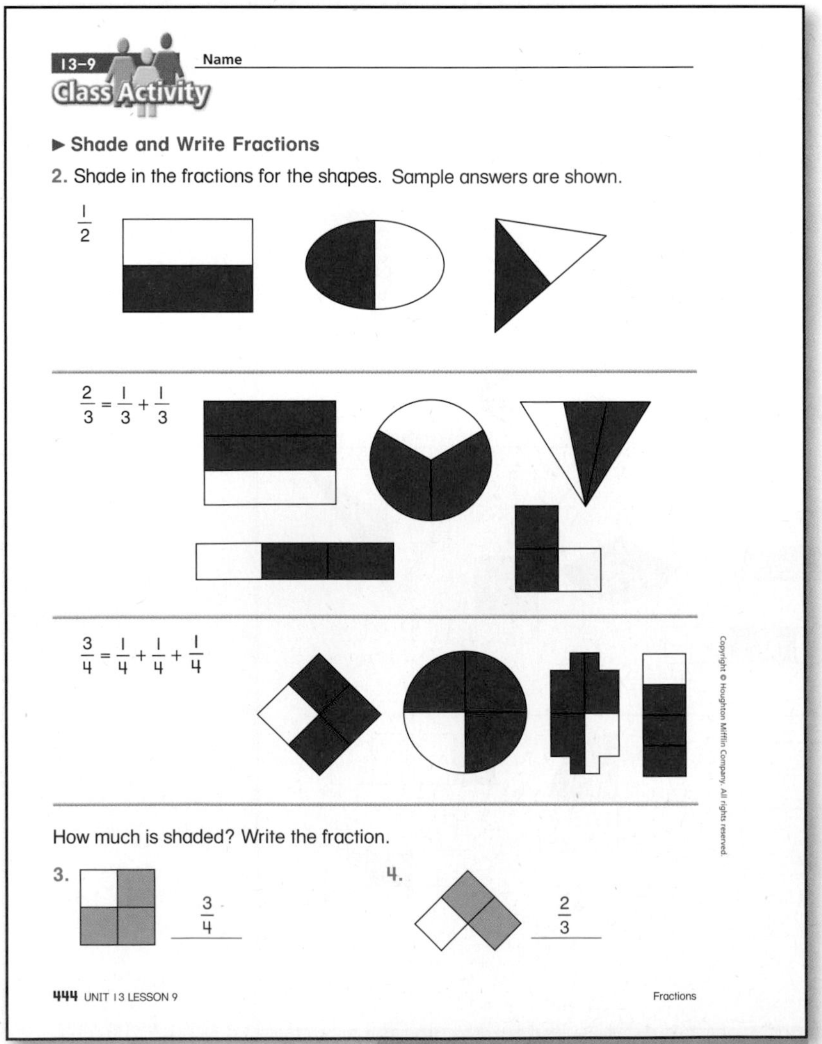

13–9 Class Activity Name

▶ Shade and Write Fractions

2. Shade in the fractions for the shapes. Sample answers are shown.

$\frac{1}{2}$

$\frac{2}{3} = \frac{1}{3} + \frac{1}{3}$

$\frac{3}{4} = \frac{1}{4} + \frac{1}{4} + \frac{1}{4}$

How much is shaded? Write the fraction.

3. $\frac{3}{4}$

4. $\frac{2}{3}$

Student Activity Book page 444

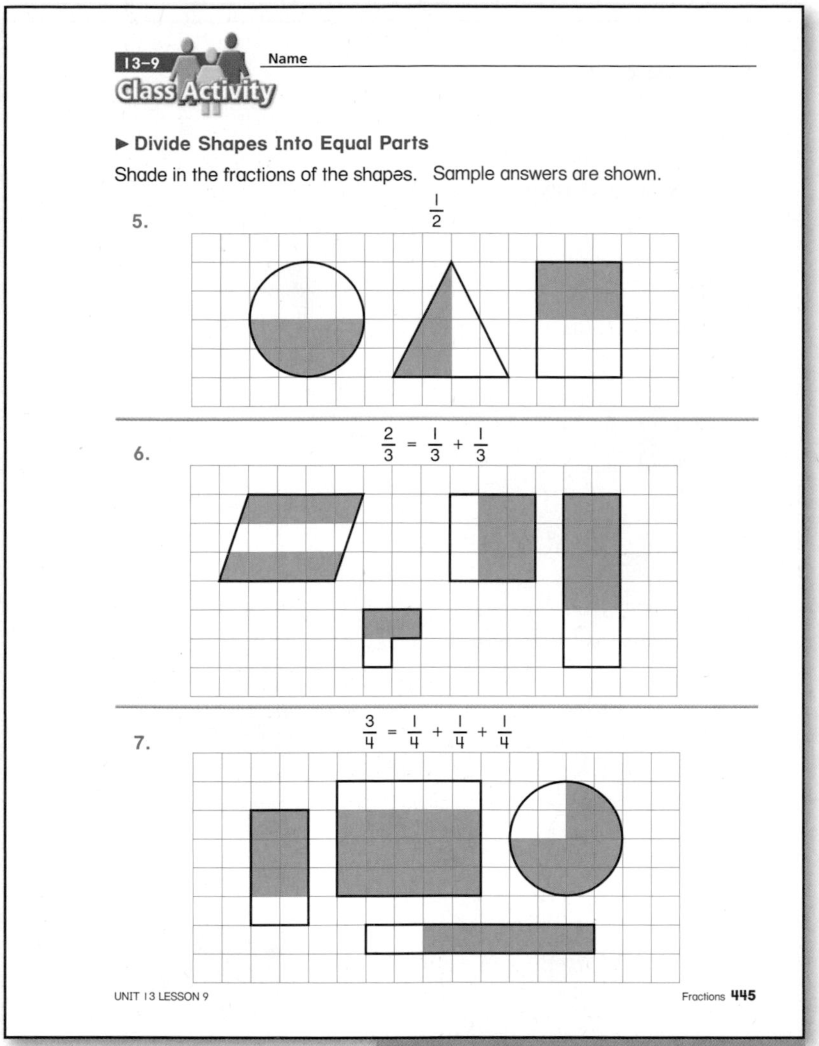

Student Activity Book page 445

► Divide Shapes into Equal Parts PAIRS

Direct children's attention to Student Activity Book page 445. Explain to children that they will need to divide each of the shapes into equal parts and then shade in $\frac{1}{2}$, $\frac{2}{3}$, or $\frac{3}{4}$ of each shape.

When children have completed the page, tell them to look at all the shapes that show $\frac{1}{2}$ and compare the size of the shaded areas. Is $\frac{1}{2}$ of each shape shaded? yes Is $\frac{1}{2}$ of the circle the same amount as $\frac{1}{2}$ of the triangle? no Is $\frac{1}{2}$ of the triangle the same amount as $\frac{1}{2}$ of the rectangle? no

Now draw one large circle and one small circle on the board. Tell children that the drawings represent a large pizza and a small pizza. Divide both pizzas into fourths and shade $\frac{3}{4}$ of each pizza.

- What fraction of the large pizza is shaded? $\frac{3}{4}$ What fraction of the small pizza is shaded? $\frac{3}{4}$ Is $\frac{3}{4}$ of a large pizza the same amount as $\frac{3}{4}$ of a small pizza? no Why or why not? $\frac{3}{4}$ of a large pizza is more than $\frac{3}{4}$ of a small pizza because the large pizza is bigger than the small pizza.

Teaching Note

Watch For! Some children may confuse numerators and denominators. Remind children that the number that tells the total number of parts goes below the fraction bar and the other number goes above it. If necessary, draw and label boxes to help children know where to write the numbers.

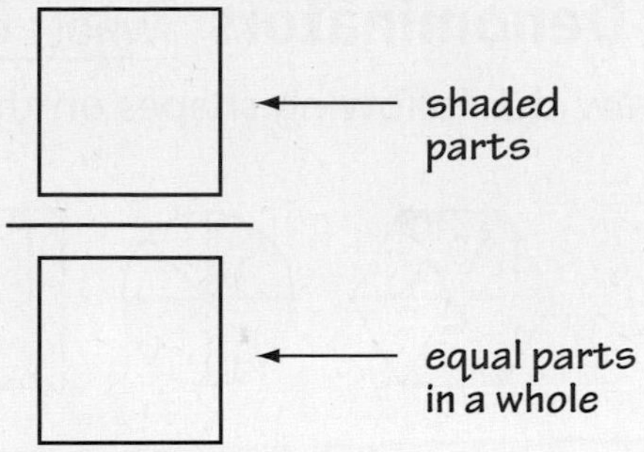

Ongoing Assessment

As children work, check that they are dividing the shapes into *equal* parts.

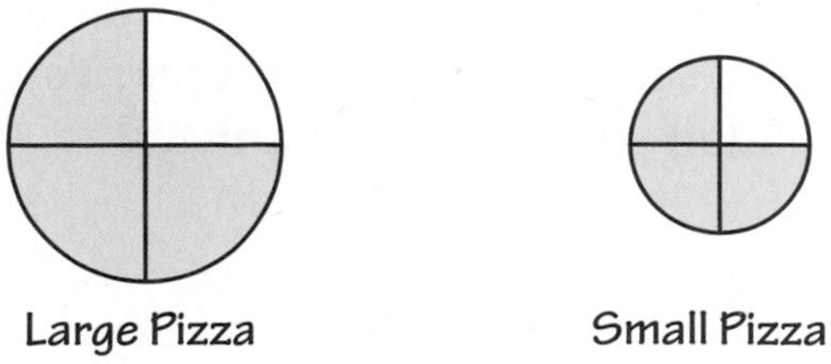

2 Going Further

Math Connection: Five or More Equal Parts

Goal: Explore fractions with denominators up to 12.

Materials: colored pencils, crayons or markers (1 per child), Student Activity Book page 446

NCTM Standards:
Number and Operations
Communication

► Introduce Fractions with Greater Denominators WHOLE CLASS

Draw the following shapes on the board.

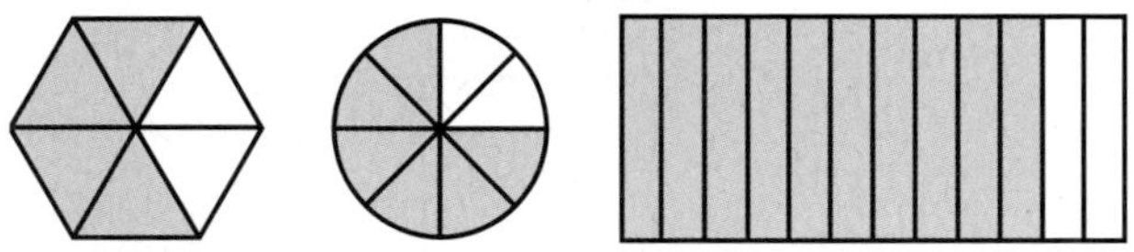

Have children discuss the hexagon.

- How many equal parts are there? 6 parts
- How many parts are shaded? 4 parts
- What is the fraction for the shaded part? $\frac{4}{6}$

Then ask the same questions for the other two shapes. circle: 8 equal parts, 6 parts shaded, $\frac{6}{8}$; rectangle: 12 equal parts, 10 parts shaded, $\frac{10}{12}$

If necessary continue with other examples until you are confident that children can identify fractions with denominators up to 12.

► Solve and Discuss

INDIVIDUALS

Math Talk

Direct children's attention to Student Activity Book page 446. Have children complete exercises 1–12. Be sure children understand that they need to color the shapes to show the fractions for exercises 1–6. For exercises 7–12 they need to write the fraction for the shaded part of each shape.

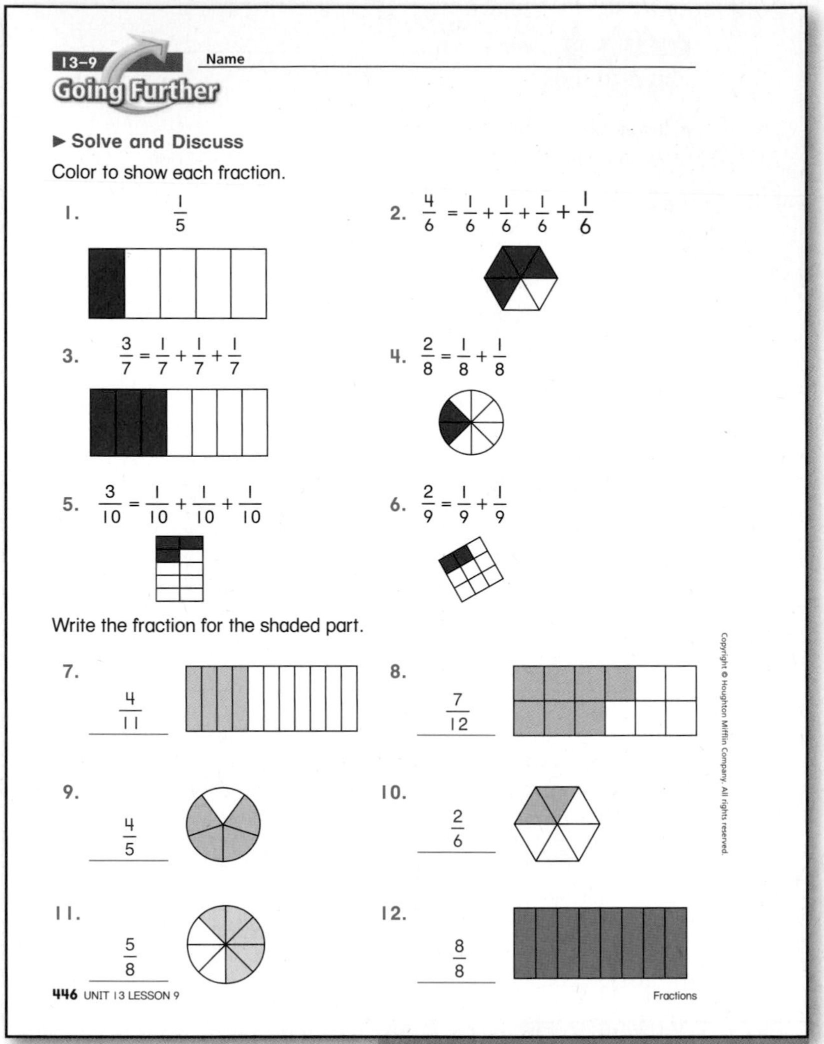

13-9 Going Further Name

► Solve and Discuss

Color to show each fraction.

1. $\frac{1}{5}$

2. $\frac{4}{6} = \frac{1}{6} + \frac{1}{6} + \frac{1}{6} + \frac{1}{6}$

3. $\frac{3}{7} = \frac{1}{7} + \frac{1}{7} + \frac{1}{7}$

4. $\frac{2}{8} = \frac{1}{8} + \frac{1}{8}$

5. $\frac{3}{10} = \frac{1}{10} + \frac{1}{10} + \frac{1}{10}$

6. $\frac{2}{9} = \frac{1}{9} + \frac{1}{9}$

Write the fraction for the shaded part.

7. $\frac{4}{11}$

8. $\frac{7}{12}$

9. $\frac{4}{5}$

10. $\frac{2}{6}$

11. $\frac{5}{8}$

12. $\frac{8}{8}$

Copyright © Houghton Mifflin Company. All rights reserved.

446 UNIT 13 LESSON 9 Fractions

Student Activity Book page 446

When children have completed the page, ask them to find the shape that is completely shaded. (Exercise 12) Ask them what they notice about the fraction. (The top and bottom numbers are the same. They are both 8.) Help children to see $\frac{8}{8}$ is another way to write 1 whole.

Intervention — Activity Card 13-9

Matching Fractions and Pictures
Activity Card 13-9

Work: (pairs)

Use:
- Fraction Match Up 1 (TRB M94)
- scissors

Choose:
- 1
- 2

1. **Work Together** Cut apart the cards on the Fraction Match Up 1 page.
2. Mix up the cards and place them face down in six rows.
3. Turn over two cards. If they match, keep the cards.

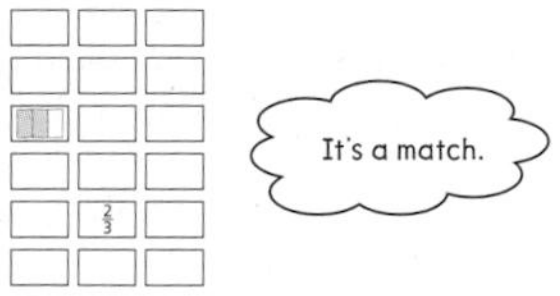

4. If the cards do not match, put them back.
5. Take turns. Play until all the matches are made. The player with the most matches wins.

Unit 13, Lesson 9

Activity Note Each pair needs Fraction Match Up 1 (TRB M94) and scissors. Have children name the fractions on the cards before they play.

Math Writing Prompt
Lunchtime Draw a picture of a sandwich divided into four equal parts. Then write about how you did it.

Soar to Success Math **Software Support**

Warm Up 5.07

On Level — Activity Card 13-9

More Matching Fractions and Pictures
Activity Card 13-9

Work: (pairs)

Use:
- Fraction Match Up 2 (TRB M95)
- scissors

Choose:
- 1
- 2

1. **Work Together** Cut apart the cards on the Fraction Match Up 2 page.
2. Mix up the cards and place them face down in six rows.
3. Turn over two cards. If they match, keep the cards.

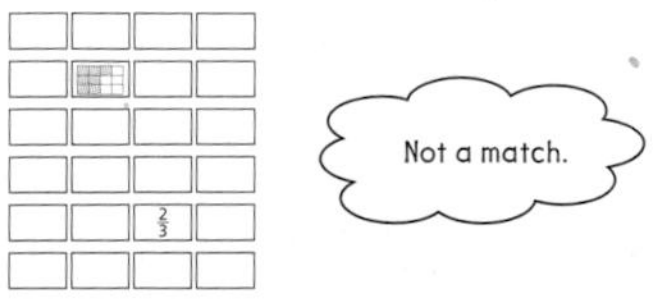

4. If the cards do not match, put them back.
5. Take turns. Play until all the matches are made. The player with the most matches wins.

Unit 13, Lesson 9

Activity Note Each pair needs Fraction Match Up 2 (TRB M95) and scissors. Have children name each fraction as they turn over each card.

Math Writing Prompt
Critical Thinking Anna ate $\frac{1}{2}$ of a pizza. Erin ate $\frac{1}{2}$ of a pizza. Erin ate more. How can this be?

Harcourt MegaMath **Software Support**

Shapes Ahoy: Ship Shapes, Level Q

Challenge — Activity Card 13-9

Match Time
Activity Card 13-9

Work: (groups)

Use:
- Fraction Match Up 2 (TRB M95)
- scissors

1. **Work Together** Cut apart the cards on the Fraction Match Up 2 page.
2. Mix up the cards and place them face down in a pile.
3. Take turns. Pick a card. Keep it. Repeat. Try to make a match with the cards you pick.

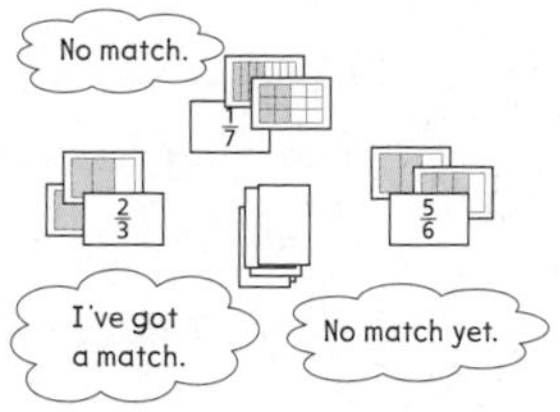

4. When all the cards have been picked, the player with the most matches wins.

Unit 13, Lesson 9

Activity Note Each group needs Fraction Match Up 2 (TRB M95) and scissors. Have children name each fraction as they make a match.

Math Writing Prompt
Investigate Math Use drawings or words to tell how you might solve this equation.

$$\frac{1}{4} + \frac{2}{4} = \square$$

Destination Math **Software Support**

Course II: Module 2: Unit 3: Fractional Parts

3 Homework and Spiral Review

13–9 Homework **Goal:** Additional Practice

✓ Include children's completed Homework page as part of their portfolios.

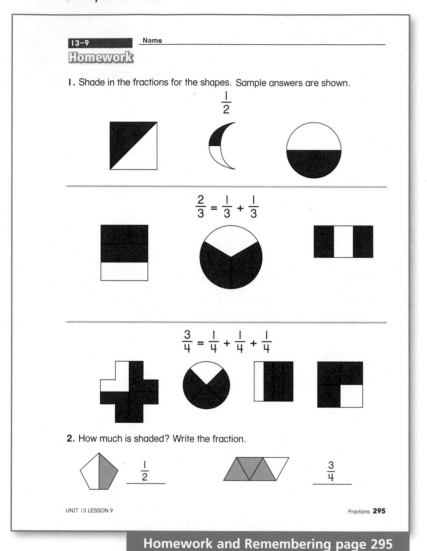

13–9 Remembering **Goal:** Spiral Review

This Remembering activity would be appropriate anytime after today's lesson.

13–9 Name ______

Homework

1. Shade in the fractions for the shapes. Sample answers are shown.

$\frac{1}{2}$

$\frac{2}{3} = \frac{1}{3} + \frac{1}{3}$

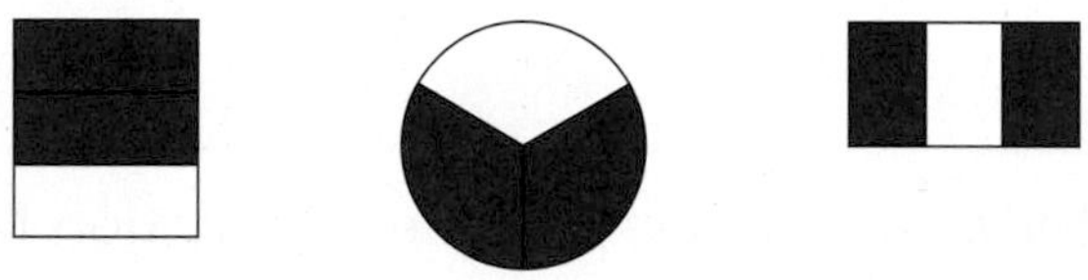

$\frac{3}{4} = \frac{1}{4} + \frac{1}{4} + \frac{1}{4}$

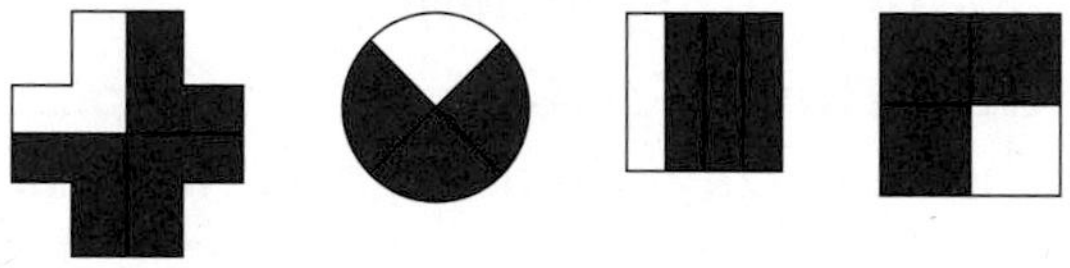

2. How much is shaded? Write the fraction.

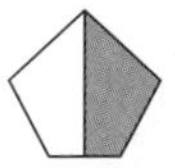 $\frac{1}{2}$

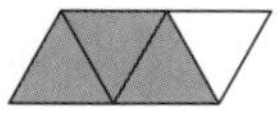 $\frac{3}{4}$

UNIT 13 LESSON 9 Fractions **295**

Homework and Remembering page 295

13–9 Name ______

Remembering

Is the figure symmetrical? Write *yes* or *no*.
If yes, draw one line of symmetry. Lines of symmetry may vary.

1. 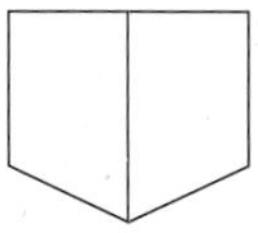 yes

2.  yes

3. 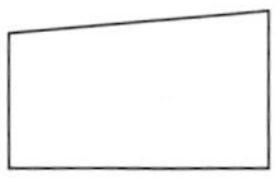 no

Add or subtract.

4. $7.21 − $4.23 = $2.98

5. 479 + 386 = 865

Draw in your answers. Write the numbers.

6. Sara has **double** the number of balloons as Ray.

Sara has 8.

Ray has 4.

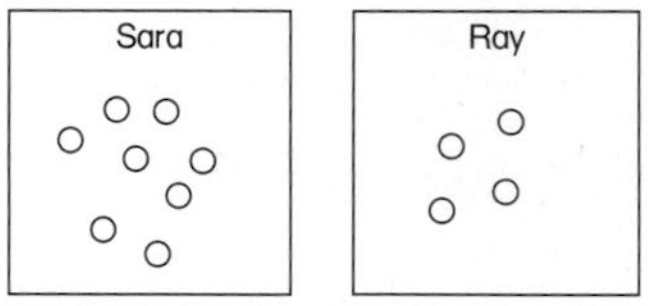

7. Luke has **half** as many chips as Leda.

Luke has 8.

Leda has 16.

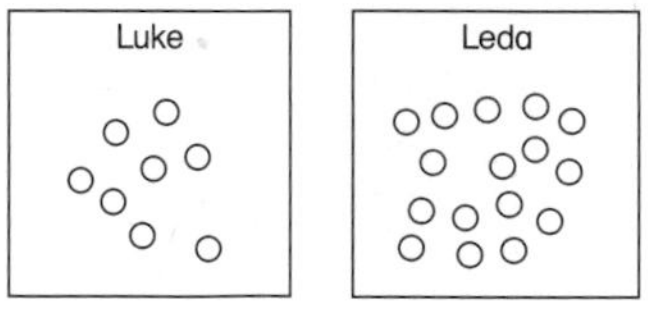

296 UNIT 13 LESSON 9 Fractions

Homework and Remembering page 296

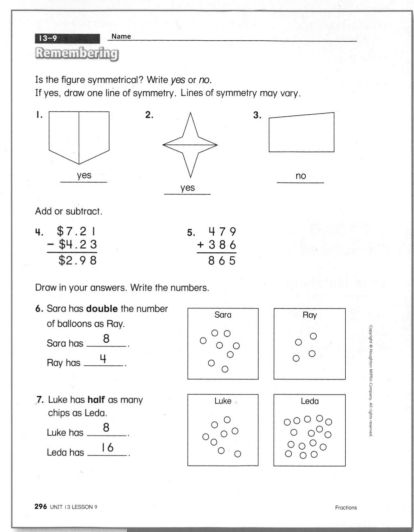

Home or School Activity

Multicultural Connection

Flags From Around the World Have children use print or approved internet resources to find pictures of flags from Austria, Indonesia, Italy, and Haiti. If possible, show children where these countries are on a world map.

Then have children secretly choose one of the flags and write a few sentences to describe what it looks like. Tell them to use fractions when describing the flag they chose. When they are finished, have children give their description to a partner to identify.

The flag has three equal parts.
$\frac{1}{3}$ of the flag is red.
What country's flag is it?

UNIT 13 LESSON 10

More on Fractions

Lesson Objectives

- Compare fractions using fraction strips.
- Write money amounts as fractions.

Vocabulary

greater than
less than
equal
estimate
order

The Day at a Glance

Today's Goals	Materials	
1 Teaching the Lesson A1: Color fraction strips to show fractions and then use the strips to compare fractions. A2: Write money amounts as fractions.	**Lesson Activities** Student Activity Book pp. 447–450 (Includes Fraction Strips) Homework and Remembering pp. 297–298 Crayons or colored pencils Scissors Quick Quiz 2 (Assessment Guide)	**Going Further** Activity Cards 13-10 Student Activity Book pp. 451–452 Fraction Strips Index cards Number Lines (TRB M93) Math Journals
2 Going Further ▸ Math Connection: Estimating with Fractions ▸ Differentiated Instruction		
3 Homework and Targeted Practice		

Use Math Talk today!

Keeping Skills Sharp

Quick Practice — 5 MINUTES

Goal: Count by 3s and 4s.

Count By 3s Divide the class into two groups. Appoint a **Student Leader** for each group or take volunteers. Have the groups count by 3s. One group starts with 3, the other follows with 6, and so on. You may wish to repeat the activity asking the second group to begin the counting.

It may be helpful to have the children use their fingers to mark off each multiple of 3 that they count. (See Unit 13 Lesson 3.)

Count By 4s Have the children practice the 4s count-bys in the same fashion. (See Unit 13 Lesson 4.)

Daily Routines

2s, 3s, and 4s Count-Bys Draw Arrays, Draw Groups on the 120 Poster, Draw Groups on the Number Path
(See pp. xxviii–xix.)

▸ Led by Student Leaders

Money Routine Using the 120 Poster, Using the Money Flip Chart, Using the Number Path, Using Secret Code Cards
(See pp. xxiii–xxv.)

▸ Led by Student Leaders

1 Teaching the Lesson

Activity 1

Compare Fractions

30 MINUTES

Goal: Color fraction strips to show fractions and then use the strips to compare fractions.

Materials: crayons or colored pencils, scissors (1 pair per child), Student Activity Book pages 447–449

NCTM Standards:
Number and Operations
Communication

Class Management

Looking Ahead Children will use these strips to compare fractions. Therefore, it is essential that they begin at the left when coloring the strips.

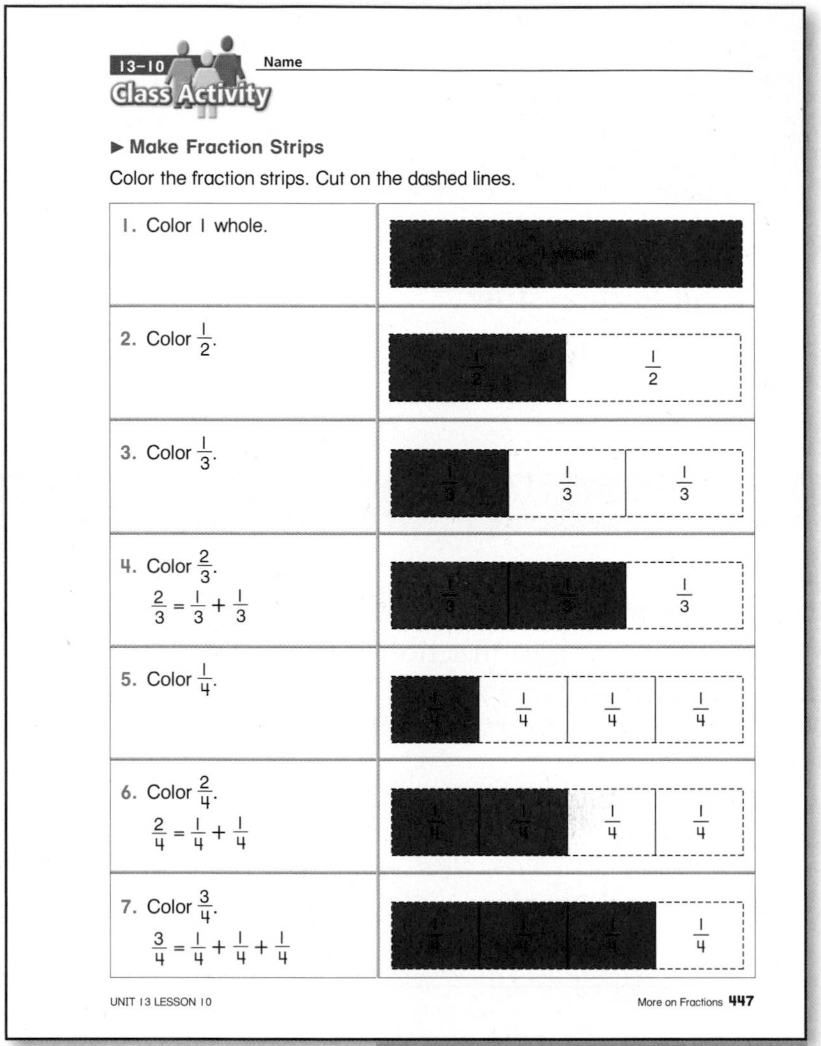

13–10 Class Activity Name

▶ **Make Fraction Strips**

Color the fraction strips. Cut on the dashed lines.

1. Color 1 whole.	1 whole
2. Color $\frac{1}{2}$.	$\frac{1}{2}$ $\frac{1}{2}$
3. Color $\frac{1}{3}$.	$\frac{1}{3}$ $\frac{1}{3}$ $\frac{1}{3}$
4. Color $\frac{2}{3}$. $\frac{2}{3} = \frac{1}{3} + \frac{1}{3}$	$\frac{1}{3}$ $\frac{1}{3}$ $\frac{1}{3}$
5. Color $\frac{1}{4}$.	$\frac{1}{4}$ $\frac{1}{4}$ $\frac{1}{4}$ $\frac{1}{4}$
6. Color $\frac{2}{4}$. $\frac{2}{4} = \frac{1}{4} + \frac{1}{4}$	$\frac{1}{4}$ $\frac{1}{4}$ $\frac{1}{4}$ $\frac{1}{4}$
7. Color $\frac{3}{4}$. $\frac{3}{4} = \frac{1}{4} + \frac{1}{4} + \frac{1}{4}$	$\frac{1}{4}$ $\frac{1}{4}$ $\frac{1}{4}$ $\frac{1}{4}$

UNIT 13 LESSON 10 More on Fractions 447

Student Activity Book page 447

▶ Make Fraction Strips WHOLE CLASS

Refer children to Student Activity Book page 447. Explain that all of the strips on the page are the same size. Point out that the first strip shows 1 whole and the other strips show the whole divided into different equal parts.

Math Talk Have children color the strip that shows 1 whole. Then work together as a class to color the remaining strips. Be sure children color the fractions one part at a time beginning on the left.

- Look at the second strip. How many equal parts are there? 2 equal parts What do we call one part? $\frac{1}{2}$ Color in $\frac{1}{2}$ of the strip.
- Look at the third strip. How many equal parts are there? 3 equal parts What do we call one part? $\frac{1}{3}$ Color in $\frac{1}{3}$ of the strip.
- Look at the fourth strip. How many equal parts are there? 3 equal parts What do we call two parts? $\frac{2}{3}$ Color in $\frac{2}{3}$ of the strip.

Repeat this process with the remaining strips on the page.

▶ Compare Fraction Strips PAIRS

Math Talk 123

After children have colored their fraction strips, tell them to carefully cut them out so that they can use them to compare different fractions. Have children work in **Helping Pairs**. Then have one child in each pair find the fraction strip that shows $\frac{1}{2}$ and the other child finds the fraction strip that shows $\frac{1}{4}$. Tell them to place the strips underneath each other and compare how much of each strip is colored.

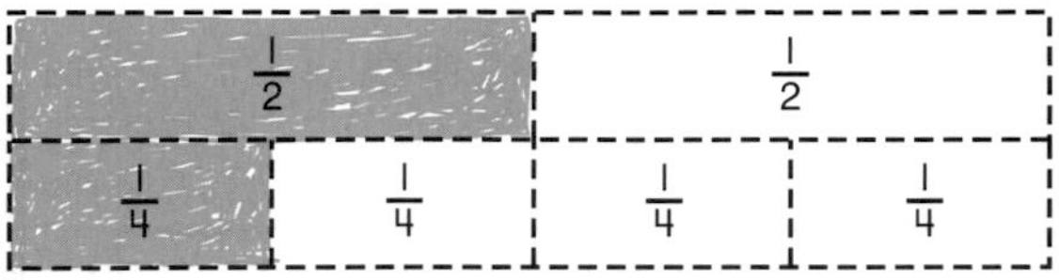

- Which strip has a greater part colored? $\frac{1}{2}$
- Which fraction is greater, $\frac{1}{2}$ or $\frac{1}{4}$? $\frac{1}{2}$

Have one child in each pair find the fraction strip that shows 1 whole and have the other child find the fraction strip that shows $\frac{1}{2}$. Tell them to place the strips underneath each other and compare them.

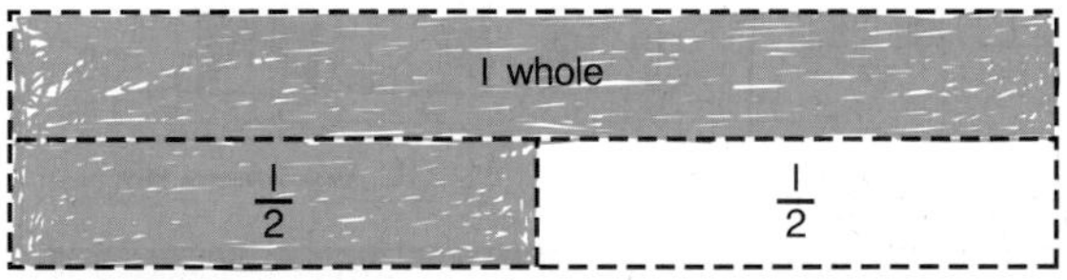

- Which strip has a greater part colored? 1 whole
- Which is greater, $\frac{1}{2}$ or 1 whole? 1 whole

Repeat the process for $\frac{1}{3}$ and $\frac{2}{4}$.

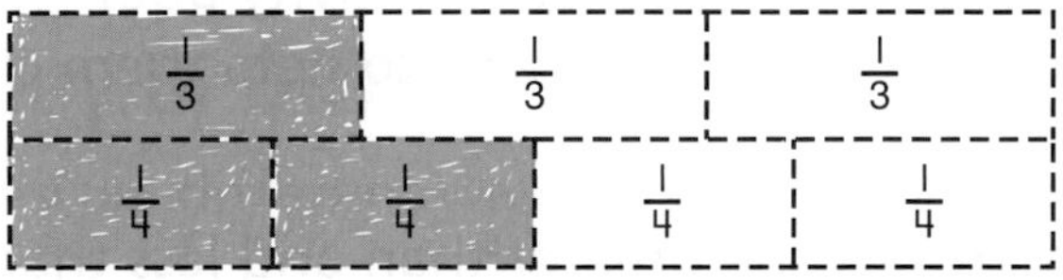

- Which strip has a greater part colored? $\frac{2}{4}$
- Which is greater, $\frac{1}{3}$ or $\frac{2}{4}$? $\frac{2}{4}$

Then repeat the process for $\frac{1}{2}$ and $\frac{2}{4}$.

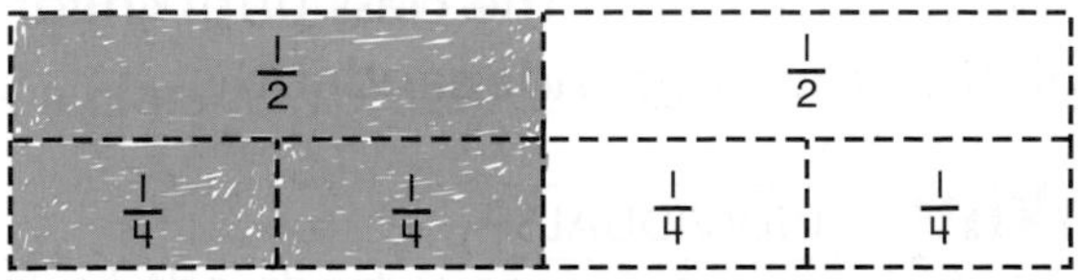

- Which strip has a greater part colored? Neither, they are the same.
- Which is greater, $\frac{1}{2}$ or $\frac{2}{4}$? Neither, the fractions are equal.

Activity continued ▶

Teaching Note

Watch For! Be sure children understand that the fractions being used in this activity are all less than 1 whole. If time permits, have children compare each of these fractions to the one whole strip to help reinforce this fact.

English Language Learners

Draw and shade $\frac{1}{2}$ of a rectangle. Draw and shade $\frac{1}{4}$ of a rectangle underneath it. Write *greater* beside the rectangles.

- **Beginning** Point and say: **$\frac{1}{2}$ is larger than $\frac{1}{4}$. It is *greater*.** Have children repeat.
- **Intermediate** Ask: **Is $\frac{1}{4}$ *greater* than $\frac{1}{2}$?** no **Is $\frac{1}{2}$ *greater* than $\frac{1}{4}$?** yes
- **Advanced** Have children identify which fraction is *greater*.

2 Going Further

Math Connection: Estimating with Fractions

Goal: Estimate with fractions.

Materials: scissors (1 pair per child), Student Activity Book pages 451–452

✓ **NCTM Standards:**
Number and Operations
Communication

▶ Estimate Fractions WHOLE CLASS

Direct children's attention to Student Activity Book page 451. Have children cut out the fraction strips. Point out that the top strip is marked 0, $\frac{1}{2}$, and 1, and should be cut out along the dashed lines. They will use this strip to estimate whether each fraction is closest to 0, $\frac{1}{2}$ or 1. Have children start with the fraction strip that shows $\frac{1}{5}$. Tell them to place the fraction strip underneath the strip that is marked 0, $\frac{1}{2}$, and 1.

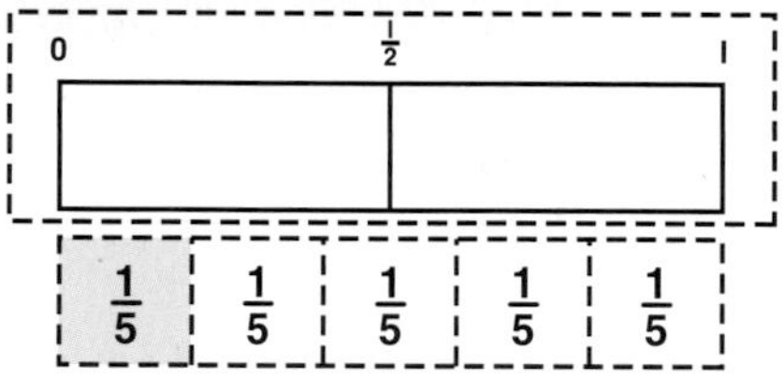

Be sure children align the 0 with the edge of the shaded fraction strip.

Now tell children to decide whether $\frac{1}{5}$ is closest to 0, $\frac{1}{2}$, or 1 and record their decision. Have children continue in this manner, estimating $\frac{3}{5}$ and $\frac{4}{5}$. Then tell children to estimate using other fractions. Give children several different fractions so that they use all the strips.

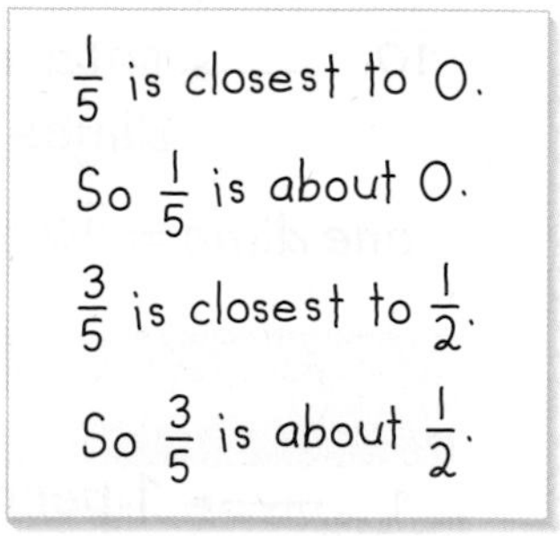

▶ Share Results WHOLE CLASS Math Talk

After children have completed the activity, ask pairs to share their results. Possible Answers: $\frac{1}{5}$ and $\frac{1}{8}$ are closest to 0; $\frac{3}{5}$ and $\frac{3}{8}$ are closest to $\frac{1}{2}$; $\frac{4}{5}$ and $\frac{7}{8}$ are closest to 1. If children had different estimates, encourage them to share their estimates and explain their reasoning.

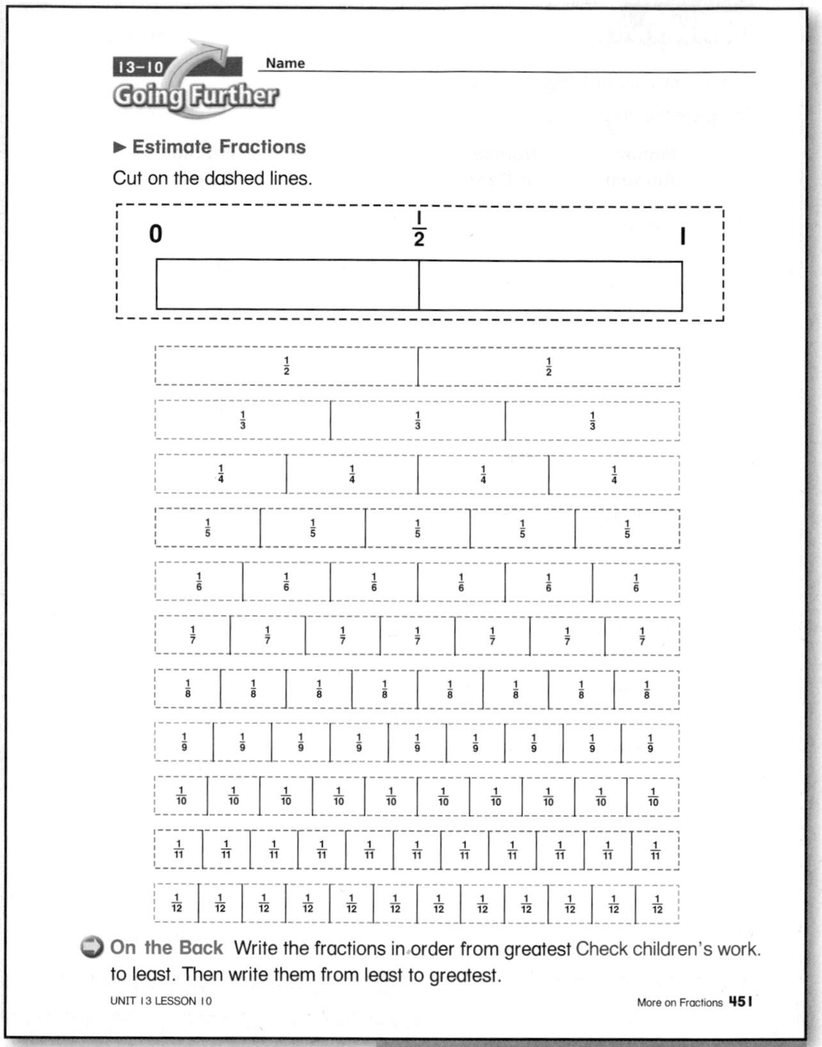
13-10 Going Further Name ____________

▶ Estimate Fractions

Cut on the dashed lines.

On the Back Write the fractions in order from greatest to least. Then write them from least to greatest. Check children's work.

UNIT 13 LESSON 10 More on Fractions 451

Student Activity Book page 451

Then ask these critical thinking questions. Elicit from children the patterns that they see from these fractions.

- Can anyone tell just by looking at the numbers in a fraction if the fraction is close to 1? If the top and bottom number are close to the same value then the fraction is close to 1. For example, $\frac{4}{5}$ and $\frac{7}{8}$ are both close to 1.
- Can anyone tell just by looking at the numbers in a fraction if the fraction is close to 0? If the top and bottom number have values that are far apart then the fraction is close to 0. For example, $\frac{1}{5}$ is close to 0. $\frac{1}{8}$ is closer to 0 than $\frac{1}{5}$.

Intervention — Activity Card 13-10

Fraction Strips

Activity Card 13-10 ●

Work: (pairs)

Use:

- 2 sets of fraction strips (Student Activity Book page 447)

1. Each (child): Take one set of fraction strips. Mix up your fraction strips and place them face down in a pile.
2. Each (child): Turn over the top fraction strip.
3. Compare the colored parts of the fraction strips. The player with the strip that shows the greater fraction keeps both strips.

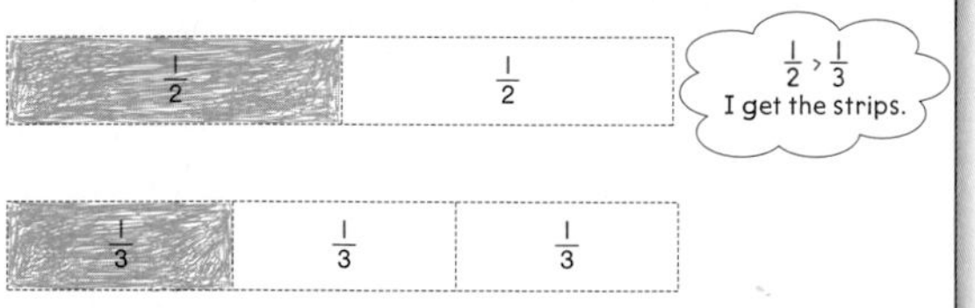

4. Repeat until all the strips are used. The player with more strips wins.

Unit 13, Lesson 10

Activity Note Each child needs the colored fraction strips from Activity 1 (Student Activity Book page 447).

Math Writing Prompt

Make a Drawing Draw a picture showing why $\frac{2}{4}$ is equal to $\frac{1}{2}$.

Soar to Success Math **Software Support**

Warm Up 5.08

On Level — Activity Card 13-10

Find the Greater Fraction

Activity Card 13-10 ▲

Work: (pairs)

Use:

- 6 index cards
- fraction strips (Student Activity Book page 447)

1. **Work Together** Write one of these fractions on each index card: $\frac{1}{2}$, $\frac{1}{3}$, $\frac{2}{3}$, $\frac{1}{4}$, $\frac{2}{4}$, and $\frac{3}{4}$.
2. Mix the index cards and place them face down in a pile. Each (child): Pick one card from the pile.
3. Compare the cards. Use the fraction strips to decide which fraction is greater.

4. The person with the greater fraction card keeps both cards.
5. Repeat until all the cards are used. The player with more cards wins.

Unit 13, Lesson 10

Activity Note Each child needs the colored fraction strips from Activity 1 (Student Activity Book page 447). Each pair needs six index cards.

Math Writing Prompt

Number Sense How do you know that $\frac{2}{3}$ is greater than $\frac{1}{3}$ without using fraction strips?

Harcourt Mega Math Grades K-6 **Software Support**

Shapes Ahoy: Ship Shapes, Level R

Challenge — Activity Card 13-10

Compare and Order Fractions

Activity Card 13-10 ■

Work: (pairs)

Use:

- Number Lines (TRB M93)

1. $\frac{1}{3}$ (>) $\frac{1}{4}$
2. $\frac{1}{2}$ (<) $\frac{2}{3}$
3. $\frac{2}{3}$ (<) $\frac{4}{5}$
4. $\frac{2}{5}$ (>) $\frac{1}{3}$
5. $\frac{1}{3}, \frac{1}{2}, \frac{1}{4}$ — $\frac{1}{4}, \frac{1}{3}, \frac{1}{2}$
6. $\frac{2}{3}, \frac{3}{4}, \frac{1}{2}$ — $\frac{1}{2}, \frac{2}{3}, \frac{3}{4}$
7. $\frac{1}{2}, \frac{1}{3}, \frac{2}{4}$ — $\frac{1}{3}, \frac{2}{5}, \frac{1}{2}$
8. $\frac{2}{5}, \frac{2}{3}, \frac{3}{4}$ — $\frac{3}{5}, \frac{2}{3}, \frac{3}{4}$

1. **Work Together** Copy the exercises above.
2. Use the Number Lines page to compare the fractions in exercises 1–4. Write < or >.
3. For exercises 5–8, order the fractions from least to greatest. Use the Number Lines page to help you.

Unit 13, Lesson 10

Activity Note Each pair needs Number Lines (TRB M93). Show pairs how to use the number lines to compare and order fractions.

Math Writing Prompt

Explain Your Thinking Explain why you can use the bottom numbers to order $\frac{1}{3}$, $\frac{1}{2}$, and $\frac{1}{4}$ from least to greatest.

DESTINATION Math® **Software Support**

Course II: Module 2: Unit 3: Fractional Parts

3 Homework and Targeted Practice

13–10 Homework **Goal:** Additional Practice

This Homework page provides practice comparing fractions and finding fractions of a dollar.

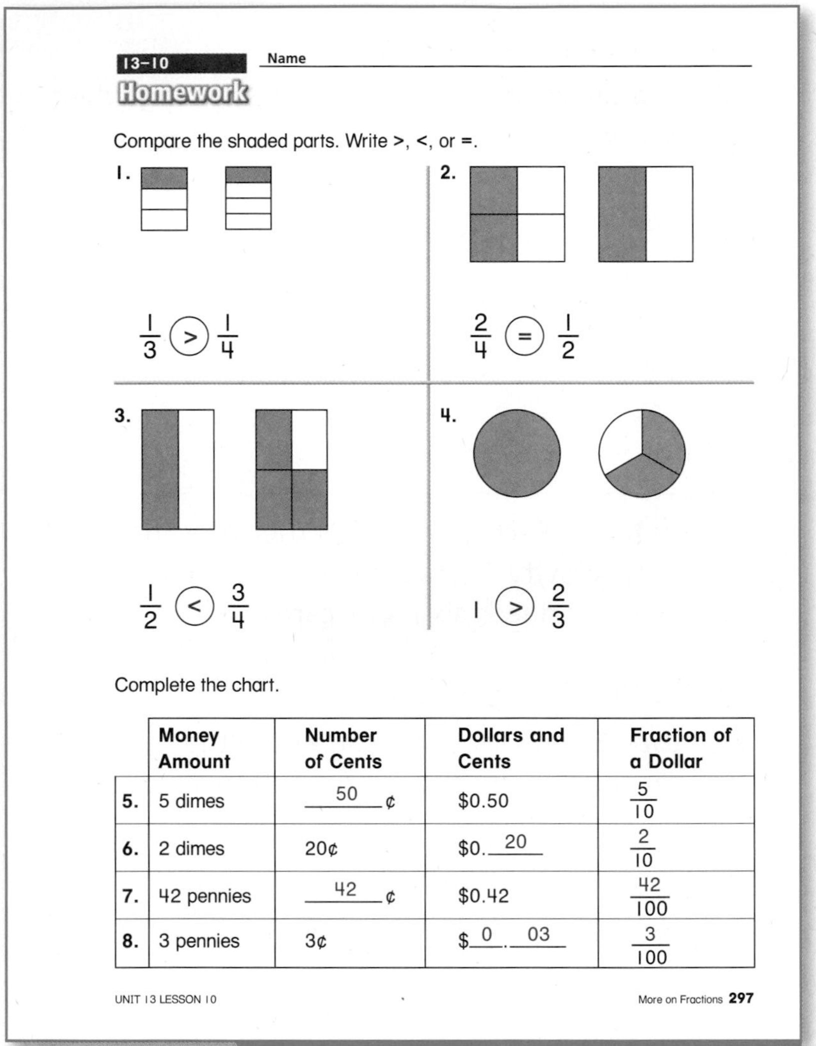

13–10 Homework Name

Compare the shaded parts. Write >, <, or =.

1. $\frac{1}{3}$ (>) $\frac{1}{4}$

2. $\frac{2}{4}$ (=) $\frac{1}{2}$

3. $\frac{1}{2}$ (<) $\frac{3}{4}$

4. 1 (>) $\frac{2}{3}$

Complete the chart.

	Money Amount	Number of Cents	Dollars and Cents	Fraction of a Dollar
5.	5 dimes	50 ¢	$0.50	$\frac{5}{10}$
6.	2 dimes	20¢	$0. 20	$\frac{2}{10}$
7.	42 pennies	42 ¢	$0.42	$\frac{42}{100}$
8.	3 pennies	3¢	$ 0 . 03	$\frac{3}{100}$

UNIT 13 LESSON 10 More on Fractions 297

Homework and Remembering page 297

13–10 Targeted Practice **Goal:** Lines of Symmetry

This Targeted Practice page can be used with children who need extra practice with symmetrical shapes.

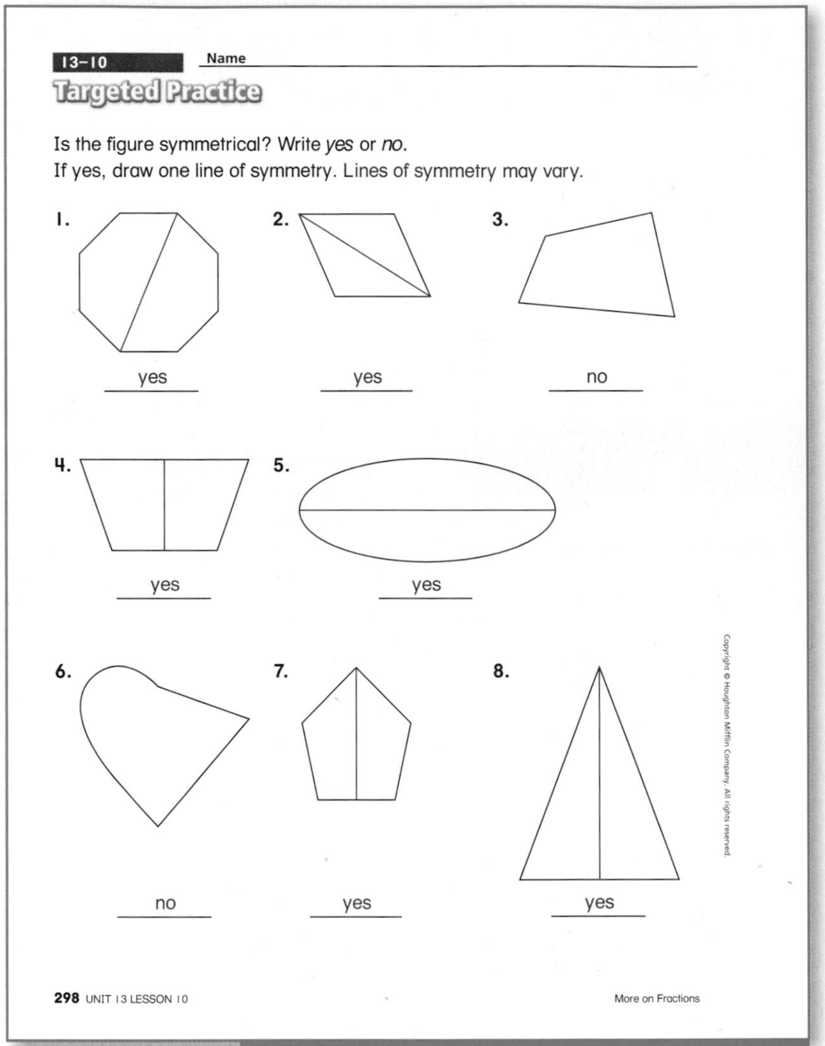

13–10 Targeted Practice Name

Is the figure symmetrical? Write *yes* or *no*.
If yes, draw one line of symmetry. Lines of symmetry may vary.

1. yes
2. yes
3. no
4. yes
5. yes
6. no
7. yes
8. yes

298 UNIT 13 LESSON 10 More on Fractions

Homework and Remembering page 298

Home or School Activity

Real-World Connection

Fractions in the Kitchen Bring in or have children bring in measuring cups or measuring spoons with fractions and half-gallon milk containers. Have volunteers use these to measure out given amounts of sand or rice.

UNIT 13 LESSON 11

Explore Probability

Lesson Objectives

- **Describe events as impossible, possible, or certain.**
- **Discuss whether a game is fair or unfair.**
- **Predict the results of a probability experiment and then do the experiment to check the prediction.**

Vocabulary	
impossible	probability
possible	prediction
certain	more likely
fair	less likely
unfair	event

The Day at a Glance

Today's Goals	Materials	
1 Teaching the Lesson **A1:** Describe events as impossible, possible, or certain. **A2:** Play a game and then discuss whether the game is fair or unfair. **A3:** Predict the results of a probability experiment and then do the experiment to check the prediction. **2 Going Further** ▶ Differentiated Instruction **3 Homework and Spiral Review**	**Lesson Activities** Student Activity Book pp. 453–454 Homework and Remembering pp. 299–300 Small brown paper bag Connecting cubes Crayons or colored pencils Paper clips Number cubes	**Going Further** Activity Cards 13-11 Crayons or colored pencils Spinners (TRB M27) Real or play money (pennies) Math Journals

Use **Math Talk** *today!*

Keeping Skills Sharp

Quick Practice — 5 MINUTES

Goal: Count by 3s and 4s.

Count By 3s Divide the class into two groups. Have the class count by 3s. The first group starts by saying the number 3. The second group responds with "6." The first group replies with "9," and so on until they have reached 30. You may wish to repeat the exercise, asking the second group to begin this time. (See Unit 13 Lesson 3.)

Have children use their fingers to mark off each multiple of 3 that they count.

Count By 4s Have children practice the 4 count-bys in the same fashion. (See Unit 13 Lesson 4.)

Daily Routines

2s, 3s, and 4s Count-Bys Draw Arrays, Draw Groups on the 120 Poster, Draw Groups on the Number Path (See pp. xxviii–xix.)

▶ Led by Student Leaders

Money Routine Using the 120 Poster, Using the Money Flip Chart, Using the Number Path, Using Secret Code Cards (See pp. xxiii–xxv.)

▶ Led by Student Leaders

1 Teaching the Lesson

Activity 1

Introduce Probability

15 MINUTES

Goal: Describe events as impossible, possible, or certain.

Materials: small brown paper bag, connecting cubes (5 blue and 3 green)

NCTM Standards:
Data Analysis and Probability
Communication

English Language Learners

Write *likely* and *unlikely* on the board. Draw 1 child eating a huge ice cream cone and 1 eating a small ice cream cone. Point to the large ice cream.

- **Beginning** Say: **It is *likely* he will get sick.** Have children repeat. Continue with the other child and *unlikely*.
- **Intermediate** Ask: **Is he *likely* to get sick?** yes Point to the other child. Ask: **Is he likely to get sick?** no Say: **It is *unlikely*.**
- **Advanced** Have children tell which child is *likely* and *unlikely* to get sick.

▶ Impossible, Possible, or Certain Events WHOLE CLASS

Introduce the term *probability*. Explain that probability is used to describe how likely it is for something to happen. Then write the words *impossible*, *possible*, and *certain* on the board and tell children that they will use these words to describe different events.

Ask for Ideas Discuss the meaning of the three words and compare them to ordinary words or phrases, such as *no way, maybe, for sure.* Then ask volunteers to describe events that are impossible, possible, and certain.

- Who can describe something that is impossible? Responses will vary. Is it really impossible, or is it possible but just not very likely to happen? Responses will vary.
- Who can describe something that is possible? Responses will vary.
- Who can describe something that is certain to happen? Responses will vary. Is it really certain, or is it just very likely to happen? Responses will vary.

Then present the events listed below and have children describe each of the events as impossible, possible, or certain. Challenge children to explain and defend their answers.

- Summer will follow spring. Certain, summer always follows spring.
- A giraffe will fly. Impossible, giraffes can't fly because they do not have wings.
- It will be a sunny day tomorrow. Possible, some days are sunny, some days are not sunny.

Finally have children watch you place five blue connecting cubes in an empty paper bag. Then ask the following questions:

- What is the likelihood of picking a blue cube? certain
- What is the likelihood of picking a green cube? impossible

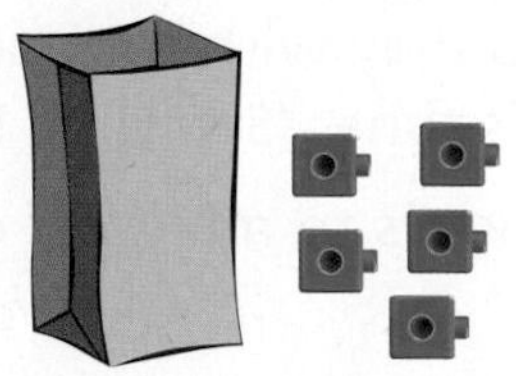

Now place three green cubes in the paper bag along with the blue cubes and ask the questions again.

- What is the likelihood of picking a blue cube? possible
- What is the likelihood of picking a green cube? possible

Activity 2

Spinners and Predictions

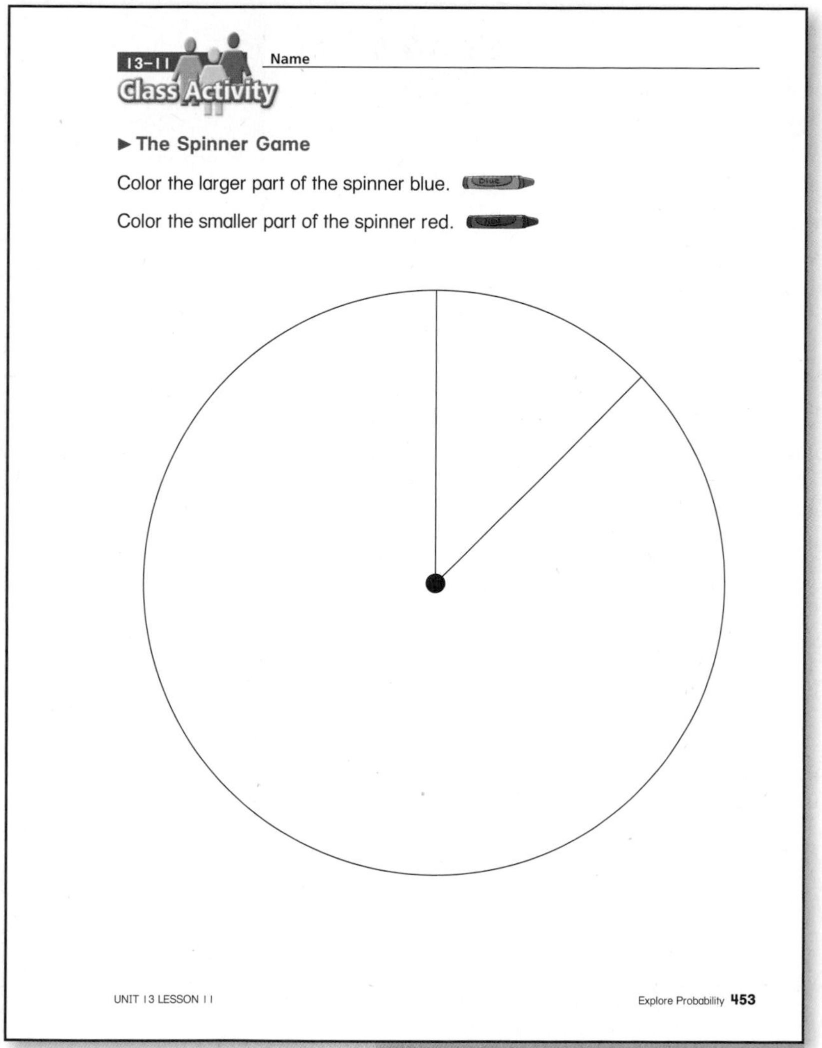

13-11 Class Activity

Name

► The Spinner Game

Color the larger part of the spinner blue.

Color the smaller part of the spinner red.

UNIT 13 LESSON 11

Explore Probability 453

Student Activity Book page 453

► The Spinner Game PAIRS

Make a Game Spinner Direct children's attention to Student Activity Book page 453. Have pairs color the larger section of the spinner red and the smaller section of the spinner blue. Show children how to use a paper clip as a pointer and a pencil as a pivot.

Play and Discuss the Game See rules at the right.

After children have played the game, discuss the game with them.

- If you were going to play the game again, which color would you rather have? red Why? It is a larger section of the spinner.
- On which color is the spinner more likely to land? red On which color is the spinner less likely to land? blue
- Do you think the game is fair or unfair? Unfair; the person who gets a point when the spinner lands on red is more likely to win. What could you do to make the game fair? Make the spinner half blue and half red.

20 MINUTES

Goal: Play a game and then discuss whether the game is fair or unfair.

Materials: Crayons or colored pencils (1 red and 1 blue crayon per pair), paper clips (1 per pair), Student Activity Book page 453

NCTM Standards:
Data Analysis and Probability
Communication

Teaching Note

Language and Vocabulary After children have finished discussing the game, help them to focus on the distinctions between the terms used in this activity and in Activity 1. Point out that *impossible* and *certain* are direct opposites (*can't happen* versus *will happen*). Likewise the terms *more likely* and *less likely* are also direct opposites (*probably will happen* versus *probably won't happen*).

Rules for *The Spinner Game*

- Have pairs take turns spinning the paper clip 10 times each.
- One child gets a point if the spinner lands on red. The other child gets a point if the spinner lands on blue.
- Children should record their points on a piece of paper.

Activity 3

Number Cubes and Predictions

20 MINUTES

Goals: Predict the results of a probability experiment and then do the experiment to check the prediction.

Materials: number cubes (2 per pair), Student Activity Book page 454

NCTM Standards:
Data Analysis and Probability
Communication

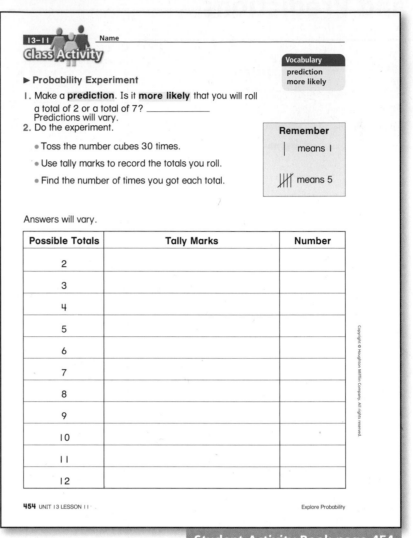

13-11 Class Activity

Name ____________

Vocabulary
prediction
more likely

▶ **Probability Experiment**

1. Make a **prediction**. Is it **more likely** that you will roll a total of 2 or a total of 7? ____________
Predictions will vary.
2. Do the experiment.
   - Toss the number cubes 30 times.
   - Use tally marks to record the totals you roll.
   - Find the number of times you got each total.

Remember
| means 1
𝍸 means 5

Answers will vary.

Possible Totals	Tally Marks	Number
2		
3		
4		
5		
6		
7		
8		
9		
10		
11		
12		

454 UNIT 13 LESSON 11 — Explore Probability

Student Activity Book page 454

▶ Probability Experiment PAIRS

Math Talk

Tell children that they will roll two number cubes 30 times and keep track of the total each time.

Explain that the table on Student Activity Book page 454 shows all the possible totals. Ask children why they think the number 1 is not listed. It is not possible to roll a total of 1.

Children will use the table to record their results as they do the probability experiment. Before they begin, have children predict whether a total of 2 or a total of 7 is more likely to be rolled. Tell them to write their prediction on the top of the student page.

When they have finished the experiment, have children share their results.

- Which numbers have a total of 2? 1 and 1 Which numbers have a total of 7 1 and 6, 2 and 5, 3 and 4 Why is a total of 7 more likely than a total of 2? because there are more ways to roll a total of 7 than a total of 2

Ongoing Assessment

Place different combinations of colored connecting cubes in a paper bag. Then ask the children to use the terms *impossible, possible,* and *certain* to describe the likelihood of choosing a particular color.

Intervention — Activity Card 13-11

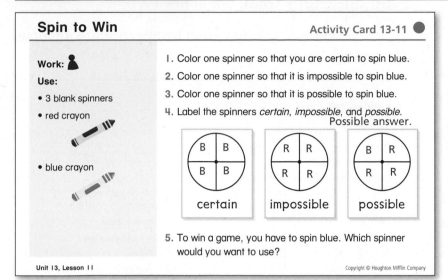

Spin to Win
Activity Card 13-11

Work:
Use:
- 3 blank spinners
- red crayon
- blue crayon

1. Color one spinner so that you are certain to spin blue.
2. Color one spinner so that it is impossible to spin blue.
3. Color one spinner so that it is possible to spin blue.
4. Label the spinners *certain*, *impossible*, and *possible*.

Possible answer.

5. To win a game, you have to spin blue. Which spinner would you want to use?

Unit 13, Lesson 11

Activity Note Each child needs three 4-part spinners (TRB M27), one red, and one blue crayon. Ask children to explain each completed spinner.

Math Writing Prompt
Write About It Suppose there are 13 red marbles and 2 green marbles in a bag. Is choosing a blue marble possible, impossible, or certain? Explain.

Soar to Success Math Software Support
Warm Up 52.05

On Level — Activity Card 13-11

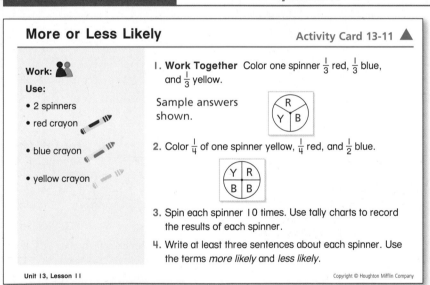

More or Less Likely
Activity Card 13-11

Work:
Use:
- 2 spinners
- red crayon
- blue crayon
- yellow crayon

1. **Work Together** Color one spinner $\frac{1}{3}$ red, $\frac{1}{3}$ blue, and $\frac{1}{3}$ yellow.

Sample answers shown.

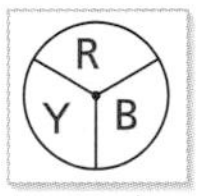

2. Color $\frac{1}{4}$ of one spinner yellow, $\frac{1}{4}$ red, and $\frac{1}{2}$ blue.

3. Spin each spinner 10 times. Use tally charts to record the results of each spinner.
4. Write at least three sentences about each spinner. Use the terms *more likely* and *less likely*.

Unit 13, Lesson 11

Activity Note Each pair needs a 3-part spinner and a 4-part spinner (TRB M27), and a red, blue, and yellow crayon.

Math Writing Prompt
It's Unfair Describe an unfair game. Use the terms *less likely* and *more likely* in your description.

Harcourt Mega Math Software Support
Numberopolis: Wash 'n Spin, Level D

Challenge — Activity Card 13-11

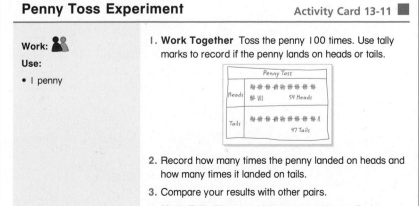

Penny Toss Experiment
Activity Card 13-11

Work:
Use:
- 1 penny

1. **Work Together** Toss the penny 100 times. Use tally marks to record if the penny lands on heads or tails.

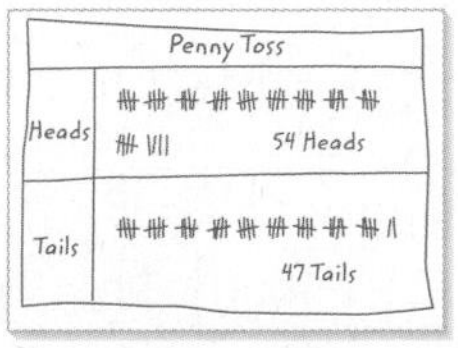

2. Record how many times the penny landed on heads and how many times it landed on tails.
3. Compare your results with other pairs.
4. **Math Talk** Discuss which event, heads or tails, is *more likely*. Which is *less likely*? Sample answer: Neither, both events are equally likely to happen.

Unit 13, Lesson 11

Activity Note Each pair needs one penny. Review the terms *more likely* and *less likely*. Then explain the term *equally likely*.

Math Writing Prompt
Write About It Describe three events—one that is *impossible*, one that is *possible*, and one that is *certain*.

Destination Math Software Support
Course II: Module 2: Unit 3: Fractional Parts

3 Homework and Spiral Review

13–11 Homework Goal: Additional Practice

✓ Include children's completed Homework page as part of their portfolios.

13–11 Name ______

Homework

Look at the bag of cubes. Circle the correct event.

1. Which event is certain?

(I will pick a black cube.) [circled]

I will pick a white cube.

2. Which event is impossible?

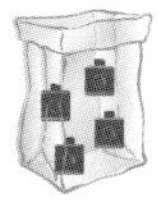

I will pick a black cube.

(I will pick a white cube.) [circled]

Look at the bag of cubes. How more likely or less likely are you to pick a  than a ?

3.

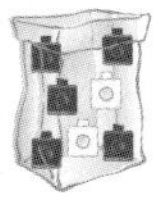

(more likely) [circled]

less likely

4.

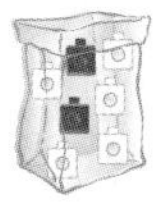

more likely

(less likely) [circled]

Color in the spinners to make the statements true. Check children's answers.

5. This is a fair spinner.

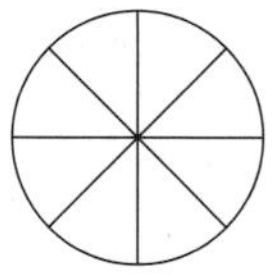

6. This is an unfair spinner.

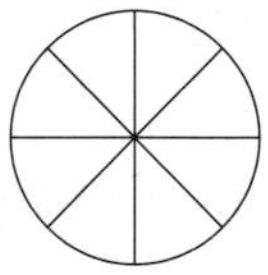

UNIT 13 LESSON 11 Explore Probability **299**

Homework and Remembering page 299

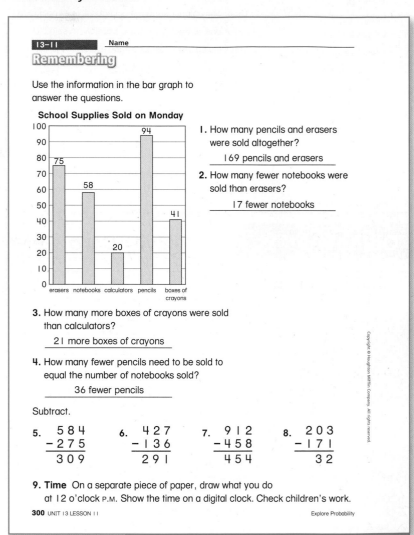

13–11 Remembering Goal: Spiral Review

This Remembering activity would be appropriate anytime after today's lesson.

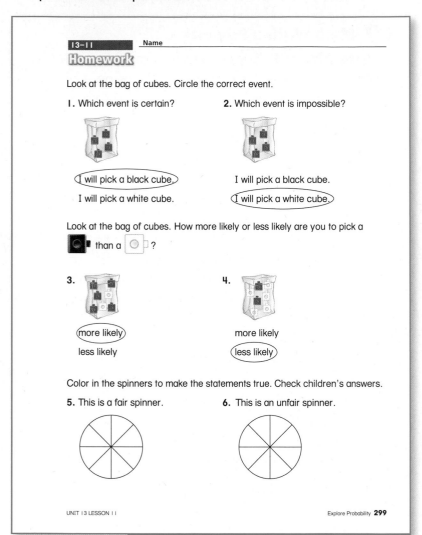

13–11 Name ______

Remembering

Use the information in the bar graph to answer the questions.

School Supplies Sold on Monday

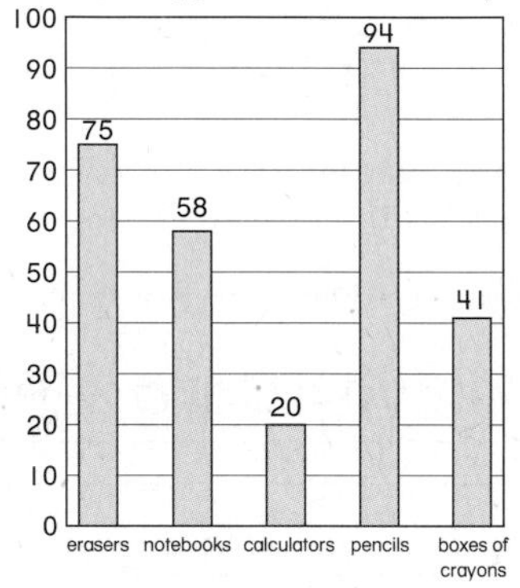

1. How many pencils and erasers were sold altogether?

169 pencils and erasers

2. How many fewer notebooks were sold than erasers?

17 fewer notebooks

3. How many more boxes of crayons were sold than calculators?

21 more boxes of crayons

4. How many fewer pencils need to be sold to equal the number of notebooks sold?

36 fewer pencils

Subtract.

5. $584 - 275 = 309$

6. $427 - 136 = 291$

7. $912 - 458 = 454$

8. $203 - 171 = 32$

9. Time On a separate piece of paper, draw what you do at 12 o'clock P.M. Show the time on a digital clock. Check children's work.

300 UNIT 13 LESSON 11 Explore Probability

Homework and Remembering page 300

Home or School Activity

Math-to-Math Connection

Fair Games Have children work in pairs to create a fair game using spinners or number cubes. Have them make a poster to describe the rules of the game. Remind children to make a game board if one is needed for their game.

If time permits, have children explain the rules of their games to the rest of the class and allow children to play the games.

Number Cube Game

- One player is ODD and one is EVEN.
- Roll the number cube 10 times.
- If the number is odd, ODD scores a point. If the number is even, EVEN scores a point.

UNIT 13 LESSON 12

Possible Outcomes

Lesson Objectives

- Identify all possible outcomes for a probability experiment and decide which is most likely and least likely to happen. Then do the experiment to check the predictions.
- Use numbers to describe the probability of an event.
- Find all the possible combinations for a given situation.

Vocabulary

outcome	event
prediction	organized list
probability	combination

The Day at a Glance

Today's Goals

1 Teaching the Lesson

A1: Identify all possible outcomes for a probability experiment and decide which is most likely and least likely. Then do the experiment to check the predictions.

A2: Use numbers to describe the probability of an event.

A3: Find all the possible combinations for a given situation.

2 Going Further

▶ Differentiated Instruction

3 Homework and Targeted Practice

Materials

Lesson Activities

Student Activity Book pp. 455–456
Homework and Remembering pp. 301–302
Small brown paper bags
Connecting cubes
MathBoard materials
Quick Quiz 3 (Assessment Guide)

Going Further

Activity Cards 13-12
Student Activity Book p. 455
Small brown paper bags
Connecting cubes
Math Journals

Use Math Talk today!

Keeping Skills Sharp

Quick Practice — 5 MINUTES

Goal: Count by 3s and 4s.

Count By 3s Divide the class into two groups. Have the class count by 3s. The first group starts by saying the number 3. The second group responds with "6." The first group replies with "9," and so on until they have reached 30. You may wish to repeat the exercise, asking the second group to begin this time. (See Unit 13 Lesson 3.)

Count By 4s Have children practice the 4 count-bys in the same fashion. (See Unit 13 Lesson 4.)

Daily Routines

2s, 3s, and 4s Count-Bys Draw Arrays, Draw Groups on the 120 Poster, Draw Groups on the Number Path (See pp. xxviii–xix.)

▶ Led by Student Leaders

Money Routine Using the 120 Poster, Using the Money Flip Chart, Using the Number Path, Using Secret Code Cards (See pp. xxiii–xxv.)

▶ Led by Student Leaders

1 Teaching the Lesson

Activity 1

Possible Outcomes

20 MINUTES

Goals: Identify all possible outcomes for a probability experiment and decide which is most likely and least likely. Then do the experiment to check the predictions.

Materials: small brown paper bag, connecting cubes (15 blue, 4 red, and 1 green), MathBoard materials

✓ **NCTM Standards:**
Data Analysis and Probability
Communication

Teaching Note

Math Background It is important to remember that there is experimental probability and theoretical (or mathematical) probability. When probability experiments are performed, the actual results will often not match the theoretical probability.

Sometimes, because of chance, outcomes are not what one would expect. However, the more an experiment is repeated, the closer the results should get to the theoretical probability. As the children do the experiments in this lesson, reassure them that it is all right if their results do not always match the theoretical probability.

▶ Discuss Outcomes WHOLE CLASS

Math Talk

Ask for Ideas Introduce the term *outcome.* Describe an outcome as the result of an experiment or as what "comes out."

- If you toss a coin, what are the possible outcomes? tossing heads or tossing tails
- If you spin a spinner that is part green and part blue, what are the possible outcomes? landing on green or landing on blue

Then tell the children that they will conduct an experiment as a class where they pick a cube from a bag without looking. Have children watch you fill a paper bag with 15 blue cubes, 4 red cubes, and 1 green cube. Then discuss the possible outcomes with children.

- What are the possible outcomes for this experiment? choosing a blue, red, or green cube
- What outcome do you think is most likely? choosing a blue cube Why? There are a lot more blue cubes in the bag than there are any other color.
- What outcome do you think is least likely? choosing a green cube Why? There is only one green cube in the bag.

▶ Conduct an Experiment WHOLE CLASS

Write children's predictions for the most likely and least likely outcomes on the board. Tell them that they will now do the experiment to test their predictions. Draw a chart like the one below and have a **Student Leader** use it to record the results of the experiment. If necessary, review how to make tally marks.

Outcomes from Experiment

Color of Cube	Tally Marks	Number of Cubes
Blue		
Red		
Green		

Have the other children come to the front of the room one at a time to pick a connecting cube from the bag and have the Student Leader record the color that is picked each time. Be sure the cube is placed back into the bag after each turn.

Repeat this process until about 40 cubes have been picked from the bag. Then have the class count the tally marks to find the total number of each color that was picked. Discuss how the results compare to their predictions.

Activity 2

Probability of an Event

▶ Use Numbers to Describe Probability WHOLE CLASS

Math Talk 123

- Tell the children that in this activity they will be using numbers to describe the chance of something happening. Show the children six connecting cubes: 3 blue, 2 red, and 1 green. Tell them that you are setting up a probability game and you want them to help you figure out the probability of picking each color from a bag.

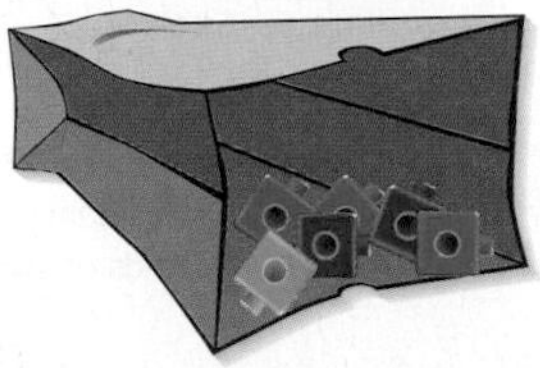

- How many cubes will be in the bag? 6 cubes
- How many of the cubes are blue? 3 cubes

Write *3 out of 6* on the board and explain that 3 out of 6 means there are 3 out of 6 chances of picking a blue cube.

- How many of the cubes are red? 2 cubes
- How could we use numbers to write the probability of picking a red cube? 2 out of 6
- How many of the cubes are green? 1 cube
- How could we use numbers to write the probability of picking a green cube? 1 out of 6

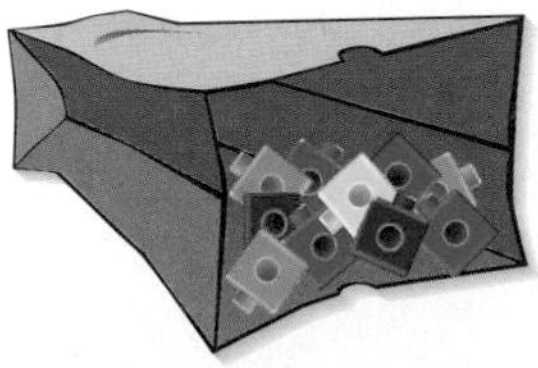

Empty out the bag and tell children that this time you want to fill the bag with 4 blue cubes, 2 red cubes, 3 green cubes, and 1 yellow cube. Then have the children identify the probability of picking each of the colors.

- How many cubes will be in the bag this time? 10 cubes
- How many of the cubes are blue? 4 cubes
- How could we write the probability of picking a blue cube? 4 out of 10
- How many of the cubes are red? 2 cubes
- How could we write the probability of picking a red cube? 2 out of 10

Repeat the questions for green 3 cubes, 3 out of 10 and yellow 1 cube, 1 out of 10. Then ask how many of the cubes are purple 0 cubes and challenge the children to write the probability of picking a purple cube. 0 out of 10 Finally, ask children to write the probability of picking a blue, red, green, or yellow cube. 10 out of 10

Repeat with other combinations of connecting cubes as time permits.

15 MINUTES

Goal: Use numbers to describe the probability of an event.

Materials: small brown paper bag, connecting cubes (4 blue, 2 red, 3 green, and 1 yellow), MathBoard materials

NCTM Standards:
Data Analysis and Probability
Communication

English Language Learners

Have children help you count 2 red cubes and 3 green cubes. Write *2 out of 5*.

- **Beginning** Say: ***2 out of 5* means 2 red cubes out of 5 total cubes.** Have children repeat.
- **Intermediate** Ask: **Does *2 out of 5* mean 2 green cubes out of 5 total cubes?** no **Does *2 out of 5* mean 2 red cubes out of 5 total cubes?** yes
- **Advanced** Have children tell what *2 out of 5* means and identify the chances of choosing a green cube.

Ongoing Assessment

Place different combinations of colored connecting cubes in a paper bag. Then ask children to use numbers to describe the probability of choosing a particular color.

Activity 3

Combinations

20 MINUTES

Goals: Find all the possible combinations for a given situation.

Materials: Student Activity Book pages 455–456

NCTM Standards:
Data Analysis and Probability
Problem Solving
Communication

Quick Quiz

See Assessment Guide for Unit 13 Quick Quiz 3.

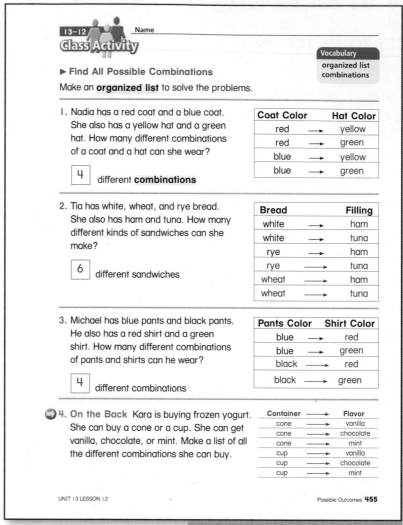

13–12 Class Activity   Name ____________________

Vocabulary
organized list
combinations

► Find All Possible Combinations

Make an **organized list** to solve the problems.

1. Nadia has a red coat and a blue coat. She also has a yellow hat and a green hat. How many different combinations of a coat and a hat can she wear?

4 different **combinations**

Coat Color		Hat Color
red	→	yellow
red	→	green
blue	→	yellow
blue	→	green

2. Tia has white, wheat, and rye bread. She also has ham and tuna. How many different kinds of sandwiches can she make?

6 different sandwiches

Bread		Filling
white	→	ham
white	→	tuna
rye	→	ham
rye	→	tuna
wheat	→	ham
wheat	→	tuna

3. Michael has blue pants and black pants. He also has a red shirt and a green shirt. How many different combinations of pants and shirts can he wear?

4 different combinations

Pants Color		Shirt Color
blue	→	red
blue	→	green
black	→	red
black	→	green

4. **On the Back** Kara is buying frozen yogurt. She can buy a cone or a cup. She can get vanilla, chocolate, or mint. Make a list of all the different combinations she can buy.

Container	→	Flavor
cone	→	vanilla
cone	→	chocolate
cone	→	mint
cup	→	vanilla
cup	→	chocolate
cup	→	mint

UNIT 13 LESSON 12   Possible Outcomes 455

Student Activity Book page 455

► Find All Possible Combinations

WHOLE CLASS   **Math Talk**

Direct children's attention to Student Activity book page 455. Have a volunteer read the first problem on the page aloud. Have children follow these steps to make an organized list to find all the combinations.

- Start with one coat and match it to each hat.
- Then match the other coat to each hat.
- Count the number of different combinations. 4 different combinations

Have children record their work on the student page and then help them see the connection to multiplication.

- How many different coats are there? 2 coats
- How many different hats are there? 2 hats
- What is 2×2? 4
- How many different combinations are there? 4 different combinations

Repeat this process for the remaining problems on the page.

Intervention Activity Card 13-12

More Red or More Blue? Activity Card 13-12

Work:
Use:
- paper bag with connecting cubes

1. There are 10 cubes in the bag. Some are red and some are blue. Do not look in the bag.
2. Reach into the bag and take out one cube.
3. Make a tally mark to record the color of the cube. Return the cube to the bag.

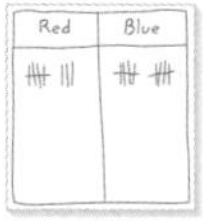

4. Take turns and repeat 30 times. Look at your results.
5. Predict if there are *more red* or *more blue* cubes in the bag. Look in the bag to check your prediction.

Unit 13, Lesson 12

Activity Note For each pair, prepare a paper bag with 2 red cubes and 8 blue cubes. Remind children to return the cube to the bag each time.

Math Writing Prompt

Draw and Explain There are five green cubes and one yellow cube in a bag. Draw the cubes. If you pick a cube from the bag without looking, what color do you think the cube will be? Explain.

Soar to Success Math Software Support

Warm Up 52.03

On Level Activity Card 13-12

Tree Diagrams Activity Card 13-12

Work:
Use:
- Student Activity Book page 455

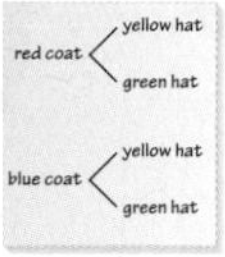

1. **Work Together** Look at problem 1 on page 455 in the Student Activity Book. The tree diagram above is another way to solve this problem.
2. **Math Talk** Discuss how the tree diagram shows the same problem and solution.
3. Make tree diagrams for problems 2–4.
4. **Look Back** Compare your tree diagrams to the organized lists. How are they the same? How are they different?

Unit 13, Lesson 12

Activity Note Each pair needs Student Activity Book p. 455. Review the tree diagram example on the card with children.

Math Writing Prompt

Explain Your Thinking A bag has five green cubes and one red cube. If you pick a cube from the bag without looking, how many outcomes are there? Which outcome is more likely? Explain your thinking.

Harcourt Mega Math Software Support

Numberopolis: Wash 'n Spin, Level F

Challenge Activity Card 13-12

What Color Are the Cubes? Activity Card 13-12

Work:
Use:
- paper bag with connecting cubes

1. **Work Together** There are 15 cubes in the bag. Some are red, some are blue, and some are yellow. Do not look in the bag. Make a chart to record the color of the cubes as you take them from the bag.
2. Reach into the bag and take out one cube.
3. Make a tally mark to record the color of the cube. Return the cube to the bag.
4. Take turns and repeat 50 times. Look at your results.
5. Predict if there are *more red*, *more blue*, or *more yellow* cubes in the bag. Look in the bag to check your prediction.

Unit 13, Lesson 12

Activity Note For each pair, prepare a paper bag with 2 red cubes, 8 blue cubes, and 5 yellow cubes. Ask children how they made their prediction.

Math Writing Prompt

How Do You Know? You roll a number cube labeled with the numbers 1 to 6. How likely is it that you will roll a 3s count-by? Explain.

Destination Math Software Support

Course II: Module 2: Unit 3: Fractional Parts

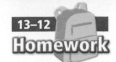

3 Homework and Targeted Practice

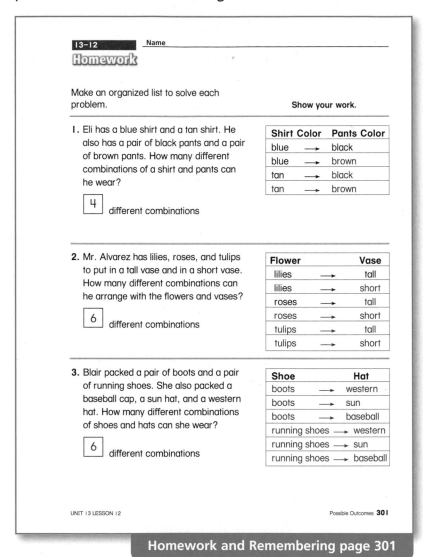

13–12 Homework Goal: Additional Practice

This Homework page provides practice in finding all possible combinations for a given event.

13–12
Name ____________________

Homework

Make an organized list to solve each problem.

Show your work.

1. Eli has a blue shirt and a tan shirt. He also has a pair of black pants and a pair of brown pants. How many different combinations of a shirt and pants can he wear?

4 different combinations

Shirt Color		Pants Color
blue	→	black
blue	→	brown
tan	→	black
tan	→	brown

2. Mr. Alvarez has lilies, roses, and tulips to put in a tall vase and in a short vase. How many different combinations can he arrange with the flowers and vases?

6 different combinations

Flower		Vase
lilies	→	tall
lilies	→	short
roses	→	tall
roses	→	short
tulips	→	tall
tulips	→	short

3. Blair packed a pair of boots and a pair of running shoes. She also packed a baseball cap, a sun hat, and a western hat. How many different combinations of shoes and hats can she wear?

6 different combinations

Shoe		Hat
boots	→	western
boots	→	sun
boots	→	baseball
running shoes	→	western
running shoes	→	sun
running shoes	→	baseball

UNIT 13 LESSON 12 Possible Outcomes 301

Homework and Remembering page 301

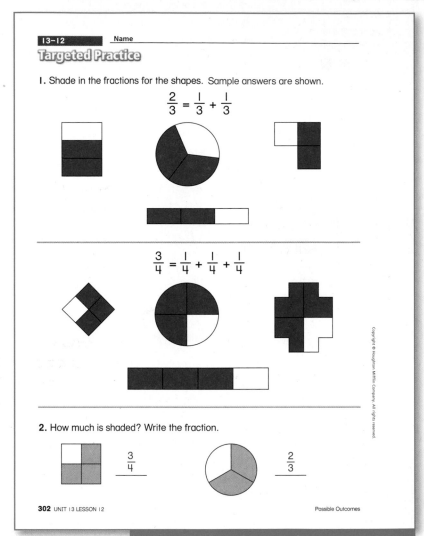

13–12 Targeted Practice Goal: Understand Fractions

This Targeted Practice page can be used with children who need extra practice with fractions.

13–12
Name ____________________

Targeted Practice

1. Shade in the fractions for the shapes. Sample answers are shown.

$$\frac{2}{3} = \frac{1}{3} + \frac{1}{3}$$

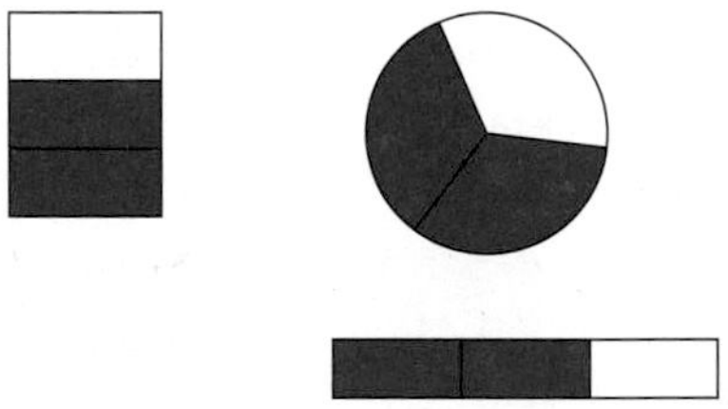

$$\frac{3}{4} = \frac{1}{4} + \frac{1}{4} + \frac{1}{4}$$

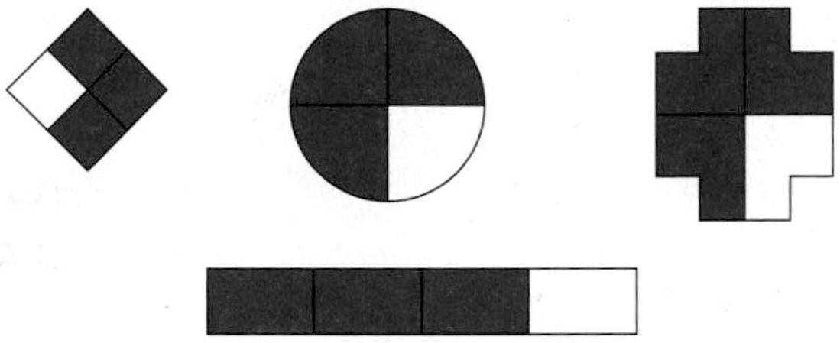

2. How much is shaded? Write the fraction.

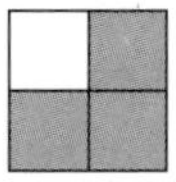

$\frac{3}{4}$

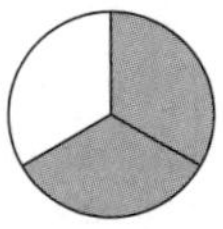

$\frac{2}{3}$

302 UNIT 13 LESSON 12 Possible Outcomes

Homework and Remembering page 302

Home or School Activity

Art Connection

Fashion Design Have children create possible combinations for 2-piece school uniforms or sports uniforms.

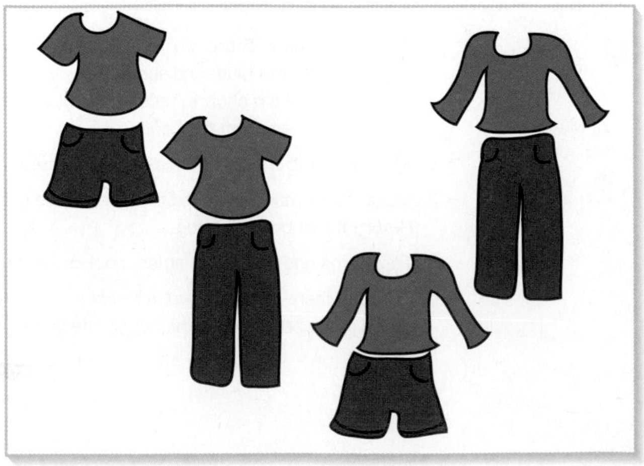

UNIT 13 LESSON 13

Use Mathematical Processes

REAL WORLD Problem Solving

Lesson Objectives

- Apply mathematical concepts and skills in meaningful contexts
- Reinforce the NCTM process skills embedded in this unit, and in previous units, with a variety of problem-solving situations.

The Day at a Glance

Today's Goals	Materials	
1 Teaching the Lesson A1: **Science Connection** Use addition and subtraction to create tables and bar graphs. A2: **Reasoning and Proof** Write a paragraph and make drawings to support a math statement. A3: **Problem Solving** Use multiplying and halving to solve a word problem. A4: **Representation** Draw a spinner to represent a likely given outcome. A5: **Communication** Explain a choice.	**Lesson Activities** Student Activity Book pp. 457–458 Homework and Remembering pp. 303–304 Crayons	**Going Further** Activity Cards 13-13 Counters Grid paper Connecting cubes Index cards Math Journals
2 Going Further ▸ Differentiated Instruction		
3 Homework and Spiral Review		

Use Math Talk today!

Keeping Skills Sharp

Quick Practice/Daily Routines	
If you wish to include Quick Practice or a Daily Routine, choose content based on the needs of your class.	**Class Management** Select activities from this lesson that support important goals and objectives, or that help children prepare for state or district tests.

1 Teaching the Lesson

Activity 1

Connections

Math and Science

45 MINUTES

Goal: Use addition and subtraction to create tables and bar graphs.

Materials: Student Activity Book page 457

NCTM Standards:
Problem Solving
Connections
Representation

13–13 Class Activity

Name ____________________

▶ **Math and Science**

Mr. Miller experiments with plants to see how many flowers bloom. He records data and makes graphs.

This first column in this table shows the number of flowers on three different plants in Week 1.

Number of Flowers on a Plant

Plant	Week 1	Week 2	Week 3
A	**2**	5	5
B	**3**	4	5
C	**5**	2	5

1. In Week 2: Plant A had 3 more flowers than it did in Week 1.
   Plant B had 1 more flower than it did in Week 1.
   Plant C had 3 fewer flowers than it did in Week 1.
   Complete the second column to show the number of flowers on each plant in Week 2.
2. In Week 3, Plant B had 1 more flower than in Week 2, and all three plants had the same number of flowers. Complete the third column to show the number of flowers on each plant in Week 3.
3. Make a bar graph to show the data in the table.

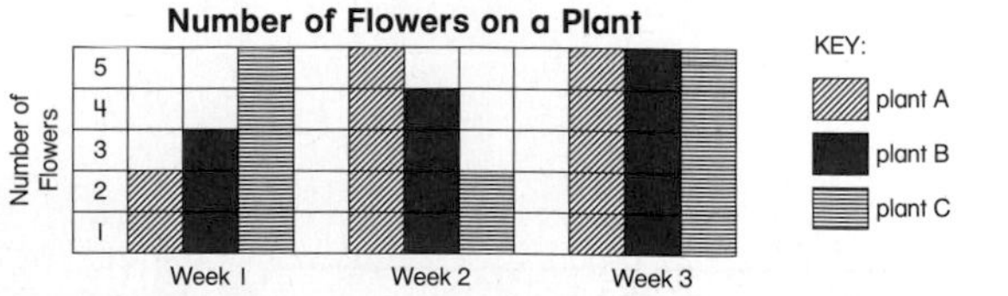

UNIT 13 LESSON 13 Use Mathematical Processes **457**

Student Activity Book page 457

▶ Science and Plants

Discuss why plants are important. Elicit from children that many foods for humans and animals come from plants, that trees provide shade, and that plants with flowers help make gardens attractive.

Task 1 and 2 Go over the information at the top of page 457. Help children see that the data in the table are for Week 1 and that there is room for more data in the table.

Go over the statements about the changes in the number of flowers from Week 1 to Week 2. Explain that they will use these statements to find the number of flowers on each plant for Week 2. Then have children complete items 1 and 2.

▶ Tables to Graphs

Check that all children have correctly identified and entered the data for weeks 2 and 3.

Task 3 Review how to use data from a table to make a bar graph. Point out that the bar graph will display information about the number of flowers on the three plants for three weeks. Guide children in making the bars for Plant A. Then let them complete the bar graph independently. Afterwards discuss whether using the table or the bar graph is better for seeing the changes in the number of flowers on each plant during the three weeks.

Alternate Approach

Class Garden Grow some flowering plants in your classroom. Have the children record changes in the number of flowers over several weeks. Create tables and graphs to show what you found.

Activity 2

Reasoning and Proof

Support Math Statements

45 MINUTES

Goals: Write a paragraph and make drawings to support a math statement.

Materials: Student Activity Book page 458

NCTM Standards:
Problem Solving
Communication
Reasoning and Proof
Representation

13–13 Class Activity

Name

▶ **Supporting Math Statements**

Support each statement. Write a paragraph and make a drawing.

1. If there is an even number of objects, equal shares for two people can always be made.

Answers may vary. Possible answer: When there is an even number of objects, you can put all the objects in pairs. Then you can give each person one object from each pair. This is what it looks like to share 6 books equally with 2 people.

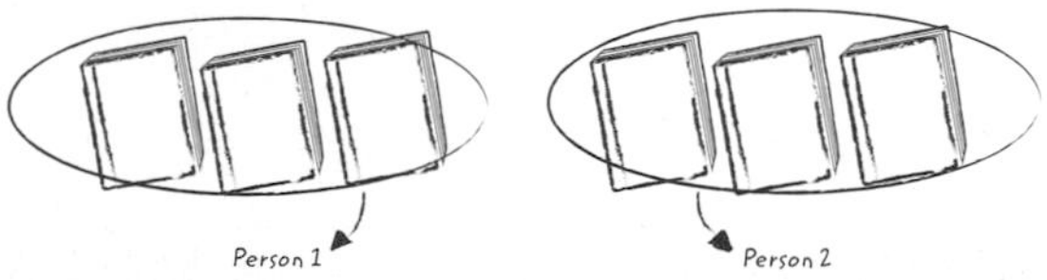

2. If a shape has four sides equal in length and four square corners, the shape is a square.

Answers may vary. Possible answer: A shape with four sides of equal length is a rhombus. A shape with four square corners is a rectangle. A shape with four sides of equal length and four square corners is a square. This drawing shows how a square is different from a rhombus or a rectangle.

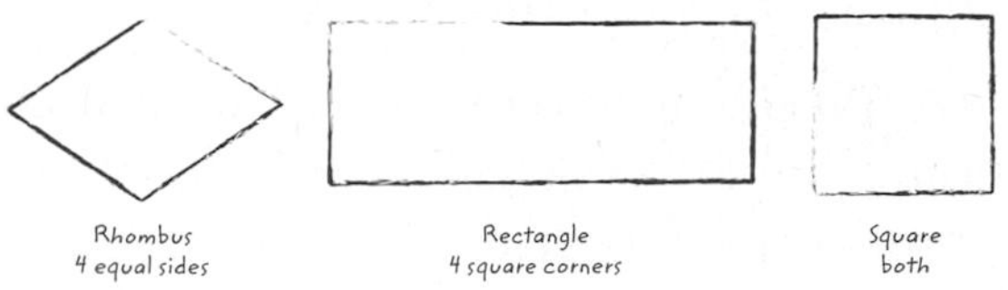

458 UNIT 13 LESSON 13 Use Mathematical Processes

Student Activity Book page 458

▶ How to Support a Statement

Tell children that one thing that mathematicians do is to find or make a statement about a mathematical idea and then support the statement by writing why they believe the statement is correct and using drawings to help make their points clear.

Tasks 1 and 2 Explain that they will be mathematicians in this activity. They will read two statements and decide how they would support these ideas with words and drawings. You may want to let children work in pairs to discuss the ideas, but all children should write paragraphs and use math drawings to support the two statements.

▶ Discuss the Statements Math Talk

Have volunteers read their statements and put their drawings on the board. Encourage discussion and sharing of ideas by eliciting and modeling questions like the following.

- ▶ What did you write to support the statement? Did you cover all the parts of the statement? Does this support the statement?
- ▶ Did you make drawings to support the statement? How did the drawings help you show your ideas? Does the drawing support the statement?

English Language Learners

Write 10 + 6 = 16 and *proof* on the board. Draw a *proof drawing*.

- **Beginning** Ask: **Does the drawing tell us 10 + 6 = 16 is true?** yes Say: **It is *proof*. Have children repeat.**
- **Intermediate and Advanced** Say: **The drawing is *proof*. It tells us the answer is __.** true

Activity 3

Problem Solving

Mato's Games

15 MINUTES

Goal: Use multiplying and halving to solve a word problem.

NCTM Standards:
Problem Solving
Reasoning and Proof
Connections

Leon has 2 games. Mina has 3 times the number of games that Leon has. Mato has half the number of games that Mina has. How many games does Mato have? 3

Hold a whole-class discussion of the problem.

► How did you figure out the number of games that Mato has? Answers will vary. Sample: I multiplied 2 × 3 to find out how many games Mina has. Mina has 6 games. Then I took half of 6 to find how many games Mato has. Half of 6 is 3 so Mato has 3 games.

Activity 4

Representation

A Spinner

15 MINUTES

Goal: Draw a spinner to represent a likely given outcome

Materials: crayons

NCTM Standards:
Problem Solving
Connections
Representation

Draw a spinner where spinning blue is twice as likely as spinning red. Drawings will vary. Use the discussion to help children see that there are many different spinners like this description.

Begin by discussing how what *twice as likely* means. Answers may vary. Possible answer: There are two ways to spin blue for every way to spin red

Continue by having children share their work.

► What does your spinner look like? Answers may vary. Have several children display their spinners.

► How did you make a spinner where you would be twice as likely to spin blue than red? Answers may vary. Possible answer: I divided a circle into thirds. I colored $\frac{1}{3}$ of the circle red and $\frac{2}{3}$ of the circle blue.

Activity 5

Communication

Choose a Spinner

15 MINUTES

Goal: Explain a choice.

NCTM Standards:
Problem Solving
Communication

Draw these spinners on the board.

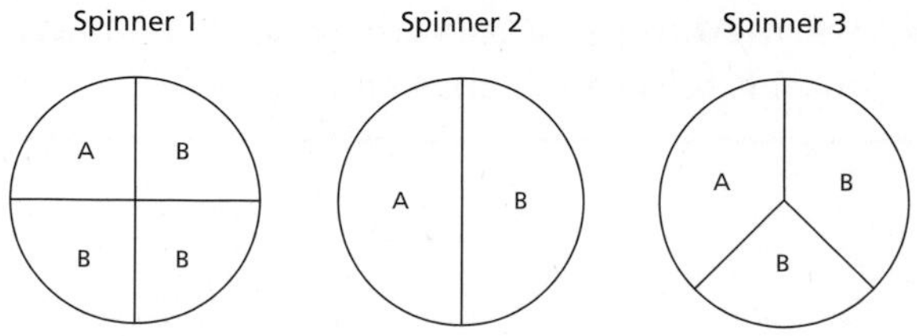

Suppose you win a prize if you spin the letter A. Which spinner would you choose? Why? Answers may vary. Possible answer: Spinner 2. I would choose Spinner 2 because $\frac{1}{2}$ of the circle is letter A. That is more than Spinner 1 where $\frac{1}{4}$ of the circle is letter A or Spinner 3 where $\frac{1}{3}$ of the circle is letter A.

Help children analyze the spinners.

► Which spinner would give you the best chance of spinning the letter A? Spinner 2 Why? In Spinner 2, $\frac{1}{2}$ of the circle is letter A. In Spinner 1 only $\frac{1}{4}$ of the circle is letter A. In Spinner 3 only $\frac{1}{3}$ of the circle is letter A.

► If you wanted to spin the letter B, which spinner would you choose? Spinner 1. Why? In Spinner 1, $\frac{3}{4}$ of the circle is letter B. In Spinner 2, $\frac{1}{2}$ of the circle is letter B. In Spinner 3, $\frac{2}{3}$ of the circle is letter B. Spinner 1 has the greatest area for the letter B.

Intervention — Activity Card 13-13

Monkey Bars

Activity Card 13-13

Work: pairs
Use:
- 5 counters
- grid paper

Choose:
- Student 1
- Student 2

The zoo has six Monkey Shows a day. There can be no more than 5 monkeys in a show. You decide how many.

1. **Work Together** Make a bar graph similar to this one.

Monkey Show

9:00						
10:00						
11:00						
1:00						
2:00						
3:00						

Number of Monkeys in Show

2. Student 1: Flip the 5 counters.
3. Color one square next to 9:00 for each red counter you flip. If none of the counters are red, flip again.
4. Student 2: Repeat steps 2 and 3. Color the squares next to 10:00.
5. Take turns until all the times have bars.
6. How many more shows had 3 monkeys than 2 monkeys?

Unit 13, Lesson 13

Activity Note You may wish to create additional questions for children to answer using their bar graph. Pairs can swap graphs and answer the questions again.

Math Writing Prompt

Understanding Bar Graphs Gwen says she can add the number of monkeys in each show to find the total number of monkeys at the zoo. Is Gwen right? Explain.

Soar to Success Math Software Support

Warm Up 66.02

On Level — Activity Card 13-13

Symmetry Squares

Activity Card 13-13

Work: pairs
Use:
- square paper

1. Fold the square in half. What shape did you make? Does the shape have a line of symmetry? rectangle or triangle, yes
2. Fold the shape in half again. What shape did you make? Does the shape have a line of symmetry? square or triangle, yes
3. Repeat step 2 as many times as you can.
4. Unfold the paper. Fold it in half to make a different shape than you made before.
5. Repeat step 2 as many times as you can.
6. **Analyze** Write a paragraph and make a drawing to support this statement.

Every time I fold a square in half, the shape I make will always have a line of symmetry.

Unit 13, Lesson 13

Activity Note Make square paper in advance by folding a sheet of notebook paper diagonally so the top edge meets the side edge. Cut off the extra.

Math Writing Prompt

Why Does It Work? Why do you always make shapes with a line of symmetry when you fold a square in half over and over again?

Harcourt Mega Math Software Support

Shapes Ahoy: Ship Shapes, Level V

Challenge — Activity Card 13-13

Probability Puzzles

Activity Card 13-13

Work: pairs
Use:
- 3 red cubes
- 3 blue cubes
- 3 yellow cubes
- index cards

1. **Work Together** Solve the probability puzzles below.

There are 7 cubes in a bag. The probability of picking a red cube is 2 out of 7. The probability of picking a blue cube is 3 out of 7. How many cubes are not red or blue?

2

There are 8 cubes in a bag. The cubes are red, yellow, and blue. The probability of picking a yellow cube is 4 out of 8. Make a list of the possible combinations of red and blue cubes that could be in the bag.

3 red and 1 blue, 2 red and 2 blue, 1 red and 3 blue

2. Each student: Write two probability puzzles on index cards. Write the answer on the back.
3. Switch cards and solve each other's puzzles.
4. Check each other's answers.

Unit 13, Lesson 13

Activity Note Suggest that children use the connecting cubes to model the probability puzzles. Children may need more cubes to model their own puzzles.

Math Writing Prompt

How Do You Know? Explain how you solved one of the probability puzzles. Prove your answer by writing a paragraph, drawing a picture, or making a list.

Destination Math Software Support

Course II: Module 2: Unit 3: Fractional Parts

3 Homework and Spiral Review

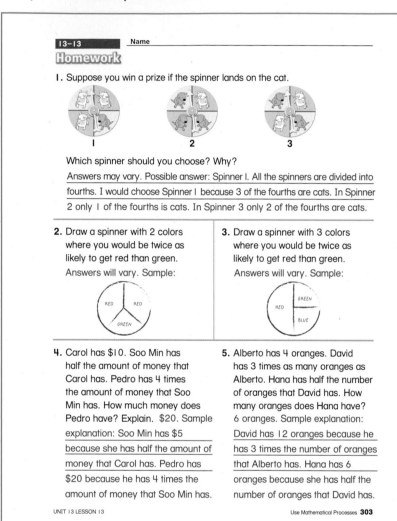

13–13
Homework **Goal:** Additional Practice

Include children's completed Homework page as part of their portfolios.

13–13 Name

Homework

1. Suppose you win a prize if the spinner lands on the cat.

Which spinner should you choose? Why?

Answers may vary. Possible answer: Spinner 1. All the spinners are divided into fourths. I would choose Spinner 1 because 3 of the fourths are cats. In Spinner 2 only 1 of the fourths is cats. In Spinner 3 only 2 of the fourths are cats.

2. Draw a spinner with 2 colors where you would be twice as likely to get red than green.

Answers will vary. Sample:

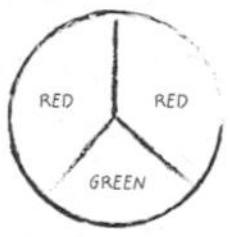

3. Draw a spinner with 3 colors where you would be twice as likely to get red than green.

Answers will vary. Sample:

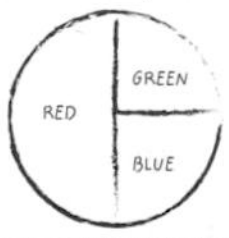

4. Carol has $10. Soo Min has half the amount of money that Carol has. Pedro has 4 times the amount of money that Soo Min has. How much money does Pedro have? Explain. $20. Sample explanation: Soo Min has $5 because she has half the amount of money that Carol has. Pedro has $20 because he has 4 times the amount of money that Soo Min has.

5. Alberto has 4 oranges. David has 3 times as many oranges as Alberto. Hana has half the number of oranges that David has. How many oranges does Hana have? 6 oranges. Sample explanation: David has 12 oranges because he has 3 times the number of oranges that Alberto has. Hana has 6 oranges because she has half the number of oranges that David has.

UNIT 13 LESSON 13 Use Mathematical Processes 303

Homework and Remembering page 303

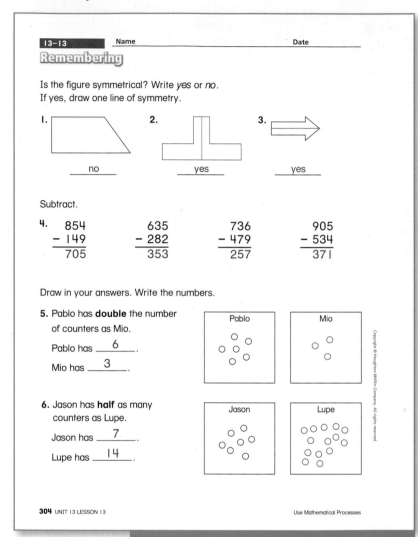

13–13
Remembering **Goal:** Spiral Review

This Remembering page would be appropriate anytime after today's lesson.

13–13 Name Date

Remembering

Is the figure symmetrical? Write *yes* or *no*.
If yes, draw one line of symmetry.

1.

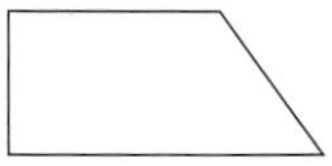

no

2.

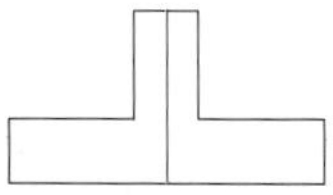

yes

3.

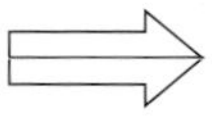

yes

Subtract.

4.

854	635	736	905
− 149	− 282	− 479	− 534
705	353	257	371

Draw in your answers. Write the numbers.

5. Pablo has **double** the number of counters as Mio.

Pablo has 6.

Mio has 3.

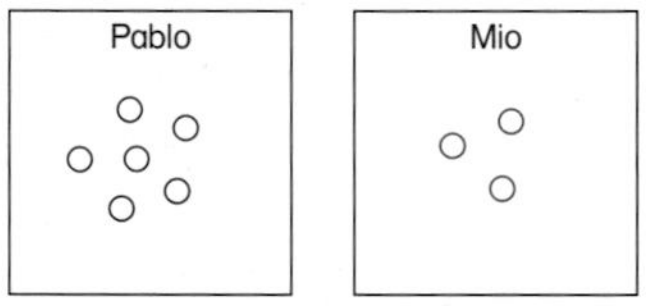

6. Jason has **half** as many counters as Lupe.

Jason has 7.

Lupe has 14.

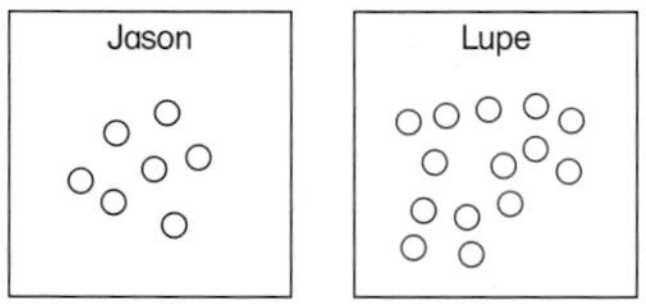

304 UNIT 13 LESSON 13 Use Mathematical Processes

Homework and Remembering page 304

Home or School Activity

Art Connection

Design a Toy Ask children to design a toy. Have them draw one picture where the toy looks symmetrical and another picture where the toy does not look symmetrical.

UNIT 13

Unit Review and Test

Lesson Objectives

- **Assess children's progress on unit objectives.**

The Day at a Glance

Today's Goals	Materials
1 Assessing the Unit ▶ Assess children's progress on unit objectives. ▶ Use activities from unit lessons to reteach content.	Unit 13 Test, Student Activity Book pages 459–462 Unit 13 Test, Form A or B, Assessment Guide (optional) Unit 13 Performance Assessment, Assessment Guide (optional)
2 Extending the Assessment ▶ Use remediation for common errors.	
There is no homework assignment on a test day.	

Keeping Skills Sharp

Quick Practice 5 MINUTES

Goal: Review any skills you choose to meet the needs of your class.

If you are doing a unit review day, use any of the Quick Practice activities that provide support for your class. If this is a test day, omit Quick Practice.

Review and Test Day You may want to choose a quiet game or other activity (reading a book or working on homework for another subject) for children who finish early.

1 Assessing the Unit

Assess Unit Objectives

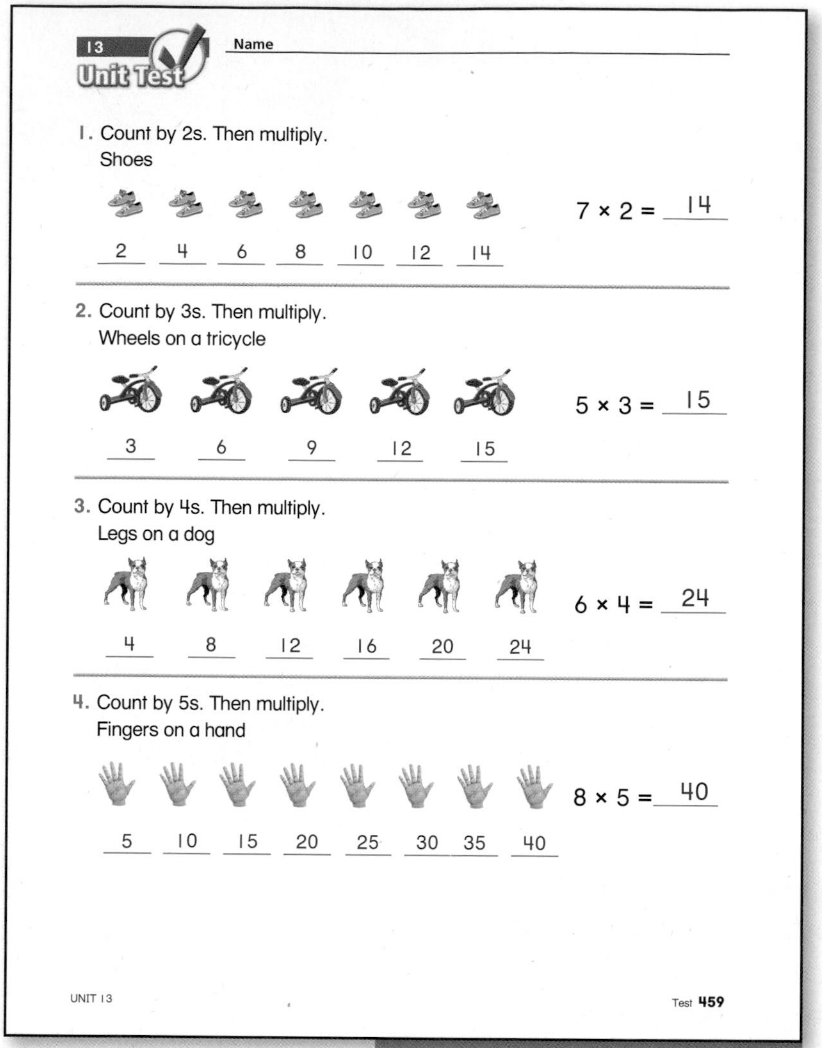

13 Unit Test Name ______

1. Count by 2s. Then multiply.
Shoes

2 4 6 8 10 12 14

7 × 2 = 14

2. Count by 3s. Then multiply.
Wheels on a tricycle

3 6 9 12 15

5 × 3 = 15

3. Count by 4s. Then multiply.
Legs on a dog

4 8 12 16 20 24

6 × 4 = 24

4. Count by 5s. Then multiply.
Fingers on a hand

5 10 15 20 25 30 35 40

8 × 5 = 40

UNIT 13 Test 459

Student Activity Book page 459

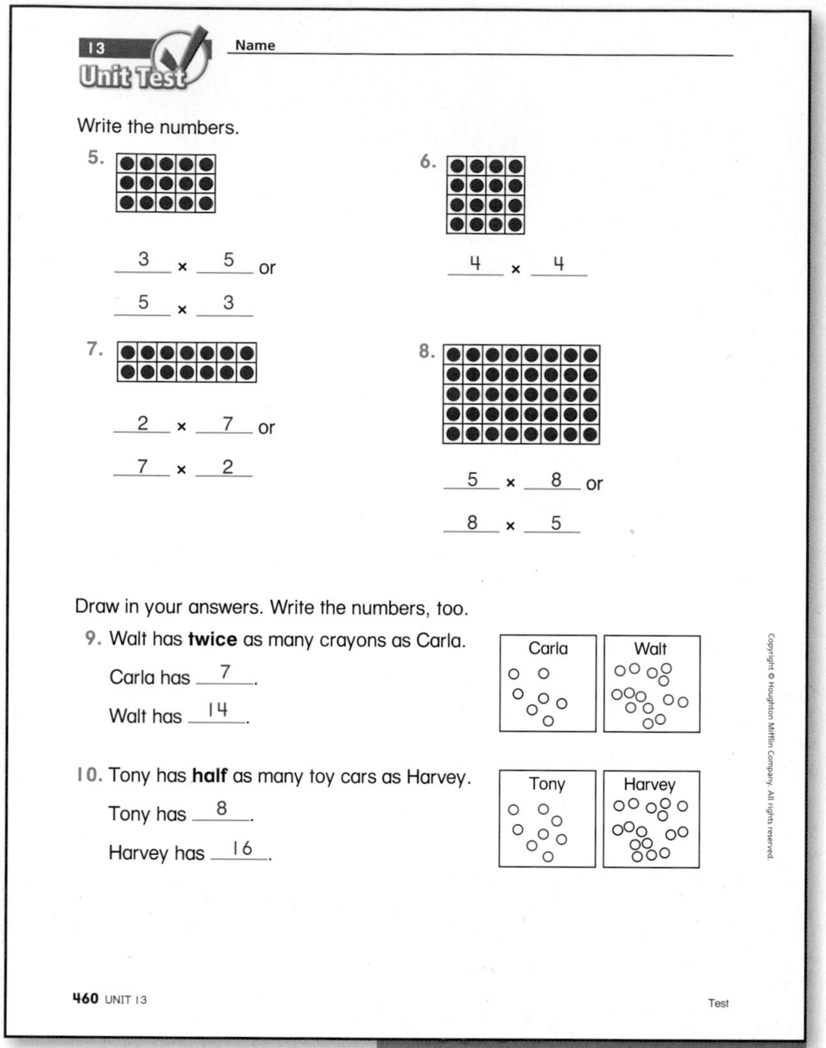

13 Unit Test Name ______

Write the numbers.

5. 3 × 5 or 5 × 3

6. 4 × 4

7. 2 × 7 or 7 × 2

8. 5 × 8 or 8 × 5

Draw in your answers. Write the numbers, too.

9. Walt has **twice** as many crayons as Carla.
Carla has 7.
Walt has 14.

Carla Walt

10. Tony has **half** as many toy cars as Harvey.
Tony has 8.
Harvey has 16.

Tony Harvey

460 UNIT 13 Test

Student Activity Book page 460

45 MINUTES (more if schedule permits)

Goal: Assess children's progress on unit objectives.

Materials: Student Activity Book pages 459–462, Assessment Guide (optional)

▶ Review and Assessment

If your students are ready for assessment on the unit objectives, use either the test on the Student Activity Book pages or one of the forms of the Unit 13 Test in the Assessment Guide to assess student progress. To assign a numerical score for all of these test forms, use 4 points for each question.

The chart to the right lists the test items, the unit objectives they cover, and the lesson activities in which the objective is covered in this unit.

▶ Reteaching Resources

Test Items	Unit Objectives Tested	Activities to Use for Reteaching
1–4	**13.1** Count by 2, 3, 4, or 5 to solve simple multiplication problems.	Lesson 1, Activity 2 Lesson 2, Activity 2 Lesson 3, Activity 2 Lesson 4, Activity 1
5–8	**13.2** Write multiplication expressions for an array.	Lesson 4, Activity 2 Lesson 5, Activity 1
9–12	**13.3** Use vocabulary (half, double, twice, equal shares).	Lesson 6, Activity 1
13–16	**13.4** Recognize lines of symmetry.	Lesson 8, Activity 1 Lesson 8, Activity 2

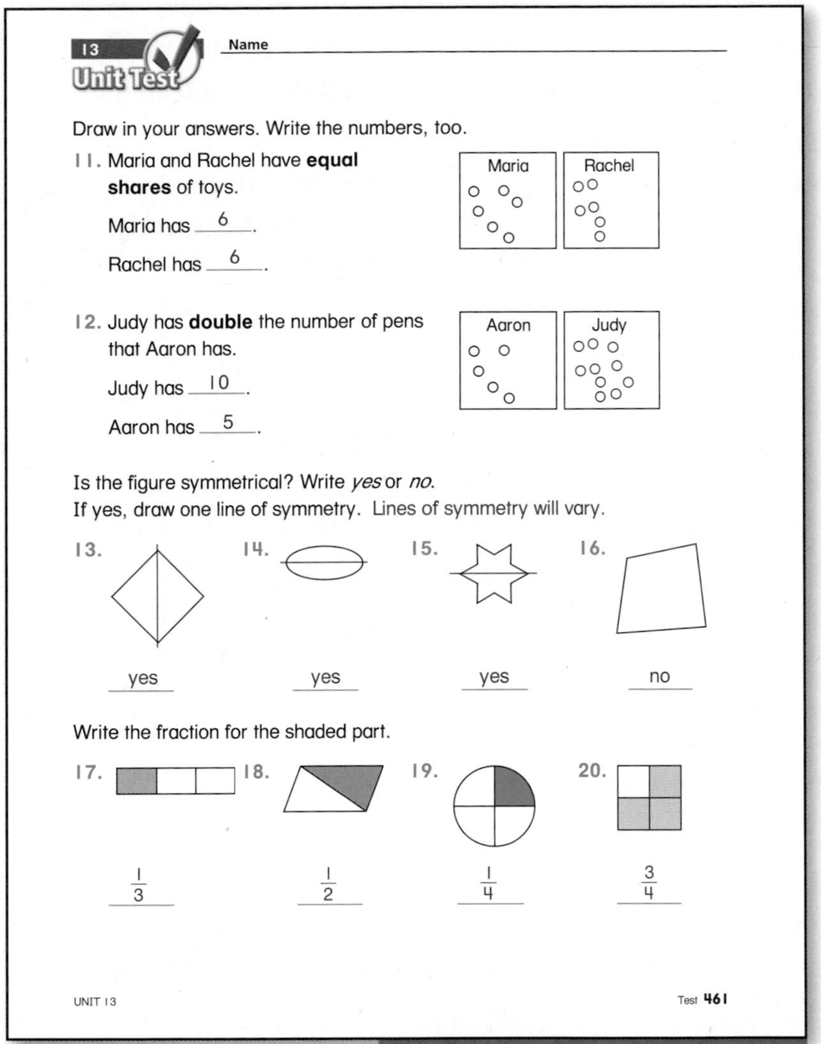

13 Unit Test Name

Draw in your answers. Write the numbers, too.

11. Maria and Rachel have **equal shares** of toys.

Maria has 6.

Rachel has 6.

12. Judy has **double** the number of pens that Aaron has.

Judy has 10.

Aaron has 5.

Is the figure symmetrical? Write *yes* or *no*.
If yes, draw one line of symmetry. Lines of symmetry will vary.

13. yes 14. yes 15. yes 16. no

Write the fraction for the shaded part.

17. $\frac{1}{3}$ 18. $\frac{1}{2}$ 19. $\frac{1}{4}$ 20. $\frac{3}{4}$

UNIT 13 Test 461

Student Activity Book page 461

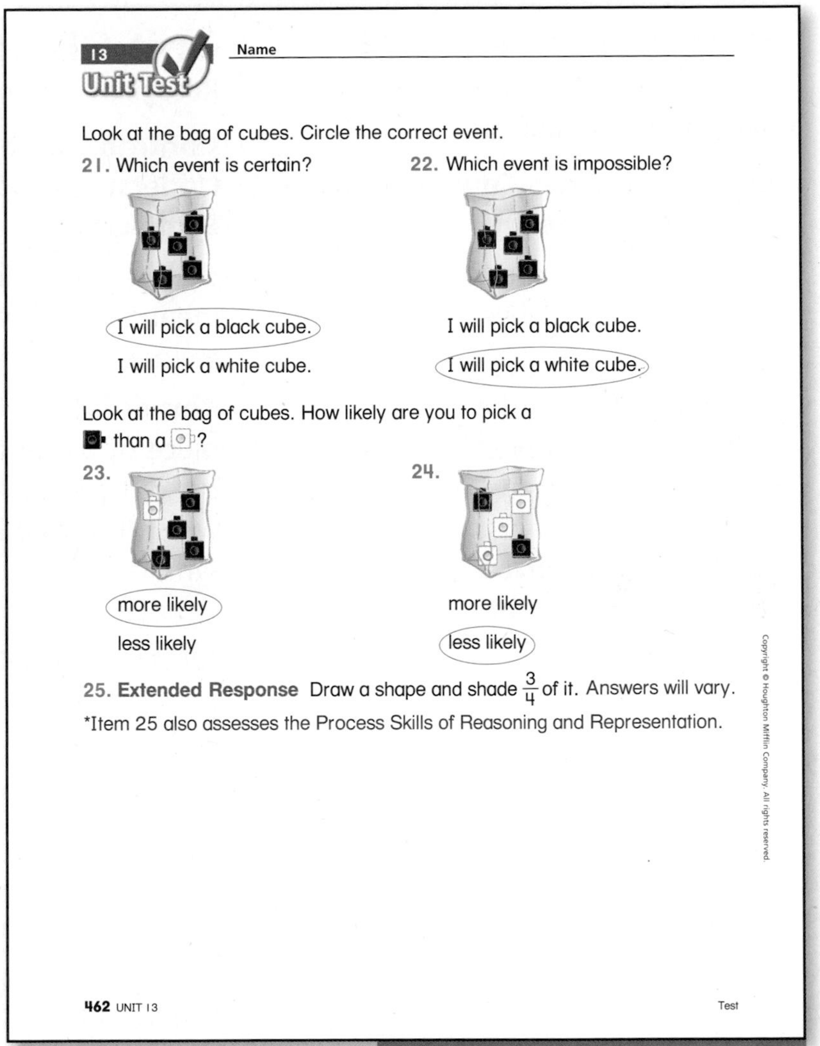

13 Unit Test Name

Look at the bag of cubes. Circle the correct event.

21. Which event is certain?

I will pick a black cube. (circled)

I will pick a white cube.

22. Which event is impossible?

I will pick a black cube.

I will pick a white cube. (circled)

Look at the bag of cubes. How likely are you to pick a ■ than a □?

23. more likely (circled) / less likely

24. more likely / less likely (circled)

25. **Extended Response** Draw a shape and shade $\frac{3}{4}$ of it. Answers will vary.

*Item 25 also assesses the Process Skills of Reasoning and Representation.

462 UNIT 13 Test

Student Activity Book page 462

Test Items	Unit Objectives Tested	Activities to Use for Reteaching
17–19	**13.5** Identify and indicate single fractional parts ($\frac{1}{2}$, $\frac{1}{3}$, $\frac{1}{4}$).	Lesson 9, Activity 1
20, 25	**13.6** Identify and indicate multiple fractional parts ($\frac{2}{3}$, $\frac{3}{4}$).	Lesson 9, Activity 2
21, 22	**13.7** Determine whether an outcome is possible, impossible, or certain.	Lesson 11, Activity 1
23, 24	**13.8** Determine whether an outcome is more likely or less likely.	Lesson 11, Activity 3 Lesson 12, Activity 1

▶ Assessment Resources

Form A, Free Response Test (Assessment Guide)
Form B, Multiple-Choice Test (Assessment Guide)
Performance Assessment (Assessment Guide)

▶ Portfolio Assessment

Teacher-selected Items for Student Portfolios:

- Homework, Lessons 5, 7, 8, 11, 13
- Class Activity work, Lessons 1, 2, 3, 4, 6

Student-selected Items for Student Portfolios:

- Favorite Home or School Activity
- Best Writing Prompt

2 Extending the Assessment

Common Errors

Activities for Remediation

Unit Objective 13.1

Count by 2, 3, 4, or 5 to solve simple multiplication problems.

Common Error: Counts By Given Numbers Incorrectly

Children may make errors when saying the count-bys.

Remediation Have children practice the counting sequences using the count-by charts with the goal of committing the counts to memory. Encourage them to memorize the correct numbers as soon as they are able.

Unit Objective 13.2

Write multiplication expressions for an array.

Common Error: Writes Incorrect Multiplication Expressions for an Array

Children may write incorrect factors for a given array.

Remediation Remind children how to read arrays by counting the numbers of rows and columns. Ask children to make an array with beans or counters and write both multiplication expressions—one with the number of rows first and one with the number of columns first.

Unit Objective 13.4

Recognize lines of symmetry.

Common Error: Does Not Understand the Meaning of Symmetry

Children may not understand the meaning of symmetry or be able to identify a line of symmetry.

Remediation Help children fold a piece of paper and use scissors to cut out a symmetrical figure for which the fold line is the line of symmetry.

Unit Objectives 13.5 and 13.6

Identify and indicate single fractional parts. Identify and indicate multiple fractional parts.

Common Error: Finds Incorrect Fractions for Given Representations

Children may write incorrect fractions for given fraction representations.

Remediation Review with children that the top number (numerator) of a fraction means the number of equal parts shaded, and the bottom number (denominator) means the total number of equal parts the figure is divided into. Tell children to be sure to check that the number they write for each part matches the figure.

Unit Objective 13.7

Determine whether an outcome is possible, impossible, or certain.

Common Error: Applies Probability Terms Incorrectly to Given Situations

Children may use the probability terms *possible, impossible,* and *certain* incorrectly to describe given situations.

Remediation Ask children to provide an example of something that is certain, possible, and impossible. For terms that children use incorrectly, provide situations that they might identify better with. For example: certain—the sun will come up tomorrow; possible—no one will be absent tomorrow; impossible—rain will fall up.

Unit Objective 13.8

Determine whether an outcome is more likely or less likely.

Common Error: Reverses Predictions for More Likely and Less Likely Outcomes

Children may incorrectly predict that an outcome is more likely (or less likely) given a probability experiment.

Remediation Have pairs of children play spinner or number cube games in which players do not have equal chances of winning. Ask questions such as "Who is more likely to win?"

Non-Standard and Standard Units of Measure

IN UNIT 14, children explore measurement concepts and propose non-standard units for length, mass, capacity, and time. After exploring non-standard units, students move to measuring with customary units. Activities include making and using a yardstick and converting between yards, feet, and inches. Children have opportunities to measure length, time, capacity, weight, mass, and temperature in metric and customary units. Activities include finding referents, converting between units, and selecting appropriate tools and units.

Skills Trace

Grade 1	Grade 2	Grade 3
• Measure and compare length to the nearest inch. • Estimate and measure length in inches.	• Use a ruler to measure a line segment to the nearest inch. • Convert between inches, feet, and yards.	• Estimate and measure length to the nearest $\frac{1}{4}$ inch. • Solve problems involving customary units.

Independent Learning Activities

Ready-Made Math Challenge Centers

53 Non-Standard Units — Pairs

Start You can measure objects using items around your classroom.

Think about different items you can use to measure.

1. Use large paper clips to measure the length of your desk. Answers will vary.
2. Use small paper clips to measure the length of your partner's desk. Answers will vary.
3. You both measured the same desk with paper clips. Did you get the same measurements? no
4. Use long straws to measure the length of your teacher's desk. Answers will vary.
5. Use short straws to measure the length of your teacher's desk. Answers will vary.
6. You both measured the same desk with straws. Did you get the same measurements? no
7. **Analyze** Why did you get different answers if you measured the same object with the same type of item? Answers will vary.
8. If you wanted a greater measurement would you use an eraser or a new pencil? Explain. Then check. an eraser; It is smaller so you would need more of them.
9. Find other items to use to measure, and predict which would give you a greater measurement and which would give a lesser measurement.

Skills: Measure and analyze — Use after Unit 14, Lesson 1.

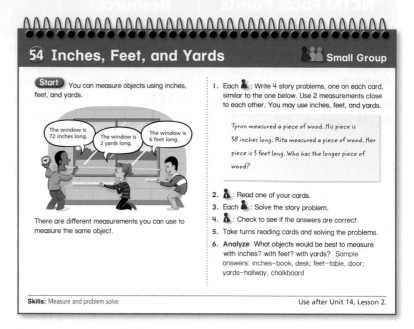

Grouping Pairs

Materials Paper clips (large and small), straws (long straws and straws cut in half), and classroom objects

Objective Children measure with 2 different non-standard units and compare measurements.

Connections Measurement and Reasoning

54 Inches, Feet, and Yards — Small Group

Start You can measure objects using inches, feet, and yards.

There are different measurements you can use to measure the same object.

1. Each: Write 4 story problems, one on each card, similar to the one below. Use 2 measurements close to each other. You may use inches, feet, and yards.

   Tyron measured a piece of wood. His piece is 38 inches long. Rita measured a piece of wood. Her piece is 3 feet long. Who has the longer piece of wood?

2. Read one of your cards.
3. Each: Solve the story problem.
4. Check to see if the answers are correct.
5. Take turns reading cards and solving the problems.
6. **Analyze** What objects would be best to measure with inches? with feet? with yards? Sample answers: inches–book, desk; feet–table, door; yards–hallway, chalkboard

Skills: Measure and problem solve — Use after Unit 14, Lesson 2.

Grouping Small Group

Materials Index cards

Objective Children compare standard measurements of inches, feet, and yards.

Connections Measurement and Problem Solving

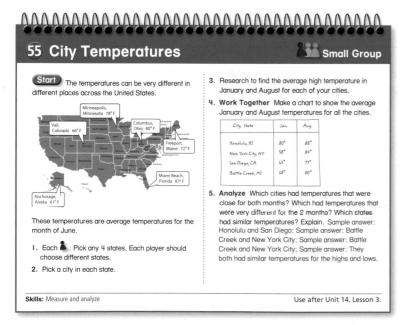

55 City Temperatures — Small Group

Start The temperatures can be very different in different places across the United States.

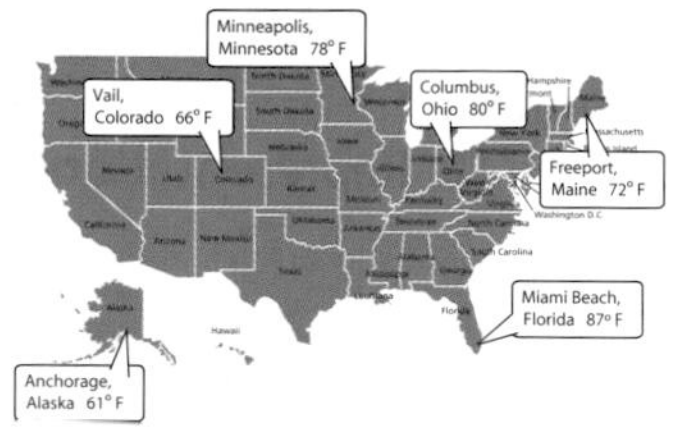

These temperatures are average temperatures for the month of June.

1. Each: Pick any 4 states. Each player should choose different states.
2. Pick a city in each state.
3. Research to find the average high temperature in January and August for each of your cities.
4. **Work Together** Make a chart to show the average January and August temperatures for all the cities.

City, State	Jan.	Aug.
Honolulu, HI	80°	88°
New York City, NY	38°	84°
San Diego, CA	65°	77°
Battle Creek, MI	28°	80°

5. **Analyze** Which cities had temperatures that were close for both months? Which had temperatures that were very different for the 2 months? Which states had similar temperatures? Explain. Sample answer: Honolulu and San Diego; Sample answer: Battle Creek and New York City; Sample answer: Battle Creek and New York City; Sample answer: They both had similar temperatures for the highs and lows.

Skills: Measure and analyze — Use after Unit 14, Lesson 3.

Grouping Small Group

Materials Research materials (books, Internet)

Objective Children find and compare temperatures for different cities.

Connections Measurement and Real World

56 Recipes — Small Group

Start These are containers used for measuring liquids.

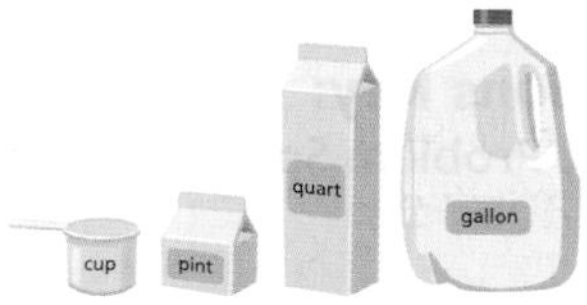

Think about making a recipe if you did not have the measuring containers you needed. Could you still make the recipe?

1. Look at the recipe card. Can you make this recipe if you only had a pint container? Explain what you would do. I could use $\frac{1}{2}$ of the pint for a cup and use 2 pints when I need a quart, and 8 pints when I need a gallon.

2. **Work Together** Rewrite the same recipe for someone who only has a cup container. 1 cup cranberry juice, 4 cups apple juice, 2 cups gingerale, 16 cups grape juice
3. Each: Write a recipe on a card using cup, pint, quart, and gallon measures.
4. Trade recipies. Write the recipe using only cups.
5. **Analyze** If you could only have one container, which would you choose and why? Answers will vary.

Skills: Measure and problem solve — Use after Unit 14, Lesson 3.

Grouping Small Group

Materials Index cards

Objective Children make measurement conversions for cup, pint, quart, and gallon.

Connections Measurement and Real World

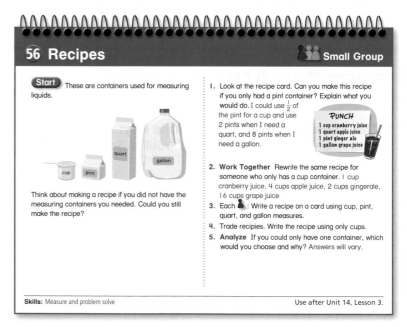

Unit 14 Teaching Resources

Differentiated Instruction

Individualizing Instruction		
	Level	Frequency
Activities	• Intervention • On Level • Challenge	All 3 in every lesson
	Level	Frequency
Math Writing Prompts	• Intervention • On Level • Challenge	All 3 in every lesson
Math Center Challenges	For advanced students	
	4 in every unit	

Reaching All Learners		
English Language Learners	Lessons	Pages
	1, 2, 3	1041, 1047, 1055
Extra Help	Lessons	Pages
	2	1052

Strategies for English Language Learners

Present this problem to all children. Offer the different levels of support to meet children's levels of language proficiency.

Objective To identify different units of measurement for length.

Problem Write *metric units, customary units, centimeters,* and *inches* on the board. Have children measure the length of their pencil in inches and centimeters.

Newcomer

- Say: **We can measure in inches or centimeters.** Have children repeat. Say: **Inches are customary units. Centimeters are metric units.**
- Guide children to measure their pencils in inches.

Beginning

- Ask: **Can we measure length in *inches* and *centimeters*?** yes Say: **Inches are *customary units*. Centimeters are *metric units*.**
- Have children measure their pencils in *centimeters* and *inches*.

Intermediate

- Ask: **What is the length of your pencil to the nearest inch? What is the length of your pencil to the nearest centimeter?**
- Ask: **Are inches *metric units*?** no Say: **They are __.** customary units Ask: **Are centimeters *metric units*?** yes

Advanced

- Have children identify the length of the pencil to the nearest inch and centimeter. Ask: **Which is a metric unit?** centimeter **What kind of unit is an inch?** customary unit

Connections

Science Connection
Lesson 3, page 1062

Social Studies Connection
Lesson 2, page 1054

Math Background

Putting Research into Practice for Unit 14

From Current Research:

Measurement

Initial student experience with a measurement system involving a particular attribute (e.g., length, area, volume, capacity, weight [mass], time, numerosity, rate, density) should include making number-free comparisons and then using non-standard units of measure (e.g., handspans, strides, index cards, jelly beans). Following these experiences, it is necessary to focus on the fundamental characteristics of any measurement system, namely the need to assign a number, to make comparisons, to recognize and use the concept of congruence, to select a unit, and to realize that, when appropriate, congruent units can be added.

Geddes, Dorothy, Robert Berkman, Iris Fearon, Michael Fishenfeld, Caroline Forlano, David J. Fuys, Jodi Goldstein, and Rosamond Welchman. *Measurement in the Middle Grades: Addenda Series, Grades 5–8.* Reston: NCTM, 1994. 4.

Estimation

It is very important to have students estimate a measurement before they make it. This is true with both informal and standard units. There are three reasons for including estimation in measurement activities:

- Estimation helps students focus on the attribute being measured and the measuring process. Think how you would estimate the area of the front of this book with standard playing cards as the unit. To do so, you have to think about what area is and how the units might be fitted into the book cover.
- Estimation provides intrinsic motivation to measurement activities. It is fun to see how close you can come to your estimate or if your team can make a better estimate than the other teams in the room.
- When standard units are used, estimation helps develop familiarity with the unit. If you estimate the height of the door in meters before measuring, you have to devise some way to think about the size of a meter.

Van de Walle, John A. *Elementary and Middle School Mathematics: Teaching Developmentally.* 4th ed. New York: Addison Wesley Longman, 2001. 280.

Other Useful References: Measurement

Dacey, Linda, Mary Cavanagh, Carol R. Findell, Carole E. Greenes, Linda Jensen Sheffield, and Marian Small. *Navigating Through Measurement in PreKindergarten–Grade 2* (with CD-ROM). Reston: NCTM, 2003.

Martinie, Sherri. "Measurement: What's the Big Idea?" *Mathematics Teaching in the Middle School* 9.8 (Apr. 2004): 430.

Preston, Ron, and Tony Thompson. "Integrating Measurement across the Curriculum." *Mathematics Teaching in the Middle School* 9.8 (Apr. 2004): 436.

Van de Walle, John A. *Elementary and Middle School Mathematics: Teaching Developmentally.* 4th ed. New York: Addison Wesley Longman, 2001 (Chapter 16).

Wilson, Patricia S., and Ruth E. Rowland. "Teaching Measurement." *Research Ideas for the Classroom: Early Childhood Mathematics.* Ed. R.J. Jensen. Old Tappan, NJ: Macmillan, 1993. 171–194.

Getting Ready to Teach Unit 14

The focus of this unit is measurement. You may use all the activities to immerse children in a hands-on exploration of this strand, or choose those that you need to fulfill district or state standards.

Linear Measurement
Lessons 1 and 2

In earlier units, children developed their linear measurement skills working with centimeter rulers. In this unit, children revisit non-standard linear units and then create and use an inch ruler and a yardstick. Activities include selecting the most appropriate customary units, rounding measures to the nearest chosen unit, and converting between units.

Mass, Capacity, Temperature and Time
Lessons 1 and 3

In the first lesson of this unit, children explore non-standard methods of measuring mass, capacity, and time. Activities include ordering objects from least to greatest mass by estimating with hands, creating a homemade balance scale, arranging containers from least to greatest capacity using estimation and then checking the order using water, measuring capacity of containers using small objects, and discussing methods of measuring time without modern clocks. In the third lesson, children have opportunities to look at the relationship between customary units of capacity, find referents for customary and metric mass and customary weight, and select the correct customary or metric tool to make a measurement.

Children have opportunities to estimate and measure in Fahrenheit and to make a table of the week's daily high and low temperatures.

Weight Versus Mass Weight is the measure of the gravitational force by which an object is attracted to Earth. The weight of an object changes with its distance from Earth's center. Mass is the measure of the amount of matter in an object; it does not change with the object's position.

Both the customary and the metric systems have units of weight and units of mass. However, the most commonly used measurement units in the customary system (ounces and pounds) are units of weight and the most commonly used measurement units in the metric system (milligrams, grams, and kilograms) are units of mass. While it is important to use these terms correctly (a ball weighs 4 ounces or a nickel has a mass of 5 grams), do not expect young children to grasp the difference between mass and weight.

MINI UNIT 14

LESSON 1

Explore Measurement Concepts

Lesson Objective

- Explore non-standard units.

Vocabulary	
length	volume
mass	time
capacity	

The Day at a Glance

Today's Goals

1 Teaching the Lesson

A: Explore measurement concepts and propose non-standard units for length, mass, capacity, and time.

2 Going Further

▸ Differentiated Instruction

3 Homework

Materials

Lesson Activities

Student Activity Book pp. 463–466 (includes Family Letter)
Homework and Remembering pp. 305–306
Wooden craft sticks
Paper clips
Real or play money (pennies)
Objects of various masses
Stick
String
Hole punch
Paper cups
Containers of various capacities
Water jug

Going Further

Activity Cards 14-1
Connecting cubes
Collection of small and large pebbles
Balance scale
Eraser
Crayon
Masking tape
Math Journals

Keeping Skills Sharp

Daily Routines

2s, 3s, and 4s Count-Bys Draw Arrays, Draw Groups on the 120 Poster, Draw Groups on the Number Path (See pp. xxviii–xix.)

▸ Led by Student Leaders

Money Routine Using the 120 Poster, Using the Money Flip Chart, Using the Number Path, Using Secret Code Cards (See pp. xxiii–xxv.)

▸ Led by Student Leaders

English Language Learners

Show an empty plastic cup. Write *capacity* and *volume* on the board.

- **Beginning** Say: ***Capacity* is the amount the cup holds. *Volume* is the space the cup takes up.** Have children repeat.
- **Intermediate** Ask: **Is *capacity* the amount the cup holds?** yes **Are *capacity* and *volume* the same?** no **Is *volume* the space the cup takes up?** yes
- **Advanced** Have children tell how *capacity* and *volume* are different.

1 Teaching the Lesson

Activity

Non-Standard Units of Measure

60 MINUTES

Goal: Explore measurement concepts and propose non-standard units for length, mass, capacity, and time.

Materials: wooden craft sticks, Student Activity Book pages 463–464, paper clips, pennies, 5 objects of varying mass, stick, string, hole punch, 2 paper cups, 5 containers of varying capacity, water jug

NCTM Standards:
Measurement
Connections

▶ Non-Standard Units of Length

WHOLE CLASS

Math Talk

Ask for Ideas Tell the class that you want to find the length of your desk but you don't have a ruler. Invite children to suggest different non-standard units of length. Record their suggestions on the board.

wooden craft sticks	unit cubes
pennies	finger widths
paper clips	pencils

Demonstrate how to measure the length of your desk using wooden craft sticks.

- Where should I place the first craft stick? Line up the craft stick with one end of your desktop.
- Where should I place the next craft stick? Place the next craft stick end-to-end with the first one. There shouldn't be any space between them.

Explain to children that you will measure to the nearest craft stick.

- If more than half of the last craft stick is on the desk, should I count it? yes
- If less than half of the last craft stick is on the desk, should I count it? no

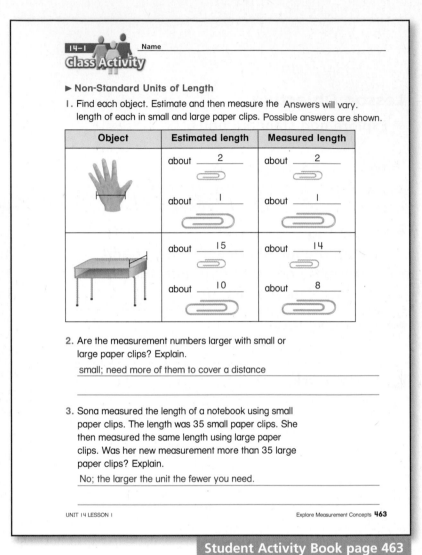

14-1 Class Activity Name ____________

▶ Non-Standard Units of Length

1. Find each object. Estimate and then measure the length of each in small and large paper clips. Answers will vary. Possible answers are shown.

Object	Estimated length	Measured length
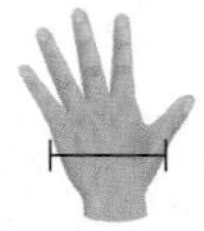	about 2 (small clips)	about 2 (small clips)
	about 1 (large clips)	about 1 (large clips)
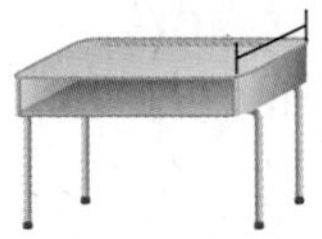	about 15 (small clips)	about 14 (small clips)
	about 10 (large clips)	about 8 (large clips)

2. Are the measurement numbers larger with small or large paper clips? Explain.
small; need more of them to cover a distance

3. Sona measured the length of a notebook using small paper clips. The length was 35 small paper clips. She then measured the same length using large paper clips. Was her new measurement more than 35 large paper clips? Explain.
No; the larger the unit the fewer you need.

UNIT 14 LESSON 1 Explore Measurement Concepts 463

Student Activity Book page 463

Count the total number of craft sticks and record the length on the board, including the unit "wooden craft sticks."

Have children work in pairs to complete exercises 1–3 on Student Activity Book page 463. For exercise 1, ensure that children estimate first. When they are finished, discuss their answers for exercises 2 and 3 as a class.

Invite children to brainstorm different non-standard units they might use to measure greater distances. Possible answers: footsteps, lengths of string, broomsticks

- If each person in the class, including me, measures the length of the schoolyard in footsteps, will we all find the same measure? no

Be sure children understand that if different people use different units, they will get different measurements, but the actual length is always the same.

Explain to children that standard units of length were developed to allow people to communicate their measures more easily. Ask children to list the standard units of length they know. inch, foot, yard, mile, meter, centimeter, decimeter, kilometer

▶ Non-Standard Units of Mass and Weight WHOLE CLASS

Math Talk 123

Ask for Ideas Ask children why they think various ways of measuring the mass or weight of objects were developed. Possible answers: to determine a fair trade; to figure out the cost of an item; to know if someone is healthy

Line up five objects of different masses.

- How can I compare the mass of two objects without using a scale? Hold one object in each hand and estimate which object is heavier.

Have children work in pairs to select five classroom objects and order them from the least mass to the greatest mass.

- How can you compare the mass of two objects without holding them in your hands? Use a balance scale.

Use a commercial balance scale or make a balance scale using a stick, a hole punch, string, and two paper cups.

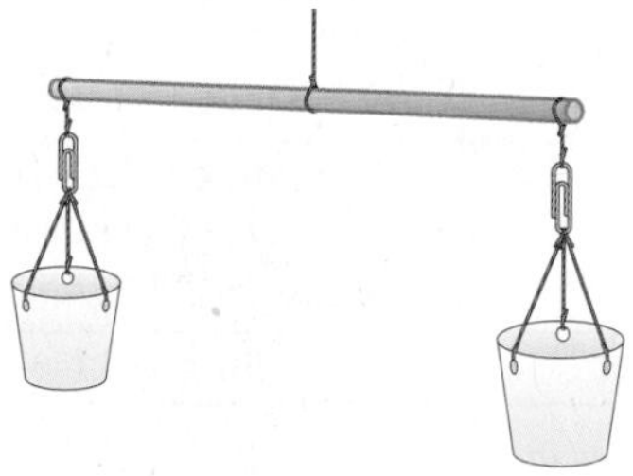

Invite children to brainstorm ideas for non-standard units of mass and ask them to complete exercise 4 on Student Activity Book page 464.

Tell children that you are going to use pennies for your unit of mass. Work together to measure the mass of various lightweight objects in the classroom using your balance scale.

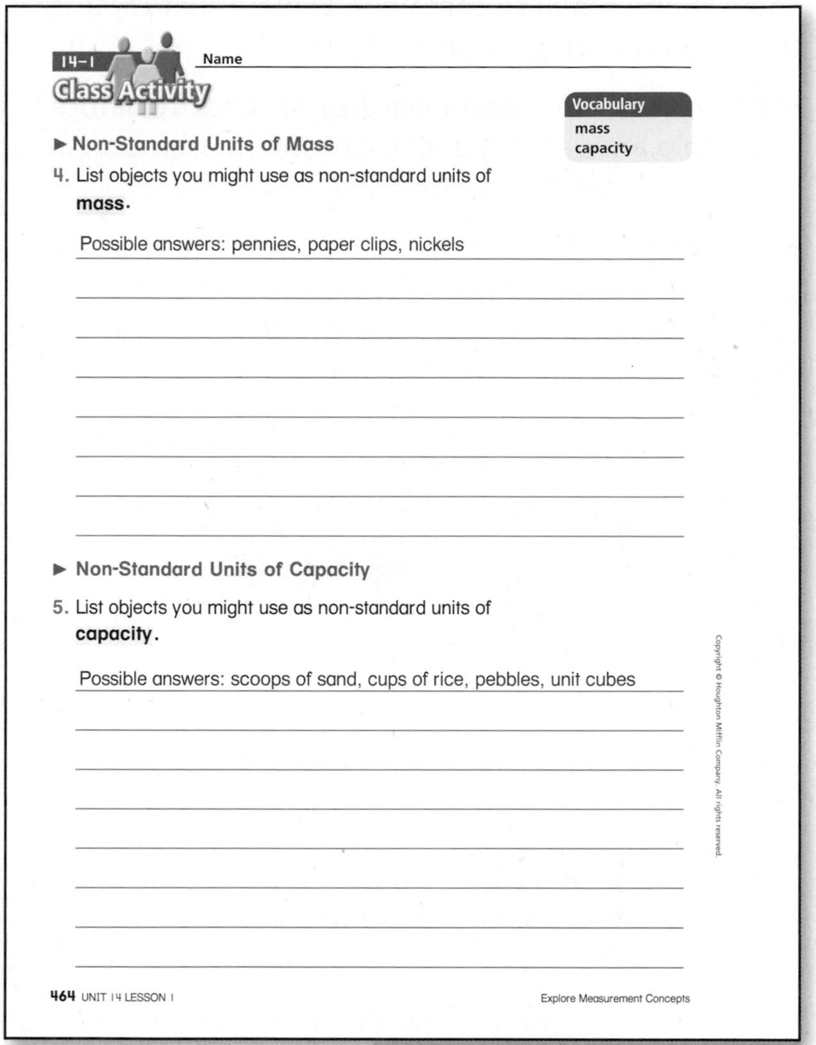

14-1 Class Activity Name

Vocabulary
mass
capacity

▶ Non-Standard Units of Mass

4. List objects you might use as non-standard units of **mass**.

Possible answers: pennies, paper clips, nickels

▶ Non-Standard Units of Capacity

5. List objects you might use as non-standard units of **capacity**.

Possible answers: scoops of sand, cups of rice, pebbles, unit cubes

Student Activity Book page 464

- If we measure the mass of these objects using paper clips, will we find the same measures? no

Point out to children that there are standard units of weight and mass.

- List the standard units of mass or weight they know. pound, ounce, gram, kilogram

Teaching Note

Math Background See page 1041F in the Unit Overview for an explanation of the difference between *mass* and *weight*.

Activity continued ▶

▶ Non-Standard Units of Capacity

WHOLE CLASS — Math Talk

Show children a juice container. Explain that *capacity* is the amount that a container will hold.

- Where have you seen measures of capacity before? Possible answers: on a milk carton; on a tin can; at the gas station; on a paint can

Ask for Ideas Present five unmarked containers of various sizes. Have children estimate the capacity of each container and place them in order from the least capacity to the greatest capacity.

- How can you use water to test whether you correctly ordered these containers from the least capacity to the greatest capacity? We can fill the first container with water and pour the water into the next one. If the water doesn't fill the next container, we know the second container has a larger capacity. We can keep repeating this.

Check children's predictions. Rearrange any containers ordered incorrectly, and test the new order.

Hold up another container.

- How can I use a non-standard unit to measure the capacity of this container? You can fill it with small objects and count them to find the capacity.

Invite children to work in pairs to think of small objects they can use to measure capacity. Have them then complete exercise 5 on Student Activity Book page 464.

- If you measure the capacity of one container using beans and another container using scoops of sand, can you compare the two capacities? no
- What standard units can you use to measure the capacity of the two containers? cup, pint, quart, gallon, liter, milliliter

▶ Non-Standard Units of Volume

Tell children that the *volume* of an object is the amount of space it occupies.

- How did you measure the volume of rectangular prisms? We counted the number of unit cubes used to make a shape.

Explain to children that they used unit cubes as non-standard units of volume. Standard units of volume are cubes with side measures like 1 in., 1 cm, 1 ft, or 1 m.

▶ Non-Standard Units of Time

Tell children that people had been measuring time long before the first clock was made.

- How could you measure time without using a clock? Possible answers: sundial, egg timer, hourglass, marked candles, pendulum, clapping hands, marking days
- List the standard units of time that you know. second, minute, hour, day, week, month, year

▶ Standard Units of Measure

Explain to children that when you use standard units, everyone knows what the measure means. Within one system, standard units also allow you to convert between units. Draw a chart on the board that shows the relationship between customary units of measure.

Customary Units of Measure

Length	12 inches = 1 foot 1 yard = 3 feet
Capacity	2 cups = 1 pint 2 pints = 1 quart 4 quarts = 1 gallon
Time	1 minute = 60 seconds 1 hour = 60 minutes 1 day = 24 hours
Weight	16 ounces = 1 pound

Ongoing Assessment

Ask children to explain in their own words the difference between standard and non-standard units of measure.

2 Going Further

Differentiated Instruction

Intervention — Activity Card 14-1

Units of Mass
Activity Card 14-1 ●

Work:

Use:
- bag of large pebbles
- bag of small pebbles
- connecting cubes
- balance scale
- eraser, crayon, roll of tape

Choose:
- 1
- 2

1. Use the small pebbles and the balance scale. Find the mass of an eraser, a crayon, and a roll of tape. To record the mass for each item count the pebbles.

2. Use the large pebbles and the balance scale. Find the mass of an eraser, a crayon, and a roll of tape. To record the mass for each item count the pebbles.
3. **Work Together** Use [cubes] and the balance scale. Find the mass of an eraser, a crayon, and a roll of tape. Record the mass for each item. Which unit is the best for measuring mass? Explain why.

Unit 14, Lesson 1

Activity Note Each pair needs different size pebbles, connecting cubes, balance scale and different objects to determine the mass.

Math Writing Prompt

You Decide Tara wants to buy a piece of lace to trim the bottom of a curtain. Should she measure the width of the curtain using straws or paper clips? Explain.

Soar to Success Math Software Support

Warm Up 39.08

On Level — Activity Card 14-1

Compare Measurements
Activity Card 14-1 ▲

Work:

Use:
- masking tape

Choose:
- 1
- 2

1. Use your steps to measure the length of the masking tape on the. Walk heel to toe. Record the number of steps.

2. Use your steps to measure the length of the masking tape on the floor. Walk heel to toe. Record the number of steps.
3. **Work Together** Compare your measurements with other pairs.
4. **Math Talk** Do you think this method is a good method for measuring the length of something? Explain why or why not.

Unit 14, Lesson 1

Activity Note Place a piece of masking tape about 10 feet long on the floor. Demonstrate for children how to measure the tape by walking heel to toe.

Math Writing Prompt

Explain Your Thinking Aisha's book has a mass of eight blocks. Ivan's book has a mass of 35 crayons. Can you tell which book is heavier? Explain why or why not.

Harcourt Mega Math Software Support

Shapes Ahoy: Made to Measure, Level D

Challenge — Activity Card 14-1

Choose a Unit
Activity Card 14-1 ■

Work:

Use:
- connecting cubes

Choose:
- 1
- 2

1. Use [cubes] to measure the length of 2 foot.

2. Use a piece of paper to measure 2 foot.
3. Trade roles and repeat.
4. **Work Together** Use [cubes] and the piece of paper to measure a classroom bulletin board or other large item.
5. **Math Talk** Which unit of measurement was best for each object? Explain your choice.

Unit 14, Lesson 1

Activity Note Each pair needs connecting cubes. Ask children to explain their conclusions about units of measure.

Math Writing Prompt

Draw a Picture People often measure a length using both a longer unit and a shorter unit. Explain why. Draw a picture in your answer.

Destination Math Software Support

Course II: Module 3: Unit 1: Area

3 Homework

14–1 Homework **Goal:** Additional Practice

On this Homework page, children measure length, capacity, and mass using non-standard units.

14–1 Homework Name ____________________

1. Use the width of your hand to measure the length of three objects. Measure the same objects using the width of a finger. Answers will vary.

Object	Length (hands)	Length (fingers)

2. Find three containers. Use small objects, like beans or cups of rice or water, to measure the capacity of each container. Remember to include units in your answers. Answers will vary.

Container	Capacity

3. Find three objects that are about the same size. Hold the objects one at a time to compare their masses. List the objects in order from least to greatest mass.

Answers will vary.

4. **On the Back** Describe how measuring length and capacity are similar. Possible answer: You can use a non-standard unit to measure them.

UNIT 14 LESSON 1 Explore Measurement Concepts **305**

Homework and Remembering page 305

Home and School Connection

Family Letter Have children take home the Family Letter on Student Activity Book page 465. This letter explains how some measurement concepts are developed in *Math Expressions.* It gives parents and guardians a better understanding of the learning that goes on in math class and creates a bridge between school and home. A Spanish translation of this letter is on the following page in the Student Activity Book.

Family Letter

Dear Family,

Your child is beginning another unit on measurement.

Children will first investigate measuring using non-standard units. They will measure length in units such as paper clips and mass in units such as pennies, using a handmade balance scale. Children will arrange containers in order of increasing capacity and test the order by transferring water from one container to another. They will also discuss ideas for measuring volume and time using non-standard units.

Children will continue to measure length in customary units. They will make their own inch ruler and yardstick to measure in inches, feet, and yards. They will also make conversions between customary units using these relationships:

1 foot = 12 inches
1 yard = 3 feet
1 yard = 36 inches

These are examples of the types of conversion they will do for homework in Lesson 2.

1 ft = 12 in. 3 ft = 36 in. 2 yd = 6 ft

In the last lesson of this unit, children will have an opportunity to measure length, mass, weight, capacity, time, and temperature using standard units.

To help bridge your child's classroom learning with home, ask your child to estimate and measure objects that he or she uses in everyday activities. For example, you might ask, "How much do you think this pot holds?" and have your child measure its capacity in cups.

If you have any questions or comments, please call or write to me.

Sincerely,
Your child's teacher

UNIT 14 LESSON 1 Explore Measurement Concepts **465**

Student Activity Book page 465

Carta a la familia

Estimada familia:

Su niño empieza otra unidad sobre las medidas.

Los niños empezarán a medir con unidades no usuales. Medirán la longitud usando sujetapapeles y la masa usando unidades tales como monedas de un centavo con una balanza que ellos harán. Los niños ordenarán recipientes según su capacidad y comprobarán el orden pasando agua de un recipiente a otro. También comentarán ideas para medir el volumen y el tiempo usando unidades no usuales.

Más adelante, los niños medirán la longitud en unidades del sistema usual. Harán su propia regla de pulgadas y su propia regla de 1 yarda para medir en pulgadas, pies y yardas. También harán conversiones entre estas unidades utilizando las siguientes relaciones:

1 pie = 12 pulgadas
1 yarda = 3 pies
1 yarda = 36 pulgadas

Estos son ejemplos de los tipos de conversiones que harán como tarea para la Lección 2.

1 pie = 12 pulg 3 pies = 36 pulg
2 yd = 6 pies

En la última lección de esta unidad los niños tendrán la oportunidad de medir la longitud, la masa, el peso, la capacidad, el tiempo y la temperatura usando unidades usuales de medida.

Para ayudar a su niño a hacer la conexión entre el aprendizaje en la escuela y la casa, pídale que estime y mida objetos que se usan en las actividades diarias. Por ejemplo, podría preguntarle, "¿Cuánto crees que cabe en esta olla?" y pedirle que mida su capacidad usando una taza.

Si tiene alguna duda o comentario, por favor comuníquese conmigo.

Atentamente,
El maestro de su niño

466 UNIT 14 LESSON 1 Explore Measurement Concepts

Student Activity Book page 466

MINI UNIT 14
LESSON 2

Customary Units of Length

Lesson Objectives

- Estimate and measure in inches.
- Measure in feet and yards.
- Select the best customary unit to measure a specific length.
- Convert between inches, feet, and yards.

Vocabulary
inch
foot
yard

The Day at a Glance

Today's Goals	Materials	
1 Teaching the Lesson **A1:** Estimate and measure lengths in inches. **A2:** Measure in customary units of length and convert between them. **2 Going Further** ▶ Differentiated Instruction **3 Homework**	**Lesson Activities** Student Activity Book pp. 467–474 (includes Inch Ruler, Yardstick) Homework and Remembering pp. 307–308 Inch Ruler (TRB M96) Yardstick (TRB M97) Scissors Tape or glue Colored pencils MathBoard materials Meter stick	**Going Further** Activity Cards 14-2 Inch Grid Paper (TRB M70) or Inch cubes Inch rulers Yardsticks Index cards Classroom objects Math Journals

123 Use Math Talk today!

Keeping Skills Sharp

Daily Routines	English Language Learners
2s, 3s, and 4s Count-Bys Draw Arrays, Draw Groups on the 120 Poster, Draw Groups on the Number Path (See pp. xxviii–xix.) ▶ Led by Student Leaders **Money Routine** Using the 120 Poster, Using the Money Flip Chart, Using the Number Path, Using Secret Code Cards (See pp. xxiii–xxv.) ▶ Led by Student Leaders	Show a 12-inch ruler and a yardstick. Write *feet* and *yards* on the board. Say: ***Feet* and *yards* are units of length.** • **Beginning** Say: **12 *inches* equals 1 *foot*. 3 *feet* equals 1 *yard*.** Have children repeat. • **Intermediate** Ask: **Do 12 inches equal 1 yard?** no **Do 12 inches equal 1 foot?** yes **Do 3 feet equal 1 yard?** yes • **Advanced** Have children tell how *inches*, *feet*, and *yards* are related.

1 Teaching the Lesson

Activity 1

Estimate and Measure in Inches

30 MINUTES

Goal: Estimate and measure lengths in inches.

Materials: Student Activity Book pages 467–470, scissors, tape or glue, colored pencils, MathBoard materials

NCTM Standards:
Measurement
Connections

▶ Make an Inch Ruler WHOLE CLASS

Hold up an inch ruler.

- Does anyone know the distance between the 0 and the 1 on this ruler? 1 inch

Write the word *inch* on the board.

- Does anyone know the short way to write inch? in.

Write the abbreviation for inch on the board. Point out the period after the "n" and explain that it helps us to distinguish between the word *in* and the abbreviation for inch.

Refer children to Student Activity Book page 467. Have them follow the instructions to make an inch ruler.

Distribute colored pencils. To help children visualize inches as lengths, have them mark the inches on their rulers with alternating colors.

Ask children to print the numbers 1 to 11 on their rulers.

Ask children to look at the shorter lines on their rulers.

- What measure does each of these shorter lines mark? half-inch

Tell children that their rulers are one foot long.

- How many inches are in one foot? 12 inches

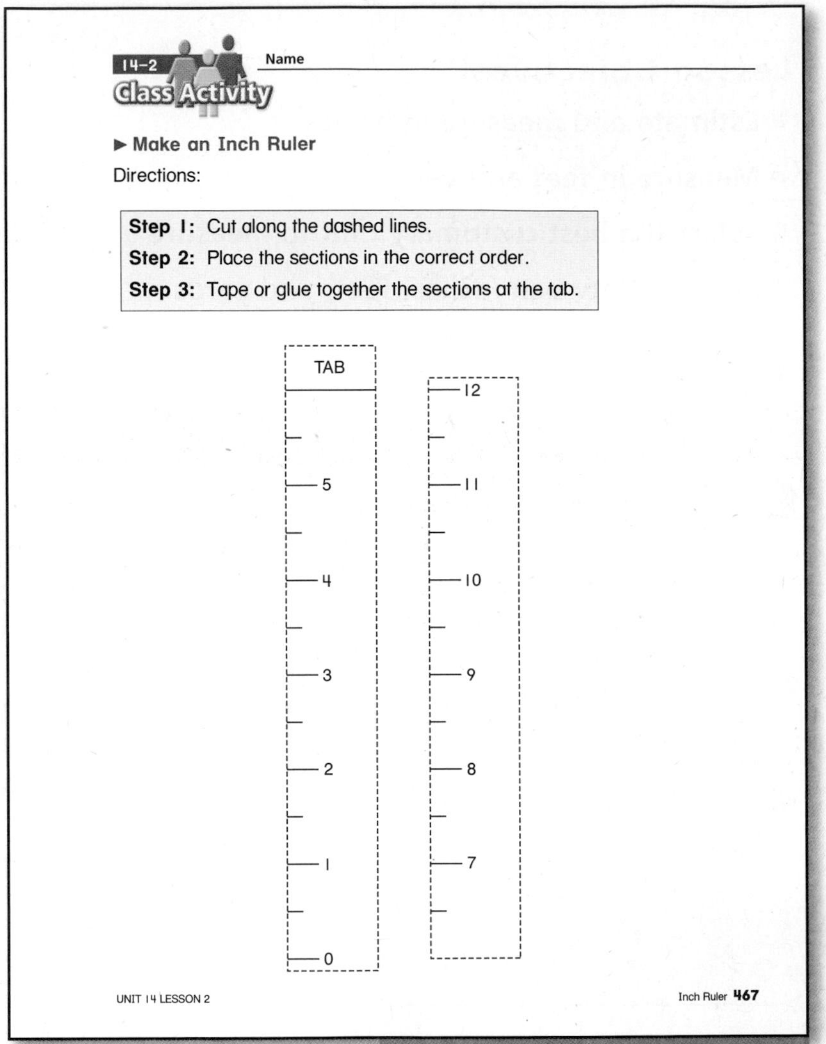
14-2 Class Activity Name

▶ Make an Inch Ruler

Directions:

Step 1: Cut along the dashed lines.
Step 2: Place the sections in the correct order.
Step 3: Tape or glue together the sections at the tab.

UNIT 14 LESSON 2 Inch Ruler 467

Student Activity Book page 467

Write the word *foot* on the board.

- What is the short way to write foot? ft

Write the abbreviation for foot on the board.

Have children use their paper inch rulers to draw line segments on their MathBoards. Ask them to draw line segments 3 in., 5 in., and 8 in. long.

14–2 Class Activity

Name

Vocabulary
inch (in.)

► **Measure to the Nearest Inch**

To measure to the nearest **inch (in.)**, place the zero mark on your ruler at the left end of the object. Find the inch mark that is closest to the right end of the object.

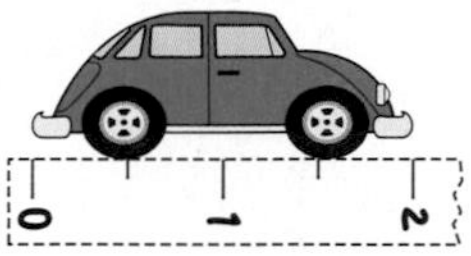

To the nearest inch, the length of this toy car is 2 inches.

Measure the length of each object to the nearest inch.

1. 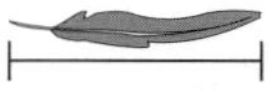 1 in.

2. 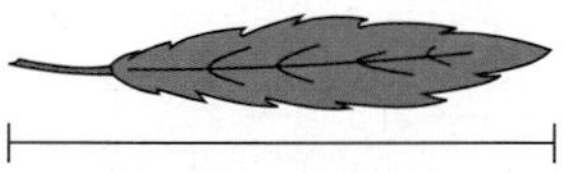 3 in.

3. 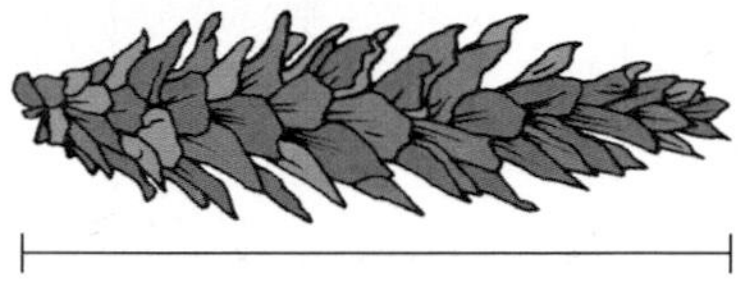 4 in.

4. Draw a horizontal line that is 2 in. long.

5. Draw a horizontal line that is 6 in. long.

UNIT 14 LESSON 2 Customary Units of Length **469**

Student Activity Book page 469

14–2 Class Activity

Name

► **Estimate and Measure in Inches**

6. Describe a part of your hand that measures about 2 in.
Possible answer: width of palm

7. Describe a part of your hand that measures about 1 in.
Possible answer: width of 2 fingers

8. Describe a part of your hand that measures about 6 in.
Possible answer: length of pinky finger to thumb when fingers are spread out

Estimate and measure the length of each line segment.

9. ______________________

Estimated length: ________

Measured length: 3 in.

10. ________________________________

Estimated length: ________

Measured length: 5 in.

11. Find four classroom objects that you can measure in inches. Estimate and then measure the length of each object to the nearest inch. Complete the table. Answers will vary.

Object	Estimated length (in.)	Measured length (in.)

470 UNIT 14 LESSON 2 Customary Units of Length

Student Activity Book page 470

► Measure to the Nearest Inch

INDIVIDUALS

Have children look at the top of Student Activity Book page 469. Read aloud the explanation of how to measure length to the nearest inch.

Ask children to complete exercises 1–5 independently. When they are finished, invite them to work in pairs to check each other's answers.

► Estimate and Measure in Inches

INDIVIDUALS

Refer children to Student Activity Book page 470 and have them complete exercises 6–8 by finding personal referents for specific lengths. Invite them to share their answers.

Then have children complete exercises 9 and 10 on their own, and exercise 11 in pairs. Discuss answers as a class when they are finished.

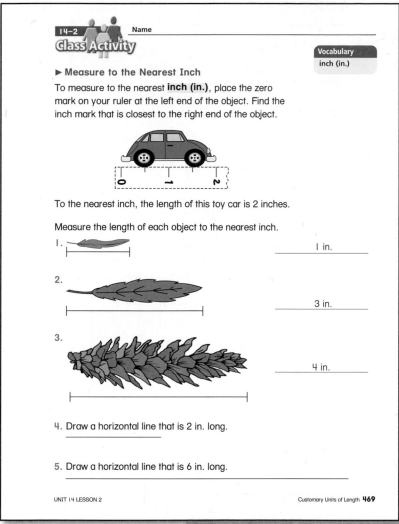

Activity 2

Inches, Feet, and Yards

30 MINUTES

Goal: Measure in customary units of length and convert between them.

Materials: yardstick, Student Activity Book pages 471–474, scissors, tape or glue, paper inch rulers from Activity 1

NCTM Standards:
Measurement
Connections

▶ Make a Yardstick WHOLE CLASS

Hold up a yardstick and ask children to identify what it is. If a child calls it a meter stick, show the class that a yardstick is a bit shorter than a meter stick and that it has inch units instead of centimeter units.

Have children follow the directions on Student Activity Book page 471 to make their own yardsticks. Have them add the numbers 6, 12, 18, 24 and 30 to their yardsticks.

When they are finished, tell children that their yardstick is 1 yard long.

Write the word *yard* on the board.

- What is the short way to write yard? yd

Write the abbreviation for yard on the board.

- How many inches are in 1 yd? 36 inches

Ask children to fold their yardsticks into three sections of equal length.

- How long is each section? 1 ft or 12 in.
- How many feet are in 1 yd? 3 feet

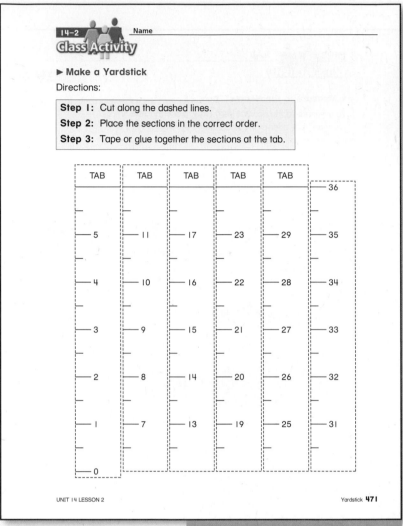

14-2 Class Activity Name

▶ Make a Yardstick

Directions:

Step 1:	Cut along the dashed lines.
Step 2:	Place the sections in the correct order.
Step 3:	Tape or glue together the sections at the tab.

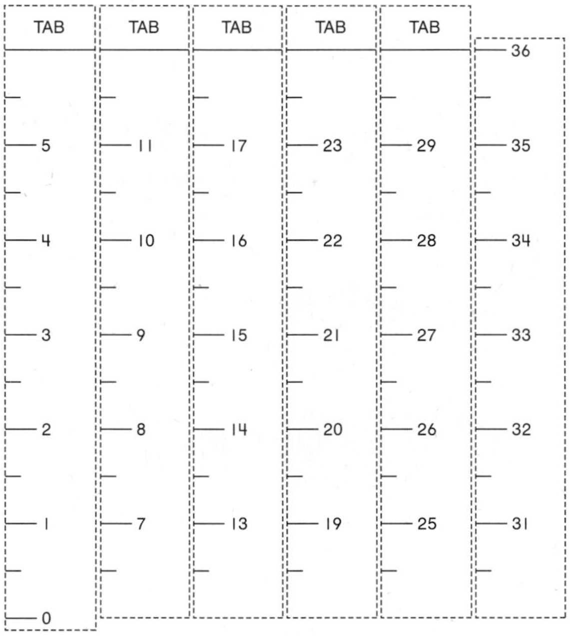

UNIT 14 LESSON 2 Yardstick 471

Student Activity Book page 471

Explain to children that you will say different lengths and they will respond by showing the lengths on their yardsticks.

- Show me 1 in.
- Show me 12 in.
- Show me 1 ft.
- Show me 20 in.
- Show me 32 in.
- Show me 24 in.
- Show me 36 in.
- Show me 1 yd.

▶ Measure in Feet and Yards PAIRS

Round Measures in Feet Draw a line segment on the board that is slightly longer than 1 ft. Demonstrate how to measure the length of the line segment using an inch ruler. Discuss how to round measures to the nearest foot.

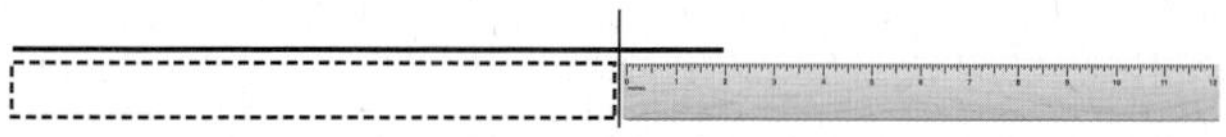

- Is this line segment closer to 1 ft or 2 ft in length? 1 ft
- Does the measure round to 1 ft or 2 ft? 1 ft

Draw another line segment on the board that is slightly less than 2 ft.

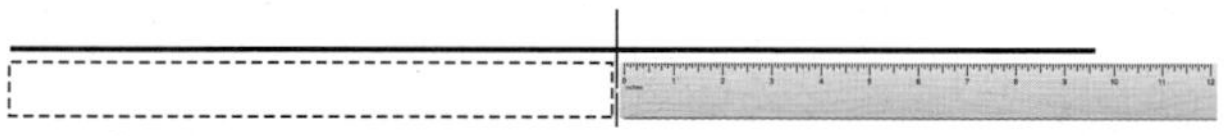

- Does this measure round to 1 ft or 2 ft? 2 ft Why? It is closer to 2 ft.

Refer children to Student Activity Book page 473 and have them complete exercises 12 and 13 using their paper inch rulers.

Round Measures in Yards Demonstrate how to measure the length of a desk to the nearest yard using a yardstick.

Have children use their paper yardsticks to complete exercises 14 and 15.

Measure in Feet and Yards Ask children to complete exercises 16 and 17 by measuring the lengths of different objects in feet and yards.

Have children complete exercise 18 and invite them to share their answers. Elicit the idea that since feet are smaller than yards, there are more of them.

Are the measures more exact when you measure in feet or in yards? feet

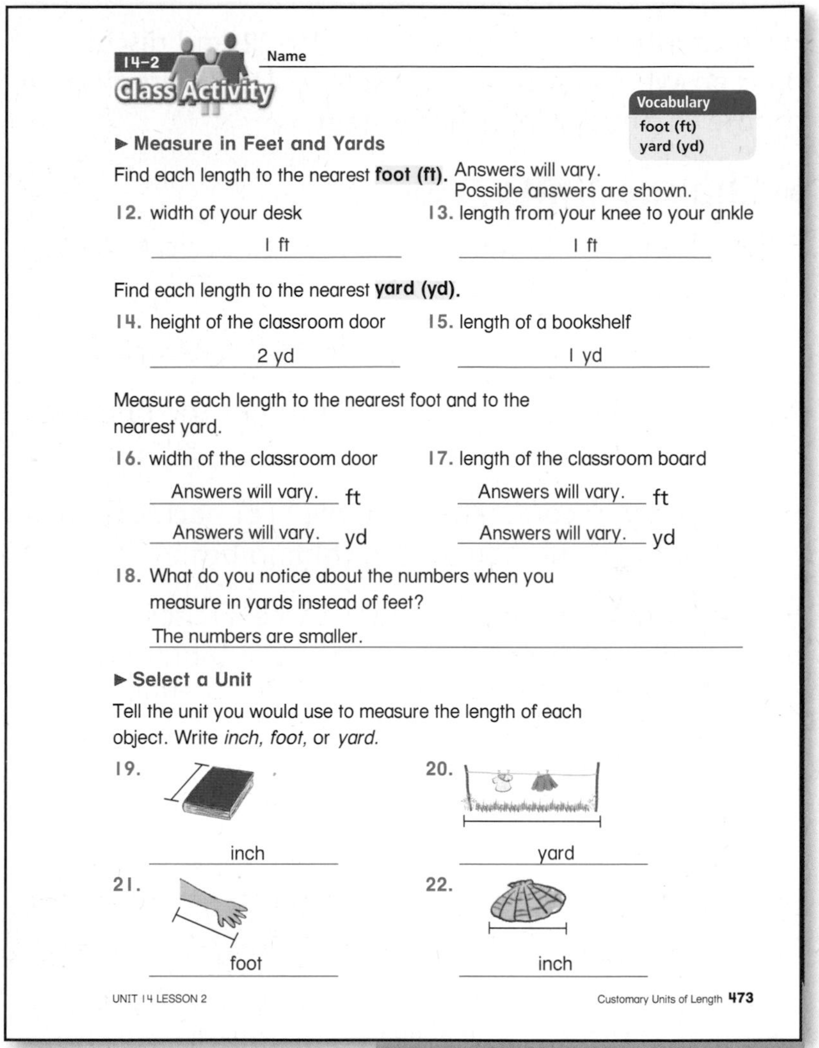
14–2 Class Activity

Name ______

Vocabulary
foot (ft)
yard (yd)

▶ **Measure in Feet and Yards**

Find each length to the nearest **foot (ft)**. Answers will vary. Possible answers are shown.

12. width of your desk — 1 ft

13. length from your knee to your ankle — 1 ft

Find each length to the nearest **yard (yd)**.

14. height of the classroom door — 2 yd

15. length of a bookshelf — 1 yd

Measure each length to the nearest foot and to the nearest yard.

16. width of the classroom door — Answers will vary. ft; Answers will vary. yd

17. length of the classroom board — Answers will vary. ft; Answers will vary. yd

18. What do you notice about the numbers when you measure in yards instead of feet?
The numbers are smaller.

▶ **Select a Unit**

Tell the unit you would use to measure the length of each object. Write *inch*, *foot*, or *yard*.

19. inch

20. yard

21. foot

22. inch

UNIT 14 LESSON 2 — Customary Units of Length 473

Student Activity Book page 473

▶ Select a Unit WHOLE CLASS **Math Talk**

Explain to children that you can use more than one unit if you want a more precise or exact measurement. For example, you might measure a person's height as 3 ft 11 in. Point out for children that you typically use only one unit when you need an approximate, not an exact, measurement.

- If you want to know about how long the classroom is, will you measure in feet, yards, or inches? yards Why? The room is very long. If I measure in inches or feet, I will have to keep track of a lot of numbers.
- If you want to know about how long a pencil is, will you measure in feet, yards, or inches? inches Why? A pencil is short. If I measure to the nearest foot or

Activity continued ▶

1 Teaching the Lesson (continued)

yard, I would not have a good idea of how long the pencil is.

Have children complete exercises 19–22 and discuss their answers as a class. For exercise 21, children can choose to answer in inches or feet.

▶ Change Units PAIRS

Refer children to Student Activity Book page 474 and ask them to look at the table in exercise 23.

- What number do you add to 12 to get 24? 12
- What number do you add to 24 to get the number of inches in 3 ft? 12
- How can you complete this table? For each column, add 12 to the number in the column before it.

Have children complete the tables in exercises 23–25 in pairs. While they are working, copy the tables on the board. When children are finished, discuss their answers and fill in the tables on the board together.

Tell children to use these tables to complete exercise 26.

Class Management

Looking Ahead Children will need an inch ruler and a yardstick to complete several homework exercises. Distribute TRB M96 and M97 so they can make an inch ruler and a yardstick for use at home.

Ongoing Assessment

Ask children to complete each conversion.

▶ Write 6 yd in feet.

▶ Write 24 in. in feet.

▶ Write 2 ft in inches.

▶ Write 9 ft in yards.

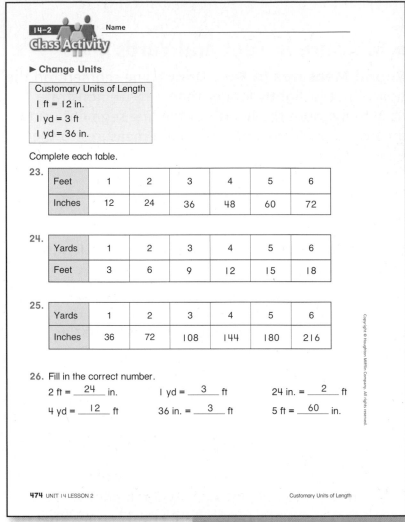

14-2 Class Activity

Name

▶ Change Units

Customary Units of Length
1 ft = 12 in.
1 yd = 3 ft
1 yd = 36 in.

Complete each table.

23.

Feet	1	2	3	4	5	6
Inches	12	24	36	48	60	72

24.

Yards	1	2	3	4	5	6
Feet	3	6	9	12	15	18

25.

Yards	1	2	3	4	5	6
Inches	36	72	108	144	180	216

26. Fill in the correct number.

2 ft = 24 in. 1 yd = 3 ft 24 in. = 2 ft

4 yd = 12 ft 36 in. = 3 ft 5 ft = 60 in.

474 UNIT 14 LESSON 2 Customary Units of Length

Student Activity Book page 474

Differentiated Instruction

Extra Help Some children may benefit from labeling feet on their paper yardsticks and then using their yardsticks to convert between customary units of length. For example, if children want to convert 2 ft to inches, they can find 24 in. on their yardsticks at the 2 ft label. To convert 3 yd to feet, several children can combine yardsticks; they can count the number of feet from the start of the first yardstick to the end of the third one.

2 Going Further

Differentiated Instruction

Intervention

Activity Card 14-2

Measure with Inch Cubes — Activity Card 14-2

Work: (pairs)

Use:

- inch ruler
- Inch Grid Paper or inch cubes

1. **Work Together** Use inch grid paper strips to measure objects in the classroom such as a notebook, a desk, a chair seat, or a book. Line up the strips along one side. Count the number of inch squares on the strip. Record your results.

2. Measure the same objects using the inch ruler. Record your results.
3. **Math Talk** Discuss which method was easier to use and why you think it was easier to use.

Unit 14, Lesson 2

Activity Note Each pair needs inch grid paper (TRB M70) or inch cubes and a 12-in. ruler. You may want to gather several items for pairs to measure and help children cut the inch grid paper into strips.

Math Writing Prompt

You Decide Would you measure the width of a CD case in inches or feet? Explain.

Soar to Success Math Software Support

Warm Up 38.15

On Level

Activity Card 14-2

Object Hunt — Activity Card 14-2

Work: (pairs)

Use:

- 8 index cards
- inch ruler
- yardstick
- classroom objects

Choose:

- 1
- 2

1. 1 Choose four classroom objects. Don't tell 2 which objects you chose.
2. Measure each object using the inch ruler or yardstick.
3. On separate index cards write two clues for each object. One clue is the measurement. The other clue is about shape, color, or location.

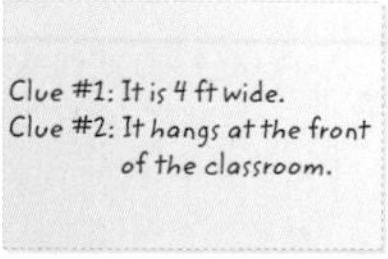
Clue #1: It is 4 ft wide.
Clue #2: It hangs at the front of the classroom.

4. 2 Repeat steps 1–3.
5. Exchange cards and use the clues to find each object.

Unit 14, Lesson 2

Activity Note Each pair needs 8 index cards, classroom objects, an inch ruler, and a yardstick. Have children provide extra clues if needed.

Math Writing Prompt

Investigate Math Emily drew a line 13 in. long. Miguel drew a line 1 ft long. Whose line is longer? How do you know?

MegaMath Software Support

Shapes Ahoy: Made to Measure, Level F

Challenge

Activity Card 14-2

Distance Between Objects — Activity Card 14-2

Work: (pairs)

Use:

- 8 index cards
- inch ruler
- yardstick
- classroom objects

Choose:

- 1
- 2

1. 1 Choose four classroom objects. Don't tell 2 which objects you chose.
2. Use the inch ruler or yardstick to measure the distance from each object to two or three other objects.
3. On separate index cards write a clue for each object. The clue should include the distance from other objects.

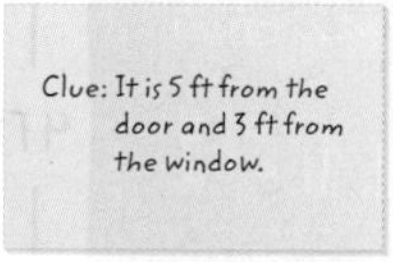
Clue: It is 5 ft from the door and 3 ft from the window.

4. 2 Repeat steps 1–3.
5. Exchange cards and use the clues to find each object.

Unit 14, Lesson 2

Activity Note Each pair needs 8 index cards, an inch ruler, and a yardstick. Have children provide extra clues if needed.

Math Writing Prompt

Explain Your Thinking Rupa has a piece of ribbon that is 28 in. long. Explain how she can write this measure as feet and inches.

Destination Math Software Support

Course II: Module 3: Unit 1: Area

1 Teaching the Lesson

Activity 1

Select Tools

10 MINUTES

Goal: Select the proper measurement tool for a given situation.

NCTM Standards:
Measurement
Connections

Teaching Note

Math Background Weight is the measure of the gravitational force by which an object is attracted to another object. On Earth, that object is Earth itself. The weight of an object changes with its distance from Earth's center. Weight is measured with spring or platform scales.

Mass is the measure of the amount of matter in an object; it does not change with the object's position. When a balance scale is used to compare two objects, it is their masses that are being compared.

So whether children use a spring scale, a bathroom scale, or a balance to compare objects in this lesson, you may use the term *weight* to refer to what they are measuring, since an object with a greater mass than another will also have a greater weight. If your science standards require that children differentiate between *weight* and mass, then you should use the term mass if children are measuring with a balance. It is not expected that young children will grasp the difference between mass and weight. Being able to compare weights is the goal for this activity

▶ Which Tool WHOLE CLASS

Begin by asking children to name measurement tools. Make a list of their responses on the board. As each tool is named ask when you would use it.

- Which tool would you use to find which is heavier: an apple or an orange? balance scale or pan balance
- Which tool would you use to find how long a table is? ruler
- Which tool would you use to find how much a bowl could hold? Sample responses: cup, pint, quart
- Which tool would you use to find the temperature? thermometer
- Which tool would you use to find the weight of something? spring or platform scale

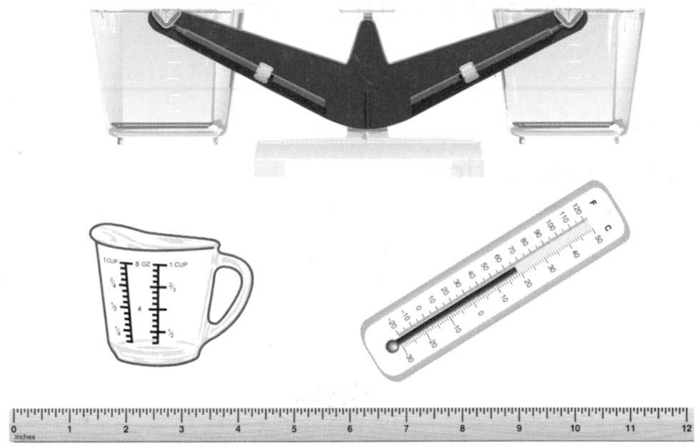

If you need to cover metric standards repeat activity using metric tools.

▶ Measurement Tools SMALL GROUPS

Have children take turns naming a measurement tool. Then have the other children each give an example of a situation when they would use the named tool.

Math Talk Have children discuss times they used measurement tools. Instruct children to explain why they needed to use the tool. Tell them to describe how they used the tools to help them.

Activity 2

Introduce Cups, Pints, Quarts, and Gallons

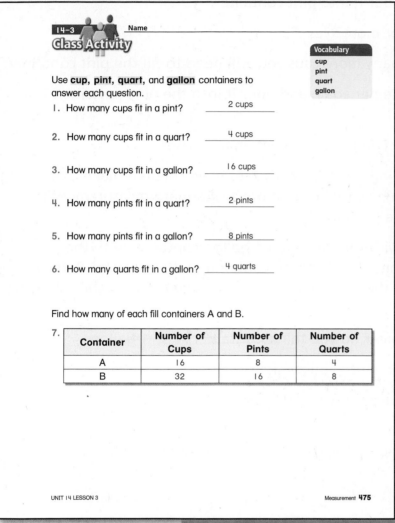

14-3 **Class Activity**

Name ______________________

Vocabulary
cup
pint
quart
gallon

Use **cup**, **pint**, **quart**, and **gallon** containers to answer each question.

1. How many cups fit in a pint? 2 cups
2. How many cups fit in a quart? 4 cups
3. How many cups fit in a gallon? 16 cups
4. How many pints fit in a quart? 2 pints
5. How many pints fit in a gallon? 8 pints
6. How many quarts fit in a gallon? 4 quarts

Find how many of each fill containers A and B.

7.

Container	Number of Cups	Number of Pints	Number of Quarts
A	16	8	4
B	32	16	8

UNIT 14 LESSON 3 Measurement 475

Student Activity Book page 475

▶ How Many Cups? SMALL GROUPS

Provide labeled containers for cups, pints, quarts, and gallon for each group. Have children predict how many of each will fit into a larger container. Then have children use water, rice, or sand to check their predictions.

▶ Cups, Pints, Quarts, and Gallons PAIRS

Direct children's attention to Student Activity Book page 475. Have children use the labeled containers to complete Exercises 1–6. Provide rice, sand, or water for children to use to measure.

Activity continued ▶

20 MINUTES

Goal: Estimate and measure with cups, pints, quarts and gallons.

Materials: labeled containers cup, pint, quart, and gallon, 1- and 2-gallon containers not labeled, sand, rice, or water, Student Activity Book page 475

NCTM Standards:
Measurement
Connections

For Exercise 1 tell children to take the cup container and fill it to the top. Instruct them to pour it into pint container.

- Is there room for more? yes
- Estimate how many more cups you will need to fill the pint container.
- Fill the cup container again and pour it into the pint container. Is it full? yes
- How many cups filled the pint container? 2 cups

Use similar questioning for Exercises 2–6. Have children make a first pour and then estimate how many more of the standard measurement they will need to fill the container.

For Exercise 7 provide an unmarked 1-gallon container with the letter *A* and an unmarked 2-gallon container with the letter *B*. Have children complete the exercise as they did above then ask the following questions.

- What size container do you think Container *A* is? 1-gallon
- What size container do you think Container *B* is? 2-gallon

Have children share how they determined the size of Containers *A* and *B*.

If you need to cover metric standards repeat activity using milliliters and liters.

Activity 3

Introduce Ounces and Pounds

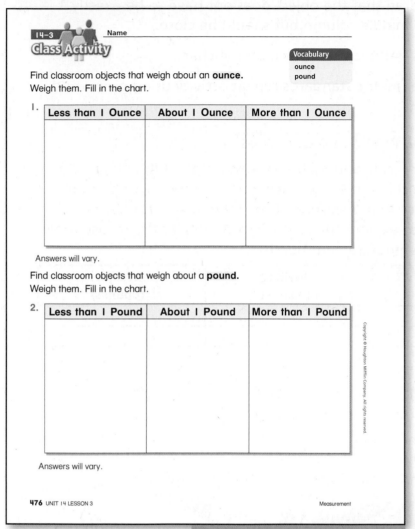

14-3 Class Activity Name ______

Vocabulary
ounce
pound

Find classroom objects that weigh about an **ounce.**
Weigh them. Fill in the chart.

1.

Less than 1 Ounce	About 1 Ounce	More than 1 Ounce

Answers will vary.

Find classroom objects that weigh about a **pound.**
Weigh them. Fill in the chart.

2.

Less than 1 Pound	About 1 Pound	More than 1 Pound

Answers will vary.

476 UNIT 14 LESSON 3 Measurement

Student Activity Book page 476

▶ Ounces and Pounds WHOLE CLASS / SMALL GROUPS

Put a small classroom object (that weighs about an ounce), such as a marker, on a scale and show the ounce reading to the children. Have the children each hold the ounce object. Put a 1-pound object (book) on the scale and show the reading. Have children each hold the 1 pound item. Have children find Student Activity Book page 476. Tell children to find other items that weigh about 1 ounce. Tell them to remember how heavy the ounce item felt when looking for other 1-ounce items. Tell children that the object does not have to be exactly 1 ounce to be in the middle column but should be close.

- You may want to use more than 1 of an object to equal 1 ounce if it is a very light object like a paper clip.
- Fill in the chart.

20 MINUTES

Goal: Estimate and measure with ounces and pounds.

Materials: Student Activity Book page 476, balance scale, Customary scale, paper bags, classroom objects (light objects and objects that weigh about 1, 2, and 3 pounds).

NCTM Standards:
Measurement
Connections

Ongoing Assessment

Assess children's understanding of measurement. Ask questions such as:

- ▶ What tool should Billy use to measure his weight? scale
- ▶ Which holds more a cup or a quart? quart

Quick Quiz

See Assessment Guide for Unit 14 Quick Quiz.

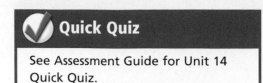

Put a 1-pound object (such as a book) on the scale and show the 1-pound reading. Have children each hold the 1 pound item. Tell them to remember how heavy the item felt when looking for other 1-pound items. Remind children that the object does not have to be exactly 1 pound to be in the middle column but should be close.

- Draw the objects in the correct place on the chart.

If you need to cover metric standards repeat activity using grams and kilograms.

▶ Which Is Heavier? SMALL GROUPS

Prepare a customary scale and 3 objects that weighs 1 lb, 2 lb, and 3 lb for each pair. Have children weigh each object in pound, and in ounces and create a table of their measures. They then look for a pattern in the table in order to explore the idea that the smaller the measurement unit, the larger the measurement number.

Object:	Weight (ounces)	Weight (pounds)

▶ Which Paper Bag Is Heavier? SMALL GROUPS

Tell children to put a combination of small objects into two paper bags. Explain that they should try to make the bags close to the same weight. Then they guess which of the bags is heavier. Have them check their guess using a balance scale. Repeat the activity a few times.

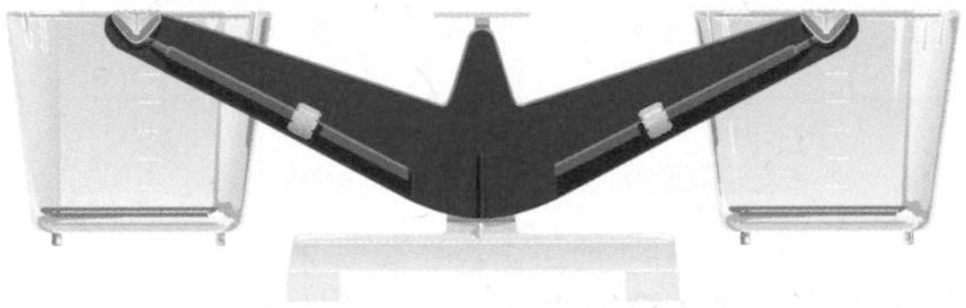

▶ Measure Many Ways SMALL GROUPS

Ask children to identify all the measurable attributes of a classroom object. For example, children might point out that you can measure the length, width, height, and capacity of the classroom fish tank. They might also notice that you can measure the temperature of the tank of water, the age of the fish, and how long it has been since the class last cleaned the tank.

Demonstrate for children how to make a picture of the object and label or list its measures, including all of those mentioned in your discussion.

Explain to children that they will select an object to measure in their classroom. Then they will draw the object on the TRB M98 and label their drawing with as many measures as possible.

Have groups take turns sharing their work with the class. The pictures can be made into a class book or displayed on a bulletin board.

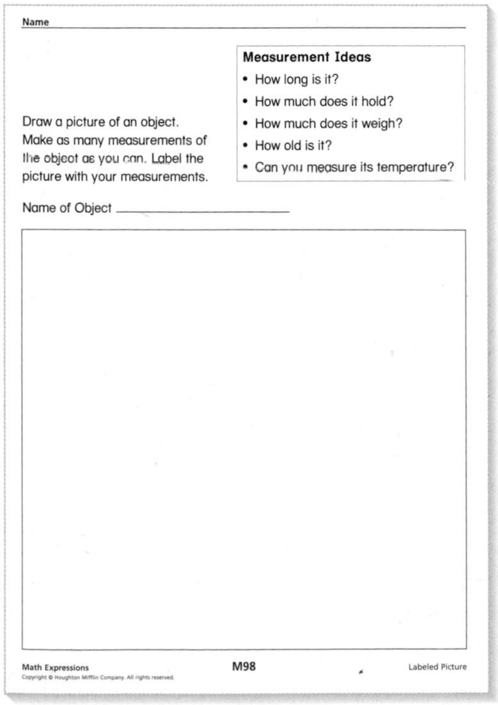
Name

Measurement Ideas
- How long is it?
- How much does it hold?
- How much does it weigh?
- How old is it?
- Can you measure its temperature?

Draw a picture of an object. Make as many measurements of the object as you can. Label the picture with your measurements.

Name of Object

Math Expressions M98 Labeled Picture
Copyright © Houghton Mifflin Company. All rights reserved.

Intervention Activity Card 14-3

Order the Containers

Activity Card 14-3

Work: pairs

Use:
- cup
- pint
- quart
- gallon
- sand, rice, or water

Choose:
- individual
- pairs

1. **Work Together** Put the containers in order from the one that holds the least amount to the one that holds the greatest amount.
2. Check your order by filling the first container with sand.
3. Then, pour that sand into the second container.
4. If the sand spills over the second container, it holds less than the first container. You will need to try another order.
5. Keep working together until you have the containers in the correct order.
6. **Math Talk** Explain how you know the containers are in order.

Unit 14, Lesson 3

Activity Note Provide something for children to use to pour (sand, rice, or water). The measurement containers should not be labeled. Children should realize the order is cup, pint, quart, and gallon.

Math Writing Prompt

Explain How can you prove that one container holds more than another container?

Soar to Success Math Software Support

Warm Up 40.06

On Level Activity Card 14-3

Ounces or Pounds

Activity Card 14-3

Work: pairs

Use:
- customary scale
- classroom objects

1. **Work Together** Estimate the weight of each object.
2. Measure and record the weight of the objects.
3. Sort the objects into 2 groups: Ounces and Pounds.
4. Draw the 2 groups.

Unit 14, Lesson 3

Activity Note Provide classroom objects for pairs. Half of the objects should have a weight in ounces and the other half should be 1–3 pounds. Tell children to use each weight they get to better help them estimate the next weight.

Math Writing Prompt

Explain Your Thinking How could you explain to a friend the difference between ounces and pounds. Give examples of each.

Harcourt MegaMath Software Support

Country Countdown: Harrison's Comparisons, Level E

Challenge Activity Card 14-3

Convert Ounces to Pounds

Activity Card 14-3

Work: individual

Use:
- Mathboard materials

1. There are 16 ounces in 1 pound.
2. Make a chart to show how many ounces are in 1, 2, 3, 4, and 5 pounds.
3. Name an object that would match each weight.

1 pound = 16 ounces box of pasta
2 pounds =

Unit 14, Lesson 3

Activity Note You may wish to weigh a 1-ounce item such as a marker and then weigh 16 of them together to demonstrate 16 ounces equals 1 pound.

Math Writing Prompt

Explain Brian has a book that weighs 3 pounds. He wants to know how many ounces it weighs but doesn't have a scale. Explain how he can find how many ounces it weighs.

Destination Math Software Support

Course II: Module 3: Unit 1: Area

3 Homework

14-3 Homework **Goal:** Additional Practice

Use this homework activity to provide children more practice with measurement.

14-3 Homework Name ____________

Ring the correct tool for each problem.

1. Paul wants to know the width of a box.

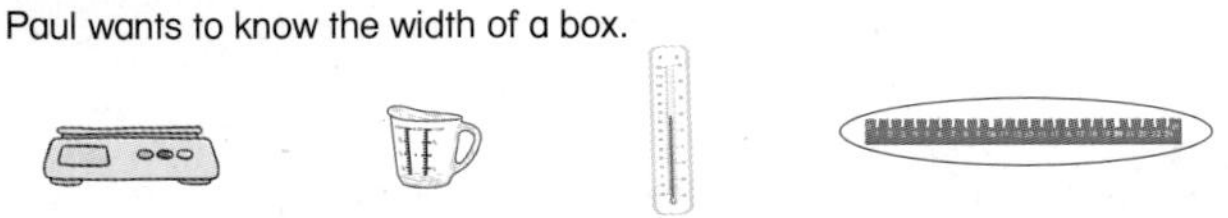

2. Ria wants to know the weight of an apple.

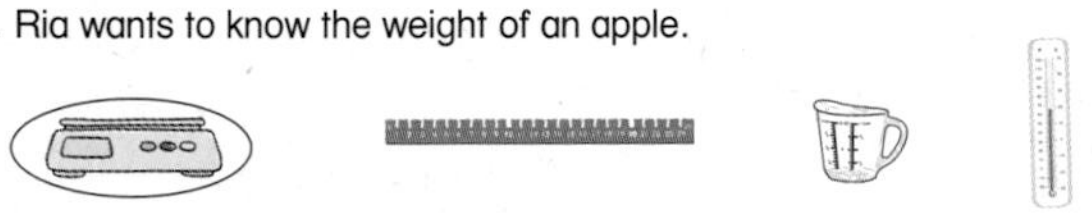

3. Dabbt wants to follow a recipe that needs 1 cup of milk.

4. Put the containers in order from the one that holds the greatest to the one that holds the least.

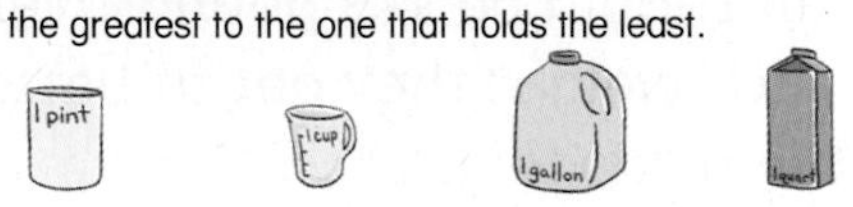

3   4   1   2

5. How many cups equal a pint? 2

6. How many pints equal a quart? 2

7. How many quarts equal a gallon? 4

8. **On the Back** Draw 3 objects that should be weighed in ounces and 3 that should be weighed in pounds.
Check children's work.

UNIT 14 LESSON 3   Measurement **309**

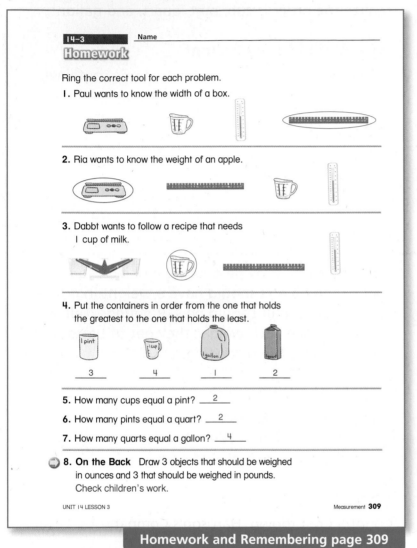

Homework and Remembering page 309

Home or School Activity

Science Connection

High and Low Temperature Review that the measurement tool used to measure temperature is called a thermometer. Discuss that thermometers can show degrees Fahrenheit. Explain that some thermometers show degrees Celsius. Have children make a table of the week's daily high and low temperatures. They should highlight the highest and lowest temperatures for the week.

Day	High	Low
Sunday	55°F	37°F
Monday	51°F	36°F
Tuesday	58°F	32°F
Wednesday	59°F	33°F
Thursday	56°F	31°F
Friday	52°F	30°F
Saturday	54°F	34°F

MINI UNIT 14

Unit Review and Test

Lesson Objectives

- Assess children's progress on unit objectives.

The Day at a Glance

Today's Goals	Materials
1 Assessing the Unit ▶ Assess children's progress on unit objectives. ▶ Use activities from unit lessons to reteach content.	Unit 14 Test, Student Activity Book pages 477–478 Unit 14 Test, Form A or B, Assessment Guide (optional) Unit 14 Performance Assessment, Assessment Guide (optional)
2 Extending the Assessment ▶ Use remediation for common errors.	
There is no homework assignment on a test day.	

Keeping Skills Sharp

Quick Practice (5 MINUTES)	
If you are doing a unit review day, go over the homework. If this is a test day, omit the homework review.	**Review and Test Day** You may want to choose a quiet game or other activity (reading a book or working on homework for another subject) for children who finish early.

1 Assessing the Unit

Assess Unit Objectives

45 MINUTES (more if schedule permits)

Goal: Assess student progress on unit objectives.

Materials: Student Activity Book pages 477–478; Assessment Guide (optional)

▶ Review and Assessment

If your students are ready for assessment on the unit objectives, you may use either the test on the Student Activity Book pages or one of the forms of the Unit 14 Test in the Assessment Guide to assess student progress.

If you feel that students need some review first, you may use the test on the Student Activity Book pages as a review of unit content, and then use one of the forms of the Unit 14 Test in the Assessment Guide to assess student progress.

To assign a numerical score for all of these test forms, use 10 points for each question.

You may also choose to use the Unit 14 Performance Assessment. Scoring for that assessment can be found in its rubric in the Assessment Guide.

▶ Reteaching Resources

The chart lists the test items, the unit objectives they cover, and the lesson activities in which the objective is covered in this unit. You may revisit these activities with students who do not show mastery of the objectives.

14 Unit Test Name

Measure the length of each object to the nearest inch.

1. 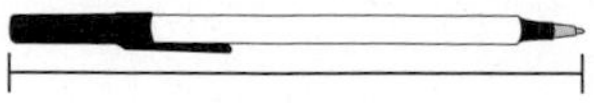 3 in.

2. 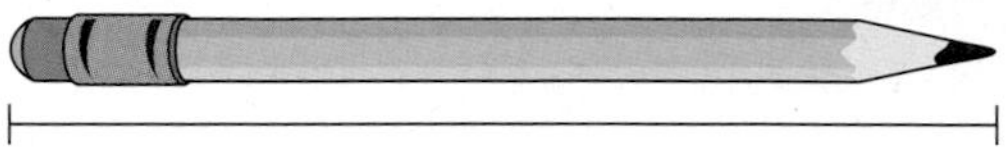 5 in.

3. 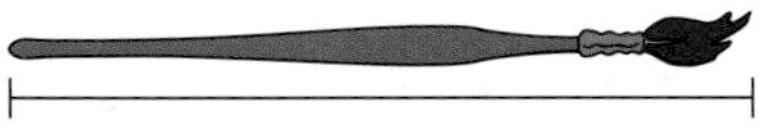 4 in.

Fill in the correct number.

4. 1 yd = 36 in.
5. 1 ft = 12 in.
6. 1 yd = 3 ft
7. 24 in. = 2 ft
8. 9 ft = 3 yd
9. 72 in. = 2 yd

UNIT 14 Test 477

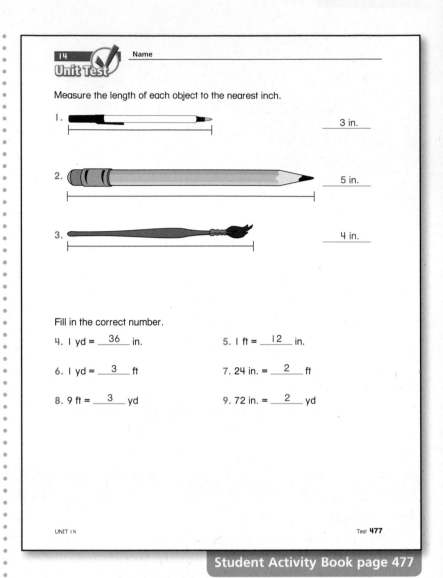

Student Activity Book page 477

Unit Test Items	Unit Objectives Tested	Activities to Use for Reteaching
10	**14.1** Relate the size of a measurement unit to the number of units.	Lesson 2, Activity 2
1, 2, 3	**14.2** Use a ruler to measure a line segment to the nearest inch.	Lesson 2, Activity 1 Lesson 2, Activity 2

14 **Unit Test** Name ______

10. **Extended Response** If you measured the length of the classroom board in inches and in yards, which measure would have a larger number? Explain.

Inches would have a larger number. Inches are smaller than yards so you would need more of them to cover a distance.

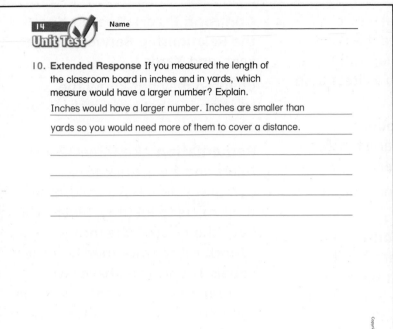

Student Activity Book page 478

Unit Test Items	Unit Objectives Tested	Activities to Use for Reteaching
4, 5, 6	**14.3** Tell the number of inches in a foot, feet in a yard, inches in a yard.	Lesson 1, Activity 1 Lesson 2, Activity 1 Lesson 2, Activity 2
7, 8, 9	**14.4** Convert between inches, feet, and yards.	Lesson 1, Activity 1 Lesson 2, Activity 2

▸ Assessment Guide Resources

Free Response Tests
Unit 14 Test, Student Activity Book pages 477–478
Unit 14 Test, Form A, Assessment Guide

Extended Response Item
The last item in the Student Activity Book test and in the Form A test will require an extended response as an answer.

Multiple-Choice Test
Unit 14 Test, Form B, Assessment Guide

Performance Assessment
Unit 14 Performance Assessment, Assessment Guide
Unit 14 Performance Assessment Rubric, Assessment Guide

▸ Portfolio Assessment

Teacher-selected Items for Student Portfolios:

- Homework, Lesson 2
- Class Activity work, Lessons 1, 2

Student-selected Items for Student Portfolios:

- Favorite Home or School Activity
- Best Writing Prompt

2 Extending the Assessment

Common Errors

Activities for Remediation

Unit Objective 14.1

Relate the size of a measurement unit to the number of units.

Common Error: Doesn't Recognize That the Larger the Unit, the Lower the Number in the Measurement Will Be

Some children may not understand why a larger unit results in a measure with a lesser number or a smaller unit results in a measure with a greater number.

Remediation Provide children with plenty of experience measuring the same length with different size units and observing the patterns in the results. Have them measure at least five different lengths greater than 1 yd in inches, feet, and yards and record their results in a table. Ask children to observe the pattern in the table to establish that smaller units result in measures with greater numbers and larger units result in measures with lesser numbers.

Unit Objective 14.2

Use a ruler to measure a line segment to the nearest inch.

Common Error: Uses a Ruler Incorrectly

In measuring with a ruler, some children may align the object with the incorrect location on their rulers.

Remediation Children must be familiar with the ruler they will be using in the classroom. The exact location of 0 may vary from one ruler to another. Make sure children know where the 0 indicator of their ruler is. If necessary have them write a 0 on the ruler itself.

Common Error: Rounds Measures to the Nearest Inch, Foot, or Yard Incorrectly

Some children may not round measures correctly.

Remediation Demonstrate rounding to the nearest inch. Draw a line segment between 4 and 5 inches long, but closer to 5 inches. Tell children that the measure to the nearest inch is 5 inches. Draw a line segment between 4 and 5 inches long, but closer to 4 inches. Tell children the measure to the nearest inch is 4 inches. Repeat with a demonstration of rounding to the nearest foot and the nearest yard.

Unit Objective 14.3

Tell the number of inches in a foot, feet in a yard, inches in a yard.

Common Error: Confuses Inches, Feet, and Yards

Some children may not distinguish between inches, feet, and yards.

Remediation If children have difficulty distinguishing between inches, feet, and yards, provide concrete examples of each. Have children work together to label objects in the classroom such as tables, windows, books, pencils, and so on with their measurements for children to use as referents.

Common Error: Doesn't Know the Relationship Between Inches, Feet, and Yards

Children may not know the relationship between inches, feet, and yards.

Remediation Use three 12-inch rulers and a yardstick for a demonstration. Have children use their rulers to identify 1 inch. Then have them count the inches on a 12-inch ruler. State that 12 inches equals 1 foot. Then have two children hold up a yardstick. Have children count the inches on the yardstick. On the board, write:

12 inches = 1 foot
3 feet = 1 yard
36 inches = 1 yard

Unit Objective 14.4

Convert between inches, feet, and yards.

Common Error: Makes Errors in Converting Between Inches, Feet, and Yards

Remediation Have children work with 3 yardsticks lined up to make conversions. To convert yards to feet, for instance, ask them to show you 2 yards on their yardsticks and then count the number of feet in the 2 yards. Repeat for conversions from inches to feet, feet to inches, feet to yards, yards to feet, inches to yards, and yards to inches.

Extension Lessons

Some state standards include content that is not generally included at this grade level. In order to cover these standards, we have provided these extension lessons. Use them only if you need to cover this content.

EXTENSION LESSON 1

Compare Money Amounts

Lesson Objectives

- Compare sets of unlike coins.
- Order sets of unlike coins.
- Compare the value of 2 sets of mixed currency.

Vocabulary

cent sign (¢)
dollar sign ($)

The Day at a Glance

Today's Goals	Materials	
1 Teaching the Lesson **A1:** Compare and order sets of unlike coins. **A2:** Compare sets of mixed currency.	**Lesson Activities** Student Activity Book pp. 479–480 Homework and Remembering pp. 311–312 Real or play money (pennies, nickels, dimes, quarters, 1-dollar bills, 5-dollar bills) Paper bags	**Going Further** Activity Cards E-1 Real or play coins (pennies, nickels, dimes, quarters) Paper bags 5-part spinners Math Journals
2 Going Further ▸ Differentiated Instruction		
3 Homework		

Use Math Talk today!

Keeping Skills Sharp

Quick Practice/Daily Routines	English Language Learners
Because you may be using this lesson at any time during the year, no specific Quick Practice or Daily Routines are recommended. Use any recent Quick Practice activities that meet the needs of your class and the Daily Routines for the unit you have been using.	Review coin names and values with children. Show children a penny, a nickel, a dime, and a quarter. • **Beginning** Point to each coin. Say the coin name and value. For example, point to the penny. Say: **This is a penny. It is worth 1 cent.** Have children repeat. • **Intermediate** Point to each coin. Have children say the name and value of each coin. • **Advanced** Pick up the nickel. Say: **This is a nickel. It is worth 5 cents. It is silver and round. It is larger than a dime and smaller than a quarter.** Have children say the names and values of the other coins and describe them using simple sentences.

1 Teaching the Lesson

Activity 1

Compare and Order Coin Sets

30 MINUTES

Goal: Compare and order sets of unlike coins.

Materials: real or play money (pennies, nickels, dimes, quarters), paper bags, Student Activity Book page 479

NCTM Standards:
Number and Operations
Measurement
Representation

Teaching Note

You may wish to take this opportunity to practice skip counting by 5s, 10s, and 25s to help children with counting coins. Remind them that when counting coins they begin skip counting by a certain number but then may switch.

► Compare Coin Sets PAIRS

Begin by asking children to name coins and their values. Make a list of their responses on the board. Provide pairs with play coins and a paper bag.

- Everyone take a few coins out of the bag without looking.
- Count your coins. Then count your partner's coins.

Remind children to count starting with the coins with the greatest value.

- Compare the values of the sets of coins.
- Which group has the greater value?
- Put the coins back and repeat the activity a few times.

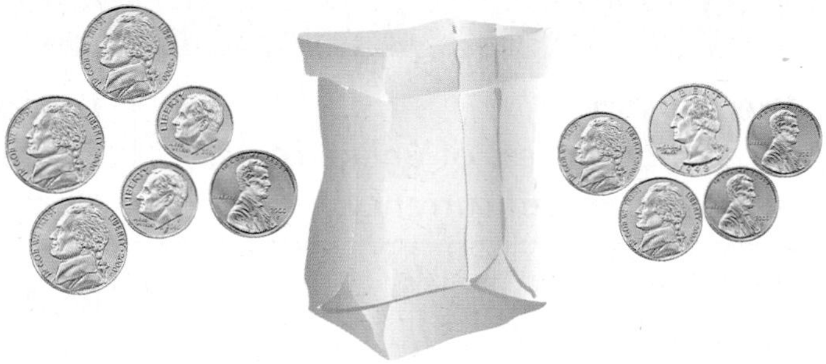

► Order Sets of Money SMALL GROUPS

Provide groups with play coins and a paper bag.

- Everyone take a few coins out of the bag without looking.
- Count your coins.
- Share your coin amounts with others.
- Order the sets from least to greatest.

Math Talk Does the set with the greatest number of coins have the greatest value? Give examples to prove your answer. Why doesn't the greatest number of coins always have the greatest value?

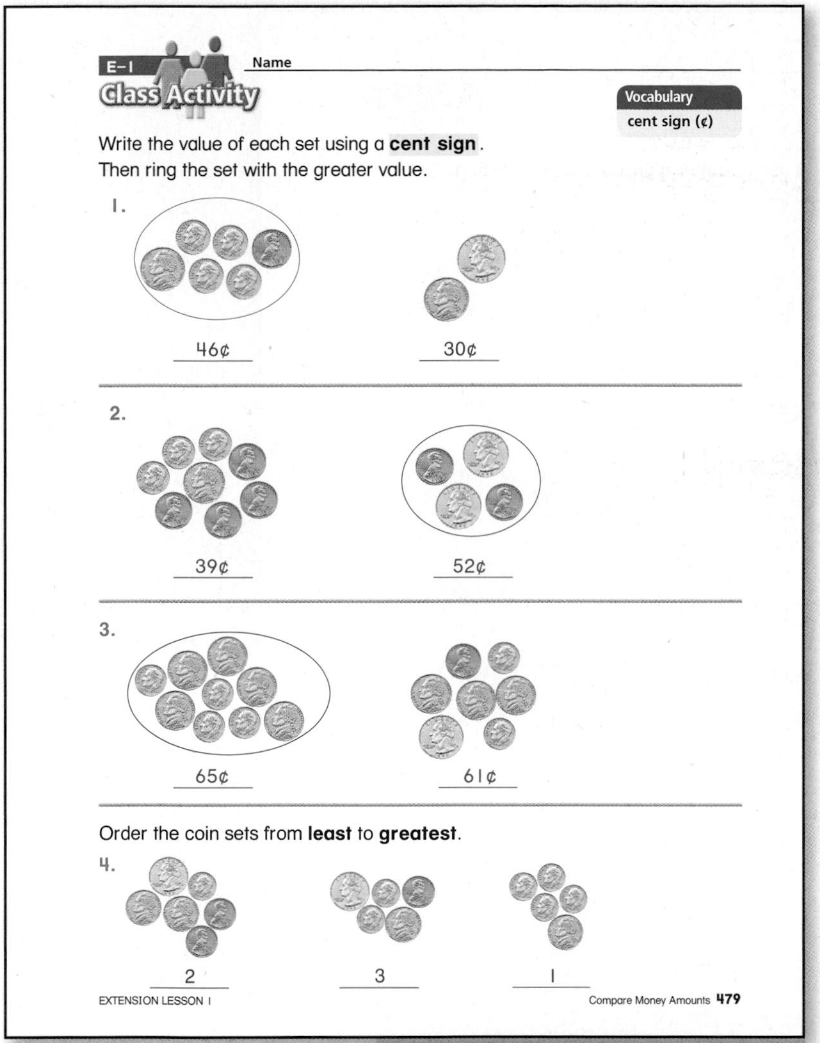
E-1 Class Activity

Name ____________

Vocabulary: cent sign (¢)

Write the value of each set using a **cent sign**.
Then ring the set with the greater value.

1. 46¢ | 30¢

2. 39¢ | 52¢

3. 65¢ | 61¢

Order the coin sets from **least** to **greatest**.

4. 2 | 3 | 1

EXTENSION LESSON 1 — Compare Money Amounts 479

Student Activity Book page 479

▸ Compare and Order Money Amounts WHOLE GROUP

Direct children's attention to Student Activity Book page 479. Tell children to cross out each coin as they count it to help them keep track.

For Exercise 1 tell children to count to find the value of each coin set.

- What coin in the first set has the greatest value? dime
- Count by tens for the dimes? 10, 20, 30, 40
- Which coin should you count next? the nickel
- Count on five. Then count on one more for the penny.
- What is the value of the money in the first set? 46¢
- What is the value of the money in the second set? 30¢
- Ring the set with the greater value. The first set.

Use similar questioning for the rest of the exercises.

Differentiated Instruction

Extra Help Provide play coins and instruct children to model the examples shown on the page. Have them group the coins by type and then put the groups in order by value. Tell children to then skip count by each coin type.

Activity 2

Compare Mixed Currency

20 MINUTES

Goal: Compare sets of mixed currency.

Materials: Student Activity Book page 480, real or play money (pennies, nickels, dimes, quarters, 1-dollar bills, 5-dollar bills)

NCTM Standards:
Number and Operations
Measurement

Ongoing Assessment

Assess children's understanding of comparing coin amounts. Ask questions such as:

- Which group of coins has a greater value: 2 nickels and 2 pennies or 2 dimes? 2 dimes
- Which group of coins has a greater value: 1 quarter and 8 pennies or 3 dimes? 1 quarter and 8 pennies

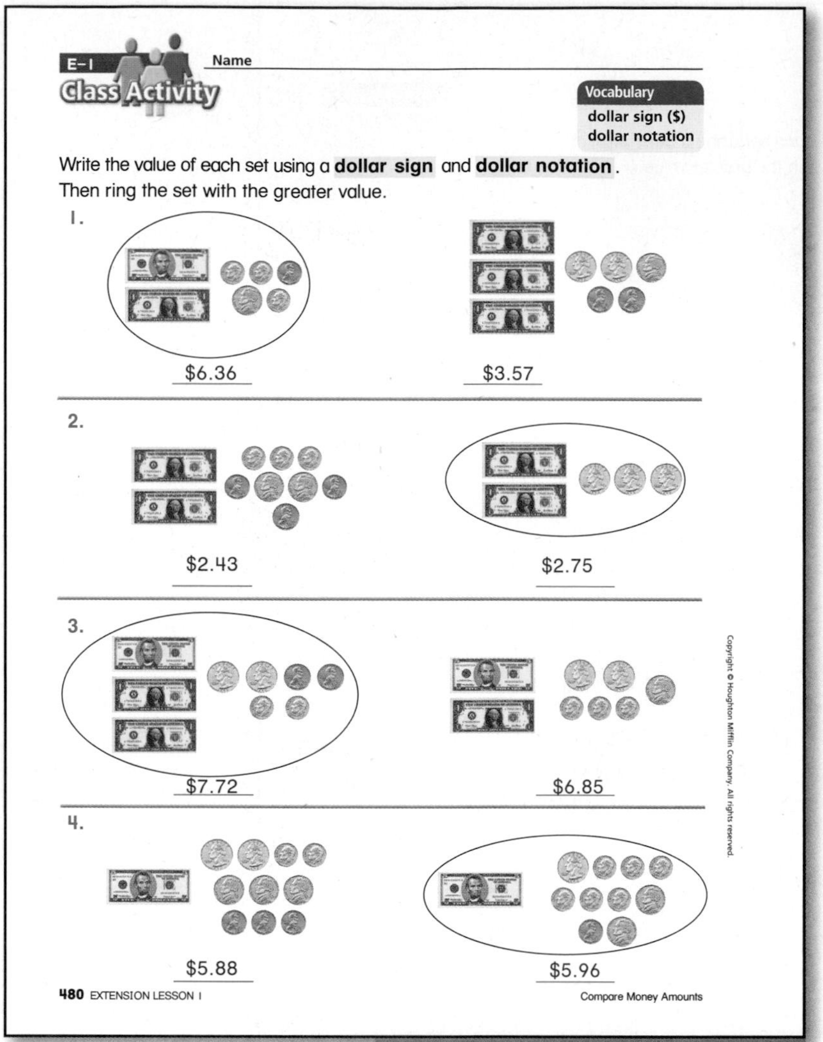

E-1 Class Activity

Name ______

Vocabulary
dollar sign ($)
dollar notation

Write the value of each set using a **dollar sign** and **dollar notation**.
Then ring the set with the greater value.

1. $6.36 $3.57

2. $2.43 $2.75

3. $7.72 $6.85

4. $5.88 $5.96

480 EXTENSION LESSON 1 Compare Money Amounts

Copyright © Houghton Mifflin Company. All rights reserved.

Student Activity Book page 480

▶ Compare Mixed Currency WHOLE CLASS

Show and review a 1-dollar bill and a 5-dollar bill. Write the value of each on the board using a dollar sign and decimal point to represent dollars and cents. Have children turn to Student Activity Book page 480. Explain that they will compare 2 sets of money to determine which has the greater value. Tell children to cross out each coin as they count it to help them keep track. You may wish to provide play money for children to use to model each exercise.

- Start with the bills of the greatest value. Then move on to the coins of the greatest value.

Discuss with children how just looking at the bills can help you determine which set has a greater value.

Intervention — Activity Card E-1

Who Has More Money?

Activity Card E-1 ●

Work: pair

Use:
- pennies, nickels, dimes, quarters
- paper bag
- 5-part spinner

Choose:
- 1
- 2

1. 1 Spin the spinner.
   Take that number of coins out of the bag.
2. 2 Spin the spinner.
   Take that number of coins out of the bag.
3. Each : Count your coins.
4. **Work Together** Compare.
   Who has more money?
5. Repeat five times.

Extension Lesson 1

Activity Note Prepare a 5-section spinner labeled 3, 4, 5, 6, 7 and a bag of coins for each pair. Remind children to start with the coins of the greatest value when counting.

Math Writing Prompt

Explain Mia has 5 coins. Joe has 3 coins. Do you know who has more money? Explain.

Soar to Success Math Software Support

Warm Up 3.15

On Level — Activity Card E-1

Estimate and Order Money

Activity Card E-1 ▲

Work: group

Use:
- pennies, nickels, dimes, quarters
- paper bag

1. Each : Take three coins out of the bag without looking.
   Estimate the value, then count.
2. **Work Together** Order the groups from the **greatest** value to the **least** value.
3. Repeat.

Extension Lesson 1

Activity Note Prepare a bag of coins for each group. Remind children not to count the coins until they have estimated the amount.

Math Writing Prompt

Explain Your Thinking Explain how to estimate the value of a set of coins. Give an example.

MegaMath Software Support

Numberopolis: Lulu's Lunch Counter, Level N

Challenge — Activity Card E-1

Equal Amounts

Activity Card E-1 ■

Work: pair

Use:
- pennies, nickels, dimes, quarters
- paper bag
- 5-part spinner

1. Each : Spin the spinner.
   Take that number of coins out of the bag.
2. Each Count your coins.
3. **Work Together** Compare. Who has less money?
4. The player with less money takes coins so both players have the same amount.
5. **Work Together** Count to check.
6. Repeat.

Extension Lesson 1

Activity Note Prepare a 5-section spinner labeled 3, 4, 5, 6, 7 and a bag of coins for each pair. Encourge children to use the fewest number of coins to make the two amounts equal.

Math Writing Prompt

You Choose Pick an amount. How could you show that amount with the greatest number of coins? with the least number of coins?

Destination Math Software Support

Course II: Module 3: Unit 1: Money

3 Homework

E–1 Homework **Goal:** Additional Practice

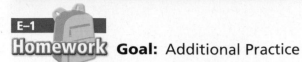

Because you may be using this lesson at any time during the year, no Spiral Review or Targeted Practice is included.

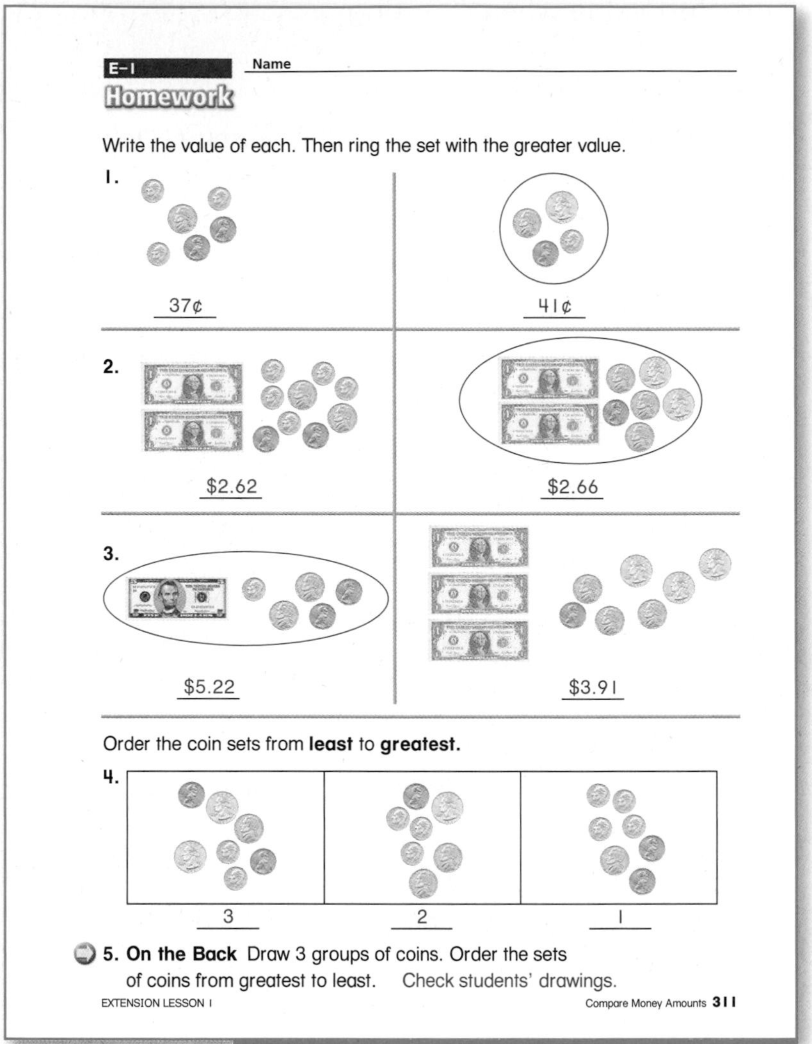

E–1 Homework

Name

Write the value of each. Then ring the set with the greater value.

1. 37¢ | 41¢

2. $2.62 | $2.66

3. $5.22 | $3.91

Order the coin sets from **least** to **greatest.**

4. 3 | 2 | 1

5. **On the Back** Draw 3 groups of coins. Order the sets of coins from greatest to least. Check students' drawings.

EXTENSION LESSON 1 — Compare Money Amounts 311

Homework and Remembering page 311

Home or School Activity

Real-World Connection

Compare Prices Look through a supermarket flyer. Use bills and coins to model two prices. Compare the amounts to see which is greater. Find three items that are less than $1.00. Model the prices and order the amounts from least to greatest.

EXTENSION LESSON 2

Count Different Ways

Lesson Objectives

- Skip count forward and backward.
- Analyze numeric patterns.
- Use a calculator for counting patterns.

Vocabulary
skip count

The Day at a Glance

Today's Goals	Materials	
1 Teaching the Lesson A1: Analyze skip-counting patterns. A2: Skip count using a calculator.	**Lesson Activities** Student Activity Book pp. 481–482 Homework and Remembering pp. 313–314 (includes 120 Poster) 120 Poster and 120 Poster (TRB M60) Crayons Calculators	**Going Further** Activity Cards E-2 120 Poster (TRB M60) Spinners (TRB M27) Calculators Paper strips Sticky notes Math Journals
2 Going Further ▶ Differentiated Instruction		
3 Homework		

Use Math Talk today!

Keeping Skills Sharp

Quick Practice/Daily Routines	English Language Learners
Because you may be using this lesson at any time during the year, no specific Quick Practice or Daily Routines are recommended. Use any recent Quick Practice activities that meet the needs of your class and the Daily Routines for the unit you have been using.	Write *forward* and *backward*. Point and say: **Let's count *forward*.** • **Beginning** Model how to step *forward* and count by 1s. Have children copy and repeat. Continue with *backward*. • **Intermediate** Have children count by 1s as they step. Point behind you. Say: **Let's count that way. Let's count backward.** • **Advanced** Have children count forward then backward by 1s as they step. Then, have them skip count by 5s to 20.

1 Teaching the Lesson

Activity 1

Count Forward and Backward

30 MINUTES

Goal: Analyze skip-counting patterns.

Materials: 120 Poster, copies of 120 Poster (TRB M60), crayons, Student Activity Book page 481

NCTM Standards:
Number and Operations
Algebra
Representation

► Number Sequences WHOLE CLASS

Write the following number sequence on the board: 0, 5, 10, 15, 20. Remind children how to state rules for sequences using *n* to stand for the *number*. Explain that if we need to add 5, we can say: "The rule is *n* plus 5." If the rule is to subtract, we can say: "The rule is *n* minus 5." Write the following sequences on the board and call on volunteers to name the rules.

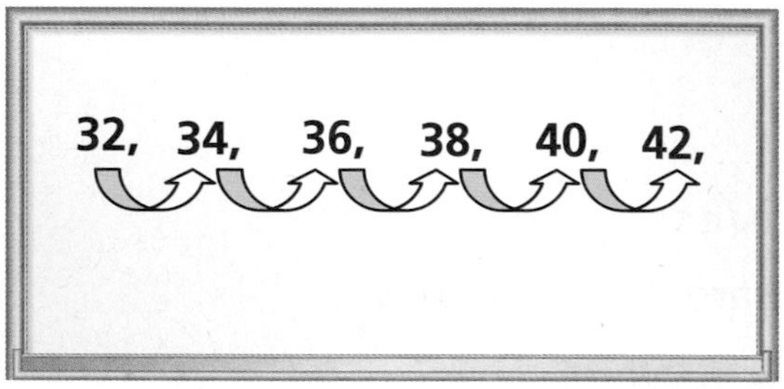

- 32, 34, 36, 38, 40, 42 *n* plus 2
- 98, 97, 96, 95, 94, 93 *n* minus 1
- 50, 60, 70, 80, 90, 100 *n* plus 10

► Skip Count WHOLE GROUP

Tell children to take turns raising one hand at a time going up and down rows as the class skip counts fingers by 5s starting from 0. Remind them that skip counting means counting by a certain number. Skip-counting would be the same as using the rule *n* plus 5 (for counting fingers on a hand). Repeat the activity with children standing and skip-counting by 10s for toes.

Math Talk Discuss times when you have used skip-counting. Have children explain why it is sometimes better to skip count than to count by ones. How would you count the arms on a starfish, the eggs in a carton, or the wheels on some bicycles?

E-2

Class Activity

Name ______________________

Vocabulary
skip count

Use the 120 Poster.

Skip count forward and backward. Check children's charts.

1. Start at 3. Skip count forward by 5s.
   Color each box green.
2. Start at 100. Skip count backward by 5s.
   Color each box blue.
3. Start at 119. Skip count backward by 5s.
   Color each box brown.
4. What pattern do you see for skip-counting by 5s?
   Sample answer: When you skip count by 5s it makes 2 rows.
5. Start at 8. Skip count forward by 10s.
   Color each box yellow.
6. Start at 100. Skip count backward by 10s.
   Circle each box.
7. Start at 92. Skip count backward by 10s.
   Color each box orange.
8. Start at 6. Skip count forward by 10s.
   Color each box red.
9. What pattern do you see for skip-counting by 10s?
   Sample answer: When you skip count by 10s it makes 1 row.

EXTENSION LESSON 2

Count Different Ways **481**

Student Activity Book page 481

▶ Skip Count WHOLE GROUP

Direct children's attention to Student Activity Book page 481. Provide each child with a copy of the 120 Poster (TRB M60). Have the children count forward and backward by 1s.

For Exercise 1 have children color box 3 green.

- To skip count forward by 5s what is the rule? add 5
- Add 5. What is 3 + 5? 8

For Exercise 2 have children color box 100 blue.

- To skip count backward by 5s what is the rule? subtract 5
- Subtract 5. What is 100 – 5? 95

Model the first few exercises on the class 120 Poster. Then have children continue on their own.

Teaching Note

Watch For! Some children may count the given number again when following a rule. For example for 2, 4, 6, 8 the rule is add 2. Children may say 8, 9 as the 2 instead of counting on 2 more: 9, 10. Explain that they must add or subtract from the given number.

1	11	21	31	41	51	61	71	81	91	101	111
2 O	12 O	22 O	32 O	42 O	52 O	62 O	72 O	82 O	92 O	102	112
3 G	13 G	23 G	33 G	43 G	53 G	63 G	73 G	83 G	93 G	103 G	113 G
4 B	14 B	24 B	34 B	44 B	54 B	64 B	74 B	84 B	94 B	104 B	114 B
5 BL	15 BL	25 BL	35 BL	45 BL	55 BL	65 BL	75 BL	85 BL	95 BL	105	115
6 R	16 R	26 R	36 R	46 R	56 R	66 R	76 R	86 R	96 R	106 R	116 R
7	17	27	37	47	57	67	77	87	97	107	117
8 Y G	18 Y G	28 Y G	38 Y G	48 Y G	58 Y G	68 Y G	78 Y G	88 Y G	98 Y G	108 Y G	118 Y G
9 B	19 B	29 B	39 B	49 B	59 B	69 B	79 B	89 B	99 B	109 B	119 B
10 BL	20 BL	30 BL	40 BL	50 BL	60 BL	70 BL	80 BL	90 BL	100 BL	110	120

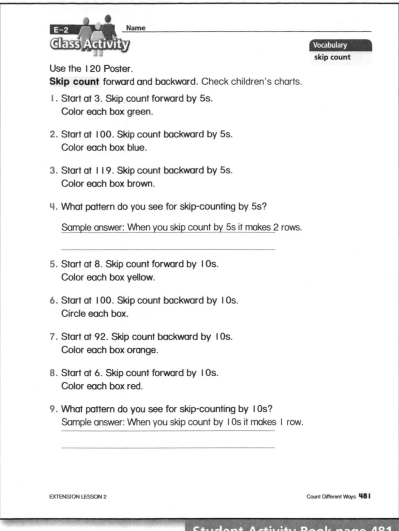

3 Homework

E–2 **Homework** **Goal:** Additional Practice

Because you may be using this lesson at any time during the year, no Spiral Review or Targeted Practice is included. A copy of the 120 Poster is provided on the back of the Homework page.

E–2 Homework Name ____________________

Use the 120 Poster on the back.
Skip count forward and backward.

1. Start at 0. Skip count forward by 5s.
Color each box yellow.

2. Start at 100. Skip count backward by 5s.
Put a blue dot in each box.

3. Start at 0. Skip count forward by 10s.
Circle each box.

4. Start at 100. Skip count backward by 10s.
X each box.

5. Start at 15. Skip count forward by 5s.
15, 20, 25, 30, 35, 40, 45, 50, 55, 60

6. Start at 95. Skip count backward by 5s.
95, 90, 85, 80, 75, 70, 65, 60, 55, 50

7. Start at 8. Skip count forward by 10s.
8, 18, 28, 38, 48, 58, 68, 78, 88, 98

8. Start at 92. Skip count backward by 10s.
92, 82, 72, 62, 52, 42, 32, 22, 12, 2

EXTENSION LESSON 2 Count Different Ways **313**

Homework and Remembering page 313

Home or School Activity

Real-World Connection

Skip Count Find things that come in 5s or 10s. Use skip-counting to count how many in all. You may want to count nickels, fingers on a hand, or starfish arms by 5s. You may count toes on a person, snacks in a box, or stickers on a page for 10s. Encourage children to look for things that are packaged as 5s or 10s.

EXTENSION LESSON 3

Change Over Time

Lesson Objectives

- **Recognize and describe change over time.**
- **Describe qualitative and quantitative change.**

Vocabulary
line graph

The Day at a Glance

Today's Goals	Materials	
1 Teaching the Lesson **A1:** Describe change over time. **A2:** Use a line graph to recognize and describe change over time.	**Lesson Activities** Student Activity Book pp. 483–484 Homework and Remembering pp. 315–316 Calculator (optional)	**Going Further** Activity Cards E-3 Line graphs (teacher-created) Centimeter Grid Paper (TRB M50) Childrens books with data Math Journals
2 Going Further ▸ Differentiated Instruction		
3 Homework		

Use Math Talk today!

Keeping Skills Sharp

Quick Practice/Daily Routines	English Language Learners
Because you may be using this lesson at any time during the year, no specific Quick Practice or Daily Routines are recommended. Use any recent Quick Practice activities that meet the needs of your class and the Daily Routines for the unit you have been using.	Draw a *line graph* showing the growth of a child over 5 years. Mark the child's height at 6 months, 3 years, and 5 years. • **Beginning** Say: **This *line graph* shows how a child grows.** Ask: **Does the child get taller or shorter?** taller • **Intermediate** Ask: **Does this *line graph* show how the child grows?** yes Say: **The child gets __.** taller • **Advanced** Ask: **What change does this *line graph* show?** the child grows taller as the child gets older

Activity 2

Use a Line Graph

20 MINUTES

Goal: Use a line graph to recognize and describe change over time.

Materials: Student Activity Book page 484, calculator (optional)

NCTM Standards:
Data Analysis and Probability
Communication

Ongoing Assessment

Assess children's understanding of change over time. Ask:

- If you recorded your height from birth to now what would you see? the height increases each year
- If you recorded the length of a banana after each bite what would you see? the length would keep decreasing

Alternate Approach

Technology If you have graphing software have children gather data and use it to show changes over time. You may also allow children to use calculators to calculate answers from given data.

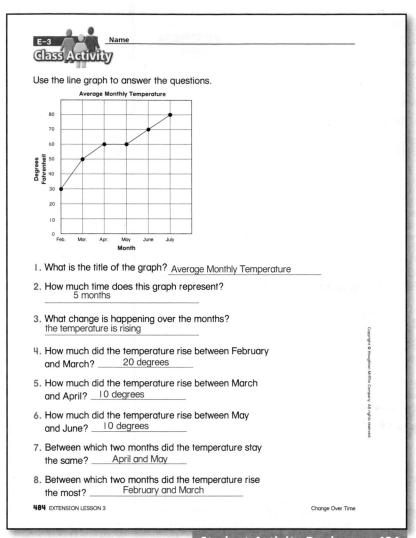

E-3 Class Activity Name ______

Use the line graph to answer the questions.

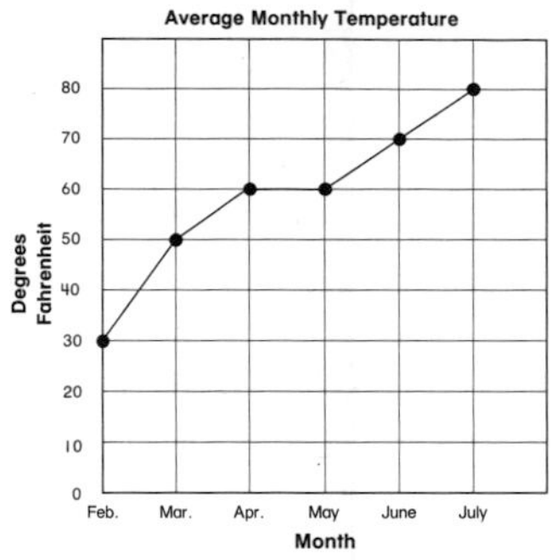

1. What is the title of the graph? Average Monthly Temperature
2. How much time does this graph represent? 5 months
3. What change is happening over the months? the temperature is rising
4. How much did the temperature rise between February and March? 20 degrees
5. How much did the temperature rise between March and April? 10 degrees
6. How much did the temperature rise between May and June? 10 degrees
7. Between which two months did the temperature stay the same? April and May
8. Between which two months did the temperature rise the most? February and March

484 EXTENSION LESSON 3 Change Over Time

Student Activity Book page 484

▶ Monthly Temperature WHOLE CLASS

Have children turn to Student Activity Book page 484. Explain that this is another line graph. Discuss what this graph shows.

- What words are written along the bottom? the months
- What is represented by the numbers on the left side of the graph? degrees Fahrenheit

Work through the first few exercises together and then have children work independently. For Exercise 7 explain that if two points are at the same level it means the temperature stayed the same.

2 Going Further

Differentiated Instruction

Intervention

Activity Card E-3

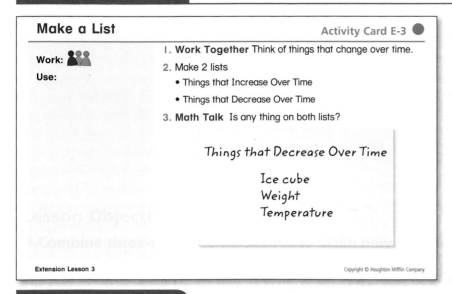

Make a List Activity Card E-3

Work:

Use:

1. **Work Together** Think of things that change over time.
2. Make 2 lists
   - Things that Increase Over Time
   - Things that Decrease Over Time
3. **Math Talk** Is any thing on both lists?

Things that Decrease Over Time

Ice cube
Weight
Temperature

Extension Lesson 3

Activity Note For step 3, suggest that children make a third list for things that could increase or decrease over time such as temperature.

Math Writing Prompt

Draw a Picture Draw a picture of something that changes over time. Use words to describe the change.

Soar to Success Math Software Support

Warm Up 48.01

On Level

Activity Card E-3

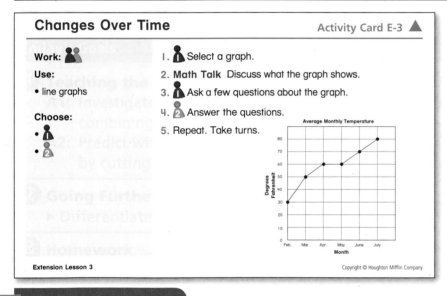

Changes Over Time Activity Card E-3

Work:

Use:
- line graphs

Choose:
- 1
- 2

1. Select a graph.
2. **Math Talk** Discuss what the graph shows.
3. Ask a few questions about the graph.
4. Answer the questions.
5. Repeat. Take turns.

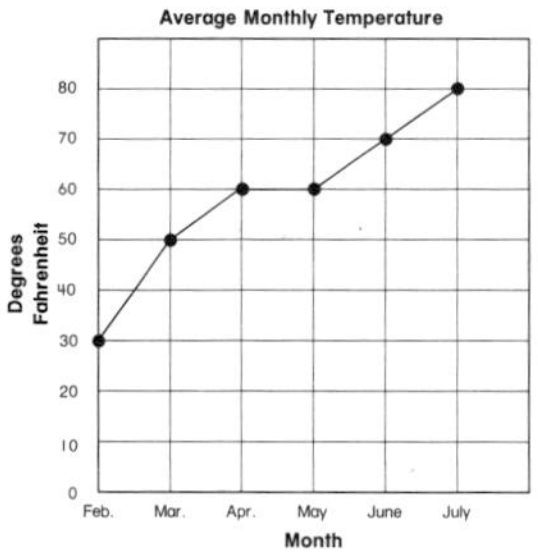

Extension Lesson 3

Activity Note Provide 4 simple line graphs for each pair. The graphs should show change over time and represent both increasing and decreasing data. Have children ask both detailed and general questions about the graphs.

Math Writing Prompt

On Your Own Describe a line graph. Give an example of when you might use a line graph in your own life.

Harcourt Mega Math Software Support

Country Countdown: White Water Graphing, Level J

Challenge

Activity Card E-3

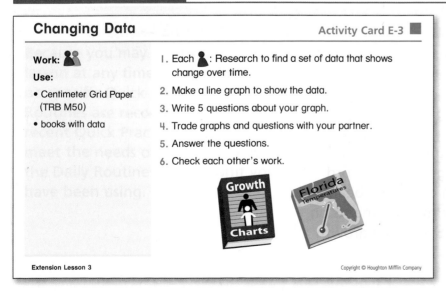

Changing Data Activity Card E-3

Work:

Use:
- Centimeter Grid Paper (TRB M50)
- books with data

1. Each : Research to find a set of data that shows change over time.
2. Make a line graph to show the data.
3. Write 5 questions about your graph.
4. Trade graphs and questions with your partner.
5. Answer the questions.
6. Check each other's work.

Extension Lesson 3

Activity Note Provide Centimeter Grid Paper (TRB M50) for children to use to make line graphs. Gather books that children can use for research.

Math Writing Prompt

Compare Compare a line graph and a bar graph. How are they the same? How are they different?

Destination Math Software Support

Course II: Module 3: Unit 2: Time

1 Teaching the Lesson

Activity 1

Combine Shapes

30 MINUTES

Goal: Investigate and predict the results of combining three-dimensional shapes.

Materials: Student Activity Book page 485, three-dimensional shapes

NCTM Standards:
Geometry
Representation

▶ Three-Dimensional Shapes WHOLE CLASS

Display a set of three-dimensional shapes. Hold up each shape (cube, sphere, rectangular prism, pyramid, and cylinder) one at a time and review the name of each shape. Allow children to hold the shapes. Ask the following about each shape.

- What can you tell me about this shape?
- Do you think this shape can roll?
- Would this be a good shape for stacking?

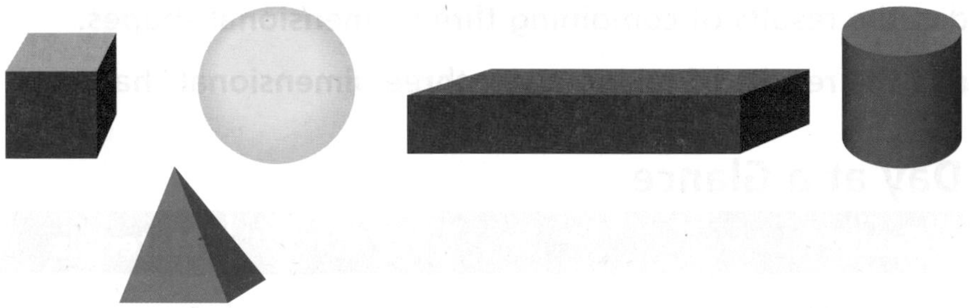

▶ Explore Combining Three-Dimensional Shapes

SMALL GROUPS

Provide three-dimensional shapes for children to work with. You may wish to use block sets or collected containers of various shapes. Allow children to take time to build with the shapes. Encourage them to try to make things, like houses and other buildings, by combining the blocks.

- Were you able to make new shapes by combining other shapes? yes
- What things were you able to make? Sample answers: house, castle, buildings

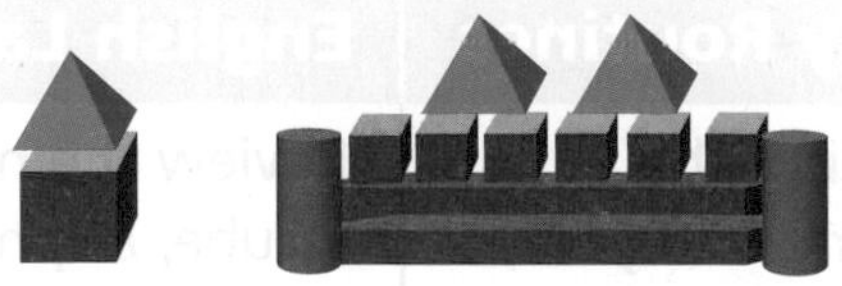

Math Talk Discuss which shapes were better to use as bottom shapes and which ones were better as top shapes. Explain why you think some were better bottom shapes and others were better top shapes.

E-4 Class Activity

Name

Vocabulary
three-dimensional shape

Use the **three-dimensional shapes** to predict and build new shapes. Predictions and drawings may vary.

1. Predict what shape you can make by combining a cube and a pyramid. Then combine the 2 shapes and draw the shape they make.

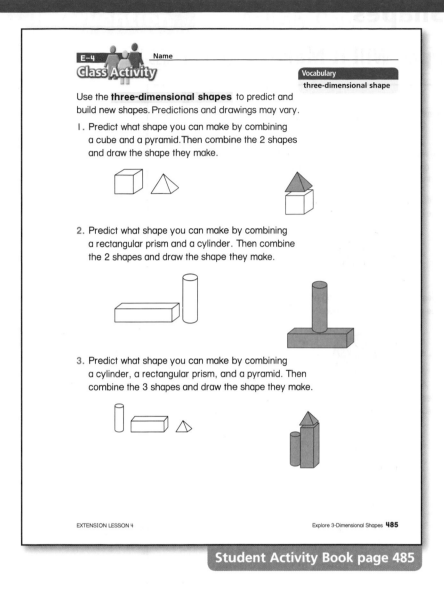

2. Predict what shape you can make by combining a rectangular prism and a cylinder. Then combine the 2 shapes and draw the shape they make.

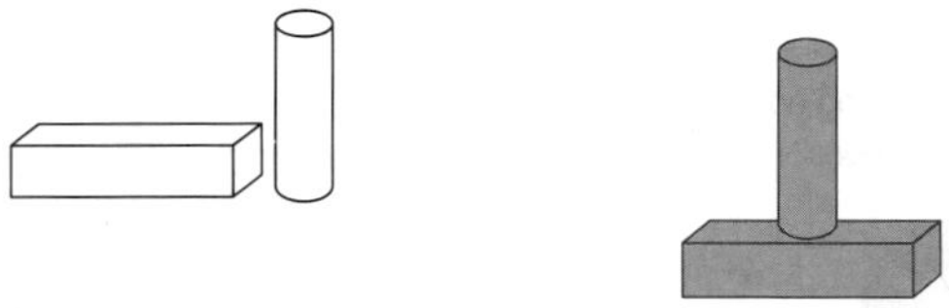

3. Predict what shape you can make by combining a cylinder, a rectangular prism, and a pyramid. Then combine the 3 shapes and draw the shape they make.

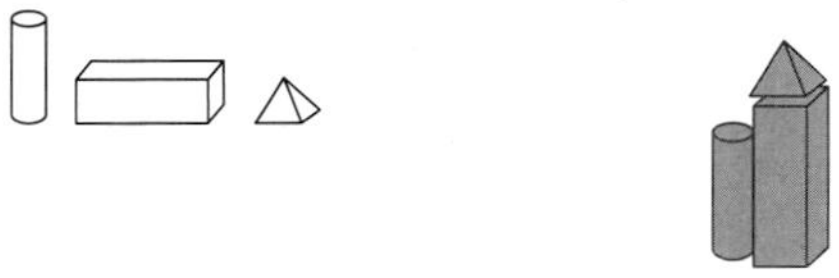

EXTENSION LESSON 4

Explore 3-Dimensional Shapes **485**

Student Activity Book page 485

▶ Predict Shapes PAIRS

Direct children's attention to Student Activity Book page 485. Review the names of each shape: sphere, cylinder, pyramid, cube, and rectangular prism. Discuss Exercise 1 as a class.

- You may want to draw your prediction on one side before you build the shape.
- After you put the shapes together draw the shape you made. Was your prediction close?

After completing the page have children work in pairs. One partner names two shapes. The other partner predicts what shape will be made if the two shapes are combined, and then combines the shapes. Children compare their predictions to the shapes they made.

Teaching Note

Watch For! Look for children trying to use a shape that does not stack as a base. Have children sort shapes by shapes that stack and shapes that do not stack. Discuss how you can stack on the ends of a cylinder but not on the curved part.

Ongoing Assessment

Ask the following questions:

- ▶ What shape will you make by combining 4 cubes? cube or rectangular prism
- ▶ What shape will you make by combining a rectangular prism and a pyramid? Sample answers: building

3 Homework

E-4 Homework **Goal:** Additional Practice

Because you may be using this lesson at any time during the year, no Spiral Review or Targeted Practice is included.

E-4 Homework Name ______________________

Use three-dimensional shapes or think about which ones you would use.

Sample answers shown.

1. Name 2 ways to make a tree.
   List the shapes you used and how many.
   1 cylinder and 1 pyramid
   1 cylinder and 1 sphere

2. Name 2 ways to make a house.
   List the shapes you used and how many.
   1 rectangular prism and 1 pyramid
   1 cube and 1 pyramid

Name the shape(s) you can cut to make the named shapes.

3. 2 rectangular prisms
   rectangular prism, cube

4. 3 cylinders
   cylinder

5. 4 cubes
   cube, rectangular prism

6. **On the Back** Draw 3 different three-dimensional shapes.
   Draw a shape you can make by combining the 3 shapes.
   Check children's work.

EXTENSION LESSON 4 Explore 3-Dimensional Shapes **317**

Homework and Remembering page 317

Home or School Activity

Social Studies Connection

Log Cabins George Washington's army used log cabins at Valley Forge during the American Revolutionary War. Log cabins are made by putting together logs. The cylinder-shaped logs are used to build homes. Today there are still people who build and live in log cabins. Think about other types of buildings that are made from putting together 3-dimesional shapes.

Student Glossary

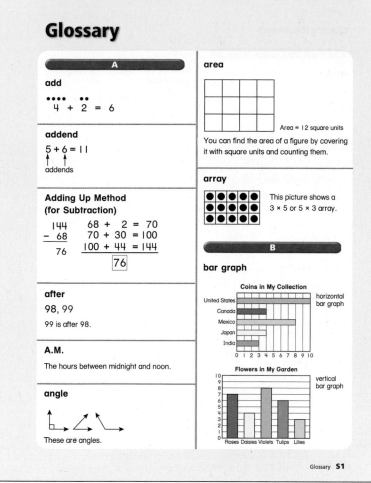

Glossary

A

add

●●●● ●●
4 + 2 = 6

addend

5 + 6 = 11
↑ ↑
addends

Adding Up Method (for Subtraction)

144 − 68 = 76	68 + 2 = 70
	70 + 30 = 100
	100 + 44 = 144
	76

after

98, 99

99 is after 98.

A.M.

The hours between midnight and noon.

angle

These are angles.

area

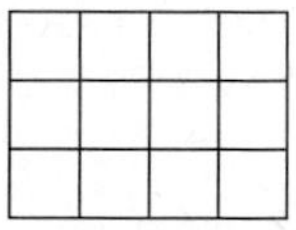

Area = 12 square units

You can find the area of a figure by covering it with square units and counting them.

array

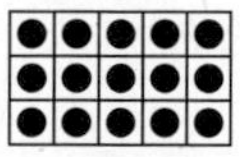

This picture shows a 3 × 5 or 5 × 3 array.

B

bar graph

horizontal bar graph

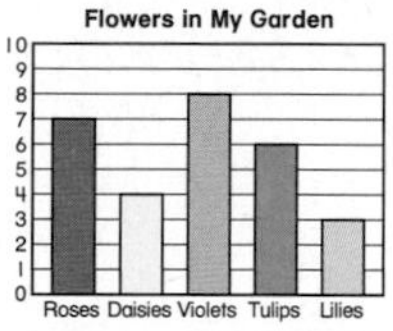

vertical bar graph

Glossary (Continued)

before

31, 32

31 is before 32.

between

81, 82, 83

82 is between 81 and 83.

break-apart

You can break apart a larger number to get two smaller amounts called break-aparts.

10
6 4
break-aparts of 10

C

calendar

capacity

Capacity is how much a container holds. This container holds 1 quart of milk.

cent

front back

1 cent or 1¢ or $0.01

centimeter (cm)

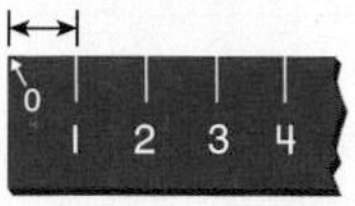

certain

You are certain to choose a black button from the jar.

change minus problem

Sarah had 12 books.
Then she loaned her friend 9 books.
How many books does Sarah have now?

12 − 9 = 3

had loaned now

Any number may be unknown.

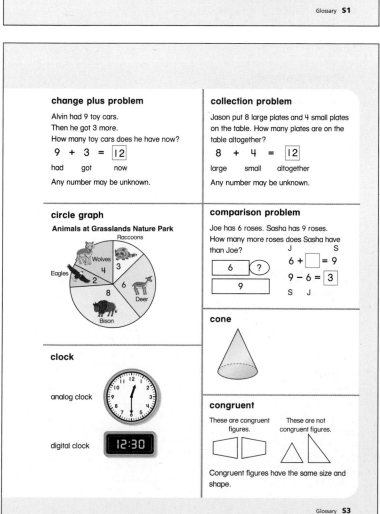

change plus problem

Alvin had 9 toy cars.
Then he got 3 more.
How many toy cars does he have now?

9 + 3 = 12

had got now

Any number may be unknown.

circle graph

Animals at Grasslands Nature Park

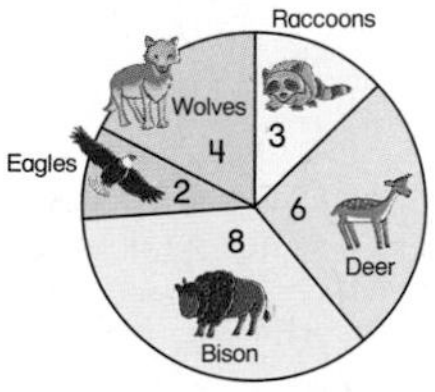

clock

analog clock

digital clock

collection problem

Jason put 8 large plates and 4 small plates on the table. How many plates are on the table altogether?

8 + 4 = 12

large small altogether

Any number may be unknown.

comparison problem

Joe has 6 roses. Sasha has 9 roses. How many more roses does Sasha have than Joe?

J: 6 ?
S: 9

6 + ☐ = 9
9 − 6 = 3

S J

cone

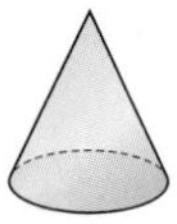

congruent

These are congruent figures. These are not congruent figures.

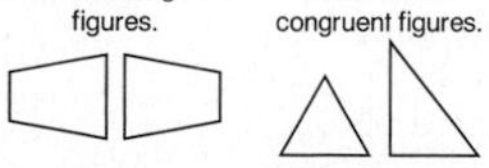

Congruent figures have the same size and shape.

Glossary (Continued)

count all

5 + 3 = ☐
1 2 3 4 5 6 7 8
● ● ● ● ● | ● ● ●
5 + 3 = 8

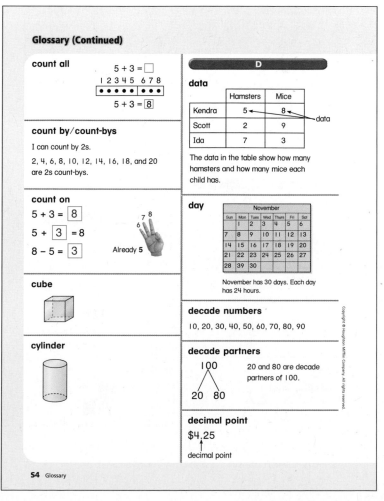

count by/count-bys

I can count by 2s.

2, 4, 6, 8, 10, 12, 14, 16, 18, and 20 are 2s count-bys.

count on

5 + 3 = 8
5 + 3 = 8
8 − 5 = 3

Already 5

cube

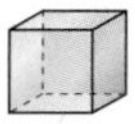

cylinder

D

data

	Hamsters	Mice
Kendra	5	8
Scott	2	9
Ida	7	3

← data

The data in the table show how many hamsters and how many mice each child has.

day

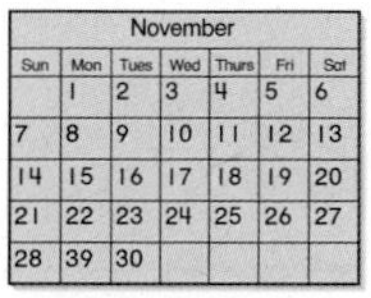

November has 30 days. Each day has 24 hours.

decade numbers

10, 20, 30, 40, 50, 60, 70, 80, 90

decade partners

100
20 80

20 and 80 are decade partners of 100.

decimal point

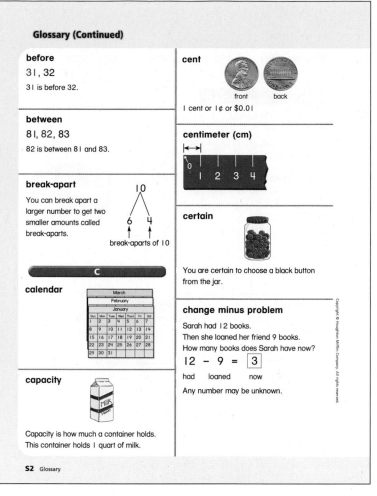

$4.25
↑
decimal point

Student Glossary (Continued)

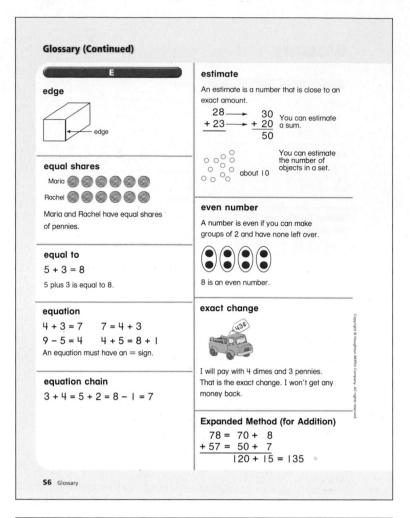

decimeter (dm)

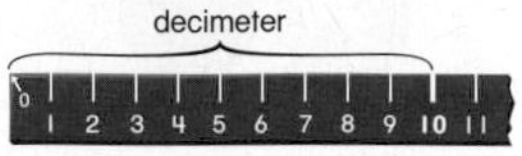

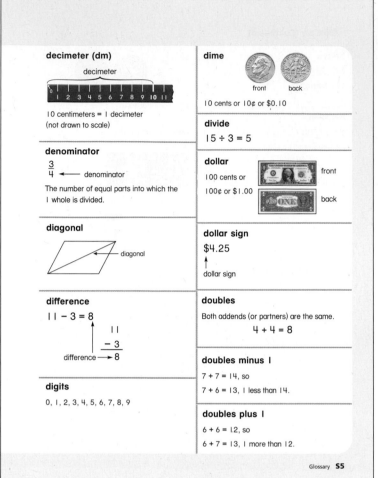

10 centimeters = 1 decimeter
(not drawn to scale)

denominator

$\frac{3}{4}$ ← denominator

The number of equal parts into which the 1 whole is divided.

diagonal

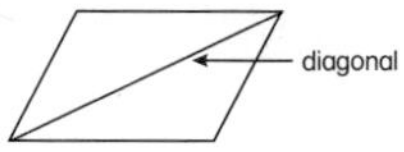

difference

11 − 3 = 8

$$\begin{array}{r} 11 \\ -\ 3 \\ \hline 8 \end{array}$$

difference → 8

digits

0, 1, 2, 3, 4, 5, 6, 7, 8, 9

dime

10 cents or 10¢ or $0.10

divide

15 ÷ 3 = 5

dollar

100 cents or 100¢ or $1.00

dollar sign

$4.25

↑ dollar sign

doubles

Both addends (or partners) are the same.

4 + 4 = 8

doubles minus 1

7 + 7 = 14, so
7 + 6 = 13, 1 less than 14.

doubles plus 1

6 + 6 = 12, so
6 + 7 = 13, 1 more than 12.

E

edge

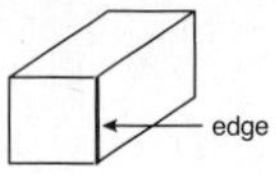

equal shares

Maria and Rachel have equal shares of pennies.

equal to

5 + 3 = 8

5 plus 3 is equal to 8.

equation

4 + 3 = 7 7 = 4 + 3
9 − 5 = 4 4 + 5 = 8 + 1

An equation must have an = sign.

equation chain

3 + 4 = 5 + 2 = 8 − 1 = 7

estimate

An estimate is a number that is close to an exact amount.

28 → 30
+ 23 → + 20
50

You can estimate a sum.

You can estimate the number of objects in a set.

even number

A number is even if you can make groups of 2 and have none left over.

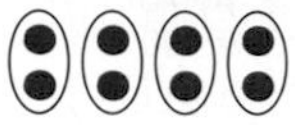

8 is an even number.

exact change

I will pay with 4 dimes and 3 pennies. That is the exact change. I won't get any money back.

Expanded Method (for Addition)

78 = 70 + 8
+ 57 = 50 + 7
120 + 15 = 135

Expanded Method (for Subtraction)

50 + 14
64 = ~~60~~ + ~~4~~
− 28 = 20 + 8
30 + 6 = 36

expanded number

283 = 200 + 80 + 3

F

face

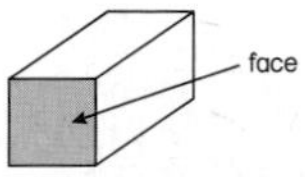

fair shares

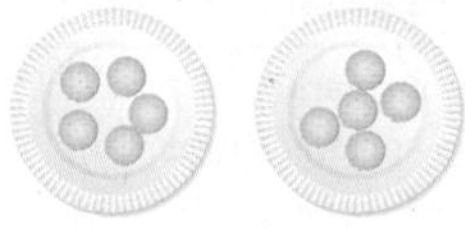

fewer

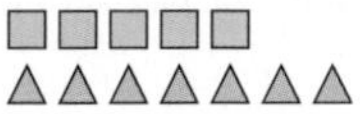

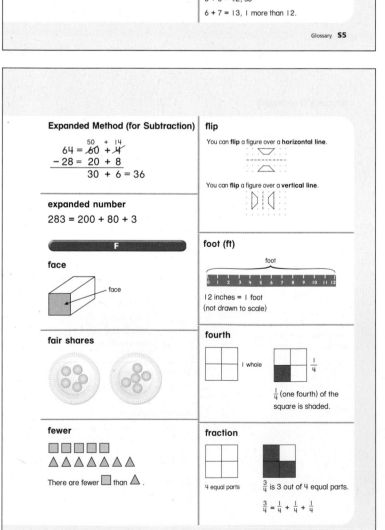

There are fewer □ than △.

flip

You can **flip** a figure over a **horizontal line**.

You can **flip** a figure over a **vertical line**.

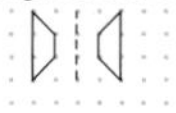

foot (ft)

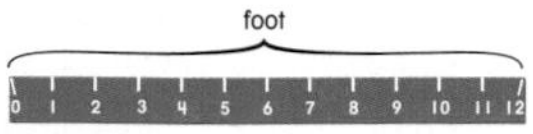

12 inches = 1 foot
(not drawn to scale)

fourth

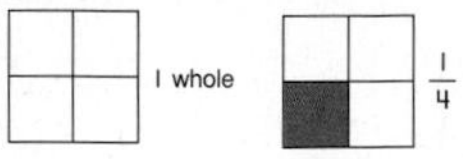

$\frac{1}{4}$ (one fourth) of the square is shaded.

fraction

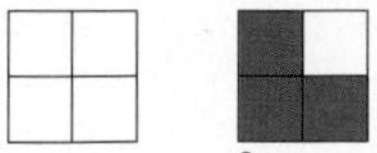

4 equal parts

$\frac{3}{4}$ is 3 out of 4 equal parts.

$\frac{3}{4} = \frac{1}{4} + \frac{1}{4} + \frac{1}{4}$

front-end estimation

(3)4 → 30
+ (1)5 → + 10
40

function table

Add 3.	
0	3
1	4
2	5
3	6

G

greater than

34 > 25

34 is greater than 25.

greatest

25 41 63

63 is the greatest number.

group name

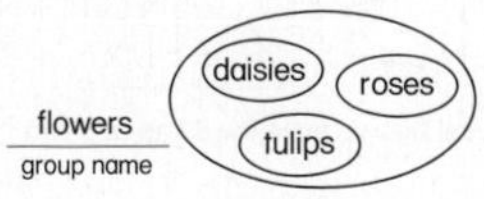

growing pattern

A number or geometric pattern that increases.

Examples: 2, 4, 6, 8, 10...
1, 2, 5, 10, 17...

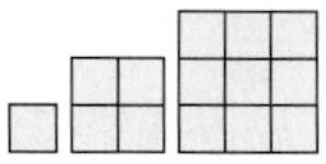

H

half

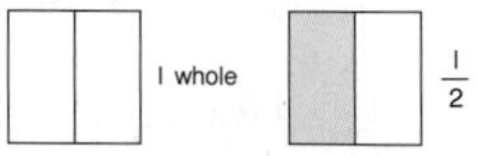

$\frac{1}{2}$ (one half) of the square is shaded.

half-hour

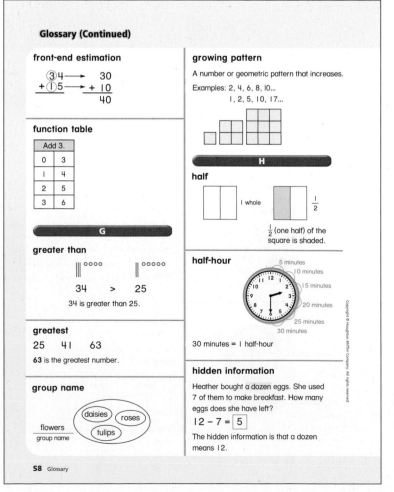

30 minutes = 1 half-hour

hidden information

Heather bought a dozen eggs. She used 7 of them to make breakfast. How many eggs does she have left?

12 − 7 = 5

The hidden information is that a dozen means 12.

horizontal

4 + 5 = 9 ←――――→

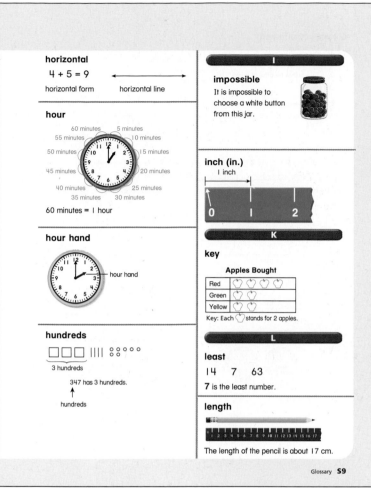

horizontal form   horizontal line

hour

60 minutes = 1 hour

hour hand

hundreds

347 has 3 hundreds.

↑

hundreds

I

impossible

It is impossible to choose a white button from this jar.

inch (in.)

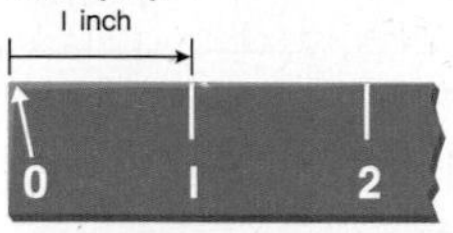

K

key

Apples Bought

Red	🍎 🍎 🍎 🍎
Green	🍎 🍎
Yellow	🍎 🍎

Key: Each 🍎 stands for 2 apples.

L

least

14 7 63

7 is the least number.

length

The length of the pencil is about 17 cm.

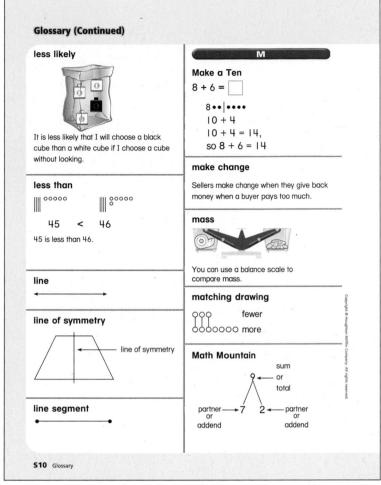

Glossary (Continued)

less likely

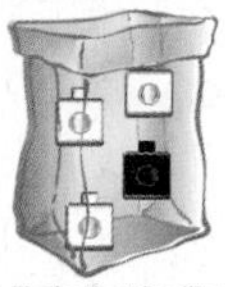

It is less likely that I will choose a black cube than a white cube if I choose a cube without looking.

less than

45 < 46

45 is less than 46.

line

←――――→

line of symmetry

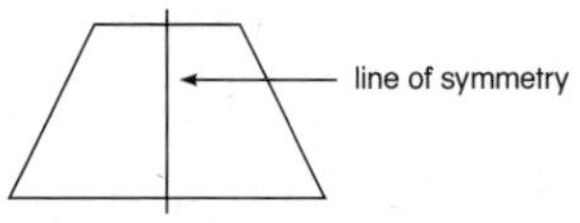

line segment

•――――•

M

Make a Ten

8 + 6 = ☐

8••|••••

10 + 4

10 + 4 = 14,

so 8 + 6 = 14

make change

Sellers make change when they give back money when a buyer pays too much.

mass

You can use a balance scale to compare mass.

matching drawing

Math Mountain

sum or total → 9

partner or addend → 7   2 ← partner or addend

measure

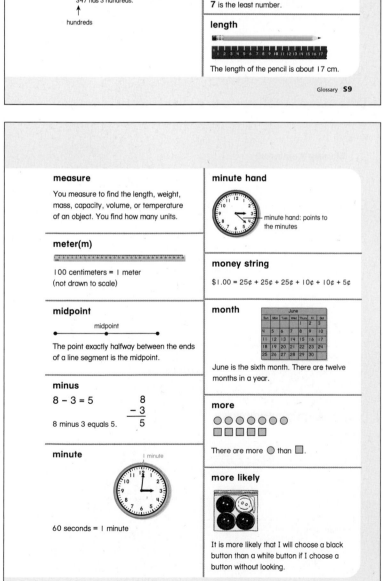

You measure to find the length, weight, mass, capacity, volume, or temperature of an object. You find how many units.

meter(m)

100 centimeters = 1 meter
(not drawn to scale)

midpoint

midpoint

•――――•――――•

The point exactly halfway between the ends of a line segment is the midpoint.

minus

8 − 3 = 5

$$\begin{array}{r} 8 \\ -\ 3 \\ \hline 5 \end{array}$$

8 minus 3 equals 5.

minute

60 seconds = 1 minute

minute hand

money string

$1.00 = 25¢ + 25¢ + 25¢ + 10¢ + 10¢ + 5¢

month

June

Sun	Mon	Tues	Wed	Thurs	Fri	Sat
				1	2	3
4	5	6	7	8	9	10
11	12	13	14	15	16	17
18	19	20	21	22	23	24
25	26	27	28	29	30	

June is the sixth month. There are twelve months in a year.

more

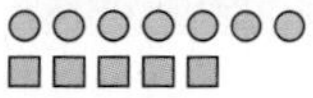

There are more ◯ than ☐.

more likely

It is more likely that I will choose a black button than a white button if I choose a button without looking.

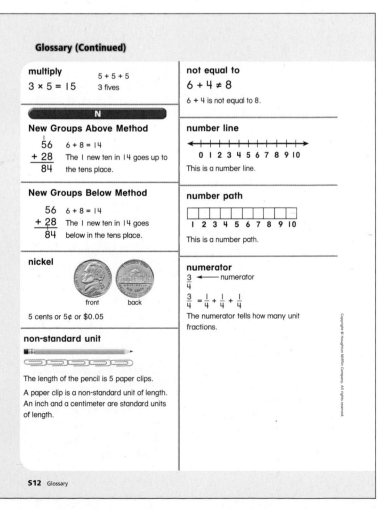

Glossary (Continued)

multiply

3 × 5 = 15   5 + 5 + 5
3 fives

N

New Groups Above Method

$$\begin{array}{r} {}^{1}\ \\ 56 \\ +\ 28 \\ \hline 84 \end{array}$$

6 + 8 = 14

The 1 new ten in 14 goes up to the tens place.

New Groups Below Method

$$\begin{array}{r} 56 \\ +\ {}_{1}28 \\ \hline 84 \end{array}$$

6 + 8 = 14

The 1 new ten in 14 goes below in the tens place.

nickel

5 cents or 5¢ or $0.05

non-standard unit

The length of the pencil is 5 paper clips.

A paper clip is a non-standard unit of length. An inch and a centimeter are standard units of length.

not equal to

6 + 4 ≠ 8

6 + 4 is not equal to 8.

number line

0 1 2 3 4 5 6 7 8 9 10

This is a number line.

number path

1 2 3 4 5 6 7 8 9 10

This is a number path.

numerator

$\frac{3}{4}$ ← numerator

$\frac{3}{4} = \frac{1}{4} + \frac{1}{4} + \frac{1}{4}$

The numerator tells how many unit fractions.

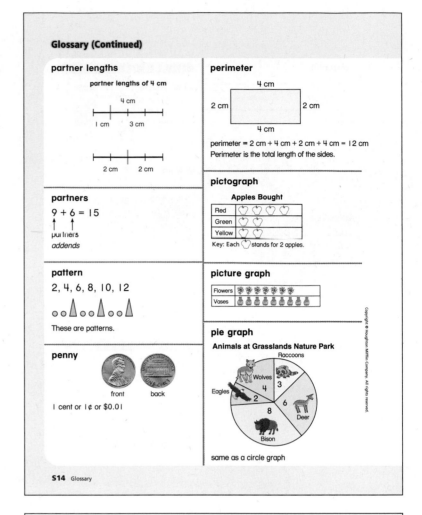

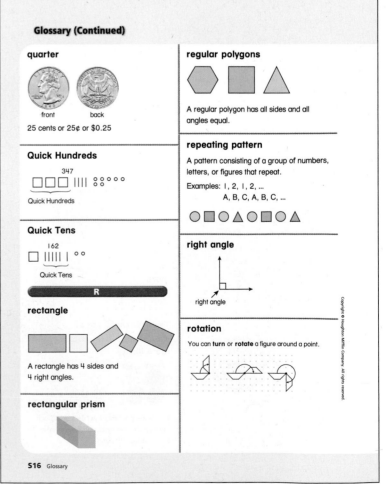

Student Glossary (Continued)

O

odd number

A number is odd if you can make groups of 2 and have one left over.

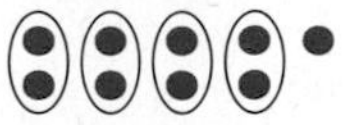

9 is an odd number.

ones

347 has 7 ones.
ones

opposite sides

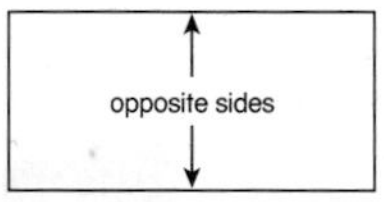

order

2, 5, 6

The numbers 2, 5, and 6 are in order from least to greatest.

ordinal number

Ordinal numbers name positions.

1st	2nd	3rd	4th
first	second	third	fourth

P

parallel

Lines or line segments that are always the same distance apart.

parallelogram

A parallelogram has 2 pairs of parallel sides.

Partner House

6	
1 + 5	5 + 1
2 + 4	4 + 2
3 + 3	

partner lengths

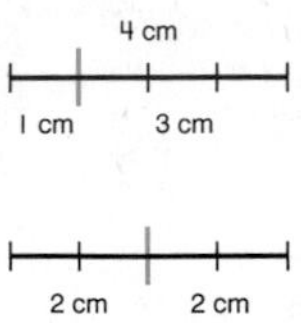

partners

9 + 6 = 15

partners
addends

pattern

2, 4, 6, 8, 10, 12

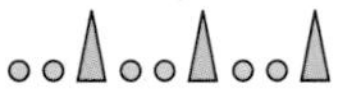

These are patterns.

penny

1 cent or 1¢ or $0.01

perimeter

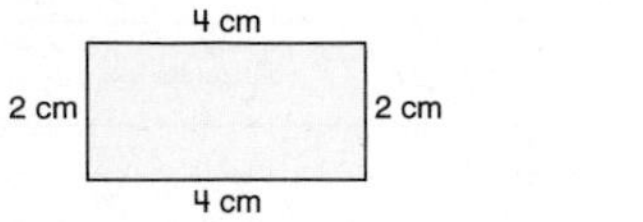

perimeter = 2 cm + 4 cm + 2 cm + 4 cm = 12 cm
Perimeter is the total length of the sides.

pictograph

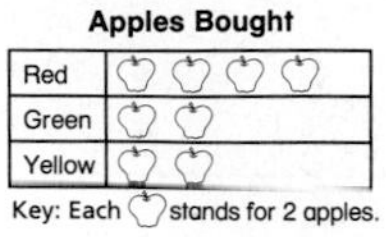

picture graph

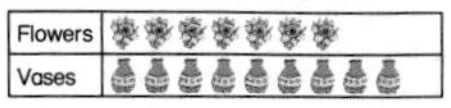

pie graph

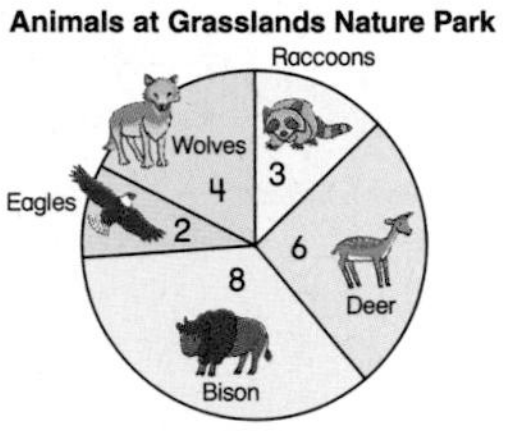

same as a circle graph

plus

3 + 2 = 5

3 plus 2 equals 5.

$$\begin{array}{r} 3 \\ +\ 2 \\ \hline 5 \end{array}$$

P.M.

The hours between noon and midnight.

polygons

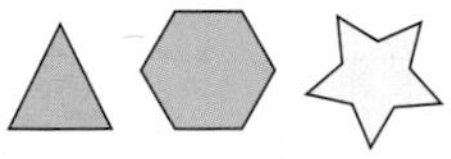

Polygons have sides that are line segments.

possible

It is possible to choose a white button.
It is possible to choose a black button.

predict

I think it will rain tomorrow.

I predict that it will rain tomorrow.

probability

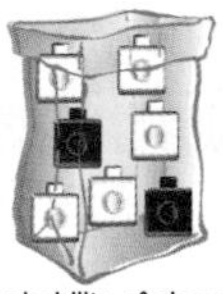

- What is the probability of choosing a white cube?
- It is likely.

proof drawing

Proof Drawing

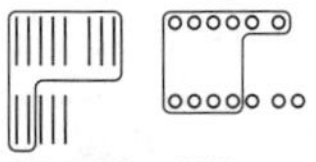

86 + 57 = 143

pyramids

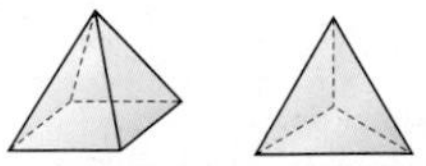

Q

quadrilateral

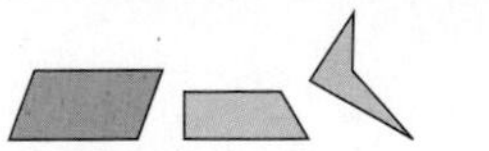

A quadrilateral has 4 sides.

quarter

25 cents or 25¢ or $0.25

Quick Hundreds

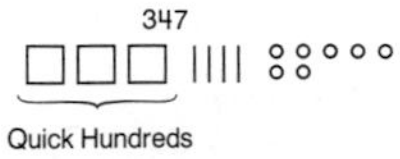

Quick Tens

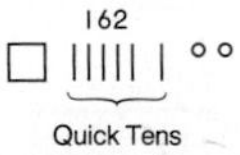

R

rectangle

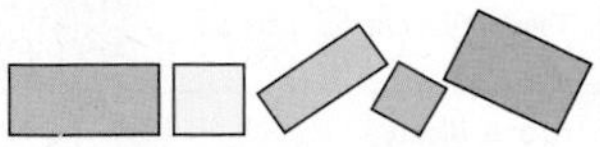

A rectangle has 4 sides and 4 right angles.

rectangular prism

regular polygons

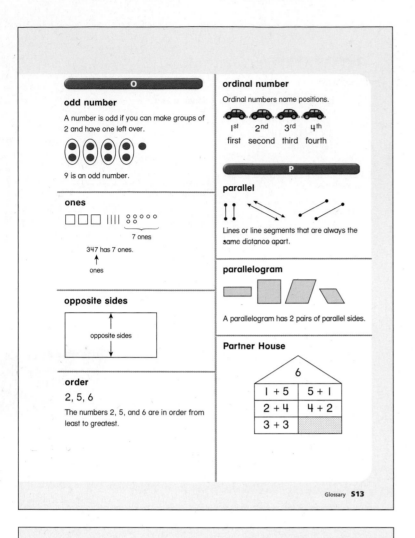

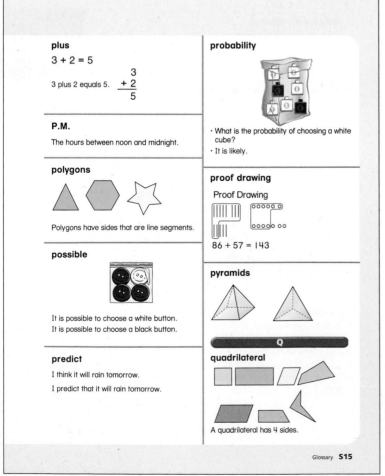

A regular polygon has all sides and all angles equal.

repeating pattern

A pattern consisting of a group of numbers, letters, or figures that repeat.

Examples: 1, 2, 1, 2, ...
A, B, C, A, B, C, ...

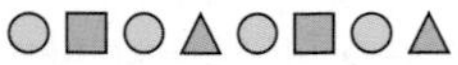

right angle

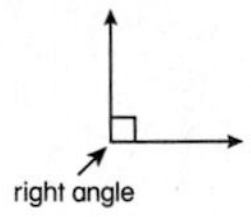

rotation

You can **turn** or **rotate** a figure around a point.

round

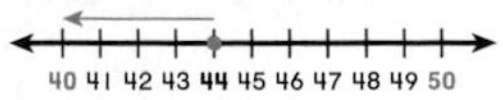

44 is closer to 40 than 50.
44 rounds to 40.

Show All Totals Method

$$\begin{array}{r} 25 \\ +\ 48 \\ \hline 60 \\ \underline{13} \\ 73 \end{array} \qquad \begin{array}{r} 724 \\ +\ 158 \\ \hline 12 \\ 70 \\ \underline{800} \\ 882 \end{array}$$

ruler

A ruler is used to measure length.

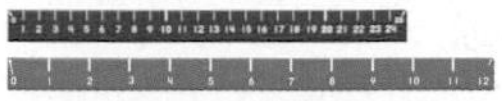

S

scale

The numbers along the side or the bottom of a graph.

sequence

Sequences follow a pattern.

2, 4, 6, . . .

9, 8, 7, . . .

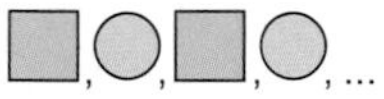

similar

Similar figures always have the same shape and sometimes have the same size.

situation equation

A baker baked 100 loaves of bread. He sold some loaves. There are 73 loaves left. How many loaves of bread did he sell?

100 − ☐ = 73

situation equation

skip count

skip count by 2s: 2, 4, 6, 8, . . .
skip count by 5s: 5, 10, 15, 20, . . .

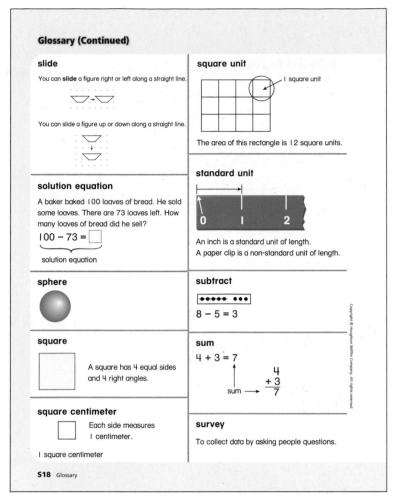

slide

You can **slide** a figure right or left along a straight line.

You can slide a figure up or down along a straight line.

solution equation

A baker baked 100 loaves of bread. He sold some loaves. There are 73 loaves left. How many loaves of bread did he sell?

100 − 73 = ☐

solution equation

sphere

square

A square has 4 equal sides and 4 right angles.

square centimeter

Each side measures 1 centimeter.

1 square centimeter

square unit

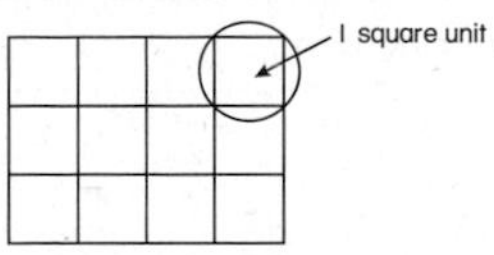

The area of this rectangle is 12 square units.

standard unit

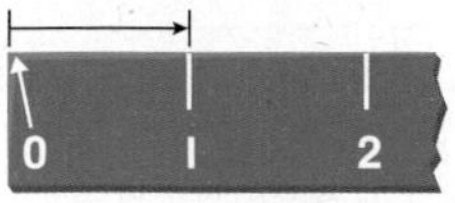

An inch is a standard unit of length.
A paper clip is a non-standard unit of length.

subtract

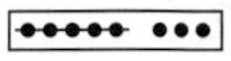

8 − 5 = 3

sum

4 + 3 = 7

sum ⟶

$$\begin{array}{r} 4 \\ +\ 3 \\ \hline 7 \end{array}$$

survey

To collect data by asking people questions.

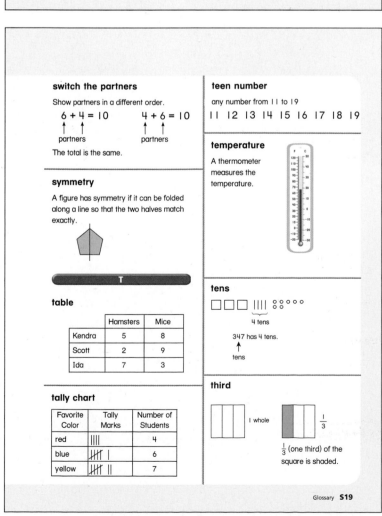

switch the partners

Show partners in a different order.

6 + 4 = 10   4 + 6 = 10

partners   partners

The total is the same.

symmetry

A figure has symmetry if it can be folded along a line so that the two halves match exactly.

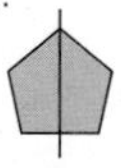

T

table

	Hamsters	Mice
Kendra	5	8
Scott	2	9
Ida	7	3

tally chart

Favorite Color	Tally Marks	Number of Students
red	||||	4
blue	卌 |	6
yellow	卌 ||	7

teen number

any number from 11 to 19

11 12 13 14 15 16 17 18 19

temperature

A thermometer measures the temperature.

tens

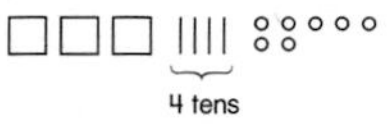

347 has 4 tens.

tens

third

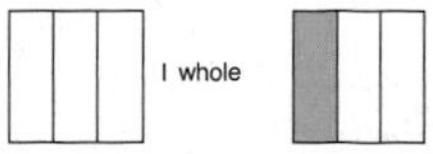

$\frac{1}{3}$ (one third) of the square is shaded.

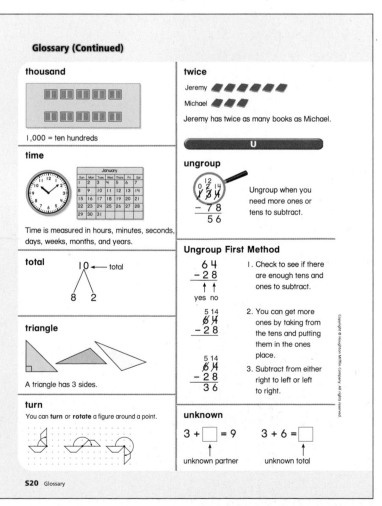

thousand

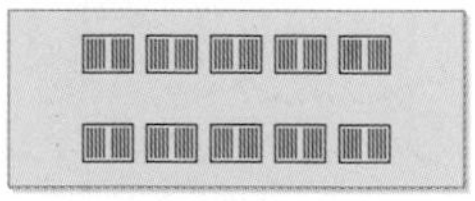

1,000 = ten hundreds

time

Time is measured in hours, minutes, seconds, days, weeks, months, and years.

total

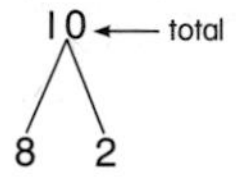

triangle

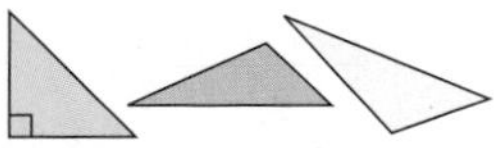

A triangle has 3 sides.

turn

You can **turn** or **rotate** a figure around a point.

twice

Jeremy has twice as many books as Michael.

U

ungroup

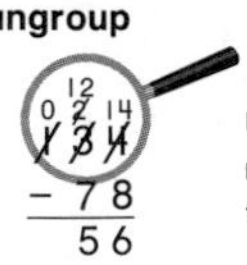

Ungroup when you need more ones or tens to subtract.

Ungroup First Method

$$\begin{array}{r} 64 \\ -\ 28 \\ \hline \end{array}$$

yes no

1. Check to see if there are enough tens and ones to subtract.

$$\begin{array}{r} {}^{5\ 14} \\ \not{6}\not{4} \\ -\ 28 \\ \hline \end{array}$$

2. You can get more ones by taking from the tens and putting them in the ones place.

$$\begin{array}{r} {}^{5\ 14} \\ \not{6}\not{4} \\ -\ 28 \\ \hline 36 \end{array}$$

3. Subtract from either right to left or left to right.

unknown

3 + ☐ = 9   3 + 6 = ☐

unknown partner   unknown total

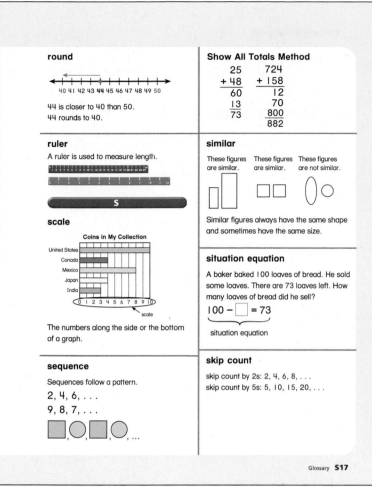

V

Venn diagram

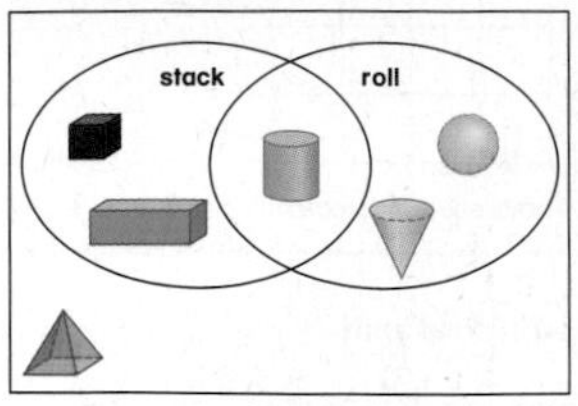

vertex

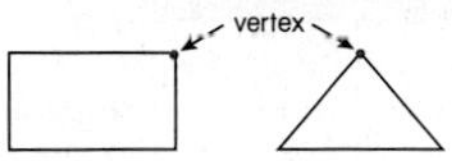

vertical

$$\begin{array}{r} 4 \\ +\,3 \\ \hline 7 \end{array}$$

vertical form   vertical line

view

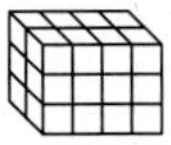

This is the side view of the rectangular prism above.

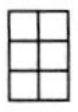

volume

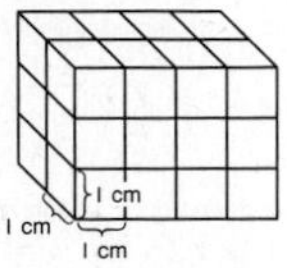

The volume of this rectangular prism is 24 cubic centimeters.

W

weight

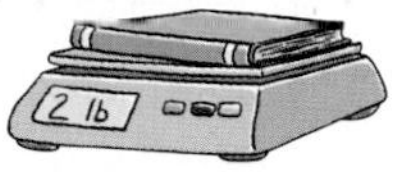

The weight of this book is 2 pounds.

width

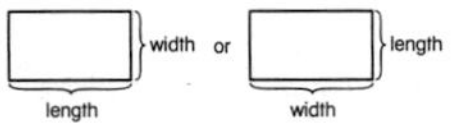

word name

12

twelve ← word name

Y

yard (yd)

3 feet = 1 yard (not drawn to scale)

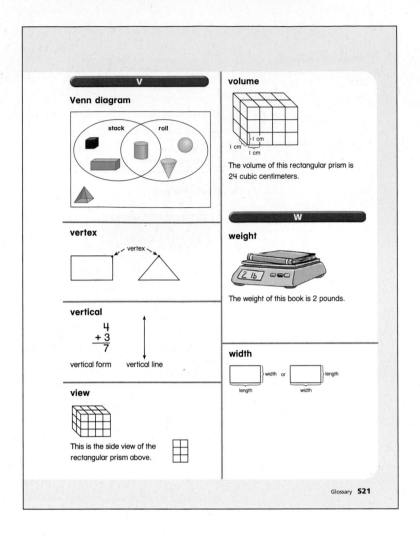

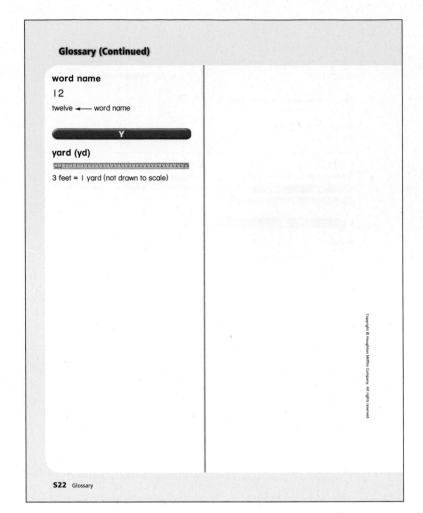

Teacher Glossary

A

actual amount The exact amount. Often found by counting or calculating after an estimate has been made.

acute angle An angle that measures less than 90°.

acute triangle A triangle in which each of the three angles is acute.

addend A number to be added in an addition equation. In the equation $7 + 4 + 8 = \square$, the numbers 7, 4 and 8 are addends.

Adding Up Method A method of finding an unknown partner or unknown addend in which children add up from the known partner until they reach the total.

$34 + \square = 73$

$73 - 34 = \square$

Start at 34 and add up to 73.

$34 + 6 = 40$
$40 + 30 = 70$
$70 + 3 = 73$
$\quad\quad\;\; 39$

after the hour The most common way of reading time where minutes are counted forward from the hour as in "38 minutes after 3 o'clock."

A.M. The abbreviation for *ante meridiem,* Latin for "before noon". Used to indicate a time between midnight and noon.

analog clock A clock displaying time by using hour and minute hands and the numbers 1 through 12.

angle A figure formed by two rays with a common endpoint.

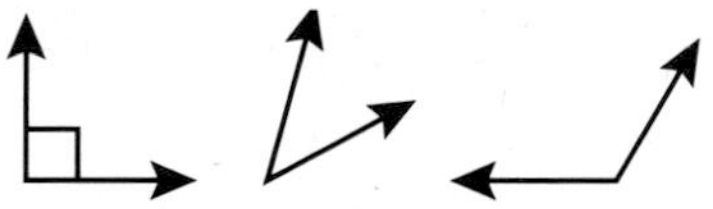

area The measure in square units of the surface of a plane figure.

array An arrangement of objects, pictures or numbers in columns and rows.

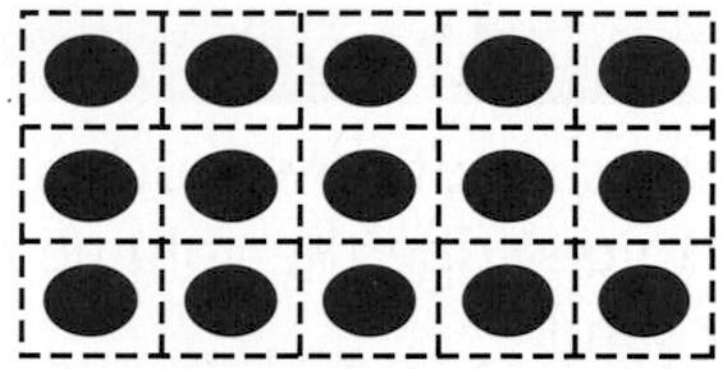

3 × 5 or 5 × 3 array

B

backward sequence A sequence of numbers that uses a subtraction rule to determine the next number.

20, 18, 16, 14, 12, 10 . . . Rule: $n - 2$

bar graph A graph that shows information using rectangular bars, either horizontally or vertically. The bars may be horizontal or vertical.

base ten blocks Blocks measured in metric units that can be used in measuring or place value. The ones block is a one centimeter cube; the tens block is one centimeter wide, 10 centimeters long, and one centimeter thick (made up of 10 ones). The hundreds block is 10 centimeters long, 10 centimeters wide, and 1 centimeter thick (made up of 100 ones).

before the hour A way of reading time where minutes are counted backward from the hour as in "20 minutes before 3 o'clock."

Blue Make-a-Ten Cards Cards used to help children become fluent in the Make a Ten strategy for subtraction.

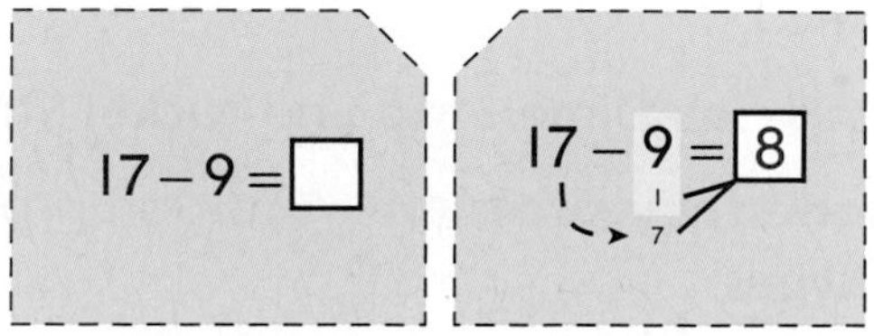

front of card   back of card

break-apart (noun or verb) You can break apart (verb) a larger number to get two smaller amounts called break-aparts (noun) or partners.

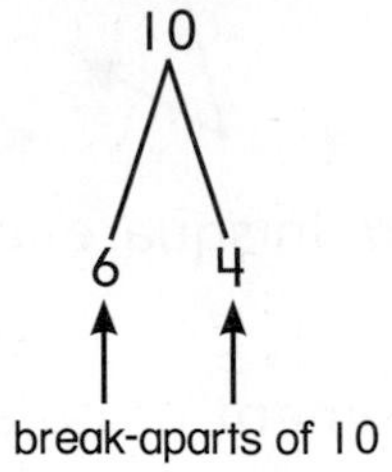

C

capacity A measure of how much a container can hold. Used to describe the volume of fluids such as water or sand.

cent The smallest unit of U.S. currency; the value of a penny; $.01.

centimeter (cm) A metric unit of length equal to 0.01 ($\frac{1}{100}$) meter.

certain Describes a probability outcome that is sure to happen.

change minus story problem A problem that begins with a given quantity which is then modified by a change—something is subtracted—that results in a new quantity.

Sarah had 12 books. She loaned her friend 9 books. How many books does Sarah have now?

Any of the three quantities can be unknown.

change plus story problem A problem that begins with a given quantity which is then modified by a change—something is added—that results in a new quantity.

Alvin had 9 toy cars. He received 3 more for his birthday. How many toy cars does Alvin have now?

Any of the three quantities can be unknown.

circle graph A graph used to display data that make up a whole. (Also called a pie graph or a pie chart.)

Coin Strip See **Dime Strip** and **Nickel Strip**.

collection story problem Addition problem of three types:

1) putting things together (putting two kinds of flowers in a vase);
2) separating a collection of things (putting some books on a shelf and some on a desk);
3) static, no action occurs (some windows are open, some windows are closed).

combine To put together; to form one group from many groups.

comparison bars A visual representation of the numbers in an additive comparison story problem; children draw different length bars to represent each number.

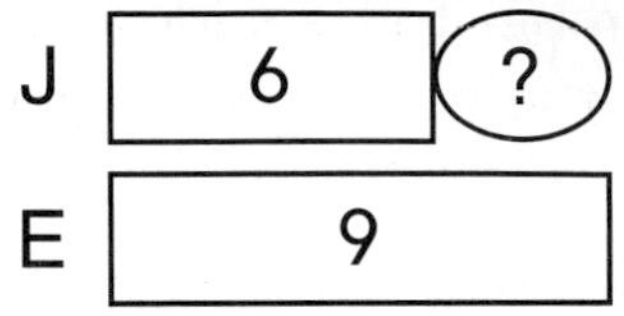

comparison drawing A drawing children make to illustrate the numbers in an additive comparison story problem.

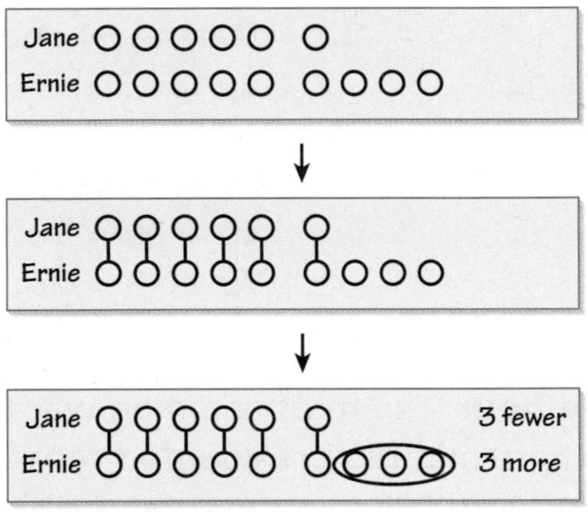

comparison language Having the same size and the same shape.

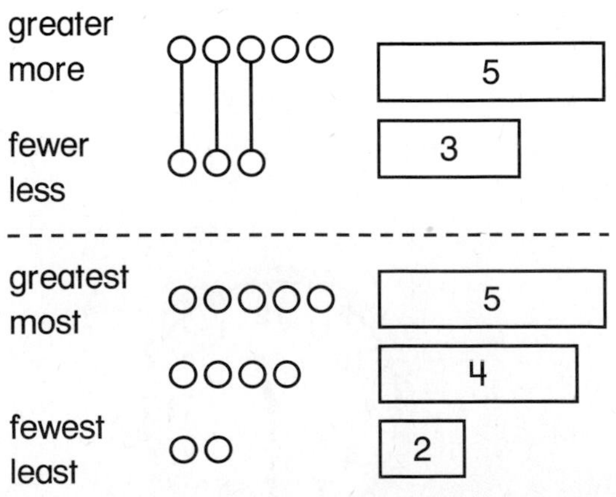

comparison story problem (additive) A problem that involves someone or something that has "more" or "less" of something than someone or something else. Comparison problems may require addition or subtraction to solve.

comparison story problem (additive) continued

Types of additive comparison problems:

1) More/Fewer Language
Manny has 5 roses. Asha has 8 roses. How many more roses does Asha have than Manny?
2) Equalizing Language
Manny has 5 roses. Asha has 8 roses. How many roses does Manny need to get to have the same amount of roses as Asha?

compose Put together.

congruent Having the same size and shape.

count all An addition strategy where children count all of something (for example, fingers on their hands or the dots on two Secret Code Cards) to find the total.

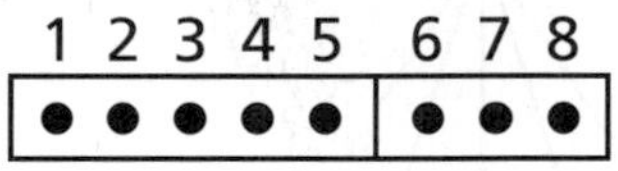

$5 + 3 = \boxed{8}$

count-bys Numbers that are found by counting by a particular number; 5s count-bys would be 5, 10, 15, 20, 25, and so on; 3s count-bys would be 3, 6, 9, 12, and so on.

count on An addition or subtraction strategy in which children begin with one partner and count on to the total. This strategy can be used to find an unknown partner or an unknown total.

$5 + 3 = \boxed{8}$

$5 + \boxed{3} = 8$

$8 - 5 = \boxed{3}$

Already **5**

D

data Pieces of information.

data table A list of data in rows and columns.

decade numbers Numbers that are multiples of 10: 10, 20, 30, 40, 50, 60, 70, 80, 90.

decade partners Decade numbers that have a sum of 100. 40 and 60 are decade partners; 30 and 70 are decade partners.

decimal notation for money A method of writing monetary values using the dollar sign symbol ($) and a decimal point (.). Fifty cents is written in decimal notation as $0.50.

decimal point In dollar notation, the symbol (.) used to separate the dollars position from the cents position; in decimal notation, the symbol used to separate the whole number position from the decimal fraction position.

decimeter (dm) A metric unit of length equal to 0.1 ($\frac{1}{10}$) meter.

decompose Take apart.

degrees Celsius (°C) The metric unit of temperature.

degrees Fahrenheit (°F) The customary unit of temperature.

Demonstration Secret Code Cards A larger version of the Secret Code Cards, for classroom use. (See **Secret Code Cards.**)

denominator In a fraction, the number below the bar. It tells the number of equal parts into which a whole is divided.

diagonal A line segment that connects two corners of a polygon and is not a side of the polygon.

difference The result of subtraction. In the subtraction equation, 5 − 2 = 3, 3 is the difference.

digit Any one of these 10 symbols: 0, 1, 2, 3, 4, 5, 6, 7, 8, 9.

digital clock A clock displaying time in hours and minutes separated by a colon.

dime A coin that has a value of 10 cents or $0.10. Ten dimes are equal to one dollar.

Dime Strip A double-sided strip of paper or cardboard displaying a dime on one side and 10 pennies on the other side.

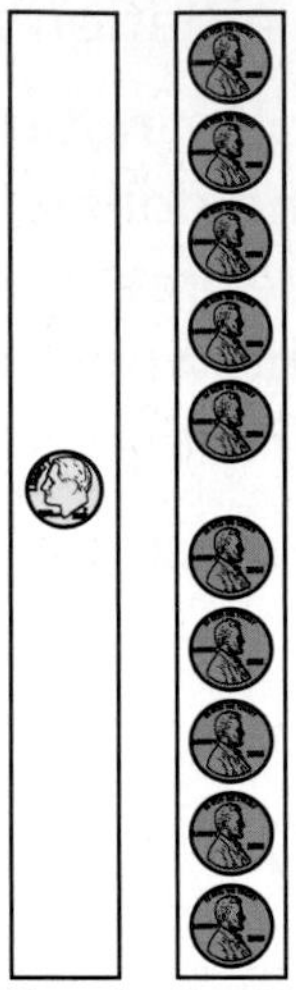

Dive the Deep A student activity used to practice subtraction with teen totals. Using columns of completed equations, children cover the answers with a strip of paper and slowly move the paper up or down the column to uncover and check the answer after solving each exercise.

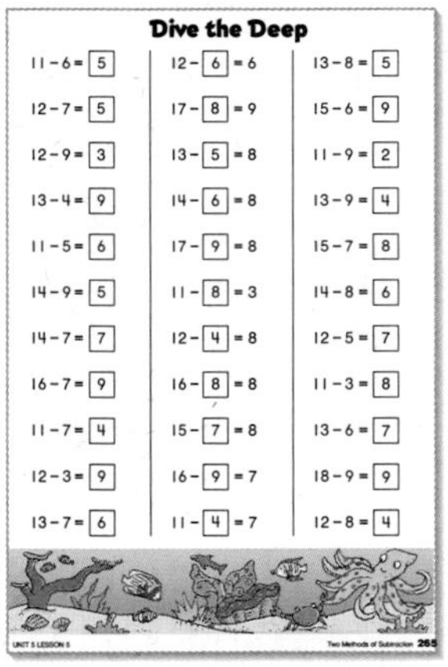

Dive the Deep

11 − 6 = 5	12 − 6 = 6	13 − 8 = 5
12 − 7 = 5	17 − 8 = 9	15 − 6 = 9
12 − 9 = 3	13 − 5 = 8	11 − 9 = 2
13 − 4 = 9	14 − 6 = 8	13 − 9 = 4
11 − 5 = 6	17 − 9 = 8	15 − 7 = 8
14 − 9 = 5	11 − 8 = 3	14 − 8 = 6
14 − 7 = 7	12 − 4 = 8	12 − 5 = 7
16 − 7 = 9	16 − 8 = 8	11 − 3 = 8
11 − 7 = 4	15 − 7 = 8	13 − 6 = 7
12 − 3 = 9	16 − 9 = 7	18 − 9 = 9
13 − 7 = 6	11 − 4 = 7	12 − 8 = 4

UNIT 5 LESSON 5 Two Methods of Subtraction 265

dollar notation A method of writing monetary values using the dollar sign symbol ($) and a decimal point (.). Two dollars and fifty cents is written in dollar notation as $2.50.

dollar The basic unit of U.S. currency. One dollar is equal to four quarters, ten dimes, twenty nickels or one hundred pennies.

dollar sign The symbol ($) used to show dollar notation.

Double Minus 1 An addition strategy using doubles (two of the same addend). Used when one addend is decreased by 1. Since 5 + **5** = 10, 5 + **4** = 9, 1 less than 10.

Double Plus 1 An addition strategy using doubles (two of the same addend) in which one addend is increased by 1. Since 5 + **5** = 10, 5 + **6** = 11, 1 more than 10.

doubles Two of the same addend. In the equation 5 + 5 = 10, the two fives are doubles.

E

equal shares Describes groups of equal size.

Equal Shares Drawing A drawing which children create that represents factors and products.

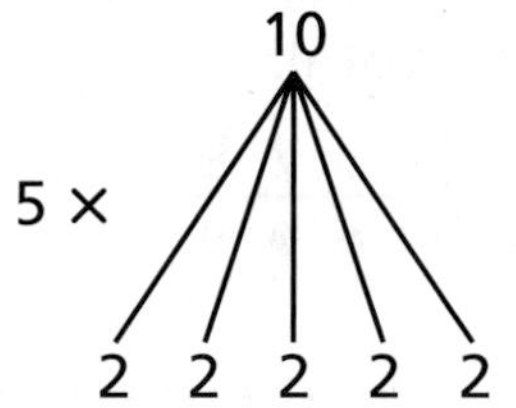

Equal Shares Drawing for 5 × 2 = 10

equation A mathematical sentence that uses an equals sign to show that two expressions are equal.

12 − 5 = 7   3 + 1 = 4   5 = 2 + 3
6 = 8 − 2   6 + 2 = 4 + 4

equation chain A series of expressions that equal the same number.

5 = 2 + 3 = 3 + 2 = 4 + 1 = 1 + 4 = 1 + 1 + 1 + 1 + 1 = 6 − 1

equilateral Describes a geometric figure that has all sides of equal length.

estimate (noun) A number close to an exact amount. An estimate tells *about* how much or *about* how many.

estimate (verb) To make a thoughtful guess or to tell *about* how much or *about* how many.

even number A number that is a multiple of 2. The ones digit of an even number is 0, 2, 4, 6 or 8. Even numbers are those that can be divided into two equal groups.

exact change The exact amount needed to purchase an item.

Expanded Method A method of subtraction in which children show the place value of each digit.

$$\begin{array}{r} 50 + 14 \\ 64 = \cancel{60} + \cancel{4} \\ \underline{-\,28} = \underline{20 + 8} \\ 30 + 6 = 36 \end{array}$$

expanded numbers or expanded notation Numbers written in a form that shows the place value of the digits.

254 = 2 hundreds + 5 tens + 4 ones or
254 = 200 + 50 + 4

expression A number, a variable, or any combination of numbers, variables, operation signs and grouping symbols.

F

face A flat surface of a solid figure.

fair game A game in which the likelihood of winning is equally likely for all players.

fair shares Describes groups of equal shares.

fewer Fewer is used to compare two quantities that can be counted. There are fewer red books than blue books. Less is used to compare two quantities that can be measured. There is less water than juice. *See* comparison language.

fewest Fewest is used to compare three or more quantities. (See fewer.)

flash ten A way for children to display the value of ten by opening and closing both hands at the same time. Flashing ten twice would represent 20.

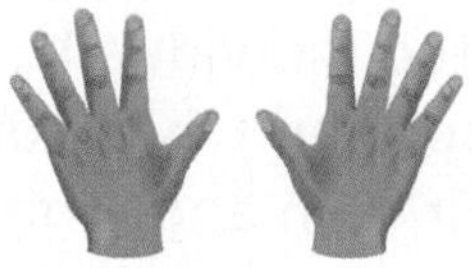

10

flip To turn a figure over a line so that the moved figure is a mirror image of the original; also referred to as a reflection.

You can **flip** a figure over a horizontal line.

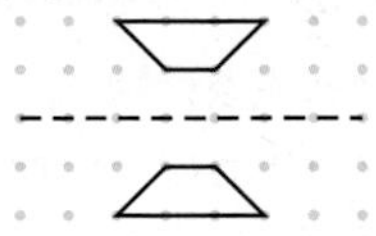

You can **flip** a figure over a vertical line.

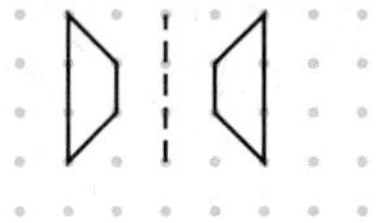

foot A customary unit of length equal to 12 inches.

forward sequence A sequence of numbers that uses an addition rule to determine the next number.

16, 20, 24, 28, 32, 36 . . . Rule: $n + 4$

fraction A number used to describe part of a whole, a whole, or more than one whole. $\frac{1}{2}$, $\frac{4}{4}$, and $\frac{6}{5}$ are fractions.

front-end estimation A method of estimation accomplished by computing with the digits in the greatest place.

$$\begin{array}{rcr} 49 & \rightarrow & 40 \\ \underline{+\,27} & \rightarrow & \underline{+\,20} \\ & & 60 \end{array} \leftarrow \text{front-end estimate}$$

function A relationship between two sets of numbers in which each number in the first set is paired with exactly one number in the second set.

function table A table that shows a function.

Subtract 4.	
9	5
10	6
7	3
8	4

G

Game Cards Cards displaying the numerals 0–9. These are on Copymaster M23.

geoboards Pegboards (usually plastic) that children use to construct geometric shapes by placing elastic bands on the pegs.

Teacher Glossary (Continued)

greater Larger or more than. Used to compare two quantities or numbers.

greatest Largest or most. Used to compare three or more quantities or numbers.

Green Make-a-Ten Cards Cards used to help children become fluent in the Make a Ten strategy for addition.

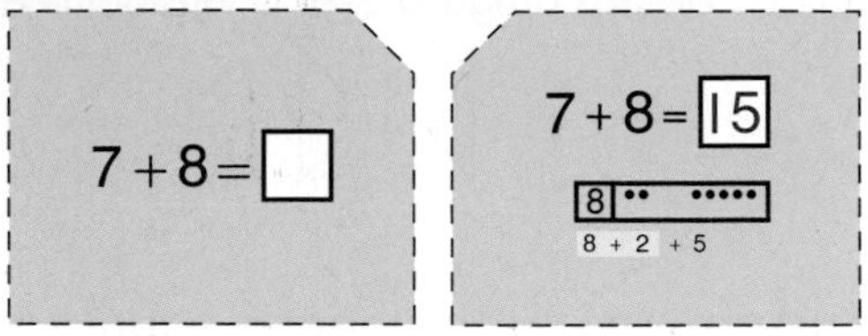

front of card back of card

group (verb) To combine ones to form tens, to combine tens to form hundreds, and so on.

group name A name used as a category or classification. Flowers is the group name for daisies and roses.

Grouping Drawing A drawing which children create that represents factors and products.

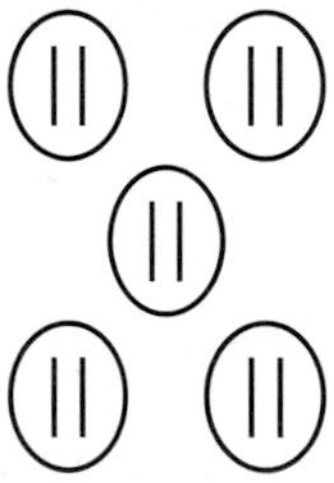

Grouping Drawing for 5 × 2 = 10

growing pattern A number or geometric pattern that increases.
Examples: 2, 4, 6, 8, 10 ...
1, 2, 5, 10, 17 ...

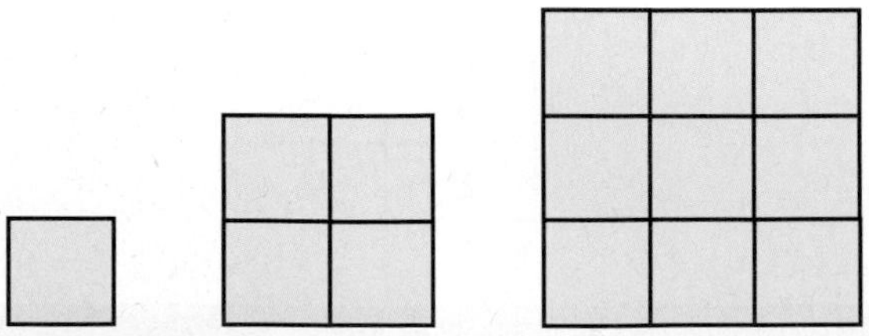

H

hidden information An implied number or implied information in a story problem: pair, dozen, double the amount.

horizontal Parallel to the horizon; going straight across.

horizontal bar graph A bar graph in which data are displayed using horizontal bars.

hundreds The name given to the third position from the right when describing whole number place value. In the number 312, 3 is in the hundreds position.

I

impossible Not able to happen (as in a particular outcome in a probability experiment).

inch A customary unit of length equal to $\frac{1}{12}$ foot.

inverse operations Opposite or reverse operations that undo each other. Addition and subtraction are inverse operations. Multiplication and division are inverse operations.

is equal to (=) Having the same value as that of another quantity or expression.

is greater than (>) Having a value that is more than that of another quantity or expression.

is less than (<) Having a value that is less than that of another quantity or expression.

is not equal to (≠) Having a value that is not the same as another quantity or expression.

isosceles triangle A triangle that has at least two sides of equal length.

K

key A part of a map, graph or chart that explains what symbols mean.

L

least Smallest amount or fewest.

length The measure of how long something is or one dimension of a two-dimensional figure.

less Word used to show a quantity smaller than another. Less is used to compare quantities that cannot be counted individually: less milk, less traffic; less is also used when comparing numbers on their own and when comparing amounts of money.

less likely Having less of a chance of happening than something else (as in an outcome in a probability experiment).

line of symmetry The line along which a figure can be folded so that the two halves match exactly.

line plot A way to show data using a number line.

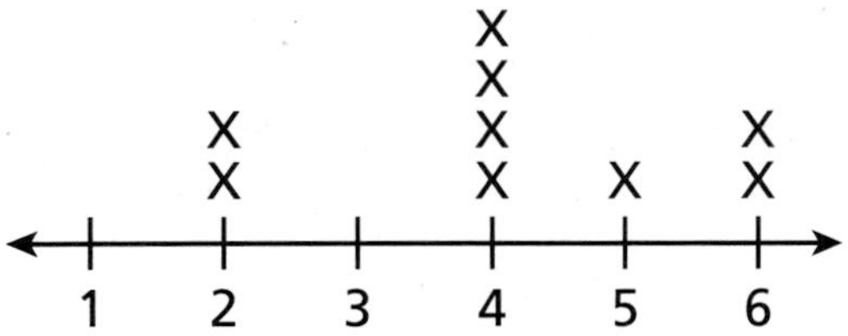

line segment A part of a line that has two endpoints.

line symmetry A property that pertains to a figure that can be folded to make two parts that are mirror images. Also called reflectional symmetry.

M

Make a Ten strategy An addition or subtraction strategy in which children count on to ten to add or subtract.

making change Finding the amount of money that needs to be returned to the buyer when the amount of money given to the seller is more than the cost of the purchase.

mass The amount of matter in an object. (Mass is constant; weight varies because weight is the effect of gravity on matter.)

matching drawing (See **comparison drawing.**)

Math Mountain A visual representation of the partners and totals of a number. The total (*sum*) appears at the top and the two partners (*addends*) that are added to produce the larger number are below to the left and right.

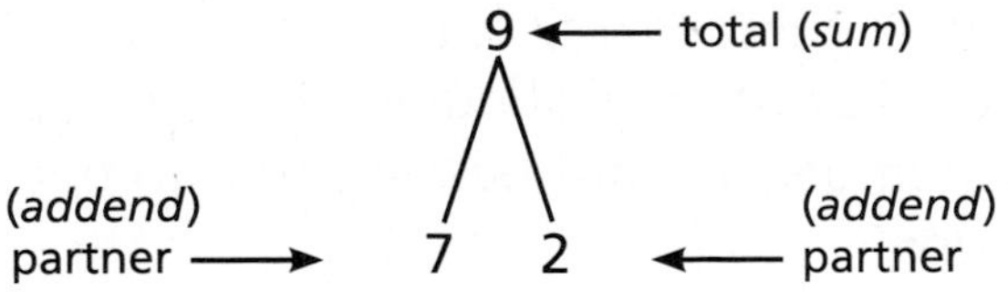

Math Mountain Cards Triangular-shaped cards used to practice addition and subtraction. Each card shows a total at the top and a pair of partners at the bottom. Yellow cards have totals of 10 or less; blue cards have teen totals.

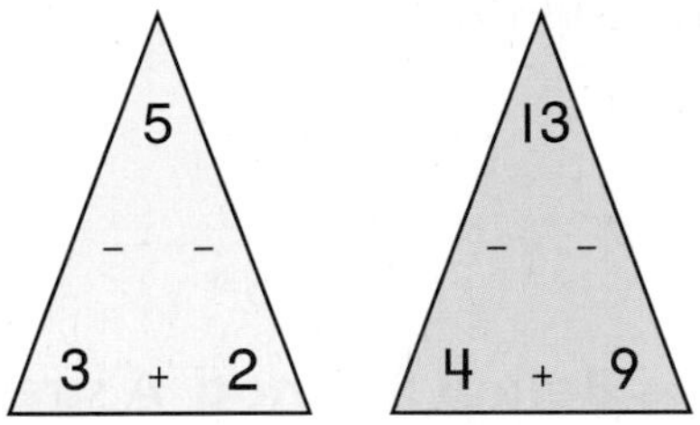

meter In the metric system, the basic unit of length or distance.

midpoint The point that divides a line segment into two congruent parts.

money string Combinations of dollars and/or coins that equal an amount.

$1.29 = $1 + 25¢ + 1¢ + 1¢ + 1¢ + 1¢ = 25¢ + 25¢ + 25¢ + 10¢ + 10¢ + 10¢ + 5¢ + 5¢ + 5¢ + 5¢ + 1¢ + 1¢ + 1¢ +1¢

more Describes an amount or quantity greater than another. *See* comparison language.

more likely Having more of a chance of happening than something else (as in an outcome in a probability experiment).

most Greatest amount or quantity.

multiple Number which is the product of a given number and any whole number. 4 is a multiple of 4 because it is the product of 4 and whole number 1; 8 is a multiple of 4 because it is the product of 4 and the whole number 2. (See **count-bys.**)

multiplication The operation of repeated addition of the same number. 3 x 5 is the same as 5 + 5 + 5.

mystery addition An addition problem in which children are asked to find an unknown addend.

$6 + \square = 10$

mystery multiplication A multiplication problem in which children are asked to find an unknown factor.

$\square \times 7 = 28$

N

New Groups Above Method A strategy for multi-digit addition. The new groups are placed above the existing groups. This is a common method of addition.

$$\begin{array}{r} {\scriptstyle 1\,1} \\ 298 \\ +\ 177 \\ \hline 475 \end{array}$$

New Groups Below Method A strategy for multi-digit addition. The new groups are placed below the existing groups on the line waiting to be added.

$$\begin{array}{r} 298 \\ +\ 177 \\ \hline {\scriptstyle 1\,1} \\ 475 \end{array}$$

nickel A coin with a value of 5 cents or \$0.05. A nickel is equal to five pennies.

Nickel Strip A double-sided strip of paper or cardboard displaying a nickel on one side and 5 pennies on the other side.

(front) (back)

non-standard unit A unit of measure not commonly recognized, such as a paper clip. An inch and a centimeter are standard units of measure.

number The word used to describe value or quantity (cardinal number: 1, 2, 3) or order (ordinal number: 1st, 2nd, 3rd).

number flash A way for children to display the value of a number by holding up the appropriate number of fingers and/or hands (See also **flash ten.**) A child would flash two by holding up two fingers; a child would flash eleven by flashing ten (opening and closing both hands once at the same time) and then moving both hands to the right, closing both and then putting up just one finger to the right. Eleven is ten and one.

number line A diagram that represents numbers as lengths on a line.

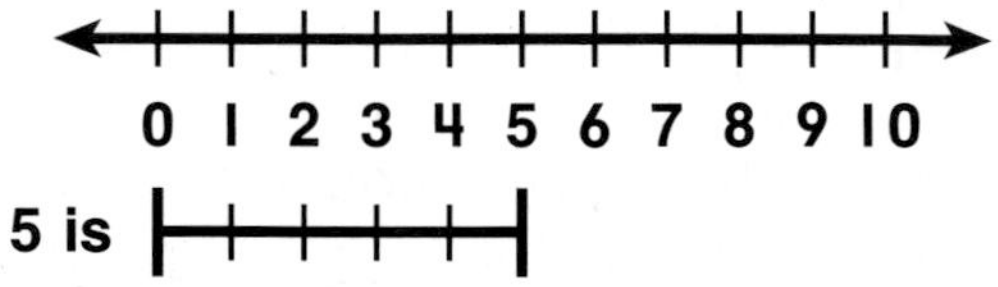

Number Path A display of the numbers 1 through 100 in groups of ten, found on the outside edge of the MathBoard or Copymaster M51.

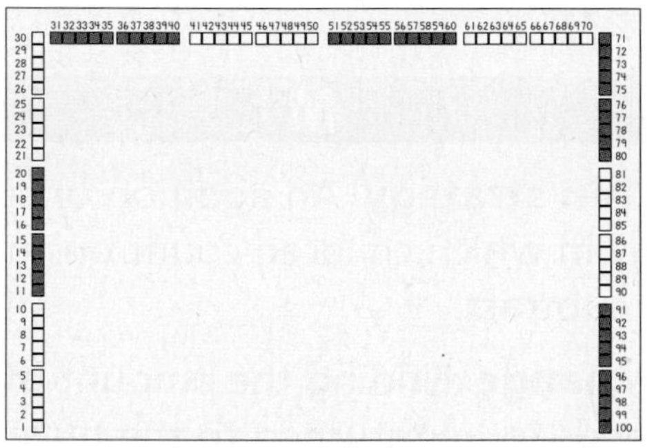

numeral A symbol used to represent a number. 7 is the numeral for seven.

numerator In a fraction, the number above the bar. The numerator tells the number of equal parts being described.

O

obtuse angle An angle that measures more than 90° and less than 180°.

obtuse triangle A triangle with one angle that measures more than 90°.

odd number A number that is not a multiple of 2. The ones digit of an odd number is 1, 3, 5, 7, or 9. Odd numbers cannot be divided into two equal groups.

ones The name given to the position furthest to the right when describing whole number place value. In the number 12, 2 is in the ones position.

Orange Count-On Cards Cards used to practice the Counting On strategy for subtraction. One side of the card shows a subtraction equation. The other side shows the answer and a counting-on drawing.

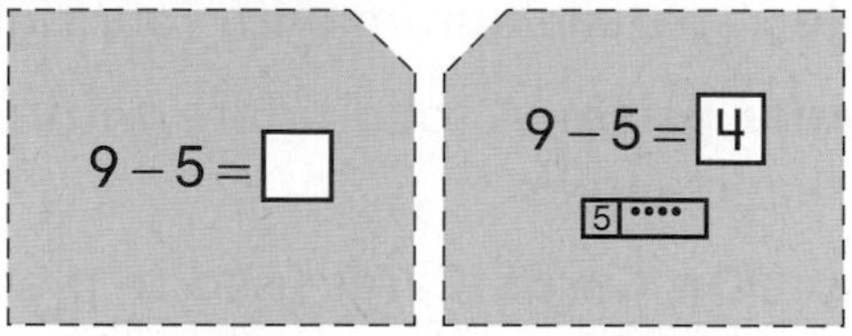

front of card back of card

ordinal number A number that describes the position in an ordered sequence of objects or events, not the quantity of them. 1st, 2nd, 3rd and 4th are ordinal numbers.

P

Parachute Drop A student activity to practice addition and subtraction with totals ≤ 10. Using columns of completed equations, children cover the answers with a strip of paper and slowly move the paper up or down the column to check their answers after solving each exercise.

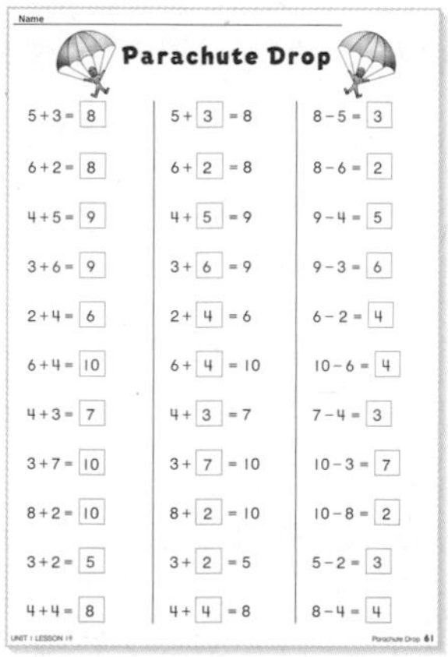
Name

Parachute Drop

5 + 3 = 8	5 + 3 = 8	8 – 5 = 3
6 + 2 = 8	6 + 2 = 8	8 – 6 = 2
4 + 5 = 9	4 + 5 = 9	9 – 4 = 5
3 + 6 = 9	3 + 6 = 9	9 – 3 = 6
2 + 4 = 6	2 + 4 = 6	6 – 2 = 4
6 + 4 = 10	6 + 4 = 10	10 – 6 = 4
4 + 3 = 7	4 + 3 = 7	7 – 4 = 3
3 + 7 = 10	3 + 7 = 10	10 – 3 = 7
8 + 2 = 10	8 + 2 = 10	10 – 8 = 2
3 + 2 = 5	3 + 2 = 5	5 – 2 = 3
4 + 4 = 8	4 + 4 = 8	8 – 4 = 4

parallel A word used to describe lines or line segments that do not intersect. The distance between the lines or line segments is the same at every point.

parallelogram A quadrilateral in which both pairs of opposite sides are parallel and opposite angles are congruent.

Partner House A pictorial representation of all the sets of partners for a total. The total is shown on the roof of the house. Each floor of the house shows a set of partners. Pairs of partners that can be "switched" are shown twice on the same floor in different order. A pair of doubles is shown only once on a floor.

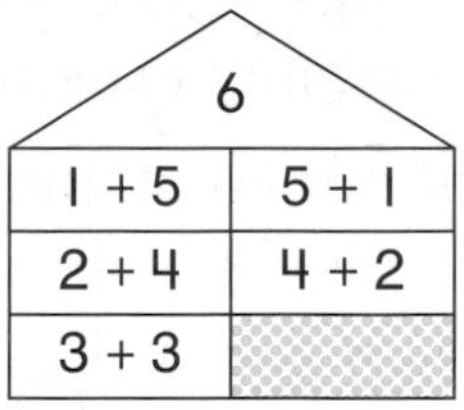

partner lengths Two lengths that add up to another length.

5 cm + 1 cm = 6 cm; 5 cm and 1 cm are partner lengths of 6 cm.

partners A pair of numbers in a break-apart.

When 10 is broken apart into 10 = 3 + 7, 3 and 7 are partners (addends).

pattern A way in which numbers or drawings are related to one another that allows predictions about the next number or drawing.

pattern blocks Small geometric shapes that children use to build other geometric shapes or to form patterns.

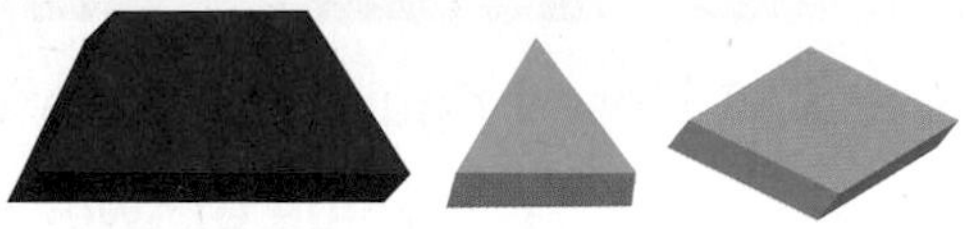

penny A coin with a value of 1 cent or $0.01.

perimeter The distance around a figure.

picture graph A graph in which data are displayed using pictures. Each picture represents one of whatever is being displayed.

pie graph or pie chart Another name for a circle graph. (See **circle graph**.)

plane A flat surface that extends in all directions without end.

plane figure A geometric figure that lies entirely in one plane.

P.M. The abbreviation for post meridiem, Latin for after noon. Used to indicate a time after noon.

point symmetry Property that pertains to a figure that can be turned less than a full turn (360°) and still look the same as it did before the turn. Also called rotational symmetry.

polygon A closed plane (two-dimensional) figure made up of three or more line segments.

possible Able to happen (as in a particular outcome in a probability experiment).

predict To think about what might happen; to guess; to anticipate what will come next.

probability The mathematical science of measuring and estimating predictability.

Proof Drawing A math drawing children create to show how to solve a problem, including the solution. It is not a formal proof.

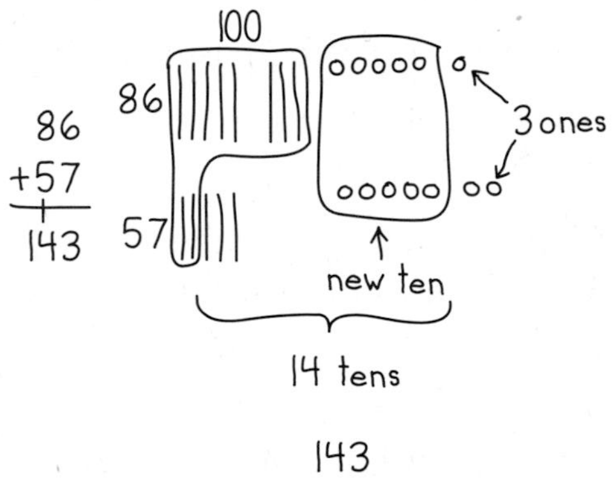

Q

quadrilateral A closed figure with four sides.

quarter A coin that has a value of twenty-five cents or $0.25.

Quick Hundred A box children draw to represent 100. The children will have first drawn 10 Quick Tens inside the box but will subsequently use only the box to represent 100.

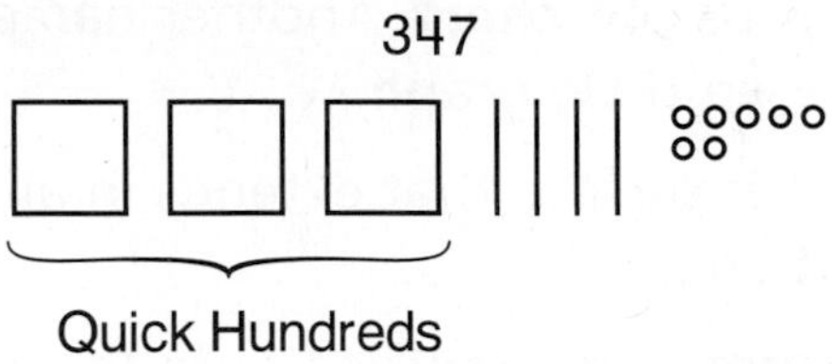

Quick Ten A vertical line children draw to represent 10.

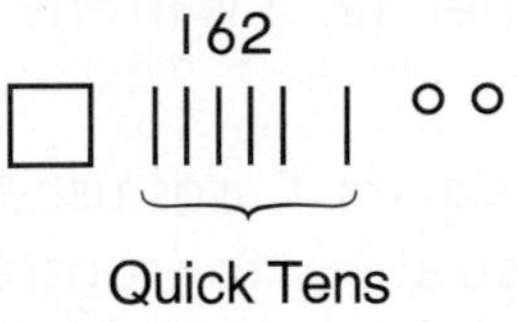

R

rectangle A parallelogram with four right angles.

rectangular prism A solid figure with six faces that are rectangles.

Red Count-On Cards Cards used to practice the Counting-On strategy for addition. One side of the card shows an addition equation with unknown total ≤ 10. The other side gives the same equation with the total. It also shows a counting-on drawing.

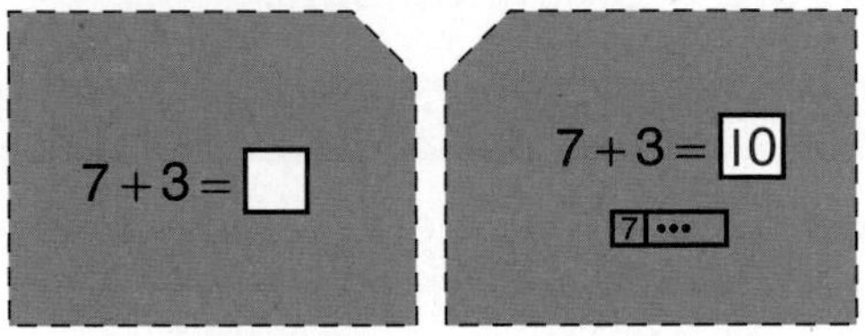

front of card back of card

reflection A transformation that produces a mirror image of a figure on the opposite side of a line; also referred to as a flip.

reflectional symmetry See **line symmetry.**

regular polygon A polygon with all sides having the same length and all angles having the same measure.

repeating pattern A pattern consisting of a group of numbers, letters, or figures that repeat.
Examples: 1, 2, 1, 2, ...
A, B, C, A, B, C, ...

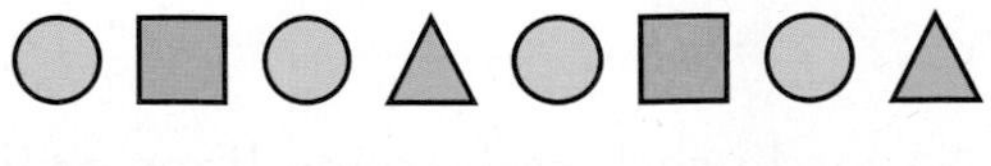

right angle An angle that measures 90°.

right triangle A triangle with one right angle.

rotation A transformation that involves a turning movement of a figure about a point, also referred to as a turn.

You can **turn** or **rotate** a figure around a point.

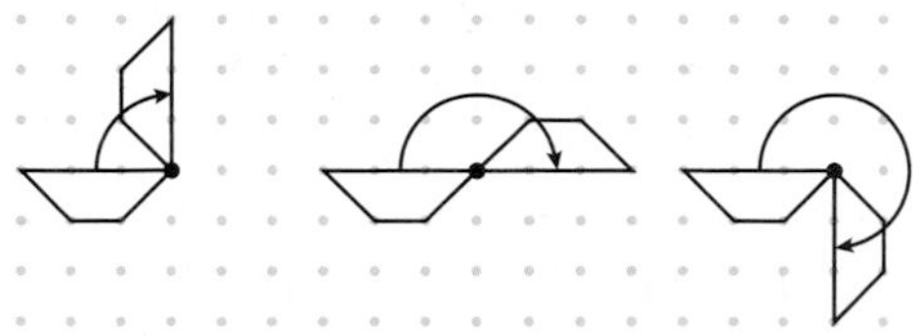

rotational symmetry See **point symmetry.**

rounding The process of finding *about* how many or *about* how much by expressing a number to the nearest unit, ten, hundred, thousand, etc.

rule In a pattern such as a function table or number sequence, what is done to the first number to get to the second number and so on. The rule *Add 3* is shown in the function table and the rule $n + 7$ is shown for the number sequence.

Function Table

Add 3.	
0	3
1	4
2	5
3	6

Number Sequence 16, 23, 30, 37, 44, 51 Rule: $n + 7$

S

scale On a graph, the numbers along the axes. The numbers are arranged in order with equal intervals.

scalene triangle A triangle whose sides are all different lengths.

Secret Code Cards Cards printed with the digits 0 through 9, multiples of 10 from 10 through 90 and multiples of 100 from 100 through 1,000. The number is represented on the back of the card by dots, sticks, or boxes. The cards are used to teach place value.

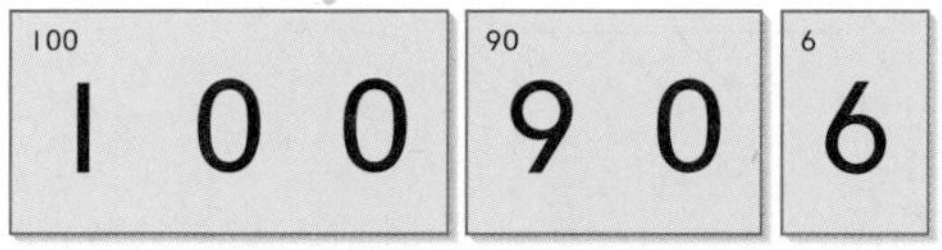

Hundreds Card Tens Card Ones Card

100 + 90 + 6

Assembled Cards

Show All Totals Method A method for finding a total of multi-digit numbers.

45
\+ 28
Add tens. → 60
Add ones. → 13
73

Find total tens. Find total ones.

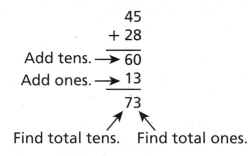

similar figures Figures that are the same shape but not necessarily the same size.

situation equation An equation children write to represent a story problem. It represents a literal translation of the problem. It may or may not have the unknown isolated on one side of the equals sign.

skip count To say the count-bys of a number. (See **count-bys.**)

Teacher Glossary (Continued)

slide A transformation in which a figure is moved along a line; also referred to as a translation. The size and shape of the figure remain the same.

You can **slide** a figure right or left along a straight line.

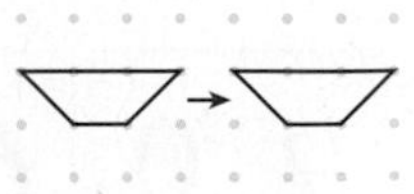

You can **slide** a figure up or down along a straight line.

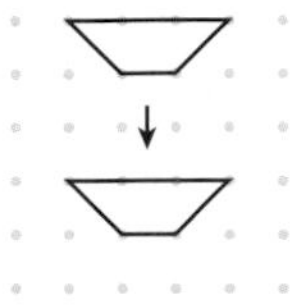

solution equation A situation equation that has been rewritten so that the unknown is on the right side of the equals sign. It is related to the operation needed to solve the problem rather than to a literal translation of the story problem.

square A figure with four right angles and four congruent sides.

square centimeter A standard metric unit for measuring area that is 1 cm on each side.

square rectangle Since a square has opposite sides parallel and four right angles, a square is also a rectangle, so it is sometimes called a square rectangle.

square unit Unit used to measure area that is 1 unit on each side. A square unit can refer to a standard or non-standard unit.

standard unit A recognized unit of measure, such as an inch or a centimeter. A non-standard unit of measure might be a paper clip.

sticks and circles A visual representation of groups of tens, as sticks and individual ones, as circles. The numbers 64 and 28 are shown.

story problem A math problem using topics from daily life and the math that is being studied.

sum The result of addition. In the addition equation, 3 + 2 = 5, 5 is the sum.

survey (noun) A method of collecting information.

survey (verb) To collect information.

Switch the Partners To change the order of the partners in an addition equation. Used to demonstrate the Commutative Property of Addition.

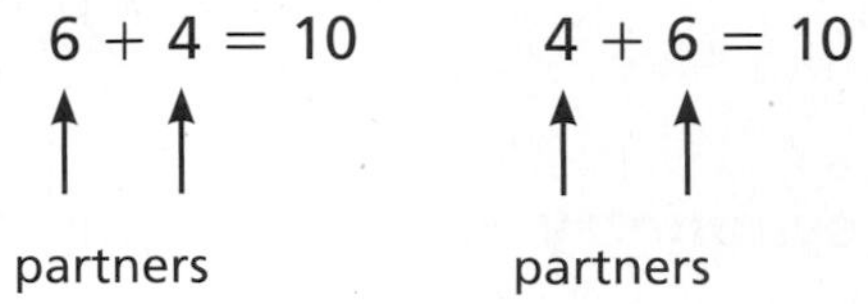

symmetry See **line symmetry** and **point symmetry.**

T

table A list of data organized in rows and columns.

tally (verb or noun) To count/record data or the type of mark that represents an individual item of data.

Colored Paper Clips

Color	Tally	Number
Pink	|||	3
White	𝍸 ||	7
Blue	𝍸	5
Green	𝍸 |	6
Yellow	|	1

teen numbers Numbers made up of one ten and some ones. In this program, the numbers 11 through 19 are referred to as teen numbers.

Ten Frame A diagram showing two rows of 5 squares that children use to practice making a ten.

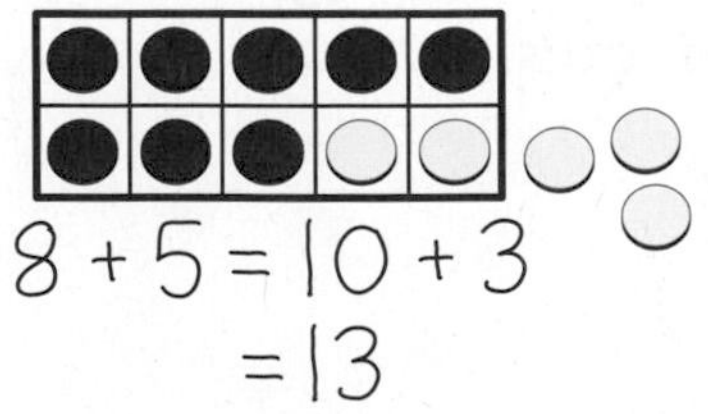

tens The name given to the second position from the right when describing whole number place value. In the number 12, 1 is in the tens position.

Time Poster

three-dimensional (3-D) Having three dimensions: length, width and height.

three-dimensional figure A figure with three dimensions.

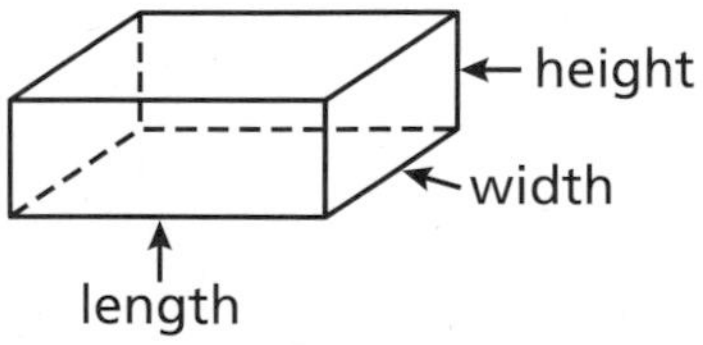

total A number that represents the combined amount of all the items added. A term used in *Math Expressions* to refer to the sum of two partners.

transformation A geometric change in the position of a figure. Transformations include slides (translations), flips (reflections) and turns (rotations).

translation See **slide.**

triangle A polygon with three sides.

turn A figure that is rotated around a point or axis; also referred to as a rotation. The size and shape of the figure remain the same. (See **rotation.**)

two-dimensional (2-D) Having two dimensions: length and width.

two-step story problem A story problem requiring two steps to arrive at the solution.

U

unfair game A game in which the likelihood of winning is not equally likely for each player.

ungroup To break into a new group in order to subtract. For example, 1 hundred can be ungrouped into 10 tens and 1 ten can be ungrouped into 10 ones.

ungrouping In subtraction, the process of breaking a number into a new group. Children may also refer to ungrouping as *trading, borrowing,* or *unpacking.*

Ungrouping First Method A method of subtraction in which children check each place to see if they need to ungroup in order to subtract. Children then complete all necessary ungrouping before they subtract.

unit fraction A fraction that is one equal part of a whole. $\frac{1}{3}$ and $\frac{1}{4}$ are unit fractions.

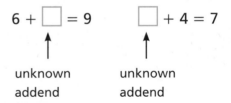

unknown addend

$6 + \square = 9$ (↑ unknown addend)

$\square + 4 = 7$ (↑ unknown addend)

unknown partner

$6 + \square = 8$

6 ↑ known partner; $\square$ ↑ unknown partner; 8 ↑ total

$8 - 6 = \square$

8 ↑ total; 6 ↑ known partner; $\square$ ↑ unknown partner

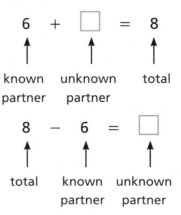

unknown start problem A change plus or change minus problem in which the starting number is the unknown number.

V

Venn diagram A pictorial way to represent relationships between sets.

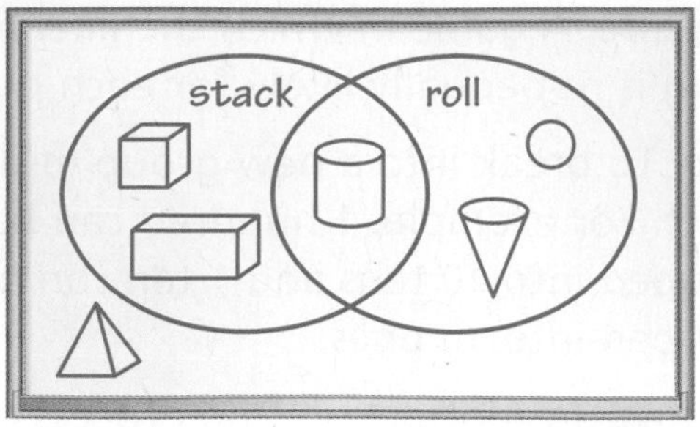

vertical Straight up and down.

vertical bar graph A bar graph in which data are displayed using vertical bars.

vertical form A way to position numbers in a problem in an up and down format.

$$\begin{array}{r} 7 \\ +\ 4 \\ \hline 11 \end{array}$$

volume The number of cubic units it takes to fill a solid.

W

word name A number represented as a word; the word name for 19 is *nineteen.*

Y

yard A customary unit for measuring length. One yard is equal to three feet; one yard is equal to thirty-six inches.

Yellow Count-On Cards Cards used to practice the Counting On strategy for addition. One side of the card shows an addition equation with an unknown partner. The other side shows the partner with a counting-on drawing.

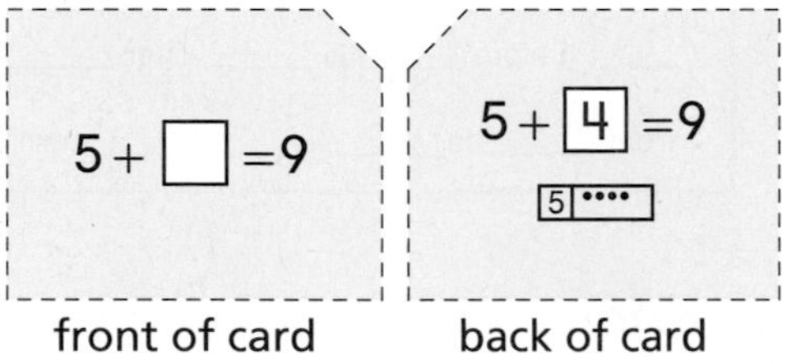

Recommended Books

Unit 1

Oliver's Party, by Jenny Fry and Angela Jolliffe (Barron's Educational Series, Inc., 2002)

Jelly Beans for Sale, by Bruce McMillan (Scholastic, 1996)

Domino Addition, by Lynette Long (Charlesbridge, 1996)

Unit 2

Racing Around, by Stuart J. Murphy, illustrated by Mike Reed (HarperTrophy, 2001)

Keep Your Distance!, by Gail Herman, illustrated by Jerry Smath (The Kane Press, 2001)

Unit 3

Even Steven and Odd Todd, by Kathryn Cristaldi, illustrated by Henry Morehouse (Cartwheel, 1996)

Count on Pablo, by Barbara deRubertis, illustrated by Rebecca Thornburgh (Kane Press, 1999)

Unit 4

Shapes (Slide 'n Seek), by Chuck Murphy (Little Simon, 2001)

Shapes, Shapes, Shapes, by Tana Hoban (HarperTrophy, 1996)

A Cloak for the Dreamer, by Aileen Friedman, illustrated by Kim Howard (Scholastic, 1994)

Unit 5

Hippos Go Berserk!, by Sandra Boynton (Little Simon, 2000)

A Place for Zero, Angeline Sparanga LoPresti, illustrated by Phyllis Hornung (Charlesbridge, 2003)

Unit 6

Clocks and More Clocks, by Pat Hutchins (Aladdin Paperbacks, Simon & Schuster, 1970)

My Grandmother's Clock, by Geraldine McCaughrean, illustrated by Stephen Lambert (Clarion Books, 2002)

How Do You Know What Time It Is?, by Robert E. Wells (Albert Whitman & Company, 2002)

Unit 7

Tiger Math: Learning to Graph from a Baby Tiger, by Ann Whitehead Nagda and Cindy Bickel (Henry Holt and Company, 2000)

Fair is Fair!, by Jennifer Dussling, illustrated by Diane Palmisciano (The Kane Press, 2003)

Recommended Books (Continued)

Unit 8

A Cloak for the Dreamer, by Aileen Friedman, illustrated by Kim Howard (Scholastic, 1994)

Unit 9

Tightwad Tod, by Daphne Skinner, illustrated by John A. Nez (Disney Press, 2005)

100th Day Worries, by Margery Cuyler, illustrated by Arthur Howard (Simon & Schuster Children's Publishing, 2000)

Pigs Will Be Pigs: Fun with Math and Money, by Amy Axelrod, illustrated by Sharon McGinley-Nally (Aladdin Picture Books, 1997)

Henry Hikes to Fitchburg, by D.B. Johnson (Houghton Mifflin Company, 2006)

Unit 10

Patterns in Nature, by Jennifer Rozines Roy and Gregory Roy (Benchmark Books, 2005)

The M.C. Escher Coloring Book, by M.C. Escher (Abrams, 1995)

Unit 11

Earth Day—Hooray!, by Stuart J. Murphy and Renee Andriani (Harper Trophy, 2004)

The 329th Friend, by Marjorie Weinman Sharmat and Cyndy Szekeres (Four Winds Press, 1979)

Hannah's Collections, by Marthe Jocelyn (Dutton Children's Books, 2000)

One Grain of Rice, by Demi (Scholastic, 1997)

Unit 12

Tell Me How Far It Is, by Shirley Willis, (Gardners Books, 2005)

Millions to Measure, by David M. Schwartz, illustrated by Steven Kellogg (HarperCollins, 2003)

Measuring Penny, by Loreen Leedy (Henry Holt and Company, 1997)

Unit 13

Each Orange Had 8 Slices: A Counting Book, by Paul Giganti, Jr. and Donald Crews (HarperTrophy, 1999)

The Doorbell Rang, by Pat Hutchins (HarperTrophy, 1989)

Let's Fly a Kite, by Stuart J. Murphy and Brian Floca (HarperTrophy, 2000)

The Grapes of Math, by Greg Tang (Scholastic, 2004)

Unit 14

Henry Hikes to Fitchburg, by D.B. Johnson (Houghton Mifflin Company, 2006)

Index

A

B

C

Index (Continued)

Index (Continued)

H

I

L

Q